Federal Criminal Procedure: Cases that Matter

3rd Edition

Charles H. Rose III
Professor of Excellence in Trial Advocacy
Director, Center for Excellence in Advocacy
Stetson University College of Law

3rd Edition

Forward

We practice, teach, and learn law in a challenging time. Technology is advancing faster than ever, the profession continues to be under stress, and the call for change in the ways in which we practice, teach and learn law has reached a crescendo. Each of us bears some responsibility for not only the current state of affairs, but for finding a way out of it while protecting the sanctity of the "Rule of Law" in a democratic society. This casebook is one small contribution to that endeavor.

Federal Criminal Procedure: Cases that Matter, 3 Edition, is a collection of edited cases, with commentary, covering the fundamental aspects of Federal Criminal Constitutional law. It is designed to be used as a stand alone casebook in a criminal procedure law school environment. It also serves as an excellent starting point for understanding the constitutional aspects of Federal Criminal Procedure and for additional research.

I created this text to properly capture the most relevant cases, while also creating a vehicle that captures the intersection of theory and practice. It is designed to work effectively for those professors adopting a "practice ready" approach, while ensuring those who approach the subject from a policy perspective also have sufficient structure and coverage to accomplish those goals as well.

I wish to extend my personal thanks to Ms. MaryAnn Jaghab and Ms. Stephanie Boussias, my research assistants. Our conversations in my office, your work in the library, and on the computer, have made this book much better than it would have otherwise been. It would have been impossible to bring this task to completion without you.

I do not pretend to have the answers to the many challenges facing the legal profession in the 21st century, but I am committed to searching for them. Drop me a line whenever you like and let me know how well we've met that goal. My email addresses are crose@law.stetson.edu and CHRoseIII@thetrialadvocate.com. Until I hear from you individually, I will continue to talk to you collectively. I hope that you enjoy the text and that it sparks within you an interest to become a lawyer that knows how to practice law, a lawyer capable of making a difference in the lives of his or her clients.

All the best,
Charles H. Rose III
December 2016

Dedication

"For Professor G. Robert Blakey — Your questions were the hammer that forged the steel of my understanding of constitutional criminal law. I will be forever grateful."

Excerpts from the Bill of Rights

The study of Federal Constitutional Criminal Law involves the application of the Bill of Rights (and occasionally relevant statutes) to specific situations. It would be remiss for us to begin our discussion without at least first reading those rights. They are provided here for you as a reference to which we will return through out the course of our study.

The Preamble to the Bill of Rights

Congress of the United States begun and held at the City of New York, on Wednesday the fourth of March, one thousand seven hundred and eighty-nine.

THE Conventions of a number of the States, having at the time of their adopting the Constitution, expressed a desire, in order to prevent misconstruction or abuse of its powers, that further declaratory and restrictive clauses should be added: And as extending the ground of public confidence in the Government, will best ensure the beneficent ends of its institution.

RESOLVED by the Senate and House of Representatives of the United States of America, in Congress assembled, two thirds of both Houses concurring, that the following Articles be proposed to the Legislatures of the several States, as Amendments to the Constitution of the United States, all, or any of which Articles, when ratified by three fourths of the said Legislatures, to be valid to all intents and purposes, as part of the said Constitution; viz.:

ARTICLES in addition to, and Amendment of the Constitution of the United States of America, proposed by Congress, and ratified by the Legislatures of the several States, pursuant to the fifth Article of the original Constitution.

Note: The following text is a transcription of the first ten amendments to the Constitution in their original form. These amendments were ratified December 15, 1791, and form what is known as the "Bill of Rights."

Amendment I

Congress shall make no law respecting an establishment of religion, or prohibiting the free exercise thereof; or abridging the freedom of speech, or of the press; or the right of the people peaceably to assemble, and to petition the Government for a redress of grievances.

Amendment II

A well regulated Militia, being necessary to the security of a free State, the right of the people to keep and bear Arms, shall not be infringed.

Amendment III

No Soldier shall, in time of peace be quartered in any house, without the consent of the Owner, nor in time of war, but in a manner to be prescribed by law.

Amendment IV

The right of the people to be secure in their persons, houses, papers, and effects, against unreasonable searches and seizures, shall not be violated, and no Warrants shall issue, but upon probable cause, supported by Oath or affirmation, and particularly describing the place to be searched, and the persons or things to be seized.

Amendment V

No person shall be held to answer for a capital, or otherwise infamous crime, unless on a presentment or indictment of a Grand Jury, except in cases arising in the land or naval forces, or in the Militia, when in actual service in time of War or public danger; nor shall any person be subject for the same offense to be twice put in jeopardy of life or limb; nor shall be compelled in any criminal case to be a witness against himself, nor be deprived of life, liberty, or property, without due process of law; nor shall private property be taken for public use, without just compensation.

Amendment VI

In all criminal prosecutions, the accused shall enjoy the right to a speedy and public trial, by an impartial jury of the State and district wherein the crime shall have been committed, which district shall have been previously ascertained by law, and to be informed of the nature and cause of the accusation; to be confronted with the witnesses against him; to have compulsory process for obtaining witnesses in his favor, and to have the Assistance of Counsel for his defense.

Amendment VII

In Suits at common law, where the value in controversy shall exceed twenty dollars, the right of trial by jury shall be preserved, and no fact tried by a jury, shall be otherwise re-examined in any Court of the United States, than according to the rules of the common law.

Amendment VIII

Excessive bail shall not be required, nor excessive fines imposed, nor cruel and unusual punishments inflicted.

Amendment IX

The enumeration in the Constitution, of certain rights, shall not be construed to deny or disparage others retained by the people.

Amendment X

The powers not delegated to the United States by the Constitution, nor prohibited by it to the States, are reserved to the States respectively, or to the people.

Introduction

This text is a practically organized, focused, and user-friendly casebook. Each chapter presents edited versions of the major cases in Federal Constitutional Criminal Law. We will read and analyze these cases together, and then discuss the holdings in light of police procedures, public policy, and jurisprudential philosophy.

My primary goal is to help you learn to evaluate the constitutional criminal issues presented in an appellate fashion and then create a practical process that you can use when practicing criminal law each and every day. From time to time, I will provide you with the types of materials and situations you will confront in practice. These real world scenarios are presented as discussion problems that put you in the shoes of the lawyer encountering the issue, making you decide what to do, and why.

To that end, we will use an approach that begins with reviewing the substantive law as developed through U.S. Supreme Court jurisprudence. Each case will be followed by a short statement of the black letter law. At the end of each section, you will find a set of discussion problems designed to develop your ability to apply the law to a specific set of facts. These problems are taken from actual cases and distinctly mirror the types of essay questions found on many exams, both during the bar and in class.

My goal is that by the time we have finished our study together you will not only know the law, but be able to apply it. This approach cross-references the skill of trial practice and constitutional criminal doctrine holistically — teaching substantive law by mirroring the way it is applied. We will deal with the same basic decisions routinely confronting practicing lawyers and judges in courts every day. To that end, let's begin by addressing a common set of facts without any prior knowledge about criminal procedure.

Consider the following introductory discussion problem and then draft a short memorandum addressing the issues raised in the call of the question.

Discussion Problem

Dan Diamond was traveling on a bus from Los Angeles to Washington D.C.. During the trip, the bus stopped for refueling at a Greyhound station. Investigator Boyer was at that Greyhound station performing drug interdiction duties. Investigator Boyer looked inside the bus's lower luggage compartments and found luggage displaying a baggage ticket with Diamond's name. He also discovered that Diamond had paid cash for his ticket on the day of travel. Investigator Boyer had law enforcement remove the luggage from the bus and take it to the rear baggage terminal.

Investigator Boyer, wearing jeans and a t-shirt displayed his badge, identified himself as a law enforcement officer, and informed Diamond he was not in trouble. Diamond then followed Investigator Boyer to a room where his luggage was being held. The room had two open doors, and one or two other officers were already inside the room. When Investigator Boyer sought permission to search the luggage, Diamond made an affirmative verbal response. During the search, Diamond claimed the luggage actually belonged to a friend. Law enforcement discovered bomb making materials and terrorist propaganda in the luggage.

Was the examination of Dan Diamond's luggage legal? Why?

Steps in Briefing a Supreme Court Case

The following seven steps should serve as a start point for students briefing the cases contained in this text. The goal is to provide a template for beginning the analytical process. These steps will get you started, your own abilities to analyze, synthesize and apply the law will bring you the rest of the way. I suggest you apply these steps in preparation for our class discussions.

1. Identify the Parties and their posture
2. Identify relevant facts: Sometimes, particularly in 4th Amendment cases, the most seemingly insignificant facts will decide the case.
3. Identify the issue(s) with specificity: What question does the Court claim to answer & do they answer it?
4. Does the case provide or apply a rule of law: What is the constitutional rule or court announced rule that applies to the facts? Is it coherent? Complete?
5. Case Analysis: What was the Court's holding? How many justices agreed with the opinion? What was the rationale that the Court used to reach its conclusion? What theoretical construct did the Court create or refer to in reaching its decision?
6. Results of the decision: Who Won?
7. Consider the Dissenting and Concurring Opinions: (There will be one or many in virtually every case.) How do these opinions articulate the case holding? What facts do they emphasize that the majority ignores? What is the theoretical basis for their opinion? Are they truer to the Court's precedent or to the language of the Constitution? What danger's do they predict for the future?

This general template will ensure that you are on the right path to understanding the development of Supreme Court jurisprudence as you analyze each individual case. Once you understand how to extract the relevant law from each case you then need to be able to place the law contextually in the overall development of the particular constitutional right(s) addressed by the case.

Chapter 1: The Exclusionary Rule

Weeks v. United States

34 S.Ct. 341

Fremont Weeks

v.

United States

No. 461. | Argued and submitted December 2 and 3, 1913. | Decided February 24, 1914.

***386** Mr. Justice Day delivered the opinion of the court:

An indictment was returned against the plaintiff in error, defendant below, and herein so designated, in the District Court of the United States for the Western District of Missouri, containing nine counts. The seventh count, upon which a conviction was had, charged the use of the mails for the purpose of transporting certain coupons or tickets representing chances or shares in a lottery or gift enterprise, in violation of §213 of the Criminal Code.[1] Sentence of fine and imprisonment was imposed. This writ of error is to review that judgment.

The defendant was arrested by a police officer, so far as the record shows, without warrant, at the Union Station in Kansas City, Missouri, where he was employed by an express company. Other police officers had gone to the house of the defendant, and after being told by a neighbor where the key was kept, found it and entered the house. They searched the defendant's room and took possession of various papers and articles found there, which were afterwards turned over to the United States marshal. Later in the same day, police officers returned with the marshal, whom they thought he might find additional evidence. Being admitted by someone in the house, probably a boarder, in response to a rap, the marshal searched the defendant's room and carried away certain letters and envelops found in the drawer of a chiffonier. Neither the marshal nor the police officer had a search warrant.

***387** The defendant filed in the cause before the time for trial the following petition:

Petition to Return Private Papers, Books, and Other Property.

Now comes defendant and states that he is a citizen and resident of Kansas City, Missouri, and that he resides, owns, and occupies a home at 1834 Penn Street in said city:

That on the 21st day of December, 1911, while plaintiff was absent at his daily vocation, certain officers of the government whose names are to plaintiff unknown, unlawfully and without warrant or authority so to do, broke open the door to plaintiff's said home and seized all of his books, letters, money, papers, notes, evidences of indebtedness, stock, certificates, insurance policies, deeds, abstracts, and other muniments of title, bonds, candies, clothes, and other property in said home, and this in violation of §§ 11 and 23 to the Constitution of Missouri, and of the 4th and 5th Amendments to the Constitution of the United States;

That the district attorney, marshal, and clerk of the United States court for the Western District of Missouri took the above-described property so seized into their possession, and have failed and refused to return to defendant portion of same, to wit:

[1] *35 Stat. at L. 1129, chap. 321, U. S. Comp. Stat. Supp. 1911, p. 1652.*

One (1) leather grip, value about $7; one (1) tin box valued at $3; one (1) Pettis County, Missouri, bond, value $500; three (3) mining stock certificates which defendant is unable to more particularly describe, valued at $12,000; and certain stock certificates in addition thereto, issued by the San Domingo Mining, Loan, & Investment Company; about $75 in currency; one (1) newspaper published about 1790, an heirloom; and certain other property which plaintiff is now unable to describe.

That said property is being unlawfully and improperly ***388** held by said district attorney, marshal, and clerk, in violation of defendant's rights under the Constitution of the United States and the state of Missouri.

That said district attorney purposes to use said books, letters, papers, certificates of stock, etc., at the trial of the above-entitled cause, and that by reason thereof and of the facts above set forth defendant's rights under the amendments aforesaid to the Constitution of Missouri and the United States have been and will be violated unless the court order the return prayed for;

Wherefore, defendant prays that said district attorney, marshal, and clerk be notified, and that the court direct and order said district attorney, marshal, and clerk, to return said property to said defendant.

Upon consideration of the petition, the court entered in the cause an order directing the return of such property as was not pertinent to the charge against the defendant, but denied the petition as to pertinent matter, reserving the right to pass upon the pertinency at a later time. In obedience to the order, the district attorney returned part of the property taken and retained the remainder, concluding a list of the latter with the statement that, "all of which last above described property is to be used in evidence in the trial of the ****343** above-entitled cause, and pertains to the alleged sale of lottery tickets of the company above named."

After the jury had been sworn and before any evidence had been given, the defendant again urged his petition for the return of his property, which was denied by the court. Upon the introduction of such papers during the trial, the defendant objected on the ground that the papers had been obtained without a search warrant, and by breaking open his home, in violation of the 4th and 5th Amendments to the Constitution of the United States, which objection was overruled by the court. Among the papers retained and put in evidence were a number of ***389** lottery tickets and statements with reference to the lottery, taken at the first visit of the police to the defendant's room, and a number of letters written to the defendant in respect to the lottery, taken by the marshal upon his search of defendant's room.

The defendant assigns error, among other things, in the court's refusal to grant his petition for the return of his property and in permitting the papers to be used at the trial.

It is thus apparent that the question presented involves the determination of the duty of the court with reference to the motion made by the defendant for the return of certain letters, as well as other papers, taken from his room by the United States marshal, tending to show his guilt. The United States Marshall, who, without authority of process(if any such could have been legally issued), visited the room of the defendant for the declared purpose of obtaining additional testimony to support the charge against the accused, and, having gained admission to the house, took from the drawer of a chiffonier there found certain letters written to the defendant. These letters were placed in the control of the district attorney and were subsequently produced by him and offered in evidence against the accused at the trial. The defendant contends that such appropriation of his private correspondence was in violation of rights secured to him by the 4th and 5th Amendments to the Constitution of the United States. We shall deal with the 4th Amendment, which provides:

"The right of the people to be secure in their persons, houses, papers, and effects, against unreasonable searches and seizures, shall not be violated, and no warrants shall issue but upon probable cause, supported by oath or affirmation, and particularly describing the place to be searched, and the persons or things to be seized."

The history of this Amendment is given with particularity in the opinion of Mr. Justice Bradley, speaking for ***390** the court in *Boyd v. United States*[2]. As was there shown, the 4th Amendment took its origin in the determination of the framers of the Amendments to provide for that instrument a Bill of Rights, securing to the American people, among other things, those safeguards which had grown up in England to protect the people from unreasonable searches and seizures. Such practices were permitted under the general warrants issued under authority of the government, by which there had been invasions of the home and privacy of the citizens, and the seizure of their private papers in support of charges, real or imaginary, made against them. Such practices had also received sanction under warrants and seizures in the so-called writs of assistance, issued in the American colonies.

Resistance to these practices had established the principle which was enacted into the fundamental law in the 4th Amendment — that a man's house was his castle, and not to be invaded by any general authority to search and seize his goods and papers. Judge Cooley, in his Constitutional Limitations,[3] said, in treating of this feature of our Constitution, "the maxim that 'every man's house is his castle' is made a part of our constitutional law in the clauses prohibiting unreasonable searches and seizures, and has always been looked upon as of high value to the citizen." 'Accordingly,' says Lieber in his work On Civil Liberty and Self-Government[4], speaking of the English law in this respect, "no man's house can be forcibly opened, or he or his goods be carried away after it has thus been forced, except in cases of felony; and then the sheriff must be furnished with a warrant, and take great care lest he commit a trespass. This principle is jealously insisted upon." In Ex parte Jackson,[5] this court recognized the principle of protection as applicable to letters and sealed packages in the mail, and held that, consistently ***391** with this guaranty of the right of the people to be secure in their papers against unreasonable searches and seizures, such matter could only be opened and examined upon warrants issued on oath or affirmation, particularly describing the thing to be seized, "as is required when papers are subjected to search in one's own household."

In *Boyd*, after citing Lord Camden's judgment in *Entick v. Carrington*,[6] Mr. Justice Bradley said:

> "The principles laid down in this opinion affect the very essence of constitutional liberty and security. They reach farther ****344** than the concrete form of the case then before the court, with its adventitious circumstances; they apply to all invasions on the part of the government and its employees of the sanctity of a man's home and the privacies of life. It is not the breaking of his doors and the rummaging of his drawers that constitutes the essence of the offense; but it is the invasion of his indefeasible right of personal security, personal liberty, and private property, where that right has never been forfeited by his conviction of some public offense, it is the invasion of this sacred right which underlies and constitutes the essence of Lord Camden's judgment."

In Bram v. United States,[7], this court, in speaking by the present Chief Justice of Boyd's case, dealing with the 4th and 5th Amendments, said:

---

[2] 116 U. S. 616, 29 L. ed. 746, 6 Sup. Ct. Rep. 524.

[3] Thomas M. Cooley, *A Treatise on the Constitutional Limitations Which Rest Upon the Legislative Power of the States of the American Union* 425-426 (1868).

[4] Francis Lieber, *On Civil Liberty and Self-Government* 62 (1853).

[5] 96 U. S. 727, 733, 24 L. ed. 877, 879.

[6] 19 How. St. Tr. 1029 (630)

[7] 168 U. S. 532, 42 L. ed. 568, 18 Sup. Ct. Rep. 183, 10 Am. Crim. Rep. 547, 544

"It was in that case demonstrated that both of these Amendments contemplated perpetuating, in their full efficacy, by means of a constitutional provision, principles of humanity and civil liberty which had been secured in the mother country only after years of struggle, so as to implant them in our institutions in the fullness of their integrity, free from the possibilities of future legislative change."

The effect of the 4th Amendment is to put the courts ***392** of the United States and Federal officials, in the exercise of their power and authority, under limitations and restraints as to the exercise of such power and authority, and to forever secure the people, their persons, houses, papers, and effects, against all unreasonable searches and seizures under the guise of law. This protection reaches all alike, whether accused of crime or not, and the duty of giving to it force and effect is obligatory upon all entrusted under our Federal system with the enforcement of the laws. The tendency of those who execute the criminal laws of the country to obtain conviction by means of unlawful seizures and enforced confessions, the latter often obtained after subjecting accused persons to unwarranted practices destructive of rights secured by the Federal Constitution, should find no sanction in the judgments of the courts, which are charged at all times with the support of the Constitution, and to which people of all conditions have a right to appeal for the maintenance of such fundamental rights.

What, then, is the present case? Before answering that inquiry specifically, it may be well by a process of exclusion to state what it is not. It is not an assertion of the right on the part of the government always recognized under English and American law, to search the person of the accused when legally arrested, to discover and seize the fruits or evidences of crime. This right has been uniformly maintained in many cases.[8] Nor is it the case of testimony offered at a trial where the court is asked to stop and consider the illegal means by which proofs, otherwise competent, were obtained, of which we shall have occasion to treat later in this opinion. Nor is it the case of burglar's tools or other proofs of guilt found upon his arrest within his control.

***393** The case in the aspect in which we are dealing with it involves the right of the court in a criminal prosecution to retain for the purposes of evidence the letters and correspondence of the accused, seized in his house in his absence and without his authority, by a United States marshal holding no warrant for his arrest and none for the search of his premises. The accused, without awaiting his trial, made timely application to the court for an order for the return of these letters, as well or other property. This application was denied, the letters retained and put in evidence, after a further application at the beginning of the trial, both applications asserting the rights of the accused under the 4th and 5th Amendments to the Constitution. If letters and private documents can thus be seized and held and used in evidence against a citizen accused of an offense, the protection of the 4th Amendment, declaring his right to be secure against such searches and seizures, is of no value, and, so far as those thus placed are concerned, might as well be stricken from the Constitution. The efforts of the courts and their officials to bring the guilty to punishment, praiseworthy as they are, are not to be aided by the sacrifice of those great principles established be years of endeavor and suffering which have resulted in their embodiment in the fundamental law of the land. The United States Marshal could only have invaded the house of the accused when armed with a warrant issued as required by the Constitution, upon sworn information, and describing with reasonable particularity the thing for which the search was to be made. Instead, he acted without sanction of law, doubtlessly prompted by the desire to bring further proof to the aid of the government, and under color of his office undertook to make a seizure of private papers in direct violation of the constitutional prohibition against such action.

---

[8] 1 Bishop. Crim. Proc. § 211; Wharton, Crim. Pl. & Pr. 8th ed. § 60; *Dillon v. O'Brien*, 16 Cox, C. C. 245, I. R. L. R. 20 C. L. 300, 7 Am. Crim. Rep. 66.

Under such circumstances, without sworn information and particular description, not **345 even an order of court would *394 have justified such procedure, much less was it within the authority of the United States marshal to thus invade the house and privacy of the accused. In *Adams v. New York*,[9] this court said that the 4th Amendment was intended to secure the citizen in person and property against unlawful invasion of the sanctity of his home by officers of the law, acting under legislative or judicial sanction. This protection is equally extended to the action of the government and officers of the law acting under it.[10]To sanction such proceedings would be to affirm by judicial decision a manifest neglect, if not an open defiance, of the prohibitions of the Constitution, intended for the protection of the people against such unauthorized action.

The court before which the application was made in this case recognized the illegal character of the seizure, and ordered the return of property not in its judgment competent to be offered at the trial, but refused the application of the accused to turn over the letters, which were afterwards put in evidence on behalf of the government. While there is no opinion in the case, the court in this proceeding doubtlessly relied upon what is now contended by the government to be the correct rule of law under such circumstances, that the letters having come into the control of the court, it would not inquire into the manner in which they were obtained, but, if competent, would keep them and permit their use in evidence. Such proposition, the government asserts, is conclusively established by certain decisions of this court, the first of which is *Adams v. New York*. In that case, the plaintiff in error had been convicted in the supreme court of the state of New York for having in his possession certain gambling paraphernalia used in the game known as policy, in violation of the Penal Code of New York.

At the trial certain papers, which had been seized by police officers executing a search warrant for the discovery and *395 seizure of policy slips, and which had been found in addition to the policy slips, were offered in evidence over his objection. The conviction was affirmed by the court of appeals of New York[11], and the case was brought here for alleged violation of the 4th and 5th Amendments to the Constitution of the United States. Pretermitting the question whether these Amendments applied to the action of the states, this court proceeded to examine the alleged violations of the 4th and 5th Amendments, and put its decision upon the ground that the papers found in the execution of the search warrant, which the warrant had a legal purpose in the attempt to find gambling paraphernalia, was competent evidence against the accused, and their offer in testimony did not violate his constitutional privilege against unlawful search or seizure, for is was held that such incriminatory documents thus discovered were not the subject of an unreasonable search and seizure, and in effect that the same were incidentally seized in the lawful execution of a warrant, and not in the wrongful invasion of the home of a citizen, and the unwarranted seizure of his papers and property. It was further held, approving in that respect the doctrine laid down in *1 Greenleaf, Ev. § 254a*, that it was no valid objection to the use of the papers that they had been thus seized, and that the courts in the course of a trial would not make an issue to determine that question, and many state cases were cited supporting that doctrine.

The same point had been ruled in *People v. Adams*,[12] from which decision the case was brought to this court, where it was held that if the papers seized in addition to the policy slips were competent evidence in the case, as the court held they were, they were admissible in evidence at the trial, the court saying:

---

[9] 192 U. S. 585, 48 L. ed. 575, 24 Sup. Ct. Rep. 372

[10] Boyd Case, 116 U. S. 616, 29 L. ed. 746, 6 Sup. Ct. Rep. 524.

[11] (176 N. Y. 351, 63 L.R.A. 406, 98 Am. St. Rep. 675, 68 N. E. 636)

[12] 176 N. Y. 351, 63 L.R.A. 406, 98 Am. St. Rep. 675, 68 N. E. 636

"The underlying principle obviously is that the court, when engaged in trying a criminal cause, will not take notice of ***396** the manner in which witnesses have possessed themselves of papers, or other articles of personal property, which are material and properly offered in evidence."[13] This doctrine thus laid down by the New York Court of Appeals and approved by this court, that a court will not, in trying a criminal cause, permit a collateral issue to be raised as to the source of competent testimony, has the sanction of so many state cases that it would be impracticable to cite or refer to them in detail. Many of them are collected in the note to *State v. Turner*.[14]After citing numerous cases the editor says: "The underlying principle of all these decisions obviously is, that the court, when engaged in the trial of a criminal action, will not take notice of the manner in which a witness has possessed himself of papers or other chattels, subjects of evidence, which are material and properly offered in evidence.'"[15]

"Such an investigation is not involved necessarily in the litigation in chief, and to pursue it would be to halt in the orderly progress of a cause, and consider incidentally a ****346** question which has happened to cross the path of such litigation, and which is wholly independent thereof."

It is therefore evident that the *Adams* case affords no authority for the action of the court in this case, when applied to in due season for the return of papers seized in violation of the Constitutional Amendment. The decision in that case rests upon incidental seizure made in the execution of a legal warrant, and in the application of the doctrine that a collateral issue will not be raised to ascertain the source from which testimony, competent in a criminal case, comes.

The government also relies upon *Hale v. Henkel*,[16] in which the previous cases of Boyd v. United States, *Adams v. New York*, ***397** *Interstate Commerce Commission v. Brimson*, [17] and *Interstate Commerce Commission v. Baird*,[18] are reviewed, and wherein it was held that a subpoena duces tecum requiring a corporation to produce all its contracts and correspondence with no less than six other companies, as well as all letters received by the corporation from thirteen other companies, located in different parts of the United States, was an unreasonable search and seizure within the 4th Amendment, and it was there stated that"an order for the production of books and papers may constitute an unreasonable search and seizure within the 4th Amendment. While a search ordinarily implies a quest by an officer of the law, and a seizure contemplates a forcible dispossession of the owner, still, as was held in Boyd, the substance of the offense is the compulsory production of private papers, whether under a search warrant or a subpoena duces tecum, against which the person, be he individual or corporation, is entitled to protection."[19] If such a seizure under the authority of a warrant supposed to be legal, constitutes a violation of the constitutional protection, a fortiori does the attempt of an officer of the United States, the United States Marshal, acting under color of his office, without even the sanction of a warrant, constitute an invasion of the rights within the protection afforded by the 4th Amendment.

Another case relied upon is *American Tobacco Co. v. Werckmeister*,[20] in which it was held that the seizure by the United States Marshal in a copyright case of certain pictures under a writ of replevin did not constitute an unreasonable search and

---

[13]Id. at 358.

[14] 136 Am. St. Rep. 129, 135 et seq.

[15] *People v. Adams, supra.*

[16] 201 U. S. 43, 50 L. ed. 652, 26 Sup. Ct. Rep. 370

[17] 154 U. S. 447, 38 L. ed. 1047, 4 Inters. Com. Rep. 545, 14 Sup. Ct. Rep. 1125

[18] 194 U. S. 25, 48 L. ed. 860, 24 Sup. Ct. Rep. 563

[19] (p. 76)

[20] 207 U. S. 284, 52 L. ed. 208, 28 Sup. Ct. Rep. 72, 12 Ann. Cas. 595

seizure. The other case from this court relied upon is *Holt v. United States*,[21] in which it was held that testimony tending to show that a certain blouse which was in evidence as incriminating him, had been put upon the prisoner, and fitted him, did not violate his constitutional right. We ***398** are at a loss to see the application of these cases to the one in hand.

The right of the court to deal with papers and documents in the possession of the district attorney and other officers of thc court, and subject to its authority, was recognized in *Wise v. Henkel*[22]. That papers wrongfully seized should be turned over to the accused has been frequently recognized in the early as well as later decisions of the courts.[23] We therefore reach the conclusion that the letters in question were taken from the house of the accused by an official of the United States, acting under color of his office, in direct violation of the constitutional rights of the defendant; that having made a seasonable application for their return, which was heard and passed upon by the court, there was involved in the order refusing the application a denial of the constitutional rights of the accused, and that the court should have restored these letters to the accused. In holding them and permitting their use upon the trial, we think prejudicial error was committed. As to the papers and property seized by the policemen, it does not appear that they acted under any claim of Federal authority such as would make the amendment applicable to such unauthorized seizures. The record shows that what they did by way of arrest and search and seizure was done before the finding of the indictment in the federal court; under what supposed right or authority does not appear. What remedies the defendant may have against them we need not inquire, as the 4th Amendment is not directed to individual misconduct of such officials. Its limitations reach the federal government and its agencies.[24] ***399** It results that the judgment of the court below must be reversed, and the case remanded for further proceedings in accordance with this opinion.

Reversed.

Black Letter Law

An accused's Fourth Amendment right to be free from unreasonable searches and seizures was violated when the Court refused to grant his petition for return of letters and papers, which were seized in his home by a United States Marshal without a valid warrant, and allowed these items to be used as evidence against him at his trial. Established the Exclusionary Rule.

[21] 218 U. S. 245, 54 L. ed. 1021, 31 Sup. Ct. Rep. 20, 20 Ann. Cas. 1138

[22] 220 U. S. 556, 55 L. ed. 581, 31 Sup. Ct. Rep. 599

[23] 1 Bishop, Crim. Proc. § 210; Rex v. Barnett, 3 Car. & P. 600; Rex v. Kinsey, 7 Car. & P. 447; United States v. Mills, 185 Fed. 318; United States v. McHie, 194 Fed. 894, 898.

[24] Boyd Case, 116 U. S. 616, 29 L. ed. 746, 6 Sup. Ct. Rep. 524, and see Twining v. New Jersey, 211 U. S. 78, 53 L. ed. 97, 29 Sup. Ct. Rep. 14.

Mapp v. Ohio

81 S.Ct. 1684

Mapp

V.

Ohio

No. 236. | Argued March 29, 1961. | Decided June 19, 1961. | Rehearing Denied Oct. 9, 1961.

Mr. Justice CLARK delivered the opinion of the Court.

Appellant stands convicted of knowingly having had in her possession and under her control certain lewd and lascivious books, pictures, and photographs in violation of §2905.34 of Ohio's Revised Code. As officially stated in the syllabus to its opinion, the Supreme Court of Ohio found that her conviction was valid though "based primarily upon the introduction in evidence of lewd and lascivious books and pictures unlawfully seized during an unlawful search of defendant's home * * *."[25]

***644** On May 23, 1957, three Cleveland police officers arrived at appellant's residence in that city pursuant to information that 'a person (was) hiding out in the home, who was wanted for questioning in connection with a recent bombing, and that there was a large amount of policy paraphernalia being hidden in the home.' Miss Mapp and her daughter by a former marriage lived on the top floor of the two-family dwelling. Upon their arrival at that house, the officers knocked on the door and demanded entrance but appellant, after telephoning her attorney, refused to admit them without a search warrant. They advised their headquarters of the situation and undertook a surveillance of the house.

The officers again sought entrance some three hours later when four or more additional officers arrived on the ****1686** scene. When Miss Mapp did not come to the door immediately, at least one of the several doors to the house was forcibly opened and the policemen gained admittance. Meanwhile, Miss Mapp's attorney arrived, but the officers, having secured their own entry, and continuing in their defiance of the law, would not permit him to see Miss Mapp nor to enter the house. It appears that Miss Mapp was halfway down the stairs from the upper floor to the front door when the officers, in this highhanded manner, broke into the hall. She demanded to see the search warrant. A paper, claimed to be a warrant, was held up by one of the officers. She grabbed the 'warrant' and placed it in her bosom. A struggle ensued in which the officers recovered the piece of paper and as a result of which they handcuffed appellant because she had been 'belligerent' ***645** in resisting their official rescue of the 'warrant' from her person. Running roughshod over appellant, a policeman 'grabbed' her, "twisted (her) hand," and she "yelled [and] pleaded with him" because "it was hurting." Appellant, in handcuffs, was then forcibly taken upstairs to her bedroom where the officers searched a dresser, a chest of drawers, a closet, and some suitcases. They also looked in a photo album and through personal papers belonging to the appellant. The search spread to the rest of the second floor including the child's bedroom, the living room, the kitchen, and a dinette. The basement of the building and a trunk found therein were also searched. The obscene materials for possession of which she was ultimately convicted were discovered in the course of that widespread search.

At the trial no search warrant was produced by the prosecution, nor was the failure to produce one explained or accounted for. At best, "There is, in the record, considerable doubt as to whether there ever was any warrant for the search of defendant's home."[26] The Ohio Supreme Court believed a 'reasonable argument' could be made that the conviction should be reversed "because the 'methods' employed to

---

[25] 170 Ohio St. 427—428, 166 N.E.2d 387, 388.

[26] 170 Ohio St. at page 430, 166 N.E.2d at page 389.

obtain the (evidence) were such as to 'offend 'a sense of justice,' but the court found determinative the fact that the evidence had not been taken 'from defendant's person by the use of brutal or offensive physical force against defendant."[27] The State says that even if the search were made without authority, or otherwise unreasonably, it is not prevented from using the unconstitutionally seized evidence at trial, citing *Wolf v. People of State of Colorado*[28], in which this Court did indeed hold "that in a prosecution in a State court for a State crime the Fourteenth Amendment ***646** does not forbid the admission of evidence obtained by an unreasonable search and seizure." On this appeal, of which we have noted probable jurisdiction[29], it is urged once again that we review that holding.

I.

Seventy-five years ago, in *Boyd v. United States*[30], considering the ****1687** Fourth and Fifth Amendments as running 'almost into each other' on the facts before it, this Court held that the doctrines of those Amendments' apply to all invasions on the part of the government and its employees of the sanctity of a man's home and the privacies of life. It is not the breaking of his doors and the rummaging of his drawers ***647** that constitutes the essence of the offense; but it is the invasion of his indefeasible right of personal security, personal liberty, and private property * * *. Breaking into a house and opening boxes and drawers are circumstances of aggravation; but any forcible and compulsory extortion of a man's own testimony or of his private papers to be used as evidence to convict him of crime or to forfeit his goods, is within the condemnation * * * (of those Amendments). The Court noted that constitutional provisions for the security of person and property should be liberally construed. * * * It is the duty of courts to be watchful for the constitutional rights of the citizen, and against any stealthy encroachments thereon.

In this jealous regard for maintaining the integrity of individual rights, the Court gave life to Madison's prediction that 'independent tribunals of justice * * * will be naturally led to resist every encroachment upon rights expressly stipulated for in the Constitution by the declaration of rights.'[31]Concluding, the Court specifically referred to the use of the evidence there seized as 'unconstitutional.'[32]

Less than 30 years after *Boyd*, this Court, in *Weeks v. United States*,[33] stated 'the 4th Amendment * * * put the courts of the United States and Federal officials, in the exercise of their power and authority, under limitations and restraints (and) * * * forever secure(d) the people, their persons, houses, papers, and effects, against all unreasonable searches and seizures under the guise of law * * * and the duty of giving it force and effect is obligatory upon all entrusted under our Federal system with the enforcement of the laws.'

***648** Specifically dealing with the use of the evidence unconstitutionally seized, the Court concluded:

> 'If letters and private documents can thus be seized and held and used in evidence against a citizen accused of an offense, the protection of the Fourth Amendment declaring his right to be secure against such searches and seizures is of no value, and, so far as those thus placed are concerned, might as well be stricken ****1688** from the Constitution. The efforts of the courts and their officials to bring the guilty to punishment,

---

[27] 170 Ohio St. at page 431, 166 N.E.2d at pages 389—390.

[28] 1949, 338 U.S. 25, at page 33, 69 S.Ct. 1359. at page 1364, 93 L.Ed. 1782.

[29] 364 U.S. 868, 81 S.Ct. 111, 5 L.Ed.2d 90

[30] 1886, 116 U.S. 616, 630, 6 S.Ct. 524, 532, 29 L.Ed. 746.

[31] I Annals of Cong. 439 (1789).

[32] At page 638 of 116 U.S., at page 536 of 6 S.Ct.

[33] 1914, 232 U.S. 383, at pages 391—392, 34 S.Ct. 341, at page 344, 58 L.Ed. 652

praiseworthy as they are, are not to be aided by the sacrifice of those great principles established by years of endeavor and suffering which have resulted in their embodiment in the fundamental law of the land.'[34]

Finally, the Court in that case clearly stated that use of the seized evidence involved 'a denial of the constitutional rights of the accused.'[35]Thus, in the year 1914, in the *Weeks* case, this Court 'for the first time' held that 'in a federal prosecution the Fourth Amendment barred the use of evidence secured through an illegal search and seizure.'[36]This Court has ever since required of federal law officers a strict adherence to that command which this Court has held to be a clear, specific, and constitutionally required—even if judicially implied—deterrent safeguard without insistence upon which the Fourth Amendment would have been reduced to 'a form of words.'[37]It meant, quite simply, that 'conviction by means of unlawful seizures and enforced confessions * * * should find no sanction in the judgments of the courts * * *,'[38], and that such evidence 'shall not be used at all.'[39]

***649** There are, in the cases of this Court, some passing references to the Weeks rule as being one of evidence. But the plain and unequivocal language of Weeks—and its later paraphrase in *Wolf*—to the effect that the *Weeks* rule is of constitutional origin, remains entirely undisturbed. In *Byars v. United States,*[40] a unanimous Court declared that evidences of crime discovered by a federal officer, in making a search without lawful warrant, may not be used against the victim of the unlawful search where a timely challenge has been interposed.' (Emphasis added.) The Court, in *Olmstead v. United States,*[41]in unmistakable language, restated the *Weeks* rule:

'The striking outcome of the *Weeks* case and those which followed it was the sweeping declaration that the Fourth Amendment, although not referring to or limiting the use of evidence in court, really forbade its introduction if obtained by government officers through a violation of the amendment.'

In *McNabb v. United States,*[42]we note this statement:

'(A) conviction in the federal courts, the foundation of which is evidence obtained in disregard of liberties deemed fundamental by the Constitution, cannot stand.[43] And this Court has, on Constitutional grounds, set aside convictions, both in the federal and state courts, which were based upon confessions 'secured by protracted and repeated questioning of ignorant and untutored persons, in whose minds the power of officers was greatly magnified' ***650** * * * or 'who have been unlawfully held incommunicado without advice of friends or counsel' * * *.'

Significantly, in *McNabb*, the Court did then pass on to formulate a rule of evidence, saying, '(i)n the view we take of ****1689** the case, however, it becomes unnecessary to reach the Constitutional issue (for) * * * (t)he principles governing the admissibility of evidence in federal criminal trials have not been restricted * * * to those derived solely from the Constitution.'[44]

[34] At page 393 of 232 U.S., at page 344 of 34 S.Ct.

[35] At page 398 of 232 U.S., at page 346 of 34 S.Ct.

[36] *Wolf v. People of State of Colorado*, supra, 338 U.S. at page 28, 69 S.Ct. at page 1361.

[37] *Holmes J., Silverthorne Lumber Co. v. United States*, 1920, 251 U.S. 385, 392, 40 S.Ct. 182, 183, 64 L.Ed. 319.

[38] *Weeks v. United States*, supra, 232 U.S. at page 392, 34 S.Ct. at page 344

[39] *Silverthorne Lumber Co. v. United States*, supra, 251 U.S. at page 392, 40 S.Ct. at page 183.

[40] 1927, 273 U.S. 28, at pages 29—30, 47 S.Ct. 248, at pages 248—249, 71 L.Ed. 520

[41] 1928, 277 U.S. 438, at page 462, 48 S.Ct. 564, 567, 72 L.Ed. 944

[42] 1943, 318 U.S. 332, at pages 339—340, 63 S.Ct. 608, at page 612, 87 L.Ed. 819

[43] Boyd v. United States * * * Weeks v. United States * * *.

[44] At pages 340—341 of 318 U.S., at page 613 of 63 S.Ct.

II.

In 1949, 35 years after *Weeks* was announced, this Court, in *Wolf v. People of State of Colorado*,[45] again for the first time, discussed the effect of the Fourth Amendment upon the States through the operation of the Due Process Clause of the Fourteenth Amendment. It said:

'(W)e have no hesitation in saying that were a State affirmatively to sanction such police incursion into privacy it would run counter to the guaranty of the Fourteenth Amendment.'[46]Nevertheless, after declaring that the 'security of one's privacy against arbitrary intrusion by the police' is 'implicit in 'the concept of ordered liberty' and as such enforceable against the States through the Due Process Clause,'[47]and announcing that it 'stoutly adhere(d)' to the *Weeks* decision, the Court decided that the *Weeks* exclusionary rule would not then be imposed upon the States as 'an essential ingredient of the right.'[48] The Court's reasons for not considering essential to the ***651** right to privacy, as a curb imposed upon the States by the Due Process Clause, that which decades before had been posited as part and parcel of the Fourth Amendment's limitations upon federal encroachment of individual privacy, were bottomed on factual considerations.

While they are not basically relevant to a decision that the exclusionary rule is an essential ingredient of the Fourth Amendment as the right it embodies is vouchsafed against the States by the Due Process Clause, we will consider the current validity of the factual grounds upon which Wolf was based.

The Court in *Wolf* first stated that '(t)he contrariety of views of the States' on the adoption of the exclusionary rule of *Weeks* was 'particularly impressive'[49]; and, in this connection that it could not 'brush aside the experience of States which deem the incidence of such conduct by the police too slight to call for a deterrent remedy * * * by overriding the (States') relevant rules of evidence.'[50] While in 1949, prior to the *Wolf* case, almost two-thirds of the States were opposed to the use of the exclusionary rule, now, despite the *Wolf* case, more than half of those since passing upon it, by their own legislative or judicial decision, have wholly or partly adopted or adhered to the Weeks rule.[51]Significantly, among those now following the rule is California, which, according to its highest court, was 'compelled to reach that conclusion because other remedies have completely failed to secure compliance with the constitutional provisions * * *.'[52] In connection with this California case, we note that the second basis elaborated in *Wolf* in support of its failure to enforce the exclusionary doctrine against the States was that 'other means of protection' have been afforded ****1690** 'the ***652** right to privacy.'[53]The experience of California that such other remedies have been worthless and futile is buttressed by the experience of other States. The obvious futility of relegating the Fourth Amendment of the protection of other remedies has, moreover, been ***653** recognized by this Court since Wolf.[54]

---

[45] *supra.*

[46] At page 28 of 338 U.S., at page 1361 of 69 S.Ct.

[47] cf. Palko v. State of Connecticut, 1937, 302 U.S. 319, 58 S.Ct. 149, 82 L.Ed. 288

[48] 338 U.S. at pages 27—29, 69 S.Ct. at page 1362.

[49] 338 U.S. at page 29, 69 S.Ct. at page 1362.

[50]At pages 31—32 of 338 U.S., at page 1363 of 69 S.Ct.

[51]See Elkins v. United States, 1960, 364 U.S. 206, Appendix, at pages 224—232, 80 S.Ct. 1437, at pages 1448—1453, 4 L.Ed.2d 1669.

[52]People v. Cahan, 1955, 44 Cal.2d 434, 445, 282 P.2d 905, 911, 50 A.L.R.2d 513.

[53] 7 338 U.S. at page 30, 69 S.Ct. at page 1362.

[54] See Irvine v. People of State of California, 1954, 347 U.S. 128, 137, 74 S.Ct. 381, 385, 98 L.Ed. 561.

Likewise, time has set its face against what Wolf called the 'weighty testimony' of *People v. Defore*.[55] There, Justice (then Judge) Cardozo, rejecting adoption of the *Weeks* exclusionary rule in New York, said that '(t)he Federal rule as it stands is either too strict or too lax.'[56] However, the force of that reasoning has been largely vitiated by later decisions of this Court. These include the recent discarding of the 'silver platter' doctrine which allowed federal judicial use of evidence seized in violation of the Constitution by state agents, *Elkins v. United States*;[57] the relaxation of the formerly strict requirements as to standing to challenge the use of evidence thus seized, so that now the procedure of exclusion, 'ultimately referable to constitutional safeguards,' is available to anyone even 'legitimately on (the) premises' unlawfully searched;[58] and finally, the formulation of a method to prevent state use of evidence unconstitutionally seized by federal agents.[59]Because there can be no fixed formula, we are admittedly met with 'recurring questions of the reasonableness of searches,' but less is not to be expected when dealing with a Constitution, and, at any rate, '(r)easonableness is in the first instance for the (trial court) to determine.' ****1691**[60]

It, therefore, plainly appears that the factual considerations supporting the failure of the *Wolf* Court to include the *Weeks* exclusionary rule when it recognized the enforceability of the right to privacy against the States in 1949, while not basically relevant to the constitutional consideration, could not, in any analysis, now be deemed controlling.

***654 III.**

Some five years after *Wolf*, in answer to a plea made here Term after Term that we overturn its doctrine on applicability of the *Weeks* exclusionary rule, this Court indicated that such should not be done until the States had 'adequate opportunity to adopt or reject the (*Weeks*) rule.'[61]There again it was said:

'Never until June of 1949 did this Court hold the basic search-and-seizure prohibition in any way applicable to the states under the Fourteenth Amendment.'[62]

And only last Term, after again carefully re-examining the *Wolf* doctrine in *Elkins v. United States*,[63] the Court pointed out that 'the controlling principles' as to search and seizure and the problem of admissibility 'seemed clear'[64] until the announcement in *Wolf* 'that the Due Process Clause of the Fourteenth Amendment does not itself require state courts to adopt the exclusionary rule' of the *Weeks* case.[65] At the same time, the Court pointed out, 'the underlying constitutional doctrine which *Wolf* established * * * that the Federal Constitution * * * prohibits unreasonable searches and seizures by state officers' had undermined the 'foundation upon which the admissibility of state seized evidence in a federal trial originally rested * * *.'[66]The Court concluded that it was therefore obliged to hold, although it chose the narrower ground on which to do so, that all evidence obtained by an unconstitutional

[55] 1926, 242 N.Y. 13, 150 N.E. 585

[56]242 N.Y. at page 22, 150 N.E. at page 588.

[57] *supra.*

[58] Jones v. United States, 1960, 362 U.S. 257, 266—267, 80 S.Ct. 725, 734, 4 L.Ed.2d 697.

[59] Rea v. United States, 1956, 350 U.S. 214, 76 S.Ct. 292, 100 L.Ed. 233.

[60]United States v. Rabinowitz, 1950, 339 U.S. 56, 63, 70 S.Ct. 430, 434, 94 L.Ed. 653.

[61] Irvine v. People of State of California, supra, 347 U.S. at page 134, 74 S.Ct. at page 384.

[62] Ibid.

[63] *supra.*

[64] 364 U.S. at page 212, 1441 of 80 S.Ct.

[65] At page 213 of 364 U.S., at page 1442 of 80 S.Ct.

[66] Ibid.

search and seizure was inadmissible in a federal court regardless of its source. Today, we once again examine *Wolf*'s constitutional documentation of the right to privacy free from unreasonable state intrusion, and, after its dozen years on our books, are led by it to close the only ***655** courtroom door remaining open to evidence secured by official lawlessness in flagrant abuse of that basic right, reserved to all persons as a specific guarantee against that very same unlawful conduct. We hold that all evidence obtained by searches and seizures in violation of the Constitution is, by that same authority, inadmissible in a state court.

IV.

Since the Fourth Amendment's right of privacy has been declared enforceable against the States through the Due Process Clause of the Fourteenth, it is enforceable against them by the same sanction of exclusion as is used against the Federal Government. Were it otherwise, then, just as without the *Weeks* rule, the assurance against unreasonable federal searches and seizures would be 'a form of words', valueless and undeserving of mention in a perpetual charter of inestimable human liberties, so too, without that rule the freedom from state invasions of privacy would be so ephemeral and so neatly severed from its conceptual nexus with the freedom from all brutish means of coercing evidence as not to merit this Court's high regard as a freedom 'implicit in 'the concept of ordered liberty.“ At the time that the Court held in *Wolf* that the Amendment was applicable to the States through the Due Process Clause, the cases of this Court, as we have seen, had steadfastly held that as to federal officers the Fourth Amendment included the exclusion of the evidence seized in violation ****1692** of its provisions. Even *Wolf* 'stoutly adhered' to that proposition. The right to privacy, when conceded operatively enforceable against the States, was not susceptible of destruction by avulsion of the sanction upon which its protection and enjoyment had always been deemed dependent under the *Boyd*, *Weeks* and *Silverthorne* cases.

Therefore, in extending the substantive protections of due process to all constitutionally unreasonable searches—state or federal—it was ***656** logically and constitutionally necessary that the exclusion doctrine—an essential part of the right to privacy—be also insisted upon as an essential ingredient of the right newly recognized by the *Wolf* case. In short, the admission of the new constitutional right by *Wolf* could not consistently tolerate denial of its most important constitutional privilege, namely, the exclusion of the evidence which an accused had been forced to give by reason of the unlawful seizure. To hold otherwise is to grant the right but in reality to withhold its privilege and enjoyment. Only last year the Court itself recognized that the purpose of the exclusionary rule 'is to deter—to compel respect for the constitutional guaranty in the only effectively available way—by removing the incentive to disregard it.'[67]

Indeed, we are aware of no restraint, similar to that rejected today, conditioning the enforcement of any other basic constitutional right. The right to privacy, no less important than any other right carefully and particularly reserved to the people, would stand in marked contrast to all other rights declared as 'basic to a free society.'[68]This Court has not hesitated to enforce as strictly against the States as it does against the Federal Government the rights of free speech and of a free press, the rights to notice and to a fair, public trial, including, as it does, the right not to be convicted by use of a coerced confession, however logically relevant it be, and without regard to its reliability.[69]And nothing could be more certain that that when a coerced confession is involved, 'the relevant rules of evidence' are overridden without regard to 'the incidence of such conduct by the police,' slight or frequent. Why should not

---

[67] *Elkins v. United States*, *supra*, 364 U.S. at page 217, 80 S.Ct. at page 1444.

[68] *Wolf v. People of State of Colorado*, *supra*, 338 U.S. at page 27, 69 S.Ct. at page 1361.

[69] *Rogers v. Richmond*, 1961, 365 U.S. 534, 81 S.Ct. 735, 5 L.Ed.2d 760.

the same rule apply to what is tantamount to coerced testimony by way of unconstitutional seizure of goods, papers, effect, documents, etc.? We find that, ***657** as to the Federal Government, the Fourth and Fifth Amendments and, as to the States, the freedom from unconscionable invasions of privacy and the freedom from convictions based upon coerced confessions do enjoy an 'intimate relation'8 in their perpetuation of 'principles of humanity and civil liberty (secured) * * * only after years of struggle.'[70] They express 'supplementing phases of the same constitutional purpose—to maintain inviolate large areas of personal privacy.'[71] The philosophy of each Amendment and of each freedom is complementary to, although not dependent upon, that of the other in its sphere of influence—the very least that together they assure in either sphere is that no man is to be convicted on unconstitutional evidence.[72]

****1693 V.**

Moreover, our holding that the exclusionary rule is an essential part of both the Fourth and Fourteenth Amendments is not only the logical dictate of prior cases, but it also makes very good sense. There is no war between the Constitution and common sense. Presently, a federal prosecutor may make no use of evidence illegally seized, but a State's attorney across the street may, although he supposedly is operating under the enforceable prohibitions of the same Amendment. Thus the State, by admitting evidence unlawfully seized, serves to encourage disobedience to the Federal Constitution which it is bound to uphold. Moreover, as was said in Elkins, '(t)he very essence of a healthy federalism depends upon the avoidance of needless conflict between ***658** state and federal courts.'[73] Such a conflict, hereafter needless, arose this very Term, in Wilson v. Schnettler,[74] in which, and in spite of the promise made by Rea, we gave full recognition to our practice in this regard by refusing to restrain a federal officer from testifying in a state court as to evidence unconstitutionally seized by him in the performance of his duties. Yet the double standard recognized until today hardly put such a thesis into practice. In non-exclusionary States, federal officers, being human, were by it invited to and did, as our cases indicate, step across the street to the State's attorney with their unconstitutionally seized evidence. Prosecution on the basis of that evidence was then had in a state court in utter disregard of the enforceable Fourth Amendment. If the fruits of an unconstitutional search had been inadmissible in both state and federal courts, this inducement to evasion would have been sooner eliminated. There would be no need to reconcile such cases as Rea and Schnettler, each pointing up the hazardous uncertainties of our heretofore ambivalent approach.

Federal-state cooperation in the solution of crime under constitutional standards will be promoted, if only by recognition of their now mutual obligation to respect the same fundamental criteria in their approaches. 'However much in a particular case insistence upon such rules may appear as a technicality that inures to the benefit of a guilty person, the history of the criminal law proves that tolerance of shortcut methods in law enforcement impairs its enduring effectiveness.'[75]Denying shortcuts to only one of two cooperating law enforcement agencies tends naturally to breed legitimate suspicion of 'working arrangements' whose results are equally tainted.[76]

---

[70] *Bram v. United States*, 1897, 168 U.S. 532, 543—544, 18 S.Ct. 183, 187, 42 L.Ed. 568.

[71] *Feldman v. United States*, 1944, 322 U.S. 487, 489—490, 64 S.Ct. 1082, 1083, 88 L.Ed. 1408.

[72] Cf. *Rochin v. People of State of California*, 1952, 342 U.S. 165, 173, 72 S.Ct. 205, 210, 96 L.Ed. 183.

[73] 364 U.S. at page 221, 80 S.Ct. at page 1446.

[74] 1961, 365 U.S. 381, 81 S.Ct. 632, 5 L.Ed.2d 620.

[75] Miller v. United States, 1958, 357 U.S. 301, 313, 78 S.Ct. 1190, 1197, 2 L.Ed.2d 1332.

[76]*Byars v. United States*, 1927, 273 U.S. 28, 47 S.Ct. 248, 71 L.Ed. 520; *Lustig v. United States*, 1949, 338 U.S. 74, 69 S.Ct. 1372, 93 L.Ed. 1819.

***659** There are those who say, as did Justice (then Judge) Cardozo, that under our constitutional exclusionary doctrine '(t)he criminal is to go free because the constable has blundered.'[77] In some cases, this will undoubtedly be the result. But, as was ****1694** said in Elkins, 'there is another consideration—the imperative of judicial integrity.'[78] The criminal goes free, if he must, but it is the law that sets him free. Nothing can destroy a government more quickly than its failure to observe its own laws, or worse, its disregard of the charter of its own existence. As Mr. Justice Brandeis, dissenting, said in Olmstead v. United States:[79] 'Our government is the potent, the omnipresent teacher. For good or for ill, it teaches the whole people by its example. * * * If the government becomes a lawbreaker, it breeds contempt for law; it invites every man to become a law unto himself; it invites anarchy.' Nor can it lightly be assumed that, as a practical matter, adoption of the exclusionary rule fetters law enforcement. Only last year this Court expressly considered that contention and found that 'pragmatic evidence of a sort' to the contrary was not wanting.[80] The Court noted that:

> 'The federal courts themselves have operated under the exclusionary rule of Weeks for almost half a century; ***660** yet it has not been suggested either that the Federal Bureau of Investigation has thereby been rendered ineffective, or that the administration of criminal justice in the federal courts has thereby been disrupted. Moreover, the experience of the states is impressive * * *. The movement towards the rule of exclusion has been halting but seemingly inexorable.'[81]

The ignoble shortcut to conviction left open to the State tends to destroy the entire system of constitutional restraints on which the liberties of the people rest. Having once recognized that the right to privacy embodied in the Fourth Amendment is enforceable against the States, and that the right to be secure against rude invasions of privacy by state officers is, therefore, constitutional in origin, we can no longer permit that right to remain an empty promise. Because it is enforceable in the same manner and to like effect as other basic rights secured by the Due Process Clause, we can no longer permit it to be revocable at the whim of any police officer who, in the name of law enforcement itself, chooses to suspend its enjoyment. Our decision, founded on reason and truth, gives to the individual no more than that which the Constitution guarantees him, to the police officer no less than that to which honest law enforcement is entitled, and, to the courts, that judicial integrity so necessary in the true administration of justice.

The judgment of the Supreme Court of Ohio is reversed and the cause remanded for further proceedings not inconsistent with this opinion.

Reversed and remanded.

***661** Mr. Justice BLACK, concurring.

For nearly fifty years, since the decision of this Court in Weeks v. United States, federal courts have refused to permit the introduction into evidence against an accused of his papers and effects obtained by 'unreasonable searches and seizures' in violation of the Fourth Amendment. In Wolf v. People of State of Colorado, decided in 1948, however, this Court held that 'in ****1695** a prosecution in a State court for a State crime the Fourteenth Amendment does not forbid the admission of evidence obtained by an unreasonable search and seizure.' I concurred in that holding on these grounds:

---

[77] *People v. Defore*, 242 N.Y. at page 21, 150 N.E. at page 587.

[78] 364 U.S. at page 222, 80 S.Ct. at page 1447.

[79] 1928, 277 U.S. 438, 485, 48 S.Ct. 564, 575, 72 L.Ed. 944.

[80] *Elkins v. United States, supra*, 364 U.S. at page 218, 80 S.Ct. at page 1444.

[81] Id., 364 U.S. at pages 218—219, 80 S.Ct. at pages 1444—1445.

'For reasons stated in my dissenting opinion in Adamson v. (People of State of) California,[82] I agree with the conclusion of the Court that the Fourth Amendment's prohibition of 'unreasonable searches and seizures' is enforceable against the states. Consequently, I should be for reversal of this case if I thought the Fourth Amendment not only prohibited 'unreasonable searches and seizures,' but also, of itself, barred the use of evidence so unlawfully obtained. But I agree with what appears to be a plain implication of the Court's opinion that the federal exclusionary rule is not a command of the Fourth Amendment but is a judicially created rule of evidence which Congress might negate.'

I am still not persuaded that the Fourth Amendment, standing alone, would be enough to bar the introduction into evidence against an accused of papers and effects seized from him in violation of its commands. For the Fourth Amendment does not itself contain any provision expressly precluding the use of such evidence, and I am ***662** extremely doubtful that such a provision could properly be inferred from nothing more than the basic command against unreasonable searches and seizures. Reflection on the problem, however, in the light of cases coming before the Court since Wolf, has led me to conclude that when the Fourth Amendment's ban against unreasonable searches and seizures is considered together with the Fifth Amendment's ban against compelled self-incrimination, a constitutional basis emerges which not only justifies but actually requires the exclusionary rule.

The close interrelationship between the Fourth and Fifth Amendments, as they apply to this problem, has long been recognized and, indeed, was expressly made the ground for this Court's holding in Boyd v. United States. There the Court fully discussed this relationship and declared itself 'unable to perceive that the seizure of a man's private books and papers to be used in evidence against him is substantially different from compelling him to be a witness against himself.' It was upon this ground that Mr. Justice Rutledge largely relied in his dissenting opinion in the Wolf case. And, although I rejected the argument at that time, its force has, for me at least, become compelling with the more thorough understanding of the problem brought on by recent cases. In the final analysis, it seems to me that the Boyd doctrine, though perhaps not required by the express language of the Constitution strictly construed, is amply justified from an historical standpoint, soundly based in ****1696** reason, ***663** and entirely consistent with what I regard to be the proper approach to interpretation of our Bill of Rights—an approach well set out by Mr. Justice Bradley in the Boyd case:

'(C)onstitutional provisions for the security of person and property should be liberally construed. A close and literal construction deprives them of half their efficacy, and leads to gradual depreciation of the right, as if it consisted more in sound than in substance. It is the duty of (the) courts to be watchful for the constitutional rights of the citizen, and against any stealthy encroachments thereon.'

The case of Rochin v. People of California, which we decided three years after the Wolf case, authenticated, I think, the soundness of Mr. Justice Bradley's and Mr. Justice Rutledge's reliance upon the interrelationship between the Fourth and Fifth Amendments as requiring the exclusion of unconstitutionally seized evidence. In Rochin, three police officers, acting with neither a judicial warrant nor probable cause, entered Rochin's home for the purpose of conducting a search and broke down the door to a bedroom occupied by Rochin and his wife. Upon their entry into the room, the officers saw Rochin pick up and swallow two small capsules. They immediately seized him and took him in handcuffs to a hospital where the capsules ***664** were recovered by use of a stomach pump. Investigation showed that the capsules contained morphine and evidence of that fact was made the basis of his conviction of a crime in a state court.

[82] 332 U.S. 46, 68 (67 S.Ct. 1672, 1683, 91 L.Ed. 1903).

When the question of the validity of that conviction was brought here, we were presented with an almost perfect example of the interrelationship between the Fourth and Fifth Amendments. Indeed, every member of this Court who participated in the decision of that case recognized this interrelationship and relied on it, to some extent at least, as justifying reversal of Rochin's conviction. The majority, though careful not to mention the Fifth Amendment's provision that '(n)o person * * * shall be compelled in any criminal case to be a witness against himself,' showed at least that it was not unaware that such a provision exists, stating: 'Coerced confessions offend the community's sense of fair play and decency. * * * It would be a stultification of the responsibility which the course of constitutional history has cast upon this Court to hold that in order to convict a man the police cannot extract by force what is in his mind but can extract what is in his stomach.' The methods used by the police thus were, according to the majority, 'too close to the rack and the screw to permit of constitutional differentiation,' and the case was reversed on the ground that these methods had violated the Due Process Clause of the Fourteenth Amendment in that the ****1697** treatment accorded Rochin was of a kind that 'shocks the conscience,' 'offend(s) 'a sense of justice" and fails to 'respect certain decencies of civilized conduct.'

I concurred in the reversal of the Rochin case, but on the ground that the Fourteenth Amendment made the Fifth Amendment's provision against self-incrimination ***665** applicable to the States and that, given a broad rather than a narrow construction, that provision barred the introduction of this 'capsule' evidence just as much as it would have forbidden the use of words Rochin might have been coerced to speak. In reaching this conclusion I cited and relied on the Boyd case, the constitutional doctrine of which was, of course, necessary to my disposition of the case. At that time, however, these views were very definitely in the minority for only Mr. Justice Douglas and I rejected the flexible and uncertain standards of the 'shock-the-conscience test' used in the majority opinion.

Two years after Rochin, in Irvine v. People of State of California, we were again called upon to consider the validity of a conviction based on evidence which had been obtained in a manner clearly unconstitutional and arguably shocking to the conscience. The five opinions written by this Court in that case demonstrate the utter confusion and uncertainty that had been brought about by the Wolf and Rochin decisions. In concurring, Mr. Justice Clark emphasized the unsatisfactory nature of the Court's 'shock-the-conscience test,' saying that this 'test' 'makes for such uncertainty and unpredictability that it would be impossible to foretell—other than by guesswork—just how brazen the invasion of the intimate privacies of one's home must be in order to shock itself into the protective arms of the Constitution. In truth, the practical result of this ad hoc approach is simply that when five Justices are sufficiently revolted by local police action, a conviction is overturned and a guilty man may go free.'

***666** Only one thing emerged with complete clarity from the Irvine case—that is that seven Justices rejected the 'shock-the-conscience' constitutional standard enunciated in the Wolf and Rochin cases. But even this did not lessen the confusion in this area of the law because the continued existence of mutually inconsistent precedents together with the Court's inability to settle upon a majority opinion in the Irvine case left the situation at least as uncertain as it had been before. Finally, today, we clear up that uncertainty. As I understand the Court's opinion in this case, we again reject the confusing 'shock-the-conscience' standard of the Wolf and Rochin cases and, instead, set aside this state conviction in reliance upon the precise, intelligible and more predictable constitutional doctrine enunciated in the Boyd case. I fully agree with Mr. Justice Bradley's opinion that the two Amendments upon which the Boyd doctrine rests are of vital importance in our constitutional scheme of liberty and that both are entitled to a liberal rather than a niggardly interpretation. The courts of the country are entitled to know with as much certainty as possible what scope they cover. The Court's opinion, in my judgment, dissipates the doubt and uncertainty in this field of constitutional law and I am persuaded, for this and other reasons stated, to depart from my prior views, to accept the Boyd doctrine ****1698** as controlling in this state case and to join the Court's judgment and opinion which are in accordance with that constitutional doctrine.

Mr. Justice DOUGLAS, concurring.

Though I have joined the opinion of the Court, I add a few words. This criminal proceeding started with a lawless search and seizure. The police entered a home ***667** forcefully, and seized documents that were later used to convict the occupant of a crime.

She lived alone with her fifteen-year-old daughter in the second-floor flat of a duplex in Cleveland. At about 1:30 in the afternoon of May 23, 1957, three policemen arrived at this house. They rang the bell, and the appellant, appearing at her window, asked them what they wanted. According to their later testimony, the policemen had come to the house on information from 'a confidential source that there was a person hiding out in the home, who was wanted for questioning in connection with a recent bombing.' To the appellant's question, however, they replied only that they wanted to question her and would not state the subject about which they wanted to talk.

The appellant, who had retained an attorney in connection with a pending civil matter, told the police she would call him to ask if she should let them in. On her attorney's advice, she told them she would let them in only when they produced a valid search warrant. For the next two and a half hours, the police laid siege to the house. At four o'clock, their number was increased to at least seven. Appellant's lawyer appeared on the scene; and one of the policemen told him that they now had a search warrant, but the officer refused to show it. Instead, going to the back door, the officer first tried to kick it in and, when that proved unsuccessful, he broke the glass in the door and opened it from the inside.

The appellant, who was on the steps going up to her flat, demanded to see the search warrant; but the officer refused to let her see it although he waved a paper in front of her face. She grabbed it and thrust it down the front of her dress. The policemen seized her, took the paper ***668** from her, and had her handcuffed to another officer. She was taken upstairs, thus bound, and into the larger of the two bedrooms in the apartment; there she was forced to sit on the bed. Meanwhile, the officers entered the house and made a complete search of the four rooms of her flat and of the basement of the house.

The testimony concerning the search is largely nonconflicting. The approach of the officers; their long wait outside the home, watching all its doors; the arrival of reinforcements armed with a paper; breaking into the house; putting their hands on appellant and handcuffing her; numerous officers ransacking through every room and piece of furniture, while the appellant sat, a prisoner in her own bedroom. There is direct conflict in the testimony, however, as to where the evidence which is the basis of this case was found. To understand the meaning of that conflict, one must understand that this case is based ****1699** on the knowing possession of four little pamphlets, a couple of photographs and a little pencil doodle—all of which are alleged to be pornographic.

According to the police officers who participated in the search, these articles were found, some in appellant's ***669** dressers and some in a suitcase found by her bed. According to appellant, most of the articles were found in a cardboard box in the basement; one in the suitcase beside her bed. All of this material, appellant—and a friend of hers—said were odds and ends belonging to a recent boarder, a man who had left suddenly for New York and had been detained there. As the Supreme Court of Ohio read the statute under which appellant is charged, she is guilty of the crime whichever story is true.

The Ohio Supreme Court sustained the conviction even though it was based on the documents obtained in the lawless search. For in Ohio evidence obtained by an unlawful search and seizure is admissible in a criminal prosecution at least where it was not taken from the 'defendant's person by the use of brutal or offensive force against defendant.'[83]This evidence would have been inadmissible in a federal prosecution.[84]For, as stated in the former decision, 'The effect of the 4th Amendment is to put the courts of the United States and Federal officials, in the exercise of their power and authority, under limitations and restraints * * *.'[85]It was therefore held that evidence obtained (which in that case was documents and correspondence) from a home without any warrant was not admissible in a federal prosecution.

We held in *Wolf v. People of State of Colorado*,[86] that the Fourth Amendment was applicable to the States by reason of the Due Process Clause of the Fourteenth Amendment. But a majority held that the exclusionary rule of the Weeks case was not required of the States, that they could apply such sanctions as they chose. That position had the necessary votes to carry the day. But with all respect it was not the voice of reason or principle. ***670** As stated in Weeks, if evidence seized in violation of the Fourth Amendment can be used against an accused, 'his right to be secure against such searches and seizures, is of no value, and * * * might as well be stricken from the Constitution.'[87]

When we allowed States to give constitutional sanction to the 'shabby business' of unlawful entry into a home (to use an expression of Mr. Justice Murphy),[88], we did indeed rob the Fourth Amendment of much meaningful force. There are, of course, other theoretical remedies. One is disciplinary action within the hierarchy of the police system, including prosecution of the police officer for a crime. Yet as Mr. Justice Murphy said in *Wolf*,'Self-scrutiny is a lofty ideal, but its exaltation reaches new heights if we expect a District Attorney to prosecute himself or his associates for well-meaning ****1700** violations of the search and seizure clause during a raid the District Attorney or his associates have ordered.'[89]

The only remaining remedy, if exclusion of the evidence is not required, is an action of trespass by the homeowner against the offending officer. Mr. Justice Murphy showed how onerous and difficult it would be for the citizen to maintain that action and how meagre the relief even if the citizen prevails.[90]The truth is that trespass actions against officers who make unlawful searches and seizures are mainly illusory remedies.

Without judicial action making the exclusionary rule applicable to the States, the *Wolf* case,in practical effect, reduced the guarantee against unreasonable searches and seizures to 'a dead letter,' as Mr. Justice Rutledge said in his dissent.[91]

---

[83] *State v. Mapp*, 170 Ohio St. 427, 166 N.E.2d 387, at page 388, syllabus 2; *State v. Lindway*, 131 Ohio St. 166, 2 N.E.2d 490.

[84] *Weeks v. United States*, 232 U.S. 383, 34 S.Ct. 341, 58 L.Ed. 652; *Elkins v. United States*, 364 U.S. 206, 80 S.Ct. 1437, 4 L.Ed. 2d 1669.

[85] Id., 232 U.S. at pages 391—392, 34 S.Ct. at page 344.

[86] 338 U.S. 25, 69 S.Ct. 1359, 93 L.Ed. 1782.

[87] 232 U.S. at page 393, 34 S.Ct. at page 344.

[88] *Wolf v. People of State of Colorado*, 338 U.S. at page 46, 69 S.Ct. at page 1371.

[89] 338 U.S. at page 42, 69 S.Ct. at page 1369.

[90] 338 U.S. 42—44, 69 S.Ct. 1369—1370.

[91] See 338 U.S. at page 47, 69 S.Ct. at page 1368.

Wolf v. People of State of Colorado[92]was decided in 1949. The immediate result was a storm of constitutional controversy which only today finds its end. I believe that this is an appropriate case in which to put an end to the asymmetry which Wolf imported into the law.[93]***671** It is an appropriate case because the facts it presents show—as would few other cases—the casual arrogance of those who have the untrammeled power to invade one's home and to seize one's person.

It is also an appropriate case in the narrower and more technical sense. The issues of the illegality of the search and the admissibility of the evidence have been presented to the state court and were duly raised here in accordance with the applicable Rule of Practice. The question was raised in the notice of appeal, the jurisdictional statement and in appellant's brief on the merits. It is true that argument was mostly directed to another issue in the case, but that is often the fact.[94]Of course, an earnest advocate of a position always believes that, had he only an additional opportunity for argument, his side would win. But, subject to the sound discretion of a court, all argument must at last come to a halt. This is especially so as to an issue about which this Court said last year that 'The arguments of its antagonists and of its proponents have been so many times marshaled as to require no lengthy elaboration here.'[95]

Moreover, continuance of *Wolf v. People of State of Colorado* in its full vigor breeds the unseemly shopping around of the kind revealed in *Wilson v. Schnettler*.[96]Once evidence, inadmissible in a federal court, is admissible in ***672** a state court a 'double standard' exists which, as the Court points out, leads to 'working arrangements' that undercut federal policy and reduce some aspects of law enforcement to shabby business. The rule that supports that practice does not have the force of reason behind it.

Black Letter Law

> Evidence obtained by way of an unconstitutional search is inadmissible. This is referred to in Constitutional Criminal Procedure as the "Exclusionary Rule." This case marks the first time that the Supreme Court applied the Exclusionary Rule to the states under the Fourteenth Amendment.

Discussion Problems:

1-1. What is the constitutional basis for the exclusionary rule found in the majority opinion? Consider the concurrence of Justice Douglas in Mapp. How do you respond to his concerns about the way in which the exclusionary rule impacts the Fourth and Fifth Amendment?

1-2. Should the exclusionary rule apply solely to the Fourth Amendment? If not, should the same rationale be applied when applying exclusionary rule doctrine to violations of the Fifth Amendment, the Fifth Amendment due process clause, and the Sixth Amendment? If the court chooses to fashion a different rule, what would you suggest? Why?

---

[92] *supra*.

[93] See *Stefanelli v. Minard*, 342 U.S. 117, 72 S.Ct. 118, 96 L.Ed. 138; *Rea v. United States*, 350 U.S. 214, 76 S.Ct. 292, 100 L.Ed. 233; *Elkins v. United States, supra*; *Monroe v. Pape*, 365 U.S. 167, 81 S.Ct. 473, 5 L.Ed.2d 492.

[94] See *Rogers v. Richmond*, 365 U.S. 534, 535—540, 81 S.Ct. 735, 736—739, 5 L.Ed.2d 760.

[95] *Elkins v. United States, supra*, 364 U.S. 216, 80 S.Ct. 1443.

[96] 365 U.S. 381, 81 S.Ct. 632, 5 L.Ed.2d 620.

1-3. Should the exclusionary rule be absolute? If not, how would you fashion a test for those exceptions to the exclusionary rule? Can you have an exception to a constitutional violation? Why or why not?

-Notes-

Chapter 2: Standing

Rakas v. Illinois

99 S.Ct. 421

Supreme Court of the United States

RAKAS et al.

v.

ILLINOIS.

No. 77–5781. | Argued Oct. 3, 1978. | Decided Dec. 5, 1978. | Rehearing Denied Jan. 15, 1979. | See 439 U.S. 1122, 99 S.Ct. 1035.

Mr. Justice REHNQUIST delivered the opinion of the Court.

Petitioners were convicted of armed robbery in the Circuit Court of Kankakee County, Ill., and their convictions were affirmed on appeal. At their trial, the prosecution offered into evidence a sawed-off rifle and rifle shells that had been seized by police during a search of an automobile in which petitioners had been passengers. Neither petitioner is the owner of the automobile and neither has ever asserted that he owned the rifle or shells seized. The Illinois Appellate Court held that petitioners lacked standing to object to the allegedly ***130** unlawful search and seizure and denied their motion to suppress the evidence. We granted certiorari in light of the obvious importance of the issues raised to the administration of criminal justice,[97], and now affirm.

I

Because we are not here concerned with the issue of probable cause, a brief description of the events leading to the search of the automobile will suffice. A police officer on a routine patrol received a radio call notifying him of a robbery of a clothing store in Bourbonnais, Illinois, and describing the getaway car. Shortly thereafter, the officer spotted an automobile which he thought might be the getaway car. After following the car for some time and after the arrival of assistance, he and several other officers stopped the vehicle. The occupants of the automobile, petitioners and two female companions, were ordered out of the car and, after the occupants had left the car, two officers searched the interior of the vehicle. They discovered a box of rifle shells in the glove compartment, which had been locked, and a sawed-off rifle under the front passenger seat.[98]After discovering the rifle and the shells, the officers took petitioners to the station and placed them under arrest.

Before trial petitioners moved to suppress the rifle and shells seized from the car on the ground that the search violated the Fourth and Fourteenth Amendments. They conceded that they did not own the automobile and were simply passengers; the owner of the car had been the driver of the vehicle at the time of the search. Nor did they assert that they owned the rifle or ****424** the shells seized.1 The prosecutor ***131** challenged petitioners' standing to object to the lawfulness of the search of the car because neither the car, the shells nor the rifle belonged to them. The trial court agreed that petitioners lacked standing and denied the motion to suppress the evidence.[99]In view of this holding, the court did not determine whether there was probable cause for the search and seizure. On appeal after petitioners' conviction, the Appellate Court of Illinois, Third Judicial District, affirmed the trial court's denial of petitioners' motion to suppress because it held that "without a proprietary or other

---

[97] 435 U.S. 922, 98 S.Ct. 1483, 55 L.Ed.2d 515 (1978).

[98] App. 10–11.

[99] App. 23–24.

similar interest in an automobile, a mere passenger therein lacks standing to challenge the legality of the search of the vehicle."[100] ***132**The court stated:

> "We believe that defendants failed to establish any prejudice to their own constitutional rights because they were not persons aggrieved by the unlawful search and seizure. . . . They wrongly seek to establish prejudice only through the use of evidence gathered as a consequence of a search and seizure directed at someone else and fail to prove an invasion of their own privacy."[101]

The Illinois Supreme Court denied petitioners leave to appeal.

II

Petitioners first urge us to relax or broaden the rule of standing enunciated in *Jones v. United States*,[102] so that any criminal defendant at whom a search was "directed" would have standing to contest the legality of that search and object to the admission at trial of evidence obtained as a result of the search. Alternatively, petitioners argue that they have standing to object to the search under Jones because they were "legitimately on [the] premises" at the time of the search.

The concept of standing discussed in Jones focuses on whether the person seeking to challenge the legality of a search as a basis for suppressing evidence was himself the "victim" of the search or seizure.[103] Adoption of ***133** the so-called "target" theory advanced by petitioners ****425** would in effect permit a defendant to assert that a violation of the Fourth Amendment rights of a third party entitled him to have evidence suppressed at his trial. If we reject petitioners' request for a broadened rule of standing such as this, and reaffirm the holding of Jones and other cases that Fourth Amendment rights are personal rights that may not be asserted vicariously, we will have occasion to re-examine the "standing" terminology emphasized in Jones. For we are not at all sure that the determination of a motion to suppress is materially aided by labeling the inquiry identified in Jones as one of standing, rather than simply recognizing it as one involving the substantive question of whether or not the proponent of the motion to suppress has had his own Fourth Amendment rights infringed by the search and seizure which he seeks to challenge. We shall therefore consider in turn petitioners' target theory, the necessity for continued adherence to the notion of standing discussed in Jones as a concept that is theoretically distinct from the merits of a defendant's Fourth Amendment claim, and, finally, the proper disposition of petitioners' ultimate claim in this case.

A

We decline to extend the rule of standing in Fourth Amendment cases in the manner suggested by petitioners. As we stated in Alderman v. United States,[104]"Fourth Amendment rights are personal rights which, like some other constitutional rights, may not be vicariously ***134** asserted."[105]A person who is aggrieved by an illegal search and seizure only through the introduction of damaging evidence secured by a search of a third person's premises or property has not had any of his Fourth Amendment rights infringed. Alderman.[106]And since the exclusionary rule

---

[100] 46 Ill.App.3d 569, 571, 4 Ill.Dec. 877, 878, 360 N.E.2d 1252, 1253 (1977).

[101] (quoting *Alderman v. United States* (1969), 394 U.S. 165, 89 S.Ct. 961, 22 L.Ed.2d 176) *Id.*, at 571–572, 4 Ill.Dec., at 879, 360 N.E.2d, at 1254.

[102] 362 U.S. 257, 80 S.Ct. 725, 4 L.Ed.2d 697 (1960).

[103] *Id.*, at 261, 80 S.Ct., at 731.

[104] 394 U.S. 165, 174, 89 S.Ct. 961, 966, 22 L.Ed.2d 176 (1969).

[105] See *Brown v. United States*, 411 U.S. 223, 230, 93 S.Ct. 1565, 1569, 36 L.Ed.2d 208 (1973); *Simmons v. United States*, 390 U.S. 377, 389, 88 S.Ct. 967, 973, 19 L.Ed.2d 1247 (1968); *Wong Sun v. United States*, 371 U.S. 471, 492, 83 S.Ct. 407, 419, 9 L.Ed.2d 441 (1963); cf. *Silverman v. United States*, 365 U.S. 505, 511, 81 S.Ct. 679, 682, 5 L.Ed.2d 734 (1961); *Gouled v. United States*, 255 U.S. 298, 304, 41 S.Ct. 261, 263, 65 L.Ed. 647 (1921).

[106] *supra*, 394 U.S., at 174, 89 S.Ct., at 966.

is an attempt to effectuate the guarantees of the Fourth Amendment, United States v. Calandra,[107]it is proper to permit only defendants whose Fourth Amendment rights have been violated to benefit from the rule's protections.[108]****426** There is no reason to think that a party whose rights have been infringed will not, if evidence is used against him, have ample motivation to move to suppress it.[109]Even if such a person is not a defendant in the action, he may be able to recover damages for the violation of his Fourth Amendment rights,[110], or seek redress under state law for invasion of privacy or trespass.

In support of their target theory, petitioners rely on the following quotation from Jones:[111]

> "In order to qualify as a 'person aggrieved by an unlawful search and seizure' one must have been a victim of a search or seizure, one against whom the search was ***135** directed, as distinguished from one who claims prejudice only through the use of evidence gathered as a consequence of a search or seizure directed at someone else."[112]

The above-quoted statement from Jones suggests that the italicized language was meant merely as a parenthetical equivalent of the previous phrase "a victim of a search or seizure." To the extent that the language might be read more broadly, it is dictum which was impliedly repudiated in Alderman v. United States,[113]and which we now expressly reject. In Jones, the Court set forth two alternative holdings: It established a rule of "automatic" standing to contest an allegedly illegal search where the same possession needed to establish standing is an essential element of the offense charged; and second, it stated that "anyone legitimately on premises where a search occurs may challenge its legality by way of a motion to suppress."[114]Had the Court intended to adopt the target theory now put forth by petitioners, neither of the above two holdings would have been necessary since Jones was the "target" of the police search in that case. Nor does United States v. Jeffers,[115] or ***136** Bumper v. North Carolina,[116] support the target theory. Standing in Jeffers was based on Jeffers' possessory interest in both the premises searched and the property seized.[117]Similarly, in Bumper, the defendant had a substantial possessory interest in both the house searched and the rifle seized.[118]

In Alderman v. United States, Mr. Justice Fortas, in a concurring and dissenting opinion, argued that the Court should "include within the category of those who may

---

[107] 414 U.S. 338, 347, 94 S.Ct. 613, 619, 38 L.Ed.2d 561 (1974).

[108] See *Simmons v. United States, supra*, 390 U.S., at 389, 88 S.Ct., at 973.

[109] *Alderman, supra*, 394 U.S., at 174, 89 S.Ct., at 966.

[110] see *Monroe v. Pape*, 365 U.S. 167, 81 S.Ct. 473, 5 L.Ed.2d 492 (1961)

[111] They also rely on *Bumper v. North Carolina*, 391 U.S. 543, 548, n. 11, 88 S.Ct. 1788, 1791, 20 L.Ed.2d 797 (1968), and *United States v. Jeffers*, 342 U.S. 48, 72 S.Ct. 93, 96 L.Ed. 59 (1951).

[112] *Jones*, 362 U.S., at 261, 80 S.Ct., at 731 (emphasis added).

[113] *supra*.

[114] 362 U.S., at 264, 267, 80 S.Ct., at 732, 734. See Combs v. United States, 408 U.S. 224, 227 n. 4, 92 S.Ct. 2284, 2286, 33 L.Ed.2d 308 (1972); Mancusi v. DeForte, 392 U.S. 364, 368 n. 5, 88 S.Ct. 2120, 2123, 20 L.Ed.2d 1154 (1968); Simmons v. United States, supra, 390 U.S., at 390, 88 S.Ct., at 974.

[115] *supra*.

[116] *supra*.

[117] 342 U.S., at 49–50, 54, 72 S.Ct., at 94–95, 96; see Mancusi v. DeForte, supra, 392 U.S., at 367–368, 88 S.Ct., at 2123–2124; Hoffa v. United States, 385 U.S. 293, 301, 87 S.Ct. 408, 413, 17 L.Ed.2d 374 (1966); Lanza v. New York, 370 U.S. 139, 143, and n. 10, 82 S.Ct. 1218, 1221, 8 L.Ed.2d 384 (1962).

[118] 391 U.S., at 548 n. 11, 88 S.Ct., at 1791.

object to the introduction of illegal evidence 'one against whom the search was directed.'"[119] **427The Court did not directly comment on Mr. Justice Fortas' suggestion, but it left no doubt that it rejected this theory by holding that persons who were not parties to unlawfully overheard conversations or who did not own the premises on which such conversations took place did not have standing to contest the legality of the surveillance, regardless of whether or not they were the "targets" of the surveillance.[120]Mr. Justice Harlan, concurring and dissenting, did squarely address Mr. Justice Fortas' arguments and declined to accept them.[121]He identified administrative problems posed by the target theory:

"[T]he [target] rule would entail very substantial administrative difficulties. In the majority of cases, I would imagine that the police plant a bug with the expectation that it may well produce leads to a large number of crimes. A lengthy hearing would, then, appear to be necessary in order to determine whether the police knew of an accused's criminal activity at the time the bug was ***137** planted and whether the police decision to plant a bug was motivated by an effort to obtain information against the accused or some other individual. I do not believe that this administrative burden is justified in any substantial degree by the hypothesized marginal increase in Fourth Amendment protection."[122]

When we are urged to grant standing to a criminal defendant to assert a violation, not of his own constitutional rights but of someone else's, we cannot but give weight to practical difficulties such as those foreseen by Mr. Justice Harlan in the quoted language.

Conferring standing to raise vicarious Fourth Amendment claims would necessarily mean a more widespread invocation of the exclusionary rule during criminal trials. The Court's opinion in Alderman counseled against such an extension of the exclusionary rule:

"The deterrent values of preventing the incrimination of those whose rights the police have violated have been considered sufficient to justify the suppression of probative evidence even though the case against the defendant is weakened or destroyed. We adhere to that judgment. But we are not convinced that the additional benefits of extending the exclusionary rule to other defendants would justify further encroachment upon the public interest in prosecuting those accused of crime and having them acquitted or convicted on the basis of all the evidence which exposes the truth."[123]

Each time the exclusionary rule is applied it exacts a substantial social cost for the vindication of Fourth Amendment rights. Relevant and reliable evidence is kept from the trier of fact and the search for truth at trial is deflected.[124]Since our cases generally ***138** have held that one whose Fourth Amendment rights are violated may successfully suppress evidence obtained in the course of an illegal search and seizure, misgivings as to the benefit of enlarging the class of persons who may invoke that rule are properly considered when deciding whether to expand standing to assert Fourth Amendment violations.

B

---

[119] 394 U.S., at 206–209, 89 S.Ct., at 985.

[120] *Id.*, at 176, 89 S.Ct., at 968.

[121] *Id.*, at 188–189, n. 1, 89 S.Ct., at 974.

[122] Ibid.

[123] *Id.*, at 174–175, 89 S.Ct., at 967.

[124] See *United States v. Ceccolini,* 435 U.S. 268, 275, 98 S.Ct. 1054, 1059, 55 L.Ed.2d 268 (1978); *Stone v. Powell,* 428 U.S. 465, 489–490, 96 S.Ct. 3037, 3050, 49 L.Ed.2d 1067 (1976); *United States v. Calandra,* 414 U.S., at 348–352, 94 S.Ct., at 620–622.

Had we accepted petitioners' request to allow persons other than those whose **428 own Fourth Amendment rights were violated by a challenged search and seizure to suppress evidence obtained in the course of such police activity, it would be appropriate to retain Jones' use of standing in Fourth Amendment analysis. Under petitioners' target theory, a court could determine that a defendant had standing to invoke the exclusionary rule without having to inquire into the substantive question of whether the challenged search or seizure violated the Fourth Amendment rights of that particular defendant. However, having rejected petitioners' target theory and reaffirmed the principle that the "rights assured by the Fourth Amendment are personal rights, [which] . . . may be enforced by exclusion of evidence only at the instance of one whose own protection was infringed by the search and seizure,"[125]the question necessarily arises whether it serves any useful analytical purpose to consider this principle a matter of standing, distinct from the merits of a defendant's Fourth *139 Amendment claim. We can think of no decided cases of this Court that would have come out differently had we concluded, as we do now, that the type of standing requirement discussed in Jones and reaffirmed today is more properly subsumed under substantive Fourth Amendment doctrine. Rigorous application of the principle that the rights secured by this Amendment are personal, in place of a notion of "standing," will produce no additional situations in which evidence must be excluded. The inquiry under either approach is the same.7 But we think the better analysis forthrightly focuses on the extent of a particular defendant's rights under the Fourth Amendment, rather than on any theoretically separate, but invariably intertwined concept of standing. The Court in Jones also may have been aware that there was a certain artificiality in analyzing this question in terms of standing because in at least three separate places in its opinion the Court placed that term within quotation marks.[126]

It should be emphasized that nothing we say here casts the least doubt on cases which recognize that, as a general proposition, the issue of standing involves two inquiries: first, whether the proponent of a particular legal right has alleged "injury in fact," and, second, whether the proponent is asserting his own legal rights and interests rather than basing his claim for relief upon the rights of third parties.[127]But this Court's long history of insistence that Fourth Amendment rights are personal in nature has already answered many of these traditional standing inquiries, and we think that definition of those rights is more properly placed within the purview of substantive Fourth Amendment law than within that of standing.[128] **429 Analyzed in these terms, the question is whether the challenged search or seizure violated the Fourth Amendment rights of a criminal defendant who seeks to exclude the evidence obtained during it. That inquiry in turn requires a determination of whether the disputed search and seizure has infringed an interest of the defendant which the Fourth Amendment was designed to protect. We are under no illusion that by dispensing with the rubric of standing used in Jones we have rendered any simpler the determination of whether the proponent of a motion to suppress is entitled to contest the legality of a search and seizure. But by frankly recognizing that this aspect of the analysis belongs more properly under the heading of substantive Fourth Amendment doctrine than under the heading of standing, we think the decision of this issue will rest on sounder logical footing.

C

[125] *Simmons v. United States,* 390 U.S., at 389, 88 S.Ct., at 974.

[126] 362 U.S., at 261, 263, 265, 80 S.Ct., at 731, 732, 733.

[127] See, *e. g., Singleton v. Wulff,* 428 U.S. 106, 112, 96 S.Ct. 2868, 2873, 49 L.Ed.2d 826 (1976); *140 *Warth v. Seldin,* 422 U.S. 490, 499, 95 S.Ct. 2197, 2205, 45 L.Ed.2d 343 (1975); *Data Processing Service v. Camp,* 397 U.S. 150, 152–153, 90 S.Ct. 827, 829–830, 25 L.Ed.2d 184 (1970).

[128] Cf. *id.*, at 153, and n. 1, 90 S.Ct., at 829; *Williams v. Jackson,* 346 U.S. 249, 256 n. 4, 73 S.Ct. 1031, 1035, 97 L.Ed. 1586 (1953); *Hale v. Henkel,* 201 U.S. 43, 69–70, 26 S.Ct. 370, 376–377, 50 L.Ed. 652 (1906).

Here petitioners, who were passengers occupying a car which they neither owned nor leased, seek to analogize their position to that of the defendant in Jones v. United States. ***141** In Jones, petitioner was present at the time of the search of an apartment which was owned by a friend. The friend had given Jones permission to use the apartment and a key to it, with which Jones had admitted himself on the day of the search. He had a suit and shirt at the apartment and had slept there "maybe a night," but his home was elsewhere. At the time of the search, Jones was the only occupant of the apartment because the lessee was away for a period of several days.[129]Under these circumstances, this Court stated that while one wrongfully on the premises could not move to suppress evidence obtained as a result of searching them, "anyone legitimately on premises where a search occurs may challenge its legality."[130]Petitioners argue that their occupancy of the automobile in question was comparable to that of Jones in the apartment and that they therefore have standing to contest the legality of the search—or as we have rephrased the inquiry, that they, like Jones, had their Fourth Amendment rights violated by the search.

We do not question the conclusion in Jones that the defendant in that case suffered a violation of his personal Fourth Amendment rights if the search in question was unlawful. ***142** Nonetheless, we believe that the phrase "legitimately on premises" coined in Jones creates too broad a gauge for measurement of Fourth Amendment rights. For example, applied literally, this ****430** statement would permit a casual visitor who has never seen, or been permitted to visit, the basement of another's house to object to a search of the basement if the visitor happened to be in the kitchen of the house at the time of the search. Likewise, a casual visitor who walks into a house one minute before a search of the house commences and leaves one minute after the search ends would be able to contest the legality of the search. The first visitor would have absolutely no interest or legitimate expectation of privacy in the basement, the second would have none in the house, and it advances no purpose served by the Fourth Amendment to permit either of them to object to the lawfulness of the search.

We think that Jones on its facts merely stands for the unremarkable proposition that a person can have a legally sufficient interest in a place other than his own home so that the Fourth Amendment protects him from unreasonable governmental intrusion into that place.[131]***143** In defining the scope of that interest, we adhere to the view expressed in Jones and echoed in later cases that arcane distinctions developed in property and tort law between guests, licensees, invitees, and the like, ought not to control.[132]But the Jones statement that a person need only be "legitimately on premises" in order to challenge the validity of the search of a dwelling place cannot be taken in its full sweep beyond the facts of that case.

Katz v. United States[133]provides guidance in defining the scope of the interest protected by the Fourth Amendment. In the course of repudiating the doctrine derived from Olmstead v. United States[134] and Goldman v. United States[135]that if police officers had not been guilty of a common-law trespass they were not prohibited by the Fourth Amendment from eavesdropping, the Court in Katz held that capacity to claim the protection of the Fourth Amendment depends not upon a property right in

[129] 362 U.S., at 259, 80 S.Ct., at 730.

[130] *Id.*, at 267, 80 S.Ct., at 734.

[131] See 362 U.S., at 263, 265, 80 S.Ct., at 732, 733.

[132] *Id.*, at 266, 80 S.Ct., at 733; see *Mancusi v. DeForte,* 392 U.S. 364, 88 S.Ct. 2120, 20 L.Ed.2d 1154 (1968); *Warden v. Hayden,* 387 U.S. 294, 87 S.Ct. 1642, 18 L.Ed.2d 782 (1967); *Silverman v. United States,* 365 U.S. 505, 81 S.Ct. 679, 5 L.Ed.2d 734 (1961).

[133] 389 U.S. 347, 88 S.Ct. 507, 19 L.Ed.2d 576 (1967).

[134] 277 U.S. 438, 48 S.Ct. 564, 72 L.Ed. 944 (1928).

[135] 316 U.S. 129, 62 S.Ct. 993, 86 L.Ed. 1322 (1942).

the invaded place but upon whether the person who claims the protection of the Amendment has a legitimate expectation of privacy in the invaded place.[136]Viewed in this manner, the holding in Jones can best be explained by the fact that Jones had a legitimate expectation of privacy in the premises he was using and therefore could claim the protection of the Fourth Amendment with respect to a governmental invasion of those premises, even though his "interest" in those premises might not have been a recognized property interest at common law.[137]

144 **431** Our Brother White in dissent expresses the view that by rejecting the phrase "legitimately on [the] premises" as the appropriate measure of Fourth Amendment rights, we are abandoning a thoroughly workable, "bright line" test in favor of a less certain analysis of whether the facts of a particular case give rise to a legitimate expectation of privacy.[138]145** If "legitimately on premises" were the successful litmus test of Fourth Amendment rights that he assumes it is, his approach would have at least the merit of easy application, whatever it lacked in fidelity to the history and purposes of the Fourth Amendment. But a reading of lower court cases that have applied the phrase "legitimately on premises," and of the dissent itself, reveals that this expression is not a shorthand summary for a bright-line rule which somehow encapsulates the "core" of the Fourth Amendment's protections.

***146 **432** The dissent itself shows that the facile consistency it is striving for is illusory. The dissenters concede that "there comes a point when use of an area is shared with so many that one simply cannot reasonably expect seclusion."[139]But surely the "point" referred to is not one demarcating a line which is black on one side and white on another; it is inevitably a point which separates one shade of gray from another. We are likewise told by the dissent that a person "legitimately on private premises . . . , though his privacy is not absolute, is entitled to expect that he is sharing it only with those persons [allowed there] and that governmental officials will intrude only with consent or by complying with the Fourth Amendment."[140]This single sentence describing the contours of the supposedly easily applied rule virtually abounds with unanswered questions: What are "private" premises? Indeed, what are the "premises?" It may be easy to describe the "premises" when one is confronted with a 1-room apartment, but what of the case of a 10-room house, or of a house with an attached garage that is searched? Also, if one's privacy is not absolute, how is it bounded? If he risks governmental intrusion "with consent," who may give that consent?

Again, we are told by the dissent that the Fourth Amendment assures that "some expectations of privacy are justified and will be protected from official intrusion."[141]But we are not told which of many possible expectations of privacy are embraced within this sentence. And our dissenting Brethren concede that "perhaps the Constitution provides some degree less protection for the ***147** personal freedom from unreasonable governmental intrusion when one does not have a possessory interest in the invaded private place." Post, at 442. But how much "less" protection is available when one does not have such a possessory interest?

Our disagreement with the dissent is not that it leaves these questions unanswered, or that the questions are necessarily irrelevant in the context of the analysis contained in this opinion. Our disagreement is rather with the dissent's bland and self-refuting assumption that there will not be fine lines to be drawn in Fourth

---

[136] 389 U.S., at 353, 88 S.Ct., at 512; see *United States v. Chadwick,* 433 U.S. 1, 7, 97 S.Ct. 2476, 2481, 53 L.Ed.2d 538 (1977); *United States v. White,* 401 U.S. 745, 752, 91 S.Ct. 1122, 1126, 28 L.Ed.2d 453 (1971).

[137] See *Jones v. United States,* 362 U.S., at 261, 80 S.Ct., at 731.

[138] *Post,* at 443.

[139] *Post,* at 441.

[140] *Ibid.* (emphasis added).

[141] *Post,* at 442 (emphasis added).

Amendment cases as in other areas of the law, and that its rubric, rather than a meaningful exegesis of Fourth Amendment doctrine, is more desirable or more easily resolves Fourth Amendment cases. In abandoning "legitimately on premises" for the doctrine that we announce today, we are not forsaking a time-tested and workable rule, which has produced consistent results when applied, solely for the sake of fidelity to the values underlying the Fourth Amendment. Rather, we are rejecting blind adherence to a phrase which at most has superficial clarity and which conceals underneath that thin veneer all of the problems of line drawing which must be faced in any conscientious effort to apply the Fourth Amendment. Where the factual premises for a rule are so generally prevalent that little would be lost and much would be gained by abandoning case-by-case analysis, we have not hesitated to do so. See United States v. Robinson, 414 U.S. 218, 235, 94 S.Ct. 467, 476, 38 L.Ed.2d 427 (1973). But the phrase "legitimately on premises" ***148** has not been shown to be an easily applicable measure of ****433** Fourth Amendment rights so much as it has proved to be simply a label placed by the courts on results which have not been subjected to careful analysis. We would not wish to be understood as saying that legitimate presence on the premises is irrelevant to one's expectation of privacy, but it cannot be deemed controlling.

D

Judged by the foregoing analysis, petitioners' claims must fail. They asserted neither a property nor a possessory interest in the automobile, nor an interest in the property seized. And as we have previously indicated, the fact that they were "legitimately on [the] premises" in the sense that they were in the car with the permission of its owner is not determinative of whether they had a legitimate expectation of privacy in the particular areas of the automobile searched. It is unnecessary for us to decide here whether the same expectations of privacy are warranted in a car as would be justified in a dwelling place in analogous circumstances. We have on numerous occasions pointed out that cars are not to be treated identically with houses or Apartments for Fourth Amendment purposes.[142] But here petitioners' claim is one which would fail even in an analogous situation in a dwelling place, since they made no showing that they had any legitimate expectation of privacy in the glove compartment or area under the seat of the car in which they were merely passengers. Like the trunk of an automobile, these are areas in which a ***149** passenger qua passenger simply would not normally have a legitimate expectation of privacy.[143]

Jones v. United States,[144]and Katz v. United States[145]involved significantly different factual circumstances. Jones not only had permission to use the apartment of his friend, but also had a key to the apartment with which he admitted himself on the day of the search and kept possessions in the apartment. Except with respect to his friend, Jones had complete dominion and control over the apartment and could exclude others from it. Likewise in Katz, the defendant occupied the telephone booth, shut the door behind him to exclude all others and paid the toll, which "entitled [him] to assume that the words he utter[ed] into the mouthpiece [would] not be broadcast to the world."[146]Katz and Jones could legitimately expect privacy in the areas which were the subject of the search and seizure each sought to contest. No such showing was made by these petitioners with respect to those portions of the automobile which were searched and from which incriminating evidence was seized.

---

[142] See *United States v. Chadwick*, 433 U.S., at 12, 97 S.Ct., at 2484; *United States v. Martinez-Fuerte*, 428 U.S. 543, 561, 96 S.Ct. 3074, 3084, 49 L.Ed.2d 1116 (1976); *Cardwell v. Lewis*, 417 U.S. 583, 590, 94 S.Ct. 2464, 2469, 41 L.Ed.2d 325 (1974) (plurality opinion).

[143] *Supra*, at 430.

[144] 362 U.S. 257, 80 S.Ct. 725, 4 L.Ed.2d 697 (1960).

[145] 389 U.S. 347, 88 S.Ct. 507, 19 L.Ed.2d 576 (1967),

[146] *Id.*, at 352, 88 S.Ct., at 512.

***150 **434 III**

The Illinois courts were therefore correct in concluding that it was unnecessary to decide whether the search of the car might have violated the rights secured to someone else by the Fourth and Fourteenth Amendments to the United States Constitution. Since it did not violate any rights of these petitioners, their judgment of conviction is

Affirmed.

*****

Mr. Justice WHITE, with whom Mr. Justice BRENNAN, Mr. Justice MARSHALL, and Mr. Justice STEVENS join, dissenting.

The Court today holds that the Fourth Amendment protects property, not people, and specifically that a legitimate occupant of an automobile may not invoke the exclusionary rule and challenge a search of that vehicle unless he happens to own or have a possessory interest in it. Though professing to acknowledge that the primary purpose of the Fourth Amendment's prohibition of unreasonable searches is the protection of privacy—not property—the Court nonetheless effectively ties the application of the Fourth Amendment and ***157** the exclusionary rule in this situation to property law concepts. Insofar as passengers are concerned, the Court's opinion today declares an "open season" on automobiles. However unlawful stopping and searching a car may be, absent a possessory or ownership interest, no "mere" passenger may object, regardless of his relationship to the owner. Because the majority's conclusion has no support in the Court's controlling decisions, in the logic of the Fourth Amendment, or in common sense, I must respectfully dissent. If the Court is troubled by the practical impact of the exclusionary rule, it should face the issue of that rule's continued validity squarely instead of distorting other doctrines in an attempt to reach what are perceived as the correct results in specific cases.[147]

I

Two intersecting doctrines long established in this Court's opinions control here. The first is the recognition of some cognizable level of privacy in the interior of an automobile. Though the reasonableness of the expectation of privacy in a vehicle may be somewhat weaker than that in a home,[148] "[a] search even of an automobile, is a substantial invasion of privacy. To protect that privacy from official arbitrariness, the Court always has regarded probable cause as the minimum requirement for a lawful search."[149]So far, the Court has not strayed from this application of the Fourth Amendment.

****438** The second tenet is that when a person is legitimately present in a private place, his right to privacy is protected from unreasonable governmental interference even if he does ***158** not own the premises. Just a few years ago, The Chief Justice, for a unanimous Court, wrote that the "[p]resence of the defendant at the search and seizure was held, in Jones, to be a sufficient source of standing in itself."[150]Brown was not the first time we had recognized that Jones established the rights of one legitimately in a private area against unreasonable governmental intrusion.[151]The

---

[147] Cf. *Stone v. Powell,* 428 U.S. 465, 536, 96 S.Ct. 3037, 3071, 49 L.Ed.2d 1067 (1976) (WHITE, J., dissenting).

[148] See *United States v. Chadwick,* 433 U.S. 1, 12–13, 97 S.Ct. 2476, 2484–2485, 53 L.Ed.2d 538 (1977).

[149] *United States v. Ortiz,* 422 U.S. 891, 896, 95 S.Ct. 2585, 2588, 45 L.Ed.2d 623 (1975) (footnote omitted).

[150] *Brown v. United States,* 411 U.S. 223, 227 n. 2, 93 S.Ct. 1565, 1568, 36 L.Ed.2d 208 (1973); accord, *id.,* at 229, 93 S.Ct., at 1569 (one basis for Fourth Amendment protection is presence "on the premises at the time of the contested search and seizure"); *Jones v. United States,* 362 U.S. 257, 80 S.Ct. 725, 4 L.Ed.2d 697 (1960) (individual legitimately present in friend's apartment may object to search of apartment).

[151] *E. g., Combs v. United States,* 408 U.S. 224, 227, and n. 4, 92 S.Ct. 2284, 2286, 33 L.Ed.2d 308 (1972); *Mancusi v. DeForte,* 392 U.S. 364, 368, 88 S.Ct. 2120, 2123, 20 L.Ed.2d 1154 and n. 5 (1968); *Simmons v. United States,* 390 U.S. 377, 390, 88 S.Ct. 967, 974, 19 L.Ed.2d 1247 (1968).

Court in Jones itself was unanimous in this regard, and its holding is not the less binding because it was an alternative one.[152]

These two fundamental aspects of Fourth Amendment law demand that petitioners be permitted to challenge the search and seizure of the automobile in this case. It is of no significance that a car is different for Fourth Amendment purposes from a house, for if there is some protection for the privacy of an automobile then the only relevant analogy is between a person legitimately in someone else's vehicle and a person legitimately in someone else's home. If both strands of the Fourth Amendment doctrine adumbrated above are valid, the Court must reach a different result. Instead, it chooses to eviscerate the Jones principle, an action in which I am unwilling to participate.

II

Though we had reserved the very issue over 50 years ago,[153]and never expressly dealt with it again until today, many of our opinions have assumed that a mere passenger in an automobile ***159** is entitled to protection against unreasonable searches occurring in his presence. In decisions upholding the validity of automobile searches, we have gone directly to the merits even though some of the petitioners did not own or possess the vehicles in question.[154]In Dyke v. Taylor Implement Mfg. Co.,[155]the Court, with seven Members agreeing, upset the admission of evidence against three petitioners though only one owned the vehicle.[156]Similarly, in Preston v. United States,[157]the Court unanimously overturned a search though the single petitioner was not the owner of the automobile. The Court's silence on this issue in light of its actions can only mean that, until now, we, like most lower courts, had assumed that Jones foreclosed the answer now supplied by the majority. That assumption was perfectly understandable, since all private premises would seem to be the same for the purposes of the analysis set out in Jones.

****439 III**

The logic of Fourth Amendment jurisprudence compels the result reached by the above decisions. Our starting point is "[t]he established principle ... that suppression of the product of a Fourth Amendment violation can be successfully urged only by those whose rights were violated by the search itself . . ."[158] Though the Amendment protects one's liberty ***160** and property interests against unreasonable seizures of self5 and effects, "the primary object of the Fourth Amendment [is] ... the protection of privacy."[159]And privacy is the ***161** interest asserted here,8 so the first step is to ascertain whether the premises searched "fall within a protected zone of privacy."[160]My Brethren in the majority assertedly do not deny that automobiles warrant at least some protection from official interference with privacy. Thus, the next step is to decide who is entitled, vis-à-vis the State, to enjoy that privacy. The answer to that question must be found by determining "whether petitioner had an interest in

---

[152] See *Combs v. United States, supra,* 408 U.S. at 227 n. 4, 92 S.Ct. at 2286.

[153] See *Carroll v. United States,* 267 U.S. 132, 162, 45 S.Ct. 280, 288, 69 L.Ed. 543 (1925).

[154] *E. g., Schneckloth v. Bustamonte,* 412 U.S. 218, 93 S.Ct. 2041, 36 L.Ed.2d 854 (1973) (sole petitioner was not owner; in fact, owner was not in the automobile at all); *Chambers v. Maroney,* 399 U.S. 42, 90 S.Ct. 1975, 26 L.Ed.2d 419 (1970) (sole petitioner was not owner); *Husty v. United States,* 282 U.S. 694, 51 S.Ct. 240, 75 L.Ed. 629 (1931).

[155] 391 U.S. 216, 88 S.Ct. 1472, 20 L.Ed.2d 538 (1968).

[156] See *id.,* at 221–222, 88 S.Ct., at 1475–1476.

[157] 376 U.S. 364, 84 S.Ct. 881, 11 L.Ed.2d 777 (1964).

[158] *Alderman v. United States,* 394 U.S. 165, 171–172, 89 S.Ct. 961, 965, 22 L.Ed.2d 176 (1969).

[159] *Cardwell v. Lewis,* 417 U.S. 583, 589, 94 S.Ct. 2464, 2469, 41 L.Ed.2d 325 (1974) (plurality opinion).

[160] *United States v. Miller,* 425 U.S. 435, 440, 96 S.Ct. 1619, 1623, 48 L.Ed.2d 71 (1976).

connection with the searched premises that gave rise to 'a reasonable expectation [on his part] of freedom from governmental intrusion' upon those premises."[161]

Not only does Combs supply the relevant inquiry, it also directs us to the proper answer. We recognized there that Jones had held that one of those protected interests is created by legitimate presence on the ****440** searched premises, even absent any possessory interest.[162]This makes unquestionable sense. We have concluded on numerous occasions that the entitlement to an expectation of privacy does not hinge on ownership:

"What a person knowingly exposes to the public, even in his own home or office, is not a subject of Fourth Amendment protection. . . . But what he seeks to preserve as private, even in an area accessible to the public, may be constitutionally protected." Katz v. United States, 389 U.S. 347, 351–352, 88 S.Ct. 507, 511, 19 L.Ed.2d 576 (1967).

In Alderman v. United States,[163]Mr. Justice Harlan, concurring in part and dissenting in part, noted that "our own past decisions . . . have decisively rejected the notion ***162** that the accused must necessarily have a possessory interest in the premises before he may assert a Fourth Amendment claim." That rejection should not have been surprising in light of our conclusion as early as 1960 that "it is unnecessary and ill-advised to import into the law surrounding the constitutional right to be free from unreasonable searches and seizures subtle distinctions, developed and refined by the common law in evolving the body of private property law which, more than almost any other branch of law, has been shaped by distinctions whose validity is largely historical."[164]The proposition today overruled was stated most directly in Mancusi v. DeForte:[165] "[T]he protection of the Amendment depends not upon a property right in the invaded place but upon whether the area was one in which there was a reasonable expectation of freedom from governmental intrusion."

Prior to Jones, the lower federal courts had based Fourth Amendment rights upon possession or ownership of the items seized or the premises searched. But Jones was foreshadowed by Mr. Justice Jackson's remark in 1948 that "even a guest may expect the shelter of the rooftree he is under against criminal intrusion."[166]Indeed, the decision today is contrary to Mr. Justice Brandeis' dissent in ***163** Olmstead v. United States[167] expressing a view of the Fourth Amendment thought to have been vindicated by Katz. The majority in Olmstead found the Fourth Amendment inapplicable absent a trespass on property rights.[168]That is exactly what the Court holds in this case; but Mr. Justice Brandeis asserted 50 years ago that more than mere property rights are involved, and the Court's opinion in Katz reemphasized that " '[t]he premise that property interests control the right of the Government to search and seize has been discredited.'"[169]That logic led us inescapably to the conclusion that "[n]o less than an individual in a business office, in a friend's apartment, or in a taxicab, a person in a telephone booth may rely upon the protection of the Fourth

[161] *Combs v. United States,* 408 U.S., at 227, 92 S.Ct., at 2286, quoting *Mancusi v. DeForte,* 392 U.S., at 368, 88 S.Ct., at 2123 (bracketed material in original).

[162] 408 U.S., at 227 n. 4, 92 S.Ct., at 2286.

[163] *supra,* 394 U.S., at 196, 89 S.Ct., at 978.

[164] *Jones v. United States,* 362 U.S., at 266, 80 S.Ct., at 733.

[165] *supra,* 392 U.S., at 368, 88 S.Ct., at 2124.

[166] *McDonald v. United States,* 335 U.S. 451, 461, 69 S.Ct. 191, 196, 93 L.Ed. 153 (1948) (Jackson, J., joined by Frankfurter, J., concurring).

[167] 277 U.S. 438, 478, 48 S.Ct. 564, 572, 72 L.Ed. 944 (1928)

[168] 277 U.S., at 466, 48 S.Ct., at 568.

[169] 389 U.S., at 353, 88 S.Ct., at 512, quoting *Warden v. Hayden,* 387 U.S. 294, 304, 87 S.Ct. 1642, 1648, 18 L.Ed.2d 782 (1967).

Amendment."[170]And if all of those situations are protected, surely a person riding in an automobile next to his friend the owner, or a **441 child or wife with the father or spouse, must have some protection as well.

The same result is reached by tracing other lines of our Fourth Amendment decisions. If a non-owner may consent to a search merely because he is a joint user or occupant of a "premises,"[171]then that same non-owner must have a protected privacy interest. The scope of the authority sufficient to grant a valid consent can hardly be broader than the contours of protected privacy. ***164** And why should the owner of a vehicle be entitled to challenge the seizure from it of evidence even if he is absent at the time of the search,[172]while a non-owner enjoying in person, and with the owner's permission, the privacy of an automobile is not so entitled?

In sum, one consistent theme in our decisions under the Fourth Amendment has been, until now, that "the Amendment does not shield only those who have title to the searched premises."[173]Though there comes a point when use of an area is shared with so many that one simply cannot reasonably expect seclusion,[174] short of that limit a person legitimately on private premises knows the others allowed there and, though his privacy is not absolute, is entitled to expect that he is sharing it only with those persons and that governmental officials will intrude only with consent or by complying with the Fourth Amendment.[175]

It is true that the Court asserts that it is not limiting the Fourth Amendment bar against unreasonable searches to the protection of property rights, but in reality it is doing exactly that. Petitioners were in a private place with the permission ***165** of the owner, but the Court states that that is not sufficient to establish entitlement to a legitimate expectation of privacy.[176]But if that is not sufficient, what would be? We are not told, and it is hard to imagine anything short of a property interest that would satisfy the majority. Insofar as the Court's rationale is concerned, no passenger in an automobile, without an ownership or possessory interest and regardless of his relationship to the owner, may claim Fourth Amendment protection against illegal stops and searches of ****442** the automobile in which he is rightfully present. The Court approves the result in Jones, but it fails to give any explanation why the facts in Jones differ, in a fashion material to the Fourth Amendment, from the facts here. More importantly, how is the Court able to avoid answering the question why presence in a private place with the owner's permission is insufficient? If it is "tautological to fall back on the notion that those expectations of privacy which are legitimate depend primarily on cases deciding exclusionary rule issues in criminal cases,"[177]then it surely must be tautological to decide that issue simply by unadorned fiat.

***166** As a control on governmental power, the Fourth Amendment assures that some expectations of privacy are justified and will be protected from official intrusion. That should be true in this instance, for if protected zones of privacy can only be purchased or obtained by possession of property, then much of our daily lives will be unshielded from unreasonable governmental prying, and the reach of the Fourth Amendment will have been narrowed to protect chiefly those with possessory inter-

---

[170] 389 U.S., at 352, 88 S.Ct., at 511 (footnotes omitted).

[171] *Frazier v. Cupp*, 394 U.S. 731, 740, 89 S.Ct. 1420, 1425, 22 L.Ed.2d 684 (1969).

[172] see *Coolidge v. New Hampshire*, 403 U.S. 443, 91 S.Ct. 2022, 29 L.Ed.2d 564 (1971),

[173] *Mancusi v. DeForte*, 392 U.S., at 367, 88 S.Ct., at 2123.

[174] See *id.*, at 377, 88 S.Ct., at 2128 (WHITE, J., dissenting); *Air Pollution Variance Bd. v. Western Alfalfa Corp.*, 416 U.S. 861, 865, 94 S.Ct. 2114, 2115, 40 L.Ed.2d 607 (1974).

[175] See *Mancusi v. DeForte, supra*, at 369–370, 88 S.Ct., at 2124–2125.

[176] *Ante*, at 433.

[177] A*nte*, at 431 n. 12.

ests in real or personal property. I had thought that Katz firmly established that the Fourth Amendment was intended as more than simply a trespass law applicable to the government. Katz had no possessory interest in the public telephone booth, at least no more than petitioners had in their friend's car; Katz was simply legitimately present. And the decision in Katz was based not on property rights, but on the theory that it was essential to securing "conditions favorable to the pursuit of happiness" that the expectation of privacy in question be recognized.

At most, one could say that perhaps the Constitution provides some degree less protection for the personal freedom from unreasonable governmental intrusion when one does not have a possessory interest in the invaded private place. But that would only change the extent of the protection; it would not free police to do the unreasonable, as does the decision today. And since the accused should be entitled to litigate the application of the Fourth Amendment where his privacy interest is merely arguable, the failure to allow such litigation here is the more incomprehensible.

***167 IV**

The Court's holding is contrary not only to our past decisions and the logic of the Fourth Amendment but also to the everyday expectations of privacy that we all share. Because of that, it is unworkable in all the various situations that arise in real life. If the owner of the car had not only invited petitioners to join her but had said to them, "I give you a temporary possessory interest in my vehicle so that you will share the right to privacy that the Supreme Court says that I own," then apparently the majority would reverse. But people seldom say such things, though they may mean their invitation to encompass them if only ****443** they had thought of the problem. If the non-owner were the spouse or child of the owner, would the Court recognize a sufficient interest? If so, would distant relatives somehow have more of an expectation of privacy than close friends? What if the non-owner were driving with the owner's permission? Would non-owning drivers have more of an expectation of privacy than mere passengers? What about a passenger in a taxicab? Katz expressly recognized protection for such passengers. Why should Fourth Amendment rights be present when one pays a cabdriver for a ride but be absent when one is given a ride by a friend?

The distinctions the Court would draw are based on relationships between private parties, but the Fourth Amendment is concerned with the relationship of one of those parties to ***168** the government. Divorced as it is from the purpose of the Fourth Amendment, the Court's essentially property-based rationale can satisfactorily answer none of the questions posed above. That is reason enough to reject it. The Jones rule is relatively easily applied by police and courts; the rule announced today will not provide law enforcement officials with a bright line between the protected and the unprotected. Only rarely will police know whether one private party has or has not been granted a sufficient possessory or other interest by another private party. Surely in this case the officers had no such knowledge. The Court's rule will ensnare defendants and police in needless litigation over factors that should not be determinative of Fourth Amendment rights.

More importantly, the ruling today undercuts the force of the exclusionary rule in the one area in which its use is most certainly justified—the deterrence of bad-faith violations of the Fourth Amendment.[178]This decision invites police to engage in patently unreasonable searches every time an automobile contains more than one occupant. Should something be found, only the owner of the vehicle, or of the item, will have standing to seek suppression, and the evidence will ***169** presumably be usable against the other occupants. The danger of such bad faith is especially high in cases such as this one where the officers are only after the passengers and can usually infer accurately that the driver is the owner. The ****444** suppression remedy for those owners in whose vehicles something is found and who are charged with crime

[178] See *Stone v. Powell*, 428 U.S., at 536–542, 96 S.Ct., at 3072–3074 (WHITE, J., dissenting).

is small consolation for all those owners and occupants whose privacy will be needlessly invaded by officers following mistaken hunches not rising to the level of probable cause but operated on in the knowledge that someone in a crowded car will probably be unprotected if contraband or incriminating evidence happens to be found. After this decision, police will have little to lose by unreasonably searching vehicles occupied by more than one person.

Of course, most police officers will decline the Court's invitation and will continue to do their jobs as best they can in accord with the Fourth Amendment. But the very purpose of the Bill of Rights was to answer the justified fear that governmental agents cannot be left totally to their own devices, and the Bill of Rights is enforceable in the courts because human experience teaches that not all such officials will otherwise adhere to the stated precepts. Some policemen simply do act in bad faith, even if for understandable ends, and some deterrent is needed. In the rush to limit the applicability of the exclusionary rule somewhere, anywhere, the Court ignores precedent, logic, and common sense to exclude the rule's operation from situations in which, paradoxically, it is justified and needed.

Black Letter Law

To assert a Fourth Amendment right the accused must have either a property or a possessory interest in the automobile searched or in the property seized. Failure to show any legitimate expectation of privacy in the glove compartment or area under the seat of the vehicle in which the defendants were merely passengers, meant they were not entitled to challenge the search of those areas.

This case worked on the principle that rights assured by the Fourth Amendment are *personal* rights which may be enforced by exclusion of evidence when your own protection has been infringed by the search and seizure. Focus should be placed on the extent of a particular defendant's rights under Fourth Amendment, rather than on any theoretically separate, but invariably intertwined concept of standing.

Minnesota v. Carter

119 S.Ct. 469

Supreme Court of the United States

MINNESOTA, Petitioner,

v.

Wayne Thomas CARTER.

No. 97-1147. | Argued Oct. 6, 1998. | Decided Dec. 1, 1998.*

***85** Chief Justice REHNQUIST delivered the opinion of the Court.

Respondents and the lessee of an apartment were sitting in one of its rooms, bagging cocaine. While so engaged they were observed by a police officer, who looked through a drawn window blind. The Supreme Court of Minnesota held that the officer's viewing was a search that violated respondents' Fourth Amendment rights. We hold that no such violation occurred.

James Thielen, a police officer in the Twin Cities' suburb of Eagan, Minnesota, went to an apartment building to investigate a tip from a confidential informant. The informant said that he had walked by the window of a ground-floor apartment and had seen people putting a white powder into bags. The officer looked in the same window through a gap in the closed blind and observed the bagging operation for several minutes. He then notified headquarters, which began preparing affidavits for a search warrant while he returned to the apartment building. When two men left the building in a previously identified Cadillac, the police stopped the car. Inside were respondents Carter and Johns. As the police opened the door of the car to let Johns out, they observed a black, zippered pouch and a handgun, later determined to be loaded, on the vehicle's floor. Carter and Johns were arrested, and a later police search of the vehicle the next day discovered pagers, a scale, and 47 grams of cocaine in plastic sandwich bags.

***86** After seizing the car, the police returned to Apartment 103 and arrested the occupant, Kimberly Thompson, who is not a party to this appeal. A search of the apartment pursuant to a warrant revealed cocaine residue on the kitchen table and plastic baggies similar to those found in the Cadillac. Thielen identified Carter, Johns, and Thompson as the three people he had observed placing the powder into baggies. The police later learned that while Thompson was the lessee of the apartment, Carter and Johns lived in Chicago and had come to the apartment for the sole purpose of packaging the cocaine. Carter and Johns had never been to the apartment before and were only in the apartment for approximately 2½ hours. In return for the use of the apartment, Carter and ****472** Johns had given Thompson one-eighth of an ounce of the cocaine.

Carter and Johns were charged with conspiracy to commit a controlled substance crime in the first degree and aiding and abetting in a controlled substance crime in the first degree, in violation of Minn.Stat. §§ 152.021, subds. 1(1), 3(a), 609.05 (1996). They moved to suppress all evidence obtained from the apartment and the Cadillac, as well as to suppress several post arrest incriminating statements they had made. They argued that Thielen's initial observation of their drug packaging activities was an unreasonable search in violation of the Fourth Amendment and that all evidence obtained as a result of this unreasonable search was inadmissible as fruit of the poisonous tree. The Minnesota trial court held that since, unlike the defendant in Minnesota v. Olson,[179]Carter and Johns were not overnight social guests but temporary out-of-state visitors, they were not entitled to claim the protection of the Fourth Amendment against the government intrusion into the apartment. The trial court also concluded that Thielen's observation was not a search within the meaning of the Fourth Amendment. After a trial, Carter and Johns were each convicted of both offenses. The Minnesota Court of Appeals ***87** held that respondent Carter did not have "standing" to object to Thielen's actions because his claim that he was predominantly a social guest was "inconsistent with the only evidence concerning his stay in the apartment, which indicates that he used it for a business purpose-to package drugs."[180]In a separate appeal, the Court of Appeals also affirmed Johns' conviction, without addressing what it termed the "standing" issue.[181]

A divided Minnesota Supreme Court reversed, holding that respondents had "standing" to claim the protection of the Fourth Amendment because they had " 'a legitimate expectation of privacy in the invaded place.'"[182]The court noted that even though "society does not recognize as valuable the task of bagging cocaine, we conclude that society does recognize as valuable the right of property owners or leaseholders to invite persons into the privacy of their homes to conduct a common task, be it legal or illegal activity. We, therefore, hold that [respondents] had standing to bring [their] motion to suppress the evidence gathered as a result of Thielen's observations."[183]Based upon its conclusion that respondents had "standing" to raise their Fourth Amendment claims, the court went on to hold that Thielen's observation con-

---

179 495 U.S. 91, 110 S.Ct. 1684, 109 L.Ed.2d 85 (1990).

180 545 N.W.2d 695, 698 (Minn.Ct.App.1996).

181 *State v. Johns,* No. C9-95-1765 (June 11, 1996), App. D-1, D-3 (unpublished).

182 569 N.W.2d 169, 174 (Minn.1997) (quoting *Rakas v. Illinois,* 439 U.S. 128, 143, 99 S.Ct. 421, 58 L.Ed.2d 387 (1978)).

183 569 N.W.2d, at 176; see also 569 N.W.2d 180, 181 (1997).

stituted a search of the apartment under the Fourth Amendment, and that the search was unreasonable.[184] We granted certiorari,[185] and now reverse.

The Minnesota courts analyzed whether respondents had a legitimate expectation of privacy under the rubric of "standing" doctrine, an analysis that this Court expressly rejected 20 years ago in Rakas.[186] In that case, we held that automobile passengers could not assert the protection of the Fourth Amendment against the ***88** seizure of incriminating evidence from a vehicle where they owned neither the vehicle nor the evidence. Ibid. Central to our analysis was the idea that in determining whether a defendant is able to show the violation of his (and not someone else's) Fourth Amendment rights, the "definition of those rights is more properly placed within the purview of substantive Fourth Amendment law than within that of standing."[187] Thus, we held that in order to claim the protection of the Fourth Amendment, a defendant must demonstrate that he personally has an expectation of privacy in the place searched, and that his expectation is reasonable; i.e., one that has "a source outside of the Fourth Amendment, either by reference to concepts of real or personal property law or to understandings that are recognized and permitted by society."[188]

****473** The Fourth Amendment guarantees: "The right of the people to be secure in their persons, houses, papers, and effects, against unreasonable searches and seizures, shall not be violated, and no Warrants shall issue, but upon probable cause, supported by Oath or affirmation, and particularly describing the place to be searched, and the persons or things to be seized." The Amendment protects persons against unreasonable searches of "their persons [and] houses" and thus indicates that the Fourth Amendment is a personal right that must be invoked by an individual.[189] But the extent to which the Fourth Amendment protects people may depend upon where those people are. We have held that "capacity to claim the protection of the Fourth Amendment depends ... upon whether the person who claims the protection of the Amendment has a legitimate expectation of privacy in the invaded place."[190]

***89** The text of the Amendment suggests that its protections extend only to people in "their" houses. But we have held that in some circumstances a person may have a legitimate expectation of privacy in the house of someone else. In Minnesota v. Olson,[191] for example, we decided that an overnight guest in a house had the sort of expectation of privacy that the Fourth Amendment protects. We said:

"To hold that an overnight guest has a legitimate expectation of privacy in his host's home merely recognizes the every day expectations of privacy that we all share. Staying overnight in another's home is a longstanding social custom that serves functions recognized as valuable by society. We stay in others' homes when we travel to a strange city for business or pleasure, when we visit our parents, children, or more distant relatives out of town, when we are in between jobs or homes, or when we house-sit for a friend…

From the overnight guest's perspective, he seeks shelter in another's home precisely because it provides him with privacy, a place where he and his possessions will not

---

[184] *Id.*, at 176-179.

[185] 523 U.S. 1003, 118 S.Ct. 1183, 140 L.Ed.2d 315 (1998).

[186] 439 U.S., at 139-140, 99 S.Ct. 421.

[187] *Id.*, at 140, 99 S.Ct. 421.

[188] *Id.*, at 143-144, and n. 12, 99 S.Ct. 421. See also *Smith v. Maryland,* 442 U.S. 735, 740-741, 99 S.Ct. 2577, 61 L.Ed.2d 220 (1979).

[189] See *Katz v. United States,* 389 U.S. 347, 351, 88 S.Ct. 507, 19 L.Ed.2d 576 (1967) ("[T]he Fourth Amendment protects people, not places").

[190] *Rakas, supra,* at 143, 99 S.Ct. 421. See also *Rawlings v. Kentucky,* 448 U.S. 98, 106, 100 S.Ct. 2556, 65 L.Ed.2d 633 (1980).

[191] 495 U.S. 91, 110 S.Ct. 1684, 109 L.Ed.2d 85 (1990).

be disturbed by anyone but his host and those his host allows inside. We are at our most vulnerable when we are asleep because we cannot monitor our own safety or the security of our belongings. It is for this reason that, although we may spend all day in public places, when we cannot sleep in our own home we seek out another private place to sleep, whether it be a hotel room, or the home of a friend."[192]

In Jones v. United States,[193]the defendant seeking to exclude evidence resulting from a search of an apartment had been given the use of the apartment by a friend. He had clothing in the apartment, had slept there " 'maybe a night,' " and at the time was the sole occupant of the apartment. But while the holding of Jones-that a search of the apartment violated the defendant's ***90** Fourth Amendment rights-is still valid, its statement that "anyone legitimately on the premises where a search occurs may challenge its legality,"[194]was expressly repudiated in Rakas v. Illinois.[195]Thus, an overnight guest in a home may claim the protection of the Fourth Amendment, but one who is merely present with the consent of the householder may not.

Respondents here were obviously not overnight guests, but were essentially present for a business transaction and were only in the home a matter of hours. There is no suggestion that they had a previous relationship with Thompson, or that there was any other purpose to their visit. Nor was there anything similar to the overnight guest relationship in Olson to suggest a degree of acceptance into the household.* While the ****474** apartment was a dwelling place for Thompson, it was for these respondents simply a place to do business.

Property used for commercial purposes is treated differently for Fourth Amendment purposes from residential property. "An expectation of privacy in commercial premises, however, is different from, and indeed less than, a similar expectation in an individual's home."[196]And while it was a "home" in which respondents were present, it was not their home. Similarly, the Court has held that in some circumstances a worker can claim Fourth Amendment protection over his ***91** own workplace.[197]But there is no indication that respondents in this case had nearly as significant a connection to Thompson's apartment as the worker in O'Connor had to his own private office.[198]

If we regard the overnight guest in Minnesota v. Olson as typifying those who may claim the protection of the Fourth Amendment in the home of another, and one merely "legitimately on the premises" as typifying those who may not do so, the present case is obviously somewhere in between. But the purely commercial nature of the transaction engaged in here, the relatively short period of time on the premises, and the lack of any previous connection between respondents and the householder, all lead us to conclude that respondents' situation is closer to that of one simply permitted on the premises. We therefore hold that any search which may have occurred did not violate their Fourth Amendment rights.

Because we conclude that respondents had no legitimate expectation of privacy in the apartment, we need not decide whether the police officer's observation constituted a "search." The judgments of the Supreme Court of Minnesota are accordingly reversed, and the cause is remanded for proceedings not inconsistent with this opinion.

---

[192] *Id.*, at 98-99, 110 S.Ct. 1684.

[193] 362 U.S. 257, 259, 80 S.Ct. 725, 4 L.Ed.2d 697 (1960).

[194] *Id.*, at 267, 80 S.Ct. 725.

[195] 439 U.S. 128, 99 S.Ct. 421, 58 L.Ed.2d 387 (1978).

[196] *New York v. Burger,* 482 U.S. 691, 700, 107 S.Ct. 2636, 96 L.Ed.2d 601 (1987).

[197] See, *e.g., O'Connor v. Ortega,* 480 U.S. 709, 107 S.Ct. 1492, 94 L.Ed.2d 714 (1987).

[198] See *id.*, at 716-717, 107 S.Ct. 1492.

It is so ordered.

******

Justice GINSBURG, with whom Justice STEVENS and Justice SOUTER join, dissenting.

The Court's decision undermines not only the security of short-term guests, but also the security of the home resident herself. In my view, when a homeowner or lessee personally invites a guest into her home to share in a common endeavor, whether it be for conversation, to engage in leisure activities, or for business purposes licit or illicit, that guest should share his host's shelter against unreasonable searches and seizures.

I do not here propose restoration of the "legitimately on the premises" criterion stated in Jones v. United States,[199]for the Court rejected that formulation in Rakas v. Illinois,[200]as it did the "automatic standing rule" in United States v. Salvucci.[201]First, the disposition I would reach in this case responds to the unique importance of the home-the most essential bastion of privacy recognized by the law.[202]Second, even within the home itself, the ***107** position to which I would adhere would not permit "a casual visitor who has never seen, or been permitted to visit, the basement of another's house to object to a search of the basement if the visitor happened to be in the kitchen of the house at the time of the search."[203]Further, I would here decide only the case of the homeowner who chooses to share the privacy of her home ****482** and her company with a guest, and would not reach classroom hypotheticals like the milkman or pizza deliverer.

My concern centers on an individual's choice to share her home and her associations there with persons she selects. Our decisions indicate that people have a reasonable expectation of privacy in their homes in part because they have the prerogative to exclude others.[204]The power to exclude implies the power to include.[205]Our Fourth Amendment decisions should reflect these complementary prerogatives.

A home dweller places her own privacy at risk, the Court's approach indicates, when she opens her home to others, uncertain whether the duration of their stay, their purpose, and their "acceptance into the household" will earn protection.[206] It remains textbook law that "[s]earches and seizures inside a home without a warrant are presumptively ***108** unreasonable absent exigent circumstances."[207]The law in practice is less secure. Human frailty suggests that today's decision will tempt police to pry into private dwellings without warrant, to find evidence incriminating guests who do

---

[199] 362 U.S. 257, 267, 80 S.Ct. 725, 4 L.Ed.2d 697 (1960),

[200] 439 U.S. 128, 142, 99 S.Ct. 421, 58 L.Ed.2d 387 (1978).

[201] 448 U.S. 83, 95, 100 S.Ct. 2547, 65 L.Ed.2d 619 (1980).

[202] See *United States v. Karo,* 468 U.S. 705, 714, 104 S.Ct. 3296, 82 L.Ed.2d 530 (1984) ("[P]rivate residences are places in which the individual normally expects privacy free of governmental intrusion not authorized by a warrant .... Our cases have not deviated from this basic Fourth Amendment principle."); *Payton v. New York,* 445 U.S. 573, 589, 100 S.Ct. 1371, 63 L.Ed.2d 639 (1980) ("The Fourth Amendment protects the individual's privacy in a variety of settings. In none is the zone of privacy more clearly defined than when bounded by the unambiguous physical dimensions of an individual's home.").

[203] *Rakas,* 439 U.S., at 142, 99 S.Ct. 421.

[204] See *id.,* at 149, 99 S.Ct. 421 (legitimate expectation of privacy turns in large part on ability to exclude others from place searched).

[205] See, *e.g.,* Coombs, Shared Privacy and the Fourth Amendment, or the Rights of Relationships, 75 Calif. L.Rev. 1593, 1618 (1987) ("One reason we protect the legal right to exclude others is to empower the owner to choose to share his home or other property with his intimates."); Alschuler, Interpersonal Privacy and the Fourth Amendment, 4 N. Ill. U.L.Rev. 1, 13 (1983) ("[O]ne of the main rights attaching to property is the right to share its shelter, its comfort and its privacy with others.").

[206] *Ante,* at 473.

[207] *Karo,* 468 U.S., at 714-715, 104 S.Ct. 3296.

not rest there through the night.[208]Rakas tolerates that temptation with respect to automobile searches.[209]I see no impelling reason to extend this risk into the home.[210]As I see it, people are not genuinely "secure in their ... houses ... against unreasonable searches and seizures,"[211] if their invitations to others increase the risk of unwarranted governmental peering and prying into their dwelling places.

Through the host's invitation, the guest gains a reasonable expectation of privacy in the home. Minnesota v. Olson,[212] so held with respect to an overnight guest. The logic of that decision extends to shorter term guests as well.[213]***109** Visiting the home of a friend, relative, or business associate, whatever the time of day, "serves functions recognized as valuable by society."[214]One need not remain overnight to anticipate privacy in another's home, "a place where [the guest] and his possessions will not be disturbed by anyone but his host and those his host allows inside."[215]In sum, when a homeowner ****483** chooses to share the privacy of her home and her company with a short-term guest, the twofold requirement "emerg[ing] from prior decisions" has been satisfied: Both host and guest "have exhibited an actual (subjective) expectation of privacy;" that "expectation [is] one [our] society is prepared to recognize as 'reasonable.'"[216]

As the Solicitor General acknowledged, the illegality of the host-guest conduct, the fact that they were partners in crime, would not alter the analysis.[217]***110** In Olson, for example, the guest whose security this Court's decision shielded stayed overnight while the police searched for him. [218]4 The Court held that the guest had Fourth Amendment protection against a warrantless arrest in his host's home despite the guest's involvement in grave crimes (first-degree murder, armed robbery, and assault). Other decisions have similarly sustained Fourth Amendment pleas despite the criminality of the defendants' activities.[219]Indeed, it must be this way. If the illegality of the activity made constitutional an otherwise unconstitutional search, such Fourth Amendment protection, reserved for the innocent only, would have little force in regulating police behavior toward either the innocent or the guilty.

Our leading decision in Katz is key to my view of this case. There, we ruled that the Government violated the petitioner's Fourth Amendment rights when it electronically recorded him transmitting wagering information while he was inside a public

---

[208] See Simien, The Interrelationship of the Scope of the Fourth Amendment and Standing to Object to Unreasonable Searches, 41 Ark. L.Rev. 487, 539 (1988) ("[I]f the police have no probable cause, they have everything to gain and nothing to lose if they search under circumstances where they know that at least one of the potential defendants will not have standing.").

[209] See Ashdown, The Fourth Amendment and the "Legitimate Expectation of Privacy," 34 Vand. L.Rev. 1289, 1321 (1981) (criticizing *Rakas* as "present[ing] a framework in which there may be nothing to lose and something to gain by the illegal search of a car that carries more than one occupant"); see also *Rakas,* 439 U.S., at 169, 99 S.Ct. 421 (White, J., dissenting) ("After this decision, police will have little to lose by unreasonably searching vehicles occupied by more than one person.").

[210] See *Silverman v. United States,* 365 U.S. 505, 511, 81 S.Ct. 679, 5 L.Ed.2d 734 (1961) ("At the very core [of the Fourth Amendment] stands the right of a man to retreat into his own home and there be free from unreasonable governmental intrusion.").

[211] U.S. Const., Amdt. 4.

[212] 495 U.S. 91, 110 S.Ct. 1684, 109 L.Ed.2d 85 (1990).

[213] See 5 W. LaFave, Search and Seizure: A Treatise on the Fourth Amendment § 11.3(b), p. 137 (3d ed. 1996) ("[I]t is fair to say that the *Olson* decision lends considerable support to the claim that shorter-term guests also have standing.").

[214] *Olson,* 495 U.S., at 98, 110 S.Ct. 1684.

[215] *Id.,* at 99, 110 S.Ct. 1684.

[216] *Katz v. United States,* 389 U.S. 347, 361, 88 S.Ct. 507, 19 L.Ed.2d 576 (1967) (Harlan, J., concurring).

[217] See Tr. of Oral Arg. 22-23.

[218] 95 U.S., at 93-94, 110 S.Ct. 1684.

[219] See, *e.g., Payton,* 445 U.S., at 583-603, 100 S.Ct. 1371 (murder and armed robbery); *Katz,* 389 U.S., at 348-359, 88 S.Ct. 507 (telephoning across state lines to place illegal wagers); *Silverman,* 365 U.S., at 508-512, 81 S.Ct. 679 (gambling offenses).

telephone booth.[220]We were mindful that "the Fourth Amendment protects people, not places,"[221]and held that this electronic monitoring of a business call "violated the privacy upon which [the caller] justifiably relied while using the telephone booth."[222]Our obligation to produce coherent results in this often visited area of the law requires us to inform our current expositions by benchmarks already established. As Justice Harlan explained in his dissent in Poe v. Ullman:[223]

"Each new claim to Constitutional protection must be considered against a background of Constitutional purposes, as they have been rationally perceived and historically developed. Though we exercise limited and ***111** sharply restrained judgment, yet there is no 'mechanical yardstick,' no 'mechanical answer.' The decision of an apparently novel claim must depend on grounds which follow closely on well-accepted principles and criteria. The new decision must take 'its place in relation to what went before and further [cut] a channel for what is to come.'"[224]

The Court's decision in this case veers sharply from the path marked in Katz. I do not agree that we have a more reasonable expectation of privacy when we place a business ****484** call to a person's home from a public telephone booth on the side of the street,[225]than when we actually enter that person's premises to engage in a common endeavor.

For the reasons stated, I dissent from the Court's judgment, and would retain judicial surveillance over the warrantless searches today's decision allows.

Black Letter Law

> Defendants who were in another person's apartment for a short time, solely for the purpose of packaging cocaine, had no legitimate expectation of privacy in the apartment, and, thus, any search which may have occurred did not violate their Fourth Amendment rights.
>
> Overnight guest in a home may claim protection of the Fourth Amendment, but one who is merely present with consent of the householder may not.

Discussion Problems:

2-1. A government agency sets up a surveillance program to record the private conversations of Allen and Bob without their knowledge. As part of this program, the government uses a special microwave microphone to record their conversations by bouncing microwaves off the surfaces of a window in the home where they are meeting. Allen and Bob discuss various criminal enterprises, and through the course of their discussions their conversation indicates that Charlie is also involved in their nefarious schemes. At his subsequent criminal trial, during a pretrial hearing, Charlie's attorney establishes that the surveillance program was conducted in violation of the fourth Amendment to the U.S. Constitution. Should the court exclude any evidence obtained from the surveillance program at Charlie's trial? Why? Why not?

As you answer this question, take the time to identify with specificity whether or not Charlie's 4th amendment right is a personal right. Is it one that only attaches when individual deprivation of that right has occurred? What is the jurisprudential basis for

---

[220] 389 U.S., at 353, 88 S.Ct. 507.

[221] *Id.*, at 351, 88 S.Ct. 507.

[222] *Id.*, at 353, 88 S.Ct. 507.

[223] 367 U.S. 497, 544, 81 S.Ct. 1752, 6 L.Ed.2d 989 (1961).

[224] *Ibid.* (quoting *Irvine v. California*, 347 U.S. 128, 147, 74 S.Ct. 381, 98 L.Ed. 561 (1954) (Frankfurter, J., dissenting)).

[225] see *Katz*, 389 U.S., at 353, 88 S.Ct. 507,

the way in which you have applied the exclusionary rule to this question? What are the potential consequences of that basis?

2-2. A large homemade bomb was detonated in the stadium of a local professional sports team. In the course of their investigation law enforcement comes to believe that a local character, Simon, has information and materials relevant to the investigation, but they do not think that he was knowingly involved in the bombing. They arrest Simon, bring him to the station, threaten him with physical harm, leave him alone with a police officer who beats him with a sock filled with sand, and then, over his requests for a lawyer, force him to tell them where his friend is and the location of the backpack his friend asked for him to keep. Eventually, Simon tells the police where his friend is located, as well as the location of the mysterious backpack, which contains a device identified as the source of the detonation command for the homemade bomb. The police arrest Simon's friend, Robert, whom they suspect of being involved in the bombing. Other than the evidence derived from their interaction with Simon the police have nothing implicating Robert in the bombing.

At his trial, Robert moves for the suppression of the backpack, as well as its contents. How should the court rule? Why?

2-3. Officer Walker received an anonymous phone call identifying Joey Alexander as one of the bank robbers who had committed a string of recent robberies. The caller was not known to Officer Walker and hung up before Officer Walker could get any additional details. Officer Walker performs a record search and identifies an address where one Joseph Alexander lives. He proceeds to the address, knocks on the door and when no one answers opens the unlocked door and steps inside. William is in the home and when he sees Officer Walker he tells him he is waiting for Joey to get home and asks him to leave. Officer Walker asks William if he lives there and William says no he just came over to play video games. Walker handcuffs William, and then searches the home, finding two shotguns matching the description of the guns used in the bank robbery. One gun has William's fingerprints on it. A GSR test subsequently identifies gunshot residue consistent with the shotgun on William's jacket sleeve.

William is now on trial for bank robbery and attempted murder. At his trial, the State attempts to admit the evidence seized by Officer Walker and when he searched the home where William was located, where the shotguns were found. The defense attorney moves for suppression of the shotguns. How should the Court rule? Why?

2-4. Linda got a text from her friend Susan, inviting her to crash at an apartment Susan was visiting. Susan told Linda it would be "fine" for her to come over and crash for the night. Linda comes over, but does not bring a toothbrush, or any other toiletries in her backpack. The backpack did contain tools for cooking crystal meth. The two begin to party with some others at the apartment. During the party the cops show up and search everyone. At trial Linda argues that she was a guest at the apartment and as such she had a reasonable expectation of privacy in the contents of her backpack.

How should the court rule on Linda's motion? Explain your reasoning.

Chapter 3: Crossing the Threshold

Olmstead v. U.S.

48 S.Ct. 564

Olmstead et al.

v.

UNITED STATES.

GREEN et al.

v.

SAME

McINNIS

v.

SAME.

No. 493.No. 532.No. 533. | Argued Feb. 20 and 21, 1928. | Decided June 4, 1928.

Opinion

***455** Mr. Chief Justice TAFT delivered the opinion of the Court.

These cases are here by certiorari from the Circuit Court of Appeals for the Ninth Circuit.[226]The petition in No. 493 Was filed August 30, 1927; in Nos. 532 and 533, September ****565** 9, 1927. They were granted with the distinct limitation that the hearing should be confined to the single question whether the use of evidence of private telephone conversations between the defendants and others, intercepted by means of wire tapping, amounted to a violation of the Fourth and Fifth Amendments.[227] The petitioners were convicted in the District Court for the Western District of Washington of a conspiracy to violate the National Prohibition Act (27 USCA) by unlawfully possessing, transporting and importing intoxicating liquors and maintaining nuisances, and by selling intoxicating liquors. Seventy-two others, in addition to the petitioners, were indicted. Some were not apprehended, some were acquitted, and others pleaded guilty.

The evidence in the records discloses a conspiracy of amazing magnitude to import, possess, and sell liquor unlawfully. ***456** It involved the employment of not less than 50 persons, of two sea-going vessels for the transportation of liquor to British Columbia, of smaller vessels for coastwise transportation to the state of Washington, the purchase and use of a branch beyond the suburban limits of Seattle, with a large underground cache for storage and a number of smaller caches in that city, the maintenance of a central office manned with operators, and the employment of executives, salesmen, deliverymen dispatchers, scouts, bookkeepers, collectors, and an attorney. In a bad month sales amounted to $176,000; the aggregate for a year must have exceeded $2,000,000.

Olmstead was the leading conspirator and the general manager of the business. He made a contribution of $10,000 to the capital; 11 others contributed $1,000 each. The profits were divided, one-half to Olmstead and the remainder to the other 11. Of the several offices in Seattle, the chief one was in a large office building. In this there were three telephones on three different lines. There were telephones in an office of the manager in his own home, at the homes of his associates, and at other places in the city. Communication was had frequently with Vancouver, British Columbia. Times were fixed for the deliveries of the 'stuff' to places along Puget Sound near Seattle, and from there the liquor was removed and deposited in the caches already

[226] 19 F.(2d) 842, 53 A. L. R. 1472, and 19 F.(2d) 850.

[227] 276 U. S. 609, 48 S. Ct. 207, 72 L. Ed.

referred to. One of the chief men was always on duty at the main office to receive orders by the telephones and to direct their filling by a corps of men stationed in another room-the 'bull pen.' The call numbers of the telephones were given to those known to be likely customers. At times the sales amounted to 200 cases of liquor per day.

The information which led to the discovery of the conspiracy and its nature and extent was largely obtained by intercepting messages on the telephones of the conspirators by four federal prohibition officers. Small ***457** wires were inserted along the ordinary telephone wires from the residences of four of the petitioners and those leading from the chief office. The insertions were made without trespass upon any property of the defendants. They were made in the basement of the large office building. The taps from house lines were made in the streets near the houses.

The gathering of evidence continued for many months. Conversations of the conspirators, of which refreshing stenographic notes were currently made, were testified to by the government witnesses. They revealed the large business transactions of the partners and their subordinates. Men at the wires heard the orders given for liquor by customers and the acceptances; they became auditors of the conversations between the partners. All this disclosed the conspiracy charged in the indictment. Many of the intercepted conversations were not merely reports, but parts of the criminal acts. The evidence also disclosed the difficulties to which the conspirators were subjected, the reported news of the capture of vessels, the arrest of their men, and the seizure of cases of liquor in garages and other places. It showed the dealing by Olmstead, the chief conspirator, with members of the Seattle police, the messages to them which secured the release of arrested members of the conspiracy, and also direct promises to officers of payments as soon as opportunity offered.

The Fourth Amendment provides:

'The right of the people to be secure in their persons, houses, papers, and effects, against unreasonable searches and seizures, shall not be violated, and no warrants shall issue, but upon probable cause, supported by oath or affirmation, and particularly describing the place to be searched, and the persons or things to be seized.'

And the Fifth:

'No person * * * shall be compelled in any criminal case to be a witness against himself.'

***458** It will be helpful to consider the chief cases in this court which bear upon the construction of these amendments.Boyd v. United States[228] was an information filed by the District Attorney in the federal court in a cause of seizure and forfeiture against 35 cases of plate glass, which charged that the owner and importer, with intent to defraud the revenue, made an entry of the imported merchandise by means of a fraudulent or false invoice. It became important to show the quantity and value of glass contained in 29 cases previously imported. The fifth section of the Act of June 22, 1874[229] provided that, in cases not criminal under the revenue laws, the United States attorney, whenever he thought an invoice, belonging ****566** to the defendant, would tend to prove any allegation made by the United States, might by a written motion, describing the invoice and setting forth the allegation which he expected to prove, secure a notice from the court to the defendant to produce the invoice, and, if the defendant refused to produce it, the allegations stated in the motion should be taken as confessed, but if produced the United States attorney should be permitted, under the direction of the court, to make an examination of the invoice, and might offer the same in evidence. This act had succeeded the act of 1867 (14 Stat. 547), which provided in such cases the District Judge, on affidavit of any person interested, might issue a warrant to the marshall to enter the premises where the invoice was

---

[228]116 U. S. 616, 6 S. Ct. 524, 29 L. Ed. 746.

[229] (19 USCA s 535)

and take possession of it and hold it subject to the order of the judge. This had been preceded by the act of 1863 (12 Stat. 740) of a similar tenor, except that it directed the warrant to the collector instead of the marshal. The United States attorney followed the act of 1874 and compelled the production of the invoice.

The court held the Act of 1874 repugnant to the Fourth and Fifth Amendments. As to the Fourth Amendment, Justice Bradley said:[230]

> ***459** 'But, in regard to the Fourth Amendment, it is contended that, whatever might have been alleged against the constitutionality of the acts of 1863 and 1867, that of 1874, under which the order in the present case was made, is free from constitutional objection, because it does not authorize the search and seizure of books and papers, but only requires the defendant or claimant to produce them. That is so; but it declares that if he does not produce them, the allegations which it is affirmed they will prove shall be taken as confessed. This is tantamount to compelling their production; for the prosecuting attorney will always be sure to state the evidence expected to be derived from them as strongly as the case will admit of. It is true that certain aggravating incidents of actual search and seizure, such as forcible entry into a man's house and searching amongst his papers, are wanting, and to this extent the proceeding under the act of 1874 is a mitigation of that which was authorized by the former acts; but it accomplishes the substantial object of those acts in forcing from a party evidence against himself. It is our opinion, therefore, that a compulsory production of a man's private papers to establish a criminal charge against him, or to forfeit his property, is within the scope of the Fourth Amendment to the Constitution, in all cases in which a search and seizure would be; because it is a material ingredient, and effects the sole object and purpose of search and seizure.'

Concurring, Mr. Justice Miller and Chief Justice Waite said that they did not think the machinery used to get this evidence amounted to a search and seizure, but they agreed that the Fifth Amendment had been violated.

The statute provided an official demand for the production of a paper of document by the defendant, for official search and use as evidence on penalty that by refusal he should be conclusively held to admit the incriminating ***460** character of the document as charged. It was certainly no straining of the language to construe the search and seizure under the Fourth Amendment to include such official procedure.

The next case, and perhaps the most important, is Weeks v. United States,[231]a conviction for using the mails to transmit coupons or tickets in a lottery enterprise. The defendant was arrested by a police officer without a warrant. After his arrest, other police officers and the United States marshal went to his house, got the key from a neighbor, entered the defendant's room, and searched it, and took possession of various papers and articles. Neither the marshal nor the police officers had a search warrant. The defendant filed a petition in court asking the return of all his property. The court ordered the return of everything not pertinent to the charge, but denied return of relevant evidence. After the jury was sworn, the defendant again made objection, and on introduction of the papers contended that the search without warrant was a violation of the Fourth and Fifth Amendments, and they were therefore inadmissible. This court held that such taking of papers by an official of the United States, acting under color of his office, was in violation of the constitutional rights of the defendant, and upon making seasonable application he was entitled to have them restored, and that by permitting their use upon the trial the trial court erred.

The opinion cited with approval language of Mr. Justice Field in Ex parte Jackson,[232]saying that the Fourth Amendment as a principle of protection was applicable to sealed letters and packages in the mail, and that, consistently with it, such

---

[230] page 621 (6 S. Ct. 527)

[231] 232 U. S. 383, 34 S. Ct. 341, 58 L. Ed. 652, L. R. A. 1915B, 834, Ann. Cas. 1815C, 1177.

[232] 96 U. S. 727, 733, 24 L. Ed. 877.

matter could only be opened and examined upon warrants issued on oath or affirmation particularly describing the thing to be seized.

In Silverthorne Lumber Co. v. United States,[233]the defendants were arrested at their homes and ***461** detained in custody. While so detained, representatives of the government without authority went to the office of their company and seized all the books, papers, and documents found there. An application for return of the things was opposed by the district attorney, who produced a subpoena for certain documents relating to the charge in the indictment then on file. The court said:

'Thus the case is not that of knowledge acquired through the wrongful act of a stranger, ****567** but it must be assumed that the government planned or at all events ratified the whole performance.'

And it held that the illegal character of the original seizure characterized the entire proceeding and under the Weeks Case the seized papers must be restored.

In Amos v. United States,[234]the defendant was convicted of concealing whisky on which the tax had not been paid. At the trial he presented a petition asking that private property seized in a search of his house and store 'within his curtilage' without warrant should be returned. This was denied. A woman, who claimed to be his wife, was told by the revenue officers that they had come to search the premises for violation of the revenue law. She opened the door; they entered and found whisky. Further searches in the house disclosed more. It was held that this action constituted a violation of the Fourth Amendment, and that the denial of the motion to restore the whisky and to exclude the testimony was error.

In Gouled v. United States,[235]the facts were these: Gouled and two others were charged with conspiracy to defraud the United States. One pleaded guilty and another was acquitted. Gouled prosecuted error. The matter was presented here on questions propounded by the lower court. The first related to the admission in evidence of a paper surreptitiously taken from the office of the defendant by one acting under the direction ***462** of an officer of the Intelligence Department of the Army of the United States. Gouled was suspected of the crime. A private in the United States Army, pretending to make a friendly call on him, gained admission to his office, and in his absence, without warrant of any character, seized and carried away several documents. One of these, belonging to Gouled, was delivered to the United States attorney and by him introduced in evidence. When produced it was a surprise to the defendant. He had had no opportunity to make a previous motion to secure a return of it. The paper had no pecuniary value, but was relevant to the issue made on the trial. Admission of the paper was considered a violation of the Fourth Amendment.

Agnello v. United States,[236]held that the Fourth and Fifth Amendments were violated by admission in evidence of contraband narcotics found in defendant's house, several blocks distant from the place of arrest, after his arrest and seized there without a warrant. Under such circumstances the seizure could not be justified as incidental to the arrest.

There is no room in the present case for applying the Fifth Amendment, unless the Fourth Amendment was first violated. There was no evidence of compulsion to induce the defendants to talk over their many telephones. They were continually and voluntarily transacting business without knowledge of the interception. Our consideration must be confined to the Fourth Amendment.

The striking outcome of the Weeks Case and those which followed it was the sweeping declaration that the Fourth Amendment, although not referring to or limit-

---

[233] 251 U. S. 385, 40 S. Ct. 182, 64 L. Ed. 319, 24 A. L. R. 1426.

[234] 255 U. S. 313, 41 S. Ct. 266, 65 L. Ed. 654.

[235] 255 U. S. 298, 41 S. Ct. 261, 65 L. Ed. 647.

[236] 269 U. S. 20, 46 S. Ct. 4, 70 L. Ed. 145, 51 A. L. R. 409.

ing the use of evidence in court, really forbade its introduction, if obtained by government officers through a violation of the amendment. Theretofore many had supposed that under the ordinary common-law rules, if the tendered evidence was pertinent, the method of obtaining it was ***463** unimportant. This was held by the Supreme Judicial Court of Massachusetts in Commonwealth v. Dana.[237] There it was ruled that the only remedy open to a defendant whose rights under a state constitutional equivalent of the Fourth Amendment had been invaded was by suit and judgment for damages, as Lord Camden held in Entick v. Carrington,[238]Mr. Justice Bradley made effective use of this case in Boyd v. United States. But in Weeks, and those which followed, this court decided with great emphasis and established as the law for the federal courts that the protection of the Fourth Amendment would be much impaired, unless it was held that not only was the official violator of the rights under the amendment subject to action at the suit of the injured defendant, but also that the evidence thereby obtained could not be received.

The well-known historical purpose of the Fourth Amendment, directed against general warrants and writs of assistance, was to prevent the use of governmental force to search a man's house, his person, his papers, and his effects, and to prevent their seizure against his will. This phase of the misuse of governmental power of compulsion is the emphasis of the opinion of the court in Boyd. This appears, too, in Weeks Case, Silverthorne, and in Amos.

Gouled v. United States carried the inhibition against unreasonable searches and seizures to the extreme limit. Its authority is not to be enlarged by implication, and must be confined to the precise state of facts disclosed by the record. A representative of the Intelligence Department of the Army, having by stealth obtained admission to the defendant's office, seized and carried away certain private papers valuable for evidential purposes. This was held an unreasonable search and seizure within the Fourth Amendment. A stealthy entrance in such circumstances ***464** became the equivalent to an entry by force. There was actual entrance into the private quarters of defendant and the taking away of something ****568** tangible. Here we have testimony only of voluntary conversations secretly overheard.

The amendment itself shows that the search is to be of material things-the person, the house, his papers, or his effects. The description of the warrant necessary to make the proceeding lawful is that it must specify the place to be searched and the person or things to be seized.

It is urged that the language of Mr. Justice Field in Ex parte Jackson, already quoted, offers an analogy to the interpretation of the Fourth Amendment in respect of wire tapping. But the analogy fails. The Fourth Amendment may have proper application to a sealed letter in the mail, because of the constitutional provision for the Postoffice Department and the relations between the government and those who pay to secure protection of their sealed letters. See Revised Statutes, ss 3978 to 3988, whereby Congress monopolizes the carriage of letters and excludes from that business everyone else, and section 3929 (39 USCA s 259), which forbids any postmaster or other person to open any letter not addressed to himself. It is plainly within the words of the amendment to say that the unlawful rifling by a government agent of a sealed letter is a search and seizure of the sender's papers of effects. The letter is a paper, an effect, and in the custody of a government that forbids carriage, except under its protection.

The United States takes no such care of telegraph or telephone messages as of mailed sealed letters. The amendment does not forbid what was done here. There was no searching. There was no seizure. The evidence was secured by the use of the

[237] 2 Metc. 329, 337.

[238] 19 Howell, State Trials, 1029.

sense of hearing and that only. There was no entry of the houses or offices of the defendants.

***465** By the invention of the telephone 50 years ago, and its application for the purpose of extending communications, one can talk with another at a far distant place.

The language of the amendment cannot be extended and expanded to include telephone wires, reaching to the whole world from the defendant's house or office. The intervening wires are not part of his house or office, any more than are the highways along which they are stretched.

____This court, in Carroll v. United States,[239]declared:

> 'The Fourth Amendment is to be construed in the light of what was deemed an unreasonable search and seizure when it was adopted, and in a manner which will conserve public interests, as well as the interest and rights of individual citizens.'

Justice Bradley, in the Boyd case, and Justice Clarke, in the Gouled case, said that the Fifth Amendment and the Fourth Amendment were to be liberally construed to effect the purpose of the framers of the Constitution in the interest of liberty. But that cannot justify enlargement of the language employed beyond the possible practical meaning of houses, persons, papers, and effects, or so to apply the words search and seizure as to forbid hearing or sight.

Hester v. United States,[240]held that the testimony of two officers of the law who trespassed on the defendant's land, concealed themselves 100 yards away from his house, and saw him come out and hand a bottle of whisky to another, was not inadmissible. While there was a trespass, there was no search of person, house, papers, or effects.[241]

Congress may, of course, protect the secrecy of telephone messages by making them, when intercepted, inadmissible in evidence in federal criminal trials, by direct legislation, ***466** and thus depart from the common law of evidence. But the courts may not adopt such a policy by attributing an enlarged and unusual meaning to the Fourth Amendment. The reasonable view is that one who installs in his house a telephone instrument with connecting wires intends to project his voice to those quite outside, and that the wires beyond his house, and messages while passing over them, are not within the protection of the Fourth Amendment. Here those who intercepted the projected voices were not in the house of either party to the conversation.

Neither the cases we have cited nor any of the many federal decisions brought to our attention hold the Fourth Amendment to have been violated as against a defendant, unless there has been an official search and seizure of his person or such a seizure of his papers or his tangible material effects or an actual physical invasion of his house 'or curtilage' for the purpose of making a seizure.

We think, therefore, that the wire tapping here disclosed did not amount to a search or seizure within the meaning of the Fourth Amendment.

What has been said disposes of the only question that comes within the terms of our order granting certiorari in these cases. But some of our number, departing from that order, have concluded that there is merit in the twofold objection, overruled in both courts below, that evidence obtained through intercepting of telephone messages by a government agents was inadmissible, because the mode of obtaining it was unethical and a misdemeanor under the law of Washington. To avoid any misapprehension of our views of that objection we shall deal with it in both of its phases.

---

[239] 267 U. S. 132, 149, 45 S. Ct. 280, 284 (69 L. Ed. 543, 39 A. L. R. 790).

[240] 265 U. S. 57, 44 S. Ct. 445, 68 L. Ed. 898.

[241] *United States v. Lee*, 274 U. S. 559, 563, 47 S. Ct. 746, 71 L. Ed. 1202; *Eversole v. State*, 106 Tex. Cr. R. 567, 294 S. W. 210.

While a territory, the English common law prevailed in Washington, and thus continued after her admission in 1889. The rules of evidence in criminal cases in courts of the **569 United States sitting there consequently are those of the common law.[242] *467

The common-law rule is that the admissibility of evidence is not affected by the illegality of the means by which it was obtained. Professor Greenleaf, in his work on Evidence,[243] says:

'It may be mentioned in this place, that though papers and other subjects of evidence may have been illegally taken from the possession of the party against whom they are offered, or otherwise unlawfully obtained, this is no valid objection to their admissibility, if they are pertinent to the issue. The court will not take notice how they were obtained, whether lawfully or unlawfully, nor will it form an issue, to determine that question.'

Mr. Jones, in his work on the same subject, refers to Mr. Greenleaf's statement, and says:'Where there is no violation of a constitutional guaranty, the verity of the above statement is absolute.'[244]

The rule is supported by many English and American cases cited by Jones,[245]and by Wigmore.[246]. It is recognized by this court in Adams v. New York.[247]The Weeks case announced an exception to the common law rule by excluding all evidence in the procuring of which government officials took part by methods forbidden by the Fourth and Fifth Amendments. Many state courts do not follow the Weeks case.[248]But those who do treat it as an exception to the general common-law rule and required by constitutional limitations.[249]***468** The common-law rule must apply in the case at bar.

Nor can we, without the sanction of congressional enactment, subscribe to the suggestion that the courts have a discretion to exclude evidence, the admission of which is not unconstitutional, because unethically secured. This would be at variance with the common-law doctrine generally supported by authority. There is no case that sustains, nor any recognized text-book that gives color to, such a view. Our general experience shows that much evidence has always been receivable, although not obtained by conformity to the highest ethics. The history of criminal trials shows numerous cases of prosecutions of oath-bound conspiracies for murder, robbery, and other crimes, where officers of the law have disguised themselves and joined the organizations, taken the oaths, and given themselves every appearance of active members engaged in the promotion of crime for the purpose of securing evidence. Evidence secured by such means has always been received.

A standard which would forbid the reception of evidence, if obtained by other than nice ethical conduct by government officials, would make society suffer and give criminals greater immunity than has been known heretofore. In the absence of

---

[242] *United States v. Reid,* 12 How. 361, 363, 366, 13 L. Ed. 1023; *Logan v. United States*, 144 U. S. 263, 301, 12 S. Ct. 617, 36 L. Ed. 429; *Rosen v. United States*, 245 U. S. 467, 38 S. Ct. 148, 62 L. Ed. 406; *Withaup v. United States* (C. C. A.) 127 F. 530, 534; *Robinson v. United States* (C. C. A.) 292 F. 683, 685.

[243] Volume 1 (12th Ed., by Redfield) s 254(a).

[244] Section 2075, note 3, vol. 5.

[245] Section 2075, note 3, and section 2076, note 6, vol. 5.

[246] Vol. 4, s 2183.

[247] 192 U. S. 585, 24 S. Ct. 372, 48 L. Ed. 575.

[248] *People v. Defore*, 242 N. Y. 13, 150 N. E. 585.

[249] *Hughes v. State*, 145 Tenn. 544, 551, 566, 238 S. W. 588, 20 A. L. R. 639; *State v. Wills*, 91 W. Va. 659, 677, 114 S. E. 261, 24 A. L. R. 1398; *State v. Slamon*, 73 Vt. 212, 214, 215, 50 A. 1097, 87 Am. St. Rep. 711; *Gindrat v. People*, 138 Ill. 103, 111, 27 N. E. 1085; *People v. Castree*, 311 Ill. 392, 396, 397, 143 N. E. 112, 32 A. L. R. 357;*State v. Gardner*, 77 Mont. 8, 21, 249 P. 574, 52 A. L. R. 454; State v. Fahn, 53 N. D. 203, 210, 205 N. W. 67.

controlling legislation by Congress, those who realize the difficulties in bringing offenders to justice may well deem it wise that the exclusion of evidence should be confined to cases where rights under the Constitution would be violated by admitting it.

The statute of Washington,[250] adopted in 1909, providesthat:

> 'Every person * * * who shall intercept, read or in any manner interrupt or delay the sending of a message over any telegraph or telephone line * * * shall be guilty of a misdemeanor.'

***469** This statute does not declare that evidence obtained by such interception shall be inadmissible, and by the common law, already referred to, it would not be.[251]Whether the state of Washington may prosecute and punish federal officers violating this law, and those whose messages were intercepted may sue them civilly, is not before us. But clearly a statute, passed 20 years after the admission of the state into the Union, cannot affect the rules of evidence applicable in courts of the United States. Chief Justice Taney, in United States v. Reid,[252]construing the thirty-fourth section of the Judiciary Act[253], said:

> 'But it could not be supposed, without very plain words to show it, that Congress intended to give to the states the power of prescribing the rules of evidence in trials for offenses against the United States. For this construction would in effect place the criminal jurisprudence of one sovereignty under the control of another.'[254]

The judgments of the Circuit Court of Appeals are affirmed. The mandates will go down forthwith under rule 31.

Affirmed.

(The dissents of Mr. Justice BRANDEIS, Mr. Justice HOLMES, Mr. Justice BUTLER and Mr. Justice STONE are omitted).

******

Black Letter Law

Held that government's activities in electronically listening to and recording defendant's words spoken into telephone receiver did not fall under the protection of the Fourth Amendment. Case decided the issue of technology and the law based upon a traditional trespass rationale forming the bedrock of Fourth Amendment jurisprudence.

The *Katz* decision did not overturn *Olmstead*, but provided an additional way to consider the interaction of the Fourth Amendment with technology.

---

250 Remington Compiled Statutes 1922, s 2656(18).

251 *People v. McDonald*, 177 App. Div. 806, 165 N. Y. S. 41.

252 12 How. 361, 363 (13 L. Ed. 1023),

253 Now 28 USCA s 77.

254 See, also, *Withaup v. United States* (C. C. A.) 127 F. 530, 534.

88 S.Ct. 507

Katz

V.

United States

No. 35. | Argued Oct. 17, 1967. | Decided Dec. 18, 1967.

MR. JUSTICE STEWART delivered the opinion of the Court.

The petitioner was convicted in the District Court for the Southern District of California under an eight-count indictment charging him with transmitting wagering information by telephone from Los Angeles to Miami and Boston in violation of a federal statute. At trial the Government was permitted, over the petitioner's objection, to introduce evidence of the petitioner's end of telephone conversations, overheard by FBI agents who had attached an electronic listening and recording device to the outside of the public telephone booth from which he had placed his calls. In affirming his conviction, the Court of Appeals rejected the contention that the recordings had been obtained in violation of the Fourth Amendment, ***349** because '(t)here was no physical entrance into the area occupied by, (the petitioner).' ****510** We granted certiorari in order to consider the constitutional questions thus presented.

The petitioner had phrased those questions as follows:

> 'A. Whether a public telephone booth is a constitutionally protected area so that evidence obtained by attaching an electronic listening recording device to the top of such a booth is obtained in violation of the right to privacy of the user of the booth.
>
> ***350** 'B. Whether physical penetration of a constitutionally protected area is necessary before a search and seizure can be said to be violative of the Fourth Amendment to the United States Constitution.'

We decline to adopt this formulation of the issues. In the first place the correct solution of Fourth Amendment problems is not necessarily promoted by incantation of the phrase 'constitutionally protected area.' Secondly, the Fourth Amendment cannot be translated into a general constitutional 'right to privacy.' That Amendment protects individual privacy against certain kinds of governmental intrusion, but its protections go further, and often have nothing to do with privacy at all. Other provisions of the Constitution protect personal privacy from other forms of governmental invasion. But the protection of a ****511** person's general right to privacy-his right to be let alone by other people-is, like the ***351** protection of his property and of his very life, left largely to the law of the individual States.

Because of the misleading way the issues have been formulated, the parties have attached great significance to the characterization of the telephone booth from which the petitioner placed his calls. The petitioner has strenuously argued that the booth was a 'constitutionally protected area.' The Government has maintained with equal vigor that it was not. But this effort to decide whether or not a given 'area,' viewed in the abstract, is 'constitutionally protected' deflects attention from the problem presented by this case. For the Fourth Amendment protects people, not places. What a person knowingly exposes to the public, even in his own home or office, is not a subject of Fourth Amendment protection.[255]But what he seeks to preserve as private, even in an area accessible to the public, may be constitutionally protected.[256] ***352**

The Government stresses the fact that the telephone booth from which the petitioner made his calls was constructed partly of glass, so that he was as visible

[255] See *Lewis v. United States*, 385 U.S. 206, 210, 87 S.Ct. 424, 427, 17 L.Ed.2d 312; *United States v. Lee*, 274 U.S. 559, 563, 47 S.Ct. 746, 748, 71 L.Ed. 1202.

[256] See *Rios v. United States*, 364 U.S. 253, 80 S.Ct. 1431, 4 L.Ed.2d 1688; *Ex parte Jackson*, 96 U.S. 727, 733, 24 L.Ed. 877.

after he entered it as he would have been if he had remained outside. But what he sought to exclude when he entered the booth was not the intruding eye-it was the uninvited ear. He did not shed his right to do so simply because he made his calls from a place where he might be seen. No less than an individual in a business office, in a friend's apartment, or in a taxicab, a person in a telephone booth may rely upon the protection of the Fourth Amendment. One who occupies it, shuts the door behind him, and pays the toll that permits ****512** him to place a call is surely entitled to assume that the words he utters into the mouthpiece will not be broadcast to the world. To read the Constitution more narrowly is to ignore the vital role that the public telephone has come to play in private communication.

The Government contends, however, that the activities of its agents in this case should not be tested by Fourth Amendment requirements, for the surveillance technique they employed involved no physical penetration of the telephone booth from which the petitioner placed his calls. It is true that the absence of such penetration was at one time thought to foreclose further Fourth Amendment inquiry,[257]for that Amendment was thought to limit only searches and seizures of tangible ***353** property. But '(t)he premise that property interests control the right of the Government to search and seize has been discredited.'[258]Thus, although a closely divided Court supposed in Olmstead that surveillance without any trespass and without the seizure of any material object fell outside the ambit of the Constitution, we have since departed from the narrow view on which that decision rested. Indeed, we have expressly held that the Fourth Amendment governs not only the seizure of tangible items, but extends as well to the recording of oral statements overheard without any 'technical trespass under * * * local property law.'[259]Once this much is acknowledged, and once it is recognized that the Fourth Amendment protects people-and not simply 'areas'-against unreasonable searches and seizures it becomes clear that the reach of that Amendment cannot turn upon the presence or absence of a physical intrusion into any given enclosure.

We conclude that the underpinnings of Olmstead and Goldman have been so eroded by our subsequent decisions that the 'trespass' doctrine there enunciated can no longer be regarded as controlling. The Government's activities in electronically listening to and recording the petitioner's words violated the privacy upon which he justifiably relied while using the telephone booth and thus constituted a 'search and seizure' within the meaning of the Fourth Amendment. The fact that the electronic device employed to achieve that end did not happen to penetrate the wall of the booth can have no constitutional significance.

The question remaining for decision, then, is whether the search and seizure conducted in this case complied with constitutional standards. In that regard, the Government's position is that its agents acted in an entirely defensible manner: They did not begin their electronic surveillance until investigation of the petitioner's activities had established a strong probability that he was using the telephone in question to transmit gambling information to persons in other States, in violation of federal law. Moreover, the surveillance was limited, both in scope and in duration, to the specific purpose of establishing the contents of the petitioner's unlawful telephonic communications. The agents confined their surveillance to the brief periods during which he used the telephone booth, and ****513** they took great care to overhear only the conversations of the petitioner himself.

Accepting this account of the Government's actions as accurate, it is clear that this surveillance was so narrowly circumscribed that a duly authorized magistrate, properly notified of the need for such investigation, specifically informed of the basis

---

[257] *Olmstead v. United States*, 277 U.S. 438, 457, 464, 466, 48 S.Ct. 564, 565, 567, 568, 72 L.Ed. 944; *Goldman v. United States*, 316 U.S. 129, 134-136, 62 S.Ct. 993, 995-997, 86 L.Ed. 1322.

[258] *Warden, Md. Penitentiary v. Hayden*, 387 U.S. 294, 304, 87 S.Ct. 1642, 1648, 18 L.Ed.2d 782.

[259] *Silverman v. United States*, 365 U.S. 505, 511, 81 S.Ct. 679, 682, 5 L.Ed.2d 734.

on which it was to proceed, and clearly apprised of the precise intrusion it would entail, could constitutionally have authorized, with appropriate safeguards, the very limited search and seizure that the Government asserts in fact took place. Only last Term we sustained the validity of ***355** such an authorization, holding that, under sufficiently 'precise and discriminate circumstances,' a federal court may empower government agents to employ a concealed electronic device 'for the narrow and particularized purpose of ascertaining the truth of the * * * allegations' of a 'detailed factual affidavit alleging the commission of a specific criminal offense.'[260]Discussing that holding, the Court in Berger v. State of New York,[261]said that 'the order authorizing the use of the electronic device' in Osborn 'afforded similar protections to those * * * of conventional warrants authorizing the seizure of tangible evidence.' Through those protections, 'no greater invasion of privacy was permitted than was necessary under the circumstances.'[262] Here, too, ****514** a similar ***356** judicial order could have accommodated 'the legitimate needs of law enforcement' by authorizing the carefully limited use of electronic surveillance.

The Government urges that, because its agents relied upon the decisions in Olmstead and Goldman, and because they did no more here than they might properly have done with prior judicial sanction, we should retroactively validate their conduct. That we cannot do. It is apparent that the agents in this case acted with restraint. Yet the inescapable fact is that this restraint was imposed by the agents themselves, not by a judicial officer. They were not required, before commencing the search, to present their estimate of probable cause for detached scrutiny by a neutral magistrate. They were not compelled, during the conduct of the search itself, to observe precise limits established in advance by a specific court order. Nor were they directed, after the search had been completed, to notify the authorizing magistrate in detail of all that had been seized. In the absence of such safeguards, this Court has never sustained a search upon the sole ground that officers reasonably expected to find evidence of a particular crime and voluntarily confined their activities to the least intrusive ***357** means consistent with that end. Searches conducted without warrants have been held unlawful 'notwithstanding facts unquestionably showing probable cause,'[263]for the Constitution requires 'that the deliberate, impartial judgment of a judicial officer * * * be interposed between the citizen and the police * * *.'[264]'Over and again this Court has emphasized that the mandate of the (Fourth) Amendment requires adherence to judicial processes,'[265]and that searches conducted outside the judicial process, without prior approval by judge or magistrate, are per se unreasonable under the Fourth Amendment18 -subject only to a few specifically established and well-delineated exceptions.

It is difficult to imagine how any of those exceptions could ever apply to the sort of search and seizure involved in this case. Even electronic surveillance substantially contemporaneous with an individual's arrest could hardly be deemed an 'incident' of that arrest. ****515 *358** Nor could the use of electronic surveillance without prior authorization be justified on grounds of 'hot pursuit.' And, of course, the very nature of electronic surveillance precludes its use pursuant to the suspect's consent.

The Government does not question these basic principles. Rather, it urges the creation of a new exception to cover this case. It argues that surveillance of a telephone booth should be exempted from the usual requirement of advance authorization by a magistrate upon a showing of probable cause. We cannot agree. Omission

[260] *Osborn v. United States*, 385 U.S. 323, 329-330, 87 S.Ct. 429, 433, 17 L.Ed.2d 394.

[261] 388 U.S. 41, 87 S.Ct. 1873, 18 L.Ed.2d 1040.

[262] Id., at 57, 87 S.Ct. at 1882.

[263] *Agnello v. United States*, 269 U.S. 20, 33, 46 S.Ct. 4, 6, 70 L.Ed. 145.

[264] *Wong Sun v. United States*, 371 U.S. 471, 481-482, 83 S.Ct. 407, 414, 9 L.Ed.2d 441.

[265] *United States v. Jeffers*, 342 U.S. 48, 51, 72 S.Ct. 93, 95, 96 L.Ed. 59.

of such authorization 'bypasses the safeguards provided by an objective predetermination of probable cause, and substitutes instead the far less reliable procedure of an after-the-event justification for the * * * search, too likely to be subtly influenced by the familiar shortcomings of hindsight judgment.'[266]And bypassing a neutral predetermination of the scope of a search leaves individuals secure from Fourth Amendment ***359** violations 'only in the discretion of the police.'[267]

These considerations do not vanish when the search in question is transferred from the setting of a home, an office, or a hotel room to that of a telephone booth. Wherever a man may be, he is entitled to know that he will remain free from unreasonable searches and seizures. The government agents here ignored 'the procedure of antecedent justification * * * that is central to the Fourth Amendment,' a procedure that we hold to be a constitutional precondition of the kind of electronic surveillance involved in this case. Because the surveillance here failed to meet that condition, and because it led to the petitioner's conviction, the judgment must be reversed.

It is so ordered.

Judgment reversed.

*****

Mr. Justice HARLAN, concurring.

I join the opinion of the Court, which I read to hold only (a) that an enclosed telephone booth is an area where, like a home,[268]and unlike a field,[269]a person has a constitutionally protected reasonable expectation of privacy; (b) that electronic as well as physical intrusion into a place that is in this sense private may constitute a violation of the Fourth Amendment; ***361** and (c) that the invasion of a constitutionally protected area by federal authorities is, as the Court has long held, presumptively unreasonable in the absence of a search warrant.

As the Court's opinion states, 'the Fourth Amendment protects people, not places.' The question, however, is what protection it affords to those people. Generally, as here, the answer to that question requires reference to a 'place.' My understanding of the rule that has emerged from prior decisions is that there is a twofold requirement, first that a person have exhibited an actual (subjective) expectation of privacy and, second, that the expectation be one that society is prepared to recognize as 'reasonable.' Thus a man's home is, for most purposes, a place where he expects privacy, but objects, activities, or statements that he exposes to the 'plain view' of outsiders are not 'protected' because no intention to keep them to himself has been exhibited. On the other hand, conversations in the open would not be protected against being overheard, for the expectation of privacy under the circumstances would be unreasonable.[270]

The critical fact in this case is that '(o)ne who occupies it, (a telephone ****517** booth) shuts the door behind him, and pays the toll that permits him to place a call is surely entitled to assume' that his conversation is not being intercepted.[271]The point is not that the booth is 'accessible to the public' at other times, ante, at 511, but that it

---

[266] *Beck v. State of Ohio*, 379 U.S. 89, 96, 85S.Ct. 223, 228, 13 L.Ed.2d 142.

[267] Id., at 97, 85 S.Ct. at 229.

[268] *Weeks v. United States*, 232 U.S. 383, 34 S.Ct. 341, 58 L.Ed. 652,

[269] *Hester v. United States*, 265 U.S. 57, 44 S.Ct. 445, 68 L.Ed. 898.

[270] Cf. *Hester v. United States, supra*.

[271] Ante, at 511.

is a temporarily private place whose momentary occupants' expectations of freedom from intrusion are recognized as reasonable.[272]

In Silverman v. United States,[273]we held that eavesdropping accomplished by means of an electronic device that penetrated the premises occupied by petitioner was a violation of the Fourth Amendment. ***362** That case established that interception of conversations reasonably intended to be private could constitute a 'search and seizure,' and that the examination or taking of physical property was not required. This view of the Fourth Amendment was followed in Wong Sun v.United States,[274]and Berger v. State of New York,[275] In Silverman we found it unnecessary to re-examine Goldman v. United States,[276]which had held that electronic surveillance accomplished without the physical penetration of petitioner's premises by a tangible object did not violate the Fourth Amendment. This case requires us to reconsider Goldman, and I agree that it should now be overruled.* Its limitation on Fourth Amendment protection is, in the present day, bad physics as well as bad law, for reasonable expectations of privacy may be defeated by electronic as well as physical invasion.

Finally, I do not read the Court's opinion to declare that no interception of a conversation one-half of which occurs in a public telephone booth can be reasonable in the absence of a warrant. As elsewhere under the Fourth Amendment, warrants are the general rule, to which the legitimate needs of law enforcement may demand specific exceptions. It will be time enough to consider any such exceptions when an appropriate occasion presents itself, and I agree with the Court that this is not one.

Mr. Justice BLACK, dissenting.

If I could agree with the Court that eavesdropping carried on by electronic means (equivalent to wiretapping) constitutes a 'search' or 'seizure,' I would be happy to join the Court's opinion. For on that premise my Brother Stewart sets out methods in accord with the Fourth Amendment to guide States in the enactment and enforcement of laws passed to regulate wiretapping by government. In this respect today's opinion differs sharply from Berger v. State of New York,[277]decided last Term, which held void on its face a New York statute authorizing wiretapping on warrants issued by magistrates on showings of probable cause. The Berger case also set up what appeared to be insuperable obstacles to the valid passage of such wiretapping laws by States. The Court's opinion in this case, however, removes the doubts about state power in this field and abates to a large extent the confusion and near-paralyzing effect of the Berger holding. Notwithstanding these good efforts of the Court, I am still unable to agree with its interpretation of the Fourth Amendment.

My basic objection is twofold: (1) I do not believe that the words of the Amendment will bear the meaning given them by today's decision, and (2) I do not believe that it is the proper role of this Court to rewrite the Amendment in order 'to bring it into harmony with the times' and thus reach a result that many people believe to be desirable.

***365** While I realize that an argument based on the meaning of words lacks the scope, and no doubt the appeal, of broad policy discussions and philosophical discourses on such nebulous subjects as privacy, for me the language of the Amendment

---

[272] *Cf. Rios v. United States*, 364 U.S. 253, 80 S.Ct. 1431, 4 L.Ed.2d 1688.

[273] 365 U.S. 505, 81 S.Ct. 679, 5 L.Ed.2d 734,

[274] 371 U.S. 471, at 485, 83 S.Ct. 407, at 416, 9 L.Ed.2d 441.

[275] 388 U.S. 41, at 51, 87 S.Ct. 1873, at 1879, 18 L.Ed.2d 1040. Also compare *Osborne v. United States*, 385 U.S. 323, at 327, 87 S.Ct. 429, at 431, 17 L.Ed.2d 394.

[276] 316 U.S. 129, 62 S.Ct. 993, 86 L.Ed. 1322.

[277] 388 U.S. 41, 87 S.Ct. 1873, 18 L.Ed.2d 1040,

is the crucial place to look in construing a written document such as our Constitution. The Fourth Amendment says that

'The right of the people to be secure in their persons, houses, papers, and effects, against unreasonable searches and seizures, shall not be violated, and no Warrants shall issue, but upon probable cause, supported by Oath or affirmation, and particularly describing the place to be searched, and the persons or things to be seized.'

The first clause protects 'persons, houses, papers, and effects, against unreasonable searches and seizures * * *.' **519 These words connote the idea of tangible things with size, form, and weight, things capable of being searched, seized, or both. The second clause of the Amendment still further establishes its Framers' purpose to limit its protection to tangible things by providing that no warrants shall issue but those 'particularly describing the place to be searched, and the persons or things to be seized.' A conversation overheard by eavesdropping, whether by plain snooping or wiretapping, is not tangible and, under the normally accepted meanings of the words, can neither be searched nor seized. In addition the language of the second clause indicates that the Amendment refers not only to something tangible so it can be seized but to something already in existence so it can be described. Yet the Court's interpretation would have the Amendment apply to overhearing future conversations which by their very nature are nonexistent until they take place. How can one 'describe' a future conversation, and, if one cannot, how can a magistrate issue a warrant to eavesdrop one in the future? It is argued that information showing what ***366** is expected to be said is sufficient to limit the boundaries of what later can be admitted into evidence; but does such general information really meet the specific language of the Amendment which says 'particularly describing'? Rather than using language in a completely artificial way, I must conclude that the Fourth Amendment simply does not apply to eavesdropping.

Tapping telephone wires, of course, was an unknown possibility at the time the Fourth Amendment was adopted. But eavesdropping (and wiretapping is nothing more than eavesdropping by telephone) was, as even the majority opinion in Berger, supra, recognized, 'an ancient practice which at common law was condemned as a nuisance.[278]In those days the eavesdropper listened by naked ear under the eaves of houses or their windows, or beyond their walls seeking out private discourse.'[279]There can be no doubt that the Framers were aware of this practice, and if they had desired to outlaw or restrict the use of evidence obtained by eavesdropping, I believe that they would have used the appropriate language to do so in the Fourth Amendment. They certainly would not have left such a task to the ingenuity of language-stretching judges. No one, it seems to me, can read the debates on the Bill of Rights without reaching the conclusion that its Framers and critics well knew the meaning of the words they used, what they would be understood to mean by others, their scope and their limitations. Under these circumstances it strikes me as a charge against their scholarship, their common sense and their candor to give to the Fourth Amendment's language the eavesdropping meaning the Court imputes to it today.

I do not deny that common sense requires and that this Court often has said that the Bill of Rights' safeguards should be given a liberal construction. This ***367** principle, however, does not justify construing the search and seizure amendment as applying to eavesdropping or the 'seizure' of conversations. The Fourth Amendment was aimed directly at the abhorred practice of breaking in, ransacking and searching homes and other buildings and seizing people's personal belongings without warrants issued by magistrates. The Amendment deserves, and this Court has given it, a liberal construction in order to protect against warrantless searches of buildings and

[278] IV Blackstone, Commentaries s 168.

[279] 388 U.S., at 45, 87 S.Ct., at 1876.

seizures of tangible personal effects. But until today this Court has refused to say that eavesdropping comes within the ambit of Fourth Amendment restrictions.[280]

****520** So far I have attempted to state why I think the words of the Fourth Amendment prevent its application to eavesdropping. It is important now to show that this has been the traditional view of the Amendment's scope since its adoption and that the Court's decision in this case, along with its amorphous holding in Berger last Term, marks the first real departure from that view.

The first case to reach this Court which actually involved a clear-cut test of the Fourth Amendment's applicability to eavesdropping through a wiretap was, of course, Olmstead.[281]In holding tha the interception of private telephone conversations by means of wiretapping was not a violation of the Fourth Amendment, this Court, speaking through Mr. Chief Justice Taft, examined the language of the Amendment and found, just as I do now, that the words could not be stretched to encompass overheard conversations:

'The amendment itself shows that the search is to be of material things-the person, the house, his papers, or his effects. The description of the warrant necessary to make the proceeding lawful is ***368** that it must specify the place to be searched and the person or things to be seized. * * *

'Justice Bradley in the Boyd case[282], and Justice Clarke in the Gouled case,[283], said that the Fifth Amendment and the Fourth Amendment were to be liberally construed to effect the purpose of the framers of the Constitution in the interest of liberty. But that can not justify enlargement of the language employed beyond the possible practical meaning of houses, persons, papers, and effects, or so to apply the words search and seizure as to forbid hearing or sight.'[284]

Goldman v. United States,[285]is an even clearer example of this Court's traditional refusal to consider eavesdropping as being covered by the Fourth Amendment. There federal agents used a 'detectaphone,' which was placed on the wall of an adjoining room, to listen to the conversation of a defendant carried on in his private office and intended to be confined within the four walls of the room. This Court, referring to Olmstead, found no Fourth Amendment violation.

It should be noted that the Court in Olmstead based its decision squarely on the fact that wiretapping or eavesdropping does not violate the Fourth Amendment. As shown, supra, in the cited quotation from the case, theCourt went to great pains to examine the actual language of the Amendment and found that the words used simply could not be stretched to cover eavesdropping. That there was no trespass was not the determinative factor, and indeed the Court in citing Hester v. United States,[286] indicated that even where there was a trespass the Fourth Amendment does not automatically apply to evidence obtained by 'hearing or ***369** sight.' The Olmstead majority characterized Hester as holding 'that the testimony of two officers of the law who trespassed on the defendant's land, concealed themselves 100 yards away from his house, and saw him come out and hand a bottle of whiskey to another, was not inadmissible. While there was a trespass, there was no search of person, house,

---

[280] See, e.g., *Olmstead v. United States*, 277 U.S. 438, 48 S.Ct. 564, 72 L.Ed. 944 (1928), and *Goldman v. United States*, 316 U.S. 129, 62 S.Ct. 993, 86 L.Ed. 1322 (1942).

[281] *supra.*

[282] *Boyd v. United States*, 116 U.S. 616, 6 S.Ct. 524, 29 L.Ed. 746.

[283] *Gouled v. United States*, 255 U.S. 298, 41 S.Ct. 261, 65 L.Ed. 647.

[284] 277 U.S., at 464-465, 48 S.Ct., at 568.

[285] 316 U.S. 129, 62 S.Ct. 993, 86 L.Ed. 1322.

[286] 265 U.S. 57, 44 S.Ct. 445, 68 L.Ed. 898.

papers, or effects.'[287]Thus the clear holding of the Olmstead and Goldman cases, undiluted by any question of trespass, is that eavesdropping, in both its original and modern forms, is not violative of the Fourth Amendment.

While my reading of the Olmstead and Goldman cases convinces me that they were decided on the basis of the inapplicability **521 of the wording of the Fourth Amendment to eavesdropping, and not on any trespass basis, this is not to say that unauthorized intrusion has not played an important role in search and seizure cases. This Court has adopted an exclusionary rule to bar evidence obtained by means of such intrusions. As I made clear in my dissenting opinion in Berger v. State of New York,[288]I continue to believe that this exclusionary rule formulated in Weeks v. United States,[289]rests on the 'supervisory power' of this Court over other federal courts and is not rooted in the Fourth Amendment.[290]This rule has caused the Court to refuse to accept evidence where there has been such an intrusion regardless of whether there has been a search or seizure in violation of the Fourth Amendment. As this Court said in Lopez v. United States,[291]'The Court has in the past sustained instances of 'electronic eavesdropping' against constitutional challenge, when devices have been used to enable government agents to overhear conversations which would have been beyond the reach of the human ear.[292]***370**It has been insisted only that the electronic device not be planted by an unlawful physical invasion of a constitutionally protected area.'[293]

To support its new interpretation of the Fourth Amendment, which in effect amounts to a rewriting of the language, the Court's opinion concludes that 'the underpinnings of Olmstead and Goldman have been * * * eroded by our subsequent decisions * * *.' But the only cases cited as accomplishing this 'eroding' are Silverman v. United States[294]and Warden, Md. Penitentiary v. Hayden.[295]Neither of these cases 'eroded' Olmstead or Goldman. Silverman is an interesting choice since there the Court expressly refused to re-examine the rationale of Olmstead or Goldman although such a re-examination was strenuously urged upon the Court by the petitioners' counsel. Also it is significant that in Silverman, as the Court described it, 'the eavesdropping was accomplished by means on an unauthorized physical penetration into the premises occupied by the petitioners,'[296] thus calling into play the supervisory exclusionary rule of evidence. As I have pointed out above, where there is an unauthorized intrusion, this Court has rejected admission of evidence obtained regardless of whether there has been an unconstitutional search and seizure. The majority's decision here relies heavily on the statement in the opinion that the Court 'need not pause to consider whether or not there was a technical trespass under the local property law relating to party walls.'[297]Yet this statement should not becloud the fact that time and again the opinion emphasizes that there has been an unauthorized intrusion: 'For a fair reading of the record in this case shows that the eaves-

---

[287] 277 U.S., at 465, 48 S.Ct., at 568.

[288] 388 U.S. 41, 76, 87 S.Ct. 1873, 1892, 18 L.Ed.2d 1040.

[289] 232 U.S. 383, 34 S.Ct. 341, 58 L.Ed. 652.

[290] See *Wolf v. People of State of Colorado*, concurring opinion, 338 U.S. 25, 39, at 40, 69 S.Ct. 1359, 1367, at 1368, 93 L.Ed. 1782. See also *Mapp v. Ohio*, concurring opinion, 367 U.S. 643, 661-666, 81 S.Ct. 1684, 1694-1698, 6 L.Ed.2d 1081.

[291] 373 U.S. 427, 438-439, 83 S.Ct. 1381, 1387, 10 L.Ed.2d 462,

[292] Citing *Olmstead* and *Goldman*.

[293] Silverman v. United States.

[294] 365 U.S. 505, 81 S.Ct. 679, 5 L.Ed.2d 734.

[295] 387 U.S. 294, 87 S.Ct. 1642, 18 L.Ed.2d 782.

[296] 365 U.S., at 509, 81 S.Ct., at 681.

[297] At 511, 81 S.Ct., at 682.

dropping was accomplished by means of an unauthorized physical penetration into the premises occupied by the petitioners.'[298]'Eavesdropping ***371** accomplished by means of such a physical intrusion is beyond the pale of even those decisions * * *.'[299]'Here * * * the officers overheard the petitioners' conversations only by usurping part of the petitioners' house or office * * *.'[300]'(D)ecision here * * * is based upon the reality of an actual intrusion * * *.'[301]'We find no occasion to re-examine Goldman ****522** here, but we decline to go beyond it, by even a fraction of an inch.'[302]As if this were not enough, Justices Clark and Whittaker concurred with the following statement: 'In view of the determination by the majority that the unauthorized physical penetration into petitioners' premises constituted sufficient trespass to remove this case from the coverage of earlier decisions, we feel obliged to join in the Court's opinion.'[303]As I made clear in my dissent in Berger, the Court in Silverman held the evidence should be excluded by virtue of the exclusionary rule and 'I would not have agreed with the Court's opinion in Silverman * * * had I thought that the result depended on finding a violation of the Fourth Amendment * * *.'[304] In light of this and the fact that the Court expressly refused to re-examine Olmstead and Goldman, I cannot read Silverman as overturning the interpretation stated very plainly in Olmstead and followed in Goldman that eavesdropping is not covered by the Fourth Amendment.

The other 'eroding' case cited in the Court's opinion is Warden, Md. Penitentiary v. Hayden,[305]It appears that this case is cited for the proposition that the Fourth Amendment applies to 'intangibles,' such as conversation, and the following ambiguous statement is quoted from the opinion: 'The premise that property interests control the right of the Government to search and seize has been discredited.'[306]But far from being concerned ***372** with eavesdropping, Warden, Md. Penitentiary v. Hayden upholds the seizure of clothes, certainly tangibles by any definition. The discussion of property interests was involved only with the common-law rule that the right to seize property depended upon proof of a superior property interest.

Thus, I think that although the Court attempts to convey the impression that for some reason today Olmstead and Goldman are no longer good law, it must face up to the fact that these cases have never been overruled or even 'eroded.' It is the Court's opinions in this case and Berger which for the first time since 1791, when the Fourth Amendment was adopted, have declared that eavesdropping is subject to Fourth Amendment restrictions and that conversation can be 'seized.'* I must align myself with all those judges who up to this year have never been able to impute such a meaning to the words of the Amendment.

***373** Since I see no way in which the words of the Fourth Amendment can be construed to apply to eavesdropping, that closes the matter for me. In interpreting the Bill of Rights, I willingly go as far ****523** as a liberal construction of the language takes me, but I simply cannot in good conscience give a meaning to words which they have never before been thought to have and which they certainly do not have in common ordinary usage. I will not distort the words of the Amendment in order to 'keep the Constitution up to date' or 'to bring it into harmony with the times.' It was

---

298 365 U.S., at 509, 81 S.Ct., at 682 emphasis added.

299 At 509, 81 S.Ct., at 682, emphasis added.

300 At 511, 81 S.Ct., at 682, emphasis added.

301 At 512, 81 S.Ct., at 683, emphasis added.

302 At 512, 81 S.Ct., at 683, emphasis added.

303 At 513, 81 S.Ct., at 684, emphasis added.

304 388 U.S., at 79-80, 87 S.Ct., at 1894.

305 387 U.S. 294, 87 S.Ct. 1642, 18 L.Ed.2d 782.

306 387 U.S., at 304, 87 S.Ct., at 1648.

never meant that this Court have such power, which in effect would make us a continuously functioning constitutional convention.

With this decision the Court has completed, I hope, its rewriting of the Fourth Amendment, which started only recently when the Court began referring incessantly to the Fourth Amendment not so much as a law against unreasonable searches and seizures as one to protect an individual's privacy. By clever word juggling the Court finds it plausible to argue that language aimed specifically at searches and seizures of things that can be searched and seized may, to protect privacy, be applied to eavesdropped evidence of conversations that can neither be searched nor seized. Few things happen to an individual that do not affect his privacy in one way or another. Thus, by arbitrarily substituting the Court's language, designed to protect privacy, for the Constitution's language, designed to protect against unreasonable searches and seizures, the Court has made the Fourth Amendment its vehicle for holding all laws violative of the Constitution which offend the Court's broadest concept of privacy. As I said in Griswold v. State of Connecticut,[307]'The Court talks about a constitutional 'right of privacy' as though there is some constitutional provision or provisions forbidding any law ever to be passed which might abridge the 'privacy' ***374** of individuals. But there is not.'[308] I made clear in that dissent my fear of the dangers involved when this Court uses the 'broad, abstract and ambiguous concept' of 'privacy' as a 'comprehensive substitute for the Fourth Amendment's guarantee against 'unreasonable searches and seizures."[309]

The Fourth Amendment protects privacy only to the extent that it prohibits unreasonable searches and seizures of 'persons, houses, papers, and effects.' No general right is created by the Amendment so as to give this Court the unlimited power to hold unconstitutional everything which affects privacy. Certainly the Framers, well acquainted as they were with the excesses of governmental power, did not intend to grant this Court such omnipotent lawmaking authority as that. The history of governments proves that it is dangerous to freedom to repose such powers in courts.

For these reasons I respectfully dissent.

Black Letter Law

Held that government's activities in electronically listening to and recording defendant's words spoken into telephone receiver in public telephone booth violated the privacy upon which defendant justifiably relied while using the telephone booth and thus constituted a 'search and seizure' within Fourth Amendment. Lack of trespass, penetration, into the phone booth by the device was held to have no constitutional significance. The court held that the search and seizure was invalid without a warrant, even if the government could show after the fact that a warrant would have been granted if requested.

Established reasonable expectation of privacy standard for 4th amendment cases.

---

[307] 381 U.S. 479, 85 S.Ct. 1678, 14 L.Ed.2d 510.

[308] Dissenting opinion, at 508, 85 S.Ct. at 1695.

[309] See generally dissenting opinion, at 507-527, 85 S.Ct., at 1694-1705.

U.S. V. White

91 S.Ct. 1122

Supreme Court of the United States

United States

v.

White

No. 13. | Argued Nov. 10, 1969. | Reargued Oct. 20, 1970. | Decided April 5, 1971. | Rehearing Denied May 17, 1971.

Mr. Justice WHITE announced the judgment of the Court and an opinion in which THE CHIEF JUSTICE, Mr. Justice STEWART, and Mr. Justice BLACKMUN join.

In 1966, respondent James A. White was tried and convicted under two consolidated indictments charging various illegal transactions in narcotics violative of 26 U.S.C. s 4705(a) and 21 U.S.C. s 174. He was fined and sentenced as a second offender to 25-year concurrent sentences. The issue before us is whether the Fourth Amendment bars from evidence the testimony of governmental agents who related certain conversations which had occurred between defendant White and a government informant, Harvey Jackson, and which the agents ***747** overheard by monitoring the frequency of a radio transmitter carried by Jackson and concealed on his person.1On four occasions ****1124** the conversations took place in Jackson's home; each of these conversations was overheard by an agent concealed in a kitchen closet with Jackson's consent and by a second agent outside the house using a radio receiver. Four other conversations-one in respondent's home, one in a restaurant, and two in Jackson's car-were overheard by the use of radio equipment. The prosecution was unable to locate and produce Jackson at the trial and the trial court overruled objections to the testimony of the agents who conducted the electronic surveillance. The jury returned a guilty verdict and defendant appealed.

The Court of Appeals read Katz v. United States,[310]as overruling On Lee v. United States,[311]and interpreting the Fourth Amendment to forbid the introduction of the agents' testimony in the circumstances of this case. Accordingly, the court reversed but without adverting to the fact that the transactions at issue here had occurred before Katz was decided in this Court. In our view, the Court of Appeals misinterpreted both the Katz case and the Fourth Amendment and in any event erred in applying the Katz case to events that occurred before that decision was rendered by this Court.

***748 I**

Until Katz v. United States, neither wiretapping nor electronic eavesdropping violated a defendant's Fourth Amendment rights 'unless there has been an official search and seizure of his person, or such a seizure of his papers or his tangible material effects, or an actual physical invasion of his house 'or curtilage' for the purpose of making a seizure.'[312]But where 'eavesdropping was accomplished by means of an unauthorized physical penetration into the premises occupied' by the defendant, although falling short of a 'technical trespass under the local property law,' the Fourth Amendment was violated and any evidence of what was seen and heard, as well as

[310] 389 U.S. 347, 88 S.Ct. 507, 19 L.Ed.2d 576 (1967).

[311] 343 U.S. 747, 72 S.Ct. 967, 96 L.Ed. 1270 (1952).

[312] *Olmstead v. United States*, 277 U.S. 438, 466, 48 S.Ct. 564, 568, 72 L.Ed. 944 (1928); *Goldman v. United States*, 316 U.S. 129, 135-136, 62 S.Ct. 993, 996-997, 86 L.Ed. 1322 (1942).

tangible objects seized, was considered the inadmissible fruit of an unlawful invasion.[313]

Katz v. United States, however, finally swept away doctrines that electronic eavesdropping is permissible under the Fourth Amendment unless physical invasion of a constitutionally protected area produced the challenged evidence. In that case government agents, without petitioner's consent or knowledge, attached a listening device to the outside of a public telephone booth and recorded the defendant's end of his telephone conversations. In declaring the recordings inadmissible in evidence in the absence of a warrant authorizing the surveillance, the Court overruled Olmstead and Goldman and held that the absence of physical intrusion into the telephone booth did not justify using electronic devices in listening to and recording Katz' words, thereby violating ***749** the privacy on which he justifiably relied while using the telephone in those circumstances.

The Court of Appeals understood Katz to render inadmissible against White the agents' testimony concerning conversations that Jackson broadcast to them. We cannot agree. Katz involved no revelation to the Government by a party to ****1125** conversations with the defendant nor did the Court indicate in any way that a defendant has a justifiable and constitutionally protected expectation that a person with whom he is conversing will not then or later reveal the conversation to the police.

Hoffa v. United States,[314]which was left undisturbed by Katz, held that however strongly a defendant may trust an apparent colleague, his expectations in this respect are not protected by the Fourth Amendment when it turns out that the colleague is a government agent regularly communicating with the authorities. In these circumstances, 'no interest legitimately protected by the Fourth Amendment is involved,' for that amendment affords no protection to 'a wrongdoer's misplaced belief that a person to whom he voluntarily confides his wrongdoing will not reveal it.'[315]No warrant to 'search and seize' is required in such circumstances, nor is it when the Government sends to defendant's home a secret agent who conceals his identity and makes a purchase of narcotics from the accused,[316]or when the same agent, unbeknown to the defendant, carries electronic equipment to record the defendant's words and the evidence so gathered is later offered in evidence.[317]

Conceding that Hoffa, Lewis, and Lopez remained unaffected by Katz, the Court of Appeals nevertheless ***750** read both Katz and the Fourth Amendment to require a different result if the agent not only records his conversations with the defendant but instantaneously transmits them electronically to other agents equipped with radio receivers. Where this occurs, the Court of Appeals held, the Fourth Amendment is violated and the testimony of the listening agents must be excluded from evidence.

To reach this result it was necessary for the Court of Appeals to hold that On Lee v. United States was no longer good law. In that case, which involved facts very similar to the case before us, the Court first rejected claims of a Fourth Amendment violation because the informer had not trespassed when he entered the defendant's premises and conversed with him. To this extent the Court's rationale cannot survive Katz.[318]But the Court announced a second and independent ground for its decision; for it went on to say that overruling Olmstead and Goldman would be of no aid to On

---

[313] *Silverman v. United States*, 365 U.S. 505, 509, 511, 81 S.Ct. 679, 681, 682, 5 L.Ed.2d 734 (1961); see also *Wong Sun v. United States*, 371 U.S. 471, 83 S.Ct. 407, 9 L.Ed.2d 441 (1963); Berger v. New York, 388 U.S. 41, 52, 87 S.Ct. 1873, 1880, 18 L.Ed.2d 1040 (1967); *Alderman v. United States*, 394 U.S. 165, 177-178, 89 S.Ct. 961, 968-969, 22 L.Ed.2d 176 (1969).

[314] 385 U.S. 293, 87 S.Ct. 408, 17 L.Ed.2d 374 (1966).

[315] *Hoffa v. United States*, at 302, 87 S.Ct., at 413.

[316] *Lewis v. United States*, 385 U.S. 206, 87 S.Ct. 424, 17 L.Ed.2d 312 (1966).

[317] *Lopez v. United States*, 373 U.S. 427, 83 S.Ct. 1381, 10 L.Ed.2d 462 (1963).

[318] See 389 U.S., at 352-353, 88 S.Ct., at 511-512.

Lee since he 'was talking confidentially and indiscreetly with one he trusted, and he was overheard. * * * It would be a dubious service to the genuine liberties protected by the Fourth Amendment to make them bedfellows with spurious liberties improvised by farfetched analogies which would liken eavesdropping on a conversation, with the connivance of one of the parties, to an unreasonable search or seizure. We find no violation of the Fourth Amendment here.'[319]We see no indication in Katz that the Court meant to disturb that understanding of the Fourth Amendment or to disturb the result reached in the On Lee case, nor are we now inclined to overturn this view of the Fourth Amendment.

***751** Concededly a police agent who conceals his police connections may write down for ****1126** official use his conversations with a defendant and testify concerning them, without a warrant authorizing his encounters with the defendant and without otherwise violating the latter's Fourth Amendment rights.[320]For constitutional purposes, no different result is required if the agent instead of immediately reporting and transcribing his conversations with defendant, either (1) simultaneously records them with electronic equipment which he is carrying on his person;[321](2) or carries radio equipment which simultaneously transmits the conversations either to recording equipment located elsewhere or to other agents monitoring the transmitting frequency.[322]If the conduct and revelations of an agent operating without electronic equipment do not invade the defendant's constitutionally justifiable expectations of privacy, neither does a simultaneous recording of the same conversations made by the agent or by others from transmissions received from the agent to whom the defendant is talking and whose trustworthiness the defendant necessarily risks.

Our problem is not what the privacy expectations of particular defendants in particular situations may be or the extent to which they may in fact have relied on the discretion of their companions. Very probably, individual defendants neither know nor suspect that their colleagues have gone or will go to the police or are carrying recorders or transmitters. Otherwise, conversation would cease and our problem with these encounters would be nonexistent or far different from those now ***752** before us. Our problem, in terms of the principles announced in Katz, is what expectations of privacy are constitutionally 'justifiable'-what expectations the Fourth Amendment will protect in the absence of a warrant. So far, the law permits the frustration of actual expectations of privacy by permitting authorities to use the testimony of those associates who for one reason or another have determined to turn to the police, as well as by authorizing the use of informants in the manner exemplified by Hoffa and Lewis. If the law gives no protection to the wrongdoer whose trusted accomplice is or becomes a police agent, neither should it protect him when that same agent has recorded or transmitted the conversations which are later offered in evidence to prove the State's case.[323]

Inescapably, one contemplating illegal activities must realize and risk that his companions may be reporting to the police. If he sufficiently doubts their trustworthiness, the association will very probably end or never materialize. But if he has no doubts, or allays them, or risks what doubt he has, the risk is his. In terms of what his course will be, what he will or will not do or say, we are unpersuaded that he would distinguish between probably informers on the one hand and probable informers with transmitters on the other. Given the possibility or probability that one of his colleagues is cooperating with the police, it is only speculation to assert that the defendant's utterances would be substantially different or his sense of security any less if

[319] 343 U.S., at 753-754, 72 S.Ct., at 972.

[320] *Hoffa v. United States*, 385 U.S., at 300-303, 87 S.Ct., at 412-414.

[321] Lopez v. United States, *supra*.

[322] On Lee v. United States, *supra*.

[323] See *Lopez v. United States*, 373 U.S. 427, 83 S.Ct. 1381, 10 L.Ed.2d 462 (1963).

he also thought it possible that the suspected colleague is wired for sound. At least there is no persuasive evidence that the difference in this respect between the electronically equipped and the unequipped agent is substantial enough to require discrete constitutional recognition, ***753** particularly under the Fourth Amendment which is ruled by fluid concepts of 'reasonableness.'

Nor should we be too ready to erect constitutional barriers to relevant and probative evidence which is also accurate and reliable. An electronic recording will many times produce a more reliable rendition of what a defendant has said than will the unaided memory of a police agent. It may also be that with the recording in existence it is less likely that the informant will change his mind, less chance that threat or injury will suppress unfavorable evidence and less chance that ****1127** cross-examination will confound the testimony. Considerations like these obviously do not favor the defendant, but we are not prepared to hold that a defendant who has no constitutional right to exclude the informer's unaided testimony nevertheless has a Fourth Amendment privilege against a more accurate version of the events in question.

It is thus untenable to consider the activities and reports of the police agent himself, though acting without a warrant, to be a 'reasonable' investigative effort and lawful under the Fourth Amendment but to view the same agent with a recorder or transmitter as conducting an 'unreasonable' and unconstitutional search and seizure. Our opinion is currently shared by Congress and the Executive Branch, Title III, Omnibus Crime Control and Safe Streets Act of 1968, 82 Stat. 212, 18 U.S.C. s 2510 et seq. (1964 ed., Supp. V), and the American Bar Association.[324]It is also the result reached by prior cases in this Court.[325]

No different result should obtain where, is in On Lee and the instant case, the informer disappears and is unavailable ***754** at trial; for the issue of whether specified events on a certain day violate the Fourth Amendment should not be determined by what later happens to the informer. His unavailability at trial and proffering the testimony of other agents may raise evidentiary problems or pose issues of prosecutorial misconduct with respect to the informer's disappearance, but they do not appear critical to deciding whether prior events invaded the defendant's Fourth Amendment rights.

It is so ordered.

The judgment of the Court of Appeals is reversed.

*****

(Dissent Omitted.)

*****

[324] Project on Standards for Criminal Justice, Electronic Surveillance s 4.1 (Approved Draft 1971).

[325] *On Lee, supra*; *Lopez v. United States, supra*.

Black Letter Law

> Held that where radio transmitter was concealed on the person of an informant with knowledge of the informant, and where conversations between the informant and defendant at various locations, including defendant's home, were overheard when the frequency of the transmitter was monitored, without warrant, by government agents, who testified as to the conversations at defendant's trial, there was no violation of defendant's Fourth Amendment right to be secure against unreasonable searches and seizures.
>
> Individuals do not have a reasonable expectation of privacy in their conversations with others.

Smith v. Maryland

99 S.Ct. 2577

Smith

V.

Maryland

No. 78–5374. | Argued March 28, 1979. | Decided June 20, 1979.

Mr. Justice BLACKMUN delivered the opinion of the Court.

This case presents the question whether the installation and use of a pen register constitutes a "search" within the meaning of the Fourth Amendment, made applicable to the States through the Fourteenth Amendment.[326]

***737 I**

On March 5, 1976, in Baltimore, Md., Patricia McDonough was robbed. She gave the police a description of the robber and of a 1975 Monte Carlo automobile she had observed near the scene of the crime.[327]After the robbery, McDonough began receiving threatening and obscene phone calls from a man identifying himself as the robber. On one occasion, the caller asked that she step out on her front porch; she did so, and saw the 1975 Monte Carlo she had earlier described to police moving slowly past her home.[328]On March 16, police spotted a man who met McDonough's description driving a 1975 Monte Carlo in her neighborhood.[329]By tracing the license plate number, police learned that the car was registered in the name of petitioner, Michael Lee Smith.[330]

The next day, the telephone company, at police request, installed a pen register at its central offices to record the numbers dialed from the telephone at petitioner's home.[331]The police did not get a warrant or court order before having the pen register installed. The register revealed that, on March 17, a call was placed ****2579** from petitioner's home to McDonough's phone.[332]On the basis of this and other evidence,

---

326 *Mapp v. Ohio*, 367 U.S. 643, 81 S.Ct. 1684, 6 L.Ed.2d 1081 (1961).

327 Tr. 66–68.

328 *Id.*, at 70.

329 *Id.*, at 71–72.

330 *Id.*, at 72.

331 *Id.*, at 73, 75.

332 *Id.*, at 74.

the police obtained a warrant to search petitioner's residence.[333]The search revealed that a page in petitioner's phone book was turned down to the name and number of Patricia McDonough; the phone book was seized.[334] Petitioner was arrested, and a six-man lineup was held on March 19. McDonough identified petitioner as the man who had robbed her.[335]

Petitioner was indicted in the Criminal Court of Baltimore for robbery. By pretrial motion, he sought to suppress "all fruits derived from the pen register" on the ground that the police had failed to secure a warrant prior to its installation.[336]The trial court denied the suppression motion, holding that the warrantless installation of the pen ***738** register did not violate the Fourth Amendment.[337]Petitioner then waived a jury, and the case was submitted to the court on an agreed statement of facts.[338]The pen register tape (evidencing the fact that a phone call had been made from petitioner's phone to McDonough's phone) and the phone book seized in the search of petitioner's residence were admitted into evidence against him.[339]Petitioner was convicted,[340]and was sentenced to six years. He appealed to the Maryland Court of Special Appeals, but the Court of Appeals of Maryland issued a writ of certiorari to the intermediate court in advance of its decision in order to consider whether the pen register evidence had been properly admitted at petitioner's trial.[341]

The Court of Appeals affirmed the judgment of conviction, holding that "there is no constitutionally protected reasonable expectation of privacy in the numbers dialed into a telephone system and hence no search within the fourth amendment is implicated by the use of a pen register installed at the central offices of the telephone company."[342]Because there was no "search," the court concluded, no warrant was needed. Three judges dissented, expressing the view that individuals do have a legitimate expectation of privacy regarding the phone numbers they dial from their homes; that the installation of a pen register thus constitutes a "search"; and that, in the absence of exigent circumstances, the failure of police to secure a warrant mandated that the pen register evidence here be excluded.[343]Certiorari was granted in order to resolve indications of conflict in the decided cases as to the restrictions imposed by the Fourth Amendment on the use of pen registers.[344]

***739 II**

A

The Fourth Amendment guarantees "[t]he right of the people to be secure in their persons, houses, papers, and effects, against unreasonable searches and seizures." In determining whether a particular form of government-initiated electronic surveillance is a "search" within the meaning of the Fourth Amendment, our lodestar ****2580** is Katz v. United States.[345]In Katz, Government agents had inter-

---

[333] *Id.*, at 75.

[334] *Ibid.*

[335] *Id.*, at 70–71.

[336] Record 14; Tr. 54–56.

[337] *Id.*, at 63.

[338] *Id.*, at 65–66.

[339] *Id.*, at 74–76.

[340] *Id.*, at 78.

[341] 283 Md. 156, 160, 389 A.2d 858, 860 (1978).

[342] *Id.*, at 173, 389 A.2d, at 867.

[343] *Id.*, at 174, 178, 389 A.2d, at 868, 870.

[344] 439 U.S. 1001, 99 S.Ct. 609, 58 L.Ed.2d 676 (1978).

[345] 389 U.S. 347, 88 S.Ct. 507, 19 L.Ed.2d 576 (1967).

cepted the contents of a telephone conversation by attaching an electronic listening device to the outside of a public phone booth. The Court rejected the argument that a "search" can occur only when there has been a "physical intrusion" into a "constitutionally protected area," noting that the Fourth Amendment "protects people, not places."[346]Because the Government's monitoring of Katz' conversation "violated the privacy upon which he justifiably relied while using the telephone booth," the Court held that ***740** it "constituted a 'search and seizure' within the meaning of the Fourth Amendment."[347] Consistently with Katz, this Court uniformly has held that the application of the Fourth Amendment depends on whether the person invoking its protection can claim a "justifiable," a "reasonable," or a "legitimate expectation of privacy" that has been invaded by government action.[348]This inquiry, as Mr. Justice Harlan aptly noted in his Katz concurrence, normally embraces two discrete questions. The first is whether the individual, by his conduct, has "exhibited an actual (subjective) expectation of privacy," 389 U.S., at 361, 88 S.Ct., at 516—whether, in the words of the Katz majority, the individual has shown that "he seeks to preserve [something] as private." Id., at 351, 88 S.Ct., at 511. The second question is whether the individual's subjective expectation of privacy is "one that society is prepared to recognize as 'reasonable,' " id., at 361, 88 S.Ct., at 516—whether, in the words of the Katz majority, the individual's expectation, viewed objectively, is "justifiable" under the circumstances.[349]

B

In applying the Katz analysis to this case, it is important to begin by specifying precisely ****2581** the nature of the state activity that is challenged. The activity here took the form of installing and using a pen register. Since the pen register was installed on telephone company property at the telephone company's central offices, petitioner obviously cannot claim that his "property" was invaded or that police intruded into a "constitutionally protected area." Petitioner's claim, rather, is that, notwithstanding the absence of a trespass, the State, as did the Government in Katz, infringed a "legitimate expectation of privacy" that petitioner held. Yet a pen register differs significantly from the listening device employed in Katz, for pen registers do not acquire the contents of communications. This Court recently noted:

> "Indeed, a law enforcement official could not even determine from the use of a pen register whether a communication existed. These devices do not hear sound. They disclose only the telephone numbers that have been dialed—a means of establishing communication. Neither the purport of any communication between the caller and the recipient of the call, their identities, nor whether the call was even completed is disclosed by pen registers."[350]

***742** Given a pen register's limited capabilities, therefore, petitioner's argument that its installation and use constituted a "search" necessarily rests upon a claim that he had a "legitimate expectation of privacy" regarding the numbers he dialed on his phone.

---

[346] *Id.*, at 351–353, 88 S.Ct., at 511–512.

[347] *Id.*, at 353, 88 S.Ct., at 512.

[348] *E. g., Rakas v. Illinois*, 439 U.S. 128, 143, 99 S.Ct. 421, 430, 58 L.Ed.2d 387, and n. 12 (1978); *id.*, at 150, 151, 99 S.Ct., at 434, 435 (concurring opinion); *id.*, at 164, 99 S.Ct., at 441 (dissenting opinion); *United States v. Chadwick*, 433 U.S. 1, 7, 97 S.Ct. 2476, 2481, 53 L.Ed.2d 538 (1977); *United States v. Miller*, 425 U.S. 435, 442, 96 S.Ct. 1619, 1623, 48 L.Ed.2d 71 (1976); *United States v. Dionisio*, 410 U.S. 1, 14, 93 S.Ct. 764, 771, 35 L.Ed.2d 67 (1973); *Couch v. United States*, 409 U.S. 322, 335–336, 93 S.Ct. 611, 619–620, 34 L.Ed.2d 548 (1973); *United States v. White*, 401 U.S. 745, 752, 91 S.Ct. 1122, 1126, 28 L.Ed.2d 453 (1971) (plurality opinion); *Mancusi v. DeForte*, 392 U.S. 364, 368, 88 S.Ct. 2120, 2123, 20 L.Ed.2d 1154 (1968); *Terry v. Ohio*, 392 U.S. 1, 9, 88 S.Ct. 1868, 1873, 20 L.Ed.2d 889 (1968).

[349] *Id.*, at 353, 88 S.Ct., at 512.5 See *741 *Rakas v. Illinois*, 439 U.S., at 143–144 n. 12, 99 S.Ct., at 430; *id.*, at 151, 99 S.Ct., at 434 (concurring opinion); *United States v. White*, 401 U.S., at 752, 91 S.Ct., at 1126 (plurality opinion).

[350] *United States v. New York Tel. Co.*, 434 U.S. 159, 167, 98 S.Ct. 364, 369, 54 L.Ed.2d 376 (1977).

This claim must be rejected. First, we doubt that people in general entertain any actual expectation of privacy in the numbers they dial. All telephone users realize that they must "convey" phone numbers to the telephone company, since it is through telephone company switching equipment that their calls are completed. All subscribers realize, moreover, that the phone company has facilities for making permanent records of the numbers they dial, for they see a list of their long-distance (toll) calls on their monthly bills. In fact, pen registers and similar devices are routinely used by telephone companies "for the purposes of checking billing operations, detecting fraud and preventing violations of law."[351]Electronic equipment is used not only to keep billing records of toll calls, but also "to keep a record of all calls dialed from a telephone which is subject to a special rate structure." [352]Pen registers are regularly employed "to determine whether a home phone is being used to conduct a business, to check for a defective dial, or to check for over billing."[353]Although most people may be oblivious to a pen register's esoteric functions, they presumably have some awareness of one common use: to aid in the identification of persons making annoying or obscene calls.[354]Most phone books tell ***743** subscribers, on a page entitled "Consumer Information," that the company "can frequently help in identifying to the authorities the origin of unwelcome and troublesome calls."[355]Telephone users, in sum, typically know that they must convey numerical information to the phone company; that the phone company has facilities for recording this information; and that the phone company does in fact record this information for a variety of legitimate business purposes. Although subjective expectations cannot be scientifically gauged, it is too much to believe that telephone subscribers, under these circumstances, harbor any general expectation that the numbers they dial will remain secret.

****2582** Petitioner argues, however, that, whatever the expectations of telephone users in general, he demonstrated an expectation of privacy by his own conduct here, since he "us[ed] the telephone in his house to the exclusion of all others."[356]But the site of the call is immaterial for purposes of analysis in this case. Although petitioner's conduct may have been calculated to keep the contents of his conversation private, his conduct was not and could not have been calculated to preserve the privacy of the number he dialed. Regardless of his location, petitioner had to convey that number to the telephone company in precisely the same way if he wished to complete his call. The fact that he dialed the number on his home phone rather than on some other phone could make no conceivable difference, nor could any subscriber rationally think that it would.

Second, even if petitioner did harbor some subjective expectation that the phone numbers he dialed would remain private, this expectation is not "one that society is prepared to recognize as 'reasonable.'"[357]This Court consistently has held that a person has no legitimate expectation of privacy in information he ***744** voluntarily turns over to third parties.[358]In Miller, for example, the Court held that a bank depositor has no "legitimate 'expectation of privacy' " in financial information "voluntarily

---

[351] *United States v. New York Tel. Co.*, 434 U.S., at 174–175, 98 S.Ct., at 373.

[352] *Hodge v. Mountain States Tel. & Tel. Co.*, 555 F.2d 254, 266 (CA9 1977) (concurring opinion).

[353] Note, The Legal Constraints upon the Use of the Pen Register as a Law Enforcement Tool, 60 Cornell L.Rev. 1028, 1029 (1975) (footnotes omitted).

[354] See, *e. g.*, *Von Lusch v. C & P Telephone Co.*, 457 F.Supp. 814, 816 (Md.1978); Note, 60 Cornell L.Rev., at 1029–1030, n. 11; Claerhout, The Pen Register, 20 Drake L.Rev. 108, 110–111 (1970).

[355] *E. g.*, Baltimore Telephone Directory 21 (1978); District of Columbia Telephone Directory 13 (1978).

[356] Brief for Petitioner 6 (emphasis added).

[357] *Katz v. United States*, 389 U.S., at 361, 88 S.Ct., at 516.

[358] *E. g.*, *United States v. Miller*, 425 U.S., at 442–444, 96 S.Ct., at 1623–1624; *Couch v. United States*, 409 U.S., at 335–336, 93 S.Ct., at 619–620; *United States v. White*, 401 U.S., at 752, 91 S.Ct., at 1126 (plurality opinion); *Hoffa v. United States*, 385 U.S. 293, 302, 87 S.Ct. 408, 413, 17 L.Ed.2d 374 (1966); *Lopez v. United States*, 373 U.S. 427, 83 S.Ct. 1381, 10 L.Ed.2d 462 (1963).

conveyed to . . . banks and exposed to their employees in the ordinary course of business."[359]The Court explained:

"The depositor takes the risk, in revealing his affairs to another, that the information will be conveyed by that person to the Government. . . . This Court has held repeatedly that the Fourth Amendment does not prohibit the obtaining of information revealed to a third party and conveyed by him to Government authorities, even if the information is revealed on the assumption that it will be used only for a limited purpose and the confidence placed in the third party will not be betrayed."[360]

Because the depositor "assumed the risk" of disclosure, the Court held that it would be unreasonable for him to expect his financial records to remain private.

This analysis dictates that petitioner can claim no legitimate expectation of privacy here. When he used his phone, petitioner voluntarily conveyed numerical information to the telephone company and "exposed" that information to its equipment in the ordinary course of business. In so doing, petitioner assumed the risk that the company would reveal to police the numbers he dialed. The switching equipment that processed those numbers is merely the modern counterpart of the operator who, in an earlier day, personally completed calls for the subscriber. Petitioner concedes that if he had placed his calls through an operator, he could claim no legitimate expectation of privacy.[361]We ***745** are not inclined to hold that a different constitutional result is required because the telephone company has decided to automate.

Petitioner argues, however, that automatic switching equipment differs from a live operator in one pertinent respect. An operator, in theory at least, is capable of remembering every number that is conveyed to him by callers. Electronic equipment, by contrast can "remember" only those numbers it is programmed to record, and telephone companies, in view of their present billing practices, usually do not record local calls. Since petitioner, in calling McDonough, was making a local call, his expectation of privacy as to her number, on this theory, would be "legitimate."

****2583** This argument does not withstand scrutiny. The fortuity of whether or not the phone company in fact elects to make a quasi-permanent record of a particular number dialed does not in our view, make any constitutional difference. Regardless of the phone company's election, petitioner voluntarily conveyed to it information that it had facilities for recording and that it was free to record. In these circumstances, petitioner assumed the risk that the information would be divulged to police. Under petitioner's theory, Fourth Amendment protection would exist, or not, depending on how the telephone company chose to define local-dialing zones, and depending on how it chose to bill its customers for local calls. Calls placed across town, or dialed directly, would be protected; calls placed across the river, or dialed with operator assistance, might not be. We are not inclined to make a crazy quilt of the Fourth Amendment, especially in circumstances where (as here) the pattern of protection would be dictated by billing practices of a private corporation.

We therefore conclude that petitioner in all probability entertained no actual expectation of privacy in the phone numbers he dialed, and that, even if he did, his expectation was not "legitimate." The installation and use of a pen register, ***746** consequently, was not a "search," and no warrant was required. The judgment of the Maryland Court of Appeals is affirmed.

It is so ordered.

*****

(Dissent of Mr. Justice STEWART, with whom Mr. Justice BRENNAN joins, dissenting, omitted.)

---

[359] 425 U.S., at 442, 96 S.Ct., at 1624.

[360] *Id.*, at 443, 96 S.Ct., at 1624.

[361] Tr. of Oral Arg. 3–5, 11–12, 32.

Mr. Justice MARSHALL, with whom Mr. Justice BRENNAN joins, dissenting.

The Court concludes that because individuals have no actual or legitimate expectation of privacy in information they voluntarily relinquish to telephone companies, the use of pen registers by government agents is immune from Fourth Amendment scrutiny. Since I remain convinced that constitutional protections are not abrogated whenever a person apprises another of facts valuable in criminal investigations,[362]I respectfully dissent.

Applying the standards set forth in Katz v. United States,[363]the Court first determines that telephone subscribers have no subjective expectations of privacy concerning the numbers they dial. To reach this conclusion, the Court posits that individuals somehow infer from the long-distance listings on their phone bills, and from the cryptic assurances of "help" in tracing obscene ***749** calls included in "most" phone books, that pen registers are regularly used for recording local calls.[364]But even assuming, as I do not, that individuals "typically know" that a phone company monitors calls for internal reasons,[365]it does ****2585** not follow that they expect this information to be made available to the public in general or the government in particular. Privacy is not a discrete commodity, possessed absolutely or not at all. Those who disclose certain facts to a bank or phone company for a limited business purpose need not assume that this information will be released to other persons for other purposes.[366]

The crux of the Court's holding, however, is that whatever expectation of privacy petitioner may in fact have entertained regarding his calls, it is not one "society is prepared to recognize as 'reasonable.'"[367]In so ruling, the Court determines that individuals who convey information to third parties have "assumed the risk" of disclosure to the government.[368]This analysis is misconceived in two critical respects.

Implicit in the concept of assumption of risk is some notion of choice. At least in the third-party consensual surveillance cases, which first incorporated risk analysis into Fourth Amendment doctrine, the defendant presumably had exercised some discretion in deciding who should enjoy his confidential communications.[369]***750** By contrast here, unless a person is prepared to forgo use of what for many has become a personal or professional necessity, he cannot help but accept the risk of surveillance.[370]It is idle to speak of "assuming" risks in contexts where, as a practical matter, individuals have no realistic alternative.

More fundamentally, to make risk analysis dispositive in assessing the reasonableness of privacy expectations would allow the government to define the scope of Fourth Amendment protections. For example, law enforcement officials, simply by announcing their intent to monitor the content of random samples of first-class mail or private phone conversations, could put the public on notice of the risks they would

---

[362] See, *e. g., United States v. White,* 401 U.S. 745, 786–790, 91 S.Ct. 1122, 1143–1145, 28 L.Ed.2d 453 (1971) (Harlan, J., dissenting); *id.,* at 795–796, 91 S.Ct., at 1147–1148 (MARSHALL, J., dissenting); *California Bankers Assn. v. Shultz,* 416 U.S. 21, 95–96, 94 S.Ct. 1494, 1534, 39 L.Ed.2d 812 (1974) (MARSHALL, J., dissenting); *United States v. Miller,* 425 U.S. 435, 455–456, 96 S.Ct. 1619, 1629–1630, 48 L.Ed.2d 71 (1976) (MARSHALL, J., dissenting).

[363] 389 U.S. 347, 361, 88 S.Ct. 507, 516, 19 L.Ed.2d 576 (1967) (Harlan, J., concurring).

[364] See *ante,* at 2581–2582.

[365] *Ante,* at 2581.

[366] See *California Bankers Assn. v. Shultz, supra,* 416 U.S., at 95–96, 94 S.Ct., at 1534 (MARSHALL, J., dissenting).

[367] *Ante,* at 2582.

[368] *Ante,* at 2582, 2583.

[369] See, *e. g., Lopez v. United States,* 373 U.S. 427, 439, 83 S.Ct. 1381, 1388, 10 L.Ed.2d 462 (1963); *Hoffa v. United States,* 385 U.S. 293, 302–303, 87 S.Ct. 408, 413–414, 17 L.Ed.2d 374 (1966); *United States v. White, supra,* 401 U.S., at 751–752, 91 S.Ct., at 1125–1126 (plurality opinion).

[370] Cf. *Lopez v. United States, supra,* 373 U.S., at 465–466, 83 S.Ct., at 1401–1402 (BRENNAN, J., dissenting).

thereafter assume in such communications. See Amsterdam.[371]Yet, although acknowledging this implication of its analysis, the Court is willing to concede only that, in some circumstances, a further "normative inquiry would be proper."[372]No meaningful effort is made to explain what those circumstances might be, or why this case is not among them.

In my view, whether privacy expectations are legitimate within the meaning of Katz depends not on the risks an individual can be presumed to accept when imparting information to third parties, but on the risks he should be forced to assume in a free and open society. By its terms, the constitutional prohibition of unreasonable searches and seizures assigns to the judiciary some prescriptive responsibility. As Mr. Justice Harlan, who formulated the standard the Court applies today, himself recognized: "[s]ince it is the task of the law to form and project, as well as mirror and reflect, we should not . . . merely recite . . . risks without examining the desirability of saddling them upon society."[373]In making this ***751** assessment, courts must evaluate the "intrinsic character" of investigative practices with reference to the basic values underlying the Fourth Amendment.[374]And for those "extensive intrusions that significantly jeopardize [individuals'] sense of security . . . . more than self-restraint by law enforcement officials is required."[375]

****2586** The use of pen registers, I believe, constitutes such an extensive intrusion. To hold otherwise ignores the vital role telephonic communication plays in our personal and professional relationships,[376]as well as the First and Fourth Amendment interests implicated by unfettered official surveillance. Privacy in placing calls is of value not only to those engaged in criminal activity. The prospect of unregulated governmental monitoring will undoubtedly prove disturbing even to those with nothing illicit to hide. Many individuals, including members of unpopular political organizations or journalists with confidential sources, may legitimately wish to avoid disclosure of their personal contacts.[377]Permitting governmental access to telephone records on less than probable cause may thus impede certain forms of political affiliation and journalistic endeavor that are the hallmark of a truly free society. Particularly given the Government's previous reliance on warrantless telephonic surveillance to trace reporters' sources and monitor protected political activity, I am unwilling to insulate use of pen registers from independent judicial review.

***752** Just as one who enters a public telephone booth is "entitled to assume that the words he utters into the mouthpiece will not be broadcast to the world,"[378]so too, he should be entitled to assume that the numbers he dials in the privacy of his home will be recorded, if at all, solely for the phone company's business purposes. Accordingly, I would require law enforcement officials to obtain a warrant before they enlist telephone companies to secure information otherwise.

---

[371] Perspectives on the Fourth Amendment, 58 Minn.L.Rev. 349, 384, 407 (1974).

[372] *Ante,* at 2580 n. 5.

[373] *United States v. White, supra,* 401 U.S., at 786, 91 S.Ct., at 1143 (dissenting opinion).

[374] *California Bankers Assn. v. Shultz,* 416 U.S., at 95, 94 S.Ct., at 1534 (MARSHALL, J., dissenting).

[375] *United States v. White, supra,* 401 U.S., at 786, 91 S.Ct., at 1143 (Harlan, J., dissenting).

[376] See *Katz v. United States,* 389 U.S., at 352, 88 S.Ct., at 511.

[377] See *NAACP v. Alabama,* 357 U.S. 449, 463, 78 S.Ct. 1163, 1172, 2 L.Ed.2d 1488 (1958); *Branzburg v. Hayes,* 408 U.S. 665, 695, 92 S.Ct. 2646, 2663, 33 L.Ed.2d 626 (1972); *id.,* at 728–734, 92 S.Ct., at 2673–2676 (STEWART, J., dissenting).

[378] *Katz v. United States, supra,* 389 U.S., at 352, 88 S.Ct., at 512.

Black Letter Law

Held that installation and use of a pen register by a telephone company does not constitute a "search" within the meaning of the Fourth Amendment. No reasonable expectation of privacy as to the means of communication.

California v. Ciraolo

106 S.Ct. 1809

Supreme Court of the United States

California

v.

Ciraolo

No. 84-1513. | Argued Dec. 10, 1985. | Decided May 19, 1986. | Rehearing Denied June 30, 1986. |

***209** Chief Justice BURGER delivered the opinion of the Court.

We granted certiorari to determine whether the Fourth Amendment is violated by aerial observation without a warrant from an altitude of 1,000 feet of a fenced-in backyard within the curtilage of a home.

I

On September 2, 1982, Santa Clara Police received an anonymous telephone tip that marijuana was growing in respondent's backyard. Police were unable to observe the contents of respondent's yard from ground level because of a 6-foot outer fence and a 10-foot inner fence completely enclosing the yard. Later that day, Officer Shutz, who was assigned to investigate, secured a private plane and flew over respondent's house at an altitude of 1,000 feet, within navigable airspace; he was accompanied by Officer Rodriguez. Both officers ****1811** were trained in marijuana identification. From the overflight, the officers readily identified marijuana plants 8 feet to 10 feet in height growing in a 15- by 25-foot plot in respondent's yard; they photographed the area with a standard 35mm camera.

On September 8, 1982, Officer Shutz obtained a search warrant on the basis of an affidavit describing the anonymous tip and their observations; a photograph depicting respondent's house, the backyard, and neighboring homes was attached to the affidavit as an exhibit. The warrant was ***210** executed the next day and 73 plants were seized; it is not disputed that these were marijuana.

After the trial court denied respondent's motion to suppress the evidence of the search, respondent pleaded guilty to a charge of cultivation of marijuana. The California Court of Appeal reversed, however, on the ground that the warrantless aerial observation of respondent's yard which led to the issuance of the warrant violated the Fourth Amendment. 161 Cal.App.3d 1081, 208 Cal.Rptr. 93 (1984). That court held first that respondent's backyard marijuana garden was within the "curtilage" of his home, under Oliver v. United States.[379]The court emphasized that the height and existence of the two fences constituted "objective criteria from which we may conclude he manifested a reasonable expectation of privacy by any standard."[380]

Examining the particular method of surveillance undertaken, the court then found it "significant" that the flyover "was not the result of a routine patrol conducted for any other legitimate law enforcement or public safety objective, but was un-

[379] 466 U.S. 170, 104 S.Ct. 1735, 80 L.Ed.2d 214 (1984).

[380] 161 Cal.App.3d, at 1089, 208 Cal.Rptr., at 97.

dertaken for the specific purpose of observing this particular enclosure within [respondent's] curtilage."[381]It held this focused observation was "a direct and unauthorized intrusion into the sanctity of the home" which violated respondent's reasonable expectation of privacy.[382]The California Supreme Court denied the State's petition for review.

We granted the State's petition for certiorari.[383]We reverse.

The State argues that respondent has "knowingly exposed" his backyard to aerial observation, because all that was seen was visible to the naked eye from any aircraft flying overhead. The State analogizes its mode of observation to a knothole or opening in a fence: if there is an opening, the police may look.

***211** The California Court of Appeal, as we noted earlier, accepted the analysis that unlike the casual observation of a private person flying overhead, this flight was focused specifically on a small suburban yard, and was not the result of any routine patrol overflight. Respondent contends he has done all that can reasonably be expected to tell the world he wishes to maintain the privacy of his garden within the curtilage without covering his yard. Such covering, he argues, would defeat its purpose as an outside living area; he asserts he has not "knowingly" exposed himself to aerial views.

II

The touchstone of Fourth Amendment analysis is whether a person has a "constitutionally protected reasonable expectation of privacy."[384]Katz posits a two-part inquiry: first, has the individual manifested a subjective expectation of privacy in the object of the challenged search? Second, is society willing to recognize that expectation as reasonable?[385]

Clearly-and understandably-respondent has met the test of manifesting his own subjective intent and desire to maintain ****1812** privacy as to his unlawful agricultural pursuits. However, we need not address that issue, for the State has not challenged the finding of the California Court of Appeal that respondent had such an expectation. It can reasonably be assumed that the 10-foot fence was placed to conceal the marijuana crop from at least street-level views. So far as the normal sidewalk traffic was concerned, this fence served that purpose, because respondent "took normal precautions to maintain his privacy."[386]

Yet a 10-foot fence might not shield these plants from the eyes of a citizen or a policeman perched on the top of a truck or a two-level bus. Whether respondent therefore manifested ***212** a subjective expectation of privacy from all observations of his backyard, or whether instead he manifested merely a hope that no one would observe his unlawful gardening pursuits, is not entirely clear in these circumstances. Respondent appears to challenge the authority of government to observe his activity from any vantage point or place if the viewing is motivated by a law enforcement purpose, and not the result of a casual, accidental observation.

We turn, therefore, to the second inquiry under Katz, i.e., whether that expectation is reasonable. In pursuing this inquiry, we must keep in mind that "[t]he test of legitimacy is not whether the individual chooses to conceal assertedly 'private' activ-

---

[381] *Ibid.*

[382] *Id.*, at 1089-1090, 208 Cal.Rptr., at 98 (footnote omitted).

[383] 471 U.S. 1134, 105 S.Ct. 2672, 86 L.Ed.2d 691 (1985).

[384] *Katz v. United States*, 389 U.S. 347, 360, 88 S.Ct. 507, 516, 19 L.Ed.2d 576 (1967) (Harlan, J., concurring).

[385] See *Smith v. Maryland*, 442 U.S. 735, 740, 99 S.Ct. 2577, 2580, 61 L.Ed.2d 220 (1979).

[386] *Rawlings v. Kentucky*, 448 U.S. 98, 105, 100 S.Ct. 2556, 2561, 65 L.Ed.2d 633 (1980).

ity," but instead "whether the government's intrusion infringes upon the personal and societal values protected by the Fourth Amendment."[387]

Respondent argues that because his yard was in the curtilage of his home, no governmental aerial observation is permissible under the Fourth Amendment without a warrant. The history and genesis of the curtilage doctrine are instructive. "At common law, the curtilage is the area to which extends the intimate activity associated with the 'sanctity of a man's home and the privacies of life.'"[388]The ***213** protection afforded the curtilage is essentially a protection of families and personal privacy in an area intimately linked to the home, both physically and psychologically, where privacy expectations are most heightened. The claimed area here was immediately adjacent to a suburban home, surrounded by high double fences. This close nexus to the home would appear to encompass this small area within the curtilage. Accepting, as the State does, that this yard and its crop fall within the curtilage, the question remains whether naked-eye observation of the curtilage by police from an aircraft lawfully operating at an altitude of 1,000 feet violates an expectation of privacy that is reasonable.

That the area is within the curtilage does not itself bar all police observation. The Fourth Amendment protection of the home has never been extended to require law enforcement officers to shield their eyes when passing by a home on public thoroughfares. Nor does the mere fact that an individual has taken measures to restrict some views of his activities preclude an officer's observations from a public vantage point where he has a right to be and which renders the activities clearly visible.[389]"What a person knowingly exposes to the public, even in his own home or office, is not a subject of Fourth Amendment protection."[390]

The observations by Officers Shutz and Rodriguez in this case took place within public navigable airspace,[391]in a physically nonintrusive manner; from this point they were able to observe plants readily discernible to the naked eye as marijuana. That the observation from aircraft was directed at identifying the plants and the officers were trained to recognize marijuana is irrelevant. Such observation is precisely what a judicial officer needs to provide a basis for a warrant. Any member of the public flying in this airspace who glanced down could have seen ***214** everything that these officers observed. On this record, we readily conclude that respondent's expectation that his garden was protected from such observation is unreasonable and is not an expectation that society is prepared to honor.

The dissent contends that the Court ignores Justice Harlan's warning in his concurrence in Katz v. United States,[392]that the Fourth Amendment should not be limited to proscribing only physical intrusions onto private property.[393]But Justice Harlan's observations about future electronic developments and the potential for electronic interference with private communications[394]were plainly not aimed at simple visual observations from a public place. Indeed, since Katz the Court has required warrants for electronic surveillance aimed at intercepting private conversations.[395]

---

[387] *Oliver, supra,* 466 U.S., at 181-183, 104 S.Ct., at 1742-1744.v

[388] *Oliver, supra,* 466 U.S., at 180, 104 S.Ct., at 1742 (quoting *Boyd v. United States,* 116 U.S. 616, 630, 6 S.Ct. 524, 532, 29 L.Ed. 746 (1886)). See 4 Blackstone, Commentaries *225.

[389] *E.g.,* **1813 *United States v. Knotts,* 460 U.S. 276, 282, 103 S.Ct. 1081, 1085-1086, 75 L.Ed.2d 55 (1983).

[390] *Katz, supra,* 389 U.S., at 351, 88 S.Ct., at 511.

[391] See 49 U.S.C.App. § 1304.

[392] 389 U.S., at 361-362, 88 S.Ct., at 516-517,

[393] *Post,* at ----.

[394] see *Katz, supra,* at 362, 88 S.Ct., at 517,

[395] See *United States v. United States District Court,* 407 U.S. 297, 92 S.Ct. 2125, 32 L.Ed.2d 752 (1972).

Justice Harlan made it crystal clear that he was resting on the reality that one who enters a telephone booth is entitled to assume that his conversation is not being intercepted. This does not translate readily into a rule of constitutional dimensions that one who grows illicit drugs in his backyard is "entitled to assume" his unlawful conduct will not be observed ***215** by a passing aircraft-or by a power company repair mechanic on a pole overlooking the yard. As Justice Harlan emphasized:

> "A man's home is, for most purposes, a place where he expects privacy, but objects, activities, or statements that he exposes to the 'plain view' of outsiders are not 'protected' because no intention to keep them to himself has been exhibited. On the other hand, conversations in the open would not be protected against being overheard, for the expectation of privacy under the circumstances would be unreasonable."[396]

One can reasonably doubt that in 1967 Justice Harlan considered an aircraft within the category of future "electronic" developments that could stealthily intrude upon an individual's privacy. In an age where private and commercial flight in the public airways is routine, it is unreasonable for respondent to expect that his marijuana plants were constitutionally protected from being observed with the naked eye from an altitude of 1,000 feet. The Fourth Amendment simply does not require the police traveling in the public airways at this altitude ****1814** to obtain a warrant in order to observe what is visible to the naked eye.

Reversed.

Justice POWELL, with whom Justice BRENNAN, Justice MARSHALL, and Justice BLACKMUN join, dissenting.

Concurring in Katz v. United States,[397], Justice Harlan warned that any decision to construe the ***216** Fourth Amendment as proscribing only physical intrusions by police onto private property "is, in the present day, bad physics as well as bad law, for reasonable expectations of privacy may be defeated by electronic as well as physical invasion."[398]Because the Court today ignores that warning in an opinion that departs significantly from the standard developed in Katz for deciding when a Fourth Amendment violation has occurred, I dissent.

I

As the Court's opinion reflects, the facts of this case are not complicated. Officer Shutz investigated an anonymous report that marijuana was growing in the backyard of respondent's home. A tall fence prevented Shutz from looking into the yard from the street. The yard was directly behind the home so that the home itself furnished one border of the fence. Shutz proceeded, without obtaining a warrant, to charter a plane and fly over the home at an altitude of 1,000 feet. Observing marijuana plants growing in the fenced-in yard, Shutz photographed respondent's home and yard, as well as homes and yards of neighbors. The photograph clearly shows that the enclosed yard also contained a small swimming pool and patio. Shutz then filed an affidavit, to which he attached the photograph, describing the anonymous tip and his aerial observation of the marijuana. A warrant issued,1 and a search of the yard confirmed Shutz' aerial observations. Respondent was arrested for cultivating marijuana, a felony under California law.

Respondent contends that the police intruded on his constitutionally protected expectation of privacy when they conducted aerial surveillance of his home and photographed his backyard without first obtaining a warrant. The Court ***217** rejects that contention, holding that respondent's expectation of privacy in the curtilage of his home, although reasonable as to intrusions on the ground, was unreasonable as to

[396] *Katz, supra,* 389 U.S., at 361, 88 S.Ct., at 516-517.

[397] 389 U.S. 347, 88 S.Ct. 507, 19 L.Ed.2d 576 (1967).

[398] *Id.,* at 362, 88 S.Ct., at 516.

surveillance from the navigable airspace. In my view, the Court's holding rests on only one obvious fact, namely, that the airspace generally is open to all persons for travel in airplanes. The Court does not explain why this single fact deprives citizens of their privacy interest in outdoor activities in an enclosed curtilage.

II

A

The Fourth Amendment protects "[t]he right of the people to be secure in their persons, houses, papers, and effects, against unreasonable searches and seizures." While the familiar history of the Amendment need not be recounted here,2 ****1815** we should remember that it reflects a choice that our society should be one in which citizens "dwell in reasonable security and freedom from surveillance."[399]Since that choice was made by the Framers of the Constitution, our cases construing the Fourth Amendment have relied in part on the common law for instruction on "what sorts of searches the Framers ... regarded as reasonable."[400]But we have repeatedly refused to freeze " 'into constitutional law those enforcement practices that existed at the time of the Fourth Amendment's passage.' "[401]Rather, we have construed the Amendment " 'in light of contemporary norms and conditions,' "[402]in order to prevent "any stealthy encroachments" on our citizens' right to be free of arbitrary official intrusion.[403]***218**. Since the landmark decision in Katz v. United States, the Court has fulfilled its duty to protect Fourth Amendment rights by asking if police surveillance has intruded on an individual's reasonable expectation of privacy.

As the decision in Katz held, and dissenting opinions written by Justices of this Court prior to Katz recognized,[404]a standard that defines a Fourth Amendment "search" by reference to whether police have physically invaded a "constitutionally protected area" provides no real protection against surveillance techniques made possible through technology. Technological advances have enabled police to see people's activities and associations, and to hear their conversations, without being in physical proximity. Moreover, the capability now exists for police to conduct intrusive surveillance without any physical penetration of the walls of homes or other structures that citizens may believe shelters their privacy.3 Looking to the Fourth Amendment for protection against such "broad and unsuspected governmental incursions" into the "cherished privacy of law-abiding citizens,"[405] ***219** the Court in Katz abandoned its inquiry into whether police had committed a physical trespass. Katz announced a standard under which the occurrence of a search turned not on the physical position of the police conducting the surveillance, but on whether the surveillance in question had invaded a constitutionally protected reasonable expectation of privacy.

Our decisions following the teaching of Katz illustrate that this inquiry "normally embraces two discrete questions."[406]****1816** "The first is whether the individual, by his conduct, has 'exhibited an actual (subjective) expectation of

---

[399] *Johnson v. United States,* 333 U.S. 10, 14, 68 S.Ct. 367, 369, 92 L.Ed. 436 (1948).

[400] *Steagald v. United States,* 451 U.S. 204, 217, 101 S.Ct. 1642, 1650, 68 L.Ed.2d 38 (1981).

[401] *Id.,* at 217, n. 10, 101 S.Ct., at 1650, n. 10, quoting *Payton v. New York,* 445 U.S. 573, 591, n. 33, 100 S.Ct. 1371, 1382-83, n. 33, 63 L.Ed.2d 639 (1980). See *United States v. United States District Court,* 407 U.S. 297, 313, 92 S.Ct. 2125, 2134-2135, 32 L.Ed.2d 752 (1972).

[402] *Steagald v. United States, supra,* 451 U.S., at 217, n. 10, 101 S.Ct., at 1650, n.10, quoting *Payton v. New York, supra,* 445 U.S., at 591, n. 33, 100 S.Ct., at 1382-1383, n. 33,

[403] *Boyd v. United States,* 116 U.S. 616, 635, 6 S.Ct. 524, 535, 29 L.Ed. 746 (1886)

[404] *E.g., Goldman v. United States,* 316 U.S. 129, 139-141, 62 S.Ct. 993, 998-999, 86 L.Ed. 1322 (1942) (Murphy, J., dissenting); *Olmstead v. United States,* 277 U.S. 438, 474, 48 S.Ct. 564, 571, 72 L.Ed. 944 (1928) (Brandeis, J., dissenting).

[405] *United States v. United States District Court, supra,* 407 U.S., at 312-313, 92 S.Ct., at 2135 (footnote omitted).

[406] *Smith v. Maryland,* 442 U.S. 735, 740, 99 S.Ct. 2577, 2580, 61 L.Ed.2d 220 (1979).

privacy.'"[407]The second is whether that subjective expectation "is 'one that society is prepared to recognize as "reasonable.'"[408]While the Court today purports to reaffirm this analytical framework, its conclusory rejection of respondent's expectation of privacy in the yard of his residence as one that "is unreasonable,"[409]represents a turning away from the principles that have guided our Fourth Amendment inquiry. The Court's rejection of respondent's Fourth Amendment claim is curiously at odds with its purported reaffirmation of the curtilage doctrine, both in this decision and its companion case,[410]and particularly with its conclusion in Dow that society is prepared to recognize as reasonable expectations of privacy in the curtilage.[411]

The second question under Katz has been described as asking whether an expectation of privacy is "legitimate in the sense required by the Fourth Amendment." [412]***220** The answer turns on "whether the government's intrusion infringes upon the personal and societal values protected by the Fourth Amendment."[413]While no single consideration has been regarded as dispositive, "the Court has given weight to such factors as the intention of the Framers of the Fourth Amendment, ... the uses to which the individual has put a location, ... and our societal understanding that certain areas deserve the most scrupulous protection from government invasion."[414] Our decisions have made clear that this inquiry often must be decided by "reference to a 'place,'"[415]and that a home is a place in which a subjective expectation of privacy virtually always will be legitimate.[416]"At the very core [of the Fourth Amendment] stands the right of a [person] to retreat into his own home and there be free from unreasonable governmental intrusion."[417]

B

This case involves surveillance of a home, for as we stated in Oliver v. United States, the curtilage "has been considered part of the home itself for Fourth Amendment purposes."[418]In Dow Chemical Co. v. United States, ***221** decided today, the Court ****1817** reaffirms that the "curtilage doctrine evolved to protect much the same kind of privacy as that covering the interior of a structure."[419]The Court in Dow emphasizes, moreover, that society accepts as reasonable citizens' expectations of privacy in the area immediately surrounding their homes. Ibid.

In deciding whether an area is within the curtilage, courts "have defined the curtilage, as did the common law, by reference to the factors that determine whether an individual reasonably may expect that an area immediately adjacent to the home

---

[407] 442 U.S., at 740, S.Ct., at 2580, quoting *Katz v. United States, supra,* 389 U.S., at 361, 88 S.Ct., at 516-517 (Harlan, J., concurring).

[408] 442 U.S., at 740, --- S.Ct., at 2580, quoting *Katz v. United States,* supra, 389 U.S., at 361, 88 S.Ct., at 516-517 (Harlan, J., concurring).

[409] *Ante,* at 1813.

[410] *Dow Chemical Co. v. United States,* 476 U.S. 227, 106 S.Ct. 1819, 90 L.Ed.2d 226.

[411] At 235, 106 S.Ct. at ----.

[412] *Oliver v. United States,* 466 U.S. 170, 182, 104 S.Ct. 1735, 1742, 80 L.Ed.2d 214 (1984).

[413] *Id.,* at 182-183, 104 S.Ct., at 1743-1744.

[414] *Id.,* at 178, 104 S.Ct., at 1741.

[415] *Katz v. United States, supra,* 389 U.S., at 361, 88 S.Ct., at 516 (Harlan, J., concurring); see *Payton v. New York,* 445 U.S., at 589, 100 S.Ct., at 1381.

[416] *Ibid.;* see, *e.g., United States v. Karo,* 468 U.S. 705, 713-715, 104 S.Ct. 3296, 3302-3303, 82 L.Ed.2d 530 (1984); *Steagald v. United States,* 451 U.S., at 211-212, 101 S.Ct., at 1647-1648.

[417] *Silverman v. United States,* 365 U.S. 505, 511, 81 S.Ct. 679, 683, 5 L.Ed.2d 734 (1961).

[418] 466 U.S., at 180, 104 S.Ct., at 1742.

[419] *Post,* at 1825.

will remain private.[420]"[421]The lower federal courts have agreed that the curtilage is "an area of domestic use immediately surrounding a dwelling and usually but not always fenced in with the dwelling."[422]Those courts also have held that whether an area is within the curtilage must be decided by looking at all of the facts.[423]Relevant facts include the proximity between the area claimed to be curtilage and the home, the nature of the uses to which the area is put, and the steps taken by the resident to protect the area from observation by people passing by.[424]

***222 III**

A

The Court begins its analysis of the Fourth Amendment issue posed here by deciding that respondent had an expectation of privacy in his backyard. I agree with that conclusion because of the close proximity of the yard to the house, the nature of some of the activities respondent conducted there, and because he had taken steps to shield those activities from the view of passersby. The Court then implicitly acknowledges that society is prepared to recognize his expectation as reasonable with respect to ground-level surveillance, holding that the yard was within the curtilage, an area in which privacy interests have been afforded the "most heightened" protection.[425]As the foregoing discussion of the curtilage doctrine demonstrates, respondent's yard unquestionably was within the curtilage. Since Officer Shutz could not see into this private family area from the street, the Court certainly would agree that he would have conducted an unreasonable search had he climbed over the fence, or used a ladder to peer into the yard without first securing a warrant.[426]

The Court concludes, nevertheless, that Shutz could use an airplane-a product of modern technology-to intrude visually into respondent's yard. The Court argues that respondent had no reasonable expectation of privacy from aerial observation. It notes that Shutz was "within public navigable airspace,"[427]when he looked into and photographed ***223** respondent's yard. It then relies on the fact that the surveillance was not accompanied by a ****1818** physical invasion of the curtilage.[428]Reliance on the manner of surveillance is directly contrary to the standard of Katz, which identifies a constitutionally protected privacy right by focusing on the interests of the individual and of a free society. Since Katz, we have consistently held that the presence or absence of physical trespass by police is constitutionally irrelevant to the question whether society is prepared to recognize an asserted privacy interest as reasonable.[429]The Court's holding, therefore, must rest solely on the fact that members of the public fly in planes and may look down at homes as they fly over them. Ante, at 1813. The Court does not explain why it finds this fact to be significant. One may assume that the Court believes that citizens bear the risk that air travelers will observe activities occurring within backyards that are open to the sun and air. This risk, the Court appears to hold, nullifies expectations of privacy in those yards even

---

420 See, *e.g.*, *United States v. Van Dyke*, 643 F.2d 992, 993-994 (CA4 1981); *United States v. Williams*, 581 F.2d 451, 453 (CA5 1978); *Care v. United States*, 231 F.2d 22, 25 (CA10), cert. denied, 351 U.S. 932, 76 S.Ct. 788, 100 L.Ed. 1461 (1956).

421 *Oliver v. United States, supra,* 466 U.S., at 180, 104 S.Ct., at 1742.

422 *United States v. LaBerge*, 267 F.Supp. 686, 692 (Md.1967); see *United States v. Van Dyke*, 643 F.2d 992, 993, n. 1 (CA4 1984).

423 *Ibid.*, citing *Care v. United States, supra,* at 25 (CA10 1956).

424 See *Care v. United States, supra,* at 25; see also *United States v. Van Dyke, supra,* at 993-994.

425 *Ante*, at 1812.

426 See *United States v. Van Dyke, supra;* see also *United States v. Williams, 581 F.2d 451 (CA 1978).*

427 *Ante*, at 1813.

428 *Ibid.*

429 *E.g.*, *United States v. United States District Court*, 407 U.S., at 313, 92 S.Ct., at 2134-2135.

as to purposeful police surveillance from the air. The Court finds support for this conclusion in United States v. Knotts.[430]

This line of reasoning is flawed. First, the actual risk to privacy from commercial or pleasure aircraft is virtually nonexistent. Travelers on commercial flights, as well as private planes used for business or personal reasons, normally obtain at most a fleeting, anonymous, and non discriminating glimpse of the landscape and buildings over which they pass. The risk that a passenger on such a plane might observe ***224** private activities, and might connect those activities with particular people, is simply too trivial to protect against. It is no accident that, as a matter of common experience, many people build fences around their residential areas, but few build roofs over their backyards. Therefore, contrary to the Court's suggestion,[431]people do not " 'knowingly expos[e]' " their residential yards "'to the public'" merely by failing to build barriers that prevent aerial surveillance.

The Court's reliance on Knotts reveals the second problem with its analysis. The activities under surveillance in Knotts took place on public streets, not in private homes.[432]Comings and goings on public streets are public matters, and the Constitution does not disable police from observing what every member of the public can see. The activity in this case, by contrast, took place within the private area immediately adjacent to a home. Yet the Court approves purposeful police surveillance of that activity and area similar to that approved in Knotts with respect to public activities and areas. The only possible basis for this holding is a judgment that the risk to privacy posed by the remote possibility that a private airplane passenger will notice outdoor activities is equivalent to the risk of official aerial surveillance. But the Court fails to acknowledge the qualitative difference between police surveillance and other uses made of the airspace. Members of the public use the airspace for travel, ****1819** business, or pleasure, not for the purpose of observing activities taking place within residential yards. Here, police conducted an overflight at low altitude solely for ***225** the purpose of discovering evidence of crime within a private enclave into which they were constitutionally forbidden to intrude at ground level without a warrant. It is not easy to believe that our society is prepared to force individuals to bear the risk of this type of warrantless police intrusion into their residential areas.

B

Since respondent had a reasonable expectation of privacy in his yard, aerial surveillance undertaken by the police for the purpose of discovering evidence of crime constituted a "search" within the meaning of the Fourth Amendment. "Warrantless searches are presumptively unreasonable, though the Court has recognized a few limited exceptions to this general rule."[433]This case presents no such exception. The indiscriminate nature of aerial surveillance, illustrated by Officer Shutz' photograph of respondent's home and enclosed yard as well as those of his neighbors, poses "far too serious a threat to privacy interests in the home to escape entirely some sort of Fourth Amendment oversight."[434]Therefore, I would affirm the judgment of the California Court of Appeal ordering suppression of the marijuana plants.

IV

Some may believe that this case, involving no physical intrusion on private property, presents "the obnoxious thing in its mildest and least repulsive form." [435]***226** But this Court recognized long ago that the essence of a Fourth Amendment

---

[430] 460 U.S. 276, 103 S.Ct. 1081, 75 L.Ed.2d 55 (1983). *Ante,* at 1812.

[431]*Ante,* at 1812.

[432] 460 U.S., at 281-282, 103 S.Ct., at 1085-1086.

[433] *United States v. Karo*, 468 U.S., at 717, 104 S.Ct., at 3304.

[434] Id., at 716, 104 S.Ct., at 3304 (footnote omitted).

[435] *Boyd v. United States*, 116 U.S., at 635, 6 S.Ct., at 535.

violation is "not the breaking of [a person's] doors, and the rummaging of his drawers," but rather is "the invasion of his indefeasible right of personal security, personal liberty and private property."[436] Rapidly advancing technology now permits police to conduct surveillance in the home itself, an area where privacy interests are most cherished in our society, without any physical trespass. While the rule in *Katz* was designed to prevent silent and unseen invasions of Fourth Amendment privacy rights in a variety of settings, we have consistently afforded heightened protection to a person's right to be left alone in the privacy of his house. The Court fails to enforce that right or to give any weight to the longstanding presumption that warrantless intrusions into the home are unreasonable. I dissent.

Black Letter Law

> Held that warrantless aerial observation of fenced-in backyard within curtilage of home was not unreasonable under the Fourth Amendment.
>
> Case defines home, curtilage, and open fields doctrine.

Bond v. U.S.

120 S.Ct. 1462

Supreme Court of the United States

BOND

v.

UNITED STATES.

No. 98–9349. | Argued Feb. 29, **2000**. | Decided April 17, **2000**.

Chief Justice REHNQUIST delivered the opinion of the Court.

This case presents the question whether a law enforcement officer's physical manipulation of a bus passenger's carry-on luggage violated the Fourth Amendment's proscription against unreasonable searches. We hold that it did.

Petitioner Steven Dewayne Bond was a passenger on a Greyhound bus that left California bound for Little Rock, Arkansas. The bus stopped, as it was required to do, at the permanent Border Patrol checkpoint in Sierra Blanca, Texas. Border Patrol Agent Cesar Cantu boarded the bus to check the immigration status of its passengers. After reaching the back of the bus, having satisfied himself that the passengers were lawfully in the United States, Agent Cantu began walking toward the front. Along the way, he squeezed the soft luggage which passengers had placed in the overhead storage space above the seats.

***336** Petitioner was seated four or five rows from the back of the bus. As Agent Cantu inspected the luggage in the compartment above petitioner's seat, he squeezed a green canvas bag and noticed that it contained a "brick-like" object. Petitioner admitted that the bag was his and agreed to allow Agent Cantu to open it. ****1464** Upon opening the bag, Agent Cantu discovered a "brick" of methamphetamine. The brick had been wrapped in duct tape until it was oval-shaped and then rolled in a pair of pants.

Petitioner was indicted for conspiracy to possess, and possession with intent to distribute, methamphetamine in violation of 84 Stat. 1260, 21 U.S.C. § 841(a)(1). He moved to suppress the drugs, arguing that Agent Cantu conducted an illegal search of his bag. Petitioner's motion was denied, and the District Court found him guilty on both counts and sentenced him to 57 months in prison. On appeal, he conceded that

[436] Id., at 630, 6 S.Ct., at 532.

other passengers had access to his bag, but contended that Agent Cantu manipulated the bag in a way that other passengers would not. The Court of Appeals rejected this argument, stating that the fact that Agent Cantu's manipulation of petitioner's bag was calculated to detect contraband is irrelevant for Fourth Amendment purposes.[437]Thus, the Court of Appeals affirmed the denial of the motion to suppress, holding that Agent Cantu's manipulation of the bag was not a search within the meaning of the Fourth Amendment. 167 F.3d, at 227. We granted certiorari,[438] and now reverse.

The Fourth Amendment provides that "[t]he right of the people to be secure in their persons, houses, papers, and effects, against unreasonable searches and seizures, shall not be violated...." A traveler's personal luggage is clearly an "effect" protected by the Amendment.[439] ***337**. Indeed, it is undisputed here that petitioner possessed a privacy interest in his bag.

But the Government asserts that by exposing his bag to the public, petitioner lost a reasonable expectation that his bag would not be physically manipulated. The Government relies on our decisions in *California v. Ciraolo*, and *Florida v. Riley*[440]for the proposition that matters open to public observation are not protected by the Fourth Amendment. In *Ciraolo*, we held that police observation of a backyard from a plane flying at an altitude of 1,000 feet did not violate a reasonable expectation of privacy. Similarly, in *Riley*, we relied on *Ciraolo* to hold that police observation of a greenhouse in a home's curtilage from a helicopter passing at an altitude of 400 feet did not violate the Fourth Amendment. We reasoned that the property was "not necessarily protected from inspection that involves no physical invasion," and determined that because any member of the public could have lawfully observed the defendants' property by flying overhead, the defendants' expectation of privacy was "not reasonable and not one 'that society is prepared to honor.'"[441]

But Ciraolo and Riley are different from this case because they involved only visual, as opposed to tactile, observation. Physically invasive inspection is simply more intrusive than purely visual inspection. For example, in *Terry v. Ohio*,[442]we stated that a "careful [tactile] exploration of the outer surfaces of a person's clothing all over his or her body" is a "serious intrusion upon the sanctity of the person, which may inflict great indignity and arouse strong resentment, and it is not to be undertaken lightly." Although Agent Cantu did not "frisk" petitioner's person, he did conduct a probing tactile examination of petitioner's carry-on luggage. Obviously, petitioner's bag was not part of his person. But travelers are particularly concerned ***338** about their carry-on luggage; they generally use it to transport ****1465** personal items that, for whatever reason, they prefer to keep close at hand.

Here, petitioner concedes that, by placing his bag in the overhead compartment, he could expect that it would be exposed to certain kinds of touching and handling. But petitioner argues that Agent Cantu's physical manipulation of his luggage "far exceeded the casual contact [petitioner] could have expected from other passengers."[443]The Government counters that it did not.

Our Fourth Amendment analysis embraces two questions. First, we ask whether the individual, by his conduct, has exhibited an actual expectation of privacy; that is,

---

[437] 167 F.3d 225, 227 (C.A.5 1999) (citing *California v. Ciraolo*, 476 U.S. 207, 106 S.Ct. 1809, 90 L.Ed.2d 210 (1986)).

[438] 528 U.S. 927, 120 S.Ct. 320, 145 L.Ed.2d 250 (1999)

[439] See *United States v. Place*, 462 U.S. 696, 707, 103 S.Ct. 2637, 77 L.Ed.2d 110 (1983)

[440] 488 U.S. 445, 109 S.Ct. 693, 102 L.Ed.2d 835 (1989),

[441] See *Riley, supra*, at 449, 109 S.Ct. 693 (explaining and relyingon Ciraolo's reasoning).

[442] 392 U.S. 1, 16–17, 88 S.Ct. 1868, 20 L.Ed.2d 889 (1968).

[443] Brief for Petitioner 18–19.

whether he has shown that "he [sought] to preserve [something] as private."[444] Here, petitioner sought to preserve privacy by using an opaque bag and placing that bag directly above his seat. Second, we inquire whether the individual's expectation of privacy is "one that society is prepared to recognize as reasonable."[445] When a bus passenger places a bag in an overhead bin, he expects that other passengers or bus employees may move it for one reason or another. Thus, a bus passenger clearly expects that his bag may be handled. He does not expect that other passengers or bus employees will, ***339** as a matter of course, feel the bag in an exploratory manner. But this is exactly what the agent did here. We therefore hold that the agent's physical manipulation of petitioner's bag violated the Fourth Amendment.

The judgment of the Court of Appeals is reversed.

(Dissent of Justice BREYER, with whom Justice SCALIA joins, omitted.)

Black Letter Law

Law enforcement officer's physical manipulation of opaque bag that passenger carried onto cross-country bus and placed in rack directly above his seat violated Fourth Amendment prohibition against unreasonable searches of effects. Although bus passenger had expectation that his bag might be handled by bus employee or other passenger, he did not have expectation that employee or other passenger would feel bag in exploratory manner. The Fourth Amendment analysis for determining whether a search was unreasonable embraces two questions: (1) whether the individual, by his conduct, has exhibited an actual expectation of privacy, and (2) whether the individual's expectation of privacy is one that society is prepared to recognize as reasonable. The subjective intent of the law enforcement officer, that is, whether he was motivated by a law enforcement purpose, is irrelevant in determining whether that officer's actions violated the Fourth Amendment.

Kyllo v. United States

121 S.Ct. 2038

Supreme Court of the United States

Danny Lee KYLLO, Petitioner,

v.

UNITED STATES.

No. 99–8508. | Argued Feb. 20, 2001. | Decided June 11, 2001.

Justice SCALIA delivered the opinion of the Court.

This case presents the question whether the use of a thermal-imaging device aimed at a private home from a public street to ****2041** detect relative amounts of heat within the home constitutes a "search" within the meaning of the Fourth Amendment.

I

[444] *Smith v. Maryland*, 442 U.S. 735, 740, 99 S.Ct. 2577, 61 L.Ed.2d 220 (1979) (internal quotation marks omitted).

[445] *Ibid.* (internal quotation marks omitted).

In 1991 Agent William Elliott of the United States Department of the Interior came to suspect that marijuana was being grown in the home belonging to petitioner Danny Kyllo, part of a triplex on Rhododendron Drive in Florence, Oregon. Indoor marijuana growth typically requires high-intensity lamps. In order to determine whether an amount of heat was emanating from petitioner's home consistent with the use of such lamps, at 3:20 a.m. on January 16, 1992, Agent Elliott and Dan Haas used an Agema Thermovision 210 thermal imager to scan the triplex. Thermal imagers detect infrared radiation, which virtually all objects emit but which is not visible to the naked eye. The imager converts radiation into images based on relative warmth—black ***30** is cool, white is hot, shades of gray connote relative differences; in that respect, it operates somewhat like a video camera showing heat images. The scan of Kyllo's home took only a few minutes and was performed from the passenger seat of Agent Elliott's vehicle across the street from the front of the house and also from the street in back of the house. The scan showed that the roof over the garage and a side wall of petitioner's home were relatively hot compared to the rest of the home and substantially warmer than neighboring homes in the triplex. Agent Elliott concluded that petitioner was using halide lights to grow marijuana in his house, which indeed he was. Based on tips from informants, utility bills, and the thermal imaging, a Federal Magistrate Judge issued a warrant authorizing a search of petitioner's home, and the agents found an indoor growing operation involving more than 100 plants. Petitioner was indicted on one count of manufacturing marijuana, in violation of 21 U.S.C. § 841(a)(1). He unsuccessfully moved to suppress the evidence seized from his home and then entered a conditional guilty plea.

The Court of Appeals for the Ninth Circuit remanded the case for an evidentiary hearing regarding the intrusiveness of thermal imaging. On remand the District Court found that the Agema 210 "is a non-intrusive device which emits no rays or beams and shows a crude visual image of the heat being radiated from the outside of the house"; it "did not show any people or activity within the walls of the structure"; "[t]he device used cannot penetrate walls or windows to reveal conversations or human activities"; and "[n]o intimate details of the home were observed."[446]Based on these findings, the District Court upheld the validity of the warrant that relied in part upon the thermal imaging, and reaffirmed its denial of the motion to suppress. A divided Court of Appeals initially reversed,[447]but that ***31** opinion was withdrawn and the panel (after a change in composition) affirmed, 190 F.3d 1041 (1999), with Judge Noonan dissenting. The court held that petitioner had shown no subjective expectation of privacy because he had made no attempt to conceal the heat escaping from his home,[448]and even if he had, there was no objectively reasonable expectation of privacy because the imager "did not expose any intimate details of Kyllo's life," only "amorphous 'hot spots' on the roof and exterior wall."[449]We granted certiorari.[450]

II

The Fourth Amendment provides that "[t]he right of the people to be secure in their persons, houses, papers, and effects, against unreasonable searches and seizures, shall not be violated." "At the very core" of the Fourth Amendment "stands the right of a man to retreat into his own home and there be free from unreasonable governmental intrusion."[451] ****2042**With few exceptions, the question whether a war-

[446] Supp.App. to Pet. for Cert. 39–40.

[447] 140 F.3d 1249 (1998).

[448] *Id.*, at 1046.

[449] *Id.*, at 1047.

[450] 530 U.S. 1305, 121 S.Ct. 29, 147 L.Ed.2d 1052 (2000).

[451] *Silverman v. United States*, 365 U.S. 505, 511, 81 S.Ct. 679, 5 L.Ed.2d 734 (1961).

rantless search of a home is reasonable and hence constitutional must be answered no.[452]

On the other hand, the antecedent question whether or not a Fourth Amendment "search" has occurred is not so simple under our precedent. The permissibility of ordinary visual surveillance of a home used to be clear because, well into the 20th century, our Fourth Amendment jurisprudence was tied to common-law trespass.[453]Visual surveillance was unquestionably lawful because " 'the ***32** eye cannot by the laws of England be guilty of a trespass.'"[454]We have since decoupled violation of a person's Fourth Amendment rights from trespassory violation of his property,[455]but the lawfulness of warrantless visual surveillance of a home has still been preserved. As we observed in *California v. Ciraolo*,[456] "[t]he Fourth Amendment protection of the home has never been extended to require law enforcement officers to shield their eyes when passing by a home on public thoroughfares."

One might think that the new validating rationale would be that examining the portion of a house that is in plain public view, while it is a "search"1 despite the absence of trespass, is not an "unreasonable" one under the Fourth Amendment.[457]But in fact we have held that visual observation is no "search" at all—perhaps in order to preserve somewhat more intact our doctrine that warrantless searches are presumptively unconstitutional.[458]In assessing when a search is not a search, we have applied somewhat in reverse the principle first enunciated in *Katz v. United States*.[459]*Katz* involved eavesdropping by means of an electronic listening device placed on the outside of a telephone booth—a location not within the catalog ("persons, houses, papers, and effects") that the Fourth Amendment protects against unreasonable searches. We held that the ***33** Fourth Amendment nonetheless protected Katz from the warrantless eavesdropping because he "justifiably relied" upon the privacy of the telephone booth.[460] As Justice Harlan's oft-quoted concurrence described it, a Fourth Amendment search occurs when the government violates a subjective expectation of privacy that society recognizes as reasonable.[461]We have subsequently applied this principle to hold that a Fourth Amendment search does not occur—even when the explicitly protected location of a house is concerned—unless "the individual manifested a subjective expectation of privacy ****2043** in the object of the challenged search," and "society [is] willing to recognize that expectation as reasonable."[462]We have applied this test in holding that it is not a search for the police to use a pen register at the phone company to determine what numbers were dialed in a private

---

[452] See *Illinois v. Rodriguez*, 497 U.S. 177, 181, 110 S.Ct. 2793, 111 L.Ed.2d 148 (1990); *Payton v. New York*, 445 U.S. 573, 586, 100 S.Ct. 1371, 63 L.Ed.2d 639 (1980).

[453] See, e.g., *Goldman v. United States*, 316 U.S. 129, 134–136, 62 S.Ct. 993, 86 L.Ed. 1322 (1942); *Olmstead v. United States*, 277 U.S. 438, 464–466, 48 S.Ct. 564, 72 L.Ed. 944 (1928). Cf. *Silverman v. United States*, *supra*, at 510–512, 81 S.Ct. 679 (technical trespass not necessary for Fourth Amendment violation; it suffices if there is "actual intrusion into a constitutionally protected area.").

[454] *Boyd v. United States*, 116 U.S. 616, 628, 6 S.Ct. 524, 29 L.Ed. 746 (1886) (quoting *Entick v. Carrington*, 19 How. St. Tr. 1029, 95 Eng. Rep. 807 (K.B.1765)).

[455] See *Rakas v. Illinois*, 439 U.S. 128, 143, 99 S.Ct. 421, 58 L.Ed.2d 387 (1978).

[456] 476 U.S. 207, 213, 106 S.Ct. 1809, 90 L.Ed.2d 210 (1986).

[457] See *Minnesota v. Carter*, 525 U.S. 83, 104, 119 S.Ct. 469, 142 L.Ed.2d 373 (1998) (BREYER, J., concurring in judgment).

[458] See *Dow Chemical Co. v. United States*, 476 U.S. 227, 234–235, 239, 106 S.Ct. 1819, 90 L.Ed.2d 226 (1986).

[459] 389 U.S. 347, 88 S.Ct. 507, 19 L.Ed.2d 576 (1967).

[460] Id., at 353, 88 S.Ct. 507.

[461] See *id*., at 361, 88 S.Ct. 507.

[462] Ciraolo, supra, at 211, 106 S.Ct. 1809.

home,[463]and we have applied the test on two different occasions in holding that aerial surveillance of private homes and surrounding areas does not constitute a search.[464]

The present case involves officers on a public street engaged in more than naked-eye surveillance of a home. We have previously reserved judgment as to how much technological enhancement of ordinary perception from such a vantage point, if any, is too much. While we upheld enhanced aerial photography of an industrial complex in *Dow Chemical*, we noted that we found "it important that this is not an area immediately adjacent to a private home, where privacy expectations are most heightened."[465]III

It would be foolish to contend that the degree of privacy secured to citizens by the Fourth Amendment has been ***34** entirely unaffected by the advance of technology. For example, as the cases discussed above make clear, the technology enabling human flight has exposed to public view (and hence, we have said, to official observation) uncovered portions of the house and its curtilage that once were private.[466]The question we confront today is what limits there are upon this power of technology to shrink the realm of guaranteed privacy.

The *Katz* test—whether the individual has an expectation of privacy that society is prepared to recognize as reasonable—has often been criticized as circular, and hence subjective and unpredictable.[467]While it may be difficult to refine Katz when the search of areas such as telephone booths, automobiles, or even the curtilage and uncovered portions of residences is at issue, in the case of the search of the interior of homes—the prototypical and hence most commonly litigated area of protected privacy—there is a ready criterion, with roots deep in the common law, of the minimal expectation of privacy that exists, and that is acknowledged to be reasonable. To withdraw protection of this minimum expectation would be to permit police technology to erode the privacy guaranteed by the Fourth Amendment. We think that obtaining by sense-enhancing technology any information regarding the interior of the home that could not otherwise have been obtained without physical "intrusion into a constitutionally protected area,"[468]constitutes a search—at least where (as here) the technology in question is not in general public use. This assures preservation of that degree of privacy against government that existed when the Fourth Amendment was adopted. On the basis of this criterion, the ***35** information obtained by the thermal imager in this case was the product of a search.

****2044** The Government maintains, however, that the thermal imaging must be upheld because it detected "only heat radiating from the external surface of the house,"[469]The dissent makes this its leading point,[470]contending that there is a fundamental difference between what it calls "off-the-wall" observations and "through-the-wall surveillance." But just as a thermal imager captures only heat emanating from a house, so also a powerful directional microphone picks up only sound emanating from a house-and a satellite capable of scanning from many miles away would pick up only visible light emanating from a house. We rejected such a mechanical interpretation of the Fourth Amendment in *Katz*, where the eavesdropping device

---

[463] *Smith v. Maryland*, 442 U.S. 735, 743–744, 99 S.Ct. 2577, 61 L.Ed.2d 220 (1979).

[464] *Ciraolo, supra*; *Florida v. Riley*, 488 U.S. 445, 109 S.Ct. 693, 102 L.Ed.2d 835 (1989).

[465] 476 U.S., at 237, n. 4, 106 S.Ct. 1819 (emphasis in original).

[466] See *Ciraolo*, supra, at 215, 106 S.Ct. 1809.

[467] See 1 W. LaFave, Search and Seizure § 2.1(d), pp. 393–394 (3d ed.1996); Posner, *The Uncertain Protection of Privacy by the Supreme Court*, 1979 S.Ct. Rev. 173, 188; Carter, supra, at 97, 119 S.Ct. 469 (SCALIA, J., concurring). But see *Rakas*, supra, at 143–144, n. 12, 99 S.Ct. 421.

[468] *Silverman*, 365 U.S., at 512, 81 S.Ct. 679.

[469] Brief for United States 26.

[470] see post, at 2047,

picked up only sound waves that reached the exterior of the phone booth. Reversing that approach would leave the homeowner at the mercy of advancing technology—including imaging technology that could discern all human ***36** activity in the home. While the technology used in the present case was relatively crude, the rule we adopt must take account of more sophisticated systems that are already in use or in development. The dissent's reliance on the distinction between "off-the-wall" and "through-the-wall" observation is entirely incompatible with the dissent's belief, which we discuss below, that thermal-imaging observations of the intimate details of a home are impermissible. The most sophisticated thermal-imaging devices continue to measure heat "off-the-wall" rather than "through-the-wall"; the dissent's disapproval of those more sophisticated thermal-imaging devices[471] is an acknowledgement that there is no substance to this distinction. As for the dissent's extraordinary assertion that anything learned through "an inference" cannot be a search[472] that would validate even the "through-the-wall" technologies that the dissent purports to disapprove. Surely the dissent does not believe that the through-the-wall radar or ultrasound technology produces an 8–by–10 Kodak glossy that needs no analysis (i.e., the making of inferences). And, of course, the novel proposition that inference insulates a search is blatantly contrary to *United States v. Karo*,[473]where the police "inferred" from the activation of a beeper that a certain can of ether was in the home. The police activity ***37** was held to be a search, and the search was held unlawful.

****2045** The Government also contends that the thermal imaging was constitutional because it did not "detect private activities occurring in private areas."[474]It points out that in *Dow Chemical* we observed that the enhanced aerial photography did not reveal any "intimate details."[475]*Dow Chemical*, however, involved enhanced aerial photography of an industrial complex, which does not share the Fourth Amendment sanctity of the home. The Fourth Amendment's protection of the home has never been tied to measurement of the quality or quantity of information obtained. In *Silverman*, for example, we made clear that any physical invasion of the structure of the home, "by even a fraction of an inch," was too much,[476]and there is certainly no exception to the warrant requirement for the officer who barely cracks open the front door and sees nothing but the non intimate rug on the vestibule floor. In the home, our cases show, all details are intimate details, because the entire area is held safe from prying government eyes. Thus, in *Karo*,[477] the only thing detected was a can of ether in the ***38** home; and in *Arizona v. Hicks*,[478]the only thing detected by a physical search that went beyond what officers lawfully present could observe in "plain view" was the registration number of a phonograph turntable. These were intimate details because they were details of the home, just as was the detail of how warm—or even how relatively warm—Kyllo was heating his residence.

Limiting the prohibition of thermal imaging to "intimate details" would not only be wrong in principle; it would be impractical in application, failing to provide "a workable accommodation between the needs of law enforcement and the interests protected by the Fourth Amendment."[479]To begin with, there is no necessary connection between the sophistication of the surveillance equipment and the "intimacy" of

---

[471] see post, at 2051

[472] see post, at 2048–2049

[473] 468 U.S. 705, 104 S.Ct. 3296, 82 L.Ed.2d 530 (1984).

[474] Brief for United States 22.

[475] 476 U.S., at 238, 106 S.Ct. 1819.

[476] 365 U.S., at 512, 81 S.Ct. 679.

[477] *supra.*

[478] 480 U.S. 321, 107 S.Ct. 1149, 94 L.Ed.2d 347 (1987).

[479] *Oliver v. United States*, 466 U.S. 170, 181, 104 S.Ct. 1735, 80 L.Ed.2d 214 (1984).

the details that it observes—which means that one cannot say (and the police cannot be assured) that use of the relatively crude equipment at issue here will always be lawful. The Agema Thermovision 210 might disclose, for example, at what hour each night the lady of the house takes her daily sauna and bath—a detail that many would consider "intimate"; and a much more sophisticated system might detect nothing more intimate than the fact that someone left a closet light on. We could not, in other words, develop a rule approving only that through-the-wall surveillance which identifies objects no smaller than 36 by 36 inches, but would have to develop a jurisprudence specifying which ***39** home activities are "intimate" and which are not. ****2046** And even when (if ever) that jurisprudence were fully developed, no police officer would be able to know in advance whether his through-the-wall surveillance picks up "intimate" details—and thus would be unable to know in advance whether it is constitutional.

The dissent's proposed standard—whether the technology offers the "functional equivalent of actual presence in the area being searched"[480]—would seem quite similar to our own at first blush. The dissent concludes that Katz was such a case, but then inexplicably asserts that if the same listening device only revealed the volume of the conversation, the surveillance would be permissible.[481] Yet if, without technology, the police could not discern volume without being actually present in the phone booth, Justice STEVENS should conclude a search has occurred.[482]

(STEVENS, J., concurring in part and dissenting in part) ("I find little comfort in the Court's notion that no invasion of privacy occurs until a listener obtains some significant information by use of the device .... A bathtub is a less private area when the plumber is present even if his back is turned"). The same should hold for the interior heat of the home if only a person present in the home could discern the heat. Thus the driving force of the dissent, despite its recitation of the above standard, appears to be a distinction among different types of information—whether the "homeowner would even care if anybody noticed."[483]The dissent offers no practical guidance for the application of this standard, and for reasons already discussed, we believe there can be none. The people in their houses, as well as the police, deserve more precision.

***40** We have said that the Fourth Amendment draws "a firm line at the entrance to the house."[484]That line, we think, must be not only firm but also bright—which requires clear specification of those methods of surveillance that require a warrant. While it is certainly possible to conclude from the videotape of the thermal imaging that occurred in this case that no "significant" compromise of the homeowner's privacy has occurred, we must take the long view, from the original meaning of the Fourth Amendment forward.

"The Fourth Amendment is to be construed in the light of what was deemed an unreasonable search and seizure when it was adopted, and in a manner which will conserve public interests as well as the interests and rights of individual citizens."[485]

Where, as here, the government uses a device that is not in general public use, to explore details of the home that would previously have been unknowable without physical intrusion, the surveillance is a "search" and is presumptively unreasonable without a warrant.

---

[480] Post, at 2050.

[481] Post, at 2051.

[482] Cf. Karo, 468 U.S., at 735, 104 S.Ct. 3296

[483] Post, at 2051.

[484] *Payton*, 445 U.S., at 590, 100 S.Ct. 1371.

[485] *Carroll v. United States*, 267 U.S. 132, 149, 45 S.Ct. 280, 69 L.Ed. 543 (1925).

Since we hold the Thermovision imaging to have been an unlawful search, it will remain for the District Court to determine whether, without the evidence it provided, the search warrant issued in this case was supported by probable cause—and if not, whether there is any other basis for supporting admission of the evidence that the search pursuant to the warrant produced.

****2047 *41** * * *

The judgment of the Court of Appeals is reversed; the case is remanded for further proceedings consistent with this opinion.

It is so ordered.

(Dissent of Justice STEVENS, with whom THE CHIEF JUSTICE, Justice O'CONNOR, and Justice KENNEDY join, omitted.)

Black Letter Law

> Obtaining by sense-enhancing technology any information regarding the interior of a home that could not otherwise have been obtained without physical intrusion into a constitutionally protected area, constitutes a "search"—at least where the technology in question is not in general public use.

United States v. Jones

132 S.Ct. 945

Supreme Court of the United States

UNITED STATES, Petitioner

v.

Antoine JONES.

No. 10–1259. | Argued Nov. 8, 2011. | Decided Jan. 23, 2012.

Justice Scalia delivered the opinion of the Court.

We decide whether the attachment of a Global–Positioning–System (GPS) tracking device to an individual's vehicle, and subsequent use of that device to monitor the vehicle's movements on public streets, constitutes a search or seizure within the meaning of the Fourth Amendment.

I

In 2004, respondent Antoine Jones, owner and operator of a nightclub in the District of Columbia, came under suspicion of trafficking in narcotics and was made the target of an investigation by a joint FBI and Metropolitan Police Department task force. Officers employed various investigative techniques, including visual surveillance of the nightclub, installation of a camera focused on the front door of the club, and a pen register and wiretap covering Jones's cellular phone.

Based in part on information gathered from these sources, in 2005 the Government applied to the United States District Court for the District of Columbia for a warrant authorizing the use of an electronic tracking device on the Jeep Grand Cherokee registered to Jones's wife. A warrant issued, authorizing installation of the device in the District of Columbia and within 10 days.

On the 11th day, and not in the District of Columbia but in Maryland,[1] agents installed a GPS tracking device on the undercarriage of the Jeep while it was parked in a public parking lot. Over the next 28 days, the Government used the device to track the vehicle's movements, and once had to replace the device's battery when the vehicle was parked in a different public lot in Maryland. By means of signals from multiple satellites, the device established the vehicle's location within 50 to 100 feet, and communicated that location by cellular phone to a Government computer. It relayed more than 2,000 pages of data over the 4–week period.

The Government ultimately obtained a multiple-count indictment charging Jones and several alleged co-conspirators with, as relevant here, conspiracy to distribute and possess with intent to distribute five kilograms or more of cocaine and 50 grams or more of cocaine base, in violation of 21 U.S.C. §§ 841 and 846. Before trial, Jones filed a motion to suppress evidence obtained through the GPS device. The District Court granted the motion only in part, suppressing the data obtained while the vehicle was parked in the garage adjoining Jones**'s** residence.[486]It held the remaining data admissible, because "'[a] person traveling in an automobile on public thoroughfares has no reasonable expectation of privacy in his movements from one place to another.'"[487]Jones's trial in October 2006 produced a hung jury on the conspiracy count.

In March 2007, a grand jury returned another indictment, charging Jones and others with the same conspiracy. The Government introduced at trial the same GPS-derived locational data admitted in the first trial, which connected Jones to the alleged conspirators' stash house that contained $850,000 in cash, 97 kilograms of ***949** cocaine, and 1 kilogram of cocaine base. The jury returned a guilty verdict, and the District Court sentenced Jones to life imprisonment.

The United States Court of Appeals for the District of Columbia Circuit reversed the conviction because of admission of the evidence obtained by warrantless use of the GPS device which, it said, violated the Fourth Amendment.[488]The D.C. Circuit denied the Government's petition for rehearing en banc, with four judges dissenting.[489]We granted certiorari.[490]II

A

The Fourth Amendment provides in relevant part that "[t]he right of the people to be secure in their persons, houses, papers, and effects, against unreasonable searches and seizures, shall not be violated." It is beyond dispute that a vehicle is an "effect" as that term is used in the Amendment.[491]We hold that the Government's installation of a GPS device on a target's vehicle,[2] and its use of that device to monitor the vehicle's movements, constitutes a "search."

It is important to be clear about what occurred in this case: The Government physically occupied private property for the purpose of obtaining information. We have no doubt that such a physical intrusion would have been considered a "search" within the meaning of the Fourth Amendment when it was adopted. *Entick v. Carrington,*[492]is a "case we have described as a 'monument of English freedom' 'undoubtedly familiar' to 'every American statesman' at the time the Constitution was adopted, and considered to be 'the true and ultimate expression of constitutional law' " with regard to search and seizure.[493]In that case, Lord Camden expressed in plain terms the significance of property rights in search-and-seizure analysis:

[486] 451 F.Supp.2d 71, 88 (2006).

[487] *Ibid.* (quoting *United States v. Knotts*, 460 U.S. 276, 281, 103 S.Ct. 1081, 75 L.Ed.2d 55 (1983)).

[488] *United States v. Maynard*, 615 F.3d 544 (2010).

[489] 625 F.3d 766 (2010).

[490] 564 U.S. ——, 131 S.Ct. 3064, 180 L.Ed.2d 885 (2011).

[491] United States v. Chadwick, 433 U.S. 1, 12, 97 S.Ct. 2476, 53 L.Ed.2d 538 (1977).

[492] 95 Eng. Rep. 807 (C.P. 1765).

[493] *Brower v. County of Inyo*, 489 U.S. 593, 596, 109 S.Ct. 1378, 103 L.Ed.2d 628 (1989) (quoting *Boyd v. United States*, 116 U.S. 616, 626, 6 S.Ct. 524, 29 L.Ed. 746 (1886)).

"[O]ur law holds the property of every man so sacred, that no man can set his foot upon his neighbor's close without his leave; if he does he is a trespasser, though he does no damage at all; if he will tread upon his neighbor's ground, he must justify it by law."[494]

The text of the Fourth Amendment reflects its close connection to property, since otherwise it would have referred simply to "the right of the people to be secure against unreasonable searches and seizures"; the phrase "in their persons, houses, papers, and effects" would have been superfluous.

Consistent with this understanding, our Fourth Amendment jurisprudence was tied to common-law trespass, at least until the latter half of the 20th century.[495]***950** Thus, in *Olmstead v. United States*,[496]we held that wiretaps attached to telephone wires on the public streets did not constitute a Fourth Amendment search because "[t]here was no entry of the houses or offices of the defendants."[497].

Our later cases, of course, have deviated from that exclusively property-based approach. In *Katz v. United States*,[498]we said that "the Fourth Amendment protects people, not places," and found a violation in attachment of an eavesdropping device to a public telephone booth. Our later cases have applied the analysis of Justice Harlan's concurrence in that case, which said that a violation occurs when government officers violate a person's "reasonable expectation of privacy."[499]

The Government contends that the Harlan standard shows that no search occurred here, since Jones had no "reasonable expectation of privacy" in the area of the Jeep accessed by Government agents (its underbody) and in the locations of the Jeep on the public roads, which were visible to all. But we need not address the Government's contentions, because Jones**'s** Fourth Amendment rights do not rise or fall with the Katz formulation. At bottom, we must "assur[e] preservation of that degree of privacy against government that existed when the Fourth Amendment was adopted."[500]As explained, for most of our history the Fourth Amendment was understood to embody a particular concern for government trespass upon the areas ("persons, houses, papers, and effects") it enumerates. *Katz* did not repudiate that understanding. Less than two years later the Court upheld defendants' contention that the Government could not introduce against them conversations between other people obtained by warrantless placement of electronic surveillance devices in their homes. The opinion rejected the dissent's contention that there was no Fourth Amendment violation "unless the conversational privacy of the homeowner himself is invaded."[501] ***951**. "[W]e [do not] believe that Katz, by holding that the Fourth Amendment protects persons and their private conversations, was intended to withdraw any of the protection which the Amendment extends to the home...."[502]

---

494 *Entick, supra*, at 817.

495 *Kyllo v. United States*, 533 U.S. 27, 31, 121 S.Ct. 2038, 150 L.Ed.2d 94 (2001); Kerr, The *950 *Fourth Amendment and New Technologies: Constitutional Myths and the Case for Caution*, 102 Mich. L.Rev. 801, 816 (2004).

496 277 U.S. 438, 48 S.Ct. 564, 72 L.Ed. 944 (1928).

497 *Id.* at 464, 48 S.Ct. 564.

498 389 U.S. 347, 351, 88 S.Ct. 507, 19 L.Ed.2d 576 (1967).

499 *Id.* at 360, 88 S.Ct. 507. See, e.g., Bond v. United States, 529 U.S. 334, 120 S.Ct. 1462, 146 L.Ed.2d 365 (2000); California v. Ciraolo, 476 U.S. 207, 106 S.Ct. 1809, 90 L.Ed.2d 210 (1986); Smith v. Maryland, 442 U.S. 735, 99 S.Ct. 2577, 61 L.Ed.2d 220 (1979).

500 *Kyllo*, supra, at 34, 121 S.Ct. 2038.

501 *Alderman v. United States*, 394 U.S. 165, 176, 89 S.Ct. 961, 22 L.Ed.2d 176 (1969)

502 Id., at 180, 89 S.Ct. 961.

More recently, in Soldal v. Cook County,[503], the Court unanimously rejected the argument that although a "seizure" had occurred "in a 'technical' sense" when a trailer home was forcibly removed,[504]no Fourth Amendment violation occurred because law enforcement had not "invade[d] the [individuals'] privacy."[505]*Katz*, the Court explained, established that "property rights are not the sole measure of Fourth Amendment violations," but did not "snuf[f] out the previously recognized protection for property."[506]As Justice Brennan explained in his concurrence in Knotts, Katz did not erode the principle "that, when the Government does engage in physical intrusion of a constitutionally protected area in order to obtain information, that intrusion may constitute a violation of the Fourth Amendment."[507]We have embodied that preservation of past rights in our very definition of "reasonable expectation of privacy" which we have said to be an expectation "that has a source outside of the Fourth Amendment, either by reference to concepts of real or personal property law or to understandings that are recognized and permitted by society."[508]*Katz* did not narrow the Fourth Amendment's scope.

The Government contends that several of our post-Katz cases foreclose the conclusion that what occurred here constituted a search. It relies principally on two cases in which we rejected Fourth Amendment challenges to "beepers," electronic tracking devices that represent another form of electronic monitoring. The first case, *Knotts*, upheld against Fourth Amendment challenge the use of a "beeper" that had been placed in a container of chloroform, allowing law enforcement to monitor the location of the container.[509]We said that there had been no infringement of Knotts' reasonable expectation of privacy since the information obtained—the location of the automobile carrying the container on public roads, and the location of the off-loaded container in open fields near Knotts' cabin—had been voluntarily conveyed to the ***952** public.[510]But as we have discussed, the *Katz* reasonable-expectation-of-privacy test has been added to, not substituted for, the common-law trespassory test. The holding in *Knotts* addressed only the former, since the latter was not at issue. The beeper had been placed in the container before it came into Knotts' possession, with the consent of the then-owner.[511]Knotts did not challenge that installation, and we specifically declined to consider its effect on the Fourth Amendment analysis.[512]Knotts would be relevant, perhaps, if the Government were making the argument that what would otherwise be an unconstitutional search is not such where it produces only public information. The Government does not make that argument, and we know of no case that would support it.

The second "beeper" case, *United States v. Karo*,[513]does not suggest a different conclusion. There we addressed the question left open by Knotts, whether the installation of a beeper in a container amounted to a search or seizure.[514]As in *Knotts*, at the time the beeper was installed the container belonged to a third party, and it did

---

[503] 506 U.S. 56, 113 S.Ct. 538, 121 L.Ed.2d 450 (1992).

[504] *Id.* at 62, 113 S.Ct. 538.

[505] *Id.* at 60, 113 S.Ct. 538.

[506] 506 U.S., at 64, 113 S.Ct. 538.

[507] 460 U.S., at 286, 103 S.Ct. 1081 (opinion concurring in judgment).

[508] *Minnesota v. Carter*, 525 U.S. 83, 88, 119 S.Ct. 469, 142 L.Ed.2d 373 (1998) (internal quotation marks omitted).

[509] 460 U.S., at 278, 103 S.Ct. 1081.

[510] Id., at 281–282, 103 S.Ct. 1081.

[511] 460 U.S., at 278, 103 S.Ct. 1081.

[512] Id., at 279, n. **, 103 S.Ct. 1081.

[513] 468 U.S. 705, 104 S.Ct. 3296, 82 L.Ed.2d 530 (1984).

[514] 468 U.S., at 713, 104 S.Ct. 3296.

not come into possession of the defendant until later.[515]Thus, the specific question we considered was whether the installation "with the consent of the original owner constitute[d] a search or seizure ... when the container is delivered to a buyer having no knowledge of the presence of the beeper."[516]We held not. The Government, we said, came into physical contact with the container only before it belonged to the defendant Karo; and the transfer of the container with the unmonitored beeper inside did not convey any information and thus did not invade Karo's privacy.[517]That conclusion is perfectly consistent with the one we reach here. Karo accepted the container as it came to him, beeper and all, and was therefore not entitled to object to the beeper's presence, even though it was used to monitor the container's location.[518]Jones, who possessed the Jeep at the time the Government trespassorily inserted the information-gathering device, is on much different footing.

The Government also points to our exposition in *New York v. Class*,[519]that "[t]he exterior of a car ... is thrust into the public eye, and thus to examine it does not constitute a 'search.'"[520]That statement is of marginal relevance here since, as the Government acknowledges, "the officers in this case did more than conduct a visual inspection of respondent's vehicle."[521]By attaching the device to the Jeep, officers encroached on a protected area. In *Class* itself we suggested that this would make a difference, for we concluded that an officer's momentary reaching into the interior of a vehicle did constitute a search.[522]

***953** Finally, the Government's position gains little support from our conclusion in Oliver v. United States,[523]that officers' information-gathering intrusion on an "open field" did not constitute a Fourth Amendment search even though it was a trespass at common law.[524]Quite simply, an open field, unlike the curtilage of a home,[525]is not one of those protected areas enumerated in the Fourth Amendment.[526]The Government's physical intrusion on such an area—unlike its intrusion on the "effect" at issue here—is of no Fourth Amendment significance.

B

The concurrence begins by accusing us of applying "18th-century tort law."[527]That is a distortion. What we apply is an 18th-century guarantee against unreasonable searches, which we believe must provide at a minimum the degree of protection it afforded when it was adopted. The concurrence does not share that belief. It would apply exclusively *Katz's* reasonable-expectation-of-privacy test, even when that eliminates rights that previously existed.

---

[515] 468 U.S., at 708, 104 S.Ct. 3296.

[516] Id., at 707, 104 S.Ct. 3296 (emphasis added).

[517] See id., at 712, 104 S.Ct. 3296.

[518] Cf. On Lee v. United States, 343 U.S. 747, 751–752, 72 S.Ct. 967, 96 L.Ed. 1270 (1952) (no search or seizure where an informant, who was wearing a concealed microphone, was invited into the defendant's business).

[519] 475 U.S. 106, 106 S.Ct. 960, 89 L.Ed.2d 81 (1986).

[520] Id., at 114, 106 S.Ct. 960.

[521] Brief for United States 41 (emphasis added).

[522] 475 U.S., at 114–115, 106 S.Ct. 960.

[523] 466 U.S. 170, 104 S.Ct. 1735, 80 L.Ed.2d 214 (1984).

[524] id., at 183, 104 S.Ct. 1735.

[525] See *United States v. Dunn*, 480 U.S. 294, 300, 107 S.Ct. 1134, 94 L.Ed.2d 326 (1987).

[526] *Oliver*, supra, at 176–177, 104 S.Ct. 1735. See also Hester v. United States, 265 U.S. 57, 59, 44 S.Ct. 445, 68 L.Ed. 898 (1924).

[527] Post, at 957.

The concurrence faults our approach for "present[ing] particularly vexing problems" in cases that do not involve physical contact, such as those that involve the transmission of electronic signals.[528]We entirely fail to understand that point. For unlike the concurrence, which would make *Katz* the exclusive test, we do not make trespass the exclusive test. Situations involving merely the transmission of electronic signals without trespass would remain subject to *Katz* analysis.

In fact, it is the concurrence's insistence on the exclusivity of the Katz test that needlessly leads us into "particularly vexing problems" in the present case. This Court has to date not deviated from the understanding that mere visual observation does not constitute a search.[529]We accordingly held in *Knotts* that "[a] person traveling in an automobile on public thoroughfares has no reasonable expectation of privacy in his movements from one place to another."[530]Thus, even assuming that the concurrence is correct to say that "[t]raditional surveillance" of Jones for a 4–week period "would have required a large team of agents, multiple vehicles, and perhaps aerial assistance,"[531]our cases suggest that such visual observation is constitutionally ***954** permissible. It may be that achieving the same result through electronic means, without an accompanying trespass, is an unconstitutional invasion of privacy, but the present case does not require us to answer that question.

And answering it affirmatively leads us needlessly into additional thorny problems. The concurrence posits that "relatively short-term monitoring of a person's movements on public streets" is okay, but that "the use of longer term GPS monitoring in investigations of most offenses " is no good.[532]That introduces yet another novelty into our jurisprudence. There is no precedent for the proposition that whether a search has occurred depends on the nature of the crime being investigated. And even accepting that novelty, it remains unexplained why a 4–week investigation is "surely" too long and why a drug-trafficking conspiracy involving substantial amounts of cash and narcotics is not an "extraordinary offens[e]" which may permit longer observation.[533]What of a 2–day monitoring of a suspected purveyor of stolen electronics? Or of a 6–month monitoring of a suspected terrorist? We may have to grapple with these "vexing problems" in some future case where a classic trespassory search is not involved and resort must be had to *Katz* analysis; but there is no reason for rushing forward to resolve them here.

III

The Government argues in the alternative that even if the attachment and use of the device was a search, it was reasonable—and thus lawful—under the Fourth Amendment because "officers had reasonable suspicion, and indeed probable cause, to believe that [Jones] was a leader in a large-scale cocaine distribution conspiracy."[534]We have no occasion to consider this argument. The Government did not raise it below, and the D.C. Circuit therefore did not address it.[535]We consider the argument forfeited.[536]

* * *

The judgment of the Court of Appeals for the D.C. Circuit is affirmed.

---

528 Post, at 962.

529 See *Kyllo*, 533 U.S., at 31–32, 121 S.Ct. 2038.

530 460 U.S., at 281, 103 S.Ct. 1081.

531 Post, at 963.

532 Post, at 964 (emphasis added).

533 See post, at 964.

534 Brief for United States 50–51.

535 See 625 F.3d, at 767 (Ginsburg, Tatel, and Griffith, JJ., concurring in denial of rehearing en banc).

536 See *Sprietsma v. Mercury Marine*, 537 U.S. 51, 56, n. 4, 123 S.Ct. 518, 154 L.Ed.2d 466 (2002).

It is so ordered.

Justice SOTOMAYOR, concurring.

I join the Court's opinion because I agree that a search within the meaning of the Fourth Amendment occurs, at a minimum, "[w]here, as here, the Government obtains information by physically intruding on a constitutionally protected area."[537]In this case, the Government installed a Global Positioning System (GPS) tracking device on respondent Antoine Jones' Jeep without a valid warrant and without Jones' consent, then used that device to monitor the Jeep's movements over the course of four weeks. The Government usurped Jones' property for the purpose of conducting surveillance on him, thereby invading privacy interests long afforded, and undoubtedly entitled to, Fourth Amendment protection.[538]

Of course, the Fourth Amendment is not concerned only with trespassory intrusions on property.[539]Rather, even in the absence of a trespass, "a Fourth Amendment search occurs when the government violates a subjective expectation of privacy that society recognizes ***955** as reasonable."[540]In *Katz*, this Court enlarged its then-prevailing focus on property rights by announcing that the reach of the Fourth Amendment does not "turn upon the presence or absence of a physical intrusion."[541]As the majority's opinion makes clear, however, *Katz's* reasonable-expectation-of-privacy test augmented, but did not displace or diminish, the common-law trespassory test that preceded it.[542]Thus, "when the government does engage in physical intrusion of a constitutionally protected area in order to obtain information, that intrusion may constitute a violation of the Fourth Amendment."[543]Justice Alito's approach, which discounts altogether the constitutional relevance of the Government's physical intrusion on Jones' Jeep, erodes that longstanding protection for privacy expectations inherent in items of property that people possess or control.[544] By contrast, the trespassory test applied in the majority's opinion reflects an irreducible constitutional minimum: When the Government physically invades personal property to gather information, a search occurs. The reaffirmation of that principle suffices to decide this case.

Nonetheless, as Justice Alito notes, physical intrusion is now unnecessary to many forms of surveillance.[545]With increasing regularity, the Government will be capable of duplicating the monitoring undertaken in this case by enlisting factory or owner installed vehicle tracking devices or GPS-enabled smartphones.[546]In cases of electronic or other novel modes of surveillance that do not depend upon a physical invasion on property, the majority opinion's trespassory test may provide little guidance. But "situations involving merely the transmission of electronic signals without trespass would remain subject to Katz analysis."[547]As Justice Alito incisively ob-

[537] Ante, at 950, n. 3.

[538] See, e.g., *Silverman v. United States*, 365 U.S. 505, 511–512, 81 S.Ct. 679, 5 L.Ed.2d 734 (1961).

[539] See, e.g., *Kyllo v. United States*, 533 U.S. 27, 31–33, 121 S.Ct. 2038, 150 L.Ed.2d 94 (2001).

[540] Id., at 33, 121 S.Ct. 2038; see also *Smith v. Maryland*, 442 U.S. 735, 740–741, 99 S.Ct. 2577, 61 L.Ed.2d 220 (1979); *Katz v. United States*, 389 U.S. 347, 361, 88 S.Ct. 507, 19 L.Ed.2d 576 (1967) (Harlan, J., concurring).

[541] Id., at 353, 88 S.Ct. 507.

[542] Ante, at 951.

[543] United States v. Knotts, 460 U.S. 276, 286, 103 S.Ct. 1081, 75 L.Ed.2d 55 (1983) (Brennan, J., concurring in judgment); see also, e.g., Rakas v. Illinois, 439 U.S. 128, 144, n. 12, 99 S.Ct. 421, 58 L.Ed.2d 387 (1978).

[544] See post, at 959 – 961 (opinion concurring in judgment).

[545] Post, at 961 – 963.

[546]

[547] Ante, at 953.

serves, the same technological advances that have made possible nontrespassory surveillance techniques will also affect the *Katz* test by shaping the evolution of societal privacy expectations.[548]Under that rubric, I agree with Justice Alito that, at the very least, "longer term GPS monitoring in investigations of most offenses impinges on expectations of privacy."[549]

In cases involving even short-term monitoring, some unique attributes of GPS surveillance relevant to the *Katz* analysis will require particular attention. GPS monitoring generates a precise, comprehensive record of a person's public movements that reflects a wealth of detail about her familial, political, professional, religious, and sexual associations.[550]The ***956** government can store such records and efficiently mine them for information years into the future.[551]And because GPS monitoring is cheap in comparison to conventional surveillance techniques and, by design, proceeds surreptitiously, it evades the ordinary checks that constrain abusive law enforcement practices: "limited police resources and community hostility."[552]

Awareness that the government may be watching chills associational and expressive freedoms. And the Government's unrestrained power to assemble data that reveal private aspects of identity is susceptible to abuse. The net result is that GPS monitoring—by making available at a relatively low cost such a substantial quantum of intimate information about any person whom the government, in its unfettered discretion, chooses to track—may "alter the relationship between citizen and government in a way that is inimical to democratic society."[553]

I would take these attributes of GPS monitoring into account when considering the existence of a reasonable societal expectation of privacy in the sum of one's public movements. I would ask whether people reasonably expect that their movements will be recorded and aggregated in a manner that enables the government to ascertain, more or less at will, their political and religious beliefs, sexual habits, and so on. I do not regard as dispositive the fact that the government might obtain the fruits of GPS monitoring through lawful conventional surveillance techniques.[554]I would also consider the appropriateness of entrusting to the Executive, in the absence of any oversight from a coordinate branch, a tool so amenable to misuse, especially in light of the Fourth Amendment's goal to curb arbitrary exercises of police power to and prevent "a too permeating police surveillance,"[555]

***957** More fundamentally, it may be necessary to reconsider the premise that an individual has no reasonable expectation of privacy in information voluntarily disclosed to third parties.[556]This approach is ill suited to the digital age, in which people reveal a great deal of information about themselves to third parties in the course of carrying out mundane tasks. People disclose the phone numbers that they dial or text to their cellular providers; the URLs that they visit and the e-mail addresses with which they correspond to their Internet service providers; and the books, groceries,

---

[548] Post, at 962 – 963.

[549] Post, at 964.

[550] See, e.g., People v. Weaver, 12 N.Y.3d 433, 441–442, 882 N.Y.S.2d 357, 909 N.E.2d 1195, 1199 (2009) ("Disclosed in [GPS] data ... will be trips the indisputably private nature of which takes little imagination to conjure: trips to the psychiatrist, the plastic surgeon, the abortion clinic, the AIDS treatment center, the strip club, the criminal defense attorney, the by-the-hour motel, the union meeting, the mosque, synagogue or church, the gay bar and on and on").

[551] Pineda–Moreno, 617 F.3d, at 1124 (opinion of Kozinski, C.J.).

[552] Illinois v. Lidster, 540 U.S. 419, 426, 124 S.Ct. 885, 157 L.Ed.2d 843 (2004).

[553] United States v. Cuevas–Perez, 640 F.3d 272, 285 (C.A.7 2011) (Flaum, J., concurring).

[554] See Kyllo, 533 U.S., at 35, n. 2, 121 S.Ct. 2038; ante, at 954 (leaving open the possibility that duplicating traditional surveillance "through electronic means, without an accompanying trespass, is an unconstitutional invasion of privacy").

[555] United States v. Di Re, 332 U.S. 581, 595, 68 S.Ct. 222, 92 L.Ed. 210 (1948).*

[556] E.g., Smith, 442 U.S., at 742, 99 S.Ct. 2577; United States v. Miller, 425 U.S. 435, 443, 96 S.Ct. 1619, 48 L.Ed.2d 71 (1976).

and medications they purchase to online retailers. Perhaps, as Justice Alitonotes, some people may find the "tradeoff" of privacy for convenience "worthwhile," or come to accept this "diminution of privacy" as "inevitable,"[557], and perhaps not. I for one doubt that people would accept without complaint the warrantless disclosure to the government of a list of every website they had visited in the last week, or month, or year. But whatever the societal expectations, they can attain constitutionally protected status only if our Fourth Amendment jurisprudence ceases to treat secrecy as a prerequisite for privacy. I would not assume that all information voluntarily disclosed to some member of the public for a limited purpose is, for that reason alone, disentitled to Fourth Amendment protection.[558]

Resolution of these difficult questions in this case is unnecessary, however, because the Government's physical intrusion on Jones' Jeep supplies a narrower basis for decision. I therefore join the majority's opinion.

Justice ALITO, with whom Justice GINSBURG, Justice BREYER, and Justice KAGAN join, concurring in the judgment.

This case requires us to apply the Fourth Amendment's prohibition of unreasonable searches and seizures to a 21st-century surveillance technique, the use of a Global Positioning System (GPS) device to monitor a vehicle's movements for an extended period of time. Ironically, the Court has chosen to decide this case based on 18th-century tort law. By attaching a small GPS device to the underside of the vehicle that respondent drove, the law enforcement officers in this case engaged in conduct that might have provided grounds in 1791 for a suit for trespass to chattels.[2] And for this reason, the Court concludes, ***958** the installation and use of the GPS device constituted a search.[559]

This holding, in my judgment, is unwise. It strains the language of the Fourth Amendment; it has little if any support in current Fourth Amendment case law; and it is highly artificial.

I would analyze the question presented in this case by asking whether respondent's reasonable expectations of privacy were violated by the long-term monitoring of the movements of the vehicle he drove.

I

A

The Fourth Amendment prohibits "unreasonable searches and seizures," and the Court makes very little effort to explain how the attachment or use of the GPS device fits within these terms. The Court does not contend that there was a seizure. A seizure of property occurs when there is "some meaningful interference with an individual's possessory interests in that property,"[560]and here there was none. Indeed, the success of the surveillance technique that the officers employed was dependent on the fact that the GPS did not interfere in any way with the operation of the vehicle, for if any such interference had been detected, the device might have been discovered.

The Court does claim that the installation and use of the GPS constituted a search,[561]but this conclusion is dependent on the questionable proposition that these

---

[557] Post, at 962.

[558] See Smith, 442 U.S., at 749, 99 S.Ct. 2577 (Marshall, J., dissenting) ("Privacy is not a discrete commodity, possessed absolutely or not at all. Those who disclose certain facts to a bank or phone company for a limited business purpose need not assume that this information will be released to other persons for other purposes"); see also Katz, 389 U.S., at 351–352, 88 S.Ct. 507 ("[W]hat [a person] seeks to preserve as private, even in an area accessible to the public, may be constitutionally protected").

[559] Ante, at 948 – 949.

[560] *United States v. Jacobsen*, 466 U.S. 109, 113, 104 S.Ct. 1652, 80 L.Ed.2d 85 (1984).

[561] see ante, at 948 – 949.

two procedures cannot be separated for purposes of Fourth Amendment analysis. If these two procedures are analyzed separately, it is not at all clear from the Court's opinion why either should be regarded as a search. It is clear that the attachment of the GPS device was not itself a search; if the device had not functioned or if the officers had not used it, no information would have been obtained. And the Court does not contend that the use of the device constituted a search either. On the contrary, the Court accepts the holding in *United States v. Knotts*,[562]that the use of a surreptitiously planted electronic device to monitor a vehicle's movements on public roads did not amount to a search. See ante, at 951.

The Court argues—and I agree—that "we must 'assur[e] preservation of that degree of privacy against government that existed when the Fourth Amendment was adopted.'"[563]But it is almost impossible to think of late–18th-century situations that are analogous to what took place in this case. (Is it possible to imagine a case in which a constable secreted himself somewhere in a coach and remained there for a period of time in order to monitor the movements of the coach's owner?[3]) The Court's theory seems to be that the concept of a search, as originally understood, comprehended any technical trespass that led to the gathering of evidence, but we know that this is incorrect. At common law, any unauthorized intrusion on private property was actionable,[564]but a trespass on open fields, as opposed to the "curtilage" of a home, does not fall within the scope of the Fourth Amendment because private property outside the curtilage ***959** is not part of a "hous[e]" within the meaning of the Fourth Amendment.[565]

B

The Court's reasoning in this case is very similar to that in the Court's early decisions involving wiretapping and electronic eavesdropping, namely, that a technical trespass followed by the gathering of evidence constitutes a search. In the early electronic surveillance cases, the Court concluded that a Fourth Amendment search occurred when private conversations were monitored as a result of an "unauthorized physical penetration into the premises occupied" by the defendant.[566]In *Silverman*, police officers listened to conversations in an attached home by inserting a "spike mike" through the wall that this house shared with the vacant house next door.[567]This procedure was held to be a search because the mike made contact with a heating duct on the other side of the wall and thus "usurp[ed] ... an integral part of the premises."[568]

By contrast, in cases in which there was no trespass, it was held that there was no search. Thus, in *Olmstead v. United States*,[569]the Court found that the Fourth Amendment did not apply because "[t]he taps from house lines were made in the streets near the houses."[570]Similarly, the Court concluded that no search occurred in *Goldman v. United States*,[571]where a "detectaphone" was placed on the outer wall of defendant's office for the purpose of overhearing conversations held within the room.

---

[562] 460 U.S. 276, 103 S.Ct. 1081, 75 L.Ed.2d 55 (1983).

[563] Ante, at 950 (quoting *Kyllo v. United States*, 533 U.S. 27, 34, 121 S.Ct. 2038, 150 L.Ed.2d 94 (2001)).

[564] See Prosser & Keeton 75.

[565] See *Oliver v. United States*, 466 U.S. 170, 104 S.Ct. 1735, 80 L.Ed.2d 214 (1984); *Hester v. United States*, 265 U.S. 57, 44 S.Ct. 445, 68 L.Ed. 898 (1924).

[566] *Silverman v. United States*, 365 U.S. 505, 509, 81 S.Ct. 679, 5 L.Ed.2d 734 (1961).

[567] Id., at 506, 81 S.Ct. 679.

[568] Id., at 511, 81 S.Ct. 679.

[569] 277 U.S. 438, 48 S.Ct. 564, 72 L.Ed. 944 (1928).

[570] Id., at 457, 48 S.Ct. 564.

[571] 316 U.S. 129, 135, 62 S.Ct. 993, 86 L.Ed. 1322 (1942).

This trespass-based rule was repeatedly criticized. In Olmstead, Justice Brandeis wrote that it was "immaterial where the physical connection with the telephone wires was made."[572]Although a private conversation transmitted by wire did not fall within the literal words of the Fourth Amendment, he argued, the Amendment should be understood as prohibiting "every unjustifiable intrusion by the government upon the privacy of the individual."[573]

Katz v. United States[574]finally did away with the old approach, holding that a trespass was not required for a Fourth Amendment violation. *Katz* involved the use of a listening device that was attached to the outside of a public telephone booth and that allowed police officers to eavesdrop on one end of the target's phone conversation. This procedure ***960** did not physically intrude on the area occupied by the target, but the *Katz* Court, "repudiate[ed]" the old doctrine, *Rakas v. Illinois*[575]and held that "[t]he fact that the electronic device employed ... did not happen to penetrate the wall of the booth can have no constitutional significance."[576]What mattered, the Court now held, was whether the conduct at issue "violated the privacy upon which [the defendant] justifiably relied while using the telephone booth."[577]

Under this approach, as the Court later put it when addressing the relevance of a technical trespass, "an actual trespass is neither necessary nor sufficient to establish a constitutional violation."[578]In *Oliver*, the Court wrote:

> "The existence of a property right is but one element in determining whether expectations of privacy are legitimate. 'The premise that property interests control the right of the Government to search and seize has been discredited.'[579]

II

The majority suggests that two post-*Katz* decisions—*Soldal v. Cook County*[580]and *Alderman v. United States*[581]—show that a technical trespass is sufficient to establish the existence of a search, but they provide little support.

In *Soldal*, the Court held that towing away a trailer home without the owner's consent constituted a seizure even if this did not invade the occupants' personal pri-

---

572 277 U.S., at 479, 48 S.Ct. 564 (dissenting opinion).

573 Id., at 478, 48 S.Ct. 564. See also, e.g., *Silverman, supra*, at 513, 81 S.Ct. 679 (Douglas, J., concurring) ("The concept of 'an unauthorized physical penetration into the premises,' on which the present decision rests seems to me beside the point. Was not the wrong ... done when the intimacies of the home were tapped, recorded, or revealed? The depth of the penetration of the electronic device—even the degree of its remoteness from the inside of the house—is not the measure of the injury"); *Goldman, supra*, at 139, 62 S.Ct. 993 (Murphy, J., dissenting) ("[T]he search of one's home or office no longer requires physical entry, for science has brought forth far more effective devices for the invasion of a person's privacy than the direct and obvious methods of oppression which were detested by our forebears and which inspired the Fourth Amendment").

574 389 U.S. 347, 88 S.Ct. 507, 19 L.Ed.2d 576 (1967),.

575 439 U.S. 128, 143, 99 S.Ct. 421, 58 L.Ed.2d 387 (1978).

576 389 U.S., at 353, 88 S.Ct. 507 ("[T]he reach of th[e] [Fourth] Amendment cannot turn upon the presence or absence of a physical intrusion into any given enclosure"); see *Rakas, supra*, at 143, 99 S.Ct. 421 (describing *Katz* as holding that the "capacity to claim the protection for the Fourth Amendment depends not upon a property right in the invaded place but upon whether the person who claims the protection of the Amendment has a legitimate expectation of privacy in the invaded place"); *Kyllo, supra*, at 32, 121 S.Ct. 2038 ("We have since decoupled violation of a person's Fourth Amendment rights from trespassory violation of his property").

577 *Katz, supra*, at 353, 88 S.Ct. 507.

578 *United States v. Karo*, 468 U.S. 705, 713, 104 S.Ct. 3296, 82 L.Ed.2d 530 (1984) (emphasis added). *Ibid.* ("Compar[ing] *Katz v. United States*, 389 U.S. 347 [88 S.Ct. 507, 19 L.Ed.2d 576] (1967) (no trespass, but Fourth Amendment violation), with *Oliver v. United States*, 466 U.S. 170 [104 S.Ct. 1735, 80 L.Ed.2d 214] (1984) (trespass, but no Fourth Amendment violation)").

579 *Katz*, 389 U.S., at 353 [88 S.Ct. 507], (quoting *Warden v. Hayden*, 387 U.S. 294, 304 [87 S.Ct. 1642, 18 L.Ed.2d 782] (1967); some internal quotation marks omitted)." 466 U.S., at 183, 104 S.Ct. 1735.

580 506 U.S. 56, 113 S.Ct. 538, 121 L.Ed.2d 450 (1992).

581 394 U.S. 165, 89 S.Ct. 961, 22 L.Ed.2d 176 (1969).

vacy. But in the present case, the Court does not find that there was a seizure, and it is clear that none occurred.

In *Alderman*, the Court held that the Fourth Amendment rights of homeowners were implicated by the use of a surreptitiously planted listening device to monitor third-party conversations that occurred within their home.[582]*Alderman* is best understood to mean that the homeowners had a legitimate expectation of privacy in all conversations that took place under their roof.[583]***961** In sum, the majority is hard pressed to find support in post-*Katz* cases for its trespass-based theory.

III

Disharmony with a substantial body of existing case law is only one of the problems with the Court's approach in this case.

I will briefly note four others. First, the Court's reasoning largely disregards what is really important (the use of a GPS for the purpose of long-term tracking) and instead attaches great significance to something that most would view as relatively minor (attaching to the bottom of a car a small, light object that does not interfere in any way with the car's operation). Attaching such an object is generally regarded as so trivial that it does not provide a basis for recovery under modern tort law.[584]But under the Court's reasoning, this conduct may violate the Fourth Amendment. By contrast, if long-term monitoring can be accomplished without committing a technical trespass—suppose, for example, that the Federal Government required or persuaded auto manufacturers to include a GPS tracking device in every car—the Court's theory would provide no protection.

Second, the Court's approach leads to incongruous results. If the police attach a GPS device to a car and use the device to follow the car for even a brief time, under the Court's theory, the Fourth Amendment applies. But if the police follow the same car for a much longer period using unmarked cars and aerial assistance, this tracking is not subject to any Fourth Amendment constraints.

In the present case, the Fourth Amendment applies, the Court concludes, because the officers installed the GPS device after respondent's wife, to whom the car was registered, turned it over to respondent for his exclusive use.[585]But if the GPS had been attached prior to that time, the Court's theory would lead to a different result. The Court proceeds on the assumption that respondent "had at least the property rights of a bailee,"[586]but a bailee may sue for a trespass to chattel only if the injury occurs during the term of the bailment.[587]So if the GPS device had been installed before respondent's wife gave him the keys, respondent would have no claim for trespass—and, presumably, no Fourth Amendment claim either.

Third, under the Court's theory, the coverage of the Fourth Amendment may vary from State to State. If the events at issue here had occurred in a community property State or a State that has adopted the Uniform Marital Property Act, respondent would likely be an owner of the vehicle, and it would not matter whether the

---

[582] See 394 U.S., at 176–180, 89 S.Ct. 961.

[583] See *Rakas*, 439 U.S., at 144, n. 12, 99 S.Ct. 421 (citing *Alderman* for the proposition that "the Court has not altogether abandoned use of property concepts in determining the presence or absence of the privacy interests protected by that Amendment"); 439 U.S., at 153, 99 S.Ct. 421 (Powell, J., concurring) (citing *Alderman* for the proposition that "property rights reflect society's explicit recognition of a person's authority to act as he wishes in certain areas, and therefore should be considered in determining whether an individual's expectations of privacy are reasonable"); *Karo*, *supra*, at 732, 104 S.Ct. 3296 (Stevens, J., concurring in part and dissenting in part) (citing Alderman in support of the proposition that "a homeowner has a reasonable expectation of privacy in the contents of his home, including items owned by others").

[584] See Prosser & Keeton § 14, at 87 (harmless or trivial contact with personal property not actionable); D. Dobbs, Law of Torts 124 (2000) (same).

[585] See ante, at 951.

[586] Ante, at 949, n. 2.

[587] See 8A Am.Jur.2d, Bailment § 166, pp. 685–686 (2009).

***962** GPS was installed before or after his wife turned over the keys. In non-community-property States, on the other hand, the registration of the vehicle in the name of respondent's wife would generally be regarded as presumptive evidence that she was the sole owner.[588]

Fourth, the Court's reliance on the law of trespass will present particularly vexing problems in cases involving surveillance that is carried out by making electronic, as opposed to physical, contact with the item to be tracked. For example, suppose that the officers in the present case had followed respondent by surreptitiously activating a stolen vehicle detection system that came with the car when it was purchased. Would the sending of a radio signal to activate this system constitute a trespass to chattels? Trespass to chattels has traditionally required a physical touching of the property.[589]In recent years, courts have wrestled with the application of this old tort in cases involving unwanted electronic contact with computer systems, and some have held that even the transmission of electrons that occurs when a communication is sent from one computer to another is enough.[590]But may such decisions be followed in applying the Court's trespass theory? Assuming that what matters under the Court's theory is the law of trespass as it existed at the time of the adoption of the Fourth Amendment, do these recent decisions represent a change in the law or simply the application of the old tort to new situations?

IV

A

The *Katz* expectation-of-privacy test avoids the problems and complications noted above, but it is not without its own difficulties. It involves a degree of circularity,[591]and judges are apt to confuse their own expectations of privacy with those of the hypothetical reasonable person to which the *Katz* test looks.[592]In addition, the *Katz* test rests on the assumption that this hypothetical reasonable person has a well-developed and stable set of privacy expectations. But technology can change those expectations. Dramatic technological change may lead to periods in which popular expectations are in flux and may ultimately produce significant changes in popular attitudes. New technology may provide increased convenience or security at the expense of privacy, and many people may find the tradeoff worthwhile. And even if the public does not welcome the diminution of privacy that new technology entails, they may eventually reconcile themselves to this development as inevitable.

On the other hand, concern about new intrusions on privacy may spur the enactment of legislation to protect against these intrusions. This is what ultimately happened ***963** with respect to wiretapping. After *Katz*, Congress did not leave it to the courts to develop a body of Fourth Amendment case law governing that complex subject. Instead, Congress promptly enacted a comprehensive statute,[593]and since that time, the regulation of wiretapping has been governed primarily by statute and not by case law. In an ironic sense, although *Katz* overruled *Olmstead*, Chief Justice Taft's suggestion in the latter case that the regulation of wiretapping was a matter better left for Congress[594]has been borne out.

B

---

[588] See 60 C.J. S., Motor Vehicles § 231, pp. 398–399 (2002); 8 Am.Jur.2d, Automobiles § 1208, pp. 859–860 (2007).

[589] See *Restatement (Second) of Torts § 217* and Comment e (1963 and 1964); *Dobbs*, *supra*, at 123.

[590] See, e.g., *CompuServe, Inc. v. Cyber Promotions, Inc.*, 962 F.Supp. 1015, 1021 (S.D.Ohio 1997); *Thrifty–Tel, Inc. v. Bezenek*, 46 Cal.App.4th 1559, 1566, n. 6, 54 Cal.Rptr.2d 468 (1996).

[591] See *Kyllo*, 533 U.S., at 34, 121 S.Ct. 2038.

[592] See *Minnesota v. Carter*, 525 U.S. 83, 97, 119 S.Ct. 469, 142 L.Ed.2d 373 (1998) (SCALIA, J., concurring).

[593] see 18 U.S.C. §§ 2510–2522 (2006 ed. and Supp. IV),

[594] See 277 U.S., at 465–466, 48 S.Ct. 564.

Recent years have seen the emergence of many new devices that permit the monitoring of a person's movements. In some locales, closed-circuit television video monitoring is becoming ubiquitous. On toll roads, automatic toll collection systems create a precise record of the movements of motorists who choose to make use of that convenience. Many motorists purchase cars that are equipped with devices that permit a central station to ascertain the car's location at any time so that roadside assistance may be provided if needed and the car may be found if it is stolen.

Perhaps most significant, cell phones and other wireless devices now permit wireless carriers to track and record the location of users—and as of June 2011, it has been reported, there were more than 322 million wireless devices in use in the United States. For older phones, the accuracy of the location information depends on the density of the tower network, but new "smart phones," which are equipped with a GPS device, permit more precise tracking. For example, when a user activates the GPS on such a phone, a provider is able to monitor the phone's location and speed of movement and can then report back real-time traffic conditions after combining ("crowdsourcing") the speed of all such phones on any particular road. Similarly, phone-location-tracking services are offered as "social" tools, allowing consumers to find (or to avoid) others who enroll in these services. The availability and use of these and other new devices will continue to shape the average person's expectations about the privacy of his or her daily movements.

V

In the pre-computer age, the greatest protections of privacy were neither constitutional nor statutory, but practical. Traditional surveillance for any extended period of time was difficult and costly and therefore rarely undertaken. The surveillance at issue in this case—constant monitoring of the location of a vehicle for four weeks —would have required a large team of agents, multiple vehicles, and perhaps aerial assistance.Only an investigation of unusual importance could have justified such an expenditure of law enforcement ***964** resources. Devices like the one used in the present case, however, make long-term monitoring relatively easy and cheap. In circumstances involving dramatic technological change, the best solution to privacy concerns may be legislative.[595]A legislative body is well situated to gauge changing public attitudes, to draw detailed lines, and to balance privacy and public safety in a comprehensive way.

To date, however, Congress and most States have not enacted statutes regulating the use of GPS tracking technology for law enforcement purposes. The best that we can do in this case is to apply existing Fourth Amendment doctrine and to ask whether the use of GPS tracking in a particular case involved a degree of intrusion that a reasonable person would not have anticipated.

Under this approach, relatively short-term monitoring of a person's movements on public streets accords with expectations of privacy that our society has recognized as reasonable.[596]But the use of longer term GPS monitoring in investigations of most offenses impinges on expectations of privacy. For such offenses, society's expectation has been that law enforcement agents and others would not—and indeed, in the main, simply could not—secretly monitor and catalogue every single movement of an individual's car for a very long period. In this case, for four weeks, law enforcement agents tracked every movement that respondent made in the vehicle he was driving. We need not identify with precision the point at which the tracking of this vehicle became a search, for the line was surely crossed before the 4–week mark. Other cases may present more difficult questions. But where uncertainty exists with respect to whether a certain period of GPS surveil lance is long enough to constitute a Fourth Amendment search, the police may always seek a warrant. We also need not

---

[595] See, e.g., Kerr, 102 Mich. L.Rev., at 805–806.

[596] See *Knotts*, 460 U.S., at 281–282, 103 S.Ct. 1081.

consider whether prolonged GPS monitoring in the context of investigations involving extraordinary offenses would similarly intrude on a constitutionally protected sphere of privacy. In such cases, long-term tracking might have been mounted using previously available techniques.

For these reasons, I conclude that the lengthy monitoring that occurred in this case constituted a search under the Fourth Amendment. I therefore agree with the majority that the decision of the Court of Appeals must be affirmed.

Black Letter Law

> The Government's installation of a Global–Positioning–System (GPS) tracking device on target's vehicle, and its use of that device to monitor vehicle's movements, constitutes a "search," within meaning of Fourth Amendment. Where the Government obtains information by physically intruding on constitutionally protected area, a "search" within original meaning of Fourth Amendment has occurred.Reasserted trespass doctrine into Fourth Amendment jurisprudence.

Florida v. Jardines

133 S.Ct. 1409

SUPREME COURT OF THE UNITED STATES

FLORIDA, PETITIONER

v.

JOELIS JARDINES

| Argued Oct. 31, 2012. | Decided March 26, 2013.

JUSTICE SCALIA delivered the opinion of the Court.

We consider whether using a drug-sniffing dog on a homeowner's porch to investigate the contents of the home is a "search" within the meaning of the Fourth Amendment.

I

In 2006, Detective William Pedraja of the Miami-Dade Police Department received an unverified tip that marijuana was being grown in the home of respondent Joelis Jardines. One month later, the Department and the Drug Enforcement Administration sent a joint surveillance team to Jardines' home. Detective Pedraja was part of that team. He watched the home for fifteen minutes and saw no vehicles in the driveway or activity around the home, and could not see inside because the blinds were drawn. Detective Pedraja then approached Jardines' home accompanied by Detective Douglas Bartelt, a trained canine handler who had just arrived at the scene with his drug-sniffing dog. The dog was trained to detect the scent of marijuana, cocaine, heroin, and several other drugs, indicating the presence of any of these substances through particular behavioral changes recognizable by his handler.

Detective Bartelt had the dog on a six-foot leash, owing in part to the dog's "wild" nature[597] and tendency to dart around erratically while search- ing. As the dog approached Jardines' front porch, he apparently sensed one of the odors he had been trained to detect, and began energetically exploring the area for the strongest point source of that odor. As Detective Bartelt explained, the dog "began tracking that airborne odor by . . . tracking back and forth," engaging in what is called "bracketing,"

[597] App. to Pet. for Cert. A– 35

"back and forth, back and forth."[598]Detective Bartelt gave the dog "the full six feet of the leash plus whatever safe distance [he could] give him" to do this—he testified that he needed to give the dog "as much distance as I can."[599]And Detective Pedraja stood back while this was occurring, so that he would not "get knocked over" when the dog was "spinning around trying to find" the source.[600]

After sniffing the base of the front door, the dog sat, which is the trained behavior upon discovering the odor's strongest point. Detective Bartelt then pulled the dog away from the door and returned to his vehicle. He left the scene after informing Detective Pedraja that there had been a positive alert for narcotics.

On the basis of what he had learned at the home, Detective Pedraja applied for and received a warrant to search the residence. When the warrant was executed later that day, Jardines attempted to flee and was arrested; the search revealed marijuana plants, and he was charged with trafficking in cannabis.

At trial, Jardines moved to suppress the marijuana plants on the ground that the canine investigation was an unreasonable search. The trial court granted the motion, and the Florida Third District Court of Appeal reversed. On a petition for discretionary review, the Florida Supreme Court quashed the decision of the Third District Court of Appeal and approved the trial court's decision to suppress, holding (as relevant here) that the use of the trained narcotics dog to investigate Jardines' home was a Fourth Amendment search unsupported by probable cause, rendering invalid the warrant based upon information gathered in that search.[601]

We granted certiorari, limited to the question of whether the officers' behavior was a search within the meaning of the Fourth Amendment.

II

The Fourth Amendment provides in relevant part that the "right of the people to be secure in their persons, houses, papers, and effects, against unreasonable searches and seizures, shall not be violated." The Amendment establishes a simple baseline, one that for much of our history formed the exclusive basis for its protections: When "the Government obtains information by physically intruding" on persons, houses, papers, or effects, "a 'search' within the original meaning of the Fourth Amendment" has "undoubtedly occurred."[602]By reason of our decision in *Katz v. United States*,[603]property rights "are not the sole measure of Fourth Amendment violations,"[604]—but though Katz may add to the baseline, it does not subtract anything from the Amendment's protections "when the Government does engage in [a] physical intrusion of a constitutionally protected area."[605] That principle renders this case a straightforward one. The officers were gathering information in an area belonging to Jardines and immediately surrounding his house— in the curtilage of the house, which we have held enjoys protection as part of the home itself. And they gathered that information by physically entering and occupying the area to engage in conduct not explicitly or implicitly permitted by the homeowner.

A

---

[598] Id., at A– 33 to A–34.

[599] Id., at A–35.

[600] Id., at A–38.

[601] 73 So. 3d 34 (2011).

[602] United States v. Jones, 565 U. S. ___, ___, n. 3 (2012) (slip op., at 6, n. 3).

[603] 389 U.S. 347 (1967).

[604] *Soldal v. Cook County*, 506 U. S. 56, 64 (1992).

[605] *United States v. Knotts*, 460 U. S. 276, 286 (1983) (Brennan, J., concurring in the judgment).

The Fourth Amendment "indicates with some precision the places and things encompassed by its protections": persons, houses, papers, and effects.[606]The Fourth Amendment does not, therefore, prevent all investigations conducted on private property; for example, an officer may (subject to *Katz*) gather information in what we have called "open fields"—even if those fields are privately owned—because such fields are not enumerated in the Amendment's text.[607]

But when it comes to the Fourth Amendment, the home is first among equals. At the Amendment's "very core" stands "the right of a man to retreat into his own home and there be free from unreasonable governmental intrusion."[608]This right would be of little practical value if the State's agents could stand in a home's porch or side garden and trawl for evidence with impunity; the right to retreat would be significantly diminished if the police could enter a man's property to observe his repose from just outside the front window.

We therefore regard the area "immediately surrounding and associated with the home"—what our cases call the curtilage—as "part of the home itself for Fourth Amendment purposes."[609]That principle has ancient and durable roots. Just as the distinction between the home and the open fields is "as old as the common law,"[610]so too is the identity of home and what Blackstone called the "curtilage or homestall," for the "house protects and privileges all its branches and appurtenants."[611]This area around the home is "intimately linked to the home, both physically and psychologically," and is where "privacy expectations are most heightened."[612]

While the boundaries of the curtilage are generally "clearly marked," the "conception defining the curtilage" is at any rate familiar enough that it is "easily understood from our daily experience."[613]Here there is no doubt that the officers entered it: The front porch is the classic exemplar of an area adjacent to the home and "to which the activity of home life extends."[614]

B

Since the officers' investigation took place in a constitutionally protected area, we turn to the question of whether it was accomplished through an unlicensed physical intrusion. While law enforcement officers need not "shield their eyes" when passing by the home "on public thoroughfares,"[615]an officer's leave to gather information is sharply circumscribed when he steps off those thoroughfares and enters the Fourth Amendment's protected areas. In permitting, for example, visual observation of the home from "public navigable airspace," we were careful to note that it was done "in a physically nonintrusive manner."[616]*Entick v. Carrington*,[617]a case "undoubtedly familiar" to "every American statesman" at the time of the Founding, *Boyd v. United States*[618]states the general rule clearly: "[O]ur law holds the property of every man so

---

[606] *Oliver v. United States*, 466 U. S. 170, 176 (1984).

[607] *Hester v. United States*, 265 U. S. 57 (1924).

[608] *Silverman v. United States*, 365 U. S. 505, 511 (1961).

[609] Oliver, supra, at 180.

[610] *Hester, supra*, at 59.

[611] 4 W. Blackstone, Commentaries on the Laws of England 223, 225 (1769).

[612] *California v. Ciraolo*, 476 U. S. 207, 213 (1986).

[613] *Oliver*, 466 U. S., at 182, n. 12.

[614] *Ibid.*

[615] *Ciraolo*, 476 U. S., at 213.

[616] *Ibid.*

[617] 2 Wils. K. B. 275, 95 Eng. Rep. 807 (K. B. 1765).

[618] 116 U. S. 616, 626 (1886).

sacred, that no man can set his foot upon his neighbour's close without his leave."[619]As it is undisputed that the detectives had all four of their feet and all four of their companion's firmly planted on the constitutionally protected extension of Jardines' home, the only question is whether he had given his leave (even implicitly) for them to do so. He had not.

"A license may be implied from the habits of the country," notwithstanding the "strict rule of the English common law as to entry upon a close."[620]We have accordingly recognized that "the knocker on the front door is treated as an invitation or license to attempt an entry, justifying ingress to the home by solicitors, hawkers and peddlers of all kinds."[621]This implicit license typically permits the visitor to approach the home by the front path, knock promptly, wait briefly to be received, and then (absent invitation to linger longer) leave. Complying with the terms of that traditional invitation does not require fine-grained legal knowledge; it is generally managed without incident by the Nation's Girl Scouts and trick-or-treaters. Thus, a police officer not armed with a warrant may approach a home and knock, precisely because that is "no more than any private citizen might do."[622]

But introducing a trained police dog to explore the area around the home in hopes of discovering incriminating evidence is something else. There is no customary invitation to do that. An invitation to engage in canine forensic investigation assuredly does not inhere in the very act of hanging a knocker. To find a visitor knocking on the door is routine (even if sometimes unwelcome); to spot that same visitor exploring the front path with a metal detector, or marching his bloodhound into the garden before saying hello and asking permission, would inspire most of us to— well, call the police. The scope of a license — express or implied—is limited not only to a particular area but also to a specific purpose. Consent at a traffic stop to an officer's checking out an anonymous tip that there is a body in the trunk does not permit the officer to rummage through the trunk for narcotics. Here, the background social norms that invite a visitor to the front door do not invite him there to conduct a search.

The State points to our decisions holding that the subjective intent of the officer is irrelevant.[623]But those cases merely hold that a stop or search that is objectively reasonable is not vitiated by the fact that the officer's real reason for making the stop or search has nothing to do with the validating reason. Thus, the defendant will not be heard to complain that although he was speeding the officer's real reason for the stop was racial harassment.[624]Here, however, the question before the court is precisely whether the officer's conduct was an objectively reasonable search. As we have described, that depends upon whether the officers had an implied license to enter the porch, which in turn depends upon the purpose for which they entered. Here, their behavior objectively reveals a purpose to conduct a search, which is not what anyone would think he had license to do.

III

The State argues that investigation by a forensic narcotics dog by definition cannot implicate any legitimate privacy interest. The State cites for authority our decisions

---

619 Wils. K. B., at 291, 95 Eng. Rep., at 817.

620 *McKee v. Gratz*, 260 U. S. 127, 136 (1922) (Holmes, J.).

621 *Breard v. Alexandria*, 341 U. S. 622, 626 (1951).

622 *Kentucky v. King*, 563 U. S. ___, ___ (2011) (slip op., at 16).

623 See *Ashcroft v. al-Kidd*, 563 U. S. ___ (2011); *Whren v. United States*, 517 U. S. 806 (1996).

624 See *id.*, at 810, 813.

in *United States v. Place*,[625] *United States v. Jacobsen*,[626] and *Illinois v. Caballes*,[627] which held, respectively, that canine inspection of luggage in an airport, chemical testing of a substance that had fallen from a parcel in transit, and canine inspection of an automobile during a lawful traffic stop, do not violate the "reasonable expectation of privacy" described in Katz.

Just last term, we considered an argument much like this. *Jones* held that tracking an automobile's whereabouts using a physically-mounted GPS receiver is a Fourth Amendment search. The Government argued that the *Katz* standard "show[ed] that no search occurred," as the defendant had "no 'reasonable expectation of privacy'" in his whereabouts on the public roads[628]—a proposition with at least as much support in our case law as the one the State marshals here.[629] But because the GPS receiver had been physically mounted on the defendant's automobile (thus intruding on his "effects"), we held that tracking the vehicle's movements was a search: a person's "Fourth Amendment rights do not rise or fall with the *Katz* formulation."[630] The *Katz* reasonable expectations test "has been added to, not substituted for," the traditional property-based understanding of the Fourth Amendment, and so is unnecessary to consider when the government gains evidence by physically intruding on constitutionally protected areas.[631]

Thus, we need not decide whether the officers' investigation of Jardines' home violated his expectation of privacy under *Katz*. One virtue of the Fourth Amendment's property-rights baseline is that it keeps easy cases easy. That the officers learned what they learned only by physically intruding on Jardines' property to gather evidence is enough to establish that a search occurred.

For a related reason we find irrelevant the State's argument (echoed by the dissent) that forensic dogs have been commonly used by police for centuries. This argument is apparently directed to our holding in *Kyllo v. United States*,[632] that surveillance of the home is a search where "the Government uses a device that is not in general public use" to "explore details of the home that would previously have been unknowable with- out physical intrusion." Id., at 40 (emphasis added). But the implication of that statement (inclusio unius est exclusio alterius) is that when the government uses a physical intrusion to explore details of the home (including its curtilage), the antiquity of the tools that they bring along is irrelevant.

***

The government's use of trained police dogs to investigate the home and its immediate surroundings is a "search" within the meaning of the Fourth Amendment. The judgment of the Supreme Court of Florida is therefore affirmed.

It is so ordered.

JUSTICE KAGAN, with whom JUSTICE GINSBURG and JUSTICE SOTOMAYOR join, concurring.

---

[625] 462 U. S. 696 (1983).

[626] 466 U. S. 109 (1984).

[627] 543 U. S. 405 (2005).

[628] Jones, 565 U. S., at ___ (slip op., at 5).

[629] See, e.g., *United States v. Knotts*, 460 U. S. 276, 278 (1983).

[630] *Jones, supra*, at ___ (slip op., at 5).

[631] *Jones, supra*, at ___ (slip op., at 8).

[632] 533 U. S. 27 (2001).

For me, a simple analogy clinches this case—and does so on privacy as well as property grounds. A stranger comes to the front door of your home carrying super high-powered binoculars.[633]He doesn't knock or say hello. Instead, he stands on the porch and uses the binoculars to peer through your windows, into your home's furthest corners. It doesn't take long (the binoculars are really very fine): In just a couple of minutes, his uncommon behavior allows him to learn details of your life you disclose to no one. Has your "visitor" trespassed on your property, exceeding the license you have granted to members of the public to, say, drop off the mail or distribute campaign flyers? Yes, he has. And has he also invaded your "reasonable expectation of privacy," by nosing into intimacies you sensibly thought protected from disclosure?[634]Yes, of course, he has done that too.

That case is this case in every way that matters. Here, police officers came to Joelis Jardines' door with a super sensitive instrument, which they deployed to detect things inside that they could not perceive unassisted. The equipment they used was animal, not mineral. But contra the dissent,[635]that is of no significance in determining whether a search occurred. Detective Bartelt's dog was not your neighbor's pet, come to your porch on a leisurely stroll. As this Court discussed earlier this term, drug-detection dogs are highly trained tools of law enforcement, geared to respond in distinctive ways to specific scents so as to convey clear and reliable information to their human partners.[636]They are to the poodle down the street as high-powered binoculars are to a piece of plain glass. Like the binoculars, a drug-detection dog is a specialized device for discovering objects not in plain view (or plain smell). And as in the hypothetical above, that device was aimed here at a home—the most private and inviolate (or so we expect) of all the places and things the Fourth Amendment protects. Was this activity a trespass? Yes, as the Court holds today. Was it also an invasion of privacy? Yes, that as well.

The Court today treats this case under a property rubric; I write separately to note that I could just as happily have decided it by looking to Jardines' privacy interests. A decision along those lines would have looked . . . well, much like this one. It would have talked about " 'the right of a man to retreat into his own home and there be free from unreasonable governmental intrusion.' "[637]It would have insisted on maintaining the "practical value" of that right by preventing police officers from standing in an adjacent space and "trawl[ing] for evidence with impunity."[638]. It would have explained that " 'privacy expectations are most heightened' " in the home and the surrounding area.[639]And it would have determined that police officers invade those shared expectations when they use trained canine assistants to reveal within the confines of a home what they could not otherwise have found there.[640]

It is not surprising that in a case involving a search of a home, property concepts and privacy concepts should so align. The law of property "naturally enough influence[s]" our "shared social expectations" of what places should be free from governmental incursions.[641]And so the sentiment "my home is my own," while originating in property law, now also denotes a common understanding—extending even beyond that law's formal protections—about an especially private sphere. Jardines'

---

633 See *ante*, at 7, n. 3.

634 *Katz v. United States*, 389 U. S. 347, 360 (1967) (Harlan, J., concurring).

635 See post, at 2 (opinion of ALITO, J.) (noting the ubiquity of dogs in American households).

636 See *Florida v. Harris*, 568 U. S. ___ (2013) (slip op. at 2–3, 7–8).

637 Ante, at 4 (quoting *Silverman v. United States*, 365 U. S. 505, 511 (1961)).

638 Ante, at 4.

639 Ante, at 4–5 (quoting *California v. Ciraolo*, 476 U. S. 207, 213 (1986)).

640 See ante, at 6–7, and nn. 2–3.

641 *Georgia v. Randolph*, 547 U. S. 103, 111 (2006); see *Rakas v. Illinois*, 439 U. S. 128, 143, n. 12 (1978).

home was his property; it was also his most intimate and familiar space. The analysis proceeding from each of those facts, as today's decision reveals, runs mostly along the same path.

I can think of only one divergence: If we had decided this case on privacy grounds, we would have realized that *Kyllo v. United States*[642]already resolved it. The *Kyllo* Court held that police officers conducted a search when they used a thermal-imaging device to detect heat emanating from a private home, even though they committed no trespass. Highlighting our intention to draw both a "firm" and a "bright" line at "the entrance to the house,"[643], we announced the following rule:

"Where, as here, the Government uses a device that is not in general public use, to explore details of the home that would previously have been unknowable without physical intrusion, the surveillance is a 'search' and is presumptively unreasonable without a warrant."[644]

That "firm" and "bright" rule governs this case: The police officers here conducted a search because they used a "device . . . not in general public use" (a trained drug detection dog) to "explore details of the home" (the presence of certain substances) that they would not otherwise have discovered without entering the premises.

And again, the dissent's argument that the device is just a dog cannot change the equation. As *Kyllo* made clear, the "sense-enhancing" tool at issue may be "crude" or "sophisticated," may be old or new (drug-detection dogs actually go back not "12,000 years" or "centuries,"[645]but only a few decades), may be either smaller or bigger than a breadbox; still, "at least where (as here)" the device is not "in general public use," training it on a home violates our "minimal expectation of privacy"—an expectation "that exists, and that is acknowledged to be reasonable."[646]That does not mean the device is off-limits, as the dissent implies, see post, at 11–12; it just means police officers cannot use it to examine a home without a warrant or exigent circumstance.[647]

With these further thoughts, suggesting that a focus on Jardines' privacy interests would make an "easy cas[e] easy" twice over, ante, at 9, I join the Court's opinion in full.

JUSTICE ALITO, with whom THE CHIEF JUSTICE, JUS- TICE KENNEDY, and JUSTICE BREYER join, dissenting.

The Court's decision in this important Fourth Amendment case is based on a putative rule of trespass law that is nowhere to be found in the annals of Anglo-American jurisprudence.

The law of trespass generally gives members of the public a license to use a walkway to approach the front door of a house and to remain there for a brief time. This license is not limited to persons who intend to speak to an occupant or who actually do so. (Mail carriers and persons delivering packages and flyers are examples of individuals who may lawfully approach a front door without intending to converse.) Nor is the license restricted to categories of visitors whom an occupant of the dwelling is likely to welcome; as the Court acknowledges, this license applies even

---

[642] 533 U. S. 27 (2001).

[643] *Id.*, at 40.

[644] *Ibid.*

[645] Post, at 2, 8, 12.

[646] 533 U. S., at 34, 36.

[647] See *Brigham City v. Stuart*, 547 U. S. 398, 403–404 (2006) (describing exigencies allowing the warrantless search of a home).

to "solicitors, hawkers and peddlers of all kinds." Ante, at 6 (internal quotation marks omitted). And the license even extends to police officers who wish to gather evidence against an occupant (by asking potentially incriminating questions).

According to the Court, however, the police officer in this case, Detective Bartelt, committed a trespass because he was accompanied during his otherwise lawful visit to the front door of respondent's house by his dog, Franky. Where is the authority evidencing such a rule? Dogs have been domesticated for about 12,000 years; they were ubiquitous in both this country and Britain at the time of the adoption of the Fourth Amendment; and their acute sense of smell has been used in law enforcement for centuries. Yet the Court has been unable to find a single case—from the United States or any other common-law nation—that supports the rule on which its decision is based. Thus, trespass law provides no support for the Court's holding today.

The Court's decision is also inconsistent with the reasonable-expectations-of-privacy test that the Court adopted in *Katz v. United States.*[648]A reasonable person understands that odors emanating from a house may be detected from locations that are open to the public, and a reasonable person will not count on the strength of those odors remaining within the range that, while detectible by a dog, cannot be smelled by a human.

For these reasons, I would hold that no search within the meaning of the Fourth Amendment took place in this case, and I would reverse the decision below.

I

The opinion of the Court may leave a reader with the mistaken impression that Detective Bartelt and Franky remained on respondent's property for a prolonged period of time and conducted a far-flung exploration of the front yard.[649]But that is not what happened.

Detective Bartelt and Franky approached the front door via the driveway and a paved path—the route that any visitor would customarily use—and Franky was on the kind of leash that any dog owner might employ. As Franky approached the door, he started to track an airborne odor. He held his head high and began "bracketing" the area (pacing back and forth) in order to determine the strongest source of the smell.[650]Detective Bartelt knew "the minute [he] observed" this behavior that Franky had detected drugs.[651] Upon locating the odor's strongest source, Franky sat at the base of the front door, and at this point, Detective Bartelt and Franky immediately returned to their patrol car.[652] A critical fact that the Court omits is that, as respondent's counsel explained at oral argument, this entire process—walking down the driveway and front path to the front door, waiting for Franky to find the strongest source of the odor, and walking back to the car—took approximately a minute or two.[653]Thus, the amount of time that Franky and the detective remained at the front porch was even less. The Court also fails to mention that, while Detective Bartelt apparently did not personally smell the odor of marijuana coming from the house, another officer who subsequently stood on the front porch, Detective Pedraja, did notice that smell and was able to identify it.[654]

---

648 389 U. S. 347 (1967).

649 See ante, at 4 ("trawl for evidence with impunity"), ("marching his bloodhound into the garden").

650 App. 95–96.

651 *Id.*, at 95.

652 *Id.*, at 98.

653 Tr. of Oral Arg. 57–58.

654 App. 81.

II

The Court concludes that the conduct in this case was a search because Detective Bartelt exceeded the boundaries of the license to approach the house that is recognized by the law of trespass, but the Court's interpretation of the scope of that license is unfounded.

A

It is said that members of the public may lawfully proceed along a walkway leading to the front door of a house because custom grants them a license to do so.[655] This rule encompasses categories of visitors whom most homeowners almost certainly wish to allow to approach their front doors—friends, relatives, mail carriers, persons making deliveries. But it also reaches categories of visitors who are less universally welcome—"solicitors," "hawkers," "peddlers," and the like. The law might attempt to draw fine lines between categories of welcome and unwelcome visitors, distinguishing, for example, between tolerable and intolerable door-to-door peddlers (Girl Scouts selling cookies versus adults selling aluminum siding) or between police officers on agreeable and disagreeable missions (gathering information about a bothersome neighbor versus asking potentially incriminating questions). But the law of trespass has not attempted such a difficult taxonomy.[656] Of course, this license has certain spatial and temporal limits. A visitor must stick to the path that is typically used to approach a front door, such as a paved walkway. A visitor cannot traipse through the garden, meander into the backyard, or take other circuitous detours that veer from the pathway that a visitor would customarily use.[657]

Nor, as a general matter, may a visitor come to the front door in the middle of the night without an express invitation.[658] Similarly, a visitor may not linger at the front door for an extended period.[659] The license is limited to the amount of time it would customarily take to approach the door, pause long enough to see if someone is home, and (if not expressly invited to stay longer), leave.

As I understand the law of trespass and the scope of the implied license, a visitor who adheres to these limitations is not necessarily required to ring the doorbell, knock on the door, or attempt to speak with an occupant. For example, mail carriers, persons making deliveries, and individuals distributing flyers may leave the items they are carrying and depart without making any attempt to converse. A pedestrian or motorist looking for a particular address may walk up to a front door in order

---

[655] *Breard v. Alexandria*, 341 U. S. 622, 626 (1951); *Lakin v. Ames*, 64 Mass. 198, 220 (1852); J. Bishop, Commentaries on the Non-Contract Law §823, p. 378 (1889).

[656] See *Desnick v. American Broadcasting Cos.*, 44 F. 3d 1345, 1351 (CA7 1995) ("[C]onsent to an entry is often given legal effect even though the entrant has intentions that if known to the owner of the property would cause him for perfectly understandable and generally ethical or at least lawful reasons to revoke his consent"); cf. Skinner v. Ogallala Public School Dist., 262 Neb. 387, 402, 631 N. W. 2d 510, 525 (2001) ("[I]n order to determine if a business invitation is implied, the inquiry is not a subjective assessment of why the visitor chose to visit the premises in a particular instance"); Crown Cork & Seal Co. v. Kane, 213 Md. 152, 159, 131 A. 2d 470, 473–474 (1957) (noting that "there are many cases in which an invitation has been implied from circumstances, such as custom," and that this test is "objective in that it stresses custom and the appearance of things" as opposed to "the undisclosed intention of the visitor").

[657] See, e.g., *Robinson v. Virginia*, 47 Va. App. 533, 549–550, 625 S. E. 2d 651, 659 (2006) (en banc); *United States v. Wells*, 648 F. 3d 671, 679–680 (CA8 2011) (police exceeded scope of their implied invitation when they bypassed the front door and proceeded directly to the back yard); *State v. Harris*, 919 S. W. 2d 619, 624 (Tenn. Crim. App. 1995) ("Any substantial and unreasonable departure from an area where the public is impliedly invited exceeds the scope of the implied invitation . . . " (internal quotation marks and brackets omitted)); 1 W. LaFave, Search and Seizure §2.3(c), p. 578 (2004) (hereinafter LaFave); id., §2.3(f), at 600–603 ("[W]hen the police come on to private property to conduct an investigation or for some other legitimate purpose and restrict their movements to places visitors could be expected to go (e.g., walkways, drive- ways, porches), observations made from such vantage points are not covered by the Fourth Amendment" (footnotes omitted)).

[658] See *State v. Cada*, 129 Idaho 224, 233, 923 P. 2d 469, 478 (App. 1996) ("Furtive intrusion late at night or in the predawn hours is not conduct that is expected from ordinary visitors. Indeed, if observed by a resident of the premises, it could be a cause for great alarm").

[659] See 9 So. 3d 1, 11 (Fla. App. 2008) (case below) (Cope, J., concurring in part and dissenting in part) ("[T]here is no such thing as squatter's rights on a front porch. A stranger may not plop down uninvited to spend the afternoon in the front porch rocking chair, or throw down a sleeping bag to spend the night, or lurk on the front porch, looking in the windows").

to check a house number that is hard to see from the sidewalk or road. A neighbor who knows that the residents are away may approach the door to retrieve an accumulation of newspapers that might signal to a potential burglar that the house is unoccupied.

As the majority acknowledges, this implied license to approach the front door extends to the police. See ante, at 6. As we recognized in *Kentucky v. King*,[660] police officers do not engage in a search when they approach the front door of a residence and seek to engage in what is termed a "knock and talk," i.e., knocking on the door and seeking to speak to an occupant for the purpose of gathering evidence.[661]
Even when the objective of a "knock and talk" is to obtain evidence that will lead to the homeowner's arrest and prosecution, the license to approach still applies. In other words, gathering evidence—even damning evidence—is a lawful activity that falls within the scope of the license to approach. And when officers walk up to the front door of a house, they are permitted to see, hear, and smell whatever can be detected from a lawful vantage point.[662]

B

Detective Bartelt did not exceed the scope of the license to approach respondent's front door. He adhered to the customary path; he did not approach in the middle of the night; and he remained at the front door for only a very short period (less than a minute or two).

The Court concludes that Detective Bartelt went too far because he had the "objectiv[e] . . . purpose to conduct a search."[663]What this means, I take it, is that anyone aware of what Detective Bartelt did would infer that his subjective purpose was to gather evidence. But if this is the Court's point, then a standard "knock and talk" and most other police visits would like-wise constitute searches. With the exception of visits to serve warrants or civil process, police almost always approach homes with a purpose of discovering information. That is certainly the objective of a "knock and talk." The Court offers no meaningful way of distinguishing the "objective purpose" of a "knock and talk" from the "objective purpose" of Detective Bartelt's conduct here.

The Court contends that a "knock and talk" is different because it involves talking, and "all are invited" to do that. Ante, at 7–8, n. 4 (emphasis deleted). But a police officer who approaches the front door of a house in accordance with the limitations already discussed may gather evidence by means other than talking. The officer may ob- serve items in plain view and smell odors coming from the house. Ciraolo, supra, at 213; Cada, 129 Idaho, at 232, 923 P. 2d, at 477; 1 LaFave §§2.2(a), 2.3(c), at 450–452, 572–577. So the Court's "objective purpose" argument cannot stand.

What the Court must fall back on, then, is the particular instrument that Detective Bartelt used to detect the odor of marijuana, namely, his dog. But in the entire body of common law decisions, the Court has not found a single case holding that a visitor to the front door of a home commits a trespass if the visitor is accompanied

---

[660] 563 U. S. ___ (2011),

[661] See id., at ___ (slip op., at 16) ("When law enforcement officers who are not armed with a warrant knock on a door, they do no more than any private citizen might do"). See also 1 LaFave §2.3(e), at 592 ("It is not objectionable for an officer to come upon that part of the property which has been opened to public common use" (internal quotation marks omitted)).

[662] *California v. Ciraolo*, 476 U. S. 207, 213 (1986) ("The Fourth Amendment protection of the home has never been extended to require law enforcement officers to shield their eyes when passing by a home on public thoroughfares"); *Cada*, *supra*, at 232, 923 P. 2d, at 477 ("[P]olice officers restricting their activity to [areas to which the public is impliedly invited] are permitted the same intrusion and the same level of observation as would be expected from a reasonably respectful citizen" (internal quotation marks omitted)); 1 LaFave §§2.2(a), 2.3(c), at 450–452, 572–577.

[663] Ante, at 8 (emphasis added).

by a dog on a leash. On the contrary, the common law allowed even unleashed dogs to wander on private property without committing a trespass.[664]

The Court responds that "[i]t is not the dog that is the problem, but the behavior that here involved use of the dog."[665]But where is the support in the law of trespass for this proposition? Dogs' keen sense of smell has been used in law enforcement for centuries. The antiquity of this practice is evidenced by a Scottish law from 1318 that made it a crime to "disturb a tracking dog or the men coming with it for pursuing thieves or seizing malefactors."[666]If bringing a tracking dog to the front door of a home constituted a trespass, one would expect at least one case to have arisen during the past 800 years. But the Court has found none.

For these reasons, the real law of trespass provides no support for the Court's holding today. While the Court claims that its reasoning has "ancient and durable roots,"[667] its trespass rule is really a newly struck counterfeit.

III

The concurring opinion attempts to provide an alternative ground for today's decision, namely, that Detective Bartelt's conduct violated respondent's reasonable expectations of privacy. But we have already rejected a very similar, if not identical argument,[668]and in any event I see no basis for concluding that the occupants of a dwelling have a reasonable expectation of privacy in odors that emanate from the dwelling and reach spots where members of the public may lawfully stand.

It is clear that the occupant of a house has no reasonable expectation of privacy with respect to odors that can be smelled by human beings who are standing in such places.[669]And I would not draw a line between odors that can be smelled by humans and those that are detectible only by dogs.

Consider the situation from the point of view of the occupant of a building in which marijuana is grown or methamphetamine is manufactured. Would such an occupant reason as follows? "I know that odors may emanate from my building and that atmospheric conditions, such as the force and direction of the wind, may affect the strength of those odors when they reach a spot where members of the public may lawfully stand. I also know that some people have a much more acute sense of smell than others, and I have no idea who might be standing in one of the spots in question when the odors from my house reach that location. In addition, I know that odors coming from my building, when they reach these locations, may be strong enough to be detected by a dog. But I am confident that they will be so faint that they cannot be smelled by any human being." Such a finely tuned expectation would be entirely unrealistic, and I see no evidence that society is prepared to recognize it as reasonable.

Contrary to the interpretation propounded by the concurrence, *Kyllo* is best understood as a decision about the use of new technology. The *Kyllo* Court focused on the fact that the thermal imaging device was a form of "sense- enhancing technology" that was "not in general public use," and it expressed concern that citizens

[664] G. Williams, Liability for Animals 136–146 (1939); J. Ingham, A Treatise on Property in Animals Wild and Domestic and the Rights and Respon- sibilities Arising Therefrom 277–278 (1900). Cf. B. Markesinis & S. Deakin, Tort Law 511 (4th ed. 1999).

[665] Ante, at 7, n. 3.

[666] K. Brown et al., The Records of the Parliaments of Scotland to 1707, (St Andrews, 2007–2013), online at http://www.rps.ac.uk/mss/1318/9.

[667] Ante, at 4.

[668] See Illinois v. Caballes, 543 U. S. 405, 409–410 (2005).

[669] See *United States v. Johns*, 469 U. S. 478, 482 (1985) ("After the officers came closer and detected the distinct odor of marijuana, they had probable cause to believe that the vehicles contained contraband"); *United States v. Ventresca*, 380 U. S. 102, 111 (1965) (scent of fermenting mash supported probable cause for warrant); *United States v. Johnston*, 497 F. 2d 397, 398 (CA9 1974) (there is no "reasonable expectation of privacy from drug agents with inquisitive nostrils").

would be "at the mercy of advancing technology" if its use was not restricted.[670] A dog, however, is not a new form of "technology or a "device." And, as noted, the use of dogs' acute sense of smell in law enforcement dates back many centuries.

The concurrence suggests that a Kyllo based decision would be "much like" the actual decision of the Court, but that is simply not so. The holding of the Court is based on what the Court sees as a "'physical intrusion of a constitutionally protected area.'"[671] As a result, it does not apply when a dog alerts while on a public sidewalk or street or in the corridor of a building to which the dog and handler have been lawfully admitted.

The concurrence's *Kyllo* based approach would have a much wider reach. When the police used the thermal imaging device in *Kyllo*, they were on a public street[672] and "committed no trespass."[673] Therefore, if a dog's nose is just like a thermal imaging device for Fourth Amendment purposes, a search would occur if a dog alerted while on a public sidewalk or in the corridor of an apartment building. And the same would be true if the dog was trained to sniff, not for marijuana, but for more dangerous quarry, such as explosives or for a violent fugitive or kidnaped child. I see no ground for hampering legitimate law enforcement in this way.

IV

The conduct of the police officer in this case did not constitute a trespass and did not violate respondent's reasonable expectations of privacy. I would hold that this conduct was not a search, and I therefore respectfully dissent.

Black Letter Law

> Though the *Katz* "reasonable expectation of privacy" test may add to the baseline, it does not subtract anything from the Amendment's protections when the Government does engage in a physical intrusion of a constitutionally protected area. The "curtilage" of a home, which is the area immediately surrounding and associated with the home, is part of the home itself for Fourth Amendment purposes. The Fourth Amendment does not prevent all investigations conducted on private property, and an officer may, subject to the *Katz* "reasonable expectation of privacy" test, gather information in open fields, even if those fields are privately owned, because such fields are not enumerated in the Amendment's text.

Maryland v. King

SUPREME COURT OF THE UNITED STATES

133 S.Ct. 1958

MARYLAND, PETITIONER

v.

ALONZO JAY KING, JR.

[June 3, 2013]

JUSTICE KENNEDY delivered the opinion of the Court.

---

[670] 533 U. S., at 34–35.

[671] Ante, at 3 (quoting *United States v. Knotts*, 460 U. S. 276, 286 (1983) (Brennan, J., concur- ring in judgment)).

[672] 533 U. S., at 29

[673] Ante, at 3.

In 2003 a man concealing his face and armed with a gun broke into a woman's home in Salisbury, Maryland. He raped her. The police were unable to identify or apprehend the assailant based on any detailed description or other evidence they then had, but they did obtain from the victim a sample of the perpetrator's DNA.

In 2009 Alonzo King was arrested in Wicomico County, Maryland, and charged with first- and second-degree assault for menacing a group of people with a shotgun. As part of a routine booking procedure for serious offenses, his DNA sample was taken by applying a cotton swab or filter paper—known as a buccal swab—to the inside of his cheeks. The DNA was found to match the DNA taken from the Salisbury rape victim. King was tried and convicted for the rape. Additional DNA samples were taken from him and used in the rape trial, but there seems to be no doubt that it was the DNA from the cheek sample taken at the time he was booked in 2009 that led to his first having been linked to the rape and charged with its commission.

The Court of Appeals of Maryland, on review of King's rape conviction, ruled that the DNA taken when King was booked for the 2009 charge was an unlawful seizure be cause obtaining and using the cheek swab was an unreasonable search of the person. It set the rape conviction aside. This Court granted certiorari and now reverses the judgment of the Maryland court.

When King was arrested on April 10, 2009, for menacing a group of people with a shotgun and charged in state court with both first- and second-degree assault, he was processed for detention in custody at the Wicomico County Central Booking facility. Booking personnel used a cheek swab to take the DNA sample from him pursuant to provisions of the Maryland DNA Collection Act (or Act).

On July 13, 2009, King's DNA record was uploaded to the Maryland DNA database, and three weeks later, on August 4, 2009, his DNA profile was matched to the DNA sample collected in the unsolved 2003 rape case. Once the DNA was matched to King, detectives presented the forensic evidence to a grand jury, which indicted him for the rape. Detectives obtained a search warrant and took a second sample of DNA from King, which again matched the evidence from the rape. He moved to suppress the DNA match on the grounds that Maryland's DNA collection law violated the Fourth Amendment. The Circuit Court Judge upheld the statute as constitutional. King pleaded not guilty to the rape charges but was convicted and sentenced to life in prison without the possibility of parole.

In a divided opinion, the Maryland Court of Appeals struck down the portions of the Act authorizing collection of DNA from felony arrestees as unconstitutional. The majority concluded that a DNA swab was an unreasonable search in violation of the Fourth Amendment because King's "expectation of privacy is greater than the State's purported interest in using King's DNA to identify him."[674]In reaching that conclusion the Maryland Court relied on the deci sions of various other courts that have concluded that DNA identification of arrestees is impermissible.[675] Both federal and state courts have reached differing conclusions as to whether the Fourth Amendment prohibits the collection and analysis of a DNA sample from persons arrested, but not yet convicted, on felony charges. This Court granted certiorari to address the question. King is the respondent here.

II

The advent of DNA technology is one of the most significant scientific advancements of our era. The full potential for use of genetic markers in medicine and science is still being explored, but the utility of DNA identification in the criminal justice system is already undisputed. Since the first use of forensic DNA analysis to

[674] 425 Md. 550, 561, 42 A. 3d 549, 556 (2012).

[675] See, e.g., People v. Buza, 129 Cal. Rptr. 3d 753 (App. 2011) (officially depublished); Mario W. v. Kaipio, 228 Ariz. 207, 265 P. 3d 389 (App. 2011).

catch a rapist and murderer in England in 1986, see J. Butler, Fundamentals of Forensic DNA Typing 5 (2009) (hereinafter Butler), law enforcement, the defense bar, and the courts have acknowledged DNA testing's "unparalleled ability both to exonerate the wrongly convicted and to identify the guilty. It has the potential to significantly improve both the criminal justice system and police investigative practices."[676]

A

The current standard for forensic DNA testing relies on an analysis of the chromosomes located within the nucleus of all human cells. "The DNA material in chromosomes is composed of 'coding' and 'noncoding' regions. The coding regions are known as genes and contain the information necessary for a cell to make proteins. . . . Non-protein coding regions . . . are not related directly to making proteins, [and] have been referred to as 'junk' DNA."[677]The adjective "junk" may mislead the layperson, for in fact this is the DNA region used with near certainty to identify a person. The term apparently is intended to indicate that this particular noncoding region, while useful and even dispositive for purposes like identity, does not show more far-reaching and complex characteristics like genetic traits.

Many of the patterns found in DNA are shared among all people, so forensic analysis focuses on "repeated DNA sequences scattered throughout the human genome," known as "short tandem repeats" (STRs).[678]The alternative possibilities for the size and frequency of these STRs at any given point along a strand of DNA are known as "alleles,"[679]and multiple alleles are analyzed in order to ensure that a DNA profile matches only one individual. Future refinements may improve present technology, but even now STR analysis makes it "possible to determine whether a biological tissue matches a suspect with near certainty."[680]

The Act authorizes Maryland law enforcement authorities to collect DNA samples from "an individual who is charged with . . . a crime of violence or an attempt to commit a crime of violence; or . . . burglary or an attempt to commit burglary."[681]Maryland law defines a crime of violence to include murder, rape, first-degree assault, kidnaping, arson, sexual assault, and a variety of other serious crimes.[682]Once taken, a DNA sample may not be processed or placed in a database before the individual is arraigned (unless the individual consents).[683]It is at this point that a judicial officer ensures that there is probable cause to detain the arrestee on a qualifying serious offense. If "all qualifying criminal charges are determined to be unsupported by probable cause . . . the DNA sample shall be immediately destroyed."[684]DNA samples are also destroyed if "a criminal action begun against the individual . . . does not result in a conviction," "the conviction is finally reversed or vacated and no new trial is permitted," or "the individual is granted an unconditional pardon."[685]

The Act also limits the information added to a DNA database and how it may be used. Specifically, "[o]nly DNA records that directly relate to the identification of

---

676 District Attorney's Office for Third Judicial Dist. v. Osborne, 557 U. S. 52, 55 (2009).

677 Butler 25.

678 *Id.*, at 147–148.

679 *Id.*, at 25.

680 Osborne, supra, at 62.

681 Md. Pub. Saf. Code Ann. §2– 504(a)(3)(i) (Lexis 2011).

682 Md. Crim. Law Code Ann. §14–101 (Lexis 2012).

683 Md. Pub. Saf. Code Ann. §2–504(d)(1) (Lexis 2011).

684 §2–504(d)(2)(i).

685 §2–511(a)(1).

individuals shall be collected and stored."[686] No purpose other than identification is permissible: "A person may not willfully test a DNA sample for information that does not relate to the identification of individuals as specified in this subtitle."[687] Tests for familial matches are also prohibited.[688] The officers involved in taking and analyzing respondent's DNA sample complied with the Act in all respects.

Respondent's DNA was collected in this case using a common procedure known as a "buccal swab." "Buccal cell collection involves wiping a small piece of filter paper or a cotton swab similar to a Q-tip against the inside cheek of an individual's mouth to collect some skin cells."[689] The procedure is quick and painless. The swab touches inside an arrestee's mouth, but it requires no "surgical intrusio[n] beneath the skin,"[690] and it poses no "threa[t] to the health or safety" of arrestees.[691]

B

Respondent's identification as the rapist resulted in part through the operation of a national project to standardize collection and storage of DNA profiles. Authorized by Congress and supervised by the Federal Bureau of Investigation, the Combined DNA Index System (CODIS) connects DNA laboratories at the local, state, and national level. Since its authorization in 1994, the CODIS system has grown to include all 50 States and a number of federal agencies. CODIS collects DNA profiles provided by local laboratories taken from arrestees, convicted offenders, and forensic evidence found at crime scenes. To participate in CODIS, a local laboratory must sign a memorandum of understanding agreeing to adhere to quality standards and submit to audits to evaluate compliance with the federal standards for scientifically rigorous DNA testing.[692]

One of the most significant aspects of CODIS is the standardization of the points of comparison in DNA analysis. The CODIS database is based on 13 loci at which the STR alleles are noted and compared. These loci make possible extreme accuracy in matching individual samples, with a "random match probability of approximately 1 in 100 trillion (assuming unrelated individuals)."[693] The CODIS loci are from the non-protein coding junk regions of DNA, and "are not known to have any association with a genetic disease or any other genetic predisposition. Thus, the information in the database is only useful for human identity testing."[694] STR information is recorded only as a "string of numbers"; and the DNA identification is accompanied only by information denoting the laboratory and the analyst responsible for the submission.[695] In short, CODIS sets uniform national standards for DNA matching and then facilitates connections between local law enforcement agencies who can share more specific information about matched STR profiles.

All 50 States require the collection of DNA from felony convicts, and respondent does not dispute the validity of that practice. See Brief for Respondent 48. Twenty-eight States and the Federal Government have adopted laws similar to the

[686] §2–505(b)(1).

[687] §2–512(c).

[688] See §2–506(d) ("A person may not perform a search of the statewide DNA data base for the purpose of identification of an offender in connection with a crime for which the offender may be a biological relative of the individual from whom the DNA sample was acquired").

[689] Butler 86.

[690] *Winston v. Lee*, 470 U. S. 753, 760 (1985).

[691] *Id.*, at 763.

[692] Butler 270.

[693] *Ibid.*

[694] *Id.*, at 279.

[695] Id., at 270.

Maryland Act authorizing the collection of DNA from some or all arrestees.[696] Although those statutes vary in their particulars, such as what charges require a DNA sample, their similarity means that this case implicates more than the specific Maryland law. At issue is a standard, expanding technology already in widespread use throughout the Nation.

III

A

Although the DNA swab procedure used here presents a question the Court has not yet addressed, the framework for deciding the issue is well established. The Fourth Amendment, binding on the States by the Fourteenth Amendment, provides that "[t]he right of the people to be secure in their persons, houses, papers, and effects, against unreasonable searches and seizures, shall not be violated." It can be agreed that using a buccal swab on the inner tissues of a person's cheek in order to obtain DNA samples is a search. Virtually any "intrusion into the human body,"[697] will work an invasion of "'cherished personal security' that is subject to constitutional scrutiny,"[698] The Court has applied the Fourth Amendment to police efforts to draw blood,[699] scraping an arrestee's fingernails to obtain trace evidence,[700] and even to "a breathalyzer test, which generally requires the production of alveolar or 'deep lung' breath for chemical analysis."[701] A buccal swab is a far more gentle process than a venipuncture to draw blood. It involves but a light touch on the inside of the cheek; and although it can be deemed a search within the body of the arrestee, it requires no "surgical intrusions beneath the skin."[702] The fact than an intrusion is negligible is of central relevance to determining reasonableness, although it is still a search as the law defines that term.

B

To say that the Fourth Amendment applies here is the beginning point, not the end of the analysis. "The Fourth Amendment's proper function is to constrain, not against all intrusions as such, but against intrusions which are not justified in the circumstances, or which are made in an improper manner."[703] "As the text of the Fourth Amendment indicates, the ultimate measure of the constitutionality of a governmental search is 'reasonableness.'"[704] In giving content to the inquiry whether an intrusion is reasonable, the Court has preferred "some quantum of individualized suspicion . . . [as] a prerequisite to a constitutional search or seizure. But the Fourth Amendment imposes no irreducible requirement of such suspicion."[705]

In some circumstances, such as "when faced with special law enforcement needs, diminished expectations of privacy, minimal intrusions, or the like, the Court has found that certain general, or individual, circumstances may render a warrantless search or seizure reasonable."[706] Those circumstances diminish the need for a war-

---

[696] See Brief for State of California etal. as Amici Curiae 4, n.1 (States Brief) (collecting state statutes).

[697] *Schmerber v. California*, 384 U. S. 757, 770 (1966).

[698] *Cupp v. Murphy*, 412 U. S. 291, 295 (1973) (quoting Terry v. Ohio, 392 U. S. 1, 24–25 (1968)).

[699] See *Schmerber*, supra; Missouri v. McNeely, 569 U. S. ___(2013).

[700] See *Cupp, supra*.

[701] *Skinner v. Railway Labor Executives' Assn.*, 489 U.S. 602, 616 (1989).

[702] *Winston*, 470 U. S., at 760.

[703] *Schmerber, supra*, at 768.

[704] Vernonia School Dist. 47J v. Acton, 515 U. S. 646, 652 (1995).

[705] *United States v. Martinez-Fuerte*, 428 U.S. 543, 560–561 (1976) (citation and footnote omitted).

[706] *Illinois v. McArthur*, 531 U. S. 326, 330 (2001).

rant, either because "the public interest is such that neither a warrant nor probable cause is required,"[707]or because an individual is already on notice, for instance because of his employment[708]or the conditions of his release from government custody[709]that some reasonable police intrusion on his privacy is to be expected. The need for a warrant is perhaps least when the search involves no discretion that could properly be limited by the "interpolation of a neutral magistrate between the citizen and the law enforcement officer."[710]

The instant case can be addressed with this background. The Maryland DNA Collection Act provides that, in order to obtain a DNA sample, all arrestees charged with serious crimes must furnish the sample on a buccal swab applied, as noted, to the inside of the cheeks. The arrestee is already in valid police custody for a serious offense supported by probable cause. The DNA collection is not subject to the judgment of officers whose perspective might be "colored by their primary involvement in 'the often competitive enterprise of ferreting out crime.'"[711]As noted by this Court in a different but still instructive context involving blood testing, "both the circumstances justifying toxicological testing and the permissible limits of such intrusions are defined narrowly and specifically in the regulations that authorize them . . . . Indeed, in light of the standardized nature of the tests and the minimal discretion vested in those charged with administering the program, there are virtually no facts for a neutral magistrate to evaluate."[712]Here, the search effected by the buccal swab of respondent falls within the category of cases this Court has analyzed by reference to the proposition that the "touchstone of the Fourth Amendment is reasonableness, not individualized suspicion."[713]

Even if a warrant is not required, a search is not beyond Fourth Amendment scrutiny; for it must be reasonable in its scope and manner of execution. Urgent government interests are not a license for indiscriminate police behavior. To say that no warrant is required is merely to acknowledge that "rather than employing a per se rule of unreasonableness, we balance the privacy-related and law enforcement-related concerns to determine if the intrusion was reasonable."[714]This application of "traditional standards of reasonableness" requires a court to weigh "the promotion of legitimate governmental interests" against "the degree to which [the search] intrudes upon an individual's privacy."[715]An assessment of reasonableness to determine the lawfulness of requiring this class of arrestees to provide a DNA sample is central to the instant case.

IV A

The legitimate government interest served by the Maryland DNA Collection Act is one that is well established: the need for law enforcement officers in a safe and accurate way to process and identify the persons and posses sions they must take into custody. It is beyond dispute that "probable cause provides legal justification for arresting a person suspected of crime, and for a brief period of detention to take the administrative steps incident to arrest."[716]

---

[707] *Maryland v. Buie*, 494 U. S. 325, 331 (1990).

[708] See *Skinner, supra*.

[709] See *Samson v. California*, 547 U. S. 843 (2006).

[710] *Treasury Employees v. Von Raab*, 489 U. S. 656, 667 (1989).

[711] Terry, supra, at 12 (quoting Johnson v. United States, 333 U. S. 10, 14 (1948)).

[712] *Skinner, supra*, at 622.

[713] *Samson, supra*, at 855, n. 4.

[714] *McArthur, supra*, at 331.

[715] *Wyoming v. Houghton*, 526 U. S. 295, 300 (1999).

[716] *Gerstein v. Pugh*, 420 U. S. 103, 113–114 (1975).

Also uncontested is the "right on the part of the Government, always recognized under English and American law, to search the person of the accused when legally arrested."[717]"The validity of the search of a person incident to a lawful arrest has been regarded as settled from its first enunciation, and has remained virtually unchallenged."[718]Even in that context, the Court has been clear that individual suspicion is not necessary, because "[t]he constitutionality of a search incident to an arrest does not depend on whether there is any indication that the person arrested possesses weapons or evidence. The fact of a lawful arrest, standing alone, authorizes a search."[719] The "routine administrative procedure[s] at a police station house incident to booking and jailing the suspect" derive from different origins and have different constitutional justifications than, say, the search of a place,[720] for the search of a place not incident to an arrest depends on the "fair probability that contraband or evidence of a crime will be found in a particular place."[721]The interests are further different when an individual is formally processed into police custody. Then "the law is in the act of subjecting the body of the accused to its physical dominion."[722]When probable cause exists to remove an individual from the normal channels of society and hold him in legal custody, DNA identification plays a critical role in serving those interests.

First, "[i]n every criminal case, it is known and must be known who has been arrested and who is being tried."[723]An individual's identity is more than just his name or Social Security number, and the government's interest in identification goes beyond ensuring that the proper name is typed on the indictment. Identity has never been considered limited to the name on the arrestee's birth certificate. In fact, a name is of little value compared to the real interest in identification at stake when an individual is brought into custody. "It is a well recognized aspect of criminal conduct that the perpetrator will take unusual steps to conceal not only his conduct, but also his identity. Disguises used while committing a crime may be supplemented or replaced by changed names, and even changed physical features."[724]An "arrestee may be carrying a false ID or lie about his identity," and "criminal history records . . . can be inaccurate or incomplete."[725]

A suspect's criminal history is a critical part of his identity that officers should know when processing him for detention. It is a common occurrence that "people detained for minor offenses can turn out to be the most devious and dangerous criminals. Hours after the Oklahoma City bombing, Timothy McVeigh was stopped by a state trooper who noticed he was driving without a license plate. Police stopped serial killer Joel Rifkin for the same reason. One of the terrorists involved in the September 11 attacks was stopped and ticketed for speeding just two days before hijacking Flight 93."[726]Police already seek this crucial identifying information. They use routine and accepted means as varied as comparing the suspect's booking photograph to sketch artists' depictions of persons of interest, showing his mugshot to potential witnesses, and of course making a computerized comparison of the arrestee's finger-

---

717 *Weeks v. United States*, 232 U. S. 383, 392 (1914), over-ruled on other grounds, *Mapp v. Ohio*, 367 U. S. 643 (1961).

718 *United States v. Robinson*, 414 U. S. 218, 224 (1973).

719 *Michigan v. DeFillippo*, 443 U. S. 31, 35 (1979).

720 *Illinois v. Lafayette*, 462 U. S. 640, 643 (1983).

721 *Illinois v. Gates*, 462 U. S. 213, 238 (1983).

722 *People v. Chiagles*, 237 N. Y. 193, 197, 142 N. E. 583, 584 (1923) (Cardozo, J.).

723 Hiibel v. Sixth Judicial Dist. Court of Nev., Humboldt Cty., 542 U. S. 177, 191 (2004).

724 *Jones v. Murray*, 962 F. 2d 302, 307 (CA4 1992).

725 *Florence v. Board of Chosen Freeholders of County of Burlington*, 566 U. S. ___, ___ (2012) (slip op., at 16).

726 Id., at ___ (slip op., at 14) (citations omitted).

prints against electronic databases of known criminals and unsolved crimes. In this respect the only difference between DNA analysis and the accepted use of fingerprint databases is the unparalleled accuracy DNA provides.

The task of identification necessarily entails searching public and police records based on the identifying information provided by the arrestee to see what is already known about him. The DNA collected from arrestees is an irrefutable identification of the person from whom it was taken. Like a fingerprint, the 13 CODIS loci are not themselves evidence of any particular crime in the way that a drug test can by itself be evidence of illegal narcotics use. A DNA profile is useful to the police because it gives them a form of identification to search the records already in their valid possession. In this respect the use of DNA for identification is no different than matching an arrestee's face to a wanted poster of a previously unidentified suspect; or matching tattoos to known gang symbols to reveal a criminal affiliation; or matching the arrestee's fingerprints to those recovered from a crime scene.[727]DNA is another metric of identification used to connect the arrestee with his or her public persona, as reflected in records of his or her actions that are available to the police. Those records may be linked to the arrestee by a variety of relevant forms of identification, including name, alias, date and time of previous convictions and the name then used, photograph, Social Security number, or CODIS profile. These data, found in official records, are checked as a routine matter to produce a more comprehensive record of the suspect's complete identity. Finding occurrences of the arrestee's CODIS profile in outstanding cases is consistent with this common practice. It uses a different form of identification than a name or fingerprint, but its function is the same.

Second, law enforcement officers bear a responsibility for ensuring that the custody of an arrestee does not create inordinate "risks for facility staff, for the existing detainee population, and for a new detainee."[728]DNA identification can provide untainted information to those charged with detaining suspects and detaining the property of any felon. For these purposes officers must know the type of person whom they are detaining, and DNA allows them to make critical choices about how to proceed.

"Knowledge of identity may inform an officer that a suspect is wanted for another offense, or has a record of violence or mental disorder. On the other hand, knowing identity may help clear a suspect and al low the police to concentrate their efforts elsewhere. Identity may prove particularly important in [certain cases, such as] where the police are investigating what appears to be a domestic assault. Officers called to investigate domestic disputes need to know whom they are dealing with in order to assess the situation, the threat to their own safety, and possible danger to the potential victim."[729]

Recognizing that a name alone cannot address this interest in identity, the Court has approved, for example, "a visual inspection for certain tattoos and other signs of gang affiliation as part of the intake process," because "[t]he identification and isolation of gang members before they are admitted protects everyone."[730]

Third, looking forward to future stages of criminal prosecution, "the Government has a substantial interest in ensuring that persons accused of crimes are available for trials."[731]A person who is arrested for one offense but knows that he has yet to answer for some past crime may be more inclined to flee the instant charges, lest continued contact with the criminal justice system expose one or more other serious

---

[727] See Tr. of Oral Arg. 19.

[728] *Florence*, *supra*, at ___ (slip op., at 10).

[729] *Hiibel*, *supra*, at 186.

[730] *Florence*, *supra*, at ___ (slip op., at 11).

[731] *Bell v. Wolfish*, 441 U. S. 520, 534 (1979).

offenses. For example, a defendant who had committed a prior sexual assault might be inclined to flee on a burglary charge, knowing that in every State a DNA sample would be taken from him after his conviction on the burglary charge that would tie him to the more serious charge of rape. In addition to subverting the administration of justice with respect to the crime of arrest, this ties back to the interest in safety; for a detainee who absconds from custody presents a risk to law enforcement officers, other detainees, victims of previous crimes, witnesses, and society at large.

Fourth, an arrestee's past conduct is essential to an assessment of the danger he poses to the public, and this will inform a court's determination whether the individual should be released on bail. "The government's interest in preventing crime by arrestees is both legitimate and compelling."[732]DNA identification of a suspect in a violent crime provides critical information to the police and judicial officials in making a determination of the arrestee's future dangerousness. This inquiry always has entailed some scrutiny beyond the name on the defendant's driver's license. For example, Maryland law requires a judge to take into account not only "the nature and circumstances of the offense charged" but also "the defendant's family ties, employment status and history, financial resources, reputation, character and mental condition, length of residence in the community."[733]Knowing that the defendant is wanted for a previous violent crime based on DNA identification is especially probative of the court's consideration of "the danger of the defendant to the alleged victim, another person, or the community."[734]

This interest is not speculative. In considering laws to require collecting DNA from arrestees, government agencies around the Nation found evidence of numerous cases in which felony arrestees would have been identified as violent through DNA identification matching them to previous crimes but who later committed additional crimes because such identification was not used to detain them.[735] Present capabilities make it possible to complete a DNA identification that provides information essential to determining whether a detained suspect can be released pending trial.[736]Regardless of when the initial bail decision is made, release is not appropriate until a further determination is made as to the person's identity in the sense not only of what his birth certificate states but also what other records and data disclose to give that identity more meaning in the whole context of who the person really is. And even when release is permitted, the back ground identity of the suspect is necessary for determining what conditions must be met before release is allowed. If release is authorized, it may take time for the conditions to be met, and so the time before actual release can be substantial. For example, in the federal system, defend ants released conditionally are detained on average for 112 days; those released on unsecured bond for 37 days; on personal recognizance for 36 days; and on other financial conditions for 27 days.[737]During this entire period, additional and supplemental data establishing more about the person's identity and background can provide critical information relevant to the conditions of release and whether to revisit an initial release determination. The facts of this case are illustrative. Though the

[732] *United States v. Salerno*, 481 U. S. 739, 749 (1987).

[733] 1 Md. Rules 4–216(f)(1)(A), (C) (2013).

[734] Rule 4–216(f)(1)(G); see also 18 U. S. C. §3142 (2006 ed. and Supp. V) (similar requirements).

[735] See Denver's Study on Preventable Crimes (2009) (three examples), online at http://www.denverda.org/DNA_ Documents / Denver%27s%20Preventable%20Crimes%20 Study.pdf (all Internet materials as visited May 31, 2013, and available in Clerk of Court's case file); Chicago's Study on Preventable Crimes (2005) (five examples), online at http://www.denverda.org/DNA_-Documents/ Arrestee_Database / Chicago%20Preventable%20Crimes- Final.pdf; Maryland Study on Preventable Crimes (2008) (three examples), online at http://www.denverda.org/DNA_ Documents/MarylandDNAarresteestudy.pdf.

[736] See, e.g., States Brief 18, n. 10 ("DNA identification database samples have been processed in as few as two days in California, although around 30 days has been average").

[737] See Dept. of Justice, Bureau of Justice Statistics, Compendium of Federal Justice Statis tics 45 (NCJ–213476, Dec. 2006) online at http://bjs.gov/ content/pub/pdf/cfjs04.pdf.

record is not clear, if some thought were being given to releasing the respondent on bail on the gun charge, a release that would take weeks or months in any event, when the DNA report linked him to the prior rape, it would be relevant to the conditions of his release. The same would be true with a supplemental fingerprint report.

Even if an arrestee is released on bail, development of DNA identification revealing the defendant's unknown violent past can and should lead to the revocation of his conditional release.[738]Pretrial release of a person charged with a dangerous crime is a most serious responsibility. It is reason able in all respects for the State to use an accepted data base to determine if an arrestee is the object of suspicion in other serious crimes, suspicion that may provide a strong incentive for the arrestee to escape and flee.

Finally, in the interests of justice, the identification of an arrestee as the perpetrator of some heinous crime may have the salutary effect of freeing a person wrongfully imprisoned for the same offense. "Prompt [DNA] testing . . . would speed up apprehension of criminals before they commit additional crimes, and prevent the grotesque detention of . . . innocent people."[739]

Because proper processing of arrestees is so important and has consequences for every stage of the criminal process, the Court has recognized that the "governmental interests underlying a station-house search of the arrestee's person and possessions may in some circumstances be even greater than those supporting a search immediately following arrest."[740]Thus, the Court has been reluctant to circumscribe the authority of the police to conduct *reasonable* booking searches. For example, "the standards traditionally governing a search *incident* to lawful arrest are not . . . commuted to the stricter Terry standards."[741]Nor are these interests in identification served only by a search of the arrestee himself. "Inspection of an arrestee's *personal* property may assist the police in ascertaining or verifying his identity."[742]And though the Fifth Amendment's protection against self-incrimination is not, as a general rule, governed by a reasonableness standard, the Court has held that "questions . . . reasonably related to the police's administrative concerns . . . fall outside the protections of Miranda [v. Arizona, 384 U. S. 436 (1966)] and the answers thereto need not be suppressed."[743]

B

DNA identification represents an important advance in the techniques used by law enforcement to serve legitimate police concerns for as long as there have been arrests, concerns the courts have acknowledged and approved for more than a century. Law enforcement agencies routinely have used scientific advancements in their standard procedures for the identification of arrestees. "Police had been using photography to capture the faces of criminals almost since its invention."[744]Courts did not dispute that practice, concluding that a "sheriff in making an arrest for a felony on a warrant has the right to exercise a discretion . . . , [if] he should deem it necessary to the safe-keeping of a prisoner, and to prevent his escape, or to enable him the more readily to retake the prisoner if he should escape, to take his photograph."[745]By the time that it had become "the daily practice of the police officers and detectives of

[738] See 18 U. S. C. §3145(a) (providing for revocation of release); see also States Brief 11–12 (discussing examples where bail and diversion determinations were reversed after DNA identified the arrestee's violent history).

[739] J. Dwyer, P. Neufeld, & B. Scheck, Actual Innocence 245 (2000).

[740] *Lafayette*, 462 U. S., at 645.

[741] *Robinson*, 414 U. S., at 234.

[742] Lafayette, *supra*, at 646.

[743] *Pennsylvania v. Muniz*, 496 U. S. 582, 601–602 (1990).

[744] S. Cole, Suspect Identities 20 (2001).

[745] *State ex rel. Bruns v. Clausmier*, 154 Ind. 599, 601, 603, 57 N. E. 541, 542 (1900).

crime to use photographic pictures for the discovery and identification of criminals," the courts likewise had come to the conclusion that "it would be a matter of regret to have its use unduly restricted upon any fanciful theory or constitutional privilege."[746]

Beginning in 1887, some police adopted more exacting means to identify arrestees, using the system of precise physical measurements pioneered by the French anthropologist Alphonse Bertillon. Bertillon identification consisted of 10 measurements of the arrestee's body, along with a "scientific analysis of the features of the face and an exact anatomical localization of the various scars, marks, of the body."[747]"When a prisoner was brought in, his photograph was taken according to the Bertillon system, and his body measurements were then made. The measurements were made... and noted down on the back of a card or a blotter, and the photograph of the prisoner was expected to be placed on the card. This card, therefore, furnished both the likeness and description of the prisoner, and was placed in the rogues' gallery, and copies were sent to various cities where similar records were kept."[748]As in the present case, the point of taking this information about each arrestee was not limited to verifying that the proper name was on the indictment. These procedures were used to "facilitate the recapture of escaped prisoners," to aid "the investigation of their past records and personal history," and "to preserve the means of identification for... future supervision after discharge."[749]

Perhaps the most direct historical analogue to the DNA technology used to identify respondent is the familiar practice of fingerprinting arrestees. From the advent of this technique, courts had no trouble determining that fingerprinting was a natural part of "the administrative steps incident to arrest."[750]In the seminal case of *United States v. Kelly*,[751]Judge Augustus Hand wrote that routine fingerprinting did not violate the Fourth Amendment precisely because it fit within the accepted means of processing an arrestee into custody:

> "Finger printing seems to be no more than an extension of methods of identification long used in dealing with persons under arrest for real or supposed violations of the criminal laws. It is known to be a very certain means devised by modern science to reach the desired end, and has become especially important in a time when increased population and vast aggregations of people in urban centers have rendered the notoriety of the individual in the community no longer a ready means of identification.We find no ground in reason or authority for interfering with a method of identifying persons charged with crime which has now become widely known and frequently practiced."[752]

By the middle of the 20th century, it was considered "elementary that a person in lawful custody may be required to submit to photographing and fingerprinting as part of routine identification processes."[753]

DNA identification is an advanced technique superior to fingerprinting in many ways, so much so that to insist on fingerprints as the norm would make little sense to either the forensic expert or a layperson. The additional intrusion upon the arrestee's

---

[746] *Shaffer v. United States*, 24 App. D. C. 417, 426 (1904).

[747] Defense of the Bertillon System, N. Y. Times, Jan. 20, 1896, p. 3.

[748] *People ex rel. Jones v. Diehl*, 53 App. Div. 645, 646, 65 N. Y. S. 801, 802 (1900).

[749] *Hodgeman v. Olsen*, 86 Wash. 615, 619, 150 P. 1122, 1124 (1915); see also *McGovern v. Van Riper*, 137 N. J. Eq. 24, 33–34, 43 A. 2d 514, 519 (Ch. 1945) ("Criminal identification is said to have two main purposes: (1) The identification of the accused as the person who committed the crime for which he is being held; and, (2) the identification of the accused as the same person who has been previously charged with, or convicted of, other offenses against the criminal law").

[750] *County of Riverside v. McLaughlin*, 500 U. S. 44, 58 (1991).

[751] 55 F. 2d 67 (CA2 1932).

[752] Id., at 69–70.

[753] *Smith v. United States*, 324 F. 2d 879, 882 (CADC 1963) (Burger, J.) (citations omitted).

privacy beyond that associated with fingerprinting is not significant, see Part V, infra, and DNA is a markedly more accurate form of identifying arrestees. A suspect who has changed his facial features to evade photographic identification or even one who has undertaken the more arduous task of altering his finger prints cannot escape the revealing power of his DNA.

The respondent's primary objection to this analogy is that DNA identification is not as fast as fingerprinting, and so it should not be considered to be the 21st-century equivalent.[754]But rapid analysis of fingerprints is itself of recent vintage. The FBI's vaunted Integrated Automated Fingerprint Identification System (IAFIS) was only "launched on July 28, 1999." "Prior to this time, the processing of... fingerprint submissions was largely a manual, labor-intensive process, taking weeks or months to process a single submission."[755]It was not the advent of this technology that rendered fingerprint analysis constitutional in a single moment. The question of how long it takes to process identifying information obtained from a valid search goes only to the efficacy of the search for its purpose of prompt identification, not the constitutionality of the search.[756]Given the importance of DNA in the identification of police records pertaining to arrestees and the need to refine and confirm that identity for its important bearing on the decision to continue release on bail or to impose of new conditions, DNA serves an essential purpose despite the existence of delays such as the one that occurred in this case. Even so, the delay in processing DNA from arrestees is being reduced to a substantial degree by rapid technical advances.[757]And the FBI has already begun testing devices that will enable police to process the DNA of arrestees within 90 minutes.[758]An assessment and understanding of the reasonableness of this minimally invasive search of a person detained for a serious crime should take account of these technical advances. Just as fingerprinting was constitutional for generations prior to the introduction of IAFIS, DNA identification of arrestees is a permissible tool of law enforcement today. New technology will only further improve its speed and therefore its effectiveness. And, as noted above, actual release of a serious offender as a routine matter takes weeks or months in any event. By identifying not only who the arrestee is but also what other available records disclose about his past to show who he is, the police can ensure that they have the proper person under arrest and that they have made the necessary arrangements for his custody; and, just as important, they can also prevent suspicion against or prosecution of the innocent.

In sum, there can be little reason to question "the legitimate interest of the government in knowing for an absolute certainty the identity of the person arrested, in knowing whether he is wanted elsewhere, and in ensuring his identification in the event he flees prosecution."[759]To that end, courts have confirmed that the Fourth Amendment allows police to take certain routine "administrative steps incident to arrest—i.e. booking, photographing, and fingerprinting."[760]DNA identification of arrestees, of the type approved by the Maryland statute here at issue, is "no more than an extension of methods of identification long used in dealing with persons un-

---

[754] See Tr. of Oral Arg. 53.

[755] Federal Bureau of Investigation, Integrated Automated Fingerprint Identification System, online at http://www.fbi.gov/about-us/cjis/ fingerprints_biometrics/iafis/iafis.

[756] Cf. Ontario v. Quon, 560 U. S. ___, ___ (2010) (slip op., at 15).

[757] See, e.g., Attorney General DeWine Announces Significant Drop in DNA Turnaround Time (Jan. 4, 2013) (DNA processing time reduced from 125 days in 2010 to 20 days in 2012), online at http://ohioattorneygeneral.gov/Media/News-Releases/January- 2013 / Attorney - General - DeWine - Announces - Significant- Drop; Gov. Jindal Announces Elimination of DNA Backlog, DNA Unit Now Operating in Real Time (Nov. 17, 2011) (average DNA report time reduced from a year or more in 2009 to 20 days in 2011), online at http:// www.gov.state.la.us/index.cfm?md=newsroom&tmp=detail &articleID=3102.

[758] See Brief for National District Attorneys Association as Amicus Curiae 20–21; Tr. of Oral Arg. 17.

[759] 3 W. LaFave, Search and Seizure §5.3(c), p. 216 (5th ed. 2012).

[760] *McLaughlin*, 500 U. S., at 58.

der arrest."[761]In the balance of reasonableness required by the Fourth Amendment, therefore, the Court must give great weight both to the significant government interest at stake in the identification of arrestees and to the unmatched potential of DNA identification to serve that interest.

V A

By comparison to this substantial government interest and the unique effectiveness of DNA identification, the intrusion of a cheek swab to obtain a DNA sample is a minimal one. True, a significant government interest does not alone suffice to justify a search. The government interest must outweigh the degree to which the search invades an individual's legitimate expectations of privacy. In considering those expectations in this case, however, the necessary predicate of a valid arrest for a serious offense is fundamental. "Although the underlying command of the Fourth Amendment is always that searches and seizures be reasonable, what is reasonable depends on the context within which a search takes place."[762]"[T]he legitimacy of certain privacy expectations vis-à-vis the State may depend upon the individual's legal relationship with the State."[763]

The reasonableness of any search must be considered in the context of the person's legitimate expectations of privacy. For example, when weighing the invasiveness of urinalysis of high school athletes, the Court noted that "legitimate privacy expectations are even less with regard to student athletes... Public school locker rooms, the usual sites for these activities, are not notable for the privacy they afford."[764]Likewise, the Court has used a context-specific benchmark inapplicable to the public at large when "the expectations of privacy of covered employees are diminished by reason of their participation in an industry that is regulated pervasively,"[765]or when "the 'operational realities of the workplace' may render entirely reasonable certain work-related intrusions by supervisors and co-workers that might be viewed as unreasonable in other contexts,"[766]

The expectations of privacy of an individual taken into police custody "necessarily [are] of a diminished scope."[767]"[B]oth the person and the property in his immediate possession may be searched at the station house."[768]A search of the detainee's person when he is booked into custody may "'involve a relatively extensive exploration,'"[769]including "requiring at least some detainees to lift their genitals or cough in a squatting position."[770]

In this critical respect, the search here at issue differs from the sort of programmatic searches of either the public at large or a particular class of regulated but otherwise law-abiding citizens that the Court has previously labeled as "'special needs'" searches.[771]When the police stop a motorist at a checkpoint,[772]or test a polit-

---

[761] *Kelly*, 55 F. 2d, at 69.

[762] *New Jersey v. T. L. O.*, 469 U. S. 325, 337 (1985).

[763] Vernonia School Dist. 47J, 515 U. S., at 654.

[764] *Id.*, at 657.

[765] *Skinner*, 489 U. S., at 627.

[766] *Von Raab*, 489 U. S., at 671.

[767] *Bell*, 441 U. S., at 557.

[768] *United States v. Edwards*, 415 U. S. 800, 803 (1974).

[769] *Robinson*, 414 U. S., at 227.

[770] *Florence*, 566 U. S., at ___ (slip op., at 13).

[771] *Chandler v. Miller*, 520 U. S. 305, 314 (1997).

[772] See *Indianapolis v. Edmond*, 531 U. S. 32 (2000).

ical candidate for illegal narcotics,[773]they intrude upon substantial expectations of privacy. So the Court has insisted on some purpose other than "to detect evidence of ordinary criminal wrongdoing" to justify these searches in the absence of individualized suspicion.[774] Once an individual has been arrested on probable cause for a dangerous offense that may require detention before trial, however, his or her expectations of privacy and freedom from police scrutiny are reduced. DNA identification like that at issue here thus does not require consideration of any unique needs that would be required to justify search ing the average citizen. The special needs cases, though in full accord with the result reached here, do not have a direct bearing on the issues presented in this case, be cause unlike the search of a citizen who has not been suspected of a wrong, a detainee has a reduced expectation of privacy.

The reasonableness inquiry here considers two other circumstances in which the Court has held that particularized suspicion is not categorically required: "diminished expectations of privacy [and] minimal intrusions."[775]This is not to suggest that any search is acceptable solely because a person is in custody. Some searches, such as invasive surgery,[776]or a search of the arrestee's home,[777]involve either greater intrusions or higher expectations of privacy than are present in this case. In those situations, when the Court must "balance the privacy-related and law enforcement related concerns to determine if the intrusion was reasonable,"[778]the privacy-related concerns are weighty enough that the search may require a warrant, notwithstanding the diminished expectations of privacy of the arrestee.

Here, by contrast to the approved standard procedures incident to any arrest detailed above, a buccal swab involves an even more brief and still minimal intrusion. A gentle rub along the inside of the cheek does not break the skin, and it "involves virtually no risk, trauma, or pain."[779]"A crucial factor in analyzing the magnitude of the intrusion . . . is the extent to which the procedure may threaten the safety or health of the individual"[780]and nothing suggests that a buccal swab poses any physical danger whatsoever. A brief intrusion of an arrestee's person is subject to the Fourth Amendment, but a swab of this nature does not increase the indignity already attendant to normal incidents of arrest.

B

In addition the processing of respondent's DNA sample's 13 CODIS loci did not intrude on respondent's privacy in a way that would make his DNA identification unconstitutional.

First, as already noted, the CODIS loci come from non coding parts of the DNA that do not reveal the genetic traits of the arrestee. While science can always progress further, and those progressions may have Fourth Amendment consequences, alleles at the CODIS loci "are not at present revealing information beyond identification."[781]The argument that the testing at issue in this case reveals any private medical information at all is open to dispute.

---

[773] See *Chandler, supra.*

[774] *Edmond, supra*, at 38.

[775] *McArthur*, 531 U. S., at 330.

[776] See *Winston*, 470 U. S. 753.

[777] See *Chimel v. California*, 395 U. S. 752 (1969).

[778] *McArthur, supra*, at 331.

[779] *Schmerber*, 384 U. S., at 771.

[780] *Winston, supra*, at 761.

[781] Katsanis & Wagner, Characterization of the Standard and Recommended CODIS Markers, 58 J. Forensic Sci. S169, S171 (2013).

And even if non-coding alleles could provide some information, they are not in fact tested for that end. It is undisputed that law enforcement officers analyze DNA for the sole purpose of generating a unique identifying number against which future samples may be matched. This parallels a similar safeguard based on actual practice in the school drug-testing context, where the Court deemed it "significant that the tests at issue here look only for drugs, and not for whether the student is, for example, epileptic, pregnant, or diabetic."[782]If in the future police analyze samples to determine, for instance, an arrestee's predisposition for a particular disease or other hereditary factors not relevant to identity, that case would present additional privacy concerns not present here.

Finally, the Act provides statutory protections that guard against further invasion of privacy. As noted above, the Act requires that "only DNA records that directly relate to the identification of individuals shall be collected and stored."[783]No purpose other than identification is permissible: "A person may not willfully test a DNA sample for information that does not relate to the identification of individuals as specified in this subtitle."[784]This Court has noted often that "a 'statutory or regulatory duty to avoid unwarranted disclosures' generally allays . . . privacy concerns."[785]The Court need not speculate about the risks posed "by a system that did not contain comparable security provisions."[786]In light of the scientific and statutory safeguards, once respondent's DNA was lawfully collected the STR analysis of respondent's DNA pursuant to CODIS procedures did not amount to a significant invasion of privacy that would render the DNA identification impermissible under the Fourth Amendment.

***

In light of the context of a valid arrest supported by probable cause respondent's expectations of privacy were not offended by the minor intrusion of a brief swab of his cheeks. By contrast, that same context of arrest gives rise to significant state interests in identifying respondent not only so that the proper name can be attached to his charges but also so that the criminal justice system can make informed decisions concerning pretrial custody. Upon these considerations the Court concludes that DNA identification of arrestees is a reasonable search that can be considered part of a routine booking procedure. When officers make an arrest supported by probable cause to hold for a serious offense and they bring the suspect to the station to be detained in custody, taking and analyzing a cheek swab of the arrestee's DNA is, like fingerprinting and photographing, a legitimate police booking procedure that is reasonable under the Fourth Amendment.

The judgment of the Court of Appeals of Maryland is reversed.

It is so ordered.

JUSTICE SCALIA, with whom JUSTICE GINSBURG, JUSTICE SOTOMAYOR, and JUSTICE KAGAN join, dissenting.

The Fourth Amendment forbids searching a person for evidence of a crime when there is no basis for believing the person is guilty of the crime or is in possession of incriminating evidence. That prohibition is categorical and without exception; it lies at the very heart of the Fourth Amendment. Whenever this Court has allowed a

[782] Vernonia School Dist. 47J, 515 U. S., at 658.

[783] Md. Pub. Saf. Code Ann. §2–505(b)(1).

[784] §2–512(c).

[785] NASA v. Nelson, 562 U. S. ___, ___ (2011) (slip op., at 20) (quoting Whalen v. Roe, 429 U. S. 589, 605 (1977)).

[786] Id., at 606.

suspicion-less search, it has insisted upon a justifying motive apart from the investigation of crime.

It is obvious that no such non-investigative motive exists in this case. The Court's assertion that DNA is being taken, not to solve crimes, but to identify those in the State's custody, taxes the credulity of the credulous. And the Court's comparison of Maryland's DNA searches to other techniques, such as fingerprinting, can seem apt only to those who know no more than today's opinion has chosen to tell them about how those DNA searches actually work.

I A

At the time of the Founding, Americans despised the British use of so-called "general warrants"—warrants not grounded upon a sworn oath of a specific infraction by a particular individual, and thus not limited in scope and application. The first Virginia Constitution declared that "general warrants, whereby any officer or messenger may be commanded to search suspected places without evidence of a fact committed," or to search a person "whose offense is not particularly described and supported by evidence," "are grievous and oppressive, and ought not be granted."[787]. The Maryland Declaration of Rights similarly provided that general warrants were "illegal."[788]In the ratification debates, Antifederalists sarcastically predicted that the general, suspicion-less warrant would be among the Constitution's "blessings."[789]"Brutus" of New York asked why the Federal Constitution contained no provision like Maryland's, Brutus II, N. Y. Journal, Nov. 1, 1787, in id., at 524,and Patrick Henry warned that the new Federal Constitution would expose the citizenry to searches and seizures "in the most arbitrary manner, without any evidence or reason."[790]

Madison's draft of what became the Fourth Amendment answered these charges by providing that the "rights of the people to be secured in their persons… from all unreasonable searches and seizures, shall not be violated by warrants issued without probable cause . . . or not particularly describing the places to be searched."[791]As ratified, the Fourth Amendment's Warrant Clause forbids a warrant to "issue" except "upon probable cause," and requires that it be "particular" (which is to say, individualized) to "the place to be searched, and the persons or things to be seized." And we have held that, even when a warrant is not constitutionally necessary, the Fourth Amendment's general prohibition of "unreasonable" searches imports the same requirement of individualized suspicion.[792] Although there is a "closely guarded category of constitutionally permissible suspicion-less searches"[793]that has never included searches designed to serve "the normal need for law enforcement."[794]Even the common name for suspicion-less searches—"special needs" searches—itself reflects that they must be justified, always, by concerns "other than crime detection."[795]We have approved random drug tests of railroad employees, yes—but only because the Government's need to "regulate the conduct of railroad employees

[787] Va. Declaration of Rights §10 (1776), in 1 B. Schwartz, The Bill of Rights: A Documentary History 234, 235 (1971)

[788] Md. Declaration of Rights §XXIII (1776), in id., at 280, 282.

[789] Blessings of the New Government, Independent Gazetteer, Oct. 6, 1787, in 13 Documentary History of the Ratification of the Constitution 345 (J. Kaminski & G. Saladino eds. 1981).

[790] 3 Debates on the Federal Constitution 588 (J. Elliot 2d ed. 1854).

[791] 1 Annals of Cong. 434–435 (1789).

[792] See *Chandler v. Miller*, 520 U. S. 305, 308 (1997).

[793] Id., at 309.

[794] *Skinner v. Railway Labor Executives' Assn.*, 489 U. S. 602, 619 (1989) (internal quotation marks omitted).

[795] *Chandler, supra*, at 313– 314. *Chandler, supra*, at 313– 314.

to ensure safety" is distinct from "normal law enforcement."[796]So too we have approved suspicion-less searches in public schools—but only because there the government acts in furtherance of its "responsibilities . . . as guardian and tutor of children entrusted to its care."[797] So while the Court is correct to note[798] that there are instances in which we have permitted searches without individualized suspicion, "[i]n none of these cases . . . did we indicate approval of a [search] whose primary purpose was to detect evidence of ordinary criminal wrongdoing."[799]That limitation is crucial. It is only when a governmental purpose aside from crime-solving is at stake that we engage in the free-form "reasonableness" inquiry that the Court indulges in at length today. To put it another way, both the legitimacy of the Court's method and the correctness of its outcome hinge entirely on the truth of a single proposition: that the primary purpose of these DNA searches is something other than simply discovering evidence of criminal wrongdoing. As I detail below, that proposition is wrong.

B

The Court eludes at several points[800]to the fact that King was an arrestee, and arrestees may be validly searched incident to their arrest. But the Court does not really rest on this principle, and for good reason: The objects of a search incident to arrest must be either (1) weapons or evidence that might easily be destroyed, or (2) evidence relevant to the crime of arrest.[801]Neither is the object of the search at issue here.

The Court hastens to clarify that it does not mean to approve invasive surgery on arrestees or warrantless searches of their homes.[802]That the Court feels the need to disclaim these consequences is as damning a criticism of its suspicion-less search regime as any I can muster. And the Court's attempt to distinguish those hypothetical searches from this real one is unconvincing. We are told that the "privacy-related concerns" in the search of a home "are weighty enough that the search may require a warrant, notwithstanding the diminished expectations of privacy of the arrestee."[803]But why are the "privacy-related concerns" not also "weighty" when an intrusion into the body is at stake? (The Fourth Amendment lists "persons" first among the entities protected against unreasonable searches and seizures.) And could the police engage, without any suspicion of wrongdoing, in a "brief and . . . minimal" intrusion into the home of an arrestee—perhaps just peeking around the curtilage a bit?[804]Obviously not.

At any rate, all this discussion is beside the point. No matter the degree of invasiveness, suspicion-less searches are never allowed if their principal end is ordinary crime solving. A search incident to arrest either serves other ends (such as officer safety, in a search for weapons) or is not suspicion-less (as when there is reason to believe the arrestee possesses evidence relevant to the crime of arrest).

---

[796] *Skinner*, *supra*, at 620.

[797] *Vernonia School Dist. 47J v. Acton*, 515 U. S. 646, 665 (1995).

[798] *Ante*, at 8–9.

[799] *Indianapolis v. Edmond*, 531 U. S. 32, 38 (2000).

[800] See ante, at 11, 25.

[801] See *Arizona v. Gant*, 556 U. S. 332, 343–344 (2009); *Thornton v. United States*, 541 U. S. 615, 632 (2004) (SCALIA, J., concurring in judgment).

[802] *Ante*, at 25.

[803] *Ante*, at 26.

[804] See *ante*, at 26.

Sensing (correctly) that it needs more, the Court elaborates at length the ways that the search here served the special purpose of "identifying" King. But that seems to me quite wrong—unless what one means by "identifying" someone is "searching for evidence that he has committed crimes unrelated to the crime of his arrest." At points the Court does appear to use "identifying" in that peculiar sense—claiming, for example, that knowing "an arrestee's past conduct is essential to an assessment of the danger he poses."[805]If identifying someone means finding out what unsolved crimes he has committed, then identification is indistinguishable from the ordinary law enforcement aims that have never been thought to justify a suspicion-less search. Searching every lawfully stopped car, for example, might turn up information about unsolved crimes the driver had committed, but no one would say that such a search was aimed at "identifying" him, and no court would hold such a search lawful. I will therefore assume that the Court means that the DNA search at issue here was useful to "identify" King in the normal sense of that word—in the sense that would identify the author of Introduction to the Principles of Morals and Legislation as Jeremy Bentham.

1

The portion of the Court's opinion that explains the identification rationale is strangely silent on the actual workings of the DNA search at issue here. To know those facts is to be instantly disabused of the notion that what happened had anything to do with identifying King.

King was arrested on April 10, 2009, on charges unrelated to the case before us. That same day, April 10, the police searched him and seized the DNA evidence at issue here. What happened next? Reading the Court's opinion, particularly its insistence that the search was necessary to know "who [had] been arrested,"[806]one might guess that King's DNA was swiftly processed and his identity thereby confirmed—perhaps against some master database of known DNA profiles, as is done for fingerprints. After all, was not the suspicion-less search here crucial to avoid "inordinate risks for facility staff" or to "existing detainee population?"[807] Surely, then— surely—the State of Maryland got cracking on those grave risks immediately, by rushing to identify King with his DNA as soon as possible.

Nothing could be further from the truth. Maryland officials did not even begin the process of testing King's DNA that day. Or, actually, the next day. Or the day after that. And that was for a simple reason: Maryland law forbids them to do so. A "DNA sample collected from an individual charged with a crime . . . may not be tested or placed in the statewide DNA data base system prior to the first scheduled arraignment date."[808]And King's first appearance in court was not until three days after his arrest. (I suspect, though, that they did not wait three days to ask his name or take his fingerprints.)

This places in a rather different light the Court's solemn declaration that the search here was necessary so that King could be identified at "every stage of the criminal process."[809]I hope that the Maryland officials who read the Court's opinion do not take it seriously. Acting on the Court's misperception of Maryland law could lead to jail time.[810]Does the Court really believe that Maryland did not know whom it was arraigning? The Court's response is to imagine that release on bail could take so

---

[805] *Ante*, at 15.

[806] *Ante*, at 11.

[807] *Ante*, at 14.

[808] Md. Pub. Saf. Code Ann. §2–504(d)(1) (Lexis 2011) (emphasis added).

[809] *Ante*, at 18.

[810] See Md. Pub. Saf. Code Ann. §2–512(c)–(e) (punishing by up to five years' imprisonment anyone who obtains or tests DNA information except as provided by statute).

long that the DNA results are returned in time, or perhaps that bail could be revoked if the DNA test turned up incriminating information.[811]That is no answer at all. If the purpose of this Act is to assess "whether [King] should be released on bail,"[812]why would it possibly forbid the DNA testing process to begin until King was arraigned? Why would Maryland resign itself to simply hoping that the bail decision will drag out long enough that the "identification" can succeed before the arrestee is released? The truth, known to Maryland and increasingly to the reader: this search had nothing to do with establishing King's identity.

It gets worse. King's DNA sample was not received by the Maryland State Police's Forensic Sciences Division until April 23, 2009—two weeks after his arrest. It sat in that office, ripening in a storage area, until the custodians got around to mailing it to a lab for testing on June 25, 2009—two months after it was received, and nearly three since King's arrest. After it was mailed, the data from the lab tests were not available for several more weeks, until July 13, 2009, which is when the test results were entered into Maryland's DNA database, together with information identifying the person from whom the sample was taken. Meanwhile, bail had been set, King had engaged in discovery, and he had requested a speedy trial—presumably not a trial of John Doe. It was not until August 4, 2009— four months after King's arrest—that the forwarded sample transmitted (without identifying information) from the Maryland DNA database to the Federal Bureau of Investigation's national database was matched with a sample taken from the scene of an unrelated crime years earlier.

A more specific description of exactly what happened at this point illustrates why, by definition, King could not have been identified by this match. The FBI's DNA database (known as CODIS) consists of two distinct collections. FBI, CODIS and NDIS Fact Sheet.[813]One of them, the one to which King's DNA was submitted, consists of DNA samples taken from known convicts or arrestees. I will refer to this as the "Convict and Arrestee Collection." The other collection consists of samples taken from crime scenes; I will refer to this as the "Unsolved Crimes Collection." The Convict and Arrestee Collection stores "no names or other personal identifiers of the offenders, arrestees, or detainees."[814]Rather, it contains only the DNA profile itself, the name of the agency that submitted it, the laboratory personnel who analyzed it, and an identification number for the specimen.[815]This is because the submitting state laboratories are expected already to know the identities of the convicts and arrestees from whom samples are taken. (And, of course, they do.)

Moreover, the CODIS system works by checking to see whether any of the samples in the Unsolved Crimes Collection match any of the samples in the Convict and Arrestee Collection.[816]That is sensible, if what one wants to do is solve those cold cases, but note what it requires: that the identity of the people whose DNA has been entered in the Convict and Arrestee Collection already be known. If one wanted to identify someone in custody using his DNA, the logical thing to do would be to compare that DNA against the Convict and Arrestee Collection: to search, in other words, the collection that could be used (by checking back with the submitting state agency) to identify people, rather than the collection of evidence from unsolved

---

811 *Ante*, at 16–17.

812 *Ante*, at 15.

813 http:// www.fbi.gov / about-us / lab / codis /codis -and- ndis-fact-sheet (all Internet materials as visited May 31, 2013, and avail- able in Clerk of Court's case file).

814 *Ibid.*

815 *Ibid.*

816 *Ibid.*

crimes, whose perpetrators are by definition unknown. But that is not what was done. And that is because this search had nothing to do with identification.

In fact, if anything was "identified" at the moment that the DNA database returned a match, it was not King—his identity was already known. (The docket for the original criminal charges lists his full name, his race, his sex, his height, his weight, his date of birth, and his address.) Rather, what the August 4 match "identified" was the previously taken sample from the earlier crime. That sample was genuinely mysterious to Maryland; the State knew that it had probably been left by the victim's attacker, but nothing else. King was not identified by his association with the sample; rather, the sample was identified by its association with King. The Court effectively destroys its own "identification" theory when it acknowledges that the object of this search was "to see what [was] already known about [King]." King was who he was, and volumes of his biography could not make him any more or any less King. No minimally competent speaker of English would say, upon noticing a known arrestee's similarity "to a wanted poster of a previously unidentified suspect,"[817]that the arrestee had thereby been identified. It was the previously unidentified suspect who had been identified—just as, here, it was the previously unidentified rapist.

2

That taking DNA samples from arrestees has nothing to do with identifying them is confirmed not just by actual practice (which the Court ignores) but by the enabling statute itself (which the Court also ignores). The Maryland Act at issue has a section helpfully entitled "Purpose of collecting and testing DNA samples."[818](One would expect such a section to play a somewhat larger role in the Court's analysis of the Act's purpose—which is to say, at least some role.) That provision lists five purposes for which DNA samples may be tested. By this point, it will not surprise the reader to learn that the Court's imagined purpose is not among them.

Instead, the law provides that DNA samples are collected and tested, as a matter of Maryland law, "as part of an official investigation into a crime."[819](Or, as our suspicion-less search cases would put it: for ordinary law-enforcement purposes.) That is certainly how everyone has always understood the Maryland Act until today. The Governor of Maryland, in commenting on our decision to hear this case, said that he was glad, because "allowing law enforcement to collect DNA samples . . . is absolutely critical to our efforts to continue driving down crime," and "bolsters our efforts to resolve open investigations and bring them to a resolution."[820]The attorney general of Maryland remarked that he "look[ed] forward to the opportunity to defend this important crime-fighting tool," and praised the DNA database for helping to "bring to justice violent perpetrators."[821]Even this Court's order staying the decision below states that the statute "provides a valuable tool for investigating unsolved crimes and thereby helping to remove violent offenders from the general population"— with, unsurprisingly, no mention of identity.[822] More devastating still for the Court's "identification" theory, the statute does enumerate two instances in which a DNA sample may be tested for the purpose of identification: "to help identify human remains,"[823]and "to help identify missing individuals."[824]No mention

[817] *Ante*, at 13.

[818] Md. Pub. Saf. Code Ann. §2–505.

[819] §2–505(a)(2).

[820] Marbella, Supreme Court Will Review Md. DNA Law, Baltimore Sun, Nov. 10, 2012, pp. 1, 14.

[821] *Ibid.*

[822] 567 U. S. ___, ___ (2012) (ROBERTS, C. J., in chambers) (slip op., at 3).

[823] §2–505(a)(3) (emphasis added).

[824] §2–505(a)(4) (emphasis added).

of identifying arrestees. Inclusio unius est exclusio alterius. And note again that Maryland forbids using DNA records "for any purposes other than those specified"—it is actually a crime to do so.[825]

The Maryland regulations implementing the Act confirm what is now monotonously obvious: These DNA searches have nothing to do with identification. For example, if someone is arrested and law enforcement determines that "a convicted offender Statewide DNA Data Base sample already exists" for that arrestee, "the agency is not required to obtain a new sample."[826]But how could the State know if an arrestee has already had his DNA sample collected, if the point of the sample is to identify who he is? Of course, if the DNA sample is instead taken in order to investigate crimes, this restriction makes perfect sense: Having previously placed an identified someone's DNA on file to check against available crime-scene evidence, there is no sense in going to the expense of taking a new sample.

Maryland's regulations further require that the "individual collecting a sample . . . verify the identity of the individual from whom a sample is taken by name and, if applicable, State identification (SID) number."[827](But how?) And after the sample is taken, it continues to be identified by the individual's name, fingerprints, etc.,[828]—rather than (as the Court believes) being used to identify individuals.[829] So, to review: DNA testing does not even begin until after arraignment and bail decisions are already made. The samples sit in storage for months, and take weeks to test. When they are tested, they are checked against the Unsolved Crimes Collection—rather than the Convict and Arrestee Collection, which could be used to identify them. The Act forbids the Court's purpose (identification), but prescribes as its purpose what our suspicion-less search cases forbid ("official investigation into a crime"). Against all of that, it is safe to say that if the Court's identification theory is not wrong, there is no such thing as error.

II

The Court also attempts to bolster its identification theory with a series of inapposite analogies.[830]

Is not taking DNA samples the same, asks the Court, as taking a person's photograph? No—because that is not a Fourth Amendment search at all. It does not involve a physical intrusion onto the person,[831]and we have never held that merely taking a person's photograph invades any recognized "expectation of privacy."[832]Thus, it is unsurprising that the cases the Court cites as authorizing photo taking do not even mention the Fourth Amendment.[833]

But is not the practice of DNA searches, the Court asks, the same as taking "Bertillon" measurements—noting an arrestee's height, shoe size, and so on, on the back of a photograph? No, because that system was not, in the ordinary case, used to solve unsolved crimes. It is possible, I suppose, to imagine situations in which such

825 §2–505(b)(2).

826 Code of Md. Regs., tit. 29, §05.01.04(B)(4) (2011).

827 §05.01.04(K).

828 See §05.01.07(B).

829 See §05.01.07(B)(2) ("Records and specimen information shall be identified by . . . [the] [n]ame of the donor" (emphasis added)).

830 See ante, at 18–23.

831 See *Florida v. Jardines*, 569 U. S. 1, ___ (2013) (slip op., at 3),

832 See *Katz v. United States*, 389 U. S. 347 (1967).

833 See *State ex rel. Bruns v. Clausmier*, 154 Ind. 599, 57 N. E. 541 (1900) (libel), *Shaffer v. United States*, 24 App. D. C. 417 (1904) (Fifth Amendment privilege against self-incrimination).

measurements might be useful to generate leads. (If witnesses described a very tall burglar, all the "tall man" cards could then be pulled.) But the obvious primary purpose of such measurements, as the Court's description of them makes clear, was to verify that, for example, the person arrested today is the same person that was arrested a year ago. Which is to say, Bertillon measurements were actually used as a system of identification, and drew their primary usefulness from that task.

It is on the fingerprinting of arrestees, however, that the Court relies most heavily.[834]The Court does not actually say whether it believes that taking a person's fingerprints is a Fourth Amendment search, and our cases provide no ready answer to that question. Even assuming so, however, law enforcement's post-arrest use of fingerprints could not be more different from its post-arrest use of DNA. Fingerprints of arrestees are taken primarily to identify them (though that process sometimes solves crimes); the DNA of arrestees is taken to solve crimes (and nothing else). Contrast CODIS, the FBI's nationwide DNA database, with IAFIS, the FBI's Integrated Automated Fingerprint Identification System.[835]

The Court asserts that the taking of fingerprints was "constitutional for generations prior to the introduction" of the FBI's rapid computer-matching system.[836]This bold statement is bereft of citation to authority because there is none for it. The "great expansion in fingerprinting came before the modern era of Fourth Amendment jurisprudence," and so we were never asked to decide the legitimacy of the practice.[837]As fingerprint databases expanded from convicted criminals, to arrestees, to civil servants, to immigrants, to everyone with a driver's license, Americans simply "became accustomed to having our fingerprints on file in some government database."[838]But it is wrong to suggest that this was uncontroversial at the time, or that this Court blessed universal fingerprinting for "generations" before it was possible to use it effectively for identification.

The Court also assures us"the delay in processing DNA from arrestees is being reduced to a substantial degree by rapid technical advances."[839]The idea, presumably, is that the snail's pace in this case is atypical, so that DNA is now readily usable for identification. The Court's proof, however, is nothing but a pair of press releases—each of which turns out to undercut this argument. We learn in them that reductions in backlog have enabled Ohio and Louisiana crime labs to analyze a submitted DNA sample in twenty days. But that is still longer than the eighteen days that Maryland needed to analyze King's sample, once it worked its way through the State's labyrinthine bureaucracy. What this illustrates is that these times do not take into account the many other sources of delay. So if the Court means to suggest that Maryland is unusual, that may be right—it may qualify in this context as a paragon of efficiency. (Indeed, the Governor of Maryland was hailing the elimination of that State's backlog more than five years ago.)[840] Meanwhile, the Court's holding will result in the dumping of a large number of arrestee samples—many from minor offenders—onto an already over-burdened system: Nearly one-third of Americans will be arrested for some offense by age 23.[841] The Court also accepts uncritically the

[834] *Ante*, at 20–23.

[835] See FBI, Integrated Automated Fingerprint Identification System, http://www.fbi.gov/about-us/cjis/fingerprints_biometrics/iafis/iafis (hereinafter IAFIS).

[836] *Ante*, at 22.

[837] *United States v. Kincade*, 379 F. 3d 813, 874 (CA9 2004) (Kozinski, J., dissenting).

[838] *Ibid.*

[839] *Ante*, at 22.

[840] See Wheeler, O'Malley Wants to Expand DNA Testing, Baltimore Sun, Jan. 11, 2008, p. 5B.

[841] See Brame, Turner, Paternoster, & Bushway, Cumulative Prevalence of Arrest From Ages 8 to 23 in a National Sample, 129 Pediatrics 21 (2011).

Government's representation at oral argument that it is developing devices that will be able to test DNA in mere minutes. At most, this demonstrates that it may one day be possible to design a program that uses DNA for a purpose other than crime-solving—not that Maryland has in fact designed such a program today. And that is the main point, which the Court's discussion of the brave new world of instant DNA analysis should not obscure. The issue before us is not whether DNA can someday be used for identification; nor even whether it can today be used for identification; but whether it was used for identification here.

Today, it can fairly be said that fingerprints really are used to identify people—so well, in fact, that there would be no need for the expense of a separate, wholly redundant DNA confirmation of the same information. What DNA adds—what makes it a valuable weapon in the law enforcement arsenal—is the ability to solve unsolved crimes, by matching old crime-scene evidence against the profiles of people whose identities are already known. That is what was going on when King's DNA was taken, and we should not disguise the fact. Solving unsolved crimes is a noble objective, but it occupies a lower place in the American pantheon of noble objectives than the protection of our people from suspicion-less law-enforcement searches. The Fourth Amendment must prevail.

***

The Court disguises the vast (and scary) scope of its holding by promising a limitation it cannot deliver. The Court repeatedly says that DNA testing, and entry into a national DNA registry, will not befall thee and me, dear reader, but only those arrested for "serious offense[s]."[842] I cannot imagine what principle could possibly justify this limitation, and the Court does not attempt to suggest any. If one believes that DNA will "identify" someone arrested for assault, he must believe that it will "identify" someone arrested for a traffic offense. This Court does not base its judgments on senseless distinctions. At the end of the day, logic will out. When there comes before us the taking of DNA from an arrestee for a traffic violation, the Court will predictably (and quite rightly) say, "We can find no significant difference between this case and King." Make no mistake about it: As an entirely predictable consequence of today's decision, your DNA can be taken and entered into a national DNA database if you are ever arrested, rightly or wrongly, and for whatever reason.

The most regrettable aspect of the suspicion-less search that occurred here is that it proved to be quite unnecessary. All parties concede that it would have been entirely permissible, as far as the Fourth Amendment is concerned, for Maryland to take a sample of King's DNA as a consequence of his conviction for second-degree assault. So the ironic result of the Court's error is this: The only arrestees to whom the outcome here will ever make a difference are those who have been acquitted of the crime of arrest (so that their DNA could not have been taken upon conviction). In other words, this Act manages to burden uniquely the sole group for whom the Fourth Amendment's protections ought to be most jealously guarded: people who are innocent of the State's accusations.

Today's judgment will, to be sure, have the beneficial effect of solving more crimes; then again, so would the taking of DNA samples from anyone who flies on an airplane (surely the Transportation Security Administration needs to know the "identity" of the flying public), applies for a driver's license, or attends a public school. Perhaps the construction of such a genetic panopticon is wise. But I doubt that the proud men who wrote the charter of our liberties would have been so eager to open their mouths for royal inspection.

I therefore dissent, and hope that today's incursion upon the Fourth Amendment, like an earlier one, will someday be repudiated.

[842] Ante, at 28; see also ante, at 1, 9, 14, 17, 22, 23, 24 (repeatedly limiting the analysis to "serious offenses").

Black Letter Law

> The Court held that when officers make an arrest supported by probable cause to hold for a serious offense and bring the suspect to the station to be detained in custody, taking and analyzing a cheek swab of the arrestee's DNA is, like fingerprinting and photographing, a legitimate police booking procedure that is reasonable under the Fourth Amendment.

Discussion Problems:

3-1. Charlotte rents the ground floor of a three story apartment building. It contains two bedrooms; one is used by her nine-year old son, David. In July, her friend, Frank, begins to use David's room to cook and cut crack cocaine. Frank pays Charlotte $100 dollars a week for the use of the bedroom, and she gives him permission to use the room for that purpose. This goes on for about 6 months, with Frank visiting the apartment to cook and cut crack cocaine at least 50 times during this period. Eventually the neighbors complain the cops, and two police officers are sent out. They walk into the side yard of the apartment, and watch through a window as Frank cuts and bags about 100K worth of crack cocaine. The window did have a privacy blind, but it was only partially closed that night. Frank does not live in the apartment, but does occasionally "visit" Charlotte. Based upon what they observed the police break into the apartment an arrest Frank.

You are the trial judge and the defense has made a motion to exclude all of the evidence based upon an argument that by looking into the window while standing in the side yard of the apartment building they intruded on the defendant's privacy, violating his Fourth Amendment rights. How do you rule? Why?

3-2. Jones and Smith are next door neighbors. Smith thinks that Jones broke into his home and stole some stuff. Smith buys a scanner that can listen in to cordless phone conversations in the hopes that he will hear something from Jones that proves he broke into Smith's house. Smith eavesdrops on Jones, but never learns that he was committing burglaries, he does, however, learn that Jones is a local drug dealer and is selling drugs out of his home.

Smith calls the cops and they tell him to continue to listen in on Jones, and to please record the conversations. Smith does so, and eventually provides enough information to the police that they arrest Jones. At trial Jones moves to suppress the evidence because the "eavesdropping" by his neighbor was a violation of his Fourth Amendment rights.

You are the trial judge. How would you rule on this motion to suppress? Explain your reasoning.

3-3. Mr. Williams and the clerk shared a computer in addition to desk space, and both used it to access records and programs. They could not, however, use the computer simultaneously. To remedy this inconvenience, Mr. Williams brought his personal computer to work. He placed the machine on the common desk and connected it via the network to the common computer. Mr. Williams informed his co-worker that this way, he and she could input data simultaneously and access files from either computer.

Thereafter, Mr. Williams conducted all of his work on his personal computer. He did not install a password shield or otherwise attempt to exclude other employees from using his machine or gaining access to his files. Indeed, he left the computer running at all times-even in the evenings and while he was away from his desk.

At approximately the time Mr. Williams networked the two computers, the clerk began to experience difficulty opening files on the office machine. She wondered whether Mr. Williams's computer had something to do with the problem. She complained about the problem to Michael, a reserve police officer who happened to be in office that afternoon to send a fax. Michael was a former computer salesman and had helped the clerk manage computer difficulties before.

Michael proceeded to open various files and delete others on the office machine in an effort to speed its operation. Still, after approximately forty-five minutes of tinkering, he found himself unable to access a file in the QuickBooks accounting program. At some point, the clerk informed Michael that Mr. Williams had networked his personal computer to the city machine, leading Michael to suspect that he could not open the file in question because it was open on the other computer.

When Michael sat down at Mr. Williams's computer, which was switched on, as usual, he noticed almost immediately that the defendant was running a file-sharing program. Michael wondered if Mr. Williams had transferred the QuickBooks file to a remote machine. Michael clicked open the file-sharing program and accessed the transfer history. When he did, he observed a series of files with sexually suggestive names. Opening two or three, he found they contained child pornography.

After Michael confirmed that at least a few of the files contained illegal pornography, he and the sheriff seized the computer and obtained a warrant to search the entire hard drive.

At trial Mr. Williams makes a motion to suppress the evidence seized from his personal computer. How should the trial judge rule? Identify the best arguments for both the admissibility an suppression of this evidence.

-Notes-

Chapter 4: Unreasonableness, Probable Cause & Informants

Draper v. U.S.

79 S.Ct. 329
Supreme Court of the United States
James Alonzo DRAPER, Petitioner,
v.
UNITED STATES of America.
No. 136. | Argued Dec. 11, 1958. | Decided Jan. 26, 1959.

Mr. Justice WHITTAKER delivered the opinion of the Court.

Petitioner was convicted of knowingly concealing and transporting narcotic drugs in Denver, Colorado, in violation of 35 Stat. 614, as amended, 21 U.S.C. § 174, 21 U.S.C.A. § 174. His conviction was based in part on the use in evidence against him of two "envelopes containing [865 grams of] heroin" and a hypodermic syringe that had been taken from his person, following his arrest, by the arresting officer. Before the trial, he moved to suppress that evidence as having been secured through an unlawful search and seizure. After hearing, the District Court found that the arresting officer had probable cause to arrest petitioner without a warrant and that the subsequent search and seizure were therefore incident to a lawful arrest, and overruled the motion to suppress.[843]At the subsequent trial, that evidence was offered and, over petitioner's renewed objection, was received in evidence, and the trial resulted, as we have said, in petitioner's conviction. The Court of Appeals affirmed the conviction,[844], and certiorari was sought on the sole ground that the search and seizure violated the Fourth Amendment1 and therefore the use of the heroin in evidence vitiated the conviction. We granted the writ to determine that question.[845]

****331 *309** The evidence offered at the hearing on the motion to suppress was not substantially disputed. It established that one Marsh, a federal narcotic agent with 29 years' experience, was stationed at Denver; that one Hereford had been engaged as a "special employee" of the Bureau of Narcotics at Denver for about six months, and from time to time gave information to Marsh regarding violations of the narcotic laws, for which Hereford was paid small sums of money, and that Marsh had always found the information given by Hereford to be accurate and reliable. On September 3, 1956, Hereford told Marsh that James Draper (petitioner) recently had taken up abode at a stated address in Denver and "was peddling narcotics to several addicts" in that city. Four days later, on September 7, Hereford told Marsh "that Draper had gone to Chicago the day before [September 6] by train [and] that he was going to bring back three ounces of heroin [and] that he would return to Denver either on the morning of the 8th of September or the morning of the 9th of September also by train." Hereford also gave Marsh a detailed physical description of Draper and of the clothing he was wearing, and said that he would be carrying "a tan zipper bag," and that he habitually "walked real fast."

On the morning of September 8, Marsh and a Denver police officer went to the Denver Union Station and kept watch over all incoming trains from Chicago, but they did not see anyone fitting the description that Hereford had given. Repeating the process on the morning of September 9, they saw a person, having the exact physical

[843] 146 F.Supp. 689.

[844] 10 Cir., 248 F.2d 295.

[845] 357 U.S. 935, 78 S.Ct. 1386, 2 L.Ed.2d 1549.

attributes and wearing the precise clothing described by Hereford, alight from an incoming Chicago train and ***310** start walking "fast" toward the exit. He was carrying a tan zipper bag in his right hand and the left was thrust in his raincoat pocket. Marsh, accompanied by the police officer, overtook, stopped and arrested him. They then searched him and found the two "envelopes containing heroin" clutched in his left hand in his raincoat pocket, and found the syringe in the tan zipper bag. Marsh then took him (petitioner) into custody. Hereford died four days after the arrest and therefore did not testify at the hearing on the motion.

26 U.S.C. (Supp. V) § 7606, added by § 104(a) of the Narcotic Control Act of 1956, 70 Stat. 570, 26 U.S.C.A. § 7607, provides, in pertinent part:

"The Commissioner * * * and agents, of the Bureau of Narcotics * * * may...make arrests without warrant for violations of any law of the United States relating to narcotic drugs * * * where the violation is committed in the presence of the person making the arrest or where such person has reasonable grounds to believe that the person to be arrested has committed or is committing such violation."

The crucial question for us then is whether knowledge of the related facts and circumstances gave Marsh "probable cause" within the meaning of the Fourth Amendment, and "reasonable grounds" within the meaning of § 104(a), supra, to believe that petitioner had committed or was committing a violation of the narcotic laws. If it did, the arrest, though without a warrant was lawful ***311** and the ****332** subsequent search of petitioner's person and the seizure of the found heroin were validly made incident to a lawful arrest, and therefore the motion to suppress was properly overruled and the heroin was competently received in evidence at the trial.[846]

Petitioner does not dispute this analysis of the question for decision. Rather, he contends (1) that the information given by Hereford to Marsh was "hearsay" and, because hearsay is not legally competent evidence in a criminal trial, could not legally have been considered, but should have been put out of mind, by Marsh in assessing whether he had "probable cause" and "reasonable grounds" to arrest petitioner without a warrant, and (2) that, even if hearsay could lawfully have been considered, Marsh's information should be held insufficient to show "probable cause" and "reasonable grounds" to believe that petitioner had violated or was violating the narcotic laws and to justify his arrest without a warrant.

Considering the first contention, we find petitioner entirely in error. *Brinegar v. United States*[847]has settled the question the other way. There, in a similar situation, the convict contended "that the factors relating to inadmissibility of the evidence [for] purposes of proving guilt at the trial, deprive[d] the evidence as a whole of sufficiency to show probable cause for the search * * *."[848]But this Court, rejecting that contention, said:

"[T]he so-called distinction places a wholly unwarranted emphasis upon the criterion of admissibility in evidence, to prove the accused's guilt, of the facts relied upon to show probable cause. That emphasis, we think, goes much too far in confusing and disregarding the difference between what is required to prove guilt in a criminal case and what is ***312** required to show probable cause for arrest or search. It approaches requiring (if it does not in practical effect require) proof sufficient to establish guilt in order to substantiate the existence of probable cause. There is a large difference between the two things to be proved [guilt and probable cause], as well as between

[846] *Weeks v. United States*, 232 U.S. 383, 392, 34 S.Ct. 341, 344, 58 L.Ed. 652; *Carroll v. United States*, 267 U.S. 132, 158, 45 S.Ct. 280, 287, 69 L.Ed. 543; *Agnello v. United States*, 269 U.S. 20, 30, 46 S.Ct. 4, 5, 70 L.Ed. 145; *Giordenello v. United States*, 357 U.S. 480, 483, 78 S.Ct. 1245, 1248, 2 L.Ed.2d 1503.

[847] 338 U.S. 160, 172-173, 69 S.Ct. 1302, 1309 93 L.Ed. 1879.

[848] *Id.*, 338 U.S. 172, 69 S.Ct. 1309. (Emphasis added.)

the tribunals which determine them, and therefore a like difference in the quanta and modes of proof required to establish them."[849]

****333** Nor can we agree with petitioner's second contention that Marsh's information was insufficient to show probable cause and reasonable grounds to believe that petitioner had violated or was violating the narcotic laws and to justify his arrest without a warrant. The information given to narcotic agent Marsh by "special employee" ***313** Hereford may have been hearsay to Marsh, but coming from one employed for that purpose and whose information had always been found accurate and reliable, it is clear that Marsh would have been derelict in his duties had he not pursued it. And when, in pursuing that information, he saw a man, having the exact physical attributes and wearing the precise clothing and carrying the tan zipper bag that Hereford had described, alight from one of the very trains from the very place stated by Hereford and start to walk at a "fast" pace toward the station exit, Marsh had personally verified every facet of the information given him by Hereford except whether petitioner had accomplished his mission and had the three ounces of heroin on his person or in his bag. And surely, with every other bit of Hereford's information being thus personally verified, Marsh had "reasonable grounds" to believe that the remaining unverified bit of Hereford's information—that Draper would have the heroin with him—was likewise true.

"In dealing with probable cause, * * as the very name implies, we deal with probabilities. These are not technical; they are the factual and practical considerations of everyday life on which reasonable and prudent men, not legal technicians, act."[850]Probable cause exists where "the facts and circumstances within their [the arresting officers'] knowledge and of which they had reasonably trustworthy information [are] sufficient in themselves to warrant a man of reasonable caution in the belief that" an offense has been or is being committed.[851]

***314** We believe that, under the facts and circumstances here, Marsh had probable cause and reasonable grounds to believe that petitioner was committing a violation of the laws of the United States relating to narcotic drugs at the time he arrested him. The arrest was therefore lawful, and the subsequent search and seizure, having been made incident to that lawful arrest, were likewise valid. It follows that petitioner's motion to suppress was properly denied and that the seized heroin was competent evidence lawfully received at the trial.

Affirmed.

Black Letter Law

Information given by an informant to a government agent leading to arrest of defendant for violation of federal narcotics laws, even though hearsay, and even though not legally competent evidence in a criminal trial, could be considered in determining whether government agent had probable cause, and reasonable grounds to arrest defendant without a warrant.

"Probable cause" for an arrest exists where the facts and circumstances within an arresting officer's knowledge and of which he had reasonably trustworthy information are sufficient in themselves to warrant a man of reasonable caution in belief that an offense has been or is being committed.

This case established hearsay-based probable cause.

[849] 338 U.S. at pages 172-173, 69 S.Ct. at page 1309.

[850] *Brinegar v. United States, supra*, 338 U.S. at page 175, 69 S.Ct. at page 1310.

[851] *Carroll v. United States*, 267 U.S. 132, 162, 45 S.Ct. 280, 288.

Spinelli v. U.S.

89 S.Ct. 584

Supreme Court of the United States

William SPINELLI, Petitioner,

v.

UNITED STATES.

No. 8. | Argued Oct. 16 and 17, 1968. | Decided Jan. 27, 1969.

Mr. Justice HARLAN delivered the opinion of the Court.

William Spinelli was convicted under 18 U.S.C. s 19521 of traveling to St. Louis, Missouri, from a nearby Illinois suburb with the intention of conducting gambling activities proscribed by Missouri law.[852]At every appropriate stage in the proceedings in the lower courts, the petitioner challenged the constitutionality of the warrant which authorized the FBI search that uncovered the evidence necessary for his conviction. At each stage, Spinelli's challenge was treated in a different way. At a pretrial suppression hearing, the United States District Court for the Eastern District of Missouri held that Spinelli ***412** lacked standing to raise a Fourth Amendment objection. A unanimous panel of the Court of Appeals for the Eighth Circuit rejected the District Court's ground, a majority holding ****587** further that the warrant was issued without probable cause. After an en banc rehearing, the Court for Appeals sustained the warrant and affirmed the conviction by a vote of six to two.[853]Both the majority and dissenting en banc opinions reflect a most conscientious effort to apply the principles we announced in *Aguilar v. Texas*,[854]to a factual situation whose basic characteristics have not been at all uncommon in recent search warrant cases. Believing it desirable that the principles of *Aguilar* should be further explicated, we granted certiorari,[855]our writ being later limited to the question of the constitutional validity of the search and seizure.[856]For reasons that follow, we reverse.

In *Aguilar*, a search warrant had issued upon an affidavit of police officers who swore only that they had 'received reliable information from a credible person and do believe' that narcotics were being illegally stored on the described premises. While recognizing that the constitutional requirement of probable cause can be satisfied by hearsay information, this Court held the ***413** affidavit inadequate for two reasons. First, the application failed to set forth any of the 'underlying circumstances' necessary to enable the magistrate independently to judge of the validity of the informant's conclusion that the narcotics were where he said they were. Second, the affiant-officers did not attempt to support their claim that their informant was "credible' or his information 'reliable." The Government is, however, quite right in saying that the FBI affidavit in the present case is more ample than that in Aguilar. Not only does it contain a report from an anonymous informant, but it also contains a report of an independent FBI investigation which is said to corroborate the informant's tip. We are then, required to delineate the manner in which Aguilar's two-pronged test should be applied in these circumstances.

In essence, the affidavit, reproduced in full in the Appendix to this opinion, contained the following allegations:

---

[852] See Mo.Rev.Stat. s 563.360 (1959), V.A.M.S.

[853] 382 F.2d 871.

[854] 378 U.S. 108, 84 S.Ct. 1509, 12 L.Ed.2d 723 (1964),

[855] 390 U.S. 942, 88 S.Ct. 1025, 19 L.Ed.2d 1130.

[856] 391 U.S. 933, 88 S.Ct. 1834, 20 L.Ed.2d 853.

1. The FBI had kept track of Spinelli's movements on five days during the month of August 1965. On four of these occasions, Spinelli was seen crossing one of two bridges leading from Illinois into St. Louis, Missouri, between 11 a.m. and 12:15 p.m. On four of the five days, Spinelli was also seen parking his car in a lot used by residents of an ****588** apartment house at 1108 Indian Circle Drive in St. Louis, between 3:30 p.m. and 4:45 p.m. ***414** On one day, Spinelli was followed further and seen to enter a particular apartment in the building.

2. An FBI check with the telephone company revealed that this apartment contained two telephones listed under the name of Grace P. Hagen, and carrying the numbers WYdown 4-0029 and WYdown 4-0136.

3. The application stated that 'William Spinelli is known to this affiant and to federal law enforcement agents and local law enforcement agents as a bookmaker, an associate of bookmakers, a gambler, and an associate of gamblers.'

4. Finally it was stated that the FBI 'has been informed by a confidential reliable informant that William Spinelli is operating a handbook and accepting wagers and disseminating wagering information by means of the telephones which have been assigned the numbers WYdown 4-0029 and WYdown 4-0136.'

There can be no question that the last item mentioned, detailing the informant's tip, has a fundamental place in this warrant application. Without it, probable cause could not be established. The first two items reflect only innocent-seeming activity and data. Spinelli's travels to and from the apartment building and his entry into a particular apartment on one occasion could hardly be taken as bespeaking gambling activity; and there is surely nothing unusual about an apartment containing two separate telephones. Many a householder indulges himself in this petty luxury. Finally, the allegation that Spinelli was 'known' to the affiant and to other federal and local law enforcement officers as a gambler and an associate of gamblers is but a bald and unilluminating assertion of suspicion that is entitled to no weight in appraising the magistrate's decision.[857]

***415** So much indeed the Government does not deny. Rather, following the reasoning of the Court of Appeals, the Government claims that the informant's tip gives a suspicious color to the FBI's reports detailing Spinelli's innocent-seeming conduct and that, conversely, the FBI's surveillance corroborates the informant's tip, thereby entitling it to more weight. It is true, of course, that the magistrate is obligated to render a judgment based upon a common-sense reading of the entire affidavit.[858] We believe, however, that the 'totality of circumstances' approach taken by the Court of Appeals paints with too broad a brush. Where, as here, the informer's tip is a necessary element in a finding of probable cause, its proper weight must be determined by a more precise analysis.

The informer's report must first be measured against Aguilar's standards so that its probative value can be assessed. If the tip is found inadequate under Aguilar, the other allegations which corroborate the information contained in the hearsay report should then be considered. At this stage as well, however, the standards enunciated in Aguilar must inform the magistrate's decision. He must ask: Can it fairly be said that the tip, even when certain parts of it have been corroborated by independent sources, is as trustworthy as a tip which would pass Aguilar's tests without independent corroboration? Aguilar is relevant at this stage of the inquiry as well because the tests it establishes were designed to implement the ****589** long-standing principle that probable cause must be determined by a 'neutral and detached magistrate,' and not by 'the officer engaged in the often competitive enterprise of ferreting out crime.'[859] A magistrate cannot be said to have properly discharged his constitutional duty if he

---

[857] *Nathanson v. United States*, 290 U.S. 41, 46, 54 S.Ct. 11, 12, 78 L.Ed. 159 (1933).

[858] *United States v. Ventresca*, 380 U.S. 102, 108, 85 S.Ct. 741, 745, 13 L.Ed.2d 684 (1965).

[859] *Johnson v. United States*, 333 U.S. 10, 14, 68 S.Ct. 367, 369, 92 L.Ed. 436 (1948).

relies on an informer's tip which-even ***416** when partially corroborated-is not as reliable as one which passes Aguilar's requirements when standing alone.

Applying these principles to the present case, we first consider the weight to be given the informer's tip when it is considered apart from the rest of the affidavit. It is clear that a Commissioner could not credit it without abdicating his constitutional function. Though the affiant swore that his confidant was 'reliable,' he offered the magistrate no reason in support of this conclusion. Perhaps even more important is the fact that Aguilar's other test has not been satisfied. The tip does not contain a sufficient statement of the underlying circumstances from which the informer concluded that Spinelli was running a bookmaking operation. We are not told how the FBI's source received his information-it is not alleged that the informant personally observed Spinelli at work or that he had ever placed a bet with him. Moreover, if the informant came by the information indirectly, he did not explain why his sources were reliable.[860]In the absence of a statement detailing the manner in which the information was gathered, it is especially important that the tip describe the accused's criminal activity in sufficient detail that the magistrate may know that he is relying on something more substantial than a casual rumor circulating in the underworld or an accusation based merely on an individual's general reputation.

The detail provided by the informant in *Draper v. United States*[861] provides a suitable benchmark. While Hereford, the Government's informer in that case did not state the way in which he had obtained his information, he reported that Draper had gone to Chicago the day before by train and that he would return to Denver by train with three ounces of heroin on one of two specified mornings. Moreover, ***417** Hereford went on to describe, with minute particularity, the clothes that Draper would be wearing upon his arrival at the Denver station. A magistrate, when confronted with such detail, could reasonably infer that the informant had gained his information in a reliable way. Such an inference cannot be made in the present case. Here, the only facts supplied were that Spinelli was using two specified telephones and that these phones were being used in gambling operations. This meager report could easily have been obtained from an offhand remark heard at a neighborhood bar.

Nor do we believe that the patent doubts Aguilar raises as to the report's reliability are adequately resolved by a consideration of the allegations detailing the FBI's independent investigative efforts. At most, these allegations indicated that Spinelli could have used the telephones specified by the informant for some purpose. This cannot by itself be said to support both the inference that the informer was generally trustworthy and that he had made his charge against Spinelli on the basis of information obtained in a reliable way. Once again, Draper provides a relevant ****590** comparison. Independent police work in that case corroborated much more than one small detail that had been provided by the informant. There, the police, upon meeting the inbound Denver train on the second morning specified by informer Hereford, saw a man whose dress corresponded precisely to Hereford's detailed description. It was then apparent that the informant had not been fabricating his report out of whole cloth; since the report was of the sort which in common experience may be recognized as having been ***418** obtained in a reliable way, it was perfectly clear that probable cause had been established.

We conclude, then, that in the present case the informant's tip-even when corroborated to the extent indicated-was not sufficient to provide the basis for a finding of probable cause. This is not to say that the tip was so insubstantial that it could not properly have counted in the magistrate's determination. Rather, it needed some further support. When we look to the other parts of the application, however, we find nothing alleged which would permit the suspicions engendered by the informant's report to ripen into a judgment that a crime was probably being committed. As we

---

[860] Cf. *Jaben v. United States*, 381 U.S. 214, 85 S.Ct. 1365, 14 L.Ed.2d 345 (1965).

[861] 358 U.S. 307, 79 S.Ct. 329, 3 L.Ed.2d 327 (1959).

have already seen, the allegations detailing the FBI's surveillance of Spinelli and its investigation of the telephone company records contain no suggestion of criminal conduct when taken by themselves-and they are not endowed with an aura of suspicion by virtue of the informer's tip. Nor do we find that the FBI's reports take on a sinister color when read in light of common knowledge that bookmaking is often carried on over the telephone and from premises ostensibly used by others for perfectly normal purposes. Such an argument would carry weight in a situation in which the premises contain an unusual number of telephones or abnormal activity is observed,[862]but it does not fit this case where neither of these factors is present. All that remains to be considered is the flat statement that Spinelli was 'known' to the FBI and others as a gambler. But just as a simple assertion of police suspicion is not itself a sufficient basis for a magistrate's finding of probable cause, we do not believe it may be used to give ***419** additional weight to allegations that would otherwise be insufficient.

The affidavit, then, falls short of the standards set forth in Aguilar, Draper, and our other decisions that give content to the notion of probable cause. In holding as we have done, we do not retreat from the established propositions that only the probability, and not a prima facie showing, of criminal activity is the standard of probable cause;[863]that affidavits of probable cause are tested by much less rigorous standards than those governing the admissibility of evidence at trial;[864]****591** that in judging probable cause issuing magistrates are not to be confined by niggardly limitations or by restrictions on the use of their common sense;[865]and that their determination of probable cause should be paid great deference by reviewing courts.[866]But we cannot sustain this warrant without diluting important safeguards that assure that the judgment of a disinterested judicial officer will interpose itself between the police and the citizenry.

***420** The judgment of the Court of Appeals is reversed and the case is remanded to that court for further proceedings consistent with this opinion.

It is so ordered.

Reversed and remanded.

Mr. Justice MARSHALL took no part in the consideration or decision of this case.

APPENDIX TO OPINION OF THE COURT.

AFFIDAVIT IN SUPPORT OF SEARCH WARRANT.

I, Robert L. Bender, being duly sworn, depose and say that I am a Special Agent of the Federal Bureau of Investigation, and as such am authorized to make searches and seizures.

That on August 6, 1965, at approximately 11:44 a.m., William Spinelli was observed by an Agent of the Federal Bureau of Investigation driving a 1964 Ford convertible, Missouri license HC3-649, onto the Eastern approach of the Veterans Bridge leading from East St. Louis, Illinois, to St. Louis, Missouri.

That on August 11, 1965, at approximately 11:16 a.m., William Spinelli was observed by an Agent of the Federal Bureau of Investigation driving a 1964 Ford convertible, Missouri license HC3-649, onto the Eastern approach of the Eads Bridge leading from East St. Louis, Illinois, to St. Louis, Missouri.

---

[862] Cf. *McCray v. Illinois*, 386 U.S. 300, 302, 87 S.Ct. 1056, 1057, 18 L.Ed.2d 62 (1967).

[863] *Beck v. Ohio*, 379 U.S. 89, 96, 85 S.Ct. 223, 228, 13 L.Ed.2d 142 (1964).

[864] *McCray v. Illinois*, 386 U.S. 300, 311, 87 S.Ct. 1056, 1062 (1967).

[865] *United States v. Ventresca*, 380 U.S. 102, 108, 85 S.Ct. 741, 745 (1965).

[866] *Jones v. United States*, 362 U.S. 257, 270-271, 80 S.Ct. 725, 735-736 (1960).

Further, at approximately 11:18 a.m. on August 11, 1965, I observed William Spinelli driving the aforesaid Ford convertible from the Western approach of the Eads Bridge into St. Louis, Missouri.

Further, at approximately 4:40 p.m. on August 11, 1965, I observed the aforesaid Ford convertible, bearing Missouri license HC3-649, parked in a parking lot used by residents of The Chieftain Manor Apartments, approximately one block east of 1108 Indian Circle Drive.

On August 12, 1965, at approximately 12:07 p.m., ***421** William Spinelli was observed by an Agent of the Federal Bureau of Investigation driving the aforesaid 1964 Ford convertible onto the Eastern approach of the Veterans Bridge from East St. Louis, Illinois, in the direction of St. Louis, Missouri.

Further, on August 12, 1965, at approximately 3:46 p.m, I observed William Spinelli driving the aforesaid 1964 Ford convertible onto the parking lot used by the residents of The Chieftain Manor Apartments approximately one block east of 1108 Indian Circle Drive.

Further, on August 12, 1965, at approximately 3:49 p.m., William Spinelli was observed by an Agent of the Federal Bureau of Investigation entering the front entrance of the two-story apartment building located at 1108 Indian Circle Drive, this building being one of The Chieftain Manor Apartments.

On August 13, 1965, at approximately 11:08 a.m., William Spinelli was observed by an Agent of the Federal Bureau of Investigation driving the aforesaid Ford convertible onto the Eastern approach of the Eads Bridge from East St. Louis, Illinois, heading towards St. Louis, Missouri.

Further, on August 13, 1965, at approximately 11:11 a.m., I observed William ****592** Spinelli driving the aforesaid Ford convertible from the Western approach of the Eads Bridge into St. Louis, Missouri.

Further, on August 13, 1965, at approximately 3:45 p.m., I observed William Spinelli driving the aforesaid 1964 Ford convertible onto the parking area used by residents of The Chieftain Manor Apartments, said parking area being approximately one block from 1108 Indian Circle Drive.

Further, on August 13, 1965, at approximately 3:55 p.m., William Spinelli was observed by an Agent of the Federal Bureau of Investigation entering the corner apartment located on the second floor in the southwest corner, known as Apartment F, of the two-story ***422** apartment building known and numbered as 1108 Indian Circle Drive.

On August 16, 1965, at approximately 3:22 p.m., I observed William Spinelli driving the aforesaid Ford convertible onto the parking lot used by the residents of The Chieftain Manor Apartments approximately one block east of 1108 Indian Circle Drive.

Further, an Agent of the F.B.I. observed William Spinelli alight from the aforesaid Ford convertible and walk toward the apartment building located at 1108 Indian Circle Drive.

The records of the Southwestern Bell Telephone Company reflect that there are two telephones located in the southwest corner apartment on the second floor of the apartment building located at 1108 Indian Circle Drive under the name of Grace P. Hagen. The numbers listed in the Southwestern Bell Telephone Company records for the aforesaid telephones are WYdown 4-0029 and WYdown 4-0136.

William Spinelli is known to this affiant and to federal law enforcement agents and local law enforcement agents as a bookmaker, an associate of bookmakers, a gambler, and an associate of gamblers.

The Federal Bureau of Investigation has been informed by a confidential reliable informant that William Spinelli is operating a handbook and accepting wagers and disseminating wagering information by means of the telephones which have been assigned the numbers WYdown 4-0029 and WYdown 4-0136.

/s/ Robert L. Bender,

Robert L. Bender,

Special Agent, Federal Bureau of Investigation.

Subscribed and sworn to before me this 18th day of August, 1965, at St. Louis, Missouri.

/s/ William R. O'Toole.

***423** Mr. Justice WHITE, concurring.

An investigator's affidavit that he has seen gambling equipment being moved into a house at a specified address will support the issuance of a search warrant. The oath affirms the honesty of the statement and negatives the lie or imagination. Personal observation attests to the facts asserted-that there is gambling equipment on the premises at the named address.

But if the officer simply avers, without more, that there is gambling paraphernalia on certain premises, the warrant should not issue, even though the belief of the officer is an honest one, as evidenced by his oath, and even though the magistrate knows him to be an experienced, intelligent officer who has been reliable in the past. This much was settled in *Nathanson v. United States*,[867]where the Court held insufficient an officer's affidavit swearing he had cause to believe that there was illegal liquor on the premises for which the warrant was sought. The unsupported assertion or belief of the officer does not satisfy the requirement of probable cause.[868]

****593** What is missing in *Nathanson* and like cases is a statement of the basis for the affiant's believing the facts contained in the affidavit-the good 'cause' which the officer in *Nathanson* said he had. If an officer swears that there is gambling equipment at a certain address, the possibilities are (1) that he has seen the equipment; (2) that he has observed or perceived facts from which the presence of the equipment may reasonably be inferred; and (3) that he has obtained the information from someone else. If (1) is true, the affidavit is good. But in (2), the affidavit is insufficient unless the perceived facts are given, for it is the magistrate, not the ***424** officer, who is to judge the existence of probable cause.[869]With respect to (3), where the officer's information is hearsay, no warrant should issue absent good cause for crediting that hearsay. Because an affidavit asserting, without more, the location of gambling equipment at a particular address does not claim personal observation of any of the facts by the officer, and because of the likelihood that the information came from an unidentified third party, affidavits of this type are unacceptable.

Neither should the warrant issue if the officer states that there is gambling equipment in a particular apartment and that his information comes from an informant, named or unnamed, since the honesty of the informant and the basis for his report are unknown. Nor would the missing elements be completely supplied by the officer's oath that the informant has often furnished reliable information in the past. This attests to the honesty of the informant, but Aguilar v. Texas, supra, requires something more-did the information come from observation, or did the informant in turn receive it from another? Absent additional facts for believing the informant's report, his assertion stands no better than the oath of the officer to the same effect.

---

[867] 290 U.S. 41, 54 S.Ct. 11, 78 L.Ed. 159 (1933).

[868] *Jones v. United States*, 362 U.S. 257, 269, 80 S.Ct. 725, 735, 4 L.Ed.2d 697 (1960); *Grau v. United States*, 287 U.S. 124, 53 S.Ct. 38, 77 L.Ed. 212 (1932); *Byars v. United States*, 273 U.S. 28, 29, 47 S.Ct. 248, 71 L.Ed. 520 (1927).

[869] *Aguilar v. Texas*, 378 U.S. 108, 84 S.Ct. 1509, 12 L.Ed.2d 723 (1964); *Giordenello v. United States*, 357 U.S. 480, 486, 78 S.Ct. 1245, 1250, 2 L.Ed.2d 1503 (1958); *Johnson v. United States*, 333 U.S. 10, 14, 68 S.Ct. 367, 369, 92 L.Ed. 436 (1948).

Indeed, if the affidavit of an officer, known by the magistrate to be honest and experienced, stating that gambling equipment is located in a certain building is unacceptable, it would be quixotic if a similar statement from an honest informant were found to furnish probable cause. A strong argument can be made that both should be acceptable under the Fourth Amendment, but under our cases neither is. The past reliability of the informant can no more furnish probable cause for believing his ***425** current report than can previous experience with the officer himself.

If the affidavit rests on hearsay-an informant's report-what is necessary under Aguilar is one of two things: the informant must declare either (1) that he has himself seen or perceived the fact or facts asserted; or (2) that his information is hearsay, but there is good reason for believing it-perhaps one of the usual grounds for crediting hearsay information. The first presents few problems: since the report, although hearsay, purports to be first-hand observation, remaining doubt centers on the honesty of the informant, and that worry is dissipated by the officer's previous experience with the informant. The other basis for accepting the informant's report is more complicated. But if, for example, the informer's hearsay comes from one of the actors in the crime in the nature of admission against interest, the affidavit giving this information should be held sufficient.

I am inclined to agree with the majority that there are limited special circumstances in which an 'honest' informant's report, if sufficiently detailed, will in effect verify itself-that is, the magistrate when confronted with such detail could reasonably infer that the informant had gained his information in a reliable way.[870]Detailed information ****594** may sometimes imply that the informant himself has observed the facts. Suppose an informant with whom an officer has had satisfactory experience states that there is gambling equipment in the living room of a specified apartment and describes in detail not only the equipment itself but also the appointments and furnishments in the apartment. Detail like this, if true at all must rest on personal observation either of the informant or of someone else. If the latter, we know nothing of the third person's honesty or ***426** sources; he may be making a wholly false report. But it is arguable that on these facts it was the informant himself who has perceived the facts, for the information reported is not usually the subject of casual day-to-day conversation. Because the informant is honest and it is probable that he has viewed the facts, there is probable cause for the issuance of a warrant.

So too in the special circumstances of *Draper v. United States*,[871]the kind of information related by the informant is not generally sent ahead of a person's arrival in a city except to those who are intimately connected with making careful arrangements for meeting him. The informant, posited as honest, somehow had the reported facts, very likely from one of the actors in the plan, or as one of them himself. The majority's suggestion is that a warrant could have been obtained based only on the informer's report. I am inclined to agree, although it seems quite plain that if it may be so easily inferred from the affidavit that the informant has himself observed the facts or has them from an actor in the event, no possible harm could come from requiring a statement to that effect, thereby removing the difficult and recurring questions which arise in such situations.

Of course, Draper itself did not proceed on this basis. Instead the Court pointed out that when the officer saw a person getting off the train at the specified time, dressed and conducting himself precisely as the informant had predicted, all but the critical fact with respect to possessing narcotics had then been verified and for that reason the officer had 'reasonable grounds' to believe also that Draper was carrying narcotics. Unquestionably, verification of arrival time, dress, and gait reinforced the honesty of the informant-he had not reported a made-up story. But if what Draper stands for is that the existence of the tenth and critical fact ***427** is made sufficiently

---

[870] See *ante*, at 589.

[871] 358 U.S. 307, 79 S.Ct. 329, 3 L.Ed.2d 327 (1959).

probable to justify the issuance of a warrant by verifying nine other facts coming from the same source, I have my doubts about that case.

In the first place, the proposition is not that the tenth fact may be logically inferred from the other nine or that the tenth fact is usually found in conjunction with the other nine. No one would suggest that just anyone getting off the 10:30 train dressed as Draper was, with a brisk walk and carrying a zippy bag, should be arrested for carrying narcotics. The thrust of Draper is not that the verified facts have independent significance with respect to proof of the tenth. The argument instead relates to the reliability of the source: because an informant is right about some things, he is more probably right about other facts, usually the critical, unverified facts.

But the Court's cases have already rejected for Fourth Amendment purposes the notion that the past reliability of an officer is sufficient reason for believing his current assertions. Nor would it suffice, I suppose, if a reliable informant states there is gambling equipment in Apartment 607 and then proceeds to describe in detail Apartment 201, a description which is verified before applying for the warrant. He was right about 201, but that hardly makes him more believable about the equipment in 607. But what if he states that there are narcotics locked in a safe in Apartment 300, which is described in detail, and the apartment manager verifies everything but the contents ****595** of the safe? I doubt that the report about the narcotics is made appreciably more believable by the verification. The informant could still have gotten his information concerning the safe from others about whom nothing is known or could have inferred the presence of narcotics from circumstances which a magistrate would find unacceptable.

The tension between *Draper* and the *Nathanson-Aguilar* line of cases is evident from the course followed ***428** by the majority opinion. First, it is held that the report from a reliable informant that Spinelli is using two telephones with specified numbers to conduct a gambling business plus Spinelli's reputation in police circles as a gambler does not add up to probable cause. This is wholly consistent with *Aguilar* and *Nathanson*: the informant did not reveal whether he had personally observed the facts or heard them from another and, if the latter, no basis for crediting the hearsay was presented. Nor were the facts, as Mr. Justice Harlan says, of such a nature that they normally would be obtainable only by the personal observation of the informant himself. The police, however, did not stop with the informant's report. Independently, they established the existence of two phones having the given numbers and located them in an apartment house which Spinelli was regularly frequenting away from his home. There remained little question but that Spinelli was using the phones, and it was a fair inference that the use was not for domestic but for business purposes. The informant had claimed the business involved gambling. Since his specific information about Spinelli using two phones with particular numbers had been verified, did not his allegation about gambling thereby become sufficiently more believable if the Draper principle is to be given any scope at all? I would think so, particularly since information from the informant which was verified was not neutral, irrelevant information but was material to proving the gambling allegation: two phones with different numbers in an apartment used away from home indicates a business use in an operation, like bookmaking, where multiple phones are needed. The *Draper* approach would reasonably justify the issuance of a warrant in this case, particularly since the police had some awareness of Spinelli's past activities. The majority, however, ***429** while seemingly embracing *Draper*, confines that case to its own facts. Pending full-scale reconsideration of that case, on the one hand, or of the *Nathanson-Aguilar* cases on the other, I join the opinion of the Court and the judgment of reversal, especially since a vote to affirm would produce an equally divided Court.

Black Letter Law

Court laid out a two prong test for establishing whether or not information from an informant meets probable cause requirements. First, there should be be sufficient information establishing the 'underlying circumstances' necessary to enable the magistrate independently to judge of the validity of the informant's information. Second, the affiant-officers must provide information supporting their claim that their informant was "credible" or his information "reliable."

Illinois v. Gates

103 S.Ct. 2317

Supreme Court of the United States

ILLINOIS, Petitioner

v.

Lance GATES et ux

No. 81-430. | Argued Oct. 13, 1982. | Reargued March 1, 1983. | Decided June 8, 1983.

***216** Justice REHNQUIST delivered the opinion of the Court.

Respondents Lance and Susan Gates were indicted for violation of state drug laws after police officers, executing a search warrant, discovered marijuana and other contraband in their automobile and home. Prior to trial the Gates' moved to suppress evidence seized during this ****2321** search. The Illinois Supreme Court,[872]affirmed the decisions of lower state courts[873]granting the motion. It held that the affidavit submitted in support of the State's application for a warrant to search the Gates' property ***217** was inadequate under this Court's decisions in *Aguilar v. Texas*[874]and *Spinelli v. United States.*[875] We granted certiorari to consider the application of the Fourth Amendment to a magistrate's issuance of a search warrant on the basis of a partially corroborated anonymous informant's tip. After receiving briefs and hearing oral argument on this question, however, we requested the parties to address an additional question:

"Whether the rule requiring the exclusion at a criminal trial of evidence obtained in violation of the Fourth Amendment, *Mapp v. Ohio*,[876] *Weeks v. United States*,[877]should to any extent be modified, so as, for example, not to require the exclusion of evidence obtained in the reasonable belief that the search and seizure at issue was consistent with the Fourth Amendment."

We decide today, with apologies to all, that the issue we framed for the parties was not presented to the Illinois courts and, accordingly, do not address it. Rather, we consider the question originally presented in the petition for certiorari, and conclude that the Illinois Supreme Court read the requirements of our Fourth Amendment decisions too restrictively. Initially, however, we set forth our reasons for not address-

[872] 85 Ill.2d 376, 53 Ill.Dec. 218, 423 N.E.2d 887 (1981)

[873] 82 Ill.App.3d 749, 38 Ill.Dec. 62, 403 N.E.2d 77 (1980)

[874] 378 U.S. 108, 84 S.Ct. 1509, 12 L.Ed.2d 723 (1964).

[875] 393 U.S. 410, 89 S.Ct. 584, 21 L.Ed.2d 637 (1969).

[876] 367 U.S. 643, 81 S.Ct. 1684, 6 L.Ed.2d 1081 (1961).

[877] 232 U.S. 383, 34 S.Ct. 341, 58 L.Ed. 652 (1914).

ing the question regarding modification of the exclusionary rule framed in our order of November 29, 1982.[878]

I

Our certiorari jurisdiction over decisions from state courts derives from 28 U.S.C. § 1257, which provides that "Final judgments or decrees rendered by the highest court of a State in which a decision could be had, may be reviewed by the Supreme Court as follows: ... (3) By writ of certiorari, ... where any title, right, privilege or immunity is specially set up or claimed under the Constitution, treaties or statutes ***218** of ... the United States."[879]

Although we have spoken frequently on the meaning of § 1257 and its predecessors, our decisions are in some respects not entirely clear. We held early on that § 25 of the Judiciary Act of 1789 furnished us with no jurisdiction unless a federal question had been both raised and decided in the state court below. As Justice Story wrote in *Crowell v. Randell*,[880]"If both of these requirements do not appear on the record, the appellate jurisdiction fails."[881]

More recently, in *McGoldrick v. Compagnie Generale*,[882]the Court observed:

> ****2322** But it is also the settled practice of this Court, in the exercise of its appellate jurisdiction, that it is only in exceptional cases, and then only in cases coming from the federal courts, that it considers questions urged by a petitioner or appellant not pressed or passed upon in the courts below.... In cases coming here from state courts in which a state statute is assailed as unconstitutional, there are reasons of peculiar force which should lead us to refrain from deciding questions not presented or decided in the highest court of the state whose judicial action we are called upon to review. Apart from the ***219** reluctance with which every court should proceed to set aside legislation as unconstitutional on grounds not properly presented, due regard for the appropriate relationship of this Court to state courts requires us to decline to consider and decide questions affecting the validity of state statutes not urged or considered there. It is for these reasons that this Court, where the constitutionality of a statute has been upheld in the state court, consistently refuses to consider any grounds of attack not raised or decided in that court.

Finally, the Court seemed to reaffirm the jurisdictional character of the rule against our deciding claims "not pressed nor passed upon" in state court in *State Farm Mutual Automobile Insurance Co. v. Duel*,[883]where we explained that "since the [state] Supreme Court did not pass on the question, we may not do so."[884]
Notwithstanding these decisions, however, several of our more recent cases have treated the so-called "not pressed or passed upon below" rule as merely a prudential restriction. In *Terminiello v. Chicago*,[885]the Court reversed a state criminal conviction on a ground not urged in state court, nor even in this Court. Likewise, in *Vachon v. New Hampshire*,[886]the Court summarily reversed a state criminal conviction on the ground, not raised in state court, or here, that it had been obtained in violation of the Due Process Clause of the Fourteenth Amendment. The Court indicated in a foot-

[878] --- U.S. ----, 103 S.Ct. 436, 74 L.Ed.2d 595.

[879] The provision derives, albeit with important alterations, see, e.g., Act of December 23, 1914, c. 2, 38 Stat. 790; Act of June 25, 1948, c. 646, 62 Stat. 929, from the Judiciary Act of 1789, c. 20, § 25, 1 Stat. 85.

[880] 10 Pet. 368, 391, 9 L.Ed. 458 (1836).

[881] See also *Owings v. Norwood's Lessee*, 5 Cranch. 344, 3 L.Ed. 120 (1809).

[882] 309 U.S. 430, 435-436, 60 S.Ct. 670, 673, 84 L.Ed. 849 (1940).

[883] 324 U.S. 154, 160, 65 S.Ct. 573, 576, 89 L.Ed. 812 (1945).

[884] See also *Hill v. California*, 401 U.S. 797, 805-806, 91 S.Ct. 1106, 1111, 1112, 28 L.Ed.2d 484 (1971).

[885] 337 U.S. 1, 69 S.Ct. 894, 93 L.Ed. 1131 (1949).

[886] 414 U.S. 478, 94 S.Ct. 664, 38 L.Ed.2d 666 (1974).

note,[887]that it possessed discretion to ignore the failure to raise in state court the question on which it decided the case.

In addition to this lack of clarity as to the character of the "not pressed or passed upon below" rule, we have recognized that it often may be unclear whether the particular federal question presented in this Court was raised or passed upon below. In *Dewey v. Des Moines*,[888]the fullest treatment of the subject, the Court said ***220** that "if the question were only an enlargement of the one mentioned in the assignment of errors, or if it were so connected with it in substance as to form but another ground or reason for alleging the invalidity of the [lower court's] judgment, we should have no hesitation in holding the assignment sufficient to permit the question to be now raised and argued. Parties are not confined here to the same arguments which were advanced in the courts below upon a Federal question there discussed." We have not attempted, and ****2323** likely would not have been able, to draw a clear-cut line between cases involving only an "enlargement" of questions presented below and those involving entirely new questions.

The application of these principles in the instant case is not entirely straightforward. It is clear in this case that respondents expressly raised, at every level of the Illinois judicial system, the claim that the Fourth Amendment had been violated by the actions of the Illinois police and that the evidence seized by the officers should be excluded from their trial. It also is clear that the State challenged, at every level of the Illinois court system, respondents' claim that the substantive requirements of the Fourth Amendment had been violated. The State never, however, raised or addressed the question whether the federal exclusionary rule should be modified in any respect, and none of the opinions of the ***221** Illinois courts give any indication that the question was considered.

The case, of course, is before us on the State's petition for a writ of certiorari. Since the Act of December 23, 1914,[889]jurisdiction has been vested in this Court to review state court decisions even when a claimed federal right has been upheld. Our prior decisions interpreting the "not pressed or passed on below" rule have not, however, involved a State's failure to raise a defense to a federal right or remedy asserted below. As explained below, however, we can see no reason to treat the State's failure to have challenged an asserted federal claim differently from the failure of the proponent of a federal claim to have raised that claim.

We have identified several purposes underlying the "not pressed or passed upon" rule: for the most part, these are as applicable to the State's failure to have opposed the assertion of a particular federal right, as to a party's failure to have asserted the claim. First, "questions not raised below are those on which the record is very likely to be inadequate since it certainly was not compiled with those questions in mind."[890]Exactly the same difficulty exists when the state urges modification of an existing constitutional right or accompanying remedy. Here, for example, the record contains little, if anything, regarding the subjective good faith of the police officers that searched the Gates' property-which might well be an important consideration in determining whether to fashion a good faith exception to the exclusionary rule. Our consideration of whether to modify the exclusionary rule plainly would benefit from a record containing such facts.

Likewise, "due regard for the appropriate relationship of this Court to state courts," *McGoldrick v. Compagnie Generale*[891]demands that those courts be given an

[887] *Id.*, at 479, n. 3, 94 S.Ct., at 665, n. 3.

[888] 173 U.S. 193, 197-198, 19 S.Ct. 379, 380-381, 43 L.Ed. 665 (1899).

[889] c. 2, 38 Stat. 790.

[890] *Cardinale v. Louisiana*, 394 U.S. 437, 439, 89 S.Ct. 1161, 1163, 22 L.Ed.2d 398 (1969).

[891] 309 U.S. 430, 435-436, 60 S.Ct. 670, 673, 84 L.Ed. 849 (1940).

opportunity to consider the constitutionality of the actions of state officials, and, equally important, proposed changes in existing remedies for unconstitutional ***222** actions. Finally, by requiring that the State first argue to the state courts that the federal exclusionary rule should be modified, we permit a state court, even if it agrees with the State as a matter of federal law, to rest its decision on an adequate and independent state ground.[892]In short, the reasons supporting our refusal to hear federal claims not raised in state court apply with equal force to the State's failure to challenge the availability of a well-settled federal remedy. Whether the "not pressed or passed upon below" rule is jurisdictional, as our earlier decisions indicate,[893]or prudential, as several of our later decisions assume, nor whether its character might be different in cases like ****2324** this from its character elsewhere, we need not decide. Whatever the character of the rule may be, consideration of the question presented in our order of November 29, 1982, would be contrary to the sound justifications for the "not pressed or passed upon below" rule, and we thus decide not to pass on the issue.

The fact that the Illinois courts affirmatively applied the federal exclusionary rule-suppressing evidence against respondents-does not affect our conclusion. In *Morrison v. Watson*,[894]the Court was asked to consider whether a state statute impaired the appellant's contract with the appellee. It declined to hear the case because the question presented here had not been pressed or passed on below. The Court acknowledged that the lower court's opinion had restated the conclusion, set forth in an earlier decision of that court, that the state statute did not impermissibly impair contractual obligations. Nonetheless, it held that there was no showing that "there was any real contest at any stage of this case upon the point,"[895]and that without such a contest, the routine restatement ***223** and application of settled law by an appellate court did not satisfy the "not pressed or passed upon below" rule. Similarly, in the present case, although the Illinois courts applied the federal exclusionary rule, there was never "any real contest" upon the point. The application of the exclusionary rule was merely a routine act, once a violation of the Fourth Amendment had been found, and not the considered judgment of the Illinois courts on the question whether application of a modified rule would be warranted on the facts of this case. In such circumstances, absent the adversarial dispute necessary to apprise the state court of the arguments for not applying the exclusionary rule, we will not consider the question whether the exclusionary rule should be modified.

Likewise, we do not believe that the State's repeated opposition to respondent's substantive Fourth Amendment claims suffices to have raised the question whether the exclusionary rule should be modified. The exclusionary rule is "a judicially created remedy designed to safeguard Fourth Amendment rights generally" and not "a personal constitutional right of the party aggrieved."[896]The question whether the exclusionary rule's remedy is appropriate in a particular context has long been regarded as an issue separate from the question whether the Fourth Amendment rights of the party seeking to invoke the rule were violated by police conduct.[897]Because of this distinction, we cannot say that modification or abolition of the exclusionary rule is "so connected with [the substantive Fourth Amendment right at issue] as to form but

---

[892] See *Cardinale*, *supra*, 394 U.S., at 439, 89 S.Ct., at 1163. Illinois, for example, adopted an exclusionary rule as early as 1923, see *People v. Brocamp*, 307 Ill. 448, 138 N.E. 728 (1923), and might adhere to its view even if it thought we would conclude that the federal rule should be modified.

[893] See 2320, *supra*.

[894] 154 U.S. 111, 14 S.Ct. 995, 138 L.Ed. 927 (1894).

[895] *Id*., at 115, 14 S.Ct., at 997.

[896] *United States v. Calandra*, 414 U.S. 338, 348, 94 S.Ct. 613, 620, 38 L.Ed.2d 561 (1974).

[897] See, e.g., *United States v. Havens*, 446 U.S. 620, 100 S.Ct. 1912, 64 L.Ed.2d 559 (1980); *United States v. Ceccolini*, 435 U.S. 268, 98 S.Ct. 1054, 55 L.Ed.2d 268 (1978); *United States v. Calandra, supra*; *Stone v. Powell*, 428 U.S. 465, 96 S.Ct. 3037, 49 L.Ed.2d 1067 (1976).

another ground or reason for alleging the invalidity" of the judgment.[898]Rather, the rule's modification was, for purposes of the "not pressed or passed upon below" rule, a separate claim that had to be specifically presented to the State courts.

***224** Finally, weighty prudential considerations militate against our considering the question presented in our order of November 29, 1982. The extent of the continued validity of the rules that have developed from our decisions in *Weeks v. United States*,[899]and *Mapp v. Ohio*,[900]is an issue of unusual significance. Sufficient evidence of this lies just in the comments on the issue that members of this Court recently have made.[901] ****2325** Where difficult issues of great public importance are involved, there are strong reasons to adhere scrupulously to the customary limitations on our discretion. By doing so we "promote respect ... for the Court's adjudicatory process [and] the stability of [our] decisions."[902]Moreover, fidelity to the rule guarantees that a factual record will be available to us, thereby discouraging the framing of broad rules, seemingly sensible on one set of facts, which may prove ill-considered in other circumstances. In Justice Harlan's words, adherence to the rule lessens the threat of "untoward practical ramifications,"[903]not foreseen at the time of decision. The public importance of our decisions in *Weeks* and *Mapp* and the emotions engendered by the debate surrounding these decisions counsel that we meticulously observe our customary procedural rules. By following this course, we promote respect for the procedures by which our decisions are rendered, as well as confidence in the stability of prior decisions. A wise exercise of the powers confided in this Court dictates that we reserve for another day the question whether the exclusionary rule should be modified.

***225 II**

We now turn to the question presented in the State's original petition for certiorari, which requires us to decide whether respondents' rights under the Fourth and Fourteenth Amendments were violated by the search of their car and house. A chronological statement of events usefully introduces the issues at stake. Bloomingdale, Ill., is a suburb of Chicago located in DuPage County. On May 3, 1978, the Bloomingdale Police Department received by mail an anonymous handwritten letter which read as follows:

"This letter is to inform you that you have a couple in your town who strictly make their living on selling drugs. They are Sue and Lance Gates, they live on Greenway, off Bloomingdale Rd. in the condominiums. Most of their buys are done in Florida. Sue his wife drives their car to Florida, where she leaves it to be loaded up with drugs, then Lance flys down and drives it back. Sue flys back after she drops the car off in Florida. May 3 she is driving down there again and Lance will be flying down in a few days to drive it back. At the time Lance drives the car back he has the trunk loaded with over $100,000.00 in drugs. Presently they have over $100,000.00 worth of drugs in their basement.

They brag about the fact they never have to work, and make their entire living on pushers.

---

[898] *Dewey v. Des Moines*, *supra*, 173 U.S., at 197-198, 19 S.Ct., at 380-381.

[899] 232 U.S. 383, 34 S.Ct. 341, 58 L.Ed. 652 (1961).

[900] 367 U.S. 643, 81 S.Ct. 1684, 6 L.Ed.2d 1081 (1961).

[901] E.g., *Bivens v. Six Unknown Named Agents*, 403 U.S. 388, 415, 91 S.Ct. 1999, 2014, 29 L.Ed.2d 619 (1971) (BURGER, C.J., dissenting); *Coolidge v. New Hampshire*, 403 U.S. 443, 490, 91 S.Ct. 2022, 2050, 29 L.Ed.2d 564 (1971) (Harlan, J., concurring); *id.*, at 502, 91 S.Ct., at 2056 (Black, J., dissenting); *Stone v. Powell*, 428 U.S. 465, 537-539, 96 S.Ct. 3037, 3072-3073, 49 L.Ed.2d 1067 (1976) (WHITE, J., dissenting); *Brewer v. Williams*, 430 U.S. 387, 413-414, 97 S.Ct. 1232, ----, 51 L.Ed.2d 424 (1977) (POWELL, J., concurring); *Robbins v. California*, 453 U.S. 420, 437, 443-444, 101 S.Ct. 2841, 2851, 2854-2855, 69 L.Ed.2d 744 (1981) (REHNQUIST, J., dissenting).

[902] *Mapp v. Ohio*, *supra*, 367 U.S., at 677, 81 S.Ct., at 1703 (Harlan, J., dissenting).

[903] *Id.*, at 676, 81 S.Ct., at 1703 (Harlan, J., dissenting).

I guarantee if you watch them carefully you will make a big catch. They are friends with some big drugs dealers, who visit their house often.

Lance & Susan Gates

Greenwayin Condominiums"

The letter was referred by the Chief of Police of the Bloomingdale Police Department to Detective Mader, who decided to pursue the tip. Mader learned, from the office of the Illinois Secretary of State, that an Illinois driver's license had ***226** been issued to one Lance Gates, residing at a stated address in Bloomingdale. He contacted a confidential informant, whose examination of certain financial records revealed a more recent address for the Gates, and he also learned from a police officer assigned to O'Hare Airport that "L. Gates" ****2326** had made a reservation on Eastern Airlines flight 245 to West Palm Beach, Fla., scheduled to depart from Chicago on May 5 at 4:15 p.m.

Mader then made arrangements with an agent of the Drug Enforcement Administration for surveillance of the May 5 Eastern Airlines flight. The agent later reported to Mader that Gates had boarded the flight, and that federal agents in Florida had observed him arrive in West Palm Beach and take a taxi to the nearby Holiday Inn. They also reported that Gates went to a room registered to one Susan Gates and that, at 7:00 a.m. the next morning, Gates and an unidentified woman left the motel in a Mercury bearing Illinois license plates and drove northbound on an interstate frequently used by travelers to the Chicago area. In addition, the DEA agent informed Mader that the license plate number on the Mercury registered to a Hornet station wagon owned by Gates. The agent also advised Mader that the driving time between West Palm Beach and Bloomingdale was approximately 22 to 24 hours.

Mader signed an affidavit setting forth the foregoing facts, and submitted it to a judge of the Circuit Court of DuPage County, together with a copy of the anonymous letter. The judge of that court thereupon issued a search warrant for the Gates' residence and for their automobile. The judge, in deciding to issue the warrant, could have determined that the modus operandi of the Gates had been substantially corroborated. As the anonymous letter predicted, Lance Gates had flown from Chicago to West Palm Beach late in the afternoon of May 5th, had checked into a hotel room registered in the name of his wife, and, at 7:00 a.m. the following morning, had headed north, accompanied by an unidentified woman, ***227** out of West Palm Beach on an interstate highway used by travelers from South Florida to Chicago in an automobile bearing a license plate issued to him.

At 5:15 a.m. on March 7th, only 36 hours after he had flown out of Chicago, Lance Gates, and his wife, returned to their home in Bloomingdale, driving the car in which they had left West Palm Beach some 22 hours earlier. The Bloomingdale police were awaiting them, searched the trunk of the Mercury, and uncovered approximately 350 pounds of marijuana. A search of the Gates' home revealed marijuana, weapons, and other contraband. The Illinois Circuit Court ordered suppression of all these items, on the ground that the affidavit submitted to the Circuit Judge failed to support the necessary determination of probable cause to believe that the Gates' automobile and home contained the contraband in question. This decision was affirmed in turn by the Illinois Appellate Court and by a divided vote of the Supreme Court of Illinois.

The Illinois Supreme Court concluded-and we are inclined to agree-that, standing alone, the anonymous letter sent to the Bloomingdale Police Department would not provide the basis for a magistrate's determination that there was probable cause to believe contraband would be found in the Gates' car and home. The letter provides virtually nothing from which one might conclude that its author is either honest or his information reliable; likewise, the letter gives absolutely no indication of the basis for the writer's predictions regarding the Gates' criminal activities. Something more was required, then, before a magistrate could conclude that there was probable cause to believe that contraband would be found in the Gates' home and car.[904]

The Illinois Supreme Court also properly recognized that Detective Mader's affidavit might be capable of supplementing ***228** the anonymous letter with information sufficient to permit a determination of probable cause.[905] ****2327** In holding that the affidavit in fact did not contain sufficient additional information to sustain a determination of probable cause, the Illinois court applied a "two-pronged test," derived from our decision in *Spinelli v. United States.*[906] The Illinois Supreme Court, like some others, apparently understood Spinelli as requiring that the anonymous letter satisfy each of two independent requirements before it could be relied on.[907]According to this view, the letter, as supplemented by Mader's affidavit, first had to adequately reveal the "basis of knowledge" of the letter writer-the particular means by which he came by the information given in his report. Second, it had to provide ***229** facts sufficiently establishing either the "veracity" of the affiant's informant, or, alternatively, the "reliability" of the informant's report in this particular case.

The Illinois court, alluding to an elaborate set of legal rules that have developed among various lower courts to enforce the "two-pronged test,"4 found that the test had not been satisfied. First, the "veracity" prong was not satisfied because, "there was simply no basis [for] ... concluding that the anonymous person [who wrote the letter to the Bloomingdale Police Department] was credible."[908]The court indicated that corroboration by police of details contained in the letter might never satisfy the "veracity" prong, and in any event, could not do so if, as in the present case, only "innocent" details are corroborated.[909] ****2328** In addition, the letter gave no indication of the basis of its writer's knowledge of the ***230** Gates' activities. The Illinois court understood Spinelli as permitting the detail contained in a tip to be used to infer that the informant had a reliable basis for his statements, but it thought that the anonymous letter failed to provide sufficient detail to permit such an inference. Thus, it concluded that no showing of probable cause had been made.

We agree with the Illinois Supreme Court that an informant's "veracity," "reliability" and "basis of knowledge" are all highly relevant in determining the value of his report. We do not agree, however, that these elements should be understood as entirely separate and independent requirements to be rigidly exacted in every case, which the opinion of the Supreme Court of Illinois would imply. Rather, as detailed below, they should be understood simply as closely intertwined issues that may usefully illuminate the commonsense, practical question whether there is "probable cause" to believe that contraband or evidence is located in a particular place.

III

This totality-of-the-circumstances approach is far more consistent with our prior treatment of probable cause than ***231** is any rigid demand that specific "tests" be satisfied by every informant's tip. Perhaps the central teaching of our decisions bearing on the probable cause standard is that it is a "practical, nontechnical conception."[910]"In dealing with probable cause, ... as the very name implies, we deal with probabilities. These are not technical; they are the factual and practical consid-

---

904 See *Aguilar v. Texas*, 378 U.S. 108, 109, n. 1, 84 S.Ct. 1509, 1511, n. 1, 12 L.Ed.2d 723 (1964); *Nathanson v. United States*, 290 U.S. 41, 54 S.Ct. 11, 78 L.Ed. 159 (1933).

905 See *Whiteley v. Warden*, 401 U.S. 560, 567, 91 S.Ct. 1031, 1036, 28 L.Ed.2d 306 (1971).

906 393 U.S. 410, 89 S.Ct. 584, 21 L.Ed.2d 637 (1969).

907 J.A., at 5.

908 J.A., at 7a.

909 J.A., at 12a.

910 *Brinegar v. United States*, 338 U.S. 160, 176, 69 S.Ct. 1302, 1311, 93 L.Ed. 1879 (1949).

erations of everyday life on which reasonable and prudent men, not legal technicians, act."[911]Our observation in *United States v. Cortez*,[912]regarding "particularized suspicion," is also applicable to the probable cause standard:

The process does not deal with hard certainties, but with probabilities. Long before the law of probabilities was articulated ****2329** as such, practical people formulated certain common-sense conclusions about human behavior; jurors as fact-finders are permitted to do the same-and ***232** so are law enforcement officers. Finally, the evidence thus collected must be seen and weighed not in terms of library analysis by scholars, but as understood by those versed in the field of law enforcement.

As these comments illustrate, probable cause is a fluid concept-turning on the assessment of probabilities in particular factual contexts-not readily, or even usefully, reduced to a neat set of legal rules. Informants' tips doubtless come in many shapes and sizes from many different types of persons. As we said in *Adams v. Williams*,[913] "informants' tips, like all other clues and evidence coming to a policeman on the scene may vary greatly in their value and reliability." Rigid legal rules are ill-suited to an area of such diversity. "One simple rule will not cover every situation."[914]

***233** Moreover, the "two-pronged test" directs analysis into two largely independent channels-the informant's "veracity" or "reliability" and his "basis of knowledge."[915]There are persuasive arguments against according these two elements such independent status. Instead, they are better understood as relevant considerations in the totality of the circumstances analysis that traditionally has guided probable cause determinations: a deficiency in one may be compensated for, in determining the overall reliability of a tip, by a strong showing as to the other, or by some other indicia of reliability.[916]

If, for example, a particular informant is known for the unusual reliability of his predictions of certain types of criminal activities in a locality, his failure, in a particular case, to thoroughly set forth the basis of his knowledge surely should not serve as an absolute bar to a finding of probable ****2330** cause based on his tip.[917]Likewise, if an unquestionably honest citizen comes forward with a report of criminal activity-which if fabricated would subject him to criminal liability, we have found ***234** rigorous scrutiny of the basis of his knowledge unnecessary.[918]Conversely, even if we entertain some doubt as to an informant's motives, his explicit and detailed description of alleged wrongdoing, along with a statement that the event was observed first-hand, entitles his tip to greater weight than might otherwise be the case. Unlike a totality of the circumstances analysis, which permits a balanced assessment of the relative weights of all the various indicia of reliability (and unreliability) attending an informant's tip, the "two-pronged test" has encouraged an excessively technical dissection of informants' tips, with undue attention ***235** being focused on isolated issues that cannot sensibly be divorced from the other facts presented to the magistrate.

---

[911] *Id.*, at 175, 69 S.Ct., at 1310.

[912] 449 U.S. 411, 418, 101 S.Ct. 690, 695, 66 L.Ed.2d 621 (1981).

[913] 407 U.S. 143, 147, 92 S.Ct. 1921, 1924, 32 L.Ed.2d 612 (1972).

[914] *Ibid.*

[915] See nn. 4 and 5 *supra*.

[916] See, e.g., *Adams v. Williams, supra*, 407 U.S., at 146-147, 92 S.Ct., at 1923-1924; *Harris v. United States*, 403 U.S. 573, 91 S.Ct. 2075, 29 L.Ed.2d 723 (1971).

[917] See *United States v. Sellers*, 483 F.2d 37 (CA5 1973).

[918] *Adams v. Williams, supra*.

As early as *Locke v. United States*,[919]Chief Justice Marshall observed, in a closely related context, that "the term 'probable cause,' according to its usual acceptation, means less than evidence which would justify condemnation... It imports a seizure made under circumstances which warrant suspicion." More recently, we said that "the quanta... of proof" appropriate in ordinary judicial proceedings are inapplicable to the decision to issue a warrant.[920]Finely tuned standards such as proof beyond a reasonable doubt or by a preponderance of the evidence, useful in formal trials, have no place in the magistrate's decision. While an effort to fix some general, numerically precise degree of certainty corresponding to "probable cause" may not be helpful, it is clear that "only the probability, and not a prima facie showing, of criminal activity is the standard of probable cause."[921] We also have recognized that affidavits "are normally drafted by non-lawyers in the midst and haste of a criminal investigation. Technical requirements of elaborate specificity once exacted under common law ****2331** pleading have no proper place in this area."[922]Likewise, search and arrest warrants long have been issued by persons who are neither lawyers nor judges, and who certainly do not remain abreast of each judicial refinement of the nature of "probable cause."[923]The rigorous inquiry into the Spinelli prongs and the complex superstructure of evidentiary and analytical rules that some have seen implicit in our Spinelli decision, cannot be reconciled with the fact that many warrants are-quite properly, ibid.-issued on the basis of nontechnical, ***236** commonsense judgments of laymen applying a standard less demanding than those used in more formal legal proceedings. Likewise, given the informal, often hurried context in which it must be applied, the "built-in subtleties"[924] of the "two-pronged test" are particularly unlikely to assist magistrates in determining probable cause.

Similarly, we have repeatedly said that after-the-fact scrutiny by courts of the sufficiency of an affidavit should not take the form of de novo review. A magistrate's "determination of probable cause should be paid great deference by reviewing courts."[925]"A grudging or negative attitude by reviewing courts toward warrants"[926] is inconsistent with the Fourth Amendment's strong preference for searches conducted pursuant to a warrant "courts should not invalidate ... warrant[s] by interpreting affidavit [s] in a hypertechnical, rather than a commonsense, manner." *Id.*, at 109, 85 S.Ct., at 746.

If the affidavits submitted by police officers are subjected to the type of scrutiny some courts have deemed appropriate, police might well resort to warrantless searches, with the hope of relying on consent or some other exception to the warrant clause that might develop at the time of the search. In addition, the possession of a warrant by officers conducting an arrest or search greatly reduces the perception of unlawful or intrusive police conduct, by assuring "the individual whose property is searched or seized of the lawful authority of the executing officer, his need to search, and the limits of his power to search."[927]Reflecting this preference for the warrant process, the traditional standard for review of an issuing magistrate's probable cause determination has been that so long as the magistrate had a "substantial basis for ...

---

919 7 Cranch. 339, 348, 3 L.Ed. 364 (1813).

920 *Brinegar, supra*, 338 U.S., at 173, 69 S.Ct., at 1309.

921 *Spinelli, supra*, 393 U.S., at 419, 89 S.Ct., at 590. See Model Code of Pre-Arraignment Procedure § 210.1(7) (Proposed Off. Draft 1972); W. LaFave, Search and Seizure, § 3.2(3) (1978).

922 *Ventresca, supra*, 380 U.S., at 108, 85 S.Ct., at 745.

923 See *Shadwick v. City of Tampa*, 407 U.S. 345, 348-350, 92 S.Ct. 2119, 2121-2122, 32 L.Ed.2d 783 (1972).

924 *Stanley v. State*, 19 Md.App. 507, 313 A.2d 847, 860 (Md.App.1974).

925 *Spinelli, supra*, 393 U.S., at 419, 89 S.Ct., at 590.

926 *Ventresca, supra*, 380 U.S., at 108, 85 S.Ct., at 745.

927 *United States v. Chadwick*, 433 U.S. 1, 9, 97 S.Ct. 2476, 2482, 53 L.Ed.2d 538 (1977).

concluding" that a search would uncover evidence of wrongdoing, the Fourth Amendment requires no more.[928]***237** We think reaffirmation of this standard better serves the purpose of encouraging recourse to the warrant procedure and is more consistent with our traditional deference to the probable cause determinations of magistrates than is the "two-pronged test."

Finally, the direction taken by decisions following Spinelli poorly serves "the ****2332** most basic function of any government": "to provide for the security of the individual and of his property."[929]The strictures that inevitably accompany the "two-pronged test" cannot avoid seriously impeding the task of law enforcement.[930] If, as the Illinois Supreme Court apparently thought, that test must be rigorously applied in every case, anonymous tips seldom would be of greatly diminished value in police work. Ordinary citizens, like ordinary witnesses,[931]generally do not provide extensive recitations of the basis of their everyday observations. Likewise, as the Illinois Supreme Court observed in this case, the veracity of persons supplying anonymous tips is by hypothesis largely unknown, and unknowable. As a result, anonymous tips seldom could survive a rigorous application of either of the Spinelli prongs. Yet, such tips, particularly when supplemented by ***238** independent police investigation, frequently contribute to the solution of otherwise "perfect crimes." While a conscientious assessment of the basis for crediting such tips is required by the Fourth Amendment, a standard that leaves virtually no place for anonymous citizen informants is not.

For all these reasons, we conclude that it is wiser to abandon the "two-pronged test" established by our decisions in *Aguilar* and *Spinelli.* In its place we reaffirm the totality-of-the-circumstances analysis that traditionally has informed probable cause determinations.[932]The task of the issuing magistrate is simply to make a practical, common-sense decision whether, given all the circumstances set forth in the affidavit before him, including the "veracity" and "basis of knowledge" of persons supplying hearsay information, there is a fair probability that contraband or evidence of a crime will be found in a particular place. And the duty of a reviewing court is simply to ensure that the magistrate had a "substantial basis for ... concluding" that probable cause ***239** existed.[933]We are convinced that this flexible, easily applied standard will better achieve the accommodation of public and private interests that the Fourth Amendment requires than does the approach that has developed from Aguilar and Spinelli.

Our earlier cases illustrate the limits beyond which a magistrate may not venture in issuing a warrant. A sworn statement of an affiant that "he has cause to suspect and does believe that" liquor illegally brought into the United States is located on certain premises will not do.[934]An affidavit must provide the magistrate with a substantial basis for determining the existence of probable cause, and the wholly conclusory statement at issue in *Nathanson* failed to meet this requirement. An ****2333** officer's statement that "affiants have received reliable information from a credible person and believe" that heroin is stored in a home, is likewise inadequate.[935]As in *Nathanson*, this is a mere conclusory statement that gives the magistrate virtually no

[928] *Jones v. United States*, 362 U.S. 257, 271, 80 S.Ct. 725, 736, 4 L.Ed.2d 697 (1960). See *United States v. Harris*, 403 U.S. 573, 577-583, 91 S.Ct. 2075, 2079-2082, 29 L.Ed.2d 723 (1971).

[929] *Miranda v. Arizona*, 384 U.S. 436, 539, 86 S.Ct. 1602, 1661, 16 L.Ed.2d 694 (1966) (WHITE, J., dissenting).

[930] See, e.g., n. 9 *supra*.

[931] See Federal Rules of Evidence 701, Advisory Committee Note (1976).

[932] See *Jones v. United States, supra*; *United States v. Ventresca, supra*; *Brinegar v. United States, supra*.

[933] *Jones v. United States, supra*, 362 U.S., at 271, 80 S.Ct., at 736.

[934] *Nathanson v. United States*, 290 U.S. 41, 54 S.Ct. 11, 78 L.Ed. 159 (1933).

[935] *Aguilar v. Texas*, 378 U.S. 108, 84 S.Ct. 1509, 12 L.Ed.2d 723 (1964).

basis at all for making a judgment regarding probable cause. Sufficient information must be presented to the magistrate to allow that official to determine probable cause; his action cannot be a mere ratification of the bare conclusions of others. In order to ensure that such an abdication of the magistrate's duty does not occur, courts must continue to conscientiously review the sufficiency of affidavits on which warrants are issued. But when we move beyond the "bare bones" affidavits present in cases such as *Nathanson* and *Aguilar*, this area simply does not lend itself to a prescribed set of rules, like that which had developed from *Spinelli*. Instead, the flexible, common-sense standard articulated in *Jones*, *Ventresca*, and *Brinegar* better serves the purposes of the Fourth Amendment's probable cause requirement.

Justice Brennan's dissent suggests in several places that the approach we take today somehow downgrades the ***240** role of the neutral magistrate, because Aguilar and Spinelli "preserve the role of magistrates as independent arbiters of probable cause...."[936]Quite the contrary, we believe, is the case. The essential protection of the warrant requirement of the Fourth Amendment, as stated in *Johnson v. United States*,[937]is in "requiring that [the usual inferences which reasonable men draw from evidence] be drawn by a neutral and detached magistrate instead of being judged by the officer engaged in the often competitive enterprise of ferreting out crime." [938]. Nothing in our opinion in any way lessens the authority of the magistrate to draw such reasonable inferences as he will from the material supplied to him by applicants for a warrant; indeed, he is freer than under the regime of *Aguilar* and *Spinelli* to draw such inferences, or to refuse to draw them if he is so minded.

The real gist of Justice Brennan's criticism seems to be a second argument, somewhat at odds with the first, that magistrates should be restricted in their authority to make probable cause determinations by the standards laid down in Aguilar and Spinelli, and that such findings "should not be authorized unless there is some assurance that the information on which they are based has been obtained in a reliable way by an honest or credible person." However, under our opinion magistrates remain perfectly free to exact such assurances as they deem necessary, as well as those required by this opinion, in making probable cause determinations. Justice Brennan would apparently prefer that magistrates be restricted in their findings of probable cause by the development of an elaborate body of case law dealing with the "veracity" prong of the Spinelli test, which in turn is broken down into two "spurs"-the informant's "credibility" and the "reliability" of his information, together with the "basis of knowledge" prong of the Spinelli test. See n. 4, supra. That such a labyrinthine body of judicial refinement bears any relationship to familiar definitions of ***241** probable cause is hard to imagine. Probable cause deals "with probabilities. These are not technical; they are the factual and practical considerations of everyday life on which reasonable and prudent men, not legal technicians, act."[939]

Justice Brennan's dissent also suggests that "words such as 'practical,' 'nontechnical,' and 'common sense,' as used in the Court's opinion, are but code words for an overly-permissive attitude towards police practices in derogation of the rights secured by the Fourth Amendment."[940]An easy, but not a complete, answer to this rather florid statement would be that nothing we know about Justice ****2334** Rutledge suggests that he would have used the words he chose in *Brinegar* in such a manner. More fundamentally, no one doubts that "under our Constitution only measures consistent with the Fourth Amendment may be employed by government to

---

[936] Post, at 2357.

[937] 333 U.S. 10, 68 S.Ct. 367, 92 L.Ed. 436 (1948),

[938] 333 U.S. 10, 68 S.Ct. 367, 92 L.Ed. 436 (1948).

[939] *Brinegar v. United States*, 338 U.S. 160, 175, 69 S.Ct. 1302, 1310, 93 L.Ed. 1879 (1949).

[940] Infra, p. 2359.

cure [the horrors of drug trafficking],"[941]but this agreement does not advance the inquiry as to which measures are, and which measures are not, consistent with the Fourth Amendment. "Fidelity" to the commands of the Constitution suggests balanced judgment rather than exhortation. The highest "fidelity" is achieved neither by the judge who instinctively goes furthest in upholding even the most bizarre claim of individual constitutional rights, any more than it is achieved by a judge who instinctively goes furthest in accepting the most restrictive claims of governmental authorities. The task of this Court, as of other courts, is to "hold the balance true," and we think we have done that in this case.

IV

Our decisions applying the totality-of-the-circumstances analysis outlined above have consistently recognized the value of corroboration of details of an informant's tip by independent police work. In *Jones v. United States*,[942]we held that an affidavit relying on hearsay "is not to ***242** be deemed insufficient on that score, so long as a substantial basis for crediting the hearsay is presented." We went on to say that even in making a warrantless arrest an officer "may rely upon information received through an informant, rather than upon his direct observations, so long as the informant's statement is reasonably corroborated by other matters within the officer's knowledge."[943]Likewise, we recognized the probative value of corroborative efforts of police officials in *Aguilar* - the source of the "two-pronged test" - by observing that if the police had made some effort to corroborate the informant's report at issue, "an entirely different case" would have been presented.[944] Our decision in *Draper v. United States*,[945]however, is the classic case on the value of corroborative efforts of police officials. There, an informant named Hereford reported that Draper would arrive in Denver on a train from Chicago on one of two days, and that he would be carrying a quantity of heroin. The informant also supplied a fairly detailed physical description of Draper, and predicted that he would be wearing a light colored raincoat, brown slacks and black shoes, and would be walking "real fast."[946]Hereford gave no indication of the basis for his information.

On one of the stated dates police officers observed a man matching this description exit a train arriving from Chicago; his attire and luggage matched Hereford's report and he was ***243** walking rapidly. We explained in *Draper* that, by this point in his investigation, the arresting officer "had personally verified every facet of the information given him by Hereford except whether petitioner had accomplished his mission and had the three ounces of heroin on his person or in his bag. And surely, with every other bit of Hereford's information being thus personally verified, [the officer] had 'reasonable grounds' to believe that the remaining unverified bit of Hereford's information - that Draper would have the heroin with him-was likewise true."[947]

****2335** The showing of probable cause in the present case was fully as compelling as that in *Draper*. Even standing alone, the facts obtained through the independent investigation of Mader and the DEA at least suggested that the Gates were involved in drug trafficking. In addition to being a popular vacation site, Florida is

---

[941] post, at 2359;

[942] *supra*, 362 U.S., at 269, 80 S.Ct., at 735,

[943] *Ibid.*

[944] *Aguilar, supra*, 378 U.S., at 109, n. 1, 84 S.Ct., at 1511, n. 1.

[945] 358 U.S. 307, 79 S.Ct. 329, 3 L.Ed.2d 327 (1959).

[946] *Id.*, at 309, 79 S.Ct., at 331.

[947] *Id.*, at 313, 79 S.Ct., at 333.

well-known as a source of narcotics and other illegal drugs.[948]Lance Gates' flight to Palm Beach, his brief, overnight stay in a motel, and apparent immediate return north to Chicago in the family car, conveniently awaiting him in West Palm Beach, is as suggestive of a pre-arranged drug run, as it is of an ordinary vacation trip.

In addition, the magistrate could rely on the anonymous letter, which had been corroborated in major part by Mader's efforts, just as had occurred in *Draper*. The Supreme Court ***244** of Illinois reasoned that *Draper* involved an informant who had given reliable information on previous occasions, while the honesty and reliability of the anonymous informant in this case were unknown to the Bloomingdale police. While this distinction might be an apt one at the time the police department received the anonymous letter, it became far less significant after Mader's independent investigative work occurred. The corroboration of the letter's predictions that the Gates' car would be in Florida, that Lance Gates would fly to Florida in the next day or so, and that he would drive the car north toward Bloomingdale all indicated, albeit not with certainty, that the informant's other assertions also were true. "Because an informant is right about some things, he is more probably right about other facts,"[949] including the claim regarding the Gates' illegal activity. This may well not be the type of "reliability" or "veracity" necessary to satisfy some views of the "veracity prong" of *Spinelli*, but we think it suffices for the practical, common-sense judgment called for in making a probable cause determination. It is enough, for purposes of assessing probable cause, that "corroboration through other sources of information reduced the ***245** chances of a reckless or prevaricating tale," thus providing "a substantial basis for crediting the hearsay."[950] Finally, the anonymous letter contained a range of details relating not just to easily obtained facts and conditions existing at the time of the tip, but to future ****2336** actions of third parties ordinarily not easily predicted. The letter writer's accurate information as to the travel plans of each of the Gates was of a character likely obtained only from the Gates themselves, or from someone familiar with their not entirely ordinary travel plans. If the informant had access to accurate information of this type a magistrate could properly conclude that it was not unlikely that he also had access to reliable information of the Gates' alleged illegal activities. Of ***246** course, the Gates' travel plans might have been learned from a talkative neighbor or travel agent; under the "two-pronged test" developed from *Spinelli*, the character of the details in the anonymous letter might well not permit a sufficiently clear inference regarding the letter writer's "basis of knowledge." But, as discussed previously,[951]probable cause does not demand the certainty we associate with formal trials. It is enough that there was a fair probability that the writer of the anonymous letter had obtained his entire story either from the Gates or someone they trusted. And corroboration of major portions of the letter's predictions provides just this probability. It is apparent, therefore, that the judge issuing the warrant had a "substantial basis for ... concluding" that probable cause to search the Gates' home and car existed. The judgment of the Supreme Court of Illinois therefore must be

Reversed.

*****

(The dissent of Justice BRENNAN, with whom Justice MARSHALL joins, omitted.)

[948] See *United States v. Mendenhall*, 446 U.S. 544, 562, 100 S.Ct. 1870, 1881, 64 L.Ed.2d 497 (1980) (POWELL, J., concurring); DEA, Narcotics Intelligence Estimate, The Supply of Drugs to the U.S. Illicit Market From Foreign and Domestic Sources 10 (1979).

[949] *Spinelli, supra*, 393 U.S., at 427, 89 S.Ct., at 594 (WHITE, J., concurring).

[950] *Jones v. United States, supra*, 362 U.S., at 269, 271, 80 S.Ct., at 735, 736.

[951] *Supra*, 2332.

(The dissent of Justice STEVENS, with whom Justice BRENNAN joins, omitted.)

Black Letter Law

Rigid "two-pronged test" under *Aguilar* and *Spinelli* for determining whether an informant's tip establishes probable cause for issuance of a warrant would be abandoned and a "totality-of-the-circumstances" approach that traditionally has informed probable-cause determinations would be substituted in its place.

Establishes the "totality of the circumstances" test for informants.

Whren v. U.S.

116 S.Ct. 1769

Supreme Court of the United States

Michael A. WHREN and James L. Brown, Petitioners,

v.

UNITED STATES.

No. 95–5841. | Argued April 17, 1996. | Decided June 10, 1996.

***808** Justice SCALIA delivered the opinion of the Court.

In this case we decide whether the temporary detention of a motorist who the police have probable cause to believe has committed a civil traffic violation is inconsistent with the Fourth Amendment's prohibition against unreasonable seizures unless a reasonable officer ****1772** would have been motivated to stop the car by a desire to enforce the traffic laws.

I

On the evening of June 10, 1993, plainclothes vice-squad officers of the District of Columbia Metropolitan Police Department were patrolling a "high drug area" of the city in an unmarked car. Their suspicions were aroused when they passed a dark Pathfinder truck with temporary license plates and youthful occupants waiting at a stop sign, the driver looking down into the lap of the passenger at his right. The truck remained stopped at the intersection for what seemed an unusually long time—more than 20 seconds. When the police car executed a U-turn in order to head back toward the truck, the Pathfinder turned suddenly to its right, without signaling, and sped off at an "unreasonable" speed. The policemen followed, and in a short while overtook the Pathfinder when it stopped behind other traffic at a red light. They pulled up alongside, and Officer Ephraim Soto stepped out and approached the driver's door, identifying himself as a police officer and directing the driver, petitioner Brown, to put the vehicle in park. When Soto drew up to the driver's ***809** window, he immediately observed two large plastic bags of what appeared to be crack cocaine in petitioner Whren's hands. Petitioners were arrested, and quantities of several types of illegal drugs were retrieved from the vehicle.

Petitioners were charged in a four-count indictment with violating various federal drug laws, including 21 U.S.C. §§ 844(a) and 860(a). At a pretrial suppression hearing, they challenged the legality of the stop and the resulting seizure of the drugs. They argued that the stop had not been justified by probable cause to believe, or even reasonable suspicion, that petitioners were engaged in illegal drug-dealing activity; and that Officer Soto's asserted ground for approaching the vehicle — to give the driver a warning concerning traffic violations — was pretextual. The District Court denied the suppression motion, concluding that "the facts of the stop were not controverted," and "[t]here was nothing to really demonstrate that the actions of the officers were contrary to a normal traffic stop."[952]

Petitioners were convicted of the counts at issue here. The Court of Appeals affirmed the convictions, holding with respect to the suppression issue that, "regardless of whether a police officer subjectively believes that the occupants of an automobile may be engaging in some other illegal behavior, a traffic stop is permissible as long as a reasonable officer in the same circumstances could have stopped the car for the suspected traffic violation."[953]We granted certiorari.[954]II

The Fourth Amendment guarantees "[t]he right of the people to be secure in their persons, houses, papers, and effects, against unreasonable searches and seizures." Temporary detention of individuals during the stop of an automobile by the police, even if only for a brief period and for a limited purpose, constitutes a "seizure" of "persons" within the ***810** meaning of this provision.[955]An automobile stop is thus subject to the constitutional imperative that it not be "unreasonable" under the circumstances. As a general matter, the decision to stop an automobile is reasonable where the police have probable cause to believe that a traffic violation has occurred.[956]

Petitioners accept that Officer Soto had probable cause to believe that various provisions of the District of Columbia traffic code had been violated.[957]****1773** They argue, however, that "in the unique context of civil traffic regulations" probable cause is not enough. Since, they contend, the use of automobiles is so heavily and minutely regulated that total compliance with traffic and safety rules is nearly impossible, a police officer will almost invariably be able to catch any given motorist in a technical violation. This creates the temptation to use traffic stops as a means of investigating other law violations, as to which no probable cause or even articulable suspicion exists. Petitioners, who are both black, further contend that police officers might decide which motorists to stop based on decidedly impermissible factors, such as the race of the car's occupants. To avoid this danger, they say, the Fourth Amendment test for traffic stops should be, not the normal one (applied by the Court of Appeals) of whether probable cause existed to justify the stop; but rather, whether a police officer, acting reasonably, would have made the stop for the reason given.

***811 A**

Petitioners contend that the standard they propose is consistent with our past cases' disapproval of police attempts to use valid bases of action against citizens as pretexts for pursuing other investigatory agendas. We are reminded that, in *Florida v. Wells*,[958]we stated that "an inventory search" must not be a ruse for a general rummaging in order to discover incriminating evidence"; that in *Colorado v. Bertine*,[959]in approving an inventory search, we apparently thought it significant that there had been "no showing that the police, who were following standardized procedures, acted in bad faith or for the sole purpose of investigation"; and that in *New York v.*

---

[952] App. 5.

[953] 53 F.3d 371, 374–375 (C.A.D.C.1995).

[954] 516 U.S. 1036, 116 S.Ct. 690, 133 L.Ed.2d 595 (1996).

[955] See *Delaware v. Prouse*, 440 U.S. 648, 653, 99 S.Ct. 1391, 1395, 59 L.Ed.2d 660 (1979); *United States v. Martinez–Fuerte*, 428 U.S. 543, 556, 96 S.Ct. 3074, 3082, 49 L.Ed.2d 1116 (1976); *United States v. Brignoni–Ponce*, 422 U.S. 873, 878, 95 S.Ct. 2574, 2578, 45 L.Ed.2d 607 (1975).

[956] See *Prouse, supra*, at 659, 99 S.Ct., at 1399; *Pennsylvania v. Mimms*, 434 U.S. 106, 109, 98 S.Ct. 330, 332, 54 L.Ed.2d 331 (1977) (per curiam).

[957] See 18 D.C. Mun. Regs. §§ 2213.4 (1995) ("An operator shall ... give full time and attention to the operation of the vehicle"); 2204.3 ("No person shall turn any vehicle ... without giving an appropriate signal"); 2200.3 ("No person shall drive a vehicle ... at a speed greater than is reasonable and prudent under the conditions").

[958] 495 U.S. 1, 4, 110 S.Ct. 1632, 1635, 109 L.Ed.2d 1 (1990).

[959] 479 U.S. 367, 372, 107 S.Ct. 738, 741, 93 L.Ed.2d 739 (1987).

Burger,[960]we observed, in upholding the constitutionality of a warrantless administrative inspection, that the search did not appear to be "a 'pretext' for obtaining evidence of... violation of... penal laws." But only an undiscerning reader would regard these cases as endorsing the principle that ulterior motives can invalidate police conduct that is justifiable on the basis of probable cause to believe that a violation of law has occurred. In each case we were addressing the validity of a search conducted in the absence of probable cause. Our quoted statements simply explain that the exemption from the need for probable cause (and warrant), which is accorded to searches made for the purpose of inventory or administrative ***812** regulation, is not accorded to searches that are not made for those purposes.[961]

Petitioners also rely upon *Colorado v. Bannister*,[962]a case which, like this one, involved a traffic stop as the prelude to a plain-view sighting and arrest on charges wholly unrelated to the basis for the stop. Petitioners point to our statement that "there was no evidence whatsoever that the officer's presence to issue a traffic citation was a pretext to confirm any other previous suspicion about the occupants" of the car.[963]That dictum at most demonstrates that the Court in Bannister found no need to inquire into the question now under discussion; not that it was certain of the answer. And it may demonstrate even less than that: If by "pretext" the Court meant that the officer really had not seen the car speeding, the statement would mean only that there was no reason to doubt probable cause for the traffic stop.

****1774** It would, moreover, be anomalous, to say the least, to treat a statement in a footnote in the per curiam Bannister opinion as indicating a reversal of our prior law. Petitioners' difficulty is not simply a lack of affirmative support for their position. Not only have we never held, outside the context of inventory search or administrative inspection (discussed above), that an officer's motive invalidates objectively justifiable behavior under the Fourth Amendment; but we have repeatedly held and asserted the contrary. In *United States v. Villamonte–Marquez*,[964]we held that an otherwise valid warrantless boarding of a vessel by customs officials was not rendered invalid "because the customs officers were accompanied by a Louisiana state policeman, and were following an informant's tip that a vessel in the ship channel was thought to be carrying marijuana." We flatly dismissed the idea that an ulterior motive might serve to strip the agents of their legal justification. In *United States v. Robinson*,[965]we held that ***813** a traffic-violation arrest (of the sort here) would not be rendered invalid by the fact that it was "a mere pretext for a narcotics search,"[966]and that a lawful post-arrest search of the person would not be rendered invalid by the fact that it was not motivated by the officer-safety concern that justifies such searches.[967]And in *Scott v. United States*,[968]in rejecting the contention that wiretap evidence was subject to exclusion because the agents conducting the tap had failed to make any effort to comply with the statutory requirement that unauthorized acquisitions be minimized, we said that "subjective intent alone... does not make otherwise lawful conduct illegal or unconstitutional." We described Robinson as having established that "the fact that the officer does not have the state of mind which is hypothecated by the reasons which provide the legal justification for the officer's

---

[960] 482 U.S. 691, 716–717, n. 27, 107 S.Ct. 2636, 2651, n. 27, 96 L.Ed.2d 601 (1987).

[961] See *Bertine, supra*, at 371–372, 107 S.Ct., at 740–741; *Burger, supra*, at 702–703, 107 S.Ct., at 2643–2644.

[962] 449 U.S. 1, 101 S.Ct. 42, 66 L.Ed.2d 1 (1980) (per curiam),

[963] *Id.*, at 4, n. 4, 101 S.Ct., at 44, n. 4.

[964] 462 U.S. 579, 584, n. 3, 103 S.Ct. 2573, 2577, n. 3, 77 L.Ed.2d 22 (1983).

[965] 414 U.S. 218, 94 S.Ct. 467, 38 L.Ed.2d 427 (1973),

[966] *Id.*, at 221, n. 1, 94 S.Ct., at 470, n. 1.

[967] See *id.*, at 236, 94 S.Ct., at 477; see also *Gustafson v. Florida*, 414 U.S. 260, 266, 94 S.Ct. 488, 492, 38 L.Ed.2d 456 (1973).

[968] 436 U.S. 128, 138, 98 S.Ct. 1717, 1723, 56 L.Ed.2d 168 (1978).

action does not invalidate the action taken as long as the circumstances, viewed objectively, justify that action."[969]

We think these cases foreclose any argument that the constitutional reasonableness of traffic stops depends on the actual motivations of the individual officers involved. We of course agree with petitioners that the Constitution prohibits selective enforcement of the law based on considerations such as race. But the constitutional basis for objecting to intentionally discriminatory application of laws is the Equal Protection Clause, not the Fourth Amendment. Subjective intentions play no role in ordinary, probable-cause Fourth Amendment analysis.

B

Recognizing that we have been unwilling to entertain Fourth Amendment challenges based on the actual motivations of individual officers, petitioners disavow any intention to make the individual officer's subjective good faith the touchstone of "reasonableness." They insist that the standard ***814** they have put forward—whether the officer's conduct deviated materially from usual police practices, so that a reasonable officer in the same circumstances would not have made the stop for the reasons given—is an "objective" one.

But although framed in empirical terms, this approach is plainly and indisputably driven by subjective considerations. Its whole purpose is to prevent the police from doing under the guise of enforcing the traffic code what they would like to do for different reasons. Petitioners' proposed standard may not use the word "pretext," but it is designed to combat nothing other than the perceived "danger" of the pretextual stop, albeit only indirectly and over the run of cases. Instead of asking whether the individual officer had the proper state of mind, the petitioners would have us ask, in effect, whether (based on general police practices) it is plausible to believe that the officer had the proper state of mind.

Why one would frame a test designed to combat pretext in such fashion that the court ****1775** cannot take into account actual and admitted pretext is a curiosity that can only be explained by the fact that our cases have foreclosed the more sensible option. If those cases were based only upon the evidentiary difficulty of establishing subjective intent, petitioners' attempt to root out subjective vices through objective means might make sense. But they were not based only upon that, or indeed even principally upon that. Their principal basis—which applies equally to attempts to reach subjective intent through ostensibly objective means—is simply that the Fourth Amendment's concern with "reasonableness" allows certain actions to be taken in certain circumstances, whatever the subjective intent.[970]But even if our concern had been only an evidentiary one, ***815** petitioners' proposal would by no means assuage it. Indeed, it seems to us somewhat easier to figure out the intent of an individual officer than to plumb the collective consciousness of law enforcement in order to determine whether a "reasonable officer" would have been moved to act upon the traffic violation. While police manuals and standard procedures may sometimes provide objective assistance, ordinarily one would be reduced to speculating about the hypothetical reaction of a hypothetical constable—an exercise that might be called virtual subjectivity.

Moreover, police enforcement practices, even if they could be practicably assessed by a judge, vary from place to place and from time to time. We cannot accept that the search and seizure protections of the Fourth Amendment are so variable[971]and can be made to turn upon such trivialities. The difficulty is illustrated by

---

[969] 436 U.S., at 136, 138, 98 S.Ct., at 1723.

[970] See, e.g., *Robinson, supra*, at 236, 94 S.Ct., at 477 ("Since it is the fact of custodial arrest which gives rise to the authority to search, it is of no moment that [the officer] did not indicate any subjective fear of the [arrestee] or that he did not himself suspect that [the arrestee] was armed") (footnotes omitted); *Gustafson, supra*, at 266, 94 S.Ct., at 492 (same).

[971] cf. *Gustafson, supra*, at 265, 94 S.Ct., at 491; *United States v. Caceres*, 440 U.S. 741, 755–756, 99 S.Ct. 1465, 1473–1474, 59 L.Ed.2d 733 (1979).

petitioners' arguments in this case. Their claim that a reasonable officer would not have made this stop is based largely on District of Columbia police regulations which permit plainclothes officers in unmarked vehicles to enforce traffic laws "only in the case of a violation that is so grave as to pose an immediate threat to the safety of others."[972]This basis of invalidation would not apply in jurisdictions that had a different practice. And it would not have applied even in the District of Columbia, if Officer Soto had been wearing a uniform or patrolling in a marked police cruiser.

Petitioners argue that our cases support insistence upon police adherence to standard practices as an objective means of rooting out pretext. They cite no holding to that effect, and dicta in only two cases. In *Abel v. United States*,[973]the petitioner had been arrested by the Immigration and Naturalization Service (INS), on the basis of ***816** an administrative warrant that, he claimed, had been issued on pretextual grounds in order to enable the Federal Bureau of Investigation (FBI) to search his room after his arrest. We regarded this as an allegation of "serious misconduct," but rejected Abel's claims on the ground that "[a] finding of bad faith is ... not open to us on th[e] record" in light of the findings below, including the finding that "'the proceedings taken by the [INS] differed in no respect from what would have been done in the case of an individual concerning whom [there was no pending FBI investigation],'"[974]But it is a long leap from the proposition that following regular procedures is some evidence of lack of pretext to the proposition that failure to follow regular procedures proves (or is an operational substitute for) pretext. *Abel*, moreover, did not involve the assertion that pretext could invalidate a search or seizure for which there was probable cause—and even what it said about pretext in other contexts is plainly inconsistent with the views we later stated in *Robinson*, *Gustafson*, *Scott*, and *Villamonte–Marquez*. In the other case claimed to contain ****1776** supportive dicta,[975]in approving a search incident to an arrest for driving without a license, we noted that the arrest was "not a departure from established police department practice."[976]That was followed, however, by the statement that "[w]e leave for another day questions which would arise on facts different from these."[977]This is not even a dictum that purports to provide an answer, but merely one that leaves the question open.

III

In what would appear to be an elaboration on the "reasonable officer" test, petitioners argue that the balancing inherent in any Fourth Amendment inquiry requires us to weigh the governmental and individual interests implicated in a traffic stop such as we have here. That balancing, petitioners claim, does not support investigation of minor traffic infractions ***817** by plainclothes police in unmarked vehicles; such investigation only minimally advances the government's interest in traffic safety, and may indeed retard it by producing motorist confusion and alarm—a view said to be supported by the Metropolitan Police Department's own regulations generally prohibiting this practice. And as for the Fourth Amendment interests of the individuals concerned, petitioners point out that our cases acknowledge that even ordinary traffic stops entail "a possibly unsettling show of authority"; that they at best "interfere with freedom of movement, are inconvenient, and consume time" and at

[972] Metropolitan Police Department, Washington, D.C., General Order 303.1, pt. 1, Objectives and Policies (A)(2)(4) (Apr. 30, 1992), reprinted as Addendum to Brief for Petitioners.

[973] 362 U.S. 217, 80 S.Ct. 683, 4 L.Ed.2d 668 (1960).

[974] *Id.*, at 226–227, 80 S.Ct., at 690–691.

[975] *United States v. Robinson*, 414 U.S. 218, 94 S.Ct. 467, 38 L.Ed.2d 427 (1973).

[976] *Id.*, at 221, n. 1, 94 S.Ct., at 470, n. 1.

[977] *Ibid.*

worst "may create substantial anxiety,[978]That anxiety is likely to be even more pronounced when the stop is conducted by plainclothes officers in unmarked cars.

It is of course true that in principle every Fourth Amendment case, since it turns upon a "reasonableness" determination, involves a balancing of all relevant factors. With rare exceptions not applicable here, however, the result of that balancing is not in doubt where the search or seizure is based upon probable cause. That is why petitioners must rely upon cases like *Prouse* to provide examples of actual "balancing" analysis. There, the police action in question was a random traffic stop for the purpose of checking a motorist's license and vehicle registration, a practice that—like the practices at issue in the inventory search and administrative inspection cases upon which petitioners rely in making their "pretext" claim—involves police intrusion without the probable cause that is its traditional justification. Our opinion in *Prouse* expressly distinguished the case from a stop based on precisely what is at issue here: "probable cause to believe that a driver is violating any one of the multitude of applicable traffic and equipment regulations."[979]It noted approvingly that "the foremost method of enforcing traffic and vehicle safety regulations ... is acting upon observed violations"[980]which afford the "'quantum of individualized suspicion'" necessary to ensure that police ***818** discretion is sufficiently constrained.[981]What is true of *Prouse* is also true of other cases that engaged in detailed "balancing" to decide the constitutionality of automobile stops, such as *Martinez–Fuerte*, which upheld checkpoint stops,[982]and *Brignoni–Ponce*, which disallowed so-called "roving patrol" stops.[983]The detailed "balancing" analysis was necessary because they involved seizures without probable cause.

Where probable cause has existed, the only cases in which we have found it necessary actually to perform the "balancing" analysis involved searches or seizures conducted in an extraordinary manner, unusually harmful to an individual's privacy or even physical interests—such as, for example, seizure by means of deadly force,[984]unannounced entry into a home,[985]entry into a home without a warrant,[986]or physical penetration of the body.[987] ****1777** The making of a traffic stop out of uniform does not remotely qualify as such an extreme practice, and so is governed by the usual rule that probable cause to believe the law has been broken "outbalances" private interest in avoiding police contact.

Petitioners urge as an extraordinary factor in this case that the "multitude of applicable traffic and equipment regulations" is so large and so difficult to obey perfectly that virtually everyone is guilty of violation, permitting the police to single out almost whomever they wish for a stop. But we are aware of no principle that would allow us to decide at what point a code of law becomes so expansive and so commonly violated that infraction itself can no longer be the ordinary measure of the lawfulness of enforcement. And even if we could identify such exorbitant codes, we do not know by what standard (or what right) we would decide, as ***819** petitioners

---

[978] *Prouse*, 440 U.S., at 657, 99 S.Ct., at 1398.

[979] *Id.*, at 661, 99 S.Ct., at 1400.

[980] *Id.*, at 659, 99 S.Ct., at 1399.

[981] *Id.*, at 654–655, 99 S.Ct., at 1396 (quoting *United States v. Martinez–Fuerte*, 428 U.S., at 560, 96 S.Ct., at 3084.)

[982] See 428 U.S., at 556–562, 96 S.Ct., at 3082–3085.

[983] See 422 U.S., at 882–884, 95 S.Ct., at 2580–2582.

[984] See *Tennessee v. Garner*, 471 U.S. 1, 105 S.Ct. 1694, 85 L.Ed.2d 1 (1985).

[985] See *Wilson v. Arkansas*, 514 U.S. 927, 115 S.Ct. 1914, 131 L.Ed.2d 976 (1995).

[986] See *Welsh v. Wisconsin*, 466 U.S. 740, 104 S.Ct. 2091, 80 L.Ed.2d 732 (1984).

[987] See *Winston v. Lee*, 470 U.S. 753, 105 S.Ct. 1611, 84 L.Ed.2d 662 (1985).

would have us do, which particular provisions are sufficiently important to merit enforcement.

For the run-of-the-mine case, which this surely is, we think there is no realistic alternative to the traditional common-law rule that probable cause justifies a search and seizure.

* * *

Here the District Court found that the officers had probable cause to believe that petitioners had violated the traffic code. That rendered the stop reasonable under the Fourth Amendment, the evidence thereby discovered admissible, and the upholding of the convictions by the Court of Appeals for the District of Columbia Circuit correct.

The judgment is affirmed.

Black Letter Law

> Automobile stop is subject to constitutional imperative that it not be unreasonable under the circumstances; as a general matter, decision to stop automobile is reasonable where police have probable cause to believe that traffic violation has occurred.
>
> Constitutional reasonableness of traffic stops does not depend on the actual motivations of the individual officers involved.

Discussion Problem:

4-1. Officer Walker received an anonymous phone call. The caller told him that 3 men had been driving around the streets of the County for the last three days in a pimped out 1993 Chevrolet Caprice. The anonymous caller told Officer Walker that the Caprice was metallic blue, with "spinners" on the rims. The caller further stated that the car is totally "tricked out," with a "wicked" sound system. The caller also claimed that they were using the Caprice as a rolling store to sell methamphetamines. The caller told Officer Walker that the Meth being sold from the Caprice was imprinted with a particular design – an Indian Arrowhead. The anonymous caller told Officer Walker that the Caprice was painted with the same design.

She claimed that you could find the Caprice in the back of the Sonic on most weeknights and weekends. Officer Walker tried to get the anonymous caller to identify herself, but she immediately hung up. Approximately eight hours after this phone call Officer Walker was on patrol in Calusa County. While on patrol he pulled into a Sonic to get a frozen coconut blueberry slushy (Sonic gives them out to cops for free), when he spotted a blue Caprice with crossed arrows painted on the hood. The car was tricked out to the max and occupied by two white males. After getting his slushy he got out of his cruiser, approached the car and identified himself as a police officer. He ordered them out of the car and separated them, placing the passenger at the front of the car and the driver at the back of the car. Officer Walker found over three pounds of methamphetamine tablets in the trunk of the car.

You are an associate in the criminal defense firm representing the driver of the Caprice. Draft a memorandum analyzing whether or not officer Walker had probable cause to stop the Caprice based upon the cases within this section and the facts above. Make sure to include the analysis under both *Aguillar-Spinelli* and under *Gates*.

Chapter 5: Unreasonableness and the Warrant Requirement

Johnson v. United States

68 S.Ct. 367

Supreme Court of the United States

JOHNSON

v.

UNITED STATES.

No. 329. | Argued Dec. 18, 1947. | Feb. 2, 1948.

Mr. Justice JACKSON delivered the opinion of the Court.

Petitioner was convicted on four counts charging violation of federal narcotic laws. The only question which brings the case here is whether it was lawful, without a warrant of any kind, to arrest petitioner and to search her living quarters. ***12** Taking the Government's version of disputed events, decision would rest on these facts:

At about 7:30 p.m. Detective Lieutenant Belland, an officer of the Seattle police force narcotic detail, received information from a confidential informer, who was also a known narcotic user, that unknown persons were smoking opium in the Europe Hotel. The informer was taken back to the hotel to interview the manager, but he returned at once saying he could smell burning opium in the hallway. Belland communicated with federal narcotic agents and between 8:30 and 9 o'clock went back to the hotel with four such agents. All were experienced in narcotic work and recognized at once a strong odor of burning opium which to them was distinctive and unmistakable. The odor led to Room 1. The officers did not know who was occupying that room. They knocked and a voice inside asked who was there. 'Lieutenant Belland,' was the reply. There was a slight delay, some 'shuffling or noise' in the room and then the defendant opened the door. The officer said, 'I want to talk to you a little bit.' She then, as he describes it, 'stepped back acquiescently and admitted us.' He said, 'I want to talk to you about the opium smell in the room here.' She denied that there was such a smell. Then he said, 'I want you to consider yourself under arrest because we are going to search the room.' The search turned up incriminating opium and smoking apparatus, the latter being warm, apparently from recent use. This evidence the District Court refused to suppress before trial and admitted over defendant's objection at the trial. Conviction resulted and the Circuit Court of Appeals affirmed.

The defendant challenged the search of her home as a violation of the rights secured to her in common with others, by the Fourth Amendment to the Constitution. ***13** The Government defends the search as legally justifiable, more particularly as incident to what it urges was a lawful arrest of the person.

I.

The Fourth Amendment to the Constitution of the United States provides:

> 'The right of the people to be secure in their persons, houses, papers, and effects, against unreasonable searches and seizures, shall not be violated, and no Warrants shall issue, but upon probable cause, supported by Oath or affirmation, and particularly describing the place to be searched, and the persons or things to be seized.'

Entry to defendant's living quarters, which was the beginning of the search, was demanded under color of office. It was granted in submission to authority rather than as an understanding and intentional waiver of a constitutional right.[988]At the time entry was demanded the officers were possessed of evidence which a magistrate

[988] Cf. *Amos v. United States*, 255 U.S. 313, 41 S.Ct. 266, 65 L.Ed. 654.

might have found to be probable cause for issuing a search warrant. We cannot sustain defendant's contention, erroneously **369 made, on the strength of *Taylor v. United States*,[989]that odors cannot be evidence sufficient to constitute probable grounds for any search. That decision held only that odors alone do not authorize a search without warrant. If the presence of odors is testified to before a magistrate and he finds the affiant qualified to know the odor, and it is one sufficiently distinctive to identify a forbidden substance, this Court has never held such a basis insufficient to justify issuance of a search warrant. Indeed it might very well be found to be evidence of most persuasive character.

The point of the Fourth Amendment, which often is not grasped by zealous officers, is not that it denies law enforcement ***14** the support of the usual inferences which reasonable men draw from evidence. Its protection consists in requiring that those inferences be drawn by a neutral and detached magistrate instead of being judged by the officer engaged in the often competitive enterprise of ferreting out crime. Any assumption that evidence sufficient to support a magistrate's disinterested determination to issue a search warrant will justify the officers in making a search without a warrant would reduce the Amendment to a nullity and leave the people's homes secure only in the discretion of police officers. Crime, even in the privacy of one's own quarters, is, of course, of grave concern to society, and the law allows such crime to be reached on proper showing. The right of officers to thrust themselves into a home is also a grave concern, not only to the individual but to a society which chooses to dwell in reasonable security and freedom from surveillance. When the right of privacy must reasonably yield to the right of search is, as a rule, to be decided by a judicial officer, not by a policeman or Government enforcement agent.

There are exceptional circumstances in which, on balancing the need for effective law enforcement against the ***15** right of privacy, it may be contended that a magistrate's warrant for search may be dispensed with. But this is not such a case. No reason is offered for not obtaining a search warrant except the inconvenience to the officers and some slight delay necessary to prepare papers and present the evidence to a magistrate. These are never very convincing reasons and, in these circumstances, certainly are not enough to bypass the constitutional requirement. No suspect was fleeing or likely to take flight. The search was of permanent premises, not of a movable vehicle. No evidence or contraband was threatened with removal or destruction, except perhaps the fumes which we suppose in time will disappear. But they were not capable at any time of being reduced to possession for presentation to court. The evidence of their existence before the search was adequate and the testimony of the officers to that effect would not perish from the delay of getting a warrant.

If the officers in this case were excused from the constitutional duty of presenting their evidence to a magistrate, it is difficult to think of a case in which it should be required.

II.

The Government contends, however, that this search without warrant ****370** must be held valid because incident to an arrest. This alleged ground of validity requires examination of the facts to determine whether the arrest itself was lawful. Since it was without warrant, it could be valid only if for a crime committed in the presence of the arresting officer or for a felony of which he had reasonable cause to believe defendant guilty. ***16** The Government, in effect, concedes that the arresting officer did not have probable cause to arrest petitioner until he had entered her room and found her to be the sole occupant. It points out specifically, referring to the time just before entry, 'For at that time the agents did not know whether there was one or several persons in the room. It was reasonable to believe that the room might have been an opium smoking den.' And it says,* * * 'that when the agents were admitted to the room and found only the petitioner present they had a reasonable basis for

[989] 286 U.S. 1, 52 S.Ct. 466, 76 L.Ed. 951.

believing that she had been smoking opium and thus illicitly possessed the narcotic.' Thus the Government quite properly stakes the right to arrest, not on the informer's tip and the smell the officers recognized before entry, but on the knowledge that she was alone in the room, gained only after, and wholly by reason of, their entry of her home. It was therefore their observations inside of her quarters, after they had obtained admission under color of their police authority, on which they made the arrest.

Thus the Government is obliged to justify the arrest by the search and at the same time to justify the search by ***17** the arrest. This will not do. An officer gaining access to private living quarters under color of his office and of the law which he personifies must then have some valid basis in law for the intrusion. Any other rule would undermine 'the right of the people to be secure in their persons, houses, papers and effects,' and would obliterate one of ****371** the most fundamental distinctions between our form of government, where officers are under the law, and the police-state where they are the law.

Reversed.

The CHIEF JUSTICE, Mr. Justice BLACK, Mr. Justice REED and Mr. Justice BURTON dissent.

United States v. Watson

96 S.Ct. 820

Supreme Court of the United States

UNITED STATES, Petitioner,

v.

Henry Ogle WATSON.

No. 74-538. | Argued Oct. 8, 1975. | Decided Jan. 26, 1976. | Rehearing Denied March 22, 1976.

Mr. Justice WHITE delivered the opinion of the Court.

This case presents questions under the Fourth Amendment as to the legality of a warrantless arrest and of an ensuing search of the arrestee's automobile carried out with his purported consent.

I

The relevant events began on August 17, 1972, when an informant, one Khoury, telephoned a postal inspector informing him that respondent Watson was in possession of a stolen credit card and had asked Khoury to cooperate in using the card to their mutual advantage. On five to ten previous occasions Khoury had provided the inspector with reliable information on postal inspection matters, some involving Watson. Later that day ***413** Khoury delivered the card to the inspector. On learning that Watson had agreed to furnish additional cards, the inspector asked Khoury to arrange to meet with Watson. Khoury did so, a meeting being scheduled for August 22. Watson canceled that engagement, but at noon on August 23, Khoury met with Watson at a restaurant designated by the latter. Khoury had been instructed that if Watson had additional stolen credit cards, Khoury was to give a designated signal. The signal was given, the officers closed in, and Watson was forthwith arrested. He was removed from the restaurant to the street where he was given the warnings required by *Miranda v. Arizona.*[990]A search having revealed that Watson had no credit cards on his person, the inspector asked if he could look inside Watson's car, which was standing within view. Watson said, "Go ahead," and repeated these words when the inspector cautioned that "if I find anything, it is going to go against you." Using keys furnished by Watson, the ****823** inspector entered the car and found under the

[990] 384 U.S. 436, 86 S.Ct. 1602, 16 L.Ed.2d 694 (1966).

floor mat an envelop containing two credit cards in the names of other persons. These cards were the basis for two counts of a four-count indictment charging Watson with possessing stolen mail in violation of 18 U.S.C. s 1708.

Prior to trial, Watson moved to suppress the cards, claiming that his arrest was illegal for want of probable cause and an arrest warrant and that his consent to search the car was involuntary and ineffective because he had not been told that he could withhold consent. ***414** The motion was denied, and Watson was convicted of illegally possessing the two cards seized from his car.

A divided panel of the Court of Appeals for the Ninth Circuit reversed,[991] ruling that the admission in evidence of the two credit cards found in the car was prohibited by the Fourth Amendment. In reaching this judgment, the court decided two issues in Watson's favor. First, notwithstanding its agreement with the District Court that Khoury was reliable and that there was probable cause for arresting Watson, the court held the arrest unconstitutional because the postal inspector had failed to secure an arrest warrant although he concededly had time to do so. Second, based on the totality of the circumstances, one of which was the illegality of the arrest, the court held Watson's consent to search had been coerced and hence was not a valid ground for the warrantless search of the automobile. We granted certiorari.[992]II

A major part of the Court of Appeals' opinion was its holding that Watson's warrantless arrest violated the Fourth Amendment. Although it did not expressly do so, it may have intended to overturn the conviction on the independent ground that the two credit cards were the inadmissible fruits of an unconstitutional arrest.[993]However that may be, the Court of Appeals treated the illegality of Watson's arrest as an important factor in determining the voluntariness of his consent to search his car. We therefore deal first with the arrest issue.

Contrary to the Court of Appeals' view, Watson's arrest was not invalid because executed without a warrant. ***415** Title 18 U.S.C. s 3061(a)(3) expressly empowers the Board of Governors of the Postal Service to authorize Postal Service officers and employees "performing duties related to the inspection of postal matters" to "make arrests without warrant for felonies cognizable under the laws of the United States if they have reasonable grounds to believe that the person to be arrested has committed or is committing such a felony."

By regulation, 39 CFR s 232.5(a)(3) (1975), and in identical language, the Board of Governors has exercised that power and authorized warrantless arrests. Because there was probable cause in this case to believe that Watson had violated s 1708, the inspector and his subordinates, in arresting Watson, were acting strictly in accordance with the governing statute and regulations. The effect of the judgment of the Court of Appeals was to invalidate the statute as applied in this case and as applied to all the situations where a court fails to find exigent circumstances justifying a warrantless arrest. We reverse that judgment.

Under the Fourth Amendment, the people are to be "secure in their persons, houses, ****824** papers, and effects, against unreasonable searches and seizures. . . and no Warrants shall issue, but upon probable cause . . . " Section 3061 represents a judgment by Congress that it is not unreasonable under the Fourth Amendment for postal inspectors to arrest without a warrant provided they have probable cause to do so. This was not an ***416** isolated or quixotic judgment of the legislative branch. Other federal law enforcement officers have been expressly authorized by statute for many years to make felony arrests on probable cause but without a warrant. This is true of United States marshals, 18 U.S.C. s 3053, and of agents of the Federal Bureau

[991] 504 F.2d 849 (1974)

[992] 420 U.S. 924, 95 S.Ct. 1117, 43 L.Ed.2d 392 (1975).

[993] Cf. *Brown v. Illinois*, 422 U.S. 590, 95 S.Ct. 2254, 45 L.Ed.2d 416 (1975).

of Investigation, 18 U.S.C. s 3052; the Drug Enforcement Administration, 84 Stat. 1273, 21 U.S.C. s 878; the Secret Service, 18 U.S.C. s 3056(a); and the Customs Service, 26 U.S.C. s 7607.

Because there is a "strong presumption of constitutionality due to an Act of Congress, especially when it turns on what is 'reasonable,' " "(o)bviously the Court should be reluctant to decide that a search thus authorized by Congress was unreasonable and that the Act was therefore unconstitutional."[994]Moreover, there is nothing in the Court's prior cases indicating that under the ***417** Fourth Amendment a warrant is required to make a valid arrest for a felony. Indeed, the relevant prior decisions are uniformly to the contrary.

"The usual rule is that a police officer may arrest without warrant one believed by the officer upon reasonable cause to have been guilty of a felony . . . "[995]In *Henry v. United States*,[996]the Court dealt with an FBI agent's warrantless arrest under 18 U.S.C. s 3052, which authorizes a warrantless arrest where there are reasonable grounds to believe that the person to be arrested has committed a felony. The Court declared that "the statute states the constitutional standard . . . "[997]The necessary inquiry, therefore, was not whether there was a warrant or whether there was time to get one, but whether there was probable cause for the arrest. In *Abel v. United States*,[998]the Court sustained an administrative arrest made without "a judicial warrant within the scope of the Fourth Amendment." The crucial question in *Draper v. United States*[999]was whether there was probable cause for the warrantless arrest. If there was, the Court said, ****825** "the arrest, though without a warrant, was lawful . . . "[1000]*Ker v. California*[1001]reiterated the rule that "the lawfulness of the arrest without warrant, in turn, must be based upon probable cause . . . " and went on to sustain the warrantless arrest over other claims going to the mode of entry. Just last Term, while recognizing that maximum protection of individual rights could be assured by requiring a magistrate's review of the factual justification prior to any arrest, we stated that "such a requirement would constitute an intolerable handicap for legitimate law enforcement" and noted that the Court "has never invalidated an arrest supported by probable cause solely ***418** because the officers failed to secure a warrant."[1002]

The cases construing the Fourth Amendment thus reflect the ancient common-law rule that a peace officer was permitted to arrest without a warrant for a misdemeanor or felony committed in his presence as well as for a felony not committed in his presence if there was reasonable ground for making the arrest.[1003]***419** This has also been the prevailing rule under state constitutions and statutes. "The rule of the common law, that a peace officer or a private citizen may arrest a felon without a warrant, has been generally held by the courts of the several States to be in force in

---

994 *United States v. Di Re*, 332 U.S. 581, 585, 68 S.Ct. 222, 224, 92 L.Ed. 210 (1948).

995 *Carroll v. United States*, 267 U.S. 132, 156, 45 S.Ct. 280, 286, 69 L.Ed. 543 (1925).

996 361 U.S. 98, 80 S.Ct. 168, 4 L.Ed.2d 134 (1959).

997 *Id.*, at 100, 80 S.Ct., at 170.

998 362 U.S. 217, 232, 80 S.Ct. 683, 693, 4 L.Ed.2d 668 (1960).

999 358 U.S. 307, 79 S.Ct. 329, 3 L.Ed.2d 327 (1959).

1000 *Id.*, at 310, 79 S.Ct., at 331.

1001 374 U.S. 23, 34-35, 83 S.Ct. 1623, 1630, 10 L.Ed.2d 726 (1963) (opinion of Clark, J.).

1002 *Gerstein v. Pugh*, 420 U.S. 103, 113, 95 S.Ct. 854, 862, 43 L.Ed.2d 54 (1975).

1003 10 Halsbury's Laws of England 344-345 (3d ed. 1955); 4 W. Blackstone, Commentaries *292; 1 J. Stephen, A History of the Criminal Law of England 193 (1883); 2 M. Hale, Pleas of the Crown *72-74; Wilgus, Arrest Without a Warrant, 22 Mich.L.Rev. 541, 547-550, 686-688 (1924); *Samuel v. Payne*, 1 Doug. 359, 99 Eng.Rep. 230 (K.B.1780); *Beckwith v. Philby*, 6 Barn. & Cress. 635, 108 Eng.Rep. 585 (K.B.1827).

cases of felony punishable by the civil tribunals."[1004] In *Rohan v. Sawin,*[1005]a false-arrest case, the Supreme Judicial Court of Massachusetts held that the common-law rule obtained in that State. Given probable cause to arrest, "the authority of a constable, to arrest without warrant, in cases of felony, is most fully established by the elementary books, and adjudicated cases."[1006]In reaching this judgment the court observed:

"It has been sometimes contended, that an arrest of this character, without a warrant, was a violation of the great fundamental principles of our national and state constitutions, forbidding unreasonable searches and arrests, except by ****826** warrant founded upon a complaint made under oath. Those provisions doubtless had another and different purpose, being in restraint of general warrants to make searches, and requiring warrants to issue only upon a complaint made under oath. They do not conflict with the authority of constables or other peace-officers, or private persons under proper limitations, to arrest without warrant those who have committed felonies. The public safety, and the due apprehension of criminals, charged with heinous offenses, imperiously require that such arrests should be made without warrant by officers of the law."[1007]

***420** Also rejected,[1008]was the trial court's view that to justify a warrantless arrest, the State must show "an immediate necessity therefor, arising from the danger, that the plaintiff would otherwise escape, or secrete the stolen property, before a warrant could be procured against him." The Supreme Judicial Court ruled that there was no "authority for thus restricting a constable in the exercise of his authority to arrest for a felony without a warrant."[1009]

Because the common law rule authorizing arrests without a warrant generally prevailed in the States, it is important for present purposes to note that in 1792 Congress invested United States marshals and their deputies with "the same powers in executing the laws of the United States, as sheriffs and their deputies in the several states have by law, in executing the laws of their respective states."[1010]The Second Congress thus saw no inconsistency between the Fourth Amendment and legislation giving United States marshals the same power as local peace officers to arrest for a felony without a warrant This provision equating the power of federal marshals ***421** with those of local sheriffs was several times re-enacted and is today s 570 of Title 28 of the United States Code. That provision, however, was supplemented in 1935 by s 504a of the Judicial Code, which in its essential elements is now 18 U.S.C. s 3053 and which expressly empowered marshals to make felony arrests without warrant and on probable cause. It was enacted to furnish a federal standard independent ****827** of the vagaries of state laws, the Committee Report remarking that under existing law a "marshal or deputy marshal may make an arrest without a warrant within his district in all cases where the sheriff might do so under the State statutes."[1011]

[1004] *Kurtz v. Moffitt*, 115 U.S. 487, 504, 6 S.Ct. 148, 154, 29 L.Ed. 458 (1885).

[1005] 59 Mass. 281 (1850).

[1006] *Id.*, at 284.

[1007] *Id.*, at 284-285.

[1008] *Id.*, at 285-286.

[1009] *Id.*, at 286. Other early cases to similar effect were *Wakely v. Hart*, 6 Bin. 316 (Pa.1814); *Holley v. Mix*, 3 Wend. 350 (N.Y.-Sup.Ct.1829); *State v. Brown*, 5 Del. 505 (Ct.Gen.Sess.1853); *Johnson v. State*, 30 Ga. 426 (1860); *Wade v. Chaffee*, 8 R.I. 224 (1865). See *Reuck v. McGregor*, 32 N.J.L. 70, 74 (Sup.Ct.1866); *Baltimore & O. R. Co. v. Cain*, 81 Md. 87, 100, 102, 31 A. 801, 803, 804 (1895).

[1010] Act of May 2, 1792, c. 28, s 9, 1 Stat. 265.

[1011] H.R.Rep.No.283, 74th Cong., 1st Sess., 1 (1935). See *United States v. Riggs*, 474 F.2d 699, 702-703, n. 2 (CA2), cert. denied, 414 U.S. 820, 94 S.Ct. 115, 38 L.Ed.2d 53 (1973).

The balance struck by the common law in generally authorizing felony arrests on probable cause, but without a warrant, has survived substantially intact. It appears ***422** in almost all of the States in the form of express statutory authorization. In 1963, the American Law Institute undertook the task of formulating a model statute governing police powers and practice in criminal law enforcement and related aspects of pretrial procedure. In 1975, after years of discussion, A Model Code of Pre-arraignment Procedure was proposed. Among its provisions was s 120.1 which authorizes an officer to take a person into custody if the officer has reasonable cause to believe that the person to be arrested has committed a felony, or has committed a misdemeanor or petty misdemeanor in his presence. The commentary to this section said: "The Code thus adopts the traditional and almost universal standard for arrest without a warrant."

423** This is the rule Congress has long directed its principal law enforcement officers to follow. Congress has plainly decided against conditioning warrantless arrest power on proof of exigent circumstances. Law enforcement officers may find it wise to seek arrest warrants where practicable to do so, and their judgments about probable cause may be more readily accepted where backed by a warrant issued by a magistrate.[1012]*828** But we decline to transform this judicial preference into a constitutional rule when the judgment of the Nation and Congress has for so long been to authorize warrantless public arrests on probable cause rather than to encumber criminal prosecutions with endless litigation with respect to the existence of exigent circumstances, whether it was practicable ***424** to get a warrant, whether the suspect was about to flee, and the like.

Watson's arrest did not violate the Fourth Amendment, and the Court of Appeals erred in holding to the contrary.

III

Because our judgment is that Watson's arrest comported with the Fourth Amendment, Watson's consent to the search of his car was not the product of an illegal arrest. To the extent that the issue of the voluntariness of Watson's consent was resolved on the premise that his arrest was illegal, the Court of Appeals was also in error.

We are satisfied in addition that the remaining factors relied upon by the Court of Appeals to invalidate Watson's consent are inadequate to demonstrate that, in the totality of the circumstances, Watson's consent was not his own "essentially free and unconstrained choice" because his "will had been overborne and his capacity for self-determination critically impaired."[1013]There was no overt act or threat of force against Watson proved or claimed. There were no promises made to him and no indication of more subtle forms of coercion that might flaw his judgment. He had been arrested and was in custody, but his consent was given while on a public street, not in the confines of the police station. Moreover, the fact of custody alone has never been enough in itself to demonstrate a coerced confession or consent to search. Similarly, under *Schneckloth*, the absence of proof that Watson knew he could withhold his consent, though it may be a factor in the overall judgment, is not to be given controlling significance. There is no indication in this record that Watson was a newcomer ***425** to the law, mentally deficient, or unable in the face of a custodial arrest to exercise a free choice. He was given Miranda warnings and was further cautioned that the results of the search of his car could be used against him. He persisted in his consent.

In these circumstances, to hold that illegal coercion is made out from the fact of arrest and the failure to inform the arrestee that he could withhold consent would not

[1012] See *United States v. Ventresca*, 380 U.S. 102, 106, 85 S.Ct. 741, 744-745, 13 L.Ed.2d 684 (1965); *Aguilar v. Texas*, 378 U.S. 108, 111, 84 S.Ct. 1509, 1512, 12 L.Ed.2d 723 (1964); *Wong Sun v. United States*, 371 U.S. 471, 479-480, 83 S.Ct. 407, 412-413, 9 L.Ed.2d 441 (1963).

[1013] *Schneckloth v. Bustamonte*, 412 U.S. 218, 225, 93 S.Ct. 2041, 2047, 36 L.Ed.2d 854 (1973).

be consistent with *Schneckloth* and would distort the voluntariness standard that we reaffirmed in that case.

In consequence, we reverse the judgment of the Court of Appeals.

So ordered.

Reversed.

Mr. Justice POWELL, concurring.

Although I concur in the opinion of the Court, I write to express additional views. I note at the outset that the case could be disposed of on the ground that respondent's consent to the search was plainly voluntary.[1014]Indeed, the evidence that his consent was the product ****829** of free will is so overwhelming that I would have held the consent voluntary even on the assumption that the preceding warrantless arrest was unconstitutional, and that the doctrine of *Wong Sun v. United States*[1015]therefore was applicable.[1016]The Court's different route to ***426** the same result requires, however, an inquiry into the validity of the arrest itself.

I

Respondent was arrested without a warrant in a public restaurant six days after postal inspectors learned from a reliable source that he possessed stolen credit cards in violation of 18 U.S.C. s 1708. The Government made no effort to show that circumstances precluded the obtaining of a warrant, relying instead for the validity of the arrest solely upon the showing of probable cause to believe that respondent had committed a felony. Respondent contends, and the Court of Appeals held, that the absence of any exigency justifying the failure to procure a warrant renders this arrest violative of the Fourth Amendment.

In reversing the Court of Appeals the Court concludes that nothing in our previous cases involving warrantless arrests supports the position of respondent and the Court of Appeals.[1017]But it is fair to say, I think, that the prior decisions of the Court have assumed the validity of such arrests without addressing in a reasoned way the analysis advanced by respondent. Today's decision is ***427** the first square holding that the Fourth Amendment permits a duly authorized law enforcement officer to make a warrantless arrest in a public place even though he had adequate opportunity to procure a warrant after developing probable cause for arrest.

On its face, our decision today creates a certain anomaly. There is no more basic constitutional rule in the Fourth Amendment area than that which makes a warrantless search unreasonable except in a few "jealously and carefully drawn" exceptional circumstances.[1018]****830** On more than one occasion this Court has rejected an argument that a law enforcement officer's own probable cause to search a private place for contraband or evidence of crime should excuse his otherwise unexplained failure to procure a warrant beforehand.[1019]***428** In short, the course of judicial development of the Fourth Amendment with respect to searches has remained true to the principles so well expressed by Mr. Justice Jackson:

> "Any assumption that evidence sufficient to support a magistrate's disinterested determination to issue a search warrant will justify the officers in making a search

---

[1014] *Schneckloth v. Bustamonte*, 412 U.S. 218, 93 S.Ct. 2041, 36 L.Ed.2d 854 (1973).

[1015] 371 U.S. 471, 83 S.Ct. 407, 9 L.Ed.2d 441 (1963).

[1016] See *Brown v. Illinois*, 422 U.S. 590, 95 S.Ct. 2254, 45 L.Ed.2d 416 (1975).

[1017] See, e. g., *Gerstein v. Pugh*, 420 U.S. 103, 113, 95 S.Ct. 854, 862, 43 L.Ed.2d 54 (1975).

[1018] *Jones v. United States*, 357 U.S. 493, 499, 78 S.Ct. 1253, 1257, 2 L.Ed.2d 1514 (1958); see *Almeida-Sanchez v. United States*, 413 U.S. 266, 279-280, 93 S.Ct. 2535, 2542-2543, 37 L.Ed.2d 596 (1973) (Powell, J., concurring); *United States v. United States District Court*, 407 U.S. 297, 314-321, 92 S.Ct. 2125, 2135-2139, 32 L.Ed.2d 752 (1972); *Coolidge v. New Hampshire*, 403 U.S. 443 454-455, 91 S.Ct. 2022, 2031-2032, 29 L.Ed.2d 564 (1971).

[1019] *Id.*, at 450, 91 S.Ct., at 2029-2030; *Katz v. United States*, 389 U.S. 347, 356-358, 88 S.Ct. 507, 514-515, 19 L.Ed.2d 576 (1967).

without a warrant would reduce the Amendment to a nullity and leave the people's homes secure only in the discretion of police officers. . . When the right of privacy must reasonably yield to the right of search is, as a rule, to be decided by a judicial officer, not by a policeman or Government enforcement agent."[1020]

Since the Fourth Amendment speaks equally to both searches and seizures, and since an arrest, the taking hold of one's person, is quintessentially a seizure, it would seem that the constitutional provision should impose the same limitations upon arrests that it does upon searches. Indeed, as an abstract matter an argument can be made that the restrictions upon arrest perhaps should be greater. A search may cause only annoyance and temporary inconvenience to the law-abiding citizen, assuming more serious dimension only when it turns up evidence of criminality. An arrest, however, is a serious personal intrusion regardless of whether the person seized is guilty or innocent. Although an arrestee cannot be held for a significant period without some neutral determination that there are grounds to do so,[1021]no decision that he should go free can come quickly enough to erase the invasion of his privacy that already will have occurred.[1022]***429** Logic, therefore, would seem to dictate that arrests be subject to the warrant requirement at least to the same extent as searches.

But logic sometimes must defer to history and experience. The Court's opinion emphasizes the historical sanction accorded warrantless felony arrests. In the early days of the common law most felony arrests were made upon personal knowledge and without warrants. So established were such arrests as the usual practice that Lord Coke seriously questioned whether a justice of the peace, receiving his information secondhand instead of from personal knowledge, even could authorize an arrest by warrant.[1023]By the late 18th century it had been firmly established by Blackstone, with an intervening assist from Sir Matthew Hale, that magistrates could issue arrest warrants upon information supplied by others.[1024]But recognition of the warrant power cast no doubt upon the validity of warrantless felony arrests, which continued to be practiced and upheld as before.[1025]There is no historical evidence that the Framers or proponents of the Fourth Amendment, outspokenly opposed to the infamous general warrants and writs of assistance, were at all concerned about warrantless arrests by local constables and other peace officers.[1026]As the Court today notes, the ****831** Second Congress' passage of an Act authorizing such arrests so soon after the adoption of the Fourth Amendment ***430** itself underscores the probability that the constitutional provision was intended to restrict entirely different practices.

The historical momentum for acceptance of warrantless arrests, already strong at the adoption of the Fourth Amendment, has gained strength during the ensuing two centuries. Both the judiciary and the legislative bodies of this Nation repeatedly have placed their imprimaturs upon the practice and, as the Government emphasizes, law enforcement agencies have developed their investigative and arrest procedures upon an assumption that warrantless arrests were valid so long as based upon probable cause. The decision of the Court of Appeals in this case was virtually unprecedented. Of course, no practice that is inconsistent with constitutional protections can be saved merely by appeal to previous uncritical acceptance. But the warrantless felony arrest, long preferred at common law and un-impeached at the passage of the Fourth

---

[1020] *Johnson v. United States*, 333 U.S. 10, 14, 68 S.Ct. 367, 369, 92 L.Ed. 436 (1948).

[1021] See *Gerstein, supra.*

[1022] See *Chimel v. California*, 395 U.S. 752, 776, 89 S.Ct. 2034, 2047, 23 L.Ed.2d 685 (1969) (White, J., dissenting); cf. *United States v. Robinson*, 414 U.S. 218, 237-238, 94 S.Ct. 467, 477-478, 38 L.Ed.2d 427 (1973) (Powell, J., concurring).

[1023] 4 E. Coke, Institutes 177 (6th ed. 1681).

[1024] 4 W. Blackstone, Commentaries *290; see 2 M. Hale, Pleas of the Crown *108-110.

[1025] 4 W. Blackstone, *supra*, at *282; 1 J. Chitty, Criminal Law *14-15.

[1026] See N. Lasson, The History and Development of the Fourth Amendment to the United States Constitution 79-105 (1937); cf. *Gerstein v. Pugh*, *supra*, 420 U.S., at 114-116, 95 S.Ct., at 863-864.

Amendment, is not such a practice. Given the revolutionary implications of such a holding, a declaration at this late date that warrantless felony arrests are constitutionally infirm would have to rest upon reasons more substantial than a desire to harmonize the rules for arrest with those governing searches.[1027]

***431** Moreover, a constitutional rule permitting felony arrests only with a warrant or in exigent circumstances could severely hamper effective law enforcement. Good police practice often requires postponing an arrest, even after probable cause has been established, in order to place the suspect under surveillance or otherwise develop further evidence necessary to prove guilt to a jury. Under the holding of the Court of Appeals, such additional investigative work could imperil the entire prosecution. Should the officers fail to obtain a warrant initially, and later be required by unforeseen circumstances to arrest immediately with no chance to procure a last-minute warrant, they would risk a court decision that the subsequent exigency did not excuse their failure to get a warrant in the interim since they first developed probable cause. If the officers attempted to meet such a ****832** contingency ***432** by procuring a warrant as soon as they had probable cause and then merely held it during their subsequent investigation, they would risk a court decision that the warrant had grown stale by the time it was used. Law enforcement personnel caught in this squeeze could ensure validity of their arrests only by obtaining a warrant and arresting as soon as probable cause existed, thereby foreclosing the possibility of gathering vital additional evidence from the suspect's continued actions.

In sum, the historical and policy reasons sketched above fully justify the Court's sustaining of a warrantless arrest upon probable cause, despite the resulting divergence between the constitutional rule governing searches and that now held applicable to seizures of the person.

II

Finally, I share the view expressed in the opinion of Mr. Justice Stewart. It makes clear that we do not today consider or decide whether or under what circumstances ***433** an officer lawfully may make a warrantless arrest in a private home or other place where the person has a reasonable expectation of privacy.

Mr. Justice STEWART, concurring in the result.

The arrest in this case was made upon probable cause in a public place in broad daylight. The Court holds that this arrest did not violate the Fourth Amendment, and I agree. The Court does not decide, nor could it decide in this case, whether or under what circumstances an officer must obtain a warrant before he may lawfully enter a private place to effect an arrest.[1028]

(The dissent of Mr. Justice MARSHALL, with whom Mr. Justice BRENNAN joins, omitted.)

[1027] Cf. *United States v. Robinson, supra*, 414 U.S., at 230, 94 S.Ct., at 474. Cf. *United States v. Robinson, supra*, 414 U.S., at 230, 94 S.Ct., at 474.

[1028] See *Gerstein v. Pugh*, 420 U.S. 103, 113 n. 13, 95 S.Ct. 854, 863, 43 L.Ed.2d 54; *Coolidge v. New Hampshire*, 403 U.S. 443, 474-481, 91 S.Ct. 2022, 2042-2046, 29 L.Ed.2d 564; *Davis v. Mississippi*, 394 U.S. 721, 728, 89 S.Ct. 1394, 1398, 22 L.Ed.2d 676; *Jones v. United States*, 357 U.S. 493, 499-500, 78 S.Ct. 1253, 1257-1258, 2 L.Ed.2d 1514.

Black Letter Law

> Where, based on information from reliable informant that defendant possessed stolen credit cards in violation of statute prohibiting possession of stolen mail, probable cause existed for arrest, warrantless arrest of defendant by postal officers in restaurant at midday was valid under statute authorizing postal service officers who are performing duties related to inspection of postal matters to make warrantless arrests for felonies if they have reasonable grounds to believe that person to be arrested has committed or is committing a felony. Defendant's consent to the search of his automobile was given while he was in custody on public street, after valid arrest and, after he had been given Miranda warnings and further cautioned that results of search could be used against him. The search was not the result of any overt act or threat of force against the defendant, and there were no indications that defendant was a newcomer to law, mentally deficient or unable to exercise free choice.

Atwater v. City of Lago Vista

121 S.Ct. 1536

Supreme Court of the United States

Gail ATWATER, et al., Petitioners,

v.

CITY OF LAGO VISTA et al.

No. 99–1408. | Argued Dec. 4, 2000. | Decided April 24, 2001.

***323** Justice SOUTER delivered the opinion of the Court.

The question is whether the Fourth Amendment forbids a warrantless arrest for a minor criminal offense, such as a misdemeanor seatbelt violation punishable only by a fine. We hold that it does not.

I

A

In Texas, if a car is equipped with safety belts, a front-seat passenger must wear one,[1029]and the driver must secure any small child riding in front.[1030]Violation of either provision is "a misdemeanor punishable by a fine not less than $25 or more than $50."[1031]Texas law expressly authorizes "[a]ny peace officer [to] arrest without warrant a person found committing a violation" of these seatbelt laws,[1032]although it permits police to issue citations in lieu of arrest.[1033]

In March 1997, petitioner Gail Atwater was driving her pickup truck in Lago Vista, Texas, with her 3–year–old son and 5–year–old daughter in the front seat. None of them was ***324** wearing a seatbelt. Respondent Bart Turek, a Lago Vista police officer at the time, observed the seatbelt violations and pulled Atwater over. According to Atwater's complaint (the allegations of which we assume to be true for present purposes), Turek approached the truck and "yell[ed]" something to the effect of "we've met before" and "you're going to jail."[1034]He then called for backup and

---

[1029] Tex. Transp.Code Ann. § 545.413(a) (1999).

[1030] § 545.413(b).

[1031] § 545.413(d).

[1032] § 543.001.

[1033] §§ 543.003–543.005.

[1034] App. 20.

asked to see Atwater's driver's license and insurance documentation, which state law required her to carry.[1035]When Atwater told Turek that she did not have the papers because her purse had been stolen the day before, Turek said that he had "heard that story two-hundred times."[1036]

Atwater asked to take her "frightened, upset, and crying" children to a friend's house nearby, but Turek told her, "you're **1542 not going anywhere."[1037]As it turned out, Atwater's friend learned what was going on and soon arrived to take charge of the children. Turek then handcuffed Atwater, placed her in his squad car, and drove her to the local police station, where booking officers had her remove her shoes, jewelry, and eyeglasses, and empty her pockets. Officers took Atwater's "mug shot" and placed her, alone, in a jail cell for about one hour, after which she was taken before a magistrate and released on $310 bond.

Atwater was charged with driving without her seatbelt fastened, failing to secure her children in seatbelts, driving without a license, and failing to provide proof of insurance. She ultimately pleaded no contest to the misdemeanor seatbelt offenses and paid a $50 fine; the other charges were dismissed.

***325 B**

Atwater and her husband, petitioner Michael Haas, filed suit in a Texas state court under 42 U.S.C. § 1983 against Turek and respondents City of Lago Vista and Chief of Police Frank Miller. So far as concerns us, petitioners (whom we will simply call Atwater) alleged that respondents (for simplicity, the City) had violated Atwater's Fourth Amendment "right to be free from unreasonable seizure,"[1038]and sought compensatory and punitive damages.

The City removed the suit to the United States District Court for the Western District of Texas. Given Atwater's admission that she had "violated the law" and the absence of any allegation "that she was harmed or detained in any way inconsistent with the law," the District Court ruled the Fourth Amendment claim "meritless" and granted the City's summary judgment motion.[1039]A panel of the United States Court of Appeals for the Fifth Circuit reversed.[1040]It concluded that "an arrest for a first-time seat belt offense" was an unreasonable seizure within the meaning of the Fourth Amendment, id., at 387, and held that Turek was not entitled to qualified immunity, id., at 389.

Sitting en banc, the Court of Appeals vacated the panel's decision and affirmed the District Court's summary judgment for the City.[1041]Relying on *Whren v. United States*,[1042]the en banc court observed that, although the Fourth Amendment generally requires a balancing of individual and governmental interests, where "an arrest is based on probable cause then 'with rare exceptions ... the result of that balancing is not in doubt.'"[1043]Because "[n]either party dispute[d] that Officer Turek had probable cause to arrest Atwater," and because "there [was] no evidence in the record that Officer Turek conducted the arrest in an 'extraordinary manner, unusually harmful'

[1035] Tex. Transp.Code Ann. §§ 521.025, 601.053 (1999).

[1036] App. 21.

[1037] *Ibid.*

[1038] App. 23.

[1039] No. A–97 CA 679 SS (WD Tex., Feb. 13, 1999), App. to Pet. for Cert. 50a–63a.

[1040] 165 F.3d 380 (1999).

[1041]

[1042] 517 U.S. 806, 116 S.Ct. 1769, 135 L.Ed.2d 89 (1996).

[1043] 195 F.3d, at 244 (quoting *Whren, supra*, at 817, 116 S.Ct. 1769).

to Atwater's ***326** privacy interests," the en banc court held that the arrest was not unreasonable for Fourth Amendment purposes.[1044]

Three judges issued dissenting opinions. On the understanding that citation is the "usual procedure" in a traffic stop situation, Judge Reynaldo Garza thought Atwater's arrest unreasonable, since there was no particular reason for taking her into custody.[1045]Judge Weiner likewise believed that "even with probable cause, [an] officer must have a plausible, articulable reason" for making a custodial arrest.[1046]Judge Dennis understood the Fourth Amendment to have incorporated an earlier, common-law prohibition on warrantless arrests for misdemeanors that do not amount to or involve a "breach of the peace."[1047]

We granted certiorari to consider whether the Fourth Amendment, either by incorporating common-law restrictions on misdemeanor arrests or otherwise, limits police officers' authority to arrest without ****1543** warrant for minor criminal offenses.[1048]We now affirm.

II

The Fourth Amendment safeguards "[t]he right of the people to be secure in their persons, houses, papers, and effects, against unreasonable searches and seizures." In reading the Amendment, we are guided by "the traditional protections against unreasonable searches and seizures afforded by the common law at the time of the framing"[1049]since "[a]n examination of the common law understanding of an officer's authority to arrest sheds light on the obviously relevant, if not entirely dispositive, consideration of what the Framers of the Amendment might have thought to be reasonable."[1050]Thus, the first step here is to assess Atwater's claim that peace officers' authority to make warrantless arrests for misdemeanors was ***327** restricted at common law (whether "common law" is understood strictly as law judicially derived or, instead, as the whole body of law extant at the time of the framing). Atwater's specific contention is that "founding-era common-law rules" forbade peace officers to make warrantless misdemeanor arrests except in cases of "breach of the peace," a category she claims was then understood narrowly as covering only those non-felony offenses "involving or tending toward violence."[1051]Although her historical argument is by no means insubstantial, it ultimately fails.

A

We begin with the state of pre-founding English common law and find that, even after making some allowance for variations in the common-law usage of the term "breach of the peace," the "founding-era ****1544** common-law rules" were not ***328** nearly as clear as Atwater claims; on the contrary, the common-law commentators (as well as the sparsely reported cases) reached divergent conclusions with respect to officers' warrantless misdemeanor arrest power. Moreover, in the years leading up to American independence, Parliament repeatedly extended express warrantless arrest authority to cover misdemeanor-level offenses not amounting to or involving any violent breach of the peace.

1

[1044] 195 F.3d, at 245–246 (quoting *Whren*, *supra*, at 818, 116 S.Ct. 1769).

[1045] 195 F.3d, at 246–247. 195 F.3d, at 246–247.

[1046] *Id.*, at 251.

[1047] *Ibid.*

[1048] 530 U.S. 1260, 120 S.Ct. 2715, 147 L.Ed.2d 981 (2000).

[1049] *Wilson v. Arkansas*, 514 U.S. 927, 931, 115 S.Ct. 1914, 131 L.Ed.2d 976 (1995),

[1050] *Payton v. New York*, 445 U.S. 573, 591, 100 S.Ct. 1371, 63 L.Ed.2d 639 (1980) (footnote omitted).

[1051] Brief for Petitioners 13.

Atwater's historical argument begins with our quotation from Halsbury in *Carroll v. United States*:[1052]

"'[I]n cases of misdemeanor, a peace officer like a private person has at common law no power of arresting without a warrant except when a breach of the peace has been committed in his presence or there is reasonable ground for supposing that a breach of peace is about to be committed or renewed in his presence.'"[1053]

***329** But the isolated quotation tends to mislead. In *Carroll* itself we spoke of the common-law rule as only "sometimes expressed" that way,[1054] and, indeed, in the very same paragraph, we conspicuously omitted any reference to a breach-of-the-peace limitation in stating that the "usual rule" at common law was that "a police officer [could] arrest without warrant ... one guilty of a misdemeanor if committed in his presence."[1055]Thus, what *Carroll* illustrates, and what others have recognized, is that statements about the common law of warrantless misdemeanor arrest simply are not uniform. Rather, "[a]t common law there is a difference of opinion among the authorities as to whether this right to arrest [without a warrant] extends to all misdemeanors."[1056]

On one side of the divide there are certainly eminent authorities supporting Atwater's position. In addition to Lord Halsbury, quoted in *Carroll*, James Fitzjames Stephen and Glanville Williams both seemed to indicate that the common law confined warrantless misdemeanor arrests to actual breaches of the peace.[1057] Sir William Blackstone and Sir Edward East might also be counted on Atwater's side, although they spoke only to the sufficiency of breach of the peace as a condition to warrantless ***330** misdemeanor arrest, not to its necessity. Blackstone recognized that at common law "[t]he constable... hath great original and inherent authority with regard to arrests," but with respect to non-felony offenses said only that "[h]e may, without warrant, arrest any one for a breach of the peace, and carry him before a justice of the peace."[1058]Not long after the framing of the Fourth Amendment, East characterized peace officers' common-law arrest power in much the same way: "A constable or other known conservator of the peace may lawfully interpose upon his own view to prevent a breach of the peace, or to quiet an ****1545** affray...."[1059]
The great commentators were not unanimous, however, and there is also considerable evidence of a broader conception of common-law misdemeanor arrest authority unlimited by any breach of the peace condition. Sir Matthew Hale, Chief Justice of King's Bench from 1671 to 1676, wrote in his History of the Pleas of the Crown that, by his "original and inherent power," a constable could arrest without a warrant "for breach of the peace and some misdemeanors, less than felony."[1060]Hale's view, posthumously published in 1736, reflected an understanding dating back at least 60

[1052] 267 U.S. 132, 45 S.Ct. 280, 69 L.Ed. 543 (1925).

[1053] *Id.*, at 157, 45 S.Ct. 280 (quoting 9 Halsbury, Laws of England § 612, p. 299 (1909)).

[1054] 267 U.S., at 157, 45 S.Ct. 280.

[1055] *Id.*, at 156–157, 45 S.Ct. 280.

[1056] American Law Institute, Code of Criminal Procedure, Commentary to § 21, p. 231 (1930).

[1057] See 1 J. Stephen, A History of the Criminal Law of England 193 (1883) ("The common law did not authorize the arrest of persons guilty or suspected of misdemeanors, except in cases of an actual breach of the peace either by an affray or by violence to an individual"); G. Williams, Arrest for Breach of the Peace, 1954 Crim. L.Rev. 578, 578 ("Apart from arrest for felony ..., the only power of arrest at common law is in respect of breach of the peace"). See also *Queen v. Tooley*, 2 Ld. Raym. 1296, 1301, 92 Eng. Rep. 349, 352 (Q.B.1710) ("[A] constable cannot arrest, but when he sees an actual breach of the peace; and if the affray be over, he cannot arrest").

[1058] 4 Blackstone 289.

[1059] 1 E. East, Pleas of the Crown § 71, p. 303 (1803).

[1060] 2 M. Hale, Pleas of the Crown 88 (1736).

years before the appearance of his Pleas yet sufficiently authoritative to sustain a momentum extending well beyond the framing era in this country. [1061] ***331**

As will be seen later, the view of warrantless arrest authority as extending to at least "some misdemeanors" beyond breaches of the peace was undoubtedly informed by statutory provisions authorizing such arrests, but it reflected common law in the strict, judge-made sense as well, for such was the holding of at least one case reported before Hale had even become a judge but which, like Hale's own commentary, continued to be cited well after the ratification of the Fourth Amendment. In *Holyday v. Oxenbridge*,[1062]the Court of King's Bench held that even a private person (and thus a fortiori a peace officer) needed no warrant to arrest a "common cheater" whom he discovered "cozen[ing] with false dice." The court expressly rejected the contention that warrantless arrests were improper "unless in felony," and said instead that "there was good cause [for] staying" the gambler and, more broadly, that "it is pro bono publico to stay such offenders."[1063]In the edition nearest to the date of the Constitution's framing, Sergeant William Hawkins's widely read Treatise of the Pleas of the Crown generalized from Holyday that "from the reason of this case it seems to follow, ***332** That the [warrantless] arrest of any other offenders ... for offenses in like manner scandalous and prejudicial to the public, may be justified."[1064]A number of other common-law commentaries shared Hawkins's broad reading of Holyday.[1065]

We thus find disagreement, not unanimity, among both the common-law jurists and the text writers who sought to pull the cases together and summarize accepted practice. Having reviewed the relevant English decisions, as well as English and colonial American legal treatises, legal dictionaries, and procedure manuals, we simply are not convinced that Atwater's is the correct, or even necessarily the better, reading of the common law history.

***333 2**

A second, and equally serious, problem for Atwater's historical argument is posed by the "Divers Statutes,"[1066]enacted by Parliament well before this Republic's founding that authorized warrantless misdemeanor arrests without reference to violence or turmoil. Quite apart from Hale and Blackstone, the legal background of any conception of reasonableness the Fourth Amendment's Framers might have entertained would have included English statutes, some centuries old, authorizing peace officers (and even private persons) to make warrantless arrests for all sorts of relatively minor offenses unaccompanied by violence. The so-called "nightwalker" statutes are perhaps the most notable examples. From the enactment of the Statute of Winchester in 1285, through its various re-adoptions and until its repeal in 1827, night watchmen were authorized and charged "as ... in Times past" to "watch the Town continually all Night, from the Sun-setting unto the Sun-rising" and were directed that "if any Stranger do pass by them, he shall be arrested until

[1061] See The Compleat Parish–Officer 11 (1744) ("[T]he Constable ... may for Breach of the Peace, and some Misdemeanors less than Felony, imprison a Man"); R. Burn, The Justice of the Peace 271 (1837) ("A constable ... may at common law, for treason, felony, breach of the peace, and some misdemeanors less than felony, committed in his view, apprehend the supposed offender without any warrant" (italics in original)); 1 J. Chitty, A Practical Treatise on the Criminal Law 20 (5th ed. 1847) ("[A constable] may for treason, felony, breach of the peace, and some misdemeanors less than felony, committed in his view, apprehend the supposed offender virtiute officii, without any warrant"); 1 W. Russell, Crimes and Misdemeanors 725 (7th ed.1909) (officer "may arrest any person who in his presence commits a misdemeanor or breach of the peace").

[1062] Cro. Car. 234, 79 Eng. Rep. 805 (1631).

[1063] *Id.*, at 805–806.

[1064] 2 Hawkins, ch. 12, § 20, at 122.

[1065] See The Law of Arrests 205 (2d ed. 1753) (In light of Holyday, "an Arrest of an Offender ... for any Crime prejudicial to the **1546 Publick, seems to be justifiable"); 1 T. Cunningham, A New and Complete Law Dictionary (1771) (definition of "arrest") (same); 1 G. Jacob, The Law Dictionary 129 (1st Am.ed., 1811) (same). See generally C. Greaves, Law of Arrest Without a Warrant, in The Criminal Law Consolidation Acts, p. lxiii (1870) ("[Holyday] is rested upon the broad ground that 'it is pro bono publico to stay such offenders,' which is equally applicable to every case of misdemeanor ... ").

[1066] M. Dalton, Country Justice, ch. 170, § 4, p. 582 (1727).

Morning...."[1067]Hawkins emphasized that the Statute of Winchester "was made" not in derogation but rather "in affirmance of the common law," for "every private person may by the common law arrest any suspicious night-walker, and detain him till he give good account of himself...."[1068] And according to Blackstone, these watchmen had virtually limitless warrantless nighttime arrest power: "Watchmen, either those appointed by the statute of Winchester ... or such as are mere assistants to the constable, may virtute officii arrest all offenders, and particularly night-walkers, and commit them to custody till the morning."[1069] ***334** The Statute of Winchester, moreover, empowered ****1547** peace officers not only to deal with night-walkers and other nighttime "offenders," but periodically to "make inquiry of all persons being lodged in the suburbs, or in foreign places of the towns." On that score, the statute provided that "if they do find any that have lodged or received any strangers or suspicious person, against the peace, the bailiffs shall do right therein,"[1070]which Hawkins understood "surely" to mean that officers could "lawfully arrest and detain any such stranger[s],"[1071]

Nor were the nightwalker statutes the only legislative sources of warrantless arrest authority absent real or threatened violence, as the parties and their amici here seem to have assumed. On the contrary, following the Edwardian legislation and throughout the period leading up to the framing, Parliament repeatedly extended warrantless arrest power to cover misdemeanor-level offenses not involving any breach of the peace. One 16th-century statute, for instance, authorized peace officers to arrest persons playing "unlawful game[s]" like bowling, tennis, dice, and cards, and for good measure extended the authority beyond players to include persons "haunting" the "houses, places and alleys where such games shall be suspected to be holden, exercised, used ***335** or occupied."[1072]A 17th-century act empowered "any person ... whatsoever to seize and detain any ... hawker, pedlar, petty chapman, or other trading person" found selling without a license.[1073]And 18th-century statutes authorized the warrantless arrest of "rogues, vagabonds, beggars, and other idle and disorderly persons" (defined broadly to include jugglers, palm readers, and unlicensed play actors);[1074]"horrid" persons who "profanely swear or curse;"[1075]individuals obstructing "publick streets, lanes or open passages" with "pipes, butts, barrels, casks or other vessels" or an "empty cart, car, dray or other carriage;"[1076]and, most significantly of all given the circumstances of the case before us, negligent carriage drivers.[1077]

The significance of these early English statutes lies not in proving that any common-law rule barring warrantless misdemeanor arrests that might have existed would have been subject to statutory override; the sovereign Parliament could of

[1067] 13 Edw. I, ch. 4, §§ 5–6, 1 Statutes at Large 232–233; see also 5 Edw. III, ch. 14, 1 Statutes at Large 448 (1331) (confirming and extending the powers of watchmen).

[1068] 2 Hawkins, ch. 13, § 6, at 130.

[1069] 4 Blackstone 289; see also 2 Hale, Pleas of the Crown, at 97 (describing broad arrest powers of watchmen even over and above those conferred by the Statute of Winchester).

[1070] 13 Edw. I, ch. 4, §§ 3–4, 1 Statutes at Large 232–233.

[1071] 2 Hawkins, ch. 13, § 12, at 134.

[1072] 33 Hen. VIII, ch. 9, §§ 11–16, 5 Statutes at Large 84–85 (1541).

[1073] 8 & 9 Wm. III, ch. 25, §§ 3, 8, 10 Statutes at Large 81–83 (1697).

[1074] 17 Geo. II, ch. 5, §§ 1–2, 5, 18 Statutes at Large 144, 145–147 (1744).

[1075] 19 Geo. II, ch. 21, § 3, 18 Statutes at Large 445 (1746).

[1076] 30 Geo. II, ch. 22, §§ 5, 13, 22 Statutes at Large 107–108, 111 (1757).

[1077] 27 Geo. II, ch. 16, § 7, 21 Statutes at Large 188 (1754). See generally S. Blackerby, The Justice of Peace: His Companion, or a Summary of all the Acts of Parliament (1723) (cataloguing statutes); S. Welch, An Essay on the Office of Constable 19–22 (1758) (describing same).

course have wiped away any judge-made rule. The point is that the statutes riddle Atwater's supposed common law rule with enough exceptions to unsettle any contention that the law of the mother country would have left the Fourth Amendment's Framers of a view that it would necessarily have been unreasonable to arrest without warrant for a misdemeanor unaccompanied by real or threatened violence.

***336 B**

An examination of specifically American evidence is to the same effect. Neither the history of the framing era nor subsequent legal development indicates that the Fourth Amendment was originally understood, ****1548** or has traditionally been read, to embrace Atwater's position.

1

To begin with, Atwater has cited no particular evidence that those who framed and ratified the Fourth Amendment sought to limit peace officers' warrantless misdemeanor arrest authority to instances of actual breach of the peace, and our own review of the recent and respected compilations of framing-era documentary history has likewise failed to reveal any such design.[1078]Nor have we found in any of the modern historical accounts of the Fourth Amendment's adoption any substantial indication that the Framers intended such a restriction.[1079]Indeed, to the extent these modern histories address the issue, their conclusions are to the contrary.[1080] ***337**

The evidence of actual practice also counsels against Atwater's position. During the period leading up to and surrounding the framing of the Bill of Rights, colonial and state legislatures, like Parliament before them[1081]regularly authorized local peace officers to make warrantless misdemeanor arrests without conditioning statutory authority on breach of the peace.[1082] ***338 **1549** What we have here, then, is just the opposite of what we had in *Wilson v. Arkansas*. There, we emphasized that during the founding era a number of States had "enacted statutes specifically embracing" the common law knock-and-announce rule;[1083]here, by contrast, those very same States passed laws extending warrantless arrest authority to a host of nonviolent misdemeanors, and in so doing acted very much inconsistently with Atwater's claims about the Fourth Amendment's object. Of course, the Fourth ***339** Amend-

---

[1078] See The Complete Bill of Rights 223–263 (N. Cogan ed.1997) (collecting original sources); 5 The Founders' Constitution 219–244 (P. Kurland & R. Lerner eds.1987) (same).

[1079] See, e.g., L. Levy, Origins of the Bill of Rights 150–179 (1999); T. Taylor, Two Studies in Constitutional Interpretation 19–93 (1969); J. Landynski, Search and Seizure and the Supreme Court 19–48 (1966); N. Lasson, History and Development of the Fourth Amendment to the United States Constitution 79–105 (1937); Davies, Recovering the Original Fourth Amendment, 98 Mich. L.Rev. 547 (1999); Amar, Fourth Amendment First Principles, 107 Harv. L.Rev. 757 (1994); Bradley, Constitutional Theory of the Fourth Amendment, 38 DePaul L.Rev. 817 (1989).

[1080] See *Landynski, supra*, at 45 (Fourth Amendment arrest rules are "based on common-law practice," which "dispensed with" a warrant requirement for misdemeanors "committed in the presence of the arresting officer"); *Davies, supra*, at 551 ("[T]he Framers did not address warrantless intrusions at all in the Fourth Amendment or in the earlier state provisions; thus, they never anticipated that 'unreasonable' might be read as a standard for warrantless intrusions").

[1081] *supra*, at 1546–1547,

[1082] See, e.g., First Laws of the State of Connecticut 214–215 (Cushing ed.1982) (1784 compilation; exact date of Act unknown) (authorizing warrantless arrests of "all Persons unnecessarily travelling on the Sabbath or Lord's Day"); id., at 23 ("such as are guilty of Drunkenness, profane Swearing, Sabbath-breaking, also vagrant Persons [and] unseasonable Night-walkers"); Digest of the Laws of the State of Georgia 1755–1800, p. 411 (H. Marbury & W. Crawford eds. 1802) (1762 Act) (breakers of the Sabbath laws); id., at 252 (1764 Act) (persons "gaming ... in any licensed public house, or other house selling liquors"); Colonial Laws of Massachusetts 139 (1889) (1646 Act) ("such as are overtaken with drink, swearing, Sabbath breaking, Lying, vagrant persons, [and] night-walkers"); Laws of the State of New Hampshire 549 (1800) (1799 Act) (persons "travelling unnecessarily" on Sunday); Digest of the Laws of New Jersey 1709–1838, pp. 585–586 (L. Elmer ed. 1838) (1799 Act) ("vagrants or vagabonds, common drunkards, common night-walkers, and common prostitutes," as well as fortune-tellers and other practitioners of "crafty science"); Laws of the State of New York, 1777–1784, pp. 358–359 (1886) (1781 Act) ("hawker[s]" and "pedlar[s]"); Earliest Printed Laws of New York, 1665–1693, p. 133 (J. Cushing ed. 1978) (Duke of York's Laws, 1665–1675) ("such as are overtaken with Drink, Swearing, Sabbath breaking, Vagrant persons or night walkers"); 3 Laws of the Commonwealth of Pennsylvania 177–183 1810) (1794 Act) (persons "profanely curs[ing]," drinking excessively, "cock-fighting," or "play[ing] at cards, dice, billiards, bowls, shuffle- boards, or any game of hazard or address, for money").

[1083] 514 U.S., at 933, 115 S.Ct. 1914.

ment did not originally apply to the States,[1084]but that does not make state practice irrelevant in unearthing the Amendment's original meaning. A number of state constitutional search-and-seizure provisions served as models for the Fourth Amendment,[1085]and the fact that many of the original States with such constitutional limitations continued to grant their own peace officers broad warrantless misdemeanor arrest authority undermines Atwater's contention that the founding generation meant to bar federal law enforcement officers from exercising the same authority. Given the early state practice, it is likewise troublesome for Atwater's view that just one year after the ratification of the Fourth Amendment, Congress vested federal marshals with "the same powers in executing the laws of the United States, as sheriffs and their deputies in the several states have by law, in executing the laws of their respective states."[1086]Thus, as we have said before in only slightly different circumstances, the Second Congress apparently "saw no inconsistency between the Fourth Amendment and legislation giving United States marshals the same power as local peace officers" to make warrantless arrests[1087] The record thus supports Justice Powell's observation that "[t]here is no historical ****1550** evidence that the Framers or proponents of the Fourth Amendment, outspokenly opposed to the infamous general warrants and writs of assistance, were at ***340** all concerned about warrantless arrests by local constables and other peace officers."[1088]We simply cannot conclude that the Fourth Amendment, as originally understood, forbade peace officers to arrest without a warrant for misdemeanors not amounting to or involving breach of the peace.

2

Nor does Atwater's argument from tradition pick up any steam from the historical record as it has unfolded since the framing, there being no indication that her claimed rule has ever become "woven ... into the fabric" of American law.[1089]The story, on the contrary, is of two centuries of uninterrupted (and largely unchallenged) state and federal practice permitting warrantless arrests for misdemeanors not amounting to or involving breach of the peace.

First, there is no support for Atwater's position in this Court's cases (apart from the isolated sentence in Carroll, already explained). Although the Court has not had much to say about warrantless misdemeanor arrest authority, what little we have said tends to cut against Atwater's argument. In discussing this authority, we have focused on the circumstance that an offense was committed in an officer's presence, to the omission of any reference to a breach-of-the-peace limitation.[1090] ***341**

Second, and again in contrast with Wilson, it is not the case here that "[e]arly American courts ... embraced" an accepted common-law rule with anything approaching unanimity.[1091]To be sure, Atwater has cited several 19th-century decisions that, at least at first glance, might seem to support her contention that "warrantless

---

[1084] See *Barron v. Mayor of Baltimore*, 7 Pet. 243, 8 L.Ed. 672 (1833).

[1085] See, e.g., N.H. Const. of 1784, pt. I, Art. XIX; Pa. Const. of 1776 (Declaration of Rights), Art. X.

[1086] Act of May 2, 1792, ch. 28, § 9, 1 Stat. 265.

[1087] *United States v. Watson*, 423 U.S. 411, 420, 96 S.Ct. 820, 46 L.Ed.2d 598 (1976).

[1088] *Id.*, at 429, 96 S.Ct. 820 (concurring opinion).

[1089] *Wilson, supra*, at 933, 115 S.Ct. 1914; see also *Payton v. New York*, 445 U.S., at 590, 100 S.Ct. 1371 (emphasizing "the clear consensus among the States adhering to [a] well-settled common-law rule").

[1090] See, e.g., *United States v. Watson, supra*, at 418, 96 S.Ct. 820 ("The cases construing the Fourth Amendment thus reflect the ancient common-law rule that a peace officer was permitted to arrest without a warrant for a misdemeanor or felony committed in his presence ..."); *Carroll*, 267 U.S., at 156–157, 45 S.Ct. 280 ("The usual rule is that a police officer may arrest without warrant one ... guilty of a misdemeanor if committed in his presence"); *Bad Elk v. United States*, 177 U.S. 529, 534, 536, n. 1, 20 S.Ct. 729, 44 L.Ed. 874 (1900) (noting common-law pedigree of state statute permitting warrantless arrest "[f]or a public offense committed or attempted in [officer's] presence"); *Kurtz v. Moffitt*, 115 U.S. 487, 499, 6 S.Ct. 148, 29 L.Ed. 458 (1885) (common-law presence requirement); cf. also *Welsh v. Wisconsin*, 466 U.S. 740, 756, 104 S.Ct. 2091, 80 L.Ed.2d 732 (1984) (White, J., dissenting) ("'[A]uthority to arrest without a warrant in misdemeanor cases may be enlarged by statute'").

[1091] *Wilson v. Arkansas*, 514 U.S., at 933, 115 S.Ct. 1914.

misdemeanor arrest was unlawful when not [for] a breach of the peace."[1092]But none is ultimately availing. Pow is fundamentally a "presence" case; it stands only for the proposition, not at issue here, see n. 11, supra, that a non-felony arrest should be made while the offense is "in [the officer's] view and ... still continuing" and not subsequently "upon vague information **1551 communicated to him."[1093]The language Atwater attributes to Carey ("[E]ven if he were a constable, he had no power to arrest for any misdemeanor without a warrant, except to stay a breach of the peace, or to prevent the commission of such an offense") is taken from the reporter's summary of one of the party's arguments, not from the opinion of the court. While the court in Carey (through Chief Justice Shaw) said that "the old established rule of the common law" was that "a constable or other peace officer could not *342 arrest one without a warrant ... if such crime were not an offense amounting in law to felony," it said just as clearly that the common law rule could be "altered by the legislature" (notwithstanding Massachusetts's own Fourth Amendment equivalent in its State Constitution).[1094]Miner, the third and final case upon which Atwater relies, was expressly overruled just six years after it was decided. In *Burroughs v. Eastman*,[1095]the Supreme Court of Michigan held that the language from Miner upon which the plaintiff there (and presumably Atwater here) relied "should not be followed," and then went on to offer the following: "[T]he question has arisen in many of our sister states, and the power to authorize arrest on view for offenses not amounting to breaches of the peace has been affirmed. Our attention has been called to no case, nor have we in our research found one, in which the contrary doctrine has been asserted."[1096]

The reports may well contain early American cases more favorable to Atwater's position than the ones she has herself invoked. But more to the point, we think, are the numerous early- and mid-19th–century decisions expressly sustaining (often against constitutional challenge) state and local laws authorizing peace officers to make warrantless arrests for misdemeanors not involving any breach of the peace.[1097]
***343 **1552**

Finally, both the legislative tradition of granting warrantless misdemeanor arrest authority and the judicial tradition of sustaining such statutes against constitutional attack are buttressed by legal commentary that, for more than a century now, has

---

[1092] Brief for Petitioners 17 (citing Pow v. Beckner, 3 Ind. 475, 478 (1852), Commonwealth v. Carey, 66 Mass. 246, 250 (1853), and Robison v. Miner, 68 Mich. 549, 556–559, 37 N.W. 21, 25 (1888)).

[1093] 3 Ind., at 478.

[1094] 66 Mass., at 252.

[1095] 101 Mich. 419, 59 N.W. 817 (1894).

[1096] 101 Mich., at 425, 59 N.W., at 819 (collecting cases from, e.g., Illinois, Indiana, Massachusetts, Minnesota, Missouri, New Hampshire, New York, Ohio, and Texas).

[1097] See, e.g., *Mayo v. Wilson*, 1 N.H. 53 (1817) (upholding statute authorizing warrantless arrests of those unnecessarily traveling on Sunday against challenge based on state due process and search-and-seizure provisions); *Holcomb v. Cornish*, 8 Conn. 375 (1831) (upholding statute permitting warrantless arrests for "drunkenness, profane swearing, cursing or sabbath-breaking," against argument that "[t]he power of a justice of the peace to arrest and detain a citizen without complaint or warrant against him, is surely not given by the common law"); *Jones v. Root*, 72 Mass. 435 (1856) (rebuffing constitutional challenge to statute authorizing officers "without a warrant [to] arrest any person or persons whom they may find in the act of illegally selling, transporting, or distributing intoxicating liquors"); *Main v. McCarty*, 15 Ill. 441, 442 (1854) (concluding that a law expressly authorizing arrests for city-ordinance violations was "not repugnant to the constitution or the general provisions of law"); *White v. Kent*, 11 Ohio St. 550 (1860) (upholding municipal ordinance permitting warrantless arrest of any person found violating any city ordinance or state law); *Davis v. American Soc. for Prevention of Cruelty to Animals*, 75 N.Y. 362 (1878) (upholding statute permitting warrantless arrest for misdemeanor violation of cruelty-to-animals prohibition). See generally Wilgus, Arrest Without a Warrant, 22 Mich. L.Rev. 541, 550, and n. 54 (1924) (collecting cases and observing that "[t]he states may, by statute, enlarge the common law right to arrest without a warrant, and have quite generally done so or authorized municipalities to do so, as for example, an officer may be authorized by statute or ordinance to arrest without a warrant for various misdemeanors and violations of ordinances, other than breaches of the peace, if committed in his presence"); id., at 706, nn. 570, 571 (collecting cases); 1 J. Bishop, New Criminal Procedure §§ 181, 183, pp. 101, n. 2, 103, n. 5 (4th ed. 1895) (same); W. Clark, Handbook of Criminal Procedure § 12, p. 50, n. 8 (2d ed.1918) (same).

almost uniformly recognized the constitutionality of extending warrantless arrest power to misdemeanors without limitation to breaches of the peace.[1098]

Small wonder, then, that today statutes in all 50 States and the District of Columbia permit warrantless misdemeanor arrests by at least some (if not all) peace officers without requiring any breach of the peace, as do a host of congressional enactments. The American Law Institute ***345** has long endorsed the validity of such legislation.[1099]This, therefore, simply is not a case in which the claimant can point to "a clear answer [that] existed in 1791 and has been generally ****1553** adhered to by the traditions of our society ever since."[1100]

III

While it is true here that history, if not unequivocal, has expressed a decided, majority view that the police need not obtain an arrest warrant merely because a misdemeanor stopped short of violence or a threat of it, Atwater does not wager all on history. Instead, she asks us to mint a new ***346** rule of constitutional law on the understanding that when historical practice fails to speak conclusively to a claim grounded on the Fourth Amendment, courts are left to strike a current balance between individual and societal interests by subjecting particular contemporary circumstances to traditional standards of reasonableness.[1101]Atwater accordingly argues for a modern arrest rule, one not necessarily requiring violent breach of the peace, but nonetheless forbidding custodial arrest, even upon probable cause, when conviction could not ultimately carry any jail time and when the government shows no compelling need for immediate detention.

If we were to derive a rule exclusively to address the uncontested facts of this case, Atwater might well prevail. She was a known and established resident of Lago Vista with no place to hide and no incentive to flee, and common sense says she would almost certainly have buckled up as a condition of driving off with a citation. In her case, the physical incidents of arrest were merely gratuitous humiliations imposed by a police officer who was (at best) exercising ***347** extremely poor judgment. Atwater's claim to live free of pointless indignity and confinement clearly outweighs anything the City can raise against it specific to her case.

But we have traditionally recognized that a responsible Fourth Amendment balance is not well served by standards requiring sensitive, case-by-case determinations of government need, lest every discretionary judgment in the field be converted

---

[1098] See, e.g., E. Fisher, Laws of Arrest § 59, p. 130 (1967) ("[I]t is generally recognized today that the common law authority to arrest without a warrant in misdemeanor cases may be enlarged by *344 statute, and this has been done in many of the states"); *Wilgus, supra*, at 705–706 ("Statutes and municipal charters have quite generally authorized an officer to arrest for any misdemeanor whether a breach of the peace or not, without a warrant, if committed in the officer's presence. Such statutes are valid" (footnote omitted)); *Clark, supra*, § 12, at 50 ("In most, if not all, the states there are statutes and city ordinances, which are clearly valid, authorizing officers to arrest for certain misdemeanors without a warrant, when committed in their presence"); J. Beale, Criminal Pleading and Practice § 21, p. 20, and n. 7 (1899) ("By statute the power of peace officers to arrest without a warrant is often extended to all misdemeanors committed in their presence." "Such a statute is constitutional"); 1 Bishop, supra, § 183, at 103 ("[T]he power of arrest extends, possibly, to any indictable wrong in [an officer's] presence.... And statutes and ordinances widely permit these arrests for violations of municipal by-laws"); J. Bassett, Criminal Pleading and Practice § 89, p. 104 (2d ed. 1885) ("[A]s to the lesser misdemeanors, except breaches of the peace, the power extends only so far as some statute gives it"). But cf. H. Vorhees, Law of Arrest § 131, pp. 78–79 (1904) (acknowledging that "by authority of statute, city charter, or ordinance, [an officer] may arrest without a warrant, one who ... commits a misdemeanor other than a breach of the peace," but suggesting that courts look with "disfavor" on such legislative enactments "as interfering with the constitutional liberties of the subject").

[1099] See American Law Institute, Code of Criminal Procedure § 21(a), p. 28 (1930); American Law Institute, Model Code of Pre-Arraignment Procedure § 120.1(1)(c), p. 13 (1975), and the consensus, as stated in the current literature, is that statutes "removing the breach of the peace limitation and thereby permit[ting] arrest without warrant for any misdemeanor committed in the arresting officer's presence" have "'never been successfully challenged and stan[d] as the law of the land.'" 3 W. LaFave, Search and Seizure § 5.1(b), pp. 13–14, and n. 76 (1996) (quoting *Higbee v. San Diego*, 911 F.2d 377, 379 (C.A.9 1990)) (emphasis in original; footnote omitted).

[1100] *County of Riverside v. McLaughlin*, 500 U.S. 44, 60, 111 S.Ct. 1661, 114 L.Ed.2d 49 (1991) (SCALIA, J., dissenting).

[1101] See *Wyoming v. Houghton*, 526 U.S. 295, 299–300, 119 S.Ct. 1297, 143 L.Ed.2d 408 (1999); Vernonia School Dist. 47J v. Acton, 515 U.S. 646, 652–653, 115 S.Ct. 2386, 132 L.Ed.2d 564 (1995).

into an occasion for constitutional review.[1102]Often enough, the Fourth Amendment has to be applied on the spur (and in the heat) of the moment, and the object in implementing its command of reasonableness is to draw standards sufficiently clear and simple to be applied with a fair prospect of surviving judicial second-guessing months and years after an arrest or **1554 search is made. Courts attempting to strike a reasonable Fourth Amendment balance thus credit the government's side with an essential interest in readily administrable rules.[1103]

At first glance, Atwater's argument may seem to respect the values of clarity and simplicity, so far as she claims that the Fourth Amendment generally forbids warrantless arrests for minor crimes not accompanied by violence or some ***348** demonstrable threat of it (whether "minor crime" be defined as a fine-only traffic offense, a fine-only offense more generally, or a misdemeanor.) But the claim is not ultimately so simple, nor could it be, for complications arise the moment we begin to think about the possible applications of the several criteria Atwater proposes for drawing a line between minor crimes with limited arrest authority and others not so restricted.

One line, she suggests, might be between "jailable" and "fine-only" offenses, between those for which conviction could result in commitment and those for which it could not. The trouble with this distinction, of course, is that an officer on the street might not be able to tell. It is not merely that we cannot expect every police officer to know the details of frequently complex penalty schemes,[1104]but that penalties for ostensibly identical conduct can vary on account of facts difficult (if not impossible) to know at the scene of an arrest. Is this the first offense or is the suspect a repeat offender? Is the weight of the marijuana a gram above or a gram below ***349** the fine-only line? Where conduct could implicate more than one criminal prohibition, which one will the ****1555** district attorney ultimately decide to charge? And so on.

But Atwater's refinements would not end there. She represents that if the line were drawn at nonjailable traffic offenses, her proposed limitation should be qualified by a proviso authorizing warrantless arrests where "necessary for enforcement of the traffic laws or when [an] offense would otherwise continue and pose a danger to others on the road."[1105](Were the line drawn at misdemeanors generally, a comparable qualification would presumably apply.) The proviso only compounds the difficulties. Would, for instance, either exception apply to speeding? At oral argument, Atwater's counsel said that "it would not be reasonable to arrest a driver for speeding unless the speeding rose to the level of reckless driving."[1106]But is it not fair to expect that the chronic speeder will speed again despite a citation in his pocket, and should that not qualify as showing that the "offense would ... continue" under Atwater's rule? And why, as a constitutional matter, should we assume that only reckless driving will "pose a danger to others on the road" while speeding will not?

***350** There is no need for more examples to show that Atwater's general rule and limiting proviso promise very little in the way of administrability. It is no answer that the police routinely make judgments on grounds like risk of immediate repetition; they surely do and should. But there is a world of difference between making that judgment in choosing between the discretionary leniency of a summons in place

---

[1102] See, e.g., *United States v. Robinson*, 414 U.S. 218, 234–235, 94 S.Ct. 467, 38 L.Ed.2d 427 (1973).

[1103] See *New York v. Belton*, 453 U.S. 454, 458, 101 S.Ct. 2860, 69 L.Ed.2d 768 (1981) (Fourth Amendment rules "'ought to be expressed in terms that are readily applicable by the police in the context of the law enforcement activities in which they are necessarily engaged'" and not "'qualified by all sorts of ifs, ands, and buts'").

[1104] See *Berkemer v. McCarty*, 468 U.S. 420, 431, n. 13, 104 S.Ct. 3138, 82 L.Ed.2d 317 (1984) ("[O]fficers in the field frequently 'have neither the time nor the competence to determine' the severity of the offense for which they are considering arresting a person").

[1105] Brief for Petitioners 46 (internal quotation marks omitted).

[1106] Tr. of Oral Arg. 16.

of a clearly lawful arrest, and making the same judgment when the question is the lawfulness of the warrantless arrest itself. It is the difference between no basis for legal action challenging the discretionary judgment, on the one hand, and the prospect of evidentiary exclusion or (as here) personal § 1983 liability for the misapplication of a constitutional standard, on the other. Atwater's rule therefore would not only place police in an almost impossible spot but would guarantee increased litigation over many of the arrests that would occur.21 For all these reasons, Atwater's various distinctions between permissible and impermissible arrests for minor crimes strike us as "very unsatisfactory line[s]" to require police officers to draw on a moment's notice.[1107] One may ask, of course, why these difficulties may not be answered by a simple tie breaker for the police to follow in the field: if in doubt, do not arrest. The first answer is that in practice the tie breaker would boil down to something akin to a least-restrictive-alternative limitation, which is itself one of those "ifs, ands, and buts" rules,[1108]generally thought inappropriate in working out Fourth Amendment protection.[1109] ***351** Beyond that, whatever ****1556** help the tie breaker might give would come at the price of a systematic disincentive to arrest in situations where even Atwater concedes that arresting would serve an important societal interest. An officer not quite sure that the drugs weighed enough to warrant jail time or not quite certain about a suspect's risk of flight would not arrest, even though it could perfectly well turn out that, in fact, the offense called for incarceration and the defendant was long gone on the day of trial. Multiplied many times over, the costs to society of such under-enforcement could easily outweigh the costs to defendants of being needlessly arrested and booked, as Atwater herself acknowledges.

Just how easily the costs could outweigh the benefits may be shown by asking, as one Member of this Court did at oral argument, "how bad the problem is out there."[1110]The very fact that the law has never jelled the way Atwater would have it leads one to wonder whether warrantless misdemeanor arrests need constitutional attention, ***352** and there is cause to think the answer is no. So far as such arrests might be thought to pose a threat to the probable-cause requirement, anyone arrested for a crime without formal process, whether for felony or misdemeanor, is entitled to a magistrate's review of probable cause within 48 hours,[1111]and there is no reason to think the procedure in this case atypical in giving the suspect a prompt opportunity to request release.[1112]Many jurisdictions, moreover, have chosen to impose more restrictive safeguards through statutes limiting warrantless arrests for minor offenses.[1113]It is of course easier to devise a minor-offense limitation by statute than to derive one through the Constitution, simply because the statute can let the arrest power turn on any sort of practical consideration without having to subsume it under a broader principle. It is, in fact, only natural that States should resort to this sort of legislative regulation, for, as Atwater's own amici emphasize, it is in the interest of the police to limit petty-offense arrests, which carry costs that are simply too great to

[1107] *Carroll v. United States*, 267 U.S., at 157, 45 S.Ct. 280.

[1108] *New York v. Belton*, 453 U.S., at 458, 101 S.Ct. 2860.

[1109] See, e.g., *Skinner v. Railway Labor Executives' Assn.*, 489 U.S. 602, 629, n. 9, 109 S.Ct. 1402, 103 L.Ed.2d 639 (1989) (collecting cases); *United States v. Martinez-Fuerte*, 428 U.S. 543, 557–558, n. 12, 96 S.Ct. 3074, 49 L.Ed.2d 1116 (1976) ("The logic of such elaborate less-restrictive-alternative arguments could raise insuperable barriers to the exercise of virtually all search-and-seizure powers").

[1110] Tr. of Oral Arg. 20.

[1111] *County of Riverside v. McLaughlin*, 500 U.S., at 55–58, 111 S.Ct. 1661.

[1112] See Tex. Transp.Code Ann. § 543.002 (1999) (persons arrested for traffic offenses to be taken "immediately" before a magistrate).

[1113] See, e.g., Ala.Code § 32–1–4 (1999); Cal. Veh.Code Ann. § 40504 (West 2000); Ky.Rev.Stat. Ann. §§ 431.015(1), (2) (Michie 1999); La.Rev.Stat. Ann. § 32:391 (West 1989); Md. Transp. Code Ann. § 26–202(a)(2) (1999); S.D. Codified Laws § 32–33–2 (1998); Tenn.Code Ann. § 40–7–118(b)(1) (1997); Va.Code Ann. § 46.2–936 (Supp.2000).

incur without good reason.[1114]Finally, and significantly, under current doctrine the preference for categorical treatment of Fourth Amendment claims gives way to individualized review when a defendant makes a colorable ***353** argument that an arrest, with or ****1557** without a warrant, was "conducted in an extraordinary manner, unusually harmful to [his] privacy or even physical interests."[1115] The upshot of all these influences, combined with the good sense (and, failing that, the political accountability) of most local lawmakers and law-enforcement officials, is a dearth of horribles demanding redress. Indeed, when Atwater's counsel was asked at oral argument for any indications of comparably foolish, warrantless misdemeanor arrests, he could offer only one. We are sure that there are others, but just as surely the country is not confronting anything like an epidemic of unnecessary minor-offense arrests. That fact caps the reasons for rejecting Atwater's request ***354** for the development of a new and distinct body of constitutional law.

Accordingly, we confirm today what our prior cases have intimated: the standard of probable cause "applies to all arrests, without the need to 'balance' the interests and circumstances involved in particular situations."[1116]If an officer has probable cause to believe that an individual has committed even a very minor criminal offense in his presence, he may, without violating the Fourth Amendment, arrest the offender.

IV

Atwater's arrest satisfied constitutional requirements. There is no dispute that Officer Turek had probable cause to believe that Atwater had committed a crime in his presence. She admits that neither she nor her children were wearing seatbelts, as required by Tex. Transp.Code Ann. § 545.413 (1999). Turek was accordingly authorized (not required, but authorized) to make a custodial arrest without balancing costs and benefits or determining whether or not Atwater's arrest was in some sense necessary.

Nor was the arrest made in an "extraordinary manner, unusually harmful to [her] privacy or ... physical interests."[1117]As our citations in *Whren* make clear, the question whether a search or seizure is "extraordinary" turns, above all else, on the manner in which the search or seizure is executed.[1118]****1558** Atwater's arrest was surely "humiliating," as she says in her brief, but it was no more "harmful to ... privacy or ... physical interests" than the normal custodial arrest. She was handcuffed, placed in a squad car, and ***355** taken to the local police station, where officers asked her to remove her shoes, jewelry, and glasses, and to empty her pockets. They then took her photograph and placed her in a cell, alone, for about an hour, after which she was taken before a magistrate, and released on $310 bond. The arrest and booking were inconvenient and embarrassing to Atwater, but not so extraordinary as to violate the Fourth Amendment.

The Court of Appeals's en banc judgment is affirmed.

It is so ordered.

******

[1114] See Brief for Institute on Criminal Justice at the University of Minnesota Law School and Eleven Leading Experts on Law Enforcement and Corrections Administration and Policy as Amici Curiae 11 (the use of custodial arrests for minor offenses "[a]ctually [c]ontradicts [l]aw [e]nforcement [i]nterests").

[1115] *Whren v. United States*, 517 U.S., at 818, 116 S.Ct. 1769; see also Graham v. Connor, 490 U.S. 386, 395–396, 109 S.Ct. 1865, 104 L.Ed.2d 443 (1989) (excessive force actionable under § 1983).

[1116] *Dunaway v. New York*, 442 U.S. 200, 208, 99 S.Ct. 2248, 60 L.Ed.2d 824 (1979).

[1117] *Whren v. United States*, 517 U.S., at 818, 116 S.Ct. 1769.

[1118] See *ibid.* (citing *Tennessee v. Garner*, 471 U.S. 1, 105 S.Ct. 1694, 85 L.Ed.2d 1 (1985) ("seizure by means of deadly force"), *Wilson v. Arkansas*, 514 U.S. 927, 115 S.Ct. 1914, 131 L.Ed.2d 976 (1995) ("unannounced entry into a home"), *Welsh v. Wisconsin*, 466 U.S. 740, 104 S.Ct. 2091, 80 L.Ed.2d 732 (1984) ("entry into a home without a warrant"), and *Winston v. Lee*, 470 U.S. 753, 105 S.Ct. 1611, 84 L.Ed.2d 662 (1985) ("physical penetration of the body")).

Justice O'CONNOR, with whom Justice STEVENS, Justice GINSBURG, and Justice BREYER join, dissenting.

The Fourth Amendment guarantees the right to be free from "unreasonable searches and seizures." The Court recognizes that the arrest of Gail Atwater was a "pointless indignity" that served no discernible state interest,[1119] and yet holds that her arrest was constitutionally permissible. Because the Court's position is inconsistent with the explicit guarantee of the Fourth Amendment, I dissent.

I

A full custodial arrest, such as the one to which Ms. Atwater was subjected, is the quintessential seizure.[1120] ****1561** When a full custodial arrest is effected without a warrant, the plain language of the Fourth Amendment requires that the arrest be reasonable.[1121]It is beyond cavil that "[t]he touchstone of our analysis under the Fourth Amendment is always 'the reasonableness in all the circumstances of the particular governmental invasion of a citizen's personal security.'"[1122] ***361**

We have "often looked to the common law in evaluating the reasonableness, for Fourth Amendment purposes, of police activity."[1123]But history is just one of the tools we use in conducting the reasonableness inquiry.[1124]And when history is inconclusive, as the majority amply demonstrates it is in this case,[1125]we will "evaluate the search or seizure under traditional standards of reasonableness by assessing, on the one hand, the degree to which it intrudes upon an individual's privacy and, on the other, the degree to which it is needed for the promotion of legitimate governmental interests."[1126]In other words, in determining reasonableness, "[e]ach case is to be decided on its own facts and circumstances."[1127]

The majority gives a brief nod to this bedrock principle of our Fourth Amendment jurisprudence, and even acknowledges that "Atwater's claim to live free of pointless indignity and confinement clearly outweighs anything the City can raise against it specific to her case."[1128]But instead of remedying this imbalance, the majority allows itself to be swayed by the worry that "every discretionary judgment in the field [will] be converted into an occasion for constitutional review."[1129]It therefore mints a new rule that "[i]f an officer has probable cause to believe that an individual ***362** has committed even a very minor criminal offense in his presence, he may, without violating the Fourth Amendment, arrest the offender."[1130]This rule is

---

[1119] *Ante*, at 1553.

[1120] See *Payton v. New York*, 445 U.S. 573, 585, 100 S.Ct. 1371, 63 L.Ed.2d 639 (1980).

[1121] See *ibid.*

[1122] *Pennsylvania v. Mimms*, 434 U.S. 106, 108–109, 98 S.Ct. 330, 54 L.Ed.2d 331 (1977) (per curiam) (quoting *Terry v. Ohio*, 392 U.S. 1, 19, 88 S.Ct. 1868, 20 L.Ed.2d 889 1968)). See also, e.g., *United States v. Ramirez*, 523 U.S. 65, 71, 118 S.Ct. 992, 140 L.Ed.2d 191 (1998); *Maryland v. Wilson*, 519 U.S. 408, 411, 117 S.Ct. 882, 137 L.Ed.2d 41 (1997); *Ohio v. Robinette*, 519 U.S. 33, 39, 117 S.Ct. 417, 136 L.Ed.2d 347 (1996); *Florida v. Jimeno*, 500 U.S. 248, 250, 111 S.Ct. 1801, 114 L.Ed.2d 297 (1991); *United States v. Chadwick*, 433 U.S. 1, 9, 97 S.Ct. 2476, 53 L.Ed.2d 538 (1977).

[1123] *Tennessee v. Garner*, 471 U.S. 1, 13, 105 S.Ct. 1694, 85 L.Ed.2d 1 (1985).

[1124] See *id.*, at 13–19, 105 S.Ct. 1694; see also *Wilson v. Arkansas*, 514 U.S. 927, 929, 115 S.Ct. 1914, 131 L.Ed.2d 976 (1995); *Wyoming v. Houghton*, 526 U.S. 295, 307, 119 S.Ct. 1297, 143 L.Ed.2d 408 (1999) (BREYER, J., concurring).

[1125] See *ante*, at 1543–1553.

[1126] *Wyoming v. Houghton, supra*, at 300, 119 S.Ct. 1297. See also, e.g., *Skinner v. Railway Labor Executives' Assn.*, 489 U.S. 602, 619, 109 S.Ct. 1402, 103 L.Ed.2d 639 (1989); *Tennessee v. Garner, supra*, at 8, 105 S.Ct. 1694; *Delaware v. Prouse*, 440 U.S. 648, 654, 99 S.Ct. 1391, 59 L.Ed.2d 660 (1979); *Pennsylvania v. Mimms, supra*, at 109, 98 S.Ct. 330.

[1127] *Go-Bart Importing Co. v. United States*, 282 U.S. 344, 357, 51 S.Ct. 153, 75 L.Ed. 374 (1931).

[1128] *Ante*, at 1553.

[1129] *Ibid.*

[1130] *Ante*, at 1557.

not only unsupported by our precedent, but runs contrary to the principles that lie at the core of the Fourth Amendment.

As the majority tacitly acknowledges, we have never considered the precise question presented here, namely, the constitutionality of a warrantless arrest for an offense punishable only by fine.[1131]Indeed, on the rare occasions that Members of this Court have contemplated such an arrest, they have indicated disapproval.[1132] ****1562**

To be sure, we have held that the existence of probable cause is a necessary condition for an arrest.[1133]And in the case of felonies punishable by a term of imprisonment, we have held that the existence of probable cause is also a sufficient condition for an arrest.[1134]In *Watson*, however, there was a clear and consistently applied common law rule permitting warrantless felony arrests.[1135]Accordingly, our inquiry ended there and we had no need to assess the reasonableness of such arrests by weighing individual liberty interests against state interests.[1136]

Here, however, we have no such luxury. The Court's thorough exegesis makes it abundantly clear that warrantless ***363** misdemeanor arrests were not the subject of a clear and consistently applied rule at common law.[1137]We therefore must engage in the balancing test required by the Fourth Amendment.[1138]While probable cause is surely a necessary condition for warrantless arrests for fine-only offenses,[1139]any realistic assessment of the interests implicated by such arrests demonstrates that probable cause alone is not a sufficient condition. See infra, at 1563–1564.

Our decision in *Whren v. United States*[1140]is not to the contrary. The specific question presented there was whether, in evaluating the Fourth Amendment reasonableness of a traffic stop, the subjective intent of the police officer is a relevant consideration.[1141]We held that it is not, and stated that "[t]he making of a traffic stop ... is governed by the usual rule that probable cause to believe the law has been broken 'outbalances' private interest in avoiding police contact."[1142]

We of course did not have occasion in *Whren* to consider the constitutional preconditions for warrantless arrests for fine-only offenses. Nor should our words be taken beyond their context. There are significant qualitative differences between a traffic stop and a full custodial arrest. While both are seizures that fall within the ambit of the Fourth Amendment, the latter entails a much greater intrusion on an

---

[1131] Cf. *ibid.*

[1132] See, e.g., *Gustafson v. Florida*, 414 U.S. 260, 266–267, 94 S.Ct. 488, 38 L.Ed.2d 456 (1973) (Stewart, J., concurring) ("[A] persuasive claim might have been made ... that the custodial arrest of the petitioner for a minor traffic offense violated his rights under the Fourth and Fourteenth Amendments. But no such claim has been made"); United States v. Robinson, 414 U.S. 218, 238, n. 2, 94 S.Ct. 467, 38 L.Ed.2d 427 (1973) (Powell, J., concurring) (the validity of a custodial arrest for a minor traffic offense is not "self-evident").

[1133] See *Dunaway v. New York*, 442 U.S. 200, 213 214, 99 S.Ct. 2248, 60 L.Ed.2d 824 (1979).

[1134] See *United States v. Watson*, 423 U.S. 411, 416–417, 96 S.Ct. 820, 46 L.Ed.2d 598 (1976).

[1135] See *id.*, at 417–422, 96 S.Ct. 820.

[1136] Cf. *Wyoming v. Houghton*, *supra*, at 299–300, 119 S.Ct. 1297; *Tennessee v. Garner*, *supra*, at 26, 105 S.Ct. 1694 (O'CONNOR, J., dissenting) (criticizing majority for disregarding undisputed common law rule).

[1137] See, e.g., *ante*, at 1546 (finding "disagreement, not unanimity, among both the common-law jurists and the text writers"); *ante*, at 1547 (acknowledging that certain early English statutes serve only to "riddle Atwater's supposed common-law rule with enough exceptions to unsettle any contention [that there was a clear common-law rule barring warrantless arrests for misdemeanors that were not breaches of the peace]").

[1138] See *Wyoming v. Houghton*, *supra*, at 299–300, 119 S.Ct. 1297.

[1139] See *Dunaway v. New York*, *supra*, at 213–214, 99 S.Ct. 2248.

[1140] 517 U.S. 806, 116 S.Ct. 1769, 135 L.Ed.2d 89 (1996).

[1141] *Id.*, at 808, 814, 116 S.Ct. 1769.

[1142] *Id.*, at 818, 116 S.Ct. 1769.

individual's liberty and privacy interests. As we have said, "[a] motorist's expectations, when he sees a policeman's light flashing behind him, are that he will be obliged to spend ***364** a short period of time answering questions and waiting while the officer checks his license and registration, that he may be given a citation, but that in the end he most likely will be allowed to continue on his way."[1143] Thus, when there is probable cause to believe that a person has violated a minor traffic law, there can be little question that the state interest in law enforcement will justify the relatively limited intrusion of a traffic stop. It is by no means certain, however, that where the offense is punishable only by fine, "probable ****1563** cause to believe the law has been broken [will] 'outbalanc [e]' private interest in avoiding" a full custodial arrest.[1144] Justifying a full arrest by the same quantum of evidence that justifies a traffic stop—even though the offender cannot ultimately be imprisoned for her conduct—defies any sense of proportionality and is in serious tension with the Fourth Amendment's proscription of unreasonable seizures.

A custodial arrest exacts an obvious toll on an individual's liberty and privacy, even when the period of custody is relatively brief. The arrestee is subject to a full search of her person and confiscation of her possessions.[1145] If the arrestee is the occupant of a car, the entire passenger compartment of the car, including packages therein, is subject to search as well.[1146] The arrestee may be detained for up to 48 hours without having a magistrate determine whether there in fact was probable cause for the arrest.[1147] Because people arrested for all types of violent and nonviolent offenses may be housed together awaiting such review, this detention period is potentially dangerous.[1148] And once the period of custody is over, the fact of the arrest is a permanent ***365** part of the public record.[1149]

We have said that "the penalty that may attach to any particular offense seems to provide the clearest and most consistent indication of the State's interest in arresting individuals suspected of committing that offense."[1150] If the State has decided that a fine, and not imprisonment, is the appropriate punishment for an offense, the State's interest in taking a person suspected of committing that offense into custody is surely limited, at best. This is not to say that the State will never have such an interest. A full custodial arrest may on occasion vindicate legitimate state interests, even if the crime is punishable only by fine. Arrest is the surest way to abate criminal conduct. It may also allow the police to verify the offender's identity and, if the offender poses a flight risk, to ensure her appearance at trial. But when such considerations are not present, a citation or summons may serve the State's remaining law enforcement interests every bit as effectively as an arrest.[1151]

Because a full custodial arrest is such a severe intrusion on an individual's liberty, its reasonableness hinges on "the degree to which it is needed for the promotion of legitimate governmental interests."[1152] In light of the availability of citations to

---

[1143] *Berkemer v. McCarty*, 468 U.S. 420, 437, 104 S.Ct. 3138, 82 L.Ed.2d 317 (1984).

[1144] *Whren v. United States, supra*, at 818, 116 S.Ct. 1769.

[1145] *United States v. Robinson, supra.*

[1146] See *New York v. Belton*, 453 U.S. 454, 101 S.Ct. 2860, 69 L.Ed.2d 768 (1981).

[1147] See *County of Riverside v. McLaughlin*, 500 U.S. 44, 111 S.Ct. 1661, 114 L.Ed.2d 49 (1991).

[1148] Rosazza & Cook, Jail Intake: Managing A Critical Function—Part One: Resources, 13 American Jails 35 (Mar./ Apr. 1999).

[1149] Cf. *Paul v. Davis*, 424 U.S. 693, 96 S.Ct. 1155, 47 L.Ed.2d 405 (1976).

[1150] *Welsh v. Wisconsin*, 466 U.S. 740, 754, n. 14, 104 S.Ct. 2091, 80 L.Ed.2d 732 (1984).

[1151] Cf. Lodging for State of Texas as Amici Curiae et al. (Texas Department of Public Safety, Student Handout, Traffic Law Enforcement 1 (1999)) ("Citations.... Definition—a means of getting violators to court without physical arrest. A citation should be used when it will serve this purpose except when by issuing a citation and releasing the violator, the safety of the public and/ or the violator might be imperiled as in the case of D.W.I.").

[1152] *Wyoming v. Houghton*, 526 U.S., at 300, 119 S.Ct. 1297.

promote a State's interests when a fine-only offense has been committed, I cannot concur in a rule which deems a full custodial arrest to be reasonable in every circumstance. Giving police ***366** officers constitutional carte blanche to effect an arrest whenever there is probable cause to believe a fine-only misdemeanor has been committed is irreconcilable with the Fourth Amendment's command that seizures be reasonable. Instead, I would require that when there is probable cause to believe that a fine-only offense has been committed, the police officer should issue a citation unless the officer is ****1564** "able to point to specific and articulable facts which, taken together with rational inferences from those facts, reasonably warrant [the additional] intrusion" of a full custodial arrest.[1153]

The majority insists that a bright-line rule focused on probable cause is necessary to vindicate the State's interest in easily administrable law enforcement rules.[1154]Probable cause itself, however, is not a model of precision. "The quantum of information which constitutes probable cause—evidence which would 'warrant a man of reasonable caution in the belief' that a [crime] has been committed—must be measured by the facts of the particular case."[1155]The rule I propose—which merely requires a legitimate reason for the decision to escalate the seizure into a full custodial arrest—thus does not undermine an otherwise "clear and simple" rule.[1156]

While clarity is certainly a value worthy of consideration in our Fourth Amendment jurisprudence, it by no means trumps the values of liberty and privacy at the heart of the Amendment's protections. What the Terry rule lacks in precision it makes up for in fidelity to the Fourth Amendment's command of reasonableness and sensitivity to the competing values protected by that Amendment. Over the past 30 years, it appears that the Terry rule has been workable and easily applied by officers on the street.

At bottom, the majority offers two related reasons why a bright-line rule is necessary: the fear that officers who arrest for fine-only offenses will be subject to "personal ***367** liability for the misapplication of a constitutional standard,"[1157]and the resulting "systematic disincentive to arrest ... where ... arresting would serve an important societal interest."[1158]These concerns are certainly valid, but they are more than adequately resolved by the doctrine of qualified immunity.

Qualified immunity was created to shield government officials from civil liability for the performance of discretionary functions so long as their conduct does not violate clearly established statutory or constitutional rights of which a reasonable person would have known.[1159]This doctrine is "the best attainable accommodan officer" and reasonably concludes that a suspect may possess more than four ounces of marijuana and thus might be guilty of a felony,[1160] the officer will be insulated from liability for arresting the suspect even if the initial assessment turns out to be factually incorrect. As we have said, "officials will not be liable for mere mistakes in judgment."[1161] ***368 **1565** Of course, even the specter of liability can entail substantial social costs, such as inhibiting public officials in the discharge of their duties.[1162] We

---

1153 *Terry v. Ohio*, 392 U.S., at 21, 88 S.Ct. 1868.

1154 See *ante*, at 1553–1556.

1155 *Wong Sun v. United States*, 371 U.S. 471, 479, 83 S.Ct. 407, 9 L.Ed.2d 441 (1963) (citation omitted).

1156 Cf. *ante*, at 1553.

1157 *Ante*, at 1555.

1158 *Ante*, at 1556.

1159 See *Harlow v. Fitzgerald*, 457 U.S. 800, 818, 102 S.Ct. 2727, 73 L.Ed.2d 396 (1982).

1160 Cf. *ante*, at 1554–1555, and n. 19, 1555–1556.

1161 *Butz v. Economou*, 438 U.S. 478, 507, 98 S.Ct. 2894, 57 L.Ed.2d 895 1978).

1162 See, e.g., *Harlow v. Fitzgerald*, *supra*, at 814, 102 S.Ct. 2727.

may not ignore the central command of the Fourth Amendment, however, to avoid these costs.

II

The record in this case makes it abundantly clear that Ms. Atwater's arrest was constitutionally unreasonable. Atwater readily admits—as she did when Officer Turek pulled her over—that she violated Texas' seatbelt law.[1163] While Turek was justified in stopping Atwater,[1164] neither law nor reason supports his decision to arrest her instead of simply giving her a citation. The officer's actions cannot sensibly be viewed as a permissible means of balancing Atwater's Fourth Amendment interests with the State's own legitimate interests.

There is no question that Officer Turek's actions severely infringed Atwater's liberty and privacy. Turek was loud and accusatory from the moment he approached Atwater's car. Atwater's young children were terrified and hysterical. Yet when Atwater asked Turek to lower his voice because he was scaring the children, he responded by jabbing his finger in Atwater's face and saying, "You're going to jail."[1165] Having made the decision to arrest, Turek did not inform Atwater of her right to remain silent.[1166] He instead asked for her license and insurance information.[1167]

Atwater asked if she could at least take her children to a friend's house down the street before going to the police station.[1168] But Turek—who had just castigated Atwater for not caring for her children—refused and said he would take the children into custody as well.[1169] Only the intervention of neighborhood ***369** children who had witnessed the scene and summoned one of Atwater's friends saved the children from being hauled to jail with their mother.[1170]

With the children gone, Officer Turek handcuffed Ms. Atwater with her hands behind her back, placed her in the police car, and drove her to the police station.[1171] Ironically, Turek did not secure Atwater in a seatbelt for the drive.[1172] At the station, Atwater was forced to remove her shoes, relinquish her possessions, and wait in a holding cell for about an hour.[1173] A judge finally informed Atwater of her rights and the charges against her, and released her when she posted bond.[1174] Atwater returned to the scene of the arrest, only to find that her car had been towed.[1175]

Ms. Atwater ultimately pleaded no contest to violating the seatbelt law and was fined $50.[1176] Even though that fine was the maximum penalty for her crime,[1177] and even though Officer Turek has never articulated any justification for his actions, the

---

[1163] Brief for Petitioners 2–3; Record 381, 384.

[1164] See *Whren v. United States*, 517 U.S., at 819, 116 S.Ct. 1769.

[1165] Record 382, 384.

[1166] *Id.*, at 390, 704.

[1167] *Id.*, at 382. But cf. *Miranda v. Arizona*, 384 U.S. 436, 86 S.Ct. 1602, 16 L.Ed.2d 694 (1966).

[1168] Record 384.

[1169] *Id.*, at 384, 427, 704–705.

[1170] *Id.*, at 382, 385–386.

[1171] *Id.*, at 386–387.

[1172] *Id.*, at 386.

[1173] *Id.*, at 387, 706.

[1174] *Id.*, at 387–388, 706.

[1175] *Id.*, at 389.

[1176] *Id.*, at 403.

[1177] Tex. Transp.Code Ann. § 545.413(d) (1999).

city contends that arresting Atwater was constitutionally reasonable because it advanced two legitimate interests: "the enforcement of child safety laws and encouraging [Atwater] to appear for trial."[1178]

It is difficult to see how arresting Atwater served either of these goals any more effectively than the issuance of a citation. With respect to the goal of law enforcement generally, Atwater did not pose a great danger to the community. She had been driving very slowly—approximately 15 miles per hour—in broad daylight on a residential street that had no other traffic.[1179] Nor was she a repeat offender; until that day, she had received one traffic citation in her life—a ticket, more than 10 years earlier, for failure to signal a lane change.[1180] Although Officer ****1566** Turek had stopped Atwater approximately three months earlier because he thought that Atwater's son was not wearing a seatbelt,[1181] Turek had been mistaken.[1182] ***370** Moreover, Atwater immediately accepted responsibility and apologized for her conduct.[1183] Thus, there was every indication that Atwater would have buckled herself and her children in had she been cited and allowed to leave.

With respect to the related goal of child welfare, the decision to arrest Atwater was nothing short of counterproductive. Atwater's children witnessed Officer Turek yell at their mother and threaten to take them all into custody. Ultimately, they were forced to leave her behind with Turek, knowing that she was being taken to jail. Understandably, the 3–year–old boy was "very, very, very traumatized."[1184] After the incident, he had to see a child psychologist regularly, who reported that the boy "felt very guilty that he couldn't stop this horrible thing ... he was powerless to help his mother or sister."[1185] Both of Atwater's children are now terrified at the sight of any police car.[1186] According to Atwater, the arrest "just never leaves us. It's a conversation we have every other day, once a week, and it's—it raises its head constantly in our lives."[1187]

Citing Atwater surely would have served the children's interests well. It would have taught Atwater to ensure that her children were buckled up in the future. It also would have taught the children an important lesson in accepting responsibility and obeying the law. Arresting Atwater, though, taught the children an entirely different lesson: that "the bad person could just as easily be the policeman as it could be the most horrible person they could imagine."[1188]

Respondents also contend that the arrest was necessary to ensure Atwater's appearance in court. Atwater, however, was far from a flight risk. A 16–year resident of Lago Vista, population 2,486, Atwater was not likely to abscond.[1189]Although she ***371** was unable to produce her driver's license because it had been stolen, she gave

---

[1178] Brief for Respondents 15.

[1179] Record 380.

[1180] *Id.*, at 378.

[1181] *id.*, at 420,

[1182] *id.*, at 379, 703.

[1183] *Id.*, at 381, 384, 420.

[1184] *Id.*, at 393.

[1185] *Id.*, at 396.

[1186] *Id.*, at 393, 395.

[1187] *Id.*, at 395.

[1188] *Ibid.*

[1189] See Record 376; Texas State Data Center, 1997 Total Population Estimates for Texas Places 15 (Sept.1998).

Officer Turek her license number and address.[1190] In addition, Officer Turek knew from their previous encounter that Atwater was a local resident.

The city's justifications fall far short of rationalizing the extraordinary intrusion on Gail Atwater and her children. Measuring "the degree to which [Atwater's custodial arrest was] needed for the promotion of legitimate governmental interests," against "the degree to which it intruded upon [her] privacy,"[1191] it can hardly be doubted that Turek's actions were disproportionate to Atwater's crime. The majority's assessment that "Atwater's claim to live free of pointless indignity and confinement clearly outweighs anything the City can raise against it specific to her case,"[1192] is quite correct. In my view, the Fourth Amendment inquiry ends there.

III

The Court's error, however, does not merely affect the disposition of this case. The per se rule that the Court creates has potentially serious consequences for the everyday lives of Americans. A broad range of conduct falls into the category of fine-only misdemeanors. In Texas alone, for example, disobeying any sort of traffic warning sign is a misdemeanor punishable only by fine,[1193] as is failing to pay a highway toll,[1194] and driving with expired license plates,[1195] Nor are fine-only crimes limited to the traffic context. In several States, for example, littering is a criminal offense punishable only by fine. [1196]****1567**

To be sure, such laws are valid and wise exercises of the States' power to protect the public health and welfare. My concern lies not with the decision to enact or enforce these ***372** laws, but rather with the manner in which they may be enforced. Under today's holding, when a police officer has probable cause to believe that a fine-only misdemeanor offense has occurred, that officer may stop the suspect, issue a citation, and let the person continue on her way.[1197] Or, if a traffic violation, the officer may stop the car, arrest the driver,[1198] search the driver,[1199] search the entire passenger compartment of the car including any purse or package inside,[1200] and impound the car and inventory all of its contents.[1201] Although the Fourth Amendment expressly requires that the latter course be a reasonable and proportional response to the circumstances of the offense, the majority gives officers unfettered discretion to choose that course without articulating a single reason why such action is appropriate.

Such unbounded discretion carries with it grave potential for abuse. The majority takes comfort in the lack of evidence of "an epidemic of unnecessary minor-offense arrests."[1202] But the relatively small number of published cases dealing with

---

[1190] Record 386.

[1191] *Wyoming v. Houghton*, 526 U.S., at 300, 119 S.Ct. 1297.

[1192] *Ante*, at 1553.

[1193] See Tex. Transp.Code Ann. § 472.022 (1999 and Supp.2000–2001).

[1194] See § 284.070.

[1195] See § 502.407.

[1196] See, e.g., Cal.Penal Code Ann. § 374.7 (West 1999); Ga.Code Ann. § 16–7–43 (1996); Iowa Code §§ 321.369, 805.8(2)(af) (Supp. 2001).

[1197] Cf. *Whren v. United States*, 517 U.S., at 806, 116 S.Ct. 1769.

[1198] See *ante*, at 1557.

[1199] See *United States v. Robinson*, 414 U.S., at 235, 94 S.Ct. 467.

[1200] See *New York v. Belton*, 453 U.S., at 460, 101 S.Ct. 2860.

[1201] See *Colorado v. Bertine*, 479 U.S. 367, 374, 107 S.Ct. 738, 93 L.Ed.2d 739 (1987); *Florida v. Wells*, 495 U.S. 1, 4–5, 110 S.Ct. 1632, 109 L.Ed.2d 1 (1990).

[1202] *Ante*, at 1557, and n. 25.

such arrests proves little and should provide little solace. Indeed, as the recent debate over racial profiling demonstrates all too clearly, a relatively minor traffic infraction may often serve as an excuse for stopping and harassing an individual. After today, the arsenal available to any officer extends to a full arrest and the searches permissible concomitant to that arrest. An officer's subjective motivations for making a traffic stop are not relevant considerations in determining the reasonableness of the stop.[1203] But it is precisely because these motivations are beyond our purview that we must vigilantly ensure that officers' poststop actions—which are properly within our reach—comport with the Fourth Amendment's guarantee of reasonableness.

***373** * * *

The Court neglects the Fourth Amendment's express command in the name of administrative ease. In so doing, it cloaks the pointless indignity that Gail Atwater suffered with the mantle of reasonableness. I respectfully dissent.

The Black Letter Law

> The police did not violate the motorist's Fourth Amendment right to be free from unreasonable seizure when she was arrested, handcuffed, and detained in jail for one hour for failing to wear her seat belt and failing to fasten her children in seat belts. The Court based its decision, at least in part, on the fact that the officer observed the behavior, the arrest was not conducted in an extraordinary manner, and was not unusually harmful to motorist's privacy interests. Under *Atwater*, when an officer has probable cause to believe that an individual has committed even very minor criminal offense in his presence, he may, without violating Fourth Amendment, arrest the offender.

Payton v. New York

100 S.Ct. 1371

Supreme Court of the United States

Theodore PAYTON, Applicant,

v.

NEW YORK.

Obie RIDDICK, Applicant,

v.

NEW YORK.

Nos. 78–5420, 78–5421. | Argued March 26, 1979. | Reargued Oct. 9, 1979. | Decided April 15, 1980.

Mr. Justice STEVENS delivered the opinion of the Court.

These appeals challenge the constitutionality of New York statutes that authorize police officers to enter a private residence without a warrant and with force, if necessary, to make a routine felony arrest. The important constitutional question presented by this challenge has been expressly left open in a number of our prior opinions. In *United States v. Watson*,[1204] we upheld a warrantless "midday public arrest," expressly noting that the case did not pose "the still unsettled question ***575** . . . 'whether and under what circumstances an officer may enter a suspect's home to make a war-

[1203] See *Whren v. United States*, *supra*, at 813, 116 S.Ct. 1769.

[1204] 423 U.S. 411, 96 S.Ct. 820, 46 L.Ed.2d 598.

rantless arrest.'"[1205] The question has been answered in different ways by other appellate courts. The Supreme Court of Florida rejected the constitutional attack, as did the New York Court of Appeals[1206] in this case. The courts of last resort in 10 other States, however, have held that unless special circumstances are present, warrantless arrests in the home are unconstitutional. Of the seven United States Courts of Appeals that have considered the question, five have expressed the opinion that such arrests are unconstitutional.

***576** Last term we noted probable jurisdiction of these appeals in order to address that question.[1207] After hearing oral argument, we set the case for re-argument this Term.[1208] We now reverse the New York Court of Appeals and hold that the Fourth Amendment to the United States Constitution, made applicable to the States by the Fourteenth Amendment,[1209] ****1375** prohibits the police from making a warrantless and nonconsensual entry into a suspect's home in order to make a routine felony arrest.

We first state the facts of both cases in some detail and put to one side certain related questions that are not presented by these records. We then explain why the New York statutes are not consistent with the Fourth Amendment and why the reasons for upholding warrantless arrests in a public place do not apply to warrantless invasions of the privacy of the home.

I

On January 14, 1970, after two days of intensive investigation, New York detectives had assembled evidence sufficient to establish probable cause to believe that Theodore Payton had murdered the manager of a gas station two days earlier. At about 7:30 a.m. on January 15, six officers went to Payton's apartment in the Bronx, intending to arrest him. They had not obtained a warrant. Although light and music emanated from the apartment, there was no response to their knock on the metal door. They summoned emergency assistance and, about 30 minutes later, used crowbars to break open the door and enter the apartment. No one was there. In plain view, however, was a .30-caliber shell casing that was ***577** seized and later admitted into evidence at Payton's murder trial.

In due course Payton surrendered to the police, was indicted for murder, and moved to suppress the evidence taken from his apartment. The trial judge held that the warrantless and forcible entry was authorized by the New York Code of Criminal Procedure, and that the evidence in plain view was properly seized. He found that exigent circumstances justified the officers' failure to announce their purpose before entering the apartment as required by the statute. He had no ***578** occasion, however, to decide whether those circumstances also ****1376** would have justified the failure to obtain a warrant, because he concluded that the warrantless entry was adequately supported by the statute without regard to the circumstances. The Appellate Division, First Department, summarily affirmed.

On March 14, 1974, Obie Riddick was arrested for the commission of two armed robberies that had occurred in 1971. He had been identified by the victims in June 1973, and in January 1974 the police had learned his address. They did not obtain a warrant for his arrest. At about noon on March 14, a detective, accompanied by three other officers, knocked on the door of the Queens house where Riddick was living. When his young son opened the door, they could see Riddick sitting in bed covered by a sheet. They entered the house and placed him under arrest. Before per-

---

[1205] *Id.*, at 418, n. 6, 96 S.Ct., at 825, n. 6.

[1206] 45 N.Y.2d 300, 408 N.Y.S.2d 395, 380 N.E.2d 224.

[1207] 439 U.S. 1044, 99 S.Ct. 718, 58 L.Ed.2d 703.

[1208] 441 U.S. 930, 99 S.Ct. 2049, 60 L.Ed.2d 658.

[1209] *Mapp v. Ohio*, 367 U.S. 643, 81 S.Ct. 1684, 6 L.Ed.2d 1081; *Wolf v. Colorado*, 338 U.S. 25, 69 S.Ct. 1359, 93 L.Ed. 1782.

mitting him to dress, they opened a chest of drawers two feet from the bed in search of weapons and found narcotics and related paraphernalia. Riddick was subsequently indicted on narcotics charges. At a suppression hearing, the trial judge held that the warrantless entry into his home was authorized by the revised New York statute, and that the search of the immediate ***579** area was reasonable under *Chimel v. California*.[1210] The Appellate Division, Second Department, affirmed the denial of the suppression motion.

The New York Court of Appeals, in a single opinion, affirmed the convictions of both Payton and Riddick.[1211] The court recognized that the question whether and under what circumstances an officer may enter a suspect's home to make a warrantless arrest had not been settled either by that court or by this Court. In answering that question, the majority of four judges relied primarily on its perception that there is a ". . . substantial difference between the intrusion which attends an entry for the purpose of searching the premises and that which results from an entry for the purpose of ***580** making an arrest, and [a] significant difference in the governmental interest in achieving the objective of the intrusion in the two instances.[1212]"

***581 **1377** The majority supported its holding by noting the "apparent historical acceptance" of warrantless entries to make felony arrests, both in the English common law and in the practice of many American States. Three members of the New York Court of Appeals dissented on this issue because they believed that the Constitution requires the police to obtain a "warrant to enter a home in order to arrest or seize a person, unless there are exigent circumstances." Starting from the premise that, except in carefully circumscribed instances, "the Fourth Amendment forbids police entry into a private home to search for and seize an object without a warrant," the dissenters reasoned that an arrest of the person involves an even greater invasion of privacy and should therefore be attended with at least as ***582** great a measure of constitutional protection. The dissenters noted "the existence ****1378** of statutes and the American Law Institute imprimatur codifying the common law rule authorizing warrantless arrests in private homes" and acknowledged that "the statutory authority of a police officer to make a warrantless arrest in this State has been in effect for almost 100 years," but concluded that "neither antiquity nor legislative unanimity can be determinative of the grave constitutional question presented" and "can never be a substitute for reasoned analysis."

Before addressing the narrow question presented by these appeals, we put to one side other related problems that are ***583** not presented today. Although it is arguable that the warrantless entry to effect Payton's arrest might have been justified by exigent circumstances, none of the New York courts relied on any such justification. The Court of Appeals majority treated both Payton's and Riddick's cases as involving routine arrests in which there was ample time to obtain a warrant, and we will do the same. Accordingly, we have no occasion to consider the sort of emergency or dangerous situation, described in our cases as "exigent circumstances," that would justify a warrantless entry into a home for the purpose of either arrest or search.

Nor do these cases raise any question concerning the authority of the police, without either a search or arrest warrant, to enter a third party's home to arrest a suspect. The police broke into Payton's apartment intending to arrest Payton, and they arrested Riddick in his own dwelling. We also note that in neither case is it argued that the police lacked probable cause to believe that the suspect was at home when they entered. Finally, in both cases we are dealing with entries into homes made without the consent of any occupant. In Payton, the police used crowbars to break

---

[1210] 395 U.S. 752, 89 S.Ct. 2034, 23 L.Ed.2d 685.

[1211] 45 N.Y.2d 300, 408 N.Y.S.2d 395, 380 N.E.2d 224 (1978).

[1212] *Id.*, at 310, 408 N.Y.S.2d, at 399, 380 N.E.2d, at 228–229.

down the door and in Riddick, although his 3-year-old son answered the door, the police entered before Riddick had an opportunity either to object or to consent.

II

It is familiar history that indiscriminate searches and seizures conducted under the authority of "general warrants" were the immediate evils that motivated the framing and adoption of the Fourth Amendment. Indeed, as originally ***584** proposed ****1379** in the House of Representatives, the draft contained only one clause, which directly imposed limitations on the issuance of warrants, but imposed no express restrictions on warrantless searches or seizures. As it was ultimately adopted, however, the Amendment contained two separate clauses, the first protecting the basic right to be free from unreasonable searches and seizures and the second requiring that warrants be particular and supported by probable cause. The Amendment provides:

"The right of the people to be secure in their persons, houses, papers, and effects, against unreasonable searches ***585** and seizures, shall not be violated, and no Warrants shall issue, but upon probable cause, supported by Oath or affirmation, and particularly describing the place to be searched, and the persons or things to be seized."

It is thus perfectly clear that the evil the Amendment was designed to prevent was broader than the abuse of a general warrant. Unreasonable searches or seizures conducted without any warrant at all are condemned by the plain language of the first clause of the Amendment. Almost a century ago the Court stated in resounding terms that the principles reflected in the Amendment "reached farther than the concrete form" of the specific cases that gave it birth, and "apply to all invasions on the part of the government and its employees of the sanctity of a man's home and the privacies of life."[1213] Without pausing to consider whether that broad language may require some qualification, it is sufficient to note that the warrantless arrest of a person is a species of seizure required by the Amendment to be reasonable.[1214] Indeed, as Mr. Justice POWELL noted in his concurrence in United States v. Watson, the arrest of a person is "quintessentially a seizure."[1215]

The simple language of the Amendment applies equally to seizures of persons and to seizures of property. Our analysis in this case may therefore properly commence with rules that have been well established in Fourth Amendment litigation involving tangible items. As the Court reiterated just a few years ago, the "physical entry of the home is the chief evil against which the wording of the Fourth Amendment is directed."[1216] ****1380 *586** And we have long adhered to the view that the warrant procedure minimizes the danger of needless intrusions of that sort.

It is a "basic principle of Fourth Amendment law" that searches and seizures inside a home without a warrant are presumptively unreasonable. Yet it is also well settled that ***587** objects such as weapons or contraband found in a public place may be seized by the police without a warrant. The seizure of property in plain view involves no invasion of privacy and is presumptively reasonable, assuming that there is probable cause to associate the property with criminal activity. The distinction between a warrantless seizure in an open area and such a seizure on private premises was plainly stated in *G. M. Leasing Corp. v. United States*:

"It is one thing to seize without a warrant property resting in an open area or seizable by levy without an intrusion into privacy, and it is quite another thing to effect a warrantless seizure of property, even that owned by a corporation, situated

---

[1213] *Boyd v. United States*, 116 U.S. 616, 630, 6 S.Ct. 524, 532, 29 L.Ed.2d 746.

[1214] *Beck v. Ohio*, 379 U.S. 89, 85 S.Ct. 223, 13 L.Ed.2d 142. Cf. *Delaware v. Prouse*, 440 U.S. 648, 99 S.Ct. 1391, 59 L.Ed.2d 660.

[1215] 423 U.S., at 428, 96 S.Ct., at 830.

[1216] *United States v. United States District Court*, 407 U.S. 297, 313, 92 S.Ct. 2125, 2134, 32 L.Ed.2d 752.

on private premises to which access is not otherwise available for the seizing officer."[1217]

As the late Judge Leventhal recognized, this distinction has equal force when the seizure of a person is involved. Writing on the constitutional issue now before us for the United States Court of Appeals for the District of Columbia Circuit sitting en banc, *Dorman v. United States*,[1218] Judge Leventhal first noted the settled rule that warrantless arrests in public places are valid. He immediately recognized, however, that "[a] greater burden is placed ... on officials who enter a home or dwelling without consent. Freedom from intrusion into the home or dwelling is the archetype of the privacy protection secured by the Fourth Amendment."[1219]

****1381** His analysis of this question then focused on the long-settled premise that, absent exigent circumstances, a warrantless ***588** entry to search for weapons or contraband is unconstitutional even when a felony has been committed and there is probable cause to believe that incriminating evidence will be found within. He reasoned that the constitutional protection afforded to the individual's interest in the privacy of his own home is equally applicable to a warrantless entry for the purpose of arresting a resident of the house; for it is inherent in such an entry that a search for the suspect may be required before he can be apprehended. Judge Leventhal concluded that an entry to arrest and an entry to search for and to seize property implicate the same interest in preserving the privacy and the sanctity of the home, and justify the same level of constitutional protection.

This reasoning has been followed in other Circuits. Thus, the Second Circuit recently summarized its position:

"To be arrested in the home involves not only the invasion ***589** attendant to all arrests but also an invasion of the sanctity of the home. This is simply too substantial an invasion to allow without a warrant, at least in the absence of exigent circumstances, even when it is accomplished under statutory authority and when probable cause is clearly present."[1220]

We find this reasoning to be persuasive and in accord with this Court's Fourth Amendment decisions.

The majority of the New York Court of Appeals, however, suggested that there is a substantial difference in the relative intrusiveness of an entry to search for property and an entry to search for a person.[1221] It is true that the area that may legally be searched is broader when executing a search warrant than when executing an arrest warrant in the home.[1222] This difference may be more theoretical than real, however, because the police may need to check the entire premises for safety reasons, and sometimes they ignore the restrictions on searches incident to arrest.

But the critical point is that any differences in the intrusiveness of entries to search and entries to arrest are merely ones of degree rather than kind. The two intrusions share this fundamental characteristic: the breach of the entrance to an individual's home. The Fourth Amendment protects the individual's privacy in a variety of settings. In none is the zone of privacy more clearly defined than when bounded by the unambiguous physical dimensions of an individual's ****1382** home—a zone that finds its roots in clear and specific constitutional terms: "The right of the people to be secure in their . . . houses . . . shall not be violated." That language unequivocally

[1217] 429 U.S. 338, 354, 97 S.Ct. 619, 629, 50 L.Ed.2d 530.

[1218] 140 U.S.App.D.C. 313, 435 F.2d 385 (1970).

[1219] *Id.*, at 317, 435 F.2d, at 389

[1220] *United States v. Reed*, 572 F.2d 412, 423 (1978), cert. denied, sub nom. *Goldsmith v. United States*, 439 U.S. 913, 99 S.Ct. 283, 58 L.Ed.2d 259.

[1221] See n. 13, *supra*.

[1222] See *Chimel v. California*, 395 U.S. 752, 89 S.Ct. 2034, 23 L.Ed.2d 685.

establishes the proposition that "[a]t the very ***590** core [of the Fourth Amendment] stands the right of a man to retreat into his own home and there be free from unreasonable governmental intrusion."[1223] In terms that apply equally to seizures of property and to seizures of persons, the Fourth Amendment has drawn a firm line at the entrance to the house. Absent exigent circumstances, that threshold may not reasonably be crossed without a warrant.

III

Without contending that *United States v. Watson*,[1224] decided the question presented by these appeals, New York argues that the reasons that support the Watson holding require a similar result here. In Watson the Court relied on (a) the well-settled common law rule that a warrantless arrest in a public place is valid if the arresting officer had probable cause to believe the suspect is a felon; (b) the clear consensus among the States adhering to that well-settled common-law rule; and (c) the expression of the judgment of Congress that such an arrest is "reasonable." We consider ***591** each of these reasons as it applies to a warrantless entry into a home for the purpose of making a routine felony arrest.

A

An examination of the common-law understanding of an officer's authority to arrest sheds light on the obviously relevant, if not entirely dispositive, consideration ****1383** of what the Framers of the Amendment might have thought to be reasonable. Initially, it should be noted that the common-law rules of arrest developed in legal contexts that substantially differ from the cases now before us. In these cases, which involve application of the exclusionary rule, the issue is whether certain ***592** evidence is admissible at trial.[1225] At common law, the question whether an arrest was authorized typically arose in civil damages actions for trespass or false arrest, in which a constable's authority to make the arrest was a defense.[1226] Additionally, if an officer was killed while attempting to effect an arrest, the question whether the person resisting the arrest was guilty of murder or manslaughter turned on whether the officer was acting within the bounds of his authority.[1227]

A study of the common law on the question whether a constable had the authority to make warrantless arrests in the home on mere suspicion of a felony—as distinguished from an officer's right to arrest for a crime committed in his presence—reveals a surprising lack of judicial decisions and a deep divergence among scholars.

The most cited evidence of the common-law rule consists of an equivocal dictum in a case actually involving the sheriff's authority to enter a home to effect service of civil process. In Semayne's case,[1228] the Court stated:

"In all cases when the King is party, the Sheriff (if the doors be not open) may break the party's house, either to arrest him, or to do other execution of the K.'s process, if otherwise he cannot enter. But before he breaks it, he ought to signify the cause of his coming, and to make request to open doors; and that appears well by the stat. of Westm. 1. c. 17. (which it but an affirmance of the common law) as hereafter appears, for the law without a default in the owner abhors the destruction ***593** or breaking of any house (which is for the habitation and safety of man) by which great damage and inconvenience might ensue to the party, when no default is in him; for

---

[1223] *Silverman v. United States*, 365 U.S. 505, 511, 81 S.Ct. 679, 683, 5 L.Ed.2d 734.

[1224] 423 U.S. 411, 96 S.Ct. 820, 46 L.Ed.2d 598.

[1225] See *Weeks v. United States*, 232 U.S. 383, 34 S.Ct. 341, 58 L.Ed. 652.

[1226] See, e. g., *Leach v. Money*, 19 How.St.Tr. 1001, 97 Eng.Rep. 1075 (K.B.1765).

[1227] See M. Foster, Crown Law 308, 312 (1762). See also *West v. Cabell*, 153 U.S. 78, 85, 14 S.Ct. 752, 753, 38 L.Ed. 643.

[1228] 5 Co.Rep. 91a, 91b, 77 Eng.Rep. 194, 195–196 (K.B.1603).

perhaps he did not know of the process, of which, if he had notice, it is to be presumed that he would obey it, and that appears by the book in 18 E. 2. Execut. 252. where it is said, that the K.'s officer who comes to do execution may open the doors which are shut, and break them, if he cannot have the keys; which proves, that he ought first to demand them."

This passage has been read by some as describing an entry without a warrant. The context strongly implies, however, that the court was describing the extent of authority in executing the King's writ. This reading is confirmed by the phrase "either to arrest him, or to do other execution of the K.'s process" and by the further point that notice was necessary because the owner may "not know of the process." In any event, the passage surely cannot be said unambiguously to endorse warrantless entries.

The common law commentators disagreed sharply on the subject. Three distinct views were expressed. Lord Coke, ***594** widely ****1384** recognized by the American colonists "as the greatest authority of his time on the laws of England," clearly viewed a warrantless entry for the purpose of arrest to be illegal. ***595** Burn, Foster, and Hawkins agreed, as did East and Russell, though the latter two qualified their opinions by stating that if an entry to arrest was made without a warrant, the officer was perhaps immune from liability for the trespass if the suspect was actually guilty. Blackstone, Chitty, and Stephen took the opposite view, that entry to arrest without a warrant was legal, though Stephen relied on ****1385** Blackstone who, along with Chitty, in turn relied exclusively on Hale. But Hale's view was not quite so unequivocally expressed. ***596** Further, Hale appears to rely solely on a statement in an early Yearbook, quoted in *Burdett v. Abbot*:

"'that for felony, or suspicion of felony, a man may break open the house to take the felon; for it is for the commonweal to take them.'"[1229]

Considering the diversity of views just described, however, it is clear that the statement was never deemed authoritative. Indeed, in *Burdett*, the statement was described as an "extrajudicial opinion."[1230]

It is obvious that the common-law rule on warrantless home arrests was not as clear as the rule on arrests in public places. Indeed, particularly considering the prominence of Lord Coke, the weight of authority as it appeared to the Framers was to the effect that a warrant was required, or at the minimum that there were substantial risks in proceeding without one. The common-law sources display a sensitivity to privacy interests that could not have been lost on the Framers. The zealous and frequent repetition of the adage that a "man's house is his castle," made it abundantly clear that both in England ***597** and in the Colonies "the freedom of one's house" was one of the most vital elements of English liberty.

****1386** Thus, our study of the relevant common law does not provide the same guidance that was present in Watson. Whereas ***598** the rule concerning the validity of an arrest in a public place was supported by cases directly in point and by the unanimous views of the commentators, we have found no direct authority supporting forcible entries into a home to make a routine arrest and the weight of the scholarly opinion is somewhat to the contrary. Indeed, the absence of any 17th- or 18th-century English cases directly in point, together with the unequivocal endorsement of the tenet that "a man's house is his castle," strongly suggests that the prevailing practice was not to make such arrests except in hot pursuit or when authorized by a warrant.[1231] In all events, the issue is not one that can be said to have been definitively settled by the common law at the time the Fourth Amendment was adopted.

[1229] 14 East 1, 155, 104 Eng.Rep. 501, 560 (K.B.1811)

[1230] *Ibid.*

[1231] Cf. *Agnello v. United States*, 269 U.S. 20, 33, 46 S.Ct. 4, 6, 70 L.Ed. 145.

B

A majority of the States that have taken a position on the question permit warrantless entry into the home to arrest even in the absence of exigent circumstances. At this time, 24 States permit such warrantless entries; 15 States clearly ***599** prohibit them, though 3 States do so on federal constitutional grounds alone; and 11 States have apparently taken no position on the question. ****1387** But these current figures reflect a significant decline during the last decade in the number of States permitting warrantless entries for arrest. Recent dicta in this Court raising questions about the practice[1232] and Federal Courts of Appeals' decisions on point,[1233] have led state courts to focus on the issue. Virtually all of the state courts that have had to confront the constitutional issue directly have held warrantless entries into the home to arrest to be invalid in the absence of exigent circumstances.[1234] Three state courts have relied on Fourth Amendment ***600** grounds alone, while seven have squarely placed their decisions on both federal and state constitutional grounds. A number of other state courts, though not having had to confront the issue directly, have recognized the serious nature of the constitutional question. Apparently, only the Supreme Court of Florida and the New York Court of Appeals in this case have expressly upheld warrantless entries to arrest in the face of a constitutional challenge.

A longstanding, widespread practice is not immune from constitutional scrutiny. But neither is it to be lightly brushed aside. This is particularly so when the constitutional standard is as amorphous as the word "reasonable," and when custom and contemporary norms necessarily play such a large role in the constitutional analysis. In this case, although the weight of state-law authority is clear, there is by no means the kind of virtual unanimity on this question that was present in *United States v. Watson*, with regard to warrantless arrests in public places.[1235] Only 24 of the 50 States currently sanction warrantless entries into the home to arrest[1236] and there is an obvious declining trend. Further, the strength of the trend is greater than the numbers alone indicate. Seven state courts have recently held that warrantless home arrests violate their respective State Constitutions.[1237] That is significant because by invoking a state constitutional provision, a state court immunizes its decision from review by this Court. This heightened degree of immutability underscores the depth of the principle underlying the result.

*601 C

No congressional determination that warrantless entries into the home are "reasonable" has been called to our attention. None of the federal statutes cited in the Watson opinion reflects any such legislative judgment. Thus, that support for the Watson holding finds no counterpart in this case.

Mr. Justice POWELL, concurring in *United States v. Watson*[1238]stated:

"But logic sometimes must defer to history and experience. The Court's opinion emphasizes the historical sanction accorded warrantless felony arrests [in public places]."

In this case, however, neither history nor this Nation's experience requires us to disregard ****1388** the overriding respect for the sanctity of the home that has been embedded in our traditions since the origins of the Republic.

[1232] See n. 1, *supra*.

[1233] See n. 4, *supra*.

[1234] See nn. 2, 3, *supra*.

[1235] See 423 U.S., at 422–423, 96 S.Ct., at 827–828.

[1236] See nn. 46–48, *supra*.

[1237] See n. 3, *supra*.

[1238] *Supra*, at 429, 96 S.Ct., at 830.

***602 IV**

The parties have argued at some length about the practical consequences of a warrant requirement as a precondition to a felony arrest in the home. In the absence of any evidence that effective law enforcement has suffered in those States that already have such a requirement,[1239] we are inclined to view such arguments with skepticism. More fundamentally, however, such arguments of policy must give way to a constitutional command that we consider to be unequivocal.

Finally, we note the State's suggestion that only a search warrant based on probable cause to believe the suspect is at home at a given time can adequately protect the privacy interests at stake, and since such a warrant requirement is manifestly impractical, there need be no warrant of any kind. We find this ingenious argument unpersuasive. It is true that an arrest warrant requirement may afford less protection than a search warrant requirement, but it will suffice to interpose the magistrate's determination of probable cause between the zealous officer and the citizen. If there is sufficient evidence of a citizen's participation in a felony to persuade a judicial officer that his arrest is justified, it is constitutionally reason able ***603** to require him to open his doors to the officers of the law. Thus, for Fourth Amendment purposes, an arrest warrant founded on probable cause implicitly carries with it the limited authority to enter a dwelling in which the suspect lives when there is reason to believe the suspect is within.

Because no arrest warrant was obtained in either of these cases, the judgments must be reversed and the cases remanded to the New York Court of Appeals for further proceedings not inconsistent with this opinion.

It is so ordered.

Mr. Justice BLACKMUN, concurring.

I joined the Court's opinion in *United States v. Watson,*[1240] upholding, on probable cause, the warrantless arrest in a public place. I, of course, am still of the view that the decision in Watson is correct. The Court's balancing of the competing governmental and individual interests properly occasioned that result. Where, however, the warrantless arrest is in the suspect's home, that same balancing requires that, absent exigent circumstances, the result be the other way. The suspect's interest in the sanctity of his home then outweighs the governmental interests.

I therefore join the Court's opinion, firm in the conviction that the result in Watson and the result here, although opposite, are fully justified by history and by the Fourth Amendment.

(The dissent of ****1389** Mr. Justice WHITE, with whom THE CHIEF JUSTICE and Mr. Justice REHNQUIST join, is omitted.)

(The dissent of Mr. Justice REHNQUIST, is omitted.)

[1239] See nn. 3, 47, *supra*.

[1240] 423 U.S. 411, 96 S.Ct. 820, 46 L.Ed.2d 598 (1976).

Black Letter Law

> The Court held that: (1) distinction between warrantless seizure in open area and such a seizure on private premises is of equal force when seizure of person is involved; (2) zone of privacy is nowhere more clearly defined than when bounded by unambiguous physical dimensions of individual's home, and at very core of Fourth Amendment stands right of man to retreat into his own home and there be free from unreasonable government intrusion, and this is true as against seizures of property and seizures of person; and (3) Fourth Amendment prohibits police from making warrantless and nonconsensual entry into suspect's home in order to make routine felony-arrest. If there is sufficient evidence of citizen's participation in felony to persuade judicial officer that his arrest is justified, it is constitutionally reasonable to require him to open his doors to officers of the law, and thus for Fourth Amendment purposes arrest warrant founded on probable cause implicitly carries with it limited authority to open dwelling in which suspect lives when there is reason to believe suspect is within.

Steagald v. United States

101 S.Ct. 1642

Supreme Court of the United States

Gary Keith STEAGALD, Petitioner,

v.

UNITED STATES.

No. 79–6777. | Argued Jan. 14, 1981. | Decided April 21, 1981.

Justice MARSHALL delivered the opinion of the Court.

The issue in this case is whether, under the Fourth Amendment, a law enforcement officer may legally search for the subject of an arrest warrant in the home of a third party without first obtaining a search warrant. Concluding that a search warrant must be obtained absent exigent circumstances ***206** or consent, we reverse the judgment of the United States Court of Appeals for the Fifth Circuit affirming petitioner's conviction.

I

In early January 1978, an agent of the Drug Enforcement Administration (DEA) was contacted in Detroit, Mich., by a confidential informant who suggested that he might be able to locate Ricky Lyons, a federal fugitive wanted on drug charges. On January 14, 1978, the informant called the agent again, and gave him a telephone number in the Atlanta, Ga., area where, according to the informant, Ricky Lyons could be reached during the next 24 hours. On January 16, 1978, the agent called fellow DEA Agent Kelly Goodowens in Atlanta and relayed the information he had obtained from the informant. Goodowens contacted Southern Bell Telephone Co., and secured the address corresponding to the telephone number obtained by the informant. Goodowens also discovered that Lyons was the subject of a 6-month-old arrest warrant.

Two days later, Goodowens and 11 other officers drove to the address supplied by the telephone company to search for Lyons. The officers observed two men standing outside the house to be searched. These men were Hoyt Gaultney and petitioner Gary Steagald. The officers approached with guns drawn, frisked both men, and, after demanding identification, determined that neither man was Lyons. Several ****1645** agents proceeded to the house. Gaultney's wife answered the door, and informed the agents that she was alone in the house. She was told to place her hands against the wall and was guarded in that position while one agent searched the house. Ricky Lyons was not found, but during the search of the house the agent observed what he believed to be cocaine. Upon being informed of this discovery, Agent Goodowens sent an officer to obtain a search warrant and in the meantime conducted a second search of the house, which uncovered ***207** additional incriminating evidence. During a third search conducted pursuant to a search warrant, the agents uncovered 43 pounds of cocaine. Petitioner was arrested and indicted on federal drug charges.

Prior to trial, petitioner moved to suppress all evidence uncovered during the various searches on the ground that it was illegally obtained because the agents had failed to secure a search warrant before entering the house. Agent Goodowens testified at the suppression hearing that there had been no "physical hinderance" preventing him from obtaining a search warrant and that he did not do so because he believed that the arrest warrant for Ricky Lyons was sufficient to justify the entry and search. The District Court agreed with this view, and denied the suppression motion. Petitioner was convicted, and renewed his challenge to the search in his appeal. A divided Court of Appeals for the Fifth Circuit affirmed the District Court's denial of petitioner's suppression motion.[1241] Because the issue presented by this case is an important one2 that has divided the Circuits, we granted certiorari.[1242]

***208 **1646 II**

The Government initially seeks to avert our consideration of the Fifth Circuit's decision by suggesting that petitioner may, regardless of the merits of that decision, lack an expectation of privacy in the house sufficient to prevail on his Fourth Amendment claim. This argument was never raised by the Government in the courts below. Moreover, in its brief in opposition to certiorari the Government represented ***209** to this Court that the house in question was "petitioner's residence" and was "occupied by petitioner, Gaultney, and Gaultney's wife."[1243] However, the Government now contends that the record does not clearly show that petitioner had a reasonable expectation of privacy in the house, and hence urges us to remand the case to the District Court for re-examination of this factual question.

We decline to follow the suggested disposition. Aside from arguing that a search warrant was not constitutionally required, the Government was initially entitled to defend against petitioner's charge of an unlawful search by asserting that petitioner lacked a reasonable expectation of privacy in the searched home, or that he consented to the search, or that exigent circumstances justified the entry. The Government, however, may lose its right to raise factual issues of this sort before this Court when it has made contrary assertions in the courts below, when it has acquiesced in contrary findings by those courts, or when it has failed to raise such questions in a timely fashion during the litigation.

We conclude that this is such a case. The Magistrate's report on petitioner's suppression motion, which was adopted by the District Court, characterized the issue as whether an arrest warrant was sufficient to justify the search of "the home of a third person" for the subject of the warrant.[1244] The Government never sought to correct this characterization on appeal, and instead acquiesced in the District Court's view of petitioner's Fourth Amendment claim.

Moreover, during both the trial and the appeal in this case the Government argued successfully that petitioner's connection with the searched home was sufficient to establish his constructive possession of the cocaine found in a suitcase in the

[1241] *United States v. Gaultney*, 606 F.2d 540 (1979).

[1242] 449 U.S. 819, 101 S.Ct. 71, 66 L.Ed.2d 21.

[1243] Brief in Opposition 1, 3.

[1244] App. 12.

closet of the house. Moreover, the Court of Appeals concluded, as ***210** had the Magistrate and the District Court, that petitioner's Fourth Amendment claim involved the type of warrant necessary to search "premises belonging to a third party."[1245] Again, the Government declined to disturb this characterization. When petitioner sought review in this Court, the Government could have filed a cross-petition for certiorari suggesting, as it does now, that the case be remanded to the District Court for further proceedings. Instead, the Government argued that further review was unnecessary. Finally, the Government in its opposition to certiorari expressly represented that the searched home was petitioner's residence.

Thus, during the course of these proceedings the Government has directly sought to connect petitioner with the house, has acquiesced in statements by the courts below characterizing the search as one of petitioner's residence, and has made similar concessions of its own. Now, two years after ****1647** petitioner's trial, the Government seeks to return the case to the District Court for a re-examination of this factual issue. ***211** The tactical advantages to the Government of this disposition are obvious, for if the Government prevailed on this claim upon a remand, it would be relieved of the task of defending the judgment of the Court of Appeals before this Court. We conclude, however, that the Government, through its assertions, concessions, and acquiescence, has lost its right to challenge petitioner's assertion that he possessed a legitimate expectation of privacy in the searched home. We therefore turn to the merits of petitioner's claim.

III

The question before us is a narrow one. The search at issue here took place in the absence of consent or exigent circumstances. Except in such special situations, we have consistently held that the entry into a home to conduct a search or make an arrest is unreasonable under the Fourth Amendment unless done pursuant to a warrant.[1246] ***212** Thus, as we recently observed: "In terms that apply equally to seizures of property and to seizures of persons, the Fourth Amendment has drawn a firm line at the entrance to the house. Absent exigent circumstances, that threshold may not reasonably be crossed without a warrant."[1247] Here, of course, the agents had a warrant—one authorizing the arrest of Ricky Lyons. However, the Fourth Amendment claim here is not being raised by Ricky Lyons. Instead, the challenge to the search is asserted by a person not named in the warrant who was convicted on the basis of evidence uncovered during a search of his residence for Ricky ****1648** Lyons. Thus, the narrow issue before us is whether an arrest warrant—as opposed to a search warrant—is adequate to protect the Fourth Amendment interests of persons not named in the warrant, when their homes are searched without their consent and in the absence of exigent circumstances.

The purpose of a warrant is to allow a neutral judicial officer to assess whether the police have probable cause to make an arrest or conduct a search. As we have often explained, the placement of this checkpoint between the Government and the citizen implicitly acknowledges that an "officer engaged in the often competitive enterprise of ferreting out crime,"[1248] may lack sufficient objectivity to weigh correctly the strength of the evidence supporting the contemplated action against the individual's interests in protecting his own liberty and the privacy of his home.[1249]

[1245] 606 F.2d, at 544.

[1246] See *Payton v. New York*, 445 U.S. 573, 100 S.Ct. 1371, 63 L.Ed.2d 639 (1980); *Johnson v. United States*, 333 U.S. 10, 13–15, 68 S.Ct. 367, 368–369, 92 L.Ed. 436 (1948).

[1247] *Payton v. New York, supra, 445 U.S., at 590, 100 S.Ct., at 1382. See, Coolidge v. New Hampshire, 403 U.S. 443, 474–475, 477–478, 91 S.Ct. 2022, 2042–2043, 2044, 29 L.Ed.2d 564 (1971); Jones v. United States, 357 U.S. 493, 497–498, 78 S.Ct. 1253, 1256–1257, 2 L.Ed.2d 514 (1958); Agnello v. United States, 269 U.S. 20, 32–33, 46 S.Ct. 4, 6, 70 L.Ed.2d 145 (1925).*

[1248] *Johnson v. United States*, supra, 333 U.S. at 14, 68 S.Ct., at 369.

[1249] *Coolidge v. New Hampshire*, *supra*, 403 U.S., at 449–451, 91 S.Ct., at 2029–2030; *McDonald v. United States*, 335 U.S. 451, 455–456, 69 S.Ct. 191, 193, 93 L.Ed. 153 (1948).

However, while an arrest warrant and a search warrant both serve to subject the probable-cause determination ***213** of the police to judicial review, the interests protected by the two warrants differ. An arrest warrant is issued by a magistrate upon a showing that probable cause exists to believe that the subject of the warrant has committed an offense and thus the warrant primarily serves to protect an individual from an unreasonable seizure. A search warrant, in contrast is issued upon a showing of probable cause to believe that the legitimate object of a search is located in a particular place, and therefore safeguards an individual's interest in the privacy of his home and possessions against the unjustified intrusion of the police.

Thus, whether the arrest warrant issued in this case adequately safeguarded the interests protected by the Fourth Amendment depends upon what the warrant authorized the agents to do. To be sure, the warrant embodied a judicial finding that there was probable cause to believe the Ricky Lyons had committed a felony, and the warrant therefore authorized the officers to seize Lyons. However, the agents sought to do more than use the warrant to arrest Lyons in a public place or in his home; instead, they relied on the warrant as legal authority to enter the home of a third person based on their belief that Ricky Lyons might be a guest there. Regardless of how reasonable this belief might have been, it was never subjected to the detached scrutiny of a judicial officer. Thus, while the warrant in this case may have protected Lyons from an unreasonable seizure, it did absolutely nothing to protect petitioner's privacy interest in being free from an unreasonable invasion and search of his home. Instead, petitioner's only protection from an illegal entry and search was the agent's personal determination of probable cause. In the absence of exigent circumstances, we have consistently held that such judicially untested determinations are not reliable enough to justify an entry into a person's home to arrest him without a warrant, or a search of a home for objects in the absence of a search warrant.[1250] ***214** We see no reason to depart from this settled course when the search of a home is for a person rather than an object.

****1649 *215** A contrary conclusion—that the police, acting alone and in the absence of exigent circumstances, may decide when there is sufficient justification for searching the home of a third party for the subject of an arrest warrant—would create a significant potential for abuse. Armed solely with an arrest warrant for a single person, the police could search all the homes of that individual's friends and acquaintances.[1251] Moreover, an arrest warrant may serve as the pretext for entering a home in which the police have a suspicion, but not probable cause to believe, that illegal activity is taking place.[1252] The Government recognizes the potential for such abuses, but contends that existing remedies—such as motions to suppress illegally procured evidence and damages actions for Fourth Amendment violations—provide adequate means of redress. We do not agree. As we observed on a previous occasion, "[t]he [Fourth] Amendment is designed to prevent, not simply to redress, unlawful police action."[1253] Indeed, if suppression motions and damages actions were sufficient to implement the Fourth Amendment's prohibition against unreasonable searches and seizures, there would be no need for the constitutional requirement that in the absence of exigent circumstances a warrant ***216** must be obtained for a home arrest or a search of a home for objects. We have instead concluded that in such cases the participation of a detached magistrate in the probable cause determination is an essential element of a reasonable search or seizure, and we believe that the same conclusion should apply here.

[1250] *Payton v. New York, supra; Johnson v. United States, supra.*

[1251] See, e. g., *Lankford v. Gelston*, 364 F.2d 197 (CA4 1966) (enjoining police practice under which 300 homes were searched pursuant to arrest warrants for two fugitives).

[1252] Cf. *Chimel v. California*, 395 U.S. 752, 767, 89 S.Ct. 2034, 2042, 23 L.Ed.2d 685 (1969).

[1253] *Chimel v. California, supra*, at 766, n. 12, 89 S.Ct., at 2042, n. 12.

In sum, two distinct interests were implicated by the search at issue here—Ricky Lyons' interest in being free from an unreasonable seizure and petitioner's interest ****1650** in being free from an unreasonable search of his home. Because the arrest warrant for Lyons addressed only the former interest, the search of petitioner's home was no more reasonable from petitioner's perspective than it would have been if conducted in the absence of any warrant. Since warrantless searches of a home are impermissible absent consent or exigent circumstances, we conclude that the instant search violated the Fourth Amendment.

IV

The government concedes that this view is "apparently logical," that it furthers the general policies underlying the Fourth Amendment, and that it "has the virtue of producing symmetry between the law of entry to conduct a search for things to be seized and the law of entry to conduct a search for persons to be seized."[1254] Yet we are informed that this conclusion is "not without its flaws" in that it is contrary to common-law precedent and creates some practical problems of law enforcement. We treat these contentions in turn.

*217 A

The common law may, within limits,10 be instructive in determining what sorts of searches the Framers of the Fourth Amendment regarded as reasonable.[1255] The Government contends that at common law an officer could forcibly enter the home of a third party to execute an arrest warrant. To be sure, several commentators do suggest that a constable could "break open doors" to effect such an arrest.[1256] As support for this proposition, these commentators all rely on a single decision.[1257] ***218** Although that case involved only the authority of a sheriff to effect civil service on a person within his own home, the court noted in dictum that a person could not "escape the ordinary process of law" by seeking refuge in the home of a third party.[1258] However, the language of the decision, while not free from ambiguity, suggests that forcible entry into a third party's house was permissible only when the person to be arrested was pursued to the house. The decision refers to a person who "flies" to another's home,[1259] ****1651** and the annotation notes that " in order to justify the breaking of the outer door; after denial on request to take a person ... in the house of a stranger, it must be understood ... that the person upon a pursuit taketh refuge in the house of another."[1260] The common-law commentators appear to have adopted this limitation.[1261] We have long recognized that such "hot pursuit" cases fall within the exigent-circumstances exception to the warrant requirement,[1262] and therefore are distinguishable from the routine search situation presented here.

More important, the general question addressed by the common-law commentators was very different from the issue presented by this case. The authorities on which the Government relies were concerned with whether the subject of the arrest

---

[1254] Brief for United States 36.

[1255] See, e. g., *Payton v. New York*, 445 U.S., at 591, 100 S.Ct., at 1382.

[1256] See 1 J. Chitty, Criminal Law *57 (Chitty); M. Foster, Crown Law 320 (1762) (Foster); 2 M. Hale, Pleas of the Crown 116–117 (1st Am. ed. 1847) (Hale). But see 4 E. Coke, Institutes *177.

[1257] Semayne's Case, 5 Co.Rep. 91a, 92b–93a, 77 Eng.Rep. 194, 198 (K.B.1603).11 See 1 Chitty *57; Foster 320; 2 Hale 116.

[1258] 5 Co.Rep., at 93a, 77 Eng.Rep., at 198.

[1259] *Ibid.*

[1260] *Id.*, at93a, n. (I), 77 Eng.Rep.,at 198,n. (I) (emphasis in original).

[1261] See 1 Chitty *57 (sheriff may enter third parties' home "if the offender fly to it for refuge"); Foster 320 ("For if a Stranger whose ordinary Residence is elsewhere, upon a Pursuit taketh Refuge in the House of another, this is not his Castle, He cannot claim the Benefit of Sanctuary in it"); 2 Hale 116, n. 20 (forcible entry permissible "only upon strong necessity").

[1262] See Warden v. Hayden, 387 U.S. 294, 87 S.Ct. 1642, 18 L.Ed.2d 782 (1967).

warrant could claim sanctuary from arrest by hiding ***219** in the home of a third party.[1263] Thus, in *Semayne's* case it was observed:

"[T]he house of any one is not a castle or privilege but for himself, and shall not extend to protect any person who flies to his house, or the goods of any other which are brought and conveyed into his house, to prevent a lawful execution, and to escape the ordinary process of law; for the privilege of his house extends only to him and his family, and to his own proper goods."[1264]

The common law thus recognized, as have our recent decisions, that rights such as those conferred by the Fourth Amendment are personal in nature, and cannot bestow vicarious protection on those who do not have a reasonable expectation of privacy in the place to be searched.[1265] The issue here, however, is not whether the subject of an arrest warrant can object to the absence of a search warrant when he is apprehended in another person's home, but rather whether the residents of that home can complain of the search. Because the authorities relied on by the Government focus on the former question without addressing the latter, we find their usefulness limited. Indeed, if anything, the little guidance that can be gleaned from common-law authorities undercuts the Government's position. The language of *Semayne's* case quoted above, for example, suggests that although the subject of an arrest warrant could not find sanctuary in the home of the third party, the home remained a "castle or privilege" for its residents. Similarly, several commentators suggested that a search warrant, rather than an arrest warrant, was necessary to fully insulate a constable from an action for trespass brought by a party whose home was searched.[1266]

***220** While the common law thus sheds relatively little light on the narrow question before us, the history of the Fourth Amendment strongly suggests that its Framers would not have sanctioned the instant search. The Fourth Amendment was intended partly to protect against the abuses of the general warrants that had occurred in England and of the writs of assistance used in the Colonies.[1267] The general warrant specified only an offense—typically seditious libel—and left to the discretion of the executing officials the decision as to ****1652** which persons should be arrested and which places should be searched. Similarly, the writs of assistance used in the Colonies noted only the object of the search—any uncustomed goods—and thus left customs officials completely free to search any place where they believed such goods might be. The central objectionable feature of both warrants was that they provided no judicial check on the determination of the executing officials that the evidence available justified an intrusion into any particular home.[1268] An arrest warrant, to the extent that it is invoked as authority to enter the homes of third parties, suffers from the same infirmity. Like a writ of assistance, it specifies only the object of a search—in this case, Ricky Lyons—and leaves to the unfettered discretion of the police the decision as to which particular homes should be searched. We do not believe that the Framers of the Fourth Amendment would have condoned such a result.

B

The Government also suggests that practical problems might arise if law enforcement officers are required to obtain ***221** a search warrant before entering the home of a third party to make an arrest. The basis of this concern is that persons, as

---

1263 See 1 Chitty *57; Foster 320; 2 Hale 116–117.

1264 5 Co.Rep., at 93a, 77 Eng.Rep., at 128.

1265 See *United States v. Salvucci*, 448 U.S. 83, 100 S.Ct. 2547, 65 L.Ed.2d 619 (1980); *Rakas v. Illinois*, 439 U.S. 128, 99 S.Ct. 421, 58 L.Ed.2d 387 (1978).

1266 See, e. g., 1 Chitty *57; 2 Hale 116–117, 151.

1267 See *Payton v. New York*, 445 U.S., at 608–609, 100 S.Ct., at 1391–1392 (WHITE, J., dissenting); *Boyd v. United States*, 116 U.S. 616, 624–629, 6 S.Ct. 524, 529–532, 29 L.Ed. 746 (1886); N. Lasson, The History and Development of the Fourth Amendment to the United States Constitution 13–78 (1937).

1268 *Stanford v. Texas*, 379 U.S. 476, 481–485, 85 S.Ct. 506, 509–512, 13 L.Ed.2d 431 (1965).

opposed to objects, are inherently mobile, and thus officers seeking to effect an arrest may be forced to return to the magistrate several times as the subject of the arrest warrant moves from place to place. We are convinced, however, that a search warrant requirement will not significantly impede effective law enforcement efforts.

First, the situations in which a search warrant will be necessary are few. As noted in *Payton v. New York*[1269] an arrest warrant alone will suffice to enter a suspect's own residence to effect his arrest. Furthermore, if probable cause exists, no warrant is required to apprehend a suspected felon in a public place.[1270] Thus, the subject of an arrest warrant can be readily seized before entering or after leaving the home of a third party.14 Finally, the exigent-circumstances doctrine significantly limits the situations in which a search warrant would be needed. For example, a warrantless entry of a home would be justified if the police were in "hot pursuit" of a fugitive.[1271] ***222** Thus, to the extent that searches for persons pose special problems, we believe that the exigent-circumstances doctrine is adequate to accommodate legitimate law enforcement needs.

Moreover, in those situations in which a search warrant is necessary, the inconvenience incurred by the police is simply not that significant. First, if the police know of the location of the felon when they obtain an arrest warrant, the additional burden of obtaining a search warrant at the same time is miniscule. The inconvenience ****1653** of obtaining such a warrant does not increase significantly when an outstanding arrest warrant already exists. In this case, for example, Agent Goodowens knew the address of the house to be searched two days in advance, and planned the raid from the federal courthouse in Atlanta where, we are informed, three full-time magistrates were on duty. In routine search cases such as this, the short time required to obtain a search warrant from a magistrate will seldom hinder efforts to apprehend a felon. Finally, if a magistrate is not nearby, a telephonic search warrant can usually be obtained.[1272]

Whatever practical problems remain, however, cannot outweigh the constitutional interests at stake. Any warrant requirement impedes to some extent the vigor with which the Government can seek to enforce its laws, yet the Fourth Amendment recognizes that this restraint is necessary in some cases to protect against unreasonable searches and seizures. We conclude that this is such a case. The additional burden imposed on the police by a warrant requirement is minimal. In contrast, the right protected—that of presumptively innocent people to be secure in their homes from unjustified, forcible intrusions by the Government—is weighty. Thus, in order to render the instant search reasonable under the Fourth Amendment, a search warrant was required.

***223** Accordingly, the judgment of the Court of Appeals is reversed, and the case is remanded to that court for further proceedings consistent with this opinion.

So ordered.

THE CHIEF JUSTICE concurs in the judgment.

(The dissent of Justice REHNQUIST, with whom Justice WHITE joins, is omitted.)

Black Letter Law

1269 *Supra*, at 602–603, 100 S.Ct., at 1388–1389.

1270 *United States v. Watson*, 423 U.S. 411, 96 S.Ct. 820, 46 L.Ed.2d 598 (1976).

1271 See *United States v. Santana*, 427 U.S. 38, 42–43, 96 S.Ct. 2406, 2409–2410, 49 L.Ed.2d 300 (1976); *Warden v. Hayden*, 387 U.S. 294, 87 S.Ct. 1642, 18 L.Ed.2d 782 1967).

1272 See Fed.Rule Crim.Proc. 41(c)(1), (2).

Held that absent exigent circumstances or consent, law enforcement officer could not legally search for subject of arrest warrant in home of third party, without first obtaining search warrant.

In terms that apply equally to seizures of property and to seizures of persons, Fourth Amendment has drawn firm line at entrance to house, and, absent exigent circumstances, that threshold may not reasonably be crossed without warrant.

United States v. Grubbs

126 S.Ct. 1494

Supreme Court of the United States

UNITED STATES, Petitioner,

v.

Jeffrey GRUBBS.

No. 04–1414. | Argued Jan. 18, 2006. | Decided March 21, 2006.

Justice SCALIA delivered the opinion of the Court.

***92** Federal law enforcement officers obtained a search warrant for respondent's house on the basis of an affidavit explaining that the warrant would be executed only after a controlled delivery of contraband to that location. We address two challenges to the constitutionality of this anticipatory warrant.

I

Respondent Jeffrey Grubbs purchased a videotape containing child pornography from a Web site operated by an undercover postal inspector. Officers from the Postal Inspection Service arranged a controlled delivery of a package containing the videotape to Grubbs' residence. A postal inspector submitted a search warrant application to a Magistrate Judge for the Eastern District of California, accompanied by an affidavit describing the proposed operation in detail. The affidavit stated:

"Execution of this search warrant will not occur unless and until the parcel has been received by a person(s) and has been physically taken into the residence.... At that time, and not before, this search warrant will be executed by me and other United States Postal inspectors, with appropriate assistance from other law enforcement officers in accordance with this warrant's command."[1273]

In addition to describing this triggering condition, the affidavit referred to two attachments, which described Grubbs' residence and the items officers would seize. These attachments, but not the body of the affidavit, were incorporated into the requested warrant. The affidavit concluded:

"Based upon the foregoing facts, I respectfully submit there exists probable cause to believe that the items set forth in Attachment B to this affidavit and the search warrant, will be found [at Grubbs' residence], which residence is ****1498** further described at Attachment A."[1274]

***93** The Magistrate Judge issued the warrant as requested. Two days later, an undercover postal inspector delivered the package. Grubbs' wife signed for it and took the unopened package inside. The inspectors detained Grubbs as he left his home a few minutes later, then entered the house and commenced the search. Roughly 30 minutes into the search, Grubbs was provided with a copy of the warrant, which included both attachments but not the supporting affidavit that explained when the warrant would be executed. Grubbs consented to interrogation by the postal in-

[1273] App. to Pet. for Cert. 72a.

[1274] *Ibid.*

spectors and admitted ordering the videotape. He was placed under arrest, and various items were seized, including the videotape.

A grand jury for the Eastern District of California indicted Grubbs on one count of receiving a visual depiction of a minor engaged in sexually explicit conduct.[1275] He moved to suppress the evidence seized during the search of his residence, arguing as relevant here that the warrant was invalid because it failed to list the triggering condition. After an evidentiary hearing, the District Court denied the motion. Grubbs pleaded guilty, but reserved his right to appeal the denial of his motion to suppress.

The Court of Appeals for the Ninth Circuit reversed.[1276] Relying on Circuit precedent, it held that "the particularity requirement of the Fourth Amendment applies with full force to the conditions precedent to an anticipatory search warrant."[1277] An anticipatory warrant defective for that reason may be "cured" if the conditions precedent are set forth in an affidavit that is incorporated in the warrant and "presented to the person whose property is being searched."[1278] Because the postal inspectors "failed to present the affidavit—the only document in which the triggering conditions were listed"—to Grubbs or ***94** his wife, the "warrant was ... inoperative, and the search was illegal."[1279] We granted certiorari.[1280]

II

Before turning to the Ninth Circuit's conclusion that the warrant at issue here ran afoul of the Fourth Amendment's particularity requirement, we address the antecedent question whether anticipatory search warrants are categorically unconstitutional.[1] An anticipatory warrant is "a warrant based upon an affidavit showing probable cause that at some future time (but not presently) certain evidence of crime will be located at a specified place."[1281] Most anticipatory warrants subject their execution to some condition precedent other than the mere passage of time—a so-called "triggering condition." The affidavit at issue here, for instance, explained that "execution of the search warrant will not occur unless ****1499** and until the parcel [containing child pornography] has been received by a person(s) and has been physically taken into the residence."[1282] If the government were to execute an anticipatory warrant before the triggering condition occurred, there would be no reason to believe the item described in the warrant could be found at the searched location; by definition, the triggering condition which establishes probable cause has not yet been satisfied when the warrant is issued. Grubbs argues that for this reason anticipatory warrants contravene the Fourth ***95** Amendment's provision that "no warrants shall issue, but upon probable cause."

We reject this view, as has every Court of Appeals to confront the issue.[1283] Probable cause exists when "there is a fair probability that contraband or evidence of a crime will be found in a particular place."[1284] Because the probable-cause requirement looks to whether evidence will be found when the search is conducted, all warrants are, in a sense, "anticipatory." In the typical case where the police seek permission to search a house for an item they believe is already located there, the magis-

---

[1275] See 18 U.S.C. § 2252(a)(2).

[1276] 377 F.3d 1072, amended, 389 F.3d 1306 (C.A.9 2004).

[1277] 377 F.3d, at 1077–1078 (citing *United States v. Hotal*, 143 F.3d 1223, 1226 (C.A.9 1998)).

[1278] 377 F.3d, at 1079.

[1279] *Ibid.*

[1280] 545 U.S. 1164, 126 S.Ct. 34, 162 L.Ed.2d 932 (2005).

[1281] 2 W. LaFave, Search and Seizure § 3.7(c), p. 398 (4th ed.2004).

[1282] App. to Pet. for Cert. 72a.

[1283] see, e.g., *United States v. Loy*, 191 F.3d 360, 364 (C.A.3 1999) (collecting cases).

[1284] *Illinois v. Gates*, 462 U.S. 213, 238, 103 S.Ct. 2317, 76 L.Ed.2d 527 (1983).

trate's determination that there is probable cause for the search amounts to a prediction that the item will still be there when the warrant is executed.[1285] The anticipatory nature of warrants is even clearer in the context of electronic surveillance.[1286] When police request approval to tap a telephone line, they do so based on the probability that, during the course of the surveillance, the subject will use the phone to engage in crime-related conversations. The relevant federal provision requires a judge authorizing "interception of wire, oral, or electronic communications" to determine that "there is probable ***96** cause for belief that particular communications concerning [one of various listed offenses] will be obtained through such interception."[1287] Thus, when an anticipatory warrant is issued, "the fact that the contraband is not presently located at the place described in the warrant is immaterial, so long as there is probable cause to believe that it will be there when the search warrant is executed."[1288]

****1500** Anticipatory warrants are, therefore, no different in principle from ordinary warrants. They require the magistrate to determine (1) that it is now probable that (2) contraband, evidence of a crime, or a fugitive will be on the described premises (3) when the warrant is executed. It should be noted, however, that where the anticipatory warrant places a condition (other than the mere passage of time) upon its execution, the first of these determinations goes not merely to what will probably be found if the condition is met. (If that were the extent of the probability determination, an anticipatory warrant could be issued for every house in the country, authorizing search and seizure if contraband should be delivered—though for any single location there is no likelihood that contraband will be delivered.) Rather, the probability determination for a conditioned anticipatory warrant looks also to the likelihood that the condition will occur, and thus that a proper object of seizure will be on the described premises. In other words, for a conditioned anticipatory warrant to comply with the Fourth Amendment's requirement of probable cause, two prerequisites of probability must be satisfied. It must be true not only that if the triggering condition occurs "there is a fair probability that contraband or evidence of a crime will be found in a particular place,"[1289] ***97** but also that there is probable cause to believe the triggering condition will occur. The supporting affidavit must provide the magistrate with sufficient information to evaluate both aspects of the probable-cause determination.[1290]

In this case, the occurrence of the triggering condition—successful delivery of the videotape to Grubbs' residence—would plainly establish probable cause for the search. In addition, the affidavit established probable cause to believe the triggering condition would be satisfied. Although it is possible that Grubbs could have refused delivery of the videotape he had ordered, that was unlikely. The Magistrate therefore "had a 'substantial basis for ... conclud[ing]' that probable cause existed."[1291]

III

The Ninth Circuit invalidated the anticipatory search warrant at issue here because the warrant failed to specify the triggering condition. The Fourth Amend-

---

[1285] See *People v. Glen*, 30 N.Y.2d 252, 258, 331 N.Y.S.2d 656, 282 N.E.2d 614, 617 (1972) ("[P]resent possession is only probative of the likelihood of future possession").

[1286] See, e.g., *Katz v. United States*, 389 U.S. 347, 88 S.Ct. 507, 19 L.Ed.2d 576 (1967).

[1287] 18 U.S.C. § 2518(3)(b) (emphasis added); see also *United States v. Ricciardelli*, 998 F.2d 8, 11, n. 3 (C.A.1 1993) ("[T]he magistrate issues the warrant on the basis of a substantial probability that crime-related conversations will ensue").

[1288] *United States v. Garcia*, 882 F.2d 699, 702 (C.A.2 1989) (quoting *United States v. Lowe*, 575 F.2d 1193, 1194 (C.A.6 1978); internal quotation marks omitted).

[1289] *Gates*, supra, at 238, 103 S.Ct. 2317,

[1290] See *Garcia*, supra, at 703.

[1291] *Gates, supra*, at 238–239, 103 S.Ct. 2317 (quoting *Jones v. United States*, 362 U.S. 257, 271, 80 S.Ct. 725, 4 L.Ed.2d 697 (1960)).

ment's particularity requirement, it held, "applies with full force to the conditions precedent to an anticipatory search warrant."[1292]

The Fourth Amendment, however, does not set forth some general "particularity requirement." It specifies only two matters that must be "particularly describ[ed]" in the warrant: "the place to be searched" and "the persons or things to be seized." We have previously rejected efforts to expand the scope of this provision to embrace unenumerated matters. In *Dalia v. United States*[1293] we considered an order authorizing the interception of oral communications by means of a "bug" installed by the police in the petitioner's office. The petitioner argued that, if a covert entry is necessary to install such a listening device, the authorizing order must "explicitly set forth its approval of such entries before the fact."[1294] This argument fell before the " 'precise and clear' " words of the Fourth ***98** Amendment: "Nothing in the language of the Constitution or in this Court's decisions interpreting that language ****1501** suggests that, in addition to the [requirements set forth in the text], search warrants also must include a specification of the precise manner in which they are to be executed."[1295] The language of the Fourth Amendment is likewise decisive here; its particularity requirement does not include the conditions precedent to execution of the warrant.

Respondent, drawing upon the Ninth Circuit's analysis below, relies primarily on two related policy rationales. First, he argues, setting forth the triggering condition in the warrant itself is necessary "to delineate the limits of the executing officer's power."[1296] This is an application, respondent asserts, of the following principle: "[I]f there is a precondition to the valid exercise of executive power, that precondition must be particularly identified on the face of the warrant."[1297] That principle is not to be found in the Constitution. The Fourth Amendment does not require that the warrant set forth the magistrate's basis for finding probable cause, even though probable cause is the quintessential "precondition to the valid exercise of executive power." Much less does it require description of a triggering condition.

Second, respondent argues that listing the triggering condition in the warrant is necessary to "'assure the individual whose property is searched or seized of the lawful authority of the executing officer, his need to search, and the limits of his power to search.'"[1298] The Ninth Circuit went even further, asserting that if the property owner were not informed of the triggering condition, he "would 'stand [no] real chance of policing the officers' conduct.'"[1299] This argument assumes that the executing officer must present the property owner with ***99** a copy of the warrant before conducting his search.[1300] In fact, however, neither the Fourth Amendment nor Federal Rule of Criminal Procedure 41 imposes such a requirement.[1301] "The absence of a constitutional requirement that the warrant be exhibited at the outset of the search, or indeed until the search has ended, is ... evidence that the requirement of particular description does not protect an interest in monitoring searches."[1302] The Constitution

---

1292 377 F.3d, at 1077–1078.

1293 441 U.S. 238, 99 S.Ct. 1682, 60 L.Ed.2d 177 (1979).

1294 *Id.*, at 255, 99 S.Ct. 1682.

1295 *Ibid.* (quoting *Stanford v. Texas*, 379 U.S. 476, 481, 85 S.Ct. 506, 13 L.Ed.2d 431 (1965)), 441 U.S., at 257, 99 S.Ct. 1682.

1296 Brief for Respondent 20.

1297 *Id.*, at 23.

1298 *Id.*, at 19 (quoting *United States v. Chadwick*, 433 U.S. 1, 9, 97 S.Ct. 2476, 53 L.Ed.2d 538 (1977)).

1299 377 F.3d, at 1079 (quoting *Ramirez v. Butte–Silver Bow County*, 298 F.3d 1022, 1027 (C.A.9 2002)).

1300 See 377 F.3d, at 1079, n. 9.

1301 See *Groh v. Ramirez*, 540 U.S. 551, 562, n. 5, 124 S.Ct. 1284, 157 L.Ed.2d 1068 (2004).

1302 *United States v. Stefonek*, 179 F.3d 1030, 1034 (C.A.7 1999) (citations omitted).

protects property owners not by giving them license to engage the police in a debate over the basis for the warrant, but by interposing, ex ante, the "deliberate, impartial judgment of a judicial officer ... between the citizen and the police,"[1303] and by providing, ex post, a right to suppress evidence improperly obtained and a cause of action for damages.

* * *

Because the Fourth Amendment does not require that the triggering condition for an anticipatory search warrant be set forth in the warrant itself, the Court of Appeals erred in invalidating the warrant at issue here. The judgment of the Court of Appeals is reversed, and the case is remanded for further proceedings consistent with this opinion.

It is so ordered.

****1502** Justice ALITO took no part in the consideration or decision of this case.

Justice SOUTER, with whom Justice STEVENS and Justice GINSBURG join, concurring in part and concurring in the judgment.

I agree with the Court that anticipatory warrants are constitutional for the reasons stated in Part II of the Court's ***100** opinion, and I join in the disposition of this case. But I would qualify some points made in Part III.

The Court notes that a warrant's failure to specify the place to be searched and the objects sought violates an express textual requirement of the Fourth Amendment, whereas the text says nothing about a condition placed by the issuing magistrate on the authorization to search (here, delivery of the package of contraband). That textual difference is, however, no authority for neglecting to specify the point or contingency intended by the magistrate to trigger authorization, and the government should beware of banking on the terms of a warrant without such specification. The notation of a starting date was an established feature even of the objectionable 18th-century writs of assistance.[1304] And it is fair to say that the very word "warrant" in the Fourth Amendment means a statement of authority that sets out the time at which (or, in the case of anticipatory warrants, the condition on which) the authorization begins.[*]

An issuing magistrate's failure to mention that condition can lead to several untoward consequences with constitutional significance. To begin with, a warrant that fails to tell the truth about what a magistrate authorized cannot inform the police officer's responsibility to respect the limits of authorization,[1305] a failing assuming real significance when the warrant is not executed by the official who applied for it and happens to know the unstated condition. The peril is that if an officer simply takes such a warrant on its face and makes the ostensibly authorized search before the unstated ***101** condition has been met, the search will be held unreasonable. It is true that we have declined to apply the exclusionary rule when a police officer reasonably relies on the product of a magistrate's faulty judgment or sloppy practice.[1306] But when a government officer obtains what the magistrate says is an anticipatory warrant, he must know or should realize when it omits the condition on which autho-

[1303] *Wong Sun v. United States*, 371 U.S. 471, 481–482, 83 S.Ct. 407, 9 L.Ed.2d 441 (1963).

[1304] See, e.g., Massachusetts Writs of Assistance Bill, 1762, reprinted in M. Smith, The Writs of Assistance Case 567–568 (1978); Writ of Assistance (English) of George III, 1761, reprinted in *id.*, at 524–527.

[1305] see *Groh v. Ramirez*, 540 U.S. 551, 560–563, and n. 4, 124 S.Ct. 1284, 157 L.Ed.2d 1068 (2004),

[1306] See *Massachusetts v. Sheppard*, 468 U.S. 981, 987–991, 104 S.Ct. 3424, 82 L.Ed.2d 737 (1984).

rization depends, and it is hard to see why the government should not be held to the condition despite the unconditional face of the warrant.[1307]

Nor does an incomplete anticipatory warrant address an owner's interest in an accurate statement of the government's **1503 authority to search property. To be sure, the extent of that interest is yet to be settled; in *Groh v. Ramirez*[1308] the Court was careful to note that the right of an owner to demand to see a copy of the warrant before making way for the police had not been determined,[1309] and it remains undetermined today. But regardless of any right on the owner's part, showing an accurate warrant reliably "assures the individual whose property is searched or seized of the lawful authority of the executing officer, his need to search, and the limits of his power to search."[1310] And if a later case holds that the homeowner has a right to inspect the warrant on request, a statement of the condition of authorization would give the owner a right to correct any misapprehension on the police's part that the condition had been met when in fact it had not been. If the police were then to enter anyway ***102** without a reasonable (albeit incorrect) justification, the search would certainly be open to serious challenge as unreasonable within the meaning of the Fourth Amendment.

******

The Black Letter Law

> Anticipatory warrants are not categorically unconstitutional under the Fourth Amendment. When an anticipatory warrant is issued, the fact that the contraband is not presently at the place described is immaterial, so long as there is probable cause to believe it will be there when the warrant is executed.
>
> Anticipatory warrants require the magistrate to determine (1) that it is now probable that (2) contraband, evidence of a crime, or a fugitive will be on the described premises (3) when the warrant is executed. Where the anticipatory warrant places a condition (other than the mere passage of time) upon its execution, the first of these determinations goes not merely to what will probably be found if the condition is met, but also to the likelihood that the condition will be met, and thus that a proper object of seizure will be on the described premises.

Wilson v. Arkansas

115 S.Ct. 1914

Supreme Court of the United States

Sharlene WILSON, Petitioner

v.

ARKANSAS.

No. 94-5707. | Argued March 28, 1995. | Decided May 22, 1995.

***929** Justice THOMAS delivered the opinion of the Court.

[1307] Cf. *Groh v. Ramirez, supra*, at 554–555, 563, and n. 6, 124 S.Ct. 1284 (declaring unconstitutional a search conducted pursuant to a warrant failing to specify the items the government asked the magistrate permission to seize in part because "officers leading a search team must 'make sure that they have a proper warrant that in fact authorizes the search and seizure they are about to conduct'" (brackets omitted)).

[1308] *Supra.*

[1309] *Id.*, at 562, n. 5, 124 S.Ct. 1284.

[1310] *United States v. Chadwick*, 433 U.S. 1, 9, 97 S.Ct. 2476, 53 L.Ed.2d 538 (1977), quoted in *Groh v. Ramirez, supra*, at 561, 124 S.Ct. 1284.

At the time of the framing, the common law of search and seizure recognized a law enforcement officer's authority to break open the doors of a dwelling, but generally indicated that he first ought to announce his presence and authority. In this case, we hold that this common-law "knock and announce" principle forms a part of the reasonableness inquiry under the Fourth Amendment.

I

During November and December 1992, petitioner Sharlene Wilson made a series of narcotics sales to an informant acting at the direction of the Arkansas State Police. In late November, the informant purchased marijuana and methamphetamine at the home that petitioner shared with Bryson Jacobs. On December 30, the informant telephoned petitioner at her home and arranged to meet her at a local store to buy some marijuana. According to testimony presented below, petitioner produced a semiautomatic pistol at this meeting and waved it in the informant's face, threatening to kill her if she turned out to be working for the police. Petitioner then sold the informant a bag of marijuana.

The next day, police officers applied for and obtained warrants to search petitioner's home and to arrest both petitioner and Jacobs. Affidavits filed in support of the warrants set forth the details of the narcotics transactions and stated that Jacobs had previously been convicted of arson and firebombing. The search was conducted later that afternoon. Police officers found the main door to petitioner's home open. While opening an unlocked screen door and entering the residence, they identified themselves as police officers and stated that they had a warrant. Once inside the home, the officers ****1916** seized marijuana, methamphetamine, valium, narcotics paraphernalia, a gun, and ammunition. They also found petitioner in the bathroom, flushing marijuana down the toilet. Petitioner and Jacobs were arrested and ***930** charged with delivery of marijuana, delivery of methamphetamine, possession of drug paraphernalia, and possession of marijuana.

Before trial, petitioner filed a motion to suppress the evidence seized during the search. Petitioner asserted that the search was invalid on various grounds, including that the officers had failed to "knock and announce" before entering her home. The trial court summarily denied the suppression motion. After a jury trial, petitioner was convicted of all charges and sentenced to 32 years in prison.

The Arkansas Supreme Court affirmed petitioner's conviction on appeal.[1311] The court noted that "the officers entered the home while they were identifying themselves," but it rejected petitioner's argument that "the Fourth Amendment requires officers to knock and announce prior to entering the residence."[1312] Finding "no authority for [petitioner's] theory that the knock and announce principle is required by the Fourth Amendment," the court concluded that neither Arkansas law nor the Fourth Amendment required suppression of the evidence.[1313]

We granted certiorari to resolve the conflict among the lower courts as to whether the common-law knock and announce principle forms a part of the Fourth Amendment reasonableness inquiry.[1314] We hold that it does, and accordingly reverse and remand.

*931 II

The Fourth Amendment to the Constitution protects "[t]he right of the people to be secure in their persons, houses, papers, and effects, against unreasonable searches and seizures." In evaluating the scope of this right, we have looked to the traditional protections against unreasonable searches and seizures afforded by the common law

[1311] 317 Ark. 548, 878 S.W.2d 755 (1994).

[1312] *Id.*, at 553, 878 S.W.2d, at 758 (emphasis added).

[1313] *Ibid.*

[1314] 513 U.S. 1014, 115 S.Ct. 571, 130 L.Ed.2d 488 (1994).

at the time of the framing.[1315] "Although the underlying command of the Fourth Amendment is always that searches and seizures be reasonable,"[1316] our effort to give content to this term may be guided by the meaning ascribed to it by the Framers of the Amendment. An examination of the common law of search and seizure leaves no doubt that the reasonableness of a search of a dwelling may depend in part on whether law enforcement officers announced their presence and authority prior to entering.

Although the common law generally protected a man's house as "his castle of defense and asylum,"[1317] ***288** common law courts long have held that "when the King is party, the sheriff (if the doors be not open) may break the party's house, either to arrest him, or to do other execution of the K[ing]'s process, if otherwise he cannot enter."[1318] To this rule, however, common-law courts appended an important qualification:

"But before he breaks it, he ought to signify the cause of his coming, and to make request to open doors ..., for the law without a default in the owner abhors the destruction or breaking of any house ****1917** (which is for the habitation and safety of man) by which great damage and inconvenience might ensue to the party, when no ***932** default is in him; for perhaps he did not know of the process, of which, if he had notice, it is to be presumed that he would obey it...."[1319]

Several prominent founding-era commentators agreed on this basic principle. According to Sir Matthew Hale, the "constant practice" at common law was that "the officer may break open the door, if he be sure the offender is there, if after acquainting them of the business, and demanding the prisoner, he refuses to open the door."[1320] ***582** William Hawkins propounded a similar principle: "the law doth never allow" an officer to break open the door of a dwelling "but in cases of necessity," that is, unless he "first signify to those in the house the cause of his coming, and request them to give him admittance."[1321] ***933** Sir William Blackstone stated simply that the sheriff may "justify breaking open doors, if the possession be not quietly delivered."[1322] ***412**

The common law knock and announce principle was woven quickly into the fabric of early American law. Most of the States that ratified the Fourth Amendment had enacted constitutional provisions or statutes generally incorporating English common law,[1323] and a few States had enacted statutes specifically embracing the common-law view that the breaking of the door of a dwelling was permitted once

---

1315 See *California v. Hodari D.*, 499 U.S. 621, 624, 111 S.Ct. 1547, 1549-50, 113 L.Ed.2d 690 (1991); *United States v. Watson*, 423 U.S. 411, 418-420, 96 S.Ct. 820, 825-26, 46 L.Ed.2d 598 (1976); *Carroll v. United States*, 267 U.S. 132, 149, 45 S.Ct. 280, 283-84, 69 L.Ed. 543 (1925).

1316 *New Jersey v. T.L.O.*, 469 U.S. 325, 337, 105 S.Ct. 733, 740, 83 L.Ed.2d 720 (1985).

1317 3 W. Blackstone, Commentaries (hereinafter Blackstone).

1318 Semayne's Case, 5 Co. Rep. 91a, 91b, 77 Eng.Rep. 194, 195 (K.B.1603).

1319 *Ibid.*, 77 Eng.Rep., at 195-196. See also Case of Richard Curtis, Fost. 135, 137, 168 Eng.Rep. 67, 68 (Crown 1757) ("[N]o precise form of words is required in a case of this kind. It is sufficient that the party hath notice, that the officer cometh not as a mere trespasser, but claiming to act under a proper authority ..."); *Lee v. Gansell*, Lofft 374, 381-382, 98 Eng.Rep. 700, 705 (K.B.1774) ("[A]s to the outer door, the law is now clearly taken" that it is privileged; but the door may be broken "when the due notification and demand has been made and refused").

1320 See 1 M. Hale, Pleas of the Crown

1321 2 W. Hawkins, Pleas of the Crown, ch. 14, § 1, p. 138 (6th ed. 1787).

1322 3 Blackstone.

1323 See, e.g., N.J. Const. of 1776, § 22, in 5 Federal and State Constitutions 2598 (F. Thorpe ed. 1909) ("[T]he common law of England ... shall still remain in force, until [it] shall be altered by a future law of the Legislature"); N.Y. Const. of 1777, Art. 35, in id., at 2635 ("[S]uch parts of the common law of England ... as ... did form the law of [New York on April 19, 1775] shall be and continue the law of this State, subject to such alterations and provisions as the legislature of this State shall, from time to time, make concerning the same"); Ordinances of May 1776, ch. 5, § 6, in 9 Statutes at Large of Virginia 127 (W. Hening ed. 1821) ("[T]he common law of England ... shall be the rule of decision, and shall be considered as in full force, until the same shall be altered by the legislative power of this colony").

admittance was refused.[1324] Early American courts similarly embraced the common-law knock and announce principle.[1325] *934

**1918 Our own cases have acknowledged that the common law principle of announcement is "embedded in Anglo-American law,"[1326] but we have never squarely held that this principle is an element of the reasonableness inquiry under the Fourth Amendment. We now so hold. Given the longstanding common law endorsement of the practice of announcement, we have little doubt that the Framers of the Fourth Amendment thought that the method of an officer's entry into a dwelling was among the factors to be considered in assessing the reasonableness of a search or seizure. Contrary to the decision below, we hold that in some circumstances an officer's unannounced entry into a home might be unreasonable under the Fourth Amendment.

This is not to say, of course, that every entry must be preceded by an announcement. The Fourth Amendment's flexible requirement of reasonableness should not be read to mandate a rigid rule of announcement that ignores countervailing law enforcement interests. As even petitioner concedes, the common law principle of announcement was never stated as an inflexible rule requiring announcement under all circumstances.[1327]

Indeed, at the time of the framing, the common-law admonition that an officer "ought to signify the cause of his coming,"[1328] had not been extended conclusively to the context of felony arrests.[1329] The common law principle gradually was applied to cases involving felonies, but at the same time the courts continued to recognize that under certain circumstances the presumption in favor of announcement necessarily would give way to contrary considerations.

Thus, because the common-law rule was justified in part by the belief that announcement generally would avoid "the destruction or breaking of any house ... by which great ***936** damage and inconvenience might ensue,"[1330] courts acknowledged that the presumption in favor of announcement would ****1919** yield under circum-

[1324] See, e.g., Act of Nov. 8, 1782, ch. 15, ¶ 6, in Acts and Laws of Massachusetts 193 (1782); Act of Apr. 13, 1782, ch. 39, § 3, in 1 Laws of the State of New York 480 (1886); Act of June 24, 1782, ch. 317, § 18, in Acts of the General Assembly of New-Jersey (1784) (reprinted in The First Laws of the State of New Jersey 293-294 (J. Cushing comp.1981)); Act of Dec. 23, 1780, ch. 925, § 5, in 10 Statutes at Large of Pennsylvania 255 (J. Mitchell & H. Flanders comp.1904).

[1325] See, e.g., Walker v. Fox, 32 Ky. 404, 405 (1834); Burton v. Wilkinson, 18 Vt. 186, 189 (1846); Howe v. Butterfield, 58 Mass. 302, 305 (1849). See generally Blakey, The Rule of Announcement and Unlawful Entry, 112 U.Pa.L.Rev. 499, 504-508 (1964) (collecting cases).

[1326] *Miller v. United States*, 357 U.S. 301, 313, 78 S.Ct. 1190, 1198, 2 L.Ed.2d 1332 (1958).

[1327] See *Ker v. California*, 374 U.S. 23, 38, 83 S.Ct. 1623, 1632, 10 L.Ed.2d 726 (1963) (plurality opinion) ("[I]t has been recognized from the early common law that ... breaking is permissible in executing an arrest under certain circumstances"); see also, e.g., *935 White & Wiltsheire, 2 Rolle 137, 138, 81 Eng.Rep. 709, 710 (K.B.*1619*) (upholding the sheriff's breaking of the door of the plaintiff's dwelling after the sheriff's bailiffs had been imprisoned in plaintiff's dwelling while they attempted an earlier execution of the seizure); *Pugh v. Griffith*, 7 Ad. & E. 827, 840-841, 112 Eng.Rep. 681, 686 (K.B.1838) (holding that "the necessity of a demand ... is obviated, because there was nobody on whom a demand could be made" and noting that White & Wiltsheire leaves open the possibility that there may be "other occasions where the outer door may be broken" without prior demand).

[1328] *Semayne's* Case, 5 Co.Rep., at 91b, 77 Eng.Rep., at 195.

[1329] See *Blakey*, *supra*, at 503 ("The full scope of the application of the rule in criminal cases ... was never judicially settled"); *Launock v. Brown*, 2 B. & Ald. 592, 593, 106 Eng.Rep. 482, 483 (K.B.1819) ("It is not at present necessary for us to decide how far, in the case of a person charged with felony, it would be necessary to make a previous demand of admittance before you could justify breaking open the outer door of his house"); W. Murfree, Law of Sheriffs and Other Ministerial Officers § 1163, p. 631 (1st ed. 1884) ("[A]lthough there has been some doubt on the question, the better opinion seems to be that, in cases of felony, no demand of admittance is necessary, especially as, in many cases, the delay incident to it would enable the prisoner to escape").

[1330] *Semayne's* Case, *supra*, at 91b, 77 Eng.Rep., at 196.

stances presenting a threat of physical violence.[1331] Similarly, courts held that an officer may dispense with announcement in cases where a prisoner escapes from him and retreats to his dwelling.[1332] Proof of "demand and refusal" was deemed unnecessary in such cases because it would be a "senseless ceremony" to require an officer in pursuit of a recently escaped arrestee to make an announcement prior to breaking the door to retake him.[1333] Finally, courts have indicated that unannounced entry may be justified where police officers have reason to believe that evidence would likely be destroyed if advance notice were given.[1334]

We need not attempt a comprehensive catalog of the relevant countervailing factors here. For now, we leave to the lower courts the task of determining the circumstances under which an unannounced entry is reasonable under the Fourth Amendment. We simply hold that although a search or seizure of a dwelling might be constitutionally defective if police officers enter without prior announcement, law enforcement interests may also establish the reasonableness of an unannounced entry.

***937 III**

Respondent contends that the judgment below should be affirmed because the unannounced entry in this case was justified for two reasons. First, respondent argues that police officers reasonably believed that a prior announcement would have placed them in peril, given their knowledge that petitioner had threatened a government informant with a semiautomatic weapon and that Mr. Jacobs had previously been convicted of arson and firebombing. Second, respondent suggests that prior announcement would have produced an unreasonable risk that petitioner would destroy easily disposable narcotics evidence.

These considerations may well provide the necessary justification for the unannounced entry in this case. Because the Arkansas Supreme Court did not address their sufficiency, however, we remand to allow the state courts to make any necessary findings of fact and to make the determination of reasonableness in the first instance. The judgment of the Arkansas Supreme Court is reversed, and the case is remanded for further proceedings not inconsistent with this opinion.

It is so ordered.

Black Letter Law

> Held that whether officers knock and announce their presence and authority before entering dwelling, as required by common law, is factor to be considered in determining reasonableness of search.

[1331] See, e.g., *Read v. Case*, 4 Conn. 166, 170 (1822) (plaintiff who "had resolved ... to resist even to the shedding of blood ... was not within the reason and spirit of the rule requiring notice"); *Mahomed v. The Queen*, 4 Moore 239, 247, 13 Eng.Rep. 293, 296 (P.C.1843) ("While he was firing pistols at them, were they to knock at the door, and to ask him to be pleased to open it for them? The law in its wisdom only requires this ceremony to be observed when it possibly may be attended with some advantage, and may render the breaking open of the outer door unnecessary").

[1332] See, e.g., *ibid.*; *Allen v. Martin*, 10 Wend. 300, 304 (N.Y.Sup.Ct.1833).

[1333] *Id.*, at 304.

[1334] See *Ker, supra*, 374 U.S., at 40-41, 83 S.Ct., at 1633-1634 (plurality opinion); *People v. Maddox*, 46 Cal.2d 301, 305-306, 294 P.2d 6, 9 (1956).

Discussion Problem:

5-1. At about 9:10 or 9:15 p.m., Officers Harder and Velloney stopped Edwards inside the hallway as he entered the building. Harder explained that Edwards exhibited no suspicious behavior but that he and Velloney stopped him because he "just happened to come in the building." They frisked Edwards, finding no weapons or drugs, and questioned him in the hallway for five to ten minutes about his identity and reason for being in the building.

Edwards cooperated with the officers, doing and saying nothing that aroused further suspicion during the five to ten minutes in the hallway. He told them his name and explained that he was visiting his girlfriend. He did not have identification with him, but said it was inside his girlfriend's apartment. The police did not place Edwards under arrest, but explained that during this period of questioning, they "probably" would not have allowed him to leave.

Still wanting verification of Edwards's identity and reason for being in the building, they accompanied Edwards to the second floor apartment where he said his girlfriend lived. Officer Harder knocked on the door but no one answered. Edwards then held up the key and Harder "grabbed" the key. When Edwards then said, "let me do it," Harder returned the key to him and Edwards opened the door. At this point, Edwards still had said and done nothing to arouse suspicion and, Harder acknowledged, his continuing investigation of Edwards related only to the general information the officers had regarding the drug dealers in the building, together with the police effort "to field interview anyone in the apartment building."

Harder said that Edwards entered the apartment indicating that he was going to check for some identification. Harder did not ask for Edwards's permission to enter, and Edwards did not ask him to come in. Harder entered anyway, without a warrant, right on the threshold approximately four to six inches maybe," "so that he couldn't slam the door shut on me."

Edwards then entered the bedroom and remained partially within Harder's view from the threshold. Harder testified: "Edwards was fumbling with something and keeping an eye on me. Now, I am suspicious." Officer Harder further testified that he became "afraid" "because I felt he was reaching for a gun. I honestly did. Just the look in his eye, just the look he had, I had an immediate fear." Harder then entered the bedroom and recovered a gun that was in plain view in the closet where Edwards had been reaching, ten bundles of cocaine from underneath the gun, and approximately $260 cash from next to the gun.

You work as an associate for Edward's defense counsel. What basis would you suggest to the senior attorney on the case to suppress the evidence from the bedroom closet? How would you structure that argument? What are its strengths and weaknesses?

-Notes-

Chapter 6: Search Incident to Arrest

Chimel v. California

89 S.Ct. 2034

Supreme Court of the United States

Ted Steven CHIMEL, Petitioner,

v.

State of CALIFORNIA

No. 770. | Argued March 27, 1969. | Decided June 23, 1969. | Rehearing Denied Oct. 13, 1969.See 90 S.Ct. 36.

Mr. Justice STEWART delivered the opinion of the Court.

This case raises basic questions concerning the permissible scope under the Fourth Amendment of a search incident to a lawful arrest.

The relevant facts are essentially undisputed. Late in the afternoon of September 13, 1965, three police officers arrived at the Santa Ana, California, home of the petitioner with a warrant authorizing his arrest for the burglary of a coin shop. The officers knocked on the door, identified themselves to the petitioner's wife, and asked if they might come inside. She ushered them into the house, where they waited 10 or 15 minutes until the petitioner returned home from work. When the petitioner entered the house, one of the officers handed him the arrest warrant and asked for permission to 'look around.' The petitioner objected, but was advised that ***754** 'on the basis of the lawful arrest,' the officers would nonetheless conduct a search. No search warrant had been issued.

Accompanied by the petitioner's wife, the officers then looked through the entire three-bedroom house, including the attic, the garage, and a small workshop. In some rooms the search was relatively cursory. In the master bedroom and sewing room, however, the officers directed the petitioner's wife to open drawers and 'to physically move contents of the drawers from side to side so that (they) might view any items that would have come from (the) burglary.' After completing the search, they seized numerous items-primarily coins, but also several medals, tokens, and a few other objects. The entire search took between 45 minutes and an hour.

At the petitioner's subsequent state trial on two charges of burglary, the items taken from his house were admitted into evidence against him, over his objection that they had been unconstitutionally seized. He was convicted, and the judgments of conviction were affirmed by both the California Court of Appeal,[1335] and the California Supreme Court.[1336] Both courts accepted the petitioner's contention that the arrest warrant was invalid because the supporting affidavit was set out in conclusory terms, but held that since the arresting officers had procured the warrant 'in good faith,' and since in any event they had had sufficient information to constitute probable cause for the petitioner's arrest, that arrest had been lawful. From this conclusion the appellate courts went on to hold that the search of the petitioner's home ***755** had been justified, despite the absence of a search warrant, on the ground that it had been incident to a valid arrest. We granted certiorari in order to consider the petitioner's substantial constitutional claims.[1337]

[1335] 61 Cal.Rptr. 714.

[1336] 68 Cal.2d 436, 67 Cal.Rptr. 421, 439 P.2d 333.

[1337] 393 U.S. 958, 89 S.Ct. 404, 21 L.Ed.2d 372.

Without deciding the question, we proceed on the hypothesis that the California **2036 courts were correct in holding that the arrest of the petitioner was valid under the Constitution. This brings us directly to the question whether the warrantless search of the petitioner's entire house can be constitutionally justified as incident to that arrest. The decisions of this Court bearing upon that question have been far from consistent, as even the most cursory review makes evident.

Approval of a warrantless search incident to a lawful arrest seems first to have been articulated by the Court in 1914 as dictum in *Weeks v. United States*,[1338] in which the Court stated:

'What then is the present case? Before answering that inquiry specifically, it may be well by a process of exclusion to state what it is not. It is not an assertion of the right on the part of the Government, always recognized under English and American law, to search the person of the accused when legally arrested to discover and seize the fruits or evidences of crime.'[1339]

That statement made no reference to any right to search the place where an arrest occurs, but was limited to a right to search the 'person.' Eleven years later the case of *Carroll v. United States*,[1340] brought the following embellishment of the Weeks statement:

'When a man is legally arrested for an offense, whatever is found upon his person or in his control which it is unlawful for him to have and which may be used to prove the offense may be seized and held ***756** as evidence in the prosecution.'[1341]

Still, that assertion too was far from a claim that the 'place' where one is arrested may be searched so long as the arrest is valid. Without explanation, however, the principle emerged in expanded form a few months later in *Agnello v. United States*[1342]-although still by way of dictum:

'The right without a search warrant contemporaneously to search persons lawfully arrested while committing crime and to search the place where the arrest is made in order to find and seize things connected with the crime as its fruits or as the means by which it was committed, as well as weapons and other things to effect an escape from custody, is not to be doubted.[1343]

And in *Marron v. United States*,[1344] two years later, the dictum of *Agnello* appeared to be the foundation of the Court's decision. In that case federal agents had secured a search warrant authorizing the seizure of liquor and certain articles used in its manufacture. When they arrived at the premises to be searched, they saw 'that the place was used for retailing and drinking intoxicating liquors.'[1345] They proceeded to arrest the person in charge and to execute the warrant. In searching a closet for the items listed in the warrant they came across an incriminating ledger, concededly not covered by the warrant, which they also seized. The Court upheld the seizure of the ledger by holding that since the agents had made a lawful arrest, '(t)hey had a right without a warrant contemporaneously to search the place in order to find and seize the things used to carry on the criminal enterprise.'[1346]

[1338] 232 U.S. 383, 34 S.Ct. 341, 58 L.Ed. 652.

[1339] *Id.*, at 392, 34 S.Ct., at 344.

[1340] 267 U.S. 132, 45 S.Ct. 280, 69 L.Ed. 543,

[1341] *Id.*, at 158, 45 S.Ct., at 287. (Emphasis added.)

[1342] 269 U.S. 20, 46 S.Ct. 4, 70 L.Ed. 145

[1343] See *Carroll v. United States*, 267 U.S. 132, 158, 45 S.Ct. 280, 69 L.Ed. 543; *Weeks v. United States*, 232 U.S. 383, 392, 34 S.Ct. 341, 58 L.Ed. 652.' 269 U.S., at 30, 46 S.Ct., at 5.

[1344] 275 U.S. 192, 48 S.Ct. 74, 72 L.Ed. 231.

[1345] *Id.*, at 194, 48 S.Ct., at 75.

[1346] *Id.*, at 199, 48 S.Ct., at 77.

***757** That the *Marron* opinion did not mean all that it seemed to say became evident, however, a few years later in *Go-Bart Importing Co. v. United States*,[1347] and *United States v. Lefkowitz.*[1348] In each of ****2037** those cases the opinion of the Court was written by Mr. Justice Butler, the author of the opinion in *Marron*. In *Go-Bart*, agents had searched the office of persons whom they had lawfully arrested, and had taken several papers from a desk, a safe, and other parts of the office. The Court noted that no crime had been committed in the agents' presence, and that although the agent in charge 'had an abundance of information and time to swear out a valid (search) warrant, he failed to do so.'[1349] In holding the search and seizure unlawful, the Court stated:

'Plainly the case before us is essentially different from *Marron v. United States.*[1350] There, officers executing a valid search warrant for intoxicating liquors found and arrested one Birdsall who in pursuance of a conspiracy was actually engaged in running a saloon. As an incident to the arrest they seized a ledger in a closet where the liquor or some of it was kept and some bills beside the cash register. These things were visible and accessible and in the offender's immediate custody. There was no threat of force or general search or rummaging of the place.'[1351] This limited characterization of *Marron* was reiterated in *Lefkowitz*, a case in which the Court held unlawful a search of desk drawers and a cabinet despite the fact that the search had accompanied a lawful arrest.[1352]

The limiting views expressed in *Go-Bart* and *Lefkowitz* were thrown to the winds, however, in ***758** *Harris v. United States*,[1353] which was decided in 1947. In that case, officers had obtained a warrant for Harris' arrest on the basis of his alleged involvement with the cashing and interstate transportation of a forged check. He was arrested in the living room of his four-room apartment, and in an attempt to recover two canceled checks thought to have been used in effecting the forgery, the officers undertook a thorough search of the entire apartment. Inside a desk drawer they found a sealed envelope marked 'George Harris, personal papers.' The envelope, which was then torn open, was found to contain altered Selective Service documents, and those documents were used to secure Harris' conviction for violating the Selective Training and Service Act of 1940. The Court rejected Harris' Fourth Amendment claim, sustaining the search as 'incident to arrest.'[1354]

Only a year after Harris, however, the pendulum swung again. In *Trupiano v. United States*[1355] agents raided the site of an illicit distillery, saw one of several conspirators operating the still, and arrested him, contemporaneously 'seiz(ing) the illicit distillery.'[1356] The Court held that the arrest and others made subsequently had been valid, but that the unexplained failure of the agents to procure a search warrant-in spite of the fact that they had had more than enough time before the raid to do so-rendered the search unlawful. The opinion stated:

'It is a cardinal rule that, in seizing goods and articles, law enforcement agents must secure and use search warrants wherever reasonably practicable. * * * This rule

---

[1347] 282 U.S. 344, 51 S.Ct. 153, 75 L.Ed. 374.

[1348] 285 U.S. 452, 52 S.Ct. 420, 76 L.Ed. 877.

[1349] 282 U.S., at 358, 51 S.Ct., at 158.

[1350] 275 U.S. 192, 48 S.Ct. 74, 72 L.Ed. 231.

[1351] 282 U.S., at 358, 51 S.Ct., at 158.

[1352] 285 U.S., at 465, 52 S.Ct., at 423.

[1353] 331 U.S. 145, 67 S.Ct. 1098, 91 L.Ed. 1399.

[1354] *Id.*, at 151, 67 S.Ct., at 1101.

[1355] 334 U.S. 699, 68 S.Ct. 1229, 92 L.Ed. 1663,

[1356] *Id.*, at 702, 68 S.Ct. at 1231.

rests upon the desirability of having magistrates rather than police officers determine when searches and seizures are permissible and what limitations should be placed upon such activities. * * * To provide the necessary security against unreasonable intrusions upon the private lives of ***759** individuals, the framers of ****2038** the Fourth Amendment required adherence to judicial processes wherever possible. And subsequent history has confirmed the wisdom of that requirement.

'A search or seizure without a warrant as an incident to a lawful arrest has always been considered to be a strictly limited right. It grows out of the inherent necessities of the situation at the time of the arrest. But there must be something more in the way of necessity than merely a lawful arrest.'[1357]

In 1950, two years after *Trupiano*, came U*nited States v. Rabinowitz*,[1358] the decision upon which California primarily relies in the case now before us. In *Rabinowitz*, federal authorities had been informed that the defendant was dealing in stamps bearing forged overprints. On the basis of that information they secured a warrant for his arrest, which they executed at his one-room business office. At the time of the arrest, the officers 'searched the desk, safe, and file cabinets in the office for about an hour and a half,'[1359] and seized 573 stamps with forged overprints. The stamps were admitted into evidence at the defendant's trial, and this Court affirmed his conviction, rejecting the contention that the warrantless search had been unlawful. The Court held that the search in its entirety fell within the principle giving law enforcement authorities '(t)he right 'to search the place where the arrest is made in order to find and seize things connected with the crime * * *.[1360] Harris was regarded as 'ample authority' for that conclusion.[1361] The opinion rejected the rule of *Trupiano* that 'in seizing goods and articles, law enforcement agents must secure and use search warrants ***760** wherever reasonably practicable.' The test, said the Court, 'is not whether it is reasonable to procure a search warrant, but whether the search was reasonable.'[1362]

Rabinowitz has come to stand for the proposition, inter alia, that a warrantless search 'incident to a lawful arrest' may generally extend to the area that is considered to be in the 'possession' or under the 'control' of the person arrested. And it was on the basis of that proposition that the California courts upheld the search of the petitioner's entire house in this case. That doctrine, however, at least in the broad sense in which it was applied by the California courts in this case, can withstand neither historical nor rational analysis.

Even limited to its own facts, the Rabinowitz decision was, as we have seen, hardly founded on an unimpeachable line of authority. As Mr. Justice Frankfurter commented in dissent in that case, the 'hint' contained in *Weeks* was, without persuasive justification, 'loosely turned into dictum and finally elevated to a decision.'[1363] And the approach taken in cases such as *Go-Bart*, *Lefkowitz*, and *Trupiano* was essentially disregarded by the *Rabinowitz* Court.

****2039** Nor is the rationale by which the State seeks here to sustain the search of the petitioner's house supported by a reasoned view of the background and purpose of the Fourth Amendment. Mr. Justice Frankfurter wisely pointed out in his Rabinowitz dissent that the Amendment's proscription of 'unreasonable searches and seizures' ***761** must be read in light of 'the history that gave rise to the words' a his-

[1357] *Id.*, at 705, 708, 68 S.Ct., at 1232, 1234.

[1358] 339 U.S. 56, 70 S.Ct. 430, 94 L.Ed. 653.

[1359] *Id.*, at 59, 70 S.Ct., at 432.

[1360] *Id.*, at 61, 70 S.Ct., at 433.

[1361] *Id.*, at 63, 70 S.Ct., at 434.

[1362] *Id.*, at 66, 70 S.Ct., at 435.

[1363] 339 U.S., at 75, 70 S.Ct., at 439.

tory of 'abuses so deeply felt by the Colonies as to be one of the potent causes of the Revolution * * *.'[1364] The Amendment was in large part a reaction to the general warrants and warrantless searches that had so alienated the colonists and had helped speed the movement for independence. In the scheme of the Amendment, therefore, the requirement that 'no Warrants shall issue, but upon probable cause,' plays a crucial part. As the Court put it in *McDonald v. United States*:[1365]

'We are not dealing with formalities. The presence of a search warrant serves a high function. Absent some grave emergency, the Fourth Amendment has interposed a magistrate between the citizen and the police. This was done not to shield criminals nor to make the home a safe haven for illegal activities. It was done so that an objective mind might weigh the need to invade that privacy in order to enforce the law. The right of privacy was deemed too precious to entrust to the discretion of those whose job is the detection of crime and the arrest of criminals. * * * And so the Constitution requires a magistrate to pass on the desires of the police before they violate the privacy of the home. We cannot be true to that constitutional requirement and excuse the absence of a search warrant without a showing by those who seek exemption from the constitutional mandate that the exigencies of the situation made that course imperative.'[1366]

***762** Even in the *Agnello* case the Court relied upon the rule the '(b)elief, however well founded, that an article sought is concealed in a dwelling house, furnishes no justification for a search of that place without a warrant. And such searches are held unlawful notwithstanding facts unquestionably showing probable cause.'[1367] Clearly, the general requirement that a search warrant be obtained is not lightly to be dispensed with, and 'the burden is on those seeking (an) exemption (from the requirement) to show the need for it * * *.'[1368]

Only last term in *Terry v. Ohio*,[1369] we emphasized that 'the police must, whenever practicable, obtain advance judicial approval of searches and seizures through the warrant procedure,'[1370] and that '(t)he scope of (a) search must be 'strictly tied to and justified by' the circumstances which rendered its initiation permissible.'[1371] ****2040** The search undertaken by the officer in that 'stop and frisk' case was sustained under that test, because it was no more than a 'protective * * * search for weapons.'[1372] But in a companion case, *Sibron v. New York*,[1373] we applied the same standard to another set of facts and reached a contrary result, holding that a policeman's action in thrusting his hand into a suspect's pocket had been neither motivated by nor limited to the objective of protection. Rather, the search had been made in order to find narcotics, which were in fact found.

A similar analysis underlies the 'search incident to arrest' principle, and marks its proper extent. When an ***763** arrest is made, it is reasonable for the arresting officer to search the person arrested in order to remove any weapons that the latter might seek to use in order to resist arrest or effect his escape. Otherwise, the officer's safety might well be endangered, and the arrest itself frustrated. In addition, it is entirely

---

[1364] 339 U.S., at 69, 70 S.Ct., at 436.

[1365] 335 U.S. 451, 69 S.Ct. 191, 93 L.Ed. 153.

[1366] *Id.*, at 455-456, 69 S.Ct., at 193.

[1367] 269 U.S., at 33, 46 S.Ct., at 6.

[1368] *United States v. Jeffers*, 342 U.S. 48, 51, 72 S.Ct. 93, 95, 96 L.Ed. 59.

[1369] 392 U.S. 1, 88 S.Ct. 1868, 20 L.Ed.2d 889.

[1370] *Id.*, at 20, 88 S.Ct. at 1879.

[1371] *Id.*, at 19, 88 S.Ct., at 1878.

[1372] *Id.*, at 29, 88 S.Ct., at 1884.

[1373] 392 U.S. 40, 88 S.Ct. 1889, 20 L.Ed.2d 917.

reasonable for the arresting officer to search for and seize any evidence on the arrestee's person in order to prevent its concealment or destruction. And the area into which an arrestee might reach in order to grab a weapon or evidentiary items must, of course, be governed by a like rule. A gun on a table or in a drawer in front of one who is arrested can be as dangerous to the arresting officer as one concealed in the clothing of the person arrested. There is ample justification, therefore, for a search of the arrestee's person and the area 'within his immediate control' construing that phrase to mean the area from within which he might gain possession of a weapon or destructible evidence.

There is no comparable justification, however, for routinely searching any room other than that in which an arrest occurs or, for that matter, for searching through all the desk drawers or other closed or concealed areas in that room itself. Such searches, in the absence of well-recognized exceptions, may be made only under the authority of a search warrant. The 'adherence to judicial processes' mandated by the Fourth Amendment requires no less.

This is the principle that underlay our decision in *Preston v. United States.*[1374] In that case three men had been arrested in a parked car, which had later been towed to a garage and searched by police. We held that search to have been unlawful under the Fourth Amendment, despite the contention that it had ***764** been incidental to a valid arrest. Our reasoning was straightforward:

'The rule allowing contemporaneous searches is justified, for example, by the need to seize weapons and other things which might be used to assault an officer or effect an escape, as well as by the need to prevent the destruction of evidence of the crime-things which might easily happen where the weapon or evidence is on the accused's person or under his immediate control. But these justifications are absent where a search is remote in time or place from the arrest.'[1375]

****2041** The same basic principle was reflected in our opinion last Term in *Sibron*. That opinion dealt with *Peters v. New York*, No. 74, as well as with Sibron's case, and *Peters* involved a search that we upheld as incident to a proper arrest. We sustained the search, however, only because its scope had been 'reasonably limited' by the 'need to seize weapons' and 'to prevent the destruction of evidence,' to which *Preston* had referred. We emphasized that the arresting officer 'did not engage in an unrestrained and thorough going examination of Peters and his personal effects. He seized him to cut short his flight, and he searched him primarily for weapons.'[1376]

It is argued in the present case that it is 'reasonable' to search a man's house when he is arrested in it. But that argument is founded on little more than a subjective view regarding the acceptability of certain sorts of police ***765** conduct, and not on consideration relevant to Fourth Amendment interests. Under such an unconfined analysis, Fourth Amendment protection in this area would approach the evaporation point. It is not easy to explain why, for instance, it is less subjectively 'reasonable' to search a man's house when he is arrested on his front lawn-or just down the street-than it is when he happens to be in the house at the time of arrest. As Mr. Justice Frankfurter put it:

'To say that the search must be reasonable is to require some criterion of reason. It is no guide at all either for a jury or for district judges or the police to say that an 'unreasonable search' is forbidden-that the search must be reasonable. What is the test of reason which makes a search reasonable? The test is the reason underlying and expressed by the Fourth Amendment: the history and experience which it em-

---

[1374] 376 U.S. 364, 84 S.Ct. 881, 11 L.Ed.2d 777.

[1375] *Id.*, at 367, 84 S.Ct., at 883.

[1376] 392 U.S., at 67, 88 S.Ct., at 1905.

bodies and the safeguards afforded by it against the evils to which it was a response.'[1377]

Thus, although '(t)he recurring questions of the reasonableness of searches' depend upon 'the facts and circumstances-the total atmosphere of the case,'[1378] those facts and circumstances must be viewed in the light of established Fourth Amendment principles.

***766** It would be possible, of course, to draw a line between *Rabinowitz* and *Harris* on the one hand, and this case on the other. For *Rabinowitz* involved a single room, and Harris a four-room apartment, while in the case before us an entire house was searched. But such a distinction would be highly artificial. The rationale that allowed the searches and seizures in *Rabinowitz* and *Harris* would allow the searches and seizures in this case. No consideration relevant to the Fourth Amendment suggests any point of rational limitation, once the search is allowed to go beyond the area from which the person arrested might obtain weapons or evidentiary items. ****2042** The only reasoned distinction is one between a search of the person arrested and the area within his reach on the one hand, and more extensive searches on the other.

***767** The petitioner correctly points out that one result of decisions such as *Rabinowitz* and *Harris* is to give law enforcement officials the opportunity to engage in searches not justified by probable cause, by the simple expedient of arranging to arrest suspects at home rather than elsewhere. We do not suggest that the petitioner is necessarily correct in his assertion that such a strategy was utilized here, but the fact remains that had he been arrested earlier in the day, at his place of employment rather than at home, no search of his house could have been made without a search warrant. In any event, even apart from the possibility of such police tactics, the general point so forcefully made by Judge Learned Hand in *United States v. Kirschenblatt*[1379] remains:

'After arresting a man in his house, to rummage at will among his papers in search of whatever will convict him, appears to us to be indistinguishable from what might be done under a general warrant; indeed, the warrant would give more protection, for presumably it must be issued by a magistrate. True, by hypothesis the power would not exist, if the supposed offender were not found on the premises; ***768** but it is small consolation to know that one's papers are safe only so long as one is not at home.'[1380]

Rabinowitz and *Harris* have been the subject of critical commentary for many years, and have been relied upon less and less in our own decisions. It is ****2043** time, for the reasons we have stated, to hold that on their own facts, and insofar as the principles they stand for are inconsistent with those that we have endorsed today, they are no longer to be followed.

Application of sound Fourth Amendment principles to the facts of this case produces a clear result. The search here went far beyond the petitioner's person and the area from within which he might have obtained either a weapon or something that could have been used as evidence against him. There was no constitutional justification, in the absence of a search warrant, for extending the search beyond that area. The scope of the search was, therefore, 'unreasonable' under the Fourth and Fourteenth Amendments and the petitioner's conviction cannot stand.

Reversed.

***769** Mr. Justice HARLAN, concurring.

[1377] *United States v. Rabinowitz*, 339 U.S., at 83, 73 S.Ct., at 443 (dissenting opinion).

[1378] *Id.*, at 63, 66, 70 S.Ct., at 434, 435 (opinion of the Court).

[1379] 2 Cir., 16 F.2d 202, 51 A.L.R. 416.

[1380] *Id.*, at 203.

I join the Court's opinion with these remarks concerning a factor to which the Court has not alluded.

The only thing that has given me pause in voting to overrule Harris and Rabinowitz is that as a result of *Mapp v. Ohio*[1381] and *Ker v. California*[1382] every change in Fourth Amendment law must now be obeyed by state officials facing widely different problems of local law enforcement. We simply do not know the extent to which cities and towns across the Nation are prepared to administer the greatly expanded warrant system which will be required by today's decision; nor can we say with assurance that in each and every local situation, the warrant requirement plays an essential role in the protection of those fundamental liberties protected against state infringement by the Fourteenth Amendment.

Thus, one is now faced with the dilemma, envisioned in my separate opinion in *Ker*,[1383] of choosing between vindicating sound Fourth Amendment principles at the possible expense of state concerns, long recognized to be consonant with the Fourteenth Amendment before *Mapp* and *Ker* came on the books, or diluting the Federal Bill of Rights in the interest of leaving the States at least some elbow room in their methods of criminal law enforcement. No comparable dilemma exists, of course, with respect to the impact of today's decision within the federal system itself.

This federal-state factor has not been an easy one for me to resolve, but in the last analysis I cannot in good conscience vote to perpetuate bad Fourth Amendment law.

I add only that this case, together with *Benton v. Maryland*,[1384] *North Carolina v. Pearce*,[1385] and *Simpson v. Rice*,[1386] all decided ***770** today, serve to ****2044** point up, as few other cases have, the profound changes that the 'incorporation doctrine' has wrought both in the workings of our federal system and upon the adjudicative processes of this Court.

Black Letter Law

Arresting officer may search person arrested and the area into which the arrestee might reach, in order to remove any weapons or seize evidence on his person. Established the wingspan rule and the twin-rationales for the SIA doctrine: officer safety and preservation of evidence.

United States v. Robinson

94 S.Ct. 467

Supreme Court of the United States

UNITED STATES, Petitioner,

v.Willie ROBINSON, Jr.

No. 72-936. | Argued Oct. 9, 1973. | Decided Dec. 11, 1973.

Mr. Justice REHNQUIST delivered the opinion of the Court.

[1381] 367 U.S. 643, 81 S.Ct. 1684, 6 L.Ed.2d 1081 (1961).

[1382] 374 U.S. 23, 83 S.Ct. 1623, 10 L.Ed.2d 726 (1963).

[1383] 374 U.S., at 45-46, 83 S.Ct., at 1646.

[1384] 395 U.S. 784, 89 S.Ct. 2056, 23 L.Ed.2d 707.

[1385] 395 U.S. 711, 89 S.Ct. 2089, 23 L.Ed.2d 656.

[1386] 395 U.S. 711, 89 S.Ct. 2072, 23 L.Ed.2d 656.

Respondent Robinson was convicted in United States District Court for the District of Columbia of the possession and facilitation of concealment of heroin in violation of 26 U.S.C. s 4704(a) (1964 ed.), and 21 U.S.C. s 174 (1964 ed.). He was sentenced to concurrent terms of imprisonment for these offenses. On his appeal to the Court of Appeals for the District of Columbia Circuit, ***220** that court first remanded the case to the District Court for an evidentiary hearing concerning the scope of the search of respondent's person which had occurred at the time of his arrest.[1387] The District Court made findings of fact and conclusions of law adverse to respondent, and he again appealed. This time the Court of Appeals en banc reversed the judgment of conviction, holding that the heroin introduced in evidence against respondent had been obtained as a result of a search which violated the Fourth Amendment to the United States Constitution.[1388] We granted certiorari[1389] and set the case for argument together with *Gustafson v. Florida*,[1390] also decided today.

On April 23, 1968, at approximately 11:00 p.m., Officer Richard Jenks, a 15-year veteran of the District of Columbia Metropolitan Police Department, observed the respondent driving a 1965 Cadillac near the intersection of 8th and C Streets, N.E., in the District of Columbia. Jenks, as a result of previous investigation following a check of respondent's operator's permit four days earlier, determined there was reason to ****470** believe that respondent was operating a motor vehicle after the revocation of his operator's permit. This is an offense defined by statute in the District of Columbia which carries a mandatory minimum jail term, a mandatory minimum fine, or both.[1391] Jenks signaled respondent to stop the automobile, which respondent did, and all three of the occupants emerged from the car. At that point Jenks informed respondent that he was under arrest for 'operating after revocation and obtaining a permit by misrepresentation.' It was assumed by the Court of Appeals, and is conceded by the respondent here, that Jenks had ***221** probable cause to arrest respondent, and that he effected a full custody arrest.

In accordance with procedures prescribed in police department instructions, Jenks then began to search ***222** respondent. He explained at a subsequent ****471** hearing that he was 'face-to-face' with the respondent, and 'placed (his) hands on (the respondent), my right-hand to his ***223** left breast like this (demonstrating) and proceeded to pat him down thus (with the right hand).' During this pat-down, Jenks felt an object in the left breast pocket of the heavy coat respondent was wearing, but testified that he 'couldn't tell what it was' and also that he 'couldn't actually tell the size of it.' Jenks then reached into the pocket and pulled out the object, which turned out to be a 'crumpled up cigarette package.' Jenks testified that at this point he still did not know what was in the package:

'As I felt the package I could feel objects in the package but I couldn't tell what they were... I knew they weren't cigarettes.'

The officer then opened the cigarette pack and found 14 gelatin capsules of white powder which he thought to be, and which later analysis proved to be, heroin. Jenks then continued his search of respondent to completion, feeling around his waist and trouser legs, and examining the remaining pockets. The heroin seized from the respondent was admitted into evidence at the trial which resulted in his conviction in the District Court.

The opinion for the plurality judges of the Court of Appeals, written by Judge Wright, the concurring opinion of Chief Judge Bazelon, and the dissenting opinion of

---

[1387] 145 U.S.App.D.C. 46, 447 F.2d 1215 (1971).

[1388] 153 U.S.App.D.C. 114, 471 F.2d 1082 (1972).

[1389] 410 U.S. 982, 93 S.Ct. 1500, 36 L.Ed.2d 177 (1973).

[1390] 414 U.S. 260, 94 S.Ct. 488, 38 L.Ed.2d 456.

[1391] D.C.Code Ann. s 40-302(d) (1967).

Judge Wilkey, concurred in by three judges, gave careful and comprehensive treatment to the authority of a police officer to search the person of one ***224** who has been validly arrested and taken into custody. We conclude that the search conducted by Jenks in this case did not offend the limits imposed by the Fourth Amendment, and we therefore reverse the judgment of the Court of Appeals.

I

It is well settled that a search incident to a lawful arrest is a traditional exception to the warrant requirement of the Fourth Amendment. This general exception has historically been formulated into two distinct propositions. The first is that a search may be made of the person of the arrestee by virtue of the lawful arrest. The second is that a search may be made of the area within the control of the arrestee.

Examination of this Court's decisions shows that these two propositions have been treated quite differently. The validity of the search of a person incident to a lawful arrest has been regarded as settled from its first enunciation, and has remained virtually unchallenged until the present case. The validity of the second proposition, while likewise conceded in principle, has been subject to differing interpretations as to the extent of the area which may be searched.

Because the rule requiring exclusion of evidence obtained in violation of the Fourth Amendment was first enunciated in *Weeks v. United States*,[1392] it is understandable that virtually all of this Court's search-and-seizure law has been ****472** developed since that time. In Weeks, the Court made clear its recognition of the validity of a search incident to a lawful arrest:

What then is the present case? Before answering that inquiry specifically, it may be well by a process of exclusion to state what it is not. It is not an assertion of the right on the part of the ***225** Government, always recognized under English and American law, to search the person of the accused when legally arrested to discover and seize the fruits or evidences of crime. This right has been uniformly maintained in many cases.[1393] *Agnello v. United States*,[1394] decided 11 years after *Weeks*, repeats the categorical recognition of the validity of a search incident to lawful arrest:

'The right without a search warrant contemporaneously to search persons lawfully arrested while committing crime and to search the place where the arrest is made in order to find and size things connected with the crime as its fruits or as the means by which it was committed, as well as weapons and other things to effect an escape from custody, is not to be doubted.'[1395]

Throughout the series of cases in which the Court has addressed the second proposition relating to a search incident to a lawful arrest-the permissible area beyond the person of the arrestee which such a search may cover-no doubt has been expressed as to the unqualified authority of the arresting authority to search the person of the arrestee.[1396] In *Chimel*, where the Court overruled *Rabinowitz* and *Harris* as to the area ***226** of permissible search incident to a lawful arrest, full recognition was again given to the authority to search the person of the arrestee:

[1392] 232 U.S. 383, 34 S.Ct. 341, 58 L.Ed. 652 (1914).

[1393] 1 Bishop on Criminal Procedure, s 211; Wharton, Crim.Plead. and Practice, 8th ed., s 60; *Dillon v. O'Brien and Davis*, 16 Cox C.C. 245.' Id., at 392, 34 S.Ct. at 344.

[1394] 269 U.S. 20, 46 S.Ct. 4, 70 L.Ed. 145 (1925).

[1395] *Id*., at 30, 46 S.Ct. at 5.

[1396] E.g., *Carroll v. United States*, 267 U.S. 132, 45 S.Ct. 280, 69 L.Ed. 543 (1925); *Marron v. United States*, 275 U.S. 192, 48 S.Ct. 74, 72 L.Ed. 231 (1927); *Go-Bart Co. v. United States*, 282 U.S. 344, 51 S.Ct. 153, 75 L.Ed. 374 (1931); *United States v. Lefkowitz*, 285 U.S. 452, 52 S.Ct. 420, 76 L.Ed. 877 (1932); *Harris v. United States*, 331 U.S. 145, 67 S.Ct. 1098, 91 L.Ed. 1399 (1947); *Trupiano v. Unit*ed States, 334 U.S. 699, 68 S.Ct. 1229, 92 L.Ed. 1663 (1948); United States v. *Rabinowitz*, 339 U.S. 56, 70 S.Ct. 430, 94 L.Ed. 653 (1950); *Preston v. United States*, 376 U.S. 364, 84 S.Ct. 881, 11 L.Ed.2d 777 (1964); *Chimel v. California*, 395 U.S. 752, 89 S.Ct. 2034, 23 L.Ed.2d 685 (1969).

'When an arrest is made, it is reasonable for the arresting officer to search the person arrested in order to remove any weapons that the latter might seek to use in order to resist arrest or effect his escape. Otherwise, the officer's safety might well be endangered, and the arrest itself frustrated. In addition, it is entirely reasonable for the arresting officer to search for and seize any evidence on the arrestee's person in order to prevent its concealment or destruction.'[1397]

Three years after the decision in *Chimel*,[1398] we upheld the validity of a search in which heroin had been taken from the person of the defendant after his arrest on a weapons charge, in *Adams v. Williams*,[1399] saying:

'Under the circumstances surrounding Williams' possession of the gun seized by Sgt. Connolly, the arrest on the weapons charge was supported by probable cause, and the search of his person and of the car incident to that arrest was lawful'[1400]

Last Term in *Cupp v. Murphy*,[1401] we again reaffirmed the traditional statement of the authority to search incident to a valid arrest.

****473** Thus the broadly stated rule, and the reasons for it, have been repeatedly affirmed in the decisions of this Court since *Weeks v. United States*,[1402] nearly 60 years ago. Since the statements in the cases speak not simply in terms of an exception to the warrant requirement, but in terms of an affirmative authority to search, they clearly imply that such searches also meet the Fourth Amendment's requirement of reasonableness.

***227 II**

In its decision of this case, the Court of Appeals decided that even after a police officer lawfully places a suspect under arrest for the purpose of taking him into custody, he may not ordinarily proceed to fully search the prisoner. He must, instead, conduct a limited frisk of the outer clothing and remove such weapons that he may, as a result of that limited frisk, reasonably believe and ascertain that the suspect has in his possession. While recognizing that *Terry v. Ohio*,[1403] dealt with a permissible 'frisk' incident to an investigative stop based on less than probable cause to arrest, the Court of Appeals felt that the principles of that case should be carried over to this probable-cause arrest for driving while one's license is revoked. Since there would be no further evidence of such a crime to be obtained in a search of the arrestee, the court held that only a search for weapons could be justified.

Terry v. Ohio,[1404] did not involve an arrest for probable cause, and it made quite clear that the 'protective frisk' for weapons which it approved might be conducted without probable cause.[1405] This Court's opinion explicitly recognized that there is a 'distinction in purpose, character, and extent between a search incident to an arrest and a limited search for weapons.'

The former, although justified in part by the acknowledged necessity to protect the arresting officer from assault with a concealed weapon, *Preston v. United*

[1397] 395 U.S., at 762-763, 89 S.Ct. at 2040.

[1398] *Supra.*

[1399] 407 U.S. 143, 92 S.Ct. 1921, 32 L.Ed.2d 612 (1972).

[1400] *Id.*, at 149, 92 S.Ct. at 1925.

[1401] 412 U.S. 291, 295, 93 S.Ct. 2000, 2003, 36 L.Ed.2d 900 (1973).

[1402] *Supra.*

[1403] 392 U.S. 1, 88 S.Ct. 1868, 20 L.Ed.2d 889 (1968).

[1404] *Supra.*

[1405] *Id.*, at 21-22, 24-25, 88 S.Ct. at 1879-1880, 1881-1882.

States,[1406] is also justified on other grounds,[1407] and can therefore involve a relatively extensive exploration of the person. A search for weapons in the absence of probable cause to arrest, however, must, like any other search, be strictly circumscribed by the exigencies ***228** which justify its initiation.[1408] Thus it must be limited to that which is necessary for the discovery of weapons which might be used to harm the officer or others nearby, and may realistically be characterized as something less than a 'full' search, even though it remains a serious intrusion.

'. . . An arrest is a wholly different kind of intrusion upon individual freedom from a limited search for weapons, and the interests each is designed to serve are likewise quite different. An arrest is the initial stage of a criminal prosecution. It is intended to vindicate society's interest in having its laws obeyed, and it is inevitably accompanied by future interference with the individual's freedom of movement, whether or not trial or conviction ultimately follows. The protective search for weapons, on the other hand, constitutes brief, though far from inconsiderable, intrusion upon the sanctity of the person.'[1409]

Terry, therefore, affords no basis to carry over to a probable-cause arrest the limitations this Court placed on a stop-and-frisk search permissible without probable cause.

The Court of Appeals also relied on language in *Peters v. New York*,[1410] a companion case to Terry. There the Court held that the police officer ****474** had authority to search Peters because he had probable cause to arrest him, and went on to say:

(T)he incident search was obviously justified 'by the need to seize weapons and other things which might be used to assault an officer or effect an escape, as well as by the need to prevent the ***229** destruction of evidence of the crime.' [1411]Moreover, it was reasonably limited in scope by these purposes. Officer Lasky did not engage in an unrestrained and thorough-going examination of Peters and his personal effects.'[1412]

It is, of course, possible to read the second sentence from this quotation as imposing a novel limitation on the established doctrine set forth in the first sentence. It is also possible to read it as did Mr. Justice Harlan in his opinion concurring in the result:

'The second possible source of confusion is the Court's statement that 'Officer Lasky did not engage in an unrestrained and thorough-going examination of Peters and his personal effects.'[1413] Since the Court found probable cause to arrest Peters, and since an officer arresting on probable cause is entitled to make a very full incident search, I assume that this is merely a factual observation. As a factual matter, I agree with it.'[1414]

We do not believe that the Court in Peters intended in one unexplained and unelaborated sentence to impose a novel and far-reaching limitation on the authority to search the person of an arrestee incident to his lawful arrest. While the language

---

[1406] 376 U.S. 364, 367 (84 S.Ct. 881, 883, 11 L.Ed.2d 777) (1964).

[1407] *Ibid*.

[1408] *Warden v. Hayden*, 387 U.S. 294, 310 (87 S.Ct. 1642, 1652, 18 L.Ed.2d 782) (1967) (Mr. Justice Fortas, concurring).

[1409] *Id*., at 25-26, 88 S.Ct., at 1882 (footnote omitted).

[1410] 392 U.S. 40, 66, 88 S.Ct. 1889, 1904, 20 L.Ed.2d 917 (1968).

[1411] *Preston v. United States*, 376 U.S. 364, 367 (84 S.Ct. 881, 11 L.Ed.2d 777) (1964).

[1412] *Id*., at 67, 88 S.Ct., at 1905.

[1413] (392 U.S., at 67, 88 S.Ct.), at 1905.

[1414] *Id*., at 77, 88 S.Ct., at 1909 (footnote omitted).

from Peters was quoted with approval in *Chimel v. California*,[1415] it is preceded by a full exposition of the traditional and unqualified authority of the arresting officer to search the arrestee's person.[1416] We do not believe that either Terry or Peters, when considered in the light of the previously discussed statements of this Court, justified the sort of limitation upon that authority which the Court of Appeals fashioned in this case.

***230 III**

Virtually all of the statements of this Court affirming the existence of an unqualified authority to search incident to a lawful arrest are dicta. We would not, therefore, be foreclosed by principles of stare decisis from further examination into history and practice in order to see whether the sort of qualifications imposed by the Court of Appeals in this case were in fact intended by the Framers of the Fourth Amendment or recognized in cases decided prior to Weeks. Unfortunately such authorities as exist are sparse. Such common-law treatises as Blackstone's Commentaries and Holmes' Common Law are simply silent on the subject. Pollock and Maitland, in their History of English Law, describe the law of arrest as 'rough and rude' before the time of Edward I, but do not address the authority to search incident to arrest.[1417]

The issue was apparently litigated in the English courts in *Dillon v. O'Brien*,.[1418] There Baron Palles said:

> 'But the interest of the State in the person charged being brought to trial in due course necessarily extends, as well to the preservation of material evidence of his guilt or innocence, as to his custody for the purpose of trial. His custody is of no value if the law is powerless to prevent the abstraction or destruction of this evidence, without which a trial would be no more than an empty form. But if there be a right to production or preservation of this evidence, I cannot see how it ****475** can be enforced otherwise than by capture.'[1419]

***231** *Spalding v. Preston*[1420] represents an early holding in this country that evidence may be seized from one who is lawfully arrested. In *Closson v. Morrison*,[1421] the Court made the following statement:

We think that an officer would also be justified in taking from a person whom he had arrested for crime, any deadly weapon he might find upon him, such as a revolver, a dirk, a knife, a sword cane, a slung shot, or a club, though it had not been used or intended to be used in the commission of the offense for which the prisoner had been arrested, and even though no threats of violence towards the officer had been made. A due regard for his own safety on the part of the officer, and also for the public safety, would justify a sufficient search to ascertain if such weapons were carried about the person of the prisoner, or were in his possession, and if found, to seize and hold them until the prisoner should be discharged, or until they could be otherwise properly disposed of.[1422]

So we think it might be with money or other articles of value, found upon the prisoner, by means of which, if left in his possession, he might procure his escape, or obtain tools, or implements, or weapons with which to effect his escape. We think the

---

[1415] 395 U.S., at 764, 89 S.Ct. at 2040.

[1416] *Id.*, at 763, 89 S.Ct. at 2040.

[1417] 2 F. Pollock & F. Maitland, The History of English Law ,582 (2d ed. 1909).

[1418] 16 Cox C.C. 245 (Exch. Ireland, 1887), cited in *Weeks v. United States, supra.*

[1419] *Id.*, at 250.

[1420] 21 Vt. 9 (1848).

[1421] 47 N.H. 482 (1867).

[1422] *Spalding v. Preston*, 21 Vt. 9, 16.

officer arresting a man for crime, not only may, but frequently should, make such searches and seizures; that in many cases they might be reasonable and proper, and courts would hold him harmless for so doing, when he acts in good faith, and from a regard to his own or the public safety, or the security of his prisoner.'[1423]

***232** Similarly, in *Holker v. Hennessey,*[1424] the Supreme Court of Missouri said:

'Generally speaking, in the absence of a statute, an officer has no right to take any property from the person of the prisoner except such as may afford evidence of the crime charged, or means of identifying the criminal, or may be helpful in making an escape.'[1425]

Then Associate Judge Cardozo of the New York Court of Appeals summarized his understanding of the historical basis for the authority to search incident to arrest in these words:

The basic principle is this: Search of the person is unlawful when the seizure of the body is a trespass, and the purpose of the search is to discover grounds as yet unknown for arrest or accusation. Search of the person becomes lawful when grounds for arrest and accusation have been discovered, and the law is in the act of subjecting the body of the accused to its physical dominion.

The distinction may seem subtle, but in truth it is founded in shrewd appreciation of the necessities of government. We are not to strain an immunity to the point at which human nature rebels against honoring it in conduct. The peace officer empowered to arrest must be empowered to disarm. If he many disarm, he may search, lest a weapon be concealed. The search being lawful, he retains what he finds if connected with the crime.[1426] While these earlier authorities are sketchy, they tend to support the broad statement of the authority to ***233** search incident to arrest found in the successive decisions of this Court, rather than the restrictive one which was applied by the Court of Appeals in this case. The scarcity of case law before *Weeks* is doubtless due in part to the fact that the exclusionary rule there enunciated had been first adopted only 11 years earlier in Iowa; but it would seem to be also ****476** due in part to the fact that the issue was regarded as well settled.

The Court of Appeals in effect determined that the only reason supporting the authority for a full search incident to lawful arrest was the possibility of discovery of evidence or fruits. Concluding that there could be no evidence or fruits in the case of an offense such as that with which respondent was charged, it held that any protective search would have to be limited by the conditions laid down in Terry for a search upon less than probable cause to arrest. Quite apart from the fact that *Terry* clearly recognized the distinction between the two types of searches, and that a different rule governed one than governed the other, we find additional reason to disagree with the Court of Appeals.

***234** The justification or reason for the authority to search incident to a lawful arrest rests quite as much on the need to disarm the suspect in order to take him into custody as it does on the need to preserve evidence on his person for later use at trial.[1427] The standards traditionally governing a search incident to lawful arrest are not, therefore, commuted to the stricter *Terry* standards by the absence of probable fruits or further evidence of the particular crime for which the arrest is made.

Nor are inclined, on the basis of what seems to us to be a rather speculative judgment, to qualify the breadth of the general authority to search incident to a law-

---

[1423] *Id.*, at 484-485.

[1424] 141 Mo. 527, 42 S.W. 1090 (1897).

[1425] *Id.*, at 539, 42 S.W., at 1093.

[1426] *People v. Chiagles*, 237 N.Y. 193, 197, 142 N.E. 583, 584 (1923).

[1427] *Agnello v. United States*, 269 U.S. 20, 46 S.Ct. 4, 70 L.Ed. 145 (1925); *Abel v. United States*, 362 U.S. 217, 80 S.Ct. 683, 4 L.Ed.2d 668 (1960).

ful custodial arrest on an assumption that persons arrested for the offense of driving while their licenses have been revoked are less likely to possess dangerous weapons than are those arrested for other crimes. It is scarcely open to doubt that the danger to an officer is far greater in the case of the extended exposure which ***235** follows the taking of a suspect into custody and transporting him to the police station than in the case of the relatively fleeting contact resulting from the typical Terry-type stop. This is an adequate basis for treating all custodial arrests alike for purposes of search justification.

****477** But quite apart from these distinctions, our more fundamental disagreement with the Court of Appeals arises from its suggestion that there must be litigated in each case the issue of whether or not there was present one of the reasons supporting the authority for a search of the person incident to a lawful arrest. We do not think the long line of authorities of this Court dating back to *Weeks*, or what we can glean from the history of practice in this country and in England, requires such a case-by-case adjudication. A police officer's determination as to how and where to search the person of a suspect whom he has arrested is necessarily a quick ad hoc judgment which the Fourth Amendment does not require to be broken down in each instance into an analysis of each step in the search. The authority to search the person incident to a lawful custodial arrest, while based upon the need to disarm and to discover evidence, does not depend on what a court may later decide was the probability in a particular arrest situation that weapons or evidence would in fact be found upon the person of the suspect. A custodial arrest of a suspect based on probable cause is a reasonable intrusion under the Fourth Amendment; that intrusion being lawful, a search incident to the arrest requires no additional justification. It is the fact of the lawful arrest which establishes the authority to search, and we hold that in the case of a lawful custodial arrest a full search of the person is not only an exception to the warrant requirement of the Fourth Amendment, but is also a 'reasonable' search under that Amendment.

***236 IV**

The search of respondent's person conducted by Officer Jenks in this case and the seizure from him of the heroin, were permissible under established Fourth Amendment law. While through, the search partook of none of the extreme or patently abusive characteristics which were held to violate the Due Process Clause of the Fourteenth Amendment in *Rochin v. California*.[1428] Since it is the fact of custodial arrest which gives rise to the authority to search,6 it is of no moment that Jenks did not indicate any subjective fear of the respondent or that he did not himself suspect that respondent was armed.7 Having in the course of a lawful search come upon the crumpled package of cigarettes, he was entitled to inspect it; and when his inspection revealed the heroin capsules, he was entitled to seize them as 'fruits, instrumentalities, or contraband' probative of criminal conduct.[1429] ***237** The judgment of the Court of Appeals holding otherwise is reversed.

Reversed.

(The dissent of Mr. Justice MARSHALL, with whom Mr. Justice DOUGLAS and Mr. Justice BRENNAN join, omitted.)

[1428] 342 U.S. 165, 72 S.Ct. 205, 96 L.Ed. 183 (1952).

[1429] *Harris v. United States*, 331 U.S., at 154-155, 67 S.Ct., at 1103-1104; *Warden v. Hayden*, 387 U.S. 294, 299, 307, 87 S.Ct. 1642, 1646, 1650 (1967); *Adams v. Williams*, 407 U.S., at 149, 92 S.Ct., at 1924.

Black Letter Law

> Where officer had probable cause to arrest a defendant for operating a motor vehicle after revocation of his operator's permit and effected a full-custody arrest, search of the defendant's person, without a search warrant, inspection of a crumpled cigarette package found on the defendant's person and seizure of heroin capsules found in the package were permissible even though officer did not indicate any subjective fear of defendant and did not suspect that defendant was armed.
>
> A search incident to a valid arrest is not limited to a frisk of suspect's outer clothing and removal of such weapons as arresting officer may, as result of such frisk, reasonably believe suspect has in his possession, and the absence of probable fruits or further evidence of particular crime for which arrest is made does not narrow standards applicable to such a search.
>
> Custodial arrest of suspect based on probable cause is a reasonable intrusion under the Fourth Amendment and requires no additional justification such as probability in a particular situation that weapons or evidence would in fact be found upon suspect's person.

New York v. Belton

101 S.Ct. 2860

Supreme Court of the United States

State of NEW YORK, Petitioner,

v.

Roger BELTON.

No. 80-328. | Argued April 27, 1981. | Decided July 1, 1981. | Rehearing Denied Sept. 23, 1981. | See 453 U.S. 950, 102 S.Ct. 26.

Justice STEWART, delivered the opinion of the Court.

When the occupant of an automobile is subjected to a lawful custodial arrest, does the constitutionally permissible scope of a search incident to his arrest include the passenger compartment of the automobile in which he was riding? That is the question at issue in the present case.

I

On April 9, 1978, Trooper Douglas Nicot, a New York State policeman driving an unmarked car on the New York Thruway, was passed by another automobile traveling at an excessive rate of speed. Nicot gave chase, overtook the speeding vehicle, and ordered its driver to pull it over to the side of the road and stop. There were four men in the car, one of whom was Roger Belton, the respondent in this case. The policeman asked to see the driver's license and automobile registration, and discovered that none of the men owned the vehicle or was related to its owner. Meanwhile, the policeman ****2862** had smelled burnt marijuana and had seen on ***456** the floor of the car an envelope marked "Supergold" that he associated with marijuana. He therefore directed the men to get out the car, and placed them under arrest for the unlawful possession of marijuana. He patted down each of the men and "split them up into four separate areas of the Thruway at this time so they would not be in physical touching area of each other." He then picked up the envelope marked "Supergold" and found that it contained marijuana. After giving the arrestees the warnings required by *Miranda v. Arizona*,[1430] the state policeman searched each one of them. He then searched the passenger compartment of the car. On the back seat he found a black leather jacket belonging to Belton. He unzipped one of the pockets of the jacket and discovered cocaine. Placing the jacket in his automobile, he drove the four arrestees to a nearby police station.

Belton was subsequently indicted for criminal possession of a controlled substance. In the trial court he moved that the cocaine the trooper had seized from the jacket pocket be suppressed. The court denied the motion. Belton then pleaded guilty to a lesser included offense, but preserved his claim that the cocaine had been seized in violation of the Fourth and Fourteenth Amendments. [1431]The Appellant Division of the New York Supreme Court upheld the constitutionality of the search and seizure, reasoning that "[o]nce defendant was validly arrested for possession of marijuana, the officer was justified in searching the immediate area for other contraband."[1432]

The New York Court of Appeals reversed, holding that "[a] warrantless search of the zippered pockets of an unaccessible jacket may not be upheld as a search incident to a lawful arrest where there is no longer any danger that the arrestee or a confederate might gain access to the article."[1433] Two judges dissented. ***457** They pointed out that the "search was conducted by a lone peace officer who was in the process of arresting four unknown individuals whom he had stopped in a speeding car owned by none of them and apparently containing an uncertain quantity of a controlled substance. The suspects were standing by the side of the car as the officer gave it a quick check to confirm his suspicions before attempting to transport them to police headquarters..."[1434] We granted certiorari to consider the constitutionally permissible scope of a search in circumstances such as these.[1435]

II

It is a first principle of Fourth Amendment jurisprudence that the police may not conduct a search unless they first convince a neutral magistrate that there is probable cause to do so. This Court has recognized, however, that "the exigencies of the situation" may sometimes make exemption from the warrant requirement "imperative."[1436] Specifically, the Court held in *Chimel v. California*[1437] that a lawful custodial arrest creates a situation which justifies the contemporaneous search without a warrant of the person arrested and of the immediately surrounding area. Such searches have long been considered valid because of the need "to remove any weapons that [the arrestee] might seek to use in order to resist arrest or effect his escape" and the need to prevent the concealment or destruction of evidence.[1438]

The Court's opinion in *Chimel* emphasized the principle that, as the Court had said in *Terry v. Ohio*,[1439] "the scope of [a] search must be 'strictly tied to and justified by' the circumstances which rendered its initiation permissible."[1440] ****2863** Thus while the Court in *Chimel* found "ample justification" for a search of "the area

[1430] 384 U.S. 436, 86 S.Ct. 1602, 16 L.Ed.2d 694.

[1431] See *Lefkowitz v. Newsome*, 420 U.S. 283, 95 S.Ct. 886, 43 L.Ed.2d 196.

[1432] 68 A.D.2d 198, 201, 416 N.Y.S.2d 922, 925.

[1433] 50 N.Y.2d 447, 449, 429 N.Y.S.2d 574, 575, 407 N.E.2d 420, 421.

[1434] *Id.*, at 454, 429 N.Y.S.2d, at 578, 407 N.E.2d, at 424.

[1435] 449 U.S. 1109, 101 S.Ct. 917, 66 L.Ed.2d 838.

[1436] *McDonald v. United States*, 335 U.S. 451, 456, 69 S.Ct. 191, 193, 93 L.Ed. 153.

[1437] 395 U.S. 752, 89 S.Ct. 2034, 23 L.Ed.2d 685.

[1438] *Id.*, at 763, 89 S.Ct., at 2040.

[1439] 392 U.S. 1, 19, 88 S.Ct. 1868, 1878, 20 L.Ed.2d 889.

[1440] Quoted in *Chimel v. California*, *supra*, at 762, 89 S.Ct., at 2039.

from within which [an arrestee] ***458** might gain possession of a weapon or destructible evidence," the Court found "no comparable justification ... for routinely searching any room other than that in which an arrest occurs-or, for that matter, for searching through all the desk drawers or other closed or concealed areas in that room itself."[1441]

Although the principle that limits a search incident to a lawful custodial arrest may be stated clearly enough, courts have discovered the principle difficult to apply in specific cases. Yet, as one commentator has pointed out, the protection of the Fourth and Fourteenth Amendments "can only be realized if the police are acting under a set of rules which, in most instances, makes it possible to reach a correct determination beforehand as to whether an invasion of privacy is justified in the interest of law enforcement."[1442] This is because "Fourth Amendment doctrine, given force and effect by the exclusionary rule, is primarily intended to regulate the police in their day-to-day activities and thus ought to be expressed in terms that are readily applicable by the police in the context of the law enforcement activities in which they are necessarily engaged. A highly sophisticated set of rules, qualified by all sorts of ifs, ands, and buts and requiring the drawing of subtle nuances and hairline distinctions, may be the sort of heady stuff upon which the facile minds of lawyers and judges eagerly feed, but they may be 'literally impossible of application by the officer in the field.'"[1443]

In short, "[a] single, familiar standard is essential to guide police officers, who have only limited time and expertise to reflect on and balance the social and individual interests involved in the specific circumstances they confront."[1444]

***459** So it was that, in *United States v. Robinson,*[1445] the Court hewed to a straightforward rule, easily applied, and predictably enforced: "[I]n the case of a lawful custodial arrest a full search of the person is not only an exception to the warrant requirement of the Fourth Amendment, but is also a 'reasonable' search under that Amendment."[1446] In so holding, the Court rejected the suggestion that "there must be litigated in each case the issue of whether or not there was present one of the reasons supporting the authority for a search of the person incident to a lawful arrest."[1447]

But no straightforward rule has emerged from the litigated cases respecting the question involved here-the question of the proper scope of a search of the interior of an automobile incident to a lawful custodial arrest of its occupants. The difficulty courts have had is reflected in the conflicting views of the New York judges who dealt with the problem in the present case, and is confirmed by a look at even a small sample drawn from the narrow class of cases in which courts have decided whether, in the course of a search incident to the lawful custodial arrest of the occupants of an automobile, police may search inside the automobile after the arrestees are no longer in it. On the one hand, decisions in some cases[1448] have upheld such warrantless searches as incident to lawful arrests. On the other hand, in other cases[1449] such

---

[1441] 395 U.S., at 763, 89 S.Ct., at 2040.

[1442] LaFave, "Case-By-Case Adjudication" Versus "Standardized Procedures": The Robinson Dilemma, 1974 S.Ct.Rev. 127, 142.

[1443] *Id.*, at 141.

[1444] *Dunaway v. New York*, 442 U.S. 200, 213-214, 99 S.Ct. 2248, 2256-57, 60 L.Ed.2d 824.

[1445] 414 U.S. 218, 94 S.Ct. 467, 38 L.Ed.2d 427.

[1446] *Id.*, at 235, 94 S.Ct., at 477.

[1447] *Ibid.*

[1448] See *United States v. Sanders*, 631 F.2d 1309 (CA8 1980); *United States v. Dixon*, 558 F.2d 919 (CA9 1977); and *United States v. Frick*, 490 F.2d 666 (CA5 1973).

[1449] See *United States v. Benson*, 631 F.2d 1336 (CA8 1980), and *United States v. Rigales*, 630 F.2d 364 (CA5 1980).

searches, in comparable factual circumstances, have been held constitutionally invalid.

****2864** When a person cannot know how a court will apply a ***460** settled principle to a recurring factual situation, that person cannot know the scope of his constitutional protection, nor can a policeman know the scope of his authority. While the *Chimel* case established that a search incident to an arrest may not stray beyond the area within the immediate control of the arrestee, courts have found no workable definition of "the area within the immediate control of the arrestee" when that area arguably includes the interior of an automobile and the arrestee is its recent occupant. Our reading of the cases suggests the generalization that articles inside the relatively narrow compass of the passenger compartment of an automobile are in fact generally, even if not inevitably, within "the area into which an arrestee might reach in order to grab a weapon or evidentiary ite[m]."[1450] In order to establish the workable rule this category of cases requires, we read *Chimel's* definition of the limits of the area that may be searched in light of that generalization. Accordingly, we hold that when a policeman has made a lawful custodial arrest of the occupant of an automobile, he may, as a contemporaneous incident of that arrest, search the passenger compartment of that automobile.

It follows from this conclusion that the police may also examine the contents of any containers found within the passenger compartment, for if the passenger compartment is within reach of the arrestee, so also will containers in it be within his reach.[1451] ***461** Such a container may, of course, be searched whether it is open or closed, since the justification for the search is not that the arrestee has no privacy interest in the container, but that the lawful custodial arrest justifies the infringement of any privacy interest the arrestee may have. Thus, while the Court in *Chimel* held that the police could not search all the drawers in an arrestee's house simply because the police had arrested him at home, the Court noted that drawers within an arrestee's reach could be searched because of the danger their contents might pose to the police.[1452]

It is true, of course, that these containers will sometimes be such that they could hold neither a weapon nor evidence of the criminal conduct for which the suspect was arrested. However, in *United States v. Robinson*, the Court rejected the argument that such a container-there a "crumpled up cigarette package"-located during a search of Robinson incident to his arrest could not be searched: "The authority to search the person incident to a lawful custodial arrest, while based upon the need to disarm and to discover evidence, does not depend on what a court may later decide was the probability in a particular arrest situation that weapons or evidence would in fact be found upon the person of the suspect. A custodial arrest of a suspect based on probable cause is a reasonable intrusion under the Fourth Amendment; that intrusion being lawful, a search incident to the arrest requires no additional justification."[1453]

The New York Court of Appeals relied upon *United States v. Chadwick*[1454] and *Arkansas* ****2865** *v. Sanders*[1455] in concluding that the search and seizure in the present case were constitutionally invalid. But neither of those ***462** cases involved an arguably valid search incident to a lawful custodial arrest. As the Court pointed out in the *Chadwick* case: "Here the search was conducted more than an hour after federal agents had gained exclusive control of the footlocker and long after respon-

[1450] *Chimel*, 395 U.S., at 763, 89 S.Ct., at 2040.

[1451] *United States v. Robinson, supra*; *Draper v. United States*, 358 U.S. 307, 79 S.Ct. 329, 3 L.Ed.2d 327.

[1452] 395 U.S., at 763, 89 S.Ct., at 2040.

[1453] 414 U.S., at 235, 94 S.Ct., at 476.

[1454] 433 U.S. 1, 97 S.Ct. 2476, 53 L.Ed.2d 538.

[1455] 442 U.S. 753, 99 S.Ct. 2586, 61 L.Ed.2d 235.

dents were securely in custody; the search therefore cannot be viewed as incidental to the arrest or as justified by any other exigency."[1456] And in the *Sanders* case, the Court explicitly stated that it did not "consider the constitutionality of searches of luggage incident to the arrest of its possessor.[1457] The State has not argued that respondent's suitcase was searched incident to his arrest, and it appears that the bag was not within his 'immediate control' at the time of the search."[1458]

III

It is not questioned that the respondent was the subject of a lawful custodial arrest on a charge of possessing marijuana. The search of the respondent's jacket followed immediately upon that arrest. The jacket was located inside the passenger compartment of the car in which the respondent had been a passenger just before he was arrested. The jacket was thus within the area which we have concluded was "within the arrestee's immediate control" within the meaning of the *Chimel* case. The search of the jacket, therefore, was a ***463** search incident to a lawful custodial arrest, and it did not violate the Fourth and Fourteenth Amendments. Accordingly, the judgment is reversed.

It is so ordered.

Justice BRENNAN, with whom Justice MARSHALL joins, dissenting.

In *Chimel v. California*,[1459] this Court carefully analyzed more than 50 years of conflicting precedent governing the permissible scope of warrantless searches incident ****2866** to custodial arrest. The Court today turns its back on the product of that analysis, formulating an arbitrary "bright-line" rule applicable to "recent" occupants of automobiles that fails to reflect *Chimel's* underlying policy justifications. While the Court claims to leave *Chimel* intact,[1460] I fear that its unwarranted abandonment of ***464** the principles underlying that decision may signal a wholesale retreat from our carefully developed search-incident-to-arrest analysis. I dissent.

I

It has long been a fundamental principle of Fourth Amendment analysis that exceptions to the warrant requirement are to be narrowly construed.[1461] Predicated on the Fourth Amendment's essential purpose of "shield[ing] the citizen from unwarranted intrusions into his privacy," *Jones v. United States*,[1462] this principle carries with it two corollaries. First, for a search to be valid under the Fourth Amendment, it must be " 'strictly tied to and justified by' the circumstances which rendered its initiation permissible."[1463] Second, in determining whether to grant an exception to the warrant requirement, courts should carefully consider the facts and circumstances of

---

[1456] 433 U.S., at 15, 97 S.Ct., at 2485.

[1457] See, e. g., *United States v. Robinson*, 414 U.S. 218, 94 S.Ct. 467, 38 L.Ed.2d 427 (1973).

[1458] 442 U.S., at 764, n. 11, 99 S.Ct., at 2593, n. 11. (The suitcase in question was in the trunk of the taxicab. See n. 4, *supra*.)

[1459] 395 U.S. 752, 89 S.Ct. 2034, 23 L.Ed.2d 685 (1969).

[1460] See *ante*, at 2864, n. 3.

[1461] *Arkansas v. Sanders*, 442 U.S. 753, 759-760, 99 S.Ct. 2586, 2590, 61 L.Ed.2d 235 (1979); *Mincey v. Arizona*, 437 U.S. 385, 393-394, 98 S.Ct. 2408, 2414, 57 L.Ed.2d 290 (1978); *Coolidge v. New Hampshire*, 403 U.S. 443, 454-455, 91 S.Ct. 2022, 2032, 29 L.Ed.2d 564 (1971); *Vale v. Louisiana*, 399 U.S. 30, 34, 90 S.Ct. 1969, 1971, 26 L.Ed.2d 409 (1970); *Katz v. United States*, 389 U.S. 347, 357, 88 S.Ct. 507, 514, 19 L.Ed.2d 576 (1967); *Jones v. United States*, 357 U.S. 493, 499, 78 S.Ct. 1253, 1257, 2 L.Ed.2d 1514 (1958).

[1462] *Supra*, at 498, 78 S.Ct., at 1256.

[1463] *Terry v. Ohio*, 392 U.S. 1, 19, 88 S.Ct. 1868, 1878, 20 L.Ed.2d 889 (1968) quoting *Warden v. Hayden*, 387 U.S. 294, 310, 87 S.Ct. 1642, 1651, 18 L.Ed.2d 782 (1967) (Fortas, J., concurring). See *Chimel v. California*, *supra*, at 762, 89 S.Ct., at 2039; *Cupp v. Murphy*, 412 U.S. 291, 295, 93 S.Ct. 2000, 2003, 36 L.Ed.2d 900 (1973).

each search and seizure, focusing on the reasons supporting the exception rather than on any bright-line rule of general application.[1464]

The *Chimel* exception to the warrant requirement was designed with two principal concerns in mind: the safety of the arresting officer and the preservation of easily concealed or destructible evidence. Recognizing that a suspect might have ***465** access to weapons or contraband at the time of arrest, the Court declared:

"When an arrest is made, it is reasonable for the arresting officer to search the person arrested in order to remove any weapons that the latter might seek to use in order to resist arrest or effect his escape. Otherwise, the officer's safety might well be endangered, and the arrest itself frustrated. In addition, it is entirely reasonable for the arresting officer to search for and seize any evidence on the arrestee's person in order to prevent its concealment or destruction. And the area into which an arrestee might reach in order to grab a weapon or evidentiary items must, of course, be governed by a like rule."[1465]

The *Chimel* standard was narrowly tailored to address these concerns: it permits police officers who have effected a custodial arrest to conduct a warrantless search "of the arrestee's person and the area 'within his immediate control'-construing that phrase to mean the area from within which he might gain possession of a weapon or destructible evidence."[1466] It thus places a temporal and a ****2867** spatial limitation on searches incident to arrest, excusing compliance with the warrant requirement only when the search "'is substantially contemporaneous with the arrest and is confined to the immediate vicinity of the arrest.'" [1467]When the arrest has been ***466** consummated and the arrestee safely taken into custody, the justifications underlying *Chimel's* limited exception to the warrant requirement cease to apply: at that point there is no possibility that the arrestee could reach weapons or contraband.[1468]

In its attempt to formulate a "'single, familiar standard ... to guide police officers, who have only limited time and expertise to reflect on and balance the social and individual interests involved in the specific circumstances they confront,'"[1469] the Court today disregards these principles, and instead adopts a fiction-that the interior of a car is always within the immediate control of an arrestee who has recently been in the car. The Court thus holds:

"[W]hen a policeman has made a lawful custodial arrest of the occupant of an automobile, he may, as a contemporaneous incident of that arrest, search the passenger compartment of that automobile ... [and] may also examine the contents of any containers found within the passenger compartment..."[1470]

In so holding, the Court ignores both precedent and principle and fails to achieve its objective of providing police officers with a more workable standard for determining the permissible scope of searches incident to arrest.

II

[1464] See *Sibron v. New York*, 392 U.S. 40, 59, 88 S.Ct. 1889, 1900, 20 L.Ed.2d 917 (1968); *Preston v. United States*, 376 U.S. 364, 367, 84 S.Ct. 881, 883, 11 L.Ed.2d 777 (1964).

[1465] 395 U.S., at 762-763, 89 S.Ct., at 2039-40.

[1466] *Id.*, at 763, 89 S.Ct., at 2040.

[1467] *Shipley v. California*, 395 U.S. 818, 819, 89 S.Ct. 2053, 2054, 23 L.Ed. 2d 732 (1969), quoting *Stoner v. California*, 376 U.S. 483, 486, 84 S.Ct. 889, 891, 11 L.Ed.2d 856 (1964). See *United States v. Chadwick*, 433 U.S. 1, 14-15, 97 S.Ct. 2476, 2485, 53 L.Ed.2d 538 (1977); *Dyke v. Taylor Implement Mfg. Co.*, 391 U.S. 216, 220, 88 S.Ct. 1472, 1474, 20 L.Ed.2d 538 (1968); *Preston v. United States*, *supra*, at 367, 84 S.Ct., at 883; *United States v. Edwards*, 415 U.S. 800, 810, 94 S.Ct. 1234, 1240, 39 L.Ed.2d 771 (1974)(STEWART, J., dissenting).

[1468] See *Chimel v. California*, *supra*, at 764, 89 S.Ct., at 2040.

[1469] *Ante*, at 2863, quoting *Dunaway v. New York*, *442 U.S.* 200, 213-214, 99 S.Ct. 2248, 2256-57, 60 L.Ed.2d 824 (1979).

[1470] *Ante*, at 2864.

As the facts of this case make clear, the Court today substantially expands the permissible scope of searches incident to arrest by permitting police officers to search areas and containers the arrestee could not possibly reach at the time of arrest. These facts demonstrate that at the time Belton and his three companions were placed under custodial arrest-which was after they had been removed from the car, patted down, and separated-none of them could have reached the jackets that had been left on the back seat of the car. The ***467** New York Court of Appeals described the sequence of events as follows:

"On April 9, 1978 defendant and three companions were traveling on the New York State Thruway in Ontario County when their car was stopped by a State trooper for speeding. Upon approaching the vehicle, the officer smelled the distinct odor of marijuana emanating from within and observed on the floor an envelope which he recognized as a type that is commonly used to sell the substance. At that point the officer ordered the occupants out of the vehicle, patted each down, removed the envelope from the floor and ascertained that it contained a small amount of marijuana."

"After the marijuana was found, the individuals, still standing outside the car, were placed under arrest. The officer then re-entered the vehicle, searched the passenger compartment and seized the ****2868** marijuana cigarette butts lying in the ashtrays. He also rifled through the pockets of five jackets on the back seat. Upon opening the zippered pocket of one of them, he discovered a small amount of cocaine and defendant's identification."[1471]

Concluding that a "warrantless search of the zippered pockets of an unaccessible jacket may not be upheld as a search incident to a lawful arrest where there is no longer any danger that the arrestee or a confederate might gain access to the article,"[1472] the court further stated:

"One searches the record in vain for support of the dissenter's claim that at the time of the arrest-the point from which the predicate for the warrantless search is measured-'the jackets were within reach of the four suspects ***468** and had not yet been reduced to the exclusive control of the officer."[1473]

By approving the constitutionality of the warrantless search in this case, the Court carves out a dangerous precedent that is not justified by the concerns underlying *Chimel.* Disregarding the principle "that the scope of a warrantless search must be commensurate with the rationale that excepts the search from the warrant requirement,"[1474] the Court for the first time grants police officers authority to conduct a warrantless "area" search under circumstances where there is no chance that the arrestee "might gain possession of a weapon or destructible evidence."[1475] Under the approach taken today, the result would presumably be the same even if Officer Nicot had handcuffed Belton and his companions in the patrol car before placing them under arrest, and even if his search had extended to locked luggage or other inaccessible containers located in the back seat of the car.

This expansion of the *Chimel* exception is both analytically unsound and inconsistent with every significant search-incident-to-arrest case we have decided in which the issue was whether the police could lawfully conduct a warrantless search

---

1471 50 N. Y.2d 447, 449, 429 N.Y.S.2d 574, 575, 407 N.E.2d 420, 421 (1980) (emphasis added).

1472 *Ibid.* (emphasis added).

1473 *Id.*, at 452, n. 2, 429 N.Y.S.2d, at 577, n. 2, 407 N.E.2d, at 423, n. 2 quoting *id.*, at 454, 429 N.Y.S.2d, at 578, 407 N.E.2d, at 424 (dissenting opinion).

1474 *Cupp v. Murphy*, 412 U.S., at 295, 93 S.Ct., at 2003.

1475 *Chimel v. California*, 395 U.S., at 763, 89 S.Ct., at 2040.

of the area surrounding the arrestee.[1476] These cases demonstrate that the crucial question under Chimel is not whether the arrestee could ever have reached the area that was searched, but whether he could have reached it at the time of arrest and search. If not, the officer's failure to obtain a warrant may not be excused. By ****2869** disregarding this settled doctrine, the Court does a great disservice not only to stare decisis, but to the policies underlying the Fourth Amendment as well.

III

The Court seeks to justify its departure from the principles underlying Chimel by proclaiming the need for a new "bright-line" rule to guide the officer in the field. As we pointed out in *Mincey v. Arizona,*[1477] however, "the mere fact that law enforcement may be made more efficient can never by itself justify disregard of the Fourth Amendment." Moreover, the Court's attempt to forge a "bright-line" rule fails on its own terms. While the "interior/trunk" distinction may provide a workable guide in certain routine cases-for example, where the officer arrests the driver of a car and then immediately searches the seats and floor-in the long run, I suspect it will create far more problems than it solves. The Court's new approach leaves open too many questions and, more important, it provides the police and the courts with too few tools with which to find the answers.

Thus, although the Court concludes that a warrantless search of a car may take place even though the suspect was ***470** arrested outside the car, it does not indicate how long after the suspect's arrest that search may validly be conducted. Would a warrantless search incident to arrest be valid if conducted five minutes after the suspect left his car? Thirty minutes? Three hours? Does it matter whether the suspect is standing in close proximity to the car when the search is conducted? Does it matter whether the police formed probable cause to arrest before or after the suspect left his car? And why is the rule announced today necessarily limited to searches of cars? What if a suspect is seen walking out of a house where the police, peering in from outside, had formed probable cause to believe a crime was being committed? Could the police then arrest that suspect and enter the house to conduct a search incident to arrest? Even assuming today's rule is limited to searches of the "interior" of cars-an assumption not demanded by logic-what is meant by "interior"? Does it include locked glove compartments, the interior of door panels, or the area under the floorboards? Are special rules necessary for station wagons and hatchbacks, where the luggage compartment may be reached through the interior, or taxicabs, where a glass panel might separate the driver's compartment from the rest of the car? Are the only containers that may be searched those that are large enough to be "capable of holding another object"? Or does the new rule apply to any container even if it "could hold neither a weapon nor evidence of the criminal conduct for which the suspect was arrested"?[1478]

The Court does not give the police any "bright-line" answers to these questions. More important, because the Court's new rule abandons the justifications underlying *Chimel*, it offers no guidance to the police officer seeking to work out these answers for himself. As we warned in *Chimel*: "No consideration relevant to the Fourth Amendment suggests any point of rational limitation, once the search is allowed to

---

[1476] See, e. g., *United States v. Chadwick*, 433 U.S., at 15, 97 S.Ct., at 2485 (search of footlocker "conducted more than an hour after federal agents had gained exclusive control of the footlocker and long after respondents were securely in custody" not incident to arrest); *Coolidge v. New Hampshire*, 403 U.S., at 456-457, and n. 11, 91 S.Ct., at 2032-33, and n. 11 (search of car in driveway not incident to arrest in house); *Chambers v. Maroney*, 399 U.S. 42, 47, 90 S.Ct. 1975, 1979, 26 L.Ed.2d 419 (1970) (warrantless search of car invalid once arrestee has been placed in police custody); *Vale v. Louisiana*, 399 U.S., at 35, 90 S.Ct., at 1972 (area of immediate control does not extend to inside of house when suspect is arrested on front step); *Dyke v. Taylor Implement Mfg. Co.*, 391 U.S., at 220, 88 S.Ct., at 1474 search of car after occupant placed in custody and taken to courthouse not valid as incident to arrest); *Preston v. United States*, 376 U.S., at 368, 84 S.Ct., at 883 (search of car not valid as incident to arrest: although suspects were in car when arrested, they were in custody at police station when car was searched).

[1477] 437 U.S., at 393, 98 S.Ct., at 2413.

[1478] Compare ante, at 2864, n. 4, with ante, at 2864.

go beyond the area from which the person arrested ***471** might obtain weapons or evidentiary items."[1479] By failing to heed this warning, the Court has undermined rather than furthered the goal of consistent law enforcement: it has failed to offer any principles to guide the police and the courts in their application of the new rule to non-routine situations.

The standard announced in *Chimel* is not nearly as difficult to apply as the Court suggests. To the contrary, I continue to believe that *Chimel* provides a sound, workable rule for determining the constitutionality of a warrantless search incident to arrest. ****2870** Under *Chimel*, searches incident to arrest may be conducted without a warrant only if limited to the person of the arrestee,[1480] or to the area within the arrestee's "immediate control." While it may be difficult in some cases to measure the exact scope of the arrestee's immediate control, relevant factors would surely include the relative number of police officers and arrestees, the manner of restraint placed on the arrestee, and the ability of the arrestee to gain access to a particular area or container. Certainly there will be some close cases, but when in doubt the police can always turn to the rationale underlying *Chimel* - the need to prevent the arrestee from reaching weapons or contraband-before ***472** exercising their judgment. A rule based on that rationale should provide more guidance than the rule announced by the Court today. Moreover, unlike the Court's rule, it would be faithful to the Fourth Amendment.

Justice WHITE, with whom Justice MARSHALL joins, dissenting.

In *Robbins v. California*,[1481] it was held that a wrapped container in the trunk of a car could not be searched without a warrant even though the trunk itself could be searched without a warrant because there was probable cause to search the car and even though there was probable cause to search the container as well. This was because of the separate interest in privacy with respect to the container. The Court now holds that as incident to the arrest of the driver or any other person in an automobile, the interior of the car and any container found therein, whether locked or not, may be not only seized but also searched even absent probable cause to believe that contraband or evidence of crime will be found. As to luggage, briefcases, or other containers this seems to me an extreme extension of Chimel and one to which I cannot subscribe. Even if the decision in *Robbins* had been otherwise and *United States v. Chadwick*[1482] and *Arkansas v. Sanders*[1483] had been overruled, luggage found in the trunk of a car could not be searched without probable cause to believe it contained contraband or evidence. Here, searches of luggage, briefcases, and other containers in the interior of an auto are authorized in the absence of any suspicion whatsoever that they contain anything in which the police have a legitimate interest. This calls for more caution than the Court today exhibits, and, with respect, I dissent.

Black Letter Law

> When a policeman has made a lawful custodial arrest of the occupants of an automobile he may, as a contemporaneous incident of that arrest, search the passenger compartment of the vehicle and may also examine the contents of any container found within the passenger compartment and such "container", i. e. an object capable of holding another object, may be searched whether it is open or closed. Allows search of passenger's compartment and containers found therein under a SIA theory.

[1479] 395 U.S., at 766, 89 S.Ct., at 2041. See also *Mincey v. Arizona*, supra, at 393, 98 S.Ct., at 2413.

[1480] see United States v. Robinson, 414 U.S. 218, 94 S.Ct. 467, 38 L.Ed.2d 427 (1973),

[1481] 453 U.S. 420, 101 S.Ct. 2841, 69 L.Ed.2d 744.

[1482] 433 U.S. 1, 97 S.Ct. 2476, 53 L.Ed.2d 538 (1977).

[1483] 442 U.S. 753, 99 S.Ct. 2586, 61 L.Ed.2d 235 (1979).

Arizona v. Gant

129 S.Ct. 1710

Supreme Court of the United States

ARIZONA, Petitioner,

v.

Rodney Joseph GANT.

No. 07–542. | Argued Oct. 7, 2008. | Decided April 21, 2009.

Justice STEVENS delivered the opinion of the Court.

***335** After Rodney Gant was arrested for driving with a suspended license, handcuffed, and locked in the back of a patrol car, police officers searched his car and discovered cocaine in the pocket of a jacket on the backseat. Because Gant could not have accessed his car to retrieve weapons or evidence at the time of the search, the Arizona Supreme Court held that the search-incident-to-arrest exception to the Fourth Amendment's warrant requirement, as defined in *Chimel v. California*[1484] and applied to vehicle searches in *New York v. Belton*,[1485] did not justify the search in this case. We agree with that conclusion.

Under *Chimel*, police may search incident to arrest only the space within an arrestee's " 'immediate control,' " meaning "the area from within which he might gain possession of a weapon or destructible evidence."[1486] The safety and evidentiary justifications underlying *Chimel's* reaching-distance rule determine *Belton's* scope. Accordingly, we hold that *Belton* does not authorize a vehicle search incident to a recent occupant's arrest after the arrestee has been secured and cannot access the interior of the vehicle. Consistent with the holding in *Thornton v. United States*,[1487] and following the suggestion in Justice SCALIA's opinion concurring in the judgment in that case,[1488] we also conclude that circumstances unique to the automobile context justify a search incident to arrest when it is reasonable to believe that evidence of the offense of arrest might be found in the vehicle.

I

On August 25, 1999, acting on an anonymous tip that the residence at 2524 North Walnut Avenue was being used to sell drugs, Tucson police officers Griffith and Reed knocked on the front door and asked to speak to the owner. Gant answered the door and, after identifying himself, stated ****1715** that ***336** he expected the owner to return later. The officers left the residence and conducted a records check, which revealed that Gant's driver's license had been suspended and there was an outstanding warrant for his arrest for driving with a suspended license.

When the officers returned to the house that evening, they found a man near the back of the house and a woman in a car parked in front of it. After a third officer arrived, they arrested the man for providing a false name and the woman for possessing drug paraphernalia. Both arrestees were handcuffed and secured in separate patrol cars when Gant arrived. The officers recognized his car as it entered the driveway, and Officer Griffith confirmed that Gant was the driver by shining a flashlight into the car as it drove by him. Gant parked at the end of the driveway, got out of his car, and shut the door. Griffith, who was about 30 feet away, called to Gant, and they

---

1484 395 U.S. 752, 89 S.Ct. 2034, 23 L.Ed.2d 685 (1969).

1485 453 U.S. 454, 101 S.Ct. 2860, 69 L.Ed.2d 768 (1981).

1486 395 U.S., at 763, 89 S.Ct. 2034.

1487 541 U.S. 615, 124 S.Ct. 2127, 158 L.Ed.2d 905 (2004).

1488 *Id.*, at 632, 124 S.Ct. 2127.

approached each other, meeting 10–to–12 feet from Gant's car. Griffith immediately arrested Gant and handcuffed him.

Because the other arrestees were secured in the only patrol cars at the scene, Griffith called for backup. When two more officers arrived, they locked Gant in the backseat of their vehicle. After Gant had been handcuffed and placed in the back of a patrol car, two officers searched his car: One of them found a gun, and the other discovered a bag of cocaine in the pocket of a jacket on the backseat.

Gant was charged with two offenses—possession of a narcotic drug for sale and possession of drug paraphernalia (i.e., the plastic bag in which the cocaine was found). He moved to suppress the evidence seized from his car on the ground that the warrantless search violated the Fourth Amendment. Among other things, Gant argued that *Belton* did not authorize the search of his vehicle because he posed no threat to the officers after he was handcuffed in the patrol car and because he was arrested for a traffic offense for which no evidence could be found in his vehicle. When asked at the ***337** suppression hearing why the search was conducted, Officer Griffith responded: "Because the law says we can do it."[1489]

The trial court rejected the State's contention that the officers had probable cause to search Gant's car for contraband when the search began,[1490] but it denied the motion to suppress. Relying on the fact that the police saw Gant commit the crime of driving without a license and apprehended him only shortly after he exited his car, the court held that the search was permissible as a search incident to arrest.[1491] A jury found Gant guilty on both drug counts, and he was sentenced to a 3–year term of imprisonment.

After protracted state-court proceedings, the Arizona Supreme Court concluded that the search of Gant's car was unreasonable within the meaning of the Fourth Amendment. The court's opinion discussed at length our decision in *Belton*, which held that police may search the passenger compartment of a vehicle and any containers therein as a contemporaneous incident of an arrest of the vehicle's recent occupant.[1492] The court distinguished *Belton* as a case concerning the permissible scope of a vehicle search incident to arrest and concluded that it did not answer "the threshold question whether the police may conduct a search incident to arrest at all once the scene is secure."[1493] Relying on our earlier decision in *Chimel*, the court observed that the search-incident-to-arrest exception to the warrant requirement is justified by ****1716** interests in officer safety and evidence preservation.[1494] When "the justifications underlying *Chimel* no longer exist because the scene is secure and the arrestee is handcuffed, secured in the back of a patrol car, and under the supervision of an officer," the court concluded, a "warrantless search of the arrestee's car cannot be justified as necessary to protect the officers at the scene or ***338** prevent the destruction of evidence."[1495] Accordingly, the court held that the search of Gant's car was unreasonable.

The dissenting justices would have upheld the search of Gant's car based on their view that "the validity of a *Belton* search ... clearly does not depend on the presence of the *Chimel* rationales in a particular case."[1496] Although they disagreed

---

[1489] App. 75.

[1490] *Id.*, at 18, 30.

[1491] *Id.*, at 37.

[1492] 216 Ariz. 1, 3–4, 162 P.3d 640, 642–643 (2007) (citing 453 U.S., at 460, 101 S.Ct. 2860).

[1493] 216 Ariz., at 4, 162 P.3d, at 643.

[1494] 216 Ariz., at 4, 162 P.3d, at 643.

[1495] *Id.*, at 5, 162 P.3d, at 644.

[1496] *Id.*, at 8, 162 P.3d, at 647.

with the majority's view of *Belton*, the dissenting justices acknowledged that "[t]he bright-line rule embraced in *Belton* has long been criticized and probably merits reconsideration."[1497] They thus "add[ed their] voice[s] to the others that have urged the Supreme Court to revisit *Belton*."[1498]

The chorus that has called for us to revisit *Belton* includes courts, scholars, and Members of this Court who have questioned that decision's clarity and its fidelity to Fourth Amendment principles. We therefore granted the State's petition for certiorari.[1499]

II

Consistent with our precedent, our analysis begins, as it should in every case addressing the reasonableness of a warrantless search, with the basic rule that "searches conducted outside the judicial process, without prior approval by judge or magistrate, are per se unreasonable under the Fourth Amendment—subject only to a few specifically established and well-delineated exceptions."[1500] Among the exceptions to the warrant requirement is a search incident to a lawful arrest.[1501] The exception derives from interests in officer safety and evidence preservation that are typically implicated in arrest situations.[1502]

***339** In *Chimel*, we held that a search incident to arrest may only include "the arrestee's person and the area 'within his immediate control'—construing that phrase to mean the area from within which he might gain possession of a weapon or destructible evidence."[1503] That limitation, which continues to define the boundaries of the exception, ensures that the scope of a search incident to arrest is commensurate with its purposes of protecting arresting officers and safeguarding any evidence of the offense of arrest that an arrestee might conceal or destroy.[1504] If there is no possibility that an arrestee could reach into the area that law enforcement officers seek to search, both justifications for the search-incident-to-arrest exception are absent and the rule does not apply.[1505]

In *Belton*, we considered *Chimel's* application to the automobile context. A lone ****1717** police officer in that case stopped a speeding car in which Belton was one of four occupants. While asking for the driver's license and registration, the officer smelled burnt marijuana and observed an envelope on the car floor marked "Supergold"—a name he associated with marijuana. Thus having probable cause to believe the occupants had committed a drug offense, the officer ordered them out of the vehicle, placed them under arrest, and patted them down. Without handcuffing the arrestees,1 the officer "'split them up into four separate areas of the Thruway ... so they would not be in physical touching area of each other'" and searched the vehicle, including the pocket of a jacket on the backseat, in which he found cocaine.[1506]

***340** The New York Court of Appeals found the search unconstitutional, concluding that after the occupants were arrested the vehicle and its contents were "safe-

[1497] 216 Ariz., at 10, 162 P.3d, at 649.

[1498] *Id.*, at 11, 163 P.3d, at 650.

[1499] 552 U.S. 1230, 128 S.Ct. 1443, 170 L.Ed.2d 274 (2008).

[1500] *Katz v. United States*, 389 U.S. 347, 357, 88 S.Ct. 507, 19 L.Ed.2d 576 (1967) (footnote omitted).

[1501] See *Weeks v. United States*, 232 U.S. 383, 392, 34 S.Ct. 341, 58 L.Ed. 652 (1914).

[1502] See *United States v. Robinson*, 414 U.S. 218, 230–234, 94 S.Ct. 467, 38 L.Ed.2d 427 (1973); Chimel, 395 U.S., at 763, 89 S.Ct. 2034.

[1503] *Ibid.*

[1504] See ibid. (noting that searches incident to arrest are reasonable "in order to remove any weapons [the arrestee] might seek to use" and "in order to prevent [the] concealment or destruction" of evidence (emphasis added)).

[1505] E.g., *Preston v. United States*, 376 U.S. 364, 367–368, 84 S.Ct. 881, 11 L.Ed.2d 777 (1964).

[1506] 453 U.S., at 456, 101 S.Ct. 2860.

ly within the exclusive custody and control of the police."[1507] The State asked this Court to consider whether the exception recognized in *Chimel* permits an officer to search "a jacket found inside an automobile while the automobile's four occupants, all under arrest, are standing unsecured around the vehicle."[1508] We granted certiorari because "courts ha[d] found no workable definition of 'the area within the immediate control of the arrestee' when that area arguably includes the interior of an automobile."[1509]

In its brief, the State argued that the Court of Appeals erred in concluding that the jacket was under the officer's exclusive control. Focusing on the number of arrestees and their proximity to the vehicle, the State asserted that it was reasonable for the officer to believe the arrestees could have accessed the vehicle and its contents, making the search permissible under *Chimel*.[1510] The United States, as amicus curiae in support of the State, argued for a more permissive standard, but it maintained that any search incident to arrest must be "'substantially contemporaneous'" with the arrest—a requirement it deemed "satisfied if the search occurs during the period in which the arrest is being consummated and before the situation has so stabilized that it could be said that the arrest was completed."[1511] There was no suggestion by the parties or amici that Chimel authorizes a vehicle search incident to arrest when there is no realistic possibility that an arrestee could access his vehicle.

After considering these arguments, we held that when an officer lawfully arrests "the occupant of an automobile, he may, as a contemporaneous incident of that arrest, search the ***341** passenger compartment of the automobile" and any containers therein.[1512] That holding was based in large part on our assumption "that articles inside the relatively narrow compass of the passenger compartment of an automobile are in fact generally, even if not inevitably, within 'the area into which an arrestee might reach.'"[1513]

The Arizona Supreme Court read our decision in *Belton* as merely delineating "the proper scope of a search of the interior of an automobile" incident to an arrest.[1514] ****1718** That is, when the passenger compartment is within an arrestee's reaching distance, *Belton* supplies the generalization that the entire compartment and any containers therein may be reached. On that view of *Belton*, the state court concluded that the search of Gant's car was unreasonable because Gant clearly could not have accessed his car at the time of the search. It also found that no other exception to the warrant requirement applied in this case.

Gant now urges us to adopt the reading of *Belton* followed by the Arizona Supreme Court.

III

Despite the textual and evidentiary support for the Arizona Supreme Court's reading of *Belton*, our opinion has been widely understood to allow a vehicle search incident to the arrest of a recent occupant even if there is no possibility the arrestee could gain access to the vehicle at the time of the search. This reading may be attributable to Justice Brennan's dissent in *Belton*, in which he characterized the Court's holding as resting on the "fiction ... that the interior of a car is always within

---

1507 *State v. Belton*, 50 N.Y.2d 447, 452, 429 N.Y.S.2d 574, 407 N.E.2d 420, 423 (1980).

1508 Brief in No. 80–328, p. i.

1509 453 U.S., at 460, 101 S.Ct. 2860.

1510 Brief in No. 80–328, at 7–8.

1511 Brief for United States as Amicus Curiae in *New York v. Belton*, O.T.1980, No. 80–328, p. 14.

1512 *Belton*, 453 U.S., at 460, 101 S.Ct. 2860 (footnote omitted).

1513 *Ibid.*

1514 *Id.*, at 459, 101 S.Ct. 2860.

the immediate control of an arrestee who has recently been in the car."[1515] Under the majority's approach, he argued, "the result would presumably be the same even if [the officer] had handcuffed Belton and his companions in the patrol car" before conducting the search.[1516]

***342** Since we decided *Belton*, Courts of Appeals have given different answers to the question whether a vehicle must be within an arrestee's reach to justify a vehicle search incident to arrest, but Justice Brennan's reading of the Court's opinion has predominated. As Justice O'Connor observed, "lower court decisions seem now to treat the ability to search a vehicle incident to the arrest of a recent occupant as a police entitlement rather than as an exception justified by the twin rationales of Chimel."[1517] Justice Scalia has similarly noted that, although it is improbable that an arrestee could gain access to weapons stored in his vehicle after he has been handcuffed and secured in the backseat of a patrol car, cases allowing a search in "this precise factual scenario ... are legion."[1518] Indeed, **1719 some courts have upheld searches ***343** under *Belton* "even when ... the handcuffed arrestee has already left the scene."[1519]

Under this broad reading of *Belton*, a vehicle search would be authorized incident to every arrest of a recent occupant notwithstanding that in most cases the vehicle's passenger compartment will not be within the arrestee's reach at the time of the search. To read *Belton* as authorizing a vehicle search incident to every recent occupant's arrest would thus untether the rule from the justifications underlying the *Chimel* exception—a result clearly incompatible with our statement in *Belton* that it "in no way alters the fundamental principles established in the *Chimel* case regarding the basic scope of searches incident to lawful custodial arrests."[1520] Accordingly, we reject this reading of *Belton* and hold that the *Chimel* rationale authorizes police to search a vehicle incident to a recent occupant's arrest only when the arrestee is unsecured and within reaching distance of the passenger compartment at the time of the search.

Although it does not follow from *Chimel*, we also conclude that circumstances unique to the vehicle context justify a search incident to a lawful arrest when it is "reasonable to believe evidence relevant to the crime of arrest might be found in the vehicle."[1521] In many cases, as when a recent occupant is arrested for a traffic violation, there will be no reasonable basis to believe the vehicle contains relevant evidence.[1522] ***344** But in others, including *Belton* and *Thornton*, the offense of arrest will supply a basis for searching the passenger compartment of an arrestee's vehicle and any containers therein.

Neither the possibility of access nor the likelihood of discovering offense-related evidence authorized the search in this case. Unlike in *Belton*, which involved a single officer confronted with four unsecured arrestees, the five officers in this case outnumbered the three arrestees, all of whom had been handcuffed and secured in separate patrol cars before the officers searched Gant's car. Under those circumstances, Gant clearly was not within reaching distance of his car at the time of the search. An evidentiary basis for the search was also lacking in this case. Whereas

[1515] 453 U.S., at 466, 101 S.Ct. 2860.

[1516] *Id.*, at 468, 101 S.Ct. 2860.

[1517] *Thornton*, 541 U.S., at 624, 124 S.Ct. 2127 (opinion concurring in part).

[1518] *Id.*, at 628, 124 S.Ct. 2127 (opinion concurring in judgment) (collecting cases).

[1519] 541 U.S., at 628, 124 S.Ct. 2127 (same).

[1520] 453 U.S., at 460, n. 3, 101 S.Ct. 2860.

[1521] *Thornton*, 541 U.S., at 632, 124 S.Ct. 2127 (SCALIA, J., concurring in judgment).

[1522] See, e.g., *Atwater v. Lago Vista*, 532 U.S. 318, 324, 121 S.Ct. 1536, 149 L.Ed.2d 549 (2001); *Knowles v. Iowa*, 525 U.S. 113, 118, 119 S.Ct. 484, 142 L.Ed.2d 492 (1998).

Belton and *Thornton* were arrested for drug offenses, Gant was arrested for driving with a suspended license—an offense for which police could not expect to find evidence in the passenger compartment of Gant's car.[1523] Because police could not reasonably have believed either that Gant could have accessed his car at the time of the search or that evidence of the offense for which he was arrested might have been found therein, the search in this case was unreasonable.

****1720** IV

The State does not seriously disagree with the Arizona Supreme Court's conclusion that Gant could not have accessed his vehicle at the time of the search, but it nevertheless asks us to uphold the search of his vehicle under the broad reading of *Belton* discussed above. The State argues that *Belton* searches are reasonable regardless of the possibility of access in a given case because that expansive rule correctly balances law enforcement interests, including the interest in a bright-line rule, with an arrestee's limited privacy interest in his vehicle.

For several reasons, we reject the State's argument. First, the State seriously undervalues the privacy interests ***345** at stake. Although we have recognized that a motorist's privacy interest in his vehicle is less substantial than in his home,[1524] the former interest is nevertheless important and deserving of constitutional protection.[1525] It is particularly significant that *Belton* searches authorize police officers to search not just the passenger compartment but every purse, briefcase, or other container within that space. A rule that gives police the power to conduct such a search whenever an individual is caught committing a traffic offense, when there is no basis for believing evidence of the offense might be found in the vehicle, creates a serious and recurring threat to the privacy of countless individuals. Indeed, the character of that threat implicates the central concern underlying the Fourth Amendment—the concern about giving police officers unbridled discretion to rummage at will among a person's private effects.

At the same time as it undervalues these privacy concerns, the State exaggerates the clarity that its reading of *Belton* provides. Courts that have read *Belton* expansively are at odds regarding how close in time to the arrest and how proximate ***346** to the arrestee's vehicle an officer's first contact with the arrestee must be to bring the encounter within *Belton's* purview and whether a search is reasonable when it commences or continues after the arrestee ****1721** has been removed from the scene. The rule has thus generated a great deal of uncertainty, particularly for a rule touted as providing a "bright line."[1526]

Contrary to the State's suggestion, a broad reading of *Belton* is also unnecessary to protect law enforcement safety and evidentiary interests. Under our view, *Belton* and *Thornton* permit an officer to conduct a vehicle search when an arrestee is within reaching distance of the vehicle or it is reasonable to believe the vehicle contains evidence of the offense of arrest. Other established exceptions to the warrant requirement authorize a vehicle search under additional circumstances when safety or evidentiary concerns demand. For instance, *Michigan v. Long*,[1527] permits an officer to search a vehicle's passenger compartment when he has reasonable suspicion that an individual, whether or not the arrestee, is "dangerous" and might access the vehicle *347 to "gain immediate control of weapons."[1528] If there is probable cause to

---

[1523] Cf. *Knowles*, 525 U.S., at 118, 119 S.Ct. 484.

[1524] See *New York v. Class*, 475 U.S. 106, 112–113, 106 S.Ct. 960, 89 L.Ed.2d 81 (1986).

[1525] see Knowles, 525 U.S., at 117, 119 S.Ct. 484.

[1526] See 3 LaFave, § 7.1(c), at 514–524.

[1527] 463 U.S. 1032, 103 S.Ct. 3469, 77 L.Ed.2d 1201 (1983),

[1528] *Id.*, at 1049, 103 S.Ct. 3469 (citing *Terry v. Ohio*, 392 U.S. 1, 21, 88 S.Ct. 1868, 20 L.Ed.2d 889 (1968)).

believe a vehicle contains evidence of criminal activity, *United States v. Ross*[1529] authorizes a search of any area of the vehicle in which the evidence might be found. Unlike the searches permitted by Justice Scalia's opinion concurring in the judgment in *Thornton*, which we conclude today are reasonable for purposes of the Fourth Amendment, *Ross* allows searches for evidence relevant to offenses other than the offense of arrest, and the scope of the search authorized is broader. Finally, there may be still other circumstances in which safety or evidentiary interests would justify a search.[1530]

These exceptions together ensure that officers may search a vehicle when genuine safety or evidentiary concerns encountered during the arrest of a vehicle's recent occupant justify a search. Construing *Belton* broadly to allow vehicle searches incident to any arrest would serve no purpose except to provide a police entitlement, and it is anathema to the Fourth Amendment to permit a warrantless search on that basis. For these reasons, we are unpersuaded by the State's arguments that a broad reading of *Belton* would meaningfully further law enforcement interests and justify a substantial intrusion on individuals' privacy.

***348 **1722** V

Our dissenting colleagues argue that the doctrine of stare decisis requires adherence to a broad reading of *Belton* even though the justifications for searching a vehicle incident to arrest are in most cases absent. The doctrine of stare decisis is of course "essential to the respect accorded to the judgments of the Court and to the stability of the law," but it does not compel us to follow a past decision when its rationale no longer withstands "careful analysis."[1531]

We have never relied on stare decisis to justify the continuance of an unconstitutional police practice. And we would be particularly loath to uphold an unconstitutional result in a case that is so easily distinguished from the decisions that arguably compel it. The safety and evidentiary interests that supported the search in *Belton* simply are not present in this case. Indeed, it is hard to imagine two cases that are factually more distinct, as *Belton* involved one officer confronted by four unsecured arrestees suspected of committing a drug offense and this case involves several officers confronted with a securely detained arrestee apprehended for driving with a suspended license. This case is also distinguishable from Thornton, in which the petitioner was ***349** arrested for a drug offense. It is thus unsurprising that Members of this Court who concurred in the judgments in *Belton* and *Thornton* also concur in the decision in this case.

We do not agree with the contention in Justice Alito's dissent (hereinafter dissent) that consideration of police reliance interests requires a different result. Although it appears that the State's reading of *Belton* has been widely taught in police academies and that law enforcement officers have relied on the rule in conducting vehicle searches during the past 28 years, many of these searches were not justified by the reasons underlying the *Chimel* exception. Countless individuals guilty of nothing more serious than a traffic violation have had their constitutional right to ****1723** the security of their private effects violated as a result. The fact that the law enforcement community may view the State's version of the *Belton* rule as an entitlement does not establish the sort of reliance interest that could outweigh the countervailing interest that all individuals share in having their constitutional rights fully protected. If it is clear that a practice is unlawful, individuals' interest in its discon-

---

[1529] 456 U.S. 798, 820–821, 102 S.Ct. 2157, 72 L.Ed.2d 572 (1982).

[1530] Cf. *Maryland v. Buie*, 494 U.S. 325, 334, 110 S.Ct. 1093, 108 L.Ed.2d 276 (1990) (holding that, incident to arrest, an officer may conduct a limited protective sweep of those areas of a house in which he reasonably suspects a dangerous person may be hiding).

[1531] *Lawrence v. Texas*, 539 U.S. 558, 577, 123 S.Ct. 2472, 156 L.Ed.2d 508 (2003).

tinuance clearly outweighs any law enforcement "entitlement" to its persistence.[1532] The dissent's reference in this regard to the reliance interests cited in *Dickerson v. United States*[1533] is misplaced.[1534] In observing ***350** that "Miranda has become embedded in routine police practice to the point where the warnings have become part of our national culture,"[1535] the Court was referring not to police reliance on a rule requiring them to provide warnings but to the broader societal reliance on that individual right.

The dissent also ignores the checkered history of the search-incident-to-arrest exception. Police authority to search the place in which a lawful arrest is made was broadly asserted in *Marron v. United States*[1536] and limited a few years later in *Go–Bart Importing Co. v. United States*[1537] and *United States v. Lefkowitz.*[1538] The limiting views expressed in *Go–Bart* and *Lefkowitz* were in turn abandoned in *Harris v. United States*,[1539] which upheld a search of a four-room apartment incident to the occupant's arrest. Only a year later the Court, in *Trupiano v. United States*,[1540] retreated from that holding, noting that the search-incident-to-arrest exception is "a strictly limited" one that must be justified by "something more in the way of necessity than merely a lawful arrest." And just two years after that, in *United States v. Rabinowitz*,[1541] the Court again reversed course and upheld the search of an entire apartment. Finally, our opinion in *Chimel* overruled *Rabinowitz* and what remained of *Harris* and established the present boundaries of the search-incident-to-arrest exception. Notably, none of the dissenters in *Chimel* or the cases that preceded it argued that law enforcement reliance interests outweighed the interest in protecting individual constitutional rights so as to warrant fidelity to an unjustifiable rule.

The experience of the 28 years since we decided *Belton* has shown that the generalization underpinning the broad reading of that decision is unfounded. We now know that articles inside the passenger compartment are rarely "within 'the area into which an arrestee might reach,'"[1542] ***351** and blind adherence to *Belton's* faulty assumption would authorize myriad unconstitutional searches. The doctrine of stare decisis does not require us to approve routine constitutional violations.

VI

Police may search a vehicle incident to a recent occupant's arrest only if the arrestee is within reaching distance of the passenger compartment at the time of the search or it is reasonable to believe the vehicle contains evidence of the offense of arrest. When these justifications are absent, a search of an arrestee's vehicle will ****1724** be unreasonable unless police obtain a warrant or show that another exception to the warrant requirement applies. The Arizona Supreme Court correctly held that this case involved an unreasonable search. Accordingly, the judgment of the State Supreme Court is affirmed.

It is so ordered.

[1532] Cf. *Mincey v. Arizona*, 437 U.S. 385, 393, 98 S.Ct. 2408, 57 L.Ed.2d 290 (1978) ("[T]he mere fact that law enforcement may be made more efficient can never by itself justify disregard of the Fourth Amendment").

[1533] 530 U.S. 428, 120 S.Ct. 2326, 147 L.Ed.2d 405 (2000).

[1534] See *post*, at 1728.

[1535] 530 U.S., at 443, 120 S.Ct. 2326.

[1536] 275 U.S. 192, 48 S.Ct. 74, 72 L.Ed. 231 (1927).

[1537] 282 U.S. 344, 51 S.Ct. 153, 75 L.Ed. 374 (1931).

[1538] 285 U.S. 452, 52 S.Ct. 420, 76 L.Ed. 877 (1932).

[1539] 331 U.S. 145, 67 S.Ct. 1098, 91 L.Ed. 1399 (1947).

[1540] 334 U.S. 699, 708, 68 S.Ct. 1229, 92 L.Ed. 1663 (1948).

[1541] 339 U.S. 56, 70 S.Ct. 430, 94 L.Ed. 653 (1950).

[1542] 453 U.S., at 460, 101 S.Ct. 2860,

Justice SCALIA, concurring.

To determine what is an "unreasonable" search within the meaning of the Fourth Amendment, we look first to the historical practices the Framers sought to preserve; if those provide inadequate guidance, we apply traditional standards of reasonableness.[1543] Since the historical scope of officers' authority to search vehicles incident to arrest is uncertain,[1544] traditional standards of reasonableness govern. It is abundantly clear that those standards do not justify what I take to be the rule set forth in [1545]*New York v. Belton* and *Thornton*: that arresting officers may always search an arrestee's vehicle in order to protect themselves from hidden weapons. When an arrest is made in connection with a roadside stop, police virtually always have a less intrusive and more effective means of ensuring their safety—and a means that is virtually ***352** always employed: ordering the arrestee away from the vehicle, patting him down in the open, handcuffing him, and placing him in the squad car.

Law enforcement officers face a risk of being shot whenever they pull a car over. But that risk is at its height at the time of the initial confrontation; and it is not at all reduced by allowing a search of the stopped vehicle after the driver has been arrested and placed in the squad car. I observed in *Thornton* that the government had failed to provide a single instance in which a formerly restrained arrestee escaped to retrieve a weapon from his own vehicle;[1546] Arizona and its amici have not remedied that significant deficiency in the present case.

It must be born in mind that we are speaking here only of a rule automatically permitting a search when the driver or an occupant is arrested. Where no arrest is made, we have held that officers may search the car if they reasonably believe "the suspect is dangerous and ... may gain immediate control of weapons."[1547] In the no-arrest case, the possibility of access to weapons in the vehicle always exists, since the driver or passenger will be allowed to return to the vehicle when the interrogation is completed. The rule of *Michigan v. Long* is not at issue here.

Justice Stevens acknowledges that an officer-safety rationale cannot justify all vehicle searches incident to arrest, but asserts that that is not the rule *Belton* and *Thornton* adopted. (As described above, I read those cases differently). Justice Stevens would therefore retain the application of *Chimel v. California*[1548] in the car-search context but would apply in the future what he believes our cases held in the past: that officers making a roadside stop may search the vehicle so long as the "arrestee is within reaching distance of the passenger compartment at the time of the search."[1549] I believe that this ***353** standard fails to provide the needed guidance to arresting officers and also leaves much room for manipulation, inviting officers to leave the scene ****1725** unsecured (at least where dangerous suspects are not involved) in order to conduct a vehicle search. In my view we should simply abandon the *Belton–Thornton* charade of officer safety and overrule those cases. I would hold that a vehicle search incident to arrest is ipso facto "reasonable" only when the object of the search is evidence of the crime for which the arrest was made, or of another crime that the officer has probable cause to believe occurred. Because respondent was arrested for driving without a license (a crime for which no evidence could

---

[1543] See *Virginia v. Moore*, 553 U.S. 164, ——, 128 S.Ct. 1598, 1602–04, 170 L.Ed.2d 559 (2008).

[1544] See *Thornton v. United States*, 541 U.S. 615, 629–631, 124 S.Ct. 2127, 158 L.Ed.2d 905 (2004) (Scalia, J., concurring in judgment).

[1545] 453 U.S. 454, 101 S.Ct. 2860, 69 L.Ed.2d 768 (1981).

[1546] 541 U.S., at 626, 124 S.Ct. 2127.

[1547] *Michigan v. Long*, 463 U.S. 1032, 1049, 103 S.Ct. 3469, 77 L.Ed.2d 1201 (1983).

[1548] 395 U.S. 752, 89 S.Ct. 2034, 23 L.Ed.2d 685 (1969),

[1549] *Ante*, at 1723.

be expected to be found in the vehicle), I would hold in the present case that the search was unlawful.

Justice Alito insists that the Court must demand a good reason for abandoning prior precedent. That is true enough, but it seems to me ample reason that the precedent was badly reasoned and produces erroneous (in this case unconstitutional) results.[1550] We should recognize *Belton;s* fanciful reliance upon officer safety for what it was: "a return to the broader sort of [evidence-gathering] search incident to arrest that we allowed before *Chimel*."[1551]

Justice Alito argues that there is no reason to adopt a rule limiting automobile-arrest searches to those cases where the search's object is evidence of the crime of arrest.[1552] I disagree. This formulation of officers' authority both preserves the outcomes of our prior cases and tethers the scope and rationale of the doctrine to the triggering event. *Belton*, by contrast, allowed searches precisely when its exigency-based rationale was least applicable: The fact of the arrest in the automobile context makes searches on exigency grounds less reasonable, not more. I also disagree with Justice Alito's conclusory ***354** assertion that this standard will be difficult to administer in practice;[1553] the ease of its application in this case would suggest otherwise.

No other Justice, however, shares my view that application of *Chimel* in this context should be entirely abandoned. It seems to me unacceptable for the Court to come forth with a 4–to–1–to–4 opinion that leaves the governing rule uncertain. I am therefore confronted with the choice of either leaving the current understanding of *Belton* and *Thornton* in effect, or acceding to what seems to me the artificial narrowing of those cases adopted by Justice Stevens. The latter, as I have said, does not provide the degree of certainty I think desirable in this field; but the former opens the field to what I think are plainly unconstitutional searches—which is the greater evil. I therefore join the opinion of the Court.

Justice BREYER, dissenting.

I agree with Justice Alito that *New York v. Belton*[1554] is best read as setting forth a bright-line rule that permits a warrantless search of the passenger compartment of an automobile incident to the lawful arrest of an occupant—regardless of the danger the arrested individual in fact poses. I also agree with Justice Stevens, however, that the rule can produce results divorced from its underlying Fourth Amendment rationale.[1555] For that reason I would look ****1726** for a better rule—were the question before us one of first impression.

The matter, however, is not one of first impression, and that fact makes a substantial difference. The *Belton* rule has been followed not only by this Court in *Thornton v. United States*,[1556] but also by numerous other courts. Principles of stare decisis must apply, and ***355** those who wish this Court to change a well-established legal precedent—where, as here, there has been considerable reliance on the legal rule in question—bear a heavy burden.[1557] I have not found that burden met. Nor do I believe that the other considerations ordinarily relevant when determining whether to

---

[1550] See *Payne v. Tennessee*, 501 U.S. 808, 827, 111 S.Ct. 2597, 115 L.Ed.2d 720 (1991).

[1551] *Thornton, supra*, at 631, 124 S.Ct. 2127 (Scalia, J., concurring in judgment; citations omitted).

[1552] *Post*, at 1731 (dissenting opinion).

[1553] *Post*, at 1729.

[1554] 453 U.S. 454, 101 S.Ct. 2860, 69 L.Ed.2d 768 (1981),.

[1555] Compare *Belton, supra*, with *Chimel v. California*, 395 U.S. 752, 764, 89 S.Ct. 2034, 23 L.Ed.2d 685 (1969) (explaining that the rule allowing contemporaneous searches is justified by the need to prevent harm to a police officer or destruction of evidence of the crime).

[1556] 541 U.S. 615, 124 S.Ct. 2127, 158 L.Ed.2d 905 (2004).

[1557] Cf. Leegin Creative Leather Products, Inc. v. PSKS, Inc., 551 U.S. 877, ——, 127 S.Ct. 2705, 2719–21, 168 L.Ed.2d 623 (2007) (Breyer, J., dissenting).

overrule a case are satisfied. I consequently join Justice ALITO's dissenting opinion with the exception of Part II–E.

Justice ALITO, with whom THE CHIEF JUSTICE and Justice KENNEDY join, and with whom Justice BREYER joins except as to Part II–E, dissenting.

Twenty-eight years ago, in *New York v. Belton*,[1558] this Court held that "when a policeman has made a lawful custodial arrest of the occupant of an automobile, he may, as a contemporaneous incident of that arrest, search the passenger compartment of that automobile."[1559] Five years ago, in *Thornton v. United States*[1560]—a case involving a situation not materially distinguishable from the situation here—the Court not only reaffirmed but extended the holding of *Belton*, making it applicable to recent occupants. Today's decision effectively overrules those important decisions, even though respondent Gant has not asked us to do so.

To take the place of the overruled precedents, the Court adopts a new two-part rule under which a police officer who arrests a vehicle occupant or recent occupant may search the passenger compartment if (1) the arrestee is within reaching distance of the vehicle at the time of the search or (2) the officer has reason to believe that the vehicle contains evidence of the offense of arrest.[1561] The first part of this new rule may endanger arresting officers and is truly endorsed by only four Justices; Justice Scalia joins solely for the purpose of avoiding a "4–to–1–to 4 opinion."[1562] ***356** The second part of the new rule is taken from Justice SCALIA's separate opinion in Thornton without any independent explanation of its origin or justification and is virtually certain to confuse law enforcement officers and judges for some time to come. The Court's decision will cause the suppression of evidence gathered in many searches carried out in good-faith reliance on well-settled case law, and although the Court purports to base its analysis on the landmark decision in *Chimel v. California*,[1563] the Court's reasoning undermines *Chimel*. I would follow *Belton*, and I therefore respectfully dissent.

I

Although the Court refuses to acknowledge that it is overruling Belton and Thornton, there can be no doubt that it does so.

In *Belton*, an officer on the New York Thruway removed the occupants from a car and placed them under arrest but did not handcuff them.[1564] The officer then searched a jacket on the ****1727** car's back seat and found drugs.[1565] By a divided vote, the New York Court of Appeals held that the search of the jacket violated *Chimel*, in which this Court held that an arresting officer may search the area within an arrestee's immediate control.[1566] The judges of the New York Court of Appeals disagreed on the factual question whether the *Belton* arrestees could have gained access to the car. The majority thought that they could not have done so,[1567] but the dissent thought that this was a real possibility.[1568]

[1558] 453 U.S. 454, 460, 101 S.Ct. 2860, 69 L.Ed.2d 768 (1981).

[1559] Footnote omitted.

[1560] 541 U.S. 615, 124 S.Ct. 2127, 158 L.Ed.2d 905 (2004).

[1561] *Ante*, at 1723 – 1724.

[1562] *Ante*, at 1725 (concurring opinion).

[1563] 395 U.S. 752, 89 S.Ct. 2034, 23 L.Ed.2d 685 (1969).

[1564] See 453 U.S., at 456, 101 S.Ct. 2860; Brief for Petitioner in *New York v. Belton*, O.T.1980, No. 80–328, p. 3.

[1565] 453 U.S., at 455, 101 S.Ct. 2860.

[1566] See *State v. Belton*, 50 N.Y.2d 447, 429 N.Y.S.2d 574, 407 N.E.2d 420 (1980).

[1567] *Id.*, at 452, n. 2, 429 N.Y.S.2d 574, 407 N.E.2d 420, 429 N.Y.S.2d 574, 407 N.E.2d, at 423, n. 2.

[1568] *Id.*, at 453, 429 N.Y.S.2d 574, 407 N.E.2d, at 424 (opinion of Gabrielli, J.).

Viewing this disagreement about the application of the *Chimel* rule as illustrative of a persistent and important problem, the *Belton* Court concluded that "'[a] single familiar ***357** standard'" was "'essential to guide police officers'" who make roadside arrests.[1569] The Court acknowledged that articles in the passenger compartment of a car are not always within an arrestee's reach, but "[i]n order to establish the workable rule this category of cases requires," the Court adopted a rule that categorically permits the search of a car's passenger compartment incident to the lawful arrest of an occupant.[1570]

The precise holding in *Belton* could not be clearer. The Court stated unequivocally: "[W]e hold that when a policeman has made a lawful custodial arrest of the occupant of an automobile, he may, as a contemporaneous incident of that arrest, search the passenger compartment of that automobile."[1571]

Despite this explicit statement, the opinion of the Court in the present case curiously suggests that *Belton* may reasonably be read as adopting a holding that is narrower than the one explicitly set out in the *Belton* opinion, namely, that an officer arresting a vehicle occupant may search the passenger compartment "when the passenger compartment is within an arrestee's reaching distance."[1572] According to the Court, the broader reading of *Belton* that has gained wide acceptance "may be attributable to Justice Brennan's dissent."[1573]

Contrary to the Court's suggestion, however, Justice Brennan's *Belton* dissent did not mischaracterize the Court's holding in that case or cause that holding to be misinterpreted. As noted, the *Belton* Court explicitly stated precisely what it held. In *Thornton*, the Court recognized the scope of *Belton's* holding.[1574] So did Justice Scalia's separate opinion.[1575] So does Justice Scalia's opinion in the present ***358** case.[1576] This "bright-line rule" has now been interred.

II

Because the Court has substantially overruled *Belton* and *Thornton*, the Court must explain why its departure from the usual rule of stare decisis is justified. I recognize that stare decisis is not an "inexorable command,"[1577] ****1728** and applies less rigidly in constitutional cases.[1578] But the Court has said that a constitutional precedent should be followed unless there is a " 'special justification' " for its abandonment.[1579] Relevant factors identified in prior cases include whether the precedent has engendered reliance,[1580] whether there has been an important change in circumstances in the outside world,[1581] whether the precedent has proved to be

---

[1569] 453 U.S., at 458, 101 S.Ct. 2860 (quoting *Dunaway v. New York*, 442 U.S. 200, 213–214, 99 S.Ct. 2248, 60 L.Ed.2d 824 (1979)).

[1570] 453 U.S., at 460, 101 S.Ct. 2860.

[1571] *Ibid.* (footnote omitted).

[1572] *Ante*, at 1717 – 1718 (emphasis in original).

[1573] *Ante*, at 1718.

[1574] See 541 U.S., at 620, 124 S.Ct. 2127.

[1575] See *id.*, at 625, 124 S.Ct. 2127 (opinion concurring in judgment) ("In [*Belton*] we set forth a bright-line rule for arrests of automobile occupants, holding that ... a search of the whole [passenger] compartment is justified in every case").

[1576] See *ante*, at 1724 (*Belton* and *Thornton* held that "arresting officers may always search an arrestee's vehicle in order to protect themselves from hidden weapons").

[1577] *Payne v. Tennessee*, 501 U.S. 808, 828, 111 S.Ct. 2597, 115 L.Ed.2d 720 (1991).

[1578] *Glidden Co. v. Zdanok*, 370 U.S. 530, 543, 82 S.Ct. 1459, 8 L.Ed.2d 671 (1962) (plurality opinion).

[1579] *Dickerson v. United States*, 530 U.S. 428, 443, 120 S.Ct. 2326, 147 L.Ed.2d 405 (2000).

[1580] *Id.*, at 442, 120 S.Ct. 2326.

[1581] *Randall v. Sorrell*, 548 U.S. 230, 244, 126 S.Ct. 2479, 165 L.Ed.2d 482 (2006) (plurality opinion); *Burnet v. Coronado Oil & Gas Co.*, 285 U.S. 393, 412, 52 S.Ct. 443, 76 L.Ed. 815 (1932) (Brandeis, J., dissenting).

unworkable,[1582] whether the precedent has been undermined by later decisions,[1583] and whether the decision was badly reasoned.[1584] These factors weigh in favor of retaining the rule established in *Belton.*

A

Reliance. While reliance is most important in "cases involving property and contract rights,"[1585] the Court has recognized that reliance by law enforcement officers is also entitled to weight. In Dickerson, the Court held that principles of stare decisis "weigh[ed]" heavily ***359** against overruling *Miranda v. Arizona,*[1586] because the *Miranda* rule had become "embedded in routine police practice."[1587]

If there was reliance in *Dickerson,* there certainly is substantial reliance here. The *Belton* rule has been taught to police officers for more than a quarter century. Many searches—almost certainly including more than a few that figure in cases now on appeal—were conducted in scrupulous reliance on that precedent. It is likely that, on the very day when this opinion is announced, numerous vehicle searches will be conducted in good faith by police officers who were taught the *Belton* rule.

The opinion of the Court recognizes that "*Belton* has been widely taught in police academies and that law enforcement officers have relied on the rule in conducting vehicle searches during the past 28 years."[1588] But for the Court, this seemingly counts for nothing. The Court states that "[w]e have never relied on stare decisis to justify the continuance of an unconstitutional police practice,"[1589] but of course the Court routinely relies on decisions sustaining the constitutionality of police practices without doing what the Court has done here—sua sponte considering whether those decisions should be overruled. And the Court cites no authority for the proposition that stare decisis may be disregarded or provides only lesser protection when the precedent that is challenged is one that sustained the constitutionality of a law enforcement practice.

The Court also errs in arguing that the reliance interest that was given heavy weight in Dickerson was not "police reliance on a rule requiring them to provide warnings but to the broader societal reliance on that individual right."[1590] The *Dickerson* opinion makes no reference to "societal reliance," and petitioner in that case contended that there had been reliance on Miranda because, ****1729** among other things, "[f]or nearly thirty-five years, Miranda's requirements ha[d] shaped law enforcement training [and] police ***360** conduct."[1591]

B

Changed circumstances. Abandonment of the *Belton* rule cannot be justified on the ground that the dangers surrounding the arrest of a vehicle occupant are different today than they were 28 years ago. The Court claims that "[w]e now know that articles inside the passenger compartment are rarely 'within "the area into which an ar-

---

[1582] *Vieth v. Jubelirer,* 541 U.S. 267, 306, 124 S.Ct. 1769, 158 L.Ed.2d 546 (2004) (plurality opinion) (citing *Payne, supra,* at 827, 111 S.Ct. 2597).

[1583] See, e.g., *Patterson v. McLean Credit Union,* 491 U.S. 164, 173–174, 109 S.Ct. 2363, 105 L.Ed.2d 132 (1989).

[1584] *Vieth, supra,* at 306, 124 S.Ct. 1769 (plurality opinion).

[1585] *Payne, supra,* at 828, 111 S.Ct. 2597.

[1586] 384 U.S. 436, 86 S.Ct. 1602, 16 L.Ed.2d 694 (1966).

[1587] 530 U.S., at 443, 120 S.Ct. 2326.

[1588] *Ante,* at 1722 – 1723.

[1589] *Ante,* at 1722.

[1590] *Ante,* at 1723.

[1591] See Brief for Petitioner in *Dickerson v. United States,* O.T.1999, No. 99–5525, p. 33.

restee might reach,"'"[1592] but surely it was well known in 1981 that a person who is taken from a vehicle, handcuffed, and placed in the back of a patrol car is unlikely to make it back into his own car to retrieve a weapon or destroy evidence.

C

Workability. The *Belton* rule has not proved to be unworkable. On the contrary, the rule was adopted for the express purpose of providing a test that would be relatively easy for police officers and judges to apply. The Court correctly notes that even the *Belton* rule is not perfectly clear in all situations. Specifically, it is sometimes debatable whether a search is or is not contemporaneous with an arrest,[1593] but that problem is small in comparison with the problems that the Court's new two-part rule will produce.

The first part of the Court's new rule—which permits the search of a vehicle's passenger compartment if it is within an arrestee's reach at the time of the search—reintroduces the same sort of case-by-case, fact specific decision-making that the *Belton* rule was adopted to avoid. As the situation in *Belton* illustrated, there are cases in which it is unclear whether an arrestee could retrieve a weapon or evidence in the passenger compartment of a car.

Even more serious problems will also result from the second part of the Court's new rule, which requires officers ***361** making roadside arrests to determine whether there is reason to believe that the vehicle contains evidence of the crime of arrest. What this rule permits in a variety of situations is entirely unclear.

D

Consistency with later cases. The *Belton* bright-line rule has not been undermined by subsequent cases. On the contrary, that rule was reaffirmed and extended just five years ago in *Thornton.*

E

Bad reasoning. The Court is harshly critical of *Belton's* reasoning, but the problem that the Court perceives cannot be remedied simply by overruling *Belton. Belton* represented only a modest—and quite defensible—extension of *Chimel*, as I understand that decision.

Prior to *Chimel*, the Court's precedents permitted an arresting officer to search the area within an arrestee's "possession" and "control" for the purpose of gathering evidence.[1594] Based on this "abstract doctrine,"[1595] the Court had sustained searches that extended far beyond an arrestee's grabbing area.[1596]

****1730** The *Chimel* Court, in an opinion written by Justice Stewart, overruled these cases. Concluding that there are only two justifications for a warrantless search incident to arrest—officer safety and the preservation of evidence—the Court stated that such a search must be confined to "the arrestee's person" and "the area from within which he might gain possession of a weapon or destructible evidence."[1597]

Unfortunately, *Chimel* did not say whether "the area from within which [an arrestee] might gain possession of a weapon or destructible evidence" is to be measured at the time of ***362** the arrest or at the time of the search, but unless the *Chimel* rule was meant to be a specialty rule, applicable to only a few unusual cases, the Court must have intended for this area to be measured at the time of arrest.

[1592] *Ante*, at 1723 – 1724.

[1593] *Ante*, at 1716 – 1718.

[1594] See 395 U.S., at 759–760, 89 S.Ct. 2034.

[1595] *Id.*, at 760, n. 4, 89 S.Ct. 2034.

[1596] See *United States v. Rabinowitz*, 339 U.S. 56, 70 S.Ct. 430, 94 L.Ed. 653 (1950) (search of entire office); *Harris v. United States*, 331 U.S. 145, 67 S.Ct. 1098, 91 L.Ed. 1399 (1947) (search of entire apartment).

[1597] 395 U.S., at 762–763, 89 S.Ct. 2034.

This is so because the Court can hardly have failed to appreciate the following two facts. First, in the great majority of cases, an officer making an arrest is able to handcuff the arrestee and remove him to a secure place before conducting a search incident to the arrest.[1598] Second, because it is safer for an arresting officer to secure an arrestee before searching, it is likely that this is what arresting officers do in the great majority of cases. (And it appears, not surprisingly, that this is in fact the prevailing practice.) Thus, if the area within an arrestee's reach were assessed, not at the time of arrest, but at the time of the search, the *Chimel* rule would rarely come into play.

Moreover, if the applicability of the *Chimel* rule turned on whether an arresting officer chooses to secure an arrestee prior to conducting a search, rather than searching first and securing the arrestee later, the rule would "create a perverse incentive for an arresting officer to prolong the period during which the arrestee is kept in an area where he could pose a danger to the officer."[1599] If this is the law, the D.C. Circuit observed, "the law would truly be, as Mr. Bumble said, 'an ass.'"[1600]

I do not think that this is what the *Chimel* Court intended. Handcuffs were in use in 1969. The ability of arresting officers ***363** to secure arrestees before conducting a search—and their incentive to do so—are facts that can hardly have escaped the Court's attention. I therefore believe that the *Chimel* Court intended that its new rule apply in cases in which the arrestee is handcuffed before the search is conducted.

The *Belton* Court, in my view, proceeded on the basis of this interpretation of *Chimel*. Again speaking through Justice Stewart, the *Belton* Court reasoned that articles in the passenger compartment of a car are "generally, even if not inevitably" within an arrestee's reach.[1601] This is undoubtedly true at the time of the arrest of a person who is seated in a car but plainly not true when the person has been removed from the car and placed in handcuffs. Accordingly, the *Belton* Court must have proceeded ****1731** on the assumption that the *Chimel* rule was to be applied at the time of arrest. And that is why the *Belton* Court was able to say that its decision "in no way alter[ed] the fundamental principles established in the *Chimel* case regarding the basic scope of searches incident to lawful custodial arrests."[1602] Viewing *Chimel* as having focused on the time of arrest, *Belton's* only new step was to eliminate the need to decide on a case-by-case basis whether a particular person seated in a car actually could have reached the part of the passenger compartment where a weapon or evidence was hidden. For this reason, if we are going to reexamine *Belton*, we should also reexamine the reasoning in *Chimel* on which *Belton* rests.

F

The Court, however, does not reexamine *Chimel* and thus leaves the law relating to searches incident to arrest in a confused and unstable state. The first part of the Court's new two-part rule—which permits an arresting officer to search the area within an arrestee's reach at the time of the search—applies, at least for now, only to vehicle occupants ***364** and recent occupants, but there is no logical reason why the same rule should not apply to all arrestees.

The second part of the Court's new rule, which the Court takes uncritically from Justice Scalia's separate opinion in *Thornton*, raises doctrinal and practical problems that the Court makes no effort to address. Why, for example, is the standard for this

---

1598 See *ante*, at 1719, n. 4 (stating that it is "the rare case" in which an arresting officer cannot secure an arrestee before conducting a search).

1599 *United States v. Abdul–Saboor*, 85 F.3d 664, 669 (C.A.D.C.1996).

1600 *Ibid.* See also *United States v. Tejada*, 524 F.3d 809, 812 (C.A.7 2008) ("[I]f the police could lawfully have searched the defendant's grabbing radius at the moment of arrest, he has no legitimate complaint if, the better to protect themselves from him, they first put him outside that radius").

1601 453 U.S., at 460, 101 S.Ct. 2860.

1602 453 U.S., at 460, n. 3, 101 S.Ct. 2860.

type of evidence-gathering search "reason to believe" rather than probable cause? And why is this type of search restricted to evidence of the offense of arrest? It is true that an arrestee's vehicle is probably more likely to contain evidence of the crime of arrest than of some other crime, but if reason-to-believe is the governing standard for an evidence-gathering search incident to arrest, it is not easy to see why an officer should not be able to search when the officer has reason to believe that the vehicle in question possesses evidence of a crime other than the crime of arrest.

Nor is it easy to see why an evidence-gathering search incident to arrest should be restricted to the passenger compartment. The *Belton* rule was limited in this way because the passenger compartment was considered to be the area that vehicle occupants can generally reach,[1603] but since the second part of the new rule is not based on officer safety or the preservation of evidence, the ground for this limitation is obscure.

***365** III

Respondent in this case has not asked us to overrule *Belton*, much less *Chimel.* Respondent's argument rests entirely on an interpretation of Belton that is plainly incorrect, an interpretation that disregards *Belton's* explicit delineation of its holding. I would therefore leave any reexamination of our prior precedents for another day, if such a reexamination is to be undertaken ****1732** at all. In this case, I would simply apply *Belton* and reverse the judgment below.

*****

Black Letter Law

> Police may search the passenger compartment of a vehicle incident to a recent occupant's arrest only if it is reasonable to believe that the arrestee migfht access the vehicle at the time of the search or that the vehicle contains evidence of the offense of arrest. However, searching a vehicle incident-to-arrest when the arrestee is handcuffed and locked in a patrol car is unreasonable under the Fourth Amendment.

Discussion Problems:

6-1. Officer Walker approaches the driver of a Caprice after pulling him over for a busted taillight. The driver identifies himself as "Bob" and asked what the problem is. Officer Williams didn't like the way "Bob" looked and told him to get out of the car slowly, walk to the back of the Caprice, and to assume the position with his hands on the trunk. Officer Williams places Bob in handcuffs, and then searches his person, discovering a 9mm Beretta tucked into the back of his trousers. He also feels a buldge in his pant's pocket. He asked for permission to place his hand's in Bob's pocket and Bob replied, "Sure, why not?" Officer Walker withdraws a cellophane bag containing approximately 150 white pills. Bob began to sputter, claiming that the speed wasn't his; he was just holding it for someone else. Officer Walker responds by telling him he is under arrest. He puts him in the backseat of the police cruiser, calls in the arrest and fills out some paperwork. About 45 minutes later he goes back to the Caprice and searches both the passenger compartment and the trunk of the car, finding another 30,000 white pills.

Assume that you are the defense attorney representing Bob. What evidence can you suppress and how?

6-2. Office Walker, working undercover, conducted a controlled purchase of methamphetamine from John Saunders. He got into contact with "Johnnie" through a con-

[1603] 453 U.S., at 460, 101 S.Ct. 2860.

fidential informant. They agreed to meet, with Walker purchasing six grams of meth for $1,000.00. They met in the back parking lot of the local Sonic Restaurant. "Johnnie" got his buddy "Eddie" to drive him to the Sonic in a red Caprice. Walker gave Saunders the money and received the meth. Eddie then drove off with Johnnie still in the car. About three blocks down the street a police car pulled them over on a pretextual traffic stop. Both were detained, and police searched the Caprice, finding the marked bills used for the transaction. The police also found two medicine bottles in the caprice, one with an orange cap and the other with a white cap. In the orange-capped bottle were five small plastic bags, two of which contained a white crystalline substance; laboratory analysis of this substance later revealed that in total it was a 2.6–gram mixture that included 1.5 grams of pure methamphetamine. The white-capped bottle had a label with the name Eddie on it. In this bottle were a small, homemade, glass smoking pipe with methamphetamine residue in it and a small piece of straw that could be used to snort methamphetamine. Also inside the bottle was a plastic bag containing a white crystalline substance; laboratory analysis of the substance revealed that it was 1.6 grams of dimethyl sulfone, a substance similar in appearance to methamphetamine that methamphetamine dealers commonly use to “cut” or add bulk to pure methamphetamine.

The cops arrested Johnnie and Eddie at the scene of the traffic stop. They searched Johnnie and seized a cell phone located in his pocket. The phone belonged to Southeast Plumbing and had been issued to Eddie for work, but Eddie was permitted to use the phone for personal purposes too. The cops took both of them to Johnnie's house where a search was being conducted pursuant to a warrant.

The cops interviewed Eddie outside the home and he admitted to past cocaine and methamphetamine use, including some methamphetamine he received from Johnnie three days ago. He also admitted to getting his friends marijuana from Johnnie on numerous occasions. But he denied any involvement in the sale of methamphetamine to Walker.

While Eddie was being interviewed another cop searched through the call records of Eddie's cell phone. The officer read the call records and text messages; several messages appeared related to narcotics use and trafficking. When Eddie was confronted with these messages he admitted to them, but said they were for marijuana drug deals, not meth. Both were indicted for possession with intent to distribute, possession, and aiding abetting. Johnnie testified against Eddie, selling him out by claiming he had sold drugs to Eddie, and that Eddie helped him out with drug deals. Johnnie claimed that Eddie came with him to the Sonic to help with the drug deal. Eddie took the stand and claimed that he did not know about the deal, but just went with him so that he could get a slushy. Eddie claimed not to know what was going on until after the sale went down.

You are the judge in this case. Eddie's counsel has made a motion to suppress the results of the search of the cell phone? How do you rule? Why?

6-3. Prior to placing Bob into the rear of the police car office Walker became concerned that the suspect might have additional contraband on his person. He called for back up to observe and once the additional officer arrived he performed a cavity search of Bob where they discovered a small sealed plastic container. Inside the container was a significant amount of pure heroin.

Assume that you are the prosecuting attorney. How will you successfully defend against the suppression of the heroin?

-Notes-

Chapter 7: Exigent Circumstances

Warden v. Hayden

87 S.Ct. 1642

Supreme Court of the United States

WARDEN, MARYLAND PENITENTIARY, Petitioner,

v.

Bennie Joe HAYDEN.

No. 480. | Argued April 12, 1967. | Decided May 29, 1967.

Mr. Justice BRENNAN delivered the opinion of the Court.

We review in this case the validity of the proposition that there is under the Fourth Amendment a 'distinction ***296** between merely evidentiary materials, on the one hand, which may not be seized either under the authority of a search warrant or during the course of a search incident to arrest, and on the other hand, those objects which may validly be seized including the instrumentalities and means by which a crime is committed, the fruits of crime such as stolen property, weapons by which escape of the person arrested might be effected, and property the possession of which is a crime. A Maryland court sitting without a jury convicted respondent of armed robbery. Items of his clothing, a cap, jacket, and trousers, among other things, were seized during a search of his home, and were admitted in evidence without objection. After unsuccessful state court proceedings, he sought and was denied federal habeas corpus relief in the District Court for Maryland. A divided panel of the Court of Appeals for the Fourth Circuit reversed.[1604] The Court of Appeals believed that *Harris v. United States*,[1605] sustained the validity of the ****1645** search, but held that respondent was correct in his contention that the clothing seized was improperly admitted in evidence because the items had 'evidential value only' and therefore were not ***297** lawfully subject to seizure. We granted certiorari.[1606] We reverse.

I.

About 8:00 a.m. on March 17, 1962, an armed robber entered the business premises of the Diamond Cab Company in Baltimore, Maryland. He took some $363 and ran. Two cab drivers in the vicinity, attracted by shouts of 'Holdup,' followed the man to 2111 Cocoa Lane. One driver notified the company dispatcher by radio that the man was a Negro about 5 8 tall, wearing a light cap and dark jacket, and that he had entered the house on Cocoa Lane. The dispatcher relayed the information to police who were proceeding to the scene of the robbery. Within minutes, police arrived at the house in a number of patrol cars. An officer knocked and announced their presence. Mrs. Hayden answered, and the officers told her they believed that a robber had entered the house, and asked to search the house. She offered no objection.

***298** The officers spread out through the first and second floors and the cellar in search of the robber. Hayden was found in an upstairs bedroom feigning sleep. He was arrested when the officers on the first floor and in the cellar reported that no other man was in the house. Meanwhile an officer was attracted to an adjoining bathroom by the noise of running water, and discovered a shotgun and a pistol in a flush tank; another officer who, according to the District Court, 'was searching the cellar for a man or the money' found in a washing machine a jacket and trousers of the type the fleeing man was said to have worn. A clip of ammunition for the pistol and a cap were found under the mattress of Hayden's bed, and ammunition for the shotgun was

---

[1604] *363 F.2d 647.*

[1605] *331 U.S. 145, 154, 67 S.Ct. 1098, 1103, 91 L.Ed. 1399.*

[1606] *385 U.S. 926, 87 S.Ct. 290, 17 L.Ed.2d 210.*

found in a bureau drawer in Hayden's room. All these items of evidence were introduced against respondent at his trial.

II.

We agree with the Court of Appeals that neither the entry without warrant to search for the robber, nor the search for him without warrant was invalid. Under the circumstances of this case, 'the exigencies of the situation made that course imperative.'[1607] ****1646** The police were informed that an armed robbery had taken place, and that the suspect had entered 2111 Cocoa Lane less than five minutes before they reached it. They acted reasonably when they entered the house and began to search for a man of the description they had been given and for weapons which he had used in the robbery or might use against them. The Fourth Amendment does not require police officers to delay in the course of an investigation ***299** if to do so would gravely endanger their lives or the lives of others. Speed here was essential, and only a thorough search of the house for persons and weapons could have insured that Hayden was the only man present and that the police had control of all weapons which could be used against them or to effect an escape.

We do not rely upon *Harris v. United States*[1608] in sustaining the validity of the search. The principal issue in *Harris* was whether the search there could properly be regarded as incident to the lawful arrest, since Harris was in custody before the search was made and the evidence seized. Here, the seizures occurred prior to or immediately contemporaneous with Hayden's arrest, as part of an effort to find a suspected felon, armed, within the house into which he had run only minutes before the police arrived. The permissible scope of search must, therefore, at the least, be as broad as may reasonably be necessary to prevent the dangers that the suspect at large in the house may resist or escape.

It is argued that, while the weapons, ammunition, and cap may have been seized in the course of a search for weapons, the officer who seized the clothing was searching neither for the suspect nor for weapons when he looked into the washing machine in which he found the clothing. But even if we assume, although we do not decide, that the exigent circumstances in this case made lawful a search without warrant only for the suspect or his weapons, it cannot be said on this record that the officer who found the clothes in the washing machine was not searching for weapons. He testified that he was searching for the man or the money, but his failure to state explicitly that he was searching for weapons, in the absence of a specific question to that effect, can hardly be accorded controlling weight. He knew that the robber was armed and he did not know that some ***300** weapons had been found at the time he opened the machine. In these circumstances the inference that he was in fact also looking for weapons is fully justified.

III.

We come, then, to the question whether, even though the search was lawful, the Court of Appeals was correct in holding that the seizure and introduction of the items of clothing violated the Fourth Amendment because they are 'mere evidence.' The distinction made by some of our cases between seizure of items of evidential value only and seizure of instrumentalities, fruits, or contraband has been criticized by courts and commentators. ****1647** The Court of Appeals, however, felt 'obligated to adhere to it.'[1609] We today reject the distinction as based on premises no longer ***301** accepted as rules governing the application of the Fourth Amendment.

We have examined on many occasions the history and purposes of the Amendment. It was a reaction to the evils of the use of the general warrant in Eng-

---

[1607] *McDonald v. United States, 335 U.S. 451, 456, 69 S.Ct. 191, 193, 93 L.Ed. 153.*

[1608] *Supra.*

[1609] *363 F.2d, at 655.*

land and the writs of assistance in the Colonies, and was intended to protect against invasions of 'the sanctity of a man's home and the privacies of life'[1610] from searches under indiscriminate, general authority. Protection of these interests was assured by prohibiting all 'unreasonable' searches and seizures, and by requiring the use of warrants, which particularly describe 'the place to be searched, and the persons or things to be seized,' thereby interposing 'a magistrate between the citizen and the police.'[1611]

Nothing in the language of the Fourth Amendment supports the distinction between 'mere evidence' and instrumentalities, fruits of crime, or contraband. On its face, the provision assures the 'right of the people to be secure in their persons, houses, papers, and effects * * *,' without regard to the use to which any of these things are applied. This 'right of the people' is certainly unrelated to the 'mere evidence' limitation. Privacy is disturbed no more by a search directed to a purely evidentiary object than it is by a search directed to an instrumentality, ***302** fruit, or contraband. A magistrate can intervene in both situations, and the requirements of probable cause and specificity can be preserved intact. Moreover, nothing in the nature of property seized as evidence renders it more private than property seized, for example, as an instrumentality; quite the opposite may be true. Indeed, the distinction is wholly irrational, since, depending on the circumstances, the same 'papers and effects' may be 'mere evidence' in one case and 'instrumentality' in another.[1612]

In *Gouled v. United States*,[1613] the Court said that search warrants 'may not be used as a means of gaining access to a man's house or office and papers solely for the purpose of making search to secure evidence to be used against him in a criminal or penal proceeding * * *.' The Court derived from *Boyd v. United States* the proposition that warrants 'may be resorted to only when a primary right to such search and seizure may be found ****1648** in the interest which the public or the complainant may have in the property to be seized, or in the right to the possession of it, or when a valid exercise of the police power renders possession of the property by the accused unlawful and provides that it may be taken;'[1614] that is, when the property is an instrumentality or fruit of crime, or contraband. Since it was 'impossible to say, on the record * * * that the government had any interest' in the papers involved 'other than as evidence against the accused * * *,' 'to permit them to be used in evidence would be, in effect, as ruled in the *Boyd* Case, to compel the defendant to become a witness against himself.'[1615]

The items of clothing involved in this case are not 'testimonial' or 'communicative' in nature, and their introduction therefore did not compel respondent to become ***303** a witness against himself in violation of the Fifth Amendment.[1616] This case thus does not require that we consider whether there are items of evidential value whose very nature precludes them from being the object of a reasonable search and seizure.

The Fourth Amendment ruling in *Gouled* was based upon the dual, related premises that historically the right to search for and seize property depended upon the assertion by the Government of a valid claim of superior interest, and that it was not enough that the purpose of the search and seizure was to obtain evidence to use in apprehending and convicting criminals. The common law of search and seizure

[1610] *Boyd v. United States, 116 U.S. 616, 630, 6 S.Ct. 524, 532, 29 L.Ed. 746.*

[1611] *McDonald v. United States, supra, 335 U.S., at 455, 69 S.Ct., at 193.*

[1612] *See Comment, 20 U.Chi.L.Rev. 319, 320—322 (1953).*

[1613] *255 U.S. 298, 309, 41 S.Ct. 261, 265, 65 L.Ed. 647.*

[1614] *255 U.S., at 309, 41 S.Ct. at 265;o*

[1615] *Id., at 311, 41 S.Ct., at 265.*

[1616] *Schmerber v. State of California, 384 U.S. 757, 86 S.Ct. 1826, 16 L.Ed.2d 908.*

after *Entick v. Carrington*[1617] reflected Lord Camden's view, derived no doubt from the political thought of his time, that the 'great end, for which men entered into society, was to secure their property.'[1618] Warrants were 'allowed only where the primary right to such a search and seizure is in the interest which the public or complainant may have in the property seized.'[1619] Thus stolen property—the fruits of crime—was always subject to seizure. And the power to search for stolen property was gradually extended to cover 'any property which the private citizen was not permitted to possess,' which included instrumentalities of crime (because of the early notion that items used in crime were forfeited to the State) and contraband.[1620] No separate governmental interest in seizing evidence to apprehend and convict criminals was recognized; it was required that some property interest be asserted. The remedial structure also reflected these dual premises. Trespass, replevin, and the other means of ***304** redress for persons aggrieved by searches and seizures, depended upon proof of a superior property interest. And since a lawful seizure presupposed a superior claim, it was inconceivable that a person could recover property lawfully seized. As Lord Camden pointed out in *Entick v. Carrington*,[1621] a general warrant enabled 'the party's own property (to be) seized before and without conviction, and he has no power to reclaim his goods, even after his innocence is cleared by acquittal.'

The premise that property interests control the right of the Government to search and seize has been discredited. Searches and seizures may be 'unreasonable' within the Fourth Amendment even though the Government asserts a superior property interest at common law. We have recognized that the principal object of the Fourth Amendment is the protection of privacy rather than property, and have increasingly discarded fictional and procedural barriers rested on property concepts.[1622] ****1649** This shift in emphasis from property to privacy has come about through a subtle interplay of substantive and procedural reform. The remedial structure at the time even of *Weeks v. United States*[1623] was arguably explainable in property terms. The Court held in *Weeks* that a defendant could petition before trial for the return of his illegally seized property, a proposition not necessarily inconsistent with *Adams v. People of State of New York*,[1624] which held in effect that the property issues involved in search and seizure are collateral to a criminal proceeding. The remedial structure finally escaped the bounds of common law property limitations in ***305** *Silverthorne Lumber Co. v. United States*[1625] and *Gouled v. United States*[1626] when it became established that suppression might be sought during a criminal trial, and under circumstances which would not sustain an action in trespass or replevin. Recognition that the role of the Fourth Amendment was to protect against invasions of privacy demanded a remedy to condemn the seizure in *Silverthorne*, although no possible common law claim existed for the return of the copies made by the Government of the papers it had seized. The remedy of suppression, necessarily involving only the limited, functional consequence of excluding the evidence from trial, satisfied that demand.

[1617] *19 How.St.Tr. 1029.*

[1618] *Id., at 1066.*

[1619] *The History and Development of the Fourth Amendment to the United States Constitution 133-134.*

[1620] *Kaplan, Search and Seizure: A No-Man's Land in the Criminal Law, 49 Calif.L.Rev. 474, 475.*

[1621] *Supra, at 1066.*

[1622] *See Jones v. United States, 362 U.S. 257, 266, 80 S.Ct. 725, 733, 4 L.Ed.2d 697; Silverman v. United States, 365 U.S. 505, 511, 81 S.Ct. 679, 682, 5 L.Ed.2d 734.*

[1623] *232 U.S. 383, 34 S.Ct. 341, 58 L.Ed. 652.*

[1624] *192 U.S. 585, 24 S.Ct. 372, 48 L.Ed. 575.*

[1625] *251 U.S. 385, 40 S.Ct. 182, 64 L.Ed. 319.*

[1626] *Supra.*

The development of search and seizure law since *Silverthorne* and *Gouled* is replete with examples of the transformation in substantive law brought about through the interaction of the felt need to protect privacy from unreasonable invasions and the flexibility in rule-making made possible by the remedy of exclusion. We have held, for example, that intangible as well as tangible evidence may be suppressed,[1627] and that an actual trespass under local property law is unnecessary to support a remediable violation of the Fourth Amendment.[1628] In determining whether someone is a 'person aggrieved by an unlawful search and seizure' we have refused 'to import into the law * * * subtle distinctions, developed and refined by the common law in evolving the body of private property law which, more than almost any other branch of law, has been shaped by distinctions whose validity is largely historical.'[1629] And with particular relevance here, we have given recognition to the interest in privacy despite the complete absence of a property claim by suppressing the very items which at ***306** common law could be seized with impunity: stolen goods,[1630] instrumentalities,[1631] and contraband.[1632]

The premise in *Gouled* that government may not seize evidence simply for the purpose of proving crime has likewise been discredited. The requirement that the Government assert in addition some property interest in material it seizes has long been a fiction, obscuring ****1650** the reality that government has an interest in solving crime. *Schmerber* settled the proposition that it is reasonable, within the terms of the Fourth Amendment, to conduct otherwise permissible searches for the purpose of obtaining evidence which would aid in apprehending and convicting criminals. The requirements of the Fourth Amendment can secure the same protection of privacy ***307** whether the search is for 'mere evidence' or for fruits, instrumentalities or contraband. There must, of course, be a nexus—automatically provided in the case of fruits, instrumentalities or contraband—between the item to be seized and criminal behavior. Thus in the case of 'mere evidence,' probable cause must be examined in terms of cause to believe that the evidence sought will aid in a particular apprehension or conviction. In so doing, consideration of police purposes will be required.[1633] But no such problem is presented in this case. The clothes found in the washing machine matched the description of those worn by the robber and the police therefore could reasonably believe that the items would aid in the identification of the culprit.

The remedy of suppression, moreover, which made possible protection of privacy from unreasonable searches without regard to proof of a superior property interest, likewise provides the procedural device necessary for allowing otherwise permissible searches and seizures conducted solely to obtain evidence of crime. For just as the suppression of evidence does not entail a declaration of superior property interest in the person aggrieved, thereby enabling him to suppress evidence unlawfully seized despite his inability to demonstrate such an interest (as with fruits, instrumentalities, contraband), the refusal to suppress evidence carries no declaration of superior property interest in the State, and should thereby enable the State to introduce evidence lawfully seized despite its inability to demonstrate such an interest. And, unlike the situation at common law, the owner of property would not be rendered remediless if 'mere evidence' could lawfully be seized to prove crime. For just as the suppression of evidence does not in itself necessarily entitle the aggrieved

---

[1627] *Wong Sun v. United States, 371 U.S. 471, 485—486, 83 S.Ct. 407, 416—417, 9 L.Ed.2d 441.*

[1628] *Silverman v. United States, supra.*

[1629] *Jones v. United States, supra, 362 U.S., at 266, 80 S.Ct., at 733.*

[1630] *Henry v. United States, 361 U.S. 98, 80 S.Ct. 168, 4 L.Ed.2d 134.*

[1631] *Beck v. State of Ohio, 379 U.S. 89, 85 S.Ct. 223, 13 L.Ed.2d 142; McDonald v. United States, supra.*

[1632] *Trupiano v. United States, 334 U.S. 699, 68 S.Ct. 1229, 92 L.Ed. 1663; Aguilar v. State of Texas, 378 U.S. 108, 84 S.Ct. 1509, 12 L.Ed.2d 723.*

[1633] *Cf. Kremen v. United States, 353 U.S. 346, 77 S.Ct. 828, 1 L.Ed.2d 876.*

person to its return (as, for example, contraband), the introduction of 'mere evidence' does not in ***308** itself entitle the State to its retention. Where public officials 'unlawfully seize or hold a citizen's realty or chattels, recoverable by appropriate action at law or in equity * * *,' the true owner may 'bring his possessory action to reclaim that which is wrongfully withheld.'[1634]

The survival of the *Gouled* distinction is attributable more to chance than considered judgment. Legislation has helped perpetuate it. Thus, Congress has never authorized the issuance of search warrants for the seizure of mere evidence of crime.[1635] ****1651** Even in the Espionage Act of 1917, where Congress for the first time granted general authority for the issuance of search warrants, the authority was limited to fruits of crime, instrumentalities, and certain contraband.[1636] *Gouled* concluded, needlessly it appears, that the Constitution virtually limited searches and seizures to these categories. After *Gouled*, pressure ***309** to test this conclusion was slow to mount. Rule 41(b) of the Federal Rules of Criminal Procedure incorporated the *Gouled* categories as limitations on federal authorities to issue warrants, and *Mapp v. Ohio*[1637] only recently made the 'mere evidence' rule a problem in the state courts. Pressure against the rule in the federal courts has taken the form rather of broadening the categories of evidence subject to seizure, thereby creating considerable confusion in the law.[1638]

The rationale most frequently suggested for the rule preventing the seizure of evidence is that 'limitations upon the fruit to be gathered tend to limit the quest itself.'[1639] But privacy 'would be just as well served by a restriction on search to the even-numbered days of the month. * * * And it would have the extra advantage of avoiding hair-splitting questions. * * *'[1640] The 'mere evidence' limitation has spawned exceptions so numerous and confusion so great, in fact, that it is questionable whether it affords meaningful protection. But if its rejection does enlarge the area of permissible searches, the intrusions are nevertheless made after fulfilling the probable cause and particularity requirements of the Fourth Amendment and after the intervention of 'a neutral and detached magistrate. ***310** * * *'[1641] The Fourth Amendment allows intrusions upon privacy under these circumstances, and there is no viable reason to distinguish intrusions to secure 'mere evidence' from intrusions to secure fruits, instrumentalities, or contraband.

****1652** The judgment of the Court of Appeals is reversed.

Reversed.

Mr. Justice FORTAS, with whom THE CHIEF JUSTICE joins, concurring.

While I agree that the Fourth Amendment should not be held to require exclusion from evidence of the clothing as well as the weapons and ammunition found by the officers during the search, I cannot join in the majority's broad—and in my judgment, totally unnecessary—repudiation of the so-called 'mere evidence' rule.

Our Constitution envisions that searches will ordinarily follow procurement by police of a valid search warrant. Such warrants are to issue only on probable cause,

---

[1634] *Land v. Dollar, 330 U.S. 731, 738, 67 S.Ct. 1009, 1012, 91 L.Ed. 1209. (Emphasis added.) See Burdeau v. McDowell, 256 U.S. 465, 474, 41 S.Ct. 574, 575, 65 L.Ed. 1048.*

[1635] *See Davis v. United States, 328 U.S. 582, 606, 66 S.Ct. 1256, 1267, 90 L.Ed. 1453 (dissenting opinion of Mr. Justice Frankfurter).*

[1636] *40 Stat. 228.*

[1637] *367 U.S. 643, 81 S.Ct. 1684, 6 L.Ed.2d 1081.*

[1638] *See, e.g., Note, 54 Geo.L.J. 593, 607—621 (1966).*

[1639] *United States v. Poller, 43 F.2d 911, 914 (C.A.2d Cir. 1930).*

[1640] *Kaplan, op. cit. supra, at 479.*

[1641] *Johnson v. United States, 333 U.S. 10, 14, 68 S.Ct. 367, 369, 92 L.Ed. 436.*

and must describe with particularity the persons or things to be seized. There are exceptions to this rule. Searches may be made incident to a lawful arrest, and—as today's decision indicates—in the course of 'hot pursuit.' But searches under each of these exceptions have, until today, been confined to those essential to fulfill the purpose of the exception: that is, we have refused to permit use of articles the seizure of which could not be strictly tied to and justified by the exigencies which excused the warrantless search. The use in evidence of weapons seized in a 'hot pursuit' search or search incident to arrest satisfies this criterion because of the need to protect the arresting officers from weapons to which the suspect might resort. The search for and seizure of fruits are, of course, justifiable on independent grounds: The fruits ***311** are an object of the pursuit or arrest of the suspect, and should be restored to their true owner. The seizure of contraband has been justified on the ground that the suspect has not even a bare possessory right to contraband.[1642]

Similarly, we have forbidden the use of articles seized in such a search unless obtained from the person of the suspect or from the immediate vicinity. Since a warrantless search is justified only as incident to an arrest or 'hot pursuit,' this Court and others have held that its scope does not include permission to search the entire building in which the arrests occurs, or to rummage through locked drawers and closets, or to search at another time or place.[1643]

In the present case, the articles of clothing admitted into evidence are not within any of the traditional categories which describe what materials may be seized, either with or without a warrant. The restrictiveness of these categories ****1653** has been subjected to telling criticism, and ***312** although I believe that we should approach expansion of these categories with the diffidence which their imposing provenance commands, I agree that the use of identifying clothing worn in the commission of a crime and seized during 'hot pursuit' is within the spirit and intendment of the 'hot pursuit' exception to the search-warrant requirement. That is because the clothing is pertinent to identification of the person hotly pursued as being, in fact, the person whose pursuit was justified by connection with the crime. I would frankly place the ruling on that basis. I would not drive an enormous and dangerous hole in the Fourth Amendment to accommodate a specific and, I think, reasonable exception.

As my Brother Douglas notes, opposition to general searches is a fundamental of our heritage and of the history of Anglo-Saxon legal principles. Such searches, pursuant to 'writs of assistance,' were one of the matters over which the American Revolution was fought. The very purpose of the Fourth Amendment was to outlaw such searches, which the Court today sanctions. I fear that in gratuitously striking down the 'mere evidence' rule, which distinguished members of this Court have acknowledged as essential to enforce the Fourth Amendment's prohibition against general searches, the Court today needlessly destroys, root and branch, a basic part of liberty's heritage.

(The dissent of Mr. Justice DOUGLAS, is omitted.)

*****

[1642] *See, e.g., Boyd v. United States, 116 U.S. 616, 623—624, 6 S.Ct. 524, 528—529, 29 L.Ed. 746 (1886); United States v. Kirschenblatt, 16 F.2d 202, 203, 51 A.L.R. 416 (C.A.2d Cir. 1926) (L. Hand, J.).*

[1643] *James v. State of Louisiana, 382 U.S. 36, 86 S.Ct. 151, 15 L.Ed.2d 30 (1965); Stoner v. State of California, 376 U.S. 483, 486—487, 84 S.Ct. 889, 891—892, 11 L.Ed.2d 856 (1964); Preston v. United States, 376 U.S. 364, 367, 84 S.Ct. 881, 883, 11 L.Ed.2d 777 (1964); United States v. Lefkowitz, 285 U.S. 452, 52 S.Ct. 420, 76 L.Ed. 877 (1932); Go-Bart Importing Co. v. United States, 282 U.S. 344, 358, 51 S.Ct. 153, 158, 75 L.Ed. 374 (1931); Agnello v. United States, 269 U.S. 20, 30—31, 46 S.Ct. 4, 5—6, 70 L.Ed. 145 (1925); United States v. Kirschenblatt, supra.*

Black Letter Law

> Where the police were informed that armed robbery had taken place and that the suspect had entered a particular house less than five minutes before they reached it, officers acted reasonably when they entered home and began to search for the man, weapons he had used in the robbery and could use against them at the house. Neither their entry without a warrant, their search of the residence for the suspect, nor their search for weapons without was invalid because their actions were justified given the exigent circumstances present.

Vale v. Louisiana

90 S.Ct. 1969

Supreme Court of the United States

Donald J. VALE, Appellant,

v.

State of LOUISIANA.

No. 727. | Argued March 4, 5, 1970. | Decided June 22, 1970.

Mr. Justice STEWART delivered the opinion of the Court.

The appellant, Donald Vale, was convicted in a Louisiana court on a charge of possessing heroin and was sentenced as a multiple offender to 15 years' imprisonment at hard labor. The Louisiana Supreme Court affirmed the conviction, rejecting the claim that evidence introduced at the trial was the product of an unlawful search and seizure.[1644] We granted Vale's motion to proceed in forma pauperis, postponed consideration of the question of jurisdiction to the hearing of the case on the merits, and limited review to the search-and-seizure question.[1645]

The evidence adduced at the pretrial hearing on a motion to suppress showed that on April 24, 1967, officers possessing two warrants for Vale's arrest and having information that he was residing at a specified address proceeded there in an unmarked car and set up a surveillance of the house. The evidence of what then took ***32** place was summarized by the Louisiana Supreme Court as follows:

'After approximately 15 minutes the officers observed a green 1958 Chevrolet drive up and sound the horn and after backing into a parking place, again blew the horn. At this juncture Donald Vale, who was well known to Officer Brady having arrested him ****1971** twice in the previous month, was seen coming out of the house and walk up to the passenger side of the Chevrolet where he had a close brief conversation with the driver; and after looking up and down the street returned inside of the house. Within a few minutes he reappeared on the porch, and again cautiously looked up and down the street before proceeding to the passenger side of the Chevrolet, leaning through the window. From this the officers were convinced a narcotics sale had taken place. They returned to their car and immediately drove toward Donald Vale, and as they reached within approximately three cars lengths from the accused, (Donald Vale) he looked up and, obviously recognizing the officers, turned around, walking quickly toward the house. At the same time the driver of the Chevrolet started to make his get away when the car was blocked by the police vehicle. The three officers promptly alighted from the car, whereupon Officers Soule and Laumann called to Donald Vale to stop as he reached the front steps of the house,

---

[1644] 252 La. 1056, 215 So.2d 811.

*[1645] 396 U.S 813, 90 S.Ct. 108, 24 L.Ed.2d 65.**

telling him he was under arrest. Officer Brady at the same time, seeing the driver of the Chevrolet, Arizzio Saucier, whom the officers knew to be a narcotic addict, place something hurriedly in his mouth, immediately placed him under arrest and joined his co-officers. Because of the transaction ***33** they had just observed they, informed Donald Vale they were going to search the house, and thereupon advised him of his constitutional rights. After they all entered the front room, Officer Laumann made a cursory inspection of the house to ascertain if anyone else was present and within about three minutes Mrs. Vale and James Vale, mother and brother of Donald Vale, returned home carrying groceries and were informed of the arrest and impending search.'[1646]

The search of a rear bedroom revealed a quantity of narcotics.

The Louisiana Supreme Court held that the search of the house did not violate the Fourth Amendment because it occurred 'in the immediate vicinity of the arrest' of Donald Vale and was 'substantially contemporaneous therewith * * *.'[1647] We cannot agree. Last Term in *Chimel v. California*,[1648] we held that when the search of a dwelling is sought to be justified as incident to a lawful arrest, it must constitutionally be confined to the area within the arrestee's reach at the time of his arrest—'the area from within which he might gain possession of a weapon or destructible evidence.'[1649] But even if *Chimel* is not accorded retroactive effect—a question on which we do not now express an opinion—no precedent of this Court can sustain the constitutional validity of the search in the case before us.

A search may be incident to an arrest "only if it is substantially contemporaneous with the arrest and is confined to the immediate vicinity of the arrest."[1650] If a search of a house is to be upheld ***34** as incident to an arrest, that arrest must take place inside the house,[1651] not somewhere outside—whether two blocks away,[1652] twenty feet away,[1653] or on the sidewalk near the front steps. 'Belief, however well founded, that an article sought is concealed in a dwelling house furnishes no justification for a search of that place without a warrant.'[1654] ****1972** That basic rule 'has never been questioned in this Court.'[1655]

The Louisiana Supreme Court thought the search independently supportable because it involved narcotics, which are easily removed, hidden, or destroyed. It would be unreasonable, the Louisiana court concluded, 'to require the officers under the facts of the case to first secure a search warrant before searching the premises, as time is of the essence inasmuch as the officers never know whether there is anyone on the premises to be searched who could very easily destroy the evidence.'[1656] Such a rationale could not apply to the present case, since by their own account the arresting officers satisfied themselves that no one else was in the house when they first entered the premises. But entirely apart from that point, our past decisions make

---

[1646] *252 La., at 1067—1068, 215 So.2d, at 815. (Footnote omitted.)*

[1647] *252 La., at 1070, 215 So.2d, at 816.*

[1648] *395 U.S. 752, 89 S.Ct. 2034, 23 L.Ed.2d 685.*

[1649] *395 U.S., at 763, 89 S.Ct. at 2040.*

[1650] *Shipley v. California, 395 U.S. 818, 819, 89 S.Ct. 2053, 23 L.Ed.2d 732; Stoner v. California, 376 U.S. 483, 486, 84 S.Ct. 889, 891, 11 L.Ed.2d 856.*

[1651] *Cf. Agnello v. United States, 269 U.S. 20, 32, 46 S.Ct. 4, 6, 70 L.Ed. 145.*

[1652] *James v. Louisiana, 382 U.S. 36, 86 S.Ct. 151, 15 L.Ed.2d 30.*

[1653] *Shipley v. California, supra.*

[1654] *Agnello v. United States, supra, 269 U.S. at 33, 46 S.Ct. at 6.*

[1655] *Stoner v. California, supra, 376 U.S. at 487 n. 5, 84 S.Ct. at 892.*

[1656] *252 La., at 1070, 215 So.2d, at 816.*

clear that only in 'a few specifically established and well-delineated' situations[1657] may a warrantless search of a dwelling withstand constitutional scrutiny, even though the authorities have probable cause to conduct it. The burden rests on the State to show the existence of such an exceptional situation.[1658] And the record before us discloses none.

***35** There is no suggestion that anyone consented to the search.[1659] The officers were not responding to an emergency.[1660] They were not in hot pursuit of a fleeing felon.[1661] The goods ultimately seized were not in the process of destruction.[1662] Nor were they about to be removed from the jurisdiction.[1663]

The officers were able to procure two warrants for Vale's arrest. They also had information that he was residing at the address where they found him. There is thus no reason, so far as anything before us appears, to suppose that it was impracticable for them to obtain a search warrant as well.[1664] We decline to hold that an arrest on the street can provide its own 'exigent circumstance' so as to justify a warrantless search of the arrestee's house.

The Louisiana courts committed constitutional error in admitting into evidence the fruits of the illegal search.[1665] ****1973** Accordingly, the judgment is ***36** reversed and the case is remanded to the Louisiana Supreme Court for further proceedings not inconsistent with this opinion. It is so ordered.

Reversed and remanded.

Mr. Justice BLACKMUN took no part in the consideration or decision of this case.

Mr. Justice BLACK, with whom THE CHIEF JUSTICE joins, dissenting.

The Fourth Amendment to the United States Constitution prohibits only 'unreasonable searches.'* A warrant has never been thought to be an absolute requirement for a constitutionally proper search. Searches, whether with or without a warrant, are to be judged by whether they are reasonable, and, as I said, speaking for the Court in *Preston v. United States*,[1666] common sense dictates that reasonableness varies with the circumstances of the search.[1667] The Louisiana Supreme Court held not only that the police action here was reasonable but also that failure to conduct an

---

[1657] *Katz v. United States, 389 U.S. 347, 357, 88 S.Ct. 507, 19 L.Ed.2d 576.*

[1658] *Chimel v. California, supra, 395 U.S. at 762, 89 S.Ct. at 2039; United States v. Jeffers, 342 U.S. 48, 51, 72 S.Ct. 93, 95, 96 L.Ed. 59; McDonald v. United States, 335 U.S. 451, 456, 69 S.Ct. 191, 193, 93 L.Ed. 153.*

[1659] *Cf. Zap v. United States, 328 U.S. 624, 628, 66 S.Ct. 1277, 1279, 90 L.Ed. 1477.*

[1660] *United States v. Jeffers, supra, 342 U.S. at 52, 72 S.Ct. at 95; McDonald v. United States, supra, 335 U.S. at 454, 69 S.Ct. at 192.*

[1661] *Warden v. Hayden, 387 U.S. 294, 298—299, 87 S.Ct. 1642, 1645—1646, 18 L.Ed.2d 782; Chapman v. United States, 365 U.S. 610, 615, 81 S.Ct. 776, 779, 5 L.Ed.2d 828; Johnson v. United States, 333 U.S. 10, 15, 68 S.Ct. 367, 369, 92 L.Ed. 436.*

[1662] *Schmerber v. California, 384 U.S. 757, 770—771, 86 S.Ct. 1826, 1835—1836, 16 L.Ed.2d 908; United States v. Jeffers, supra; McDonald v. United States, supra, 335 U.S. at 455, 69 S.Ct. at 193.*

[1663] *Chapman v. United States, supra; Johnson v. United States, supra; United States v. Jeffers, supra.*

[1664] *Cf. McDonald v. United States, supra, 335 U.S. at 454—455, 69 S.Ct. at 192—193; Trupiano v. United States, 334 U.S. 699, 705—706, 68 S.Ct. 1229, 1232—1233, 92 L.Ed. 1663; Johnson v. United States, supra; Taylor v. United States, 286 U.S. 1, 6, 52 S.Ct. 466, 467, 76 L.Ed. 928; Go-Bart Importing Co. v. United States, 282 U.S. 344, 358, 51 S.Ct. 153, 158, 75 L.Ed. 374; Carroll v. United States, 267 U.S. 132, 156, 45 S.Ct. 280, 286, 69 L.Ed. 543; cf. Ker v. California, 374 U.S. 23, 42, 83 S.Ct. 1623, 10 L.Ed.2d 726 (opinion of Clark, J.).*

[1665] *Shipley v. California, supra, 395 U.S. at 819, 89 S.Ct. at 2054; James v. Louisiana, supra, 382 U.S. at 37, 86 S.Ct. at 151; Ker v. California, supra, 374 U.S. at 30—34, 83 S.Ct. at 1628—1630; Mapp v. Ohio, 367 U.S. 643, 81 S.Ct. 1684, 6 L.Ed.2d 1081.*

[1666] *376 U.S. 364, 366—367, 84 S.Ct. 881, 882—883, 11 L.Ed.2d 777 (1964).*

[1667] *See, e.g., Henry v. United States, 361 U.S. 98, 80 S.Ct. 168, 4 L.Ed.2d 134 (1959); Brinegar v. United States, 338 U.S. 160, 69 S.Ct. 1302, 93 L.Ed. 1879 (1949).*

immediate search would have been unreasonable.[1668] With that view I am in complete agreement, for the following reasons.

The police, having warrants for Vale's arrest, were watching his mother's house from a short distance away. Not long after they began their vigil a car arrived, ***37** sounded its horn, and backed into a parking space near the house. The driver did not get out, but instead honked the car horn again. Vale, who had been arrested twice the month before and against whom an indictment for a narcotics offense was then pending, came out of his mother's house and talked to the driver of the car. At the conclusion of the conversation Vale looked both ways, up and down the street, and then went back inside the house. When he reappeared he stopped before going to the car and stood, as one of the officers testified, looking back and forth like to see who might be coming or who was in the neighborhood.' He then walked to the car and leaned in.

From this behavior the officers were convinced that a narcotics transaction was taking place at that very moment. They drove down the street toward Vale and the parked car. When they came within a few car lengths of the two men Vale saw them and began to walk quickly back toward the house. At the same time the driver of the car attempted to pull away. The police brought both parties to the transaction to a stop. They then saw that the driver of the car was one Saucier, a known narcotics addict. He hurriedly placed something in his mouth, and apparently swallowed it. The police placed both Vale and Saucier under arrest.

At this point the police had probable cause to believe that Vale was engaged in a narcotics transfer, and that a supply of narcotics would be found in the house, to which Vale had returned after his first conversation, from which he had emerged furtively bearing what the police could readily deduce was a supply of narcotics, and toward which he hurried after seeing the police. But the police did not know then who else might be in the house. Vale's arrest took place ****1974** near the house, and anyone observing from inside would surely have been alerted to destroy the stocks of contraband which ***38** the police believed Vale had left there. The police had already seen Saucier, the narcotics addict, apparently swallow what Vale had given him. Believing that some evidence had already been destroyed and that other evidence might well be, the police were faced with the choice of risking the immediate destruction of evidence or entering the house and conducting a search. I cannot say that their decision to search was unreasonable. Delay in order to obtain a warrant would have given an accomplice just the time he needed.

That the arresting officers did, in fact, believe that others might be in the house is attested to by their actions upon entering the door left open by Vale. The police at once checked the small house to determine if anyone else was present. Just as they discovered the house was empty, however, Vale's mother and brother arrived. Now what had been a suspicion became a certainty: Vale's relatives were in possession and knew of his arrest. To have abandoned the search at this point, and left the house with Vale, would not have been the action of reasonable police officers. As Mr. Justice White said, dissenting in *Chimel v. California*:[1669]

'For the police to search the house while the evidence they had probable cause to search out and seize was still there cannot be considered unreasonable.'

In my view, whether a search incident to a lawful arrest is reasonable should still be determined by the facts and circumstances of each case.[1670] For the reasons given above I am convinced that the search here was reasonable, even though Vale had not yet crossed the threshold of the house toward which he was headed.

[1668] *252 La. 1056, 1070, 215 So.2d 811, 816.*

[1669] *395 U.S. 752, 775, 89 S.Ct. 2034, 23 L.Ed.2d 685 (1969).*

[1670] *Ker v. California, 374 U.S. 23, 34—36, 83 S.Ct. 1623, 1630—1631, 10 L.Ed.2d 726 (1963); United States v. Rabinowitz, 339 U.S. 56, 63—64, 70 S.Ct. 430, 434, 94 L.Ed. 653 (1950).*

***39** Moreover, the circumstances here were sufficiently exceptional to justify a search, even if the search was not strictly 'incidental' to an arrest. The Court recognizes that searches to prevent the destruction or removal of evidence have long been held reasonable by this Court.[1671] Whether the 'exceptional circumstances' justifying such a search exist or not is a question that may be, as it is here, quite distinct from whether or not the search was incident to a valid arrest. [1672]It is thus unnecessary to determine whether the search was valid as incident to the arrest under either *Chimel v. United States*,[1673] or under the pre-*Chimel* standard as interpreted in *Shipley v. California*.[1674] It is only necessary to find that, given Vale's arrest in a spot readily visible to anyone in the house and the probable existence of narcotics inside, it was reasonable for the police to conduct an immediate search of the premises.

The Court, however, finds the search here unreasonable. First, the Court suggests that the contraband was not 'in the process of destruction.' None of the cases cited by the Court supports the proposition that 'exceptional circumstances' exist only when the process of destruction has already begun. On the contrary we implied that those circumstances did exist when 'evidence or contraband was threatened with removal or destruction.'[1675] ****1975**

***40** Second, the Court seems to argue that the search was unreasonable because the police officers had time to obtain a warrant. I agree that the opportunity to obtain a warrant is one of the factors to be weighed in determining reasonableness.[1676] But the record conclusively shows that there was no such opportunity here. As I noted above, once the officers had observed Vale's conduct in front of the house they had probable cause to believe that a felony had been committed and that immediate action was necessary. At no time after the events in from of Mrs. Vale's house would it have been prudent for the officers to leave the house in order to secure a warrant.

The Court asserts, however, that because the police obtained two warrants for Vale's arrest there is 'no reason * * * to suppose that it was impracticable for them to obtain a search warrant as well.' The difficulty is that the two arrest warrants on which the Court seems to rely so heavily were not issued because of any present misconduct of Vale's; they were issued because the bond had been increased for an earlier narcotics charge then pending against Vale. When the police came to arrest Vale, they knew only that his bond had been increased. There is nothing in the record to indicate that, absent the increased bond, there would have been probable cause for an arrest, much less a search. Probable cause for the search arose for the first time when the police observed the activity of Vale and Saucier in and around the house.

I do not suggest that all arrests necessarily provide the basis for a search of the arrestee's house. In this case there is far more than a mere street arrest. The police also observed Vale's use of the house as a base of operations for his commercial business, his attempt to ***41** return hurriedly to the house on seeing the officers, and the apparent destruction of evidence by the man with whom Vale was dealing. Furthermore the police arrival and Vale's arrest were plainly visible to anyone within the house, and the police had every reason to believe that someone in the house was likely to destroy the contraband if the search were postponed.

[1671] *Preston v. United States, supra; McDonald v. United States, 335 U.S. 451, 455, 69 S.Ct. 191, 193, 93 L.Ed. 153 (1948); Carroll v. United States, 267 U.S. 132, 45 S.Ct. 280, 69 L.Ed. 543 (1925).*

[1672] *See United States v. Jeffers, 342 U.S. 48, 51, 72 S.Ct. 93, 95, 96 L.Ed. 59 (1951); Johnson v. United States, 333 U.S. 10, 68 S.Ct. 367, 92 L.Ed.2d 436 (1948).*

[1673] *Supra.*

[1674] *395 U.S. 818, 89 S.Ct. 2053, 23 L.Ed.2d 732 (1969).*

[1675] *Johnson v. United States, supra, 333 U.S. at 15, 68 S.Ct. at 369 (emphasis added). See also Chapman v. United States, 365 U.S. 610, 615, 81 S.Ct. 776, 779, 5 L.Ed.2d 828 (1961); Hernandez v. United States, 353 F.2d 624 (C.A.9th Cir. 1965), cert. denied, 384 U.S. 1008, 86 S.Ct. 1972, 16 L.Ed.2d 1021 (1966).*

[1676] *Trupiano v. United States, 334 U.S. 699, 68 S.Ct. 1229, 92 L.Ed. 1663 (1948); United States v. Rabinowitz, supra, 339 U.S. at 66, 70 S.Ct. at 435 (Black, J., dissenting).*

This case raises most graphically the question how does a policeman protect evidence necessary to the State if he must leave the premises to get a warrant, allowing the evidence he seeks to be destroyed. The Court's answer to that question makes unnecessarily difficult the conviction of those who prey upon society.

Black Letter Law

> Held that where defendant was arrested on front steps of his premises, immediately after arresting officers had observed what they believed to have been sale of narcotics to known drug addict, with transaction being consummated in addict's automobile parked near curb, and officers had two warrants for defendant's arrest and had satisfied themselves that no one was in premises when they entered, warrantless search of premises was illegal and could not be justified as incident to arrest. Admission of heroin found in search of rear bedroom was constitutional error. If search of a house is to be upheld as incident to arrest, arrest must take place inside house, not somewhere outside—whether two blocks away, twenty feet away or on sidewalk near front steps.

Discussion Problems:

7-1. George and Harry were roommates who worked construction together. While on a job site George asked Harry to take his car to the local supermarket and buy some beer for everyone. The car was titled in George's name, but Harry had his own key for the car and routinely drove it when George did not need it. Harry was pulled over for speeding on his way to the supermarket. The officer asked Harry for his driver's license. When Harry gave him his license his hands were shaking violently and he sounded upset. The officer asked for proof of insurance, but Harry could not find it. The officer went back to his car to write the ticket and run Harry's information through the system. He found prior charges for both theft and narcotics. Harry disappeared from view several times during this timeframe and the officer became nervous and called for backup.

Concerned that Harry might be attempting to hide drugs, the officer returned and asked Harry to step out of the car so that he could show him the radar reading and explain the tickets. Once he was out of the car, the officer conducted a Terry stop and began to question Harry about his suspicions.

He then asked Harry if he could search the car. The officer claims Harry consented to the search, Harry maintains otherwise. The officer discovered drug paraphernalia and drugs in the passenger compartment under both the seat and in the glove compartment. Harry was then arrested.

The police then sent a squad car to the job site where the interviewed George, discovered drugs on his person and arrested him as well.

At trial, George's counsel has challenged the constitutionality of the search of George's car when Harry was driving it. He is arguing that the search was illegal and therefore all subsequent evidence derived from that search should be excluded.

What is the best argument the state attorney should make to overcome the motion to suppress? How would you structure the brief and subsequent oral argument?

7-2. On April 15, 2013, two young men wearing baseball caps and carrying backpacks were walking alongside Gulfport Drive during the Gulfport Marathon. The Gulfport Marathon draws thousands of spectators each year, who gather along the 26.2 mile track to cheer on and watch the competitors. These two young men left their backpacks unattended on the ground, amongst a crowd and disappeared. Several minutes later, two large blasts followed; injuring close to 300 spectators and killing three of them. Local and federal law enforcement reviewed nearby surveillance videos and were able to identify two men who had dropped off backpacks in temporal proximity to the blasts and with the help of the public were able to identify the two bombers as Mikah and Noah Transvia, brothers from the Czech Republic. After reviewing the contents of the backpacks, the police learned that the destructive bombs were home-made from pressure cookers and feared that the brothers would make new bombs and place them throughout the city.

The two brothers created a YouTube video the following morning, praising Allah and threatening additional attacks on the city of Gulfport starting "tonight."

The police received an anonymous tip from a local resident who claimed that she believed her next-door neighbors were the now notorious marathon bombers. She claimed that in the past 24 hours, she had heard them making a lot of "racket," "speaking in foreign tongues," and playing Middle-Eastern music. The police responded to the reported apartment with a squat team and in fact did hear a lot of ruckus and Middle-Eastern music playing loudly. Fearing that the bombers were inside with additional bombs, the police escorted all of the residents of the apartment complex away from the building to a nearby parking lot. The SWAT team kicked down the door and arrested the two occupants of the apartment, Mikah and Noah Transvia, without a valid warrant and without announcing their presence. The police conducted a thorough search of the apartment and it yielded no C4, dynamite, or other explosive materials. The police did find five pressure cookers in the brothers' apartment as well as baseball caps and clothing matching what the brothers were seen wearing in the surveillance video.

At their trial, their defense attorneys sought to exclude the evidence of the pressure cookers and the clothing based upon the unlawful search.

How should the Court rule and why?

7-3. Officer Lockte, a fifteen-year veteran of the City of New London Police Department and former marine, was primarily tasked with ensuring the safety of Matthew Phelps, an undercover officer, during the Hide Park protests. These protests were part of an organized movement to "occupy" Hide Park. Hundreds of protestors participated in the Hide Park movement, joining the multitude of protests in cities nationwide. This occupy movement often posted videos and organizational tips on a website called "99percent.com." Officer Phelps, under the directive of the NLPD, infiltrated the protests by posing as a retired civil servant and assumed a role within the movement's hierarchy. In this leadership role, Officer Phelps provided the NLPD with information about the protests, while also utilizing his position to keep the protests relatively peaceful. Officer Phelps had been instrumental in discouraging the movement from occupying other areas of New London. This was particularly vital since similar protests in other cities were becoming increasingly violent. Officer Lockte recognized that similar violence would likely occur in Hide Park if the protestors discovered Officer Phelps' true identity.

Although Officer Phelps was sometimes videotaped giving speeches to the protestors, on September 28, 2011, Officer Lockte observed Michael Franklin videotape a private conversation between Officer Phelps and a uniformed police officer. Fearing that Officer Phelps' cover would be compromised and that violence would ensue, Officer Lockte stopped Franklin and began to ask him questions. Under the City of New London's Wiretapping Statute, it is illegal to record the conversation of another without their consent. After Franklin was stopped, he yelled: "So he IS one of you!" Officer Lockte detained Franklin and confiscated his cell phone. Fearing that the iPhone had been used to post the video to the web, therefore exposing Officer Phelps' identity as an undercover office to hundreds, if not millions of persons using

99percent.com, Officer Lockte briefly inspected the phone and saw that its video application was still open. After reviewing the application, Lockte learned that fortunately the video had not yet been posted. Officer Lockte found the video in draft form with a caption saying: "Why is Phelps so friendly with the NLPD?"

At Franklin's trial for violating the Wiretapping Statute, he sought to suppress any evidence obtained from the cellphone claiming that the search was illegal and therefore the evidence should be excluded.

What is the best argument the state attorney should make to overcome the motion to suppress?

-Notes-

Chapter 8: Vehicle and Container Searches

Chambers v. Maroney

90 S.Ct. 1975

Supreme Court of the United States

Frank CHAMBERS, Petitioner,

v.

James F. MARONEY, Superintendent, State Correctional Institution.

No. 830. | Argued April 27, 1970. | Decided June 22, 1970. | Rehearing Denied Oct. 12, 1970.

Mr. Justice WHITE delivered the opinion of the Court.

The principal question in this case concerns the admissibility of evidence seized from an automobile, in which petitioner was riding at the time of his arrest, after the automobile was taken to a police station and was there thoroughly searched without a warrant. The Court of Appeals for the Third Circuit found no violation of petitioner's Fourth Amendment rights. We affirm.

***44 I**

During the night of May 20, 1963, a Gulf service station in North Braddock, Pennsylvania, was robbed by two men, each of whom carried and displayed a gun. The robbers took the currency from the cash register; the service station attendant, one Stephen Kovacich, was directed to place the coins in his right-hand glove, which was then taken by the robbers. Two teen-agers, who had earlier noticed a blue compact station wagon circling the block in the vicinity of the Gulf station, then saw the station wagon speed away from a parking lot close to the Gulf station. About the same time, they learned that the Gulf station had been robbed. They reported to police, who arrived immediately, that four men were in the station wagon and one was wearing a green sweater. Kovacich told the police that one of the men who robbed him was wearing a green sweater and the other was wearing a trench coat. A description of the car and the two robbers was broadcast over the police radio. Within an hour, a light blue compact station wagon answering the description and carrying four men was stopped by the police about two miles from the Gulf station. Petitioner was one of the men in the station wagon. He was wearing a green sweater and there was a trench coat in the car. The occupants were arrested and the car was driven to the police station. In the course of a thorough search of the car at the station, the police found concealed in a compartment under the dashboard two .38-caliber revolvers (one loaded with dumdum bullets), a right-hand glove containing small change, and certain cards bearing the name of Raymond Havicon, the attendant at a Boron service station in McKeesport, Pennsylvania, who had been robbed at gunpoint on May 13, 1963. In the course of a warrant-authorized search of petitioner's home the day after petitioner's arrest, police found and ***45** seized certain .38-caliber ammunition, including some dumdum bullets similar to those found in one of the guns taken from the station wagon.

****1978** Petitioner was indicted for both robberies. His first trial ended in a mistrial but he was convicted of both robberies at the second trial. Both Kovacich and Havicon identified petitioner as one of the robbers. The materials taken from the station wagon were introduced into evidence, Kovacich identifying his glove and Havicon the cards taken in the May 13 robbery. The bullets seized at petitioner's house were also introduced over objections of petitioner's counsel. Petitioner was sentenced to a term of four to eight years' imprisonment for the May 13 robbery and to a term of two to seven years' imprisonment for the May 20 robbery, the sentences to run consecutively.Petitioner did not take a direct appeal from these convictions. In 1965, petitioner sought a writ of habeas corpus in the state court, which denied the writ after a brief evidentiary hearing; the denial of ***46** the writ was affirmed on appeal in the Pennsylvania appellate courts. Habeas corpus proceedings were then commenced in the United States District Court for the Western District of Pennsylvania. An order to show cause was issued. Based on the State's response and the state court record, the petition for habeas corpus was denied without a hearing. The Court of Appeals for the Third Circuit affirmed,[1677] and we granted certiorari.[1678]

II

We pass quickly the claim that the search of the automobile was the fruit of an unlawful arrest. Both the ****1979** courts below thought the arresting officers had probable cause to make the arrest. We agree. Having talked to the teen-age observers and to the victim Kovacich, the police had ample cause to stop a light blue compact station wagon carrying four men and to arrest the occupants, one of whom was wearing a green sweater ***47** and one of whom had a trench coat with him in the car.

Even so, the search that produced the incriminating evidence was made at the police station some time after the arrest and cannot be justified as a search incident to an arrest: 'Once an accused is under arrest and in custody, then a search made at another place, without a warrant, is simply not incident to the arrest.'[1679] *Dyke v. Taylor Implement Mfg. Co.*[1680] is to the same effect; the reasons that have been thought sufficient to justify warrantless searches carried out in connection with an arrest no longer obtain when the accused is safely in custody at the station house.

There are, however alternative grounds arguably justifying the search of the car in this case. In *Preston*,[1681] the arrest was for vagrancy; it was apparent that the officers had no cause to believe that evidence of crime was concealed in the auto. In *Dyke*,[1682] the Court expressly rejected the suggestion that there was probable cause to search the car.[1683] Here the situation is different, for the police had probable cause to believe that the robbers, carrying guns and the fruits of the crime, had fled the scene in a light blue compact station wagon which would be carrying four men, one wearing a green sweater and another wearing a trench coat. As the state courts correctly held, there was probable cause to arrest the occupants of the station wagon that the officers stopped; just as obviously was ***48** there probable cause to search the car for guns and stolen money.

In terms of the circumstances justifying a warrantless search, the Court has long distinguished between an automobile and a home or office. In *Carroll v. United States*,[1684] the issue was the admissibility in evidence of contraband liquor seized in a warrantless search of a car on the highway. After surveying the law from the time of the adoption of the Fourth Amendment onward, the Court held that automobiles and other conveyances may be searched without a warrant in circumstances that would not justify the search without a warrant of a house or an office, provided that there is probable cause to believe that the car contains articles that the officers are entitled to seize. The Court expressed its holding as follows:

'We have made a somewhat extended reference to these statutes to show that the guaranty of freedom from unreasonable searches and seizures by the Fourth Amendment has been construed, practically since the beginning of the government,

---

[1677] *408 F.2d 1186.*

[1678] *396 U.S. 900, 90 S.Ct. 225, 24 L.Ed.2d 177 (1969).*

[1679] *Preston v. United States, 376 U.S. 364, 367, 84 S.Ct. 881, 883, 11 L.Ed.2d 777 (1964).*

[1680] *391 U.S. 216, 88 S.Ct. 1472, 20 L.Ed.2d 538 (1968).*

[1681] *Supra.*

[1682] *Supra.*

[1683] *391 U.S., at 221-222, 88 S.Ct. 1475-1476.*

[1684] *267 U.S. 132, 45 S.Ct. 280, 69 L.Ed. 543 (1925).*

as recognizing a necessary difference between a search of a store, dwelling house, or other structure in respect of which a proper official warrant readily may be obtained and a search of a ship, motor boat, wagon, or automobile for contraband goods, where it is not practicable to secure a warrant, because the vehicle can be quickly moved out of the locality or jurisdiction in which the warrant must be sought.

****1980** 'Having thus established that contraband goods concealed and illegally transported in an automobile or other vehicle may be searched for without a warrant, we come now to consider under what circumstances such search may be made. * * * Those lawfully within the country, entitled to use ***49** the public highways, have a right to free passage without interruption or search unless there is known to a competent official, authorized to search, probable cause for believing that their vehicles are carrying contraband or illegal merchandise. * * *

'The measure of legality of such a seizure is, therefore, that the seizing officer shall have reasonable or probable cause for believing that the automobile which he stops and seizes has contraband liquor therein which is being illegally transported.'[1685]

The Court also noted that the search of an auto on probable cause proceeds on a theory wholly different from that justifying the search incident to an arrest:

> 'The right to search and the validity of the seizure are not dependent on the right to arrest. They are dependent on the reasonable cause the seizing officer has for belief that the contents of the automobile offend against the law.'[1686]

Finding that there was probable cause for the search and seizure at issue before it, the Court affirmed the convictions. *Carroll* was followed and applied in *Husty v. United States*[1687] and *Scher v. United States.*[1688] It was reaffirmed and followed in *Brinegar v. United States.*[1689] In 1964, the opinion in *Preston*[1690] cited both *Brinegar* and *Carroll* with approval.[1691] In *Cooper v. California,*[1692] ***50** the Court read *Preston* as dealing primarily with a search incident to arrest and cited that case for the proposition that the mobility of a car may make the search of a car without a warrant reasonable 'although the result might be the opposite in a search of a home, a store, or other fixed piece of property.'[1693] The Court's opinion in *Dyke*[1694] recognized that 'automobiles, because of their mobility, may be searched without a warrant upon facts not justifying a warrantless search of a residence or office,' citing *Brinegar* and *Carroll.*[1695] However, because there was insufficient reason to search the car involved in the *Dyke* case, the Court did not reach the question of whether those cases 'extend to a warrantless search, based upon probable cause, of an automobile which, having been stopped originally on a highway, is parked outside a courthouse.'[1696]

[1685] *267 U.S., at 153-154, 155-156, 45 S.Ct. at 285-286.*

[1686] *267 U.S., at 158-159, 45 S.Ct. at 287.*

[1687] *282 U.S. 694, 51 S.Ct. 240, 75 L.Ed. 629 (1931).*

[1688] *305 U.S. 251, 59 S.Ct. 174, 83 L.Ed. 151 (1938).*

[1689] *338 U.S. 160, 69 S.Ct. 1302, 93 L.Ed. 1879 (1949).*

[1690] *Supra.*

[1691] *376 U.S., at 366-367, 84 S.Ct. at 882-883.*

[1692] *386 U.S. 58, 87 S.Ct. 788, 17 L.Ed.2d 730 (1967).*

[1693] *386 U.S., at 59, 87 S.Ct. at 790.*

[1694] *391 U.S., at 221, 88 S.Ct. at 1475.*

[1695] *Supra.*

[1696] *391 U.S., at 222, 88 S.Ct. at 1476.*

Neither *Carroll*[1697] nor other cases in this Court require or suggest that in **1981 every conceivable circumstance the search of an auto even with probable cause may be made without the extra protection for privacy that a warrant affords. But the circumstances that *51 furnish probable cause to search a particular auto for particular articles are most often unforeseeable; moreover, the opportunity to search is fleeting since a car is readily movable. Where this is true, as in *Carroll* and the case before us now, if an effective search is to be made at any time, either the search must be made immediately without a warrant or the car itself must be seized and held without a warrant for whatever period is necessary to obtain a warrant for the search.

In enforcing the Fourth Amendment's prohibition against unreasonable searches and seizures, the Court has insisted upon probable cause as a minimum requirement for a reasonable search permitted by the Constitution. As a general rule, it has also required the judgment of a magistrate on the probable-cause issue and the issuance of a warrant before a search is made. Only in exigent circumstances will the judgment of the police as to probable cause serve as a sufficient authorization for a search. *Carroll*[1698] holds a search warrant unnecessary where there is probable cause to search an automobile stopped on the highway; the car is movable, the occupants are alerted, and the car's contents may never be found again if a warrant must be obtained. Hence an immediate search is constitutionally permissible.

Arguably, because of the preference for a magistrate's judgment, only the immobilization of the car should be permitted until a search warrant is obtained; arguably, only the 'lesser' intrusion is permissible until the magistrate authorizes the 'greater.' But which is the 'greater' and which the 'lesser' intrusion is itself a debatable question and the answer may depend on a variety *52 of circumstances. For constitutional purposes, we see no difference between on the one hand seizing and holding a car before presenting the probable cause issue to a magistrate and on the other hand carrying out an immediate search without a warrant. Given probable cause to search, either course is reasonable under the Fourth Amendment.

On the facts before us, the blue station wagon could have been searched on the spot when it was stopped since there was probable cause to search and it was a fleeting target for a search. The probable-cause factor still obtained at the station house and so did the mobility of the car unless the Fourth Amendment permits a warrantless seizure of the car and the denial of its use to anyone until a warrant is secured. In that event there is little to choose in terms of practical consequences between an immediate search without a warrant and the car's immobilization until a warrant is obtained. The same consequences **1982 may not follow where there is unforeseeable cause to search a house.[1699] But as *Carroll*, supra, held, for the purposes of the Fourth Amendment there is a constitutional difference between houses and cars.

III

Neither of petitioner's remaining contentions warrants reversal of the judgment of the Court of Appeals. One of them challenges the admissibility at trial of the .38-caliber ammunition seized in the course of a search of petitioner's house. The circumstances relevant to this *53 issue are somewhat confused, involving as they do questions of probable cause, a lost search warrant, and the Pennsylvania procedure for challenging the admissibility of evidence seized. Both the District Court and the Court of Appeals, however, after careful examination of the record, found that if there was error in admitting the ammunition, the error was harmless beyond a rea-

---

[1697] *Supra.*

[1698] *Supra.*

[1699] *Compare Vale v. Louisiana, ante, 399 U.S. 30, 90 S.Ct. 1969, 26 L.Ed.2d 409.*

sonable doubt. Having ourselves studied this record, we are not prepared to differ with the two courts below.[1700]

The final claim is that petitioner was not afforded the effective assistance of counsel. The facts pertinent to this claim are these: The Legal Aid Society of Allegheny County was appointed to represent petitioner prior to his first trial. A representative of the society conferred with petitioner, and a member of its staff, Mr. Middleman, appeared for petitioner at the first trial. There is no claim that petitioner was not then adequately represented by fully prepared counsel. The difficulty arises out of the second trial. Apparently no one from the Legal Aid Society again conferred with petitioner until a few minutes before the second trial began. The attorney who then appeared to represent petitioner was not Mr. Middleman but Mr. Tamburo, another Legal Aid Society attorney. No charge is made that Mr. Tamburo was incompetent or inexperienced; rather the claim is that his appearance for petitioner was so belated that he could not have furnished effective legal assistance at the second trial. Without granting an evidentiary hearing, the District Court rejected petitioner's claim. The Court of Appeals dealt with the matter in an extensive opinion. After carefully examining the state court record, which it had before it, the court found ample grounds for holding that the appearance of a different attorney at the second trial had not resulted in prejudice to petitioner. The claim that Mr. Tamburo ***54** was unprepared centered around his allegedly inadequate efforts to have the guns and ammunition excluded from evidence. But the Court of Appeals found harmless any error in the admission of the bullets and ruled that the guns and other materials seized from the car were admissible evidence. Hence the claim of prejudice from the substitution of counsel was without substantial basis. In this posture of the case we are not inclined to disturb the judgment of the Court of Appeals as to what the state record shows with respect to the adequacy of counsel. Unquestionably, the courts should make every effort to effect early appointments of counsel in all cases. But we are not disposed to fashion a per se rule requiring reversal of every ****1983** conviction following tardy appointment of counsel or to hold that, whenever a habeas corpus petition alleges a belated appointment, an evidentiary hearing must be held to determine whether the defendant has been denied his constitutional right to counsel. The Court of Appeals reached the right result in denying a hearing in this case.

Affirmed.

Mr. Justice BLACKMUN took no part in the consideration or decision of this case.

Mr. Justice STEWART, concurring.

I adhere to the view that the admission at trial of evidence acquired in alleged violation of Fourth Amendment ***55** standards is not of itself sufficient ground for a collateral attack upon an otherwise valid criminal conviction, state or federal.[1701] But until the Court adopts that view, I regard myself as obligated to consider the merits of the Fourth and Fourteenth Amendment claims in a case of this kind. Upon that premise I join the opinion and judgment of the Court.

Mr. Justice HARLAN, concurring in part and dissenting in part.

I find myself in disagreement with the Court's disposition of this case in two respects.

I

I cannot join the Court's casual treatment of the issue that has been presented by both parties as the major issue in this case: petitioner's claim that he received ineffective assistance of counsel at his trial. As the Court acknowledges, petitioner met Mr. Tamburo, his trial counsel, for the first time en route to the courtroom on the morning of trial. Although a different Legal Aid Society attorney had represented

---

[1700] *See Harrington v. California, 395 U.S. 250, 89 S.Ct. 1726, 23 L.Ed.2d 284 (1969).*

[1701] *See Harris v. Nelson, 394 U.S. 286, 307, 89 S.Ct. 1082, 1094-1095, 22 L.Ed.2d 281 (dissenting opinion); Kaufman v. United States, 394 U.S. 217, 242, 89 S.Ct. 1068, 1082, 22 L.Ed.2d 227 (dissenting opinion).*

petitioner at his first trial, apparently neither he nor anyone else from the society had conferred with petitioner in the interval between trials. Because the District Court did not hold an evidentiary hearing on the habeas petition, there is no indication in the record of the extent to which Mr. Tamburo may have consulted petitioner's previous attorney, the attorneys for the other defendants, or the files of the Legal Aid Society. What the record does disclose on this claim is essentially a combination of two factors: the entry of counsel into the case immediately ***56** before trial, and his handling of the issues that arose during the trial.

As respondent must concede, counsel's last-minute entry into the case precluded his compliance with the state rule requiring that motions to suppress evidence be made before trial, even assuming that he had sufficient acquaintance with the case to know what arguments were worth making. Furthermore, the record suggests that he may have had virtually no such acquaintance.

****1984** In the first place, he made no objection to the admission in evidence of the objects found during the search of the car at the station house after the arrest of its occupants, although that search was of questionable validity under Fourth Amendment standards, see infra.

Second, when the prosecution offered in evidence the bullets found in the search of petitioner's home, which had been excluded on defense objection at the first trial, Mr. Tamburo objected to their admission, but in a manner that suggested that he was a stranger to the facts of the case. While he indicated that he did know of the earlier exclusion, he apparently did not know on what ground the bullets had been excluded, and based his ***57** objection only on their asserted irrelevance. Later in the trial he renewed his objection on the basis of the inadequacy of the warrant, stating, 'I didn't know a thing about the search Warrant until this morning.'[1702]

Third, when prosecution witness Havicon made an in-court identification of petitioner as the man who had ***58** threatened him with a gun during one of the robberies, Mr. Tamburo asked questions in cross-examination that suggested that he had not had time to settle upon a trial strategy or even to consider whether petitioner would take the stand. Mr. Tamburo asked whether, at a pretrial lineup, a detective had not told Havicon that petitioner 'was the man with the gun.' After Havicon's negative answer, this colloquy ensued:

'THE COURT: I take it you will be able to disprove that, will you?

'MR. TAMBURO: What?

'THE COURT: You shouldn't ask that question unless you are prepared to disprove that, contradict him.

'MR. TAMBURO: I have the defendant's testimony.

'THE COUT: Disprove it in any way at all.

'MR. MEANS (the prosecutor): I don't understand how the defendant would know what the detectives told him.

'THE COURT: He said he is going to disprove it by the defendant, that's all right, go ahead.'[1703]

****1985** The next witness was a police officer who had been present at the lineup, and who testified that no one had told Havicon whom to pick out. Petitioner's counsel did not cross-examine, and petitioner never took the stand.

On this state of the record the Court of Appeals ruled that, although the late appointment of counsel necessitated close scrutiny into the effectiveness of his representation, petitioner 'was not prejudiced by the late appointment of counsel' because neither of the Fourth Amendment claims belatedly raised justified reversal of

---

[1702] *App. 130.*

[1703] *App. 34.*

***59** the conviction.[1704] I agree that the strength of the search-and-seizure claims is an element to be considered in the assessment of whether counsel was adequately prepared to make an effective defense, but I cannot agree that the relevance of those claims in this regard disappears upon a conclusion by an appellate court that they do not invalidate the conviction.

This Court recognized long ago that they duty to provide counsel 'is not discharged by an assignment at such a time or under such circumstances as to preclude the giving of effective aid in the preparation and trial of the case.'[1705] While 'the Constitution nowhere specifies any period which must intervene between the required appointment of counsel and trial,' the Court has recognized that 'the denial of opportunity for appointed counsel to confer, to consult with the accused and to prepare his defense, could convert the appointment of counsel into a sham and nothing more than a formal compliance with the Constitution's requirement that an accused be given the assistance of counsel.'[1706]

Where counsel has no acquaintance with the facts of the case and no opportunity to plan a defense, the result is that the defendant is effectively denied his constitutional right to assistance of counsel.

It seems to me that what this record reveals about counsel's handling of the search and seizure claims and about the tenor of his cross-examination of the government witness Havicon, when coupled with his late entry into the case, called for more exploration by the District Court before petitioner's ineffective assistance of counsel claim could be dismissed. Such an exploration should ***60** have been directed to ascertaining whether the circumstances under which Mr. Tamburo was required to undertake petitioner's defense at the second trial were such as to send him into the courtroom with so little knowledge of the case as to render him incapable of affording his client adequate representation. The event of that exploration would turn, not on a mere assessment of particular missteps or omissions of counsel, whether or not caused by negligence,[1707] but on the District Court's evaluation of the total picture, with the objective of determining whether petitioner was deprived of rudimentary legal assistance.[1708] And, of course, such an exploration would not be confined to the three episodes that, in my opinion, triggered the necessity for a hearing.

It is not an answer to petitioner's claim for a reviewing court simply to conclude that he has failed after the fact to show that, with adequate assistance, he would have prevailed at trial.[1709] Further inquiry might show, of course, that counsel's opportunity for preparation was adequate to protect petitioner's ****1986** interests, but petitioner did, in my view, raise a sufficient doubt on that score to be entitled to an evidentiary hearing.

***61 II**

In sustaining the search of the automobile I believe the Court ignores the framework of our past decisions circumscribing the scope of permissible search without a warrant. The Court has long read the Fourth Amendment's proscription of 'unreasonable' searches as imposing a general principle that a search without a warrant is not justified by the mere knowledge by the searching officers of facts showing probable cause. The 'general requirement that a search warrant be obtained' is basic

---

[1704] *408 F.2d 1186, 1196.*

[1705] *Powell v. Alabama, 287 U.S. 45, 71, 53 S.Ct. 55, 65, 77 L.Ed. 158 (1932); Hawk v. Olson, 326 U.S. 271, 278, 66 S.Ct. 116, 322, 90 L.Ed. 61 (1945).*

[1706] *Avery v. Alabama, 308 U.S. 444, 446, 60 S.Ct. 321, 322, 84 L.Ed. 377 (1940).*

[1707] *Cf. McMann v. Richardson, 397 U.S. 759, 90 S.Ct. 1441, 25 L.Ed.2d 763 (1970),*

[1708] *See Williams v. Beto, 354 F.2d 698 (C.A.5th Cir. 1965).*

[1709] *Glasser v. United States, 315 U.S. 60, 75-76, 62 S.Ct. 457, 467, 86 L.Ed. 680 (1942); cf. White v. Maryland, 373 U.S. 59, 83 S.Ct. 1050, 10 L.Ed.2d 193 (1963); Reynolds v. Cochran, 365 U.S. 525, 530-533, 81 S.Ct. 723, 726-727, 5 L.Ed.2d 754 (1961).*

to the Amendment's protection of privacy, and "the burden is on those seeking (an) exemption * * * to show the need for it."[1710]

Fidelity to this established principle requires that, where exceptions are made to accommodate the exigencies of particular situations, those exceptions be no broader than necessitated by the circumstances presented. For example, the Court has recognized that an arrest creates an emergency situation justifying a warrantless search of the arrestee's person and of 'the area from within which he might gain possession of a weapon or destructible evidence'; however, because the exigency giving rise to this exception extends only that far, the search may go no further.[1711] Similarly, we held in *Terry v. Ohio*[1712] that a warrantless search in a 'stop and frisk' situation must 'be strictly circumscribed ***62** by the exigencies which justify its initiation.'[1713] Any intrusion beyond what is necessary for the personal safety of the officer or others nearby is forbidden.

Where officers have probable cause to search a vehicle on a public way, a further limited exception to the warrant requirement is reasonable because 'the vehicle can be quickly moved out of the locality or jurisdiction in which the warrant must be sought.'[1714] Because the officers might be deprived of valuable evidence if required to obtain a warrant before effecting any search or seizure, I agree with the Court that they should be permitted to take the steps necessary to preserve evidence and to make a search possible.[1715] ****1987** The Court holds that those steps include making a warrantless search of the entire vehicle on the highway-a conclusion reached by the Court in *Carroll* without discussion and indeed appears to go further and to condone the removal of the car to the police station for a warrantless search at the convenience of the police. I cannot agree that this result is consistent ***63** with our insistence in other areas that departures from the warrant requirement strictly conform to the exigency presented.

The Court concedes that the police could prevent removal of the evidence by temporarily seizing the car for the time necessary to obtain a warrant. It does not dispute that such a course would fully protect the interests of effective law enforcement; rather it states that whether temporary seizure is a 'lesser' intrusion than warrantless search 'is itself a debatable question and the answer may depend on a variety of circumstances.'[1716] I believe it clear that a warrantless search involves the greater sacrifice of Fourth Amendment values.

The Fourth Amendment proscribes, to be sure, unreasonable 'seizures' as well as 'searches.' However, in the circumstances in which this problem is likely to occur, the lesser intrusion will almost always be the simple seizure of the car for the period-perhaps a day-necessary to enable the officers to obtain a search warrant. In the first place, as this case shows, the very facts establishing probable cause to search will often ***64** also justify arrest of the occupants of the vehicle. Since the occupants themselves are to be taken into custody, they will suffer minimal further inconvenience from the temporary immobilization of their vehicle. Even where no arrests are

---

[1710] *E.g., Chimel v. California, 395 U.S. 752, 762, 89 S.Ct. 2034, 2039 (1969); Katz v. United States, 389 U.S. 347, 356-358, 88 S.Ct. 507, 514-515, 19 L.Ed.2d 576 (1967); Warden v. Hayden, 387 U.S. 294, 299, 87 S.Ct. 1642, 1646, 18 L.Ed.2d 782 (1967); Preston v. United States, 376 U.S. 364, 367, 84 S.Ct. 881, 883, 11 L.Ed.2d 777 (1964); United States v. Jeffers, 342 U.S. 48, 51, 72 S.Ct. 93, 95, 96 L.Ed. 59 (1951); McDonald v. United States, 335 U.S. 451, 455-456, 69 S.Ct. 191, 193-194, 93 L.Ed. 153 (1948); Agnello v. United States, 269 U.S. 20, 33 46 S.Ct. 4, 6-7, 70 L.Ed. 145 (1925).*

[1711] *Chimel v. California, 395 U.S., at 763, 89 S.Ct. at 2040; Trupiano v. United States, 334 U.S. 699, 705, 708, 68 S.Ct. 1229, 1232-1234, 92 L.Ed. 1663 (1948).*

[1712] *392 U.S. 1, 88 S.Ct. 1868, 20 L.Ed.2d 889 (1968).*

[1713] *Id., at 26, 88 S.Ct. at 1882.*

[1714] *Carroll v. United States, 267 U.S. 132, 153, 45 S.Ct. 280, 285, 69 L.Ed. 543 (1925).*

[1715] *Cf. ALI, Model Code of Pre-Arraignment Procedure s 6.03 (Tent. Draft No. 3, 1970).*

[1716] *Ante, at 1981.*

made, persons who wish to avoid a search-either to protect their privacy or to conceal incriminating evidence-will almost certainly prefer a brief loss of the use of the vehicle in exchange for the opportunity to have a magistrate pass upon the justification for the search. To be sure, one can conceive of instances in which the occupant, ****1988** having nothing to hide and lacking concern for the privacy of the automobile, would be more deeply offended by a temporary immobilization of his vehicle than by a prompt search of it. However, such a person always remains free to consent to an immediate search, thus avoiding any delay. Where consent is not forthcoming, the occupants of the car have an interest in privacy that is protected by the Fourth Amendment even where the circumstances justify a temporary seizure.[1717] The Court's endorsement of a warrantless invasion of that privacy where another course would suffice is simply inconsistent with our repeated stress on the Fourth Amendment's mandate of "adherence to judicial processes."[1718]

Indeed, I believe this conclusion is implicit in the opinion of the unanimous Court in ***65** *Preston v. United States*.[1719] The Court there purported to decide whether a factual situation virtually identical to the one now before us was 'such as to fall within any of the exceptions to the constitutional rule that a search warrant must be had before a search may be made.'[1720] The Court concluded that no exception was available, stating that 'since the men were under arrest at the police station and the car was in police custody at a garage, (there was no) danger that the car would be moved out of the locality or jurisdiction.'[1721] The Court's reliance on the police custody of the car as its reason for holding 'that the search of the car without a warrant failed to meet the test of reasonableness under the Fourth Amendment'[1722] can only have been based on the premise that the more reasonable course was for the police to retain custody of the car for the short time necessary to obtain a warrant. The Court expressly did not rely, as suggested today, on the fact that an arrest for vagrancy provided 'no cause to believe that evidence of crime was concealed in the auto.'[1723] The Court now discards the approach taken in *Preston*, and creates a special rule for automobile searches that is seriously at odds with generally applied Fourth Amendment principles.

III

The Court accepts the conclusion of the two courts below that the introduction of the bullets found in petitioner's home, if error, was harmless. Although, as explained above, I do not agree that this destroys the relevance of the issue to the ineffectiveness of counsel claim, I agree that the record supports the lower courts' conclusion that this item of evidence, taken alone, was harmless beyond a reasonable doubt.

*****

[1717] *Terry v. Ohio, supra.*

[1718] *E.g., Katz v. United States, 389 U.S., at 357, 88 S.Ct., at 514.*

[1719] *376 U.S. 364, 84 S.Ct. 881 (1964).*

[1720] *Id., at 367, 84 S.Ct., at 883 (emphasis added).*

[1721] *Id., at 368, 84 S.Ct., at 884.*

[1722] *ibid.,*

[1723] *Ante, at 1979; see 376 U.S., at 368; Wood v. Crouse, 417 F.2d 394, 397-398 (C.A.10th Cir. 1969).*

Black Letter Law

> The Court held that where police, as result of talking to victim and teenage observers, had probable cause to believe that robbers, carrying guns and fruits of crime, had fled scene in light blue compact station wagon carrying four men, one wearing a green sweater and another wearing a trench coat, officers had probable cause to stop automobile and search it for guns and stolen money, and search of automobile at station house without warrant was not improper. Automobiles and other conveyances may be searched without a warrant in circumstances that would not justify search without warrant of house or office, provided that there is probable cause to believe that automobile contains articles that officers are entitled to seize.

United States v. Chadwick

97 S.Ct. 2476

Supreme Court of the United States

UNITED STATES, Petitioner,

v.

Joseph A. CHADWICK et al., Respondents.

No. 75-1721. | Argued April 26, 1977. | Decided June 21, 1977.

Mr. Chief Justice BURGER delivered the opinion of the Court.

We granted certiorari in this case to decide whether a search warrant is required before federal agents may open a locked footlocker which they have lawfully seized at the time of the arrest of its owners, when there is probable cause to believe the footlocker contains contraband.

(1)

On May 8, 1973, Amtrak railroad officials in San Diego observed respondents Gregory Machado and Bridget Leary load a brown footlocker onto a train bound for Boston. Their suspicions were aroused when they noticed that the trunk was unusually heavy for its size, and that it was leaking talcum power, a substance often used to mask the odor of marijuana or hashish. Because Machado matched a profile used to spot drug traffickers, the railroad officials reported these circumstances to federal agents in San Diego, who in turn relayed the information, together with detailed descriptions of Machado and the footlocker, to their counterparts in Boston.

When the train arrived in Boston two days later, federal narcotics agents were on hand. Though the officers had not obtained an arrest or search warrant, they had with them a police dog trained to detect marijuana. The agents identified Machado and Leary and kept them under surveillance as they claimed their suitcases and the footlocker, which had been ***4** transported by baggage cart from the train to the departure area. Machado and Leary lifted the footlocker from the baggage cart, placed it on the floor and sat down on it.

The agents then released the dog near the footlocker. Without alerting respondents, the dog signaled the presence of a controlled substance inside. Respondent Chadwick then joined Machado and Leary, and they engaged an attendant to move the footlocker outside to Chadwick's waiting automobile. Machado, Chadwick, and the attendant together lifted the 200-pound footlocker into the trunk of the car, while Leary waited in the front seat. At that ****2480** point, while the trunk of the car was still open and before the car engine had been started, the officers arrested all three. A search disclosed no weapons, but the keys to the footlocker were apparently taken from Machado.

Respondents were taken to the Federal Building in Boston; the agents followed with Chadwick's car and the footlocker. As the Government concedes, from the moment of respondents' arrests at about 9 p. m., the footlocker remained under the exclusive control of law enforcement officers at all times. The footlocker and luggage were placed in the Federal Building, where, as one of the agents later testified, "there was no risk that whatever was contained in the footlocker trunk would be removed by the defendants or their associates."[1724] The agents had no reason to believe that the footlocker contained explosives or other inherently dangerous items, or that it contained evidence which would lose its value unless the footlocker were opened at once. Facilities were readily available in which the footlocker could have been stored securely; it is not contended that there was any exigency calling for an immediate search.

At the Federal Building an hour and a half after the arrests, the agents opened the footlocker and luggage. They did not obtain respondents' consent; they did not secure a search warrant. The footlocker was locked with a padlock and a ***5** regular trunk lock. It is unclear whether it was opened with the keys taken from respondent Machado, or by other means. Large amounts of marijuana were found in the footlocker.

Respondents were indicted for possession of marijuana with intent to distribute it, in violation of 21 U.S.C. s 841(a)(1), and for conspiracy, in violation of 21 U.S.C. s 846. Before trial, they moved to suppress the marijuana obtained from the footlocker. In the District Court, the Government sought to justify its failure to secure a search warrant under the "automobile exception" of *Chambers v. Maroney*[1725] and as a search incident to the arrests. Holding that "warrantless searches are per se unreasonable, subject to a few carefully delineated and limited exceptions," the District Court rejected both justifications.[1726] The court saw the relationship between the footlocker and Chadwick's automobile as merely coincidental, and held that the double-locked, 200-pound footlocker was not part of "the area from within which (respondents) might gain possession of a weapon or destructible evidence."[1727]

A divided Court of Appeals for the First Circuit affirmed the suppression of the seized marijuana. The court held that the footlocker had been properly taken into federal custody after respondents' lawful arrest; it also agreed that the agents had probable cause to believe that the footlocker contained a controlled substance when they opened it. But probable cause alone was held not enough to sustain the warrantless search. ***6** On the premise that warrantless searches are per se unreasonable unless they fall within some established exception to the warrant requirement, the Court of Appeals agreed with the District Court that the footlocker search was not justified either under the "automobile exception" or as a search incident to a lawful arrest.

The Court of Appeals then responded to an argument, suggested by the Government for the first time on appeal, that movable personalty lawfully seized in a public place should be subject to search without a warrant ****2481** if there exists probable cause to believe it contains evidence of a crime. Conceding that such personalty shares some characteristics of mobility which support warrantless automobile searches, the court nevertheless concluded that a rule permitting a search of personalty on probable cause alone had not yet "received sufficient recognition by the Supreme Court outside the automobile area, or generally, for us to recognize it as a

---

[1724] *App. 44.*

[1725] *399 U.S. 42, 90 S.Ct. 1975, 26 L.Ed.2d 419 (1970),*

[1726] *393 F.Supp. 763, 771 (Mass.1975).*

[1727] *Chimel v. California, 395 U.S. 752, 763, 89 S.Ct. 2034, 2040, 23 L.Ed.2d 685 (1969).*

valid exception to the fourth amendment warrant requirement."[1728] We granted certiorari.[1729] We affirm.

(2)

In this Court the Government again contends that the Fourth Amendment Warrant Clause protects only interests traditionally identified with the home. Recalling the colonial writs of assistance, which were often executed in searches of private dwellings, the Government claims that the Warrant Clause was adopted primarily, if not exclusively, in response to unjustified intrusions into private homes on the authority of general warrants. The Government argues there is no evidence that the Framers of the Fourth Amendment intended ***7** to disturb the established practice of permitting warrantless searches outside the home, or to modify the initial clause of the Fourth Amendment by making warrantless searches supported by probable cause per se unreasonable.

Drawing on its reading of history, the Government argues that only homes, offices, and private communications implicate interests which lie at the core of the Fourth Amendment. Accordingly, it is only in these contexts that the determination whether a search or seizure is reasonable should turn on whether a warrant has been obtained. In all other situations, the Government contends, less significant privacy values are at stake, and the reasonableness of a government intrusion should depend solely on whether there is probable cause to believe evidence of criminal conduct is present. Where personal effects are lawfully seized outside the home on probable cause, the Government would thus regard searches without a warrant as not "unreasonable."

We do not agree that the Warrant Clause protects only dwellings and other specifically designated locales. As we have noted before, the Fourth Amendment "protects people, not places;"[1730] more particularly, it protects people from unreasonable government intrusions into their legitimate expectations of privacy. In this case, the Warrant Clause makes a significant contribution to that protection. The question, then, is whether a warrantless search in these circumstances was unreasonable.

(3)

It cannot be doubted that the Fourth Amendment's commands grew in large measure out of the colonists' experience ***8** with the writs of assistance and their memories of the general warrants formerly in use in England. These writs, which were issued on executive rather than judicial authority, granted sweeping power to customs officials and other agents of the King to search at large for smuggled goods. Though the authority to search granted by the writs was not limited to the home, searches conducted pursuant to them often were carried out in private residences.[1731]
****2482**

Although the searches and seizures which deeply concerned the colonists, and which were foremost in the minds of the Framers, were those involving invasions of the home, it would be a mistake to conclude, as the Government contends, that the Warrant Clause was therefore intended to guard only against intrusions into the home. First, the Warrant Clause does not in terms distinguish between searches conducted in private homes and other searches. There is also a strong historical connection between the Warrant Clause and the initial clause of the Fourth Amendment,

---

[1728] *532 F.2d 773, 781 (1976).*

[1729] *429 U.S. 814, 97 S.Ct. 54, 50 L.Ed.2d 74 (1976).*

[1730] *Katz v. United States, 389 U.S. 347, 351, 88 S.Ct. 507, 511, 19 L.Ed.2d 576 (1967).*

[1731] *See generally Stanford v. Texas, 379 U.S. 476, 481-485, 85 S.Ct. 506, 509-511, 13 L.Ed.2d 431 (1965); Marcus v. Search Warrant, 367 U.S. 717, 724-729, 81 S.Ct. 1708, 1712-1714, 6 L.Ed.2d 1127 (1961); Frank v. Maryland, 359 U.S. 360, 79 S.Ct. 804, 3 L.Ed.2d 877 (1959).*

which draws no distinctions among "persons, houses, papers, and effects" in safeguarding against unreasonable searches and seizures.[1732]

Moreover, if there is little evidence that the Framers intended the Warrant Clause to operate outside the home, there is no evidence at all that they intended to exclude from protection of the Clause all searches occurring outside the home. The absence of a contemporary outcry against warrantless searches in public places was because, aside from searches incident to arrest, such warrantless searches were not a large issue in colonial America. Thus, silence in the historical record tells us little about the Framers' attitude toward application of the Warrant Clause to the search of respondents' footlocker. ***9**

Moreover, in this area we do not write on a clean slate. Our fundamental inquiry in considering Fourth Amendment issues is whether or not a search or seizure is reasonable under all the circumstances.[1733] The judicial warrant has a significant role to play in that it provides the detached scrutiny of a neutral magistrate, which is a more reliable safeguard against improper searches than the hurried judgment of a law enforcement officer "engaged in the often competitive enterprise of ferreting out crime."[1734] Once a lawful search has begun, it is also far more likely that it will not exceed proper bounds when it is done pursuant to a judicial authorization "particularly describing the place to be searched and the persons or things to be seized." Further, a warrant assures the individual whose property is searched or seized of the lawful authority of the executing officer, his need to search, and the limits of his power to search.[1735]

Just as the Fourth Amendment "protects people, not places," the protections a judicial warrant offers against erroneous ***10** governmental intrusions are effective whether applied in or out of the home. Accordingly, we have held warrantless searches unreasonable, and therefore unconstitutional, in a variety of settings. A century ago, Mr. ****2483** Justice Field, speaking for the Court, included within the reach of the Warrant Clause printed matter traveling through the mails within the United States:

> "Letters and sealed packages of this kind in the mail are as fully guarded from examination and inspection, except as to their outward form and weight, as if they were retained by the parties forwarding them in their own domiciles. The constitutional guaranty of the right of the people to be secure in their papers against unreasonable searches and seizures extends to their papers, thus closed against inspection, wherever they may be. Whilst in the mail, they can only be opened and examined under like warrant, issued upon similar oath or affirmation, particularly describing the thing to be seized, as is required when papers are subjected to search in one's own household."[1736]

We reaffirmed *Jackson* in *United States v. Van Leeuwen*,[1737] where a search warrant was obtained to open two packages which, on mailing, the sender had declared contained only coins. Judicial warrants have been required for other searches conducted

---

[1732] *See United States v. Rabinowitz, 339 U.S. 56, 68, 70 S.Ct. 430, 445, 94 L.Ed. 653 (1950) (Frankfurter, J., dissenting).*

[1733] *Cooper v. California, 386 U.S. 58, 87 S.Ct. 788, 17 L.Ed.2d 730 (1967).*

[1734] *Johnson v. United States, 333 U.S. 10, 14, 68 S.Ct. 367, 369, 92 L.Ed. 436 (1948).*

[1735] *Camara v. Municipal Court, 387 U.S. 523, 532, 87 S.Ct. 1727, 1732, 18 L.Ed.2d 930 (1967).*

[1736] *Ex parte Jackson, 96 U.S. 727, 733, 24 L.Ed. 877 (1878).*

[1737] *397 U.S. 249, 90 S.Ct. 1029, 25 L.Ed.2d 282 (1970).*

outside the home.[1738] These cases illustrate the applicability of the Warrant Clause beyond the narrow limits suggested by the Government. They also reflect the settled constitutional principle, discussed earlier, that a fundamental purpose of the Fourth Amendment is to safeguard individuals from unreasonable government invasions of legitimate privacy interests,6 and not simply those interests found inside the four walls of the home.[1739]

In this case, important Fourth Amendment privacy interests were at stake. By placing personal effects inside a double-locked footlocker, respondents manifested an expectation that the contents would remain free from public examination. No less than one who locks the doors of his home against intruders, one who safeguards his personal possessions in this manner is due the protection of the Fourth Amendment Warrant Clause. There being no exigency, it was unreasonable for the Government to conduct this search without the safeguards a judicial warrant provides.

(4)

The Government does not contend that the footlocker's brief contact with Chadwick's car makes this an automobile search, ****2484** but it is argued that the rationale of our automobile ***12** search cases demonstrates the reasonableness of permitting warrantless searches of luggage; the Government views such luggage as analogous to motor vehicles for Fourth Amendment purposes. It is true that, like the footlocker in issue here, automobiles are "effects" under the Fourth Amendment, and searches and seizures of automobiles are therefore subject to the constitutional standard of reasonableness. But this Court has recognized significant differences between motor vehicles and other property which permit warrantless searches of automobiles in circumstances in which warrantless searches would not be reasonable in other contexts.[1740]

Our treatment of automobiles has been based in part on their inherent mobility, which often makes obtaining a judicial warrant impracticable. Nevertheless, we have also sustained "warrantless searches of vehicles . . . in cases in which the possibilities of the vehicle's being removed or evidence in it destroyed were remote, if not nonexistent."[1741]

The answer lies in the diminished expectation of privacy which surrounds the automobile:

"One has a lesser expectation of privacy in a motor vehicle because its function is transportation and it seldom serves as one's residence or as the repository of personal effects . . . It travels public thoroughfares where both its occupants and its contents are in plain view."[1742]

Other factors reduce automobile privacy. "All States require ***13** vehicles to be registered and operators to be licensed. States and localities have enacted extensive and detailed codes regulating the condition and manner in which motor vehicles may

---

[1738] E. g., Katz v. United States, 389 U.S. 347, 88 S.Ct. 507, 19 L.Ed.2d 576 (1967) (electronic interception of conversation in public telephone booth); Coolidge v. New Hampshire, 403 U.S. 443, 91 S.Ct. 2022, 29 L.Ed.2d 564 (1971) (automobile on private ****11*** *premises); Preston v. United States, 376 U.S. 364, 84 S.Ct. 881, 11 L.Ed.2d 777 (1964) (automobile in custody); United States v. Jeffers, 342 U.S. 48, 72 S.Ct. 93, 96 L.Ed. 59 (1951) (hotel room); G. M. Leasing Corp. v. United States, 429 U.S. 338, 97 S.Ct. 619, 50 L.Ed.2d 530 (1977) (office); Mancusi v. DeForte, 392 U.S. 364, 88 S.Ct. 2120, 20 L.Ed.2d 1154 (1968) (office).*

[1739] Wolf v. Colorado, 338 U.S. 25, 27, 69 S.Ct. 1359, 1361, 93 L.Ed. 1782 (1949).

[1740] Carroll v. United States, 267 U.S. 132, 45 S.Ct. 280, 69 L.Ed. 543 (1925); Preston v. United States, supra, 376 U.S., at 366-367, 84 S.Ct., at 882-883; Chambers v. Maroney, 399 U.S. 42, 90 S.Ct. 1975, 26 L.Ed.2d 419 (1970). See also South Dakota v. Opperman, 428 U.S. 364, 367, 96 S.Ct. 3092, 3095, 49 L.Ed.2d 1000 (1976).

[1741] Cady v. Dombrowski, 413 U.S. 433, 441-442, 93 S.Ct. 2523, 2528, 37 L.Ed.2d 706 (1973); accord, South Dakota v. Opperman, supra, 428 U.S., at 367, 96 S.Ct., at 3095; see Texas v. White, 423 U.S. 67, 96 S.Ct. 304, 46 L.Ed.2d 209 (1975); Chambers v. Maroney, supra ; Cooper v. California, 386 U.S. 58, 87 S.Ct. 788, 17 L.Ed.2d 730 (1967).

[1742] Cardwell v. Lewis, 417 U.S. 583, 590, 94 S.Ct. 2464, 2469, 41 L.Ed.2d 325 (1974) (plurality opinion).

be operated on public streets and highways."[1743] Automobiles periodically undergo official inspection, and they are often taken into police custody in the interests of public safety.[1744]

The factors which diminish the privacy aspects of an automobile do not apply to respondents' footlocker. Luggage contents are not open to public view, except as a condition to a border entry or common carrier travel; nor is luggage subject to regular inspections and official scrutiny on a continuing basis. Unlike an automobile, whose primary function is transportation, luggage is intended as a repository of personal effects. In sum, a person's expectations of privacy in personal luggage are substantially greater than in an automobile.

Nor does the footlocker's mobility justify dispensing with the added protections of the Warrant Clause. Once the federal agents had seized it at the railroad station and had safely transferred it to the Boston Federal Building under their exclusive control, there was not the slightest danger that the footlocker or its contents could have been removed before a valid search warrant could be obtained. The ****2485** initial seizure and detention of the footlocker, the validity of which respondents do not contest, were sufficient to guard against any risk that evidence might be lost. With the footlocker safely immobilized, it was unreasonable to undertake the additional and greater intrusion of a search without a warrant.

***14** Finally, the Government urges that the Constitution permits the warrantless search of any property in the possession of a person arrested in public, so long as there is probable cause to believe that the property contains contraband or evidence of crime. Although recognizing that the footlocker was not within respondents' immediate control, the Government insists that the search was reasonable because the footlocker was seized contemporaneously with respondents' arrests and was searched as soon thereafter as was practicable. The reasons justifying search in a custodial arrest are quite different. When a custodial arrest is made, there is always some danger that the person arrested may seek to use a weapon , or that evidence may be concealed or destroyed. To safeguard himself and others, and to prevent the loss of evidence, it has been held reasonable for the arresting officer to conduct a prompt, warrantless "search of the arrestee's person and the area 'within his immediate control' construing that phrase to mean the area from within which he might gain possession of a weapon or destructible evidence."[1745]

Such searches may be conducted without a warrant, and they may also be made whether or not there is probable cause to believe that the person arrested may have a weapon or is about to destroy evidence. The potential dangers lurking in ***15** all custodial arrests make warrantless searches of items within the "immediate control" area reasonable without requiring the arresting officer to calculate the probability that weapons or destructible evidence may be involved.[1746] However, warrantless searches of luggage or other property seized at the time of an arrest cannot be justified as incident to that arrest either if the "search is remote in time or place from the arrest"[1747] or no exigency exists. Once law enforcement officers have reduced luggage or other personal property not immediately associated with the person of the arrestee to their exclusive control, and there is no longer any danger that the arrestee might gain access to the property to seize a weapon or destroy evidence, a search of that property is no longer an incident of the arrest.

[1743] *Cady v. Dombrowski, supra, 413 U.S., at 441, 93 S.Ct., at 2528.*

[1744] *South Dakota v. Opperman, supra, 428 U.S., at 368, 96 S.Ct., at 3096.*

[1745] *Chimel v. California, 395 U.S., at 763, 89 S.Ct., at 2040. See also Terry v. Ohio, 392 U.S. 1, 88 S.Ct. 1868, 20 L.Ed.2d 889 (1968).*

[1746] *United States v. Robinson, 414 U.S. 218, 94 S.Ct. 467, 38 L.Ed.2d 427 (1973); Terry v. Ohio, supra.*

[1747] *Preston v. United States, 376 U.S., at 367, 84 S.Ct., at 883.*

Here the search was conducted more than an hour after federal agents had gained exclusive control of the footlocker and long after respondents were securely in **2486 custody; the search therefore cannot be viewed as incidental to the arrest or as justified by any other exigency. Even though on this record the issuance of a warrant by a judicial officer was reasonably predictable, a line must be drawn. In our view, when no exigency is shown to support the need for an immediate search, the Warrant Clause places the line at the point where the property to be searched comes under the exclusive dominion of police authority. Respondents were therefore entitled to the protection of the Warrant Clause with the *16 evaluation of a neutral magistrate, before their privacy interests in the contents of the footlocker were invaded.

Accordingly, the judgment is affirmed.

Mr. Justice BRENNAN, concurring.

I fully join the Chief Justice's thorough opinion for the Court. I write only to comment upon two points made by my Brother Blackmun's dissent.

First, I agree wholeheartedly with my Brother Blackmun that it is "unfortunate" that the Government in this case "sought . . . to vindicate an extreme view of the Fourth Amendment."[1748] It is unfortunate, in my view, not because this argument somehow "distract(ed)" the Court from other more meritorious arguments made by the Government these arguments are addressed and convincingly rejected in the Court's opinion but because it is deeply distressing that the Department of Justice, whose mission is to protect the constitutional liberties of the people of the United States, should even appear to be seeking to subvert them by extreme and dubious legal arguments. It is gratifying that the Court today unanimously rejects the Government's position.

Second, it should be noted that while Part II of the dissent suggests a number of possible alternative courses of action that the agents could have followed without violating the Constitution, no decision of this Court is cited to support the constitutionality of these courses, but only some decisions of Courts of Appeals.[1749] In my view, it is not at all obvious that the agents could *17 legally have searched the footlocker had they seized it after Machado and Leary had driven away with it in their car1 or "at the time and place of the arrests."

Mr. Justice BLACKMUN, with whom Mr. Justice REHNQUIST joins, dissenting.

I think it somewhat unfortunate that the Government sought a reversal in this case primarily to vindicate an extreme view of the Fourth Amendment that would restrict the protection of the Warrant Clause to private dwellings and a few other "high privacy" areas. I reject this argument for **2487 the reasons stated in Parts (2) and (3) of the Court's opinion, with which I am in general agreement. The overbroad nature of the Government's principal argument, however, has served to distract the Court from the more important task of defining the proper scope of a search incident to an arrest. The Court fails to accept the opportunity this case presents to apply the rationale of recent decisions and develop a clear doctrine concerning the proper consequences *18 of custodial arrest. Accordingly, I dissent from the judgment.

I

One line of recent decisions establishes that no warrant is required for the arresting officer to search the clothing and effects of one placed in custodial arrest. The rationale for this was explained in *United States v. Robinson*:[1750]

> "A police officer's determination as to how and where to search the person of a suspect whom he has arrested is necessarily a quick ad hoc judgment which the Fourth Amendment does not require to be broken down in each instance into an

---

[1748] *Post, at 2486.*

[1749] *Post, at 2489-2490 nn. 4 and 5.*

[1750] *414 U.S. 218, 94 S.Ct. 467, 38 L.Ed.2d 427 (1973).*

analysis of each step in the search. The authority to search the person incident to a lawful custodial arrest, while based upon the need to disarm and to discover evidence, does not depend on what a court may later decide was the probability in a particular arrest situation that weapons or evidence would in fact be found upon the person of the suspect. A custodial arrest of a suspect based on probable cause is a reasonable intrusion under the Fourth Amendment; that intrusion being lawful, a search incident to the arrest requires no additional justification. It is the fact of the lawful arrest which establishes the authority to search, and we hold that in the case of a lawful custodial arrest a full search of the person is not only an exception to the warrant requirement of the Fourth Amendment, but is also a 'reasonable' search under that Amendment."[1751]

Under this doctrine, a search of personal effects need not be contemporaneous with the arrest, and indeed may be delayed a number of hours while the suspect remains in lawful custody.[1752]

A second series of decisions concerns the consequences of custodial arrest of a person driving an automobile. The car ***19** may be impounded and, with probable cause, its contents (including locked compartments) subsequently examined without a warrant.[1753] Moreover, once a car has been properly impounded for any reason, the police may follow a standard procedure of inventorying its contents without any showing of probable cause.[1754]

I would apply the rationale of these two lines of authority and hold generally that a warrant is not required to seize and search any movable property in the possession of a person properly arrested in a public place. A person arrested in a public place is likely to have various kinds of property with him: items inside his clothing, a briefcase or suitcase, packages, or a vehicle. In such instances the police cannot very well leave the property on the sidewalk or street while they go to get a warrant. The items may be stolen by a passer-by or removed by the suspect's confederates. Rather than requiring the police to "post a guard" over such property, I think it is surely reasonable for the police to take the items along to the station with the arrested person.

In the present case the Court of Appeals held, and respondents do not contest, that it was proper for the federal agents to seize the footlocker and take it to their office. Given the propriety of seizing the footlocker, ****2488** there is some reason to believe that the subsequent search a fortiori was permissible.[1755] I acknowledge, however, that impounding the footlocker without searching it would have been a less intrusive alternative in this case. The police could have waited to conduct their search until after a warrant had been obtained. Nevertheless, the mere fact that a warrant could have been obtained while the footlocker was safely impounded does not necessarily make the warrantless search unreasonable.[1756] ***20**

As the Court in Robinson recognized, custodial arrest is such a serious deprivation that various lesser invasions of privacy may be fairly regarded as incidental. An arrested person, of course, has an additional privacy interest in the objects in his possession at the time of arrest. To be sure, allowing impoundment of those objects pursuant to arrest, but requiring a warrant for examination of their contents, would protect that incremental privacy interest in cases where the police assessment of

---

[1751] *Id., at 235, 94 S.Ct., at 477. Accord, Gustafson v. Florida, 414 U.S. 260, 94 S.Ct. 488, 38 L.Ed.2d 456 (1973).*

[1752] *United States v. Edwards, 415 U.S. 800, 94 S.Ct. 1234, 39 L.Ed.2d 771 (1974).*

[1753] *Texas v. White, 423 U.S. 67, 96 S.Ct. 304, 46 L.Ed.2d 209 (1975); Cady v. Dombrowski, 413 U.S. 433, 439-448, 93 S.Ct. 2523, 2527-2531, 37 L.Ed.2d 706 (1973); Chambers v. Maroney, 399 U.S. 42, 47-52, 90 S.Ct. 1975, 1979-1981, 26 L.Ed.2d 419 (1970).*

[1754] *South Dakota v. Opperman, 428 U.S. 364, 96 S.Ct. 3092, 49 L.Ed.2d 1000 (1976).*

[1755] *See Chambers v. Maroney, 399 U.S., at 51-52, 90 S.Ct., at 1981.*

[1756] *See, e. g., United States v. Edwards, 415 U.S., at 805, 94 S.Ct., at 1238; Cardwell v. Lewis, 417 U.S. 583, 595-596, 94 S.Ct. 2464, 2471-2472, 41 L.Ed.2d 325 (1974) (plurality opinion).*

probable cause is subsequently rejected by a magistrate. But a countervailing consideration is that a warrant would be routinely forthcoming in the vast majority of situations where the property has been seized in conjunction with the valid arrest of a person in a public place. I therefore doubt that requiring the authorities to go through the formality of obtaining a warrant in this situation would have much practical effect in protecting Fourth Amendment values.

I believe this sort of practical evaluation underlies the Court's decision permitting clothing, personal effects, and automobiles to be searched without a warrant as an incident of arrest, even though it would be possible simply to impound these items until a warrant could be obtained. The Court's opinion does not explain why a wallet carried in the arrested person's clothing, but not the footlocker in the present case, is subject to "reduced expectations of privacy caused by ***21** the arrest."[1757] Nor does the Court explain how such items as purses or briefcases fit into the dichotomy. Perhaps the holding in the present case will be limited in the future to objects that are relatively immobile by virtue of their size or absence of a means of propulsion.

It is also possible that today's decision will not have much impact because other doctrines often will be available to sustain warrantless searches of objects in police custody. As the Court acknowledges,[1758] no warrant is necessary when the authorities suspect the object they have impounded has dangerous contents. Moreover, police may establish a routine procedure of inventorying the contents of any container taken into custody, for reasons of security and property conservation.[1759] ****2489** Law enforcement officers should not be precluded from conducting an inventory search when they take a potential "Trojan horse" into their office. Finally, exigent circumstances may often justify an immediate search of property seized in conjunction with an arrest, in order to facilitate the apprehension of confederates or the termination of continuing criminal activity.[1760]

Since one of the preceding special circumstances is likely to be available in most instances, and since the suspect's expectations of privacy are properly abated by the fact of arrest itself, it would be better, in my view, to adopt a clearcut rule permitting property seized in conjunction with a valid arrest in a public place to be searched without a warrant. ***22** Such an approach would simplify the constitutional law of criminal procedure without seriously derogating from the values protected by the Fourth Amendment's prohibition of unreasonable searches and seizures.

II

The approach taken by the Court has the perverse result of allowing fortuitous circumstances to control the outcome of the present case. The agents probably could have avoided having the footlocker search held unconstitutional either by delaying the arrest for a few minutes or by conducting the search on the spot rather than back at their office. Probable cause for the arrest was present from the time respondents Machado and Leary were seated on the footlocker inside Boston's South Station and the agents' dog signaled the presence of marijuana. Rather than make an arrest at this moment, the agents commendably sought to determine the possible involvement of others in the illegal scheme. They waited a short time until respondent Chadwick arrived and the footlocker had been loaded into the trunk of his car, and then made the arrest. But if the agents had postponed the arrest just a few minutes longer until the respondents started to drive away, then the car could have been ***23** seized, taken to the agents' office, and all its contents including the footlocker searched without a warrant.

[1757] *Ante, at 2486 n. 10.*

[1758] *Ante, at 2485 n. 9.*

[1759] *Cf. South Dakota v. Opperman, 428 U.S. 364, 96 S.Ct. 3092, 49 L.Ed.2d 1000 (1976).*

[1760] *Cf. Warden v. Hayden, 387 U.S. 294, 298-300, 87 S.Ct. 1642, 1645-1646, 18 L.Ed.2d 782 (1967).*

Alternatively, the agents could have made a search of the footlocker at the time and place of the arrests. Machado and Leary were standing next to an open automobile trunk containing the footlocker, and thus it was within the area of their "immediate control." And certainly the footlocker would have been properly subject to search at the time if the arrest had occurred ****2490** a few minutes earlier while Machado and Leary were seated on it.

***24** In many cases, of course, small variations in the facts are determinative of the legal outcome. Criminal law necessarily involves some line drawing. But I see no way that these alternative courses of conduct, which likely would have been held constitutional under the Fourth Amendment, would have been any more solicitous of the privacy or well-being of the respondents. Indeed, as Judge Thomsen observed in dissenting from this aspect of the Court of Appeals' decision that is today affirmed, the course of conduct followed by the agents in this case was good police procedure. It is decisions of the kind made by the Court today that make criminal law a trap for the unwary policeman and detract from the important activities of detecting criminal activity and protecting the public safety.

Black Letter Law

> The Court held that: (1) the warrant requirement of the Fourth Amendment is not limited in its protection only to dwellings and other specifically designated locales; (2) by placing personal effects inside a double-locked footlocker, defendants manifested an expectation that the contents would remain free from public examination, and there being no exigency, it was unreasonable for Government to conduct search of footlocker without the safeguards that a judicial warrant provides, even where agents lawfully seized the footlocker at the time of the arrest of its owners and there was probable cause to believe that it contained contraband; (3) footlocker's mobility did not justify dispensing with the warrant requirement, as the footlocker was not analogous to an automobile, and (4) warrantless search of luggage or other property seized at the time of an arrest cannot be justified as incident to that arrest either if the search is remote in time or place from the arrest or if no exigency exists.Abrogated by California v. Acevedo, 500 U.S. 565, 111 S. Ct. 1982, 114 L. Ed. 2d 619 (1991)

Texas v. White

96 S.Ct. 304

Supreme Court of the United States

State of TEXAS

v.

Earl Elmer WHITE

No. 75-124. | Dec. 1, 1975. | Rehearing Denied Jan. 19, 1976. See 423 U.S. 1081, 96 S.Ct. 869.

***67 **305** PER CURIAM.

Respondent was arrested at 1:30 p. m. by Amarillo, Tex., police officers while attempting to pass fraudulent checks at a drive-in window of the First National Bank of Amarillo. Only 10 minutes earlier, the officers had been informed by another bank that a man answering respondent's description and driving an automobile exactly matching that of respondent had tried to negotiate four checks drawn on a nonexistent account. Upon arrival at the First National Bank pursuant to a telephone call from that bank, the officers obtained from the drive-in teller other checks that respondent had attempted to pass there. The officers directed respondent to park his automobile at the curb. While parking the car, respondent was observed by a bank employee and one of the officers attempting to "stuff" something between the seats. Respondent was arrested and one officer drove him to the station house while the other drove respondent's car there. At the station house, the ***68** officers questioned respondent for 30 to 45 minutes and, pursuant to their normal procedure, requested consent to search the automobile. Respondent refused to consent to the search. The officers then proceeded to search the automobile anyway. During the search, an officer discovered four wrinkled checks that corresponded to those respondent had attempted to pass at the first bank. The trial judge, relying on *Chambers v. Maroney*,[1761] admitted over respondent's objection the four checks seized during the search of respondent's automobile at the station house. The judge expressly found probable cause both for the arrest and for the search of the vehicle, either at the scene or at the station house. Respondent was convicted after a jury trial of knowingly attempting to pass a forged instrument. The Texas Court of Criminal Appeals, in a 3-2 decision, reversed respondent's conviction on the ground that the four wrinkled checks used in evidence were obtained without a warrant in violation of respondent's Fourth Amendment rights.[1762] We reverse.

In *Chambers v. Maroney* we held that police officers with probable cause to search an automobile at the scene where it was stopped could constitutionally do so later at the station house without first obtaining a warrant. There, as here, "(t)he probable-cause factor" that developed at the scene "still obtained at the station house."[1763] The Court of Criminal Appeals erroneously excluded the evidence seized from the search at the station house in light of the trial judge's finding, undisturbed by the appellate court, that there was probable cause to search respondent's car.

The petition for certiorari and the motion of respondent to proceed in forma pauperis are granted, the judgment of the Court of Criminal Appeals is reversed, and ***69** the case is remanded to that court for further proceedings not inconsistent with this opinion.

It is so ordered. Reversed and remanded.

Mr. Justice MARSHALL, with whom Mr. Justice BRENNAN concurs, dissenting.

Only by misstating the holding of *Chambers v. Maroney*[1764] can the Court make that case appear dispositive of this one. The Court in its brief per curiam opinion today extends Chambers to a clearly distinguishable factual setting, without having afforded the opportunity for full briefing and oral argument. I respectfully dissent.

Chambers did not hold, as the Court suggests, that "police officers with probable cause to search an automobile at the scene where it was stopped could constitutionally ****306** do so later at the station house without first obtaining a warrant." Ante, this page. Chambers simply held that to be the rule when it is reasonable to take the car to the station house in the first place.

In *Chambers* the Court took as its departure point this Court's holding in *Carroll v. United States*:[1765]

"Carroll . . . holds a search warrant unnecessary where there is probable cause to search an automobile stopped on the highway; the car is movable, the occupants are

---

[1761] 399 U.S. 42, 90 S.Ct. 1975, 26 L.Ed.2d 419 (1970).

[1762] 521 S.W.2d 255 (1975).

[1763] 399 U.S., at 52, 90 S.Ct., at 1981.

[1764] 399 U.S. 42, 90 S.Ct. 1975, 26 L.Ed.2d 419 (1970).

[1765] 267 U.S. 132, 45 S.Ct. 280, 69 L.Ed. 543 (1925).

alerted, and the car's contents may never be found again if a warrant must be obtained. Hence an immediate search is constitutionally permissible."[1766]

Carroll, however, did not dispose of *Chambers*, for in *Chambers*, as in this case, the police did not conduct an "immediate search," but rather seized the car and took it to the station house before searching it. The Court in Chambers went on to hold that once the car was ***70** legitimately at the station house a prompt search could be conducted. But in recognition of the need to justify the seizure and removal of the car to the station house, the Court added:

"It was not unreasonable in this case to take the car to the station house. All occupants in the car were arrested in a dark parking lot in the middle of the night. A careful search at that point was impractical and perhaps not safe for the officers, and it would serve the owner's convenience and the safety of his car to have the vehicle and the keys together at the station house."[1767]

In this case, the arrest took place at 1:30 in the afternoon, and there is no indication that an immediate search would have been either impractical or unsafe for the arresting officers. It may be, of course, that respondent preferred to have his car brought to the station house, but if his convenience was the concern of the police they should have consulted with him. Surely a seizure cannot be justified on the sole ground that a citizen might have consented to it as a matter of convenience. Since, then, there was no apparent justification for the warrantless removal of respondent's car, it is clear that this is a different case from Chambers.

It might be argued that the taking of respondent's car to the police station was neither more of a seizure, nor in practical terms more of an intrusion, than would have been involved in an immediate at-the-scene search, which was clearly permissible. Such a contention may well be substantial enough to warrant full briefing and argument, but it is not so clearly meritorious as to warrant adoption in the summary fashion in which the Court proceeds. Indeed, a reading of Chambers itself suggests that this contention is without merit.

***71** In Chambers the Court considered and rejected the argument that Carroll was wrong in permitting a warrantless search of an automobile that the immobilization of a car until a search warrant is obtained is a "lesser" intrusion and should therefore be the outer bounds of what is permitted. The Court noted that "which is the 'greater' and which the 'lesser' intrusion is itself a debatable question,"[1768] and concluded:

"For constitutional purposes, we see no difference between on the one hand seizing and holding a car before presenting the probable cause issue to a magistrate and on the other hand carrying out an immediate search without a warrant."[1769]

In the Court's view, then, the intrusion involved in initially seizing a car on the highway and holding it for the short time required to seek a warrant is so substantial as to be constitutionally indistinguishable from the intrusion involved in a search of ****307** the vehicle. But the Court did not stop with that observation. It went on to note that once a car is legitimately brought to the station house, the additional intrusion involved in simply immobilizing the car until a warrant can be sought is no less significant than that involved in a station house search: "(T)here is little to choose in terms of practical consequences between an immediate search without a warrant and the car's immobilization until a warrant is obtained."[1770] It was because such tempo-

---

[1766] *399 U.S., at 51, 90 S.Ct., at 1981.*

[1767] *Id., at 52 n. 10, 90 S.Ct., at 1981.*

[1768] *399 U.S., at 51, 90 S.Ct., at 1981.*

[1769] *Id., at 52, 90 S.Ct., at 1981.*

[1770] *Ibid.*

rary seizures were deemed no less intrusive than searches themselves that Chambers approved searches when temporary seizures would have been justified.

In short, the basic premise of Chambers' conclusion that seizures pending the seeking of a warrant are not constitutionally preferred to warrantless ***72** searches was that temporary seizures are themselves intrusive. That same premise suggests that the seizure and removal of respondent's car in this case were quite apart from the subsequent search, an intrusion of constitutional dimension that must be independently justified. The seizure and removal here were not for the purpose of immobilizing the car until a warrant could be secured, nor were they for the purpose of facilitating a safe and thorough search of the car. In the absence of any other justification, I would hold the seizure of petitioner's car unlawful and exclude the evidence seized in the subsequent search.

I would have denied the petition for certiorari, but now that the writ has been granted I would affirm the judgment of the Court of Criminal Appeals, or at least set the case for oral argument. In any event, it should be clear to the court below that nothing this Court does today precludes it from reaching the result it did under applicable state law.[1771]

Black Letter Law

> Held that where police had probable cause to search automobile of defendant at scene where he was arrested, after which one officer drove defendant to the station while the other officer drove defendant's automobile there, officer had authority, after questioning of defendant, to search automobile without a warrant and over objection of defendant, since probable cause factor that developed on the scene was still present at the station house.

California v. Carney

105 S.Ct. 2066

Supreme Court of the United States

CALIFORNIA, Petitioner

v.

Charles R. CARNEY.

No. 83-859. | Argued Oct. 30, 1984. | Decided May 13, 1985.

Chief Justice BURGER delivered the opinion of the Court.

We granted certiorari to decide whether law enforcement agents violated the Fourth Amendment when they conducted a warrantless search, based on probable cause, of a fully mobile "motor home" located in a public place.

I

On May 31, 1979, Drug Enforcement Agency Agent Robert Williams watched respondent, Charles Carney, approach ***388** a youth in downtown San Diego. The youth accompanied Carney to a Dodge Mini Motor Home parked in a nearby lot. Carney and the youth closed the window shades in the motor home, including one across the front window. Agent Williams had previously received uncorroborated information that the same motor home was used by another person who was exchanging marijuana for sex. Williams, with assistance from other agents, kept the

[1771] *See Oregon v. Hass, 420 U.S. 714, 726, 95 S.Ct. 1215, 1222, 43 L.Ed.2d 570 (1975) (Marshall, J., dissenting).*

motor home under surveillance for the entire one and one-quarter hours that Carney and the youth remained inside. When the youth left the motor home, the agents followed and stopped him. The youth told the agents that he had received marijuana in return for allowing Carney sexual contacts.

At the agents' request, the youth returned to the motor home and knocked on its door; Carney stepped out. The agents identified themselves as law enforcement officers. Without a warrant or consent, one agent entered the motor home and observed marijuana, plastic bags, and a scale of the kind used in weighing drugs on a table. Agent Williams took Carney into custody and took possession of the motor home. A subsequent search of the motor home at the police station revealed additional marijuana in the cupboards and refrigerator.

Respondent was charged with possession of marijuana for sale. At a preliminary hearing, he moved to suppress the evidence ****2068** discovered in the motor home. The Magistrate denied the motion, upholding the initial search as a justifiable search for other persons, and the subsequent search as a routine inventory search.

Respondent renewed his suppression motion in the Superior Court. The Superior Court also rejected the claim, holding that there was probable cause to arrest respondent, that the search of the motor home was authorized under the automobile exception to the Fourth Amendment's warrant requirement, and that the motor home itself could be seized without a warrant as an instrumentality of the crime. Respondent ***389** then pleaded nolo contendere to the charges against him, and was placed on probation for three years.

Respondent appealed from the order placing him on probation. The California Court of Appeal affirmed, reasoning that the vehicle exception applied to respondent's motor home.[1772]

The California Supreme Court reversed the conviction.[1773] The Supreme Court did not disagree with the conclusion of the trial court that the agents had probable cause to arrest respondent and to believe that the vehicle contained evidence of a crime; however, the court held that the search was unreasonable because no warrant was obtained, rejecting the State's argument that the vehicle exception to the warrant requirement should apply. That court reached its decision by concluding that the mobility of a vehicle "is no longer the prime justification for the automobile exception; rather, 'the answer lies in the diminished expectation of privacy which surrounds the automobile.'"[1774] The California Supreme Court held that the expectations of privacy in a motor home are more like those in a dwelling than in an automobile because the primary function of motor homes is not to provide transportation but to "provide the occupant with living quarters."[1775]

We granted certiorari.[1776] We reverse.

***390 II**

The Fourth Amendment protects the "right of the people to be secure in their persons, houses, papers, and effects, against unreasonable searches and seizures." This fundamental right is preserved by a requirement that searches be conducted pursuant to a warrant issued by an independent judicial officer. There are, of course, exceptions to the general rule that a warrant must be secured before a search is undertaken; one is the so-called "automobile exception" at issue in this case. This exception to the warrant requirement was first set forth by the Court 60 years ago in

---

[1772] *117 Cal.App.3d 36, 172 Cal.Rptr. 430 (1981).*

[1773] *34 Cal.3d 597, 194 Cal.Rptr. 500, 668 P.2d 807 (1983).*

[1774] *Id., at 605, 194 Cal.Rptr., at 504, 668 P.2d, at 811.*

[1775] *Id., at 606, 194 Cal.Rptr., at 505, 668 P.2d, at 812.*

[1776] *465 U.S. 1098, 104 S.Ct. 1589, 80 L.Ed.2d 122 (1984).*

Carroll v. United States.[1777] There, the Court recognized that the privacy interests in an automobile are constitutionally protected; however, it held that the ready mobility of the automobile justifies a lesser degree of protection of those interests. The Court rested this exception on a long-recognized distinction between stationary structures and vehicles:

"The guaranty of freedom from unreasonable searches and seizures by the Fourth Amendment has been construed, practically since the beginning of Government, as recognizing a necessary ****2069** difference between a search of a store, dwelling house or other structure in respect of which a proper official warrant readily may be obtained, and a search of a ship, motor boat, wagon or automobile, for contraband goods, where it is not practicable to secure a warrant because the vehicle can be quickly moved out of the locality or jurisdiction in which the warrant must be sought."[1778]

The capacity to be "quickly moved" was clearly the basis of the holding in Carroll, and our cases have consistently recognized ready mobility as one of the principal bases of the automobile exception.[1779] ***391** In *Chambers*, for example, commenting on the rationale for the vehicle exception, we noted that "the opportunity to search is fleeting since a car is readily movable."[1780] More recently, in *United States v. Ross*,[1781] we once again emphasized that "an immediate intrusion is necessary" because of "the nature of an automobile in transit..." The mobility of automobiles, we have observed, "creates circumstances of such exigency that, as a practical necessity, rigorous enforcement of the warrant requirement is impossible."[1782].

However, although ready mobility alone was perhaps the original justification for the vehicle exception, our later cases have made clear that ready mobility is not the only basis for the exception. The reasons for the vehicle exception, we have said, are twofold.[1783] "Besides the element of mobility, less rigorous warrant requirements govern because the expectation of privacy with respect to one's automobile is significantly less than that relating to one's home or office."[1784]

Even in cases where an automobile was not immediately mobile, the lesser expectation of privacy resulting from its use as a readily mobile vehicle justified application of the vehicular exception.[1785] In some cases, the configuration of the vehicle contributed to the lower expectations of privacy; for example, we held in *Cardwell v. Lewis*[1786] that, because the passenger compartment of a standard automobile is relatively open to plain view, there are lesser expectations of privacy. But even when enclosed "repository" areas have been involved, we have concluded that the lesser expectations of privacy warrant application of the exception. We have applied the exception in the context of a locked car trunk,[1787] a sealed package in a car

---

[1777] *267 U.S. 132, 45 S.Ct. 280, 69 L.Ed. 543 (1925).*

[1778] *Id., at 153, 45 S.Ct., at 285 (emphasis added).*

[1779] *See, e.g., Cooper v. California, 386 U.S. 58, 59, 87 S.Ct. 788, 789, 17 L.Ed.2d 730 (1967); Chambers v. Maroney, 399 U.S. 42, 52, 90 S.Ct. 1975, 1981, 26 L.Ed.2d 419 (1970); Cady v. Dombrowski, 413 U.S. 433, 442, 93 S.Ct. 2523, 2528, 37 L.Ed.2d 706 (1973); Cardwell v. Lewis, 417 U.S. 583, 588, 94 S.Ct. 2464, 2468, 41 L.Ed.2d 325 (1974); South Dakota v. Opperman, 428 U.S. 364, 367, 96 S.Ct. 3092, 3096, 49 L.Ed.2d 1000 (1976).*

[1780] *399 U.S., at 51, 90 S.Ct., at 1981.*

[1781] *456 U.S. 798, 806, 102 S.Ct. 2157, 2163, 72 L.Ed.2d 572 (1982).*

[1782] *South Dakota v. Opperman, supra, 428 U.S., at 367, 96 S.Ct., at 3096.*

[1783] *428 U.S., at 367, 96 S.Ct., at 3096.*

[1784] *Ibid.*

[1785] *See, e.g., Cady v. Dombrowski, supra.*

[1786] *Supra, 417 U.S., at 590, 94 S.Ct., at 2469.*

[1787] *Cady v. Dombrowski, supra.*

trunk,[1788] a closed compartment under the dashboard,[1789] ***392** the interior of a vehicle's upholstery,[1790] or sealed packages inside a covered pickup truck.[1791]

These reduced expectations of privacy derive not from the fact that the area to be searched is in plain view, but from the pervasive regulation of vehicles capable of traveling on the public highways.[1792] As we explained in *South Dakota v. Opperman*, an inventory search case:

"Automobiles, unlike homes, are subjected to pervasive and continuing governmental regulation and controls, including periodic inspection and licensing requirements. As an everyday occurrence, police stop and examine vehicles when license plates or inspection stickers have expired, or if other violations, such as exhaust fumes or excessive noise, are ****2070** noted, or if headlights or other safety equipment are not in proper working order."[1793]

The public is fully aware that it is accorded less privacy in its automobiles because of this compelling governmental need for regulation. Historically, "individuals always [have] been on notice that movable vessels may be stopped and searched on facts giving rise to probable cause that the vehicle contains contraband, without the protection afforded by a magistrate's prior evaluation of those facts."[1794] In short, the pervasive schemes of regulation, which necessarily lead to reduced expectations of privacy, and the exigencies attendant to ready mobility justify searches without prior recourse to the authority of a magistrate so long as the overriding standard of probable cause is met.

When a vehicle is being used on the highways, or if it is readily capable of such use and is found stationary in a place not regularly used for residential purposes-temporary or otherwise-the two justifications for the vehicle exception ***393** come into play. First, the vehicle is obviously readily mobile by the turn of an ignition key, if not actually moving. Second, there is a reduced expectation of privacy stemming from its use as a licensed motor vehicle subject to a range of police regulation inapplicable to a fixed dwelling. At least in these circumstances, the overriding societal interests in effective law enforcement justify an immediate search before the vehicle and its occupants become unavailable.

While it is true that respondent's vehicle possessed some, if not many of the attributes of a home, it is equally clear that the vehicle falls clearly within the scope of the exception laid down in *Carroll* and applied in succeeding cases. Like the automobile in *Carroll*, respondent's motor home was readily mobile. Absent the prompt search and seizure, it could readily have been moved beyond the reach of the police. Furthermore, the vehicle was licensed to "operate on public streets; [was] serviced in public places; ... and [was] subject to extensive regulation and inspection."[1795] And the vehicle was so situated that an objective observer would conclude that it was being used not as a residence, but as a vehicle.

Respondent urges us to distinguish his vehicle from other vehicles within the exception because it was capable of functioning as a home. In our increasingly mobile society, many vehicles used for transportation can be and are being used not only for transportation but for shelter, i.e., as a "home" or "residence." To distinguish

---

[1788] *Ross, supra.*

[1789] *Chambers v. Maroney, supra.*

[1790] *Carroll, supra.*

[1791] *United States v. Johns, 469 U.S. 478, 105 S.Ct. 881, 83 L.Ed.2d 890 (1985).*

[1792] *Cady v. Dombrowski, supra, 413 U.S., at 440-441, 93 S.Ct., at 2527-2528.*

[1793] *428 U.S., at 368, 96 S.Ct., at 3096.*

[1794] *Ross, supra, 456 U.S., at 806, n. 8, 102 S.Ct., at 2163, n. 8.*

[1795] *Rakas v. Illinois, 439 U.S. 128, 154, n. 2, 99 S.Ct. 421, 436, n. 2, 58 L.Ed.2d 387 (1978) (POWELL, J., concurring).*

between respondent's motor home and an ordinary sedan for purposes of the vehicle exception would require that we apply the exception depending upon the size of the vehicle and the quality of its appointments. Moreover, to fail to apply the exception to vehicles ***394** such as a motor home ignores the fact that a motor home lends itself easily to use as an instrument of illicit drug traffic and other illegal activity. In *United States v. Ross,*[1796] we declined to distinguish between "worthy" and "unworthy" containers, noting that "the central purpose of the Fourth Amendment forecloses such a distinction." We decline today to distinguish between "worthy" and "unworthy" vehicles which are either on the public roads and highways, or situated such that it is reasonable to conclude that the vehicle is not being used as a residence.

Our application of the vehicle exception has never turned on the other uses to which a vehicle might be put. The exception has historically turned on the ready mobility of the vehicle, and on the presence of the vehicle in a setting that objectively indicates that the vehicle is being used for ****2071** transportation. These two requirements for application of the exception ensure that law enforcement officials are not unnecessarily hamstrung in their efforts to detect and prosecute criminal activity, and that the legitimate privacy interests of the public are protected. Applying the vehicle exception in these circumstances allows the essential purposes served by the exception to be fulfilled, while assuring that the exception will acknowledge legitimate privacy interests.

III

The question remains whether, apart from the lack of a warrant, this search was unreasonable. Under the vehicle exception to the warrant requirement, "[o]nly the prior approval of the magistrate is waived; the search otherwise [must be such] as the magistrate could authorize."[1797]

***395** This search was not unreasonable; it was plainly one that the magistrate could authorize if presented with these facts. The DEA agents had fresh, direct, uncontradicted evidence that the respondent was distributing a controlled substance from the vehicle, apart from evidence of other possible offenses. The agents thus had abundant probable cause to enter and search the vehicle for evidence of a crime notwithstanding its possible use as a dwelling place.

The judgment of the California Supreme Court is reversed, and the case is remanded for further proceedings not inconsistent with this opinion.

It is so ordered.

(The dissent of Justice STEVENS, with whom Justice BRENNAN and Justice MARSHALL join, is omitted.)

*****

Black Letter Law

> The Court held that the warrantless search of defendant's motor home did not violate the Fourth Amendment because the automobile exception applied. The Court maintained that the motor home was a vehicle because it was capable of highway-use and was found in a place not regularly used for business purposes. The Court discussed the two rationales for the automobile exception, mobility and reduced expectation of privacy in vehicles.

[1796] *456 U.S., at 822, 102 S.Ct., at 2171.*

[1797] *Ross, supra, at 823, 102 S.Ct., at 2172.*

California v. Acevedo

111 S.Ct. 1982

Supreme Court of the United States

CALIFORNIA, Petitioner

v.

Charles Steven ACEVEDO.

No. 89-1690. | Argued Jan. 8, 1991. | Decided May 30, 1991.

Justice BLACKMUN delivered the opinion of the Court.

This case requires us once again to consider the so-called "automobile exception" to the warrant requirement of the Fourth Amendment and its application to the search of a closed container in the trunk of a car.

I

On October 28, 1987, Officer Coleman of the Santa Ana, Cal., Police Department received a telephone call from a federal ***567** drug enforcement agent in Hawaii. The agent informed Coleman that he had seized a package containing marijuana which was to have been delivered to the Federal Express Office in Santa Ana and which was addressed to J.R. Daza at 805 West Stevens Avenue in that city. The agent arranged to send the package to Coleman instead. Coleman then was to take the package to the Federal Express office and arrest the person who arrived to claim it.

Coleman received the package on October 29, verified its contents, and took it to the Senior Operations Manager at the Federal Express office. At about 10:30 a.m. on October 30, a man, who identified himself as Jamie Daza, arrived to claim the package. He accepted it and drove to his apartment on West Stevens. He carried the package into the apartment.

At 11:45 a.m., officers observed Daza leave the apartment and drop the box and paper that had contained the marijuana into a trash bin. Coleman at that point left the scene to get a search warrant. About 12:05 p.m., the officers saw Richard St. George leave the apartment carrying a blue knapsack which appeared to be half full. The officers stopped him as he was driving off, searched the knapsack, and found 1 ½ pounds of marijuana.

At 12:30 p.m., respondent Charles Steven Acevedo arrived. He entered Daza's apartment, stayed for about 10 minutes, and reappeared carrying a brown paper bag that looked full. The officers noticed that the bag was the size of one of the wrapped marijuana packages sent from Hawaii. Acevedo walked to a silver Honda in the parking lot. He placed the bag in the trunk of the car and ****1985** started to drive away. Fearing the loss of evidence, officers in a marked police car stopped him. They opened the trunk and the bag, and found marijuana.

***568** Respondent was charged in state court with possession of marijuana for sale, in violation of Cal. Health & Safety Code Ann. § 11359.[1798] He moved to suppress the marijuana found in the car. The motion was denied. He then pleaded guilty but appealed the denial of the suppression motion.

The California Court of Appeal, Fourth District, concluded that the marijuana found in the paper bag in the car's trunk should have been suppressed.[1799] The court concluded that the officers had probable cause to believe that the paper bag contained drugs but lacked probable cause to suspect that Acevedo's car, itself, otherwise contained contraband. Because the officers' probable cause was directed specif-

[1798] *(West Supp.1991). App. 2.*

[1799] *216 Cal.App.3d 586, 265 Cal.Rptr. 23 (1990).*

ically at the bag, the court held that the case was controlled by *United States v. Chadwick,*[1800] rather than by *United States v. Ross.*[1801] Although the court agreed that the officers could seize the paper bag, it held that, under Chadwick, they could not open the bag without first obtaining a warrant for that purpose. The court then recognized "the anomalous nature" of the dichotomy between the rule in Chadwick and the rule in Ross.[1802] That dichotomy dictates that if there is probable cause to search a car, then the entire car-including any closed container found therein-may be searched without a warrant, but if there is probable cause only as to a container in the car, the container may be held but not searched until a warrant is obtained.

The Supreme Court of California denied the State's petition for review.[1803] On May 14, 1990, Justice O'Connor stayed enforcement of the Court of Appeal's judgment pending the disposition of the State's petition for certiorari, and, if that petition were granted, the issuance of the mandate of this Court.

We granted certiorari[1804] to reexamine the law applicable to a closed container in an automobile, a ***569** subject that has troubled courts and law enforcement officers since it was first considered in Chadwick.

II

The Fourth Amendment protects the "right of the people to be secure in their persons, houses, papers, and effects, against unreasonable searches and seizures." Contemporaneously with the adoption of the Fourth Amendment, the First Congress, and, later, the Second and Fourth Congresses, distinguished between the need for a warrant to search for contraband concealed in "a dwelling house or similar place" and the need for a warrant to search for contraband concealed in a movable vessel.[1805] In *Carroll*, this Court established an exception to the warrant requirement for moving vehicles, for it recognized "a necessary difference between a search of a store, dwelling house or other structure in respect of which a proper official warrant readily may be obtained, and a search of a ship, motor boat, wagon or automobile, for contraband goods, where it is not practicable to secure a warrant because the vehicle can be quickly moved out of the locality or jurisdiction in which the warrant must be sought."[1806]

****1986** It therefore held that a warrantless search of an automobile, based upon probable cause to believe that the vehicle contained evidence of crime in the light of an exigency arising out of the likely disappearance of the vehicle, did not contravene the Warrant Clause of the Fourth Amendment.[1807]

The Court refined the exigency requirement in *Chambers v. Maroney*[1808] when it held that the existence of exigent circumstances was to be determined at the time the automobile is seized. The car search at issue in ***570** *Chambers* took place at the police station, where the vehicle was immobilized, some time after the driver had been arrested. Given probable cause and exigent circumstances at the time the vehicle was first stopped, the Court held that the later warrantless search at the station passed constitutional muster. The validity of the later search derived from the ruling

---

[1800] *433 U.S. 1, 97 S.Ct. 2476, 53 L.Ed.2d 538 (1977).*

[1801] *456 U.S. 798, 102 S.Ct. 2157, 72 L.Ed.2d 572 (1982).*

[1802] *216 Cal.App.3d, at 592, 265 Cal.Rptr., at 27.*

[1803] *App. E to Pet. for Cert. 33.*

[1804] *498 U.S. 807, 111 S.Ct. 39, 112 L.Ed.2d 15 (1990).*

[1805] *See Carroll v. United States, 267 U.S. 132, 151, 45 S.Ct. 280, 284, 69 L.Ed. 543 (1925). See also Boyd v. United States, 116 U.S. 616, 623-624, 6 S.Ct. 524, 528-529, 29 L.Ed. 746 (1886).*

[1806] *267 U.S., at 153, 45 S.Ct., at 285.*

[1807] *See id., at 158-159, 45 S.Ct., at 287.*

[1808] *399 U.S. 42, 90 S.Ct. 1975, 26 L.Ed.2d 419 (1970).*

in *Carroll* that an immediate search without a warrant at the moment of seizure would have been permissible.[1809] The Court reasoned in *Chambers* that the police could search later whenever they could have searched earlier, had they so chosen.[1810] Following *Chambers*, if the police have probable cause to justify a warrantless seizure of an automobile on a public roadway, they may conduct either an immediate or a delayed search of the vehicle.

In *United States v. Ross*,[1811] decided in 1982, we held that a warrantless search of an automobile under the Carroll doctrine could include a search of a container or package found inside the car when such a search was supported by probable cause. The warrantless search of Ross' car occurred after an informant told the police that he had seen Ross complete a drug transaction using drugs stored in the trunk of his car. The police stopped the car, searched it, and discovered in the trunk a brown paper bag containing drugs. We decided that the search of Ross' car was not unreasonable under the Fourth Amendment: "The scope of a warrantless search based on probable cause is no narrower-and no broader-than the scope of a search authorized by a warrant supported by probable cause."[1812] Thus, "[i]f probable cause justifies the search of a lawfully stopped vehicle, it justifies the search of every part of the vehicle and its contents that may conceal the object of the search."[1813] In *Ross*, therefore, we clarified the scope of the *Carroll* doctrine as properly including a "probing search" of compartments and containers within the automobile so long as the search is supported by probable cause.[1814]

***571** In addition to this clarification, *Ross* distinguished the *Carroll* doctrine from the separate rule that governed the search of closed containers.[1815] The Court had announced this separate rule, unique to luggage and other closed packages, bags, and containers, in *United States v. Chadwick.*[1816] In *Chadwick*, federal narcotics agents had probable cause to believe that a 200-pound double-locked footlocker contained marijuana. The agents tracked the locker as the defendants removed it from a train and carried it through the station to a waiting car. As soon as the defendants lifted the locker into the trunk of the car, the agents arrested them, seized the locker, and searched it. In this Court, the United States did not contend that the locker's brief contact with the automobile's trunk sufficed to make the *Carroll* doctrine applicable. Rather, the United States urged that the search of movable luggage could be considered analogous to the search of an automobile.[1817]

The Court rejected this argument because, it reasoned, a person expects more privacy in his luggage and personal effects than he does in his automobile.[1818] Moreover, it concluded that as "may ****1987** often not be the case when automobiles are seized," secure storage facilities are usually available when the police seize luggage.[1819]

[1809] *See Chambers, 399 U.S., at 51, 90 S.Ct., at 1981.*

[1810] *Id., at 51-52, 90 S.Ct., at 1981.*

[1811] *456 U.S. 798, 102 S.Ct. 2157, 72 L.Ed.2d 572.*

[1812] *Id., at 823, 102 S.Ct., at 2172.*

[1813] *Id., at 825, 102 S.Ct., at 2173.*

[1814] *Id., at 800, 102 S.Ct., at 2160.*

[1815] *See 456 U.S., at 817, 102 S.Ct., at 2169.*

[1816] *433 U.S. 1, 97 S.Ct. 2476, 53 L.Ed.2d 538 (1977).*

[1817] *433 U.S., at 11-12, 97 S.Ct., at 2483-2484.*

[1818] *Id., at 13, 97 S.Ct., at 2484.*

[1819] *Id., at 13, n. 7, 97 S.Ct., at 2484, n. 7.*

In *Arkansas v. Sanders*,[1820] the Court extended Chadwick 's rule to apply to a suitcase actually being transported in the trunk of a car. In *Sanders*, the police had probable cause to believe a suitcase contained marijuana. They watched as the defendant placed the suitcase in the trunk of a taxi and was driven away. The police pursued the taxi for several blocks, stopped it, found the suitcase in the trunk, and searched it. Although the Court had applied the *Carroll* doctrine to searches of integral parts of the automobile itself, (indeed, in *Carroll*, contraband whiskey was in the upholstery of the seats),[1821] it did not extend the doctrine to the warrantless search of personal luggage ***572** "merely because it was located in an automobile lawfully stopped by the police."[1822] Again, the *Sanders* majority stressed the heightened privacy expectation in personal luggage and concluded that the presence of luggage in an automobile did not diminish the owner's expectation of privacy in his personal items.[1823]

In *Ross*, the Court endeavored to distinguish between *Carroll*, which governed the *Ross* automobile search, and *Chadwick*, which governed the *Sanders* automobile search. It held that the *Carroll* doctrine covered searches of automobiles when the police had probable cause to search an entire vehicle, but that the *Chadwick* doctrine governed searches of luggage when the officers had probable cause to search only a container within the vehicle. Thus, in a *Ross* situation, the police could conduct a reasonable search under the Fourth Amendment without obtaining a warrant, whereas in a *Sanders* situation, the police had to obtain a warrant before they searched.

Justice Stevens is correct, of course, that Ross involved the scope of an automobile search.[1824] *Ross* held that closed containers encountered by the police during a warrantless search of a car pursuant to the automobile exception could also be searched. Thus, this Court in *Ross* took the critical step of saying that closed containers in cars could be searched without a warrant because of their presence within the automobile. Despite the protection that *Sanders* purported to extend to closed containers, the privacy interest in those closed containers yielded to the broad scope of an automobile search.

III

The facts in this case closely resemble the facts in *Ross*. In *Ross*, the police had probable cause to believe that drugs were stored in the trunk of a particular car. [1825]Here, the California Court of Appeal concluded that the police had probable cause to believe that respondent was ***573** carrying marijuana in a bag in his car's trunk.[1826] Furthermore, for what it is worth, in *Ross*, as here, the drugs in the trunk were contained in a brown paper bag.

This Court in Ross rejected Chadwick 's distinction between containers and cars. It concluded that the expectation of privacy in one's vehicle is equal to one's expectation of privacy in the container, and noted that "the ****1988** privacy interests in a car's trunk or glove compartment may be no less than those in a movable container."[1827] It also recognized that it was arguable that the same exigent circumstances that permit a warrantless search of an automobile would justify the warrant-

---

[1820] *442 U.S. 753, 99 S.Ct. 2586, 61 L.Ed.2d 235 (1979).*

[1821] *see 267 U.S., at 136, 45 S.Ct., at 281.*

[1822] *442 U.S., at 765, 99 S.Ct., at 2594.*

[1823] *Id., at 764-765, 99 S.Ct., at 2593-2594. Cf. California v. Carney, 471 U.S. 386, 105 S.Ct. 2066, 85 L.Ed.2d 406 (1985).*

[1824] *See post, at 1998.*

[1825] *See 456 U.S., at 800, 102 S.Ct., at 2160.*

[1826] *216 Cal.App.3d, at 590, 265 Cal.Rptr., at 25.*

[1827] *456 U.S., at 823, 102 S.Ct., at 2172.*

less search of a movable container.[1828] In deference to the rule of Chadwick and Sanders, however, the Court put that question to one side.[1829] It concluded that the time and expense of the warrant process would be misdirected if the police could search every cubic inch of an automobile until they discovered a paper sack, at which point the Fourth Amendment required them to take the sack to a magistrate for permission to look inside. We now must decide the question deferred in *Ross*: whether the Fourth Amendment requires the police to obtain a warrant to open the sack in a movable vehicle simply because they lack probable cause to search the entire car. We conclude that it does not.

IV

Dissenters in *Ross* asked why the suitcase in *Sanders* was "more private, less difficult for police to seize and store, or in ***574** any other relevant respect more properly subject to the warrant requirement, than a container that police discover in a probable-cause search of an entire automobile?"[1830] We now agree that a container found after a general search of the automobile and a container found in a car after a limited search for the container are equally easy for the police to store and for the suspect to hide or destroy. In fact, we see no principled distinction in terms of either the privacy expectation or the exigent circumstances between the paper bag found by the police in *Ross* and the paper bag found by the police here. Furthermore, by attempting to distinguish between a container for which the police are specifically searching and a container which they come across in a car, we have provided only minimal protection for privacy and have impeded effective law enforcement.

The line between probable cause to search a vehicle and probable cause to search a package in that vehicle is not always clear, and separate rules that govern the two objects to be searched may enable the police to broaden their power to make warrantless searches and deserve privacy interests. We noted this in *Ross* in the context of a search of an entire vehicle. Recognizing that under *Carroll*, the "entire vehicle itself ... could be searched without a warrant," we concluded that "prohibiting police from opening immediately a container in which the object of the search is most likely to be found and instead forcing them first to comb the entire vehicle would actually exacerbate the intrusion on privacy interests."[1831] At the moment when officers stop an automobile, it may be less than clear whether they suspect with a high degree of certainty that the vehicle contains drugs in a bag or simply contains drugs. If the police know that they may open a bag only if they are actually searching the entire car, they may search more extensively ***575** than they otherwise would in order to establish the general probable cause required by *Ross*.

Such a situation is not farfetched. In *United States v. Johns*,[1832] customs agents saw two trucks drive to a private airstrip and approach two small planes. The agents drew near the trucks, smelled marijuana, and then saw in the backs of the trucks packages wrapped in a manner that marijuana smugglers customarily employed. The agents took the trucks to headquarters and searched the packages without a warrant.[1833] Relying on *Chadwick*, the defendants argued that the search was unlawful.[1834] The defendants contended that *Ross* was inapplicable because the agents lacked probable cause to search anything but the packages themselves and supported this contention ****1989** by noting that a search of the entire vehicle never

[1828] *Id., at 809, 102 S.Ct., at 2165.*

[1829] *Id., at 809-810, 102 S.Ct., at 2165.*

[1830] *Id., 456 U.S., at 839-840, 102 S.Ct., at 2180-2181.*

[1831] *456 U.S., at 821, n. 28, 102 S.Ct., at 2171, n. 28.*

[1832] *469 U.S. 478, 105 S.Ct. 881, 83 L.Ed.2d 890 (1985).*

[1833] *Id., at 481, 105 S.Ct., at 883.*

[1834] *Id., at 482, 105 S.Ct., at 884.*

occurred.[1835] We rejected that argument and found *Chadwick* and *Sanders* inapposite because the agents had probable cause to search the entire body of each truck, although they had chosen not to do so. We cannot see the benefit of a rule that requires law enforcement officers to conduct a more intrusive search in order to justify a less intrusive one.

To the extent that the *Chadwick-Sanders* rule protects privacy, its protection is minimal. Law enforcement officers may seize a container and hold it until they obtain a search warrant.[1836] "Since the police, by hypothesis, have probable cause to seize the property, we can assume that a warrant will be routinely forthcoming in the overwhelming majority of cases."[1837] And the police often will be able to search containers without a warrant, despite the *Chadwick-Sanders* rule, as a search incident to a lawful arrest. In *New York v. Belton*,[1838] the Court said:

***576** "[W]e hold that when a policeman has made a lawful custodial arrest of the occupant of an automobile, he may, as a contemporaneous incident of that arrest, search the passenger compartment of that automobile. It follows from this conclusion that the police may also examine the contents of any containers found within the passenger compartment."[1839]

Under *Belton*, the same probable cause to believe that a container holds drugs will allow the police to arrest the person transporting the container and search it.

Finally, the search of a paper bag intrudes far less on individual privacy than does the incursion sanctioned long ago in *Carroll*. In that case, prohibition agents slashed the upholstery of the automobile. This Court nonetheless found their search to be reasonable under the Fourth Amendment. If destroying the interior of an automobile is not unreasonable, we cannot conclude that looking inside a closed container is. In light of the minimal protection to privacy afforded by the *Chadwick-Sanders* rule, and our serious doubt whether that rule substantially serves privacy interests, we now hold that the Fourth Amendment does not compel separate treatment for an automobile search that extends only to a container within the vehicle.

V

The *Chadwick-Sanders* rule not only has failed to protect privacy but also has confused courts and police officers and impeded effective law enforcement. The conflict between the *Carroll* doctrine cases and the *Chadwick-Sanders* line has been criticized in academic commentary.[1840] One leading authority on the Fourth Amendment, after comparing Chadwick and Sanders with Carroll and its progeny, observed: "These two lines of authority cannot be completely reconciled, and thus how one comes out in the container-in-the-car situation depends upon which line of authority is used as a point of departure."[1841]

The discrepancy between the two rules has led to confusion for law enforcement officers. For example, when an officer, who has developed probable cause to believe that a vehicle contains drugs, begins to search the vehicle and immediately discovers a closed container, ****1990** which rule applies? The defendant will argue that the fact that the officer first chose to search the container indicates that his probable cause

---

[1835] *Id., at 483, 105 S.Ct., at 884.*

[1836] *Chadwick, 433 U.S., at 13, 97 S.Ct., at 2484.*

[1837] *Sanders, 442 U.S., at 770, 99 S.Ct., at 2596 (dissenting opinion).*

[1838] *453 U.S. 454, 101 S.Ct. 2860, 69 L.Ed.2d 768 (1981).*

[1839] *Id., at 460, 101 S.Ct., at 2864 (footnote omitted).*

[1840] *See, e.g., Gardner, Searches and Seizures of Automobiles and Their Contents: Fourth Amendment Considerations in a Post-Ross World, 62 Neb.L.Rev. 1 (1983); Latzer, Searching Cars and Their Contents: United States v. Ross, 18 Crim.L.Bull. 381 (1982); Kamisar, The "Automobile Search" Cases: The Court Does Little to Clarify the "Labyrinth" of Judicial Uncertainty,* ***577** *in 3 The Supreme Court: Trends and Developments 1980-1981, p. 69 (D. Opperman ed. 1982).*

[1841] *3 W. LaFave, Search and Seizure 53 (2d ed. 1987).*

extended only to the container and that *Chadwick* and *Sanders* therefore require a warrant. On the other hand, the fact that the officer first chose to search in the most obvious location should not restrict the propriety of the search. The *Chadwick* rule, as applied in *Sanders*, has devolved into an anomaly such that the more likely the police are to discover drugs in a container, the less authority they have to search it. We have noted the virtue of providing ""'clear and unequivocal" guidelines to the law enforcement profession.'"[1842] The *Chadwick-Sanders* rule is the antithesis of a "'clear and unequivocal' guideline."

Justice Stevens argues that the decisions of this Court evince a lack of confusion about the automobile exception.[1843] The first case cited by the dissent,[1844] however, did not involve an automobile at all. We considered in Place the temporary detention of luggage in an airport. Not only was no automobile involved, but the defendant, Place, was waiting ***578** at the airport to board his plane rather than preparing to leave the airport in a car. Any similarity to *Sanders*, in which the defendant was leaving the airport in a car, is remote at best. Place had nothing to do with the automobile exception and is inapposite.

Nor does Justice Stevens' citation of *Oklahoma v. Castleberry*[1845] support his contention. *Castleberry* presented the same question about the application of the automobile exception to the search of a closed container that we face here. In *Castleberry*, we affirmed by an equally divided court. That result illustrates this Court's continued struggle with the scope of the automobile exception rather than the absence of confusion in applying it.

Justice Stevens also argues that law enforcement has not been impeded because the Court has decided 29 Fourth Amendment cases since Ross in favor of the government.[1846] In each of these cases, the government appeared as the petitioner. The dissent fails to explain how the loss of 29 cases below, not to mention the many others which this Court did not hear, did not interfere with law enforcement. The fact that the state courts and the Federal Courts of Appeals have been reversed in their Fourth Amendment holdings 29 times since 1982 further demonstrates the extent to which our Fourth Amendment jurisprudence has confused the courts.

Most important, with the exception of *United States v. Johns*[1847] and *Texas v. Brown*,[1848] the Fourth Amendment cases cited by the dissent do not concern automobiles or the automobile exception. From *Carroll* through *Ross*, this Court has explained that automobile searches differ from other searches. The dissent fails to acknowledge this basic principle and so misconstrues and misapplies our Fourth Amendment case law.

The *Chadwick* dissenters predicted that the container rule would have "the perverse result of allowing fortuitous circumstances to control the outcome" of various searches.[1849] ***579** The rule also was so confusing that within two years after Chadwick, this Court found it necessary to expound on the meaning of that decision and explain its application to luggage in general.[1850] Again, dissenters bemoaned the

---

[1842] *Minnick v. Mississippi, 498 U.S. 146, 151, 111 S.Ct. 486, 489, 112 L.Ed.2d 489 (1990) quoting Arizona v. Roberson, 486 U.S. 675, 682, 108 S.Ct. 2093, 2098, 100 L.Ed.2d 704 (1988).*

[1843] *See post, at 1998-1999.*

[1844] *United States v. Place, 462 U.S. 696, 103 S.Ct. 2637, 77 L.Ed.2d 110 (1983).*

[1845] *471 U.S. 146, 105 S.Ct. 1859, 85 L.Ed.2d 112 (1985).*

[1846] *See post, at 2002.*

[1847] *469 U.S. 478, 105 S.Ct. 881, 83 L.Ed.2d 890 (1985).*

[1848] *460 U.S. 730, 103 S.Ct. 1535, 75 L.Ed.2d 502 (1983).*

[1849] *433 U.S., at 22, 97 S.Ct., at 2489.*

[1850] *Sanders, 442 U.S., at 761-764, 99 S.Ct., at 2591-2593.*

"inherent opaqueness" of the difference between the *Carroll* and *Chadwick* principles and noted "the confusion to be created for all concerned."[1851] ****1991** Three years after *Sanders*, we returned in *Ross* to "this troubled area"[1852] in order to assert that *Sanders* had not cut back on *Carroll*.

Although we have recognized firmly that the doctrine of stare decisis serves profoundly important purposes in our legal system, this Court has overruled a prior case on the comparatively rare occasion when it has bred confusion or been a derelict or led to anomalous results.[1853] *Sanders* was explicitly undermined in *Ross*,[1854] and the existence of the dual regimes for automobile searches that uncover containers has proven as confusing as the *Chadwick* and *Sanders* dissenters predicted. We conclude that it is better to adopt one clear-cut rule to govern automobile searches and eliminate the warrant requirement for closed containers set forth in *Sanders*.

VI

The interpretation of the *Carroll* doctrine set forth in *Ross* now applies to all searches of containers found in an automobile. In other words, the police may search without a warrant if their search is supported by probable cause. The Court in *Ross* put it this way:

"The scope of a warrantless search of an automobile ... is not defined by the nature of the container in which the contraband is secreted. Rather, it is defined by the object ***580** of the search and the places in which there is probable cause to believe that it may be found."[1855]

It went on to note: "Probable cause to believe that a container placed in the trunk of a taxi contains contraband or evidence does not justify a search of the entire cab."[1856] We reaffirm that principle. In the case before us, the police had probable cause to believe that the paper bag in the automobile's trunk contained marijuana. That probable cause now allows a warrantless search of the paper bag. The facts in the record reveal that the police did not have probable cause to believe that contraband was hidden in any other part of the automobile and a search of the entire vehicle would have been without probable cause and unreasonable under the Fourth Amendment.

Our holding today neither extends the *Carroll* doctrine nor broadens the scope of the permissible automobile search delineated in *Carroll*, *Chambers*, and *Ross*. It remains a "cardinal principle that 'searches conducted outside the judicial process, without prior approval by judge or magistrate, are per se unreasonable under the Fourth Amendment-subject only to a few specifically established and well-delineated exceptions.'"[1857] We held in *Ross*: "The exception recognized in *Carroll* is unquestionably one that is 'specifically established and well delineated.'"[1858]

Until today, this Court has drawn a curious line between the search of an automobile that coincidentally turns up a container and the search of a container that coincidentally turns up in an automobile. The protections of the Fourth Amendment must not turn on such coincidences. We therefore interpret *Carroll* as providing one

---

[1851] *Id., at 771, 90 S.Ct., at 2597. See also Robbins v. California, 453 U.S. 420, 425-426, 101 S.Ct. 2841, 2845-2846, 69 L.Ed.2d 744 (1981) (listing cases decided by Federal Courts of Appeals since Chadwick had been announced).*

[1852] *456 U.S., at 817, 102 S.Ct., at 2169.*

[1853] *See, e.g., Complete Auto Transit, Inc. v. Brady, 430 U.S. 274, 288-289, 97 S.Ct. 1076, 1084, 51 L.Ed.2d 326 (1977).*

[1854] *456 U.S., at 824, 102 S.Ct., at 2172.*

[1855] *456 U.S., at 824, 102 S.Ct., at 2172.*

[1856] *Ibid.*

[1857] *Mincey v. Arizona, 437 U.S. 385, 390, 98 S.Ct. 2408, 2412, 57 L.Ed.2d 290 (1978), quoting Katz v. United States, 389 U.S. 347, 357, 88 S.Ct. 507, 514, 19 L.Ed.2d 576 (1967) (footnotes omitted).*

[1858] *456 U.S., at 825, 102 S.Ct., at 514.*

rule to govern all automobile searches. The police may search an automobile and the containers within it where they have probable cause to believe contraband or evidence is contained.

***581** The judgment of the California Court of Appeal is reversed, and the case is remanded to that court for further proceedings not inconsistent with this opinion.

It is so ordered.

****1992** Justice SCALIA, concurring in the judgment.

I agree with the dissent that it is anomalous for a briefcase to be protected by the "general requirement" of a prior warrant when it is being carried along the street, but for that same briefcase to become unprotected as soon as it is carried into an automobile. On the other hand, I agree with the Court that it would be anomalous for a locked compartment in an automobile to be unprotected by the "general requirement" of a prior warrant, but for an unlocked briefcase within the automobile to be protected. I join in the judgment of the Court because I think its holding is more faithful to the text and tradition of the Fourth Amendment, and if these anomalies in our jurisprudence are ever to be eliminated that is the direction in which we should travel.

The Fourth Amendment does not by its terms require a prior warrant for searches and seizures; it merely prohibits searches and seizures that are "unreasonable." What it explicitly states regarding warrants is by way of limitation upon their issuance rather than requirement of their use.[1859] For the warrant was a means of insulating officials from personal liability assessed by colonial juries. An officer who searched or seized without a warrant did so at his own risk; he would be liable for trespass, including exemplary damages, unless the jury found that his action was "reasonable."[1860] If, however, the officer acted pursuant to a proper warrant, he would be absolutely immune.[1861] By restricting the issuance of warrants, ***582** the Framers endeavored to preserve the jury's role in regulating searches and seizures.[1862]

Although the Fourth Amendment does not explicitly impose the requirement of a warrant, it is of course textually possible to consider that implicit within the requirement of reasonableness. For some years after the explosion in Fourth Amendment litigation that followed our announcement of the exclusionary rule in *Weeks v. United States*,[1863] our jurisprudence lurched back and forth between imposing a categorical warrant requirement and looking to reasonableness alone. (The opinions preferring a warrant involved searches of structures.)[1864] By the late 1960's, the preference for a warrant had won out, at least rhetorically.[1865]

The victory was illusory. Even before today's decision, the "warrant requirement" had become so riddled with exceptions that it was basically unrecognizable. In 1985, one commentator cataloged nearly 20 such exceptions, including "searches incident to arrest ... automobile searches ... border searches ... administrative search-

---

[1859] See Wakely v. Hart, 6 Binney 316, 318 (Pa.1814).

[1860] Amar, The Bill of Rights as a Constitution, 100 Yale L.J. 1131, 1178-1180 (1991); Huckle v. Money, 2 Wils. 205, 95 Eng.Rep. 768 (K.B.1763).

[1861] See Bell v. Clapp, 10 Johns. 263 (N.Y.1813); 4 W. Blackstone, Commentaries 288 (1769).

[1862] Amar, supra; Posner, Rethinking the Fourth Amendment, 1981 S.Ct.Rev. 49, 72-73; see also T. Taylor, Two Studies in Constitutional Interpretation 41 (1969).

[1863] 232 U.S. 383, 34 S.Ct. 341, 58 L.Ed. 652 (1914).

[1864] Compare Harris v. United States, 331 U.S. 145, 67 S.Ct. 1098, 91 L.Ed. 1399 (1947), with Johnson v. United States, 333 U.S. 10, 68 S.Ct. 367, 92 L.Ed. 436 (1948); compare Trupiano v. United States, 334 U.S. 699, 68 S.Ct. 1229, 92 L.Ed. 1663 (1948), with United States v. Rabinowitz, 339 U.S. 56, 70 S.Ct. 430, 94 L.Ed. 653 (1950). See generally Chimel v. California, 395 U.S. 752, 89 S.Ct. 2034, 23 L.Ed.2d 685 (1969).

[1865] See Chimel; Coolidge v. New Hampshire, 403 U.S. 443, 91 S.Ct. 2022, 29 L.Ed.2d 564 (1971).

es of regulated businesses ... exigent circumstances ... search[es] incident to nonarrest when there is probable cause to arrest ... boat boarding for document checks ... welfare searches ... inventory searches ... airport searches ... school search[es]...."[1866] Since then, we have added at least two more.[1867] ***583 **1993** Our intricate body of law regarding "reasonable expectation of privacy" has been developed largely as a means of creating these exceptions, enabling a search to be denominated not a Fourth Amendment "search" and therefore not subject to the general warrant requirement.[1868]

Unlike the dissent, therefore, I do not regard today's holding as some momentous departure, but rather as merely the continuation of an inconsistent jurisprudence that has been with us for years. Cases like *United States v. Chadwick* and *Arkansas v. Sanders* have taken the "preference for a warrant" seriously, while cases like *United States v. Ross* and *Carroll v. United States* have not. There can be no clarity in this area unless we make up our minds, and unless the principles we express comport with the actions we take.

In my view, the path out of this confusion should be sought by returning to the first principle that the "reasonableness" requirement of the Fourth Amendment affords the protection that the common law afforded.[1869] I have no difficulty with the proposition that that includes the requirement of a warrant, where the common law required a warrant; and it may even be that changes in the surrounding legal rules (for example, elimination of the common-law rule that reasonable, good-faith belief was no defense to absolute liability for trespass)[1870] may make a warrant indispensable to reasonableness where it once was not. But the supposed "general ***584** rule" that a warrant is always required does not appear to have any basis in the common law[1871] and confuses rather than facilitates any attempt to develop rules of reasonableness in light of changed legal circumstances, as the anomaly eliminated and the anomaly created by today's holding both demonstrate.

And there are more anomalies still. Under our precedents (as at common law), a person may be arrested outside the home on the basis of probable cause, without an arrest warrant.[1872] Upon arrest, the person, as well as the area within his grasp, may be searched for evidence related to the crime.[1873] Under these principles, if a known drug dealer is carrying a briefcase reasonably believed to contain marijuana (the unauthorized possession of which is a crime), the police may arrest him and search his person on the basis of probable cause alone. And, under our precedents, upon arrival at the station house, the police may inventory his possessions, including the briefcase, even if there is no reason to suspect that they contain contraband.[1874] According to our current law, however, the police may not, on the basis of the same probable cause, take the less intrusive step of stopping the individual on the street

---

[1866] *Bradley, Two Models of the Fourth Amendment, 83 Mich.L.Rev. 1468, 1473-1474 (footnotes omitted).*

[1867] *California v. Carney, 471 U.S. 386, 105 S.Ct. 2066, 85 L.Ed.2d 406 (1985) (searches of mobile homes); O'Connor v. Ortega, 480 U.S. 709, 107 S.Ct. 1492, 94 L.Ed.2d 714 (1987) (searches of offices of government employees).*

[1868] *Cf. id., at 729, 107 S.Ct., at 1504 (Scalia, J., concurring in judgment).*

[1869] *See County of Riverside v. McLaughlin, 500 U.S. 44, 60, 111 S.Ct. 1661, 1672, 114 L.Ed.2d 49 (1991) (Scalia, J., dissenting); People v. Chiagles, 237 N.Y. 193, 195, 142 N.E. 583 (1923) (Cardozo, J.). Cf. California v. Hodari D., 499 U.S. 621, 624-627, 111 S.Ct. 1547, 1549-1551, 113 L.Ed.2d 690 (1991).*

[1870] *Little v. Barreme, 2 Cranch 170, 2 L.Ed. 243 (1804) (Marshall, C.J.); see generally Amar, Of Sovereignty and Federalism, 96 Yale L.J. 1425, 1486-1487 (1987),*

[1871] *See, e.g., Carroll, supra, 267 U.S., at 150-153, 45 S.Ct., at 284-85; Gelston v. Hoyt, 3 Wheat. 246, 310-311, 4 L.Ed. 381 (1818) (Story, J.); Wakely, supra.*

[1872] *United States v. Watson, 423 U.S. 411, 418-421, 96 S.Ct. 820, 825-826, 46 L.Ed.2d 598 (1976); Rohan v. Sawin, 59 Mass. 281 (1851).*

[1873] *Chimel v. California, supra, 395 U.S., at 762-763, 89 S.Ct., at 2039-2040; People v. Chiagles, supra (collecting authority).*

[1874] *Illinois v. Lafayette, 462 U.S. 640, 103 S.Ct. 2605, 77 L.Ed.2d 65 (1983).*

and demanding to see the contents of his briefcase. That makes no sense a priori, and in the absence of any **1994 common-law tradition supporting such a distinction, I see no reason to continue it.

I would reverse the judgment in the present case, not because a closed container carried inside a car becomes subject to the "automobile" exception to the general warrant requirement, *585 but because the search of a closed container, outside a privately owned building, with probable cause to believe that the container contains contraband, and when it in fact does contain contraband, is not one of those searches whose Fourth Amendment reasonableness depends upon a warrant. For that reason I concur in the judgment of the Court.

(The dissent of Justice STEVENS, with whom Justice MARSHALL joins, is omitted.)

Black Letter Law

Held that police may search container located within automobile and need not hold container pending issuance of search warrant, even though they lack probable cause to search vehicle as whole and have probable cause to believe only that container itself holds contraband or evidence.

Discussion Problems:

8-1. While on patrol Officer Williams pulled into a Sonic to get a frozen coconut blueberry slushy (Sonic gives them out to cops for free), when he spotted a blue Caprice with crossed arrows painted on the hood. The car was tricked out to the max and occupied by two white males. The music from the Caprice was so loud he could not hear the lady on the drive through speaker. After getting his slushy, he got out of his cruiser, approached the car and identified himself as a police officer. He then asked them to turn down the music. Something about the way the occupants of the Caprice responded to his request upset Officer Williams. He ordered them out of the car and separated them, placing the passenger at the front of the car and the driver at the back of the car.

The driver of the Caprice identified himself as "Bob" and asked what the problem was. Officer Williams didn't like the way "Bob" looked and told him to assume the position with his hands on the trunk of the blue Caprice. Officer Williams conducted a frisk of "Bob," discovering a 9mm Beretta tucked into the back of his trousers. He also felt a budge in his pant's pocket. He asked for permission to place his hand's in Bob's pocket and Bob replied, "Sure, why not?" Officer Williams then withdrew a cellophane bag containing approximately 150 white pills with the imprint of an arrowhead on them. Bob began to sputter, claiming that the speed wasn't his; he was just holding it for someone else. Officer Williams responded by placing Bob in handcuffs and having him sit down on the hot Florida parking lot.

Officer Williams then approached the guy standing by the front end of the Caprice. The fellow identified himself as Johnny Rae and claimed to be the cousin of "Bob." He told Officer Williams that he was here in Florida to look for work and that his home of record was in Charlottesville, Virginia. Officer Williams asked Johnny Rae to empty his pockets onto the hood of the car. Johnny Rae did so, and Officer Williams went through the pile of objects, finding nothing of interest other than a cell phone and a key ring with the words "Caprice" on it and what appeared to be a driver's key. Johnny Rae asked Officer Williams how he liked "his ride?" Officer Williams told Johnny Rae to shut up and remain by the hood of the Caprice and proceeded to the rear of the Caprice to check on Billy Bob.

Officer Williams smelled a suspicious odor coming from the trunk. He asked Billy Bob if he could look in the trunk and Billy Bob said "no." While inspecting the outside of the trunk Officer Williams heard a sound like crunching gravel. He looked up to see Johnny Rae beating feet across the next parking lot and head into a residential area. At the same time he could hear Bob screaming at Johnny Rae to "keep his head down" and to "start plan B." Officer Williams pulled his weapon and fired off one round. Johnny Rae staggered briefly, but then disappeared into the neighborhood. Officer Williams went to check the area, but couldn't find any blood. He did see some transmission fluid, and bent down to cover his hand with the transmission fluid from the street.

Officer Williams approached "Bob" showing him his red hand and screaming at him that if he wanted to save Johnny Rae's life he better tell him where Johnny Rae was headed. Bob begin to sob and told Officer Williams that Johnny Rae was going to the motel room where he had been staying. He then told Officer Williams they had a crystal meth lab there. Bob told him the address was room 101 at the Lonely Mermaid Inn in Calusa Park – just down the street. Officer Williams called in the report to dispatch, asking for back up. He asked them to tell Officer Walker that he had discovered Meth on Billy Bob, and that the drugs had an arrowhead imprinted on them. While waiting for backup to arrive, Officer Williams put both Bob and Bubba into the back of his police cruiser. He also secured the items that Johnny Rae had left on the hood of the car, to include a wallet filled with receipts, one of them from the Lonely Mermaid Inn, and Johnny Rae's cell phone. He turned the cell phone on and began to scroll through the messages. In the text message storage he found reference to a "job," "shotguns," and talk about how great it was to be a living on Foxworthy Blvd. He then placed all of the items in an evidence bag and put the bag into the front of his police cruiser.

After making sure Billy Bob was locked in the backseat of his cruiser, Officer Williams took the keys from the ignition of the Caprice and opened the trunk, discovering boxes of chemicals normally used to manufacture Methamphetamines. He also discovered a sealed container. Upon opening it he found over 30,000 methamphetamine tablets. While moving the boxes around in the trunk he inadvertently broke some of the bottles. The rising fumes made Officer Williams sick. The last thing he remembered before losing consciousness were the flashing lights of another police cruiser as it pulled into the Sonic parking lot.

The defense has moved to suppress all of the evidence found in the car based upon an unlawful search. Prepare a memorandum of talking points for the senior state counsel who will argue this motion to the trial judge. Include case law as necessary to support your suggested positions.

Chapter 9: Inventories

South Dakota v. Opperman

96 S.Ct. 3092

Supreme Court of the United States

SOUTH DAKOTA, Petitioner,

v.

Donald OPPERMAN.

No. 75-76. | Argued March 29, 1976. | Decided July 6, 1976.

***365** Mr. Chief Justice BURGER delivered the opinion of the Court.

We review the judgment of the Supreme Court of South Dakota, holding that local police violated the Fourth Amendment to the Federal Constitution, as applicable to the States under the Fourteenth Amendment, when they conducted a routine inventory search of an automobile lawfully impounded by police for violations of municipal parking ordinances.

(1)

Local ordinances prohibit parking in certain areas of downtown Vermillion, S. D., between the hours of 2:00 a.m. and 6:00 a.m. During the early morning hours of December 10, 1973, a Vermillion police officer observed respondent's unoccupied vehicle illegally parked in the restricted zone. At approximately 3:00 a.m., the officer issued an overtime parking ticket and placed it on the car's windshield. The citation warned: "Vehicles in violation of any parking ordinance may be towed from the area."

At approximately 10 o'clock on the same morning, another ***366** officer issued a second ticket for an overtime parking violation. These circumstances were routinely reported to police headquarters, and after the vehicle was inspected, the car was towed to the city impound lot.

From outside the car at the impound lot, a police officer observed a watch on the dashboard and other items of personal property located on the back seat and back floorboard. At the officer's direction, the car door was then unlocked and, using a standard inventory form pursuant to standard police procedures, the officer inventoried the contents of the car, including the contents of the glove compartment which was unlocked. There he found marijuana contained in a plastic bag. All items, including the contraband, were removed to the police department for safekeeping. During the late afternoon of December 10, respondent appeared at the police department to claim his property. The marijuana was retained by police.

Respondent was subsequently arrested on charges of possession of marijuana. His motion to suppress the evidence yielded by ****3096** the inventory search was denied; he was convicted after a jury trial and sentenced to a fine of $100 and 14 days' incarceration in the county jail. On appeal, the Supreme Court of South Dakota reversed ***367** the conviction.[1875] The court concluded that the evidence had been obtained in violation of the Fourth Amendment prohibition against unreasonable searches and seizures. We granted certiorari[1876] and reverse.

(2)

This Court has traditionally drawn a distinction between automobiles and homes or offices in relation to the Fourth Amendment. Although automobiles are "effects"

[1875] *228 N.W.2d 152.*

[1876] *423 U.S. 923, 96 Ct. 264, 46 L.Ed.2d 248 (1975).*

and thus within the reach of the Fourth Amendment,[1877] warrantless examinations of automobiles have been upheld in circumstances in which a search of a home or office would not.[1878]

The reason for this well-settled distinction is twofold. First, the inherent mobility of automobiles creates circumstances of such exigency that, as a practical necessity, rigorous enforcement of the warrant requirement is impossible.[1879] But the Court has also upheld warrantless searches where no immediate danger was presented that the car would be removed from the jurisdiction.[1880] Besides the element of mobility, less rigorous warrant requirements govern because the expectation of privacy with respect to one's automobile is significantly less than that relating to one's home or office. In discharging their varied responsibilities ***368** for ensuring the bloc safety, law enforcement officials are necessarily brought into frequent contact with automobiles. Most of this contact is distinctly noncriminal in nature.[1881] Automobiles, unlike homes, are subjected to pervasive and continuing governmental regulation and controls, including periodic inspection and licensing requirements. As an everyday occurrence, police stop and examine vehicles when license plates or inspection stickers have expired, or if other violations, such as exhaust fumes or excessive noise, are noted, or if headlights or other safety equipment are not in proper working order.

The expectation of privacy as to automobiles is further diminished by the obviously public nature of automobile travel. Only two terms ago, the Court noted: "One has a lesser expectation of privacy in a motor vehicle because its function is transportation and it seldom serves as one's residence or as the repository of personal effects. . . A car has little capacity for escaping public scrutiny. It travels public thoroughfares where both its occupants and its contents are in plain view."[1882]

****3097** In the interests of public safety and as part of what the Court has called "community care-taking functions,"[1883] automobiles are frequently taken into police custody. Vehicle accidents present one such occasion. To permit the uninterrupted flow of traffic and in some circumstances to preserve evidence, disabled or damaged vehicles will often be removed from the highways or streets at the behest of police engaged solely in care-taking and traffic-control activities. Police ***369** will also frequently remove and impound automobiles which violate parking ordinances and which thereby jeopardize both the public safety and the efficient movement of vehicular traffic. The authority of police to seize and remove from the streets vehicles impeding traffic or threatening public safety and convenience is beyond challenge.

When vehicles are impounded, local police departments generally follow a routine practice of securing and inventorying the automobiles' contents. These procedures developed in response to three distinct needs: the protection of the owner's property while it remains in police custody;[1884] the protection the police against claims or disputes over lost or stolen property;[1885] and the protection of the police

---

[1877] *Cady v. Dombrowski, 413 U.S. 433, 439, 93 S.Ct. 2523, 2527, 37 L.Ed.2d 706 (1973).*

[1878] *Cardwell v. Lewis, 417 U.S. 583, 589, 94 S.Ct. 2464, 2468, 41 L.Ed.2d 325 (1974); Cady v. Dombrowski, supra, 413 U.S., at 439-440, 93 S.Ct. at 2527; Chambers v. Maroney, 399 U.S. 42, 48, 90 S.Ct. 1975, 1979, 26 L.Ed.2d 419 (1970).*

[1879] *Carroll v. United States, 267 U.S. 132, 153-154, 45 S.Ct. 280, 69 L.Ed. 543 (1925); Coolidge v. New Hampshire, 403 U.S. 443, 459-460, 91 S.Ct. 2022, 2034, 29 L.Ed.2d 564 (1971).*

[1880] *Chambers v. Maroney, supra, 399 U.S., at 51-52, 90 S.Ct. at 1981; Cooper v. California, 386 U.S. 58, 87 S.Ct. 788, 17 L.Ed. 2d 730 (1967).*

[1881] *Cady v. Dombrowski, supra, 413 U.S. at 442, 93 S.Ct. at 2528.*

[1882] *Cardwell v. Lewis, supra, 417 U.S., at 590, 94 S.Ct. at 2469.*

[1883] *Cady v. Dombrowski, supra, 413 U.S. at 441, 93 S.Ct. at 2528.*

[1884] *United States v. Mitchell, 458 F.2d 960, 961 (CA9 1972).*

[1885] *United States v. Kelehar, 470 F.2d 176, 178 (CA5 1972).*

from potential danger.[1886] The practice has been viewed as essential to respond to incidents of theft or vandalism.[1887] In addition, police frequently attempt to determine whether a vehicle has been stolen and thereafter abandoned.

These care-taking procedures have almost uniformly been upheld by the state courts, which by virtue of the localized nature of traffic regulation have had considerable occasion to deal with the issue. Applying the ***370** Fourth Amendment standard of "reasonableness," the state courts have overwhelmingly concluded that, even if an inventory is characterized as a "search," ****3098** the ***371** intrusion is constitutionally permissible.[1888] Even the seminal state decision relied on by the South Dakota Supreme Court in reaching the contrary result[1889] expressly approved police caretaking activities resulting in the securing of property within the officer's plain view.

The majority of the Federal Courts of Appeals have likewise sustained inventory procedures as reasonable police intrusions. As Judge Wisdom has observed:

"(W)hen the police take custody of any sort of container (such as) an automobile . . . it is reasonable to search the container to itemize the property to be held by the police. (This reflects) the underlying principle that the fourth amendment proscribes only Unreasonable searches."[1890] ***372** These cases have recognized that standard inventories often include an examination of the glove compartment, since it is a customary place for documents of ownership and registration,[1891] as well as a place for the temporary storage of valuables.

(3)

The decisions of this Court point unmistakably to the conclusion reached by both federal and state courts that inventories pursuant to standard police procedures ****3099** are reasonable. In the first such case, Mr. Justice Black made plain the nature of the inquiry before us:

"But the question here is not whether the search was authorized by state law. The question is rather whether the search was reasonable under the Fourth Amendment."[1892] And, in his last writing on the Fourth Amendment, Mr. Justice Black said:

"(T)he Fourth Amendment does not require that every search be made pursuant to a warrant. It ***373** prohibits only 'unreasonable searches and seizures.' The relevant test is not the reasonableness of the opportunity to procure a warrant, but the

---

[1886] *Cooper v. California, supra, 386 U.S., at 61-62, 87 S.Ct., at 790.*

[1887] *See Cabbler v. Commonwealth, 212 Va. 520, 522, 184 S.E.2d 781, 782 (1971), cert. denied, 405 U.S. 1073, 92 S.Ct. 1501, 31 L.Ed.2d 807 (1972); Warrix v. State, 50 Wis.2d 368, 376, 184 N.W.2d 189, 194 (1971).*

[1888] *See, E. g., City of St. Paul v. Myles, 298 Minn. 298, 300-301, 218 N.W.2d 697, 699 (1974); State v. Tully, 166 Conn. 126, 136, 348 A.2d 603, 609 (1974); People v. Trusty, 183 Colo. 291, 292-297, 516 P.2d 423, 425-426 (1973); People v. Sullivan, 29 N.Y.2d 69, 73, 323 N.Y.S.2d 945, 948, 272 N.E.2d 464, 466 (1971); Cabbler v. Commonwealth, supra; Warrix v. State, supra; State v. Wallen, 185 Neb. 44, 173 N.W.2d 372, cert. denied, 399 U.S. 912, 90 S.Ct. 2211, 26 L.Ed.2d 568 (1970); State v. Criscola, 21 Utah 2d 272, 444 P.2d 517 (1968); State v. Montague, 73 Wash.2d 381, 438 P.2d 571 (1968); People v. Clark, 32 Ill.App. 3d 898, 336 N.E.2d 892 (1975); State v. Achter, 512 S.W.2d 894 (Mo.Ct.App.1974); Bennett v. State, 507 P.2d 1252 (Okl.Cr.App. 1973); People v. Willis, 46 Mich.App. 436, 208 N.W.2d 204 (1973); State v. All, 17 N.C.App. 284, 193 S.E.2d 770, cert. denied, 414 U.S. 866, 94 S.Ct. 51, 38 L.Ed.2d 85 (1973); Godbee v. State, 224 So.2d 441 (Fla.Dist.Ct.App.1969).*

[1889] *Mozzetti v. Superior Court, 4 Cal.3d 699, 94 Cal.Rptr. 412, 484 P.2d 84 (1971).*

[1890] *United States v. Gravitt, 484 F.2d 375, 378 (CA5 1973), cert. denied, 414 U.S. 1135, 94 S.Ct. 879, 38 L.Ed.2d 761 (1974) (emphasis in original). See also Cabbler v. Superintendent, 528 F.2d 1142 (CA4 1975), cert. pending, No. 75-1463; Barker v. Johnson, 484 F.2d 941 (CA6 1973); United States v. Mitchell, 458 F.2d 960 (CA9 1972); United States v. Lipscomb, 435 F.2d 795 (CA5 1970), cert. denied, 401 U.S. 980, 91 S.Ct. 1213, 28 L.Ed.2d 331 (1971); United States v. Pennington, 441 F.2d 249 (CA5), cert. denied, 404 U.S. 854, 92 S.Ct. 97, 30 L.Ed.2d 94 (1971); United States v. Boyd, 436 F.2d 1203 (CA5 1971); Cotton v. United States, 371 F.2d 385 (CA9 1967). Accord, Lowe v. Hopper, 400 F.Supp. 970, 976-977 (SD Ga.1975); United States v. Spitalieri, 391 F.Supp. 167, 169-170 (ND Ohio 1975); United States v. Smith, 340 F.Supp. 1023 (Conn.1972); United States v. Fuller, 277 F.Supp. 97 (DC 1967), conviction aff'd, 139 U.S.App.D.C. 375, 433 F.2d 533 (1970).*

[1891] *United States v. Pennington, supra, at 251.*

[1892] *Cooper v. California, 386 U.S. at 61, 87 S.Ct., at 790 (emphasis added).*

reasonableness of the seizure under all the circumstances. The test of reasonableness cannot be fixed by Per se Rules; each case must be decided on its own facts."[1893]

In applying the reasonableness standard adopted by the Framers, this Court has consistently sustained police intrusions into automobiles impounded or otherwise in lawful police custody where the process is aimed at securing or protecting the car and its contents. In *Cooper v. California*, the Court upheld the inventory of a car impounded under the authority of a state forfeiture statute. Even though the inventory was conducted in a distinctly criminal setting and carried out a week after the car had been impounded, the Court nonetheless found that the car search, including examination of the glove compartment where contraband was found, was reasonable under the circumstances. This conclusion was reached despite the fact that no warrant had issued and probable cause to search for the contraband in the vehicle had not been established. The Court said in language explicitly applicable here:

"It would be unreasonable to hold that the police, having to retain the car in their custody for such a length of time, had no right, even for their own protection, to search it."[1894]

***374** In the following term, the *Court in Harris v. United States*,[1895] upheld the introduction of evidence, seized by an officer who, after conducting an inventory search of a car and while taking means to safeguard it, observed a car registration card lying on the metal stripping of the car door. Rejecting the argument that a warrant was necessary, the Court held that the intrusion was justifiable since it was "taken to protect the car while it was in police custody."[1896]

Finally, in *Cady v. Dombrowski*, the Court upheld a warrantless search of an automobile towed to a private garage even ****3100** though no probable cause existed to believe that the vehicle contained fruits of a crime. The sole justification for the warrantless incursion was that it was incident to the care-taking function of the local police to protect the community's safety. Indeed, the protective search was instituted solely because the local police "were under the impression" that the incapacitated driver, a Chicago police officer, was required to carry his service revolver at all times; the police had reasonable grounds to believe a weapon might be in the car, and thus available to vandals.[1897] The Court carefully noted that the protective search was ***375** carried out in accordance with standard procedures in the local police department,, a factor tending to ensure that the intrusion would be limited in scope to the extent necessary to carry out the caretaking function.[1898] In reaching this result, the Court in *Cady* distinguished *Preston v. United States*,[1899] on the grounds that the holding, invalidating a car search conducted after a vagrancy arrest, "stands only for the proposition that the search challenged there could not be justified as one incident to an arrest."[1900] Preston therefore did not raise the issue of the constitutionality of a protective inventory of a car lawfully within police custody.

The holdings in *Cooper*, *Harris*, And *Cady* point the way to the correct resolution of this case. None of the three cases, of course, involves the precise situation presented here; but, as in all Fourth Amendment cases, we are obliged to look to all

---

[1893] *Coolidge v. New Hampshire, 403 U.S., at 509-510, 91 S.Ct. 2022, 2059, 29 L.Ed.2d 564 (concurring and dissenting) (emphasis added).*

[1894] *386 U.S., at 61-62, 87 S.Ct. at 791.*

[1895] *390 U.S. 234, 88 S.Ct. 992, 19 L.Ed.2d 1067 (1968).*

[1896] *Id., at 236, 88 S.Ct. at 993.*

[1897] *413 U.S., at 436, 93 S.Ct. at 2525.*

[1898] *See United States v. Spitalieri, 391 F.Supp., at 169.*

[1899] *376 U.S. 364, 84 S.Ct. 881, 11 L.Ed.2d 777 (1964).*

[1900] *413 U.S., at 444, 93 S.Ct. at 2529.*

the facts and circumstances of this case in light of the principles set forth in these prior decisions.

"Whether a search and seizure is unreasonable within the meaning of the Fourth Amendment depends upon the facts and circumstances of each case . . ."[1901]

The Vermillion police were indisputably engaged in a care-taking search of a lawfully impounded automobile.[1902] The inventory was conducted only after the car had been impounded for multiple parking violations. The owner, having left his car illegally parked for an extended period, and thus subject to impoundment, was not present to make other arrangements for the safekeeping of his belongings. The inventory itself was prompted by the presence in plain view of a number of ***376** valuables inside the car. As in *Cady*, there is no suggestion whatever that this standard procedure, essentially like that followed throughout the country, was a pretext concealing an investigatory police motive.

On this record we conclude that in following standard police procedures, prevailing throughout the country and approved by the overwhelming majority of courts, the conduct of the police was not "unreasonable" under the Fourth Amendment.

The judgment of the South Dakota Supreme Court is therefore reversed, and the ****3101** case is remanded for further proceedings not inconsistent with this opinion.

Reversed and remanded.

Mr. Justice POWELL, concurring.

While I join the opinion of the Court, I add this opinion to express additional views as to why the search conducted in this case is valid under the Fourth and Fourteenth Amendments. This inquiry involves two distinct questions: (i) whether routine inventory searches are impermissible, and (ii) if not, whether they must be conducted pursuant to a warrant.

***377 I**

The central purpose of the Fourth Amendment is to safeguard the privacy and security of individuals against arbitrary invasions by government officials.[1903] None of our prior decisions is dispositive of the issue whether the Amendment permits routine inventory "searches"1 of automobiles. Resolution of this ***378** question requires a weighing of the governmental and societal interests advanced to justify such intrusions against the constitutionally protected interest of the individual citizen in the privacy of his effects.[1904] As noted in the Court's opinion, three interests generally have been advanced in support of inventory searches: (i) protection of the police from danger; (ii) protection of the police against claims and disputes over lost or stolen property; and (iii) protection of the owner's property while it remains in police custody.

Except in rare cases, there is little danger associated with impounding unsearched automobiles. But the occasional danger that may exist cannot be discounted entirely.[1905] ****3102** The harmful consequences in those rare cases may be great, and there does not appear to be any effective way of identifying in advance those circum-

---

[1901] *Cooper v. California, 386 U.S., at 59, 87 S.Ct., at 790.*

[1902] *Cf. United States v. Lawson, 487 F.2d 468, 471 (CA8 1973).*

[1903] *See, e.g., United States v. Brignoni-Ponce, 422 U.S. 873, 878, 95 S.Ct. 2574, 2573, 45 L.Ed.2d 607 (1975); Camara v. Municipal Court, 387 U.S. 523, 528, 87 S.Ct. 1727, 1730, 18 L.Ed.2d 930 (1967).*

[1904] *United States v. Martinez-Fuerte, 428 U.S. 543, at 555, 96 S.Ct. 3074, at 3081, 49 L.Ed.2d 1116; United States v. Brignoni-Ponce, supra, 422 U.S. at 878-879, 95 S.Ct. at 2573 (1975); United States v. Ortiz, 422 U.S. 891, 892, 95 S.Ct. 2585, 2573, 45 L.Ed.2d 623 (1975); Cady v. Dombrowski, 413 U.S. 433, 447-448, 93 S.Ct. 2523, 2531, 37 L.Ed.2d 706 (1973); Terry v. Ohio, 392 U.S. 1, 20-21, 88 S.Ct. 1868, 1879, 20 L.Ed.2d 889 (1968). Cf. Camara v. Municipal Court, supra, 387 U.S. at 534-535, 87 S.Ct. at 1734.*

[1905] *See Cooper v. California, 386 U.S. 58, 61-62, 87 S.Ct. 788, 791, 17 L.Ed.2d 730 (1967).*

stances or classes of automobile impoundments which represent a greater risk. Society also has an important interest in minimizing the number of false claims filed against police since they may diminish the community's respect for law enforcement generally and lower department morale, thereby impairing the effectiveness of the police. It ***379** is not clear, however, that inventories are a completely effective means of discouraging false claims, since there remains the possibility of accompanying such claims with an assertion that an item was stolen prior to the inventory or was intentionally omitted from the police records.

The protection of the owner's property is a significant interest for both t he policeman and the citizen. It is argued that an inventory is not necessary since locked doors and rolled-up windows afford the same protection that the contents of a parked automobile normally enjoy. But many owners might leave valuables in their automobile temporarily that they would not leave there unattended for the several days that police custody may last. There is thus a substantial grain in security if automobiles were inventoried and valuable items removed for storage. And, while the same security could be attained by posting a guard at the storage lot, that alternative may be prohibitively expensive, especially for smaller jurisdictions.

Against these interests must be weighed the citizen's interest in the privacy of the contents of his automobile. Although the expectation of privacy in an automobile is significantly less than the traditional expectation of privacy in an automobile is significantly less than the traditional expectation of privacy associated with the home,[1906] the unrestrained search ***380** of an automobile and its contents would constitute a serious intrusion upon the privacy of the individual in many circumstances. But such a search is not at issue in this case. As the Court's opinion emphasizes, the search here was limited to an inventory of the unoccupied automobile and was conducted strictly in accord with the regulations of the Vermillion Police Department. Upholding searches of this type provides no general license for the police to examine all the contents of such automobiles.

****3103** I agree with the Court that the Constitution permits routine inventory searches, and turn next to the question whether they must be conducted pursuant to a warrant.

***381 II**

While the Fourth Amendment speaks broadly in terms of "unreasonable searches and seizures," the decisions of this Court have recognized that the definition of "reasonableness" turns, at least in part, on the more specific dictates of the Warrant Clause.[1907] As the Court explained in Katz v. United States, supra, 389 U.S. at 357, 88 S.Ct. at 514, "(s)earches conducted without warrants have been held unlawful 'notwithstanding facts unquestionably showing probable cause,' Agnello v. United States, 269 U.S. 20, 33, 46 S.Ct. 4, 6, 70 L.Ed. 145, for the Constitution requires 'that the deliberate, impartial judgment of a judicial officer . . . be interposed between the citizen and the police . . ..' Wong Sun v. United States, 371 U.S. 471, 481-482, 83 S.Ct. 407, 414, 9 L.Ed.2d 441." Thus, although "(s)ome have argued that '(t)he relevant test is not whether it is reasonable to procure a search warrant, but whether the search was reasonable,' United States v. Rabinowitz, 339 U.S. 56, 66, 70 S.Ct. 430, 435, 94 L.Ed. 653 (1950)," "(t)his view has not been accepted." United States v. United States District Court, supra, 407 U.S., at 315, and n. 16, 92 S.Ct., at 2136. See Chimel v. California, 395 U.S. 752, 89 S.Ct. 2034, 23 L.Ed.2d 685 (1969). Except in a few carefully defined classes of cases, a search of private property with-

---

[1906] *United States v. Martinez-Fuerte, 428 U.S., at 561-562, 96 S.Ct., at 3084; United States v. Ortiz, supra, 422 U.S., at 896 n. 2, 95 S.Ct., at 2588; see Cardwell v. Lewis, 417 U.S. 583, 590-591, 94 S.Ct. 2464, 2469, 41 L.Ed.2d 325 (1974) (plurality opinion).*

[1907] *See United States v. United States District Court, 407 U.S. 297, 315, 92 S.Ct. 2125, 2135, 32 L.Ed.2d 752 (1972); Katz v. United States, 389 U.S. 347, 356, 88 S.Ct. 507, 514, 19 L.Ed.2d 576 (1967); Camara v. Municipal Court, 387 U.S., at 528, 87 S.Ct. at 1730.*

out valid consent is "unreasonable" unless it has been authorized by a valid search warrant.[1908] ***382**

Although the Court has validated warrantless searches of automobiles in circumstances that would not justify a search of a home or office, *Cady v. Dombrowski*, 413 U.S. 433, 93 S.Ct. 2523, 37 L.Ed.2d 706 (1973); *Chambers v. Maroney*, 399 U.S. 42, 90 S.Ct. 1975, 26 L.Ed.2d 419 (1970); *Carroll v. United States*, 267 U.S. 132, 45 S.Ct. 280, 69 L.Ed. 543 (1925), these decisions establish no general "automobile exception" to the warrant requirement. See *Preston v. United States*, 376 U.S. 364, 84 S.Ct. 881, 11 L.Ed.2d 777 (1964). Rather, they demonstrate that " 'for the purposes of the Fourth Amendment there is a constitutional difference between houses and cars,' "[1909] a difference that may in some cases justify a warrantless search.

****3104** The routine inventory search under consideration in this case does not fall within any of the established exceptions to the warrant requirement.10 But examination of the interests which are protected when searches are *383 conditioned on warrants issued by a judicial officer reveals that none of these is implicated here. A warrant may issue only upon "probable cause." In the criminal context the requirement of a warrant protects the individual's legitimate expectation of privacy against the overzealous police officer. "Its protection consists in requiring that those inferences (concerning probable cause) be drawn by a neutral and detached magistrate instead of being judged by the officer engaged in the often competitive enterprise of ferreting out crime."[1910] Inventory searches, however, are not conducted in order to discover evidence of crime. The officer does not make a discretionary determination to search based on a judgment that certain conditions are present. Inventory searches are conducted in accordance with established police department rules or policy and occur whenever an automobile is seized. There are thus no special facts for a neutral magistrate to evaluate.

A related purpose of the warrant requirement is to prevent hindsight from affecting the evaluation of the reasonableness of a search.[1911] In the case of an inventory search conducted in accordance with standard police department procedures, there is no significant danger of hindsight justification. The absence of a warrant will not impair the effectiveness of post-search review of the reasonableness of a particular inventory search.

Warrants also have been required outside the context of a criminal investigation. In *Camara v. Municipal Court*, the Court held that, absent consent, a warrant was necessary to conduct an areawide building code inspection, *384 even though the search could be made absent cause to believe that there were violations in t particular buildings being searched. In requiring a warrant the Court emphasized that "(t)he practical effect of (the existing warrantless search procedures had been) to leave the occupant subject to the discretion of the official in the field," "when (an) inspector demands entry, the occupant ha(d) no way of knowing whether enforcement of the municipal code involved require(d) inspection of his premises, no way of knowing the lawful limits of the inspector's power to search, and no way of knowing whether the inspector himself (was) acting under proper authorization."[1912]

[1908] *See, e.g., Almeida-Sanchez v. United States, 413 U.S. 266, 269, 93 S.Ct. 2535, 2537, 37 L.Ed.2d 596 (1973); Stoner v. California, 376 U.S. 483, 486, 84 S.Ct. 889, 891, 11 L.Ed.2d 856 (1964); Camara v. Municipal Court, supra, 387 U.S., at 528, 87 S.C at 1730; United States v. Jeffers, 342 U.S. 48, 51, 72 S.Ct. 93, 95, 96 L.Ed. 59 (1951); Agnello v. United States, 269 U.S. 20, 30, 46 S.Ct. 4, 10, 70 L.Ed. 145 (1925).*

[1909] *Cady v. Dombrowski, supra, 413 U.S., at 439, 93 S.Ct. at 2527, quoting Chambers v. Maroney, supra, 399 U.S. at 52, 90 S.Ct. at 1981.*

[1910] *Johnson v. United States, 333 U.S. 10, 14, 68 S.Ct. 367, 369, 92 L.Ed. 436 (1948). See, e.g., United States v. United States District Court, supra, 407 U.S. at 316-318, 92 S.Ct. at 2136.*

[1911] *See United States v. Martinez-Fuerte, 428 U.S., at 565, 96 S.Ct., at 3086; cf. United States v. Watson, 423 U.S. 411, 455 n. 22, 96 S.Ct. 820, 843, 46 L.Ed.2d 598 (1976) (Marshall, J., dissenting).*

[1912] *387 U.S., at 532, 87 S.Ct. at 1732.*

In the inventory search context these concerns are absent. The owner or prior occupant of the automobile is not present, nor, in many cases, is there any real likelihood that he could be located within a reasonable period of time. More importantly, no significant discretion is placed in the hands of the individual officer: he usually has no **3105** choice as to the subject of the search or its scope.

In sum, I agree with the Court that the routine inventory search in this case is constitutional.

(The dissent of Mr. Justice MARSHALL, with whom Mr. Justice BRENNAN and Mr. Justice STEWART join, is omitted.)

(The Statement of Mr. Justice WHITE is omitted.)

Black Letter Law

> The Court held that routine inventory search of defendant's locked automobile, which had been lawfully impounded for multiple violations of municipal parking ordinances, did not involve an "unreasonable" search in violation of the Fourth Amendment. The Court pointed out that the inventory was prompted by placement of a number of valuables inside the vehicle in plain view, and there was no suggestion that the standard procedure utilized was a pretext concealing investigatory police motive, and that once the officer was lawfully inside the vehicle to secure the personal property in plain view, it was not unreasonable to open the unlocked glove compartment, to which vandals would have had ready and unobstructed access once inside the vehicle and in which the subject marijuana was discovered.

Illinois v. Lafayette

103 S.Ct. 2605

Supreme Court of the United States

ILLINOIS, Petitioner

v.

Ralph LAFAYETTE.

No. 81-1859. | Argued April 20, 1983. | Decided June 20, 1983.

Chief Justice BURGER delivered the opinion of the Court.

The question presented is whether, at the time an arrested person arrives at a police station, the police may, without obtaining a warrant, search a shoulder bag carried by that person.

I

On September 1, 1980, at about 10 p.m., Officer Maurice Mietzner of the Kankakee City Police arrived at the Town Cinema in Kankakee, Illinois, in response to a call about a disturbance. There he found respondent involved in an altercation with the theatre manager. He arrested respondent for disturbing the peace, handcuffed him, and took him to the police station. Respondent carried a purse-type shoulder bag on the trip to the station.

At the police station respondent was taken to the booking room; there, Officer Mietzner removed the handcuffs from respondent and ordered him to empty his pockets and place ***642** the contents on the counter. After doing so, respondent took a package of cigarettes from his shoulder bag and placed the bag on the counter. Mietzner then removed the contents of the bag, and found ten amphetamine pills inside a cigarette case package.

Respondent was subsequently charged with violating Section 402(b) of the Illinois Controlled Substances Act, Ill.Rev.Stat., ch. 56 ½, ¶ 1402(b), on the basis of the controlled substances found in his shoulder bag. A pretrial suppression hearing was held at which the State argued that the search of the shoulder bag was a valid inventory search under *South Dakota v. Opperman.*[1913] Officer Mietzner testified that he examined the bag's contents because it was standard procedure to inventory "everything" in the possession of an arrested person.[1914] He testified that he was not seeking and did not expect to find drugs or weapons when he searched the bag and he conceded that the shoulder bag was small enough that it could have been placed and sealed in a bag, container or locker for protective purposes.[1915] After the hearing, but before any ruling, the State submitted a brief in which it argued for the first time that the search was valid as a delayed search incident to arrest. Thereafter, the trial court ordered the suppression of the amphetamine pills.[1916]

On appeal, the Illinois Appellate Court affirmed.[1917] It first held that the State had waived the argument that the search was incident to a valid arrest by failing to raise that argument at the suppression hearing.[1918] However, the court went on to discuss and reject the State's argument: "[E]ven assuming, arguendo, that the State has not waived this argument, the stationhouse search of the shoulder bag did not constitute a valid search incident to a lawful ****2608** arrest."[1919]

The State court also held that the search was not a valid inventory of respondent's belongings. It purported to distinguish ***643** *South Dakota v. Opperman*, on the basis that there is a greater privacy interest in a purse-type shoulder bag than in an automobile, and that the State's legitimate interests could have been met in a less intrusive manner, by "sealing [the shoulder bag] within a plastic bag or box and placing it in a secured locker."[1920] The Illinois court concluded:

"Therefore, the postponed warrantless search of the [respondent's] shoulder bag was neither incident to his lawful arrest nor a valid inventory of his belongings, and thus, violated the fourth amendment."[1921]

The Illinois Supreme Court denied discretionary review. We granted certiorari, because of the frequency with which this question confronts police and courts, and we reverse.

II

The question here is whether, consistent with the Fourth Amendment, it is reasonable for police to search the personal effects of a person under lawful arrest as part of the routine administrative procedure at a police stationhouse incident to booking and jailing the suspect. The justification for such searches does not rest on probable cause, and hence the absence of a warrant is immaterial to the reasonableness of the search. Indeed, we have previously established that the inventory search consti-

---

[1913] *428 U.S. 364, 96 S.Ct. 3092, 49 L.Ed.2d 1000 (1976).*

[1914] *App. 15, 16.*

[1915] *Id., at 15.*

[1916] *Id., at 22.*

[1917] *99 Ill.App.3d 830, 55 Ill.Dec. 210, 425 N.E.2d 1383 (3d Dist.1981).*

[1918] *Id., at 832, 55 Ill.Dec., at 212, 425 N.E.2d, at 1385.*

[1919] *Id.*, at 833, 55 Ill.Dec., at 212, 425 N.E.2d, at 1385.

[1920] 99 Ill.App.3d, at 834-835, 55 Ill.Dec., at 213, 425 N.E.2d, at 1386.

[1921] *Id.*, at 835, 55 Ill.Dec., at 213, 425 N.E.2d, at 1386.

tutes a well-defined exception to the warrant requirement.[1922] The Illinois court and respondent rely on *United States v. Chadwick,*[1923] and *Arkansa v. Sanders;*[1924] in the former, we noted that "probable cause to search is irrelevant" in inventory searches and went on to state:

"This is so because the salutary functions of a warrant simply have no application in that context; the constitutional ***644** reasonableness of inventory searches must be determined on other bases."[1925]

A so-called inventory search is not an independent legal concept but rather an incidental administrative step following arrest and preceding incarceration. To determine whether the search of respondent's shoulder bag was unreasonable we must "balance its intrusion on the individual's Fourth Amendment interests against its promotion of legitimate governmental interests."[1926]

In order to see an inventory search in proper perspective, it is necessary to study the evolution of interests along the continuum from arrest to incarceration. We have held that immediately upon arrest an officer may lawfully search the person of an arrestee,[1927] he may also search the area within the arrestee's immediate control.[1928] We explained the basis for this doctrine in *United States v. Robinson* where we said:

"A police officer's determination as to how and where to search the person of a suspect whom he has arrested is necessarily a quick ad hoc judgment which the ****2609** Fourth Amendment does not require to be broken down in each instance into an analysis of each step in the search. The authority to search the person incident to a lawful custodial arrest, while based upon the need to disarm and to discover evidence, does not depend on what a court may later decide was the probability in a particular arrest ***645** situation that weapons or evidence would in fact be found upon the person of the suspect. A custodial arrest of a suspect based on probable cause is a reasonable intrusion under the Fourth Amendment; that intrusion being lawful, a search incident to the arrest requires no additional justification. It is the fact of the lawful arrest which establishes the authority to search, and we hold that in the case of a lawful custodial arrest a full search of the person is not only an exception to the warrant requirement of the Fourth Amendment, but is also a 'reasonable' search under that Amendment."[1929]

An arrested person is not invariably taken to a police station or confined; if an arrestee is taken to the police station, that is no more than a continuation of the custody inherent in the arrest status. Nonetheless, the factors justifying a search of the person and personal effects of an arrestee upon reaching a police station but prior to being placed in confinement are somewhat different from the factors justifying an immediate search at the time and place of arrest.

The governmental interests underlying a station house search of the arrestee's person and possessions may in some circumstances be even greater than those supporting a search immediately following arrest. Consequently, the scope of a station house search will often vary from that made at the time of arrest. Police conduct that would be impractical or unreasonable-or embarrassingly intrusive-on the street can more readily and privately be performed at the station. For example, the interests

[1922] See *South Dakota v. Opperman, supra.*

[1923] 433 U.S. 1, 97 S.Ct. 2476, 53 L.Ed.2d 538 (1977).

[1924] 442 U.S. 753, 99 S.Ct. 2586, 61 L.Ed.2d 235 (1979).

[1925] *Id.,* 433 U.S., at 10 n. 5, 97 S.Ct., at 2483 n. 5.

[1926] *Delaware v. Prouse,* 440 U.S. 648, 654, 99 S.Ct. 1391, 1396, 59 L.Ed.2d 660 (1979).

[1927] *United States v. Robinson,* 414 U.S. 218, 94 S.Ct. 467, 38 L.Ed.2d 427 (1973);

[1928] *Chimel v. California,* 395 U.S. 752, 89 S.Ct. 2034, 23 L.Ed.2d 685 (1969).

[1929] 414 U.S., at 235, 94 S.Ct., at 477 *(emphasis added).*

supporting a search incident to arrest would hardly justify disrobing an arrestee on the street, but the practical necessities of routine jail administration may even justify taking a prisoner's clothes before confining him, although that step would be rare. This was made clear in *United States v. Edwards*: "With or without probable cause, the authorities were entitled [at the station house] not only to search [the ***646** arrestee's] clothing but also to take it from him and keep it in official custody."[1930]

At the station house, it is entirely proper for police to remove and list or inventory property found on the person or in the possession of an arrested person who is to be jailed. A range of governmental interests support an inventory process. It is not unheard of for persons employed in police activities to steal property taken from arrested persons; similarly, arrested persons have been known to make false claims regarding what was taken from their possession at the station house. A standardized procedure for making a list or inventory as soon as reasonable after reaching the station house not only deters false claims but also inhibits theft or careless handling of articles taken from the arrested person. Arrested persons have also been known to injure themselves-or others-with belts, knives, drugs or other items on their person while being detained. Dangerous instrumentalities-such as razor blades, bombs, or weapons can be concealed in innocent-looking articles taken from the arrestee's possession. The bare recital of these mundane realities justifies reasonable measures by police to limit these risks either while the items are in police possession or at the time they are returned to the arrestee upon his release. Examining all the items removed from the arrestee's person or possession and listing ****2610** or inventorying them is an entirely reasonable administrative procedure. It is immaterial whether the police actually fear any particular package or container; the need to protect against such risks arises independent of a particular officer's subjective concerns.[1931] Finally, inspection of an arrestee's personal property may assist the police in ascertaining or verifying his identity.[1932] In short, ***647** every consideration of orderly police administration benefiting both police and the public points toward the appropriateness of the examination of respondent's shoulder bag prior to his incarceration.

Our prior cases amply support this conclusion. In *South Dakota v. Opperman*, we upheld a search of the contents of the glove compartment of an abandoned automobile lawfully impounded by the police. We held that the search was reasonable because it served legitimate governmental interests that outweighed the individual's privacy interests in the contents of his car. Those measures protected the owner's property while it was in the custody of the police and protected police against possible false claims of theft. We found no need to consider the existence of less intrusive means of protecting the police and the property in their custody-such as locking the car and impounding it in safe storage under guard. Similarly, standardized inventory procedures are appropriate to serve legitimate governmental interests at stake here.

The Illinois court held that the search of respondent's shoulder bag was unreasonable because "preservation of the defendant's property and protection of police from claims of lost or stolen property, 'could have been achieved in a less intrusive manner.' For example, ... the defendant's shoulder bag could easily have been secured by sealing it within a plastic bag or box and placing it in a secured locker."[1933] Perhaps so, but the real question is not what "could have been achieved," but whether the Fourth Amendment requires such steps; it is not our function to write a manual on administering routine, neutral procedures of the station house. Our role is to assure against violations of the Constitution.

[1930] *Supra, 415 U.S., at 804, 94 S.Ct., at 1237-123.*

[1931] *See United States v. Robinson, supra, 414 U.S., at 235, 94 S.Ct., at 476-477.*

[1932] *See 2 W. LaFave, Search and Seizure § 5.3, at 306-307 (1978).*

[1933] *99 Ill.App.3d, at 835, 55 Ill.Dec., at 213, 425 N.E.2d, at 1386 (citation omitted).*

The reasonableness of any particular governmental activity does not necessarily or invariably turn on the existence of alternative "less intrusive" means. In *Cady v. Dombrowski,*[1934] for example, we upheld the search of *648 the trunk of a car to find a revolver suspected of being there. We rejected the contention that the public could equally well have been protected by the posting of a guard over the automobile. In language equally applicable to this case, we held, "[t]he fact that the protection of the public might, in the abstract, have been accomplished by 'less intrusive' means does not, by itself, render the search unreasonable."[1935] We are hardly in a position to second-guess police departments as to what practical administrative method will best deter theft by and false claims against its employees and preserve the security of the station house. It is evident that a station house search of every item carried on or by a person who has lawfully been taken into custody by the police will amply serve the important and legitimate governmental interests involved.

Even if less intrusive means existed of protecting some particular types of property, it would be unreasonable to expect police officers in the everyday course of business to make fine and subtle distinctions in deciding which containers or items may be searched and which must be sealed as a unit. Only recently in *New York v. Belton,*[1936] we stated: "'[a] **2611 single familiar standard is essential to guide police officers, who have only limited time and expertise to reflect on and balance the social and individual interests involved in the specific circumstances they confront.'"[1937]

Applying these principles, we hold that it is not "unreasonable" for police, as part of the routine procedure incident to incarcerating an arrested person, to search any container or article in his possession, in accordance with established inventory procedures.

***649** The judgment of the Illinois Appellate Court is reversed and the case is remanded for proceedings not inconsistent with this opinion.

It is so ordered.

Justice MARSHALL, with whom Justice BRENNAN joins, concurring in the judgment.

I agree that the police do not need a warrant or probable cause to conduct an inventory search prior to incarcerating a suspect, and I therefore concur in the judgment. The practical necessities of securing persons and property in a jailhouse setting justify an inventory search as part of the standard procedure incident to incarceration.

A very different case would be presented if the State had relied solely on the fact of arrest to justify the search of respondent's shoulder bag. A warrantless search incident to arrest must be justified by a need to remove weapons or prevent the destruction of evidence.[1938] Officer Mietzner did not in fact deem it necessary to search the bag when he arrested respondent, and I seriously doubt that such a search would have been lawful. A search at the time of respondent's arrest could not have been justified by a need to prevent the destruction of evidence, for there is no evidence or fruits of the offense-disturbing the peace-of which respondent was suspected. Moreover, although a concern about weapons might have justified seizure of the bag, such

---

[1934] *413 U.S. 433, 93 S.Ct. 2523, 37 L.Ed.2d 706 (1973),.*

[1935] *Id., at 447, 93 S.Ct., at 2531. See also United States v. Martinez-Fuerte, 428 U.S. 543, 557 n. 12, 96 S.Ct. 3074, 3082 n. 12, 49 L.Ed.2d 1116 (1976).*

[1936] *453 U.S. 454, 101 S.Ct. 2860, 69 L.Ed.2d 768 (1981),*

[1937] *Id., at 458-460, 101 S.Ct., at 2863-2864, quoting Dunaway v. New York, 442 U.S. 200, 213-214, 99 S.Ct. 2248, 2257-2258, 60 L.Ed.2d 824 (1979). See also United States v. Ross, 456 U.S. 798, 821, 102 S.Ct. 2157, 2170, 72 L.Ed.2d 572 (1982).*

[1938] *See United States v. Robinson, 414 U.S. 218, 251, 94 S.Ct. 467, 484, 38 L.Ed.2d 427 (1973) (Marshall, J., dissenting); Chimel v. California, 395 U.S. 752, 763, 89 S.Ct. 2034, 2040, 23 L.Ed.2d 685 (1969); United States v. Rabinowitz, 339 U.S. 56, 72, 70 S.Ct. 430, 437, 94 L.Ed. 653 (1950) (Frankfurter, J., dissenting).*

a concern could not have justified the further step of searching the bag following its seizure.[1939]

Black Letter Law

> Court held that the search of a shoulder bag was an inventory search, and as such was consistent with the Fourth Amendment. Routine police administrative procedures applying to lawful arrests need not rest on probable cause, and therefore the lack of warrant does not matter.

Colorado v. Bertine

107 S.Ct. 738

Supreme Court of the United States

COLORADO, Petitioner

v.

Steven Lee BERTINE.

No. 85–889. | Argued Nov. 10, 1986. | Decided Jan. 14, 1987.

Chief Justice REHNQUIST delivered the opinion of the Court.

On February 10, 1984, a police officer in Boulder, Colorado, arrested respondent Steven Lee Bertine for driving while under the influence of alcohol. After Bertine was taken into custody and before the arrival of a tow truck to take Bertine's van to an impoundment lot, a backup officer ***369** inventoried the contents of the van. The officer opened a closed backpack in which he found controlled substances, cocaine paraphernalia, and a large amount of cash. Bertine was subsequently charged with driving while under the influence of alcohol, unlawful possession of cocaine with intent to dispense, sell, and distribute, and unlawful possession of methaqualone. We ****740** are asked to decide whether the Fourth Amendment prohibits the State from proving these charges with the evidence discovered during the inventory of Bertine's van. We hold that it does not.

The backup officer inventoried the van in accordance with local police procedures, which require a detailed inspection and inventory of impounded vehicles. He found the backpack directly behind the frontseat of the van. Inside the pack, the officer observed a nylon bag containing metal canisters. Opening the canisters, the officer discovered that they contained cocaine, methaqualone tablets, cocaine paraphernalia, and $700 in cash. In an outside zippered pouch of the backpack, he also found $210 in cash in a sealed envelope. After completing the inventory of the van, the officer had the van towed to an impound lot and brought the backpack, money, and contraband to the police station.

After Bertine was charged with the offenses described above, he moved to suppress the evidence found during the inventory search on the ground, inter alia, that the search of the closed backpack and containers exceeded the permissible scope of such a search under the Fourth Amendment. The Colorado trial court ruled that probable cause supported Bertine's arrest and that the police officers had made the decisions to impound the vehicle and to conduct a thorough inventory search in good faith. Although noting that the inventory of the vehicle was performed in a "somewhat slipshod" manner, the District Court concluded that "the search of the backpack was done for the purpose of protecting the *370 owner's property, protection of the

[1939] *Cf. United States v. Chadwick, 433 U.S. 1, 15, 97 S.Ct. 2476, 2485, 53 L.Ed.2d 538 (1977); id., at 17 and n. 2, 97 S.Ct., at 2486 (Brennan, J., concurring).*

police from subsequent claims of loss or stolen property, and the protection of the police from dangerous instrumentalities." The court observed that the standard procedures for impounding vehicles mandated a "detailed inventory involving the opening of containers and the listing of [their] contents." Based on these findings, the court determined that the inventory search did not violate Bertine's rights under the Fourth Amendment of the United States Constitution. The court, nevertheless, granted Bertine's motion to suppress, holding that the inventory search violated the Colorado Constitution.

On the State's interlocutory appeal, the Supreme Court of Colorado affirmed.[1940] In contrast to the District Court, however, the Colorado Supreme Court premised its ruling on the United States Constitution. The court recognized that in *South Dakota v. Opperman*,[1941] we had held inventory searches of automobiles to be consistent with the Fourth Amendment, and that in *Illinois v. Lafayette*,[1942] we had held that the inventory search of personal effects of an arrestee at a police station was also permissible under that Amendment. The Supreme Court of Colorado felt, however, that our decisions in *Arkansas v. Sanders*[1943] and *United States v. Chadwick*,[1944] holding searches of closed trunks and suitcases to violate the Fourth Amendment, meant that *Opperman* and Lafayette did not govern this case.

We granted certiorari to consider the important and recurring question of federal law decided by the ***371 **741** Colorado Supreme Court.[1945] As that court recognized, inventory searches are now a well-defined exception to the warrant requirement of the Fourth Amendment.[1946] The policies behind the warrant requirement are not implicated in an inventory search,[1947] nor is the related concept of probable cause:

"The standard of probable cause is peculiarly related to criminal investigations, not routine, noncriminal procedures.... The probable-cause approach is unhelpful when analysis centers upon the reasonableness of routine administrative care-taking functions, particularly when no claim is made that the protective procedures are a subterfuge for criminal investigations."[1948] For these reasons, the Colorado Supreme Court's reliance on *Arkansas v. Sanders*,, and *United States v. Chadwick*, was incorrect. Both of these cases concerned searches solely for the purpose of investigating criminal conduct, with the validity of the searches therefore dependent on the application of the probable cause and warrant requirements of the Fourth Amendment.

By contrast, an inventory search may be "reasonable" under the Fourth Amendment even though it is not conducted pursuant to a warrant based upon probable cause. In ***372** *Opperman*, this Court assessed the reasonableness of an inventory search of the glove compartment in an abandoned automobile impounded by the police. We found that inventory procedures serve to protect an owner's property while it is in the custody of the police, to insure against claims of lost, stolen, or vandalized property, and to guard the police from danger. In light of these strong governmental interests and the diminished expectation of privacy in an automobile, we upheld the search. In reaching this decision, we observed that our cases accorded

---

[1940] *706 P.2d 411 (1985).*

[1941] *428 U.S. 364, 96 S.Ct. 3092, 49 L.Ed.2d 1000 (1976),*

[1942] *462 U.S. 640, 103 S.Ct. 2605, 77 L.Ed.2d 65 (1983).*

[1943] *442 U.S. 753, 99 S.Ct. 2586, 61 L.Ed.2d 235 (1979).*

[1944] *433 U.S. 1, 97 S.Ct. 2476, 53 L.Ed.2d 538 (1977),*

[1945] *475 U.S. 1081, 106 S.Ct. 1457, 89 L.Ed.2d 715 (1986).*

[1946] *See Lafayette, supra, 462 U.S., at 643, 103 S.Ct., at 2608; Opperman, supra, 428 U.S., at 367–376, 96 S.Ct., at 3096–3100.*

[1947] *Opperman, 428 U.S., at 370, n. 5, 96 S.Ct., at 3097, n. 5,*

[1948] *Ibid. See also United States v. Chadwick, supra, 433 U.S., at 10, n. 5, 97 S.Ct., at 2482, n. 5.*

deference to police care-taking procedures designed to secure and protect vehicles and their contents within police custody.[1949]

In our more recent decision, *Lafayette*, a police officer conducted an inventory search of the contents of a shoulder bag in the possession of an individual being taken into custody. In deciding whether this search was reasonable, we recognized that the search served legitimate governmental interests similar to those identified in *Opperman*. We determined that those interests outweighed the individual's Fourth Amendment interests and upheld the search.

In the present case, as in *Opperman* and *Lafayette*, there was no showing that the police, who were following standardized procedures, acted in bad faith or for the sole purpose of investigation. In addition, the governmental interests justifying the inventory searches in *Opperman* and *Lafayette* are ***373** nearly the same as ****742** those which obtain here. In each case, the police were potentially responsible for the property taken into their custody. By securing the property, the police protected the property from unauthorized interference. Knowledge of the precise nature of the property helped guard against claims of theft, vandalism, or negligence. Such knowledge also helped to avert any danger to police or others that may have been posed by the property.

The Supreme Court of Colorado opined that *Lafayette* was not controlling here because there was no danger of introducing contraband or weapons into a jail facility. Our opinion in *Lafayette*, however, did not suggest that the station-house setting of the inventory search was critical to our holding in that case. Both in the present case and in *Lafayette*, the common governmental interests described above were served by the inventory searches.

The Supreme Court of Colorado also expressed the view that the search in this case was unreasonable because Bertine's van was towed to a secure, lighted facility and because Bertine himself could have been offered the opportunity to make other arrangements for the safekeeping of his property. But the security of the storage facility does not completely eliminate the need for inventorying; the police may still wish to protect themselves or the owners of the lot against false claims of theft or dangerous instrumentalities. And while giving Bertine an opportunity to make alternative ***374** arrangements would undoubtedly have been possible, we said in *Lafayette*:

"The real question is not what 'could have been achieved,' but whether the Fourth Amendment requires such steps ... "The reasonableness of any particular governmental activity does not necessarily or invariably turn on the existence of alternative 'less intrusive' means."[1950] We conclude that here, as in *Lafayette*, reasonable police regulations relating to inventory procedures administered in good faith satisfy the Fourth Amendment, even though courts might as a matter of hindsight be able to devise equally reasonable rules requiring a different procedure.

The Supreme Court of Colorado also thought it necessary to require that police, before inventorying a container, weigh the strength of the individual's privacy interest in the container against the possibility that the container might serve as a repository for dangerous or valuable items. We think that such a requirement is contrary to our decisions in ***375** *Opperman* and *Lafayette*, and by analogy to our decision in *United* ****743** *States v. Ross*:[1951]

[1949] *See Cooper v. California, 386 U.S. 58, 61–62, 87 S.Ct. 788, 790–791, 17 L.Ed.2d 730 (1967); Harris v. United States, 390 U.S. 234, 236, 88 S.Ct. 992, 993, 19 L.Ed.2d 1067 (1968); Cady v. Dombrowski, 413 U.S. 433, 447–448, 93 S.Ct. 2523, 2530–2531, 37 L.Ed.2d 706 (1973).*

[1950] *Lafayette, 462 U.S., at 647, 103 S.Ct., at 2610 (emphasis in original). See Cady v. Dombrowski, supra, 413 U.S., at 447, 93 S.Ct., at 2530; United States v. Martinez-Fuerte, 428 U.S. 543, 557, n. 12, 96 S.Ct. 3074, 3082, n. 12, 49 L.Ed.2d 1116 (1976).*

[1951] *456 U.S. 798, 102 S.Ct. 2157, 72 L.Ed.2d 572 (1982).*

"Even if less intrusive means existed of protecting some particular types of property, it would be unreasonable to expect police officers in the everyday course of business to make fine and subtle distinctions in deciding which containers or items may be searched and which must be sealed as a unit."[1952]

"When a legitimate search is under way, and when its purpose and its limits have been precisely defined, nice distinctions between closets, drawers, and containers, in the case of a home, or between glove compartments, upholstered seats, trunks, and wrapped packages, in the case of a vehicle, must give way to the interest in the prompt and efficient completion of the task at hand."[1953]

We reaffirm these principles here: "'[a] single familiar standard is essential to guide police officers, who have only limited time and expertise to reflect on and balance the social and individual interests involved in the specific circumstances they confront.'"[1954]

Bertine finally argues that the inventory search of his van was unconstitutional because departmental regulations gave the police officers discretion to choose between impounding his van and parking and locking it in a public parking place. The Supreme Court of Colorado did not rely on this argument in reaching its conclusion, and we reject it. Nothing in *Opperman* or *Lafayette* prohibits the exercise of police discretion so long as that discretion is exercised according to standard criteria and on the basis of something other than suspicion of evidence of criminal activity. Here, the discretion afforded the Boulder police was exercised in light of ***376** standardized criteria, related to the feasibility and appropriateness of parking and locking a vehicle rather than impounding it. There was no showing that the police chose to impound Bertine's van in order to investigate suspected criminal activity.

While both *Opperman* and *Lafayette* are distinguishable from the present case on their facts, we think that the principles enunciated in those cases govern the present one. The judgment of the Supreme Court of Colorado is therefore

Reversed.

Justice BLACKMUN, with whom Justice POWELL and Justice O'CONNOR join, concurring.

The Court today holds that police officers may open closed containers while conducting a routine inventory search of an impounded vehicle. I join the Court's opinion, but write separately to underscore the importance of having such inventories conducted only pursuant to standardized police procedures. The underlying rationale for allowing an inventory exception to the Fourth Amendment warrant rule is that police officers are not vested with discretion to determine the scope of the inventory search.[1955] This absence of discretion ensures that inventory searches will not be used as a purposeful and general means of discovering evidence of crime. Thus, it is ****744** permissible ***377** for police officers to open closed containers in an inventory search only if they are following standard police procedures that mandate the opening of such containers in every impounded vehicle. As the Court emphasizes, the trial court in this case found that the Police Department's standard procedures did mandate the opening of closed containers and the listing of their contents.

[1952] *Lafayette, supra, 462 U.S., at 648, 103 S.Ct., at 2610.*

[1953] *United States v. Ross, supra, 456 U.S., at 821, 102 S.Ct., at 2170.*

[1954] *Lafayette, supra, 462 U.S., at 648, 103 S.Ct., at 2610 (quoting New York v. Belton, 453 U.S. 454, 458, 101 S.Ct. 2860, 2863, 69 L.Ed.2d 768 (1981)).*

[1955] *See South Dakota v. Opperman, 428 U.S. 364, 382–383, 96 S.Ct. 3092, 3103–3104, 49 L.Ed.2d 1000 (1976) (Powell, J., concurring).*

(The dissent of Justice MARSHALL, with whom Justice BRENNAN joins, is omitted.)

Black Letter Law

> Court held that the policies behind the warrant requirement and the related concept of probable cause are not implicated in an inventory search, which serves the strong governmental interests in protecting an owner's property while it is in police custody, insuring against claims of lost, stolen, or vandalized property, and guarding the police from danger. There was no showing here that the police, who were following standardized caretaking procedures, acted in bad faith or for the sole purpose of investigation.

Discussion Problems:

9-1. Officer Eric Jennings noticed the defendant in an area of town where narcotics were frequently used and sold at all times of the day and night. Jennings was aware that the defendant had an arrest history for narcotics-related offenses. Despite the fact the defendant lived 58 blocks away, Jennings had previously seen defendant in the area. Each time he was riding his bicycle. The officer stopped the defendant about two weeks before and confiscated food stamps that belonged to someone else. Jennings had seen "instances" in that neighborhood when food stamps were illicitly traded for narcotics, alcohol and numerous other things. Defendant was released, but his companion was arrested for possessing heroin. Thereafter, Jennings again stopped defendant, this time for running a stop sign while riding his bicycle.

On the date at issue here, defendant again rode his bicycle through a stop sign. The officers pulled up next to defendant and told him to stop. Defendant looked at the officers but continued to ride. As he did so, defendant moved his right hand to the right handlebar and used his thumb to push something inside. About 25 feet thereafter and 100 feet after ignoring the officer's order, defendant stopped his bicycle.

After Jennings seized a knife from the defendant and patted him down for other weapons, defendant became nervous when Jennings started to look at the bicycle. Jennings then searched the handlebar by turning the bicycle upside down and tapping on it. Three small rocks of cocaine dropped out. Defendant was then arrested.

At trial the defense moves to suppress the rock cocaine taken from the bicycle under the theory that it is the fruit of an unlawful search.

Draft a response to the defense motion to suppress the evidence.

9-2. At approximately 2:30 a.m. on October 9, Kelly, the Defendant's wife, called the Calusa County Sheriff's Office. Kelly reported that Defendant was in her house, in violation of a no-contact order. The Sheriff's Office confirmed that a state court had issued a valid no-contact order on September 20, and dispatched two deputies to Kelly's house. State law requires that if a law enforcement officer has probable cause to believe that someone has violated such a no-contact order, the officer must arrest that person.

While the officers were on their way to Kelly's house, Kelly told the Sheriff's Office that Defendant had left her house in a blue 1986 Ford Escort and was likely headed to his parents' house at 1312 Grove Road. The deputies, who were driving separate vehicles, switched routes and went to 1312 Grove Road to arrest Defendant.

At approximately 2:45 a.m., the deputies arrived at 1312 Grove Road, which is a farm. The two entered the property on a gravel lane. They traveled eastward on the gravel lane for approximately one-quarter mile, until they reached a gravel circular drive. There was a machine shed and a house on the gravel drive. The deputies continued eastward, driving past both buildings.

They drove around the farm on various gravel and dirt pathways that connected the buildings on the property, looking for the Escort, finding it just east of the house. The Escort was parked east of a number of outbuildings on the far (east) side of four cylindrical grain bins. A dirt path led between the far side of the grain bins and the Escort. The Escort was parked next to a field in some tall weeds. The Escort was not visible from either a public road or from the circular drive next to the farmhouse. The Escort only became visible once the deputies drove around the far side of the grain bins. The Escort was, however, visible from an open field east of the grain bins. A 4.5 foot high barbed-wire fence surrounded the entire compound, i.e., the house, the outbuildings and the grain bins (but not the open field east of the grain bins). The Escort was parked inside the fence.

Upon discovering the Escort, the deputies got out of their vehicle and walked over to the Escort. Each used his flashlight to look inside the windows of the Escort. No one was in the vehicle.

A gray conversion van was parked approximately five to six feet away from the Escort. The van was parked in one to two-feet tall weeds. The van's front tires were flat and the front of it was badly damaged. The van did not have license plates and was not registered. The van was not operational. A month and a half before the date in question, the van was in an accident, "totaled," and towed to the farm.

One deputy looked through the van's windows inside the front passenger compartment of the van, but did not find Defendant. The van was completely silent and dark. The second deputy opened one of the van's doors. Upon opening the door, he saw a plugged-in cell phone cord. The deputy called out Defendant's name. Defendant answered. The deputy then drew his weapon, ordered the Defendant out of the van, handcuffed, and arrested him. The Defendant was dressed in boxer shorts, a t-shirt, and socks.

The deputies then searched the van, finding a loaded Remington twenty-gauge shotgun. They also found three cases of empty beer cans and a case of full beer cans. It was apparent to the deputy that someone had been living in the van or was at least sleeping in it. There were a lot of blankets in the van and the back seat was folded down to make a bed. At some unknown point in time, Defendant told the deputies he had gone to the van to sleep.

Your boss, the defendant's senior defense counsel, has tasked you with drafting a motion to exclude the evidence seized from the van. Be sure to address all of the relevant constitutional issues.

Chapter 10: Consent & Plainview

Schnecklothe v. Bustamonte

93 S.Ct. 2041

Supreme Court of the United States

Merle R. SCHNECKLOTH, Superintendent, California Conservation Center, Petitioner,

v.

Robert Clyde BUSTAMONTE.

No. 71—732. | Argued Oct. 10, 1972. | Decided May 29, 1973.

***219** Mr. Justice STEWART delivered the opinion of the Court.

It is well settled under the Fourth and Fourteenth Amendments that a search conducted without a warrant issued upon probable cause is 'per se unreasonable. . . subject only to a few specifically established and well-delineated exceptions.'[1956] It is equally well settled that one of the specifically established exceptions to the requirements of both a warrant and probable cause is a search that is ****2044** conducted pursuant to consent.[1957] The constitutional question in the present case concerns the definition of 'consent' in this Fourth and Fourteenth Amendment context.

I

The respondent was brought to trial in a California court upon a charge of possessing a check with intent to defraud. He moved to suppress the introduction of certain material as evidence against him on the ground that the material had been acquired through an unconstitutional search and seizure. In response to the motion, the trial judge conducted an evidentiary hearing ***220** where it was established that the material in question had been acquired by the State under the following circumstances:

While on routine patrol in Sunnyvale, California, at approximately 2:40 in the morning, Police Officer James Rand stopped an automobile when he observed that one headlight and its license plate light were burned out. Six men were in the vehicle. Joe Alcala and the respondent, Robert Bustamonte, were in the front seat with Joe Gonzales, the driver. Three older men were seated in the rear. When, in response to the policeman's question, Gonzales could not produce a driver's license, Officer Rand asked if any of the other five had any evidence of identification. Only Alcala produced a license, and he explained that the car was his brother's. After the six occupants had stepped out of the car at the officer's request and after two additional policemen had arrived, Officer Rand asked Alcala if he could search the car. Alcala replied, 'Sure, go ahead.' Prior to the search no one was threatened with arrest and, according to Officer Rand's uncontradicted testimony, it 'was all very congenial at this time.' Gonzales testified that Alcala actually helped in the search of the car, by opening the trunk and glove compartment. In Gonzales' words: '(T)he police officer asked Joe (Alcala), he goes, 'Does the trunk open?' And Joe said, 'Yes.' He went to the car and got the keys and opened up the trunk.' Wadded up under the left rear seat, the police officers found three checks that had previously been stolen from a car wash.

The trial judge denied the motion to suppress, and the checks in question were admitted in evidence at Bustamonte's trial. On the basis of this and other evidence he

---

[1956] *Katz v. United States, 389 U.S. 347, 357, 88 S.Ct. 507, 514, 19 L.Ed.2d 576; Coolidge v. New Hampshire, 403 U.S. 443, 454-455, 91 S.Ct. 2022, 2031—2032, 29 L.Ed.2d 564; Chambers v. Maroney, 399 U.S. 42, 51, 90 S.Ct. 1975, 1981, 26 L.Ed.2d 419.*

[1957] *Davis v. United States, 328 U.S. 582, 593—594, 66 S.Ct. 1256, 1261—1262, 90 L.Ed. 1453; Zap v. United States, 328 U.S. 624, 630, 66 S.Ct. 1277, 1280, 90 L.Ed. 1477.*

was convicted, and the California Court of Appeal for the First Appellate District affirmed the conviction.[1958] ***221** In agreeing that the search and seizure were constitutionally valid, the appellate court applied the standard earlier formulated by the Supreme Court of California in an opinion by then Justice Traynor: 'Whether in a particular case an apparent consent was in fact voluntarily given or was in submission to an express or implied assertion of authority, is a question of fact to be determined in the light of all the circumstances.'[1959] The appellate court found that '(i)n the instant case the prosecution met the necessary burden of showing consent . . . since there were clearly circumstances from which the trial court could ascertain that consent had been freely given without coercion or submission to authority. Not only officer Rand, but Gonzales, the driver of the automobile, testified that Alcala's assent to the search of his brother's automobile was freely, even casually given. At the time of the request to search the automobile the atmosphere, according to Rand, was 'congenital' and there has been no discussion of any crime. As noted, Gonzales said Alcala even attempted to aid in the search.'[1960] ****2045** The California Supreme Court denied review.

Thereafter, the respondent sought a writ of habeas corpus in a federal district court. It was denied. On appeal, the Court of Appeals for the Ninth Circuit, relying on its prior decisions in *Cipres v. United States*[1961] and *Schoepflin v. United States*,[1962] set aside the District Court's order. The appellate court reasoned that a consent was a waiver of a person's Fourth and Fourteenth Amendment rights, and that the State was under an obligation to demonstrate, ***222** not only that the consent had been uncoerced, but that it had been given with an understanding that it could be freely and effectively withhold. Consent could not be found, the court held, solely from the absence of coercion and a verbal expression of assent. Since the District Court had not determined that Alcala had known that his consent could have been withheld and that he could have refused to have his vehicle searched, the Court of Appeals vacated the order denying the writ and remanded the case for further proceedings. We granted certiorari to determine whether the Fourth and Fourteenth Amendments require the showing thought necessary by the Court of Appeals.[1963]

II

It is important to make it clear at the outset what is not involved in this case. The respondent concedes that a search conducted pursuant to a valid consent is constitutionally permissible. In *Katz v. United States*,[1964] and more recently in *Vale v. Louisiana*,[1965] we recognized that a search authorized by consent is wholly valid.[1966] And similarly the State concedes that '(w)hen a prosecutor seeks to rely upon consent to justify the lawfulness of a search, he has the burden of proving that the consent was, in fact, freely and voluntarily given.'[1967]

[1958] *270 Cal.App.2d 648, 76 Cal.Rptr. 17.*

[1959] *People v. Michael, 45 Cal.2d 751, 753, 290 P.2d 852, 854.*

[1960] *270 Cal.App.2d, at 652, 76 Cal.Rptr., at 20.*

[1961] *343 F.2d 95.*

[1962] *391 F.2d 390.*

[1963] *405 U.S. 953, 92 S.Ct. 1168, 31 L.Ed.2d 230.*

[1964] *389 U.S., at 358, 88 S.Ct., at 515.*

[1965] *399 U.S. 30, 35, 90 S.Ct. 1969, 1972, 26 L.Ed.2d 409.*

[1966] *See also Davis v. United States, 328 U.S., at 593—594, 66 S.Ct., at 1261—1262; Zap v. United States, 328 U.S., at 630, 66 S.Ct., at 1280.*

[1967] *Bumper v. North Carolina, 391 U.S. 543, 548, 88 S.Ct. 1788, 1792, 20 L.Ed.2d 797. See also Johnson v. United States, 333 U.S. 10, 68 S.Ct. 367, 92 L.Ed. 436; Amos v. United States, 255 U.S. 313, 41 S.Ct. 266, 65 L.Ed. 654.*

***223** The precise question in this case, then, is what must the prosecution prove to demonstrate that a consent was 'voluntarily' given. And upon that question there is a square conflict of views between the state and federal courts that have reviewed the search involved in the case before us. The Court of Appeals for the Ninth Circuit concluded that it is an essential part of the State's initial burden to prove that a person knows he has a right to refuse consent. The California courts have followed the rule that voluntariness is a question of fact to be determined from the totality of all the circumstances, and that the state of a defendant's knowledge is only one factor to be taken into account in assessing the voluntariness of a consent.[1968]

A

The most extensive judicial exposition of the meaning of 'voluntariness' has been developed in those cases in which ****2046** the Court has had to determine the 'voluntariness' of a defendant's confession for purposes of the Fourteenth Amendment. Almost 40 years ago, in *Brown v. Mississippi*,[1969] the Court held that a criminal conviction based upon a confession obtained by brutality and violence was constitutionally invalid under the Due Process Clause of the Fourteenth Amendment. In some 30 different cases decided during the era that intervened between *Brown* and *Escobedo v. Illinois*,[1970] the Court was faced with the necessity of determining whether in fact the confessions in issue had been 'voluntarily' given. It is to that body ***224** of case law to which we turn for initial guidance on the meaning of 'voluntariness' in the present context.

Those cases yield no talismanic definition of 'voluntariness,' mechanically applicable to the host of situations where the question has arisen. 'The notion of 'voluntariness," Mr. Justice Frankfurter once wrote, 'is itself an amphibian.'[1971] It cannot be taken literally to mean a 'knowing' choice. 'Except where a person is unconscious or drugged or otherwise lacks capacity for conscious choice, all incriminating statements—even those made under brutal treatment—are 'voluntary' in the sense of representing a choice of alternatives. On the other hand, if 'voluntariness' incorporates notions of 'but-for' cause, the question should be whether the statement would have been made even absent inquiry or other official action. Under such a test, virtually no statement would be voluntary because very few people give incriminating statements in the absence of official action of some kind.' It is thus evident that neither linguistics nor epistemology will provide a ready definition of the meaning of 'voluntariness.'

Rather, 'voluntariness' has reflected an accommodation of the complex of values implicated in police questioning ***225** of a suspect. At one end of the spectrum is the acknowledged need for police questioning as a tool for the effective enforcement of criminal laws.[1972] Without such investigation, those who were innocent might be falsely accused, those who were guilty might wholly escape prosecution, and many crimes would go unsolved. In short, the security of all would be diminished.[1973] At the other end of the spectrum is the set of values reflecting society's deeply felt belief that the criminal law cannot be used as an instrument of unfairness, and that the possibility of unfair and even brutal police tactics poses a real and serious threat to civilized notions of justice. '(I)n cases involving involuntary confessions, this Court enforces the strongly felt attitude of our society that important hu-

---

[1968] *See, e.g., People v. Tremayne, 20 Cal.App.3d 1006, 98 Cal.Rptr. 193; People v. Roberts, 246 Cal.App.2d 715, 55 Cal.Rptr. 62.*

[1969] *297 U.S. 278, 56 S.Ct. 461, 80 L.Ed. 682.*

[1970] *378 U.S. 478, 84 S.Ct. 1758, 12 L.Ed.2d 977.*

[1971] *Culombe v. Connecticut, 367 U.S. 568, 604—605, 81 S.Ct. 1860, 1880—1881, 6 L.Ed.2d 1037.*

[1972] *See Culombe v. Connecticut, supra, at 578—580, 81 S.Ct., at 1865—1866.*

[1973] *Haynes v. Washington, 373 U.S. 503, 515, 83 S.Ct. 1336, 1344, 10 L.Ed.2d 513.*

man values are sacrificed where an agency of the government, in the course of securing a conviction, ****2047** wrings a confession out of an accused against his will.'[1974]

This Court's decisions reflect a frank recognition that the Constitution requires the sacrifice of neither security nor liberty. The Due Process Clause does not mandate that the police forgo all questioning, or that they be given carte blanche to extract what they can from a suspect. 'The ultimate test remains that which has been the only clearly established test in Anglo-American courts for two hundred years: the test of voluntariness. Is the confession the product of an essentially free and unconstrained choice by its maker? If it is, if he has willed to confess, it may be used against him. If it is not, if his will has been overborne and his capacity for self-determination critically impaired, the use of his ***226** confession offends due process.'[1975]

In determining whether a defendant's will was overborne in a particular case, the Court has assessed the totality of all the surrounding circumstances—both the characteristics of the accused and the details of the interrogation. Some of the factors taken into account have included the youth of the accused;[1976] his lack of education;[1977] or his low intelligence;[1978] the lack of any advice to the accused of his constitutional rights;[1979] the length of detention;[1980] the repeated and prolonged nature of the questioning,;[1981] and the use of physical punishment such as the deprivation of food or sleep,[1982] In all of these cases, the Court determined the factual circumstances surrounding the confession, assessed the psychological impact on the accused, and evaluated the legal significance of how the accused reacted.[1983]

The significant fact about all of these decisions is that none of them turned on the presence or absence of a single controlling criterion; each reflected a careful scrutiny of all the surrounding circumstances.[1984] In none of them did the Court rule that the Due Process Clause required the prosecution to prove as part of its ***227** initial burden that the defendant knew he had a right to refuse to answer the questions that were put. While the state of the accused's mind, and the failure of the police to advise the accused of his rights, were certainly factors to be evaluated in assessing the 'voluntariness' of an accused's responses, they were not in and of themselves determinative.[1985]

B

Similar considerations lead us to agree with the courts of California that the question whether a consent to a ****2048** search was in fact 'voluntary' or was the

[1974] *Blackburn v. Alabama, 361 U.S. 199, 206—207, 80 S.Ct. 274, 280, 4 L.Ed.2d 242. See also Culombe v. Connecticut, supra, 367 U.S., at 581—584, 81 S.Ct., at 1867—1869; Chambers v. Florida, 309 U.S. 227, 235—238, 60 S.Ct. 472, 476—478, 84 L.Ed. 716.*

[1975] *Culombe v. Connecticut, supra, 367 U.S., at 602, 81 S.Ct., at 1879.*

[1976] *E.g., Haley v. Ohio, 332 U.S. 596, 68 S.Ct. 302, 92 L.Ed. 224.*

[1977] *E.g., Payne v. Arkansas, 356 U.S. 560, 78 S.Ct. 844, 2 L.Ed.2d 975.*

[1978] *E.g., Fikes v. Alabama, 352 U.S. 191, 77 S.Ct. 281, 1 L.Ed.2d 246.*

[1979] *E.g., Davis v. North Carolina, 384 U.S. 737, 86 S.Ct. 1761, 16 L.Ed.2d 895.*

[1980] *E.g., Chambers v. Florida, supra.*

[1981] *E.g., Ashcraft v. Tennessee, 322 U.S. 143, 64 S.Ct. 921, 88 L.Ed. 1192.*

[1982] *E.g., Reck v. Pate, 367 U.S. 433, 81 S.Ct. 1541, 6 L.Ed.2d 948.*

[1983] *Culombe v. Connecticut, supra, 367 U.S., at 603, 81 S.Ct., at 1879.*

[1984] *See Miranda v. Arizona, 384 U.S. 436, 508, 86 S.Ct. 1602, 1645, 16 L.Ed.2d 694 (Harlan, J., dissenting); id., at 534—535, 86 S.Ct., at 1659—1660 (White, J., dissenting).*

[1985] *See, e.g., Davis v. North Carolina, supra; Haynes v. Washington, supra, 373 U.S., at 510—511, 83 S.Ct., at 1341—1342; Culombe v. Connecticut, supra, 367 U.S., at 610, 81 S.Ct., at 1883; Turner v. Pennsylvania, 338 U.S. 62, 64, 69 S.Ct. 1352, 93 L.Ed. 1810.*

product of duress or coercion, express or implied, is a question of fact to be determined from the totality of all the circumstances. While knowledge of the right to refuse consent is one factor to be taken into account, the government need not establish such knowledge as the sine qua non of an effective consent. As with police questioning, two competing concerns must be accommodated in determining the meaning of a 'voluntary' consent—the legitimate need for such searches and the equally important requirement of assuring the absence of coercion.

In situations where the police have some evidence of illicit activity, but lack probable cause to arrest or search, a search authorized by a valid consent may be the only means of obtaining important and reliable evidence. In the present case for example, while the police had reason to stop the car for traffic violations, the State does not contend that there was probable cause to search the vehicle or that the search was incident to a valid arrest ***228** of any of the occupants. Yet, the search yielded tangible evidence that served as a basis for a prosecution, and provided some assurance that others, wholly innocent of the crime, were not mistakenly brought to trial. And in those cases where there is probable cause to arrest or search, but where the police lack a warrant, a consent search may still be valuable. If the search is conducted and proves fruitless, that in itself may convince the police that an arrest with its possible stigma and embarrassment is unnecessary, or that a far more extensive search pursuant to a warrant is not justified. In short, a search pursuant to consent may result in considerably less inconvenience for the subject of the search, and, properly conducted, is a constitutionally permissible and wholly legitimate aspect of effective police activity.

But the Fourth and Fourteenth Amendments require that a consent not be coerced, by explicit or implicit means, by implied threat or covert force. For, no matter how subtly the coercion was applied, the resulting 'consent' would be no more than a pretext for the unjustified police intrusion against which the Fourth Amendment is directed. In the words of the classic admonition in *Boyd v. United States*:[1986]

'It may be that it is the obnoxious thing in its mildest and least repulsive form; but illegitimate and unconstitutional practices get their first footing in that way, namely, by silent approaches and slight deviations from legal modes of procedure. This can only be obviated by adhering to the rule that constitutional provisions for the security of person and property should be liberally construed. A close ***229** and literal construction deprives them of half their efficacy, and leads to gradual depreciation of the right, as if it consisted more in sound than in substance. It is the duty of courts to be watchful for the constitutional rights of the citizen, and against any stealthy encroachments thereon.'

The problem of reconciling the recognized legitimacy of consent searches with the requirement that they be free from any aspect of official coercion cannot be resolved by any infallible touchstone. To approve such searches without the most careful scrutiny would sanction the possibility of official coercion; to place artificial restrictions upon such searches would jeopardize their basic validity. Just as was true with confessions, the requirement of a 'voluntary' consent reflects a fair accommodation ****2049** of the constitutional requirements involved. In examining all the surrounding circumstances to determine if in fact the consent to search was coerced, account must be taken of subtly coercive police questions, as well as the possibly vulnerable subjective state of the person who consents. Those searches that are the product of police coercion can thus be filtered out without undermining the continuing validity of consent searches. In sum, there is no reason for us to depart in the area of consent searches, from the traditional definition of 'voluntariness.'

The approach of the Court of Appeals for the Ninth Circuit finds no support in any of our decisions that have attempted to define the meaning of 'voluntariness.' Its ruling, that the State must affirmatively prove that the subject of the search knew that

---

[1986] *116 U.S. 616, 635, 6 S.Ct. 524, 535, 29 L.Ed. 746.*

he had a right to refuse consent, would, in practice, create serious doubt whether consent searches could continue to be conducted. There might be rare cases where it could be proved from the record that a person in fact affirmatively knew of his ***230** right to refuse—such as a case where he announced to the police that if he didn't sign the consent form, 'you (police) are going to get a search warrant;' or a case where by prior experience and training a person had clearly and convincingly demonstrated such knowledge. But more commonly where there was no evidence of any coercion, explicit or implicit, the prosecution would nevertheless be unable to demonstrate that the subject of the search in fact had known of his right to refuse consent.

The very object of the inquiry—the nature of a person's subjective understanding—underlines the difficulty of the prosecution's burden under the rule applied by the Court of Appeals in this case. Any defendant who was the subject of a search authorized solely by his consent could effectively frustrate the introduction into evidence of the fruits of that search by simply failing to testify that he in fact knew he could refuse to consent. And the near impossibility of meeting this prosecutorial burden suggests why this Court has never accepted any such litmus-paper test of voluntariness. It is instructive to recall the fears of then Justice Traynor of the California Supreme Court:

'(I)t is not unreasonable for officers to seek interviews with suspects or witnesses or to call upon them at their homes for such purposes. Such inquiries, although courteously made and not accompanied with any assertion of a right to enter or search or secure answers, would permit the criminal to defeat his prosecution by voluntarily revealing all of the evidence against him and then contending that he acted only in response to an implied assertion of ***231** unlawful authority.'[1987]

One alternative that would go far toward proving that the subject of a search did know he had a right to refuse consent would be to advise him of that right before eliciting his consent. That, however, is a suggestion that has been almost universally repudiated by both federal and state courts, and, ****2050** we think, rightly so. For it would be thoroughly impractical to impose on the normal consent search the detailed requirements of an effective warning. Consent searches are part of the standard investigatory techniques of law enforcement ***232** agencies. They normally occur on the highway, or in a person's home or office, and under informal and unstructured conditions. The circumstances that prompt the initial request to search may develop quickly or be a logical extension of investigative police questioning. The police may seek to investigate further suspicious circumstances or to follow up leads developed in questioning persons at the scene of a crime. These situations are a far cry from the structured atmosphere of a trial where, assisted by counsel if he chooses, a defendant is informed of his trial rights.[1988] And, while surely a closer question, these situations are still immeasurably, far removed from 'custodial interrogation' where, in *Miranda v. Arizona* we found that the Constitution required certain now familiar warnings as a prerequisite to police interrogation. Indeed, in language applicable to the typical consent search, we refused to extend the need for warnings:

'Our decision is not intended to hamper the traditional function of police officers in investigating crime. . . . When an individual is in custody on probable cause, the police may, of course, seek out evidence in the field to be used at trial against him. Such investigation may include inquiry of persons not under restraint. General on-the-scene questioning as to facts surrounding a crime or other general questioning of citizens in the fact-finding process is not affected by our holding. It is an act of

[1987] *People v. Michael, 45 Cal.2d, at 754, 290 P.2d, at 854.*

[1988] *Cf. Boykin v. Alabama, 395 U.S. 238, 243, 89 S.Ct. 1709, 1712, 23 L.Ed.2d 274.*

responsible citizenship for individuals to give whatever information they may have to aid in law enforcement.'[1989]

Consequently, we cannot accept the position of the Court of Appeals in this case that proof of knowledge of the right to refuse consent is a necessary prerequisite ***233** to demonstrating a 'voluntary' consent. Rather it is only by analyzing all the circumstances of an individual consent that it can be ascertained whether in fact it was voluntary or coerced. It is this careful sifting of the unique facts and circumstances of each case that is evidenced in our prior decisions involving consent searches.

For example, in *Davis v. United States*,[1990] federal agents enforcing wartime gasoline-rationing regulations, arrested a filling station operator and asked to see his rationing coupons. He eventually unlocked a room where the agents discovered the coupons that formed the basis for his conviction. The District Court found that the petitioner had consented to the search—that although he had at first refused to turn the coupons over, he had soon been persuaded to do so and that force or threat of force had not been employed to persuade ****2051** him. Concluding that it could not be said that this finding was erroneous, this Court, in an opinion by Mr. Justice Douglas that looked to all the circumstances surrounding the consent, affirmed the judgment of conviction: 'The public character of the property, the fact that the demand was made during business hours at the place of business where the coupons were required to be kept, the existence of the right to inspect, the nature of the request, the fact that the initial refusal to turn the coupons over was soon followed by acquiescence in the demand—these circumstances all support the conclusion of the District Court.'[1991]

Conversely, if under all the circumstances it has appeared that the consent was not given voluntarily—that it was coerced by threats or force, or granted only in submission to a claim of lawful authority—then we have found the consent invalid and the search unreasonable.[1992] ***234** In *Bumper*, a 66-year-old Negro widow, who lived in a house located in a rural area at the end of an isolated mile-long dirt road, allowed four white law enforcement officials to search her home after they asserted they had a warrant to search the house. We held the alleged consent to be invalid, noting that '(w)hen a law enforcement officer claims authority to search a home under a warrant, he announces in effect that the occupant has no right to resist the search. The situation is instinct with coercion—albeit colorably lawful coercion. Where there is coercion there cannot be consent.'[1993]

Implicit in all of these cases is the recognition that knowledge of a right to refuse is not a prerequisite of a voluntary consent. If the prosecution were required to demonstrate such knowledge, *Davis* and *Zap* could not have found consent without evidence of that knowledge. And similarly if the failure to prove such knowledge were sufficient to show an ineffective consent, the Amos, Johnson, and Bumper opinions would surely have focused upon the subjective mental state of the person who consented. Yet they did not.

In short, neither this Court's prior cases, nor the traditional definition of 'voluntariness' requires proof of knowledge of a right to refuse as the sine qua non of an effective consent to a search.

***235 C**

[1989] 384 U.S., at 477—478, 86 S.Ct., at 1629—1630.

[1990] 328 U.S. 582, 66 S.Ct. 1256, 90 L.Ed. 1453,

[1991] Id., 328 U.S., at 593—594, 66 S.Ct., at 1261—1262, 90 L.Ed. 1453. See also Zap v. United States, 328 U.S. 624, 66 S.Ct. 1277, 90 L.Ed. 1477.

[1992] See, e.g., Bumper v. North Carolina, 391 U.S., at 548—549, 88 S.Ct., at 1791—1792; Johnson v. United States, 333 U.S. 10, 68 S.Ct. 367, 92 L.Ed. 436; Amos v. United States, 255 U.S. 313, 41 S.Ct. 266, 65 L.Ed. 654.

[1993] 391 U.S., at 550, 88 S.Ct., at 1792.

It is said, however, that a 'consent' is a 'waiver' of a person's rights under the Fourth and Fourteenth Amendments. The argument is that by allowing the police to conduct a search, a person 'waives' whatever right he had to prevent the police from searching. It is argued that under the doctrine of ****2052** *Johnson v. Zerbst*[1994] to establish such a 'waiver' the State must demonstrate 'an intentional relinquishment or abandonment of a known right or privilege.'

But these standards were enunciated in Johnson in the context of the safeguards of a fair criminal trial. Our cases do not reflect an uncritical demand for a knowing and intelligent waiver in every situation where a person has failed to invoke a constitutional protection. As Mr. Justice Black once observed for the Court: "Waiver' is a vague term used for a great variety of purposes, good and bad, in the law.'[1995] With respect to procedural due process, for example, the Court has acknowledged that waiver is possible, while explicitly leaving open the question whether a 'knowing and intelligent' waiver need be shown.[1996] ***236**

The requirement of a 'knowing' and 'intelligent' waiver was articulated in a case involving the validity of a defendant's decision to forego a right constitutionally guaranteed to protect a fair trial and the reliability of the truth-determining process. *Zerbst* dealt with the denial of counsel in a federal criminal trial. There the Court held that under the Sixth Amendment a criminal defendant is entitled to the assistance of counsel, and that if he lacks sufficient funds to retain counsel, it is the Government's obligation to furnish him with a lawyer. As Mr. Justice Black wrote for the Court: 'The Sixth Amendment stands as a constant admonition that if the constitutional safeguards it provides be lost, justice will not 'still be done.' It embodies a realistic recognition of the obvious truth that the average defendant does not have the professional legal skill to protect himself when brought before a tribunal with power to take his life or liberty, wherein the prosecution is presented by experienced and learned counsel. That which is simple, orderly, and necessary to the lawyer—to the untrained layman may appear intricate, complex and mysterious.'[1997] To preserve the fairness of the trial process the Court established an appropriately heavy burden on the Government before waiver could be found—'an intentional ***237** relinquishment or abandonment of a known right or privilege.'[1998]

Almost without exception, the requirement of a knowing and intelligent waiver has been applied only to those rights which the Constitution guarantees to a criminal defendant in ****2053** order to preserve a fair trial. Hence, and hardly surprisingly in view of the facts of Johnson itself, the standard of a knowing and intelligent waiver has most often been applied to test the validity of a waiver of counsel, either at trial, or upon a guilty plea. And the Court has also applied the Johnson criteria to assess the effectiveness of a waiver of other trial rights such as the right to confrontation, to a jury trial, and to a speedy trial, and the right to be free from ***238** twice being placed in jeopardy. Guilty pleas have been carefully scrutinized to determine whether the accused knew and understood all the rights to which he would be entitled at trial, and that he had intentionally chosen to forgo them. And the Court has evaluated the knowing and intelligent nature of the waiver of trial rights in trial-type situations, such as the waiver of the privilege against compulsory self-incrimination before an administrative agency or a congressional committee, or the waiver of counsel in a juvenile proceeding.

[1994] *304 U.S. 458, 464, 58 S.Ct. 1019, 1023, 82 L.Ed. 1461.*

[1995] *Green v. United States, 355 U.S. 184, 191, 78 S.Ct. 221, 226, 2 L.Ed.2d 199.*

[1996] *See D. H. Overmyer Co., Inc. v. Frick Co., 405 U.S. 174, 185—186, 92 S.Ct. 775, 782, 31 L.Ed.2d 124; Fuentes v. Shevin, 407 U.S. 67, 94—96, 92 S.Ct. 1983, 2001—2002, 32 L.Ed.2d 556.*

[1997] *304 U.S., at 462—463, 58 S.Ct., at 1022 (footnote omitted).*

[1998] *Id., at 464, 58 S.Ct., at 1023.*

**2054 The guarantees afforded a criminal defendant at trial also protect him at certain stages before the actual trial, and any alleged waiver must meet the strict standard of an intentional relinquishment of a 'known' right. But the 'trial' guarantees that have been applied to the 'pretrial' *239 stage of the criminal process are similarly designed to protect the fairness of the trial itself.

Hence, in *United States v. Wade*,[1999] the Court held 'that a post-indictment pretrial lineup at which the accused is exhibited to identifying witnesses is a critical stage of the criminal prosecution; that police conduct of such a lineup without notice to and in the absence of his counsel denies the accused his Sixth (and Fourteenth) Amendment right to counsel . . .'[2000] Accordingly, the Court indicated that the standard of a knowing and intelligent waiver must be applied to test the waiver of counsel at such a lineup.[2001] The Court stressed the necessary interrelationship between the presence of counsel at a post-indictment lineup before trial and the protection of the trial process itself:

'Insofar as the accused's conviction may rest on a courtroom identification in fact the fruit of a suspect pretrial identification which the accused is helpless the subject to effective scrutiny at trial, the accused is deprived of that right of cross-examination which is an essential safeguard to his right to confront the witnesses against him.[2002] And even though cross-examination is a precious safeguard to a fair trial, it cannot be viewed as an absolute assurance of accuracy and reliability. Thus in the present context, where so many variables and pitfalls exist, the first line of defense must be the prevention of unfairness and the lessening of the hazards of eyewitness identification at the lineup itself. The trial which might determine the accused's fate may well not be that in the courtroom but that at the pretrial confrontation, with the State aligned against the accused, the *240 witness the sole jury, and the accused unprotected against the overreaching, intentional or unintentional, and with little or no effective appeal from the judgment there rendered by the witness—'that's the man.''[2003]

And in *Miranda v. Arizona*,[2004] the Court found that custodial interrogation by the police was inherently coercive, and consequently held that detailed warnings were required to protect the privilege against compulsory self-incrimination. The Court made it clear that the basis for decision was the need to protect the fairness of the trial itself:

"That counsel is present when statements are taken from an individual during interrogation obviously enhances the integrity of the fact-finding processes in court. The presence of an attorney, and the warnings delivered to the individual, enable the defendant under otherwise compelling circumstances to tell his story without fear, effectively, and in a way that eliminates the evils in the interrogation process. Without the protections flowing from adequate warnings and the rights of counsel, 'all the careful safeguards erected around the giving of testimony, whether by an accused or any other witness, would become empty formalities in a procedure where the most compelling possible evidence of guilt, a confession, would have already been obtained at the unsupervised pleasure of the police."[2005]

[1999] *388 U.S. 218, 87 S.Ct. 1926, 18 L.Ed.2d 1149, and Gilbert v. California, 388 U.S. 263, 87 S.Ct. 1951, 18 L.Ed.2d 1178,.*

[2000] *Id., at 272, 87 S.Ct., at 1956.*

[2001] *See United States v. Wade, supra, 388 U.S., at 237, 87 S.Ct., at 1937.*

[2002] *Pointer v. Texas, 380 U.S. 400, 85 S.Ct. 1065, 13 L.Ed.2d 923.*

[2003] *Id., at 235—236, 87 S.Ct., at 1936—1937.*

[2004] *384 U.S. 436, 86 S.Ct. 1602, 16 L.Ed.2d 694.*

[2005] *Id., at 466, 86 S.Ct., at 1623.*

The standards of Johnson were, therefore, found to be a necessary prerequisite to a finding of a valid waiver.[2006] ****2055**

***241** There is a vast difference between those rights that protect a fair criminal trial and the rights guaranteed under the Fourth Amendment. Nothing, either in the purposes behind requiring a 'knowing' and 'intelligent' waiver of trial rights, or in the practical application of such a requirement suggests that it ought to be extended to the constitutional guarantee against unreasonable searches and seizures.

A strict standard of waiver has been applied to those rights guaranteed to a criminal defendant to insure that he will be accorded the greatest possible opportunity to utilize every facet of the constitutional model of a fair criminal trial. Any trial conducted in derogation of that model leaves open the possibility that the trial reached an unfair result precisely because all the protections specified in the Constitution were not provided. A prime example is the right to counsel. For without that right, a wholly innocent accused faces the real and substantial danger that simply because of his lack of legal expertise he may be convicted. As Mr. Justice Harlan once wrote: 'The sound reason why (the right to counsel) is so freely extended for a criminal trial is the severe injustice risked by confronting an untrained defendant with a range of technical points of law, evidence, and tactics familiar to the prosecutor but not to ***242** himself.'[2007] The Constitution requires that every effort be made to see to it that a defendant in a criminal case has not unknowingly relinquished the basic protections that the Framers thought indispensable to a fair trial.

The protections of the Fourth Amendment are of a wholly different order, and have nothing whatever to do with promoting the fair ascertainment of truth at a criminal trial. Rather, as Mr. Justice Frankfurter's opinion for the Court put it in *Wolf v. Colorado*,[2008] the Fourth Amendment protects the 'security of one's privacy against arbitrary intrusion by the police . . ..' In declining to apply the exclusionary rule of *Mapp v. Ohio*[2009] to convictions that had become final before rendition of that decision, the Court emphasized that 'there is no likelihood of unreliability or coercion present in a search-and-seizure case.'[2010] In *Linkletter*, the Court indicated that those cases that had been given retroactive effect went to 'the fairness of the trial—the very integrity of the fact-finding process. Here . . . the fairness of the trial is not under attack.'[2011] The Fourth Amendment 'is not an adjunct to the ascertainment of truth.' The guarantees of the ****2056** Fourth Amendment stand 'as a protection of quite different constitutional values—values reflecting the concern of our society for the right of each individual to be let alone. To recognize this is no more than to accord those values undiluted respect.'[2012]

Nor can it even be said that a search, as opposed to an eventual trial, is somehow 'unfair' if a person consents to a search. While the Fourth and Fourteenth ***243** Amendments limit the circumstances under which the police can conduct a search, there is nothing constitutionally suspect in a person's voluntarily allowing a search. The actual conduct of the search may be precisely the same as if the police had obtained a warrant. And, unlike those constitutional guarantees that protect a defendant at trial, it cannot be said every reasonable presumption ought to be indulged against voluntary relinquishment. We have only recently stated: '(I)t is no part of the policy underlying the Fourth and Fourteenth Amendments to discourage citizens from aid-

---

[2006] *See 384 U.S., at 475—479, 86 S.Ct., at 1628—1631. Cf. Escobedo v. Illinois, 378 U.S., at 490 n. 14, 84 S.Ct., at 1765.*

[2007] *Miranda v. Arizona, supra, 384 U.S., at 514, 86 S.Ct., at 1649 (dissenting opinion).*

[2008] *338 U.S. 25, 27, 69 S.Ct. 1359, 1361, 93 L.Ed. 1782.*

[2009] *367 U.S. 643, 81 S.Ct. 1684, 6 L.Ed.2d 1081.*

[2010] *Linkletter v. Walker, 381 U.S. 618, 638, 85 S.Ct. 1731, 1742, 14 L.Ed.2d 601.*

[2011] *Id., at 639, 85 S.Ct., at 1743.*

[2012] *Tehan v. United States ex rel. Shott, 382 U.S. 406, 416, 86 S.Ct. 459, 465, 15 L.Ed.2d 453.*

ing to the utmost of their ability in the apprehension of criminals.'[2013] Rather, the community has a real interest in encouraging consent, for the resulting search may yield necessary evidence for the solution and prosecution of crime, evidence that may insure that a wholly innocent person is not wrongly charged with a criminal offense.

Those cases that have dealt with the application of the *Johnson v. Zerbst* rule make clear that it would be next to impossible to apply to a consent search the standard of 'an intentional relinquishment or abandonment of a known right or privilege.' To be true to *Johnson* ***244** and its progeny, there must be examination into the knowing and understanding nature of the waiver, an examination that was designed for a trial judge in the structured atmosphere of a courtroom. As the Court expressed it in *Johnson*:

'The constitutional right of an accused to be represented by counsel invokes, of itself, the protection of a trial court, in which the accused—whose life or liberty is at stake—is without counsel. This protecting duty imposes the serious and weighty responsibility upon the trial judge of determining whether there is an intelligent and competent waiver by the accused. While an accused may waive the right to counsel, whether there is a proper waiver should be clearly determined by the trial court, and it would be fitting and appropriate for that determination to appear upon the record.'[2014]

****2057 *245** It would be unrealistic to expect that in the informal, unstructured context of a consent search, a policeman, upon pain of tainting the evidence obtained, could make the detailed type of examination demanded by Johnson. And, if for this reason a diluted form of 'waiver' were found acceptable, that would itself be ample recognition of the fact that there is no universal standard that must be applied in every situation where a person foregoes a constitutional right.

Similarly, a 'waiver' approach to consent searches would be thoroughly inconsistent with our decisions that have approved 'third party consents.' In *Coolidge v. New Hampshire*, where a wife surrendered to the police guns and clothing belonging to her husband, we found nothing constitutionally impermissible in the admission of that evidence at trial since the wife had not been coerced. *Frazier v. Cupp*[2015] held that evidence seized from the defendant's duffel bag in a search authorized by his cousin's consent was admissible at trial. We found that the defendant had assumed the risk that his cousin, with whom he shared the bag, would allow the police to search it.[2016] And ***246** in *Hill v. California*,[2017] we held that the police had validly seized evidence from the petitioner's apartment incident to the arrest of a third party, since the police had probable cause to arrest the petitioner and reasonably, though mistakenly, believed the man they had arrested was he. Yet it is inconceivable that the Constitution could countenance the waiver of a defendant's right to counsel by a third party, or that a waiver could be found because a trial judge reasonably, though mistakenly, believed a defendant had waived his right to plead not guilty.

In short, there is nothing in the purposes or application of the waiver requirements of *Johnson v. Zerbst* that justifies, much less compels, the easy equation of a knowing waiver with a consent search. To make such an equation is to generalize from the broad rhetoric of some of our decisions, and to ignore the substance of the differing constitutional guarantees. We decline to follow what one judicial scholar has termed 'the domino method of constitutional ****2058** adjudication . . . wherein

---

[2013] *Coolidge v. New Hampshire, 403 U.S., at 488, 91 S.Ct., at 2049.*

[2014] *304 U.S., at 465, 58 S.Ct., at 1023, 82 L.Ed. 1461.*

[2015] *394 U.S. 731, 740, 89 S.Ct. 1420, 1425, 22 L.Ed.2d 684.*

[2016] *See also Abel v. United States, 362 U.S. 217, 80 S.Ct. 683, 4 L.Ed.2d 668.*

[2017] *401 U.S. 797, 802—805, 91 S.Ct. 1106, 1110—1111, 28 L.Ed.2d 484.*

every explanatory statement in a previous opinion is made the basis for extension to a wholly different situation.'

D

Much of what has already been said disposes of the argument that the Court's decision in the Miranda case requires the conclusion that knowledge of a right to refuse is an indispensable element of a valid consent. The considerations that informed the Court's holding in *Miranda* are simply inapplicable in the present case. ***247** In *Miranda* the Court found that the techniques of police questioning and the nature of custodial surroundings produce an inherently coercive situation. The Court concluded that '(u)nless adequate protective devices are employed to dispel the compulsion inherent in custodial surroundings, no statement obtained from the defendant can truly be the product of his free choice.' [2018] And at another point the Court noted that 'without proper safeguards the process of in-custody interrogation of persons suspected or accused of crime contains inherently compelling pressures which work to undermine the individual's will to resist and to compel him to speak where he would not otherwise do so freely.'[2019]

In this case, there is no evidence of any inherently coercive tactics—either from the nature of the police questioning or the environment in which it took place. Indeed, since consent searches will normally occur on a person's own familiar territory, the specter of incommunicado police interrogation in some remote station house is simply inapposite. There is no reason to believe, under circumstances such as are present here, that the response to a policeman's question is presumptively coerced; and there is, therefore, no reason to reject the traditional test for determining the voluntariness of a person's response. *Miranda*, of course, did not reach investigative questioning of a person not in custody, which is most directly analogous to the situation of a consent search, and it assuredly did not indicate that such questioning ought to be deemed inherently coercive.

It is also argued that the failure to require the Government to establish knowledge as a prerequisite to a valid ***248** consent, will relegate the Fourth Amendment to the special province of 'the sophisticated, v. knowledgeable and the privileged.' We cannot agree. The traditional definition of voluntariness we accept today has always taken into account evidence of minimal schooling, low intelligence, and the lack of any effective warnings to a person of his rights; and the voluntariness of any statement taken under those conditions has been carefully scrutinized to determine whether it was in fact voluntarily given.

****2059 E**

Our decision today is a narrow one. We hold only that when the subject of a search is not in custody and the State attempts to justify a search on the basis of his consent, the Fourth and Fourteenth Amendments require that it demonstrate that the consent was in fact voluntarily given, and not the result of duress or coercion, express or implied. Voluntariness is a question of fact ***249** to be determined from all the circumstances, and while the subject's knowledge of a right to refuse is a factor to be taken into account, the prosecution is not required to demonstrate such knowledge as a prerequisite to establishing a voluntary consent. Because the California court followed these principles in affirming the respondent's conviction, and because the Court of Appeals for the Ninth Circuit in remanding for an evidentiary hearing required more, its judgment must be reversed.

It is so ordered.

Judgment of Court of Appeals reversed.

[2018] *384 U.S., at 458, 86 S.Ct., at 1619.*

[2019] *Id., at 467, 86 S.Ct., at 1624.*

(The dissent of Mr. Justice DOUGLAS, is omitted.)
(The dissent of Mr. Justice BRENNAN, is omitted.)
(The dissent of Mr. Justice MARSHALL, is omitted.)

Black Letter Law

> Held that when the subject of a search is not in custody and the state attempts to justify a search on basis of his consent, state must demonstrate that the consent was in fact voluntarily given; that voluntariness is a question of fact to be determined from the totality of the circumstances; and that, while the subject's knowledge of his right to refuse is a factor to be taken into account, the prosecution is not required to demonstrate such knowledge as a prerequisite to establishing a voluntary consent.

United States v. Matlock

94 S.Ct. 988
Supreme Court of the United States
UNITED STATES, Petitioner,
v.
William Earl MATLOCK.
No. 72—1355. | Argued Dec. 10—11, 1973. | Decided Feb. 20, 1974.

Mr. Justice WHITE delivered the opinion of the Court.

In *Schneckloth v. Bustamonte*,[2020] the Court reaffirmed the principle that the search of property, without warrant and without probable cause, ***166** but with proper consent voluntarily given, is valid under the Fourth Amendment. The question now before us is whether the evidence presented by the United States with respect to the voluntary consent of a third party to search the living quarters of the respondent was legally sufficient to render the seized materials admissible in evidence at the respondent's criminal trial.

I

Respondent Matlock was indicted in February 1971 for the robbery of a federally insured bank in Wisconsin, in violation of 18 U.S.C. s 2113. A week later, ****991** he filed a motion to suppress evidence seized by law enforcement officers from a home in the town of Pardeeville, Wisconsin, in which he had been living. Suppression hearings followed. As found by the District Court, the facts were that respondent was arrested in the yard in front of the Pardeeville home on November 12, 1970. The home was leased from the owner by Mr. and Mrs. Marshall. Living in the home were Mrs. Marshall, several of her children, including her daughter Mrs. Gayle Graff, Gayle's three-year-old son, and respondent. Although the officers were aware at the time of the arrest that respondent lived in the house, they did not ask him which room he occupied or whether he would consent to a search. Three of the arresting officers went to the door of the house and were admitted by Mrs. Graff, who was dressed in a robe and was holding her son in her arms. The officers told her they were looking for money and a gun and asked if they could search the house. Although denied by Mrs. Graff at the suppression hearings, it was found that she consented voluntarily to the search of the house, including the east bedroom on the

---

[2020] *412 U.S. 218, 93 S.Ct. 2041, 36 L.Ed.2d 854 (1973).*

second floor which she said was jointly occupied by Matlock and herself. The east bedroom was searched and the evidence at issue here, $4,995.00 in cash, was found in a diaper ***167** bag in the only closet in the room. The issue came to be whether Mrs. Graff's relationship to the east bedroom was sufficient to make her consent to the search valid against respondent Matlock.

The District Court ruled that before the seized evidence could be admitted at trial, the Government had to prove, first, that it reasonably appeared to the searching officers 'just prior to the search, that facts exist which will render the consenter's consent binding on the putative defendant,' and, second, that 'just prior to the search, facts do exist which render the consenter's consent binding on the putative defendant. There was no requirement that express permission from respondent to Mrs. Graff to allow the officers to search be shown; it was sufficient to show her authority to consent in her own right, by reason of her relationship to the premises. The first requirement was held satisfied because of respondent's presence in the yard of the house at the time of his arrest, because of Gayle Graff's residence in the house for some time and her presence in the house just prior to the search, and because of her statement to the officers that she and the respondent occupied the east bedroom.

The District Court concluded, however, that the Government had failed to satisfy the second requirement and ***168** had not satisfactorily proved Mrs. Graff's actual authority to consent to the search. To arrive at this result, the District Court held that although Gayle Graff's statements to the officers that she and the respondent occupied the east bedroom were admissible to prove the good-faith belief of the officers, they were nevertheless extrajudicial statements inadmissible to prove the truth of the facts therein averred. The same was true of Mrs. Graff's additional statements to the officers later on November 12 that she and the respondent had been sleeping together in the east bedroom regularly, including the early morning of November 12, and that she and respondent shared the use of a dresser in the room. There was also testimony that both Gayle Graff and respondent, ****992** at various times and places and to various persons, had made statements that they were wife and husband. These statements were deemed inadmissible to prove that respondent and Gayle Graff were married, which they were not, or that they were sleeping together as a husband and wife might be expected to do. Having excluded these declarations, the District Court then concluded that the remaining evidence was insufficient to prove 'to a reasonable certainty, by the greater weight of the credible evidence, that at the time of the search, and for some period of reasonable length theretofore, Gayle Graff and the defendant were living together in the east bedroom.' The remaining evidence, briefly stated, was that Mrs. Graff and respondent had lived together in a one-bedroom apartment in Florida from April to August 1970; that they lived at the Marshall home in Pardeeville from August to November 12, 1970; that they were several times seen going up or down stairs in the house together; and that the east bedroom, which respondent was shown to have rented from Mr. and Mrs. Marshall, contained evidence that it was also lived in by ***169** a man and a woman. The District Court thought these items of evidence created an 'inference' or at least a 'mild inference' that respondent and Gayle Graff at times slept together in the east bedroom, but it deemed them insufficient to satisfy the Government's burden of proof. The District Court also rejected the Government's claim that it was required to prove only that at the time of the search the officers could reasonably have concluded that Gayle Graff's relationship to the east bedroom was sufficient to make her consent binding on respondent.

The Court of Appeals affirmed the judgment of the District Court in all respects.[2021] We granted certiorari,[2022] and now reverse the Court of Appeals.

II

[2021] *7 Cir., 476 F.2d 1083.*

[2022] *412 U.S. 917, 94 S.Ct. 2734, 37 L.Ed.2d 143.*

It has been assumed by the parties and the courts below that the voluntary consent of any joint occupant of a residence to search the premises jointly occupied is valid against the co-occupant, permitting evidence discovered in the search to be used against him at a criminal trial. This basic proposition was accepted by the Seventh Circuit in this case, as it had been in prior cases, and has generally been applied ***170** in similar circumstances by other courts of appeals, and ****993** various state courts. This Court left open, in *Amos v. United States*,[2023] the question whether wife's permission to search the residence in which she lived with her husband could 'waive his constitutional rights,' but more recent authority here clearly indicates that the consent of one who possesses common authority over premises or effects is valid as against the absent, non-consenting person with whom that authority is shared. In *Frazier v. Cupp*,[2024] the Court 'dismissed rather quickly' the contention that the consent of the petitioner's cousin to the search of a duffel bag, which was being used jointly by both men and had been left in the cousin's home, would not justify the seizure of petitioner's clothing ***171** found inside; joint use of the bag rendered the cousin's authority to consent to its search clear. Indeed, the Court was unwilling to engage in the 'metaphysical subtleties' raised by Frazier's claim that his cousin only had permission to use one compartment within the bag. By allowing the cousin the use of the bag, and by leaving it in his house, Frazier was held to have assumed the risk that his cousin would allow someone else to look inside. More generally, in *Schneckloth v. Bustamonte*,[2025] we noted that our prior recognition of the constitutional validity of 'third party consent' searches in cases like *Frazier* and *Coolidge v. New Hampshire*[2026] supported the view that a consent search is fundamentally different in nature from the waiver of a trial right. These cases at least make clear that when the prosecution seeks to justify a warrantless search by proof of voluntary consent, it is not limited to proof that consent was given by the defendant, but may show that permission to search was obtained from a third party who possessed common authority over or other sufficient relationship to the premises or effects sought to be inspected. The ***172** issue now before us is whether the Government made the requisite showing in this case.

III

The District Court excluded from evidence at the suppression hearings, as inadmissible hearsay, the out-of-court statements of Mrs. Graff with respect to her and respondent's joint occupancy and use of the east bedroom, as well as the evidence that both respondent and Mrs. Graff at various times and to various persons had represented themselves as husband and wife. The Court of Appeals affirmed the ruling. Both courts were in error.

****994** As an initial matter we fail to understand why, on any approach to the case, the out-of-court representations of respondent himself that he and Gayle Graff were husband and wife were considered to be inadmissible against him. Whether or not Mrs. Graff's statements were hearsay, the respondent's own out-of-court admissions would surmount all objections based on the hearsay rule both at the suppression hearings and at the trial itself, and would be admissible for whatever inferences the trial judge could reasonably draw concerning joint occupancy of the east bedroom.[2027]

As for Mrs. Graff's statements to the searching officers, it should be recalled that the rules of evidence normally applicable in criminal trials do not operate with full force at hearings before the judge to determine the admissibility *173 of evi-

---

[2023] *255 U.S. 313, 317, 41 S.Ct. 266, 267, 65 L.Ed. 654 (1921).*

[2024] *394 U.S. 731, 740, 89 S.Ct. 1420, 1425, 22 L.Ed.2d 684 (1969).*

[2025] *412 U.S., at 245—246, 93 S.Ct., at 2057.*

[2026] *403 U.S. 443, 487—490, 91 S.Ct. 2022, 2048, 29 L.Ed.2d 564 (1971).*

[2027] *See 4 J. Wigmore, Evidence s 1048 (J. Chadbourn rev. 1972); C. McCormick, Evidence s 262 (2d ed. 1972).*

dence. In *Brinegar v. United States*,[2028] it was objected that hearsay had been used at the hearing on a challenge to the admissibility of evidence seized when a car was searched and that other evidence used at the hearing was held inadmissible at the trial itself. The Court sustained the trial court's rulings. It distinguished between the rules applicable to proceedings to determine probable cause for arrest and search and those governing the criminal trial itself—' There is a large difference between the two things to be proved, as well as between the tribunals which determine them, and therefore a like difference in the quanta and modes of proof required to establish them.'[2029] That certain evidence was admitted in preliminary proceedings but excluded at the trial—and the Court thought both rulings proper—was thought merely to 'illustrate the difference in standards and latitude allowed in passing upon the distinct issues of probable cause and guilt.'[2030]

That the same rules of evidence governing criminal jury trials are not generally thought to govern hearings before a judge to determine evidentiary questions was confirmed on November 20 last year when the Court transmitted to Congress the proposed Federal Rules of Evidence. Rule 104(a) provides that preliminary questions concerning admissibility are matters for ***174** the judge and that in performing this function he is not bound by the Rules of Evidence except those with respect to privileges. Essentially the same language on the scope of the proposed Rules is repeated in Rule 1101(d)(1). The Rules in this respect reflect the general views of various authorities on evidence.[2031] ****995**

Search warrants are repeatedly issued on ex parte affidavits containing out-of-court statements of identified and unidentified persons.[2032] An arrest and search without a warrant were involved in *McCray v. Illinois.*[2033] At the initial suppression hearing, the police proved probable cause for the arrest by testifying to the out-of-court statements of an unidentified informer. The Government would have been obligated to produce the informer and to put him on the stand had it wanted to use his testimony at defendant's trial, but we sustained the use of his out-of-court statements at the suppression hearing, as well as the Government's ***175** refusal to identify him. In the course of the opinion, we specifically rejected the claim that defendant's right to confrontation under the Sixth Amendment and Due Process Clause of the Fourteenth Amendment had in any way been violated. We also made clear that there was no contrary rule governing proceedings in the federal courts.

There is, therefore, much to be said for the proposition that in proceedings where the judge himself is considering the admissibility of evidence, the exclusionary rules, aside from rules of privilege, should not be applicable; and the judge should receive the evidence and give it such weight as his judgment and experience counsel. However that may be, certainly there should be no automatic rule against the reception of hearsay evidence in such proceedings, and it seems equally clear to us that the trial judge should not have excluded Mrs. Graff's statements in the circumstances present here.

In the first place, the court was quite satisfied that the statements had in fact been made. Second, there is nothing in the record to raise serious doubts about the truthfulness of the statements themselves. Mrs. Graff harbored no hostility or bias against respondent that might call her statements into question. Indeed, she testified on his behalf at the suppression hearings. Mrs. Graff responded to inquiry at the time

---

[2028] *338 U.S. 160, 69 S.Ct. 1302, 93 L.Ed. 1879 (1949).*

[2029] *Id., at 173, 69 S.Ct., at 1309.*

[2030] *Id., at 174, 69 S.Ct., at 1310.*

[2031] *5 J. Wigmore, Evidence s 1385 (3d ed. 1940); C. McCormick, Evidence s 53, p. 122 n. 91 (2d ed. 1972). See also Maguire & Epstein, Rules of Evidence in Preliminary Controversies as to Admissibility, 36 Yale L.J. 1101 (1927).*

[2032] *United States v. Ventresca, 380 U.S. 102, 108, 85 S.Ct. 741, 745, 13 L.Ed.2d 684 (1965).*

[2033] *386 U.S. 300, 87 S.Ct. 1056, 18 L.Ed.2d 62 (1967).*

of the search that she and respondent occupied the east bedroom together. A few minutes later, having led the officers to the bedroom, she stated that she and respondent shared the one dresser in the room and that the woman's clothing in the ***176** room was hers. Later the same day, she stated to the officers that she and respondent had slept together regularly in the room, including the early morning of that very day. These statements were consistent with one another. They were also corroborated by other evidence received at the suppression hearings: Mrs. Graff and respondent had lived together in Florida for several months immediately prior to coming to Wisconsin, where they lived in the house in question and where they were seen going upstairs together in the evening; respondent was the tenant of the east bedroom and that room bore every evidence that it was also occupied by a woman; respondent indicated in prior statements to various people that he and Mrs. Graff were husband and wife. Under circumstances there was no apparent reason for the judge to distrust the evidence and to exclude Mrs. Graff's declarations from his own consideration ****996** for whatever they might be worth in resolving, one way or another, the issues raised at the suppression hearings.

If there is remaining doubt about the matter, it should be dispelled by another consideration: cohabitation out of wedlock would not seem to be a relationship that one would falsely confess. Respondent and Gayle Graff were not married, and cohabitation out of wedlock is a crime in the State of Wisconsin. Mrs. Graff's statements were against her penal interest and they carried their own indicia of reliability. This was sufficient in itself, we think, to warrant admitting them to evidence for consideration by the trial judge. This ***177** is the case even if they would be inadmissible hearsay at respondent's trial either because statements against penal interest are to be excluded under *Donnelly v. United States*[2034] or because, if Rule 804(b)(4) of the proposed Federal Rules of Evidence becomes the law, such declarations would be admissible only if the declarant is unavailable at the time of the trial.

Finally, we note that Mrs. Graff was a witness for the respondent at the suppression hearings. As such, she was available for cross-examination, and the risk of prejudice, if there was any, from the use of hearsay was reduced. Indeed, she entirely denied that she either gave consent or made the November 12 statements to the officers that the District Court excluded from evidence. When asked whether in fact she and respondent had lived together, she claimed her privilege against self-incrimination and declined to answer.

IV

It appears to us, given the admissibility of Mrs. Graff's and respondent's out-of-court statements, that the Government sustained its burden of proving by the preponderance of the evidence that Mrs. Graff's voluntary consent to search the east bedroom was legally sufficient to warrant admitting into evidence the $4,995.00 found in the diaper bag. But we prefer that the District Court ***178** first reconsider the sufficiency of the evidence in the light of this decision and opinion. The judgment of the Court of Appeals is reversed and the case is remanded to the Court of Appeals with directions to remand the case to the District Court for further proceedings consistent with this opinion.

So ordered.

Reversed and remanded.

(THe dissent of Mr. Justice DOUGLAS is omitted.)

(The dissent of Mr. Justice BRENNAN, with whom Mr. Justice MARSHALL joins, is omitted.)

[2034] *228 U.S. 243, 272—277, 33 S.Ct. 449, 57 L.Ed. 820 (1913).*

Black Letter Law

> The Court held that consent to warrantless search by one who possesses common authority over the premises or effect is valid as against absent, nonconsenting person with whom that authority is shared.

Georgia v. Randolph

126 S.Ct. 1515

Supreme Court of the United States

GEORGIA, Petitioner,

v.

Scott Fitz RANDOLPH.

No. 04-1067. | Argued Nov. 8, 2005. | Decided March 22, 2006.

Justice SOUTER delivered the opinion of the Court.

***106** The Fourth Amendment recognizes a valid warrantless entry and search of premises when police obtain the voluntary consent of an occupant who shares, or is reasonably believed to share, authority over the area in common with a co-occupant who later objects to the use of evidence so obtained.[2035] The question here is whether such an evidentiary seizure is likewise lawful ****1519** with the permission of one occupant when the other, who later seeks to suppress the evidence, is present at the scene and expressly refuses to consent. We hold that, in the circumstances here at issue, a physically present co-occupant's stated refusal to permit entry prevails, rendering the warrantless search unreasonable and invalid as to him.

I

Respondent Scott Randolph and his wife, Janet, separated in late May 2001, when she left the marital residence in Americus, Georgia, and went to stay with her parents in Canada, taking their son and some belongings. In July, she returned to the Americus house with the child, though the record does not reveal whether her object was reconciliation or retrieval of remaining possessions.

***107** On the morning of July 6, she complained to the police that after a domestic dispute her husband took their son away, and when officers reached the house she told them that her husband was a cocaine user whose habit had caused financial troubles. She mentioned the marital problems and said that she and their son had only recently returned after a stay of several weeks with her parents. Shortly after the police arrived, Scott Randolph returned and explained that he had removed the child to a neighbor's house out of concern that his wife might take the boy out of the country again; he denied cocaine use, and countered that it was in fact his wife who abused drugs and alcohol.

One of the officers, Sergeant Murray, went with Janet Randolph to reclaim the child, and when they returned she not only renewed her complaints about her husband's drug use, but also volunteered that there were "'items of drug evidence'" in the house. Sergeant Murray asked Scott Randolph for permission to search the house, which he unequivocally refused.

The sergeant turned to Janet Randolph for consent to search, which she readily gave. She led the officer upstairs to a bedroom that she identified as Scott's, where the sergeant noticed a section of a drinking straw with a powdery residue he suspect-

[2035] *Illinois v. Rodriguez, 497 U.S. 177, 110 S.Ct. 2793, 111 L.Ed.2d 148 (1990); United States v. Matlock, 415 U.S. 164, 94 S.Ct. 988, 39 L.Ed.2d 242 (1974).*

ed was cocaine. He then left the house to get an evidence bag from his car and to call the district attorney's office, which instructed him to stop the search and apply for a warrant. When Sergeant Murray returned to the house, Janet Randolph withdrew her consent. The police took the straw to the police station, along with the Randolphs. After getting a search warrant, they returned to the house and seized further evidence of drug use, on the basis of which Scott Randolph was indicted for possession of cocaine.

He moved to suppress the evidence, as products of a warrantless search of his house unauthorized by his wife's consent over his express refusal. The trial court denied the ***108** motion, ruling that Janet Randolph had common authority to consent to the search.

The Court of Appeals of Georgia reversed, 264 Ga.App. 396, 590 S.E.2d 834 (2003), and was itself sustained by the State Supreme Court, principally on the ground that "the consent to conduct a warrantless search of a residence given by one occupant is not valid in the face of the refusal of another occupant who is physically present at the scene to permit a warrantless search," 278 Ga. 614, 604 S.E.2d 835, 836 (2004). The Supreme Court of Georgia acknowledged this Court's holding in Matlock, 415 U.S. 164, 94 S.Ct. 988, 39 L.Ed.2d 242, that "the consent of one who possesses common authority over premises or effects is valid as against the absent, nonconsenting person with whom that authority is shared," **1520 id., at 170, 94 S.Ct. 988, and found Matlock distinguishable just because Scott Randolph was not "absent" from the colloquy on which the police relied for consent to make the search. The State Supreme Court stressed that the officers in Matlock had not been "faced with the physical presence of joint occupants, with one consenting to the search and the other objecting." 278 Ga., at 615, 604 S.E.2d, at 837. It held that an individual who chooses to live with another assumes a risk no greater than " 'an inability to control access to the premises during [his] absence,' " ibid. (quoting 3 W. LaFave, Search and Seizure § 8.3(d), p. 731 (3d ed.1996) (hereinafter LaFave)), and does not contemplate that his objection to a request to search commonly shared premises, if made, will be overlooked.

We granted certiorari to resolve a split of authority on whether one occupant may give law enforcement effective consent to search shared premises, as against a co-tenant who is present and states a refusal to permit the search. 544 U.S. 973, 125 S.Ct. 1840, 161 L.Ed.2d 722 (2005). We now affirm.

*109 II

To the Fourth Amendment rule ordinarily prohibiting the warrantless entry of a person's house as unreasonable per se, Payton v. New York, 445 U.S. 573, 586, 100 S.Ct. 1371, 63 L.Ed.2d 639 (1980); Coolidge v. New Hampshire, 403 U.S. 443, 454-455, 91 S.Ct. 2022, 29 L.Ed.2d 564 (1971), one "jealously and carefully drawn" exception, Jones v. United States, 357 U.S. 493, 499, 78 S.Ct. 1253, 2 L.Ed.2d 1514 (1958), recognizes the validity of searches with the voluntary consent of an individual possessing authority, Rodriguez, 497 U.S., at 181, 110 S.Ct. 2793. That person might be the householder against whom evidence is sought, Schneckloth v. Bustamonte, 412 U.S. 218, 222, 93 S.Ct. 2041, 36 L.Ed.2d 854 (1973), or a fellow occupant who shares common authority over property, when the suspect is absent, Matlock, supra, at 170, 94 S.Ct. 988, and the exception for consent extends even to entries and searches with the permission of a co-occupant whom the police reasonably, but erroneously, believe to possess shared authority as an occupant, Rodriguez, supra, at 186, 110 S.Ct. 2793. None of our co-occupant consent-to-search cases, however, has presented the further fact of a second occupant physically present and refusing permission to search, and later moving to suppress evidence so obtained. The significance of such a refusal turns on the underpinnings of the co-occupant consent rule, as recognized since Matlock.

A

The defendant in that case was arrested in the yard of a house where he lived with a Mrs. Graff and several of her **1521 *110 relatives, and was detained in a squad car parked nearby. When the police went to the door, Mrs. Graff admitted them and consented to a search of the house. 415 U.S., at 166, 94 S.Ct. 988. In resolving the defendant's objection to use of the evidence taken in the warrantless search, we said that "the consent of one who possesses common authority over premises or effects is valid as against the absent, nonconsenting person with whom that authority is shared." Id., at 170, 94 S.Ct. 988. Consistent with our prior understanding that Fourth Amendment rights are not limited by the law of property, cf. Katz v. United States, 389 U.S. 347, 352-353, 88 S.Ct. 507, 19 L.Ed.2d 576 (1967), we explained that the third party's "common authority" is not synonymous with a technical property interest:

"The authority which justifies the third-party consent does not rest upon the law of property, with its attendant historical and legal refinements, but rests rather on mutual use of the property by persons generally having joint access or control for most purposes, so that it is reasonable to recognize that any of the co-inhabitants has the right to permit the inspection in his own right and that the others have assumed the risk that one of their number might permit the common area to be searched." 415 U.S., at 171, n. 7, 94 S.Ct. 988 (citations omitted).

See also Frazier v. Cupp, 394 U.S. 731, 740, 89 S.Ct. 1420, 22 L.Ed.2d 684 (1969) ("[I]n allowing [his cousin to share use of a duffel bag] and in leaving it in his house, [the suspect] must be taken to have assumed the risk that [the cousin] would allow someone else to look inside"). The common authority that counts under the Fourth Amendment may thus be broader than the rights accorded by property law, see Rodriguez, supra, at 181-182, 110 S.Ct. 2793 (consent is sufficient when given by a person who reasonably appears to have common authority but who, in fact, has no property interest in the premises searched), although its limits, too, reflect specialized tenancy arrangements apparent to the police, see *111 Chapman v. United States, 365 U.S. 610, 81 S.Ct. 776, 5 L.Ed.2d 828 (1961) (landlord could not consent to search of tenant's home).

The constant element in assessing Fourth Amendment reasonableness in the consent cases, then, is the great significance given to widely shared social expectations, which are naturally enough influenced by the law of property, but not controlled by its rules. Cf. Rakas v. Illinois, 439 U.S. 128, 144, n. 12, 99 S.Ct. 421, 58 L.Ed.2d 387 (1978) (an expectation of privacy is reasonable if it has "a source outside of the Fourth Amendment, either by reference to concepts of real or personal property law or to understandings that are recognized and permitted by society"). Matlock accordingly not only holds that a solitary co-inhabitant may sometimes consent to a search of shared premises, but stands for the proposition that the reasonableness of such a search is in significant part a function of commonly held understanding about the authority that co-inhabitants may exercise in ways that affect each other's interests.

B

Matlock's example of common understanding is readily apparent. When someone comes to the door of a domestic dwelling with a baby at her hip, as Mrs. Graff did, she shows that she belongs there, and that fact standing alone is enough to tell a law enforcement officer or any other visitor that if she occupies the place along with others, she probably lives there subject to the assumption tenants usually make about their common authority when they share quarters. They understand that any one of them may admit visitors, with the consequence that a guest obnoxious **1522 to one may nevertheless be admitted in his absence by another. As Matlock put it, shared tenancy is understood to include an "assumption of risk," on which police officers are entitled to rely, and although some group living together might make an exceptional arrangement that no one could admit a guest without the agreement of all, the chance of such an eccentric scheme is too remote to expect visitors to investigate a particular *112 household's rules before accepting an invitation to come in. So, Matlock relied on what was usual and placed no burden on the police to eliminate the possibility of atypical arrangements, in the absence of reason to doubt that the regular scheme was in place.

It is also easy to imagine different facts on which, if known, no common authority could sensibly be suspected. A person on the scene who identifies himself, say, as a landlord or a hotel manager calls up no customary understanding of authority to admit guests without the consent of the current occupant. See Chapman v. United States, supra (landlord); Stoner v. California, 376 U.S. 483, 84 S.Ct. 889, 11 L.Ed.2d 856 (1964) (hotel manager). A tenant in the ordinary course does not take rented premises subject to any formal or informal agreement that the landlord may let visitors into the dwelling, Chapman, supra, at 617, 81 S.Ct. 776, and a hotel guest customarily has no reason to expect the manager to allow anyone but his own employees into his room, see Stoner, supra, at 489, 84 S.Ct. 889; see also United States v. Jeffers, 342 U.S. 48, 51, 72 S.Ct. 93, 96 L.Ed. 59 (1951) (hotel staff had access to room for purposes of cleaning and maintenance, but no authority to admit police). In these circumstances, neither state-law property rights, nor common contractual arrangements, nor any other source points to a common understanding of authority to admit third parties generally without the consent of a person occupying the premises. And when it comes to searching through bureau drawers, there will be instances in which even a person clearly belonging on premises as an occupant may lack any perceived authority to consent; "a child of eight might well be considered to have the power to consent to the police crossing the threshold into that part of the house where any caller, such as a pollster or salesman, might well be admitted," 4 LaFave § 8.4(c), at 207 (4th ed.2004), but no one would reasonably expect such a child to be in a position to authorize anyone to rummage through his parents' bedroom.

***113 C**

Although we have not dealt directly with the reasonableness of police entry in reliance on consent by one occupant subject to immediate challenge by another, we took a step toward the issue in an earlier case dealing with the Fourth Amendment rights of a social guest arrested at premises the police entered without a warrant or the benefit of any exception to the warrant requirement. Minnesota v. Olson, 495 U.S. 91, 110 S.Ct. 1684, 109 L.Ed.2d 85 (1990), held that overnight houseguests have a legitimate expectation of privacy in their temporary quarters because "it is unlikely that [the host] will admit someone who wants to see or meet with the guest over the objection of the guest," id., at 99, 110 S.Ct. 1684. If that customary expectation of courtesy or deference is a foundation of Fourth Amendment rights of a houseguest, it presumably should follow that an inhabitant of shared premises may claim at least as much, and it turns out that the co-inhabitant naturally has an even stronger claim.

To begin with, it is fair to say that a caller standing at the door of shared premises would have no confidence that one occupant's invitation was a sufficiently **1523 good reason to enter when a fellow tenant stood there saying, "stay out." Without some very good reason, no sensible person would go inside under those conditions. Fear for the safety of the occupant issuing the invitation, or of someone else inside, would be thought to justify entry, but the justification then would be the personal risk, the threats to life or limb, not the disputed invitation.

The visitor's reticence without some such good reason would show not timidity but a realization that when people living together disagree over the use of their common quarters, *114 a resolution must come through voluntary accommodation, not by appeals to authority. Unless the people living together fall within some recognized hierarchy, like a household of parent and child or barracks housing military personnel of different grades, there is no societal understanding of superior and inferior, a fact reflected in a standard formulation of domestic property law, that "[e]ach cotenant ... has the right to use and enjoy the entire property as if he or she were the sole owner, limited only by the same right in the other cotenants." 7 R. Powell, Powell on Real Property § 50.03[1], p. 50-14 (M. Wolf gen. ed.2005). The want of any recognized superior authority among disagreeing tenants is also reflected in the law's response when the disagreements cannot be resolved. The law does not ask who has the better side of the conflict; it simply provides a right to any co-tenant, even the most unreasonable, to obtain a decree partitioning the property (when the relationship is one of co-ownership) and terminating the relationship. See, e.g., 2 H. Tiffany, Real Property §§ 468, 473, 474, pp. 297, 307-309 (3d ed.1939 and 2006 Cum.Supp.). And while a decree of partition is not the answer to disagreement among rental tenants, this situation resembles co-ownership in lacking the benefit of any understanding that one or the other rental co-tenant has a superior claim to control the use of the quarters they occupy together. In sum, there is no common understanding that one co-tenant generally has a right or authority to prevail over the express wishes of another, whether the issue is the color of the curtains or invitations to outsiders.

D

Since the co-tenant wishing to open the door to a third party has no recognized authority in law or social practice to prevail over a present and objecting co-tenant, his disputed invitation, without more, gives a police officer no better claim to reasonableness in entering than the officer would have in the absence of any consent at all. Accordingly, in the balancing *115 of competing individual and governmental interests entailed by the bar to unreasonable searches, Camara v. Municipal Court of City and County of San Francisco, 387 U.S. 523, 536-537, 87 S.Ct. 1727, 18 L.Ed.2d 930 (1967), the cooperative occupant's invitation adds nothing to the government's side to counter the force of an objecting individual's claim to security against the government's intrusion into his dwelling place. Since we hold to the "centuries-old principle of respect for the privacy of the home," Wilson v. Layne, 526 U.S. 603, 610, 119 S.Ct. 1692, 143 L.Ed.2d 818 (1999), "it is beyond dispute that the home is entitled to special protection as the center of the private lives of our people," Minnesota v. Carter, 525 U.S. 83, 99, 119 S.Ct. 469, 142 L.Ed.2d 373 (1998) **1524 (KENNEDY, J., concurring). We have, after all, lived our whole national history with an understanding of "the ancient adage that a man's house is his castle [to the point that t]he poorest man may in his cottage bid defiance to all the forces of the Crown," Miller v. United States, 357 U.S. 301, 307, 78 S.Ct. 1190, 2 L.Ed.2d 1332 (1958) (internal quotation marks omitted).

Disputed permission is thus no match for this central value of the Fourth Amendment, and the State's other countervailing claims do not add up to outweigh it. Yes, we recognize the consenting tenant's interest as a citizen in bringing criminal *116 activity to light, see Coolidge, 403 U.S., at 488, 91 S.Ct. 2022 ("[I]t is no part of the policy underlying the Fourth ... Amendmen[t] to discourage citizens from aiding to the utmost of their ability in the apprehension of criminals"). And we understand a co-tenant's legitimate self-interest in siding with the police to deflect suspicion raised by sharing quarters with a criminal, see 4 LaFave § 8.3(d), at 162, n. 72 ("The risk of being convicted of possession of drugs one knows are present and has tried to get the other occupant to remove is by no means insignificant"); cf. Schneckloth, 412 U.S., at 243, 93 S.Ct. 2041 (evidence obtained pursuant to a consent search "may insure that a wholly innocent person is not wrongly charged with a criminal offense").

But society can often have the benefit of these interests without relying on a theory of consent that ignores an inhabitant's refusal to allow a warrantless search. The co-tenant acting on his own initiative may be able to deliver evidence to the police, Coolidge, supra, at 487-489, 91 S.Ct. 2022 (suspect's wife retrieved his guns from the couple's house and turned them over to the police), and can tell the police what he knows, for use before a magistrate in getting a warrant. The reliance *117 on a co- **1525 tenant's information instead of disputed consent accords with the law's general partiality toward "police action taken under a warrant [as against] searches and seizures without one," United States v. Ventresca, 380 U.S. 102, 107, 85 S.Ct. 741, 13 L.Ed.2d 684 (1965); "the informed and deliberate determinations of magistrates empowered to issue warrants as to what searches and seizures are permissible under the Constitution are to be preferred over the hurried action of officers," United States v. Lefkowitz, 285 U.S. 452, 464, 52 S.Ct. 420, 76 L.Ed. 877 (1932).

Nor should this established policy of Fourth Amendment law be undermined by the principal dissent's claim that it shields spousal abusers and other violent co-tenants who will refuse to allow the police to enter a dwelling when their victims ask the police for help, post, at 1537 (opinion of ROBERTS, C.J.) (hereinafter the dissent). It is not that the dissent exaggerates violence in the home; we recognize that domestic abuse is a serious problem in the United States. See U.S. Dept. of Justice, National Institute of Justice, P. Tjaden & N. Thoennes, Full Report of the Prevalence, Incidence, and Consequences of Violence Against Women 25-26 (2000) (noting that over 20 million women and 6 million men will, in the course of their lifetimes, be the victims of intimate-partner abuse); U.S. Dept. of Health and Human Services, Centers for Disease Control and Prevention, National Center for Injury Prevention and Control, Costs of Intimate Partner Violence Against Women in the United States 19 (2003) (finding that nearly 5.3 million intimate-partner victimizations, which result in close to 2 million injuries and 1,300 deaths, occur among women in the United States each year); U.S. Dept. of Justice, Bureau of Justice Statistics, Crime Data Brief, C. Rennison, Intimate Partner Violence, 1993-2001 (Feb.2003) (noting that in 2001 intimate-partner violence made up 20% of violent crime against women); see also Becker, The *118 Politics of Women's Wrongs and the Bill of "Rights": A Bicentennial Perspective, 59 U. Chi. L.Rev. 453, 507-508 (1992) (noting that women may feel physical insecurity in their homes as a result of abuse from domestic partners).

But this case has no bearing on the capacity of the police to protect domestic victims. The dissent's argument rests on the failure to distinguish two different issues: when the police may enter without committing a trespass, and when the police may enter to search for evidence. No question has been raised, or reasonably could be, about the authority of the police to enter a dwelling to protect a resident from domestic violence; so long as they have good reason to believe such a threat exists, it would be silly to suggest that the police would commit a tort by entering, say, to give a complaining tenant the opportunity to collect belongings and get out safely, or to determine whether violence (or threat of violence) has just occurred or is about to (or soon will) occur, however much a spouse or other co-tenant objected. (And since the police would then be lawfully in the premises, there is no question that they could seize any evidence in plain view or take further action supported by any consequent probable cause, see Texas v. Brown, 460 U.S. 730, 737-739, 103 S.Ct. 1535, 75 L.Ed.2d 502 (1983) (plurality opinion).) Thus, the question whether the police might lawfully enter over objection in order to provide any protection that might be reasonable is easily answered yes. See **1526 4 LaFave § 8.3(d), at 161 ("[E]ven when ... two persons quite clearly have equal rights in the place, as where two individuals are sharing an apartment on an equal basis, there may nonetheless sometimes exist a basis for giving greater recognition to the interests of one over the other.... [W]here the defendant has victimized the third-party ... the emergency nature of the situation is such that the third-party consent should validate a warrantless search despite defendant's objections" (internal quotation marks omitted; third omission in original)). The undoubted right of the police *119 to enter in order to protect a victim, however, has nothing to do with the question in this case, whether a search with the consent of one co-tenant is good against another, standing at the door and expressly refusing consent.

None of the cases cited by the dissent support its improbable view that recognizing limits on merely evidentiary searches would compromise the capacity to protect a fearful occupant. In the circumstances of those cases, there is no danger that the fearful occupant will be kept behind the closed door of the house simply because the abusive tenant refuses to consent to a search. See United States v. Donlin, 982 F.2d 31, 32 (C.A.1 1992) (victimized individual was already outside of her apartment when police arrived and, for all intents and purposes, within the protective custody of law enforcement officers); United States v. Hendrix, 595 F.2d 883, 885-886 (C.A.D.C.1979) (per curiam) (even if the consent of the threatened co-occupant did not justify a warrantless search, the police entry was nevertheless allowable on exigent circumstances grounds); People v. Sanders, 904 P.2d 1311, 1313-1315 (Colo. 1995) (en banc) (victimized individual gave her consent to search away from her home and was not present at the time of the police visit; alternatively, exigent circumstances existed to satisfy the warrantless exception); Brandon v. State, 778 P.2d 221, 223-224 (Alaska App.1989) (victimized individual consented away from her home and was not present at the time of the police visit); United States v. Davis, 290 F.3d 1239, 1241 (C.A.10 2002) (immediate harm extinguished after husband "order[ed]" wife out of the home).

*120 The dissent's red herring aside, we know, of course, that alternatives to disputed consent will not always open the door to search for evidence that the police suspect is inside. The consenting tenant may simply not disclose enough information, or information factual enough, to add up to a showing of probable cause, and there may be no exigency to justify fast action. But nothing in social custom or its reflection in private law argues for placing a higher value on delving into private premises to search for evidence in the face of disputed consent, than on requiring clear justification before the government searches private living quarters over a resident's objection. We therefore hold that a warrantless search of a shared dwelling for evidence over the express refusal of consent by a physically present resident cannot be justified as reasonable as to him on the basis of consent given to the police by another resident.

****1527 E**

There are two loose ends, the first being the explanation given in Matlock for the constitutional sufficiency of a co-tenant's consent to enter and search: it "rests ... on mutual use of the property by persons generally having joint access or control for most purposes, so that it is reasonable to recognize that any of the co-inhabitants has the right to permit the inspection in his own right ...." 415 U.S., at 171, n. 7, 94 S.Ct. 988. If Matlock's co-tenant is giving permission "in his own right," how can his "own right" be eliminated by another tenant's objection? The answer appears in the very footnote from which the quoted statement is taken: the "right" to admit the police to which Matlock refers is not an enduring and enforceable ownership right as understood by the *121 private law of property, but is instead the authority recognized by customary social usage as having a substantial bearing on Fourth Amendment reasonableness in specific circumstances. Thus, to ask whether the consenting tenant has the right to admit the police when a physically present fellow tenant objects is not to question whether some property right may be divested by the mere objection of another. It is, rather, the question whether customary social understanding accords the consenting tenant authority powerful enough to prevail over the cotenant's objection. The Matlock Court did not purport to answer this question, a point made clear by another statement (which the dissent does not quote): the Court described the co-tenant's consent as good against "the absent, nonconsenting" resident. Id., at 170, 94 S.Ct. 988.

The second loose end is the significance of Matlock and Rodriguez after today's decision. Although the Matlock defendant was not present with the opportunity to object, he was in a squad car not far away; the Rodriguez defendant was actually asleep in the apartment, and the police might have roused him with a knock on the door before they entered with only the consent of an apparent co-tenant. If those cases are not to be undercut by today's holding, we have to admit that we are drawing a fine line; if a potential defendant with self-interest in objecting is in fact at the door and objects, the co-tenant's permission does not suffice for a reasonable search, whereas the potential objector, nearby but not invited to take part in the threshold colloquy, loses out.

This is the line we draw, and we think the formalism is justified. So long as there is no evidence that the police have removed the potentially objecting tenant from the entrance for the sake of avoiding a possible objection, there is practical value in the simple clarity of complementary rules, one recognizing the co-tenant's permission when there is no fellow occupant on hand, the other according dispositive weight to the fellow occupant's contrary indication when he *122 expresses it. For the very reason that Rodriguez held it would be unjustifiably impractical to require the police to take affirmative steps to confirm the actual authority of a consenting individual whose authority was apparent, we think it would needlessly limit the capacity of the police to respond to ostensibly legitimate opportunities in the field if we were to hold that reasonableness required the police to take affirmative steps to find a potentially objecting co-tenant before acting on the permission they had already received. There is no ready reason to believe that efforts to invite a refusal would make a difference in many cases, whereas every co-tenant consent case **1528 would turn into a test about the adequacy of the police's efforts to consult with a potential objector. Better to accept the formalism of distinguishing Matlock from this case than to impose a requirement, time consuming in the field and in the courtroom, with no apparent systemic justification. The pragmatic decision to accept the simplicity of this line is, moreover, supported by the substantial number of instances in which suspects who are asked for permission to search actually consent, albeit imprudently, a fact that undercuts any argument that the police should try to locate a suspected inhabitant because his denial of consent would be a foregone conclusion.

III

This case invites a straightforward application of the rule that a physically present inhabitant's express refusal of consent to a police search is dispositive as to him, regardless of *123 the consent of a fellow occupant. Scott Randolph's refusal is clear, and nothing in the record justifies the search on grounds independent of Janet Randolph's consent. The State does not argue that she gave any indication to the police of a need for protection inside the house that might have justified entry into the portion of the premises where the police found the powdery straw (which, if lawfully seized, could have been used when attempting to establish probable cause for the warrant issued later). Nor does the State claim that the entry and search should be upheld under the rubric of exigent circumstances, owing to some apprehension by the police officers that Scott Randolph would destroy evidence of drug use before any warrant could be obtained.

The judgment of the Supreme Court of Georgia is therefore affirmed.

It is so ordered.

Justice ALITO took no part in the consideration or decision of this case.

Justice STEVENS, concurring.

The study of history for the purpose of ascertaining the original understanding of constitutional provisions is much like the study of legislative history for the purpose of ascertaining the intent of the lawmakers who enact statutes. In both situations the facts uncovered by the study are usually relevant but not necessarily dispositive. This case illustrates why even the most dedicated adherent to an approach to constitutional interpretation that places primary reliance on the search for original understanding would recognize the relevance of changes in our society.

At least since 1604 it has been settled that in the absence of exigent circumstances, a government agent has no right to enter a "house" or "castle" unless authorized to do so by a valid warrant. See Semayne's Case, 5 Co. Rep. 91a, 77 Eng. Rep. 194 (K.B.). Every occupant of the home has a *124 right-protected by the common law for centuries and by the Fourth Amendment since 1791-to refuse entry. When an occupant gives his or her consent to enter, he or she is waiving a valuable constitutional right. To be sure that the waiver is voluntary, it is sound practice-a practice some Justices of this Court thought necessary to make the waiver **1529 voluntary1-for the officer to advise the occupant of that right.2 The issue in this case relates to the content of the advice that the officer should provide when met at the door by a man and a woman who are apparently joint tenants or joint owners of the property.

In the 18th century, when the Fourth Amendment was adopted, the advice would have been quite different from what is appropriate today. Given the then-prevailing dramatic differences between the property rights of the husband and the far lesser rights of the wife, only the consent of the husband would matter. Whether "the master of the house" consented or objected, his decision would control. Thus if "original understanding" were to govern the outcome of this case, the search was clearly invalid because the husband did not consent. History, however, is not dispositive because it is now clear, as a matter of constitutional law, that *125 the male and the female are equal partners. Reed v. Reed, 404 U.S. 71, 92 S.Ct. 251, 30 L.Ed.2d 225 (1971).

In today's world the only advice that an officer could properly give should make it clear that each of the partners has a constitutional right that he or she may independently assert or waive. Assuming that both spouses are competent, neither one is a master possessing the power to override the other's constitutional right to deny entry to their castle.

With these observations, I join the Court's opinion.

Justice BREYER, concurring.

If Fourth Amendment law forced us to choose between two bright-line rules, (1) a rule that always found one tenant's consent sufficient to justify a search without a warrant and (2) a rule that never did, I believe we should choose the first. That is because, as THE CHIEF JUSTICE'S dissent points out, a rule permitting such searches can serve important law enforcement needs (for example, in domestic abuse cases), and the consenting party's joint tenancy diminishes the objecting party's reasonable expectation of privacy.

But the Fourth Amendment does not insist upon bright-line rules. Rather, it recognizes that no single set of legal rules can capture the ever-changing complexity of human life. It consequently uses the general terms "unreasonable searches and seizures." And this Court has continuously emphasized that "[r]easonableness ... is measured ... by examining the totality of the circumstances." Ohio v. Robinette, 519 U.S. 33, 39, 117 S.Ct. 417, 136 L.Ed.2d 347 (1996); see also Illinois v. Wardlow, 528 U.S. 119, 136, 120 S.Ct. 673, 145 L.Ed.2d 570 (2000) (STEVENS, J., concurring in part and dissenting in part); Florida v. Bostick, 501 U.S. 429, 439, 111 S.Ct. 2382, 115 L.Ed.2d 389 (1991); Michigan v. **1530 Chesternut, 486 U.S. 567, 572-573, 108 S.Ct. 1975, 100 L.Ed.2d 565 (1988); Florida v. Royer, 460 U.S. 491, 506, 103 S.Ct. 1319, 75 L.Ed.2d 229 (1983) (plurality opinion).

The circumstances here include the following: The search at issue was a search solely for evidence. The objecting *126 party was present and made his objection known clearly and directly to the officers seeking to enter the house. The officers did not justify their search on grounds of possible evidence destruction. Cf. Thornton v. United States, 541 U.S. 615, 620-622, 124 S.Ct. 2127, 158 L.Ed.2d 905 (2004); Skinner v. Railway Labor Executives' Assn., 489 U.S. 602, 623, 109 S.Ct. 1402, 103 L.Ed.2d 639 (1989); Schmerber v. California, 384 U.S. 757, 770-771, 86 S.Ct. 1826, 16 L.Ed.2d 908 (1966). And, as far as the record reveals, the officers might easily have secured the premises and sought a warrant permitting them to enter. See Illinois v. McArthur, 531 U.S. 326, 121 S.Ct. 946, 148 L.Ed.2d 838 (2001). Thus, the "totality of the circumstances" present here do not suffice to justify abandoning the Fourth Amendment's traditional hostility to police entry into a home without a warrant.

I stress the totality of the circumstances, however, because, were the circumstances to change significantly, so should the result. The Court's opinion does not apply where the objector is not present "and object[ing]." Ante, at 1527.

Moreover, the risk of an ongoing crime or other exigent circumstance can make a critical difference. Consider, for example, instances of domestic abuse. See ante, at 1525. "Family disturbance calls ... constitute the largest single category of calls received by police departments each year." Mederer & Gelles, Compassion or Control: Intervention in Cases of Wife Abuse, 4 J. of Interpersonal Violence 25 (Mar.1989) (emphasis deleted); see also, e.g., Office of the Attorney General, California Criminal Justice Statistics Center, Domestic Violence Related Calls for Assistance, 1987-2003, County by Year, http://ag.ca.gov/cjsc/publications/misc/dvsr/tabs/8703.pdf (as visited Mar. 1, 2006, and available in Clerk of Court's case file) (providing data showing that California police received an average of 207,848 domestic violence related calls each year); Cessato, Defenders Against Domestic Abuse, Washington Post, Aug. 25, 2002, p. B8 ("In the District [of Columbia], police report that almost half of roughly 39,000 violent crime calls received in 2000 involved domestic violence"); Zorza, Women Battering: High Costs *127 and the State of the Law, Clearinghouse Review, 383, 385 (Special Issue 1994) ("One-third of all police time is spent responding to domestic disturbance calls"). And, law enforcement officers must be able to respond effectively when confronted with the possibility of abuse.

If a possible abuse victim invites a responding officer to enter a home or consents to the officer's entry request, that invitation (or consent) itself could reflect the victim's fear about being left alone with an abuser. It could also indicate the availability of evidence, in the form of an immediate willingness to speak, that might not otherwise exist. In that context, an invitation (or consent) would provide a special reason for immediate, rather than later, police entry. And, entry following invitation or consent by one party ordinarily would be reasonable even in the face of direct objection by the other. That being so, contrary to THE CHIEF JUSTICE'S suggestion, post, at 1537, today's decision will not adversely affect ordinary law enforcement practices.

**1531 Given the case-specific nature of the Court's holding, and with these understandings, I join the Court's holding and its opinion.

(The dissent of Chief Justice ROBERTS, with whom Justice SCALIA joins, is omitted.)

(The dissent of Justice SCALIA, is omitted.)

(The dissent of Justice THOMAS, is omitted.)

Black Letter Law

> Court held that a physically present co-occupant's stated refusal to permit entry renders warrantless entry and search unreasonable and invalid as to him. While the Fourth Amendment recognizes a valid warrantless entry and search of a premises when the police obtain the voluntary consent of an occupant who shares, or is reasonably believed to share, common authority over the property, and no present co-tenant objects. On the other hand, earlier case law established that a solitary co-inhabitant may sometimes consent to a search of shared premises, the reasonableness of such a search is in significant part a function of commonly held understandings about the authority that co-inhabitants may exercise in ways that affect each other's interests. When one co-habitant refuses entry, the permission of the other will not be sufficient.

Illinois v. Rodriguez

110 S.Ct. 2793

Supreme Court of the United States

ILLINOIS, Petitioner

v.

Edward RODRIGUEZ.

No. 88–2018. | Argued March 20, 1990. | Decided June 21, 1990.

*179 Justice SCALIA delivered the opinion of the Court.

In United States v. Matlock, 415 U.S. 164, 94 S.Ct. 988, 39 L.Ed.2d 242 (1974), this Court reaffirmed that a warrantless entry and search by law enforcement officers does not violate the Fourth Amendment's proscription of "unreasonable searches and seizures" if the officers have obtained the consent of a third party who possesses common authority over the premises. The present case presents an issue we expressly reserved in Matlock, see id., at 177, n. 14, 94 S.Ct., at 996, n. 14: Whether a warrantless entry is valid when based upon the consent of a third party whom the police, at the time of the entry, reasonably believe to possess common authority over the premises, but who in fact does not do so.

I

Respondent Edward Rodriguez was arrested in his apartment by law enforcement officers and charged with possession of illegal drugs. The police gained entry to the apartment with the consent and assistance of Gail Fischer, who had lived there with respondent for several months. The relevant facts leading to the arrest are as follows.

On July 26, 1985, police were summoned to the residence of Dorothy Jackson on South Wolcott in Chicago. They were met by Ms. Jackson's daughter, Gail Fischer, who showed signs of a severe beating. She told the officers that she had been assaulted by respondent Edward Rodriguez earlier that day in an apartment on South California. **2797 Fischer stated that Rodriguez was then asleep in the apartment, and she consented to travel there with the police in order to unlock the door with her key so that the officers could enter and arrest him. During this conversation, Fischer several times referred to the apartment on South California as "our" apartment, and said that she had clothes and furniture there. It is unclear whether she indicated that she currently lived at the apartment, or only that she used to live there.

*180 The police officers drove to the apartment on South California, accompanied by Fischer. They did not obtain an arrest warrant for Rodriguez, nor did they seek a search warrant for the apartment. At the apartment, Fischer unlocked the door with her key and gave the officers permission to enter. They moved through the door into the living room, where they observed in plain view drug paraphernalia and containers filled with white powder that they believed (correctly, as later analysis showed) to be cocaine. They proceeded to the bedroom, where they found Rodriguez asleep and discovered additional containers of white powder in two open attaché cases. The officers arrested Rodriguez and seized the drugs and related paraphernalia.

Rodriguez was charged with possession of a controlled substance with intent to deliver. He moved to suppress all evidence seized at the time of his arrest, claiming that Fischer had vacated the apartment several weeks earlier and had no authority to consent to the entry. The Cook County Circuit Court granted the motion, holding that at the time she consented to the entry Fischer did not have common authority over the apartment. The Court concluded that Fischer was not a "usual resident" but rather an "infrequent visitor" at the apartment on South California, based upon its findings that Fischer's name was not on the lease, that she did not contribute to the rent, that she was not allowed to invite others to the apartment on her own, that she did not have access to the apartment when respondent was away, and that she had moved some of her possessions from the apartment. The Circuit Court also rejected the State's contention that, even if Fischer did not possess common authority over the premises, there was no Fourth Amendment violation if the police reasonably believed at the time of their entry that Fischer possessed the authority to consent.

The Appellate Court of Illinois affirmed the Circuit Court in all respects. The Illinois Supreme Court denied the State's petition for leave to appeal, *181 125 Ill.2d 572, 130 Ill.Dec. 487, 537 N.E.2d 816 (1989), and we granted certiorari. 493 U.S. 932, 110 S.Ct. 320, 107 L.Ed.2d 311 (1989).

II

The Fourth Amendment generally prohibits the warrantless entry of a person's home, whether to make an arrest or to search for specific objects. Payton v. New York, 445 U.S. 573, 100 S.Ct. 1371, 63 L.Ed.2d 639 (1980); Johnson v. United States, 333 U.S. 10, 68 S.Ct. 367, 92 L.Ed. 436 (1948). The prohibition does not apply, however, to situations in which voluntary consent has been obtained, either from the individual whose property is searched, see Schneckloth v. Bustamonte, 412 U.S. 218, 93 S.Ct. 2041, 36 L.Ed.2d 854 (1973), or from a third party who possesses common authority over the premises, see United States v. Matlock, supra, 415 U.S., at 171, 94 S.Ct., at 993. The State of Illinois contends that that exception applies in the present case.

As we stated in Matlock, supra, at 171, n. 7, 94 S.Ct., at 993, n. 7, "[c]ommon authority" rests "on mutual use of the property by persons generally having joint access or control for most purposes...." The burden of establishing that common authority rests upon the State. On the basis of this record, it is clear that burden was not sustained. The evidence showed that although Fischer, with her two small children, had lived with Rodriguez beginning in December 1984, she had moved out on July 1, 1985, almost a month before the search at issue **2798 here, and had gone to live with her mother. She took her and her children's clothing with her, though leaving behind some furniture and household effects. During the period after July 1 she sometimes spent the night at Rodriguez's apartment, but never invited her friends there, and never went there herself when he was not home. Her name was not on the lease nor did she contribute to the rent. She had a key to the apartment, which she said at trial she had taken without Rodriguez's knowledge (though she testified at the preliminary hearing that Rodriguez had given her the key). On these facts the State has not established that, with respect to the South California apartment, Fischer had *182 "joint access or control for most purposes." To the contrary, the Appellate Court's determination of no common authority over the apartment was obviously correct.

III

A

The State contends that, even if Fischer did not in fact have authority to give consent, it suffices to validate the entry that the law enforcement officers reasonably believed she did. Before reaching the merits of that contention, we must consider a jurisdictional objection: that the decision below rests on an adequate and independent state ground. Respondent asserts that the Illinois Constitution provides greater protection than is afforded under the Fourth Amendment, and that the Appellate Court relied upon this when it determined that a reasonable belief by the police officers was insufficient.

When a state-court decision is clearly based on state law that is both adequate and independent, we will not review the decision. Michigan v. Long, 463 U.S. 1032, 1041, 103 S.Ct. 3469, 3476–77, 77 L.Ed.2d 1201 (1983). But when "a state court decision fairly appears to rest primarily on federal law, or to be interwoven with the federal law," we require that it contain a " 'plain statement' that [it] rests upon adequate and independent state grounds," id., at 1040, 1042, 103 S.Ct., at 3476, 3477; otherwise, "we will accept as the most reasonable explanation that the state court decided the case the way it did because it believed that federal law required it to do so." Id., at 1041, 103 S.Ct., at 3476. Here, the Appellate Court's opinion contains no "plain statement" that its decision rests on state law. The opinion does not rely on (or even mention) any specific provision of the Illinois Constitution, nor even the Illinois Constitution generally. Even the Illinois cases cited by the opinion rely upon no constitutional provisions other than the Fourth and Fourteenth Amendments of the United States Constitution. We conclude that the Appellate Court of Illinois rested its decision on federal law.

*183 B

On the merits of the issue, respondent asserts that permitting a reasonable belief of common authority to validate an entry would cause a defendant's Fourth Amendment rights to be "vicariously waived." Brief for Respondent 32. We disagree.

We have been unyielding in our insistence that a defendant's waiver of his trial rights cannot be given effect unless it is "knowing" and "intelligent." Colorado v. Spring, 479 U.S. 564, 574–575, 107 S.Ct. 851, 857–858, 93 L.Ed.2d 954 (1987); Johnson v. Zerbst, 304 U.S. 458, 58 S.Ct. 1019, 82 L.Ed. 1461 (1938). We would assuredly not permit, therefore, evidence seized in violation of the Fourth Amendment to be introduced on the basis of a trial court's mere "reasonable belief"—derived from statements by unauthorized persons—that the defendant has waived his objection. But one must make a distinction between, on the one hand, trial rights that derive from the violation of constitutional guarantees and, on the other hand, the nature of those constitutional guarantees themselves. As we said in Schneckloth:

**2799 "There is a vast difference between those rights that protect a fair criminal trial and the rights guaranteed under the Fourth Amendment. Nothing, either in the purposes behind requiring a 'knowing' and 'intelligent' waiver of trial rights, or in the practical application of such a requirement suggests that it ought to be extended to the constitutional guarantee against unreasonable searches and seizures." 412 U.S., at 241, 93 S.Ct., at 2055.

What Rodriguez is assured by the trial right of the exclusionary rule, where it applies, is that no evidence seized in violation of the Fourth Amendment will be introduced at his trial unless he consents. What he is assured by the Fourth Amendment itself, however, is not that no government search of his house will occur unless he consents; but that no such search will occur that is "unreasonable." U.S. Const., Amdt. 4. There are various elements, of course, *184 that can make a search of a person's house "reasonable"—one of which is the consent of the person or his cotenant. The essence of respondent's argument is that we should impose upon this element a requirement that we have not imposed upon other elements that regularly compel government officers to exercise judgment regarding the facts: namely, the requirement that their judgment be not only responsible but correct.

The fundamental objective that alone validates all unconsented government searches is, of course, the seizure of persons who have committed or are about to commit crimes, or of evidence related to crimes. But "reasonableness," with respect to this necessary element, does not demand that the government be factually correct in its assessment that that is what a search will produce. Warrants need only be supported by "probable cause," which demands no more than a proper "assessment of probabilities in particular factual contexts...." Illinois v. Gates, 462 U.S. 213, 232, 103 S.Ct. 2317, 2329, 76 L.Ed.2d 527 (1983). If a magistrate, based upon seemingly reliable but factually inaccurate information, issues a warrant for the search of a house in which the sought-after felon is not present, has never been present, and was never likely to have been present, the owner of that house suffers one of the inconveniences we all expose ourselves to as the cost of living in a safe society; he does not suffer a violation of the Fourth Amendment.

Another element often, though not invariably, required in order to render an unconsented search "reasonable" is, of course, that the officer be authorized by a valid warrant. Here also we have not held that "reasonableness" precludes error with respect to those factual judgments that law enforcement officials are expected to make. In Maryland v. Garrison, 480 U.S. 79, 107 S.Ct. 1013, 94 L.Ed.2d 72 (1987), a warrant supported by probable cause with respect to one apartment was erroneously issued for an entire floor that was divided (though not clearly) into two apartments. We upheld the search of the apartment not properly covered by the warrant. We said:

*185 "[T]he validity of the search of respondent's apartment pursuant to a warrant authorizing the search of the entire third floor depends on whether the officers' failure to realize the overbreadth of the warrant was objectively understandable and reasonable. Here it unquestionably was. The objective facts available to the officers at the time suggested no distinction between [the suspect's] apartment and the third-floor premises." Id., at 88, 107 S.Ct., at 1018.

The ordinary requirement of a warrant is sometimes supplanted by other elements that render the unconsented search "reasonable." Here also we have not held that the Fourth Amendment requires factual accuracy. A warrant is not needed, for example, where the search is incident to an arrest. In Hill v. California, 401 U.S. 797, 91 S.Ct. 1106, 28 L.Ed.2d 484 (1971), we upheld a search incident to an arrest, even **2800 though the arrest was made of the wrong person. We said:

"The upshot was that the officers in good faith believed Miller was Hill and arrested him. They were quite wrong as it turned out, and subjective good-faith belief would not in itself justify either the arrest or the subsequent search. But sufficient probability, not certainty, is the touchstone of reasonableness under the Fourth Amendment and on the record before us the officers' mistake was understandable and the arrest a reasonable response to the situation facing them at the time." Id., at 803–804, 91 S.Ct., at 1110–1111.

It would be superfluous to multiply these examples. It is apparent that in order to satisfy the "reasonableness" requirement of the Fourth Amendment, what is generally demanded of the many factual determinations that must regularly be made by agents of the government—whether the magistrate issuing a warrant, the police officer executing a warrant, or the police officer conducting a search or seizure under one of the exceptions to the warrant requirement—is not that they always be correct, but that they always be reasonable. *186 As we put it in Brinegar v. United States, 338 U.S. 160, 176, 69 S.Ct. 1302, 1311, 93 L.Ed. 1879 (1949):

"Because many situations which confront officers in the course of executing their duties are more or less ambiguous, room must be allowed for some mistakes on their part. But the mistakes must be those of reasonable men, acting on facts leading sensibly to their conclusions of probability."

We see no reason to depart from this general rule with respect to facts bearing upon the authority to consent to a search. Whether the basis for such authority exists is the sort of recurring factual question to which law enforcement officials must be expected to apply their judgment; and all the Fourth Amendment requires is that they answer it reasonably. The Constitution is no more violated when officers enter without a warrant because they reasonably (though erroneously) believe that the person who has consented to their entry is a resident of the premises, than it is violated when they enter without a warrant because they reasonably (though erroneously) believe they are in pursuit of a violent felon who is about to escape. See Archibald v. Mosel, 677 F.2d 5 (CA1 1982).*

*187 Stoner v. California, 376 U.S. 483, 84 S.Ct. 889, 11 L.Ed.2d 856 (1964), is in our view not to the contrary. There, in holding that police had improperly entered the defendant's hotel room based on the consent of a hotel clerk, we stated that "the rights protected by the Fourth Amendment are not to be eroded ... by unrealistic doctrines of 'apparent authority.' " Id., at 488, 84 S.Ct. at 892. It is ambiguous, of course, whether the word "unrealistic" is descriptive or limiting—that is, whether we were condemning as unrealistic all reliance upon apparent authority, or whether we were condemning only such reliance upon apparent authority as is unrealistic.

**2801 Similarly ambiguous is the opinion's earlier statement that "there [is no] substance to the claim that the search was reasonable because the police, relying upon the night clerk's expressions of consent, had a reasonable basis for the belief that the clerk had authority to consent to the search." Ibid. Was there no substance to it because it failed as a matter of law, or because the facts could not possibly support it? At one point the opinion does seem to speak clearly:

"It is important to bear in mind that it was the petitioner's constitutional right which was at stake here, and not the night clerk's nor the hotel's. It was a right, therefore, which only the petitioner could waive by word or deed, either directly or through an agent." Id., at 489, 84 S.Ct., at 893.

But as we have discussed, what is at issue when a claim of apparent consent is raised is not whether the right to be free of searches has been waived, but whether the right to be free of unreasonable searches has been violated. Even if one does not think the Stoner opinion had this subtlety in mind, the supposed clarity of its foregoing statement is immediately compromised, as follows:

*188 "It is true that the night clerk clearly and unambiguously consented to the search. But there is nothing in the record to indicate that the police had any basis whatsoever to believe that the night clerk had been authorized by the petitioner to permit the police to search the petitioner's room." Ibid. (emphasis added). The italicized language should have been deleted, of course, if the statement two sentences earlier meant that an appearance of authority could never validate a search. In the last analysis, one must admit that the rationale of Stoner was ambiguous—and perhaps deliberately so. It is at least a reasonable reading of the case, and perhaps a preferable one, that the police could not rely upon the obtained consent because they knew it came from a hotel clerk, knew that the room was rented and exclusively occupied by the defendant, and could not reasonably have believed that the former had general access to or control over the latter. Similarly ambiguous in its implications (the Court's opinion does not even allude to, much less discuss the effects of, "reasonable belief") is Chapman v. United States, 365 U.S. 610, 81 S.Ct. 776, 5 L.Ed.2d 828 (1961). In sum, we were correct in Matlock, 415 U.S., at 177, n. 14, 94 S.Ct., at 996, n. 14, when we regarded the present issue as unresolved.

As Stoner demonstrates, what we hold today does not suggest that law enforcement officers may always accept a person's invitation to enter premises. Even when the invitation is accompanied by an explicit assertion that the person lives there, the surrounding circumstances could conceivably be such that a reasonable person would doubt its truth and not act upon it without further inquiry. As with other factual determinations bearing upon search and seizure, determination of consent to enter must "be judged against an objective standard: would the facts available to the officer at the moment ... 'warrant a man of reasonable caution in the belief' " that the consenting party had authority over the premises? Terry v. Ohio, 392 U.S. 1, 21–22, 88 S.Ct. 1868, 1880, 20 L.Ed.2d 889 (1968). If not, then warrantless *189 entry without further inquiry is unlawful unless authority actually exists. But if so, the search is valid.

* * *

In the present case, the Appellate Court found it unnecessary to determine whether the officers reasonably believed that Fischer had the authority to consent, because it ruled as a matter of law that a reasonable belief could not validate the entry. Since we find that ruling to be in error, we remand for consideration of that question. The judgment of the Illinois Appellate Court is reversed, and the case is remanded for further **2802 proceedings not inconsistent with this opinion.

So ordered.

(The dissents of Justice MARSHALL, with whom Justice BRENNAN and Justice STEVENS join, are omitted.)

Black Letter Law

> The Court held that a former cotenant did not have common authority over defendant's premises and could not give consent to search those premises; nonetheless, the warrantless entry is still valid if based upon the consent of such third party to possess common authority over premises, even when in fact they did not have such common authority.

Horton v. California

110 S.Ct. 2301

Supreme Court of the United States

Terry Brice HORTON, Petitioner

v.

CALIFORNIA

No. 88-7164. | Argued Feb. 21, 1990. | Decided June 4, 1990.

Justice STEVENS delivered the opinion of the Court.

In this case we revisit an issue that was considered, but not conclusively resolved, in Coolidge v. New Hampshire, 403 U.S. 443, 91 S.Ct. 2022, 29 L.Ed.2d 564 (1971): Whether the warrantless seizure of evidence of crime in plain view is prohibited by the Fourth Amendment if the discovery of the evidence was not inadvertent. We conclude that even though inadvertence is a characteristic of most legitimate "plain-view" seizures, it is not a necessary condition.

I

Petitioner was convicted of the armed robbery of Erwin Wallaker, the treasurer of the San Jose Coin Club. When Wallaker returned to his home after the Club's annual show, he entered his garage and was accosted by two masked men, one armed with a machine gun and the other with an electrical shocking device, sometimes referred to as a "stun gun." The two men shocked Wallaker, bound and handcuffed him, and robbed him of jewelry and cash. During the encounter sufficient conversation took place to enable Wallaker subsequently to identify petitioner's distinctive voice. His identification was partially corroborated by a witness who saw the robbers leaving the scene and by evidence that petitioner had attended the coin show.

Sergeant LaRault, an experienced police officer, investigated the crime and determined that there was probable cause to search petitioner's home for the proceeds of the robbery ***131** and for the weapons used by the robbers. His affidavit for a search warrant referred to police reports that described the weapons as well as the proceeds, but the warrant issued by the Magistrate only authorized a search for the proceeds, including three specifically described rings.

Pursuant to the warrant, LaRault searched petitioner's residence, but he did not find the stolen property. During the course of the search, however, he discovered the weapons ****2305** in plain view and seized them. Specifically, he seized an Uzi machine gun, a .38-caliber revolver, two stun guns, a handcuff key, a San Jose Coin Club advertising brochure, and a few items of clothing identified by the victim.1 LaRault testified that while he was searching for the rings, he also was interested in finding other evidence connecting petitioner to the robbery. Thus, the seized evidence was not discovered "inadvertently."

The trial court refused to suppress the evidence found in petitioner's home and, after a jury trial, petitioner was found guilty and sentenced to prison. The California Court of Appeal affirmed. App. 43. It rejected petitioner's argument that our decision in Coolidge required suppression of the seized evidence that had not been listed in the warrant because its discovery was not inadvertent. App. 52-53. The court relied on the California Supreme Court's decision in North v. Superior Court, 8 Cal.3d 301, 104 Cal.Rptr. 833, 502 P.2d 1305 (1972). In that case the court noted that the discussion of the inadvertence limitation on the "plain-view" doctrine in Justice Stewart's opinion in Coolidge had been joined by only three other Members of this Court and therefore was not binding on it.2 The California Supreme Court denied petitioner's request for review. App. 78.

***132** Because the California courts' interpretation of the "plain-view" doctrine conflicts with the view of other courts,3 and because the unresolved issue is important, we granted certiorari, 493 U.S. 889, 110 S.Ct. 231, 107 L.Ed.2d 183 (1989).

***133 II**

The Fourth Amendment provides:

"The right of the people to be secure in their persons, houses, papers, and effects, against unreasonable searches and seizures, ****2306** shall not be violated, and no Warrants shall issue, but upon probable cause, supported by Oath or affirmation, and particularly describing the place to be searched, and the persons or things to be seized."

The right to security in person and property protected by the Fourth Amendment may be invaded in quite different ways by searches and seizures. A search compromises the individual interest in privacy; a seizure deprives the individual of dominion over his or her person or property. United States v. Jacobsen, 466 U.S. 109, 113, 104 S.Ct. 1652, 1656, 80 L.Ed.2d 85 (1984). The "plain-view" doctrine is often considered an exception to the general rule that warrantless searches are presumptively unreasonable,4 but this characterization overlooks the important difference between searches and seizures.5 If an article is already in plain view, neither its observation nor its seizure would involve any invasion of privacy. ***134** Arizona v. Hicks, 480 U.S. 321, 325, 107 S.Ct. 1149, 1152, 94 L.Ed.2d 347 (1987); Illinois v. Andreas, 463 U.S. 765, 771, 103 S.Ct. 3319, 3324, 77 L.Ed.2d 1003 (1983). A seizure of the article, however, would obviously invade the owner's possessory interest. Maryland v. Macon, 472 U.S. 463, 469, 105 S.Ct. 2778, 2782, 86 L.Ed.2d 370 (1985); Jacobsen, 466 U.S., at 113, 104 S.Ct., at 1652. If "plain view" justifies an exception from an otherwise applicable warrant requirement, therefore, it must be an exception that is addressed to the concerns that are implicated by seizures rather than by searches.

The criteria that generally guide "plain-view" seizures were set forth in Coolidge v. New Hampshire, 403 U.S. 443, 91 S.Ct. 2022, 29 L.Ed.2d 564 (1971). The Court held that the police, in seizing two automobiles parked in plain view on the defendant's driveway in the course of arresting the defendant, violated the Fourth Amendment. Accordingly, particles of gunpowder that had been subsequently found in vacuum sweepings from one of the cars could not be introduced in evidence against the defendant. The State endeavored to justify the seizure of the automobiles, and their subsequent search at the police station, on four different grounds, including the "plain-view" doctrine.6 The scope of that doctrine as it had developed in earlier cases was fairly summarized in these three paragraphs from Justice Stewart's opinion:

"It is well established that under certain circumstances the police may seize evidence in plain view without a warrant. But it is important to keep in mind that, in the vast majority of cases, any evidence seized by the police will be in plain view, at least at the moment of seizure. The problem ****2307** with the 'plain view' doctrine has been to identify the circumstances in which plain view ***135** has legal significance rather than being simply the normal concomitant of any search, legal or illegal.

"An example of the applicability of the 'plain view' doctrine is the situation in which the police have a warrant to search a given area for specified objects, and in the course of the search come across some other article of incriminating character. Cf. Go-Bart Importing Co. v. United States, 282 U.S. 344, 358 [51 S.Ct. 153, 158, 75

L.Ed. 374 (1931)]; United States v. Lefkowitz, 285 U.S. 452, 465 [52 S.Ct. 420, 423, 76 L.Ed. 877 (1932)]; Steele v. United States, 267 U.S. 498 [45 S.Ct. 414, 69 L.Ed. 757 (1925)]; Stanley v. Georgia, 394 U.S. 557, 571 [89 S.Ct. 1243, 1251, 22 L.Ed.2d 542 (1969)] (STEWART, J., concurring in result). Where the initial intrusion that brings the police within plain view of such an article is supported, not by a warrant, but by one of the recognized exceptions to the warrant requirement, the seizure is also legitimate. Thus the police may inadvertently come across evidence while in 'hot pursuit' of a fleeing suspect. Warden v. Hayden [387 U.S. 294, 87 S.Ct. 1642, 18 L.Ed.2d 782 (1967)]; cf. Hester v. United States, 265 U.S. 57 [44 S.Ct. 445, 68 L.Ed. 898 (1924)]. And an object that comes into view during a search incident to arrest that is appropriately limited in scope under existing law may be seized without a warrant. Chimel v. California, 395 U.S. [752,] 762-763 [89 S.Ct. 2034, 2039-2040 (1969)]. Finally, the 'plain view' doctrine has been applied where a police officer is not searching for evidence against the accused, but nonetheless inadvertently comes across an incriminating object. Harris v. United States, 390 U.S. 234 [88 S.Ct. 992, 19 L.Ed.2d 1067 (1968)]; Frazier v. Cupp, 394 U.S. 731 [89 S.Ct. 1420, 22 L.Ed.2d 684 (1969)]; Ker v. California, 374 U.S. [23,] 43 [83 S.Ct. 1623, 1635, 10 L.Ed.2d 726 (1963)]. Cf. Lewis v. United States, 385 U.S. 206 [87 S.Ct. 424, 17 L.Ed.2d 312 (1966)].

"What the 'plain view' cases have in common is that the police officer in each of them had a prior justification for an intrusion in the course of which he came inadvertently across a piece of evidence incriminating the accused. The doctrine serves to supplement the prior justification-whether it be a warrant for another object, ***136** hot pursuit, search incident to lawful arrest, or some other legitimate reason for being present unconnected with a search directed against the accused-and permits the warrantless seizure. Of course, the extension of the original justification is legitimate only where it is immediately apparent to the police that they have evidence before them; the 'plain view' doctrine may not be used to extend a general exploratory search from one object to another until something incriminating at last emerges." Id., at 465-466, 91 S.Ct., at 2037-2038 (footnote omitted).

Justice Stewart then described the two limitations on the doctrine that he found implicit in its rationale: First, that "plain view alone is never enough to justify the warrantless seizure of evidence," id., at 468, 91 S.Ct., at 2039; and second, that "the discovery of evidence in plain view must be inadvertent." Id., at 469, 91 S.Ct., at 2040.

Justice Stewart's analysis of the "plain-view" doctrine did not command a majority, and a plurality of the Court has since made clear that the discussion is "not a binding precedent." Texas v. Brown, 460 U.S. 730, 737, 103 S.Ct. 1535, 1541, 75 L.Ed.2d 502 (1983) (opinion of REHNQUIST, J.). Justice Harlan, who concurred in the Court's judgment and in its response to the dissenting opinions, 403 U.S., at 473-484, 490-493, 91 S.Ct., at 2042-2047, 2050-2051, did not join the plurality's discussion of the "plain-view" doctrine. See id., at 464-473, 91 S.Ct., at 2037-2042. The decision nonetheless is a ****2308** binding precedent. Before discussing the second limitation, which is implicated in this case, it is therefore necessary to explain why the first adequately supports the Court's judgment.

It is, of course, an essential predicate to any valid warrantless seizure of incriminating evidence that the officer did not violate the Fourth Amendment in arriving at the place from which the evidence could be plainly viewed. There are, moreover, two additional conditions that must be satisfied to justify the warrantless seizure. First, not only must the item be in plain view; its incriminating character must also be "immediately apparent." Id., at 466, 91 S.Ct., at 2038; see also Arizona v. ***137** Hicks, 480 U.S., at 326-327, 107 S.Ct., at 1153. Thus, in Coolidge, the cars were obviously in plain view, but their probative value remained uncertain until after the interiors were swept and examined microscopically. Second, not only must the officer be lawfully located in a place from which the object can be plainly seen, but he or she must also have a lawful right of access to the object itself. As the United

States has suggested, Justice Harlan's vote in Coolidge may have rested on the fact that the seizure of the cars was accomplished by means of a warrantless trespass on the defendant's property. In all events, we are satisfied that the absence of inadvertence was not essential to the Court's rejection of the State's "plain-view" argument in Coolidge.

III

Justice Stewart concluded that the inadvertence requirement was necessary to avoid a violation of the express constitutional requirement that a valid warrant must particularly describe the things to be seized. He explained:

"The rationale of the exception to the warrant requirement, as just stated, is that a plain-view seizure will not turn an initially valid (and therefore limited) search into ***138** a 'general' one, while the inconvenience of procuring a warrant to cover an inadvertent discovery is great. But where the discovery is anticipated, where the police know in advance the location of the evidence and intend to seize it, the situation is altogether different. The requirement of a warrant to seize imposes no inconvenience whatever, or at least none which is constitutionally cognizable in a legal system that regards warrantless searches as 'per se unreasonable' in the absence of 'exigent circumstances.'

"If the initial intrusion is bottomed upon a warrant that fails to mention a particular object, though the police know its location and intend to seize it, then there is a violation of the express constitutional requirement of 'Warrants ... particularly describing ... [the] things to be seized.' " 403 U.S., at 469-471, 91 S.Ct., at 2040-2041.

We find two flaws in this reasoning. First, evenhanded law enforcement is best achieved by the application of objective standards of conduct, rather than standards that ****2309** depend upon the subjective state of mind of the officer. The fact that an officer is interested in an item of evidence and fully expects to find it in the course of a search should not invalidate its seizure if the search is confined in area and duration by the terms of a warrant or a valid exception to the warrant requirement. If the officer has knowledge approaching certainty that the item will be found, we see no reason why he or she would deliberately omit a particular description of the item to be seized from the application for a search warrant.9 Specification of the additional item could only permit the officer ***139** to expand the scope of the search. On the other hand, if he or she has a valid warrant to search for one item and merely a suspicion concerning the second, whether or not it amounts to probable cause, we fail to see why that suspicion should immunize the second item from seizure if it is found during a lawful search for the first. The hypothetical case put by Justice WHITE in his concurring and dissenting opinion in Coolidge is instructive:

"Let us suppose officers secure a warrant to search a house for a rifle. While staying well within the range of a rifle search, they discover two photographs of the murder victim, both in plain sight in the bedroom. Assume also that the discovery of the one photograph was inadvertent but finding the other was anticipated. The Court would permit the seizure of only one of the photographs. But in terms of the 'minor' peril to Fourth Amendment values there is surely no difference between these two photographs: the interference with possession is the same in each case and the officers' appraisal of the photograph they expected to see is no less reliable than their judgment about the other. And in both situations the actual inconvenience and danger to evidence remain identical if the officers must depart and secure a warrant." Id., at 516, 91 S.Ct., at 2063.

Second, the suggestion that the inadvertence requirement is necessary to prevent the police from conducting general searches, or from converting specific warrants into general warrants, is not persuasive because that interest is already served by the requirements that no warrant issue unless it "particularly describ[es] the place to be searched and the persons or things to be seized," see Maryland v. Garrison, 480 U.S. 79, 84, 107 S.Ct. 1013, 1016, 94 L.Ed.2d 72 (1987); Steele v. United States No. 1,

267 U.S. 498, 503, 45 S.Ct. 414, 416, 69 L.Ed. 757 (1925),10 and that a warrantless search be circumscribed *140 by the exigencies which justify its initiation. See, e.g., Maryland v. Buie, 494 U.S. 325, 332-334, 110 S.Ct. 1093, 1098-1099, 108 L.Ed.2d 276 (1990); Mincey v. Arizona, 437 U.S. 385, 393, 98 S.Ct. 2408, 2413, 57 L.Ed.2d 290 (1978). Scrupulous adherence to these requirements serves the interests in limiting the area and duration of the search that the inadvertence requirement inadequately protects. Once those commands have been satisfied and the officer has a lawful right of access, however, no additional **2310 Fourth Amendment interest is furthered by requiring that the discovery of evidence be inadvertent. If the scope of the search exceeds that permitted by the terms of a validly issued warrant or the character of the relevant exception from the warrant requirement, the subsequent seizure is unconstitutional without more. Thus, in the case of a search incident to a lawful arrest, "[i]f the police stray outside the scope of an authorized Chimel search they are already in violation of the Fourth Amendment, and evidence so seized will be excluded; adding a second reason for excluding evidence hardly seems worth the candle." Coolidge, 403 U.S., at 517, 91 S.Ct., at 2063 (WHITE, J., concurring and dissenting). Similarly, the object of a warrantless search of an automobile also defines its scope:

"The scope of a warrantless search of an automobile thus is not defined by the nature of the container in which the contraband is secreted. Rather, it is defined by the object of the search and the places in which there is probable cause to believe that it may be found. Just as probable cause to believe that a stolen lawnmower may be found in a garage will not support a warrant to search an upstairs bedroom, probable cause to believe *141 that undocumented aliens are being transported in a van will not justify a warrantless search of a suitcase. Probable cause to believe that a container placed in the trunk of a taxi contains contraband or evidence does not justify a search of the entire cab." United States v. Ross, 456 U.S. 798, 824, 102 S.Ct. 2157, 2172, 72 L.Ed.2d 572 (1982).

In this case, the scope of the search was not enlarged in the slightest by the omission of any reference to the weapons in the warrant. Indeed, if the three rings and other items named in the warrant had been found at the outset-or if petitioner had them in his possession and had responded to the warrant by producing them immediately-no search for weapons could have taken place. Again, Justice WHITE's concurring and dissenting opinion in Coolidge is instructive:

"Police with a warrant for a rifle may search only places where rifles might be and must terminate the search once the rifle is found; the inadvertence rule will in no way reduce the number of places into which they may lawfully look." 403 U.S., at 517, 91 S.Ct., at 2063.

As we have already suggested, by hypothesis the seizure of an object in plain view does not involve an intrusion on privacy. If the interest in privacy has been invaded, the violation must have occurred before the object came into plain view and there is no need for an inadvertence limitation on seizures to condemn it. The prohibition against general searches and general warrants serves primarily as a protection against unjustified intrusions on privacy. But reliance *142 on privacy concerns that support that prohibition is misplaced when the inquiry concerns the scope of an exception that merely authorizes an officer with a lawful right of access to an item to seize it without a warrant.

In this case the items seized from petitioner's home were discovered during a lawful search authorized by a valid warrant. When they were discovered, it was immediately apparent to the officer that they constituted incriminating evidence. He had probable cause, not only to obtain a warrant to search for the stolen property, but also to believe that the weapons and handguns had **2311 been used in the crime he was investigating. The search was authorized by the warrant; the seizure was authorized by the "plain-view" doctrine. The judgment is affirmed.

It is so ordered.

Justice BRENNAN, with whom Justice MARSHALL joins, dissenting.

I remain convinced that Justice Stewart correctly articulated the plain-view doctrine in Coolidge v. New Hampshire, 403 U.S. 443, 91 S.Ct. 2022, 29 L.Ed.2d 564 (1971). The Fourth Amendment permits law enforcement officers to seize items for which they do not have a warrant when those items are found in plain view and (1) the officers are lawfully in a position to observe the items, (2) the discovery of the items is "inadvertent," and (3) it is immediately apparent to the officers that the items are evidence of a crime, contraband, or otherwise subject to seizure. In eschewing the inadvertent discovery requirement, the majority ignores the Fourth Amendment's express command that warrants particularly describe not only the places to be searched, but also the things to be seized. I respectfully dissent from this rewriting of the Fourth Amendment.

I

The Fourth Amendment states:

"The right of the people to be secure in their persons, houses, papers, and effects, against unreasonable ***143** searches and seizures, shall not be violated, and no Warrants shall issue, but upon probable cause, supported by Oath or affirmation, and particularly describing the place to be searched, and the persons or things to be seized."

The Amendment protects two distinct interests. The prohibition against unreasonable searches and the requirement that a warrant "particularly describ [e] the place to be searched" protect an interest in privacy. The prohibition against unreasonable seizures and the requirement that a warrant "particularly describ[e] ... the ... things to be seized" protect a possessory interest in property.1 See ante, at 2306; Texas v. Brown, 460 U.S. 730, 747, 103 S.Ct. 1535, 1546, 75 L.Ed.2d 502 (1983) (STEVENS, J., concurring in judgment). The Fourth Amendment, by its terms, declares the privacy and possessory interests to be equally important. As this Court recently stated: "Although the interest protected by the Fourth Amendment injunction against unreasonable searches is quite different from that protected by its injunction against unreasonable seizures, neither the one nor the other is of inferior worth or necessarily requires only lesser protection." Arizona v. Hicks, 480 U.S. 321, 328, 107 S.Ct. 1149, 1154, 94 L.Ed.2d 347 (1987) (citation omitted).

The Amendment protects these equally important interests in precisely the same manner: by requiring a neutral and detached magistrate to evaluate, before the search or seizure, the government's showing of probable cause and its particular description of the place to be searched and the items to be seized. Accordingly, just as a warrantless ***144** search is per se unreasonable absent exigent circumstances, so too a seizure of personal property is "per se unreasonable within the meaning of the Fourth Amendment unless it is accomplished pursuant to a judicial warrant issued upon probable cause and particularly describing the items to be seized." United States v. Place, 462 U.S. 696, 701, 103 S.Ct. 2637, 2641, 77 L.Ed.2d 110 (1983) (footnote omitted) (citing ****2312** Marron v. United States, 275 U.S. 192, 196, 48 S.Ct. 74, 76, 72 L.Ed. 231 (1927)). "Prior review by a neutral and detached magistrate is the time-tested means of effectuating Fourth Amendment rights." United States v. United States District Court, Eastern District of Michigan, 407 U.S. 297, 318, 92 S.Ct. 2125, 2137, 32 L.Ed.2d 752 (1972). A decision to invade a possessory interest in property is too important to be left to the discretion of zealous officers "engaged in the often competitive enterprise of ferreting out crime." Johnson v. United States, 333 U.S. 10, 14, 68 S.Ct. 367, 369, 92 L.Ed. 436 (1948). "The requirement that warrants shall particularly describe the things to be seized makes general searches under them impossible and prevents the seizure of one thing under a warrant describing another. As to what is to be taken, nothing is left to the discretion of the officer executing the warrant." Marron, supra, at 196, 48 S.Ct., at 76.

The plain-view doctrine is an exception to the general rule that a seizure of personal property must be authorized by a warrant. As Justice Stewart explained in Coolidge, 403 U.S., at 470, 91 S.Ct., at 2040, we accept a warrantless seizure when an officer is lawfully in a location and inadvertently sees evidence of a crime because of "the inconvenience of procuring a warrant" to seize this newly discovered piece of evidence. But "where the discovery is anticipated, where the police know in advance the location of the evidence and intend to seize it," the argument that procuring a warrant would be "inconvenient" loses much, if not all, of its force. Ibid. Barring an exigency, there is no reason why the police officers could not have obtained a warrant to seize this evidence before entering the premises. The rationale behind the inadvertent discovery requirement is simply that we will not excuse officers ***145** from the general requirement of a warrant to seize if the officers know the location of evidence, have probable cause to seize it, intend to seize it, and yet do not bother to obtain a warrant particularly describing that evidence. To do so would violate "the express constitutional requirement of 'Warrants ... particularly describing ... [the] things to be seized,' " and would "fly in the face of the basic rule that no amount of probable cause can justify a warrantless seizure." Id., at 471, 91 S.Ct., at 2040.

Although joined by only three other Members of the Court, Justice Stewart's discussion of the inadvertent discovery requirement has become widely accepted. See Texas v. Brown, supra, at 746, 103 S.Ct., at 1546 (Powell, J., concurring in judgment) ("Whatever my view might have been when Coolidge was decided, I see no reason at this late date to imply criticism of its articulation of this exception. It has been accepted generally for over a decade"). Forty-six States and the District of Columbia and 12 United States Courts of Appeals3 now require plain-view seizures to be inadvertent. There has been no outcry from law enforcement officials that the inadvertent discovery requirement unduly burdens their efforts. Given that the requirement is inescapably rooted in the plain language of the Fourth Amendment, I cannot fathom the Court's enthusiasm for discarding this element of the plain-view doctrine.

The Court posits two "flaws" in Justice Stewart's reasoning that it believes demonstrate the inappropriateness of the inadvertent discovery requirement. But these flaws are illusory. First, the majority explains that it can see no reason ***146** why an officer who "has knowledge approaching certainty" that an item will be found in a particular ****2313** location "would deliberately omit a particular description of the item to be seized from the application for a search warrant." Ante, at 2309. But to the individual whose possessory interest has been invaded, it matters not why the police officer decided to omit a particular item from his application for a search warrant. When an officer with probable cause to seize an item fails to mention that item in his application for a search warrant-for whatever reason-and then seizes the item anyway, his conduct is per se unreasonable. Suppression of the evidence so seized will encourage officers to be more precise and complete in future warrant applications.

Furthermore, there are a number of instances in which a law enforcement officer might deliberately choose to omit certain items from a warrant application even though he has probable cause to seize them, knows they are on the premises, and intends to seize them when they are discovered in plain view. For example, the warrant application process can often be time consuming, especially when the police attempt to seize a large number of items. An officer interested in conducting a search as soon as possible might decide to save time by listing only one or two hard-to-find items, such as the stolen rings in this case, confident that he will find in plain view all of the other evidence he is looking for before he discovers the listed items. Because rings could be located almost anywhere inside or outside a house, it is unlikely that a warrant to search for and seize the rings would restrict the scope of the search. An officer might rationally find the risk of immediately discovering the items listed in the warrant-thereby forcing him to conclude the search immediately-outweighed by the time saved in the application process.

The majority also contends that, once an officer is lawfully in a house and the scope of his search is adequately circumscribed by a warrant, "no additional Fourth Amendment ***147** interest is furthered by requiring that the discovery of evidence be inadvertent." Ante, at 2310. Put another way, " 'the inadvertence rule will in no way reduce the number of places into which [law enforcement officers] may lawfully look.' " Ante, at 2310 (quoting Coolidge, 403 U.S., at 517, 91 S.Ct., at 2063 (WHITE, J., concurring and dissenting)). The majority is correct, but it has asked the wrong question. It is true that the inadvertent discovery requirement furthers no privacy interests. The requirement in no way reduces the scope of a search or the number of places into which officers may look. But it does protect possessory interests. Cf. Illinois v. Andreas, 463 U.S. 765, 771, 103 S.Ct. 3319, 3324, 77 L.Ed.2d 1003 (1983) ("The plain-view doctrine is grounded on the proposition that once police are lawfully in a position to observe an item first-hand, its owner's privacy interest in that item is lost; the owner may retain the incidents of title and possession but not privacy") (emphasis added). The inadvertent discovery requirement is essential if we are to take seriously the Fourth Amendment's protection of possessory interests as well as privacy interests. See supra, at 2304. The Court today eliminates a rule designed to further possessory interests on the ground that it fails to further privacy interests. I cannot countenance such constitutional legerdemain.

II

Fortunately, this decision should have only a limited impact, for the Court is not confronted today with what lower courts have described as a "pretextual" search. See, e.g., State v. Lair, 95 Wash.2d 706, 717-718, 630 P.2d 427, 434 (1981) (en banc) (holding pretextual searches invalid). For example, if an officer enters a house pursuant to a warrant to search for evidence of one crime when he is really interested only in seizing evidence relating to another crime, for which he does not have a warrant, his search is "pretextual" and the fruits of that search should be suppressed. See, e.g., State v. Kelsey, 592 S.W.2d 509 (Mo.App.1979) (evidence suppressed because officers, who had ample opportunity ****2314** to obtain ***148** warrant relating to murder investigation, entered the premises instead pursuant to a warrant relating to a drug investigation, and searched only the hiding place of the murder weapon, rather than conducting a "top to bottom" search for drugs). Similarly, an officer might use an exception to the generally applicable warrant requirement, such as "hot pursuit," as a pretext to enter a home to seize items he knows he will find in plain view. Such conduct would be a deliberate attempt to circumvent the constitutional requirement of a warrant "particularly describing the place to be searched, and the persons or things to be seized," and cannot be condoned.

The discovery of evidence in pretextual searches is not "inadvertent" and should be suppressed for that reason. But even state courts that have rejected the inadvertent discovery requirement have held that the Fourth Amendment prohibits pretextual searches. See State v. Bussard, 114 Idaho 781, 788, n. 2, 760 P.2d 1197, 1204, n. 2 (1988); State v. Kelly, 718 P.2d 385, 389, n. 1 (Utah 1986). The Court's opinion today does not address pretextual searches, but I have no doubt that such searches violate the Fourth Amendment.

III

The Fourth Amendment demands that an individual's possessory interest in property be protected from unreasonable governmental seizures, not just by requiring a showing of probable cause, but also by requiring a neutral and detached ***149** magistrate to authorize the seizure in advance. The Court today ignores the explicit language of the Fourth Amendment, which protects possessory interests in the same manner as it protects privacy interests, in order to eliminate a generally accepted element of the plain-view doctrine that has caused no apparent difficulties for law enforcement officers. I am confident, however, that when confronted with more egregious police conduct than that found in this case, ante, at 2304-2305, such as pretextual searches, the Court's interpretation of the Constitution will be less parsimonious than it is today. I respectfully dissent.

Black Letter Law

> Held that Fourth Amendment does not prohibit warrantless seizure of evidence of crime in plain view, even if discovery of evidence was not inadvertent. To justify warrantless seizure of item in plain view, not only must police officer be lawfully located in place from which object can be plainly seen, but he or she must also have lawful right or access to object itself.

Arizona v. Hicks

107 S.Ct. 1149

Supreme Court of the United States

ARIZONA, Petitioner

v.

James Thomas HICKS.

No. 85–1027. | Argued Dec. 8, 1986. | Decided March 3, 1987.

***323** Justice SCALIA delivered the opinion of the Court.

In Coolidge v. New Hampshire, 403 U.S. 443, 91 S.Ct. 2022, 29 L.Ed.2d 564 (1971), we said that in certain circumstances a warrantless seizure by police of an item that comes within plain view during their lawful search of a private area may be reasonable under the Fourth Amendment. See id., at 465–471, 91 S.Ct. at 2037–2041 (plurality opinion); id., at 505–506, 91 S.Ct. at 2057–2058 (Black, J., concurring and dissenting); id., at 521–522, 91 S.Ct. at 2065–2066 (WHITE, J., concurring and dissenting). We granted certiorari, 475 U.S. 1107, 106 S.Ct. 1512, 89 L.Ed.2d 912 (1986), in the present case to decide whether this "plain view" doctrine may be invoked when the police have less than probable cause to believe that the item in question is evidence of a crime or is contraband.

I

On April 18, 1984, a bullet was fired through the floor of respondent's apartment, striking and injuring a man in the ****1152** apartment below. Police officers arrived and entered respondent's apartment to search for the shooter, for other victims, and for weapons. They found and seized three weapons, including a sawed-off rifle, and in the course of their search also discovered a stocking-cap mask.

One of the policemen, Officer Nelson, noticed two sets of expensive stereo components, which seemed out of place in the squalid and otherwise ill-appointed four-room apartment. Suspecting that they were stolen, he read and recorded their serial numbers—moving some of the components, including a Bang and Olufsen turntable, in order to do so—which he then reported by phone to his headquarters. On being advised that the turntable had been taken in an armed robbery, he seized it immediately. It was later determined that some of the other serial numbers matched those on other stereo equipment taken in the same armed robbery, and a warrant ***324** was obtained and executed to seize that equipment as well. Respondent was subsequently indicted for the robbery.

The state trial court granted respondent's motion to suppress the evidence that had been seized. The Court of Appeals of Arizona affirmed. It was conceded that the initial entry and search, although warrantless, were justified by the exigent circumstance of the shooting. The Court of Appeals viewed the obtaining of the serial numbers, however, as an additional search, unrelated to that exigency. Relying upon a statement in Mincey v. Arizona, 437 U.S. 385, 98 S.Ct. 2408, 57 L.Ed.2d 290 (1978), that a "warrantless search must be 'strictly circumscribed by the exigencies which justify its initiation,' " id., at 393, 98 S.Ct. at 2413 (citation omitted), the Court of Appeals held that the police conduct violated the Fourth Amendment, requiring the evidence derived from that conduct to be excluded. 146 Ariz. 533, 534–535, 707 P.2d 331, 332–333 (1985). Both courts—the trial court explicitly and the Court of Appeals by necessary implication—rejected the State's contention that Officer Nelson's actions were justified under the "plain view" doctrine of Coolidge v. New Hampshire, supra. The Arizona Supreme Court denied review, and the State filed this petition.

II

As an initial matter, the State argues that Officer Nelson's actions constituted neither a "search" nor a "seizure" within the meaning of the Fourth Amendment. We agree that the mere recording of the serial numbers did not constitute a seizure. To be sure, that was the first step in a process by which respondent was eventually deprived of the stereo equipment. In and of itself, however, it did not "meaningfully interfere" with respondent's possessory interest in either the serial numbers or the equipment, and therefore did not amount to a seizure. See Maryland v. Macon, 472 U.S. 463, 469, 105 S.Ct. 2778, 2782, 86 L.Ed.2d 370 (1985).

Officer Nelson's moving of the equipment, however, did constitute a "search" separate and apart from the search for ***325** the shooter, victims, and weapons that was the lawful objective of his entry into the apartment. Merely inspecting those parts of the turntable that came into view during the latter search would not have constituted an independent search, because it would have produced no additional invasion of respondent's privacy interest. See Illinois v. Andreas, 463 U.S. 765, 771, 103 S.Ct. 3319, 3324, 77 L.Ed.2d 1003 (1983). But taking action, unrelated to the objectives of the authorized intrusion, which exposed to view concealed portions of the apartment or its contents, did produce a new invasion of respondent's privacy unjustified by the exigent circumstance that validated the entry. This is why, contrary to Justice POWELL's suggestion, post, at 1156, the "distinction between 'looking' at a suspicious object in plain view and 'moving' it even a few inches" is much more than trivial for purposes of the Fourth Amendment. It matters not that the search uncovered nothing of any great personal value to respondent—serial numbers rather than (what ****1153** might conceivably have been hidden behind or under the equipment) letters or photographs. A search is a search, even if it happens to disclose nothing but the bottom of a turntable.

III

The remaining question is whether the search was "reasonable" under the Fourth Amendment.

On this aspect of the case we reject, at the outset, the apparent position of the Arizona Court of Appeals that because the officers' action directed to the stereo equipment was unrelated to the justification for their entry into respondent's apartment, it was ipso facto unreasonable. That lack of relationship always exists with regard to action validated under the "plain view" doctrine; where action is taken for the purpose justifying the entry, invocation of the doctrine is superfluous. Mincey v. Arizona, supra, in saying that a warrantless search must be "strictly circumscribed by the exigencies which justify its initiation," 437 U.S., at 393, 98 S.Ct. at 2413 (citation omitted), was addressing only the scope of the primary ***326** search itself, and was not overruling by implication the many cases acknowledging that the "plain view" doctrine can legitimate action beyond that scope.

We turn, then, to application of the doctrine to the facts of this case. "It is well established that under certain circumstances the police may seize evidence in plain view without a warrant," Coolidge v. New Hampshire, 403 U.S., at 465, 91 S.Ct. at 2037 (plurality opinion) (emphasis added). Those circumstances include situations "[w]here the initial intrusion that brings the police within plain view of such [evidence] is supported ... by one of the recognized exceptions to the warrant requirement," ibid., such as the exigent-circumstances intrusion here. It would be absurd to say that an object could lawfully be seized and taken from the premises, but could not be moved for closer examination. It is clear, therefore, that the search here was valid if the "plain view" doctrine would have sustained a seizure of the equipment.

There is no doubt it would have done so if Officer Nelson had probable cause to believe that the equipment was stolen. The State has conceded, however, that he had only a "reasonable suspicion," by which it means something less than probable cause. See Brief for Petitioner 18–19.* We have not ruled on the question whether probable cause is required in order to invoke the "plain view" doctrine. Dicta in Payton v. New York, 445 U.S. 573, 587, 100 S.Ct. 1371, 1380, 63 L.Ed.2d 639 (1980), suggested that the standard of probable cause must be met, but our later opinions in Texas v. Brown, 460 U.S. 730, 103 S.Ct. 1535, 75 L.Ed.2d 502 (1983), explicitly regarded the issue as unresolved, see id., at 742, n. 7, 103 S.Ct. at 1543 n. 7 (plurality opinion); id., at 746, 103 S.Ct. at 1545 (STEVENS, J., concurring in judgment).

We now hold that probable cause is required. To say otherwise would be to cut the "plain view" doctrine loose from its theoretical and practical moorings. The theory of that doctrine consists of extending to nonpublic places such as the ***327** home, where searches and seizures without a warrant are presumptively unreasonable, the police's longstanding authority to make warrantless seizures in public places of such objects as weapons and contraband. See Payton v. New York, supra, at 586–587, 100 S.Ct. at 1380. And the practical justification for that extension is the desirability of sparing police, whose viewing of the object in the course of a lawful search is as legitimate as it would have been in a public place, the inconvenience and the risk—to themselves or to preservation of the evidence—of going to obtain a warrant. See Coolidge v. New Hampshire, supra, at 468, 91 S.Ct. at 2039 (plurality opinion). Dispensing with the need for a warrant is ****1154** worlds apart from permitting a lesser standard of cause for the seizure than a warrant would require, i.e., the standard of probable cause. No reason is apparent why an object should routinely be seizable on lesser grounds, during an unrelated search and seizure, than would have been needed to obtain a warrant for that same object if it had been known to be on the premises.

We do not say, of course, that a seizure can never be justified on less than probable cause. We have held that it can—where, for example, the seizure is minimally intrusive and operational necessities render it the only practicable means of detecting certain types of crime. See, e.g., United States v. Cortez, 449 U.S. 411, 101 S.Ct. 690, 66 L.Ed.2d 621 (1981) (investigative detention of vehicle suspected to be transporting illegal aliens); United States v. Brignoni-Ponce, 422 U.S. 873, 95 S.Ct. 2574, 45 L.Ed.2d 607 (1975) (same); United States v. Place, 462 U.S. 696, 709, and n. 9, 103 S.Ct. 2637, 2645 and n. 9, 77 L.Ed.2d 110 (1983) (dictum) (seizure of suspected drug dealer's luggage at airport to permit exposure to specially trained dog). No special operational necessities are relied on here, however—but rather the mere fact that the items in question came lawfully within the officer's plain view. That alone cannot supplant the requirement of probable cause.

The same considerations preclude us from holding that, even though probable cause would have been necessary for a seizure, the search of objects in plain view that occurred here ***328** could be sustained on lesser grounds. A dwelling-place search, no less than a dwelling-place seizure, requires probable cause, and there is no reason in theory or practicality why application of the "plain view" doctrine would supplant that requirement. Although the interest protected by the Fourth Amendment injunction against unreasonable searches is quite different from that protected by its injunction against unreasonable seizures, see Texas v. Brown, supra, 460 U.S., at 747–748, 103 S.Ct., at 1546 (STEVENS, J., concurring in judgment), neither the one nor the other is of inferior worth or necessarily requires only lesser protection. We have not elsewhere drawn a categorical distinction between the two insofar as concerns the degree of justification needed to establish the reasonableness of police action, and we see no reason for a distinction in the particular circumstances before us here. Indeed, to treat searches more liberally would especially erode the plurality's warning in Coolidge that "the 'plain view' doctrine may not be used to extend a general exploratory search from one object to another until something incriminating at last emerges." 403 U.S., at 466, 91 S.Ct. at 2038. In short, whether legal authority to move the equipment could be found only as an inevitable concomitant of the authority to seize it, or also as a consequence of some independent power to search certain objects in plain view, probable cause to believe the equipment was stolen was required.

Justice O'CONNOR's dissent suggests that we uphold the action here on the ground that it was a "cursory inspection" rather than a "full-blown search," and could therefore be justified by reasonable suspicion instead of probable cause. As already noted, a truly cursory inspection—one that involves merely looking at what is already exposed to view, without disturbing it—is not a "search" for Fourth Amendment purposes, and therefore does not even require reasonable suspicion. We are unwilling to send police and judges into a new thicket of Fourth Amendment law, to seek a creature of uncertain description that is neither a "plain view" inspection nor ***329** yet a "full-blown search." Nothing in the prior opinions of this Court supports such a distinction, not even the dictum from Justice Stewart's concurrence in Stanley v. Georgia, 394 U.S. 557, 571, 89 S.Ct. 1243, 1251, 22 L.Ed.2d 542 (1969), whose reference to a "mere inspection" describes, in our view, close observation of what lies in plain sight.

****1155** Justice POWELL's dissent reasonably asks what it is we would have had Officer Nelson do in these circumstances. Post, at ——. The answer depends, of course, upon whether he had probable cause to conduct a search, a question that was not preserved in this case. If he had, then he should have done precisely what he did. If not, then he should have followed up his suspicions, if possible, by means other than a search—just as he would have had to do if, while walking along the street, he had noticed the same suspicious stereo equipment sitting inside a house a few feet away from him, beneath an open window. It may well be that, in such circumstances, no effective means short of a search exist. But there is nothing new in the realization that the Constitution sometimes insulates the criminality of a few in order to protect the privacy of us all. Our disagreement with the dissenters pertains to where the proper balance should be struck; we choose to adhere to the textual and traditional standard of probable cause.

The State contends that, even if Officer Nelson's search violated the Fourth Amendment, the court below should have admitted the evidence thus obtained under the "good faith" exception to the exclusionary rule. That was not the question on which certiorari was granted, and we decline to consider it.

For the reasons stated, the judgment of the Court of Appeals of Arizona is

Affirmed.

Justice WHITE, concurring.

I write only to emphasize that this case does not present, and we have no occasion to address, the so-called "inadvertent ***330** discovery" prong of the plain-view exception to the Warrant Clause. See Coolidge v. New Hampshire, 403 U.S. 443, 469–471, 91 S.Ct. 2022, 2040–2041, 29 L.Ed.2d 564 (1971) (plurality opinion). This "requirement" of the plain-view doctrine has never been accepted by a judgment supported by a majority of this Court, and I therefore do not accept Justice O'CONNOR's dissent's assertion that evidence seized in plain view must have been inadvertently discovered in order to satisfy the dictates of the Fourth Amendment. See post, at ——. I join the majority opinion today without regard to the inadvertence of the officers' discovery of the stereo components' serial numbers. The police officers conducted a search of respondent's stereo equipment absent probable cause that the equipment was stolen. It is for this reason that the judgment of the Court of Appeals of Arizona must be affirmed.

Justice POWELL, with whom THE CHIEF JUSTICE and Justice O'CONNOR join, dissenting.

I join Justice O'CONNOR's dissenting opinion, and write briefly to highlight what seem to me the unfortunate consequences of the Court's decision.

Today the Court holds for the first time that the requirement of probable cause operates as a separate limitation on the application of the plain-view doctrine.1 The plurality opinion in Coolidge v. New Hampshire, 403 U.S. 443, 91 S.Ct. 2022, 29 L.Ed. 2d 564 (1971), ***331** required only that it be "immediately apparent to the police that they have evidence before them; the 'plain view' doctrine may not be used to extend a ****1156** general exploratory search from one object to another until something incriminating at last emerges." Id., at 466, 91 S.Ct. at 2038 (citation omitted). There was no general exploratory search in this case, and I would not approve such a search. All the pertinent objects were in plain view and could be identified as objects frequently stolen. There was no looking into closets, opening of drawers or trunks, or other "rummaging around." Justice O'CONNOR properly emphasizes that the moving of a suspicious object in plain view results in a minimal invasion of privacy. Post, at ——. The Court nevertheless holds that "merely looking at" an object in plain view is lawful, ante, at 1154, but "moving" or "disturbing" the object to investigate a reasonable suspicion is not, ante, at 1153, 1154. The facts of this case well illustrate the unreasonableness of this distinction.

The officers' suspicion that the stereo components at issue were stolen was both reasonable and based on specific, articulable facts. Indeed, the State was unwise to concede the absence of probable cause. The police lawfully entered respondent's apartment under exigent circumstances that arose when a bullet fired through the floor of the apartment struck a man in the apartment below. What they saw in the apartment hardly suggested that it was occupied by law-abiding citizens. A .25–caliber automatic pistol lay in plain view on the living room floor. During a concededly lawful search, the officers found a .45–caliber automatic, a .22–caliber, sawed-off rifle, and a stocking-cap mask. The apartment was littered with drug paraphernalia. App. 29. The officers also observed two sets of expensive stereo components of a type that frequently was stolen.

***332** It is fair to ask what Officer Nelson should have done in these circumstances. Accepting the State's concession that he lacked probable cause, he could not have obtained a warrant to seize the stereo components. Neither could he have remained on the premises and forcibly prevented their removal. Officer Nelson's testimony indicates that he was able to read some of the serial numbers without moving the components. To read the serial number on a Bang and Olufsen turntable, however, he had to "turn it around or turn it upside down." Id., at 19. Officer Nelson noted the serial numbers on the stereo components and telephoned the National Crime Information Center to check them against the Center's computerized listing of stolen property. The computer confirmed his suspicion that at least the Bang and Olufsen turntable had been stolen. On the basis of this information, the officers obtained a warrant to seize the turntable and other stereo components that also proved to be stolen.

The Court holds that there was an unlawful search of the turntable. It agrees that the "mere recording of the serial numbers did not constitute a seizure." Ante, at 1152. Thus, if the computer had identified as stolen property a component with a visible serial number, the evidence would have been admissible. But the Court further holds that "Officer Nelson's moving of the equipment ... did constitute a 'search'...." Ibid. It perceives a constitutional distinction between reading a serial number on an object and moving or picking up an identical object to see its serial number. To make its position unmistakably clear, the Court concludes that a "search is a search, even if it happens to disclose nothing but the bottom of a turntable." Ante, at 1153. With ***333** all respect, ****1157** this distinction between "looking" at a suspicious object in plain view and "moving" it even a few inches trivializes the Fourth Amendment. The Court's new rule will cause uncertainty, and could deter conscientious police officers from lawfully obtaining evidence necessary to convict guilty persons. Apart from the importance of rationality in the interpretation of the Fourth Amendment, today's decision may handicap law enforcement without enhancing privacy interests. Accordingly, I dissent.

Justice O'CONNOR, with whom THE CHIEF JUSTICE and Justice Powell join, dissenting.

The Court today gives the right answer to the wrong question. The Court asks whether the police must have probable cause before either seizing an object in plain view or conducting a full-blown search of that object, and concludes that they must. I agree. In my view, however, this case presents a different question: whether police must have probable cause before conducting a cursory inspection of an item in plain view. Because I conclude that such an inspection is reasonable if the police are aware of facts or circumstances that justify a reasonable suspicion that the item is evidence of a crime, I would reverse the judgment of the Arizona Court of Appeals, and therefore dissent.

***334** In Coolidge v. New Hampshire, 403 U.S. 443, 91 S.Ct. 2022, 29 L.Ed.2d 564 (1971), Justice Stewart summarized three requirements that the plurality thought must be satisfied for a plain-view search or seizure. First, the police must lawfully make an initial intrusion or otherwise be in a position from which they can view a particular area. Second, the officer must discover incriminating evidence "inadvertently." Third, it must be "immediately apparent" to the police that the items they observe may be evidence of a crime, contraband, or otherwise subject to seizure. As another plurality observed in Texas v. Brown, 460 U.S. 730, 737, 103 S.Ct. 1535, 1540–1541, 75 L.Ed.2d 502 (1983), these three requirements have never been expressly adopted by a majority of this Court, but "as the considered opinion of four Members of this Court [the Coolidge plurality] should obviously be the point of reference for further discussion of the issue." There is no dispute in this case that the first two requirements have been satisfied. The officers were lawfully in the apartment pursuant to exigent circumstances, and the discovery of the stereo was inadvertent—the officers did not " 'know in advance the location of [certain] evidence and intend to seize it,' relying on the plain-view doctrine only as a pretext." Ibid. (quoting Coolidge v. New Hampshire, supra, at 470, 91 S.Ct. at 2040). Instead, the dispute in this case focuses on the application of the "immediately apparent" requirement; at issue is whether a police officer's reasonable suspicion is adequate to justify a cursory examination of an item in plain view.

The purpose of the "immediately apparent" requirement is to prevent "general, exploratory rummaging in a person's belongings." Coolidge v. New Hampshire, 403 U.S., at 467, 91 S.Ct. at 2038. If an officer could indiscriminately search every item in plain view, a search justified by a limited purpose—such as exigent circumstances—could be used to eviscerate the protections of the Fourth Amendment. In ****1158** order to prevent such a general search, therefore, we require that the relevance of the item be "immediately apparent." As Justice Stewart explained:

***335** "Of course, the extension of the original justification [for being present] is legitimate only where it is immediately apparent to the police that they have evidence before them; the 'plain view' doctrine may not be used to extend a general exploratory search from one object to another until something incriminating at last emerges. Cf. Stanley v. Georgia, [394 U.S. 557], 571–572 [89 S.Ct. 1243, 1251–1252, 22 L.Ed.2d 542] [(1969)] (Stewart, J., concurring in result)." Id., at 466–467, 91 S.Ct. at 2038–2039.

Thus, I agree with the Court that even under the plain-view doctrine, probable cause is required before the police seize an item, or conduct a full-blown search of evidence in plain view. Ante, at ——. Such a requirement of probable cause will prevent the plain-view doctrine from authorizing general searches. This is not to say, however, that even a mere inspection of a suspicious item must be supported by probable cause. When a police officer makes a cursory inspection of a suspicious item in plain view in order to determine whether it is indeed evidence of a crime, there is no "exploratory rummaging." Only those items that the police officer "reasonably suspects" as evidence of a crime may be inspected, and perhaps more importantly, the scope of such an inspection is quite limited. In short, if police officers have a reasonable, articulable suspicion that an object they come across during the course of a lawful search is evidence of crime, in my view they may make a cursory examination of the object to verify their suspicion. If the officers wish to go beyond such a cursory examination of the object, however, they must have probable cause.

This distinction between a full-blown search and seizure of an item and a mere inspection of the item was first suggested by Justice Stewart. In his concurrence in Stanley v. Georgia, 394 U.S. 557, 89 S.Ct. 1243, 22 L.Ed.2d 542 (1969), which is cited in Coolidge, Justice Stewart observed that the federal agents there had acted within the scope of a lawful warrant in opening the drawers of the defendant's desk. When they found in one of the drawers not the gambling material described in the warrant ***336** but movie films, they proceeded to exhibit the films on the defendant's projector, and thereafter arrested the defendant for possession of obscene matter. Justice Stewart agreed with the majority that the film had to be suppressed, but in doing so he suggested that a less intrusive inspection of evidence in plain view would present a different case: "This is not a case where agents in the course of a lawful search came upon contraband, criminal activity, or criminal evidence in plain view. For the record makes clear that the contents of the films could not be determined by mere inspection." Id., at 571, 89 S.Ct. at 1251 (emphasis added) (footnote omitted).

Following Justice Stewart's suggestion, the overwhelming majority of both state and federal courts have held that probable cause is not required for a minimal inspection of an item in plain view. As Professor LaFave summarizes the view of these courts, "the minimal additional intrusion which results from an inspection or examination of an object in plain view is reasonable if the officer was first aware of some facts and circumstances which justify a reasonable suspicion (not probable cause, in the traditional sense) that the object is or contains a fruit, instrumentality, or evidence of crime." 2 W. LaFave, Search and Seizure § 6.7(b), p. 717 (2d ed. 1987); see also id., at 345 ("It is generally assumed that there is nothing improper in merely picking up an unnamed article for the purpose of noting its brand name or serial number or other identifying characteristics to be found on the surface"). Thus, while courts require probable cause for more extensive examination, cursory inspections—including picking up or moving objects for a better view—require only a reasonable ****1159** suspicion. See, e.g., United States v. Marbury, 732 F.2d 390, 399 (CA5 1984) (police may inspect an item found in plain view to determine whether it is evidence of crime if they have a reasonable suspicion to believe that the item is evidence); United States v. Hillyard, 677 F.2d 1336, 1342 (CA9 1982) (police may give suspicious documents brief perusal if they have a "reasonable suspicion"); ***337** United States v. Wright, 667 F.2d 793, 798 (CA9 1982) ("[A]n officer may conduct such an examination if he at least has a 'reasonable suspicion' to believe that the discovered item is evidence"); United States v. Roberts, 619 F.2d 379, 381 (CA5 1980) ("Police officers are not required to ignore the significance of items in plain view even when the full import of the objects cannot be positively ascertained without some examination"); United States v. Ochs, 595 F.2d 1247, 1257–1258, and n. 8 (CA2 1979) (Friendly, J.) (same).

Indeed, several state courts have applied a reasonable-suspicion standard in factual circumstances almost identical to this case. See, e.g., State v. Noll, 116 Wis.2d 443, 343 N.W.2d 391 (1984) (officer, upon seeing television, could check serial numbers);

State v. Riedinger, 374 N.W.2d 866 (ND 1985) (police, in executing warrant for drugs, could check serial number of microwave oven); People v. Dorris, 110 Ill.App. 3d 660, 66 Ill.Dec. 390, 442 N.E.2d 951 (1982) (police may note account number of deposit slip because, when the police have a reasonable suspicion that an item in plain view is stolen property, the minimal additional intrusion of checking external identification numbers is proper); State v. Proctor, 12 Wash.App. 274, 529 P.2d 472 (1974) (upholding police notation of serial numbers on calculators); People v. Eddington, 23 Mich.App. 210, 178 N.W.2d 686 (1970) (upholding examination of the heels of shoes), rev'd on other grounds, 387 Mich. 551, 198 N.W.2d 297 (1972).

This distinction between searches based on their relative intrusiveness—and its subsequent adoption by a consensus of American courts—is entirely consistent with our Fourth Amendment jurisprudence. We have long recognized that searches can vary in intrusiveness, and that some brief searches "may be so minimally intrusive of Fourth Amendment interests that strong countervailing governmental interests will justify a [search] based only on specific articulable facts" that the item in question is contraband or evidence of a crime. ***338** United States v. Place, 462 U.S. 696, 706, 103 S.Ct. 2637, 2644, 77 L.Ed.2d 110 1983). In Delaware v. Prouse, 440 U.S. 648, 654, 99 S.Ct. 1391, 1396, 59 L.Ed.2d 660 (1979), we held that the permissibility of a particular law enforcement practice should be judged by balancing its intrusion on the individual's Fourth Amendment interests against its promotion of legitimate governmental interests. Thus, "[w]here a careful balancing of governmental and private interests suggests that the public interest is best served by a Fourth Amendment standard of reasonableness that stops short of probable cause, we have not hesitated to adopt such a standard." New Jersey v. T.L.O., 469 U.S. 325, 341, 105 S.Ct. 733, 743, 83 L.Ed.2d 720 (1985). The governmental interests considered include crime prevention and detection. Terry v. Ohio, 392 U.S. 1, 22, 88 S.Ct. 1868, 1880, 20 L.Ed.2d 889 (1968). The test is whether these law enforcement interests are sufficiently "substantial," not, as the Court would have it, whether "operational necessities render [a standard less than probable cause] the only practicable means of detecting certain types of crimes." Ante, at ——. See United States v. Place, supra, at 704, 103 S.Ct. at 2643.

In my view, the balance of the governmental and privacy interests strongly supports a reasonable-suspicion standard for the cursory examination of items in plain view. The additional intrusion caused by an inspection of an item in plain view for its serial number is miniscule. Indeed, the intrusion in this case was even more transitory and less intrusive than the seizure of luggage from a suspected drug dealer in United States v. Place, supra, and the "severe, though brief, intrusion upon cherished ****1160** personal security" in Terry v. Ohio, supra, at 24–25, 88 S.Ct. at 1881–1882.

Weighed against this minimal additional invasion of privacy are rather major gains in law enforcement. The use of identification numbers in tracing stolen property is a powerful law enforcement tool. Serial numbers are far more helpful and accurate in detecting stolen property than simple police recollection of the evidence. Cf. New York v. Class, 475 U.S. 106, 111, 106 S.Ct. 960, 964, 89 L.Ed.2d 81 (1986) (observing importance of vehicle identification numbers). Given the prevalence of mass produced ***339** goods in our national economy, a serial number is often the only sure method of detecting stolen property. The balance of governmental and private interests strongly supports the view accepted by a majority of courts that a standard of reasonable suspicion meets the requirements of the Fourth Amendment.

Unfortunately, in its desire to establish a "bright-line" test, the Court has taken a step that ignores a substantial body of precedent and that places serious roadblocks to reasonable law enforcement practices. Indeed, in this case no warrant to search the stereo equipment for its serial number could have been obtained by the officers based on reasonable suspicion alone, and in the Court's view the officers may not even move the stereo turntable to examine its serial number. The theoretical advantages of the "search is a search" approach adopted by the Court today are simply too remote to justify the tangible and severe damage it inflicts on legitimate and effective law enforcement.

Even if probable cause were the appropriate standard, I have little doubt that it was satisfied here. When police officers, during the course of a search inquiring into grievously unlawful activity, discover the tools of a thief (a sawed-off rifle and a stocking mask) and observe in a small apartment two sets of stereo equipment that are both inordinately expensive in relation to their surroundings and known to be favored targets of larcenous activity, the "flexible, common-sense standard" of probable cause has been satisfied. Texas v. Brown, 460 U.S., at 742, 103 S.Ct. at 1543 (plurality opinion).

Because the Court today ignores the existence of probable cause, and in doing so upsets a widely accepted body of precedent on the standard of reasonableness for the cursory examination of evidence in plain view, I respectfully dissent.

Black Letter Law

> The Court held that: (1) no "seizure" occurred for purposes of Fourth Amendment, when officer merely recorded serial numbers of stereo equipment he observed in plain view, but (2) officer's actions in moving equipment to locate serial numbers constituted "search," which had to be supported by probable cause, notwithstanding that officer was lawfully present in apartment where equipment was located.

Discussion Problem:

10-1. Jack and Jill had been dating for several months. During this period of courtship, Jill would occasionally stay at Jack's house and visa versa. Each of them had several belongings at each other's apartments including clothing, toiletries, a toothbrush and household items. On May 5th, the couple went out to celebrate Cinco de Mayo with some friends. At this celebration, the two became extremely intoxicated. Upon returning to Jack's apartment, the couple engaged in a heated argument. The neighbors feared that violence may ensue and called the Gulfport police department. Jack went to take a walk outside to "cool off" and give Jill some space.

While he was gone, two police officers from the Gulfport police department came to the door, and Jill greeted them. When the police officers saw her, her hair was messy, her eyes were bloodshot, she was still in tears and her right cheek looked particularly red, as though she had been slapped. The police officers informed her that they were there responding to a call about domestic violence and asked if they could enter. Jill told the police that they could enter but that this was not her apartment, it belonged to her boyfriend and he would be back shortly. The police officers asked Jill what happened and she said: "Oh nothing, Jack just went on one of this 'roid-rages' again and lost his temper." Knowing that possession of certain performance-enhancing chemicals were illegal, the officer's asked Jill for her consent to search the apartment and she said yes.

As the Officers stood up from the coffee table, Jack returned. As soon as he opened the door, he saw the officers and yelled at Jill: "You stupid bitch!" One of the officers escorted Jack out of the apartment to have a word. As soon as Jack started conversing with the officer he stated, "She doesn't live here. I want her out. Kick her out. And if she told you that you could search my place she's wrong, get out now." The other Officer continued to search the apartment and found illegal performance enhancing drugs, a bong and several ounces of marijuana exposed on the dresser in the master bedroom. At this trial for drug possession, Jack moved to exclude the evidence obtained, claiming it was a product of an unlawful search and seizure.

If you're the state attorney on the case, how do you respond to the defendant's motion? Please explain your reasoning.

10-2. In the early morning hours of October 31, a detective and a team of officers from his unit were at the Greyhound Trailways bus station in Washington, D.C. Their assignment was to interrogate passengers arriving in or passing through Washington, D.C. from New York City and presumably to search them if there was cause or if police secured their consent. At about 2:30 a.m., a bus arrived from New York en route to various points to the south, one of which was Wilmington, North Carolina. After the driver announced a ten-minute rest stop, The detective and two other officers, who were all dressed in civilian clothes, boarded the bus.

The detective took control of the intercom without first asking the bus driver for authority to do so. He announced that he was a member of a police drug interdiction unit, and that he and his colleagues interviewed passengers arriving from New York because that city was a "source supply of drugs." He explained that other members of the unit were also on the bus at the time.

There were at least fifteen passengers on the bus. After questioning several passengers, the Detective approached the defendant, who was occupying a window seat approximately three-quarters of the way to the rear. He inquired where the defendant had boarded the bus and where he was going, and requested to see the defendant's ticket. The defendant responded to these questions and showed the detective his ticket, which reflected a trip from New York to Wilmington. The detective then asked whether he was carrying drugs or weapons; the defendant said no. The detective asked if he could search the defendant's bag; he agreed, but the search revealed nothing.

The defendant undoubtedly hoped, and may well have believed, that his ordeal was now over and that he would escape the encounter without the police discovering the contraband which was concealed on his person, but it was not to be. The detective next asked the defendant if he could pat him down. In response the defendant raised his arms. The detective felt a large lump next to the defendant's rib cage, lifted his shirt, and discovered a clear plastic bag containing 110 grams of rock cocaine.

The defendant testified that he was fourteen years old at the time of the incident and that he had recently begun the ninth grade. There was no evidence was adduced that he had ever had any prior encounter with the law. The defendant said he was afraid when the police boarded the bus but he could not leave because there was not enough room to get by the cops. One of the police was also standing in a way that blocked the exit. He also testified that he was afraid that the police would become suspicious if he did not agree to allow the detective to search his bag. He insisted that he raised his hands to facilitate the patdown because he felt he had no choice, and because any non-cooperation on his part would have made the police even more suspicious of him. He admitted that he had told the detective that he had no drugs on his person, and that this statement was not true.

The defendant acknowledged that the detective spoke to him in a polite and conversational tone of voice and did not abuse or threaten him. There was no overt intimidation, and he did not claim that the detective ever drew his weapon.

The defense has moved to exclude evidence of the patdown on the grounds that the consent was not valid. You are the clerk who must draft the court's order. Be sure to include your reasoning in the order.

Chapter 11: Encounters on the Street

Terry v. Ohio

88 S.Ct. 1868

Supreme Court of the United States

John W. TERRY, Petitioner,

v.

STATE OF OHIO.

No. 67. | Argued Dec. 12, 1967. | Decided June 10, 1968.

Mr. Chief Justice WARREN delivered the opinion of the Court.

This case presents serious questions concerning the role of the Fourth Amendment in the confrontation on the street between the citizen and the policeman investigating suspicious circumstances.

Petitioner Terry was convicted of carrying a concealed weapon and sentenced to the statutorily prescribed term of one to three years in the penitentiary. Following the denial of a pretrial motion to suppress, the prosecution introduced in evidence two revolvers and a number of bullets seized from Terry and a codefendant, Richard Chilton, by Cleveland Police Detective Martin McFadden. At the hearing on the motion to suppress this evidence, Officer McFadden testified that while he was patrolling in plain clothes in downtown Cleveland at approximately 2:30 in the afternoon of October 31, 1963, his attention was attracted by two men, Chilton and Terry, standing on the corner of Huron Road and Euclid Avenue. He had never seen the two men before, and he was unable to say precisely what first drew his eye to them. However, he testified that he had been a policeman for 39 years and a detective for 35 and that he had been assigned to patrol this vicinity of downtown Cleveland for shoplifters and pickpockets for 30 years. He explained that he had developed routine habits of observation over the years and that he would 'stand and watch people or walk and watch people at many intervals of the day.' He added: 'Now, in this case when I looked over they didn't look right to me at the time.'

His interest aroused, Officer McFadden took up a post of observation in the ****1872** entrance to a store 300 to 400 feet away from the two men. 'I get more purpose to watch them when I seen their movements,' he testified. He saw one of the men leave the other one and walk southwest on Huron Road, past some stores. The man paused for a moment and looked in a store window, then walked on a short distance, turned around and walked back toward the corner, pausing once again to look in the same store window. He rejoined his companion at the corner, and the two conferred briefly. Then the second man went through the same series of motions, strolling down Huron Road, looking in the same window, walking on a short distance, turning back, peering in the store window again, and returning to confer with the first man at the corner. The two men repeated this ritual alternately between five and six times apiece—in all, roughly a dozen trips. At one point, while the two were standing together on the corner, a third man approached them and engaged them briefly in conversation. This man then left the two others and walked west on Euclid Avenue. Chilton and Terry resumed their measured pacing, peering and conferring. After this had gone on for 10 to 12 minutes, the two men walked off together, heading west on Euclid Avenue, following the path taken earlier by the third man.

By this time Officer McFadden had become thoroughly suspicious. He testified that after observing their elaborately casual and oft-repeated reconnaissance of the store window on Huron Road, he suspected the two men of 'casing a job, a stick-up,' and that he considered it his duty as a police officer to investigate further. He added that he feared 'they may have a gun.' Thus, Officer McFadden followed Chilton and Terry and saw them stop in front of Zucker's store to talk to the same man who had conferred with them earlier on the street corner. Deciding that the situation was ripe for direct action, Officer McFadden approached the three men, identified *7 himself as a police officer and asked for their names. At this point his knowledge was confined to what he had observed. He was not acquainted with any of the three men by name or by sight, and he had received no information concerning them from any other source. When the men 'mumbled something' in response to his inquiries, Officer McFadden grabbed petitioner Terry, spun him around so that they were facing the other two, with Terry between McFadden and the others, and patted down the outside of his clothing. In the left breast pocket of Terry's overcoat Officer McFadden felt a pistol. He reached inside the overcoat pocket, but was unable to remove the gun. At this point, keeping Terry between himself and the others, the officer ordered all three men to enter Zucker's store. As they went in, he removed Terry's overcoat completely, removed a .38-caliber revolver from the pocket and ordered all three men to face the wall with their hands raised. Officer McFadden proceeded to pat down the outer clothing of Chilton and the third man, Katz. He discovered another revolver in the outer pocket of Chilton's overcoat, but no weapons were found on Katz. The officer testified that he only patted the men down to see whether they had weapons, and that he did not put his hands beneath the outer garments of either Terry or Chilton until he felt their guns. So far as appears from the record, he never placed his hands beneath Katz' outer garments. Officer McFadden seized Chilton's gun, asked the proprietor of the store to call a police wagon, and took all three men to the station, where Chilton and Terry were formally charged with carrying concealed weapons.

On the motion to suppress the guns the prosecution took the position that they had been seized following a search incident to a lawful arrest. The trial court rejected this theory, stating that it 'would be stretching the facts beyond reasonable comprehension' to find that Officer McFadden had had probable **1873 cause to arrest the men before he patted them down for weapons. However, the court denied the defendants' motion on the ground that Officer McFadden, on the basis of his experience, 'had reasonable cause to believe * * * that the defendants were conducting themselves suspiciously, and some interrogation should be made of their action.' Purely for his own protection, the court held, the officer had the right to pat down the outer clothing of these men, who he had reasonable cause to believe might be armed. The court distinguished between an investigatory 'stop' and an arrest, and between a 'frisk' of the outer clothing for weapons and a full-blown search for evidence of crime. The frisk, it held, was essential to the proper performance of the officer's investigatory duties, for without it 'the answer to the police officer may be a bullet, and a loaded pistol discovered during the frisk is admissible.'

After the court denied their motion to suppress, Chilton and Terry waived jury trial and pleaded not guilty. The court adjudged them guilty, and the Court of Appeals for the Eighth Judicial District, Cuyahoga County, affirmed. State v. Terry, 5 Ohio App. 2d 122, 214 N.E.2d 114 (1966). The Supreme Court of Ohio dismissed their appeal on the ground that no 'substantial constitutional question' was involved. We granted certiorari, 387 U.S. 929, 87 S.Ct. 2050, 18 L.Ed.2d 989 (1967), to determine whether the admission of the revolvers in evidence violated petitioner's rights under the Fourth Amendment, made applicable to the States by the Fourteenth. Mapp v. Ohio, 367 U.S. 643, 81 S.Ct. 1684, 6 L.Ed.2d 1081 (1961). We affirm the conviction.

The Fourth Amendment provides that 'the right of the people to be secure in their persons, houses, papers, and effects, against unreasonable searches and seizures, shall not be violated * * *.' This inestimable right of personal security belongs as much to the citizen on the streets of our cities as to the homeowner closeted in his study to dispose of his secret affairs. For, as this Court has always recognized,

'No right is held more sacred, or is more carefully guarded, by the common law, than the right of every individual to the possession and control of his own person, free from all restraint or interference of others, unless by clear and unquestionable authority of law.' Union Pac. R. Co. v. Botsford, 141 U.S. 250, 251, 11 S.Ct. 1000, 1001, 35 L.Ed. 734 (1891).

We have recently held that 'the Fourth Amendment protects people, not places,' Katz v. United States, 389 U.S. 347, 351, 88 S.Ct. 507, 511, 19 L.Ed.2d 576 (1967), and wherever an individual may harbor a reasonable 'expectation of privacy,' id., at 361, 88 S.Ct. at 507, (Mr. Justice Harlan, concurring), he is entitled to be free from unreasonable governmental intrusion. Of course, the specific content and incidents of this right must be shaped by the context in which it is asserted. For 'what the Constitution forbids is not all searches and seizures, but unreasonable searches and seizures.' Elkins v. United States, 364 U.S. 206, 222, 80 S.Ct. 1437, 1446, 4 L.Ed.2d 1669 (1960). Unquestionably petitioner was entitled to the protection of the Fourth Amendment as he walked down the street in Cleveland. Beck v. State of Ohio, 379 U.S. 89, 85 S.Ct. 223, 13 L.Ed.2d 142 (1964); Rios v. United States, 364 U.S. 253, 80 S.Ct. 1431, 4 L.Ed.2d 1688 (1960); Henry v. United States, 361 U.S. 98, 80 S.Ct. 168, 4 L.Ed.2d 134 (1959); United States v. Di Re, 332 U.S. 581, 68 S.Ct. 222, 92 L.Ed. 210 (1948); Carroll v. United States, 267 U.S. 132, 45 S.Ct. 280, 69 L.Ed. 543 (1925). The question is whether in all the circumstances of this on-the-street encounter, his right to personal security was violated by an unreasonable search and seizure.

****1874** We would be less than candid if we did not acknowledge that this question thrusts to the fore difficult and troublesome issues regarding a sensitive area of police activity—issues which have never before been squarely presented to this Court. Reflective of the tensions involved are the practical and constitutional arguments pressed with great vigor on both sides of the public debate over the power of the police to 'stop and frisk' —as it is sometimes euphemistically termed—suspicious persons.

On the one hand, it is frequently argued that in dealing with the rapidly unfolding and often dangerous situations on city streets the police are in need of an escalating set of flexible responses, graduated in relation to the amount of information they possess. For this purpose it is urged that distinctions should be made between a 'stop' and an 'arrest' (or a 'seizure' of a person), and between a 'frisk' and a 'search.' Thus, it is argued, the police should be allowed to 'stop' a person and detain him briefly for questioning upon suspicion that he may be connected with criminal activity. Upon suspicion that the person may be armed, the police should have the power to 'frisk' him for weapons. If the 'stop' and the 'frisk' give rise to probable cause to believe that the suspect has committed a crime, then the police should be empowered to make a formal 'arrest,' and a full incident 'search' of the person. This scheme is justified in part upon the notion that a 'stop' and a 'frisk' amount to a mere 'minor inconvenience and petty indignity,' which can properly be imposed upon the citizen in the interest of effective law enforcement on the basis of a police officer's suspicion.

On the other side the argument is made that the authority of the police must be strictly circumscribed by the law of arrest and search as it has developed to date in the traditional jurisprudence of the Fourth Amendment. It is contended with some force that there is not—and cannot be—a variety of police activity which does not depend solely upon the voluntary cooperation of the citizen and yet which stops short of an arrest based upon probable cause to make such an arrest. The heart of the Fourth Amendment, the argument ****1875** runs, is a severe requirement of specific justification for any intrusion upon protected personal security, coupled with a highly developed system of judicial controls to enforce upon the agents of the State the commands of the Constitution. Acquiescence by the courts in the compulsion inherent in the field interrogation practices at issue here, it is urged, would constitute an abdication of judicial control over, and indeed an encouragement of, substantial interference with liberty and personal security by police officers whose judgment is necessarily colored by their primary involvement in 'the often competitive enterprise of ferreting out crime.' Johnson v. United States, 333 U.S. 10, 14, 68 S.Ct. 367, 369, 92

L.Ed. 436 (1948). This, it is argued, can only serve to exacerbate police-community tensions in the crowded centers of our Nation's cities.

In this context we approach the issues in this case mindful of the limitations of the judicial function in controlling the myriad daily situations in which policemen and citizens confront each other on the street. The State has characterized the issue here as 'the right of a police officer * * * to make an on-the-street stop, interrogate and pat down for weapons (known in street vernacular as 'stop and frisk').' But this is only partly accurate. For the issue is not the abstract propriety of the police conduct, but the admissibility against petitioner of the evidence uncovered by the search and seizure. Ever since its inception, the rule excluding evidence seized in violation of the Fourth Amendment has been recognized as a principal mode of discouraging lawless police conduct. See Weeks v. United States, 232 U.S. 383, 391—393, 34 S.Ct. 341, 344, 58 L.Ed. 652 (1914). Thus its major thrust is a deterrent one, see Linkletter v. Walker, 381 U.S. 618, 629—635, 85 S.Ct. 1731, 1741, 14 L.Ed.2d 601 (1965), and experience has taught that it is the only effective deterrent to police misconduct in the criminal context, and that without it the constitutional guarantee against unreasonable searches and seizures would be a mere 'form of words.' Mapp v. Ohio, 367 U.S. 643, 655, 81 S.Ct. 1684, 1692, 6 L.Ed.2d 1081 (1961). The rule also serves another vital function—'the imperative of judicial integrity.' Elkins v. United States, 364 U.S. 206, 222, 80 S.Ct. 1437, 1447, 4 L.Ed.2d 1669 (1960). Courts which sit under our Constitution cannot and will not be made party to lawless invasions of the constitutional rights of citizens by permitting unhindered governmental use of the fruits of such invasions. Thus in our system evidentiary rulings provide the context in which the judicial process of inclusion and exclusion approves some conduct as comporting with constitutional guarantees and disapproves other actions by state agents. A ruling admitting evidence in a criminal trial, we recognize, has the necessary effect of legitimizing the conduct which produced the evidence, while an application of the exclusionary rule withholds the constitutional imprimatur.

The exclusionary rule has its limitations, however, as a tool of judicial control. It cannot properly be invoked to exclude the products of legitimate police investigative techniques on the ground that much conduct which is closely similar involves unwarranted intrusions upon constitutional protections. Moreover, in some contexts the rule is ineffective as a deterrent. Street encounters between citizens and police officers are incredibly rich in diversity. They range from wholly friendly exchanges of pleasantries or mutually useful information to hostile confrontations of armed men involving arrests, or injuries, or loss of life. Moreover, hostile confrontations are not all of a piece. Some of them begin in a friendly enough manner, only to take a ****1876** different turn upon the injection of some unexpected element into the conversation. Encounters are initiated by the police for a wide variety of purposes, some of which are wholly unrelated to a desire to prosecute for crime. Doubtless some police 'field interrogation' conduct violates the Fourth Amendment. But a stern refusal by this Court to condone such activity does not necessarily render it responsive to the exclusionary rule. Regardless of how effective the rule may be where obtaining convictions is an important objective of the police, it is powerless to deter invasions of constitutionally guaranteed rights where the police either have no interest in prosecuting or are willing to forgo successful prosecution in the interest of serving some other goal.

Proper adjudication of cases in which the exclusionary rule is invoked demands a constant awareness of these limitations. The wholesale harassment by certain elements of the police community, of which minority groups, particularly Negroes, frequently complain, will not be stopped by the exclusion of any evidence from any criminal trial. Yet a rigid and unthinking application of the exclusionary rule, in futile protest against practices which it can never be used effectively to control, may exact a high toll in human injury and frustration of efforts to prevent crime. No judicial opinion can comprehend the protean variety of the street encounter, and we can only judge the facts of the case before us. Nothing we say today is to be taken as indicating approval of police conduct outside the legitimate investigative sphere. Under our decision, courts still retain their traditional responsibility to guard against police conduct which is over-bearing or harassing, or which trenches upon personal security without the objective evidentiary justification which the Constitution requires. When such conduct is identified, it must be condemned by the judiciary and its fruits must be excluded from evidence in criminal trials. And, of course, our approval of legitimate and restrained investigative conduct undertaken **1877** on the basis of ample factual justification should in no way discourage the employment of other remedies than the exclusionary rule to curtail abuses for which that sanction may prove inappropriate.

Having thus roughly sketched the perimeters of the constitutional debate over the limits on police investigative conduct in general and the background against which this case presents itself, we turn our attention to the quite narrow question posed by the facts before us: whether it is always unreasonable for a policeman to seize a person and subject him to a limited search for weapons unless there is probable cause for an arrest. Given the narrowness of this question, we have no occasion to canvass in detail the constitutional limitations upon the scope of a policeman's power when he confronts a citizen without probable cause to arrest him.

II.

Our first task is to establish at what point in this encounter the Fourth Amendment becomes relevant. That is, we must decide whether and when Officer McFadden 'seized' Terry and whether and when he conducted a 'search.' There is some suggestion in the use of such terms as 'stop' and 'frisk' that such police conduct is outside the purview of the Fourth Amendment because neither action rises to the level of a 'search' or 'seizure' within the meaning of the Constitution. We emphatically reject this notion. It is quite plain that the Fourth Amendment governs 'seizures' of the person which do not eventuate in a trip to the station house and prosecution for crime—'arrests' in traditional terminology. It must be recognized that whenever a police officer accosts an individual and restrains his freedom to walk away, he has 'seized' that person. And it is nothing less than sheer torture of the English language to suggest that a careful exploration of the outer surfaces of a person's clothing all over his or her body in an attempt to find weapons is not a 'search,' Moreover, it is simply fantastic to urge that such a procedure performed in public by a policeman while the citizen stands helpless, perhaps facing a wall with his hands raised, is a 'petty indignity.' It is a serious intrusion upon the sanctity of the person, which may inflict great indignity and arouse strong resentment, and it is not to be undertaken lightly.

The danger in the logic which proceeds upon distinctions between **1878** a 'stop' and an 'arrest,' or 'seizure' of the person, and between a 'frisk' and a 'search' is twofold. It seeks to isolate from constitutional scrutiny the initial stages of the contact between the policeman and the citizen. And by suggesting a rigid all-or-nothing model of justification and regulation under the Amendment, it obscures the utility of limitations upon the scope, as well as the initiation, of police action as a means of constitutional regulation.15 This Court has held in the past that a search which is reasonable at its inception may violate the Fourth Amendment by virtue of its intolerable intensity and scope. Kremen v. United States, 353 U.S. 346, 77 S.Ct. 828, 1 L.Ed.2d 876 (1957); Go-Bart Importing Co. v. United States, 282 U.S. 344, 356—358, 51 S.Ct. 153, 158, 75 L.Ed. 374 (1931); see United States v. Di Re, 332 U.S. 581, 586—587, 68 S.Ct. 222, 225, 92 L.Ed. 210 (1948). The scope of the search must be 'strictly tied to and justified by' the circumstances which rendered its initiation permissible. Warden v. Hayden, 387 U.S. 294, 310, 87 S.Ct. 1642, 1652 (1967) (Mr. Justice Fortas, concurring); see e.g., Preston v. United States, 376 U.S. 364, 367—368, 84 S.Ct. 881, 884, 11 L.Ed.2d 777 (1964); Agnello v. United States, 269 U.S. 20, 30—31, 46 S.Ct. 4, 6, 70 L.Ed. 145 (1925).

The distinctions of classical 'stop-and-frisk' theory thus serve to divert attention from the central inquiry under the Fourth Amendment—the reasonableness in all the circumstances of the particular ****1879** governmental invasion of a citizen's personal security. 'Search' and 'seizure' are not talismans. We therefore reject the notions that the Fourth Amendment does not come into play at all as a limitation upon police conduct if the officers stop short of something called a 'technical arrest' or a 'full-blown search.'

In this case there can be no question, then, that Officer McFadden 'seized' petitioner and subjected him to a 'search' when he took hold of him and patted down the outer surfaces of his clothing. We must decide whether at that point it was reasonable for Officer McFadden to have interfered with petitioner's personal security as he did. And in determining whether the seizure and search were 'unreasonable' our inquiry is a dual one—whether the officer's action was justified at its inception, and whether it was reasonably related in scope to the circumstances which justified the interference in the first place.

III.

If this case involved police conduct subject to the Warrant Clause of the Fourth Amendment, we would have to ascertain whether 'probable cause' existed to justify the search and seizure which took place. However, that is not the case. We do not retreat from our holdings that the police must, whenever practicable, obtain advance judicial approval of searches and seizures through the warrant procedure, see e.g., Katz v. United States, 389 U.S. 347, 88 S.Ct. 507, 19 L.Ed.2d 576 (1967); Beck v. State of Ohio, 379 U.S. 89, 96, 85 S.Ct. 223, 228, 13 L.Ed.2d 142 (1964); Chapman v. United States, 365 U.S. 610, 81 S.Ct. 776, 5 L.Ed.2d 828 (1961), or that in most instances failure to comply with the warrant requirement can only be excused by exigent circumstances, see, e.g., Warden v. Hayden, 387 U.S. 294, 87 S.Ct. 1642, 18 L.Ed.2d 782 (1967) (hot pursuit); cf. Preston v. United States, 376 U.S. 364, 367—368, 84 S.Ct. 881, 884, 11 L.Ed.2d 777 (1964). But we deal here with an entire rubric of police conduct—necessarily swift action predicated upon the on-the-spot observations of the officer on the beat—which historically has not been, and as a practical matter could not be, subjected to the warrant procedure. Instead, the conduct involved in this case must be tested by the Fourth Amendment's general proscription against unreasonable searches and seizures.

Nonetheless, the notions which underlie both the warrant procedure and the requirement of probable cause remain fully relevant in this context. In order to assess the reasonableness of Officer McFadden's conduct as a general proposition, it is necessary 'first to focus upon the governmental interest which allegedly justifies official intrusion upon the constitutionally protected interests of the private citizen,' for there is 'no ready test for determining reasonableness other than by balancing the need to search (or seize) against the invasion which the search (or seizure) entails.' ****1880** Camara v. Municipal Court, 387 U.S. 523, 534—535, 536—537, 87 S.Ct. 1727, 1735, 18 L.Ed.2d 930 (1967). And in justifying the particular intrusion the police officer must be able to point to specific and articulable facts which, taken together with rational inferences from those facts, reasonably warrant that intrusion.18 The scheme of the Fourth Amendment becomes meaningful only when it is assured that at some point the conduct of those charged with enforcing the laws can be subjected to the more detached, neutral scrutiny of a judge who must evaluate the reasonableness of a particular search or seizure in light of the particular circumstances.19 And in making that assessment it is imperative that the facts be judged against an objective standard: would the facts available to the officer at the moment of the seizure or the search 'warrant a man of reasonable caution in the belief' that the action taken was appropriate? Cf. Carroll v. United States, 267 U.S. 132, 45 S.Ct. 280, 69 L.Ed. 543 (1925); Beck v. State of Ohio, 379 U.S. 89, 96—97, 85 S.Ct. 223, 229, 13 L.Ed. 2d 142 (1964).20 Anything less would invite intrusions upon constitutionally guaranteed rights based on nothing more substantial than inarticulate hunches, a result this

Court has consistently refused to sanction. See, e.g., Beck v. Ohio, supra; Rios v. United States, 364 U.S. 253, 80 S.Ct. 1431, 4 L.Ed.2d 1688 (1960); Henry v. United States, 361 U.S. 98, 80 S.Ct. 168, 4 L.Ed.2d 134 (1959). And simple "good faith on the part of the arresting officer is not enough.' * * * If subjective good faith alone were the test, the protections of the Fourth Amendment would evaporate, and the people would be 'secure in their persons, houses, papers and effects,' only in the discretion of the police.' Beck v. Ohio, supra, at 97, 85 S.Ct. at 229.

Applying these principles to this case, we consider first the nature and extent of the governmental interests involved. One general interest is of course that of effective crime prevention and detection; it is this interest which underlies the recognition that a police officer may in appropriate circumstances and in an appropriate manner approach a person for purposes of investigating possibly criminal behavior even though there is no probable cause to make an arrest. It was this legitimate investigative function Officer McFadden was discharging when he decided to approach petitioner and his companions. He had observed Terry, Chilton, and Katz go Through a series of acts, each of them perhaps innocent **1881 in itself, but which taken together warranted further investigation. There is nothing unusual in two men standing together on a street corner, perhaps waiting for someone. Nor is there anything suspicious about people in such circumstances strolling up and down the street, singly or in pairs. Store windows, moreover, are made to be looked in. But the story is quite different where, as here, two men hover about a street corner for an extended period of time, at the end of which it becomes apparent that they are not waiting for anyone or anything; where these men pace alternately along an identical route, pausing to stare in the same store window roughly 24 times; where each completion of this route is followed immediately by a conference between the two men on the corner; where they are joined in one of these conferences by a third man who leaves swiftly; and where the two men finally follow the third and rejoin him a couple of blocks away. It would have been poor police work indeed for an officer of 30 years' experience in the detection of thievery from stores in this same neighborhood to have failed to investigate this behavior further.

The crux of this case, however, is not the propriety of Officer McFadden's taking steps to investigate petitioner's suspicious behavior, but rather, whether there was justification for McFadden's invasion of Terry's personal security by searching him for weapons in the course of that investigation. We are now concerned with more than the governmental interest in investigating crime; in addition, there is the more immediate interest of the police officer in taking steps to assure himself that the person with whom he is dealing is not armed with a weapon that could unexpectedly and fatally be used against him. Certainly it would be unreasonable to require that police officers take unnecessary risks in the performance of their duties. American criminals have a long tradition of armed violence, and every year in this country many law enforcement officers are killed in the line of duty, and thousands more are wounded. Virtually all of these deaths and a substantial portion of the injurics are inflicted with guns and knives.

In view of these facts, we cannot blind ourselves to the need for law enforcement officers to protect themselves and other prospective victims of violence in situations where they may lack probable cause for an arrest. When an officer is justified in believing that the individual whose suspicious behavior he is investigating at close range is armed and presently dangerous to the officer or to others, it would appear to be clearly unreasonable to deny the officer the power to take necessary measures to determine whether the person is in fact carrying a weapon and to neutralize the threat of physical harm.

We must still consider, however, the nature and quality of the intrusion on individual rights which must be accepted if police officers are to be conceded the right to search for weapons in situations where probable cause to arrest for crime is lacking. Even a limited search of the **1882 outer clothing for weapons constitutes a severe, though brief, intrusion upon cherished personal security, and it must surely be an annoying, frightening, and perhaps humiliating experience. Petitioner contends that such an intrusion is permissible only incident to a lawful arrest, either for a crime involving the possession of weapons or for a crime the commission of which led the officer to investigate in the first place. However, this argument must be closely examined.

Petitioner does not argue that a police officer should refrain from making any investigation of suspicious circumstances until such time as he has probable cause to make an arrest; nor does he deny that police officers in properly discharging their investigative function may find themselves confronting persons who might well be armed and dangerous. Moreover, he does not say that an officer is always unjustified in searching a suspect to discover weapons. Rather, he says it is unreasonable for the policeman to take that step until such time as the situation evolves to a point where there is probable cause to make an arrest. When that point has been reached, petitioner would concede the officer's right to conduct a search of the suspect for weapons, fruits or instrumentalities of the crime, or 'mere' evidence, incident to the arrest.

There are two weaknesses in this line of reasoning however. First, it fails to take account of traditional limitations upon the scope of searches, and thus recognizes no distinction in purpose, character, and extent between a search incident to an arrest and a limited search for weapons. The former, although justified in part by the acknowledged necessity to protect the arresting officer from assault with a concealed weapon, Preston v. United States, 376 U.S. 364, 367, 84 S.Ct. 881, 883, 11 L.Ed.2d 777 (1964), is also justified on other grounds, ibid., and can therefore involve a relatively extensive exploration of the person. A search for weapons in the absence of probable cause to arrest, however, must, like any other search, be strictly circumscribed by the exigencies which justify its initiation. Warden v. Hayden, 387 U.S. 294, 310, 87 S.Ct. 1642, 1652, 18 L.Ed.2d 782 (1967) (Mr. Justice Fortas, concurring). Thus it must be limited to that which is necessary for the discovery of weapons which might be used to harm the officer or others nearby, and may realistically be characterized as something less than a 'full' search, even though it remains a serious intrusion.

A second, and related, objection to petitioner's argument is that it assumes that the law of arrest has already worked out the balance between the particular interests involved here—the neutralization of danger to the policeman in the investigative circumstance and the sanctity of the individual. But this is not so. An arrest is a wholly different kind of intrusion upon individual freedom from a limited search for weapons, and the interests each is designed to serve are likewise quite different. An arrest is the initial stage of a criminal prosecution. It is intended to vindicate society's interest in having its laws obeyed, and it is inevitably accompanied by future interference with the individual's freedom of movement, whether or not trial or conviction ultimately follows. The protective search for weapons, on the other hand, constitutes a brief, though far from inconsiderable, intrusion upon the sanctity of the person. It does not follow that because an officer may lawfully arrest a person only when he is apprised of facts sufficient to warrant a belief that the person has committed or is committing a crime, the officer is equally unjustified, absent that kind of evidence, in making any intrusions short of an arrest. Moreover, a perfectly reasonable apprehension of danger may arise long before the officer is possessed of **1883 adequate information to justify taking a person into custody for the purpose of prosecuting him for a crime. Petitioner's reliance on cases which have worked out standards of reasonableness with regard to 'seizures' constituting arrests and searches incident thereto is thus misplaced. It assumes that the interests sought to be vindicated and the invasions of personal security may be equated in the two cases, and thereby ignores a vital aspect of the analysis of the reasonableness of particular types of conduct under the Fourth Amendment. See Camara v. Municipal Court, supra.

Our evaluation of the proper balance that has to be struck in this type of case leads us to conclude that there must be a narrowly drawn authority to permit a reasonable search for weapons for the protection of the police officer, where he has reason to believe that he is dealing with an armed and dangerous individual, regardless of whether he has probable cause to arrest the individual for a crime. The officer need not be absolutely certain that the individual is armed; the issue is whether a reasonably prudent man in the circumstances would be warranted in the belief that his safety or that of others was in danger. Cf. Beck v. State of Ohio, 379 U.S. 89, 91, 85 S.Ct. 223, 226, 13 L.Ed.2d 142 (1964); Brinegar v. United States, 338 U.S. 160, 174—176, 69 S.Ct. 1302, 1311, 93 L.Ed. 1879 (1949); Stacey v. Emery, 97 U.S. 642, 645, 24 L.Ed. 1035 (1878).23 And in determining whether the officer acted reasonably in such circumstances, due weight must be given, not to his inchoate and unparticularized suspicion or 'hunch,' but to the specific reasonable inferences which he is entitled to draw from the facts in light of his experience. Cf. Brinegar v. United States, supra.

IV.

We must now examine the conduct of Officer McFadden in this case to determine whether his search and seizure of petitioner were reasonable, both at their inception and as conducted. He had observed Terry, together with Chilton and another man, acting in a manner he took to be preface to a 'stick-up.' We think on the facts and circumstances Officer McFadden detailed before the trial judge a reasonably prudent man would have been warranted in believing petitioner was armed and thus presented a threat to the officer's safety while he was investigating his suspicious behavior. The actions of Terry and Chilton were consistent with McFadden's hypothesis that these men were contemplating a daylight robbery—which, it is reasonable to assume, would be likely to involve the use of weapons—and nothing in their conduct from the time he first noticed them until the time he confronted them and identified himself as a police officer gave him sufficient reason to negate that hypothesis. Although the trio had departed the original scene, there was nothing to indicate abandonment of an intent to commit a robbery at some point. Thus, when Officer McFadden approached the three men gathered before the display window at Zucker's store he had observed enough to make it quite reasonable to fear that they were armed; and nothing in their response to his hailing them, identifying himself as a police officer, and asking their names served to dispel that reasonable belief. We cannot say his decision at that point to seize Terry and pat his clothing for weapons was the product of a volatile or inventive imagination, or was undertaken simply as an act of harassment; the record evidences the tempered act of a policeman who in the course of an investigation had to make a quick decision as to how to protect himself and others from possible danger, and took limited steps to do so.

The manner in which the seizure and search were conducted is, of course, as vital a part of the inquiry as whether they were warranted at all. The Fourth Amendment proceeds as much by limitations upon the scope of governmental ****1884** action as by imposing preconditions upon its initiation. Compare Katz v. United States, 389 U.S. 347, 354—356, 88 S.Ct. 507, 514, 19 L.Ed.2d 576 (1967). The entire deterrent purpose of the rule excluding evidence seized in violation of the Fourth Amendment rests on the assumption that 'limitations upon the fruit to be gathered tend to limit the quest itself.' United States v. Poller, 43 F.2d 911, 914, 74 A.L.R. 1382 (C.A.2d Cir. 1930); see, e.g., Linkletter v. Walker, 381 U.S. 618, 629—635, 85 S.Ct. 1731, 1741, 14 L.Ed.2d 601 (1965); Mapp v. Ohio, 367 U.S. 643, 81 S.Ct. 1684, 6 L.Ed.2d 1081 (1961); Elkins v. United States, 364 U.S. 206, 216—221, 80 S.Ct. 1437, 1446, 4 L.Ed.2d 1669 (1960). Thus, evidence may not be introduced if it was discovered by means of a seizure and search which were not reasonably related in scope to the justification for their initiation Warden v. Hayden, 387 U.S. 294, 310, 87 S.Ct. 1642, 1652, 18 L.Ed.2d 782 (1967) (Mr. Justice Fortas, concurring).

We need not develop at length in this case, however, the limitations which the Fourth Amendment places upon a protective seizure and search for weapons. These limitations will have to be developed in the concrete factual circumstances of individual cases. See Sibron v. New York, 392 U.S. 40, 88 S.Ct. 1889, 1912, 20 L.Ed.2d 917 decided today. Suffice it to note that such a search, unlike a search without a warrant incident to a lawful arrest, is not justified by any need to prevent the disappearance or destruction of evidence of crime. See Preston v. United States, 376 U.S. 364, 367, 84 S.Ct. 1642, 1652, 18 L.Ed.2d 782 (1964). The sole justification of the search in the present situation is the protection of the police officer and others nearby, and it must therefore be confined in scope to an intrusion reasonably designed to discover guns, knives, clubs, or other hidden instruments for the assault of the police officer.

The scope of the search in this case presents no serious problem in light of these standards. Officer McFadden patted down the outer clothing of petitioner and his two companions. He did not place his hands in their pockets or under the outer surface of their garments until he had felt weapons, and then he merely reached for and removed the guns. He never did invade Katz' person beyond the outer surfaces of his clothes, since he discovered nothing in his pat down which might have been a weapon. Officer McFadden confined his search strictly to what was minimally necessary to learn whether the men were armed and to disarm them once he discovered the weapons. He did not conduct a general exploratory search for whatever evidence of criminal activity he might find.

V.

We conclude that the revolver seized from Terry was properly admitted in evidence against him. At the time he seized petitioner and searched him for weapons, Officer McFadden had reasonable grounds to believe that petitioner was armed and dangerous, and it was necessary for the protection of himself and others to take swift measures to discover the true facts and neutralize the threat of harm if it materialized. The policeman carefully restricted his search to what was appropriate to the discovery of the particular items which he sought. Each case of this sort will, of course, have to be decided on its own facts. We merely hold today that where a police officer observes unusual conduct which leads him reasonably to conclude in light of his experience that criminal activity may be afoot and that the persons with whom he is dealing may be armed and presently dangerous, where in the course of investigating this behavior he identifies himself as a policeman and makes reasonable inquiries, and where nothing in the initial stages of the encounter serves to dispel his reasonable fear for his own or others' safety, he is entitled for the protection of himself and ****1885** others in the area to conduct a carefully limited search of the outer clothing of such persons in an attempt to discover weapons which might be used to assault him. Such a search is a reasonable search under the Fourth Amendment, and any weapons seized may properly be introduced in evidence against the person from whom they were taken.

Affirmed.

Mr. Justice HARLAN, concurring.

While I unreservedly agree with the Court's ultimate holding in this case, I am constrained to fill in a few gaps, as I see them, in its opinion. I do this because what is said by this Court today will serve as initial guidelines for law enforcement authorities and courts throughout the land as this important new field of law develops.

A police officer's right to make an on-the-street 'stop' and an accompanying 'frisk' for weapons is of course bounded by the protections afforded by the Fourth and Fourteenth Amendments. The Court holds, and I agree, that while the right does not depend upon possession by the officer of a valid warrant, nor upon the existence of probable cause, such activities must be reasonable under the circumstances as the officer credibly relates them in court. Since the question in this and most cases is whether evidence produced by a frisk is admissible, the problem is to determine what makes a frisk reasonable.

If the State of Ohio were to provide that police officers could, on articulable suspicion less than probable cause, forcibly frisk and disarm persons thought to be carrying concealed weapons, I would have little doubt that action taken pursuant to such authority could be constitutionally reasonable. Concealed weapons create an immediate and severe danger to the public, and though that danger might not warrant routine general weapons checks, it could well warrant action on less than a 'probability.' I mention this line of analysis because I think it vital to point out that it cannot be applied in this case. On the record before us Ohio has not clothed its policemen with routine authority to frisk and disarm on suspicion; in the absence of state authority, policemen have no more right to 'pat down' the outer clothing of passers-by, or of persons to whom they address casual questions, than does any other citizen. Consequently, the Ohio courts did not rest the constitutionality of this frisk upon any general authority in Officer McFadden to take reasonable steps to protect the citizenry, including himself, from dangerous weapons.

The state courts held, instead, that when an officer is lawfully confronting a possibly hostile person in the line of duty he has a right, springing only from the necessity of the situation and not from any broader right to disarm, to frisk for his own protection. This holding, with which I agree and with which I think the Court agrees, offers the only satisfactory basis I can think of for affirming this conviction. The holding has, however, two logical corollaries that I do not think the Court has fully expressed.

In the first place, if the frisk is justified in order to protect the officer during an encounter with a citizen, the officer must first have constitutional grounds to insist on an encounter, to make a forcible stop. Any person, including a policeman, is at liberty to avoid a person he considers dangerous. If and when a policeman has a right instead to disarm such a person for his own protection, he must first have a right not to avoid him but to be in his presence. That right must be more than the liberty (again, possessed by every citizen) to address questions to other persons, for ordinarily the person addressed has an ****1886** equal right to ignore his interrogator and walk away; he certainly need not submit to a frisk for the questioner's protection. I would make it perfectly clear that the right to frisk in this case depends upon the reasonableness of a forcible stop to investigate a suspected crime.

Where such a stop is reasonable, however, the right to frisk must be immediate and automatic if the reason for the stop is, as here, an articulable suspicion of a crime of violence. Just as a full search incident to a lawful arrest requires no additional justification, a limited frisk incident to a lawful stop must often be rapid and routine. There is no reason why an officer, rightfully but forcibly confronting a person suspected of a serious crime, should have to ask one question and take the risk that the answer might be a bullet.

The facts of this case are illustrative of a proper stop and an incident frisk. Officer McFadden had no probable cause to arrest Terry for anything, but he had observed circumstances that would reasonably lead an experienced, prudent policeman to suspect that Terry was about to engage in burglary or robbery. His justifiable suspicion afforded a proper constitutional basis for accosting Terry, restraining his liberty of movement briefly, and addressing questions to him, and Officer McFadden did so. When he did, he had no reason whatever to suppose that Terry might be armed, apart from the fact that he suspected him of planning a violent crime. McFadden asked Terry his name, to which Terry 'mumbled something.' Whereupon McFadden, without asking Terry to speak louder and without giving him any chance to explain his presence or his actions, forcibly frisked him.

I would affirm this conviction for what I believe to be the same reasons the Court relies on. I would, however, make explicit what I think is implicit in affirmance on the present facts. Officer McFadden's right to interrupt Terry's freedom of movement and invade his privacy arose only because circumstances warranted forcing an encounter with Terry in an effort to prevent or investigate a crime. Once that forced encounter was justified, however, the officer's right to take suitable measures for his own safety followed automatically.

Upon the foregoing premises, I join the opinion of the Court.

*****

Mr. Justice DOUGLAS, dissenting.

I agree that petitioner was 'seized' within the meaning of the Fourth Amendment. I also agree that frisking petitioner and his companions for guns was a 'search.' But it is a mystery how that 'search' and that 'seizure' can be constitutional by Fourth Amendment standards, unless there was 'probable cause' to believe that (1) a crime had been committed or (2) a crime was in the process of being committed or (3) a crime was about to be committed.

The opinion of the Court disclaims the existence of 'probable cause.' If loitering were in issue and that was the offense charged, there would be 'probable cause' shown. But the crime here is carrying concealed weapons; and there is no basis for concluding that the officer had 'probable cause' for believing that that crime was being committed. Had a warrant been sought, a magistrate would, therefore, have been unauthorized to issue one, for he can act only if there is a showing of 'probable cause.' We hold today that the police have greater authority to make a 'seizure' and conduct a 'search' than a judge has to authorize such action. We have said precisely the opposite over and over again.

In other words, police officers up to today have been permitted to effect arrests **1888** or searches without warrants only when the facts within their personal knowledge would satisfy the constitutional standard of probable cause. At the time of their 'seizure' without a warrant they must possess facts concerning the person arrested that would have satisfied a magistrate that 'probable cause' was indeed present. The term 'probable cause' rings a bell of certainty that is not sounded by phrases such as 'reasonable suspicion.' Moreover, the meaning of 'probable cause' is deeply imbedded in our constitutional history. As we stated in Henry v. United States, 361 U.S. 98, 100—102, 80 S.Ct. 168, 170:

'The requirement of probable cause has roots that are deep in our history. The general warrant, in which the name of the person to be arrested was left blank, and the writs of assistance, against which James Otis inveighed, both perpetuated the oppressive practice of allowing the police to arrest and search on suspicion. Police control took the place of judicial control, since no showing of 'probable cause' before a magistrate was required.

'That philosophy (rebelling against these practices) later was reflected in the Fourth Amendment. And as the early American decisions both before and immediately after its adoption show, common rumor or report, suspicion, or even 'strong reason to suspect' was not adequate to support a warrant for arrest. And that principle has survived to this day. * * *

'* * * It is important, we think, that this requirement (of probable cause) be strictly enforced, for the standard set by the Constitution protects both the officer and the citizen. If the officer acts with probable cause, he is protected even though it turns out that the citizen is innocent. * * * And while a search without a warrant is, within limits, permissible if incident to a lawful arrest, if an arrest without a warrant is to support an incidental search, it must be made with probable cause. * * * This immunity of officers cannot fairly be enlarged without jeopardizing the privacy or security of the citizen.'

The infringement on personal liberty of any 'seizure' of a person can only be 'reasonable' under the Fourth Amendment if we require the police to possess 'probable cause' before they seize him. Only that line draws a meaningful distinction between an officer's mere inkling and the presence of facts within the officer's personal knowledge which would convince a reasonable man that the person seized has committed, is committing, or is about to commit a particular crime. 'In dealing with probable cause, * * * as the very name implies, we deal with probabilities. These are not technical; they are the factual and practical considerations of everyday life on which reasonable and prudent men, not legal technicians, act.' Brinegar v. United States, 338 U.S. 160, 175, 69 S.Ct. 1302, 1310.

To give the police greater power than a magistrate is to take a long step down the totalitarian path. Perhaps such a step is desirable to cope with modern forms of lawlessness. But if it is taken, it should be the deliberate choice of the people through a constitutional amendment. Until the Fourth Amendment, **1889 which is closely allied with the Fifth, is rewritten, the person and the effects of the individual are beyond the reach of all government agencies until there are reasonable grounds to believe (probable cause) that a criminal venture has been launched or is about to be launched.

There have been powerful hydraulic pressures throughout our history that bear heavily on the Court to water down constitutional guarantees and give the police the upper hand. That hydraulic pressure has probably never been greater than it is today.

Yet if the individual is no longer to be sovereign, if the police can pick him up whenever they do not like the cut of his jib, if they can 'seize' and 'search' him in their discretion, we enter a new regime. The decision to enter it should be made only after a full debate by the people of this country.

Black Letter Law

> Court held that a police officer did not exceed the reasonable scope of a search when they patted down the outer clothing of the defendants without placing hands in the pockets or under the outer surface garments until such time as he felt weapons, and then only secured and removed the guns discovered. The actions of the officer were reasonable in that the officer first saw the defendant and another individual act in a way that was consistent with someone planning a daylight robbery. After observing this the office approached, identified himself as a cop, and ask their names before patting them down. To justify a particular intrusion, the officer must be able to point to specific and articulable facts which, taken together with rational inferences from those facts, reasonably warrant that intrusion; facts must be judged against objective standard of whether facts available to officer at moment of seizure or search would warrant man of reasonable caution in belief that action taken was appropriate.

Dunaway v. New York

99 S.Ct. 2248

Supreme Court of the United States

Irving Jerome DUNAWAY, Petitioner,

v.

State of NEW YORK.

Mr. Justice BRENNAN delivered the opinion of the Court.

We decide in this case the question reserved 10 years ago in Morales v. New York, 396 U.S. 102, 90 S.Ct. 291, 24 L.Ed.2d 299 (1969), namely, "the question of the legality of custodial questioning on less than probable cause for a full-fledged arrest." Id., at 106, 90 S.Ct., at 293.

I

On March 26, 1971, the proprietor of a pizza parlor in Rochester, N.Y., was killed during an attempted robbery. On August 10, 1971, Detective Anthony Fantigrossi of the Rochester Police was told by another officer that an informant had supplied a possible lead implicating petitioner in the crime. Fantigrossi questioned the supposed source of the lead—a jail inmate awaiting trial for burglary—but learned nothing that supplied "enough information to get a warrant" for petitioner's arrest. App. 60. Nevertheless, Fantigrossi ordered other detectives to "pick up" petitioner and "bring him in." Id., at 54. Three detectives located ****2252** petitioner at a neighbor's house on the morning of August 11. Petitioner was taken into custody; although he was not told he was under arrest, he would have been physically restrained if he had attempted to leave. Opinion in People v. Dunaway (Monroe County Ct., Mar. 11, 1977), App. 116, 117. He was driven to police headquarters in a police car and placed in an interrogation room, where he was questioned by officers after being given the warnings required by Miranda v. Arizona, 384 U.S. 436, 86 S.Ct. 1602, 16 L.Ed.2d 694 (1966). Petitioner waived counsel and eventually made statements and drew sketches that incriminated him in the crime.

At petitioner's jury trial for attempted robbery and felony murder, his motions to suppress the statements and sketches were denied, and he was convicted. On appeal, both the Appellate Division of the Fourth Department and the New York Court of Appeals initially affirmed the conviction without opinion. 42 A.D.2d 689, 346 N.Y.S. 2d 779 (1973), aff'd 35 N.Y.2d 741, 361 N.Y.S.2d 912, 320 N.E.2d 646 (1974). However, this Court granted certiorari, vacated the judgment, and remanded the case for further consideration in light of the Court's supervening decision in Brown v. Illinois, 422 U.S. 590, 95 S.Ct. 2254, 45 L.Ed.2d 416 (1975). 422 U.S. 1053, 95 S.Ct. 2674, 45 L.Ed.2d 705 (1975). The petitioner in Brown, like petitioner Dunaway, made inculpatory statements after receiving Miranda warnings during custodial interrogation following his seizure—in that case a formal arrest—on less than probable cause. Brown's motion to suppress the statements was also denied and the statements were used to convict him. Although the Illinois Supreme Court recognized that Brown's arrest was unlawful, it affirmed the admission of the statements on the ground that the giving of Miranda warnings served to break the causal connection between the illegal arrest and the giving of the statements. This Court reversed, holding that the Illinois courts erred in adopting a per se rule that Miranda warnings in and of themselves sufficed to cure the Fourth Amendment violation; rather the Court held that in order to use such statements, the prosecution must show not only that the statements meet the Fifth Amendment voluntariness standard, but also that the causal connection between the statements and the illegal arrest is broken sufficiently to purge the primary taint of the illegal arrest in light of the distinct policies and interests of the Fourth Amendment.

In compliance with the remand, the New York Court of Appeals directed the Monroe County Court to make further factual findings as to whether there was a detention of petitioner, whether the police had probable cause, "and, in the event there was a detention and probable cause is not found for such detention, to determine the further question as to whether the making of the confessions was rendered infirm by the illegal arrest (see Brown v. Illinois, 422 U.S. 590, 95 S.Ct. 2254, 45 L.Ed.2d 416, supra)." People v. Dunaway, 38 N.Y.2d 812, 813–814, 382 N.Y.S.2d 40, 41, 345 N.E.2d 583, 584 (1975).

The County Court determined after a supplementary suppression hearing that Dunaway's motion to suppress should have been granted. Although reaffirming that there had been "full compliance with the mandate of Miranda v. Arizona," the County Court found that "this case does not involve a situation where the defendant voluntarily appeared at police headquarters in response to a request of the police . . . ."

App. 117. The State's attempt to justify petitioner's involuntary investigatory detention on the authority of People v. Morales, 22 N.Y.2d 55, 290 N.Y.S.2d 898, 238 N.E.2d 307 (1968)—which upheld a similar detention on the basis of information amounting to less than probable cause for arrest—was rejected on the grounds that ****2253** the precedential value of Morales was questionable, and that the controlling authority was the "strong language" in Brown v. Illinois indicating "disdain for custodial questioning without probable cause to arrest."4 The County Court further held that "the factual predicate in this case did not amount to probable cause sufficient to support the arrest of the defendant," that "the Miranda warnings by themselves did not purge the taint of the defendant's illegal seizure[,] Brown v. Illinois, supra, and [that] there was no claim or showing by the People of any attenuation of the defendant's illegal detention," App. 121. Accordingly petitioner's motion to suppress was granted. Ibid.

A divided Appellate Division reversed. Although agreeing that the police lacked probable cause to arrest petitioner, the majority relied on the Court of Appeals' reaffirmation, subsequent to the County Court's decision, that " '[l]aw enforcement officials may detain an individual upon reasonable suspicion for questioning for a reasonable and brief period of time under carefully controlled conditions which are ample to protect the individual's Fifth and Sixth Amendment rights'." 61 A.D.2d 299, 302, 402 N.Y.S.2d 490, 492 (1978), quoting People v. Morales, 42 N.Y.2d 129, 135, 397 N.Y.S.2d 587, 590, 366 N.E.2d 248, 251 (1977). The Appellate Division also held that even if petitioner's detention were illegal, the taint of his illegal detention was sufficiently attenuated to allow the admission of his statements and sketches. The Appellate Division emphasized that petitioner was never threatened or abused by the police and purported to distinguish Brown v. Illinois. The Court of Appeals dismissed petitioner's application for leave to appeal. App. 134.

We granted certiorari, 439 U.S. 979, 99 S.Ct. 563, 58 L.Ed.2d 649 (1978), to clarify the Fourth Amendment's requirements as to the permissible grounds for custodial interrogation and to review the New York court's application of Brown v. Illinois. We reverse.

II

We first consider whether the Rochester police violated the Fourth and Fourteenth Amendments when, without probable cause to arrest, they took petitioner into custody, transported him to the police station, and detained him there for interrogation.

The Fourth Amendment, applicable to the States through the Fourteenth Amendment, Mapp v. Ohio, 367 U.S. 643, 81 S.Ct. 1684, 6 L.Ed.2d 1081 (1961), provides: "The right of the people to be secure in their persons . . . against unreasonable searches and seizures, shall not be violated, and no Warrants shall issue but upon probable cause . . . ." There can be little doubt that petitioner was "seized" in the Fourth Amendment sense when he was taken involuntarily to the police station. ****2254** And respondent State concedes that the police lacked probable cause to arrest petitioner before his incriminating statement during interrogation. Nevertheless respondent contends that the seizure of petitioner did not amount to an arrest and was therefore permissible under the Fourth Amendment because the police had a "reasonable suspicion" that petitioner possessed "intimate knowledge about a serious and unsolved crime." Brief for Respondent 10. We disagree.

Before Terry v. Ohio, 392 U.S. 1, 88 S.Ct. 1868, 20 L.Ed.2d 889 (1968), the Fourth Amendment's guarantee against unreasonable seizures of persons was analyzed in terms of arrest, probable cause for arrest, and warrants based on such probable cause. The basic principles were relatively simple and straightforward: The term "arrest" was synonymous with those seizures governed by the Fourth Amendment. While warrants were not required in all circumstances, the requirement of probable cause, as elaborated in numerous precedents, was treated as absolute. The "long-prevailing standards" of probable cause embodied "the best compromise that has been found for accommodating [the] often opposing interests" in "safeguard[ing] citizens from rash and unreasonable interferences with privacy" and in "seek [ing] to give fair leeway for enforcing the law in the community's protection." Brinegar v. United States, 338 U.S. 160, 176, 69 S.Ct. 1302, 1311, 93 L.Ed. 1879 (1949). The standard of probable cause thus represented the accumulated wisdom of precedent and experience as to the minimum justification necessary to make the kind of intrusion involved in an arrest "reasonable" under the Fourth Amendment. The standard applied to all arrests, without the need to "balance" the interests and circumstances involved in particular situations. Cf. Camara v. Municipal Court, 387 U.S. 523, 87 S.Ct. 1727, 18 L.Ed.2d 930 (1967).

Terry for the first time recognized an exception to the requirement that Fourth Amendment seizures of persons must be based on probable cause. That case involved a brief, on-the-spot stop on the street and a frisk for weapons, a situation that did not fit comfortably within the traditional concept of an "arrest." Nevertheless, the Court held that even this type of "necessarily swift action predicated upon the on-the-spot observations of the officer on the beat" constituted a "serious intrusion ****2255** upon the sanctity of the person, which may inflict great indignity and arouse strong resentment," 392 U.S., at 20, 17, 88 S.Ct., at 1879, 1877, and therefore "must be tested by the Fourth Amendment's general proscription against unreasonable searches and seizures." Id., at 20, 88 S.Ct., at 1879. However, since the intrusion involved in a "stop and frisk" was so much less severe than that involved in traditional "arrests," the Court declined to stretch the concept of "arrest"—and the general rule requiring probable cause to make arrests "reasonable" under the Fourth Amendment—to cover such intrusions. Instead, the Court treated the stop-and-frisk intrusion as a sui generis "rubric of police conduct," ibid. And to determine the justification necessary to make this specially limited intrusion "reasonable" under the Fourth Amendment, the Court balanced the limited violation of individual privacy involved against the opposing interests in crime prevention and detection and in the police officer's safety. Id., at 22–27, 88 S.Ct., at 1880–1883. As a consequence, the Court established "a narrowly drawn authority to permit a reasonable search for weapons for the protection of the police officer, where he has reason to believe that he is dealing with an armed and dangerous individual, regardless of whether he has probable cause to arrest the individual for a crime." Id., at 27, 88 S.Ct., at 1883.11 Thus, Terry departed from traditional Fourth Amendment analysis in two respects. First, it defined a special category of Fourth Amendment "seizures" so substantially less intrusive than arrests that the general rule requiring probable cause to make Fourth Amendment "seizures" reasonable could be replaced by a balancing test. Second, the application of this balancing test led the Court to approve this narrowly defined less intrusive seizure on grounds less rigorous than probable cause, but only for the purpose of a pat-down for weapons.

Because Terry involved an exception to the general rule requiring probable cause, this Court has been careful to maintain its narrow scope. Terry itself involved a limited, on-the-street frisk for weapons. Two subsequent cases which applied Terry also involved limited weapons frisks. See Adams v. Williams, 407 U.S. 143, 92 S.Ct. 1921, 32 L.Ed.2d 612 (1972) (frisk for weapons on basis of reasonable suspicion); Pennsylvania v. Mimms, 434 U.S. 106, 98 S.Ct. 330, 54 L.Ed.2d 331 (1977) (order to get out of car is permissible "de minimis" intrusion after car is lawfully detained for traffic violations; frisk for weapons justified after "bulge" observed in jacket). United States v. Brignoni-Ponce, 422 U.S. 873, 95 S.Ct. 2574, 45 L.Ed.2d 607 (1975), applied Terry in the special context of roving border patrols stopping automobiles to check for illegal immigrants. The investigative stops usually consumed ***211** less than a minute and involved "a brief question or two." 422 U.S., at 880, 95 S.Ct., at 2579. The Court stated that "[b]ecause of the limited nature of the ****2256** intrusion, stops of this sort may be justified on facts that do not amount to the probable cause required for an arrest." Ibid.13 See alsoUnited States v. Martinez-Fuerte, 428 U.S. 543, 96 S.Ct. 3074, 49 L.Ed.2d 1116 (1976) (fixed checkpoint to stop and check vehicles for aliens); Delaware v. Prouse, 440 U.S. 648, 99 S.Ct. 1391, 59

L.Ed.2d 660 (1979) (random checks for drivers' licenses and proper vehicle registration not permitted on less than articulable reasonable suspicion).

Respondent State now urges the Court to apply a balancing test, rather than the general rule, to custodial interrogations, and to hold that "seizures" such as that in this case may be justified by mere "reasonable suspicion." Terry and its progeny clearly do not support such a result. The narrow intrusions involved in those cases were judged by a balancing test rather than by the general principle that Fourth Amendment seizures must be supported by the "long-prevailing standards" of probable cause, Brinegar v. United States, 338 U.S., at 176, 69 S.Ct., at 1311, only because these intrusions fell far short of the kind of intrusion associated with an arrest. Indeed, Brignoni-Ponce expressly refused to extend Terry in the manner respondent now urges. The Court there stated: "The officer may question the driver and passengers about their citizenship and immigration status, and he may ask them to explain suspicious circumstances, but any further detention or search must be based on consent or probable cause." 422 U.S., at 881–882, 95 S.Ct., at 2580. (emphasis added). Accord, United States v. Martinez-Fuerte, supra, 428 U.S., at 567, 96 S.Ct., at 3087.

In contrast to the brief and narrowly circumscribed intrusions involved in those cases, the detention of petitioner was in important respects indistinguishable from a traditional arrest. Petitioner was not questioned briefly where he was found. Instead, he was taken from a neighbor's home to a police car, transported to a police station, and placed in an interrogation room. He was never informed that he was "free to go"; indeed, he would have been physically restrained if he had refused to accompany the officers or had tried to escape their custody. The application of the Fourth Amendment's requirement of probable cause does not depend on whether an intrusion of this magnitude is termed an "arrest" under state law. The mere facts that petitioner was not told he was under arrest, was not "booked," and would not have had an arrest record if the interrogation had proved fruitless, while not insignificant for all purposes, see ****2257** Cupp v. Murphy, 412 U.S. 291, 93 S.Ct. 2000, 36 L.Ed.2d 900 (1973), obviously do not make petitioner's seizure even roughly analogous to the narrowly defined intrusions involved in Terry and its progeny. Indeed, any "exception" that could cover a seizure as intrusive as that in this case would threaten to swallow the general rule that Fourth Amendment seizures are "reasonable" only if based on probable cause.

The central importance of the probable-cause requirement to the protection of a citizen's privacy afforded by the Fourth Amendment's guarantees cannot be compromised in this fashion. "The requirement of probable cause has roots that are deep in our history." Henry v. United States, 361 U.S. 98, 100, 80 S.Ct. 168, 170, 4 L.Ed.2d 134 (1959). Hostility to seizures based on mere suspicion was a prime motivation for the adoption of the Fourth Amendment, and decisions immediately after its adoption affirmed that "common rumor or report, suspicion, or even 'strong reason to suspect' was not adequate to support a warrant for arrest." Id., at 101, 80 S.Ct., at 170 (footnotes omitted). The familiar threshold standard of probable cause for Fourth Amendment seizures reflects the benefit of extensive experience accommodating the factors relevant to the "reasonableness" requirement of the Fourth Amendment, and provides the relative simplicity and clarity necessary to the implementation of a workable rule. See Brinegar v. United States, supra, 338 U.S., at 175–176, 69 S.Ct., at 1310–1311.

In effect, respondent urges us to adopt a multifactor balancing test of "reasonable police conduct under the circumstances" to cover all seizures that do not amount to technical arrests. But the protections intended by the Framers could all too easily disappear in the consideration and balancing of the multifarious circumstances presented by different cases, especially when that balancing may be done in the first instance by police officers engaged in the "often competitive enterprise of ferreting out crime." Johnson v. United States, 333 U.S. 10, 14, 68 S.Ct. 367, 369, 92 L.Ed. 436 (1948). A single, familiar standard is essential to guide police officers, who have only limited time and expertise to reflect on and balance the social and individual interests involved in the specific circumstances they confront. Indeed, our recognition of these dangers, and our consequent reluctance to depart from the proved protections afforded by the general rule, are reflected in the narrow limitations emphasized in the cases employing the balancing test. For all but those narrowly defined intrusions, the requisite "balancing" has been performed in centuries of precedent and is embodied in the principle that seizures are "reasonable" only if supported by probable cause.

Moreover, two important decisions since Terry confirm the conclusion that the treatment of petitioner, whether or not it is technically characterized as an arrest, must be supported by probable cause. Davis v. Mississippi, 394 U.S. 721, 89 S.Ct. 1394, 22 L.Ed.2d 679 (1969), decided the Term after Terry, considered whether fingerprints taken from a suspect detained without probable cause must be excluded from evidence. The State argued that the detention "was of a type which does not require probable cause," 394 U.S., at 726, 89 S.Ct., at 1397, because it occurred during an investigative, rather than accusatory, stage, and because it was for the sole purpose of taking fingerprints. Rejecting the State's first argument, the Court warned:

"[T]o argue that the Fourth Amendment does not apply to the investigatory stage is fundamentally to misconceive the purposes of the Fourth Amendment. Investigatory seizures would subject unlimited ****2258** numbers of innocent persons to the harassment and ignominy incident to involuntary detention. Nothing is more clear than that the Fourth Amendment was meant to prevent wholesale intrusions upon the personal security of our citizenry, whether these intrusions be termed 'arrests' or 'investigatory detentions.' " Id., at 726–727, 89 S.Ct., at 1397.

The State's second argument in Davis was more substantial, largely because of the distinctions between taking fingerprints and interrogation:

"Fingerprinting involves none of the probing into an individual's private life and thoughts that marks an interrogation or search. Nor can fingerprint detention be employed repeatedly to harass any individual, since the police need only one set of each person's prints. Furthermore, fingerprinting is an inherently more reliable and effective crime-solving tool than eye witness identifications or confessions and is not subject to such abuses as the improper line-up and the 'third degree.' Finally, because there is no danger of destruction of fingerprints, the limited detention need not come unexpectedly or at an inconvenient time." Id., at 727, 89 S.Ct., at 1398.

In Davis, however, the Court found it unnecessary to decide the validity of a "narrowly circumscribed procedure for obtaining" the fingerprints of suspects without probable cause—in part because, as the Court emphasized, "petitioner was not merely fingerprinted during the . . . detention but also subjected to interrogation." Id., at 728, 89 S.Ct., at 1398 (emphasis added). The detention therefore violated the Fourth Amendment.

Brown v. Illinois, 422 U.S. 590, 95 S.Ct. 2254, 45 L.Ed.2d 416 (1975), similarly disapproved arrests made for "investigatory" purposes on less than probable cause. Although Brown's arrest had more of the trappings of a technical formal arrest than petitioner's, such differences in form must not be exalted over substance. Once in the police station, Brown was taken to an interrogation room, and his experience was indistinguishable from petitioner's. Our condemnation of the police conduct in Brown fits equally the police conduct in this case:

"The impropriety of the arrest was obvious; awareness of the fact was virtually conceded by the two detectives when they repeatedly acknowledged, in their testimony, that the purpose of their action was 'for investigation' or for 'questioning.' . . . The arrest, both in design and in execution, was investigatory. The detectives embarked upon this expedition for evidence in the hope that something might turn up." Id., at 605, 95 S.Ct., at 2262.

See also, id., at 602, 95 S.Ct., at 2261.

These passages from Davis and Brown reflect the conclusion that detention for custodial interrogation—regardless of its label—intrudes so severely on interests protected by the Fourth Amendment as necessarily to trigger the traditional safeguards against illegal arrest. We accordingly hold that the Rochester police violated the Fourth and Fourteenth Amendments when, without probable cause, they seized petitioner and transported him to the police station for interrogation.

III

There remains the question whether the connection between this unconstitutional police conduct and the incriminating statements and sketches obtained during petitioner's illegal detention was nevertheless sufficiently attenuated to permit the use at trial of the statements and sketches. See ****2259** Wong Sun v. United States, 371 U.S. 471, 83 S.Ct. 407, 9 L.Ed.2d 441 (1963); Nardone v. United States, 308 U.S. 338, 60 S.Ct. 266, 84 L.Ed. 307 (1939); Silverthorne Lumber Co. v. United States, 251 U.S. 385, 40 S.Ct. 182, 64 L.Ed. 319 (1920).

The New York courts have consistently held, and petitioner does not contest, that proper Miranda warnings were given and that his statements were "voluntary" for purposes of the Fifth Amendment. But Brown v. Illinois, supra, settled that "[t]he exclusionary rule, . . . when utilized to effectuate the Fourth Amendment, serves interests and policies that are distinct from those it serves under the Fifth," 422 U.S., at 601, 95 S.Ct., at 2260, and held therefore that "Miranda warnings, and the exclusion of a confession made without them, do not alone sufficiently deter a Fourth Amendment violation." Ibid.

"If Miranda warnings, by themselves, were held to attenuate the taint of an unconstitutional arrest, regardless of how wanton and purposeful the Fourth Amendment violation, the effect of the exclusionary rule would be substantially diluted. . . . Arrests made without warrant or without probable cause, for questioning or 'investigation,' would be encouraged by the knowledge that evidence derived therefrom could well be made admissible at trial by the simple expedient of giving Miranda warnings." Id., at 602, 95 S.Ct., at 2261.

Consequently, although a confession after proper Miranda warnings may be found "voluntary" for purposes of the Fifth Amendment, this type of "voluntariness" is merely a "threshold requirement" for Fourth Amendment analysis, 422 U.S., at 604, 95 S.Ct., at 2262. Indeed, if the Fifth Amendment has been violated, the Fourth Amendment issue would not have to be reached.

Beyond this threshold requirement, Brown articulated a test designed to vindicate the "distinct policies and interests of the Fourth Amendment." Id., at 602, 95 S.Ct., at 2261. Following Wong Sun, the Court eschewed any per se or "but for" rule, and identified the relevant inquiry as "whether Brown's statements were obtained by exploitation of the illegality of his arrest," 422 U.S., at 600, 95 S.Ct., at 2260; see Wong Sun v. United States, supra, 371 U.S., at 488, 83 S.Ct., at 417. Brown's focus on "the causal connection between the illegality and the confession," 422 U.S., at 603, 95 S.Ct., at 2261, reflected the two policies behind the use of the exclusionary rule to effectuate the Fourth Amendment. When there is a close causal connection between the illegal seizure and the confession, not only is exclusion of the evidence more likely to deter similar police misconduct in the future, but also use of the evidence is more likely to compromise the integrity of the courts.

Brown identified several factors to be considered "in determining whether the confession is obtained by exploitation of an illegal arrest[:t]he temporal proximity of the arrest and the confession, the presence of intervening circumstances, . . . and, particularly, the purpose and flagrancy of the official misconduct . . . . And the burden of showing admissibility rests, of course, on the prosecution." Id., at 603–604, 95 S.Ct., at 2261–62. Examining the case before it, the Court readily concluded that the State had failed to sustain its burden of showing the confession was admissible. In the "less than two hours" that elapsed between the arrest and the confession "there was no intervening event of significance whatsoever." Ibid. Furthermore, the arrest without probable cause had a "quality of purposefulness" in that it was an "expedition for evidence" admittedly undertaken "in the hope that something might turn up." Id., at 605, 95 S.Ct., at 2262.

****2260** The situation in this case is virtually a replica of the situation in Brown. Petitioner was also admittedly seized without probable cause in the hope that something might turn up, and confessed without any intervening event of significance. Nevertheless, three members of the Appellate Division purported to distinguish Brown on the ground that the police did not threaten or abuse petitioner (presumably putting aside his illegal seizure and detention) and that the police conduct was "highly protective of defendant's Fifth and Sixth Amendment rights." 61 A.D.2d, at 303, 402 N.Y.S.2d, at 493. This betrays a lingering confusion between "voluntariness" for purposes of the Fifth Amendment and the "causal connection" test established in Brown. Satisfying the Fifth Amendment is only the "threshold" condition of the Fourth Amendment analysis required by Brown. No intervening events broke the connection between petitioner's illegal detention and his confession. To admit petitioner's confession in such a case would allow "law enforcement officers to violate the Fourth Amendment with impunity, safe in the knowledge that they could wash their hands in the 'procedural safeguards' of the Fifth."

Reversed.

Mr. Justice WHITE, concurring.

The opinion of the Court might be read to indicate that Terry v. Ohio, 392 U.S. 1, 88 S.Ct. 1868, 20 L.Ed.2d 889 (1968), is an almost unique exception to a hard-and-fast standard of probable cause. As our prior cases hold, however, the key principle of the Fourth Amendment is reasonableness—the balancing of competing interests. E. g., Delaware v. Prouse, 440 U.S. 648, 653–654, 99 S.Ct. 1391, 1396, 59 L.Ed.2d 660 (1979); Michigan v. Tyler, 436 U.S. 499, 506, 98 S.Ct. 1942, 1948, 56 L.Ed.2d 486 (1978); Marshall v. Barlow's, Inc., 436 U.S. 307, 321–322, 98 S.Ct. 1816, 1825, 56 L.Ed.2d 305 (1978); United States v. Martinez-Fuerte, 428 U.S. 543, 555, 96 S.Ct. 3074, 3081, 49 L.Ed.2d 1116 (1976); United States v. Brignoni-Ponce, 422 U.S. 873, 878, 95 S.Ct. 2574, 2578, 45 L.Ed.2d 607 (1975); Terry v. Ohio, supra, 392 U.S., at 20–21, 88 S.Ct., at 1879; Camara v. Municipal Court, 387 U.S. 523, 536–537, 87 S.Ct. 1727, 1734–1735, 18 L.Ed.2d 930 (1967). But if courts and law enforcement officials are to have workable rules, see Rakas v. Illinois, 439 U.S. 128, 168, 99 S.Ct. 421, 443, 58 L.Ed.2d 387 (1978) (dissenting opinion), this balancing must in large part be done on a categorical basis—not in an ad hoc, case-by-case fashion by individual police officers. Cf. Mincey v. Arizona, 437 U.S. 385, 394–395, 98 S.Ct. 2408, 2414–2415, 57 L.Ed.2d 290 (1978). On the other hand, the need for rules of general applicability precludes neither the recognition in particular cases of extraordinary private or public interests, cf. Zurcher v. Stanford Daily, 436 U.S. 547, 564–565, 98 S.Ct. 1970, 1981, 56 L.Ed.2d 525 (1978), nor the generic recognition of certain exceptions to the normal rule of probable cause where more flexibility is essential. Cf., e. g., Terry v. Ohio, supra. It is enough, for me, that the police conduct here is similar enough to an arrest that the normal level of probable cause is necessary before the interests of privacy and personal security must give way.

Mr. Justice STEVENS, concurring.

Although I join the Court's opinion, I add this comment on the significance of two factors that may be considered when determining whether a confession has been obtained by exploitation of an illegal arrest.

The temporal relationship between the arrest and the confession may be an ambiguous ****2261** factor. If there are no relevant intervening circumstances, a prolonged detention may well be a more serious exploitation of an illegal arrest than a short one. Conversely, even an immediate confession may have been motivated by a prearrest event such as a visit with a minister.

The flagrancy of the official misconduct is relevant, in my judgment, only insofar as it has a tendency to motivate the defendant. A midnight arrest with drawn guns will be equally frightening whether the police acted recklessly or in good faith. Conversely, a courteous command has the same effect on the arrestee whether the officer thinks he has probable cause or knows that he does not. In either event, if the Fourth Amendment is violated, the admissibility question will turn on the causal relationship between that violation and the defendant's subsequent confession.

I recognize that the deterrence rationale for the exclusionary rule is sometimes interpreted quite differently. Under that interpretation, exclusion is applied as a substitute for punishment of the offending officer; if he acted recklessly or flagrantly, punishment is appropriate, but if he acted in good faith, it is not. But when evidence is excluded at a criminal trial, it is the broad societal interest in effective law enforcement that suffers. The justification for the exclusion of evidence obtained by improper methods is to motivate the law enforcement profession as a whole—not the aberrant individual officer—to adopt and enforce regular procedures that will avoid the future invasion of the citizen's constitutional rights. For that reason, exclusionary rules should embody objective criteria rather than subjective considerations.

(The dissent of Mr. Justice REHNQUIST, with whom THE CHIEF JUSTICE joins, is omitted.)

Black Letter Law

> When determining whether the actions of the police should be viewed under *Terry*, the Court held that a defendant was "seized" for Fourth Amendment purposes when he was arrested and taken to the police station for questioning; seizure without probable cause violated the Fourth Amendment, and confession given following the seizure and interrogation was inadmissible. Application of Fourth Amendment's requirement of probable cause for seizure of defendant did not depend upon whether the intrusion, which occurred when he was taken involuntarily to the police station, was termed an arrest under state law; his seizure, transportation to a police station, and placement in interrogation room and questioning under conditions in which he was not free to go and would have been physically restrained if he had refused to accompany the officers was not analogous to the narrowly defined intrusions approved in *Terry.*

United States v. Mendenhall

100 S.Ct. 1870

Supreme Court of the United States

UNITED STATES, Petitioner,

v.

Sylvia L. MENDENHALL.

No. 78–1821. | Argued Feb. 19, 1980. | Decided May 27, 1980. | Rehearing Denied June 30, 1980. | See 448 U.S. 908, 100 S.Ct. 3051.

Mr. Justice STEWART announced the judgment of the Court and delivered an opinion, in which Mr. Justice REHNQUIST joined.**

The respondent was brought to trial in the United States District Court for the Eastern District of Michigan on a charge of possessing heroin with intent to distribute it. She moved to suppress the introduction at trial of the heroin as evidence against her on the ground that it had been acquired from her through an unconstitutional search and seizure by agents of the Drug Enforcement Administration (DEA). The District Court denied the respondent's motion, and she was convicted after a trial upon stipulated facts. The Court of Appeals, 596 F.2d 706, reversed, finding the search of the respondent's person to have been unlawful. We granted certiorari to consider whether any right of the respondent guaranteed by the Fourth Amendment was violated in the circumstances presented by this case. 444 U.S. 822, 100 S.Ct. 42, 62 L.Ed.2d 29.

I

At the hearing in the trial court on the respondent's motion to suppress, it was established how the heroin she was charged with possessing had been obtained from her. The respondent arrived at the Detroit Metropolitan Airport on a commercial airline flight from Los Angeles early in the morning on February 10, 1976. As she disembarked from the airplane, she was observed by two agents of the DEA, who were present at the airport for the purpose of detecting unlawful traffic in narcotics. After observing the respondent's conduct, which appeared to the agents to be characteristic of persons unlawfully carrying narcotics, the agents approached her as she was walking through the concourse, identified themselves as federal agents, and asked to see her identification and airline ticket. The respondent produced her driver's ****1874** license, which was in the name of Sylvia Mendenhall, and, in answer to a question of one of the agents, stated that she resided at the address appearing on the license. The airline ticket was issued in the name of "Annette Ford." When asked why the ticket bore a name different from her own, the respondent stated that she "just felt like using that name." In response to a further question, the respondent indicated that she had been in California only two days. Agent Anderson then specifically identified himself as a federal narcotics agent and, according to his testimony, the respondent "became quite shaken, extremely nervous. She had a hard time speaking."

After returning the airline ticket and driver's license to her, Agent Anderson asked the respondent if she would accompany him to the airport DEA office for further questions. She did so, although the record does not indicate a verbal response to the request. The office, which was located up one flight of stairs about 50 feet from where the respondent had first been approached, consisted of a reception area adjoined by three other rooms. At the office the agent asked the respondent if she would allow a search of her person and handbag and told her that she had the right to decline the search if she desired. She responded: "Go ahead." She then handed Agent Anderson her purse, which contained a receipt for an airline ticket that had been issued to "F. Bush" three days earlier for a flight from Pittsburgh through Chicago to Los Angeles. The agent asked whether this was the ticket that she had used for her flight to California, and the respondent stated that it was.

A female police officer then arrived to conduct the search of the respondent's person. She asked the agents if the respondent had consented to be searched. The agents said that she had, and the respondent followed the policewoman into a private room. There the policewoman again asked the respondent if she consented to the search, and the respondent replied that she did. The policewoman explained that the search would require that the respondent remove her clothing. The respondent stated that she had a plane to catch and was assured by the policewoman that if she were carrying no narcotics, there would be no problem. The respondent then began to disrobe without further comment. As the respondent removed her clothing, she took from her undergarments two small packages, one of which appeared to contain heroin, and handed both to the policewoman. The agents then arrested the respondent for possessing heroin.

It was on the basis of this evidence that the District Court denied the respondent's motion to suppress. The court concluded that the agents' conduct in initially approaching the respondent and asking to see her ticket and identification was a permissible investigative stop under the standards of Terry v. Ohio, 392 U.S. 1, 88 S.Ct. 1868, 20 L.Ed.2d 889 and United States v. Brignoni-Ponce, 422 U.S. 873, 95 S.Ct. 2574, 45 L.Ed.2d 607, finding that this conduct was based on specific and articulable facts that justified a suspicion of criminal activity. The court also found that the respondent had not been placed under arrest or otherwise detained when she was asked to accompany the agents to the DEA office, but had accompanied the agents " 'voluntarily in a spirit of apparent cooperation.' " It was the court's view that no arrest occurred until after the heroin had been found. Finally, the trial court found that the respondent "gave her consent to the search [in the DEA office] and . . . such consent was freely and voluntarily given."

The Court of Appeals reversed the respondent's subsequent conviction, stating only that "the court concludes that this case is indistinguishable from United States v. McCaleb," 552 F.2d 717 (CA6 1977). In McCaleb the Court of Appeals had suppressed ****1875** heroin seized by DEA agents at the Detroit Airport in circumstances substantially similar to those in the present case. The Court of Appeals there disapproved the Government's reliance on the so-called "drug courier profile," and held that the agents could not reasonably have suspected criminal activity in that case, for the reason that "the activities of the [persons] observed by DEA agents, were consistent with innocent behavior," id., at 720. The Court of Appeals further concluded in McCaleb that, even if the initial approach had been permissible, asking the suspects to accompany the agents to a private room for further questioning constituted an arrest requiring probable cause. Finally, the court in McCaleb held that the consent to the search in that case had not been voluntarily given, principally because it was the fruit of what the court believed to have been an unconstitutional detention.

On rehearing en banc of the present case, the Court of Appeals reaffirmed its original decision, stating simply that the respondent had not validly consented to the search "within the meaning of [McCaleb]." 596 F.2d 706, 707.

II

The Fourth Amendment provides that "the right of the people to be secure in their persons, houses, papers, and effects, against unreasonable searches and seizures, shall not be violated . . . ." There is no question in this case that the respondent possessed this constitutional right of personal security as she walked through the Detroit Airport, for "the Fourth Amendment protects people, not places," Katz v. United States, 389 U.S. 347, 351, 88 S.Ct. 507, 511, 19 L.Ed.2d 576. Here the Government concedes that its agents had neither a warrant nor probable cause to believe that the respondent was carrying narcotics when the agents conducted a search of the respondent's person. It is the Government's position, however, that the search was conducted pursuant to the respondent's consent, and thus was excepted from the requirements of both a warrant and probable cause. See Schneckloth v. Bustamonte, 412 U.S. 218, 93 S.Ct. 2041, 36 L.Ed.2d 854. Evidently, the Court of Appeals concluded that the respondent's apparent consent to the search was in fact not voluntarily given and was in any event the product of earlier official conduct violative of the Fourth Amendment. We must first consider, therefore, whether such conduct occurred, either on the concourse or in the DEA office at the airport.

A

The Fourth Amendment's requirement that searches and seizures be founded upon an objective justification, governs all seizures of the person, "including seizures that involve only a brief detention short of traditional arrest. Davis v. Mississippi, 394 U.S. 721 [89 S.Ct. 1394, 22 L.Ed.2d 676] (1969); Terry v. Ohio, 392 U.S. 1, 16–19 [88 S.Ct. 1868, 1877, 20 L.Ed.2d 889] (1968)." United States v. Brignoni-Ponce, supra, at 878, 95 S.Ct., at 2578.5 Accordingly, if the respondent ****1876** was "seized" when the DEA agents approached her on the concourse and asked questions of her, the agents' conduct in doing so was constitutional only if they reasonably suspected the respondent of wrongdoing. But "[o]bviously, not all personal intercourse between policemen and citizens involves 'seizures' of persons. Only when the officer, by means of physical force or show of authority, has in some way restrained the liberty of a citizen may we conclude that a 'seizure' has occurred." Terry v. Ohio, 392 U.S., at 19, n. 16, 88 S.Ct., at 1879, n. 16.

The distinction between an intrusion amounting to a "seizure" of the person and an encounter that intrudes upon no constitutionally protected interest is illustrated by the facts of Terry v. Ohio, which the Court recounted as follows: "Officer McFadden approached the three men, identified himself as a police officer and asked for their names. . . . When the men 'mumbled something' in response to his inquiries, Officer McFadden grabbed petitioner Terry, spun him around so that they were facing the other two, with Terry between McFadden and the others, and patted down the outside of his clothing." Id., at 6–7, 88 S.Ct., at 1872. Obviously the officer "seized" Terry and subjected him to a "search" when he took hold of him, spun him around, and patted down the outer surfaces of his clothing, id., at 19, 88 S.Ct., at 1879. What was not determined in that case, however, was that a seizure had taken place before the officer physically restrained Terry for purposes of searching his person for weapons. The Court "assume[d] that up to that point no intrusion upon constitutionally protected rights had occurred." Id., at 19, n. 16, 88 S.Ct., at 1879, n. 16. The Court's assumption appears entirely correct in view of the fact, noted in the concurring opinion of Mr. Justice WHITE, that "[t]here is nothing in the Constitution which prevents a policeman from addressing questions to anyone on the streets," id., at 34, 88 S.Ct., at 1886. Police officers enjoy "the liberty (again, possessed by every citizen) to address questions to other persons," id., at 31, 32–33, 88 S.Ct., at 1885–1886 (Harlan, J., concurring), although "ordinarily the person addressed has an equal right to ignore his interrogator and walk away." Ibid.

Similarly, the Court in Sibron v. New York, 392 U.S. 40, 88 S.Ct. 1889, 20 L.Ed.2d 917, a case decided the same day as Terry v. Ohio, indicated that not every encounter between a police officer and a citizen is an intrusion requiring an objective justification. In that case, a police officer, before conducting what was later found to have been an unlawful search, approached Sibron in a restaurant and told him to come outside, which Sibron did. The Court had no occasion to decide whether there was a "seizure" of Sibron inside the restaurant antecedent to the seizure that accompanied the search. The record was "barren of any ****1877** indication whether Sibron accompanied [the officer] outside in submission to a show of force or authority which left him no choice, or whether he went voluntarily in a spirit of apparent cooperation with the officer's investigation." 392 U.S., at 63, 88 S.Ct., at 1903 (emphasis added). Plainly, in the latter event, there was no seizure until the police officer in some way demonstrably curtailed Sibron's liberty.

We adhere to the view that a person is "seized" only when, by means of physical force or a show of authority, his freedom of movement is restrained. Only when such restraint is imposed is there any foundation whatever for invoking constitutional safeguards. The purpose of the Fourth Amendment is not to eliminate all contact between the police and the citizenry, but "to prevent arbitrary and oppressive interference by enforcement officials with the privacy and personal security of individuals." United States v. Martinez-Fuerte, 428 U.S. 543, 554, 96 S.Ct. 3074, 3081, 49 L.Ed.2d 1116. As long as the person to whom questions are put remains free to disregard the questions and walk away, there has been no intrusion upon that person's liberty or privacy as would under the Constitution require some particularized and objective justification.

Moreover, characterizing every street encounter between a citizen and the police as a "seizure," while not enhancing any interest secured by the Fourth Amendment, would impose wholly unrealistic restrictions upon a wide variety of legitimate law enforcement practices. The Court has on other occasions referred to the acknowledged need for police questioning as a tool in the effective enforcement of the criminal laws. "Without such investigation, those who were innocent might be falsely accused, those who were guilty might wholly escape prosecution, and many crimes would go unsolved. In short, the security of all would be diminished. Haynes v. Washington, 373 U.S. 503, 515, [83 S.Ct. 1336, 1344, 10 L.Ed.2d 513]." Schneckloth v. Bustamonte, 412 U.S., at 225, 93 S.Ct., at 2046.

We conclude that a person has been "seized" within the meaning of the Fourth Amendment only if, in view of all of the circumstances surrounding the incident, a reasonable person would have believed that he was not free to leave. Examples of circumstances that might indicate a seizure, even where the person did not attempt to leave, would be the threatening presence of several officers, the display of a weapon by an officer, some physical touching of the person of the citizen, or the use of language or tone of voice indicating that compliance with the officer's request might be compelled. See Terry v. Ohio, supra, 392 U.S., at 19, n. 16, 88 S.Ct., at 1879, n. 16; Dunaway v. New York, 442 U.S. 200, 207, and n. 6, 99 S.Ct. 2248, 2253, 60 L.Ed.2d 824; 3 W. LaFave, Search and Seizure 53–55 (1978). In the absence of some such evidence, otherwise inoffensive contact between a member of the public and the police cannot, as a matter of law, amount to a seizure of that person.

On the facts of this case, no "seizure" of the respondent occurred. The events took place in the public concourse. The agents wore no uniforms and displayed no weapons. They did not summon the respondent to their presence, but instead approached her and identified themselves as federal agents. They requested, but did not demand to see the respondent's identification and ticket. Such conduct without more, did not amount to an intrusion upon any constitutionally protected interest. The respondent was not seized simply by reason of the fact that the agents approached her, asked her if she would show them her ticket and identification, and posed to her a few questions. Nor was it enough to establish a seizure that the person asking the questions was a law enforcement official. See ****1878** Terry v. Ohio, 392 U.S., at 31, 32–33, 88 S.Ct., at 1885–1886 (Harlan, J., concurring). See also ALI, Model Code of Pre-Arraignment Procedure § 110.1(1) and commentary, at 257–261 (1975). In short, nothing in the record suggests that the respondent had any objective reason to believe that she was not free to end the conversation in the concourse and proceed on her way, and for that reason we conclude that the agents' initial approach to her was not a seizure.

Our conclusion that no seizure occurred is not affected by the fact that the respondent was not expressly told by the agents that she was free to decline to cooperate with their inquiry, for the voluntariness of her responses does not depend upon her having been so informed. See Schneckloth v. Bustamonte, supra. We also reject the argument that the only inference to be drawn from the fact that the respondent acted in a manner so contrary to her self-interest is that she was compelled to answer the agents' questions. It may happen that a person makes statements to law enforcement officials that he later regrets, but the issue in such cases is not whether the statement was self-protective, but rather whether it was made voluntarily.

The Court's decision last Term in Brown v. Texas, 443 U.S. 47, 99 S.Ct. 2637, 61 L.Ed.2d 357, on which the respondent relies, is not apposite. It could not have been plainer under the circumstances there presented that Brown was forcibly detained by the officers. In that case, two police officers approached Brown in an alley, and asked him to identify himself and to explain his reason for being there. Brown "refused to identify himself and angrily asserted that the officers had no right to stop him," id., at 49, 99 S.Ct., at 2639. Up to this point there was no seizure. But after continuing to protest the officers' power to interrogate him, Brown was first frisked, and then arrested for violation of a state statute making it a criminal offense for a person to refuse to give his name and address to an officer "who has lawfully stopped him and requested the information." The Court simply held in that case that because the officers had no reason to suspect Brown of wrongdoing, there was no basis for detaining him, and therefore no permissible foundation for applying the state statute in the circumstances there presented. Id., at 52–53, 99 S.Ct., at 2641–2642.

The Court's decisions involving investigatory stops of automobiles do not point in any different direction. In United States v. Brignoni-Ponce, 422 U.S. 873, 95 S.Ct. 2574, 45 L.Ed.2d 607, the Court held that a roving patrol of law enforcement officers could stop motorists in the general area of an international border for brief inquiry into their residence status only if the officers reasonably suspected that the vehicle might contain aliens who were illegally in the country. Id., at 881–882, 95 S.Ct., at 2580. The Government did not contend in that case that the persons whose automobiles were detained were not seized. Indeed, the Government acknowledged that the occupants of a detained vehicle were required to respond to the officers' questions and on some occasions to produce documents evidencing their eligibility to be in the United States. Id., at 880, 95 S.Ct., at 2579. Moreover, stopping or diverting an automobile in transit, with the attendant opportunity for a visual inspection of areas of the passenger compartment not otherwise observable, is materially more intrusive than a question put to a passing pedestrian, and the fact that the former amounts to a seizure tells very little about the constitutional status of the latter. See also Delaware v. Prouse, 440 U.S. 648, 99 S.Ct. 1391, 59 L.Ed.2d 660; United States v. Martinez-Fuerte, 428 U.S., at 556–559, 96 S.Ct., at 3082–3083.

B

Although we have concluded that the initial encounter between the DEA agents and the respondent on the concourse at the Detroit Airport did not constitute an unlawful seizure, it is still arguable that the respondent's Fourth Amendment protections were violated when she went from the concourse to the DEA office. Such a violation might in turn infect the subsequent search of the respondent's person.

****1879** The District Court specifically found that the respondent accompanied the agents to the office " 'voluntarily in a spirit of apparent cooperation,' " quoting Sibron v. New York, 392 U.S., at 63, 88 S.Ct., at 1903. Notwithstanding this determination by the trial court, the Court of Appeals evidently concluded that the agents' request that the respondent accompany them converted the situation into an arrest requiring probable cause in order to be found lawful. But because the trial court's finding was sustained by the record, the Court of Appeals was mistaken in substituting for that finding its view of the evidence. See Jackson v. United States, 122 U.S.App.D.C. 324, 353 F.2d 862 (1965).

The question whether the respondent's consent to accompany the agents was in fact voluntary or was the product of duress or coercion, express or implied, is to be determined by the totality of all the circumstances, Schneckloth v. Bustamonte, 412 U.S., at 227, 93 S.Ct., at 2047, and is a matter which the Government has the burden of proving. Id., at 222, 93 S.Ct., at 2045, citing Bumper v. North Carolina, 391 U.S. 543, 548, 88 S.Ct. 1788, 1791, 20 L.Ed.2d 797. The respondent herself did not testify at the hearing. The Government's evidence showed that the respondent was not told that she had to go to the office, but was simply asked if she would accompany the officers. There were neither threats nor any show of force. The respondent had been questioned only briefly, and her ticket and identification were returned to her before she was asked to accompany the officers.

On the other hand, it is argued that the incident would reasonably have appeared coercive to the respondent, who was 22 years old and had not been graduated from high school. It is additionally suggested that the respondent, a female and a Negro, may have felt unusually threatened by the officers, who were white males. While these factors were not irrelevant, see Schneckloth v. Bustamonte, supra, 412 U.S., at 226, 93 S.Ct., at 2047, neither were they decisive, and the totality of the evidence in this case was plainly adequate to support the District Court's finding that the respondent voluntarily consented to accompany the officers to the DEA office.

C

Because the search of the respondent's person was not preceded by an impermissible seizure of her person, it cannot be contended that her apparent consent to the subsequent search was infected by an unlawful detention. There remains to be considered whether the respondent's consent to the search was for any other reason invalid. The District Court explicitly credited the officers' testimony and found that the "consent was freely and voluntarily given," citing Schneckloth v. Bustamonte, supra. There was more than enough evidence in this case to sustain that view. First, we note that the respondent, who was 22 years old and had an 11th-grade education, was plainly capable of a knowing consent. Second, it is especially significant that the respondent was twice expressly told that she was free to decline to consent to the search, and only thereafter explicitly consented to it. Although the Constitution does not require "proof of knowledge of a right to refuse as the sine qua non of an effective consent to a search," id., at 234, 93 S.Ct., at 2051 (footnote omitted), such knowledge was highly relevant to the determination that there had been consent. And, perhaps more important for present purposes, the fact that the officers themselves informed the respondent that she was free to withhold her consent substantially lessened the probability that their conduct could reasonably have appeared to her to be coercive.

Counsel for the respondent has argued that she did in fact resist the search, relying principally on the testimony that when she was told that the search would require the removal of her clothing, she stated to the female police officer that "she had a plane to catch." But the trial court was entitled to view the statement as simply an expression of concern that the search be conducted quickly. The respondent had twice unequivocally indicated her consent to the ****1880** search, and when assured by the police officer that there would be no problem if nothing were turned up by the search, she began to undress without further comment.

Counsel for the respondent has also argued that because she was within the DEA office when she consented to the search, her consent may have resulted from the inherently coercive nature of those surroundings. But in view of the District Court's finding that the respondent's presence in the office was voluntary, the fact that she was there is little or no evidence that she was in any way coerced. And in response to the argument that the respondent would not voluntarily have consented to a search that was likely to disclose the narcotics that she carried, we repeat that the question is not whether the respondent acted in her ultimate self-interest, but whether she acted voluntarily.

III

We conclude that the District Court's determination that the respondent consented to the search of her person "freely and voluntarily" was sustained by the evidence and that the Court of Appeals was, therefore, in error in setting it aside. Accordingly, the judgment of the Court of Appeals is reversed, and the case is remanded to that court for further proceedings.

It is so ordered.

Mr. Justice POWELL, with whom THE CHIEF JUSTICE and Mr. Justice BLACKMUN join, concurring in part and concurring in the judgment.

I join Parts I, II–B, II–C, and III of the Court's opinion. Because neither of the courts below considered the question, I do not reach the Government's contention that the agents did not "seize" the respondent within the meaning of the Fourth Amendment. In my view, we may assume for present purposes that the stop did constitute a seizure.1 I would hold—as did the District Court—that the federal agents had reasonable suspicion that the respondent was engaging in criminal activity, and, therefore, that they did not violate the Fourth Amendment by stopping the respondent for routine questioning.

I

The relevant facts may be stated briefly. The respondent arrived at the Detroit Metropolitan Airport on a flight from Los Angeles. She was the last passenger to leave the aircraft. Two agents of the Drug Enforcement Administration watched the respondent enter the terminal, walk to the baggage area, then change directions and proceed to an Eastern Airlines ticket counter. After the respondent accepted a boarding pass for a flight to Pittsburgh, the two agents approached her. They identified themselves as federal officers, and requested some identification. The respondent gave them her driver's license and airline ticket. The agents asked the respondent several brief questions. The respondent accompanied the agents to an airport office where a body search conducted by a female police officer revealed two plastic bags of heroin.

II

Terry v. Ohio, 392 U.S. 1, 88 S.Ct. 1868, 20 L.Ed.2d 889 (1968), establishes that a reasonable ****1881** investigative stop does not offend the Fourth Amendment. The reasonableness of a stop turns on the facts and circumstances of each case. In particular, the Court has emphasized (i) the public interest served by the seizure, (ii) the nature and scope of the intrusion, and (iii) the objective facts upon which the law enforcement officer relied in light of his knowledge and expertise. See Brown v. Texas, 443 U.S. 47, 50–51, 99 S.Ct. 2637, 2640, 2641, 61 L.Ed.2d 357 (1979); Delaware v. Prouse, 440 U.S. 648, 654–655, 99 S.Ct. 1391, 1396, 1397, 59 L.Ed.2d 660 (1979); United States v. Brignoni-Ponce, 422 U.S. 873, 879–883, 95 S.Ct. 2574, 2579–2581, 45 L.Ed.2d 607 (1975); Terry v. Ohio, supra, 392 U.S., at 20–22, 88 S.Ct., at 1879, 1880.

A

The public has a compelling interest in detecting those who would traffic in deadly drugs for personal profit. Few problems affecting the health and welfare of our population, particularly our young, cause greater concern than the escalating use of controlled substances. Much of the drug traffic is highly organized and conducted by sophisticated criminal syndicates. The profits are enormous. And many drugs, including heroin, may be easily concealed. As a result, the obstacles to detection of illegal conduct may be unmatched in any other area of law enforcement.

To meet this pressing concern, the Drug Enforcement Administration since 1974 has assigned highly skilled agents to the Detroit Airport as part of a nationwide program to intercept drug couriers transporting narcotics between major drug sources and distribution centers in the United States. Federal agents have developed "drug courier profiles" that describe the characteristics generally associated with narcotics traffickers. For example, because the Drug Enforcement Administration believes that most drugs enter Detroit from one of four "source" cites (Los Angeles, San Diego, Miami, or New York), agents pay particular attention to passengers who arrive from those places. See United States v. Van Lewis, 409 F.Supp. 535, 538 (ED Mich.1976), aff'd, 556 F.2d 385 (CA6 1977). During the first 18 months of the program, agents watching the Detroit Airport searched 141 persons in 96 encounters. They found controlled substances in 77 of the encounters and arrested 122 persons. 409 F.Supp., at 539. When two of these agents stopped the respondent in February 1976, they were carrying out a highly specialized law enforcement operation designed to combat the serious societal threat posed by narcotics distribution.

B

Our cases demonstrate that "the scope of [a] particular intrusion, in light of all the exigencies of the case, [is] a central element in the analysis of reasonableness." Terry v. Ohio, supra, 392 U.S., at 18, n. 15, 88 S.Ct., at 1878, n. 15.3 The intrusion in this case ****1882** was quite modest. Two plainclothes agents approached the respondent as she walked through a public area. The respondent was near airline employees from whom she could have sought aid had she been accosted by strangers. The agents identified themselves and asked to see some identification. One officer asked the respondent why her airline ticket and her driver's license bore different names. The agent also inquired how long the respondent had been in California. Unlike the petitioner in Terry, supra, at 7, 88 S.Ct., at 1872, the respondent was not physically restrained. The agents did not display weapons. The questioning was brief. In these circumstances, the respondent could not reasonably have felt frightened or isolated from assistance.

C

In reviewing the factors that led the agents to stop and question the respondent, it is important to recall that a trained law enforcement agent may be "able to perceive and articulate meaning in given conduct which would be wholly innocent to the untrained observer." Brown v. Texas, supra, at 52, n. 2, 99 S.Ct., at 2641, n. 2. Among the circumstances that can give rise to reasonable suspicion are the agent's knowledge of the methods used in recent criminal activity and the characteristics of persons engaged in such illegal practices. Law enforcement officers may rely on the "characteristics of the area," and the behavior of a suspect who appears to be evading police contact. United States v. Brignoni-Ponce, 422 U.S., at 884–885, 95 S.Ct., at 2581–2582. "In all situations the officer is entitled to assess the facts in light of his experience." Id., at 885, 95 S.Ct., at 2582.

The two officers who stopped the respondent were federal agents assigned to the Drug Enforcement Administration. Agent Anderson, who initiated the stop and questioned the respondent, had 10 years of experience and special training in drug enforcement. He had been assigned to the Detroit Airport, known to be a cross roads for illicit narcotics traffic, for over a year and he had been involved in approximately 100 drug-related arrests. App. 7–8.

The agents observed the respondent as she arrived in Detroit from Los Angeles. The respondent, who appeared very nervous, engaged in behavior that the agents believed was designed to evade detection. She deplaned only after all other passengers had left the aircraft. Agent Anderson testified that drug couriers often disembark last in order to have a clear view of the terminal so that they more easily can detect government agents. Id., at 9. Once inside the terminal, the respondent scanned the entire gate area and walked "very, very slowly" toward the baggage area. Id., at 10 (testimony of Agent Anderson). When she arrived there, she claimed no baggage. Instead, she asked a skycap for directions to the Eastern Airlines ticket counter located in a different terminal. Agent Anderson stood in line immediately behind the respondent at the ticket counter. Although she carried an American Airlines ticket for a flight from Detroit to Pittsburgh, she asked for an Eastern Airlines ticket. An airline employee gave her an Eastern Airlines boarding pass. Id., at 10–11. Agent Anderson testified that drug couriers frequently travel without ***565** baggage and change flights en route to avoid surveillance. Ibid. On the basis of these observations, the agents stopped and questioned the respondent.

III

The District Court, which had an opportunity to hear Agent Anderson's testimony and judge his credibility, concluded that the decision to stop the respondent was reasonable. I agree. The public interest in preventing ****1883** drug traffic is great, and the intrusion upon the respondent's privacy was minimal. The specially trained agents acted pursuant to a well-planned, and effective, federal law enforcement program. They observed respondent engaging in conduct that they reasonably associated with criminal activity. Furthermore, the events occurred in an airport known to be frequented by drug couriers. In light of all of the circumstances, I would hold that the agents possessed reasonable and articulable suspicion of criminal activity when they stopped the respondent in a public place and asked her for identification.

The jurisprudence of the Fourth Amendment demands consideration of the public's interest in effective law enforcement as well as each person's constitutionally secured right to be free from unreasonable searches and seizures. In applying a test of "reasonableness," courts need not ignore the considerable expertise that law enforcement officials have gained from their special training and experience. The careful and commendable police work that led to the criminal conviction at issue in this case satisfies the requirements of the Fourth Amendment.

Mr. Justice WHITE, with whom Mr. Justice BRENNAN, Mr. Justice MARSHALL, and Mr. Justice STEVENS join, dissenting.

The Court today concludes that agents of the Drug Enforcement Administration (DEA) acted lawfully in stopping a traveler changing planes in an airport terminal and escorting her to a DEA office for a strip-search of her person. This result is particularly curious because a majority of the Members of the Court refuse to reject the conclusion that Ms. Mendenhall was "seized," while a separate majority decline to hold that there were reasonable grounds to justify a seizure. Mr. Justice STEWART concludes that the DEA agents acted lawfully, regardless of whether there were any reasonable grounds for suspecting Ms. Mendenhall of criminal activity, because he finds that Ms. Mendenhall was not "seized" by the DEA agents, even though throughout the proceedings below the Government never questioned the fact that a seizure had occurred necessitating a showing of antecedent reasonable suspicion. Mr. Justice POWELL's opinion concludes that even though Ms. Mendenhall may have been "seized," the seizure was lawful because her behavior while changing planes in the airport provided reasonable suspicion that she was engaging in criminal activity. The Court then concludes, based on the absence of evidence that Ms. Mendenhall resisted her detention, that she voluntarily consented to being taken to the DEA office, even though she in fact had no choice in the matter. This conclusion is inconsistent with our recognition that consent cannot be presumed from a showing of acquiescence to authority, and it cannot be reconciled with our decision last Term in Dunaway v. New York, 442 U.S. 200, 99 S.Ct. 2248, 60 L.Ed.2d 824 (1979).

I

Beginning with Terry v. Ohio, 392 U.S. 1, 16, 88 S.Ct. 1868, 1877, 20 L.Ed.2d 889 (1968), the Court has recognized repeatedly that the Fourth Amendment's proscription of unreasonable "seizures" protects individuals during encounters with police that do not give rise to an arrest. ****1884** United States v. Brignoni-Ponce, 422 U.S. 873, 878, 95 S.Ct. 2574, 2578, 45 L.Ed.2d 607 (1975); United States v. Martinez-Fuerte, 428 U.S. 543, 556, 96 S.Ct. 3074, 3082, 49 L.Ed.2d 1116 (1976); Delaware v. Prouse, 440 U.S. 648, 653, 99 S.Ct. 1391, 1396, 59 L.Ed.2d 660 (1979). In Terry we "emphatically reject[ed]" the notion that a "stop" "is outside the purview of the Fourth Amendment because . . . [it is not a] 'seizure' within the meaning of the Constitution." 392 U.S., at 16, 88 S.Ct., at 1877. We concluded that "the sounder course is to recognize that the Fourth Amendment governs all intrusions by agents of the public upon personal security, and to make the scope of the particular intrusion, in light of all the exigencies of the case, a central element in the analysis of reasonableness." Id., at 18, n. 15, 88 S.Ct., at 1878. Applying this principle,

"[w]e have recognized that in some circumstances an officer may detain a suspect briefly for questioning although he does not have 'probable cause' to believe that the suspect is involved in criminal activity, as is required for a traditional arrest. However, we have required the officers to have a reasonable suspicion, based on objective facts, that the individual is involved in criminal activity." Brown v. Texas, 443 U.S. 47, 51, 99 S.Ct. 2637, 2641, 61 L.Ed.2d 357 (1979) (citations omitted).

Throughout the lower court proceedings in this case, the Government never questioned that the initial stop of Ms. Mendenhall was a "seizure" that required reasonable suspicion. Rather, the Government sought to justify the stop by arguing that Ms. Mendenhall's behavior had given rise to reasonable suspicion because it was consistent with portions of the so-called "drug courier profile," an informal amalgam of characteristics thought to be associated with persons carrying illegal drugs. Having failed to convince the Court of Appeals that the DEA agents had reasonable suspicion for the stop, the Government seeks reversal here by arguing for the first time that no “seizure” occurred, an argument that Mr. Justice STEWART now accepts, thereby pretermitting the question whether there was reasonable suspicion to stop Ms. Mendenhall. Mr. Justice STEWART’s opinion not only is inconsistent with our usual refusal to reverse judgments on grounds not raised below, but it also addresses a fact-bound question with a totality-of-circumstances assessment that is best left in the first instance to the trial court, particularly since the question was not litigated **1885 below and hence we cannot be sure is adequately addressed by the record before us.

Mr. Justice STEWART believes that a “seizure” within the meaning of the Fourth Amendment occurs when an individual’s freedom of movement is restrained by means of physical force or a show of authority. Although it is undisputed that Ms. Mendenhall was not free to leave after the DEA agents stopped her and inspected her identification, App. 19, Mr. Justice STEWART concludes that she was not “seized” because he finds that, under the totality of the circumstances, a reasonable person would have believed that she was free to leave. While basing this finding on an alleged absence from the record of objective evidence indicating that Ms. Mendenhall was not free to ignore the officer’s inquiries and continue on her way, Mr. Justice STEWART’S opinion brushes off the fact that this asserted evidentiary deficiency may be largely attributable to the fact that the “seizure” question was never raised below. In assessing what the record does reveal, the opinion discounts certain objective factors that would tend to support a “seizure” finding, while relying on contrary factors inconclusive even under its own illustrations of how a “seizure” may be established. Moreover, although Mr. Justice STEWART’S opinion purports to make its “seizure” finding turn on objective factors known to the person accosted, in distinguishing prior decisions holding that investigatory stops constitute “seizures,” it does not rely on differences in the extent to which persons accosted could reasonably believe that they were free to leave. Even if one believes the Government should be permitted **1886 to raise the “seizure” question in this Court, the proper course would be to direct a remand to the District Court for an evidentiary hearing on the question, rather than to decide it in the first instance in this Court.

II

Assuming, as we should, that Ms. Mendenhall was “seized” within the meaning of the Fourth Amendment when she was stopped by the DEA agents, the legality of that stop turns on whether there were reasonable grounds for suspecting her of criminal activity at the time of the stop. Brown v. Texas, 443 U.S., at 51, 99 S.Ct., at 2641. To establish that there was reasonable suspicion for the stop, it was necessary for the police at least to “be able to point to specific and articulable facts which, taken together with rational inferences from those facts, reasonably warrant that intrusion.” Terry v. Ohio, 392 U.S., at 21, 88 S.Ct., at 1880.

At the time they stopped Ms. Mendenhall, the DEA agents’ suspicion that she was engaged in criminal activity was based solely on their brief observations of her conduct at the airport.7 The officers had no advance information that Ms. Mendenhall, or anyone on her flight, would be carrying drugs. What the agents observed Ms. Mendenhall do in the airport was not “unusual conduct” which would lead an experienced officer reasonably to conclude that criminal activity was afoot, id., at 30, 88 S.Ct., at 1884, but rather the kind of behavior that could reasonably be expected of anyone changing planes in an airport terminal.

None of the aspects of Ms. Mendenhall’s conduct, either alone or in combination, were sufficient to provide reasonable suspicion that she was engaged in criminal activity. The fact that Ms. Mendenhall was the last person to alight from a flight originating in Los Angeles was plainly insufficient to provide a basis for stopping her. Nor was the fact that her flight originated from a “major source city,” for the mere proximity of a person to areas with a high incidence of drug activity or to persons known to be drug addicts, does not provide the necessary reasonable suspicion for an investigatory stop. Ybarra v. Illinois, 444 U.S. 85, 100 S.Ct. 338, 62 L.Ed.2d 238

(1979); Brown v. Texas, supra ; Sibron v. New York, 392 U.S. 40, 62, 88 S.Ct. 1889, 1902, 20 L.Ed.2d 917 (1968). Under the circumstances of this case, the DEA agents' observations that Ms. Mendenhall claimed no luggage and changed airlines were also insufficient to provide reasonable suspicion. Unlike the situation in **1887 Terry v. Ohio, 392 U.S., at 28, 88 S.Ct., at 1883, where "nothing in [the suspects'] conduct from the time [the officer] first noticed them until the time he confronted them and identified himself as a police officer gave him sufficient reason to negate [his] hypothesis" of criminal behavior, Ms. Mendenhall's subsequent conduct negated any reasonable inference that she was traveling a long distance without luggage or changing her ticket to a different airline to avoid detection. Agent Anderson testified that he heard the ticket agent tell Ms. Mendenhall that her ticket to Pittsburgh already was in order and that all she needed was a boarding pass for the flight. Thus it should have been plain to an experienced observer that Ms. Mendenhall's failure to claim luggage was attributable to the fact that she was already ticketed through to Pittsburgh on a different airline. Because Agent Anderson's suspicion that Ms. Mendenhall was transporting narcotics could be based only on "his inchoate and unparticularized suspicion or 'hunch,' " rather than "specific reasonable inferences which he is entitled to draw from the facts in light of his experience," id., at 27, 88 S.Ct., at 1883, he was not justified in "seizing" Ms. Mendenhall.

III

Whatever doubt there may be concerning whether Ms. Mendenhall's Fourth Amendment interests were implicated during the initial stages of her confrontation with the DEA agents, she undoubtedly was "seized" within the meaning of the Fourth Amendment when the agents escorted her from the public area of the terminal to the DEA office for questioning and a strip-search of her person. In Dunaway v. New York, 442 U.S. 200, 99 S.Ct. 2248, 60 L.Ed.2d 824 (1979), we held that a person who accompanied police officers to a police station for purposes of interrogation undoubtedly "was 'seized' in the Fourth Amendment sense," even though "he was not told he was under arrest." Id., at 207, 203, 99 S.Ct., at 2253, 2251. We found it significant that the suspect was taken to a police station, "was never informed that he was 'free to go,' " and "would have been physically restrained if he had refused to accompany the officers or had tried to escape their custody." Id., at 212, 99 S.Ct., at 2256. Like the "seizure" in Dunaway, the nature of the intrusion to which Ms. Mendenhall was subjected when she was escorted by DEA agents to their office and detained there for questioning and a strip-search was so great that it "was in important respects indistinguishable from a traditional arrest." Ibid. Although Ms. Mendenhall was not told that she was under arrest, she in fact was not free to refuse to go to the DEA office and was not **1888 told that she was. Furthermore, once inside the office, Ms. Mendenhall would not have been permitted to leave without submitting to a strip-search. Thus, as in Dunaway,

"[t]he mere facts that [the suspect] was not told he was under arrest, was not 'booked,' and would not have had an arrest record if the interrogation had proved fruitless, while not insignificant for all purposes, . . . obviously do not make [the suspect's] seizure even roughly analogous to the narrowly defined intrusions involved in Terry and its progeny." Id., at 212–213, 99 S.Ct., at 2256 (citation omitted). Because the intrusion to which Ms. Mendenhall was subjected when she was escorted to the DEA office is of the same character as that involved in Dunaway, probable cause, which concededly was absent, was required to support the intrusion.

The Court's suggestion that no Fourth Amendment interest possessed by Ms. Mendenhall was implicated because she consented to go to the DEA office is inconsistent with Dunaway and unsupported in the record. There was no evidence in the record to support the District Court's speculation, made before Dunaway was decided, that Ms. Mendenhall accompanied "Agent Anderson to the airport DEA Office 'voluntarily in a spirit of apparent cooperation with the [agent's] investigation,' Sibron v. New York, 392 U.S. 40, 63 [88 S.Ct. 1889, 1902, 20 L.Ed.2d 917] (1968)."

App. to Pet. for Cert. 16a. Ms. Mendenhall did not testify at the suppression hearing and the officers presented no testimony concerning what she said, if anything, when informed that the officers wanted her to come with them to the DEA office. Indeed, the only testimony concerning what occurred between Agent Anderson's "request" and Ms. Mendenhall's arrival at the DEA office is the agent's testimony that if Ms. Mendenhall had wanted to leave at that point she would have been forcibly restrained. The evidence of consent here is even flimsier than that we rejected in Dunaway where it was claimed that the suspect made an affirmative response when asked if he would accompany the officers to the police station. Dunaway v. New York, supra, at 223, 99 S.Ct., at 2261 (REHNQUIST, J., dissenting). Also in Sibron v. New York, from which the District Court culled its description of Ms. Mendenhall's "consent," we described a record in a similar state as "totally barren of any indication whether Sibron accompanied Patrolman Martin outside in submission to a show of force or authority which left him no choice, or whether he went voluntarily in a spirit of apparent cooperation with the officer's investigation." 392 U.S., at 63, 88 S.Ct., at 1903.

The Court recognizes that the Government has the burden of proving that Ms. Mendenhall consented to accompany the officers, but it nevertheless holds that the "totality of evidence was plainly adequate" to support a finding of consent. On the record before us, the Court's conclusion can only be based on the notion that consent ****1889** can be assumed from the absence of proof that a suspect resisted police authority. This is a notion that we have squarely rejected. In Bumper v. North Carolina, 391 U.S. 543, 548–549, 88 S.Ct. 1788, 1792, 20 L.Ed.2d 797 (1968), the Court held that the prosecution's "burden of proving that the consent was, in fact, freely and voluntarily given . . . cannot be discharged by showing no more than acquiescence to a claim of lawful authority." (Footnotes omitted.) Johnson v. United States, 333 U.S. 10, 68 S.Ct. 367, 92 L.Ed. 436 (1948); Amos v. United States, 255 U.S. 313, 41 S.Ct. 266, 65 L.Ed. 654 (1921). While the Government need not prove that Ms. Mendenhall knew that she had a right to refuse to accompany the officers,Schneckloth v. Bustamonte, 412 U.S. 218, 93 S.Ct. 2041, 36 L.Ed.2d 854 (1973), it cannot rely solely on acquiescence to the officers' wishes to establish the requisite consent. The Court of Appeals properly understood this in rejecting the District Court's "findings" of consent.

Since the defendant was not present to testify at the suppression hearing, we can only speculate about her state of mind as her encounter with the DEA agents progressed from surveillance, to detention, to questioning, to seclusion in a private office, to the female officer's command to remove her clothing. Nevertheless, it is unbelievable15 that this sequence of events involved no invasion of a citizen's constitutionally protected interest in privacy. The rule of law requires a different conclusion.

Because Ms. Mendenhall was being illegally detained at the time of the search of her person, her suppression motion should have been granted in the absence of evidence to dissipate the taint.

Black Letter Law

> Where agents approached defendant in a public concourse at an airport, without summoning her to their presence and without displaying their weapons and in plain clothes, and identified themselves as federal agents and requested to see defendant's identification and airline ticket, agents' conduct did not amount to intrusion upon any constitutionally protected interest and agents' initial approach to defendant was not a "seizure," even though defendant was not expressly told by agents that she was free to decline to cooperate with their inquiry. The Court held that: (1) evidence was sufficient to support finding that defendant voluntarily accompanied agents from airport concourse to Drug Enforcement Administration office, and (2) evidence was sufficient to support finding that defendant voluntarily consented to search of her person, despite defendant's statement to female police officer that "she had a plane to catch."

Florida v. Bostick

111 S.Ct. 2382

Supreme Court of the United States

FLORIDA, Petitioner,

v.

Terrance BOSTICK.

No. 89–1717. | Argued Feb. 26, 1991. | Decided June 20, 1991.

***431** Justice O'CONNOR delivered the opinion of the Court.

We have held that the Fourth Amendment permits police officers to approach individuals at random in airport lobbies and other public places to ask them questions and to request consent to search their luggage, so long as a reasonable person would understand that he or she could refuse to cooperate. This case requires us to determine whether the same rule applies to police encounters that take place on a bus.

I

Drug interdiction efforts have led to the use of police surveillance at airports, train stations, and bus depots. Law enforcement officers stationed at such locations routinely approach individuals, either randomly or because they suspect in some vague way that the individuals may be engaged in criminal activity, and ask them potentially incriminating questions. Broward County has adopted such a program. County Sheriff's Department officers routinely board buses at scheduled stops and ask passengers for permission to search their luggage.

In this case, two officers discovered cocaine when they searched a suitcase belonging to Terrance Bostick. The underlying facts of the search are in dispute, but the Florida Supreme Court, whose decision we review here, stated explicitly the factual premise for its decision:

" 'Two officers, complete with badges, insignia and one of them holding a recognizable zipper pouch, containing a pistol, boarded a bus bound from Miami to Atlanta during a stopover in Fort Lauderdale. Eyeing the passengers, the officers, admittedly without articulable suspicion, picked ****2385** out the defendant passenger and asked to inspect his ticket and identification. The ticket, from Miami to Atlanta, matched the defendant's identification and both were immediately returned to him as unremarkable. However, the two police officers persisted and explained their presence as narcotics agents on the ***432** lookout for illegal drugs. In pursuit of that aim, they then requested the defendant's consent to search his luggage. Needless to say, there is a conflict in the evidence about whether the defendant consented to the search of the second bag in which the contraband was found and as to whether he was informed of his right to refuse consent. However, any conflict must be resolved in favor of the state, it being a question of fact decided by the trial judge.' " 554 So.2d 1153, 1154–1155 (1989), quoting 510 So.2d 321, 322 (Fla.App.1987) (Letts, J., dissenting in part).

Two facts are particularly worth noting. First, the police specifically advised Bostick that he had the right to refuse consent. Bostick appears to have disputed the point, but, as the Florida Supreme Court noted explicitly, the trial court resolved this evidentiary conflict in the State's favor. Second, at no time did the officers threaten Bostick with a gun. The Florida Supreme Court indicated that one officer carried a zipper pouch containing a pistol—the equivalent of carrying a gun in a holster—but the court did not suggest that the gun was ever removed from its pouch, pointed at Bostick, or otherwise used in a threatening manner. The dissent's characterization of the officers as "gun-wielding inquisitor[s]," post, at 2393, is colorful, but lacks any basis in fact.

Bostick was arrested and charged with trafficking in cocaine. He moved to suppress the cocaine on the grounds that it had been seized in violation of his Fourth Amendment rights. The trial court denied the motion but made no factual findings. Bostick subsequently entered a plea of guilty, but reserved the right to appeal the denial of the motion to suppress.

The Florida District Court of Appeal affirmed, but considered the issue sufficiently important that it certified a question to the Florida Supreme Court. 510 So.2d, at 322. The ***433** Supreme Court reasoned that Bostick had been seized because a reasonable passenger in his situation would not have felt free to leave the bus to avoid questioning by the police. 554 So.2d, at 1154. It rephrased and answered the certified question so as to make the bus setting dispositive in every case. It ruled categorically that " 'an impermissible seizure result[s] when police mount a drug search on buses during scheduled stops and question boarded passengers without articulable reasons for doing so, thereby obtaining consent to search the passengers' luggage.' " Ibid. The Florida Supreme Court thus adopted a per se rule that the Broward County Sheriff's practice of "working the buses" is unconstitutional.* The result of this decision is that police in Florida, as elsewhere, may approach persons at random in most public places, ask them questions and seek consent to a search, see id., at 1156; but they may not engage in the same behavior on a bus. Id., at 1157. We granted certiorari, 498 U.S. 894, 111 S.Ct. 241, 112 L.Ed.2d 201 (1990), to determine whether the Florida Supreme Court's per se rule is consistent with our Fourth Amendment jurisprudence.

****2386 II**

The sole issue presented for our review is whether a police encounter on a bus of the type described above necessarily constitutes a "seizure" within the meaning of the Fourth Amendment. The State concedes, and we accept for purposes of this decision, that the officers lacked the reasonable ***434** suspicion required to justify a seizure and that, if a seizure took place, the drugs found in Bostick's suitcase must be suppressed as tainted fruit.

Our cases make it clear that a seizure does not occur simply because a police officer approaches an individual and asks a few questions. So long as a reasonable person would feel free "to disregard the police and go about his business," California v. Hodari D., 499 U.S. 621, 628, 111 S.Ct. 1547, 1552, 113 L.Ed.2d 690 (1991), the encounter is consensual and no reasonable suspicion is required. The encounter will not trigger Fourth Amendment scrutiny unless it loses its consensual nature. The Court made precisely this point in Terry v. Ohio, 392 U.S. 1, 19, n. 16, 88 S.Ct. 1868, 1879, n. 16, 20 L.Ed.2d 889 (1968): "Obviously, not all personal intercourse between policemen and citizens involves 'seizures' of persons. Only when the officer, by means of physical force or show of authority, has in some way restrained the liberty of a citizen may we conclude that a 'seizure' has occurred."

Since Terry, we have held repeatedly that mere police questioning does not constitute a seizure. In Florida v. Royer, 460 U.S. 491, 103 S.Ct. 1319, 75 L.Ed.2d 229 (1983) (plurality opinion), for example, we explained that "law enforcement officers do not violate the Fourth Amendment by merely approaching an individual on the street or in another public place, by asking him if he is willing to answer some questions, by putting questions to him if the person is willing to listen, or by offering in evidence in a criminal prosecution his voluntary answers to such questions." Id., at 497, 103 S.Ct., at 1324; see id., at 523, n. 3, 103 S.Ct., at 1338 n. 3 (REHNQUIST, J., dissenting).

There is no doubt that if this same encounter had taken place before Bostick boarded the bus or in the lobby of the bus terminal, it would not rise to the level of a seizure. The Court has dealt with similar encounters in airports and has found them to be "the sort of consensual encounter[s] that implicat[e] no Fourth Amendment interest." Florida v. Rodriguez, 469 U.S. 1, 5–6, 105 S.Ct. 308, 310–311, 83 L.Ed.2d 165 (1984). We have stated that even ***435** when officers have no basis for suspecting a particular individual, they may generally ask questions of that individual, see INS v. Delgado, 466 U.S. 210, 216, 104 S.Ct. 1758, 1762, 80 L.Ed.2d 247 (1984); Rodriguez, supra, 469 U.S., at 5–6, 105 S.Ct., at 310–311; ask to examine the individual's identification, see Delgado, supra, 466 U.S., at 216, 104 S.Ct., at 1762; Royer, supra, 460 U.S., at 501, 103 S.Ct., at 1326 (plurality opinion); United States v. Mendenhall, 446 U.S. 544, 557–558, 100 S.Ct. 1870, 1878–1879, 64 L.Ed.2d 497 (1980); and request consent to search his or her luggage, see Royer, supra, 460 U.S., at 501, 103 S.Ct., at 1326 (plurality opinion)—as long as the police do not convey a message that compliance with their requests is required.

Bostick insists that this case is different because it took place in the cramped confines of a bus. A police encounter is much more intimidating in this setting, he argues, because police tower over a seated passenger and there is little room to move around. Bostick claims to find support in language from Michigan v. Chesternut, 486 U.S. 567, 573, 108 S.Ct. 1975, 1979, 100 L.Ed.2d 565 (1988), and other cases, indicating that a seizure occurs when a reasonable person would believe that he or she is not "free to leave." Bostick maintains that a reasonable bus passenger would not have felt free to leave under the circumstances of this case because there is nowhere to go on a bus. Also, the bus was about to depart. Had Bostick disembarked, he would have risked being stranded and losing whatever baggage ****2387** he had locked away in the luggage compartment.

The Florida Supreme Court found this argument persuasive, so much so that it adopted a per se rule prohibiting the police from randomly boarding buses as a means of drug interdiction. The state court erred, however, in focusing on whether Bostick was "free to leave" rather than on the principle that those words were intended to capture. When police attempt to question a person who is walking down the street or through an airport lobby, it makes sense to inquire whether a reasonable person would feel free to continue walking. But when the person is seated on a bus and has no desire to leave, the degree to which a reasonable person ***436** would feel that he or she could leave is not an accurate measure of the coercive effect of the encounter.

Here, for example, the mere fact that Bostick did not feel free to leave the bus does not mean that the police seized him. Bostick was a passenger on a bus that was scheduled to depart. He would not have felt free to leave the bus even if the police had not been present. Bostick's movements were "confined" in a sense, but this was the natural result of his decision to take the bus; it says nothing about whether or not the police conduct at issue was coercive.

In this respect, the Court's decision in INS v. Delgado, supra, is dispositive. At issue there was the INS' practice of visiting factories at random and questioning employees to determine whether any were illegal aliens. Several INS agents would stand near the building's exits, while other agents walked through the factory questioning workers. The Court acknowledged that the workers may not have been free to leave their worksite, but explained that this was not the result of police activity: "Ordinarily, when people are at work their freedom to move about has been meaningfully restricted, not by the actions of law enforcement officials, but by the workers' voluntary obligations to their employers." Id., 466 U.S., at 218, 104 S.Ct., at 1763. We concluded that there was no seizure because, even though the workers were not free to leave the building without being questioned, the agents' conduct should have given employees "no reason to believe that they would be detained if they gave truthful answers to the questions put to them or if they simply refused to answer." Ibid.

The present case is analytically indistinguishable from Delgado. Like the workers in that case, Bostick's freedom of movement was restricted by a factor independent of police conduct—i.e., by his being a passenger on a bus. Accordingly, the "free to leave" analysis on which Bostick relies is inapplicable. In such a situation, the appropriate inquiry is whether a reasonable person would feel free to decline the officers' requests or otherwise terminate the encounter. This ***437** formulation follows logically from prior cases and breaks no new ground. We have said before that the crucial test is whether, taking into account all of the circumstances surrounding the encounter, the police conduct would "have communicated to a reasonable person that he was not at liberty to ignore the police presence and go about his business." Chesternut, supra, 486 U.S., at 569, 108 S.Ct., at 1977. See also Hodari D., 499 U.S., at 628, 111 S.Ct., at 1552. Where the encounter takes place is one factor, but it is not the only one. And, as the Solicitor General correctly observes, an individual may decline an officer's request without fearing prosecution. See Brief for United States as Amicus Curiae 25. We have consistently held that a refusal to cooperate, without more, does not furnish the minimal level of objective justification needed for a detention or seizure. See Delgado, supra, 466 U.S., at 216–217, 104 S.Ct., at 1762–1763; Royer, 460 U.S., at 498, 103 S.Ct., at 1324 (plurality opinion); Brown v. Texas, 443 U.S. 47, 52–53, 99 S.Ct. 2637, 2641–2642, 61 L.Ed.2d 357 (1979).

The facts of this case, as described by the Florida Supreme Court, leave some doubt ****2388** whether a seizure occurred. Two officers walked up to Bostick on the bus, asked him a few questions, and asked if they could search his bags. As we have explained, no seizure occurs when police ask questions of an individual, ask to examine the individual's identification, and request consent to search his or her luggage—so long as the officers do not convey a message that compliance with their requests is required. Here, the facts recited by the Florida Supreme Court indicate that the officers did not point guns at Bostick or otherwise threaten him and that they specifically advised Bostick that he could refuse consent.

Nevertheless, we refrain from deciding whether or not a seizure occurred in this case. The trial court made no express findings of fact, and the Florida Supreme Court rested its decision on a single fact—that the encounter took place on a bus—rather than on the totality of the circumstances. We remand so that the Florida courts may evaluate the seizure question under the correct legal standard. We do reject, however, Bostick's argument that he must have been seized ***438** because no reasonable person would freely consent to a search of luggage that he or she knows contains drugs. This argument cannot prevail because the "reasonable person" test presupposes an innocent person. See Royer, supra, 460 U.S., at 519, n. 4, 103 S.Ct., at 1335, n. 4 (BLACKMUN, J., dissenting) ("The fact that [respondent] knew the search was likely to turn up contraband is of course irrelevant; the potential intrusiveness of the officers' conduct must be judged from the viewpoint of an innocent person in [his] position"). Accord, Chesternut, 486 U.S., at 574, 108 S.Ct., at 1980 ("This 'reasonable person' standard ... ensures that the scope of Fourth Amendment protection does not vary with the state of mind of the particular individual being approached").

The dissent characterizes our decision as holding that police may board buses and by an "intimidating show of authority," post, at 2393 (emphasis added), demand of passengers their "voluntary" cooperation. That characterization is incorrect. Clearly, a bus passenger's decision to cooperate with law enforcement officers authorizes the police to conduct a search without first obtaining a warrant only if the cooperation is voluntary. "Consent" that is the product of official intimidation or harassment is not consent at all. Citizens do not forfeit their constitutional rights when they are coerced to comply with a request that they would prefer to refuse. The question to be decided by the Florida courts on remand is whether Bostick chose to permit the search of his luggage.

The dissent also attempts to characterize our decision as applying a lesser degree of constitutional protection to those individuals who travel by bus, rather than by other forms of transportation. This, too, is an erroneous characterization. Our Fourth Amendment inquiry in this case—whether a reasonable person would have felt free to decline the officers' requests or otherwise terminate the encounter—applies equally to police encounters that take place on trains, planes, and city streets. It is the dissent that would single out this particular ***439** mode of travel for differential treatment by adopting a per se rule that random bus searches are unconstitutional.

The dissent reserves its strongest criticism for the proposition that police officers can approach individuals as to whom they have no reasonable suspicion and ask them potentially incriminating questions. But this proposition is by no means novel; it has been endorsed by the Court any number of times. Terry, Royer, Rodriguez, and Delgado are just a few examples. As we have explained, today's decision follows logically from those decisions and breaks no new ground. Unless the dissent advocates overruling a long, unbroken line of decisions dating back more than 20 years, its criticism is not well taken.

****2389** This Court, as the dissent correctly observes, is not empowered to suspend constitutional guarantees so that the Government may more effectively wage a "war on drugs." See post, at 2389, 2394–2395. If that war is to be fought, those who fight it must respect the rights of individuals, whether or not those individuals are suspected of having committed a crime. By the same token, this Court is not empowered to forbid law enforcement practices simply because it considers them distasteful. The Fourth Amendment proscribes unreasonable searches and seizures; it does not proscribe voluntary cooperation. The cramped confines of a bus are one relevant factor that should be considered in evaluating whether a passenger's consent is voluntary. We cannot agree, however, with the Florida Supreme Court that this single factor will be dispositive in every case.

We adhere to the rule that, in order to determine whether a particular encounter constitutes a seizure, a court must consider all the circumstances surrounding the encounter to determine whether the police conduct would have communicated to a reasonable person that the person was not free to decline the officers' requests or otherwise terminate the encounter. That rule applies to encounters that take place on a city street or in an airport lobby, and it applies equally to ***440** encounters on a bus. The Florida Supreme Court erred in adopting a per se rule.

The judgment of the Florida Supreme Court is reversed, and the case is remanded for further proceedings not inconsistent with this opinion.

It is so ordered.

Justice MARSHALL, with whom Justice BLACKMUN and Justice STEVENS join, dissenting.

Our Nation, we are told, is engaged in a "war on drugs." No one disputes that it is the job of law-enforcement officials to devise effective weapons for fighting this war. But the effectiveness of a law-enforcement technique is not proof of its constitutionality. The general warrant, for example, was certainly an effective means of law enforcement. Yet it was one of the primary aims of the Fourth Amendment to protect citizens from the tyranny of being singled out for search and seizure without particularized suspicion notwithstanding the effectiveness of this method. See Boyd v. United States, 116 U.S. 616, 625–630, 6 S.Ct. 524, 529–532, 29 L.Ed. 746 (1886); see also Harris v. United States, 331 U.S. 145, 171, 67 S.Ct. 1098, 1111, 91 L.Ed. 1399 (1947) (Frankfurter, J., dissenting). In my view, the law-enforcement technique with which we are confronted in this case—the suspicionless police sweep of buses in intrastate or interstate travel—bears all of the indicia of coercion and unjustified intrusion associated with the general warrant. Because I believe that the bus sweep at issue in this case violates the core values of the Fourth Amendment, I dissent.

I

At issue in this case is a "new and increasingly common tactic in the war on drugs": the suspicionless police sweep of buses in interstate or intrastate travel. United States v. Lewis, 287 U.S.App.D.C. 306, 307, 921 F.2d 1294, 1295 (1990); see United States v. Flowers, 912 F.2d 707, 710 (CA4 1990) (describing technique in Charlotte, North Carolina); United States v. Madison, 936 F.2d 90, 91 (CA 2 1991) (describing ***441** technique in Port Authority terminal in New York City); United States v. Chandler, 744 F.Supp. 333, 335 (DC 1990) ("[I]t has become routine to subject interstate travelers to warrantless searches and intimidating interviews while sitting aboard a bus stopped for a short layover in the Capital"); 554 So.2d 1153, 1156–1157 (Fla.1989) (describing Florida police policy of " 'working the buses' "); see also ante, at 2384. Typically under this technique, a group of state or federal officers will board a bus while it is stopped at an intermediate ****2390** point on its route. Often displaying badges, weapons or other indicia of authority, the officers identify themselves and announce their purpose to intercept drug traffickers. They proceed to approach individual passengers, requesting them to show identification, produce their tickets, and explain the purpose of their travels. Never do the officers advise the passengers that they are free not to speak with the officers. An "interview" of this type ordinarily culminates in a request for consent to search the passenger's luggage. See generally United States v. Lewis, supra, 287 U.S.App.D.C., at 308, 921 F.2d, at 1296; United States v. Flowers, supra, at 708–709; United States v. Madison, supra, at 91; 554 So. 2d, at 1154.

These sweeps are conducted in "dragnet" style. The police admittedly act without an "articulable suspicion" in deciding which buses to board and which passengers to approach for interviewing.1 By proceeding systematically in this ***442** fashion, the police are able to engage in a tremendously high volume of searches. See, e.g., Florida v. Kerwick, 512 So.2d 347, 348–349 (Fla.App.1987) (single officer employing sweep technique able to search over 3,000 bags in nine-month period). The percentage of successful drug interdictions is low. See United States v. Flowers, supra, at 710 (sweep of 100 buses resulted in seven arrests).

To put it mildly, these sweeps "are inconvenient, intrusive, and intimidating." United States v. Chandler, 744 F.Supp., at 335. They occur within cramped confines, with officers typically placing themselves in between the passenger selected for an interview and the exit of the bus. See, e.g., id., at 336. Because the bus is only temporarily stationed at a point short of its destination, the passengers are in no position to leave as a means of evading the officers' questioning. Undoubtedly, such a sweep holds up the progress of the bus. See United States v. Fields, 909 F.2d 470, 474 n. 2 (CA11 1990); cf. United States v. Rembert, 694 F.Supp. 163, 175 (WDNC 1988) (reporting testimony of officer that he makes " 'every effort in the world not to delay the bus' " but that the driver does not leave terminal until sweep is complete). Thus, this "new and increasingly common tactic," United States v. Lewis, supra, 287 U.S.App.D.C., at 307, 921 F.2d, at 1295, burdens the experience of traveling by bus with a degree of governmental interference to which, until now, our society has been proudly unaccustomed. See, e.g., State ex rel. Ekstrom v. Justice Court, 136 Ariz. 1, 6, 663 P.2d 992, 997 (1983) (Feldman, J., concurring) ("The thought that an American can be compelled to 'show his papers' before exercising his right to walk the streets, drive the highways or board the trains is repugnant to American institutions and ideals").

***443** This aspect of the suspicionless sweep has not been lost on many of the lower courts called upon to review the constitutionality of this practice. Remarkably, the courts located at the heart of the "drug war" have been the most adamant in condemning this technique. As one Florida court put it:

****2391** " '[T]he evidence in this cause has evoked images of other days, under other flags, when no man traveled his nation's roads or railways without fear of unwarranted interruption, by individuals who held temporary power in the Government. The spectre of American citizens being asked, by badge-wielding police, for identification, travel papers—in short a raison d'etre—is foreign to any fair reading of the Constitution, and its guarantee of human liberties. This is not Hitler's Berlin, nor Stalin's Moscow, nor is it white supremacist South Africa. Yet in Broward County, Florida, these police officers approach every person on board buses and trains ("that time permits") and check identification [and] tickets, [and] ask to search luggage—all in the name of "voluntary cooperation" with law enforcement....' " 554 So.2d, at 1158, quoting State v. Kerwick, supra, at 348–349 (quoting trial court order).

The District Court for the District of Columbia spoke in equally pointed words:

"It seems rather incongruous at this point in the world's history that we find totalitarian states becoming more like our free society while we in this nation are taking on their former trappings of suppressed liberties and freedoms."

. . . . .

"The random indiscriminate stopping and questioning of individuals on interstate busses seems to have gone too far. If this Court approves such 'bus stops' and allows prosecutions to be based on evidence seized as a result of such 'stops,' then we will have stripped our ***444** citizens of basic Constitutional protections. Such action would be inconsistent with what this nation has stood for during its 200 years of existence. If passengers on a bus passing through the Capital of this great nation cannot be free from police interference where there is absolutely no basis for the police officers to stop and question them, then the police will be free to accost people on our streets without any reason or cause. In this 'anything goes' war on drugs, random knocks on the doors of our citizens' homes seeking 'consent' to search for drugs cannot be far away. This is not America." United States v. Lewis, 728 F.Supp. 784, 788–789, rev'd, 287 U.S.App.D.C. 306, 921 F.2d 1294 (1990).

See also United States v. Alexander, 755 F.Supp. 448, 453 (DC 1991); United States v. Madison, 744 F.Supp. 490, 495–497 (SDNY 1990), rev'd, 936 F.2d 90 (CA2 1991); United States v. Chandler, supra, at 335–336; United States v. Mark, 742 F.-Supp. 17, 18–19 (DC 1990); United States v. Alston, 742 F.Supp. 13, 15 (DC 1990); United States v. Cothran, 729 F.Supp. 153, 156–158 (DC 1990), rev'd, 287 U.S.Ap-p.D.C. 306, 921 F.2d 1294 (1990); United States v. Felder, 732 F.Supp. 204, 209 (DC 1990).

The question for this Court, then, is whether the suspicionless, dragnet-style sweep of buses in intrastate and interstate travel is consistent with the Fourth Amendment. The majority suggests that this latest tactic in the drug war is perfectly compatible with the Constitution. I disagree.

II

I have no objection to the manner in which the majority frames the test for determining whether a suspicionless bus sweep amounts to a Fourth Amendment "seizure." I agree that the appropriate question is whether a passenger who is approached during such a sweep "would feel free to decline the officers' requests or otherwise terminate the encounter." ***445** Ante, at 2387. What I cannot understand is how the majority can possibly suggest an affirmative answer to this question.

The majority reverses what it characterizes as the Florida Supreme Court's "per se rule" against suspicionless encounters between the police and bus passengers, see ante, at 2385, 2386–2389, suggesting only in dictum its "doubt" that a seizure occurred on the facts of this case, see ante, at 2387. However, the notion that the Florida Supreme **2392 Court decided this case on the basis of any "per se rule" independent of the facts of this case is wholly a product of the majority's imagination. As the majority acknowledges, the Florida Supreme Court "stated explicitly the factual premise for its decision." Ante, at 2384. This factual premise contained all of the details of the encounter between respondent and the police. See 554 So.2d, at 1154; ante, at 2384–2385. The lower court's analysis of whether respondent was seized drew heavily on these facts, and the court repeatedly emphasized that its conclusion was based on "all the circumstances" of this case. 554 So.2d, at 1157 (emphasis added); see ibid. ("Here, the circumstances indicate that the officers effectively 'seized' [respondent]" (emphasis added)).

The majority's conclusion that the Florida Supreme Court, contrary to all appearances, ignored these facts is based solely on the failure of the lower court to expressly incorporate all of the facts into its reformulation of the certified question on which respondent took his appeal. See ante, at 2385.2 The majority never explains the basis of its implausible assumption that the Florida Supreme Court intended its phrasing of the certified question to trump its opinion's careful treatment of the facts in this case. Certainly, when this Court issues an opinion, it does not intend lower courts and *446 parties to treat as irrelevant the analysis of facts that the parties neglected to cram into the question presented in the petition for certiorari. But in any case, because the issue whether a seizure has occurred in any given factual setting is a question of law, see United States v. Mendenhall, 446 U.S. 544, 554–555, 100 S.Ct. 1870, 1877–1878, 64 L.Ed.2d 497 (1980) (opinion of Stewart, J.); United States v. Maragh, 282 U.S.App.D.C. 256, 258–259, 894 F.2d 415, 417–418 (CADC), cert. denied, 498 U.S. 880, 111 S.Ct. 214, 112 L.Ed.2d 174 (1990), nothing prevents this Court from deciding on its own whether a seizure occurred based on all of the facts of this case as they appear in the opinion of the Florida Supreme Court.

These facts exhibit all of the elements of coercion associated with a typical bus sweep. Two officers boarded the Greyhound bus on which respondent was a passenger while the bus, en route from Miami to Atlanta, was on a brief stop to pick up passengers in Fort Lauderdale. The officers made a visible display of their badges and wore bright green "raid" jackets bearing the insignia of the Broward County Sheriff's Department; one held a gun in a recognizable weapons pouch. See 554 So. 2d, at 1154, 1157. These facts alone constitute an intimidating "show of authority." See Michigan v. Chesternut, 486 U.S. 567, 575, 108 S.Ct. 1975, 1980, 100 L.Ed.2d 565 (1988) (display of weapon contributes to coercive environment); United States v. Mendenhall, supra, 446 U.S., at 554, 100 S.Ct., at 1877 (opinion of Stewart, J.) ("threatening presence of several officers" and "display of a weapon"); id., at 555, 100 S.Ct., at 1877 (uniformed attire). Once on board, the officers approached respondent, who was sitting in the back of the bus, identified themselves as narcotics officers and began to question him. See 554 So.2d, at 1154. One officer stood in front of respondent's seat, partially blocking the narrow aisle through which respondent would have been required to pass to reach the exit of the bus. See id., at 1157.

As far as is revealed by facts on which the Florida Supreme Court premised its decision, the officers did not advise respondent that he was free to break off this "interview." Inexplicably, the majority repeatedly stresses the trial court's *447 implicit finding that the police officers advised respondent that he was free to refuse permission to search his travel bag. **2393 See ante, at 2385, 2387–2388. This aspect of the exchange between respondent and the police is completely irrelevant to the issue before us. For as the State concedes, and as the majority purports to "accept," id., at 2385–2386, if respondent was unlawfully seized when the officers approached him and initiated questioning, the resulting search was likewise unlawful no matter how well advised respondent was of his right to refuse it. See Florida v. Royer, 460 U.S. 491, 501, 507–508, 103 S.Ct. 1319, 1326, 1329–1330, 75 L.Ed.2d 229 (1983) (plurality opinion); Wong Sun v. United States, 371 U.S. 471, 83 S.Ct. 407, 9 L.Ed.2d 441 (1963). Consequently, the issue is not whether a passenger in respondent's position would have felt free to deny consent to the search of his bag, but whether such a passenger—without being apprised of his rights—would have felt free to terminate the antecedent encounter with the police.

Unlike the majority, I have no doubt that the answer to this question is no. Apart from trying to accommodate the officers, respondent had only two options. First, he could have remained seated while obstinately refusing to respond to the officers' questioning. But in light of the intimidating show of authority that the officers made upon boarding the bus, respondent reasonably could have believed that such behavior would only arouse the officers' suspicions and intensify their interrogation. Indeed, officers who carry out bus sweeps like the one at issue here frequently admit that this is the effect of a passenger's refusal to cooperate. See, e.g., United States v. Cothran, 729 F.Supp., at 156; United States v. Felder, 732 F.Supp., at 205. The majority's observation that a mere refusal to answer questions, "without more," does not give rise to a reasonable basis for seizing a passenger, ante, at 2387, is utterly beside the point, because a passenger unadvised of his rights and otherwise unversed in constitutional law has no reason to know that the police cannot hold his refusal to cooperate against him.

***448** Second, respondent could have tried to escape the officers' presence by leaving the bus altogether. But because doing so would have required respondent to squeeze past the gun-wielding inquisitor who was blocking the aisle of the bus, this hardly seems like a course that respondent reasonably would have viewed as available to him.3 The majority lamely protests that nothing in the stipulated facts shows that the questioning officer "point [ed] [his] gu[n] at [respondent] or otherwise threaten [ed] him" with the weapon. Ante, at 2388 (emphasis added). Our decisions recognize the obvious point, however, that the choice of the police to "display" their weapons during an encounter exerts significant coercive pressure on the confronted citizen. E.g., Michigan v. Chesternut, supra, 486 U.S., at 575, 108 S.Ct., at 1980; United States v. Mendenhall, supra, 446 U.S., at 554, 100 S.Ct., at 1877. We have never suggested that the police must go so far as to put a citizen in immediate apprehension of being shot before a court can take account of the intimidating effect of being questioned by an officer with weapon in hand.

Even if respondent had perceived that the officers would let him leave the bus, moreover, he could not reasonably have been expected to resort to this means of evading their intrusive questioning. For so far as respondent knew, the bus's departure from the terminal was imminent. Unlike a person approached by the police on the street, see Michigan v. Chesternut, supra, or at a bus or airport terminal after reaching his destination, see United States v. Mendenhall, supra, a passenger approached by the police at an intermediate point in a long bus journey cannot simply leave the scene and repair to a safe haven to avoid unwanted probing by law-enforcement officials. The vulnerability ****2394** that an intrastate or interstate traveler experiences when confronted by the police outside of his "own familiar territory" surely aggravates ***449** the coercive quality of such an encounter. See Schneckloth v. Bustamonte, 412 U.S. 218, 247, 93 S.Ct. 2041, 2058, 36 L.Ed.2d 854 (1973).

The case on which the majority primarily relies, INS v. Delgado, 466 U.S. 210, 104 S.Ct. 1758, 80 L.Ed.2d 247 (1984), is distinguishable in every relevant respect. In Delgado, this Court held that workers approached by law-enforcement officials inside of a factory were not "seized" for purposes of the Fourth Amendment. The Court was careful to point out, however, that the presence of the agents did not furnish the workers with a reasonable basis for believing that they were not free to leave the factory, as at least some of them did. See id., at 218–219, and n. 7, 104 S.Ct., at 1763–1764, and n. 7. Unlike passengers confronted by law-enforcement officials on a bus stopped temporarily at an intermediate point in its journey, workers approached by law-enforcement officials at their workplace need not abandon personal belongings and venture into unfamiliar environs in order to avoid unwanted questioning. Moreover, the workers who did not leave the building in Delgado remained free to move about the entire factory, see id., at 218, 104 S.Ct., at 1763, a considerably less confining environment than a bus. Finally, contrary to the officer who confronted respondent, the law-enforcement officials in Delgado did not conduct their interviews with guns in hand. See id., at 212, 104 S.Ct., at 1760.

Rather than requiring the police to justify the coercive tactics employed here, the majority blames respondent for his own sensation of constraint. The majority concedes that respondent "did not feel free to leave the bus" as a means of breaking off the interrogation by the Broward County officers. Ante, at 2387. But this experience of confinement, the majority explains, "was the natural result of his decision to take the bus." Ibid. (emphasis added). Thus, in the majority's view, because respondent's "freedom of movement was restricted by a factor independent of police conduct—i.e., by his being a passenger on a bus," ante, at 2387—respondent was not seized for purposes of the Fourth Amendment.

***450** This reasoning borders on sophism and trivializes the values that underlie the Fourth Amendment. Obviously, a person's "voluntary decision" to place himself in a room with only one exit does not authorize the police to force an encounter upon him by placing themselves in front of the exit. It is no more acceptable for the police to force an encounter on a person by exploiting his "voluntary decision" to expose himself to perfectly legitimate personal or social constraints. By consciously deciding to single out persons who have undertaken interstate or intrastate travel, officers who conduct suspicionless, dragnet-style sweeps put passengers to the choice of cooperating or of exiting their buses and possibly being stranded in unfamiliar locations. It is exactly because this "choice" is no "choice" at all that police engage this technique.

In my view, the Fourth Amendment clearly condemns the suspicionless, dragnet-style sweep of intrastate or interstate buses. Withdrawing this particular weapon from the government's drug-war arsenal would hardly leave the police without any means of combatting the use of buses as instrumentalities of the drug trade. The police would remain free, for example, to approach passengers whom they have a reasonable, articulable basis to suspect of criminal wrongdoing.4 Alternatively, they could continue to confront passengers without suspicion so long as they took simple steps, like advising the passengers confronted of their right to decline to be questioned, to dispel the aura of coercion and ****2395** intimidation that pervades such encounters. There is no reason to expect that such requirements would render the Nation's buses law-enforcement-free zones.

III

The majority attempts to gloss over the violence that today's decision does to the Fourth Amendment with empty admonitions. "If th[e] [war on drugs] is to be fought," the majority ***451** intones, "those who fight it must respect the rights of individuals, whether or not those individuals are suspected of having committed a crime." Ante, at 2389. The majority's actions, however, speak louder than its words.

I dissent.

Black Letter Law

> The Court held that random bus searches conducted pursuant to passenger's consent are not per-se unconstitutional, and the question of whether police, without articulable suspicion, could board bus and ask at random for and receive consent to search passenger's luggage when they advised passenger that he had right to refuse consent to search depended upon whether or not the officer's request to search bus passenger's luggage was so coercive as to vitiate that consent. The Court did not focus on whether or not a reasonable person would feel free to leave, but rather whether he would feel free to decline officer's requests or otherwise to terminate encounter; "free to leave" test does not apply where party's freedom of movement is restricted by factor independent of police conduct, e.g., by his being a passenger on bus.

California v. Hodari

111 S.Ct. 1547

Supreme Court of the United States

CALIFORNIA, Petitioner

v.

HODARI D.

No. 89–1632. | Argued Jan. 14, 1991. | Decided April 23, 1991.

Justice SCALIA delivered the opinion of the Court.

Late one evening in April 1988, Officers Brian McColgin and Jerry Pertoso were on patrol in a high-crime area of Oakland, California. They were dressed in street clothes but wearing jackets with "Police" embossed on both front and back. Their unmarked car proceeded west on Foothill Boulevard, and turned south onto 63rd Avenue. As they rounded the corner, they saw four or five youths huddled around a small red car parked at the curb. When the youths saw the officers' car approaching they apparently panicked, and took flight. The respondent here, Hodari D., and one companion ran west through an alley; the others fled south. The red car also headed south, at a high rate of speed.

The officers were suspicious and gave chase. McColgin remained in the car and continued south on 63rd Avenue; Pertoso left the car, ran back north along 63rd, then west on Foothill Boulevard, and turned south on 62nd Avenue. Hodari, meanwhile, emerged from the alley onto 62nd and ran north. Looking behind as he ran, he did not turn and see Pertoso until the officer was almost upon him, whereupon he tossed away what appeared to be a small rock. A moment later, Pertoso tackled Hodari, handcuffed him, and radioed for assistance. Hodari was found to be carrying $130 in cash and a pager; and the rock he had discarded was found to be crack cocaine.

In the juvenile proceeding brought against him, Hodari moved to suppress the evidence relating to the cocaine. The court denied the motion without opinion. The California Court of Appeal reversed, holding that Hodari had been "seized" when he saw Officer Pertoso running towards him, that this seizure was unreasonable under the Fourth Amendment, and that the evidence of cocaine had to be suppressed as the fruit of that illegal seizure. The California Supreme Court denied the State's application for review. We granted certiorari. 498 U.S. 807, 111 S.Ct. 38, 112 L.Ed.2d 15 (1990).

As this case comes to us, the only issue presented is whether, at the time he dropped the drugs, Hodari had been "seized" within the meaning of the Fourth Amendment.

If so, respondent argues, the drugs were the fruit of that seizure and the evidence concerning them was properly excluded. If not, the drugs were abandoned by Hodari and lawfully recovered by the police, and the evidence should have been admitted. (In addition, of course, Pertoso's seeing the rock of cocaine, at least if he recognized it as such, would provide reasonable suspicion for the unquestioned seizure that occurred when he tackled Hodari. Cf. Rios v. United States, 364 U.S. 253, 80 S.Ct. 1431, 4 L.Ed.2d 1688 (1960).)

We have long understood that the Fourth Amendment's protection against "unreasonable ... seizures" includes seizure of the person, see Henry v. United States, 361 U.S. 98, 100, 80 S.Ct. 168, 170, 4 L.Ed.2d 134 (1959). From the time of the founding to the present, the word "seizure" has meant a "taking possession," 2 N. Webster, An American Dictionary of the English Language 67 (1828); 2 J. Bouvier, A Law Dictionary 510 (6th ed. 1856); Webster's Third New International Dictionary 2057 (1981). For most purposes at common law, the word connoted not merely grasping, or applying physical force to, the animate or inanimate object in ****1550** question, but actually bringing it within physical control. A ship still fleeing, even though under attack, would not be considered to have been seized as a war prize. Cf. The Josefa Segunda, 10 Wheat. 312, 325–326, 6 L.Ed. 320 (1825). A res capable of manual delivery was not seized until "tak[en] into custody." Pelham v. Rose, 9 Wall. 103, 106, 19 L.Ed. 602 (1870). To constitute an arrest, however—the quintessential "seizure of the person" under our Fourth Amendment jurisprudence—the mere grasping or application of physical force with lawful authority, whether or not it succeeded in subduing the arrestee, was sufficient. See, e.g., Whitehead v. Keyes, 85 Mass. 495, 501 (1862) ("[A]n officer effects an arrest of a person whom he has authority to arrest, by laying his hand on him for the purpose of arresting him, though he may not succeed in stopping and holding him"); 1 Restatement of Torts § 41, Comment h (1934). As one commentator has described it:

"There can be constructive detention, which will constitute an arrest, although the party is never actually brought within the physical control of the party making an arrest. This is accomplished by merely touching, however slightly, the body of the accused, by the party making the arrest and for that purpose, although he does not succeed in stopping or holding him even for an instant; as where the bailiff had tried to arrest one who fought him off by a fork, the court said, 'If the bailiff had touched him, that had been an arrest....' " A. Cornelius, Search and Seizure 163–164 (2d ed. 1930) (footnote omitted).

To say that an arrest is effected by the slightest application of physical force, despite the arrestee's escape, is not to say that for Fourth Amendment purposes there is a continuing arrest during the period of fugitivity. If, for example, Pertoso had laid his hands upon Hodari to arrest him, but Hodari had broken away and had then cast away the cocaine, it would hardly be realistic to say that that disclosure had been made during the course of an arrest. Cf. Thompson v. Whitman, 18 Wall. 457, 471, 21 L.Ed. 897 (1874) ("A seizure is a single act, and not a continuous fact"). The present case, however, is even one step further removed. It does not involve the application of any physical force; Hodari was untouched by Officer Pertoso at the time he discarded the cocaine. His defense relies instead upon the proposition that a seizure occurs "when the officer, by means of physical force or show of authority, has in some way restrained the liberty of a citizen." Terry v. Ohio, 392 U.S. 1, 19, n. 16, 88 S.Ct. 1868, 1879, n. 16, 20 L.Ed.2d 889 (1968) (emphasis added). Hodari contends (and we accept as true for purposes of this decision) that Pertoso's pursuit qualified as a "show of authority" calling upon Hodari to halt. The narrow question before us is whether, with respect to a show of authority as with respect to application of physical force, a seizure occurs even though the subject does not yield. We hold that it does not.

The language of the Fourth Amendment, of course, cannot sustain respondent's contention. The word "seizure" readily bears the meaning of a laying on of hands or application of physical force to restrain movement, even when it is ultimately unsuccessful. ("She seized the purse-snatcher, but he broke out of her grasp.") It does not remotely apply, however, to the prospect of a policeman yelling "Stop, in the name of the law!" at a fleeing form that continues to flee. That is no seizure. Nor can the result respondent wishes to achieve be produced— **1551 indirectly, as it were—by suggesting that Pertoso's uncomplied-with show of authority was a common-law arrest, and then appealing to the principle that all common-law arrests are seizures. An arrest requires either physical force (as described above) or, where that is absent, submission to the assertion of authority.

"Mere words will not constitute an arrest, while, on the other hand, no actual, physical touching is essential. The apparent inconsistency in the two parts of this statement is explained by the fact that an assertion of authority and purpose to arrest followed by submission of the arrestee constitutes an arrest. There can be no arrest without either touching or submission." Perkins, The Law of Arrest, 25 Iowa L.Rev. 201, 206 (1940) (footnotes omitted).

We do not think it desirable, even as a policy matter, to stretch the Fourth Amendment beyond its words and beyond the meaning of arrest, as respondent urges.3 Street pursuits always place the public at some risk, and compliance with police orders to stop should therefore be encouraged. Only a few of those orders, we must presume, will be without adequate basis, and since the addressee has no ready means of identifying the deficient ones it almost invariably is the responsible course to comply. Unlawful orders will not be deterred, moreover, by sanctioning through the exclusionary rule those of them that are not obeyed. Since policemen do not command "Stop!" expecting to be ignored, or give chase hoping to be outrun, it fully suffices to apply the deterrent to their genuine, successful seizures.

Respondent contends that his position is sustained by the so-called Mendenhall test, formulated by Justice Stewart's opinion in United States v. Mendenhall, 446 U.S. 544, 554, 100 S.Ct. 1870, 1877, 64 L.Ed.2d 497 (1980), and adopted by the Court in later cases, see Michigan v. Chesternut, 486 U.S. 567, 573, 108 S.Ct. 1975, 1979, 100 L.Ed.2d 565 (1988); INS v. Delgado, 466 U.S. 210, 215, 104 S.Ct. 1758, 1762, 80 L.Ed.2d 247 (1984): "[A] person has been 'seized' within the meaning of the Fourth Amendment only if, in view of all the circumstances surrounding the incident, a reasonable person would have believed that he was not free to leave." 446 U.S., at 554, 100 S.Ct., at 1877. See also Florida v. Royer, 460 U.S. 491, 502, 103 S.Ct. 1319, 1326–1327, 75 L.Ed.2d 229 (1983) (opinion of WHITE, J.). In seeking to rely upon that test here, respondent fails to read it carefully. It says that a person has been seized "only if," not that he has been seized "whenever"; it states a necessary, but not a sufficient, condition for seizure—or, more precisely, for seizure effected through a "show of authority." Mendenhall establishes that the test for existence of a "show of authority" is an objective one: not whether the citizen perceived that he was being ordered to restrict his movement, but whether the officer's words and actions would have conveyed that to a reasonable person. Application of this objective test was the basis for our decision in the other case principally **1552 relied upon by respondent, Chesternut, supra, where we concluded that the police cruiser's slow following of the defendant did not convey the message that he was not free to disregard the police and go about his business. We did not address in Chesternut, however, the question whether, if the Mendenhall test was met—if the message that the defendant was not free to leave had been conveyed—a Fourth Amendment seizure would have occurred. See 486 U.S., at 577, 108 S.Ct., at 1981 (KENNEDY, J., concurring).

Quite relevant to the present case, however, was our decision in Brower v. Inyo County, 489 U.S. 593, 596, 109 S.Ct. 1378, 1381, 103 L.Ed.2d 628 (1989). In that case, police cars with flashing lights had chased the decedent for 20 miles—surely an adequate "show of authority"—but he did not stop until his fatal crash into a police-erected blockade. The issue was whether his death could be held to be the consequence of an unreasonable seizure in violation of the Fourth Amendment. We did not even consider the possibility that a seizure could have occurred during the course of the chase because, as we explained, that "show of authority" did not produce his stop. Id., at 597, 109 S.Ct., at 1381. And we discussed, ibid., an opinion of Justice Holmes, involving a situation not much different from the present case, where revenue agents had picked up containers dropped by moonshiners whom they were pursuing without adequate warrant. The containers were not excluded as the product of an unlawful seizure because "[t]he defendant's own acts, and those of his associates, disclosed the jug, the jar and the bottle—and there was no seizure in the sense of the law when the officers examined the contents of each after they had been abandoned." Hester v. United States, 265 U.S. 57, 58, 44 S.Ct. 445, 446, 68 L.Ed. 898 (1924). The same is true here.

In sum, assuming that Pertoso's pursuit in the present case constituted a "show of authority" enjoining Hodari to halt, since Hodari did not comply with that injunction he was not seized until he was tackled. The cocaine abandoned while he was running was in this case not the fruit of a seizure, and his motion to exclude evidence of it was properly denied. We reverse the decision of the California Court of Appeal, and remand for further proceedings not inconsistent with this opinion.

It is so ordered.

(The dissent of Justice STEVENS, with whom Justice MARSHALL joins, is omitted.)

Black Letter Law

> The Court held that juvenile was not seized until police officer tackled him because even though police officer demonstrated a show of authority when he chased the defendant in pursuit, the defendant did not submit to the show of authority until he was tackled. Therefore, the cocaine abandoned while juvenile was running was not fruit of the seizure. In order for "seizure" to have occurred, there must either be some application of physical force, even if extremely slight, or a show of authority to which the subject yields; a show of authority, without any application of physical force, to which the subject does not yield is not a "seizure."

Michigan v. Long

103 S.Ct. 3469

Supreme Court of the United States

MICHIGAN, Petitioner

v.

David Kerk LONG.

No. 82–256. | Argued Feb. 23, 1983. | Decided July 6, 1983.

Justice O'CONNOR delivered the opinion of the Court.

In Terry v. Ohio, 392 U.S. 1, 88 S.Ct. 1868, 20 L.Ed.2d 889 (1968), we upheld the validity of a protective search for weapons in the absence of probable cause to arrest because it is unreasonable to deny a police officer the right "to neutralize the threat of physical harm," id., at 24, 88 S.Ct., at 1881, when he possesses an articulable suspicion that an individual is armed and dangerous. We did not, however, expressly address whether such a protective search for weapons could extend to an area beyond the person in the absence of probable cause to arrest. In the present case, respondent David Long was convicted for possession of marijuana found by police in the passenger compartment and trunk of the ***1035** automobile that he was driving. The police searched the passenger compartment because they had reason to believe that the vehicle contained weapons potentially dangerous to the officers. We hold that the protective search of the passenger compartment was reasonable under the principles articulated in Terry and other decisions of this Court. We also examine Long's argument that the decision below rests upon an adequate and independent state ground, and we decide in favor of our jurisdiction.

I

Deputies Howell and Lewis were on patrol in a rural area one evening when, shortly after midnight, they observed a car traveling erratically and at excessive speed.1 The officers observed the car turning down a side road, where it swerved off into a shallow ditch. The officers stopped to investigate. Long, the only occupant of the automobile, met the deputies at the rear of the car, which was protruding ***1036** from the ditch onto the road. The door on the driver's side of the vehicle was left open.

Deputy Howell requested Long to produce his operator's license, but he did not respond. After the request was repeated, Long produced his license. Long again failed to respond when Howell requested him to produce the vehicle registration. After another repeated request, Long, whom Howell thought "appeared to be under the ****3474** influence of something," 413 Mich. 461, 469, 320 N.W.2d 866, 868 (1982), turned from the officers and began walking toward the open door of the vehicle. The officers followed Long and both observed a large hunting knife on the floorboard of the driver's side of the car. The officers then stopped Long's progress and subjected him to a Terry protective pat-down, which revealed no weapons.

Long and Deputy Lewis then stood by the rear of the vehicle while Deputy Howell shined his flashlight into the interior of the vehicle, but did not actually enter it. The purpose of Howell's action was "to search for other weapons." Id., 413 Mich. at 469, 320 N.W.2d, at 868. The officer noticed that something was protruding from under the armrest on the front seat. He knelt in the vehicle and lifted the armrest. He saw an open pouch on the front seat, and upon flashing his light on the pouch, determined that it contained what appeared to be marijuana. After Deputy Howell showed the pouch and its contents to Deputy Lewis, Long was arrested for possession of marijuana. A further search of the interior of the vehicle, including the glovebox, revealed neither more contraband nor the vehicle registration. The officers decided to impound the vehicle. Deputy Howell opened the trunk, which did not have a lock, and discovered inside it approximately 75 pounds of marijuana.

The Barry County Circuit Court denied Long's motion to suppress the marijuana taken from both the interior of the car and its trunk. He was subsequently convicted of possession of marijuana. The Michigan Court of Appeals affirmed Long's conviction, holding that the search of the passenger ***1037** compartment was valid as a protective search under Terry, supra, and that the search of the trunk was valid as an inventory search under South Dakota v. Opperman, 428 U.S. 364, 96 S.Ct. 3092, 49 L.Ed.2d 1000 (1976). See 94 Mich.App. 338, 288 N.W.2d 629 (1979). The Michigan Supreme Court reversed. The court held that "the sole justification of the Terry search, protection of the police officers and others nearby, cannot justify the search in this case." 413 Mich., at 472, 320 N.W.2d, at 869. The marijuana found in Long's trunk was considered by the court below to be the "fruit" of the illegal search of the interior, and was also suppressed.

We granted certiorari in this case to consider the important question of the authority of a police officer to protect himself by conducting a Terry-type search of the passenger compartment of a motor vehicle during the lawful investigatory stop of the occupant of the vehicle. 459 U.S. 904, 103 S.Ct. 205, 74 L.Ed.2d 164 (1982).

II

Before reaching the merits, we must consider Long's argument that we are without jurisdiction to decide this case because the decision below rests on an adequate and independent state ground. The court below referred twice to the state constitution in its opinion, but otherwise relied exclusively on federal law. Long argues that the Michigan ***1038** courts have provided greater protection from searches and seizures under the state constitution than is afforded under the Fourth Amendment, and the references to the state constitution therefore establish an adequate and independent ground for the decision below.

****3475** It is, of course, "incumbent upon this Court ... to ascertain for itself ... whether the asserted non-federal ground independently and adequately supports the judgment." Abie State Bank v. Bryan, 282 U.S. 765, 773, 51 S.Ct. 252, 255, 75 L.Ed. 690 (1931). Although we have announced a number of principles in order to help us determine whether various forms of references to state law constitute adequate and independent state grounds,4 we openly admit that we have thus far not developed a satisfying and consistent approach for resolving this vexing issue. In some instances, we have taken the strict view that if the ground of decision was at all unclear, we would dismiss the case. See, e.g., Lynch v. New York, 293 U.S. 52, 55 S.Ct. 16, 79 L.Ed. 191 (1934). In other instances, we have vacated, ***1039** see, e.g., Minnesota v. National Tea Co., 309 U.S. 551, 60 S.Ct. 676, 84 L.Ed. 20 (1940), or continued a case, see e.g., Herb v. Pitcairn, 324 U.S. 117, 65 S.Ct. 459, 89 L.Ed. 789 (1945), in order to obtain clarification about the nature of a state court decision. See also California v. Krivda, 409 U.S. 33, 93 S.Ct. 32, 34 L.Ed.2d 45 (1972). In more recent cases, we have ourselves examined state law to determine whether state courts have used federal law to guide their application of state law or to provide the actual basis for the decision that was reached. See Texas v. Brown, — U.S. ——, ——, 103 S.Ct. 1535, 1538, 75 L.Ed.2d 502 (1983) (plurality opinion). Cf. South Dakota v. Neville, ——U.S. ——, ——, 103 S.Ct. 916, 925, 74 L.Ed.2d 748 (1983) (STEVENS, J., dissenting). In Oregon v. Kennedy, 456 U.S. 667, 670–671, 102 S.Ct. 2083, 2086–2087, 72 L.Ed.2d 416 (1982), we rejected an invitation to remand to the state court for clarification even when the decision rested in part on a case from the state court, because we determined that the state case itself rested upon federal grounds. We added that "[e]ven if the case admitted of more doubt as to whether federal and state grounds for decision were intermixed, the fact that the state court relied to the extent it did on federal grounds requires us to reach the merits." Id., at 671, 102 S.Ct., at 2087.

This ad hoc method of dealing with cases that involve possible adequate and independent state grounds is antithetical to the doctrinal consistency that is required when sensitive issues of federal-state relations are involved. Moreover, none of the various methods of disposition that we have employed thus far recommends itself as the preferred method that we should apply to the exclusion of others, and we therefore determine that it is appropriate to reexamine our treatment of this jurisdictional issue in order to achieve the consistency that is necessary.

The process of examining state law is unsatisfactory because it requires us to interpret state laws with which we are generally unfamiliar, and which often, as in this case, have not been discussed at length ****3476** by the parties. Vacation and continuance for clarification have also been unsatisfactory both because of the delay and decrease in efficiency of judicial ***1040** administration, see Dixon v. Duffy, 344 U.S. 143, 73 S.Ct. 193, 97 L.Ed. 153 (1952),5 and, more important, because these methods of disposition place significant burdens on state courts to demonstrate the presence or absence of our jurisdiction. See Philadelphia Newspapers, Inc. v. Jerome, 434 U.S. 241, 244, 98 S.Ct. 546, 548, 54 L.Ed.2d 506 (1978) (REHNQUIST, J., dissenting); Department of Motor Vehicles v. Rios, 410 U.S. 425, 427, 93 S.Ct. 1019, 1021, 35 L.Ed.2d 398 (1973) (Douglas, J., dissenting). Finally, outright dismissal of cases is clearly not a panacea because it cannot be doubted that there is an important need for uniformity in federal law, and that this need goes unsatisfied when we fail to review an opinion that rests primarily upon federal grounds and where the independence of an alleged state ground is not apparent from the four corners of the opinion. We have long recognized that dismissal is inappropriate "where there is strong indication ... that the federal constitution as judicially construed controlled the decision below." National Tea Co., supra, 309 U.S., at 556, 60 S.Ct., at 679 (1940).

Respect for the independence of state courts, as well as avoidance of rendering advisory opinions, have been the cornerstones of this Court's refusal to decide cases where there is an adequate and independent state ground. It is precisely because of this respect for state courts, and this desire to avoid advisory opinions, that we do not wish to continue to decide issues of state law that go beyond the opinion that we review, or to require state courts to reconsider cases to clarify the grounds of their decisions. Accordingly, when, as in this case, a state court decision fairly appears to rest primarily on federal law, or to be interwoven with the federal law, and when the adequacy and independence of any possible ***1041** state law ground is not clear from the face of the opinion, we will accept as the most reasonable explanation that the state court decided the case the way it did because it believed that federal law required it to do so. If a state court chooses merely to rely on federal precedents as it would on the precedents of all other jurisdictions, then it need only make clear by a plain statement in its judgment or opinion that the federal cases are being used only for the purpose of guidance, and do not themselves compel the result that the court has reached. In this way, both justice and judicial administration will be greatly improved. If the state court decision indicates clearly and expressly that it is alternatively based on bona fide separate, adequate, and independent grounds, we, of course, will not undertake to review the decision.

This approach obviates in most instances the need to examine state law in order to decide the nature of the state court decision, and will at the same time avoid the danger of our rendering advisory opinions. It also avoids the unsatisfactory and intrusive practice of requiring state courts to clarify their decisions to the satisfaction of this Court. We believe that such an approach will provide state judges with a clearer opportunity to develop state jurisprudence unimpeded by federal interference, and yet will preserve the integrity of federal law. "It is fundamental that state courts be left free and unfettered by us in interpreting their state constitutions. But it is equally important that ambiguous or ****3477** obscure adjudications by state courts do not stand as barriers to a determination by this Court of the validity under the federal constitution of state action." National Tea Co., supra, 309 U.S., at 557, 60 S.Ct., at 679.

The principle that we will not review judgments of state courts that rest on adequate and independent state grounds ***1042** is based, in part, on "the limitations of our own jurisdiction." Herb v. Pitcairn, 324 U.S. 117, 125, 65 S.Ct. 459, 463, 89 L.Ed. 789 (1945).7 The jurisdictional concern is that we not "render an advisory opinion, and if the same judgment would be rendered by the state court after we corrected its views of federal laws, our review could amount to nothing more than an advisory opinion." Id., at 126, 65 S.Ct., at 463. Our requirement of a "plain statement" that a decision rests upon adequate and independent state grounds does not in any way authorize the rendering of advisory opinions. Rather, in determining, as we must, whether we have jurisdiction to review a case that is alleged to rest on adequate and independent state grounds, see Abie State Bank v. Bryan, supra, 282 U.S., at 773, 51 S.Ct., at 255, we merely assume that there are no such grounds when it is not clear from the opinion itself that the state court relied upon an adequate and independent state ground and when it fairly appears that the state court rested its decision primarily on federal law.

****3478 *1043** Our review of the decision below under this framework leaves us unconvinced that it rests upon an independent state ground. Apart from its two citations to the state constitution, the court below relied exclusively on its understanding of Terry and other federal cases. Not a single state case was cited to support the state court's holding that the search of the passenger compartment was unconstitutional.9 Indeed, ***1044** the court declared that the search in this case was unconstitutional because "[t]he Court of Appeals erroneously applied the principles of Terry v. Ohio ... to the search of the interior of the vehicle in this case." 413 Mich., at 471, 320 N.W.2d, at 869. The references to the state constitution in no way indicate that the decision below rested on grounds in any way independent from the state court's interpretation of federal law. Even if we accept that the Michigan constitution has been interpreted to provide independent protection for certain rights also secured under the Fourth Amendment, it fairly appears in this case that the Michigan Supreme Court rested its decision primarily on federal law.

Rather than dismissing the case, or requiring that the state court reconsider its decision on our behalf solely because of a mere possibility that an adequate and independent ground supports the judgment, we find that we have jurisdiction in the absence of a plain statement that the decision below rested on an adequate and independent state ground. It appears to us that the state court "felt compelled by what it understood to be federal constitutional considerations to construe ... its own law in the manner it did." Zacchini v. Scripps-Howard Broadcasting Co., 433 U.S. 562, 568, 97 S.Ct. 2849, 2854, 53 L.Ed.2d 965 (1977).10

***1045 **3479 III**

The court below held, and respondent Long contends, that Deputy Howell's entry into the vehicle cannot be justified under the principles set forth in Terry because "Terry authorized only a limited pat-down search of a person suspected of criminal activity" rather than a search of an area. ***1046** 413 Mich., at 472, 320 N.W.2d, at 869 (footnote omitted). Brief for Respondent, p. 10. Although Terry did involve the protective frisk of a person, we believe that the police action in this case is justified by the principles that we have already established in Terry and other cases.

In Terry, the Court examined the validity of a "stop and frisk" in the absence of probable cause and a warrant. The police officer in Terry detained several suspects to ascertain their identities after the officer had observed the suspects for a brief period of time and formed the conclusion that they were about to engage in criminal activity. Because the officer feared that the suspects were armed, he patted down the outside of the suspects' clothing and discovered two revolvers.

Examining the reasonableness of the officer's conduct in Terry,11 we held that there is " 'no ready test for determining reasonableness other than by balancing the need to search [or seize] against the invasion which the search [or seizure] entails.' " 392 U.S., at 21, 88 S.Ct., at 1879 (quoting Camara v. Municipal Court, 387 U.S. 523, 536–537, 87 S.Ct. 1727, 1734–1735, 18 L.Ed.2d 930 (1967)). Although the conduct of the officer in Terry involved a "severe, though brief, intrusion upon cherished personal security," 392 U.S., at 24–25, 88 S.Ct., at 1881–1882, ***1047** we found that the conduct was reasonable when we weighed the interest of the individual against the legitimate interest in "crime prevention and detection," id., at 22, 88 S.Ct., at 1880, and the "need for law enforcement officers to protect themselves and other prospective victims of violence in situations where they lack probable cause for an arrest." Id., at 24, 88 S.Ct., at 1881. When the officer has a reasonable belief "that the individual whose suspicious behavior he is investigating at close range is armed and presently dangerous to the officer or to others, it would appear to be clearly unreasonable to deny the officer the power to take necessary measures to determine whether the person is in fact carrying a weapon and to neutralize the threat of physical harm." Ibid.

Although Terry itself involved the stop and subsequent pat-down search of a person, we were careful to note that "[w]e need not develop at length in this case, however, the limitations which the Fourth Amendment places upon a protective search and seizure for weapons. These limitations will have to be developed in the ****3480** concrete factual circumstances of individual cases." Id., at 29, 88 S.Ct., at 1884. Contrary to Long's view, Terry need not be read as restricting the preventative search to the person of the detained suspect.

In two cases in which we applied Terry to specific factual situations, we recognized that investigative detentions involving suspects in vehicles are especially fraught with danger to police officers. In Pennsylvania v. Mimms, 434 U.S. 106, 98 S.Ct. 330, 54 L.Ed.2d 331 (1977), we held that police may order persons out of ***1048** an automobile during a stop for a traffic violation, and may frisk those persons for weapons if there is a reasonable belief that they are armed and dangerous. Our decision rested in part on the "inordinate risk confronting an officer as he approaches a person seated in an automobile." Id., at 110, 98 S.Ct., at 333. In Adams v. Williams, 407 U.S. 143, 92 S.Ct. 1921, 32 L.Ed.2d 612 (1972), we held that the police, acting on an informant's tip, may reach into the passenger compartment of an automobile to remove a gun from a driver's waistband even where the gun was not apparent to police from outside the car and the police knew of its existence only because of the tip. Again, our decision rested in part on our view of the danger presented to police officers in "traffic stop" and automobile situations.

Finally, we have also expressly recognized that suspects may injure police officers and others by virtue of their access to weapons, even though they may not themselves be armed. In the Term following Terry, we decided Chimel v. California, 395 U.S. 752, 89 S.Ct. 2034, 23 L.Ed.2d 685 (1969), which involved the limitations imposed on police authority to conduct a search incident to a valid arrest. Relying explicitly on Terry, we held that when an arrest is made, it is reasonable for the arresting officer to search "the arrestee's person and the area 'within his immediate control'—construing that phrase to mean the area from within which he might gain possession of a weapon or destructible evidence." Id., at 763, 89 S.Ct., at 2040. We reasoned that "[a] gun on a table or in a drawer in front of one who is arrested can be as dangerous to the arresting officer as one concealed in the clothing of the person arrested." Ibid. In New York v. Belton, 453 U.S. 454, 101 S.Ct. 2860, 69 L.Ed.2d 768 (1981), we determined that the lower courts "have found no workable definition of 'the area within the immediate control of the arrestee' when ***1049** that area arguably includes the interior of an automobile and the arrestee is its recent occupant." Id., at 460, 101 S.Ct., at 2864. In order to provide a "workable rule," ibid., we held that "articles inside the relatively narrow compass of the passenger compartment of an automobile are in fact generally, even if not inevitably, within 'the area into which an arrestee might reach in order to grab a weapon'...." Ibid. (quoting Chimel, supra, 395 U.S., at 763, 89 S.Ct., at 2040). We also held that the police may examine the contents of any open or closed container found within the passenger compartment, "for if the passenger compartment is within the reach of the arrestee, so will containers in it be within his reach." 453 U.S., at 460, 101 S.Ct., at 2864. (footnote omitted). See also Michigan v. Summers, 452 U.S. 692, 702, 101 S.Ct. 2587, 2594, 69 L.Ed.2d 340 (1981).

Our past cases indicate then that protection of police and others can ****3481** justify protective searches when police have a reasonable belief that the suspect poses a danger, that roadside encounters between police and suspects are especially hazardous, and that danger may arise from the possible presence of weapons in the area surrounding a suspect. These principles compel our conclusion that the search of the passenger compartment of an automobile, limited to those areas in which a weapon may be placed or hidden, is permissible if the police officer possesses a reasonable belief based on "specific and articulable facts which, taken together with the rational inferences from those facts, reasonably warrant" the officers in believing that the suspect is dangerous and the suspect may gain immediate control of weapons.14 See ***1050** Terry, 392 U.S., at 21, 88 S.Ct., at 1880. "[T]he issue is whether a reasonably prudent man in the circumstances would be warranted in the belief that his safety or that of others was in danger." Id., at 27, 88 S.Ct., at 1883. If a suspect is "dangerous," he is no less dangerous simply because he is not arrested. If, while conducting a legitimate Terry search of the interior of the automobile, the officer should, as here, discover contraband other than weapons, he clearly cannot be required to ignore the contraband, and the Fourth Amendment does not require its suppression in such circumstances. Coolidge v. New Hampshire, 403 U.S. 443, 465, 91 S.Ct. 2022, 2037, 29 L.Ed.2d 564 (1971); Michigan v. Tyler, 436 U.S. 499, 509, 98 S.Ct. 1942, 1949, 56 L.Ed.2d 486 (1978); Texas v. Brown, —— U.S. ——, ——, ——, 103 S.Ct. 1535, 1541, 1544, 75 L.Ed.2d 502 (1983) (plurality opinion by REHNQUIST, J., and opinion concurring in the judgment by POWELL, J.).

The circumstances of this case clearly justified Deputies Howell and Lewis in their reasonable belief that Long posed a danger if he were permitted to reenter his vehicle. The hour was late and the area rural. Long was driving his automobile at excessive speed, and his car swerved into a ditch. The officers had to repeat their questions to Long, who appeared to be "under the influence" of some intoxicant. Long was not frisked until the officers observed that there was a large knife in the interior of the car into which Long was about to reenter. The subsequent search of the car was restricted to those areas to which Long would generally have immediate control, and that could contain a weapon. The trial court determined that the leather pouch containing ***1051** marijuana could have contained a weapon. App. 64a.15 It is clear that the intrusion was "strictly circumscribed by the exigencies which justifi[ed] its initiation." Terry, supra, 392 U.S., at 26, 88 S.Ct., at 1882.

In evaluating the validity of an officer's investigative or protective conduct under Terry, the "[t]ouchstone of our analysis ... is always 'the reasonableness in all circumstances of the particular governmental intrusion of a citizen's personal security.' ****3482** " Pennsylvania v. Mimms, supra, 434 U.S., at 108–109, 98 S.Ct., at 332–333 (quoting Terry, supra, 392 U.S., at 19, 88 S.Ct., at 1879). In this case, the officers did not act unreasonably in taking preventive measures to ensure that there were no other weapons within Long's immediate grasp before permitting him to reenter his automobile. Therefore, the balancing required by Terry clearly weighs in favor of allowing the police to conduct an area search of the passenger compartment to uncover weapons, as long as they possess an articulable and objectively reasonable belief that the suspect is potentially dangerous.

The Michigan Supreme Court appeared to believe that it was not reasonable for the officers to fear that Long could injure them, because he was effectively under their control during the investigative stop and could not get access to any weapons that might have been located in the automobile. See 413 Mich., at 472, 320 N.W.2d, at 869. This reasoning is mistaken in several respects. During any investigative detention, the suspect is "in the control" of the officers in the sense that he "may be briefly detained against his will ...." Terry, supra, 392 U.S., at 34, 88 S.Ct., at 1886 (WHITE, J., concurring). Just as a Terry suspect on the street may, despite being under the brief control of a police officer, reach into his clothing and retrieve a weapon, so might a Terry suspect in Long's position break away from police control and retrieve a weapon from his automobile. See

United States v. Rainone, 586 F.2d 1132, 1134 (CA7 1978), cert. denied, 440 U.S. 980, 99 S.Ct. 1787, 60 L.Ed.2d 239 (1979). In addition, ***1052** if the suspect is not placed under arrest, he will be permitted to reenter his automobile, and he will then have access to any weapons inside. United States v. Powless, 546 F.2d 792, 795–796 (CA8), cert. denied, 430 U.S. 910, 97 S.Ct. 1185, 51 L.Ed.2d 588 (1977). Or, as here, the suspect may be permitted to reenter the vehicle before the Terry investigation is over, and again, may have access to weapons. In any event, we stress that a Terry investigation, such as the one that occurred here, involves a police investigation "at close range," Terry, supra, 392 U.S., at 24, 88 S.Ct., at 1881, when the officer remains particularly vulnerable in part because a full custodial arrest has not been effected, and the officer must make a "quick decision as to how to protect himself and others from possible danger ...." Id., at 28, 88 S.Ct., at 1883. In such circumstances, we have not required that officers adopt alternate means to ensure their safety in order to avoid the intrusion involved in a Terry encounter.

***1053 **3483 IV**

The trial court and the court of appeals upheld the search of the trunk as a valid inventory search under this Court's decision in South Dakota v. Opperman, 428 U.S. 364, 96 S.Ct. 3092, 49 L.Ed.2d 1000 (1976). The Michigan Supreme Court did not address this holding, and instead suppressed the marijuana taken from the trunk as a fruit of the illegal search of the interior of the automobile. Our holding that the initial search was justified under Terry makes it necessary to determine whether the trunk search was permissible under the Fourth Amendment. However, we decline to address this question because it was not passed upon by the Michigan Supreme Court, whose decision we review in this case. See Cardinale v. Louisiana, 394 U.S. 437, 438, 89 S.Ct. 1161, 1162, 22 L.Ed.2d 398 (1969). We remand this issue to the court below, to enable it to determine whether the trunk search was permissible under Opperman, supra, or other decisions of this Court. See, e.g., United States v. Ross, 456 U.S. 798, 102 S.Ct. 2157, 72 L.Ed.2d 572 (1982).

***1054 V**

The decision of the Michigan Supreme Court is reversed, and the case is remanded for further proceedings not inconsistent with this opinion.

It is so ordered.

Justice BLACKMUN, concurring in part and concurring in the judgment.

I join Parts I, III, IV, and V of the Court's opinion. While I am satisfied that the Court has jurisdiction in this particular case, I do not join the Court, in Part II of its opinion, in fashioning a new presumption of jurisdiction over cases coming here from state courts. Although I agree with the Court that uniformity in federal criminal law is desirable, I see little efficiency and an increased danger of advisory opinions in the Court's new approach.

Justice BRENNAN, with whom Justice MARSHALL joins, dissenting.

The Court today holds that "the protective search of the passenger compartment" of the automobile involved in this case "was reasonable under the principles articulated in Terry and other decisions of this Court." Ante, at 3472. I disagree. Terry v. Ohio, 392 U.S. 1, 88 S.Ct. 1868, 20 L.Ed.2d 889 (1968), does not support the Court's conclusion and the reliance on "other decisions" is patently misplaced. Plainly, the Court is simply continuing the process of distorting Terry beyond recognition and forcing it into service as an unlikely weapon against the Fourth Amendment's fundamental requirement that searches and seizures be based on probable cause. See United States v. Place, — U.S. —, —, 103 S.Ct. 2637, 2646, 75 L.Ed.2d — (1983) (BRENNAN, J., concurring in the result). I, therefore, dissent.

***1055** On three occasions this Term I have discussed the limited scope of the exception to the probable cause requirement created by Terry and its progeny. See Florida v. Royer, —— U.S. ——, ——, 103 S.Ct. 1319, 1330, 75 L.Ed.2d 229 (1983) (BRENNAN, J., concurring in the result); ****3484** Kolender v. Lawson, —— U.S. ——, ——, 103 S.Ct. 1855, 1861, 75 L.Ed.2d 903 (1983) (BRENNAN, J., concurring); United States v. Place, 462 U.S., at ——, 103 S.Ct., at 2646 (BRENNAN, J., concurring in the result). I will not repeat those discussions here and note only that "Terry, and the cases that followed it, permit only brief investigative stops and extremely limited searches based on reasonable suspicion." Id., at ——, 103 S.Ct., at 2648. However, the Court's opinion compels a detailed review of Terry itself.

In Terry, the Court confronted the "quite narrow question" of "whether it is always unreasonable for a policeman to seize a person and subject him to a limited search for weapons unless there is probable cause for an arrest." 392 U.S., at 15, 88 S.Ct., at 1877 (emphasis supplied). Because the Court was dealing "with an entire rubric of police conduct ... which historically [had] not been, and as a practical matter could not be, subjected to the warrant procedure," id., at 20, 88 S.Ct., at 1879, the Court tested the conduct at issue "by the Fourth Amendment's general proscription against unreasonable searches and seizures." Ibid. (footnote omitted). In considering the "reasonableness" of the conduct, the Court balanced " 'the need to search [or seize] against the invasion which the search [or seizure] entails.' " Id., at 21, 88 S.Ct., at 1879, quoting Camara v. Municipal Court, 387 U.S. 523, 534–535, 536–537, 87 S.Ct. 1727, 1733–1734, 1735, 18 L.Ed.2d 930 (1967). It deserves emphasis that in discussing the "invasion" at issue, the Court stated that "[e]ven a limited search of the outer clothing for weapons constitutes a severe, though brief, intrusion upon cherished personal security ...." Id., at 24–25, 88 S.Ct., at 1881–1882 (emphasis supplied). Ultimately, the Court concluded that "there must be a narrowly drawn authority to permit a reasonable search for weapons for the protection of the police officer, where he has reason to believe that he is dealing with an armed and dangerous individual, regardless of whether he has probable ***1056** cause to arrest the individual for a crime." Id., at 27, 88 S.Ct., at 1883 (emphasis supplied). The Court expressed its holding as follows:

"We merely hold today that where a police officer observes unusual conduct which leads him reasonably to conclude in light of his experience that criminal activity may be afoot and that the persons with whom he is dealing may be armed and presently dangerous, where in the course of investigating this behavior he identifies himself as a policeman and makes reasonable inquiries, and where nothing in the initial stages of the encounter serves to dispel his reasonable fear for his own or others' safety, he is entitled for the protection of himself and others in the area to conduct a carefully limited search of the outer clothing of such persons in an attempt to discover weapons which might be used to assault him." Id., at 30, 88 S.Ct., at 1884–1885 (emphasis supplied).

It is clear that Terry authorized only limited searches of the person for weapons. In light of what Terry said, relevant portions of which the Court neglects to quote, the Court's suggestion that "Terry need not be read as restricting the preventive search to the person of the detained suspect," ante, at 3479 (footnote omitted), can only be described as disingenuous. Nothing in Terry authorized police officers to search a suspect's car based on reasonable suspicion. The Court confirmed this this very Term in United States v. Place, supra, where it described the search authorized by Terry as a "limited search for weapons, or 'frisk' ...." 462 U.S., at ——, 103 S.Ct., at 2642. The search at issue in this case is a far cry from a "frisk" and certainly was not "limited."

***1057** ****3485** The Court's reliance on Chimel v. California, 395 U.S. 752, 89 S.Ct. 2034, 23 L.Ed.2d 685 (1969), and New York v. Belton, 453 U.S. 454, 101 S.Ct. 2860, 69 L.Ed.2d 768 (1981), as support for its new "area search" rule within the context of a Terry stop is misplaced. In Chimel, the Court addressed the scope of a search incident to a lawful arrest, 395 U.S., at 753, 89 S.Ct., at 2035, and held invalid the search at issue there because it "went far beyond the petitioner's person and the area from within which he might have obtained a weapon or something that could have been used as evidence against him." Id., at 768, 89 S.Ct., at 2043. Chimel stressed the need to limit the scope of searches incident to arrest and overruled two prior decisions of this Court validating overly broad searches. Ibid.

In Belton, the Court considered the scope of a search incident to the lawful custodial arrest of an occupant of an automobile. 453 U.S., at 455, 101 S.Ct., at 2861. In this "particular and problematic context," id., at 460, n. 3, 101 S.Ct., at 2864, n. 3, the Court held that "when a policeman has made a lawful custodial arrest of the occupant of an automobile, he may, as a contemporaneous incident of that arrest, search the passenger compartment of that automobile." Id., at 460, 101 S.Ct., at 2864 (footnote omitted).

The critical distinction between this case and Terry on the one hand, and Chimel and Belton on the other, is that the latter two cases arose within the context of lawful custodial arrests supported by probable cause.4 The Court in Terry expressly recognized the difference between a search incident to arrest and the "limited search for weapons," 392 U.S., at 25, 88 S.Ct., at 1882, involved in that case. The Court stated:

***1058** "[A search incident to arrest], although justified in part by the acknowledged necessity to protect the arresting officer from assault with a concealed weapon, ... is also justified on other grounds, ... and can therefore involve a relatively extensive exploration of the person. A search for weapons in the absence of probable cause to arrest, however, must, like any other search, be strictly circumscribed by the exigencies which justify its initiation.... Thus it must be limited to that which is necessary for the discovery of weapons which might be used to harm the officer or others nearby, and may realistically be characterized as something less than a 'full' search, even though it remains a serious intrusion.

"... An arrest is a wholly different kind of intrusion upon individual freedom from a limited search for weapons, and the interests each is designed to serve are likewise quite different. An arrest is the initial stage of a criminal prosecution. It is intended to vindicate society's interest in having its laws obeyed, and it is inevitably accompanied by future interference with the individual's freedom of movement, whether or not trial or conviction ultimately follows. The protective search for weapons, on the other hand, constitutes a brief, though far from inconsiderable, intrusion upon the sanctity of the person." Id., 392 U.S., at 25–26, 88 S.Ct., at 1882–1883 (footnote omitted).

In United States v. Robinson, 414 U.S. 218, 94 S.Ct. 467, 38 L.Ed.2d 427 (1973), the Court relied on the differences between searches incident to lawful custodial arrests and Terry "stop-and-frisk" searches to reject an argument that the limitations ****3486** established in Terry should be applied to a search incident to arrest. Id., at 228, 94 S.Ct., at 473. The Court noted that "Terry clearly recognized the distinction between the two types of searches, and that a different rule governed one than governed the other," id., at 233, 94 S.Ct., at 476, and described Terry as involving "stricter ... standards," id., at 234, 94 S.Ct., at 476, than those governing searches incident to arrest. The Court went on to state:

***1059** "A custodial arrest of a suspect based on probable cause is a reasonable intrusion under the Fourth Amendment; that intrusion being lawful, a search incident to the arrest requires no additional justification. It is the fact of the lawful arrest which establishes the authority to search, and we hold that in the case of a lawful custodial arrest a full search of the person is not only an exception to the warrant requirement of the Fourth Amendment, but is also a 'reasonable' search under that Amendment." Id., at 235, 94 S.Ct., at 477.

See also id., at 237–238, 94 S.Ct., at 477–478 (POWELL, J., concurring) ("The search incident to arrest is reasonable under the Fourth Amendment because the privacy interest protected by that constitutional guarantee is legitimately abated by the fact of arrest." (footnote omitted)); Gustafson v. Florida, 414 U.S. 260, 264, 94 S.Ct. 488, 491, 38 L.Ed.2d 456 (1973).

As these cases recognize, there is a vital difference between searches incident to lawful custodial arrests and Terry protective searches. The Court deliberately ignores that difference in relying on principles developed within the context of intrusions supported by probable cause to arrest to construct an "area search" rule within the context of a Terry stop.

The Court denies that an "area search" is fundamentally inconsistent with Terry, see ante, at 3482, n. 16, stating:

"We have recognized that Terry searches are limited insofar as they may not be conducted in the absence of an articulable suspicion that the intrusion is justified, see e.g., Sibron v. New York, 392 U.S. 40, 65 [88 S.Ct. 1889, 1904, 20 L.Ed.2d 917] (1968), and that they are protective in nature and limited to weapons, see Ybarra v. Illinois, 444 U.S. 85, 93–94 [100 S.Ct. 338, 343–344, 62 L.Ed.2d 238] (1979). However, neither of these concerns is violated by our decision. To engage in an area search, which is limited to seeking weapons, the officer must have an articulable suspicion that the suspect is potentially dangerous." Ante, at 3482, n. 16.

***1060** This patently is no answer: respondent's argument relates to the scope of the search, not to the standard that justifies it. The Court flouts Terry 's holding that Terry searches must be carefully limited in scope. See supra, at 3474. Indeed, the page in Sibron cited by the Court states:

"Even assuming arguendo that there were adequate grounds to search Sibron for weapons, the nature and scope of the search conducted by Patrolman Martin were so clearly unrelated to that justification as to render the heroin inadmissible. The search for weapons approved in Terry consisted solely of a limited patting of the outer clothing of the suspect for concealed objects which might be used as instruments of assault. Only when he discovered such objects did the officer in Terry place his hands in the pockets of the men he searched. In this case, with no attempt at an initial limited exploration for arms, Patrolman Martin thrust his hand into Sibron's pocket and took from him envelopes of heroin. His testimony shows that he was looking for narcotics, and he found them. The search was not reasonably limited in scope to the accomplishment of the only goal which might conceivably have justified its inception—the protection of the officer by disarming a potentially dangerous ****3487** man." 392 U.S., at 65, 88 S.Ct., at 1904 (emphasis supplied).

As this passage makes clear, the scope of a search is determined not only by reference to its purpose, but also by reference to its intrusiveness. Yet the Court today holds that a search of a car (and the containers within it) that is not even occupied by the suspect is only as intrusive as, or perhaps less intrusive than, thrusting a hand into a pocket after an ***1061** initial patdown has suggested the presence of concealed objects that might be used as weapons.

The Court suggests no limit on the "area search" it now authorizes. The Court states that a "search of the passenger compartment of an automobile, limited to those areas in which a weapon may be placed or hidden, is permissible if the police officer possesses a reasonable belief based on 'specific and articulable facts which, taken together with the rational inferences from those facts, reasonably warrant' the officers to believe that the suspect is dangerous and the suspect may gain immediate control of weapons." Ante, at 3480 (footnote omitted). Presumably a weapon "may be placed or hidden" anywhere in a car. A weapon also might be hidden in a container in the car. In this case, the Court upholds the officer's search of a leather pouch because it "could have contained a weapon." Id., at 3481 (footnote omitted). In addition, the Court's requirement that an officer have a reasonable suspicion that a suspect is armed and dangerous does little to check the initiation of an area search. In this case, the officers saw a hunting knife in the car, see ante, at 3473, 3481, but the Court does not base its holding that the subsequent search was permissible on the ground that possession of the knife may have been illegal under state law. See ante, at 3482, n. 16. An individual can lawfully possess many things that can be used as weapons. A hammer, or a baseball bat, can be used as a very effective weapon. Finally, the Court relies on the following facts to conclude that the officers had a reasonable suspicion that respondent was presently dangerous: the hour was late; the area was rural; respondent had been driving at an excessive speed; he had been involved in an accident; he was not immediately responsive to the officers' questions; and he appeared to be under the influence of some intoxicant. Id., at 3481. Based on these facts, one might reasonably conclude that respondent was drunk. A drunk driver is indeed dangerous while driving, but not while stopped on the roadside by ***1062** the police. Even when an intoxicated person lawfully has in his car an object that could be used as a weapon, it requires imagination to conclude that he is presently dangerous. Even assuming that the facts in this case justified the officers' initial "frisk" of respondent, see ante, at 3473, 3481, n. 15, they hardly provide adequate justification for a search of a suspect's car and the containers within it. This represents an intrusion not just different in degree, but in kind, from the intrusion sanctioned by Terry. In short, the implications of the Court's decision are frightening.

The Court also rejects the Michigan Supreme Court's view that it "was not reasonable for the officers to fear that [respondent] could injure them, because he was effectively under their control during the investigative stop and could not get access to any weapons that might have been located in the automobile." Ante, at 3481. In this regard, the Court states:

"[W]e stress that a Terry investigation, such as the one that occurred here, involves a police investigation 'at close range,' ... when the officer remains particularly vulnerable in part because a full custodial arrest has not been effected, and the officer must make a 'quick decision as to how to protect himself and others from possible danger.' ... In ****3488** such circumstances, we have not required that officers adopt alternate means to ensure their safety in order to avoid the intrusion involved in a Terry encounter." Ante, at 3482 (footnote omitted) (emphasis in original).

Putting aside the fact that the search at issue here involved a far more serious intrusion than that "involved in a Terry encounter," see supra, at 3482, and as such might suggest the need for resort to "alternate means," the Court's reasoning is perverse. The Court's argument in essence is that the absence of probable cause to arrest compels the conclusion that a broad search, traditionally associated in scope with a search incident to arrest, must be permitted based on reasonable suspicion. But United States v. Robinson, supra, stated: "It is ***1063** scarcely open to doubt that the danger to an officer is far greater in the case of the extended exposure which follows the taking of a suspect into custody and transporting him to the police station than in the case of the relatively fleeting contact resulting from the typical Terry -type stop." 414 U.S., at 234–235, 94 S.Ct., at 476–477. In light of Robinson 's observation, today's holding leaves in grave doubt the question of whether the Court's assessment of the relative dangers posed by given confrontations is based on any principled standard.

Moreover, the Court's reliance on a "balancing" of the relevant interests to justify its decision, see ante, at 3481, is certainly inappropriate. In Dunaway v. New York, 442 U.S. 200, 99 S.Ct. 2248, 60 L.Ed.2d 824 (1979), the Court stated that "[t]he narrow intrusions involved in [Terry and its progeny] were judged by a balancing test rather than by the general principle that Fourth Amendment seizures must be supported by the 'long-prevailing standards' of probable cause, ... only because these intrusions fell far short of the kind of intrusion associated with an arrest." Id., at 212, 99 S.Ct., at 2256. The intrusion involved in this case is precisely "the kind of intrusion associated with an arrest." Ibid. There is no justification, therefore, for "balancing" the relevant interests.

In sum, today's decision reflects once again the threat to Fourth Amendment values posed by "balancing." See United States v. Place, 462 U.S., at ——, 103 S.Ct., at 2647 (1983) (BRENNAN, J., concurring in the result). As Justice Frankfurter stated in United States v. Rabinowitz, 339 U.S. 56, 70 S.Ct. 430, 94 L.Ed. 653 (1950):

"To say that the search must be reasonable is to require some criterion of reason. It is no guide at all either for a jury or for district judges or the police to say that an 'unreasonable search' is forbidden—that the search must be reasonable. What is the test of reason which makes a search reasonable? The test is the reason underlying and expressed by the Fourth Amendment: the history and the experience which it embodies and the safeguards afforded by it against the evils to which it was a response." Id., at 83, 70 S.Ct., at 443 (dissenting opinion).

***1064** Hornbook law has been that "the police may not conduct a search unless they first convince a neutral magistrate that there is probable cause to do so." New York v. Belton, 453 U.S., at 457, 101 S.Ct., at 2862. While under some circumstances the police may search a car without a warrant, see e.g., Carroll v. United States, 267 U.S. 132, 45 S.Ct. 280, 69 L.Ed. 543 (1925), "the exception to the warrant requirement established in Carroll ... applies only to searches of vehicles that are supported by probable cause." United States v. Ross, 456 U.S. 798, 809, 102 S.Ct. 2157, 2165, 72 L.Ed.2d 572 (1982) (footnote omitted). "[T]he Court in Carroll emphasized the importance of the requirement that officers have probable cause to believe that the vehicle contains contraband." Id., at 807–808, 102 S.Ct., at 2163–2164. See also Almeida-Sanchez v. United States, 413 U.S. 266, 269, 93 S.Ct. 2535, 2537, 37 L.Ed.2d 596 (1973) ("Automobile or no automobile, there must be probable cause for the search." (footnote omitted)). Today the Court discards these basic principles and employs the very narrow exception established by Terry "to swallow the general ****3489** rule that Fourth Amendment [searches of cars] are 'reasonable' only if based on probable cause."6 Dunaway v. New York, 442 U.S., at 213, 99 S.Ct., at 2257. See also United States v. Place, 462 U.S., at ——, 103 S.Ct., at 2646 (BRENNAN, J., concurring in the result).

Today's decision disregards the Court's warning in Almeida-Sanchez: "The needs of law enforcement stand in constant tension with the Constitution's protections of the individual against certain exercises of official power. It is precisely the predictability of these pressures that counsels a resolute loyalty to constitutional safeguards." 413 U.S., at 273, 93 S.Ct., at 2540. Of course, police should not be exposed to unnecessary danger in the performance of their duties. But a search of a car and the containers within it based on nothing more than reasonable suspicion, even under the circumstances present ***1065** here, cannot be sustained without doing violence to the requirements of the Fourth Amendment. There is no reason in this case why the officers could not have pursued less intrusive, but equally effective, means of insuring their safety.7 Cf. United States v. Place, 462 U.S., at ——, 103 S.Ct., at 2647; Florida v. Royer, 460 U.S., at ——, 103 S.Ct., at 1325 (plurality opinion). The Court takes a long step today toward "balancing" into oblivion the protections the Fourth Amendment affords. I dissent, for as Justice Jackson said in Brinegar v. United States, 338 U.S. 160, 69 S.Ct. 1302, 93 L.Ed. 1879 (1949):

"[Fourth Amendment rights] are not mere second-class rights but belong in the catalog of indispensable freedoms. Among deprivations of rights, none is so effective in cowing a population, crushing the spirit of the individual and putting terror in every heart. Uncontrolled search and seizure is one of the first and most effective weapons in the arsenal of every arbitrary government." Id., at 180, 69 S.Ct., at 1313 (dissenting opinion).

(The dissent of Justice STEVENS is omitted.)

Black Letter Law

> The Court found reasonable a protective search of passenger compartment of motor vehicle during lawful investigatory stop of occupant of vehicle. Search of passenger compartment of automobile, limited to those areas in which weapon may be placed or hidden, is permissible if police officer possesses reasonable belief based on specific and articulable facts which, taken together with rational inferences from those facts, reasonably warrant officers in believing that suspect is dangerous and may gain immediate control of weapons; issue is whether reasonably prudent man in the circumstances would be warranted in belief that his safety or that of others was in danger.

Discussion Problems:

11-1. On September 9, two undercover cops were working as uniformed officers in the special operations section of the Police Department. The officers were driving the last car of a four car caravan converging on an area known for heavy narcotics trafficking in order to investigate drug transactions. The officers were traveling together because they expected to find a crowd of people in the area, including lookouts and customers.

As the caravan passed Seminole Drive, one of the officers observed the defendant standing next to the building holding an opaque bag. The defendant looked in the direction of the officers and fled. The undercover cops turned their car southbound, watched him as he ran through the gangway and an alley, and eventually cornered him on the street. One officer then exited his car and stopped the defendant. He immediately conducted a protective patdown search for weapons because in his experience it was common for there to be weapons in the near vicinity of narcotics transactions. During the frisk, the officer squeezed the bag the defendant was carrying and felt a heavy, hard object similar to the shape of a gun. The officer then opened the bag and discovered a .38–caliber handgun with five live rounds of ammunition.

At trial, the defendant moves to suppress the results of the patdown. The senior state's attorney on the case has tasked you with drafting a response to the defendant's motion. Prepare your talking points for the meeting with the senior attorney to discuss strategies for responding to the defense's position.

11-2. On October 13, an anonymous caller reported to the Police that a young black male standing at a particular bus stop and wearing a plaid shirt was carrying a gun. There is no audio recording of the tip, and nothing is known about the informant. Sometime after the police received the tip—two officers were instructed to respond. They arrived at the bus stop about six minutes later and saw three black males "just hanging out." One of the three, the defendant, was wearing a plaid shirt. Apart from the tip, the officers had no reason to suspect any of the three of illegal conduct. The officers did not see a firearm, and the defendant made no threatening or otherwise unusual movements. One of the officers approached the defendant and told him to put his hands up on the bus stop, frisked him, and seized a gun from the defendant. The second officer frisked the other two individuals, against whom no allegations had been made, and found nothing. A the time of the frisk the defendant was just ten days shy of his sixteenth birthday.

The defendant was charged under state law with carrying a concealed firearm without a license and possessing a firearm while under the age of 18. He moved to suppress the gun as the fruit of an unlawful search.

Your senior supervising attorney has asked you to address the applicability of the Terry "Stop and Frisk" doctrine to the this situation. They want you to draft a short legal memorandum outlining the relevant standards under the doctrine and applying it to these facts.

11-3. On April 22, at approximately 3 p.m., a Corporal in the Police Department received a telephone call from an anonymous person, stating that the defendant would be leaving the Terrace Apartments at a particular time in a brown Plymouth station wagon with the right taillight lens broken, that she would be going to Mowery Motel, and that she would be in possession of about an ounce of cocaine inside a brown attaché case. The Corporal went to the Terrace Apartments. The officers saw a brown Plymouth station wagon with a broken right taillight in the parking lot in front of the building. The officers observed the defendant leave the building, carrying nothing in her hands, and enter the station wagon. They followed the vehicle as it drove the most direct route to Mowery Motel. When the vehicle reached the Highway, on which Mowery Motel is located, the Corporal requested a patrol unit to stop the vehicle. The vehicle was stopped at approximately 4:18 p.m., just short of the Motel. The Corporal asked the defendant to step to the rear of her car, where he informed her that she had been stopped because she was suspected of carrying cocaine in the vehicle. He asked if they could look for cocaine, and respondent said they could look. The officers found a locked brown attaché case in the car, and, upon request, respondent provided the combination to the lock. The officers found marijuana in the attaché case and placed the defendant under arrest. During processing at the station, the officers found three milligrams of cocaine in her purse. She was was charged in Montgomery County Court with possession of marijuana and possession of cocaine. At trial, her defense counsel makes a motion to suppress the drugs.

Outline the best argument for suppressing the evidence seized. Pay particular attention to the issues surrounding informants, cars and reasonableness.

11-4. Officer Walker was sitting in the dining area of the local donut shop when he observed "Johnnie Rae" jaywalk across a four lane divided street towards the donut shop. Officer Walker left his donuts on the table, went outside and stopped Johnnie Rae just as he reached the area right outside the donut shop. The local municipal ordinance requires pedestrians to use crosswalks when crossing divided roads. After stopping Johnnie Rae Officer Walker decides to frisk him for his own safety. He discovers an armed hand grenade in Johnnie Rae's pant pocket.

Will the hand grenade be admissible in court if Johnnie Rae is charged with possession of an unlawful explosive device?

-Notes-

Chapter 12: Confessions & Identifications

Ashcraft v. Tennessee

64 S.Ct. 921

Supreme Court of the United States.

ASHCRAFT et al.

v.

STATE OF TENNESSEE.

No. 391. | Argued Feb. 28, 1944. | Decided May 1, 1944.

Mr. Justice BLACK delivered the opinion of the Court.

About three o'clock on the morning of Thursday, June 5, 1941, Mrs. Zelma Ida Ashcraft got in her automobile at her **922 home in Memphis, Tennessee, and set out on a trip to visit her mother's home in Kentucky. Late in the afternoon of the same day her car was observed a few miles out of Memphis, standing on the wrong side of a road which she would likely have taken on her journey. Just off the road, in a slough, her lifeless body was found. On her head were cut places inflicted by blows sufficient to have caused her death. Petitioner Ware, age 20, a Negro, was indicted in a state court and found guilty of her murder. Petitioner Ashcraft, age 45, a white man, husband of the deceased, charged with having hired Ware to commit the murder, was tried jointly with Ware and convicted as an accessory before the fact. Both were sentenced to ninety-nine years in the state penitentiary. *145 The Supreme Court of Tennessee affirmed the convictions.

In applying to us for certiorari, Ware and Ashcraft urged that alleged confessions were used at their trial which had been extorted from them by state law enforcement officers in violation of the Fourteenth Amendment, and that 'solely and alone' on the basis of these confessions they had been convicted. Their contentions raised a federal question which the record showed to be substantial and we brought both cases here for review. Upon oral argument before this Court Tennessee's legal representatives conceded that the convictions could not be sustained without the confessions but defended their use upon the ground that they were not compelled but were 'freely and voluntarily made.'

The record discloses that neither the trial court nor the Tennessee Supreme Court actually held as a matter of fact that petitioners' confessions were 'freely and voluntarily made.' The trial court heard evidence on the issue out of the jury's hearing, but did not itself determine from that evidence that the confessions were voluntary. Instead it over-ruled Ashcraft's objection to the use of his alleged confession with the statement that, 'This Court is not able to hold, as a matter of law, that reasonable minds might not differ on the question of whether or not that alleged confession was voluntarily obtained.' And it likewise over-ruled Ware's objection to use of his alleged confession, stating that 'the reasonable minds of twelve men might * * * differ as to * * * whether Ware's confession was voluntary, and * * * therefore, that is a question of fact for the jury to pass on.' Nor did the *146 State Supreme Court review the evidence pertaining to the confessions and affirmatively hold them voluntary. In sustaining the petitioners' convictions, one Justice dissenting, it went no further than to point out that, 'The trial judge * * * held * * * he could not say that the confessions were not voluntarily made and, therefore, permitted them to go to the jury', and to declare that it, likewise, was 'unable to say that the confessions were not freely and voluntarily made.'

If, therefore, the question of the voluntariness of the two confessions was actually decided at all it was by the jury. And the jury was charged generally on the subject of the two confessions as follows:

**923 'I further charge you that if verbal or written statements made by the defendants freely and voluntarily and without fear of punishment or hope of reward, have been proven to you in this case, you may take them into consideration with all of the other facts and circumstances in the case. * * * In statements made at the time of the arrest, you may take into consideration the condition of the minds of the prisoners owing to their arrest and *147 whether they were influenced by motives of hope or fear, to make the statements. Such a statement is competent evidence against the defendant who makes it and is not competent evidence against the other defendant. * * * You cannot consider it for any purpose against the other defendant.'

Concerning Ashcraft's alleged confession this general charge constituted the sole instruction to the jury.3 But with regard to Ware's alleged confession the jury further was instructed:

'It is his (Ware's) further theory that he was induced by the fear of violence at the hands of a mob and by fear of the officers of the law to confess his guilt of the crime charged against him, but that such confession was false and that he had nothing whatsoever to do with, and no knowledge of the alleged crime. If you believe the theory of the defendant, Ware, * * * it is your duty to acquit him.'

Having submitted the two alleged confessions to the jury in this manner, the trial court instructed the jury that:

'what the proof may show you, if anything, that the defendants have said against themselves, the law presumes to be true, but anything the defendants have said in their own behalf, you are not obliged to believe. * * *'This treatment of the confessions by the two State courts, the manner of the confessions' submission to the jury, and the emphasis upon the great weight to be given confessions make all the more important the kind of 'independent examination' of petitioners' claims which, in *148 any event, we are bound to make. Lisenba v. California, 314 U.S. 219, 237, 238, 62 S.Ct. 280, 290, 86 L.Ed. 166. Our duty to make that examination could not have been 'foreclosed by the finding of a court, or the verdict of a jury, or both.' Id. We proceed therefore to consider the evidence relating to the circumstances out of which the alleged confessions came.

First, as to Ashcraft. Ashcraft was born on an Arkansas farm. At the age of eleven he left the farm and became a farm hand working for others. Years later he gravitated into construction work, finally becoming a skilled dragline and steam shovel operator. Uncontradicted evidence in the record was that he had acquired for himself 'an excellent reputation.' In 1929 he married the deceased Zelma Ida Ashcraft. Childless, they accumulated, apparently through Ashcraft's earnings, a very modest amount of jointly held property including bank accounts and an equity in the home in which they lived. The Supreme Court of Tennessee found 'nothing to show but what the home life of Ashcraft and the deceased was pleasant and happy.' Several of Mrs. Ashcraft's friends who were guests at the Ashcraft home on the night before her tragic death testified that both husband and wife appeared to be in a happy frame of mind.

The officers first talked to Ashcraft about 6 P.M. on the day of his wife's murder as he was returning home from work. Informed by them of the tragedy, he was taken to an undertaking establishment to identify her body which previously had been identified only by a driver's license. From there he was taken to the county jail where he conferred with the officers until about 2 A.M. No clues of ultimate value came from this conference, though it did result in the officers' holding and interrogating the Ashcrafts' maid and several of her friends. During the following week the officers made extensive investigations in Ashcraft's neighborhood and *149 elsewhere **924 and further conferred with Ashcraft himself on several occasions, but none of these activities produced tangible evidence pointing to the identity of the murderer.

Then, early in the evening of Saturday, June 14, the officers came to Ashcraft's home and 'took him into custody.' In the words of the Tennessee Supreme Court, 'They took him to an office or room on the northwest corner of the fifth Floor of the Shelby County jail. This office is equipped with all sorts of crime and detective devices such as a fingerprint outfit, cameras, high-powered lights, and such other devices as might be found in a homicide investigating office. * * * It appears that the officers placed Ashcraft at a table in this room on the fifth floor of the county jail with a light over his head and began to quiz him. They questioned him in relays until the following Monday morning, June 16, 1941, around nine-thirty or ten o'clock. It appears that Ashcraft from Saturday evening at seven o'clock until Monday morning at approximately nine-thirty never left this homicide room of the fifth floor.'

Testimony of the officers shows that the reason they questioned Ashcraft 'in relays' was that they became so tired they were compelled to rest. But from 7:00 Saturday evening until 9:30 Monday morning Ashcraft had no rest. One officer did say that he gave the suspect a single five minutes respite, but except for this five minutes the procedure consisted of one continuous stream of questions.

As to what happened in the fifth-floor jail room during this thirty-six hour secret examination the testimony *150 follows the usual pattern and is in hopeless conflict. Ashcraft swears that the first thing said to him when he was taken into custody was, 'Why in hell did you kill your wife?'; that during the course of the examination he was threatened and abused in various ways; and that as the hours passed his eyes became blinded by a powerful electric light, his body became weary, and the strain on his nerves became unbearable. The officers, on the other hand, swear that throughout the questioning they were kind and considerate. They say that they did not accuse Ashcraft of the murder until four hours after he was brought to the jail building, though they freely admit that from that time on their barrage of questions was constantly directed at him on the assumption that he was *151 the murderer. Together with other persons whom they brought in on Monday morning to witness the culmination of the thirty-six hour ordeal **925 the officers declare that at that time Ashcraft was 'cool', 'calm', 'collected,' 'normal'; that his vision was unimpaired and his eyes not bloodshot; and that he showed no outward signs of being tired or sleepy.

As to whether Ashcraft actually confessed there is a similar conflict of testimony. Ashcraft maintains that although the officers incessantly attempted by various tactics of intimidation to entrap him into a confession, not once did he admit knowledge concerning or participation in the crime. And he specifically denies the officers' statements that he accused Ware of the crime, insisting that in response to their questions he merely gave them the name of Ware as one of several men who occasionally had ridden with him to work. The officers' version of what happened, however, is that about 11 P.M. on Sunday night, after twenty-eight hours' constant questioning, Ashcraft made a statement that Ware had overpowered him at his home and abducted the deceased, and was probably the killer. About midnight the officers found Ware and took him into custody, and, according to their testimony, Ware made a self-incriminating statement as of early Monday morning, and at 5:40 A.M. signed by mark a written confession in which appeared the statement that Ashcraft had hired him to commit the murder. This alleged confession of Ware was read to Ashcraft about six o'clock Monday morning, whereupon Ashcraft is said substantially to have admitted its truth in a detailed statement taken down by a reporter. About 9:30 Monday morning a transcript of Ashcraft's purported statement was read to him. The State's position is that he affirmed its truth but refused to sign the transcript, saying that he first wanted to consult his lawyer. As to *152 this latter 9:30 episode the officers' testimony is reinforced by testimony of the several persons whom they brought in to witness the end of the examination.

In reaching our conclusion as to the validity of Ashcraft's confession we do not resolve any of the disputed questions of fact relating to the details of what transpired within the confession chamber of the jail or whether Ashcraft actually did confess. Such disputes, we may say, are an inescapable consequence of secret inquisitorial practices. And always evidence concerning the inner details of secret inquisitions is weighted against an accused, *153 particularly where, as here, he is **926 charged with a brutal crime, or where, as in many other cases, his supposed offense bears relation to an unpopular economic, political, or religious cause.

Our conclusion is that if Ashcraft made a confession it was not voluntary but compelled. We reach this conclusion from facts which are not in dispute at all. Ashcraft, a citizen of excellent reputation, was taken into custody by police officers. Ten days' examination of the Ashcrafts' maid, and of several others, in jail where they were held, had revealed nothing whatever against Ashcraft. Inquiries among his neighbors and business associates likewise had failed to unearth one single tangible clue pointing to his guilt. For thirty-six hours after Ashcraft's seizure during which period he was held incommunicado, without sleep or rest, relays of officers, experienced investigators, and highly trained lawyers questioned him without respite. From the beginning of the questioning at 7 o'clock on Saturday evening until 6 o'clock on Monday morning Ashcraft denied that he had anything to do with the murder of his wife. And at a hearing *154 before a magistrate about 8:30 Monday morning Ashcraft pleaded not guilty to the charge of murder which the officers had sought to make him confess during the previous thirty-six hours.

We think a situation such as that here shown by uncontradicted evidence is so inherently coercive that its very existence is irreconcilable with the possession of mental freedom by a lone suspect against whom its full coercive force is brought to bear. It is inconceivable that any court of justice in the land, conducted as our courts are, open to the public, would permit prosecutors serving in relays to keep a defendant witness under continuous cross examination for thirty-six hours without rest or sleep in an effort to extract a 'voluntary' confession. Nor can we, consistently with Constitutional due process of law, hold voluntary a confession where prosecutors do the same thing away from the restraining influences of a public trial in an open court room.

**927 *155 The Constitution of the United States stands as a bar against the conviction of any individual in an American court by means of a coerced confession. There have been, and are now, certain foreign nations with governments dedicated to an opposite policy: governments which convict individuals with testimony obtained by police organizations possessed of an unrestrained power to seize persons suspected of crimes against the state, hold them in secret custody, and wring from them confessions by physical or mental torture. So long as the Constitution remains the basic law of our Republic, America will not have that kind of government.

Second, as to Ware. Ashcraft and Ware were jointly tried, and were convicted on the theory that Ashcraft hired Ware to perform the murder. Ware's conviction was sustained by the Tennessee Supreme Court on the assumption that Ashcraft's confession was properly admitted and his conviction valid. Whether it would have been sustained had the court reached the conclusion we have reached as to Ashcraft we cannot know. Doubt as to what the State court would have done under the changed *156 circumstances brought about by our reversal of its decision as to Ashcraft is emphasized by the position of the State's representatives in this Court. They have asked that if we reverse Ashcraft's conviction we also reverse Ware's.

In disposing of cases before us it is our responsibility to make such disposition as justice may require. 'And in determining what justice does require, the Court is bound to consider any change, either in fact or in law, which has supervened since the judgment was entered.' Patterson v. Alabama, 294 U.S. 600, 607, 55 S.Ct. 575, 578, 79 L.Ed. 1082; State Tax Commission v. Van Cott, 306 U.S. 511, 515, 516, 59 S.Ct. 605, 607, 83 L.Ed. 950. Application of this guiding principle to the case at hand requires that we send Ware's case back to the Tennessee Supreme Court. Should that Court in passing on Ware's conviction in the light of our ruling as to Ashcraft adopt the State Attorney General's view and reverse the conviction there then would be no occasion for our passing on the federal question here raised by Ware. Under these circumstances we vacate the judgment of the Tennessee Supreme Court affirming Ware's conviction, and remand his case to that court for further proceedings.

The judgment affirming Ashcraft's conviction is reversed and the cause is remanded to the Supreme Court of Tennessee for proceedings not inconsistent with this opinion. It is so ordered.

Judgment of Tennessee Supreme Court affirming defendant Ware's conviction vacated and case remanded with directions and judgment of Tennessee Supreme Court affirming Ashcraft's conviction reversed and ause remanded with directions.

(The dissent of Mr. Justice JACKSON, is omitted.)

Mr. Justice ROBERTS and Mr. Justice FRANKFURTER join in this opinion.

Black Letter Law

> A confession is not voluntary when it is given: (1) while the defendant has been in custody for 36 hours, (2) during a period of time when he was held incommunicado, (3) when he was held without sleep or rest and (4) subjected to questioning by officers, experienced investigators and highly trained lawyers. The Court found that the questioning, which commenced at 7 pm on Saturday evening and ceased at 6:00 am on Monday morning, constituted a denial of "due process of law" and the conviction could not be sustained.

Spano v. New York

79 S.Ct. 1202

Supreme Court of the United States

Vincent Joseph SPANO, Petitioner,

v.

PEOPLE OF THE STATE OF NEW YORK.

No. 582. | Argued April 27, 1959. | Decided June 22, 1959.

Mr. Chief Justice WARREN delivered the opinion of the Court.

This is another in the long line of cases presenting the question whether a confession was properly admitted into evidence under the Fourteenth Amendment. As in all such cases, we are forced to resolve a conflict between two fundamental interests of society; its interest in prompt and efficient law enforcement, and its interest in preventing the rights of its individual members from being abridged by unconstitutional methods of law enforcement. *316 Because of the delicate nature of the constitutional determination which we must make, we cannot escape the responsibility of making our own examination of the record. Norris v. State of Alabama, 294 U.S. 587, 55 S.Ct. 579, 79 L.Ed. 1074.

The State's evidence reveals the following: Petitioner Vincent Joseph Spano is a derivative citizen of this country, having been born in Messina, Italy. He was 25 years old at the time of the shooting in question and had graduated from junior high school. He had a record of regular employment. The shooting took place on January 22, 1957.

On that day, petitioner was drinking in a bar. The decedent, a former professional boxer weighing almost 200 pounds who had fought in Madison Square Garden, took some of petitioner's money from the bar. Petitioner followed him out of the bar to recover it. A fight ensued, with the decedent knocking petitioner down and then kicking him in the head three or four times. Shock from the force of these blow caused petitioner to vomit. After the bartender applied some ice to his head, petitioner left the bar, walked to his apartment, secured a gun, and walked eight or nine blocks to a candy store where the decedent was frequently to be found. He entered the store in which decedent, three friends of decedent, at least two of whom were ex-convicts, and a boy who was supervising the store were present. He fired five shots, two of which entered the decedent's body, causing his death. The boy was the only eyewitness; the three friends of decedent did not see the person who fired the shot. Petitioner then disappeared for the next week or so.

On February 1, 1957, the Bronx County Grand Jury returned an indictment for first-degree murder against petitioner. Accordingly, a bench warrant was issued for his arrest, commanding that he be forthwith brought before the court to answer the indictment, or, if the court had adjourned for the term, that he be delivered into the *317 custody of the Sheriff of Bronx County. See N.Y. Code Crim.Proc. s 301.

**1204 On February 3, 1957, petitioner called one Gaspar Bruno, a close friend of 8 or 10 years' standing who had attended school with him. Bruno was a fledgling police officer, having at that time not yet finished attending police academy. According to Bruno's testimony, petitioner told him 'that he took a terrific beating, that the deceased hurt him real bad and he dropped him a couple of times and he was dazed; he didn't know what he was doing and that he went and shot at him.' Petitioner told Bruno that he intended to get a lawyer and give himself up. Bruno relayed this information to his superiors.

The following day, February 4, at 7:10 p.m., petitioner, accompanied by counsel, surrendered himself to the authorities in front of the Bronx County Building, where both the office of the Assistant District Attorney who ultimately prosecuted his case and the court-room in which he was ultimately tried were located. His attorney had cautioned him to answer no questions, and left him in the custody of the officers. He was promptly taken to the office of the Assistant District Attorney and at 7:15 p.m. the questioning began, being conducted by Assistant District Attorney Goldsmith, Lt. Gannon, Detectives Farrell, Lehrer and Motta, and Sgt. Clarke. The record reveals that the questioning was both persistent and continuous. Petitioner, in accordance with his attorney's instructions, steadfastly refused to answer. Detective Motta testified: 'He refused to talk to me.' 'He just looked up to the ceiling and refused to talk to me.' Detective Farrell testified:

'Q. And you started to interrogate him? A. That is right.

'Q. What did he say? *318 A. He said 'you would have to see my attorney. I tell you nothing but my name.'

'Q. Did you continue to examine him? A. Verbally, yes, sir.'

He asked one officer, Detective Ciccone, if he could speak to his attorney, but that request was denied. Detective Ciccone testified that he could not find the attorney's name in the telephone book.1 He was given two sandwiches, coffee and cake at 11 p.m.

At 12:15 a.m. on the morning of February 5, after five hours of questioning in which it became evident that petitioner was following his attorney's instructions, on the Assistant District Attorney's orders petitioner was transferred to the 46th Squad, Ryer Avenue Police Station. The Assistant District Attorney also went to the police station and to some extent continued to participate in the interrogation. Petitioner arrived at 12:30 and questioning was resumed at 12:40. The character of the questioning is revealed by the testimony of Detective Farrell:

'Q. Who did you leave him in the room with? A. With Detective Lehrer and Sergeant Clarke came in and Mr. Goldsmith came in or Inspector Halk came in. It was back and forth. People just came in, spoke a few words to the defendant or they listened a few minutes and they left.'

But petitioner persisted in his refusal to answer, and again requested permission to see his attorney, this time from Detective Lehrer. His request was again denied.

It was then that those in charge of the investigation decided that petitioner's close friend, Bruno, could be of *319 use. He had been called out on the case around 10 or 11 p.m., although he was not connected with the 46th Squad or Precinct in any way. Although, in fact, his job was in no way threatened, Bruno was **1205 told to tell petitioner that petitioner's telephone call had gotten him 'in a lot of trouble,' and that he should seek to extract sympathy from petitioner for Bruno's pregnant wife and three children. Bruno developed this theme with petitioner without success, and petitioner, also without success, again sought to see his attorney, a request which Bruno relayed unavailingly to his superiors. After this first session with petitioner, Bruno was again directed by Lt. Gannon to play on petitioner's sympathies, but again no confession was forthcoming. But the Lieutenant a third time ordered Bruno falsely to importune his friend to confess but again petitioner clung to his attorney's advice. Inevitably, in the fourth such session directed by the Lieutenant, lasting a full hour, petitioner succumbed to his friend's prevarications and agreed to make a statement. Accordingly, at 3:25 a.m. the Assistant District Attorney, a stenographer, and several other law enforcement officials entered the room where petitioner was being questioned, and took his statement in question and answer form with the Assistant District Attorney asking the questions. The statement was completed at 4:05 a.m.

But this was not the end. At 4:30 a.m. three detectives took petitioner to Police Headquarters in Manhattan. On the way they attempted to find the bridge from which petitioner said he had thrown the murder weapon. They crossed the Triborough Bridge into Manhattan, arriving at Police Headquarters at 5 a.m., and left Manhattan for the Bronx at 5:40 a.m. via the Willis Avenue Bridge. When petitioner recognized neither bridge as the one from which he had thrown the weapon, they reentered Manhattan via the Third Avenue Bridge, which petitioner stated was the right one, and then returned to *320 the Bronx well after 6 a.m. During that trip the officers also elicited a statement from petitioner that the deceased was always 'on (his) back,' 'always pushing' him and that he was 'not sorry' he had shot the deceased. All three detectives testified to that statement at the trial.

Court opened at 10 a.m. that morning, and petitioner was arraigned at 10:15.

At the trial, the confession was introduced in evidence over appropriate objections. The jury was instructed that it could rely on it only if it was found to be voluntary. The jury returned a guilty verdict and petitioner was sentenced to death. The New York Court of Appeals affirmed the conviction over three dissents, 4 N.Y.2d 256, 173 N.Y.S.2d 793, 150 N.E.2d 226, and we granted certiorari to resolve the serious problem presented under the Fourteenth Amendment. 358 U.S. 919, 79 S.Ct. 293, 3 L.Ed. 2d 238.

Petitioner's first contention is that his absolute right to counsel in a capital case, Powell v. State of Alabama, 287 U.S. 45, 53 S.Ct. 55, 77 L.Ed. 158, became operative on the return of an indictment against him, for at that time he was in every sense a defendant in a criminal case, the grand jury having found sufficient cause to believe that he had committed the crime. He argues accordingly that following indictment no confession obtained in the absence of counsel can be used without violating the Fourteenth Amendment. He seeks to distinguish Crooker v. State of California, 357 U.S. 433, 78 S.Ct. 1287, 2 L.Ed.2d 1448, and Cicenia v. Lagay, 357 U.S. 504, 78 S.Ct. 1297, 2 L.Ed.2d 1523, on the ground that in those cases no indictment had been returned. We find it unnecessary to reach that contention, for we find use of the confession obtained here inconsistent with the Fourteenth Amendment under traditional principles.

The abhorrence of society to the use of involuntary confessions does not turn alone on their inherent untrustworthiness. It also turns on the deep-rooted feeling that the police must obey **1206 the law while enforcing the law; that in the end life and liberty can be as much endangered *321 from illegal methods used to convict those thought to be criminals as from the actual criminals themselves. Accordingly, the actions of police in obtaining confessions have come under scrutiny in a long series of cases. Those cases suggest that in recent years law enforcement officials have become increasingly aware of the burden which they share, along with our courts, in protecting fundamental rights of our citizenry, including that portion of our citizenry suspected of crime. The facts of no case recently in this Court have quite approached the brutal beatings in Brown v. State of Mississippi, 1936, 297 U.S. 278, 56 S.Ct. 461, 80 L.Ed. 682, or the 36 consecutive hours of questioning present in Ashcraft v. State of Tennessee, 1944, 322 U.S. 143, 64 S.Ct. 921, 88 L.Ed. 1192. But as law enforcement officers become more responsible, and the methods used to extract confessions more sophisticated, our duty to enforce federal constitutional protections does not cease. It only becomes more difficult because of the more delicate judgments to be made. Our judgment here is that, on all the facts, this conviction cannot stand.

Petitioner was a foreign-born young man of 25 with no past history of law violation or of subjection to official interrogation, at least insofar as the record shows. He *322 had progressed only one-half year into high school and the record indicates that he had a history of emotional instability. He did not make a narrative statement, but was subject to the leading questions of a skillful prosecutor in a question and answer confession. He was subjected to questioning **1207 not by a few men, but by many. They included Assistant District Attorney Goldsmith, one Hyland of the District Attorney's Office, Deputy Inspector Halks, Lieutenant Gannon, Detective Ciccone, Detective Motta, Detective Lehrer, Detective Marshal, Detective Farrell, Detective Leira, Detective Murphy, Detective Murtha, Sergeant Clarke, Patrolman Bruno and Stenographer Baldwin. All played some part, and the effect of such massive official interrogation must have been felt. Petitioner was questioned for virtually eight straight hours before he confessed, with his only respite being a transfer to an arena presumably considered more appropriate by the police for the task at hand. Nor was the questioning conducted during normal business hours, but began in early evening, continued into the night, and did not bear fruition until the not-too-early morning. The drama was not played out, with the final admissions obtained, until almost sunrise. In such circumstances slowly mounting fatigue does, and is calculated to, play its part. The questioners persisted in the face of his repeated refusals to answer on the advice of his *323 attorney, and they ignored his reasonable requests to contact the local attorney whom he had already retained and who had personally delivered him into the custody of these officers in obedience to the bench warrant.

The use of Bruno, characterized in this Court by counsel for the State as a 'childhood friend' of petitioner's, is another factor which deserves mention in the totality of the situation. Bruno's was the one face visible to petitioner in which he could put some trust. There was a bond of friendship between them going back a decade into adolescence. It was with this material that the officers felt that they could overcome petitioner's will. They instructed Bruno falsely to state that petitioner's telephone call had gotten him into trouble, that his job was in jeopardy, and that loss of his job would be disastrous to his three children, his wife and his unborn child. And Bruno played this part of a worried father, harried by his superiors, in not one, but four different acts, the final one lasting an hour. Cf. Leyra v. Denno, 347 U.S. 556, 74 S.Ct. 716, 98 L.Ed. 948. Petitioner was apparently unaware of John Gay's famous couplet:

'An open foe may prove a curse, But a pretended friend is worse,'

and he yielded to his false friend's entreaties.

We conclude that petitioner's will was overborne by official pressure, fatigue and sympathy falsely aroused after considering all the facts in their post-indictment setting.6 Here a grand jury had already found sufficient cause to require petitioner to face trial on a charge of first-degree murder, and the police had an eyewitness to the shooting. The police were not therefore merely trying to solve a crime, or even to absolve a suspect. Compare *324 Crooker v. State of California, supra, and Cicenia

v. Lagay, supra. They were rather concerned primarily with securing a statement from defendant on which they could convict him. The undeviating intent of the officers to extract a confession from petitioner is therefore patent. When such an intent is shown, this Court has held that the confession obtained must be examined with the most careful scrutiny, and has reversed a conviction on facts less compelling than these. **1208 Malinski v. People of State of New York, 324 U.S. 401, 65 S.Ct. 781, 89 L.Ed. 1029. Accordingly, we hold that petitioner's conviction cannot stand under the Fourteenth Amendment.

The State suggests, however, that we are not free to reverse this conviction, since there is sufficient other evidence in the record from which the jury might have found guilt, relying on Stein v. People of State of New York, 346 U.S. 156, 73 S.Ct. 1077, 97 L.Ed. 1522. But Payne v. State of Arkansas, 356 U.S. 560, 568, 78 S.Ct. 844, 850, 2 L.Ed.2d 975, authoritatively establishes that Stein did not hold that a conviction may be sustained on the basis of other evidence if a confession found to be involuntary by this Court was used, even though limiting instructions were given. Stein held only that when a confession is not found by this Court to be involuntary, this Court will not reverse on the ground that the jury might have found it involuntary and might have relied on it. The judgment must be reversed.

Reversed.

Mr. Justice DOUGLAS, with whom Mr. Justice BLACK and Mr. Justice BRENNAN join, concurring.

While I join the opinion of the Court, I add what for me is an even more important ground of decision.

We have often divided on whether state authorities may question a suspect for hours on end when he has no lawyer present and when he has demanded that he have the benefit of legal advice. See Crooker v. State of California, 357 U.S. 433, 78 S.Ct. 1287, 2 L.Ed.2d 1448, and cases cited. But here we deal not with a suspect but with a man who has been formally charged *325 with a crime. The question is whether after the indictment and before the trial the Government can interrogate the accused in secret when he asked for his lawyer and when his request was denied. This is a capital case; and under the rule of Powell v. State of Alabama, 287 U.S. 45, 53 S.Ct. 55, 77 L.Ed. 158, the defendant was entitled to be represented by counsel. This representation by counsel is not restricted to the trial. As stated in Powell v. State of Alabama, supra, 287 U.S. at page 57, 53 S.Ct. at page 59:

'during perhaps the most critical period of the proceedings against these defendants, that is to say, from the time of their arraignment until the beginning of their trial, when consultation, thorough-going investigation and preparation were vitally important, the defendants did not have the aid of counsel in any real sense, although they were as much entitled to such aid during that period as at the trial itself.'

Depriving a person, formally charged with a crime, of counsel during the period prior to trial may be more damaging than denial of counsel during the trial itself.

We do not have here mere suspects who are being secretly interrogated by the police as in Crooker v. State of California, supra, nor witnesses who are being questioned in secret administrative or judicial proceedings as in In re Groban, 352 U.S. 330, 77 S.Ct. 510, 1 L.Ed.2d 376, and Anonymous Nos. 6 & 7 v. Baker, 360 U.S. 287, 79 S.Ct. 1157. This is a case of an accused, who is scheduled to be tried by a judge and jury, being tried in a preliminary way by the police. This is a kangaroo court procedure whereby the police produce the vital evidence in the form of a confession which is useful or necessary to obtain a conviction. They in effect deny him effective representation by counsel. This seems to me to be a flagrant violation of the principle announced in Powell v. State of Alabama, supra, that the right of counsel extends to the preparation for trial, as well as **1209 to the trial itself. As Professor Chafee once said, 'A person accused of crime *326 needs a lawyer right after his arrest probably more than at any other time.' Chafee, Documents on Fundamental Human Rights,

Pamphlet 2 (1951—1952), p. 541. When he is deprived of that right after indictment and before trial, he may indeed be denied effective representation by counsel at the only stage when legal aid and advice would help him. This secret inquisition by the police when defendant asked for and was denied counsel was as serious an invasion of his constitutional rights as the denial of a continuance in order to employ counsel was held to be in Chandler v. Fretag, 348 U.S. 3, 10, 75 S.Ct. 1, 5, 99 L.Ed. 4. What we said in Avery v. State of Albama, 308 U.S. 444, 446, 60 S.Ct. 321, 322, 84 L.Ed. 377, has relevance here:

'* * * the denial of opportunity for appointed counsel to confer, to consult with the accused and to prepare his defense, could convert the appointment of counsel into a sham and nothing more than a formal compliance with the Constitution's requirement that an accused be given the assistance of counsel.'

I join with Judges Desmond, Fuld, and Van Voorhis of the New York Court of Appeals (4 N.Y.2d 256, 266, 173 N.Y.S.2d 793, 801, 150 N.E.2d 226, 232—233), in asking, what use is a defendant's right to effective counsel at every stage of a criminal case if, while he is held awaiting trial, he can be questioned in the absence of counsel until he confesses? In that event the secret trial in the police precincts effectively supplants the public trial guaranteed by the Bill of Rights.

Mr. Justice STEWART, whom Mr. Justice DOUGLAS and Mr. Justice BRENNAN join, concurring.

While I concur in the opinion of the Court, it is my view that the absence of counsel when this confession was elicited was alone enough to render it inadmissible under the Fourteenth Amendment.

*327 Let it be emphasized at the outset that this is not a case where the police were questioning a suspect in the course of investigating an unsolved crime. See Crooker v. State of California, 357 U.S. 433, 78 S.Ct. 1287, 2 L.Ed.2d 1448; Cicenia v. Lagay, 357 U.S. 504, 78 S.Ct. 1297, 2 L.Ed.2d 1523. When the petitioner surrendered to the New York authorities he was under indictment for first degree murder

Under our system of justice an indictment is supposed to be followed by an arraignment and a trial. At every stage in those proceedings the accused has an absolute right to a lawyer's help if the case is one in which a death sentence may be imposed. Powell v. State of Alabama, 287 U.S. 45, 53 S.Ct. 55, 77 L.Ed. 158. Indeed the right to the assistance of counsel whom the accused has himself retained is absolute, whatever the offense for which he is on trial. Chandler v. Fretag, 348 U.S. 3, 75 S.Ct. 1, 99 L.Ed. 4.

What followed the petitioner's surrender in this case was not arraignment in a court of law, but an all-night inquisition in a prosecutor's office, a police station, and an automobile. Throughout the night the petitioner repeatedly asked to be allowed to send for his lawyer, and his requests were repeatedly denied. He finally was induced to make a confession. That confession was used to secure a verdict sending him to the electric chair.

Our Constitution guarantees the assistance of counsel to a man on trial for his life in an orderly courtroom, presided over by a judge, open to the public, and protected by all the procedural safeguards of the law. Surely a Constitution which promises that much can vouchsafe no less to the same man under midnight inquisition in the squad room of a police station.

Black Letter Law

> The Court held that the interrogation violated the defendant's Fourteenth Amendment due process rights because his confession was not voluntary when the defendant admitted to a policeman friend over the telephone prior to his surrender that he had killed the decedent and the following day he surrender to police officers who began questioning him, ignored his requests to contact his retained lawyer, and continued to question him for eight hours until the early morning.

Colorado v. Conelly

107 S.Ct. 515

Supreme Court of the United States

COLORADO, Petitioner

v.

Francis Barry CONNELLY.

No. 85–660. | Argued Oct. 8, 1986. | Decided Dec. 10, 1986.

*159 Chief Justice REHNQUIST delivered the opinion of the Court.

In this case, the Supreme Court of Colorado held that the United States Constitution **518 requires a court to suppress a confession when the mental state of the defendant, at the time he made the confession, interfered with his "rational intellect" and his "free will." Because this decision seemed to conflict with prior holdings of this Court, we granted certiorari. 474 U.S. 1050, 106 S.Ct. 785, 88 L.Ed.2d 763 (1986). We conclude that the admissibility of this kind of statement is governed by state rules of evidence, rather than by our previous decisions regarding coerced confessions and Miranda waivers. We therefore reverse.

*160 On August 18, 1983, Officer Patrick Anderson of the Denver Police Department was in uniform, working in an off-duty capacity in downtown Denver. Respondent Francis Connelly approached Officer Anderson and, without any prompting, stated that he had murdered someone and wanted to talk about it. Anderson immediately advised respondent that he had the right to remain silent, that anything he said could be used against him in court, and that he had the right to an attorney prior to any police questioning. See Miranda v. Arizona, 384 U.S. 436, 86 S.Ct. 1602, 16 L.Ed.2d 694 (1966). Respondent stated that he understood these rights but he still wanted to talk about the murder. Understandably bewildered by this confession, Officer Anderson asked respondent several questions. Connelly denied that he had been drinking, denied that he had been taking any drugs, and stated that, in the past, he had been a patient in several mental hospitals. Officer Anderson again told Connelly that he was under no obligation to say anything. Connelly replied that it was "all right," and that he would talk to Officer Anderson because his conscience had been bothering him. To Officer Anderson, respondent appeared to understand fully the nature of his acts. Tr. 19.

Shortly thereafter, Homicide Detective Stephen Antuna arrived. Respondent was again advised of his rights, and Detective Antuna asked him "what he had on his mind." Id., at 24. Respondent answered that he had come all the way from Boston to confess to the murder of Mary Ann Junta, a young girl whom he had killed in Denver sometime during November 1982. Respondent was taken to police headquarters, and a search of police records revealed that the body of an unidentified female had been found in April 1983. Respondent openly detailed his story to Detective Antuna and Sergeant Thomas Haney, and readily agreed to take the officers to the scene of the killing. Under Connelly's sole direction, the two officers and respondent proceeded *161 in a police vehicle to the location of the crime. Respondent pointed out the exact location of the murder. Throughout this episode, Detective Antuna perceived no indication whatsoever that respondent was suffering from any kind of mental illness. Id., at 33–34.

Respondent was held overnight. During an interview with the public defender's office the following morning, he became visibly disoriented. He began giving confused answers to questions, and for the first time, stated that "voices" had told him to come to Denver and that he had followed the directions of these voices in confessing. Id., at 42. Respondent was sent to a state hospital for evaluation. He was initially found incompetent to assist in his own defense. By March 1984, however, the doctors evaluating respondent determined that he was competent to proceed to trial.

At a preliminary hearing, respondent moved to suppress all of his statements. Dr. Jeffrey Metzner, a psychiatrist employed by the state hospital, testified that respondent was suffering from chronic schizophrenia and was in a psychotic state at least as of August 17, 1983, the day before he confessed. Metzner's interviews with respondent revealed that respondent was following the "voice of God." This voice instructed respondent to withdraw money from the bank, to buy an airplane ticket, and to fly from Boston to Denver. When respondent arrived from Boston, God's voice became stronger and told respondent **519 either to confess to the killing or to commit suicide. Reluctantly following the command of the voices, respondent approached Officer Anderson and confessed.

Dr. Metzner testified that, in his expert opinion, respondent was experiencing "command hallucinations." Id., at 56. This condition interfered with respondent's "volitional abilities; that is, his ability to make free and rational choices." Ibid. Dr. Metzner further testified that Connelly's illness did not significantly impair his cognitive abilities. Thus, respondent understood the rights he had when Officer Anderson *162 and Detective Antuna advised him that he need not speak. Id., at 56–57. Dr. Metzner admitted that the "voices" could in reality be Connelly's interpretation of his own guilt, but explained that in his opinion, Connelly's psychosis motivated his confession.

On the basis of this evidence the Colorado trial court decided that respondent's statements must be suppressed because they were "involuntary." Relying on our decisions in Townsend v. Sain, 372 U.S. 293, 83 S.Ct. 745, 9 L.Ed.2d 770 (1963), and Culombe v. Connecticut, 367 U.S. 568, 81 S.Ct. 1860, 6 L.Ed.2d 1037 (1961), the court ruled that a confession is admissible only if it is a product of the defendant's rational intellect and "free will." Tr. 88. Although the court found that the police had done nothing wrong or coercive in securing respondent's confession, Connelly's illness destroyed his volition and compelled him to confess. Id., at 89. The trial court also found that Connelly's mental state vitiated his attempted waiver of the right to counsel and the privilege against compulsory self-incrimination. Accordingly, respondent's initial statements and his custodial confession were suppressed. Id., at 90.

The Colorado Supreme Court affirmed. 702 P.2d 722 (1985). In that court's view, the proper test for admissibility is whether the statements are "the product of a rational intellect and a free will." Id., at 728. Indeed, "the absence of police coercion or duress does not foreclose a finding of involuntariness. One's capacity for rational judgment and free choice may be overborne as much by certain forms of severe mental illness as by external pressure." Ibid. The court found that the very admission of the evidence in a court of law was sufficient state action to implicate the Due Process Clause of the Fourteenth Amendment to the United States Constitution. The evidence fully supported the conclusion that respondent's initial statement was not the product of a rational intellect and a free will. The court then considered respondent's attempted waiver of his constitutional rights and found that respondent's mental condition precluded his *163 ability to make a valid waiver. Id., at 729. The Colorado Supreme Court thus affirmed the trial court's decision to suppress all of Connelly's statements.

The Due Process Clause of the Fourteenth Amendment provides that no State shall "deprive any person of life, liberty, or property, without due process of law." Just last Term, in Miller v. Fenton, 474 U.S. 104, 109, 106 S.Ct. 445, 449, 88 L.Ed.2d 405 (1985), we held that by virtue of the Due Process Clause "certain interrogation techniques, either in isolation or as applied to the unique characteristics of a particular suspect, are so offensive to a civilized system of justice that they must be condemned." See also Moran v. Burbine, 475 U.S. 412, 432–434, 106 S.Ct. 1135, 1147, 89 L.Ed.2d 410 (1986).

Indeed, coercive government misconduct was the catalyst for this Court's seminal confession case, Brown v. Mississippi, 297 U.S. 278, 56 S.Ct. 461, 80 L.Ed. 682 (1936). In that case, police officers extracted confessions from the accused through brutal torture. The Court had little difficulty concluding that even though the Fifth Amendment did not at that time apply to the States, the actions of the police were "revolting to the sense of justice." Id., at 286, 56 S.Ct., at 465. The Court has retained this due process focus, even after holding, in **520 Malloy v. Hogan, 378 U.S. 1, 84 S.Ct. 1489, 12 L.Ed.2d 653 (1964), that the Fifth Amendment privilege against compulsory self-incrimination applies to the States. See Miller v. Fenton, supra, 474 U.S., at 109–110, 106 S.Ct., at 449.

Thus the cases considered by this Court over the 50 years since Brown v. Mississippi have focused upon the crucial element of police overreaching.1 While each confession case *164 has turned on its own set of factors justifying the conclusion that police conduct was oppressive, all have contained a substantial element of coercive police conduct. Absent police conduct causally related to the confession, there is simply no basis for concluding that any state actor has deprived a criminal defendant of due process of law. Respondent correctly notes that as interrogators have turned to more subtle forms of psychological persuasion, courts have found the mental condition of the defendant a more significant factor in the "voluntariness" calculus. See Spano v. New York, 360 U.S. 315, 79 S.Ct. 1202, 3 L.Ed.2d 1265 (1959). But this fact does not justify a conclusion that a defendant's mental condition, by itself and apart from its relation to official coercion, should ever dispose of the inquiry into constitutional "voluntariness."

Respondent relies on Blackburn v. Alabama, 361 U.S. 199, 80 S.Ct. 274, 4 L.Ed.2d 242 (1960), and Townsend v. Sain, 372 U.S. 293, 83 S.Ct. 745, 9 L.Ed.2d 770 (1963), for the proposition that the "deficient mental condition of the defendants in those cases was sufficient to render their confessions involuntary." Brief for Respondent 20. But respondent's reading of Blackburn and Townsend ignores the integral element of police overreaching present in both cases. In Blackburn, the Court found that the petitioner was probably insane at the time of his confession and the police learned during the interrogation that he had a history of mental problems. *165 The police exploited this weakness with coercive tactics: "the eight- to nine-hour sustained interrogation in a tiny room which was upon occasion literally filled with police officers; the absence of Blackburn's friends, relatives, or legal counsel; [and] the composition of the confession by the Deputy Sheriff rather than by Blackburn." 361 U.S., at 207–208, 80 S.Ct., at 280. These tactics supported a finding that the confession was involuntary. Indeed, the Court specifically condemned police activity that "wrings a confession out of an accused against his will." Id., at 206–207, 80 S.Ct., at 280. Townsend presented a similar instance of police wrongdoing. In that case, a police physician had given Townsend a drug with truth-serum properties. 372 U.S., at 298–299, 83 S.Ct., at 749–750. The subsequent confession, obtained by officers who knew that Townsend had been given drugs, was held involuntary. These two cases demonstrate that while mental **521 condition is surely relevant to an individual's susceptibility to police coercion, mere examination of the confessant's state of mind can never conclude the due process inquiry.

Our "involuntary confession" jurisprudence is entirely consistent with the settled law requiring some sort of "state action" to support a claim of violation of the Due Process Clause of the Fourteenth Amendment. The Colorado trial court, of course, found that the police committed no wrongful acts, and that finding has been neither challenged by respondent nor disturbed by the Supreme Court of Colorado. The latter court, however, concluded that sufficient state action was present by virtue of the admission of the confession into evidence in a court of the State. 702 P.2d, at 728–729.

The difficulty with the approach of the Supreme Court of Colorado is that it fails to recognize the essential link between coercive activity of the State, on the one hand, and a resulting confession by a defendant, on the other. The flaw in respondent's constitutional argument is that it would expand our previous line of "voluntariness" cases into a far-ranging requirement that courts must divine a defendant's *166 motivation for speaking or acting as he did even though there be no claim that governmental conduct coerced his decision.

The most outrageous behavior by a private party seeking to secure evidence against a defendant does not make that evidence inadmissible under the Due Process Clause. See Walter v. United States, 447 U.S. 649, 656, 100 S.Ct. 2395, 2401, 65 L.Ed.2d 410 (1980); Coolidge v. New Hampshire, 403 U.S. 443, 487–488, 91 S.Ct. 2022, 2048–49, 29 L.Ed.2d 564 (1971); Burdeau v. McDowell, 256 U.S. 465, 476, 41 S.Ct. 574, 576, 65 L.Ed. 1048 (1921). We have also observed that "[j]urists and scholars uniformly have recognized that the exclusionary rule imposes a substantial cost on the societal interest in law enforcement by its proscription of what concededly is relevant evidence." United States v. Janis, 428 U.S. 433, 448–449, 96 S.Ct. 3021, 3029, 49 L.Ed.2d 1046 (1976). See also United States v. Havens, 446 U.S. 620, 627, 100 S.Ct. 1912, 1916, 64 L.Ed.2d 559 (1980); United States v. Calandra, 414 U.S. 338, 94 S.Ct. 613, 38 L.Ed.2d 561 (1974). Moreover, suppressing respondent's statements would serve absolutely no purpose in enforcing constitutional guarantees. The purpose of excluding evidence seized in violation of the Constitution is to substantially deter future violations of the Constitution. See United States v. Leon, 468 U.S. 897, 906–913, 104 S.Ct. 3405, 3411–3415, 82 L.Ed.2d 677 (1984). Only if we were to establish a brand new constitutional right—the right of a criminal defendant to confess to his crime only when totally rational and properly motivated—could respondent's present claim be sustained.

We have previously cautioned against expanding "currently applicable exclusionary rules by erecting additional barriers to placing truthful and probative evidence before state juries...." Lego v. Twomey, 404 U.S. 477, 488–489, 92 S.Ct. 619, 626, 30 L.Ed. 2d 618 (1972). We abide by that counsel now. "[T]he central purpose of a criminal trial is to decide the factual question of the defendant's guilt or innocence," Delaware v. Van Arsdall, 475 U.S. 673, 681, 106 S.Ct. 1431, 1436, 89 L.Ed.2d 674 (1986), and while we have previously held that exclusion of evidence may be necessary to protect constitutional guarantees, both the necessity for the collateral inquiry and the exclusion of evidence deflect a criminal trial from its basic purpose. Respondent would now have us require *167 sweeping inquiries into the state of mind of a criminal defendant who has confessed, inquiries quite divorced from any coercion brought to bear on the defendant by the State. We think the Constitution rightly leaves this sort of inquiry to be resolved by state laws governing the admission of evidence and erects no standard of its own in this area. A statement rendered by one in the condition of respondent might be proved to be quite unreliable, but this is a **522 matter to be governed by the evidentiary laws of the forum, see, e.g., Fed.Rule Evid. 601, and not by the Due Process Clause of the Fourteenth Amendment. "The aim of the requirement of due process is not to exclude presumptively false evidence, but to prevent fundamental unfairness in the use of evidence, whether true or false." Lisenba v. California, 314 U.S. 219, 236, 62 S.Ct. 280, 290, 86 L.Ed. 166 (1941).

We hold that coercive police activity is a necessary predicate to the finding that a confession is not "voluntary" within the meaning of the Due Process Clause of the Fourteenth Amendment. We also conclude that the taking of respondent's statements, and their admission into evidence, constitute no violation of that Clause.

III

A

The Supreme Court of Colorado went on to affirm the trial court's ruling that respondent's later statements made while in custody should be suppressed because respondent had not waived his right to consult an attorney and his right to remain silent. That court held that the State must bear its burden of proving waiver of these Miranda rights by "clear and convincing evidence." 702 P.2d, at 729. Although we have stated in passing that the State bears a "heavy" burden in proving waiver, Tague v. Louisiana, 444 U.S. 469, 100 S.Ct. 652, 62 L.Ed.2d 622 (1980) (per curiam); North Carolina v. Butler 441 U.S. 369, 373, 99 S.Ct. 1755, 1757, 60 L.Ed.2d 286 (1979); Miranda v. Arizona, 384 U.S., at 475, 86 S.Ct., at 1628, we have never *168 held that the "clear and convincing evidence" standard is the appropriate one.

In Lego v. Twomey, supra, this Court upheld a procedure in which the State established the voluntariness of a confession by no more than a preponderance of the evidence. We upheld it for two reasons. First, the voluntariness determination has nothing to do with the reliability of jury verdicts; rather, it is designed to determine the presence of police coercion. Thus, voluntariness is irrelevant to the presence or absence of the elements of a crime, which must be proved beyond a reasonable doubt. See In re Winship, 397 U.S. 358, 90 S.Ct. 1068, 25 L.Ed.2d 368 (1970). Second, we rejected Lego's assertion that a high burden of proof was required to serve the values protected by the exclusionary rule. We surveyed the various reasons for excluding evidence, including a violation of the requirements of Miranda v. Arizona, supra, and we stated that "[i]n each instance, and without regard to its probative value, evidence is kept from the trier of guilt or innocence for reasons wholly apart from enhancing the reliability of verdicts." Lego v. Twomey, 404 U.S., at 488, 92 S.Ct., at 626. Moreover, we rejected the argument that "the importance of the values served by exclusionary rules is itself sufficient demonstration that the Constitution also requires admissibility to be proved beyond a reasonable doubt." Ibid. Indeed, the Court found that "no substantial evidence has accumulated that federal rights have suffered from determining admissibility by a preponderance of the evidence." Ibid.

We now reaffirm our holding in Lego: Whenever the State bears the burden of proof in a motion to suppress a statement that the defendant claims was obtained in violation of our Miranda doctrine, the State need prove waiver only by a preponderance of the evidence. See Nix v. Williams, 467 U.S. 431, 444, and n. 5, 104 S.Ct. 2501, 2509, and n. 5, 81 L.Ed.2d 377 (1984); United States v. Matlock, 415 U.S. 164, 178, n. 14, 94 S.Ct. 988, 996, n. 14, 39 L.Ed.2d 242 (1974) ("[T]he controlling burden of proof at suppression hearings should impose no greater burden than proof by a preponderance of the evidence ..."). *169 Cf. Moore v. Michigan, 355 U.S. 155, 161–162, 78 S.Ct. 191, 195, 2 L.Ed.2d 167 (1957). If, as we held in Lego v. Twomey, supra, the voluntariness of a confession need be established only by a preponderance of the evidence, then a waiver of the auxiliary protections established in MIRANDA **523 should require no higher burden of proof. "[E]xclusionary rules are very much aimed at deterring lawless conduct by police and prosecution and it is very doubtful that escalating the prosecution's burden of proof in ... suppression hearings would be sufficiently productive in this respect to outweigh the public interest in placing probative evidence before juries for the purpose of arriving at truthful decisions about guilt or innocence." Lego v. Twomey, supra, 404 U.S., at 489, 92 S.Ct., at 626. See also United States v. Leon, 468 U.S., at 906–913, 104 S.Ct., at 3411–3415.

B

We also think that the Supreme Court of Colorado was mistaken in its analysis of the question whether respondent had waived his Miranda rights in this case. Of course, a waiver must at a minimum be "voluntary" to be effective against an accused. Miranda, supra, 384 U.S., at 444, 476, 86 S.Ct., at 1612, 1628; North Carolina v. Butler, supra, 441 U.S., at 373, 99 S.Ct., at 1757. The Supreme Court of Colorado in addressing this question relied on the testimony of the court-appointed psychiatrist to the effect that respondent was not capable of making a "free decision with respect to his constitutional right of silence ... and his constitutional right to confer with a lawyer before talking to the police." 702 P.2d, at 729.

We think that the Supreme Court of Colorado erred in importing into this area of constitutional law notions of "free will" that have no place there. There is obviously no reason to require more in the way of a "voluntariness" inquiry in the *170 Miranda waiver context than in the Fourteenth Amendment confession context. The sole concern of the Fifth Amendment, on which Miranda was based, is governmental coercion. See United States v. Washington, 431 U.S. 181, 187, 97 S.Ct. 1814, 1818, 52 L.Ed.2d 238 (1977); Miranda, supra, 384 U.S., at 460, 86 S.Ct., at 1620. Indeed, the Fifth Amendment privilege is not concerned "with moral and psychological pressures to confess emanating from sources other than official coercion." Oregon v. Elstad, 470 U.S. 298, 305, 105 S.Ct. 1285, 1290, 84 L.Ed.2d 222 (1985). The voluntariness of a waiver of this privilege has always depended on the absence of police overreaching, not on "free choice" in any broader sense of the word. See Moran v. Burbine, 475 U.S., at 421, 106 S.Ct., at 1141 ("[T]he relinquishment of the right must have been voluntary in the sense that it was the product of a free and deliberate choice rather than intimidation, coercion or deception.... [T]he record is devoid of any suggestion that police resorted to physical or psychological pressure to elicit the statements"); Fare v. Michael C., 442 U.S. 707, 726–727, 99 S.Ct. 2560, 2572–2573, 61 L.Ed.2d 197 (1979) (The defendant was "not worn down by improper interrogation tactics or lengthy questioning or by trickery or deceit.... The officers did not intimidate or threaten respondent in any way. Their questioning was restrained and free from the abuses that so concerned the Court in Miranda").

Respondent urges this Court to adopt his "free will" rationale, and to find an attempted waiver invalid whenever the defendant feels compelled to waive his rights by reason of any compulsion, even if the compulsion does not flow from the police. But such a treatment of the waiver issue would "cut this Court's holding in [Miranda] completely loose from its own explicitly stated rationale." Beckwith v. United States, 425 U.S. 341, 345, 96 S.Ct. 1612, 1615, 48 L.Ed.2d 1 (1976). Miranda protects defendants against government coercion leading them to surrender rights protected by the Fifth Amendment; it goes no further than that. Respondent's perception **524 of coercion flowing from the "voice of God," however important or significant such a *171 perception may be in other disciplines, is a matter to which the United States Constitution does not speak.

IV

The judgment of the Supreme Court of Colorado is accordingly reversed, and the cause is remanded for further proceedings not inconsistent with this opinion.4

It is so ordered.

Justice BLACKMUN, concurring in part and concurring in the judgment.

I join Parts I, II, III–B, and IV of the Court's opinion and its judgment.

I refrain, however, from joining Part III–A of the opinion. Whatever may be the merits of the issue discussed there, which concerns the level of the State's burden of proof in showing that respondent had waived his rights under Miranda v. Arizona, 384 U.S. 436, 86 S.Ct. 1602, 16 L.Ed. 694 (1966), that issue was neither raised nor briefed by the parties, and, in my view, it is not necessary to the decision.

Justice STEVENS, concurring in the judgment in part and dissenting in part.

Respondent made incriminatory statements both before and after he was handcuffed and taken into custody. The only question presented by the Colorado District Attorney in his certiorari petition concerned the admissibility of respondent's precustodial statements. Pet. for Cert. i, 14–15.1 I *172 agree with the State of Colorado that the United States Constitution does not require suppression of those statements, but in reaching that conclusion, unlike the Court, I am perfectly willing to accept the state trial court's finding that the statements were involuntary.

The state trial court found that, in view of the "overwhelming evidence presented by the Defense," the prosecution did not meet its burden of demonstrating that respondent's initial statements to Officer Anderson were voluntary. App. 47–48. Nevertheless, in my opinion, the use of these involuntary precustodial statements does not violate the Fifth Amendment because they were not the product of state compulsion. Although they may well be so unreliable that they could not support a conviction, at this stage of the proceeding I could not say that they have no probative force whatever. The fact that the statements were involuntary—just as the product of Lady Macbeth's nightmare was involuntary2—does not mean that their use for whatever evidentiary value they may have is fundamentally unfair or a denial of due process.

The postcustodial statements raise an entirely distinct question. When the officer whom respondent approached elected to handcuff him and to take him into custody, the police assumed a fundamentally different relationship with him. Prior to that moment, the police had no duty to give respondent Miranda warnings and had every right to continue their exploratory conversation with him.3 Once the custodial relationship was established, however, the **525 questioning assumed *173 a presumptively coercive character. Miranda v. Arizona, 384 U.S. 436, 467, 86 S.Ct. 1602, 1624, 16 L.Ed.2d 694 (1966). In my opinion the questioning could not thereafter go forward in the absence of a valid waiver of respondent's constitutional rights unless he was provided with counsel. Since it is undisputed that respondent was not then competent to stand trial, I would also conclude that he was not competent to waive his constitutional right to remain silent.

The Court seems to believe that a waiver can be voluntary even if it is not the product of an exercise of the defendant's " 'free will.' " Ante, at 523. The Court's position is not only incomprehensible to me; it is also foreclosed by the Court's recent pronouncement in Moran v. Burbine, 475 U.S. 412, 421, 106 S.Ct. 1135, 1141, 89 L.Ed. 2d 410 (1986), that "the relinquishment of the right must have been voluntary in the sense that it was the product of a free and deliberate choice...."5 Because respondent's waiver was not voluntary in that sense, his custodial interrogation was presumptively coercive. The Colorado Supreme Court was unquestionably correct in concluding that his post-custodial incriminatory statements were inadmissible.

Accordingly, I concur in the judgment insofar as it applies to respondent's precustodial statements but respectfully dissent *174 from the Court's disposition of the question that was not presented by the certiorari petition.

(The dissent of Justice BRENNAN, with whom Justice MARSHALL joins, is omitted.)

Black Letter Law

> The Court held that coercive police activity is a necessary predicate to finding that confession is not voluntary within meaning of due process clause of Fourteenth Amendment; statements made by defendant when he approached police officer and stated that he wanted to confess to murder and then did so after receiving his *Miranda* rights could be admitted without violation of due process clause regardless of defendant's mental health. The state must prove waiver of *Miranda* rights only by a preponderance of the evidence, and voluntariness of waiver of privilege of Fifth Amendment depends upon absence of police overreaching not on "free choice" in any broader sense of the term.

Stovall v. Deno

87 S.Ct. 1967

Supreme Court of the United States

Theodore STOVALL, Petitioner,

v.

Wilfred DENNO, Warden.

No. 254. | Argued Feb. 16, 1967. | Decided June 12, 1967.

Mr. Justice BRENNAN delivered the opinion of the Court.

This federal habeas corpus proceeding attacks collaterally a state criminal conviction for the same alleged constitutional errors in the admission of allegedly tainted identification evidence that were before us on direct review of the convictions involved in United States v. Wade, 388 U.S. 218, 87 S.Ct. 1926, 18 L.Ed.2d 1149, and Gilbert v. State of California, 388 U.S. 263, 87 S.Ct. 1951, 18 L.Ed.2d 1178. This case therefore provides a vehicle for deciding the extent to which the rules announced in Wade and Gilbert-requiring the exclusion of identification evidence which is tainted by exhibiting the accused to identifying witnesses before trial in the absence of his counsel-are to be applied retroactively. See Linkletter v. Walker, 381 U.S. 618, 85 S.Ct. 1731, 14 L.Ed.2d 601; Tehan v. United States ex rel. Shott, 382 U.S. 406, 86 S.Ct. 459, 15 L.Ed.2d 453; Johnson v. State of New Jersey, 384 U.S. 719, 86 S.Ct. 1772, 16 L.Ed.2d 882.1 A further question is whether in any event, on the facts of the particular confrontation ***295** involved in this case, petitioner was denied due process of law in violation of ****1969** the Fourteenth Amendment. Cf. Davis v. State of North Carolina, 384 U.S. 737, 86 S.Ct. 1761, 16 L.Ed.2d 895.

Dr. Paul Behrendt was stabbed to death in the kitchen of his home in Garden City, Long Island, about midnight August 23, 1961. Dr. Behrendt's wife, also a physician, had followed her husband to the kitchen and jumped at the assailant. He knocked her to the floor and stabbed her 11 times. The police found a shirt on the kitchen floor and keys in a pocket which they traced to petitioner. They arrested him on the afternoon of August 24. An arraignment was promptly held but was postponed until petitioner could retain counsel.

Mrs. Behrendt was hospitalized for major surgery to save her life. The police, without affording petitioner time to retain counsel, arranged with her surgeon to permit them to bring petitioner to her hospital room about noon of August 25, the day after the surgery. Petitioner was handcuffed to one of five police officers who, with two members of the staff of the District Attorney, brought him to the hospital room. Petitioner was the only Negro in the room. Mrs. Behrendt identified him from her hospital bed after being asked by an officer whether he 'was the man' and after petitioner repeated at the direction of an officer a 'few words for voice identification.' None of the witnesses could recall the words that were used. Mrs. Behrendt and the officers testified at the trial to her identification of the petitioner in the hospital room, and she also made an in-court identification of petitioner in the courtroom.

Petitioner was convicted and sentenced to death. The New York Court of Appeals affirmed without opinion. People v. Stovall, 13 N.Y.2d 1094, 246 N.Y.S.2d 410, 196 N.E.2d 65. Petitioner pro se sought federal habeas corpus in the District Court for the Southern District of New York. He claimed that among other constitutional rights allegedly denied him ***296** at his trial, the admission of Mrs. Behrendt's identification testimony violated his rights under the Fifth, Sixth, and Fourteenth Amendments because he had been compelled to submit to the hospital room confrontation without the help of counsel and under circumstances which unfairly focused the witness' attention on him as the man believed by the police to be the guilty person. The District Court dismissed the petition after hearing argument on an unrelated claim of an alleged invalid search and seizure. On appeal to the Court of Appeals for the Second Circuit a panel of that court initially reversed the dismissal after reaching the issue of the admissibility of Mrs. Behrendt's identification evidence and holding it inadmissible on the ground that the hospital room identification violated petitioner's constitutional right to the assistance of counsel. The Court of Appeals thereafter heard the case en banc, vacated the panel decision, and affirmed the District Court. 355 F.2d 731. We granted certiorari, 384 U.S. 1000, 86 S.Ct. 1983, 16 L.Ed.2d 1014, and set the case for argument with Wade and Gilbert. We hold that Wade and Gilbert affect only those cases and all future cases which involve confrontations for identification purposes conducted in the absence of counsel after this date. The rulings of Wade and Gilbert are therefore inapplicable in the present case. We think also that on the facts of this case petitioner was not deprived of due process of law in violation of the Fourteenth Amendment. The judgment of the Court of Appeals is, therefore, affirmed.

I.

Our recent discussions of the retroactivity of the constitutional rules of criminal procedure make unnecessary any detailed treatment of that question here. Linkletter v. Walker, supra; Tehan v. United States ex rel. Shott, supra; Johnson v. State of New Jersey, supra. 'These cases establish the principle that in criminal litigation concerning constitutional ****1970 *297** claims, 'the Court may in the interest of justice make the rule prospective * * * where the exigencies of the situation require such an application' * * *.' Johnson, supra, 384 U.S., at 726-727, 86 S.Ct., at 1777. The criteria guiding resolution of the question implicates (a) the purpose to be served by the new standards, (b) the extent of the reliance by law enforcement authorities on the old standards, and (c) the effect on the administration of justice of a retroactive application of the new standards. '(T)he retroactivity or nonretroactivity of a rule is not automatically determined by the provision of the Constitution on which the dictate is based. Each constitutional rule of criminal procedure has its own distinct functions, its own background of precedent, and its own impact on the administration of justice, and the way in which these factors combine must inevitably vary with the dictate involved.' Johnson, supra, at 728, 86 S.Ct. at 1778.

Wade and Gilbert fashion exclusionary rules to deter law enforcement authorities from exhibiting an accused to witnesses before trial for identification purposes without notice to and in the absence of counsel. A conviction which rests on a mistaken identification is a gross miscarriage of justice. The Wade and Gilbert rules are aimed at minimizing that possibility by preventing the unfairness at the pretrial confrontation that experience has proved can occur and assuring meaningful examination of the identification witness' testimony at trial. Does it follow that the rules should be applied retroactively? We do not think so.

It is true that the right to the assistance of counsel has been applied retroactively at stages of the prosecution where denial of the right must almost invariably deny a fair trial, for example, at the trial itself, Gideon v. Wainwright, 372 U.S. 335, 83 S.Ct. 792, 9 L.Ed.2d 799, or at some forms of arraignment, Hamilton v. State of Alabama, 368 U.S. 52, 82 S.Ct. 157, 7 L.Ed.2d 114, or on appeal, Douglas v. People of State of California, 372 U.S. 353, 83 S.Ct. 814, 9 L.Ed.2d 811. 'The basic purpose ***298** of a trial is the determination of truth, and it is self-evident that to deny a lawyer's help through the technical intricacies of a criminal trial or to deny a full opportunity to appeal a conviction because the accused is poor is to impede that purpose and to infect a criminal proceeding with the clear danger of convicting the innocent.' Tehan v. United States ex rel. Shott, supra, 382 U.S., at 416, 86 S.Ct., at 465. We have also retroactively applied rules of criminal procedure fashioned to correct serious flaws in the fact-finding process at trial. See for example Jackson v. Denno, 378 U.S. 368, 84 S.Ct. 1774, 12 L.Ed.2d 908. Although the Wade and Gilbert rules also are aimed at avoiding unfairness at the trial by enhancing the reliability of the fact-finding process in the area of identification evidence, 'the question whether a constitutional rule of criminal procedure does or does not enhance the reliability of the fact-finding process at trial is necessarily a matter of degree.' Johnson v. State of New Jersey, supra, 384 U.S., at 729, 86 S.Ct., at 1778. The extent to which a condemned practice infects the integrity of the truth-determining process at trial is a 'question of probabilities.' Ibid. Such probabilities must in turn be weighed against the prior justified reliance upon the old standards and the impact of retroactivity upon the administration of justice.

We have outlined in Wade the dangers and unfairness inherent in confrontations for identification. The possibility of unfairness at that point is great, both because of the manner in which confrontations are frequently conducted, and because of the likelihood that the accused will often be precluded from reconstructing what occurred and thereby from obtaining a full hearing on the ****1971** identification issue at trial. The presence of counsel will significantly promote fairness at the confrontation and a full hearing at trial on the issue of identification. We have, therefore, concluded that the confrontation is a 'critical stage,' and that counsel is required at all confrontations. It must be recognized, however, that, unlike ***299** cases in which counsel is absent at trial or on appeal, it may confidently be assumed that confrontations for identification can be and often have been conducted in the absence of counsel with scrupulous fairness and without prejudice to the accused at trial. Therefore, while we feel that the exclusionary rules set forth in Wade and Gilbert are justified by the need to assure the integrity and reliability of our system of justice, they undoubtedly will affect cases in which no unfairness will be present. Of course, we should also assume there have been injustices in the past which could have been averted by having counsel present at the confrontation for identification, just as there are injustices when counsel is absent at trial. But the certainty and frequency with which we can say in the confrontation cases that no injustice occurred differs greatly enough from the cases involving absence of counsel at trial or on appeal to justify treating the situations as different in kind for the purpose of retroactive application, especially in light of the strong countervailing interests outlined below, and because it remains open to all persons to allege and prove, as Stovall attempts to do in this case, that the confrontation resulted in such unfairness that it infringed his right to due process of law. See Palmer v. Peyton, 359 F.2d 199 (C.A.4th Cir. 1966).

The unusual force of the countervailing considerations strengthens our conclusion in favor of prospective application. The law enforcement officials of the Federal Government and of all 50 States have heretofore proceeded on the premise that the Constitution did not require the presence of counsel at pretrial confrontations for identification. Today's rulings were not foreshadowed in our cases; no court announced such a requirement until Wade was decided by the Court of Appeals for the Fifth Circuit, 358 F.2d 557. The overwhelming majority of American courts have always treated the evidence question ***300** not as one of admissibility but as one of credibility for the jury. Wall, Eye-Witness Identification in Criminal Cases 38. Law enforcement authorities fairly relied on this virtually unanimous weight of authority, now no longer valid, in conducting pretrial confrontations in the absence of counsel. It is, therefore, very clear that retroactive application of Wade and Gilbert 'would seriously disrupt the administration of our criminal laws.' Johnson v. State of New Jersey, supra, at 731, 86 S.Ct., at 1780. In Tehan v. United States ex rel. Shott, supra, we thought it persuasive against retroactive application of the no-comment rule of Griffin v. State of California, 380 U.S. 609, 85 S.Ct. 1229, 14 L.Ed.2d 106, that such application would have a serious impact on the six States that allowed comment on an accused's failure to take the stand. We said, 'To require all of those States now to void the conviction of every person who did not testify at his trial would have an impact upon the administration of their criminal law so devastating as to need no elaboration.' 382 U.S., at 419, 86 S.Ct., at 467. That impact is insignificant compared to the impact to be expected from retroactivity of the Wade and Gilbert rules. At the very least, the processing of current criminal calendars would be disrupted while hearings were conducted to determine taint, if any, in identification evidence, and whether in any event the admission of the evidence was harmless error. Doubtless, too, inquiry would be handicapped by the unavailability of witnesses and dim memories. We conclude, therefore, that the Wade and Gilbert rules should not be made retroactive.

****1972** We also conclude that, for these purposes, no distinction is justified between convictions now final, as in the instant case, and convictions at various stages of trial and direct review. We regard the factors of reliance and burden on the administration of justice as entitled to such overriding significance as to make that distinction ***301** unsupportable. We recognize that Wade and Gilbert are, therefore, the only victims of pretrial confrontations in the absence of their counsel to have the benefit of the rules established in their cases. That they must be given that benefit is, however, an unavoidable consequence of the necessity that constitutional adjudications not stand as mere dictum. Sound policies of decision-making, rooted in the command of Article III of the Constitution that we resolve issues solely in concrete cases or controversies, and in the possible effect upon the incentive of counsel to advance contentions requiring a change in the law, militate against denying Wade and Gilbert the benefit of today's decisions. Inequity arguably results from according the benefit of a new rule to the parties in the case in which it is announced but not to other litigants similarly situated in the trial or appellate process who have raised the same issue. But we regard the fact that the parties involved are chance beneficiaries as an insignificant cost for adherence to sound principles of decision-making.

II.

We turn now to the question whether petitioner, although not entitled to the application of Wade and Gilbert to his case, is entitled to relief on his claim that in any event the confrontation conducted in this ***302** case was so unnecessarily suggestive and conducive to irreparable mistaken identification that he was denied due process of law. This is a recognized ground of attack upon a conviction independent of any right to counsel claim. Palmer v. Peyton, 359 F.2d 199 (C.A.4th Cir. 1966). The practice of showing suspects singly to persons for the purpose of identification, and not as part of a lineup, has been widely condemned. However, a claimed violation of due process of law in the conduct of a confrontation depends on the totality of the circumstances surrounding it, and the record in the present case reveals that the showing of Stovall to Mrs. Behrendt in an immediate hospital confrontation was imperative. The Court of Appeals, en banc, stated, 355 F.2d at 735,

'Here was the only person in the world who could possibly exonerate Stovall. Her words, and only her words, 'He is not the man' could have resulted in freedom for Stovall. The hospital was not far distant from the courthouse and jail. No one knew how long Mrs. Behrendt might live. Faced with the responsibility of identifying the attacker, with the need for immediate action and with the knowledge that Mrs.

Behrendt could not visit the jail, the police followed the only feasible procedure and took Stovall to the hospital room. Under these circumstances, the usual police station line-up, ****1973** which Stovall now argues he should have had, was out of the question.'

The judgment of the Court of Appeals is affirmed. It is so ordered.

Affirmed.

Mr. Justice DOUGLAS is of the view that the deprivation of the right to counsel in the setting of this case ***303** should be given retroactive effect as it was in Gideon v. Wainwright, 372 U.S. 335, 83 S.Ct. 792, and in Douglas v. People of State of California, 372 U.S. 353, 83 S.Ct. 814. And see Linkletter v. Walker, 381 U.S. 618, 640, 85 S.Ct. 1731, 1745 (dissenting opinion); Johnson v. State of New Jersey, 384 U.S. 719, 736, 86 S.Ct. 1772, 1782 (dissenting opinion).

Mr. Justice FORTAS would reverse and remand for a new trial on the ground that the State's reference at trial to the improper hospital identification violated petitioner's Fourteenth Amendment rights and was prejudicial. He would not reach the question of retroactivity of Wade and Gilbert.

Mr. Justice WHITE, whom Mr. Justice HARLAN and Mr. Justice STEWART join.

For the reasons stated in my separate opinion in United States v. Wade, 388 U.S. 250, 87 S.Ct. 1944. I perceive no constitutional error in the identification procedure to which the petitioner was subjected. I concur in the result and in that portion of the Court's opinion which limits application of the new Sixth Amendment rule.

(The dissent of Mr. Justice Black is omitted.)

Black Letter Law

> The Court held that rules requiring exclusion of identification evidence, which is obtained by exhibiting accused to identifying witnesses before trial in absence of his counsel, are not to be applied retroactively. The Court further held that the defendant was not deprived of due process when he was brought to the identifying witness' hospital room because she was not physically capable to visit jail, where defendant was detained, and required hospitalization for life-saving surgery.

Manson v. Braithwaithe

97 S.Ct. 2243

Supreme Court of the United States

John R. MANSON, Commissioner of Correction of Connecticut, Petitioner,

v.

Nowell A. BRATHWAITE.

No. 75-871. | Argued Nov. 29, 1976. | Decided June 16, 1977.

Mr. Justice BLACKMUN delivered the opinion of the Court.

This case presents the issue as to whether the Due Process Clause of the Fourteenth Amendment compels the exclusion, in a state criminal trial, apart from any consideration of reliability, of pretrial identification evidence obtained by a police procedure that was both suggestive and unnecessary. This Court's decisions in Stovall v. Denno, 388 U.S. 293, 87 S.Ct. 1967, 18 L.Ed.2d 1199 (1967), and Neil v. Biggers, 409 U.S. 188, 93 S.Ct. 375, 34 L.Ed.2d 401 (1972), are particularly implicated.

I

Jimmy D. Glover, a full-time trooper of the Connecticut State Police, in 1970 was assigned to the Narcotics Division in an undercover capacity. On May 5 of that year, about ***100** 7:45 p. m., e.d.t., and while there was still daylight, Glover and Henry Alton Brown, an informant, went to an apartment building at 201 Westland, in Hartford, for the purpose of purchasing narcotics from "Dickie Boy" Cicero, a known narcotics dealer. Cicero, it was thought, lived on the third floor of that ****2246** apartment building. Tr. 45-46, 68. Glover and Brown entered the building, observed by back-up Officers D'Onofrio and Gaffey, and proceeded by stairs to the third floor. Glover knocked at the door of one of the two apartments served by the stairway. The area was illuminated by natural light from a window in the third floor hallway. Id., at 27-28. The door was opened 12 to 18 inches in response to the knock. Glover observed a man standing at the door and, behind him, a woman. Brown identified himself. Glover then asked for "two things" of narcotics. Id., at 29. The man at the door held out his hand, and Glover gave him two $10 bills. The door closed. Soon the man returned and handed Glover two glassine bags. While the door was open, Glover stood within two feet of the person from whom he made the purchase and observed his face. Five to seven minutes elapsed from the ***101** time the door first opened until it closed the second time. Id., at 30-33.

Glover and Brown then left the building. This was about eight minutes after their arrival. Glover drove to headquarters where he described the seller to D'Onofrio and Gaffey. Glover at that time did not know the identity of the seller. Id., at 36. He described him as being "a colored man, approximately five feet eleven inches tall, dark complexion, black hair, short Afro style, and having high cheekbones, and of heavy build. He was wearing at the time blue pants and a plaid shirt." Id., at 36-37. D'Onofrio, suspecting from this description that respondent might be the seller, obtained a photograph of respondent from the Records Division of the Hartford Police Department. He left it at Glover's office. D'Onofrio was not acquainted with respondent personally but did know him by sight and had seen him "(s)everal times" prior to May 5. Id., at 63-65. Glover, when alone, viewed the photograph for the first time upon his return to headquarters on May 7; he identified the person shown as the one from whom he had purchased the narcotics. Id., at 36-38.

The toxicological report on the contents of the glassine bags revealed the presence of heroin. The report was dated July 16, 1970. Id., at 75-76. Respondent was arrested on July 27 while visiting at the apartment of a Mrs. Ramsey on the third floor of 201 Westland. This was the apartment at which the narcotics sale had taken place on May 5.

Respondent was charged, in a two-count information, with possession and sale of heroin, in violation of Conn.Gen.Stat. (Rev. of 1958, as amended in 1969), ss 19-481a and 19-480a ***102** 1977). At his trial in January ****2247** 1971, the photograph from which Glover had identified respondent was received in evidence without objection on the part of the defense. Tr. 38. Glover also testified that, although he had not seen respondent in the eight months that had elapsed since the sale, "there (was) no doubt whatsoever" in his mind that the person shown on the photograph was respondent. Id., at 41-42. Glover also made a positive in-court identification without objection. Id., at 37-38.

No explanation was offered by the prosecution for the failure to utilize a photographic array or to conduct a lineup.

Respondent, who took the stand in his own defense, testified that on May 5, the day in question, he had been ill at his Albany Avenue apartment ("a lot of back pains, muscle spasms . . . a bad heart . . . high blood pressure . . . neuralgia in my face, and sinus," id., at 106), and that at no time on that particular day had he been at 201 Westland. Id., at 106, 113-114. His wife testified that she recalled, after her husband had refreshed her memory, that he was home all day on May 5. Id., at 164-165. Doctor Wesley M. Vietzke, an internist and assistant professor of medicine at the University of Connecticut, testified that respondent had consulted him on April 15, 1970, and that he took a medical history from him, heard his complaints about his back and facial pain, and discovered that he had high blood pressure. Id., at 129-131. The physician found respondent, subjectively, "in great discomfort." Id., at 135. Respondent in fact underwent surgery for a herniated disc at L5 and S1 on August 17. Id., at 157.

The jury found respondent guilty on both counts of the information. He received a sentence of not less than six nor ***103** more than nine years. His conviction was affirmed per curiam by the Supreme Court of Connecticut. State v. Brathwaite, 164 Conn. 617, 325 A.2d 284 (1973). That court noted the absence of an objection to Glover's in-court identification and concluded that respondent "has not shown that substantial injustice resulted from the admission of this evidence." Id., at 619, 325 A. 2d, at 285. Under Connecticut law, substantial injustice must be shown before a claim of error not made or passed on by the trial court will be considered on appeal. Ibid.

Fourteen months later, respondent filed a petition for habeas corpus in the United States District Court for the District of Connecticut. He alleged that the admission of the identification testimony at his state trial deprived him of due process of law to which he was entitled under the Fourteenth Amendment. The District Court, by an unreported written opinion based on the court's review of the state trial transcript, dismissed respondent's petition. On appeal, the United States Court of Appeals for the Second Circuit reversed, with instructions to issue the writ unless the State gave notice of a desire to retry respondent and the new trial occurred within a reasonable time to be fixed by the District Judge.7 527 F.2d 363 (1975).

In brief summary, the court felt that evidence as to the photograph should have been excluded, regardless of reliability, ***104** because the examination of the single photograph was unnecessary and suggestive. And, in the court's view, the evidence was unreliable in any event. We granted certiorari. 425 U.S. 957, 96 S.Ct. 1737, 48 L.Ed. 2d 202 (1976).

II

Stovall v. Denno, supra, decided in 1967, concerned a petitioner who had been convicted ****2248** in a New York court of murder. He was arrested the day following the crime and was taken by the police to a hospital where the victim's wife, also wounded in the assault, was a patient. After observing Stovall and hearing him speak, she identified him as the murderer. She later made an in-court identification. On federal habeas, Stovall claimed the identification testimony violated his Fifth, Sixth, and Fourteenth Amendment rights. The District Court dismissed the petition, and the Court of Appeals, en banc, affirmed. This Court also affirmed. On the identification issue, the Court reviewed the practice of showing a suspect singly for purposes of identification, and the claim that this was so unnecessarily suggestive and conducive to irreparable mistaken identification that it constituted a denial of due process of law. The Court noted that the practice "has been widely condemned," 388 U.S., at 302, 87 S.Ct., at 1972, but it concluded that "a claimed violation of due process of law in the conduct of a confrontation depends on the totality of the circumstances surrounding it." Ibid. In that case, showing Stovall to the victim's spouse "was imperative." The Court then quoted the observations of the Court of Appeals, 2 Cir., 355 F.2d 731, 735 (CA2 1966), to the effect that the spouse was the only person who could possibly exonerate the accused; that the hospital was not far from the courthouse and jail; that no one knew how long she might live; that she was not able to visit the jail; and that taking Stovall to the hospital room was the only feasible procedure, and, under the circumstances, " 'the usual police station line-up . . . was out of the question.' " 388 U.S., at 302, 87 S.Ct., at 1972-1973.

***105** Neil v. Biggers, supra, decided in 1972, concerned a respondent who had been convicted in a Tennessee court of rape, on evidence consisting in part of the victim's visual and voice identification of Biggers at a station-house showup seven months after the crime. The victim had been in her assailant's presence for some time and had directly observed him indoors and under a full moon outdoors. She testified that she had "no doubt" that Biggers was her assailant. She previously had given the police a description of the assailant. She had made no identification of others presented at previous showups, lineups, or through photographs. On federal habeas, the District Court held that the confrontation was so suggestive as to violate due process. The Court of Appeals affirmed. This Court reversed on that issue, and held that the evidence properly had been allowed to go to the jury. The Court reviewed Stovall and certain later cases where it had considered the scope of due process protection against the admission of evidence derived from suggestive identification procedures, namely, Simmons v. United States, 390 U.S. 377, 88 S.Ct. 967, 19 L.Ed.2d 1247 (1968); Foster v. California, 394 U.S. 440, 89 S.Ct. 1127, 22 L.Ed.2d 402 (1969); and Coleman v. Alabama, 399 U.S. 1, 90 S.Ct. 1999, 26 L.Ed.2d 387 (1970).8 The Court concluded that ***106** general ****2249** guidelines emerged from these cases "as to the relationship between suggestiveness and misidentification." The "admission of evidence of a showup without more does not violate due process." 409 U.S., at 198, 93 S.Ct., at 382. The Court expressed concern about the lapse of seven months between the crime and the confrontation and observed that this "would be a seriously negative factor in most cases." Id., at 201, 93 S.Ct., at 383. The "central question," however, was "whether under the 'totality of the circumstances' the identification was reliable even though the confrontation procedure was suggestive." Id., at 199, 93 S.Ct., at 382. Applying that test, the Court found "no substantial likelihood of misidentification. The evidence was properly allowed to go to the jury." Id., at 201, 93 S.Ct., at 383.

Biggers well might be seen to provide an unambiguous answer to the question before us: The admission of testimony concerning a suggestive and unnecessary identification procedure does not violate due process so long as the identification possesses sufficient aspects of reliability. In one passage, ***107** however, the Court observed that the challenged procedure occurred pre-Stovall and that a strict rule would make little sense with regard to a confrontation that preceded the Court's first indication that a suggestive procedure might lead to the exclusion of evidence. Id., at 199, 93 S.Ct., at 382. One perhaps might argue that, by implication, the Court suggested that a different rule could apply post-Stovall. The question before us, then, is simply whether the Biggers analysis applies to post-Stovall confrontations as well to those pre-Stovall.

III

In the present case the District Court observed that the "sole evidence tying Brathwaite to the possession and sale of the heroin consisted in his identifications by the police undercover agent, Jimmy Glover." App. to Pet. for Cert. 6a. On the constitutional issue, the court stated that the first inquiry was whether the police used an impermissibly suggestive procedure in obtaining the out-of-court identification. If so, the second inquiry is whether, under all the circumstances, that suggestive procedure gave rise to a substantial likelihood of irreparable misidentification. Id., at 9a. Biggers and Simmons were cited. The court noted that in the Second Circuit, its controlling court, it was clear that "this type of identification procedure (display of a single photograph) is impermissibly ***108** suggestive," and turned to the second inquiry. App. to Pet. for Cert. 9a. The factors Biggers specified for consideration were recited ****2250** and applied. The court concluded that there was no substantial likelihood of irreparable misidentification. It referred to the facts: Glover was within two feet of the seller. The duration of the confrontation was at least a "couple of minutes." There was natural light from a window or skylight and there was adequate light to see clearly in the hall. Glover "certainly was paying attention to identify the seller." Id., at 10a. He was a trained police officer who realized that later he would have to find and arrest the person with whom he was dealing. He gave a detailed description to D'Onofrio. The reliability of this description was supported by the fact that it enabled D'Onofrio to pick out a single photograph that was thereafter positively identified by Glover. Only two days elapsed between the crime and the photographic identification. Despite the fact that another eight months passed before the in-court identification, Glover had "no doubt" that Brathwaite was the person who had sold him heroin.

The Court of Appeals confirmed that the exhibition of the single photograph to Glover was "impermissibly suggestive," 527 F.2d, at 366, and felt that, in addition, "it was unnecessarily so." Id., at 367. There was no emergency and little urgency. The court said that prior to the decision in Biggers, except in cases of harmless error, "a conviction secured as the result of admitting an identification obtained by impermissibly suggestive and unnecessary measures could not stand." Ibid. It noted what it felt might be opposing inferences to be drawn from passages in Biggers, but concluded that the case preserved the principle "requiring the exclusion of identifications resulting from 'unnecessarily suggestive confrontation' " in post-Stovall situations. 527 F.2d, at 368. The court also concluded that for post-Stovall identifications, Biggers had not changed the existing rule. Thus: "Evidence of an identification unnecessarily obtained by impermissibly ***109** suggestive means must be excluded under Stovall . . . . No rules less stringent than these can force police administrators and prosecutors to adopt procedures that will give fair assurance against the awful risks of misidentification." 527 F.2d, at 371. Finally, the court said, even if this conclusion were wrong, the writ, nevertheless, should issue. It took judicial notice that on May 5, 1970, sunset at Hartford was at 7:53 p. m. It characterized Glover's duty as an undercover agent as one "to cause arrests to be made," and his description of the suspect as one that "could have applied to hundreds of Hartford black males." Ibid. The in-court identification had "little meaning," for Brathwaite was at the counsel table. The fact that respondent was arrested in the very apartment where the sale was made was subject to a "not implausible" explanation from the respondent, "although evidently not credited by the jury." And the court was troubled by "the long and unexplained delay" in the arrest. It was too great a danger that the respondent was convicted because he was a man D'Onofrio had previously observed near the scene, was thought to be a likely offender, and was arrested when he was known to be in Mrs. Ramsey's apartment, rather than because Glover "really remembered him as the seller." Id., at 371-372.

IV

Petitioner at the outset acknowledges that "the procedure in the instant case was suggestive (because only one photograph was used) and unnecessary" (because there was no emergency or exigent circumstance). Brief for Petitioner 10; Tr. of Oral Arg. 7. The respondent, in agreement with the Court of Appeals, proposes a per se rule of exclusion that he claims is dictated by the demands of the Fourteenth Amendment's guarantee of due process. He rightly observes that this is the first case in which this Court has had occasion to rule upon strictly post-Stovall out-of-court identification evidence of the challenged kind.

***110** Since the decision in Biggers, the Courts of Appeals appear to have developed at least two approaches to such evidence. See ****2251** Pulaski, Neil v. Biggers : The Supreme Court Dismantles the Wade Trilogy's Due Process Protection, 26 Stan.L.Rev. 1097, 1111-1114 (1974). The first, or per se approach, employed by the Second Circuit in the present case, focuses on the procedures employed and requires exclusion of the out-of-court identification evidence, without regard to reliability, whenever it has been obtained through unnecessarily suggested confrontation procedures.10 The justifications advanced are the elimination of evidence of uncertain reliability, deterrence of the police and prosecutors, and the stated "fair assurance against the awful risks of misidentification." 527 F.2d, at 371. See Smith v. Coiner, 473 F.2d 877, 882 (CA4), cert. denied sub nom. Wallace v. Smith, 414 U.S. 1115, 94 S.Ct. 848, 38 L.Ed.2d 743 (1973).

The second, or more lenient, approach is one that continues to rely on the totality of the circumstances. It permits the admission of the confrontation evidence if, despite the suggestive aspect, the out-of-court identification possesses certain features of reliability. Its adherents feel that the per se approach is not mandated by the Due Process Clause of the Fourteenth Amendment. This second approach, in contrast to the other, is ad hoc and serves to limit the societal costs imposed by a sanction that excludes relevant evidence from consideration and evaluation by the trier of fact. See United States ex rel. Kirby v. Sturges, 510 F.2d 397, 407-408 (CA7) (opinion by Judge, now Mr. Justice, Stevens), cert. denied, 421 U.S. 1016, 95 S.Ct. 2424, 44 L.Ed.2d 685 (1975); ***111** Stanley v. Cox, 486 F.2d 48 (CA4 1973), cert. denied sub nom. Stanley v. Slayton, 416 U.S. 958, 94 S.Ct. 1975, 40 L.Ed.2d 309 (1974).11

Mr. Justice Stevens, in writing for the Seventh Circuit in Kirby, supra, observed: "There is surprising unanimity among scholars in regarding such a rule (the per se approach) as essential to avoid serious risk of miscarriage of justice." 510 F.2d, at 405. He pointed out that well-known federal judges have taken the position that "evidence of, or derived from, a showup identification should be inadmissible unless the prosecutor can justify his failure to use a more reliable identification procedure." Id., at 406. Indeed, the ALI Model Code of Pre-Arraignment Procedure ss 160.1 and 160.2 (1975) (hereafter Model Code), frowns upon the use of a showup or the display of only a single photograph.

The respondent here stresses the same theme and the need for deterrence of improper identification practice, a factor he regards as pre-eminent. Photographic identification, it is said, continues to be needlessly employed. He notes that the legislative regulation "the Court had hoped (United States v.) Wade (, 388 U.S. 218, 239, 87 S.Ct. 1926, 1938-1939, 18 L.Ed.2d 1149 (1967),) would engender," Brief for Respondent 15, has not been forthcoming. He argues that a totality rule cannot be expected to have a significant deterrent impact; only a strict rule of exclusion will have direct and immediate impact on law enforcement agents. Identification evidence is so convincing to the jury that sweeping exclusionary rules are required. Fairness of the trial is threatened by suggestive confrontation evidence, and thus, it is said, an exclusionary rule has an established constitutional predicate.

There are, of course, several interests to be considered and taken into account. The driving force behind United States v. Wade, 388 U.S. 218, 87 S.Ct. 1926, 18 L.Ed.2d 1149 (1967), ***112** Gilbert v. California, 388 U.S. 263, 87 S.Ct. 1951, 18 L.Ed.2d 1178 (1967) (right ****2252** to counsel at a post-indictment line-up), and Stovall, all decided on the same day, was the Court's concern with the problems of eyewitness identification. Usually the witness must testify about an encounter with a total stranger under circumstances of emergency or emotional stress. The witness' recollection of the stranger can be distorted easily by the circumstances or by later actions of the police. Thus, Wade and its companion cases reflect the concern that the jury not hear eyewitness testimony unless that evidence has aspects of reliability. It must be observed that both approaches before us are responsive to this concern. The per se rule, however, goes too far since its application automatically and peremptorily, and without consideration of alleviating factors, keeps evidence from the jury that is reliable and relevant.

The second factor is deterrence. Although the per se approach has the more significant deterrent effect, the totality approach also has an influence on police behavior. The police will guard against unnecessarily suggestive procedures under the totality rule, as well as the per se one, for fear that their actions will lead to the exclusion of identifications as unreliable.

The third factor is the effect on the administration of justice. Here the per se approach suffers serious drawbacks. Since it denies the trier reliable evidence, it may result, on occasion, in the guilty going free. Also, because of its rigidity, the per se approach may make error by the trial judge more likely than the totality approach. And in those cases in which the admission of identification evidence is error under the per se approach but not under the totality approach ***113** cases in which the identification is reliable despite an unnecessarily suggestive identification procedure reversal is a Draconian sanction. Certainly, inflexible rules of exclusion that may frustrate rather than promote justice have not been viewed recently by this Court with unlimited enthusiasm. See, for example, the several opinions in Brewer v. Williams, 430 U.S. 387, 97 S.Ct. 1232, 51 L.Ed.2d 424 (1977). See also United States v. Janis, 428 U.S. 433, 96 S.Ct. 3021, 49 L.Ed.2d 1046 (1976).

It is true, as has been noted, that the Court in Biggers referred to the pre-Stovall character of the confrontation in that case. 409 U.S., at 199, 93 S.Ct., at 382. But that observation was only one factor in the judgmental process. It does not translate into a holding that post-Stovall confrontation evidence automatically is to be excluded.

The standard, after all, is that of fairness as required by the Due Process Clause of the Fourteenth Amendment. See United States v. Lovasco, 431 U.S. 783, 790, 97 S.Ct. 2044, 2049, 52 L.Ed.2d 752 (1977); Rochin v. California, 342 U.S. 165, 170-172, 72 S.Ct. 205, 208-209, 96 L.Ed. 183 (1952). Stovall, with its reference to "the totality of the circumstances," 388 U.S., at 302, 87 S.Ct., at 1972, and Biggers, with its continuing stress on the same totality, 409 U.S., at 199, 93 S.Ct., at 382, did not, singly or together, establish a strict exclusionary rule or new standard of due process. Judge Leventhal, although speaking pre-Biggers and of a pre-Wade situation, correctly has described Stovall as protecting an evidentiary interest and, at the same time, as recognizing the limited extent of that interest in our adversary system. 14

****2253*114** We therefore conclude that reliability is the linchpin in determining the admissibility of identification testimony for both pre- and post-Stovall confrontations. The factors to be considered are set out in Biggers. 409 U.S., at 199-200, 93 S.Ct., at 382. These include the opportunity of the witness to view the criminal at the time of the crime, the witness' degree of attention, the accuracy of his prior description of the criminal, the level of certainty demonstrated at the confrontation, and the time between the crime and the confrontation. Against these factors is to be weighed the corrupting effect of the suggestive identification itself.

V

We turn, then, to the facts of this case and apply the analysis:

1. The opportunity to view. Glover testified that for two to three minutes he stood at the apartment door, within two feet of the respondent. The door opened twice, and each time the man stood at the door. The moments passed, the conversation took place, and payment was made. Glover looked directly at his vendor. It was near sunset, to be sure, but the sun had not yet set, so it was not dark or even dusk or twilight. Natural light from outside entered the hallway through a window. There was natural light, as well, from inside the apartment.

***115** 2. The degree of attention. Glover was not a casual or passing observer, as is so often the case with eyewitness identification. Trooper Glover was a trained police officer on duty and specialized and dangerous duty when he called at the third floor of 201 Westland in Hartford on May 5, 1970. Glover himself was a Negro and unlikely to perceive only general features of "hundreds of Hartford black males," as the Court of Appeals stated. 527 F.2d, at 371. It is true that Glover's duty was that of ferreting out narcotics offenders and that he would be expected in his work to produce results. But it is also true that, as a specially trained, assigned, and experienced officer, he could be expected to pay scrupulous attention to detail, for he knew that subsequently he would have to find and arrest his vendor. In addition, he knew that his claimed observations would be subject later to close scrutiny and examination at any trial.

3. The accuracy of the description. Glover's description was given to D'Onofrio within minutes after the transaction. It included the vendor's race, his height, his build, the color and style of his hair, and the high cheekbone facial feature. It also included clothing the vendor wore. No claim has been made that respondent did not possess the physical characteristics so described. D'Onofrio reacted positively at

once. Two days later, when Glover was alone, he viewed the photograph D'Onofrio produced and identified its subject as the narcotics seller.

4. The witness' level of certainty. There is no dispute that the photograph in question was that of respondent. Glover, in response to a question whether the photograph was that of the person from whom he made the purchase, testified: "There is no question whatsoever." Tr. 38. This positive assurance was repeated. Id., at 41-42.

5. The time between the crime and the confrontation. Glover's description of his vendor was given to D'Onofrio ***116** within minutes of the crime. The photographic identification took place only two days later. We ****2254** do not have here the passage of weeks or months between the crime and the viewing of the photograph.

These indicators of Glover's ability to make an accurate identification are hardly outweighed by the corrupting effect of the challenged identification itself. Although identifications arising from single-photograph displays may be viewed in general with suspicion, see Simmons v. United States, 390 U.S., at 383, 88 S.Ct., at 970-971, we find in the instant case little pressure on the witness to acquiesce in the suggestion that such a display entails. D'Onofrio had left the photograph at Glover's office and was not present when Glover first viewed it two days after the event. There thus was little urgency and Glover could view the photograph at his leisure. And since Glover examined the photograph alone, there was no coercive pressure to make an identification arising from the presence of another. The identification was made in circumstances allowing care and reflection.

Although it plays no part in our analysis, all this assurance as to the reliability of the identification is hardly undermined by the facts that respondent was arrested in the very apartment where the sale had taken place, and that he acknowledged his frequent visits to that apartment.

Surely, we cannot say that under all the circumstances of this case there is "a very substantial likelihood of irreparable misidentification." Id., at 384, 88 S.Ct., at 971. Short of that point, such evidence is for the jury to weigh. We are content to rely upon the good sense and judgment of American juries, for evidence with some element of untrustworthiness is customary grist for the jury mill. Juries are not so susceptible that they cannot measure intelligently the weight of identification testimony that has some questionable feature.

***117** Of course, it would have been better had D'Onofrio presented Glover with a photographic array including "so far as practicable . . . a reasonable number of persons similar to any person then suspected whose likeness is included in the array." Model Code, s 160.2(2). The use of that procedure would have enhanced the force of the identification at trial and would have avoided the risk that the evidence would be excluded as unreliable. But we are not disposed to view D'Onofrio's failure as one of constitutional dimension to be enforced by a rigorous and unbending exclusionary rule. The defect, if there be one, goes to weight and not to substance.

We conclude that the criteria laid down in Biggers are to be applied in determining the admissibility of evidence offered by the prosecution concerning a post-Stovall identification, and that those criteria are satisfactorily met and complied with here.

The judgment of the Court of Appeals is reversed. It is so ordered.

Mr. Justice STEVENS, concurring.

While I join the Court's opinion, I would emphasize two points.

First, as I indicated in my opinion in United States ex rel. Kirby v. Sturges, 510 F.2d 397, 405-406 (CA7 1975), the arguments in favor of fashioning new rules to minimize the danger of convicting the innocent on the basis of unreliable eyewitness testimony carry substantial force. Nevertheless, ***118** for the reasons stated in that opinion, as well as those stated by the Court today. I am persuaded that this rulemaking function can be performed "more effectively by the legislative process than by a somewhat clumsy judicial fiat," id., at 408, ****2255** and that the Federal Constitution does not foreclose experimentation by the States in the development of such rules.

Second, in evaluating the admissibility of particular identification testimony it is sometimes difficult to put other evidence of guilt entirely to one side.* Mr. Justice BLACKMUN'S opinion for the Court carefully avoids this pitfall and correctly relies only on appropriate indicia of the reliability of the identification itself. Although I consider the factual question in this case extremely close, I am persuaded that the Court has resolved it properly.

(The dissent of Mr. Justice MARSHALL, with whom Mr. Justice BRENNAN joins, is omitted.)

Black Letter Law

Dealt with identification procedures in light of *Stovall*, where there was some issue of taint in the identification process and held that a suggestive single-photo line-up was not so corruptive as to be inadmissible. The Court held that reliability is the linchpin when determining the admissibility of identification testimony of confrontation occurring both prior to and after *Stovall.* The factors to consider in assessing reliability of identification include: (1) the opportunity of the witness to view the perpetrator at the time of the crime, (2) the witness' degree of attention, (3) the accuracy of his prior description of the criminal, (4) the level of certainty demonstrated at the confrontation, and (5) the time between the crime and the confrontation.

Discussion Problems:

12-1. Around midnight on February 14, Brandi visited the home of Chris Alexander, her former boyfriend and the father of her son. Chris and Brandi talked in his driveway for approximately 35–40 minutes. Brandi got into her car to leave, however, when Nikki Long, Alexander's current girlfriend, walked out of the house. As Nikki stood on Chris's lawn, Brandi's car pulled forward and hit her. Long became trapped under the car and died.

Police officers escorted Brandi to the police station around 1:30 a.m. Officers informed Brandi of her Miranda rights, and Brandi signed a waiver form. Brandi stated that she had no medical problems, was not under the influence of alcohol or drugs, and understood English. Brandi was twenty-seven years old and had never been in jail before. She was a high school graduate.

Between approximately 5:00 a.m. and 7:30 a.m., Detectives Record and Baxter-White interrogated Brandi. The interrogation began with Brandi giving her version of how Long died. Brandi told the detectives that Long's death was an accident. Brandi stated that she had only attempted to back her car out of the driveway. She thought that she put the car into reverse, but instead she accidentally put it into drive. When Brandi pressed the gas pedal, her car lunged forward and hit Long. After the first forty-five minutes of the interrogation, the detectives allowed Brandi a twenty-minute break. Brandi drank coffee.

When the interrogation resumed, the detectives had Brandi repeat her story. During this portion of the interrogation, the detectives permitted Brandi to take several breaks. Brandi was able to use the restroom and call her mother. Before ending the interrogation, the detectives had Brandi write down her version of what happened that night. Brandi's story never changed during this stage of the interrogation.

Detective Baxter-White then took over the interrogation for approximately the next one and one-half hours. Brandi declined any food, coffee, or water. For the first thirty to forty-five minutes, Brandi continued to maintain that Long's death was an accident. During this time, however, Baxter-White became more confrontational. He told Brandi that the officers did not believe her. He gave her a "hook," a question that aims to get a defendant to admit to a crime while simultaneously shifting the blame away, by asking Brandi if she had merely tried to scare Long by driving towards her. Brandi testified at her trial that Baxter-White told her that if she changed her story, the prosecutor might drop the charges. She also testified that Baxter-White told her that she could go home if she changed her story to say that she had intended to only scare Long. Baxter-White never admitted to promising Brandi anything, but he testified that he told Brandi that if she went to prison for first-degree murder, she would spend the rest of her life in prison and would not have contact with her family, including her children.

According to Baxter-White, Brandi suddenly looked at him and said, "I did it." Brandi stated that she drove her car towards Long to scare her. Baxter-White then reduced Brandi's admissions to written questions and answers. According to Baxter-White, he never threatened Brandi or told her what to write. He maintained that Brandi was "quite unemotional" during the interrogation. Before the interrogation ended at approximately 10:00 a.m., Brandi had not asked for the interrogation to stop.

Brandi was charged with first-degree murder, and a jury trial began in September.

The defense counsel makes a motion, prior to trial, to suppress the statement of Brandi because it was not voluntary. Identify the strongest argument for this defense position. Draft the talking points you will use in arguing the motion. After you have drafted the strongest argument for the defense motion, identify the potential points the state will raise in response and identify how you will reduce the strength of their argument during the motion hearing.

12-2. In November, Mr. Antonio was arrested pursuant to a state warrant for the robbery of a store. During the course of the investigation of the robbery, the detective engaged in a variety of tactics designed to allegedly wrongfully implicate Mr. Antonio for the crime for which he stood accused.

The detective's activities included falsely indicating to Mr. Antonio that Mr. Antonio's fingerprints were recovered from the scene of the robbery, falsely indicating that the license tag numbers belonging to Mr. Antonio's car were seen on the vehicle leaving the scene of the robbery, taking a number of photographs of Mr. Antonio that resulted in an improper and unduly suggestive photographic array for identification by the store manager of Mr. Antonio, and pointing and identifying Mr. Antonio to the victim of the robbery during his preliminary hearing to assist the victim in any future identifications of Mr. Antonio that he might have been called upon to make.

The defendant made a motion to suppress the confession at trial and was denied. After the motion was denied he plead guilty. He is now appealing his conviction pro se from prison.

You are the clerk for an appellate judge and she has asked you to craft an order reversing the conviction of Mr. Antonio. She instructs you to draft the holding portion, focusing on the substantive law and its application in light of these facts.

-Notes-

Chapter 13: Basis for Privilege Against Self Incrimination & the Right to Counsel

Miranda v. Arizona

86 S.Ct. 1602
Supreme Court of the United States
Ernesto A. MIRANDA, Petitioner,
v.
STATE OF ARIZONA.
Michael VIGNERA, Petitioner,
v.
STATE OF NEW YORK.
Carl Calvin WESTOVER, Petitioner,
v.
UNITED STATES.
STATE OF CALIFORNIA, Petitioner,
v.
Roy Allen STEWART.
Nos. 759—761, 584. | Argued Feb. 28, March 1 and 2, 1966. | Decided June 13, 1966. | Rehearing Denied No. 584 Oct. 10, 1966.

***439** Mr. Chief Justice WARREN delivered the opinion of the Court.

The cases before us raise questions which go to the roots of our concepts of American criminal jurisprudence: the restraints society must observe consistent with the Federal Constitution in prosecuting individuals for crime. More specifically, we deal with the admissibility of statements obtained from an individual who is subjected to custodial police interrogation and the necessity for procedures which assure that the individual is accorded his privilege under the Fifth Amendment to the Constitution not to be compelled to incriminate himself.

***440** We dealt with certain phases of this problem recently in ****1610** Escobedo v. State of Illinois,[2036] There, as in the four cases before us, law enforcement officials took the defendant into custody and interrogated him in a police station for the purpose of obtaining a confession. The police did not effectively advise him of his right to remain silent or of his right to consult with his attorney. Rather, they confronted him with an alleged accomplice who accused him of having perpetrated a murder. When the defendant denied the accusation and said 'I didn't shoot Manuel, you did it,' they handcuffed him and took him to an interrogation room. There, while handcuffed and standing, he was questioned for four hours until he confessed. During this interrogation, the police denied his request to speak to his attorney, and they prevented his retained attorney, who had come to the police station, from consulting with him. At his trial, the State, over his objection, introduced the confession against him. We held that the statements thus made were constitutionally inadmissible.

This case has been the subject of judicial interpretation and spirited legal debate since it was decided two years ago. Both state and federal courts, in assessing its implications, have arrived at varying conclusions. A wealth of scholarly material has been written tracing its ramifications and underpinnings. Police and prosecutor ***441**

[2036] *378 U.S. 478, 84 S.Ct. 1758, 12 L.Ed.2d 977 (1964)*

have speculated on its range and desirability. We granted **1611 certiorari in these cases[2037] in order further to explore some facets of the problems, thus exposed, of applying the privilege against self-incrimination to in-custody interrogation, and to give *442 concrete constitutional guidelines for law enforcement agencies and courts to follow.

We start here, as we did in Escobedo, with the premise that our holding is not an innovation in our jurisprudence, but is an application of principles long recognized and applied in other settings. We have undertaken a thorough re-examination of the Escobedo decision and the principles it announced, and we reaffirm it. That case was but an explication of basic rights that are enshrined in our Constitution—that 'No person * * * shall be compelled in any criminal case to be a witness against himself,' and that 'the accused shall * * * have the Assistance of Counsel'—rights which were put in jeopardy in that case through official overbearing. These precious rights were fixed in our Constitution only after centuries of persecution and struggle. And in the words of Chief Justice Marshall, they were secured 'for ages to come, and * * * designed to approach immortality as nearly as human institutions can approach it,' Cohens v. Commonwealth of Virginia, 6 Wheat. 264, 387, 5 L.Ed. 257 (1821).[2038]

Over 70 years ago, our predecessors on this Court eloquently stated:

> 'The maxim 'Nemo tenetur seipsum accusare,' had its origin in a protest against the inquisitorial and manifestly unjust methods of interrogating accused persons, which (have) long obtained in the continental system, and, until the expulsion of the Stuarts from the British throne in 1688, and the erection of additional barriers for the protection of the people against the exercise of arbitrary power, (were) not uncommon even in England. While the admissions or confessions of the prisoner, when voluntarily and freely made, have always ranked high in the scale of incriminating evidence, if an accused person be asked to explain his apparent connection with a crime under investigation, the ease with which the *443 questions put to him may assume an inquisitorial character, the temptation to press the witness unduly, to browbeat him if he be timid or reluctant, to push him into a corner, and to entrap him into fatal contradictions, which is so painfully evident in many of the earlier state trials, notably in those of Sir Nicholas Throckmorton, and Udal, the Puritan minister, made the system so odious as to give rise to a demand for its total abolition. The change in the English criminal procedure in that particular seems to be founded upon no statute and no judicial opinion, but upon a general and silent acquiescence of the courts in a popular demand. But, however adopted, it has become firmly embedded in English, as well as in American jurisprudence. So deeply did the iniquities of the ancient system impress themselves upon the minds of the American colonists that the States, with one accord, made a denial of the right to question an accused person a part of their fundamental law, so that a maxim, which in England was a mere rule of evidence, became clothed in this country with the impregnability of a constitutional enactment.[2039]

In stating the obligation of the judiciary to apply these constitutional rights, this Court declared in Weems v. United States[2040]:

[2037] *382 U.S. 924, 925, 937, 86 S.Ct. 318, 320, 395, 15 L.Ed.2d 338, 339, 348*

[2038] *Cohens v. Commonwealth of Virginia, 6 Wheat. 264, 387, 5 L.Ed. 257 (1821)*

[2039] *Brown v. Walker, 161 U.S. 591, 596—597, 16 S.Ct. 644, 646, 40 L.Ed. 819 (1896)*

[2040] *217 U.S. 349, 373, 30 S.Ct. 544, 551, 54 L.Ed. 793 (1910)*

> * * * our contemplation cannot be only of what has been, but of what may be. Under any other rule a constitution would indeed be as easy of application as it would be deficient in efficacy and power. Its general principles would have little value, and be converted ****1612** by precedent into important and lifeless formulas. Rights declared in words might be lost in reality. And this has been recognized. The ***444** meaning and vitality of the Constitution have developed against narrow and restrictive construction.

This was the spirit in which we delineated, in meaningful language, the manner in which the constitutional rights of the individual could be enforced against overzealous police practices. It was necessary in Escobedo, as here, to insure that what was proclaimed in the Constitution had not become but a 'form of words,'[2041] in the hands of government officials. And it is in this spirit, consistent with our role as judges, that we adhere to the principles of Escobedo today.

Our holding will be spelled out with some specificity in the pages which follow but briefly stated it is this: the prosecution may not use statements, whether exculpatory or inculpatory, stemming from custodial interrogation of the defendant unless it demonstrates the use of procedural safeguards effective to secure the privilege against self-incrimination. By custodial interrogation, we mean questioning initiated by law enforcement officers after a person has been taken into custody or otherwise deprived of his freedom of action in any significant way. As for the procedural safeguards to be employed, unless other fully effective means are devised to inform accused persons of their right of silence and to assure a continuous opportunity to exercise it, the following measures are required. Prior to any questioning, the person must be warned that he has a right to remain silent, that any statement he does make may be used as evidence against him, and that he has a right to the presence of an attorney, either retained or appointed. The defendant may waive effectuation of these rights, provided the waiver is made voluntarily, knowingly and intelligently. If, however, he indicates in any manner and at any stage of the ***445** process that he wishes to consult with an attorney before speaking there can be no questioning. Likewise, if the individual is alone and indicates in any manner that he does not wish to be interrogated, the police may not question him. The mere fact that he may have answered some questions or volunteered some statements on his own does not deprive him of the right to refrain from answering any further inquiries until he has consulted with an attorney and thereafter consents to be questioned.

1

The constitutional issue we decide in each of these cases is the admissibility of statements obtained from a defendant questioned while in custody or otherwise deprived of his freedom of action in any significant way. In each, the defendant was questioned by police officers, detectives, or a prosecuting attorney in a room in which he was cut off from the outside world. In none of these cases was the defendant given a full and effective warning of his rights at the outset of the interrogation process. In all the cases, the questioning elicited oral admissions, and in three of them, signed statements as well which were admitted at their trials. They all thus share salient features—incommunicado interrogation of individuals in a police-dominated atmosphere, resulting in self-incriminating statements without full warnings of constitutional rights.

An understanding of the nature and setting of this in-custody interrogation is essential to our decisions today. The difficulty in depicting what transpires at such

[2041] *Silverthorn Lumber Co. v. United States, 251 U.S. 385, 392, 40 S.Ct. 182, 64 L.Ed. 319 (1920)*

interrogations stems from the fact **1613 that in this country they have largely taken place incommunicado. From extensive factual studies undertaken in the early 1930's, including the famous Wickersham Report to Congress by a Presidential Commission, it is clear that police violence and the 'third degree' flourished at that time. *446 In a series of cases decided by this Court long after these studies, the police resorted to physical brutality—beatings, hanging, whipping—and to sustained and protracted questioning incommunicado in order to extort confessions. The Commission on Civil Rights in 1961 found much evidence to indicate that 'some policemen still resort to physical force to obtain confessions.'[2042] The use of physical brutality and violence is not, unfortunately, relegated to the past or to any part of the country. Only recently in Kings County, New York, the police brutally beat, kicked and placed lighted cigarette butts on the back of a potential witness under interrogation for the purpose of securing a statement incriminating a third party.[2043]

***447** The examples given above are undoubtedly the exception now, but they are sufficiently widespread to be the object of concern. Unless a proper limitation upon custodial interrogation is achieved—such as these decisions will advance—there can be no assurance that practices of this nature will be eradicated in the foreseeable future. The conclusion of the Wickersham **1614 Commission Report, made over 30 years ago, is still pertinent:

> To the contention that the third degree is necessary to get the facts, the reporters aptly reply in the language of the present Lord Chancellor of England (Lord Sankey): 'It is not admissible to do a great right by doing a little wrong. * * * It is not sufficient to do justice by obtaining a proper result by irregular or improper means.' Not only does the use of the third degree involve a flagrant violation of law by the officers of the law, but it involves also the dangers of false confessions, and it tends to make police and prosecutors less zealous in the search for objective evidence. As the New York prosecutor quoted in the report said, 'It is a short cut and makes the police lazy and unenterprising.' Or, as another official quoted remarked: 'If you use your fists, you *448 are not so likely to use your wits.' We agree with the conclusion expressed in the report, that 'The third degree brutalizes the police, hardens the prisoner against society, and lowers the esteem in which the administration of justice is held by the public.'[2044]

Again we stress that the modern practice of in-custody interrogation is psychologically rather than physically oriented. As we have stated before, 'Since Chambers v. State of Florida,[2045] this Court has recognized that coercion can be mental as well as physical, and that the blood of the accused is not the only hallmark of an unconstitutional inquisition.'[2046] Interrogation still takes place in privacy. Privacy results in secrecy and this in turn results in a gap in our knowledge as to what in fact goes on in the interrogation rooms. A valuable source of information about present police practices, however, may be found in various police manuals and texts which document procedures employed with success in the past, and which recommend various other effective tactics. These *449 texts are used by law enforcement agencies themselves as guides. It should be noted that these texts professedly present the most

---

[2042] *1961 Comm'n on Civil Rights Rep., Justice, pt. 5, 17*

[2043] *People v. Portelli, 15 N.Y.2d 235, 257 N.Y.S.2d 931, 205 N.E.2d 857 (1965)*

[2044] *IV National Commission on Law Observance and Enforcement, Report on Lawlessness in Law Enforcement 5 (1931)*

[2045] *309 U.S. 227, 60 S.Ct. 472, 84 L.Ed. 716*

[2046] *Blackburn v. State of Alabama, 361 U.S. 199, 206, 80 S.Ct. 274, 279, 4 L.Ed.2d 242 (1960)*

enlightened and effective means presently used to obtain statements through custodial interrogation. By considering these texts and other **1615 data, it is possible to describe procedures observed and noted around the country.

The officers are told by the manuals that the 'principal psychological factor contributing to a successful interrogation is privacy—being alone with the person under interrogation.' The efficacy of this tactic has been explained as follows:

> If at all practicable, the interrogation should take place in the investigator's office or at least in a room of his own choice. The subject should be deprived of every psychological advantage. In his own home he may be confident, indignant, or recalcitrant. He is more keenly aware of his rights and *450 more reluctant to tell of his indiscretions of criminal behavior within the walls of his home. Moreover his family and other friends are nearby, their presence lending moral support. In his office, the investigator possesses all the advantages. The atmosphere suggests the invincibility of the forces of the law.

To highlight the isolation and unfamiliar surroundings, the manuals instruct the police to display an air of confidence in the suspect's guilt and from outward appearance to maintain only an interest in confirming certain details. The guilt of the subject is to be posited as a fact. The interrogator should direct his comments toward the reasons why the subject committed the act, rather than court failure by asking the subject whether he did it. Like other men, perhaps the subject has had a bad family life, had an unhappy childhood, had too much to drink, had an unrequited desire for women. The officers are instructed to minimize the moral seriousness of the offense, to cast blame on the victim or on society. These tactics are designed to put the subject in a psychological state where his story is but an elaboration of what the police purport to know already—that he is guilty. Explanations to the contrary are dismissed and discouraged.

The texts thus stress that the major qualities an interrogator should possess are patience and perseverance. *451 One writer describes the efficacy of these characteristics in this manner:

> In the preceding paragraphs emphasis has been placed on kindness and stratagems. The investigator will, however, encounter many situations where the sheer weight of his personality will be the deciding factor. Where emotional appeals and tricks are employed to no avail, he must rely on an oppressive atmosphere of dogged persistence. He must interrogate steadily and without relent, leaving the subject no prospect of surcease. He must dominate his subject and overwhelm him with his inexorable will to obtain the truth. He should interrogate for a spell of several hours pausing only for the subject's necessities in acknowledgment of the need to avoid a charge of duress that can be technically substantiated. In a serious case, the interrogation may continue for days, with the required intervals for food and sleep, but with no respite from the atmosphere of domination. It is possible in this way to induce the subject to talk without resorting to duress or coercion. The method should be used only when the guilt of **1616 the subject appears highly probable.

The manuals suggest that the suspect be offered legal excuses for his actions in order to obtain an initial admission of guilt. Where there is a suspected revenge-killing, for example, the interrogator may say:

> Joe, you probably didn't go out looking for this fellow with the purpose of shooting him. My guess is, however, that you expected something from him and that's why you carried a gun—for your own protection. You knew him for what he was, no good. Then when you met him he probably started using foul, abusive language and he gave some indication ***452** that he was about to pull a gun on you, and that's when you had to act to save your own life. That's about it, isn't it, Joe?

Having then obtained the admission of shooting, the interrogator is advised to refer to circumstantial evidence which negates the self-defense explanation. This should enable him to secure the entire story. One text notes that 'Even if he fails to do so, the inconsistency between the subject's original denial of the shooting and his present admission of at least doing the shooting will serve to deprive him of a self-defense 'out' at the time of trial.'

When the techniques described above prove unavailing, the texts recommend they be alternated with a show of some hostility. One ploy often used has been termed the 'friendly-unfriendly' or the 'Mutt and Jeff' act:

> * * * In this technique, two agents are employed. Mutt, the relentless investigator, who knows the subject is guilty and is not going to waste any time. He's sent a dozen men away for this crime and he's going to send the subject away for the full term. Jeff, on the other hand, is obviously a kindhearted man. He has a family himself. He has a brother who was involved in a little scrape like this. He disapproves of Mutt and his tactics and will arrange to get him off the case if the subject will cooperate. He can't hold Mutt off for very long. The subject would be wise to make a quick decision. The technique is applied by having both investigators present while Mutt acts out his role. Jeff may stand by quietly and demur at some of Mutt's tactics. When Jeff makes his plea for cooperation, Mutt is not present in the room.

***453** The interrogators sometimes are instructed to induce a confession out of trickery. The technique here is quite effective in crimes which require identification or which run in series. In the identification situation, the interrogator may take a break in his questioning to place the subject among a group of men in a line-up. 'The witness or complainant (previously coached, if necessary) studies the line-up and confidently points out the subject as the guilty party.' Then the questioning resumes 'as though there were now no doubt about the guilt ****1617** of the subject.' A variation on this technique is called the 'reverse line-up':

> The accused is placed in a line-up, but this time he is identified by several fictitious witnesses or victims who associated him with different offenses. It is expected that the subject will become desperate and confess to the offense under investigation in order to escape from the false accusations.

The manuals also contain instructions for police on how to handle the individual who refuses to discuss the matter entirely, or who asks for an attorney or relatives. The examiner is to concede him the right to remain silent. 'This usually has a very undermining effect. First of all, he is disappointed in his expectation of an unfavorable reaction on the part of the interrogator. Secondly, a concession of this right to remain silent impresses ***454** the subject with the apparent fairness of his interrogator.' After this psychological conditioning, however, the officer is told to point out the incriminating significance of the suspect's refusal to talk:

> Joe, you have a right to remain silent. That's your privilege and I'm the last person in the world who'll try to take it away from you. If that's the way you want to leave this, O.K. But let me ask you this. Suppose you were in my shoes and I were in yours and you called me in to ask me about this and I told you, 'I don't want to answer any of your questions.' You'd think I had something to hide, and you'd probably be right in thinking that. That's exactly what I'll have to think about you, and so will everybody else. So let's sit here and talk this whole thing over.

Few will persist in their initial refusal to talk, it is said, if this monologue is employed correctly.

In the event that the subject wishes to speak to a relative or an attorney, the following advice is tendered:

> (T)he interrogator should respond by suggesting that the subject first tell the truth to the interrogator himself rather than get anyone else involved in the matter. If the request is for an attorney, the interrogator may suggest that the subject save himself or his family the expense of any such professional service, particularly if he is innocent of the offense under investigation. The interrogator may also add, 'Joe, I'm only looking for the truth, and if you're telling the truth, that's it. You can handle this by yourself.'

***455** From these representative samples of interrogation techniques, the setting prescribed by the manuals and observed in practice becomes clear. In essence, it is this: To be alone with the subject is essential to prevent distraction and to deprive him of any outside support. The aura of confidence in his guilt undermines his will to resist. He merely confirms the preconceived story the police seek to have him describe. Patience and persistence, at times relentless questioning, are employed. To obtain a confession, the interrogator must 'patiently maneuver himself or his quarry into a position from which the desired objective may be attained.' When normal procedures fail to produce the needed result, the police may resort to deceptive stratagems such as giving false legal advice. It is important to keep the subject off balance, for example, by trading on his insecurity about himself or his surroundings. The police then persuade, trick, or cajole him out of exercising his constitutional rights.

Even without employing brutality, the 'third degree' or the specific stratagems ****1618** described above, the very fact of custodial interrogation exacts a heavy toll on individual liberty and trades on the weakness of individuals. ***456** This fact may be illustrated simply by referring to three confession cases decided by this Court in the Term immediately preceding our Escobedo decision. In Townsend v. Sain,[2047] the defendant was a 19-year-old heroin addict, described as a 'near mental defective.'[2048] The defendant in Lynumn v. State of Illinois,[2049] was a woman who confessed to the arresting officer after being importuned to 'cooperate' in order to prevent her children from being taken by relief authorities. This Court as in those cases reversed the conviction of a defendant in Haynes v. State of Washington,[2050] whose persistent request during his interrogation was to phone his wife or attorney.25 In other settings, these individuals might have exercised their constitutional rights. In the incommunicado police-dominated atmosphere, they succumbed.

[2047] *372 U.S. 293, 83 S.Ct. 745, 9 L.Ed.2d 770 (1963)*

[2048] *Id., at 307—310, 83 S.Ct. at 754—755*

[2049] *372 U.S. 528, 83 S.Ct. 917, 9 L.Ed.2d 922 (1963)*

[2050] *373 U.S. 503, 83 S.Ct. 1336, 10 L.Ed.2d 513 (1963)*

In the cases before us today, given this background, we concern ourselves primarily with this interrogation atmosphere and the evils it can bring. In No. 759, Miranda v. Arizona, the police arrested the defendant and took him to a special interrogation room where they secured a confession. In No. 760, Vignera v. New York, the defendant made oral admissions to the police after interrogation in the afternoon, and then signed an inculpatory statement upon being questioned by an assistant district attorney later the same evening. In No. 761, Westover v. United States, the defendant was handed over to the Federal Bureau of Investigation by ***457** local authorities after they had detained and interrogated him for a lengthy period, both at night and the following morning. After some two hours of questioning, the federal officers had obtained signed statements from the defendant. Lastly, in No. 584, California v. Stewart, the local police held the defendant five days in the station and interrogated him on nine separate occasions before they secured his inculpatory statement.

In these cases, we might not find the defendants' statements to have been involuntary in traditional terms. Our concern for adequate safeguards to protect precious Fifth Amendment rights is, of course, not lessened in the slightest. In each of the cases, the defendant was thrust into an unfamiliar atmosphere and run through menacing police interrogation procedures. The potentiality for compulsion is forcefully apparent, for example, in Miranda, where the indigent Mexican defendant was a seriously disturbed individual with pronounced sexual ****1619** fantasies, and in Stewart, in which the defendant was an indigent Los Angeles Negro who had dropped out of school in the sixth grade. To be sure, the records do not evince overt physical coercion or patent psychological ploys. The fact remains that in none of these cases did the officers undertake to afford appropriate safeguards at the outset of the interrogation to insure that the statements were truly the product of free choice.

It is obvious that such an interrogation environment is created for no purpose other than to subjugate the individual to the will of his examiner. This atmosphere carries its own badge of intimidation. To be sure, this is not physical intimidation, but it is equally destructive of human dignity. The current practice of incommunicado interrogation is at odds with one of our ***458** Nation's most cherished principles—that the individual may not be compelled to incriminate himself. Unless adequate protective devices are employed to dispel the compulsion inherent in custodial surroundings, no statement obtained from the defendant can truly be the product of his free choice.

From the foregoing, we can readily perceive an intimate connection between the privilege against self-incrimination and police custodial questioning. It is fitting to turn to history and precedent underlying the Self-Incrimination Clause to determine its applicability in this situation.

II

We sometimes forget how long it has taken to establish the privilege against self-incrimination, the sources from which it came and the fervor with which it was defended. Its roots go back into ancient times. Perhaps ***459** the critical historical event shedding light on its origins and evolution was the trial of one John Lilburn, a vocal anti-Stuart Leveller, who was made to take the Star Chamber Oath in 1637. The oath would have bound him to answer to all questions posed to him on any subject. The Trial of John Lilburn and John Wharton.[2051] He resisted the oath and declaimed the proceedings, stating: 'Another fundamental right I then contended for, was, that no man's conscience ought to be racked by oaths imposed, to answer to questions concerning himself in matters criminal, or pretended to be so.'[2052]

[2051] *3 How.St.Tr. 1315 (1637)*

[2052] *Haller & Davies, The Leveller Tracts 1647—1653, p. 454 (1944)*

On account of the Lilburn Trial, Parliament abolished the inquisitorial Court of Star Chamber and went further in giving him generous reparation. The lofty principles to which Lilburn had appealed ****1620** during his trial gained popular acceptance in England. These sentiments worked their way over to the Colonies and were implanted after great struggle into the Bill of Rights. Those who framed our Constitution and the Bill of Rights were ever aware of subtle encroachments on individual liberty. They knew that 'illegitimate and unconstitutional practices get their first footing * * * by silent approaches and slight deviations from legal modes of procedure.'[2053] The privilege was elevated to constitutional status and has always been 'as broad ad the mischief ***460** against which it seeks to guard.'[2054] We cannot depart from this noble heritage.

Thus we may view the historical development of the privilege as one which groped for the proper scope of governmental power over the citizen. As a 'noble principle often transcends its origins,' the privilege has come right-fully to be recognized in part as an individual's substantive right, a 'right to a private enclave where he may lead a private life. That right is the hallmark of our democracy.'[2055] We have recently noted that the privilege against self-incrimination—the essential mainstay of our adversary system—is founded on a complex of values.[2056] All these policies point to one overriding thought: the constitutional foundation underlying the privilege is the respect a government—state or federal—must accord to the dignity and integrity of its citizens. To maintain a 'fair state-individual balance,' to require the government 'to shoulder the entire load,'[2057] to respect the inviolability of the human personality, our accusatory system of criminal justice demands that the government seeking to punish an individual produce the evidence against him by its own independent labors, rather than by the cruel, simple expedient of compelling it from his own mouth.[2058] In sum, the privilege is fulfilled only when the person is guaranteed the right 'to remain silent unless he chooses to speak in the unfettered exercise of his own will.'[2059]

The question in these cases is whether the privilege is fully applicable during a period of custodial interrogation. ***461** In this Court, the privilege has consistently been accorded a liberal construction.[2060] We are satisfied that all the principles embodied in the privilege apply to informal compulsion exerted by ****1621** law-enforcement officers during in-custody questioning. An individual swept from familiar surroundings into police custody, surrounded by antagonistic forces, and subjected to the techniques of persuasion described above cannot be otherwise than under compulsion to speak. As a practical matter, the compulsion to speak in the isolated setting of the police station may well be greater than in courts or other official investigations, where there are often impartial observers to guard against intimidation or trickery.

[2053] *Boyd v. United States, 116 U.S. 616, 635, 6 S.Ct. 524, 535, 29 L.Ed. 746 (1886)*

[2054] *Counselman v. Hitchcock, 142 U.S. 547, 562, 12 S.Ct. 195, 198, 35 L.Ed. 1110 (1892)*

[2055] *United States v. Grunewald, 233 F.2d 556, 579, 581—582 (Frank, J., dissenting), rev'd, 353 U.S. 391, 77 S.Ct. 963, 1 L.Ed. 2d 931 (1957)*

[2056] *Murphy v. Waterfront Comm. of New York Harbor, 378 U.S. 52, 55—57, n. 5, 84 S.Ct. 1594, 1596—1597, 12 L.Ed.2d 678 (1964); Tehan v. United States ex rel. Shott, 382 U.S. 406, 414—415, n. 12, 86 S.Ct. 459, 464, 15 L.Ed.2d 453 (1966)*

[2057] *8 Wigmore, Evidence 317 (McNaughton rev. 1961)*

[2058] *Chambers v. State of Florida, 309 U.S. 227, 235—238, 60 S.Ct. 472, 476—477, 84 L.Ed. 716 (1940)*

[2059] *Malloy v. Hogan, 378 U.S. 1, 8, 84 S.Ct. 1489, 1493, 12 L.Ed.2d 653 (1964)*

[2060] *Albertson v. Subversive Activities Control Board, 382 U.S. 70, 81, 86 S.Ct. 194, 200, 15 L.Ed.2d 165 (1965); Hoffman v. United States, 341 U.S. 479, 486, 71 S.Ct. 814, 818, 95 L.Ed.2d 1118 (1951); Arnstein v. McCarthy, 254 U.S. 71, 72—73, 41 S.Ct. 26, 65 L.Ed. 138 (1920); Counselman v. Hitchcock, 142 U.S. 547, 562, 12 S.Ct. 195, 197, 35 L.Ed. 1110 (1892)*

This question, in fact, could have been taken as settled in federal courts almost 70 years ago, when, in Bram v. United States,[2061] this Court held:

> In criminal trials, in the courts of the United States, wherever a question arises whether a confession is incompetent because not voluntary, the issue is controlled by that portion of the fifth amendment * * * commanding that no person 'shall be compelled in any criminal case to be a witness against himself.'

In Bram, the Court reviewed the British and American history and case law and set down the Fifth Amendment standard for compulsion which we implement today:

> Much of the confusion which has resulted from the effort to deduce from the adjudged cases what ***462** would be a sufficient quantum of proof to show that a confession was or was not voluntary has arisen from a misconception of the subject to which the proof must address itself. The rule is not that, in order to render a statement admissible, the proof must be adequate to establish that the particular communications contained in a statement were voluntarily made, but it must be sufficient to establish that the making of the statement was voluntary; that is to say, that, from the causes which the law treats as legally sufficient to engender in the mind of the accused hope or fear in respect to the crime charged, the accused was not involuntarily impelled to make a statement when but for the improper influences he would have remained silent. * * *[2062]

The Court has adhered to this reasoning. In 1924, Mr. Justice Brandeis wrote for a unanimous Court in reversing a conviction resting on a compelled confession, Ziang Sung Wan v. United States.[2063] He stated:

> In the federal courts, the requisite of voluntariness is not satisfied by establishing merely that the confession was not induced by a promise or a threat. A confession is voluntary in law if, and only if, it was, in fact, voluntarily made. A confession may have been given voluntarily, although it was made to police officers, while in custody, and in answer to an examination conducted by them. But a confession obtained by compulsion must be excluded whatever may have been the character of the compulsion, and whether the compulsion was applied in a judicial proceeding or otherwise. Bram v. United States.[2064]

In addition to the expansive historical development of the privilege and the sound policies which have nurtured ***463** its evolution, judicial precedent thus clearly establishes its application to incommunicado interrogation. In fact, the Government concedes this point as well established in No. 761, Westover v. United States, stating: 'We have no doubt * * * that it is possible for a suspect's Fifth ****1622** Amendment right to be violated during in-custody questioning by a law-enforcement officer.'

[2061] *168 U.S. 532, 542, 18 S.Ct. 183, 187, 42 L.Ed. 568 (1897)*

[2062] *168 U.S., at 549, 18 S.Ct. at 189. And see, id., at 542, 18 S.Ct. at 186*

[2063] *266 U.S. 1, 45 S.Ct. 1, 69 L.Ed. 131*

[2064] *168 U.S. 532, 18 S.Ct. 183, 42 L.Ed. 568.' 266 U.S., at 14—15, 45 S.Ct. at 3*

Because of the adoption by Congress of Rule 5(a) of the Federal Rules of Criminal Procedure, and the Court's effectuation of that Rule in McNabb v. United States,[2065] and Mallory v. United States,[2066] we have had little occasion in the past quarter century to reach the constitutional issues in dealing with federal interrogations. These supervisory rules, requiring production of an arrested person before a commissioner 'without unnecessary delay' and excluding evidence obtained in default of that statutory obligation, were nonetheless responsive to the same considerations of Fifth Amendment policy that unavoidably face us now as to the States. In McNabb,[2067] and in Mallory,[2068] we recognized both the dangers of interrogation and the appropriateness of prophylaxis stemming from the very fact of interrogation itself.

Our decision in Malloy v. Hogan,[2069] necessitates an examination of the scope of the privilege in state cases as well. In Malloy, we squarely held the ***464** privilege applicable to the States, and held that the substantive standards underlying the privilege applied with full force to state court proceedings. There, as in Murphy v. Waterfront Comm. of New York Harbor,[2070] and Griffin v. State of California,[2071] we applied the existing Fifth Amendment standards to the case before us. Aside from the holding itself, the reasoning in Malloy made clear what had already become apparent—that the substantive and procedural safeguards surrounding admissibility of confessions in state cases had become exceedingly exacting, reflecting all the policies embedded in the privilege.[2072] The voluntariness ****1623** doctrine in the state cases, as Malloy indicates, encompasses all interrogation practices which are likely to exert such pressure upon an individual as to disable him from ***465** making a free and rational choice. The implications of this proposition were elaborated in our decision in Escobedo v. State of Illinois,[2073] decided one week after Malloy applied the privilege to the States.

Our holding there stressed the fact that the police had not advised the defendant of his constitutional privilege to remain silent at the outset of the interrogation, and we drew attention to that fact at several points in the decision.[2074] This was no isolated factor, but an essential ingredient in our decision. The entire thrust of police interrogation there, as in all the cases today, was to put the defendant in such an emotional state as to impair his capacity for rational judgment. The abdication of the constitutional privilege—the choice on his part to speak to the police—was not made knowingly or competently because of the failure to apprise him of his rights; the compelling atmosphere of the in-custody interrogation, and not an independent decision on his part, caused the defendant to speak.

A different phase of the Escobedo decision was significant in its attention to the absence of counsel during the questioning. There, as in the cases today, we sought a protective device to dispel the compelling atmosphere of the interrogation. In Escobedo, however, the police did not relieve the defendant of the anxieties which they had created in the interrogation rooms. Rather, they denied his request for the as-

---

[2065] *318 U.S. 332, 63 S.Ct. 608, 87 L.Ed. 819 (1943)*

[2066] *354 U.S. 449, 77 S.Ct. 1356, 1 L.Ed.2d 1479 (1957)*

[2067] *318 U.S., at 343—344, 63 S.Ct. at 614*

[2068] *354 U.S., at 455—456, 77 S.Ct. at 1359—1360*

[2069] *378 U.S. 1, 84 S.Ct. 1489, 12 L.Ed.2d 653 (1964)*

[2070] *378 U.S. 52, 84 S.Ct. 1594, 12 L.Ed.2d 678 (1964)*

[2071] *380 U.S. 609, 85 S.Ct. 1229, 14 L.Ed.2d 106 (1965)*

[2072] *378 U.S., at 7—8, 84 S.Ct. at 1493*

[2073] *378 U.S. 478, 84 S.Ct. 1758, 12 L.Ed.2d 977*

[2074] *378 U.S., at 483, 485, 491, 84 S.Ct. at 1761, 1762, 1765*

sistance of counsel.[2075] This heightened his dilemma, and ***466** made his later statements the product of this compulsion.[2076] The denial of the defendant's request for his attorney thus undermined his ability to exercise the privilege—to remain silent if he chose or to speak without any intimidation, blatant or subtle. The presence of counsel, in all the cases before us today, would be the adequate protective device necessary to make the process of police interrogation conform to the dictates of the privilege. His presence would insure that statements made in the government-established atmosphere are not the product of compulsion.

It was in this manner that Escobedo explicated another facet of the pre-trial privilege, noted in many of the Court's prior decisions: the protection of rights at trial. That counsel is present when ****1624** statements are taken from an individual during interrogation obviously enhances the integrity of the fact-finding processes in court. The presence of an attorney, and the warnings delivered to the individual, enable the defendant under otherwise compelling circumstances to tell his story without fear, effectively, and in a way that eliminates the evils in the interrogation process. Without the protections flowing from adequate warning and the rights of counsel, 'all the careful safeguards erected around the giving of testimony, whether by an accused or any other witness, would become empty formalities in a procedure where the most compelling possible evidence of guilt, a confession, would have already been obtained at the unsupervised pleasure of the police.'[2077]

*467 III

Today, then, there can be no doubt that the Fifth Amendment privilege is available outside of criminal court proceedings and serves to protect persons in all settings in which their freedom of action is curtailed in any significant way from being compelled to incriminate themselves. We have concluded that without proper safeguards the process of in-custody interrogation of persons suspected or accused of crime contains inherently compelling pressures which work to undermine the individual's will to resist and to compel him to speak where he would not otherwise do so freely. In order to combat these pressures and to permit a full opportunity to exercise the privilege against self-incrimination, the accused must be adequately and effectively apprised of his rights and the exercise of those rights must be fully honored.

It is impossible for us to foresee the potential alternatives for protecting the privilege which might be devised by Congress or the States in the exercise of their creative rule-making capacities. Therefore we cannot say that the Constitution necessarily requires adherence to any particular solution for the inherent compulsions of the interrogation process as it is presently conducted. Our decision in no way creates a constitutional straitjacket which will handicap sound efforts at reform, nor is it intended to have this effect. We encourage Congress and the States to continue their laudable search for increasingly effective ways of protecting the rights of the individual while promoting efficient enforcement of our criminal laws. However, unless we are shown other procedures which are at least as effective in apprising accused persons of their right of silence and in assuring a continuous opportunity to exercise it, the following safeguards must be observed.

At the outset, if a person in custody is to be subjected to interrogation, he must first be informed in clear and ***468** unequivocal terms that he has the right to remain silent. For those unaware of the privilege, the warning is needed simply to make them aware of it—the threshold requirement for an intelligent decision as to its exercise. More important, such a warning is an absolute prerequisite in overcoming the

---

[2075] *378 U.S., at 481, 488, 491, 84 S.Ct. at 1760, 1763, 1765*

[2076] *Cf. Haynes v. State of Washington, 373 U.S. 503, 514, 83 S.Ct. 1336, 1343 (1963)*

[2077] *Mapp v. Ohio, 367 U.S. 643, 685, 81 S.Ct. 1684, 1707, 6 L.Ed.2d 1081 (1961) (Harlan, J., dissenting). Cf. Pointer v. State of Texas, 380 U.S. 400, 85 S.Ct. 1065, 13 L.Ed.2d 923 (1965)*

inherent pressures of the interrogation atmosphere. It is not just the subnormal or woefully ignorant who succumb to an interrogator's imprecations, whether implied or expressly stated, that the interrogation will continue until a confession is obtained or that silence in the face of accusation is itself damning and will bode ill when presented to a jury. Further, **1625 the warning will show the individual that his interrogators are prepared to recognize his privilege should he choose to exercise it.

The Fifth Amendment privilege is so fundamental to our system of constitutional rule and the expedient of giving an adequate warning as to the availability of the privilege so simple, we will not pause to inquire in individual cases whether the defendant was aware of his rights without a warning being given. Assessments of the knowledge the defendant possessed, based on information *469 as to his age, education, intelligence, or prior contact with authorities, can never be more than speculation;38 a warning is a clearcut fact. More important, whatever the background of the person interrogated, a warning at the time of the interrogation is indispensable to overcome its pressures and to insure that the individual knows he is free to exercise the privilege at that point in time.

The warning of the right to remain silent must be accompanied by the explanation that anything said can and will be used against the individual in court. This warning is needed in order to make him aware not only of the privilege, but also of the consequences of forgoing it. It is only through an awareness of these consequences that there can be any assurance of real understanding and intelligent exercise of the privilege. Moreover, this warning may serve to make the individual more acutely aware that he is faced with a phase of the adversary system—that he is not in the presence of persons acting solely in his interest.

The circumstances surrounding in-custody interrogation can operate very quickly to overbear the will of one merely made aware of his privilege by his interrogators. Therefore, the right to have counsel present at the interrogation is indispensable to the protection of the Fifth Amendment privilege under the system we delineate today. Our aim is to assure that the individual's right to choose between silence and speech remains unfettered throughout the interrogation process. A once-stated warning, delivered by those who will conduct the interrogation, cannot itself suffice to that end among those who most require knowledge of their rights. A mere *470 warning given by the interrogators is not alone sufficient to accomplish that end. Prosecutors themselves claim that the admonishment of the right to remain silent without more 'will benefit only the recidivist and the professional.'[2078] Even preliminary advice given to the accused by his own attorney can be swiftly overcome by the secret interrogation process.[2079] Thus, the need for counsel to protect **1626 the Fifth Amendment privilege comprehends not merely a right to consult with counsel prior to questioning, but also to have counsel present during any questioning if the defendant so desires.

The presence of counsel at the interrogation may serve several significant subsidiary functions as well. If the accused decides to talk to his interrogators, the assistance of counsel can mitigate the dangers of untrustworthiness. With a lawyer present the likelihood that the police will practice coercion is reduced, and if coercion is nevertheless exercised the lawyer can testify to it in court. The presence of a lawyer can also help to guarantee that the accused gives a fully accurate statement to the police and that the statement is rightly reported by the prosecution at trial.[2080]

An individual need not make a pre-interrogation request for a lawyer. While such request affirmatively secures his right to have one, his failure to ask for a

---

[2078] *Brief for the National District Attorneys Association as amicus curiae, p. 14*

[2079] *Cf. Escobedo v. State of Illinois, 378 U.S. 478, 485, n. 5, 84 S.Ct. 1758, 1762*

[2080] *See Crooker v. State of California, 357 U.S. 433, 443—448, 78 S.Ct. 1287, 1293—1296, 2 L.Ed.2d 1448 (1958) (Douglas, J., dissenting)*

lawyer does not constitute a waiver. No effective waiver of the right to counsel during interrogation can be recognized unless specifically made after the warnings we here delineate have been given. The accused who does not know his rights and therefore does not make a request ***471** may be the person who most needs counsel. As the California Supreme Court has aptly put it:

> Finally, we must recognize that the imposition of the requirement for the request would discriminate against the defendant who does not know his rights. The defendant who does not ask for counsel is the very defendant who most needs counsel. We cannot penalize a defendant who, not understanding his constitutional rights, does not make the formal request and by such failure demonstrates his helplessness. To require the request would be to favor the defendant whose sophistication or status had fortuitously prompted him to make it.[2081]

In Carnley v. Cochran,[2082] we stated: '(I)t is settled that where the assistance of counsel is a constitutional requisite, the right to be furnished counsel does not depend on a request.' This proposition applies with equal force in the context of providing counsel to protect an accused's Fifth Amendment privilege in the face of interrogation. Although the role of counsel at trial differs from the role during interrogation, the differences are not relevant to the question whether a request is a prerequisite.

Accordingly we hold that an individual held for interrogation must be clearly informed that he has the right to consult with a lawyer and to have the lawyer with him during interrogation under the system for protecting the privilege we delineate today. As with the warnings of the right to remain silent and that anything stated can be used in evidence against him, this warning is an absolute prerequisite to interrogation. No amount of ***472** circumstantial evidence that the person may have been aware of this right will suffice to stand in its stead. Only through such a warning is there ascertainable assurance that the accused was aware of this right.

If an individual indicates that he wishes the assistance of counsel before any interrogation occurs, the authorities cannot rationally ignore or deny his request on the basis that the individual does not have or cannot afford a retained attorney. The financial ability ****1627** of the individual has no relationship to the scope of the rights involved here. The privilege against self-incrimination secured by the Constitution applies to all individuals. The need for counsel in order to protect the privilege exists for the indigent as well as the affluent. In fact, were we to limit these constitutional rights to those who can retain an attorney, our decisions today would be of little significance. The cases before us as well as the vast majority of confession cases with which we have dealt in the past involve those unable to retain counsel. While authorities are not required to relieve the accused of his poverty, they have the obligation not to take advantage of indigence in the administration of justice. Denial ***473** of counsel to the indigent at the time of interrogation while allowing an attorney to those who can afford one would be no more supportable by reason or logic than the similar situation at trial and on appeal struck down in Gideon v. Wainwright[2083] and Douglas v. People of State of California.[2084]

In order fully to apprise a person interrogated of the extent of his rights under this system then, it is necessary to warn him not only that he has the right to consult with an attorney, but also that if he is indigent a lawyer will be appointed to represent

---

[2081] *People v. Dorado, 62 Cal.2d 338, 351, 42 Cal.Rptr. 169, 177—178, 398 P.2d 361, 369—370, (1965) (Tobriner, J.)*

[2082] *369 U.S. 506, 513, 82 S.Ct. 884, 889, 8 L.Ed.2d 70 (1962)*

[2083] *372 U.S. 335, 83 S.Ct. 792, 9 L.Ed.2d 799 (1963)*

[2084] *372 U.S. 353, 83 S.Ct. 814, 9 L.Ed.2d 811 (1963)*

him. Without this additional warning, the admonition of the right to consult with counsel would often be understood as meaning only that he can consult with a lawyer if he has one or has the funds to obtain one. The warning of a right to counsel would be hollow if not couched in terms that would convey to the indigent—the person most often subjected to interrogation—the knowledge that he too has a right to have counsel present. As with the warnings of the right to remain silent and of the general right to counsel, only by effective and express explanation to the indigent of this right can there be assurance that he was truly in a position to exercise it.

Once warnings have been given, the subsequent procedure is clear. If the individual indicates in any manner, ***474** at any time prior to or during questioning, that he wishes to remain silent, the interrogation must cease.44 At this ****1628** point he has shown that he intends to exercise his Fifth Amendment privilege; any statement taken after the person invokes his privilege cannot be other than the product of compulsion, subtle or otherwise. Without the right to cut off questioning, the setting of in-custody interrogation operates on the individual to overcome free choice in producing a statement after the privilege has been once invoked. If the individual states that he wants an attorney, the interrogation must cease until an attorney is present. At that time, the individual must have an opportunity to confer with the attorney and to have him present during any subsequent questioning. If the individual cannot obtain an attorney and he indicates that he wants one before speaking to police, they must respect his decision to remain silent.

This does not mean, as some have suggested, that each police station must have a 'station house lawyer' present at all times to advise prisoners. It does mean, however, that if police propose to interrogate a person they must make known to him that he is entitled to a lawyer and that if he cannot afford one, a lawyer will be provided for him prior to any interrogation. If authorities conclude that they will not provide counsel during a reasonable period of time in which investigation in the field is carried out, they may refrain from doing so without violating the person's Fifth Amendment privilege so long as they do not question him during that time.

***475** If the interrogation continues without the presence of an attorney and a statement is taken, a heavy burden rests on the government to demonstrate that the defendant knowingly and intelligently waived his privilege against self-incrimination and his right to retained or appointed counsel. Escobedo v. State of Illinois.[2085] This Court has always set high standards of proof for the waiver of constitutional rights, Johnson v. Zerbst,[2086] and we reassert these standards as applied to in-custody interrogation. Since the State is responsible for establishing the isolated circumstances under which the interrogation takes place and has the only means of making available corroborated evidence of warnings given during incommunicado interrogation, the burden is rightly on its shoulders.

An express statement that the individual is willing to make a statement and does not want an attorney followed closely by a statement could constitute a waiver. But a valid waiver will not be presumed simply from the silence of the accused after warnings are given or simply from the fact that a confession was in fact eventually obtained. A statement we made in Carnley v. Cochran,[2087] is applicable here:

> Presuming waiver from a silent record is impermissible. The record must show, or there must be an allegation and evidence which show, that an

[2085] *378 U.S. 478, 490, n. 14, 84 S.Ct. 1758, 1764, 12 L.Ed.2d 977*

[2086] *304 U.S. 458, 58 S.Ct. 1019, 82 L.Ed. 1461 (1938)*

[2087] *369 U.S. 506, 516, 82 S.Ct. 884, 890, 8 L.Ed.2d 70 (1962)*

> accused was offered counsel but intelligently and understandingly rejected the offer. Anything less is not waiver.[2088]

Moreover, where in-custody interrogation is involved, there is no room for the contention that the privilege is waived if the individual answers some questions or gives ***476** some information on his own prior to invoking his right to remain silent when interrogated.

****1629** Whatever the testimony of the authorities as to waiver of rights by an accused, the fact of lengthy interrogation or incommunicado incarceration before a statement is made is strong evidence that the accused did not validly waive his rights. In these circumstances the fact that the individual eventually made a statement is consistent with the conclusion that the compelling influence of the interrogation finally forced him to do so. It is inconsistent with any notion of a voluntary relinquishment of the privilege. Moreover, any evidence that the accused was threatened, tricked, or cajoled into a waiver will, of course, show that the defendant did not voluntarily waive his privilege. The requirement of warnings and waiver of rights is a fundamental with respect to the Fifth Amendment privilege and not simply a preliminary ritual to existing methods of interrogation.

The warnings required and the waiver necessary in accordance with our opinion today are, in the absence of a fully effective equivalent, prerequisites to the admissibility of any statement made by a defendant. No distinction can be drawn between statements which are direct confessions and statements which amount to 'admissions' of part or all of an offense. The privilege against self-incrimination protects the individual from being compelled to incriminate himself in any manner; it does not distinguish degrees of incrimination. Similarly, ***477** for precisely the same reason, no distinction may be drawn between inculpatory statements and statements alleged to be merely 'exculpatory.' If a statement made were in fact truly exculpatory it would, of course, never be used by the prosecution. In fact, statements merely intended to be exculpatory by the defendant are often used to impeach his testimony at trial or to demonstrate untruths in the statement given under interrogation and thus to prove guilt by implication. These statements are incriminating in any meaningful sense of the word and may not be used without the full warnings and effective waiver required for any other statement. In Escobedo itself, the defendant fully intended his accusation of another as the slayer to be exculpatory as to himself.

The principles announced today deal with the protection which must be given to the privilege against self-incrimination when the individual is first subjected to police interrogation while in custody at the station or otherwise deprived of his freedom of action in any significant way. It is at this point that our adversary system of criminal proceedings commences, distinguishing itself at the outset from the inquisitorial system recognized in some countries. Under the system of warnings we delineate today or under any other system which may be devised and found effective, the safeguards to be erected about the privilege must come into play at this point.

Our decision is not intended to hamper the traditional function of police officers in investigating crime.[2089] When an individual is in custody on probable cause, the police may, of course, seek out evidence in the field to be used at trial against him. Such investigation may include inquiry of persons not under restraint. General on-the-scene questioning as to facts surrounding a crime or other general questioning of citizens in the fact-finding process is not affected by our holding. It is an act of ***478** responsible citizenship for individuals to give whatever information they may have to aid in ****1630** law enforcement. In such situations the compelling atmosphere inherent in the process of in-custody interrogation is not necessarily present.

[2088] *See also Glasser v. United States, 315 U.S. 60, 62 S.Ct. 457, 86 L.Ed. 680 (1942)*

[2089] *See Escobedo v. State of Illinois, 378 U.S. 478, 492, 84 S.Ct. 1758, 1765*

In dealing with statements obtained through interrogation, we do not purport to find all confessions inadmissible. Confessions remain a proper element in law enforcement. Any statement given freely and voluntarily without any compelling influences is, of course, admissible in evidence. The fundamental import of the privilege while an individual is in custody is not whether he is allowed to talk to the police without the benefit of warnings and counsel, but whether he can be interrogated. There is no requirement that police stop a person who enters a police station and states that he wishes to confess to a crime, or a person who calls the police to offer a confession or any other statement he desires to make. Volunteered statements of any kind are not barred by the Fifth Amendment and their admissibility is not affected by our holding today.

To summarize, we hold that when an individual is taken into custody or otherwise deprived of his freedom by the authorities in any significant way and is subjected to questioning, the privilege against self-incrimination is jeopardized. Procedural safeguards must be employed to ***479** protect the privilege and unless other fully effective means are adopted to notify the person of his right of silence and to assure that the exercise of the right will be scrupulously honored, the following measures are required. He must be warned prior to any questioning that he has the right to remain silent, that anything he says can be used against him in a court of law, that he has the right to the presence of an attorney, and that if he cannot afford an attorney one will be appointed for him prior to any questioning if he so desires. Opportunity to exercise these rights must be afforded to him throughout the interrogation. After such warnings have been given, and such opportunity afforded him, the individual may knowingly and intelligently waive these rights and agree to answer questions or make a statement. But unless and until such warnings and waiver are demonstrated by the prosecution at trial, no evidence obtained as a result of interrogation can be used against him.

IV

A recurrent argument made in these cases is that society's need for interrogation outweighs the privilege. This argument is not unfamiliar to this Court.[2090] The whole thrust of our foregoing discussion demonstrates that the Constitution has prescribed the rights of the individual when confronted with the power of government when it provided in the Fifth Amendment that an individual cannot be compelled to be a witness against himself. That right cannot be abridged. As Mr. Justice Brandeis once observed:

> Decency, security, and liberty alike demand that government officials shall ****1631** be subjected to the same ***480** rules of conduct that are commands to the citizen. In a government of laws, existence of the government will be imperiled if it fails to observe the law scrupulously. Our government is the potent, the omnipresent teacher. For good or for ill, it teaches the whole people by its example. Crime is contagious. If the government becomes a lawbreaker, it breeds contempt for law; it invites every man to become a law unto himself; it invites anarchy. To declare that in the administration of the criminal law the end justifies the means * * * would bring terrible retribution. Against that pernicious doctrine this court should resolutely set its face.[2091]

[2090] *See, e.g., Chambers v. State of Florida, 309 U.S. 227, 240—241, 60 S.Ct. 472, 478—479, 84 L.Ed. 716 (1940)*

[2091] *Olmstead v. United States, 277 U.S. 438, 485, 48 S.Ct. 564, 575, 72 L.Ed. 944 (1928) (dissenting opinion)*

In this connection, one of our country's distinguished jurists has pointed out: 'The quality of a nation's civilization can be largely measured by the methods it uses in the enforcement of its criminal law.'

If the individual desires to exercise his privilege, he has the right to do so. This is not for the authorities to decide. An attorney may advise his client not to talk to police until he has had an opportunity to investigate the case, or he may wish to be present with his client during any police questioning. In doing so an attorney is merely exercising the good professional judgment he has been taught. This is not cause for considering the attorney a menace to law enforcement. He is merely carrying out what he is sworn to do under his oath—to protect to the extent of his ability the rights of his ***481** client. In fulfilling this responsibility the attorney plays a vital role in the administration of criminal justice under our Constitution.

In announcing these principles, we are not unmindful of the burdens which law enforcement officials must bear, often under trying circumstances. We also fully recognize the obligation of all citizens to aid in enforcing the criminal laws. This Court, while protecting individual rights, has always given ample latitude to law enforcement agencies in the legitimate exercise of their duties. The limits we have placed on the interrogation process should not constitute an undue interference with a proper system of law enforcement. As we have noted, our decision does not in any way preclude police from carrying out their traditional investigatory functions. Although confessions may play an important role in some convictions, the cases before us present graphic examples of the overstatement of the 'need' for confessions. In each case authorities conducted interrogations ranging up to five days in duration despite the presence, through standard investigating practices, of considerable evidence against each defendant. Further examples are chronicled in our prior cases.[2092]

****1632 *482** It is also urged that an unfettered right to detention for interrogation should be allowed because it will often redound to the benefit of the person questioned. When police inquiry determines that there is no reason to believe that the person has committed any crime, it is said, he will be released without need for further formal procedures. The person who has committed no offense, however, will be better able to clear himself after warnings with counsel present than without. It can be assumed that in such circumstances a lawyer would advise his client to talk freely to police in order to clear himself.

Custodial interrogation, by contrast, does not necessarily afford the innocent an opportunity to clear themselves. A serious consequence of the present practice of the interrogation alleged to be beneficial for the innocent is that many arrests 'for investigation' subject large numbers of innocent persons to detention and interrogation. In one of the cases before us, No. 584, California v. Stewart, police held four persons, who were in the defendant's house at the time of the arrest, in jail for five days until defendant confessed. At that time they were finally released. Police stated that there was 'no evidence to connect them with any crime.' Available statistics on the extent of this practice where it is condoned indicate that these four are far from alone in being subjected to arrest, prolonged detention, and interrogation without the requisite probable cause.

***483** Over the years the Federal Bureau of Investigation has compiled an exemplary record of effective law enforcement while advising any suspect or arrested person, at the outset of an interview, that he is not required to make a statement, that any statement may be used against him in court, that the individual may obtain the services of an attorney of his own choice and, more recently, that he has a right to free counsel if he is unable to pay. A ****1633** letter received from the Solicitor General in response to a question from the Bench makes it clear that the present pattern

---

[2092] *See, e.g., Haynes v. State of Washington, 373 U.S. 503, 518—519, 83 S.Ct. 1336, 1345, 1346, 10 L.Ed.2d 513 (1963); Rogers v. Richmond, 365 U.S. 534, 541, 81 S.Ct. 735, 739, 5 L.Ed.2d 760 (1961); Malinski v. People of State of New York, 324 U.S. 401, 402, 65 S.Ct. 781, 782 (1945)*

of warnings and respect for the ***484** rights of the individual followed as a practice by the FBI is consistent with the procedure which we delineate today. It states:

> At the oral argument of the above cause, Mr. Justice Fortas asked whether I could provide certain information as to the practices followed by the Federal Bureau of Investigation. I have directed these questions to the attention of the Director of the Federal Bureau of Investigation and am submitting herewith a statement of the questions and of the answers which we have received.
>
> "(1) When an individual is interviewed by agents of the Bureau, what warning is given to him?"
>
> "The standard warning long given by Special Agents of the FBI to both suspects and persons under arrest is that the person has a right to say nothing and a right to counsel, and that any statement he does make may be used against him in court."[2093]
>
> "After passage of the Criminal Justice Act of 1964, which provides free counsel for Federal defendants unable to pay, we added to our instructions to Special Agents the requirement that any person who is under arrest for an offense under FBI jurisdiction, or whose arrest is contemplated following the interview, must also be advised of his right to free counsel if he is unable to pay, and the fact that such counsel will be assigned by the Judge. At the same time, we broadened the right to counsel warning ***485** to read counsel of his own choice, or anyone else with whom he might wish to speak."
>
> "(2) When is the warning given?"
>
> "The FBI warning is given to a suspect at the very outset of the interview, as shown in the Westover case, cited above. The warning may be given to a person arrested as soon as practicable after the arrest, as shown in the Jackson case, also cited above, and in U.S. v. Konigsberg,[2094] but in any event it must precede the interview with the person for a confession or admission of his own guilt."
>
> "(3) What is the Bureau's practice in the event that (a) the individual requests counsel and (b) counsel appears?"
>
> "When the person who has been warned of his right to counsel decides that he wishes to consult with counsel before making a statement, the interview is terminated at that point.[2095] It may be continued, however, as to all matters other than the person's own guilt or innocence. If he is indecisive in his request for counsel, there may be some question on whether he did or did not waive counsel. Situations of this kind must necessarily be left to the judgment of the interviewing Agent. For example, in Hiram v. U.S.,[2096] the Agent's conclusion that the person arrested had waived his right to counsel was upheld by the courts."

[2093] *Examples of this warning are to be found in the Westover case at 342 F.2d 684 (1965), and Jackson v. U.S., (119 U.S.App.D.C. 100) 337 F.2d 136 (1964), cert. den. 380 U.S. 935, 85 S.Ct. 1353*

[2094] *336 F.2d 844 (1964), cert. den. (Celso v. United States) 379 U.S. 933 (85 S.Ct. 327, 13 L.Ed.2d 342)*

[2095] *Shultz v. U.S., 351 F.2d 287 ((10 Cir.) 1965)*

[2096] *354 F.2d 4 ((9 Cir.) 1965)*

> "A person being interviewed and desiring to consult counsel by telephone must be permitted to do so, as shown in Caldwell v. U.S.[2097] When counsel **1634** appears in person, he is permitted to confer with his client in private."
>
> *486 "(4) What is the Bureau's practice if the individual requests counsel, but cannot afford to retain an attorney?"
>
> "If any person being interviewed after warning of counsel decides that he wishes to consult with counsel before proceeding further the interview is terminated, as shown above. FBI Agents do not pass judgment on the ability of the person to pay for counsel. They do, however, advise those who have been arrested for an offense under FBI jurisdiction, or whose arrest is contemplated following the interview, of a right to free counsel if they are unable to pay, and the availability of such counsel from the Judge."

The practice of the FBI can readily be emulated by state and local enforcement agencies. The argument that the FBI deals with different crimes than are dealt with by state authorities does not mitigate the significance of the FBI experience.

The experience in some other countries also suggests that the danger to law enforcement in curbs on interrogation is overplayed. The English procedure since 1912 under the Judges' Rules is significant. As recently ***487** strengthened, the Rules require that a cautionary warning be given an accused by a police officer as soon as he has evidence that affords reasonable grounds for suspicion; they also require that any statement made be given by the accused without questioning by police. ***488** The right of the individual to ****1635** consult with an attorney during this period is expressly recognized.

The safeguards present under Scottish law may be even greater than in England. Scottish judicial decisions bar use in evidence of most confessions obtained through police interrogation. In India, confessions made to police not in the presence of a magistrate have been excluded ***489** by rule of evidence since 1872, at a time when it operated under British law. Identical provisions appear in the Evidence Ordinance of Ceylon, enacted in 1895. Similarly, in our country the Uniform Code of Military Justice has long provided that no suspect may be interrogated without first being warned of his right not to make a statement and that any statement he makes may be used against him. Denial of the right to consult counsel during interrogation has also been proscribed by military tribunals. ****1636** There appears to have been no marked detrimental effect on criminal law enforcement in these jurisdictions as a result of these rules. Conditions of law enforcement in our country are sufficiently similar to permit reference to this experience as assurance that lawlessness will not result from warning an individual of his rights or allowing him to exercise them. Moreover, it is consistent with our legal system that we give at least as much protection to these rights as is given in the jurisdictions described. We deal in our country with rights grounded in a specific requirement of the Fifth Amendment of the Constitution, ***490** whereas other jurisdictions arrived at their conclusions on the basis of principles of justice not so specifically defined.

It is also urged upon us that we withhold decision on this issue until state legislative bodies and advisory groups have had an opportunity to deal with these problems by rule making. We have already pointed out that the Constitution does not require any specific code of procedures for protecting the privilege against self-incrimination during custodial interrogation. Congress and the States are free to develop their own safeguards for the privilege, so long as they are fully as effective as those described above in informing accused persons of their right of silence and in afford-

[2097] *351 F.2d 459 ((1 Cir.) 1965)*

ing a continuous opportunity to exercise it. In any event, however, the issues presented are of constitutional dimensions and must be determined by the courts. The admissibility of a statement in the face of a claim that it was obtained in violation of the defendant's constitutional rights is an issue the resolution of which has long since been undertaken by this Court.[2098] Judicial solutions to problems of constitutional dimension have evolved decade by decade. As courts have been presented with the need to enforce constitutional rights, they have found means of doing so. That was our responsibility when Escobedo was before us and it is our ***491** responsibility today. Where rights secured by the Constitution are involved, there can be no rule making or legislation which would abrogate them.

V

Because of the nature of the problem and because of its recurrent significance in numerous cases, we have to this point discussed the relationship of the Fifth Amendment privilege to police interrogation without specific concentration on the facts of the cases before us. We turn now to these facts to consider the application to these cases of the constitutional principles discussed above. In each instance, we have concluded that statements were obtained from the defendant under circumstances that did not meet constitutional standards for protection of the privilege.

No. 759. Miranda v. Arizona.

On March 13, 1963, petitioner, Ernesto Miranda, was arrested at his home and taken in custody to a Phoenix police station. He was there identified by the complaining witness. The police then took him to 'Interrogation Room No. 2' of the detective bureau. There he was questioned by two police officers. The officers admitted at trial that Miranda was ****1637** not advised that he had a right to have an attorney present. Two hours later, the ***492** officers emerged from the interrogation room with a written confession signed by Miranda. At the top of the statement was a typed paragraph stating that the confession was made voluntarily, without threats or promises of immunity and 'with full knowledge of my legal rights, understanding any statement I make may be used against me.'

At his trial before a jury, the written confession was admitted into evidence over the objection of defense counsel, and the officers testified to the prior oral confession made by Miranda during the interrogation. Miranda was found guilty of kidnapping and rape. He was sentenced to 20 to 30 years' imprisonment on each count, the sentences to run concurrently. On appeal, the Supreme Court of Arizona held that Miranda's constitutional rights were not violated in obtaining the confession and affirmed the conviction.[2099] In reaching its decision, the court emphasized heavily the fact that Miranda did not specifically request counsel.

We reverse. From the testimony of the officers and by the admission of respondent, it is clear that Miranda was not in any way apprised of his right to consult with an attorney and to have one present during the interrogation, nor was his right not to be compelled to incriminate himself effectively protected in any other manner. Without these warnings the statements were inadmissible. The mere fact that he signed a statement which contained a typed-in clause stating that he had 'full knowledge' of his 'legal rights' does not approach the knowing and intelligent waiver required to relinquish constitutional rights.[2100]

[2098] *See Hopt v. People of Territory of Utah, 110 U.S. 574, 4 S.Ct. 202, 28 L.Ed. 262 (1884)*

[2099] *98 Ariz. 18, 401 P.2d 721*

[2100] *Cf. Haynes v. State of Washington, 373 U.S. 503, 512—513, 83 S.Ct. 1336, 1342, 10 L.Ed.2d 513 (1963); Haley v. State of Ohio, 332 U.S. 596, 601, 68 S.Ct. 302, 304, 92 L.Ed. 224 (1948) (opinion of Mr. Justice Douglas)*

***493 No. 760. Vignera v. New York.**

Petitioner, Michael Vignera, was picked up by New York police on October 14, 1960, in connection with the robbery three days earlier of a Brooklyn dress shop. They took him to the 17th Detective Squad headquarters in Manhattan. Sometime thereafter he was taken to the 66th Detective Squad. There a detective questioned Vignera with respect to the robbery. Vignera orally admitted the robbery to the detective. The detective was asked on cross-examination at trial by defense counsel whether Vignera was warned of his right to counsel before being interrogated. The prosecution objected to the question and the trial judge sustained the objection. Thus, the defense was precluded from making any showing that warnings had not been given. While at the 66th Detective Squad, Vignera was identified by the store owner and a saleslady as the man who robbed the dress shop. At about 3 p.m. he was formally arrested. The police then transported him to still another station, the 70th Precinct in Brooklyn, 'for detention.' At 11 p.m. Vignera was questioned by an assistant district attorney in the presence of a hearing reporter who transcribed the questions and Vignera's answers. This verbatim account of these proceedings ****1638** contains no statement of any warnings given by the assistant district attorney. At Vignera's trial on a charge of first degree robbery, the detective testified as to the oral confession. The transcription of the statement taken was also introduced in evidence. At the conclusion of the testimony, the trial judge charged the jury in part as follows: 'The law doesn't say that the confession is void or invalidated because the police officer didn't advise the defendant as to his rights. Did you hear what ***494** I said? I am telling you what the law of the State of New York is.'

Vignera was found guilty of first degree robbery. He was subsequently adjudged a third-felony offender and sentenced to 30 to 60 years' imprisonment. The conviction was affirmed without opinion by the Appellate Division,[2101] and by the Court of Appeals, also without opinion.[2102] In argument to the Court of Appeals, the State contended that Vignera had no constitutional right to be advised of his right to counsel or his privilege against self-incrimination.

We reverse. The foregoing indicates that Vignera was not warned of any of his rights before the questioning by the detective and by the assistant district attorney. No other steps were taken to protect these rights. Thus he was not effectively apprised of his Fifth Amendment privilege or of his right to have counsel present and his statements are inadmissible.

No. 761. Westover v. United States.

At approximately 9:45 p.m. on March 20, 1963, petitioner, Carl Calvin Westover, was arrested by local police in Kansas City as a suspect in two Kansas City robberies. A report was also received from the FBI that he was wanted on a felony charge in California. The local authorities took him to a police station and placed him in a line-up on the local charges, and at about 11:45 p.m. he was booked. Kansas City police interrogated Westover ***495** on the night of his arrest. He denied any knowledge of criminal activities. The next day local officers interrogated him again throughout the morning. Shortly before noon they informed the FBI that they were through interrogating Westover and that the FBI could proceed to interrogate him. There is nothing in the record to indicate that Westover was ever given any warning as to his rights by local police. At noon, three special agents of the FBI continued the interrogation in a private interview room of the Kansas City Police Department, this time with respect to the robbery of a savings and loan association and a bank in Sacramento, California. After two or two and one-half hours, Westover signed separate confessions to each of these two robberies which had been prepared by one of

---

[2101] *Second Department, 21 A.D.2d 752, 252 N.Y.S.2d 19*

[2102] *15 N.Y.2d 970, 259 N.Y.S.2d 857, 207 N.E.2d 527, remittitur amended, 16 N.y.2d 614, 261 N.Y.S.2d 65, 209 N.E.2d 110*

the agents during the interrogation. At trial one of the agents testified, and a paragraph on each of the statements states, that the agents advised Westover that he did not have to make a statement, that any statement he made could be used against him, and that he had the right to see an attorney.

Westover was tried by a jury in federal court and convicted of the California robberies. His statements were introduced at trial. He was sentenced to 15 years' imprisonment on each count, the sentences to run consecutively. On appeal, the conviction was affirmed by the Court of Appeals for the Ninth Circuit.[2103]

****1639** We reverse. On the facts of this case we cannot find that Westover knowingly and intelligently waived his right to remain silent and his right to consult with counsel prior to the time he made the statement. At the ***496** time the FBI agents began questioning Westover, he had been in custody for over 14 hours and had been interrogated at length during that period. The FBI interrogation began immediately upon the conclusion of the interrogation by Kansas City police and was conducted in local police headquarters. Although the two law enforcement authorities are legally distinct and the crimes for which they interrogated Westover were different, the impact on him was that of a continuous period of questioning. There is no evidence of any warning given prior to the FBI interrogation nor is there any evidence of an articulated waiver of rights after the FBI commenced its interrogation. The record simply shows that the defendant did in fact confess a short time after being turned over to the FBI following interrogation by local police. Despite the fact that the FBI agents gave warnings at the outset of their interview, from Westover's point of view the warnings came at the end of the interrogation process. In these circumstances an intelligent waiver of constitutional rights cannot be assumed.

We do not suggest that law enforcement authorities are precluded from questioning any individual who has been held for a period of time by other authorities and interrogated by them without appropriate warnings. A different case would be presented if an accused were taken into custody by the second authority, removed both in time and place from his original surroundings, and then adequately advised of his rights and given an opportunity to exercise them. But here the FBI interrogation was conducted immediately following the state interrogation in the same police station—in the same compelling surroundings. Thus, in obtaining a confession from Westover ***497** the federal authorities were the beneficiaries of the pressure applied by the local in-custody interrogation. In these circumstances the giving of warnings alone was not sufficient to protect the privilege.

No. 584. California v. Stewart.

In the course of investigating a series of purse-snatch robberies in which one of the victims had died of injuries inflicted by her assailant, respondent, Roy Allen Stewart, was pointed out to Los Angeles police as the endorser of dividend checks taken in one of the robberies. At about 7:15 p.m., January 31, 1963, police officers went to Stewart's house and arrested him. One of the officers asked Stewart if they could search the house, to which he replied, 'Go ahead.' The search turned up various items taken from the five robbery victims. At the time of Stewart's arrest, police also arrested Stewart's wife and three other persons who were visiting him. These four were jailed along with Stewart and were interrogated. Stewart was taken to the University Station of the Los Angeles Police Department where he was placed in a cell. During the next five days, police interrogated Stewart on nine different occasions. Except during the first interrogation session, when he was confronted with an accusing witness, Stewart was isolated with his interrogators.

****1640** During the ninth interrogation session, Stewart admitted that he had robbed the deceased and stated that he had not meant to hurt her. Police then brought

[2103] *342 F.2d 684*

Stewart before a magistrate for the first time. Since there was no evidence to connect them with any crime, the police then released the other four persons arrested with him.

Nothing in the record specifically indicates whether Stewart was or was not advised of his right to remain silent or his right to counsel. In a number of instances, ***498** however, the interrogating officers were asked to recount everything that was said during the interrogations. None indicated that Stewart was ever advised of his rights.

Stewart was charged with kidnapping to commit robbery, rape, and murder. At his trial, transcripts of the first interrogation and the confession at the last interrogation were introduced in evidence. The jury found Stewart guilty of robbery and first degree murder and fixed the penalty as death. On appeal, the Supreme Court of California reversed.[2104] It held that under this Court's decision in Escobedo, Stewart should have been advised of his right to remain silent and of his right to counsel and that it would not presume in the face of a silent record that the police advised Stewart of his rights.

We affirm. In dealing with custodial interrogation, we will not presume that a defendant has been effectively apprised of his rights and that his privilege against self-incrimination has been adequately safeguarded on a record that does not show that any warnings have been given or that any effective alternative has been employed. Nor can a knowing and intelligent waiver of ***499** these rights be assumed on a silent record. Furthermore, Stewart's steadfast denial of the alleged offenses through eight of the nine interrogations over a period of five days is subject to no other construction than that he was compelled by persistent interrogation to forgo his Fifth Amendment privilege.

Therefore, in accordance with the foregoing, the judgments of the Supreme Court of Arizona in No. 759, of the New York Court of Appeals in No. 760, and of the Court of Appeals for the Ninth Circuit in No. 761 are reversed. The judgment of the Supreme Court of California in No. 584 is affirmed. It is so ordered.

Judgments of Supreme Court of Arizona in No. 759, of New York Court of Appeals in No. 760, and of the Court of Appeals for the Ninth Circuit in No. 761 reversed.

Judgment of Supreme Court of California in No. 584 affirmed.

(The dissent of Mr. Justice HARLAN, whom Mr. Justice STEWART and Mr. Justice WHITE join, is omitted.)

Mr. Justice WHITE, with whom Mr. Justice HARLAN and Mr. Justice STEWART join, dissenting.

I

The proposition that the privilege against self-incrimination forbids in-custody interrogation without the warnings specified in the majority opinion and without a clear waiver of counsel has no significant support in the history of the privilege or in the language of the Fifth Amendment. As for the English authorities and the common-law history, the privilege, firmly established in the second half of the seventeenth century, was never applied except to prohibit compelled judicial interrogations. The rule excluding coerced confessions matured about 100 years later, '(b)ut there is nothing in the reports to suggest that the theory has its roots in the privilege against self-incrimination. And so far as the cases reveal, the privilege, as such,

[2104] *62 Cal.2d 571, 43 Cal.Rptr. 201, 400 P.2d 97*

seems to have been given effect only in judicial proceedings, including the preliminary examinations by authorized magistrates.'[2105]

Our own constitutional provision provides that no person 'shall be compelled in any criminal case to be a witness against himself.' These words, when '(c)onsidered in the light to be shed by grammar and the dictionary * * * appear to signify simply that nobody shall be ***527** compelled to give oral testimony against himself in a criminal proceeding under way in which he is defendant.'[2106] And there is very little in the surrounding circumstances of the adoption of the Fifth Amendment or in the provisions of the then existing state constitutions or in state practice which would give the constitutional provision any broader meaning.[2107] Such a construction, however, was considerably narrower than the privilege at common law, and when eventually faced with the issues, the Court extended the constitutional privilege to the compulsory production of books and papers, to the ordinary witness before the grand jury and to witnesses generally.[2108] Both rules had solid support in common-law history, if not in the history of our own constitutional provision.

A few years later the Fifth Amendment privilege was similarly extended to encompass the then well-established rule against coerced confessions: 'In criminal trials, in the courts of the United States, wherever a question arises whether a confession is incompetent because not voluntary, the issue is controlled by that portion of the fifth amendment to the constitution of the United States, commanding that no person 'shall be compelled in any criminal case to be a witness against himself.''[2109] Although this view has found approval in other cases,[2110] it has also been questioned,[2111] ***528** and finds scant support in either the English or American authorities.[2112] ****1656** Whatever the source of the rule excluding coerced confessions, it is clear that prior to the application of the privilege itself to state courts,[2113] the admissibility of a confession in a state criminal prosecution was tested by the same standards as were applied in federal prosecutions.[2114]

Bram, however, itself rejected the proposition which the Court now espouses. The question in Bram was whether a confession, obtained during custodial interrogation, had been compelled, and if such interrogation was to be deemed inherently vulnerable the Court's inquiry could have ended there. After examining the English and American authorities, however, the Court declared that:

> In this court also it has been settled that the mere fact that the confession is made to a police officer, while the accused was under arrest in or out of prison, or was drawn out by his questions, does not necessarily render

---

[2105] *Morgan, The Privilege Against Self-Incrimination, 34 Minn.L.Rev. 1, 18 (1949)*

[2106] *Corwin, The Supreme Court's Construction of the Self-Incrimination Clause, 29 Mich.L.Rev. 1, 2*

[2107] *Mayers, The Federal Witness' Privilege Against Self-Incrimination: Constitutional or Common-Law? 4 American Journal of Legal History 107 (1960)*

[2108] *Boyd v. United States, 116 U.S. 616, 6 S.Ct. 524, 29 L.Ed. 746, and Counselman v. Hitchcock, 142 U.S. 547, 12 S.Ct. 195, 35 L.Ed. 1110*

[2109] *Bram v. United States, 168 U.S. 532, 542, 18 S.Ct. 183, 187, 42 L.Ed. 568*

[2110] *Burdeau v. McDowell, 256 U.S. 465, 475, 41 S.Ct. 574, 576, 65 L.Ed. 1048; Powers v. United States, 223 U.S. 303, 313, 32 S.Ct. 281, 283, 56 L.Ed. 448; Shotwell Mfg. Co. v. United States, 371 U.S. 341, 347, 83 S.Ct. 448, 453, 9 L.Ed.2d 357*

[2111] *See Brown v. State of Mississippi, 297 U.S. 278, 285, 56 S.Ct. 461, 464, 80 L.Ed. 682; United States v. Carignan, 342 U.S. 36, 41, 72 S.Ct. 97, 100, 96 L.Ed. 48; Stein v. People of State of New York, 346 U.S. 156, 191, n. 35, 73 S.Ct. 1077, 1095, 97 L.Ed. 1522*

[2112] *See generally Regina v. Scott, Dears. & Bell 47; 3. Wigmore, Evidence s 823 (3d ed. 1940), at 249 ('a confession is not rejected because of any connection with the privilege against self-crimination'), and 250, n. 5 (particularly criticizing Bram); 8 Wigmore, Evidence s 2266, at 400—401 (McNaughton rev. 1961)*

[2113] *Malloy v. Hogan, 378 U.S. 1, 84 S.Ct. 1489, 12 L.Ed.2d 653*

[2114] *Id., at 6—7, 10, 84 S.Ct., at 1492—1493, 1494*

> the confession involuntary; but, as one of the circumstances, such imprisonment or interrogation may be taken into account in determining whether or not the statements of the prisoner were voluntary.[2115]

In this respect the Court was wholly consistent with prior and subsequent pronouncements in this Court.

Thus prior to Bram the Court, in Hopt v. People of Territory of Utah,[2116] had upheld the admissibility of a ***529** confession made to police officers following arrest, the record being silent concerning what conversation had occurred between the officers and the defendant in the short period preceding the confession. Relying on Hopt, the Court ruled squarely on the issue in Sparf and Hansen v. United States[2117]:

> Counsel for the accused insist that there cannot be a voluntary statement, a free, open confession, while a defendant is confined and in irons, under an accusation of having committed a capital offense. We have not been referred to any authority in support of that position. It is true that the fact of a prisoner being in custody at the time he makes a confession is a circumstance not to be overlooked, because it bears upon the inquiry whether the confession was voluntarily made, or was extorted by threats or violence or made under the influence of fear. But confinement or imprisonment is not in itself sufficient to justify the exclusion of a confession, if it appears to have been voluntary and was not obtained by putting the prisoner in fear or by promises.[2118]

And in Wilson v. United States,[2119] the Court had considered the significance of custodial interrogation without any antecedent warnings regarding the right to remain silent or the right to counsel. There the defendant had answered questions posed by a Commissioner, who had filed to advise him of his rights, and his answers were held admissible over his claim of involuntariness. 'The fact that (a defendant) is in custody and manacled does not necessarily render his statement involuntary, nor is that necessarily the effect of popular excitement shortly preceding. * * * And it is laid down ***530** that it is not essential to the admissibility of a confession ****1657** that it should appear that the person was warned that what he said would be used against him; but, on the contrary, if the confession was voluntary, it is sufficient, though it appear that he was not so warned.'

Since Bram, the admissibility of statements made during custodial interrogation has been frequently reiterated. Powers v. United States[2120] cited Wilson approvingly and held admissible as voluntary statements the accused's testimony at a preliminary hearing even though he was not warned that what he said might be used against him. Without any discussion of the presence or absence of warnings, presumably because such discussion was deemed unnecessary, numerous other cases have declared that '(t) he mere fact that a confession was made while in the custody of the police does

---

[2115] *168 U.S., at 558, 18 S.Ct., at 192*

[2116] *110 U.S. 574, 583—587, 4 S.Ct. 202, 206, 28 L.Ed. 262*

[2117] *156 U.S. 51, 55, 15 S.Ct. 273, 275, 39 L.Ed. 343*

[2118] *Whart(on's) Cr.Ev. (9th Ed.) ss 661, 663, and authorities cited. Accord, Pierce v. United States, 160 U.S. 355, 357, 16 S.Ct. 321, 322, 40 L.Ed. 454*

[2119] *162 U.S. 613, 623, 16 S.Ct. 895, 899, 40 L.Ed. 1090*

[2120] *223 U.S. 303, 32 S.Ct. 281*

not render it inadmissible,'[2121] despite its having been elicited by police examination.[2122] Likewise, in Crooker v. State of California,[2123] the Court said that '(t)he bare fact of police 'detention and police examination in private of one in official state custody' does not render involuntary a confession by the one so detained.' And finally, in Cicenia v. La Gay,[2124] a confession obtained by police interrogation after arrest was held voluntary even though the authorities refused to permit the defendant to consult with his attorney.[2125]

Only a tiny minority of our judges who have dealt with the question, including today's majority, have considered incustody interrogation, without more, to be a violation of the Fifth Amendment. And this Court, as ***531** every member knows, has left standing literally thousands of criminal convictions that rested at least in part on confessions taken in the course of interrogation by the police after arrest.

II

That the Court's holding today is neither compelled nor even strongly suggested by the language of the Fifth Amendment, is at odds with American and English legal history, and involves a departure from a long line of precedent does not prove either that the Court has exceeded its powers or that the Court is wrong or unwise in its present reinterpretation of the Fifth Amendment. It does, however, underscore the obvious—that the Court has not discovered or found the law in making today's decision, nor has it derived it from some irrefutable sources; what it has done is to make new law and new public policy in much the same way that it has in the course of interpreting other great clauses of the Constitution. This is what the Court historically has done. Indeed, it is what it must do and will continue to do until and unless there is some fundamental change in the constitutional distribution of governmental powers.

But if the Court is here and now to announce new and fundamental policy to govern certain aspects of our affairs, it is wholly legitimate to examine the mode of this or any other constitutional decision in this Court and to inquire into the advisability of its end product in ****1658** terms of the long-range interest of the country. At the very least, the Court's text and reasoning should withstand analysis and be a fair exposition of the constitutional provision which its opinion interprets. Decisions ***532** like these cannot rest alone on syllogism, metaphysics or some ill-defined notions of natural justice, although each will perhaps play its part. In proceeding to such constructions as it now announces, the Court should also duly consider all the factors and interests bearing upon the cases, at least insofar as the relevant materials are available; and if the necessary considerations are not treated in the record or obtainable from some other reliable source, the Court should not proceed to formulate fundamental policies based on speculation alone.

III

First, we may inquire what are the textual and factual bases of this new fundamental rule. To reach the result announced on the grounds it does, the Court must stay within the confines of the Fifth Amendment, which forbids self-incrimination only if compelled. Hence the core of the Court's opinion is that because of the 'com-

---

[2121] *McNabb v. United States, 318 U.S. 332, 346, 63 S.Ct. 608, 615, 87 L.Ed. 819; accord, United States v. Mitchell, 322 U.S. 65, 64 S.Ct. 896, 88 L.Ed. 1140*

[2122] *Ziang Sung Wan v. United States, 266 U.S. 1, 14, 45 S.Ct. 3; United States v. Carignan, 342 U.S. 36, 39, 72 S.Ct. 97, 99*

[2123] *357 U.S. 433, 437, 78 S.Ct. 1287, 1290, 2 L.Ed.2d 1448*

[2124] *357 U.S. 504, 78 S.Ct. 1297, 2 L.Ed.2d 1523*

[2125] *See generally Culombe v. Connecticut, 367 U.S. 568, 587—602, 81 S.Ct. 1860, 1870, 6 L.Ed.2d 1037 (opinion of Frankfurter, J.); 3 Wigmore, Evidence s 851, at 313 (3d ed. 1940); see also Joy, Admissibility of Confessions 38, 46 (1842)*

pulsion inherent in custodial surroundings, no statement obtained from (a) defendant (in custody) can truly be the product of his free choice,'[2126] absent the use of adequate protective devices as described by the Court. However, the Court does not point to any sudden inrush of new knowledge requiring the rejection of 70 years' experience. Nor does it assert that its novel conclusion reflects a changing consensus among state courts,[2127] or that a succession of cases had steadily eroded the old rule and proved it unworkable.[2128] Rather than asserting new knowledge, the Court concedes that it cannot truly know what occurs during custodial questioning, because of the innate secrecy of such proceedings. It extrapolates a picture of what it conceives to be the norm from police investigatorial manuals, published in 1959 and 1962 or earlier, without any attempt to allow for adjustments in police practices that may ***533** have occurred in the wake of more recent decisions of state appellate tribunals or this Court. But even if the relentless application of the described procedures could lead to involuntary confessions, it most assuredly does not follow that each and every case will disclose this kind of interrogation or this kind of consequence. Insofar as appears from the Court's opinion, it has not examined a single transcript of any police interrogation, let alone the interrogation that took place in any one of these cases which it decides today. Judged by any of the standards for empirical investigation utilized in the social sciences the factual basis for the Court's premise is patently inadequate.

Although in the Court's view in-custody interrogation is inherently coercive, the Court says that the spontaneous product of the coercion of arrest and detention is still to be deemed voluntary. An accused, arrested on probable cause, may blurt out a confession which will be admissible despite the fact that he is alone and in custody, without any showing that ****1659** he had any notion of his right to remain silent or of the consequences of his admission. Yet, under the Court's rule, if the police ask him a single question such as 'Do you have anything to say?' or 'Did you kill your wife?' his response, if there is one, has somehow been compelled, even if the accused has ***534** been clearly warned of his right to remain silent. Common sense informs us to the contrary. While one may say that the response was 'involuntary' in the sense the question provoked or was the occasion for the response and thus the defendant was induced to speak out when he might have remained silent if not arrested and not questioned, it is patently unsound to say the response is compelled.

Today's result would not follow even if it were agreed that to some extent custodial interrogation is inherently coercive.[2129] The test has been whether the totality of circumstances deprived the defendant of a 'free choice to admit, to deny, or to refuse to answer,'[2130] and whether physical or psychological coercion was of such a degree that 'the defendant's will was overborne at the time he confessed.'[2131] The duration and nature of incommunicado custody, the presence or absence of advice concerning the defendant's constitutional rights, and the granting or refusal of requests to communicate with lawyers, relatives or friends have all been rightly regarded as important data bearing on the basic inquiry.[2132] ***535** But it has never been suggested, until today, that such questioning was so coercive and accused persons so lacking in hardihood that the very first response to the very first question following

---

[2126] *Ante, at 1619*

[2127] *See Mapp v. Ohio, 367 U.S. 643, 81 S.Ct. 1684, 6 L.Ed.2d 1081*

[2128] *See Gideon v. Wainwright, 372 U.S. 335, 83 S.Ct. 792, 9 L.Ed.2d 799*

[2129] *See Ashcraft v. State of Tennessee, 322 U.S. 143, 161, 64 S.Ct. 921, 929, 88 L.Ed. 1192 (Jackson, J., dissenting)*

[2130] *Lisenba v. People of State of California, 314 U.S. 219, 241, 62 S.Ct. 280, 292, 86 L.Ed. 166*

[2131] *Haynes v. State of Washington, 373 U.S. 503, 513, 83 S.Ct. 1336, 1343, 10 L.Ed.2d 513; Lynumn v. State of Illinois, 372 U.S. 528, 534, 83 S.Ct. 917, 920, 9 L.Ed.2d 922*

[2132] *See, e.g., Ashcraft v. State of Tennessee, 322 U.S. 143, 64 S.Ct. 921; Haynes v. State of Washington, 373 U.S. 503, 83 S.Ct. 1336*

the commencement of custody must be conclusively presumed to be the product of an overborne will.

If the rule announced today were truly based on a conclusion that all confessions resulting from custodial interrogation are coerced, then it would simply have no rational foundation.[2133] A fortiori that would be true of the extension of the rule to exculpatory statements, which the Court effects after a brief discussion of why, in the Court's view, they must be deemed incriminatory but without any discussion of why they must be deemed coerced.[2134] Even if one were to postulate that the Court's concern is not that all confessions induced by police interrogation are coerced but rather that some such confessions are coerced and present judicial procedures are believed to be inadequate to identify the confessions that are coerced ****1660** and those that are not, it would still not be essential to impose the rule that the Court has now fashioned. Transcripts or observers could be required, specific time limits, tailored to fit the cause, could be imposed, or other devices could be utilized to reduce the chances that otherwise indiscernible coercion will produce an inadmissible confession.

On the other hand, even if one assumed that there was an adequate factual basis for the conclusion that all confessions obtained during in-custody interrogation are the product of compulsion, the rule propounded by ***536** the Court will still be irrational, for, apparently, it is only if the accused is also warned of his right to counsel and waives both that right and the right against self-incrimination that the inherent compulsiveness of interrogation disappears. But if the defendant may not answer without a warning a question such as 'Where were you last night?' without having his answer be a compelled one, how can the Court ever accept his negative answer to the question of whether he wants to consult his retained counsel or counsel whom the court will appoint? And why if counsel is present and the accused nevertheless confesses, or counsel tells the accused to tell the truth, and that is what the accused does, is the situation any less coercive insofar as the accused is concerned? The Court apparently realizes its dilemma of foreclosing questioning without the necessary warnings but at the same time permitting the accused, sitting in the same chair in front of the same policemen, to waive his right to consult an attorney. It expects, however, that the accused will not often waive the right; and if it is claimed that he has, the State faces a severe, if not impossible burden of proof.

All of this makes very little sense in terms of the compulsion which the Fifth Amendment proscribes. That amendment deals with compelling the accused himself. It is his free will that is involved. Confessions and incriminating admissions, as such, are not forbidden evidence; only those which are compelled are banned. I doubt that the Court observes these distinctions today. By considering any answers to any interrogation to be compelled regardless of the content and course of examination and by escalating the requirements to prove waiver, the Court not only prevents the use of compelled confessions but for all practical purposes forbids interrogation except in the presence of counsel. That is, instead of confining itself to protection of the right against compelled ***537** self-incrimination the Court has created a limited Fifth Amendment right to counsel—or, as the Court expresses it, a 'need for counsel to protect the Fifth Amendment privilege * * *.'[2135] The focus then is not on the will of the accused but on the will of counsel and how much influence he can have on the accused. Obviously there is no warrant in the Fifth Amendment for thus installing counsel as the arbiter of the privilege.

In sum, for all the Court's expounding on the menacing atmosphere of police interrogation procedures, it has failed to supply any foundation for the conclusions it draws or the measures it adopts.

[2133] *Compare Tot v. United States, 319 U.S. 463, 466, 63 S.Ct. 1241, 1244, 87 L.Ed. 1519; United States v. Romano, 382 U.S. 136, 86 S.Ct. 279, 15 L.Ed.2d 210*

[2134] *See Wilson v. United States, 162 U.S. 613, 624, 16 S.Ct. 895, 900, 40 L.Ed. 1090*

[2135] *Ante, at 1625*

IV.

Criticism of the Court's opinion, however, cannot stop with a demonstration that the factual and textual bases for the rule it proponds are, at best, less than compelling. Equally relevant is an assessment of the rule's consequences measured against community values. The Court's duty to assess the consequences of its action is not satisfied by the utterance of the truth that a value of our system of criminal justice is 'to respect the inviolability of the human personality' and to require government to produce the evidence against the accused by its own independent labors.[2136] More than the human dignity of the accused is involved; the human personality of others in the society must also be preserved. ****1661** Thus the values reflected by the privilege are not the sole desideratum; society's interest in the general security is of equal weight.

The obvious underpinning of the Court's decision is a deep-seated distrust of all confessions. As the Court declares that the accused may not be interrogated without counsel present, absent a waiver of the right to counsel, and as the Court all but admonishes the lawyer to ***538** advise the accused to remain silent, the result adds up to a judicial judgment that evidence from the accused should not be used against him in any way, whether compelled or not. This is the not so subtle overtone of the opinion—that it is inherently wrong for the police to gather evidence from the accused himself. And this is precisely the nub of this dissent. I see nothing wrong or immoral, and certainly nothing unconstitutional, in the police's asking a suspect whom they have reasonable cause to arrest whether or not he killed his wife or in confronting him with the evidence on which the arrest was based, at least where he has been plainly advised that he may remain completely silent.[2137] Until today, 'the admissions or confessions of the prisoner, when voluntarily and freely made, have always ranked high in the scale of incriminating evidence.'[2138] Particularly when corroborated, as where the police have confirmed the accused's disclosure of the hiding place of implements or fruits of the crime, such confessions have the highest reliability and significantly contribute to the certitude with which we may believe the accused is guilty. Moreover, it is by no means certain that the process of confessing is injurious to the accused. To the contrary it may provide psychological relief and enhance the prospects for rehabilitation.

This is not to say that the value of respect for the inviolability of the accused's individual personality should be accorded no weight or that all confessions should be indiscriminately admitted. This Court has long read the Constitution to proscribe compelled confessions, a salutary rule from which there should be no retreat. But I see no sound basis, factual or otherwise, and the Court gives none, for concluding that the present rule against the receipt of coerced confessions is inadequate for the ***539** task of sorting out inadmissible evidence and must be replaced by the per se rule which is now imposed. Even if the new concept can be said to have advantages of some sort over the present law, they are far outweighed by its likely undesirable impact on other very relevant and important interests.

The most basic function of any government is to provide for the security of the individual and of his property.[2139] These ends of society are served by the criminal laws which for the most part are aimed at the prevention of crime. Without the rea-

---

[2136] *Ante, at 1620*

[2137] *See Escobedo v. State of Illinois, 378 U.S. 478, 499, 84 S.Ct. 1758, 1769, 12 L.Ed.2d 977 (dissenting opinion)*

[2138] *Brown v. Walker, 161 U.S. 591, 596, 16 S.Ct. 644, 646, 40 L.Ed. 819, see also Hopt v. People of Territory of Utah, 110 U.S. 574, 584—585, 4 S.Ct. 202, 207*

[2139] *Lanzetta v. State of New Jersey, 306 U.S. 451, 455, 59 S.Ct. 618, 619, 83 L.Ed. 888*

sonably effective performance of the task of preventing private violence and retaliation, it is idle to talk about human dignity and civilized values.

The modes by which the criminal laws serve the interest in general security are many. First the murderer who has taken the life of another is removed from the streets, deprived of his liberty and thereby prevented from repeating his offense. In view of the statistics on recidivism in this country and of the number of instances ****1662 *540** in which apprehension occurs only after repeated offenses, no one can sensibly claim that this aspect of the criminal law does not prevent crime or contribute significantly to the personal security of the ordinary citizen.

Secondly, the swift and sure apprehension of those who refuse to respect the personal security and dignity of their neighbor unquestionably has its impact on others who might be similarly tempted. That the criminal law is wholly or partly ineffective with a segment of the population or with many of those who have been apprehended and convicted is a very faulty basis for concluding that it is not effective with respect to the great bulk of our citizens or for thinking that without the criminal laws, ***541** or in the absence of their enforcement, there would be no increase in crime. Arguments of this nature are not borne out by any kind of reliable evidence that I have been to this date.

Thirdly, the law concerns itself with those whom it has confined. The hope and aim of modern penology, fortunately, is as soon as possible to return the convict to society a better and more law-abiding man than when he left. Sometimes there is success, sometimes failure. But at least the effort is made, and it should be made to the very maximum extent of our present and future capabilities.

The rule announced today will measurably weaken the ability of the criminal law to perform these tasks. It is a deliberate calculus to prevent interrogations, to reduce the incidence of confessions and pleas of guilty and to increase the number of trials. Criminal trials, ****1663** no ***542** matter how efficient the police are, are not sure bets for the prosecution, nor should they be if the evidence is not forthcoming. Under the present law, the prosecution fails to prove its case in about 30% of the criminal cases actually tried in the federal courts.[2140] But it is something else again to remove from the ordinary criminal case all those confessions which heretofore have been held to be free and voluntary acts of the accused and to thus establish a new constitutional barrier to the ascertainment of truth by the judicial process. There is, in my view, every reason to believe that a good many criminal defendants who otherwise would have been convicted on what this Court has previously thought to be the most satisfactory kind of evidence will now under this new version of the Fifth Amendment, either not be tried at all or will be acquitted if the State's evidence, minus the confession, is put to the test of litigation.

I have no desire whatsoever to share the responsibility for any such impact on the present criminal process.

In some unknown number of cases the Court's rule will return a killer, a rapist or other criminal to the streets and to the environment which produced him, to repeat his crime whenever it pleases him. As a consequence, there will not be a gain, but a loss, in human dignity. The real concern is not the unfortunate consequences of this new decision on the criminal law as an abstract, disembodied series of authoritative proscriptions, but the impact on those who rely on the public authority for protection and who without it can only engage in violent self-help with guns, knives and the help of their neighbors similarly inclined. There is, of ***543** course, a saving factor: the next victims are uncertain, unnamed and unrepresented in this case.

Nor can this decision do other than have a corrosive effect on the criminal laws as an effective device to prevent crime. A major component in its effectiveness in

---

[2140] *See Federal Offenders: 1964, supra, note 4, at 6 (Table 4), 59 (Table 1); Federal Offenders; 1963, supra, note 4, at 5 (Table 3); District of Columbia Offenders: 1963, supra, note 4, at 2 (Table 1)*

this regard is its swift and sure enforcement. The easier it is to get away with rape and murder, the less the deterrent effect on those who are inclined to attempt it. This is still good common sense. If it were not, we should posthaste liquidate the whole law enforcement establishment as a useless, misguided effort to control human conduct.

And what about the accused who has confessed or would confess in response to simple, non-coercive questioning and whose guilt could not otherwise be proved? Is it so clear that release is the best thing for him in every case? Has it so unquestionably been resolved that in ****1664** each and every case it would be better for him not to confess and to return to his environment with no attempt whatsoever to help him? I think not. It may well be that in many cases it will be no less than a callous disregard for his own welfare as well as for the interests of his next victim.

There is another aspect to the effect of the Court's rule on the person whom the police have arrested on probable cause. The fact is that he may not be guilty at all and may be able to extricate himself quickly and simply if he were told the circumstances of his arrest and were asked to explain. This effort, and his release, must now await the hiring of a lawyer or his appointment by the court, consultation with counsel and then a session with the police or the prosecutor. Similarly, where probable cause exists to arrest several suspects, as where the body of the victim is discovered in a house having several residents,[2141] it will often ***544** be true that a suspect may be cleared only through the results of interrogation of other suspects. Here too the release of the innocent may be delayed by the Court's rule.

Much of the trouble with the Court's new rule is that it will operate indiscriminately in all criminal cases, regardless of the severity of the crime or the circumstances involved. It applies to every defendant, whether the professional criminal or one committing a crime of momentary passion who is not part and parcel of organized crime. It will slow down the investigation and the apprehension of confederates in those cases where time is of the essence, such as kidnapping,[2142] and some of those involving organized crime. In the latter context the lawyer who arrives may also be the lawyer for the defendant's colleagues and can be relied upon to insure that no breach of the organization's security takes place even though the accused may feel that the best thing he can do is to cooperate.

At the same time, the Court's per se approach may not be justified on the ground that it provides a 'bright line' permitting the authorities to judge in advance whether interrogation may safely be pursued without jeopardizing the admissibility of any information obtained as a consequence. Nor can it be claimed that judicial time and effort, assuming that is a relevant consideration, ***545** will be conserved because of the ease of application of the new rule. Today's decision leaves open such questions as whether the accused was in custody, whether his statements were spontaneous or the product of interrogation, whether the accused has effectively waived his rights, and whether non-testimonial evidence introduced at trial is the fruit of statements made during a prohibited interrogation, all of which are certain to prove productive of uncertainty during investigation and litigation during prosecution. For all these reasons, if further restrictions on police interrogation are desirable at this time, a more flexible approach makes much more sense than the Court's constitutional straitjacket which forecloses more discriminating treatment by legislative or rule-making pronouncements.

[2141] *Compare Johnson v. State, 238 Md. 140, 207 A.2d 643 (1965), cert. denied, 382 U.S. 1013, 86 S.Ct. 623, 15 L.Ed.2d 528*

[2142] *See Brinegar v. United States, 338 U.S. 160, 183, 69 S.Ct. 1302, 1314, 93 L.Ed. 1879 (Jackson, J., dissenting); People v. Modesto, 62 Cal.2d 436, 446, 42 Cal.Rptr. 417, 423, 398 P.2d 753, 759 (1965), those involving the national security, see United States v. Drummond, 354 F.2d 132, 147 (C.A.2d Cir. 1965) (en banc) (espionage case), pet. for cert. pending, No. 1203, Misc., O.T. 1965; cf. Gessner v. United States, 354 F.2d 726, 730, n. 10 (C.A.10th Cir. 1965) (upholding, in espionage case, trial ruling that Government need not submit classified portions of interrogation transcript)*

**1665 Applying the traditional standards to the cases before the Court, I would hold these confessions voluntary. I would therefore affirm in Nos. 759, 760, and 761, and reverse in No. 584.

Black Letter Law

> Held that statements obtained from defendants during incommunicado interrogation in police-dominated atmosphere, without full warning of constitutional rights, were inadmissible as having been obtained in violation of Fifth Amendment privilege against self-incrimination. Prosecution may not use statements, whether exculpatory or inculpatory, stemming from custodial interrogation of defendant unless it demonstrates use of procedural safeguards effective to secure privilege against self-incrimination. PASI for 5th Amendment purposes is created by custodial interrogation.

New York v. Quarles

104 S.Ct. 2626

Supreme Court of the United States

NEW YORK

v.

Benjamin QUARLES.

No. 82-1213. | Argued Jan. 18, 1984. | Decided June 12, 1984.

***651** Justice REHNQUIST delivered the opinion of the Court.

Respondent Benjamin Quarles was charged in the New York trial court with criminal possession of a weapon. The trial court suppressed the gun in question, and a statement made by respondent, because the **2629 statement was obtained by police before they read respondent his "Miranda rights." That ruling was affirmed on appeal through the New York Court of Appeals. We granted certiorari,[2143] and we now reverse. We conclude that under the circumstances involved in this case, overriding considerations of public safety justify the officer's failure to provide Miranda warnings before he asked questions devoted to locating the abandoned weapon.

On September 11, 1980, at approximately 12:30 a.m., Officer Frank Kraft and Officer Sal Scarring were on road patrol in Queens, N.Y., when a young woman approached their car. She told them that she had just been raped by a black male, approximately six feet tall, who was wearing a black jacket with the name "Big Ben" printed in yellow letters on the back. She told the officers that the man had just entered ***652** an A & P supermarket located nearby and that the man was carrying a gun.

The officers drove the woman to the supermarket, and Officer Kraft entered the store while Officer Scarring radioed for assistance. Officer Kraft quickly spotted respondent, who matched the description given by the woman, approaching a checkout counter. Apparently upon seeing the officer, respondent turned and ran toward the rear of the store, and Officer Kraft pursued him with a drawn gun. When respondent turned the corner at the end of an aisle, Officer Kraft lost sight of him for several seconds, and upon regaining sight of respondent, ordered him to stop and put his hands over his head.

[2143] *461 U.S. 942, 103 S.Ct. 2118, 77 L.Ed.2d 1299 (1983)*

Although more than three other officers had arrived on the scene by that time, Officer Kraft was the first to reach respondent. He frisked him and discovered that he was wearing a shoulder holster which was then empty. After handcuffing him, Officer Kraft asked him where the gun was. Respondent nodded in the direction of some empty cartons and responded, "the gun is over there." Officer Kraft thereafter retrieved a loaded .38–caliber revolver from one of the cartons, formally placed respondent under arrest, and read him his Miranda rights from a printed card. Respondent indicated that he would be willing to answer questions without an attorney present. Officer Kraft then asked respondent if he owned the gun and where he had purchased it. Respondent answered that he did own it and that he had purchased it in Miami, Fla.

In the subsequent prosecution of respondent for criminal possession of a weapon, the judge excluded the statement, "the gun is over there," and the gun because the officer had not given respondent the warnings required by our decision in Miranda v. Arizona,[2144] before asking ***653** him where the gun was located. The judge excluded the other statements about respondent's ownership of the gun and the place of purchase, as evidence tainted by the prior Miranda violation. The Appellate ****2630** Division of the Supreme Court of New York affirmed without opinion.[2145]

The Court of Appeals granted leave to appeal and affirmed by a 4–3 vote.[2146] It concluded that respondent was in "custody" within the meaning of Miranda during all questioning and rejected the State's argument that the exigencies of the situation justified Officer Kraft's failure to read respondent his Miranda rights until after he had located the gun. The court declined to recognize an exigency exception to the usual requirements of Miranda because it found no indication from Officer Kraft's testimony at the suppression hearing that his subjective motivation in asking the question was to protect his own safety or the safety of the public.[2147] For the reasons which follow, we believe that this case presents a situation where concern for public safety must be paramount to adherence to the literal language of the prophylactic rules enunciated in Miranda.

***654** The Fifth Amendment guarantees that "[n]o person ... shall be compelled in any criminal case to be a witness against himself." In Miranda this Court for the first time extended the Fifth Amendment privilege against compulsory self-incrimination to individuals subjected to custodial interrogation by the police.[2148] The Fifth Amendment itself does not prohibit all incriminating admissions; "[a]bsent some officially coerced self-accusation, the Fifth Amendment privilege is not violated by even the most damning admissions."[2149] The Miranda Court, however, presumed that interrogation in certain custodial circumstances is inherently coercive and held that statements made under those circumstances are inadmissible unless the suspect is specifically informed of his Miranda rights and freely decides to forgo those rights. The prophylactic Miranda warnings therefore are "not themselves rights protected by the Constitution but [are] instead measures to insure that the right against compulsory self-incrimination [is] protected."[2150] Requiring Miranda warnings before custodi-

---

[2144] *384 U.S. 436, 86 S.Ct. 1602, 16 L.Ed.2d 694 (1966)*

[2145] *85 A.D.2d 936, 447 N.Y.S.2d 84 (1981)*

[2146] *58 N.Y.2d 664, 458 N.Y.S.2d 520, 444 N.E.2d 984 (1982)*

[2147] *58 N.Y.2d, at 666, 458 N.Y.S.2d, at 521, 444 N.E.2d, at 985*

[2148] *384 U.S., at 460–461, 467, 86 S.Ct., at 1620–1621, 1624*

[2149] *United States v. Washington, 431 U.S. 181, 187, 97 S.Ct. 1814, 1818, 52 L.Ed.2d 238 (1977) (emphasis added)*

[2150] *Michigan v. Tucker, 417 U.S. 433, 444, 94 S.Ct. 2357, 2364, 41 L.Ed.2d 182 (1974); see Edwards v. Arizona, 451 U.S. 477, 492, 101 S.Ct. 1880, 1888, 68 L.Ed.2d 378 (1981) (POWELL, J., concurring)*

al interrogation provides "practical reinforcement" for the Fifth Amendment right.[2151]

In this case we have before us no claim that respondent's statements were actually **2631 compelled by police conduct which overcame his will to resist.[2152] Thus the only issue before us is whether *655 Officer Kraft was justified in failing to make available to respondent the procedural safeguards associated with the privilege against compulsory self-incrimination since Miranda.

The New York Court of Appeals was undoubtedly correct in deciding that the facts of this case come within the ambit of the Miranda decision as we have subsequently interpreted it. We agree that respondent was in police custody because we have noted that "the ultimate inquiry is simply whether there is a 'formal arrest or restraint on freedom of movement' of the degree associated with a formal arrest."[2153] Here Quarles was surrounded by at least four police officers and was handcuffed when the questioning at issue took place. As the New York Court of Appeals observed, there was nothing to suggest that any of the officers were any longer concerned for their own physical safety.[2154] The New York Court of Appeals' majority declined to express an opinion as to whether there might be an exception to the Miranda rule if the police had been acting to protect the public, because the lower courts in New York had made no factual determination that the police had acted with that motive.[2155]

We hold that on these facts there is a "public safety" exception to the requirement that Miranda warnings be given before a suspect's answers may be admitted into evidence, *656 and that the availability of that exception does not depend upon the motivation of the individual officers involved. In a kaleidoscopic situation such as the one confronting these officers, where spontaneity rather than adherence to a police manual is necessarily the order of the day, the application of the exception which we recognize today should not be made to depend on post hoc findings at a suppression hearing concerning the subjective motivation of the arresting officer. Undoubtedly most police officers, if placed in Officer Kraft's position, would act out of a host of different, instinctive, and largely unverifiable motives—their own safety, the safety of others, and perhaps as well the desire to obtain incriminating evidence from the suspect.

Whatever the motivation of individual officers in such a situation, we do not believe that the doctrinal underpinnings of **2632 Miranda require that it be applied in all its rigor to a situation in which police officers ask questions reasonably prompted by a concern for the public safety. The Miranda decision was based in large part on this Court's view that the warnings which it required police to give to suspects in custody would reduce the likelihood that the suspects would fall victim to constitutionally impermissible practices of police interrogation in the presumptively coercive environment of the station house.[2156] The dissenters warned that the requirement of Miranda warnings would have the effect of decreasing the number of suspects who respond to police questioning.[2157] The Miranda majority, however, apparently felt that whatever the *657 cost to society in terms of fewer convictions of

---

[2151] *Michigan v. Tucker, supra, 417 U.S., at 444, 94 S.Ct., at 2364*

[2152] *See Beckwith v. United States, 425 U.S. 341, 347–348, 96 S.Ct. 1612, 1616–1617, 48 L.Ed.2d 1 (1976); Davis v. North Carolina, 384 U.S. 737, 738, 86 S.Ct. 1761, 1763, 16 L.Ed.2d 895 (1966)*

[2153] *California v. Beheler, 463 U.S. 1121, 1125, 103 S.Ct. 3517, 3519, 77 L.Ed.2d 1275 (1983) (per curiam), quoting Oregon v. Mathiason, 429 U.S. 492, 495, 97 S.Ct. 711, 714, 50 L.Ed.2d 714 (1977) (per curiam)*

[2154] *58 N.Y.2d, at 666, 458 N.Y.S.2d, at 521, 444 N.E.2d, at 985*

[2155] *Ibid.*

[2156] *384 U.S., at 455–458, 86 S.Ct., at 1617–1619*

[2157] *Id., at 504, 516–517, 86 S.Ct., at 1643, 1649–1650 (Harlan, J., joined by Stewart and WHITE, JJ., dissenting)*

guilty suspects, that cost would simply have to be borne in the interest of enlarged protection for the Fifth Amendment privilege.

The police in this case, in the very act of apprehending a suspect, were confronted with the immediate necessity of ascertaining the whereabouts of a gun which they had every reason to believe the suspect had just removed from his empty holster and discarded in the supermarket. So long as the gun was concealed somewhere in the supermarket, with its actual whereabouts unknown, it obviously posed more than one danger to the public safety: an accomplice might make use of it, a customer or employee might later come upon it.

In such a situation, if the police are required to recite the familiar Miranda warnings before asking the whereabouts of the gun, suspects in Quarles' position might well be deterred from responding. Procedural safeguards which deter a suspect from responding were deemed acceptable in Miranda in order to protect the Fifth Amendment privilege; when the primary social cost of those added protections is the possibility of fewer convictions, the Miranda majority was willing to bear that cost. Here, had Miranda warnings deterred Quarles from responding to Officer Kraft's question about the whereabouts of the gun, the cost would have been something more than merely the failure to obtain evidence useful in convicting Quarles. Officer Kraft needed an answer to his question not simply to make his case against Quarles but to insure that further danger to the public did not result from the concealment of the gun in a public area.

We conclude that the need for answers to questions in a situation posing a threat to the public safety outweighs the need for the prophylactic rule protecting the Fifth Amendment's privilege against self-incrimination. We decline to place officers such as Officer Kraft in the untenable position of having to consider, often in a matter of seconds, whether it best serves society for them to ask the necessary questions without the Miranda warnings and render whatever probative ***658** evidence they uncover inadmissible, or for them to give the warnings in order to preserve the admissibility of evidence they might uncover but possibly damage or destroy their ability to obtain that evidence and neutralize the volatile situation confronting them.

In recognizing a narrow exception to the Miranda rule in this case, we acknowledge that to some degree we lessen the desirable clarity of that rule. At least in part in order to preserve its clarity, we have over ****2633** the years refused to sanction attempts to expand our Miranda holding.[2158] As we have in other contexts, we recognize here the importance of a workable rule "to guide police officers, who have only limited time and expertise to reflect on and balance the social and individual interests involved in the specific circumstances they confront."[2159] But as we have pointed out, we believe that the exception which we recognize today lessens the necessity of that on-the-scene balancing process. The exception will not be difficult for police officers to apply because in each case it will be circumscribed by the exigency which justifies it. We think police officers can and will distinguish almost instinctively ***659** between questions necessary to secure their own safety or the safety of the public and questions designed solely to elicit testimonial evidence from a suspect.

The facts of this case clearly demonstrate that distinction and an officer's ability to recognize it. Officer Kraft asked only the question necessary to locate the missing gun before advising respondent of his rights. It was only after securing the loaded revolver and giving the warnings that he continued with investigatory questions about the ownership and place of purchase of the gun. The exception which we recognize today, far from complicating the thought processes and the on-the-scene

---

[2158] *See, e.g., Minnesota v. Murphy, 465 U.S. 420, 104 S.Ct. 1136, 79 L.Ed.2d 409 (1984) (refusal to extend Miranda requirements to interviews with probation officers); Fare v. Michael C., i442 U.S. 707, 99 S.Ct. 2560, 61 L.Ed.2d 197 (1979) (refusal to equate request to see a probation officer with request to see a lawyer for Miranda purposes); Beckwith v. United States, 425 U.S. 341, 96 S.Ct. 1612, 48 L.Ed.2d 1 (1976) (refusal to extend Miranda requirements to questioning in noncustodial circumstances)*

[2159] *Dunaway v. New York, 442 U.S. 200, 213–214, 99 S.Ct. 2248, 2257, 60 L.Ed.2d 824 (1979)*

judgments of police officers, will simply free them to follow their legitimate instincts when confronting situations presenting a danger to the public safety.

We hold that the Court of Appeals in this case erred in excluding the statement, "the gun is over there," and the gun because of the officer's failure to read respondent his Miranda rights before attempting to locate the weapon. Accordingly ***660** we hold that it also erred in excluding the subsequent statements as illegal fruits of a Miranda violation. We therefore reverse and remand for further proceedings not inconsistent with this opinion.

It is so ordered.

Justice O'CONNOR, concurring in the judgment in part and dissenting in part.

In Miranda v. Arizona,[2160] the Court ****2634** held unconstitutional, because inherently compelled, the admission of statements derived from in-custody questioning not preceded by an explanation of the privilege against self-incrimination and the consequences of forgoing it. Today, the Court concludes that overriding considerations of public safety justify the admission of evidence—oral statements and a gun—secured without the benefit of such warnings.[2161] In so holding, the Court acknowledges that it is departing from prior precedent,[2162] and that it is "lessen[ing] the desirable clarity of [the Miranda] rule."[2163] Were the Court writing from a clean slate, I could agree with its holding. But Miranda is now the law and, in my view, the Court has not provided sufficient justification for departing from it or for blurring its now clear strictures. Accordingly, I would require suppression of the initial statement taken from respondent in this case. On the other hand, nothing in Miranda or the privilege itself requires exclusion of non-testimonial evidence derived from informal custodial interrogation, and I therefore agree with the Court that admission of the gun in evidence is proper.

***661 I**

Prior to Miranda, the privilege against self-incrimination had not been applied to an accused's statements secured during custodial police interrogation. In these circumstances, the issue of admissibility turned, not on whether the accused had waived his privilege against self-incrimination, but on whether his statements were "voluntary" within the meaning of the Due Process Clause.[2164] Under this approach, the "totality of the circumstances" were assessed. If the interrogation was deemed unreasonable or shocking, or if the accused clearly did not have an opportunity to make a rational or intelligent choice, the statements received would be inadmissible.

The Miranda Court for the first time made the Self–Incrimination Clause applicable to responses induced by informal custodial police interrogation, thereby requiring suppression of many admissions that, under traditional due process principles, would have been admissible. More specifically, the Court held that "the prosecution may not use statements, whether exculpatory or inculpatory, stemming from custodial interrogation of the defendant unless it demonstrates the use of ***662** procedural safeguards effective to secure the privilege against self-incrimination."[2165]

[2160] *384 U.S. 436, 86 S.Ct. 1602, 16 L.Ed.2d 694 (1966)*

[2161] *Ante, at 2633*

[2162] *See ante, at 2630*

[2163] *Ante, at 2633*

[2164] *See, e.g., Haynes v. Washington, 373 U.S. 503, 83 S.Ct. 1336, 10 L.Ed.2d 513 (1963); Payne v. Arkansas, 356 U.S. 560, 78 S.Ct. 844, 2 L.Ed.2d 975 (1958); Chambers v. Florida, 309 U.S. 227, 60 S.Ct. 472, 84 L.Ed. 716 (1940); Brown v. Mississippi, 297 U.S. 278, 56 S.Ct. 461, 80 L.Ed. 682 (1936)*

[2165] *Miranda v. Arizona, 384 U.S., at 444, 86 S.Ct., at 1612*

Those safeguards included the now familiar Miranda warnings—namely, that the defendant must be informed,

> [T]hat he has the right to remain silent, that anything he says can be used against him in a court of law, that he has the right to the presence of an attorney, and that if he cannot afford an attorney ****2635** one will be appointed for him prior to any questioning if he so desires.[2166]

The defendant could waive these rights, but any waiver had to be made "knowingly and intelligently,"[2167] and the burden was placed on the prosecution to prove that such a waiver had voluntarily been made.[2168] If the Miranda warnings were not properly administered or if no valid waiver could be shown, then all responses to interrogation made by the accused "while in custody ... or otherwise deprived of his freedom of action in any significant way" were to be presumed coerced and excluded from evidence at trial.[2169]

The Miranda Court itself considered objections akin to those raised by the Court today. In dissent, Justice WHITE protested that the Miranda rules would "operate indiscriminately in all criminal cases, regardless of the severity of the crime or the circumstances involved."[2170] But the Miranda Court would not accept any suggestion that "society's need for interrogation [could] outweig[h] the privilege." To that Court, the privilege against self-incrimination was absolute and therefore could not be "abridged."[2171]

Since the time Miranda was decided, the Court has repeatedly refused to bend the literal terms of that decision. To be sure, the Court has been sensitive to the substantial burden ***663** the Miranda rules place on local law enforcement efforts, and consequently has refused to extend the decision or to increase its strictures on law enforcement agencies in almost any way.[2172] Similarly, where "statements taken in violation of the Miranda principles [have] not be[en] used to prove the prosecution's case at trial," the Court has allowed evidence derived from those statements to be admitted.[2173] But wherever an accused has been taken into "custody" and subjected to "interrogation" without warnings, the Court has consistently prohibited the use of his responses for prosecutorial purposes at trial.[2174]

In my view, a "public safety" exception unnecessarily blurs the edges of the clear line heretofore established and makes Miranda's requirements more difficult to understand. In some cases, police will benefit because a reviewing court will find

---

[2166] *Id., at 479, 86 S.Ct., at 1630*

[2167] *Id., at 475, 86 S.Ct., at 1628*

[2168] *Ibid.*

[2169] *Id., at 476, 479, 86 S.Ct., at 1628, 1630*

[2170] *Id., at 544, 86 S.Ct., at 1664*

[2171] *Id., at 479, 86 S.Ct., at 1630*

[2172] *See, e.g., California v. Beheler, 463 U.S. 112, 103 S.Ct. 3517, 77 L.Ed.2d 1275 (1983) (per curiam); Oregon v. Mathiason, 429 U.S. 492, 97 S.Ct. 711, 50 L.Ed.2d 714 (1977); Beckwith v. United States, 425 U.S. 341, 96 S.Ct. 1612, 48 L.Ed.2d 1 (1976); Michigan v. Mosley, 423 U.S. 96, 96 S.Ct. 321, 46 L.Ed.2d 313 (1975); but cf. Edwards v. Arizona, 451 U.S. 477, 101 S.Ct. 1880, 68 L.Ed.2d 378 (1981)*

[2173] *Michigan v. Tucker, 417 U.S. 433, 445, 94 S.Ct. 2357, 2364, 41 L.Ed.2d 182 (1974)*

[2174] *See, e.g., Estelle v. Smith, 451 U.S. 454, 101 S.Ct. 1866, 68 L.Ed.2d 359 (1981); Orozco v. Texas, 394 U.S. 324, 89 S.Ct. 1095, 22 L.Ed.2d 311 (1969); Mathis v. United States, 391 U.S. 1, 88 S.Ct. 1503, 20 L.Ed.2d 381 (1968); cf. Harris v. New York, 401 U.S. 222, 91 S.Ct. 643, 28 L.Ed.2d 1 (1971) (statements may be used for impeachment purposes). As a consequence, the "meaning of Miranda has become reasonably clear and law enforcement practices have adjusted to its strictures." Rhode Island v. Innis, 446 U.S. 291, 304, 100 S.Ct. 1682, 1691, 64 L.Ed.2d 297 (1980) (BURGER, C.J., concurring); see generally Stephens, Flanders, & Cannon, Law Enforcement and the Supreme Court: Police Perceptions of the Miranda Requirements, 39 Tenn.L.Rev. 407 (1972)*

that an exigency excused their failure to administer the required warnings. But in other cases, police will suffer because, though they thought an exigency excused their noncompliance, a reviewing court will view the "objective" circumstances differently and require exclusion of admissions thereby obtained. The end result will be a finespun new ***664** doctrine on public safety exigencies incident to custodial interrogation, complete with the hair-splitting distinctions that currently plague our Fourth Amendment jurisprudence. "While the rigidity of ****2636** the prophylactic rules was a principal weakness in the view of dissenters and critics outside the Court, ... that rigidity [has also been called a] strength of the decision. It [has] afforded police and courts clear guidance on the manner in which to conduct a custodial investigation: if it was rigid, it was also precise.... [T]his core virtue of Miranda would be eviscerated if the prophylactic rules were freely [ignored] by ... courts under the guise of [reinterpreting] Miranda...."[2175]

The justification the Court provides for upsetting the equilibrium that has finally been achieved—that police cannot and should not balance considerations of public safety against the individual's interest in avoiding compulsory testimonial self-incrimination—really misses the critical question to be decided.[2176] Miranda has never been read to prohibit the police from asking questions to secure the public safety. Rather, the critical question Miranda addresses is who shall bear the cost of securing the public safety when such questions are asked and answered: the defendant or the State. Miranda, for better or worse, found the resolution of that question implicit in the prohibition against compulsory self-incrimination and placed the burden on the State. When police ask custodial questions without administering the required warnings, Miranda quite clearly requires that the answers received be presumed compelled and that they be excluded from evidence at trial.[2177]

The Court concedes, as it must, both that respondent was in "custody" and subject to "interrogation" and that his statement "the gun is over there" was compelled within the meaning of our precedent.[2178] In my view, ***665** since there is nothing about an exigency that makes custodial interrogation any less compelling, a principled application of Miranda requires that respondent's statement be suppressed.

II

The court below assumed, without discussion, that the privilege against self-incrimination required that the gun derived from respondent's statement also be suppressed, whether or not the State could independently link it to him. That conclusion was, in my view, incorrect.

A

Citizens in our society have a deeply rooted social obligation "to give whatever information they may have to aid in law enforcement."[2179] ****2637 *666** Except where a recognized exception applies, "the criminal defendant no less than any other citizen is obliged to assist the authorities."[2180] The privilege against compulsory self-incrimination is one recognized exception, but it is an exception nonetheless. Only the introduction of a defendant's own testimony is proscribed by the Fifth Amend-

---

[2175] *Fare v. Michael C., 439 U.S. 1310, 1314, 99 S.Ct. 3, 5, 58 L.Ed.2d 19 (1978) (REHNQUIST, J., in chambers on application for stay)*

[2176] *See ante, at 2632–2633*

[2177] *See Michigan v. Tucker, supra, 417 U.S., at 445, 447–448, 451, 452, and n. 26, 94 S.Ct., at 2364, 2365–2366, 2367, 2368, and n. 26; Orozco v. Texas, supra, 394 U.S., at 326, 89 S.Ct., at 1096*

[2178] *See ante, at 2630–2631*

[2179] *Miranda v. Arizona, 384 U.S., at 478, 86 S.Ct., at 1629–30*

[2180] *Roberts v. United States, 445 U.S. 552, 558, 100 S.Ct. 1358, 1363, 63 L.Ed.2d 622 (1980)*

ment's mandate that no person "shall be compelled in any criminal case to be a witness against himself." That mandate does not protect an accused from being compelled to surrender non-testimonial evidence against himself.[2181]

The distinction between testimonial and non-testimonial evidence was explored in some detail in Schmerber v. California,[2182] a decision this Court handed down a week after of deciding Miranda. The defendant in Schmerber had argued that the privilege against self-incrimination barred the State from compelling him to submit to a blood test, the results of which would be used to prove his guilt at trial. The State, on the other hand, had urged that the privilege prohibited it only from compelling the accused to make a formal testimonial statement against himself in an official legal proceeding. This Court rejected both positions. It favored an approach that protected the "accused only from being compelled to testify against himself, or otherwise provide the State with evidence of a testimonial or communicative nature."[2183] The blood tests were admissible because they were neither testimonial nor communicative in nature.[2184]

In subsequent decisions, the Court relied on Schmerber in holding the privilege inapplicable to situations where the accused was compelled to stand in a lineup and utter words that allegedly had been spoken by the robber,[2185] to provide handwriting samples, see Gilbert v. California,[2186] and to supply voice exemplars.[2187] ***667** "The distinction which ... emerged [in these cases], often expressed in different ways, [was] that the privilege is a bar against compelling 'communications' or 'testimony,' but that compulsion which makes a suspect or accused the source of 'real or physical evidence' does not violate it."[2188]

B

The gun respondent was compelled to supply is clearly evidence of the "real or physical" sort. What makes the question of its admissibility difficult is the fact that, in asking respondent to produce the gun, the police also "compelled" him, in the Miranda sense, to create an incriminating testimonial response. In other words, the case is problematic because police compelled respondent not only to provide the gun but also to admit that he knew where it was and that it was his.

It is settled that Miranda did not itself determine whether physical evidence obtained in this manner would be admissible.[2189] But the Court in Schmerber, with Miranda fresh on its mind, did address the issue. In concluding that the privilege did not require suppression of compelled blood tests, the Court noted:

This conclusion would not necessarily govern had the State tried to show that the accused had incriminated himself when told that he would have to be tested. Such incriminating evidence may be an unavoidable by-product of the compulsion to take the test, especially for an ****2638** individual who fears the extraction or opposes it on

---

[2181] *See Fisher v. United States, 425 U.S. 391, 408, 96 S.Ct. 1569, 1579, 48 L.Ed.2d 39 (1976)*

[2182] *384 U.S. 757, 86 S.Ct. 1826, 16 L.Ed.2d 908 (1966)*

[2183] *384 U.S., at 761, 86 S.Ct., at 1830*

[2184] *Id., at 765, 86 S.Ct., at 1832*

[2185] *See United States v. Wade, 388 U.S. 218, 221–223, 87 S.Ct. 1926, 1929–1930, 18 L.Ed.2d 1149 (1967)*

[2186] *388 U.S. 263, 265–266, 87 S.Ct. 1951, 1952–1953, 18 L.Ed.2d 1178 (1967)*

[2187] *See United States v. Dionisio, 410 U.S. 1, 5–7, 93 S.Ct. 764, 767–768, 35 L.Ed.2d 67 (1973); see also United States v. Mara, 410 U.S. 19, 21–22, 93 S.Ct. 774, 775–776, 35 L.Ed.2d 99 (1973)*

[2188] *Schmerber v. California, supra, 384 U.S., at 764, 86 S.Ct., at 1832*

[2189] *See Michigan v. Tucker, 417 U.S., at 445–446, 447, 452, and n. 26, 94 S.Ct., at 2364–2365, 2365, 2368, and n. 26*

religious grounds. If it wishes to compel persons to submit to such attempts to discover evidence, the State may have to forgo the advantage of any testimonial products of administering the test—products which would fall within the privilege.[2190]

***668** Thus, Schmerber resolved the dilemma by allowing admission of the non-testimonial, but not the testimonial, products of the State's compulsion.

The Court has applied this bifurcated approach in its subsequent cases as well. For example, in United States v. Wade,[2191] where admission of a lineup identification was approved, the Court emphasized that no question was presented as to the admissibility of anything said or done at the lineup. Likewise, in Michigan v. Tucker, where evidence derived from a technical Miranda violation was admitted, the Court noted that no statement taken without Miranda warnings was being admitted into evidence.[2192] Thus, based on the distinction first articulated in Schmerber, "a strong analytical argument can be made for an intermediate rule whereby[,] although [the police] cannot require the suspect to speak by punishment or force, the non-testimonial [evidence derived from] speech that is [itself] excludable for failure to comply with the Miranda code could still be used."[2193]

To be sure, admission of non-testimonial evidence secured through informal custodial interrogation will reduce the incentives to enforce the Miranda code. But that fact simply begs the question of how much enforcement is appropriate. There are some situations, as the Court's struggle to accommodate a "public safety" exception demonstrates, in which the societal cost of administering the Miranda warnings is very high indeed. The Miranda decision quite practically does not express any societal interest in having those warning ***669** administered for their own sake. Rather, the warnings and waiver are only required to ensure that "testimony" used against the accused at trial is voluntarily given. Therefore, if the testimonial aspects of the accused's custodial communications are suppressed, the failure to administer the Miranda warnings should cease to be of concern.[2194] The harm caused by failure to administer Miranda warnings relates only to admission of testimonial self-incriminations, and the suppression of such incriminations should by itself produce the optimal enforcement of the Miranda rule.

There are, of course, decisions of this Court which suggest that the privilege against self-incrimination requires suppression not only of compelled statements but also of all evidence derived therefrom.[2195] In each of these cases, however, the Court was responding to the dilemma that confronts persons asserting their Fifth Amendment privilege to a court or other tribunal vested with the contempt ****2639** power. In each instance, the tribunal can require witnesses to appear without any showing of probable cause to believe they have committed an offense or that they have relevant information to convey, and require the witnesses to testify even if they have formally and expressly asserted a privilege of silence. Individuals in this situation are faced with what Justice Goldberg once described as "the cruel trilemma of self-accusation, perjury, or contempt."[2196] If the witness' invocation of the privilege at trial is not to

[2190] *384 U.S., at 765, and n. 9, 86 S.Ct., at 1832, and n. 9 (emphasis in original)*

[2191] *388 U.S. 218, 223, 87 S.Ct. 1926, 1930, 18 L.Ed.2d 1149 (1967)*

[2192] *See 417 U.S., at 445, 94 S.Ct., at 2364; cf. California v. Byers, 402 U.S. 424, 431–433, 91 S.Ct. 1535, 1539–1540, 29 L.Ed. 2d 9 (1971) (opinion of BURGER, C.J.)*

[2193] *H. Friendly, Benchmarks 280 (1967)*

[2194] *Cf. Weatherford v. Bursey, 429 U.S. 545, 97 S.Ct. 837, 51 L.Ed.2d 30 (1977) (where interference with assistance of counsel has no effect on trial, no Sixth Amendment violation lies)*

[2195] *See, e.g., Maness v. Meyers, 419 U.S. 449, 95 S.Ct. 584, 42 L.Ed.2d 574 (1975); Kastigar v. United States, 406 U.S. 441, 92 S.Ct. 1653, 32 L.Ed.2d 212 (1972); McCarthy v. Arndstein, 266 U.S. 34, 45 S.Ct. 16, 69 L.Ed. 158 (1924); Counselman v. Hitchcock, 142 U.S. 547, 12 S.Ct. 195, 35 L.Ed. 1110 (1892)*

[2196] *Murphy v. Waterfront Comm'n, 378 U.S. 52, 55, 84 S.Ct. 1594, 1596, 12 L.Ed.2d 678 (1964)*

be defeated by the State's refusal to let him remain silent at an earlier proceeding, the witness has to ***670** be protected "against the use of his compelled answers and evidence derived therefrom in any subsequent criminal case...."[2197]

By contrast, suspects subject to informal custodial police interrogation of the type involved in this case are not in the same position as witnesses required to appear before a court, grand jury, or other such formal tribunal. Where independent evidence leads police to a suspect, and probable cause justifies his arrest, the suspect cannot seriously urge that the police have somehow unfairly infringed on his right "to a private enclave where he may lead a private life."[2198] Moreover, when a suspect interjects not the privilege itself but a post hoc complaint that the police failed to administer Miranda warnings, he invokes only an irrebuttable presumption that the interrogation was coercive. He does not show that a privilege was raised and that the police actually or overtly coerced him to provide testimony and other evidence to be used against him at trial.[2199] He could have remained silent and the interrogator could not have punished him for refusing to speak. Indeed, the accused is in the unique position of seeking the protection of the privilege without having timely asserted it.[2200] The person in police custody surely may sense that he is in "trouble,"[2201] but he is in no position to protest that he faced the Hobson's choice of self-accusation, perjury, or contempt. He therefore has a much less sympathetic case for obtaining the benefit of a broad suppression ruling.[2202]

Indeed, whatever case can be made for suppression evaporates when the statements themselves are not admitted, given the rationale of the Schmerber line of cases. Certainly ***671** interrogation which provides leads to other evidence does not offend the values underlying the Fifth Amendment privilege any more than the compulsory taking of blood samples, fingerprints, or voice exemplars, all of which may be compelled in an "attempt to discover evidence that might be used to prosecute [a defendant] for a criminal offense."[2203] Use of a suspect's answers "merely to find other evidence establishing his connection with the crime [simply] differs only by a shade from the permitted use for that purpose of his body or his blood."[2204]
The values underlying the privilege may justify exclusion of an unwarned person's out-of-court statements, as perhaps they may justify exclusion of statements and derivative evidence compelled under the threat of contempt. But when the only evidence to be admitted is derivative evidence such as a gun—derived not from actual compulsion but from a statement taken in the absence of Miranda warnings—those values simply cannot require ****2640** suppression, at least no more so than they would for other such non-testimonial evidence.

***672** On the other hand, if a suspect is subject to abusive police practices and actually or overtly compelled to speak, it is reasonable to infer both an unwillingness to speak and a perceptible assertion of the privilege.[2205] Thus, when the Miranda violation consists of a deliberate and flagrant abuse of the accused's constitutional rights, amounting to a denial of due process, application of a broader exclusionary

---

[2197] *Lefkowitz v. Turley, 414 U.S. 70, 78, 94 S.Ct. 316, 322, 38 L.Ed.2d 274 (1973)*

[2198] *Murphy v. Waterfront Comm'n, supra, 378 U.S., at 55, 84 S.Ct., at 1597*

[2199] *See Johnson v. New Jersey, 384 U.S. 719, 730, 86 S.Ct. 1772, 1779, 16 L.Ed.2d 882 (1966)*

[2200] *Cf. United States v. Kordel, 397 U.S. 1, 10, 90 S.Ct. 763, 768, 25 L.Ed.2d 1 (1970) (failure to assert waives right to complain about testimonial compulsion)*

[2201] *Oregon v. Hass, 420 U.S. 714, 722, 95 S.Ct. 1215, 1221, 43 L.Ed.2d 570 (1975)*

[2202] *See Michigan v. Tucker, 417 U.S., at 444–451, 94 S.Ct., at 2363–2367; cf. New Jersey v. Portash, 440 U.S. 450, 458–459, 99 S.Ct. 1292, 1296–1297, 59 L.Ed.2d 501 (1979)*

[2203] *Schmerber v. California, 384 U.S., at 761, 86 S.Ct., at 1831*

[2204] *H. Friendly, Benchmarks 280 (1967)*

[2205] *See Mincey v. Arizona, 437 U.S. 385, 396–402, 98 S.Ct. 2408, 2415–2418, 57 L.Ed.2d 290 (1978)*

rule is warranted. Of course, "a defendant raising [such] a coerced-confession claim ... must first prevail in a voluntariness hearing before his confession and evidence derived from it [will] become inadmissible."[2206] By contrast, where the accused proves only that the police failed to administer the Miranda warnings, exclusion of the statement itself is all that will and should be required.5 Limitation of the Miranda prohibition to testimonial use of the statements themselves adequately serves the purposes of the privilege against self-incrimination.

III

In Miranda, the Court looked to the experience of countries like England, India, Scotland, and Ceylon in developing its code to regulate custodial interrogations.[2207] ***673** Those countries had also adopted procedural rules to regulate the manner in which police secured confessions to be used against accused persons at trial.[2208] Confessions induced by trickery or physical abuse were never admissible at trial, and any confession secured without the required procedural safeguards could, in the courts' discretion, be excluded on grounds of fairness or prejudice.[2209] But non-testimonial evidence derived from all confessions "not blatantly coerced" was and still is admitted. Admission of non-testimonial evidence of this type is based on the very sensible view ****2641** that procedural errors should not cause entire investigations and prosecutions to be lost.[2210]

The learning of these countries was important to development of the initial Miranda rule. It therefore should be of equal importance in establishing the scope of the Miranda exclusionary rule today. I would apply that learning in this case and adhere to our precedents requiring that statements elicited in the absence of Miranda warnings be suppressed. But because non-testimonial evidence such as the gun should not be suppressed, I join in that part of the Court's judgment ***674** that reverses and remands for further proceedings with the gun admissible as evidence against the accused.

(The dissent of Justice MARSHALL, with whom Justice BRENNAN and Justice STEVENS join, is omitted.)

Black Letter Law

> Where suspect, when detained and frisked by police officer in supermarket, was discovered to be wearing an empty shoulder holster, and confronting officer, who had been informed suspect was carrying a gun, who had every reason to believe suspect had just removed from his holster and discarded it in supermarket, where an accomplice might make use of it or a customer or employee come upon it, was justified in his questions as to whereabouts of gun. The Court held that suspect's incriminating response fell within "public safety" exception to requirement that Miranda warnings be given before a suspect's answers may be admitted into evidence, since officer needed answer to question not simply to make case against suspect but to insure that danger to public did not result "from concealment of gun in public area."
>
> This case establishes the "public safety" exception to Miranda warnings and does not condition the use of the exception on the motivation of individual officers involved."

[2206] *Kastigar v. United States, 406 U.S., at 462, 92 S.Ct., at 1665*

[2207] *See Miranda v. Arizona, 384 U.S., at 486–489, 86 S.Ct., at 1634–1635*

[2208] *See Note, Developments in the Law—Confessions, 79 Harv.L.Rev. 935, 1090–1114 (1966)*

[2209] *See Gotlieb, Confirmation by Subsequent Facts, 72 L.Q.Rev. 209, 223–224 (1956)*

[2210] *See Enker & Elsen, Counsel For the Suspect: Massiah v. United States and Escobedo v. Illinois, 49 Minn.L.Rev. 47, 80 (1964)*

Massiah v. United States

84 S.Ct. 1199
Supreme Court of the United States
Winston **MASSIAH**, Petitioner,
v.
UNITED STATES.
No. 199. | Argued March 3, 1964. | Decided May 18, 1964.

Mr. Justice STEWART delivered the opinion of the Court.

The petitioner was indicted for violating the federal narcotics laws. He retained a lawyer, pleaded not guilty, and was released on bail. While he was free on bail a federal agent succeeded by surreptitious means in listening to incriminating statements made by him. Evidence of these statements was introduced against the petitioner at his trial over his objection. He was convicted, and the Court of Appeals affirmed. We granted certiorari to ***202** consider whether, under the circumstances here presented, the prosecution's use at the trial of evidence of the petitioner's own incriminating statements deprived him of any right secured to him under the Federal Constitution.[2211]

****1201** The petitioner, a merchant seaman, was in 1958 a member of the crew of the S. S. Santa Maria. In April of that year federal customs officials in New York received information that he was going to transport a quantity of narcotics aboard that ship from South America to the United States. As a result of this and other information, the agents searched the Santa Maria upon its arrival in New York and found in the afterpeak of the vessel five packages containing about three and a half pounds of cocaine. They also learned of circumstances, not here relevant, tending to connect the petitioner with the cocaine. He was arrested, promptly arraigned, and subsequently indicted for possession of narcotics aboard a United States vessel. In July a superseding indictment was returned, charging the petitioner and a man named Colson with the same substantive offense, and in separate counts charging the petitioner, Colson, and others with having conspired to possess narcotics aboard a United States vessel, and to import, conceal, and facilitate the sale of narcotics. The petitioner, who had retained a lawyer, pleaded not guilty and was released on bail, along with Colson.

A few days later, and quite without the petitioner's knowledge, Colson decided to cooperate with the government agents in their continuing investigation of the nacotics activities in which the petitioner, Colson, and others had allegedly been engaged. Colson permitted an agent named Murphy to install a Schmidt radio transmitter ***203** under the front seat of Colson's automobile, by means of which Murphy, equipped with an appropriate receiving device, could overhear from some distance away conversations carried on in Colson's car.

On the evening of November 19, 1959, Colson and the petitioner held a lengthy conversation while sitting in Colson's automobile, parked on a New York street. By prearrangement with Colson, and totally unbeknown to the petitioner, the agent Murphy sat in a car parked out of sight down the street and listened over the radio to the entire conversation. The petitioner made several incriminating statements during the course of this conversation. At the petitioner's trial these incriminating statements were brought before the jury through Murphy's testimony, despite the insistent objection of defense counsel. The jury convicted the petitioner of several related narcotics offenses, and the convictions were affirmed by the Court of Appeals.

The petitioner argues that it was an error of constitutional dimensions to permit the agent Murphy at the trial to testify to the petitioner's incriminating statements

[2211] *374 U.S. 805, 83 S.Ct. 1698, 10 L.Ed.2d 1030*

which Murphy had overheard under the circumstances disclosed by this record. This argument is based upon two distinct and independent grounds. First, we are told that Murphy's use of the radio equipment violated the petitioner's rights under the Fourth Amendment, and, consequently, that all evidence which Murphy thereby obtained was, under the rule of Weeks v. United States,[2212] inadmissible against the petitioner at the trial. Secondly, it is said that the petitioner's ***204** Fifth and Sixth Amendment rights were violated by the use in evidence against him of incriminating statements which government agents had deliberately elicited from him after he had been indicted and in the absence of his retained counsel. Because of the way ****1202** we dispose of the case, we do not reach the Fourth Amendment issue.

In Spano v. New York,[2213] this Court reversed a state criminal conviction because a confession had been wrongly admitted into evidence against the defendant at his trial. In that case the defendant had already been indicted for first-degree murder at the time he confessed. The Court held that the defendant's conviction could not stand under the Fourteenth Amendment. While the Court's opinion relied upon the totality of the circumstances under which the confession had been obtained, four concurring Justices pointed out that the Constitution required reversal of the conviction upon the sole and specific ground that the confession had been deliberately elicited by the police after the defendant had been indicted, and therefore at a time when he was clearly entitled to a lawyer's help. It was pointed out that under our system of justice the most elemental concepts of due process of law contemplate that an indictment be followed by a trial, 'in an orderly courtroom, presided over by a judge, open to the public, and protected by all the procedural safeguards of the law.'[2214] It was said that a Constitution which guarantees a defendant the aid of counsel at such a trial could surely vouchsafe no less to an indicted defendant under interrogation by the police in a completely extrajudicial proceeding. Anything less, it was said, might deny a defendant 'effective representation by counsel at the only stage when legal aid and advice would help him.'[2215]

Ever since this Court's decision in the Spano case, the New York courts have unequivocally followed this constitutional ***205** rule. 'Any secret interrogation of the defendant, from and after the finding of the indictment, without the protection afforded by the presence of counsel, contravenes the basic dictates of fairness in the conduct of criminal causes and the fundamental rights of persons charged with crime.'[2216]

This view no more than reflects a constitutional principle established as long ago as Powell v. Alabama,[2217] where the Court noted that '* * * during perhaps the most critical period of the proceedings * * * that is to say, from the time of their arraignment until the beginning of their trial, when consultation, thorough-going investigation and preparation (are) vitally important, the defendants * * * (are) as much entitled to such aid (of counsel) during that period as at the trial itself.'[2218] And since the Spano decision the same basic constitutional principle has been broadly reaffirmed by this Court.[2219]

[2212] *232 U.S. 383, 34 S.Ct. 341, 58 L.Ed. 652*

[2213] *360 U.S. 315, 79 S.Ct. 1202, 3 L.Ed.2d 1265*

[2214] *360 U.S., at 327, 79 S.Ct. at 1209, 3 L.Ed.2d 1265 (STEWART, J., concurring)*

[2215] *360 U.S., at 326, 79 S.Ct., at 1209, 3 L.Ed.2d 1265 (DOUGLAS, J., concurring)*

[2216] *People v. Waterman, 9 N.Y.2d 561, 565, 216 N.Y.S.2d 70, 75, 175 N.E.2d 445, 448*

[2217] *287 U.S. 45, 53 S.Ct. 55, 77 L.Ed. 158*

[2218] *Id., 287 U.S., at 57, 53 S.Ct., at 59, 77 L.Ed. 158*

[2219] *Hamilton v. Alabama, 368 U.S. 52, 82 S.Ct. 157, 7 L.Ed.2d 114; White v. Maryland, 373 U.S. 59, 83 S.Ct. 1050, 10 L.Ed.2d 193. See Gideon v. Wainwright, 372 U.S. 335, 83 S.Ct. 792, 9 L.Ed.2d 799*

Here we deal not with a state court conviction, but with a federal case, where the specific guarantee of the Sixth **1203 Amendment directly applies.[2220] *206 We hold that the petitioner was denied the basic protections of that guarantee when there was used against him at his trial evidence of his own incriminating words, which federal agents had deliberately elicited from him after he had been indicted and in the absence of his counsel. It is true that in the Spano case the defendant was interrogated in a police station, while here the damaging testimony was elicited from the defendant without his knowledge while he was free on bail. But, as Judge Hays pointed out in his dissent in the Court of Appeals, 'if such a rule is to have any efficacy it must apply to indirect and surreptitious interrogations as well as those conducted in the jailhouse. In this case, Massiah was more seriously imposed upon * * * because he did not even know that he was under interrogation by a government agent.'[2221]

The Solicitor General, in his brief and oral argument, has strenuously contended that the federal law enforcement agents had the right, if not indeed the duty, to continue their investigation of the petitioner and his alleged criminal associates even though the petitioner had been indicted. He points out that the Government was continuing its investigation in order to uncover not only the source of narcotics found on the S. S. Santa Maria, but also their intended buyer. He says that the quantity of narcotics involved was such as to suggest that the petitioner was part of a large and well-organized ring, and indeed that the continuing investigation confirmed this suspicion, since it resulted in criminal charges against many defendants. Under these circumstances the Solicitor General concludes that the Government agents were completely 'justified in making use of Colson's cooperation by having Colson continue his normal associations and by surveilling them.'

We may accept and, at least for present purposes, completely approve all that this argument implies, Fourth *207 Amendment problems to one side. We do not question that in this case, as in many cases, it was entirely proper to continue an investigation of the suspected criminal activities of the defendant and his alleged confederates, even though the defendant had already been indicted. All that we hold is that the defendant's own incriminating statements, obtained by federal agents under the circumstances here disclosed, could not constitutionally be used by the prosecution as evidence against him at his trial.

Reversed.

(The dissent of Mr. Justice WHITE, with whom Mr. Justice CLARK and Mr. Justice HARLAN join, is omitted.)

Black Letter Law

> The use of the defendant's statements, that were overheard on the radio by law enforcement after he and his co-defendant were indicted and released on bail, in absence of defendant's retained counsel, and without defendant's knowledge, constituted a violation of his Fifth and Sixth Amendment rights, and should not have been used against him at trial.

[2220] *Johnson v. Zerbst, 304 U.S. 458, 58 S.Ct. 1019, 82 L.Ed. 1461*

[2221] *307 F.2d at 72—73*

Scott v. Illinois

99 S.Ct. 1158

Supreme Court of the United States

Aubrey SCOTT, Petitioner,

v.

State of ILLINOIS.

No. 77-1177. | Argued Dec. 4, 1978. | Decided March 5, 1979.

Justice REHNQUIST delivered the opinion of the Court.

We granted certiorari in this case to resolve a conflict among state and lower federal courts regarding the proper application of our decision in Argersinger v. Hamlin,[2222] Petitioner Scott was convicted of theft and fined $50 after a bench trial in the Circuit Court of Cook County, Ill. His conviction was affirmed by the state intermediate appellate court and then by the Supreme Court of Illinois, over Scott's contention that the Sixth and Fourteenth Amendments to the United States Constitution required that Illinois provide trial counsel to him at its expense.

Petitioner Scott was convicted of shoplifting merchandise valued at less than $150. The applicable Illinois statute set the maximum penalty for such an offense at a $500 fine or one year in jail, or both. The petitioner argues that a line of this Court's cases culminating in Argersinger v. Hamlin,[2223] requires state provision of counsel whenever imprisonment is an authorized penalty.

***369** The Supreme Court of Illinois rejected this contention, quoting the following language from Argersinger :

> ****1160** We hold, therefore, that absent a knowing and intelligent waiver, no person may be imprisoned for any offense, whether classified as petty, misdemeanor, or felony, unless he was represented by counsel at his trial.[2224]
>
> Under the rule we announce today, every judge will know when the trial of a misdemeanor starts that no imprisonment may be imposed, even though local law permits it, unless the accused is represented by counsel. He will have a measure of the seriousness and gravity of the offense and therefore know when to name a lawyer to represent the accused before the trial starts.[2225]

The Supreme Court of Illinois went on to state that it was "not inclined to extend Argersinger " to the case where a defendant is charged with a statutory offense for which imprisonment upon conviction is authorized but not actually imposed upon the defendant.[2226] We agree with the Supreme Court of Illinois that the Federal Constitution does not require a state trial court to appoint counsel for a criminal defendant such as petitioner, and we therefore affirm its judgment.

[2222] *407 U.S. 25, 92 S.Ct. 2006, 32 L.Ed.2d 530 (1972). 436 U.S. 925, 98 S.Ct. 2817, 56 L.Ed.2d 767.*

[2223] *Supra.*

[2224] *407 U.S., at 37, 92 S.Ct., at 2012*

[2225] *Id., at 40, 92 S.Ct., at 2014*

[2226] *68 Ill.2d 269, 272, 12 Ill.Dec. 174, 177, 369 N.E.2d 881, 882 (1977)*

In his petition for certiorari, petitioner referred to the issue in this case as "the question left open in Argersinger v. Hamlin.[2227]"[2228] Whether this question was indeed "left open" in Argersinger depends upon whether one considers that opinion to be a point in a moving line or a holding that the States are required to go only so far in furnishing counsel to indigent defendants. The Supreme Court of Illinois, in quoting the above language from Argersinger, clearly viewed the latter as Argersinger's holding. ***370** Additional support for this proposition may be derived from the concluding paragraph of the opinion in that case: "The run of misdemeanors will not be affected by today's ruling. But in those that end up in the actual deprivation of a person's liberty, the accused will receive the benefit of 'the guiding hand of counsel' so necessary where one's liberty is in jeopardy."[2229]

Petitioner, on the other hand, refers to language in the Court's opinion, responding to the opinion of Mr. Justice Powell, which states that the Court "need not consider the requirements of the Sixth Amendment as regards the right to counsel where loss of liberty is not involved . . . for here petitioner was in fact sentenced to jail."[2230]

T here is considerable doubt that the Sixth Amendment itself, as originally drafted by the Framers of the Bill of Rights, contemplated any guarantee other than the right of an accused in a criminal prosecution in a federal court to employ a lawyer to assist in his defense.[2231] In Powell v. Alabama,[2232] the Court held that Alabama was obligated to appoint counsel for the Scottsboro defendants, phrasing the inquiry as "whether the defendants were in substance denied the right of counsel, and if so, whether such denial infringes the due process clause of the Fourteenth Amendment."[2233] It concluded its opinion with the following language:

The United States by statute and every state in the Union by express provision of law, or by the determination of its courts, make it the duty of the trial judge, where the accused is unable to employ counsel, to appoint counsel for him. In most states the rule applies broadly to all criminal prosecutions, in others it is limited to the more serious crimes, and in a very limited number, to capital cases. A rule adopted with such unanimous ***371** accord reflects, if it does not establish, the inherent right to have counsel appointed, at least in cases like the present, and lends convincing support to the conclusion we have reached as to the ****1161** fundamental nature of that right.[2234]

Betts v. Brady[2235] held that not every indigent defendant accused in a state criminal prosecution was entitled to appointment of counsel. A determination had to be made in each individual case whether failure to appoint counsel was a denial of fundamental fairness. Betts was in turn overruled in Gideon v. Wainwright.[2236] In Gideon, Betts was described as holding "that a refusal to appoint counsel for an indi-

---

[2227] *407 U.S. 25, 92 S.Ct. 2006, 32 L.Ed.2d 530 (1972)*

[2228] *Pet. for Cert. 5*

[2229] *407 U.S., at 40, 92 S.Ct., at 2014*

[2230] *Id., at 37, 92 S.Ct., at 2012*

[2231] *W. Beaney, The Right to Counsel in American Courts 27-30 (1955)*

[2232] *287 U.S. 45, 53 S.Ct. 55, 77 L.Ed. 158 (1932)*

[2233] *Id., at 52, 53 S.Ct., at 58*

[2234] *Id., at 73, 53 S.Ct., at 65*

[2235] *316 U.S. 455, 62 S.Ct. 1252, 86 L.Ed. 1595 (1942)*

[2236] *372 U.S. 335, 83 S.Ct. 792, 9 L.Ed.2d 799 (1963)*

gent defendant charged with a felony did not necessarily violate the Due Process Clause of the Fourteenth Amendment . . . ."[2237]

Several Terms later the Court held in Duncan v. Louisiana,[2238] that the right to jury trial in federal court guaranteed by the Sixth Amendment was applicable to the States by virtue of the Fourteenth Amendment. The Court held, however: "It is doubtless true that there is a category of petty crimes or offenses which is not subject to the Sixth Amendment jury trial provision and should not be subject to the Fourteenth Amendment jury trial requirement here applied to the States. Crimes carrying possible penalties up to six months do not require a jury trial if they otherwise qualify as petty offenses . . . ."[2239] In Baldwin v. New York,[2240] the controlling opinion of Mr. Justice White concluded that "no offense can be deemed 'petty' for purposes of the right to trial by jury where imprisonment for more than six months is authorized."

In Argersinger the State of Florida urged that a similar dichotomy be employed in the right-to-counsel area: Any offense punishable by less than six months in jail should not ***372** require appointment of counsel for an indigent defendant. The Argersinger Court rejected this analogy, however, observing that "the right to trial by jury has a different genealogy and is brigaded with a system of trial to a judge alone."[2241]

The number of separate opinions in Gideon, Duncan, Baldwin, and Argersinger, suggests that constitutional line drawing becomes more difficult as the reach of the Constitution is extended further, and as efforts are made to transpose lines from one area of Sixth Amendment jurisprudence to another. The process of incorporation creates special difficulties, for the state and federal contexts are often different and application of the same principle may have ramifications distinct in degree and kind. The range of human conduct regulated by state criminal laws is much broader than that of the federal criminal laws, particularly on the "petty" offense part of the spectrum. As a matter of constitutional adjudication, we are, therefore, less willing to extrapolate an already extended line when, although the general nature of the principle sought to be applied is clear, its precise limits and their ramifications become less so. We have now in our decided cases departed from the literal meaning of the Sixth Amendment. And we cannot fall back on the common law as it existed prior to the enactment of that Amendment, since it perversely gave less in the way of right to counsel to accused felons than to those accused of misdemeanors.[2242]

In Argersinger the Court rejected arguments that social cost or a lack of available lawyers militated against its holding, in some part because it thought these arguments were factually incorrect.[2243] But they were rejected in much larger part because of the Court's conclusion that incarceration was so severe a sanction that it should not be imposed as a result of a criminal trial unless an indigent ***373** defendant had been offered appointed counsel to assist in his defense, ****1162** regardless of the cost to the States implicit in such a rule. The Court in its opinion repeatedly referred to trials "where an accused is deprived of his liberty,"[2244] and to "a case that

---

[2237] *Id., at 339, 83 S.Ct., at 793*

[2238] *391 U.S. 145, 88 S.Ct. 1444, 20 L.Ed.2d 491 (1968)*

[2239] *Id., at 159, 88 S.Ct., at 1453 (footnote omitted)*

[2240] *399 U.S. 66, 69, 90 S.Ct. 1886, 1888, 26 L.Ed.2d 437 (1970)*

[2241] *407 U.S., at 29, 92 S.Ct., at 2008*

[2242] *See Powell v. Alabama, supra, 287 U.S., at 60, 53 S.Ct., at 61*

[2243] *407 U.S., at 37 n. 7, 92 S.Ct., at 2012*

[2244] *Id., at 32, 92 S.Ct., at 2010*

actually leads to imprisonment even for a brief period."[2245] The Chief Justice in his opinion concurring in the result also observed that "any deprivation of liberty is a serious matter."[2246]

Although the intentions of the Argersinger Court are not unmistakably clear from its opinion, we conclude today that Argersinger did indeed delimit the constitutional right to appointed counsel in state criminal proceedings. Even were the matter res nova, we believe that the central premise of Argersinger -that actual imprisonment is a penalty different in kind from fines or the mere threat of imprisonment-is eminently sound and warrants adoption of actual imprisonment as the line defining the constitutional right to appointment of counsel. Argersinger has proved reasonably workable, whereas any extension would create confusion and impose unpredictable, but necessarily substantial, costs on 50 quite diverse States. We therefore hold that the Sixth ***374** and Fourteenth Amendments to the United States Constitution require only that no indigent criminal defendant be sentenced to a term of imprisonment unless the State has afforded him the right to assistance of appointed counsel in his defense. The judgment of the Supreme Court of Illinois is accordingly

Affirmed.

Mr. Justice POWELL, concurring.

For the reasons stated in my opinion in Argersinger v. Hamlin,[2247] I do not think the rule adopted by the Court in that case is required by the Constitution. Moreover, the drawing of a line based on whether there is imprisonment (even for overnight) can have the practical effect of precluding provision of counsel in other types of cases in which conviction can have more serious consequences. The Argersinger rule also tends to impair the proper functioning of the criminal justice system in that trial judges, in advance of hearing any evidence and before knowing anything about the case except the charge, all too often will be compelled to forgo the legislatively granted option to impose a sentence of imprisonment upon conviction. Preserving this option by providing counsel often will be impossible or impracticable-particularly in congested urban courts where scores of cases are heard in a single sitting, and in small and rural communities where lawyers may not be available.

Despite my continuing reservations about the Argersinger rule, it was approved by the Court in the 1972 opinion and four Justices have reaffirmed it today. It is important that this Court provide clear guidance to the hundreds of courts across the country that confront this problem daily. Accordingly, and mindful of stare decisis, I join the opinion of the ***375** Court. I do so, however, with the hope that in due time a ****1163** majority will recognize that a more flexible rule is consistent with due process and will better serve the cause of justice.

(The dissent of Mr. Justice BRENNAN, with whom Mr. Justice MARSHALL and Mr. Justice STEVENS join, is omitted.)

(The dissent of Mr. Justice BLACKMUN is omitted.)

[2245] *Id., at 33, 92 S.Ct., at 2010*

[2246] *Id., at 41, 92 S.Ct., at 2014*

[2247] *407 U.S. 25, 44, 92 S.Ct. 2006, 2015, 32 L.Ed.2d 530 (1972)*

Black Letter Law

> The Court declined to extend the Sixth Amendment right to counsel to those cases where a prison sentence is not contemplated. The Court held that the Sixth and Fourteenth Amendments to the United States Constitution require the States to afford the assistance of defense counsel only to indigent criminal defendants facing a term of imprisonment.

Dickerson v. United States

120 S.Ct. 2326

Supreme Court of the United States

Charles Thomas DICKERSON, Petitioner,

v.

UNITED STATES.

No. 99–5525. | Argued April 19, 2000. | Decided June 26, 2000.

***431** Chief Justice REHNQUIST delivered the opinion of the Court.

In Miranda v. Arizona,[2248] we held that certain warnings must be given before a suspect's statement made during custodial interrogation could be admitted in ***432** evidence. In the wake of that decision, Congress enacted 18 U.S.C. § 3501, which in essence laid down a rule that the admissibility of such statements should turn only on whether or not they were voluntarily made. We hold that Miranda, being a constitutional decision of this Court, may not be in effect overruled by an Act of Congress, and we decline to overrule Miranda ourselves. We therefore hold that Miranda and its progeny in this Court govern the admissibility of statements ****2330** made during custodial interrogation in both state and federal courts.

Petitioner Dickerson was indicted for bank robbery, conspiracy to commit bank robbery, and using a firearm in the course of committing a crime of violence, all in violation of the applicable provisions of Title 18 of the United States Code. Before trial, Dickerson moved to suppress a statement he had made at a Federal Bureau of Investigation field office, on the grounds that he had not received "Miranda warnings" before being interrogated. The District Court granted his motion to suppress, and the Government took an interlocutory appeal to the United States Court of Appeals for the Fourth Circuit. That court, by a divided vote, reversed the District Court's suppression order. It agreed with the District Court's conclusion that petitioner had not received Miranda warnings before making his statement. But it went on to hold that § 3501, which in effect makes the admissibility of statements such as Dickerson's turn solely on whether they were made voluntarily, was satisfied in this case. It then concluded that our decision in Miranda was not a constitutional holding, and that, therefore, Congress could by statute have the final say on the question of admissibility. 166 F.3d 667 (1999).

Because of the importance of the questions raised by the Court of Appeals' decision, we granted certiorari,[2249] and now reverse.

We begin with a brief historical account of the law governing the admission of confessions. Prior to Miranda, we ***433** evaluated the admissibility of a suspect's confession under a voluntariness test. The roots of this test developed in the common law, as the courts of England and then the United States recognized that coerced con-

---

[2248] *384 U.S. 436, 86 S.Ct. 1602, 16 L.Ed.2d 694 (1966)*

[2249] *528 U.S. 1045, 120 S.Ct. 578, 145 L.Ed.2d 481 (1999)*

fessions are inherently untrustworthy.[2250] Over time, our cases recognized two constitutional bases for the requirement that a confession be voluntary to be admitted into evidence: the Fifth Amendment right against self-incrimination and the Due Process Clause of the Fourteenth Amendment.[2251]

While Bram was decided before Brown and its progeny, for the middle third of the 20th century our cases based the rule against admitting coerced confessions primarily, if not exclusively, on notions of due process. We applied the ***434** due process voluntariness test in "some 30 different cases decided during the era that intervened between Brown and Escobedo v. Illinois.[2252]"[2253] ****2331** Those cases refined the test into an inquiry that examines "whether a defendant's will was overborne" by the circumstances surrounding the giving of a confession.[2254] The due process test takes into consideration "the totality of all the surrounding circumstances—both the characteristics of the accused and the details of the interrogation."[2255] The determination "depend[s] upon a weighing of the circumstances of pressure against the power of resistance of the person confessing."[2256]

We have never abandoned this due process jurisprudence, and thus continue to exclude confessions that were obtained involuntarily. But our decisions in Malloy v. Hogan,[2257] and Miranda changed the focus of much of the inquiry in determining the admissibility of suspects' incriminating statements. In Malloy, we held that the Fifth Amendment's Self–Incrimination Clause is incorporated in the Due Process Clause of the Fourteenth Amendment and thus applies to the States.[2258] We decided Miranda on the heels of Malloy.

In Miranda, we noted that the advent of modern custodial police interrogation brought with it an increased concern ***435** about confessions obtained by coercion.[2259] Because custodial police interrogation, by its very nature, isolates and pressures the individual, we stated that "[e]ven without employing brutality, the 'third degree' or [other] specific stratagems, ... custodial interrogation exacts a heavy toll on individual liberty and trades on the weakness of individuals."[2260] We concluded that the coercion inherent in custodial interrogation blurs the line between volun-

---

[2250] *See, e.g., King v. Rudd, 1 Leach 115, 117–118, 122–123, 168 Eng. Rep. 160, 161, 164 (K.B.1783) (Lord Mansfield, C.J.) (stating that the English courts excluded confessions obtained by threats and promises); King v. Warickshall, 1 Leach 262, 263–264, 168 Eng. Rep. 234, 235 (K.B.1783) ("A free and voluntary confession is deserving of the highest credit, because it is presumed to flow from the strongest sense of guilt ... but a confession forced from the mind by the flattery of hope, or by the torture of fear, comes in so questionable a shape ... that no credit ought to be given to it; and therefore it is rejected"); King v. Parratt, 4 Car. & P. 570, 172 Eng. Rep. 829 (N.P. 1831); Queen v. Garner, 1 Den. 329, 169 Eng. Rep. 267 (Ct.Crim.App.1848); Queen v. Baldry, 2 Den. 430, 169 Eng. Rep. 568 (Ct.Crim.App.1852); Hopt v. Territory of Utah, 110 U.S. 574, 4 S.Ct. 202, 28 L.Ed. 262 (1884); Pierce v. United States, 160 U.S. 355, 357, 16 S.Ct. 321, 40 L.Ed. 454 (1896)*

[2251] *See, e.g., Bram v. United States, 168 U.S. 532, 542, 18 S.Ct. 183, 42 L.Ed. 568 (1897) (stating that the voluntariness test "is controlled by that portion of the Fifth Amendment ... commanding that no person 'shall be compelled in any criminal case to be a witness against himself' "); Brown v. Mississippi, 297 U.S. 278, 56 S.Ct. 461, 80 L.Ed. 682 (1936) (reversing a criminal conviction under the Due Process Clause because it was based on a confession obtained by physical coercion)*

[2252] *378 U.S. 478, 84 S.Ct. 1758, 12 L.Ed.2d 977 [(1964)]*

[2253] *Schneckloth v. Bustamonte, 412 U.S. 218, 223, 93 S.Ct. 2041, 36 L.Ed.2d 854 (1973). See, e.g., Haynes v. Washington, 373 U.S. 503, 83 S.Ct. 1336, 10 L.Ed.2d 513 (1963); Ashcraft v. Tennessee, 322 U.S. 143, 64 S.Ct. 921, 88 L.Ed. 1192 (1944); Chambers v. Florida, 309 U.S. 227, 60 S.Ct. 472, 84 L.Ed. 716 (1940)*

[2254] *Schneckloth, 412 U.S., at 226, 93 S.Ct. 2041*

[2255] *Ibid. See also Haynes, supra, at 513, 83 S.Ct. 1336; Gallegos v. Colorado, 370 U.S. 49, 55, 82 S.Ct. 1209, 8 L.Ed.2d 325 (1962); Reck v. Pate, 367 U.S. 433, 440, 81 S.Ct. 1541, 6 L.Ed.2d 948 (1961) ("[A]ll the circumstances attendant upon the confession must be taken into account"); Malinski v. New York, 324 U.S. 401, 404, 65 S.Ct. 781, 89 L.Ed. 1029 (1945) ("If all the attendant circumstances indicate that the confession was coerced or compelled, it may not be used to convict a defendant")*

[2256] *Stein v. New York, 346 U.S. 156, 185, 73 S.Ct. 1077, 97 L.Ed. 1522 (1953)*

[2257] *378 U.S. 1, 84 S.Ct. 1489, 12 L.Ed.2d 653 (1964)*

[2258] *378 U.S., at 6–11, 84 S.Ct. 1489*

[2259] *384 U.S., at 445–458, 86 S.Ct. 1602*

[2260] *Id., at 455, 86 S.Ct. 1602*

tary and involuntary statements, and thus heightens the risk that an individual will not be "accorded his privilege under the Fifth Amendment ... not to be compelled to incriminate himself."[2261] Accordingly, we laid down "concrete constitutional guidelines for law enforcement agencies and courts to follow."[2262] Those guidelines established that the admissibility in evidence of any statement given during custodial interrogation of a suspect would depend on whether the police provided the suspect with four warnings. These warnings (which have come to be known colloquially as "Miranda rights") are: a suspect "has the right to remain silent, that anything he says can be used against him in a court of law, that he has the right to the presence of an attorney, and that if he cannot afford an attorney one will be appointed for him prior to any questioning if he so desires."[2263]

Two years after Miranda was decided, Congress enacted § 3501. That section provides, in relevant part:

> ****2332** (a) In any criminal prosecution brought by the United States or by the District of Columbia, a confession ... shall be admissible in evidence if it is voluntarily given. Before such confession is received in evidence, the trial ***436** judge shall, out of the presence of the jury, determine any issue as to voluntariness. If the trial judge determines that the confession was voluntarily made it shall be admitted in evidence and the trial judge shall permit the jury to hear relevant evidence on the issue of voluntariness and shall instruct the jury to give such weight to the confession as the jury feels it deserves under all the circumstances. (b) The trial judge in determining the issue of voluntariness shall take into consideration all the circumstances surrounding the giving of the confession, including (1) the time elapsing between arrest and arraignment of the defendant making the confession, if it was made after arrest and before arraignment, (2) whether such defendant knew the nature of the offense with which he was charged or of which he was suspected at the time of making the confession, (3) whether or not such defendant was advised or knew that he was not required to make any statement and that any such statement could be used against him, (4) whether or not such defendant had been advised prior to questioning of his right to the assistance of counsel; and (5) whether or not such defendant was without the assistance of counsel when questioned and when giving such confession.
>
> The presence or absence of any of the above—mentioned factors to be taken into consideration by the judge need not be conclusive on the issue of voluntariness of the confession.

Given § 3501's express designation of voluntariness as the touchstone of admissibility, its omission of any warning requirement, and the instruction for trial courts to consider a nonexclusive list of factors relevant to the circumstances of a confession, we agree with the Court of Appeals that Congress intended by its enactment to overrule Miranda.[2264] ***437** Because of the obvious conflict between our decision in Miranda and § 3501, we must address whether Congress has constitutional

[2261] *Id., at 439, 86 S.Ct. 1602*

[2262] *Id., at 442, 86 S.Ct. 1602*

[2263] *Id., at 479, 86 S.Ct. 1602*

[2264] *See also Davis v. United States, 512 U.S. 452, 464, 114 S.Ct. 2350, 129 L.Ed.2d 362 (1994) (SCALIA, J., concurring) (stating that, prior to Miranda, "voluntariness vel non was the touchstone of admissibility of confessions")*

authority to thus supersede Miranda. If Congress has such authority, § 3501's totality-of-the-circumstances approach must prevail over Miranda's requirement of warnings; if not, that section must yield to Miranda's more specific requirements.

The law in this area is clear. This Court has supervisory authority over the federal courts, and we may use that authority to prescribe rules of evidence and procedure that are binding in those tribunals.[2265] However, the power to judicially create and enforce non-constitutional "rules of procedure and evidence for the federal courts exists only in the absence of a relevant Act of Congress."[2266] Congress retains the ultimate authority to modify or set aside any judicially created rules of evidence and procedure that are not required by the Constitution.[2267]

But Congress may not legislatively supersede our decisions interpreting and applying the Constitution.[2268] This case therefore turns on whether the Miranda Court announced a constitutional rule or merely exercised its supervisory authority to regulate evidence in the absence of congressional direction. Recognizing this point, the Court of Appeals surveyed Miranda and its progeny to determine the constitutional status of the Miranda decision.[2269] Relying on the fact that we have created several exceptions to Miranda's warnings requirement and that we have repeatedly referred to the Miranda warnings as "prophylactic,"[2270] ***438** and "not themselves rights protected by the Constitution,"[2271] the Court of Appeals concluded that the protections announced in Miranda are not constitutionally required.[2272]

We disagree with the Court of Appeals' conclusion, although we concede that there is language in some of our opinions that supports the view taken by that court. But first and foremost of the factors on the other side—that Miranda is a constitutional decision—is that both Miranda and two of its companion cases applied the rule to proceedings in state courts—to wit, Arizona, California, and New York.[2273] Since that time, we have consistently applied Miranda 's rule to prosecutions arising in state courts.[2274] It is beyond dispute that we do not hold a supervisory power over the courts of the several States.[2275] With respect to proceedings in state courts, our "authority is limited to enforcing the commands of the United States Constitution."[2276] ***439**

[2265] *Carlisle v. United States, 517 U.S. 416, 426, 116 S.Ct. 1460, 134 L.Ed.2d 613 (1996)*

[2266] *Palermo v. United States, 360 U.S. 343, 353, n. 11, 79 S.Ct. 1217, 3 L.Ed.2d 1287 (1959) (citing Funk v. United States, 290 U.S. 371, 382, 54 S.Ct. 212, 78 L.Ed. 369 (1933), and Gordon v. United States, 344 U.S. 414, 418, 73 S.Ct. 369, 97 L.Ed. 447 (1953))*

[2267] *Palermo, supra, at 345–348, 79 S.Ct. 1217; Carlisle, supra, at 426, 116 S.Ct. 1460; Vance v. Terrazas, 444 U.S. 252, 265, 100 S.Ct. 540, 62 L.Ed.2d 461 (1980)*

[2268] *See, e.g., ****2333** City of Boerne v. Flores, 521 U.S. 507, 517–521, 117 S.Ct. 2157, 138 L.Ed.2d 624 (1997)*

[2269] *166 F.3d, at 687–692*

[2270] *New York v. Quarles, 467 U.S. 649, 653, 104 S.Ct. 2626, 81 L.Ed.2d 550 1984)*

[2271] *Michigan v. Tucker, 417 U.S. 433, 444, 94 S.Ct. 2357, 41 L.Ed.2d 182 (1974)*

[2272] *166 F.3d, at 687–690*

[2273] *See 384 U.S., at 491–494, 497–499*

[2274] *See, e.g., Stansbury v. California, 511 U.S. 318, 114 S.Ct. 1526, 128 L.Ed.2d 293 (1994) (per curiam); Minnick v. Mississippi, 498 U.S. 146, 111 S.Ct. 486, 112 L.Ed.2d 489 (1990); Arizona v. Roberson, 486 U.S. 675, 108 S.Ct. 2093, 100 L.Ed.2d 704 (1988); Edwards v. Arizona, 451 U.S. 477, 481–482, 101 S.Ct. 1880, 68 L.Ed.2d 378 (1981)*

[2275] *Smith v. Phillips, 455 U.S. 209, 221, 102 S.Ct. 940, 71 L.Ed.2d 78 (1982) ("Federal courts hold no supervisory authority over state judicial proceedings and may intervene only to correct wrongs of constitutional dimension"); Cicenia v. La Gay, 357 U.S. 504, 508–509, 78 S.Ct. 1297, 2 L.Ed.2d 1523 (1958)*

[2276] *Mu'Min v. Virginia, 500 U.S. 415, 422, 111 S.Ct. 1899, 114 L.Ed.2d 493 (1991). See also Harris v. Rivera, 454 U.S. 339, 344–345, 102 S.Ct. 460, 70 L.Ed.2d 530 (1981) (per curiam) (stating that "[f]ederal judges ... may not require the observance of any special procedures" in state courts "except when necessary to assure compliance with the dictates of the Federal Constitution")*

The Miranda opinion itself begins by stating that the Court granted certiorari "to explore some facets of the problems ... of applying the privilege against self-incrimination to in-custody interrogation, **2334 and to give concrete constitutional guidelines for law enforcement agencies and courts to follow."[2277] In fact, the majority opinion is replete with statements indicating that the majority thought it was announcing a constitutional rule. Indeed, the Court's ultimate conclusion was that the *440 unwarned confessions obtained in the four cases before the Court in Miranda "were obtained from the defendant under circumstances that did not meet constitutional standards for protection of the privilege."[2278]

Additional support for our conclusion that Miranda is constitutionally based is found in the Miranda Court's invitation for legislative action to protect the constitutional right against coerced self-incrimination. After discussing the "compelling pressures" inherent in custodial police interrogation, the Miranda Court concluded that, "[i]n order to combat these pressures and to permit a full opportunity to exercise the privilege against self-incrimination, the accused must be adequately and effectively apprised of his rights and the exercise of those rights must be fully honored."[2279] However, the Court emphasized that it could not foresee "the potential alternatives for protecting the privilege which might be devised by Congress or the States," and it accordingly opined that the Constitution would not preclude legislative solutions that differed from the prescribed Miranda warnings but which were "at least as effective in apprising accused persons of their right of silence and in assuring a continuous opportunity to exercise it."[2280]

*441 The Court of Appeals also relied on the fact that we have, after our Miranda **2335 decision, made exceptions from its rule in cases such as New York v. Quarles.[2281] But we have also broadened the application of the Miranda doctrine in cases such as Doyle v. Ohio,[2282] and Arizona v. Roberson.[2283] These decisions illustrate the principle—not that Miranda is not a constitutional rule—but that no constitutional rule is immutable. No court laying down a general rule can possibly foresee the various circumstances in which counsel will seek to apply it, and the sort of modifications represented by these cases are as much a normal part of constitutional law as the original decision.

The Court of Appeals also noted that in Oregon v. Elstad,[2284] we stated that "'[t]he Miranda exclusionary rule ... serves the Fifth Amendment and sweeps more broadly than the Fifth Amendment itself.'"[2285] Our decision in that case—refusing to apply the traditional "fruits" doctrine developed in Fourth Amendment cases—does not prove that Miranda is a non-constitutional decision, but simply recognizes the fact that unreasonable searches under the Fourth Amendment are different from unwarned interrogation under the Fifth Amendment.

As an alternative argument for sustaining the Court of Appeals' decision, the court-invited amicus curiae contends that the section complies with the requirement that a legislative alternative to Miranda be equally as effective in preventing coerced

[2277] *384 U.S., at 441–442, 86 S.Ct. 1602 (emphasis added)*

[2278] *Id., at 491, 86 S.Ct. 1602*

[2279] *Id., at 467, 86 S.Ct. 1602*

[2280] *Ibid.*

[2281] *467 U.S. 649, 104 S.Ct. 2626, 81 L.Ed.2d 550 (1984), and Harris v. New York, 401 U.S. 222, 91 S.Ct. 643, 28 L.Ed.2d 1 (1971). See 166 F.3d, at 672, 689–691*

[2282] *426 U.S. 610, 96 S.Ct. 2240, 49 L.Ed.2d 91 (1976)*

[2283] *486 U.S. 675, 108 S.Ct. 2093, 100 L.Ed.2d 704 (1988)*

[2284] *470 U.S. 298, 105 S.Ct. 1285, 84 L.Ed.2d 222 (1985)*

[2285] *166 F.3d, at 690 (quoting Elstad, supra, at 306, 105 S.Ct. 1285)*

confessions.[2286] ***442** We agree with the amicus 'contention that there are more remedies available for abusive police conduct than there were at the time Miranda was decided,[2287] to hold that a suspect may bring a federal cause of action under the Due Process Clause for police misconduct during custodial interrogation). But we do not agree that these additional measures supplement § 3501's protections sufficiently to meet the constitutional minimum. Miranda requires procedures that will warn a suspect in custody of his right to remain silent and which will assure the suspect that the exercise of that right will be honored.[2288] As discussed above, § 3501 explicitly eschews a requirement of pre-interrogation warnings in favor of an approach that looks to the administration of such warnings as only one factor in determining the voluntariness of a suspect's confession. The additional remedies cited by amicus do not, in our view, render them, together with § 3501, an adequate substitute for the warnings required by Miranda.

The dissent argues that it is judicial overreaching for this Court to hold § 3501 unconstitutional unless we hold that the Miranda warnings are required by the Constitution, in the sense that nothing else will suffice to satisfy constitutional requirements.[2289] But we need not go further than Miranda to decide this case. In Miranda, the Court noted that reliance on the traditional totality-of-the-circumstances test raised a risk of overlooking an involuntary custodial confession,[2290] a risk that the Court found unacceptably great when the confession is offered in the case in chief to prove guilt. The Court therefore concluded that something more ****2336** than the totality test was necessary.[2291] As discussed above, § 3501 reinstates the totality test as ***443** sufficient. Section 3501 therefore cannot be sustained if Miranda is to remain the law.

Whether or not we would agree with Miranda's reasoning and its resulting rule, were we addressing the issue in the first instance, the principles of stare decisis weigh heavily against overruling it now.[2292] While "'stare decisis is not an inexorable command,'"[2293] particularly when we are interpreting the Constitution,[2294] "even in constitutional cases, the doctrine carries such persuasive force that we have always required a departure from precedent to be supported by some 'special justification.'"[2295]

We do not think there is such justification for overruling Miranda. Miranda has become embedded in routine police practice to the point where the warnings have become part of our national culture.[2296] While we have overruled our precedents

---

[2286] *See Brief for Paul G. Cassell as Amicus Curiae 28–39.*

[2287] *See, e.g., Wilkins v. May, 872 F.2d 190, 194 (C.A.7 1989) (applying Bivens v. Six Unknown Fed. Narcotics Agents, 403 U.S. 388, 91 S.Ct. 1999, 29 L.Ed.2d 619 (1971)*

[2288] *See, e.g., 384 U.S., at 467, 86 S.Ct. 1602*

[2289] *Post, at 2341–2342, 2347–2348 (opinion of SCALIA, J.)*

[2290] *384 U.S., at 457, 86 S.Ct. 1602*

[2291] *See ibid.; see also id., at 467, 490–491, 86 S.Ct. 1602*

[2292] *See, e.g., Rhode Island v. Innis, 446 U.S. 291, 304, 100 S.Ct. 1682, 64 L.Ed.2d 297 (1980) (Burger, C. J., concurring in judgment) ("The meaning of Miranda has become reasonably clear and law enforcement practices have adjusted to its strictures; I would neither overrule Miranda, disparage it, nor extend it at this late date")*

[2293] *State Oil Co. v. Khan, 522 U.S. 3, 20, 118 S.Ct. 275, 139 L.Ed.2d 199 (1997) (quoting Payne v. Tennessee, 501 U.S. 808, 828, 111 S.Ct. 2597, 115 L.Ed.2d 720 (1991))*

[2294] *Agostini v. Felton, 521 U.S. 203, 235, 117 S.Ct. 1997, 138 L.Ed.2d 391 (1997)*

[2295] *United States v. International Business Machines Corp., 517 U.S. 843, 856, 116 S.Ct. 1793, 135 L.Ed.2d 124 (1996) (quoting Payne, supra, at 842, 111 S.Ct. 2597 (SOUTER, J., concurring), in turn quoting Arizona v. Rumsey, 467 U.S. 203, 212, 104 S.Ct. 2305, 81 L.Ed.2d 164 (1984))*

[2296] *See Mitchell v. United States, 526 U.S. 314, 331–332, 119 S.Ct. 1307, 143 L.Ed.2d 424 (1999) (SCALIA, J., dissenting) (stating that the fact that a rule has found " 'wide acceptance in the legal culture' " is "adequate reason not to overrule" it)*

when subsequent cases have undermined their doctrinal underpinnings,[2297] we do not believe that this has happened to the Miranda decision. If anything, our subsequent cases have reduced the impact of the Miranda rule on legitimate law enforcement while reaffirming the decision's core ruling that unwarned ***444** statements may not be used as evidence in the prosecution's case in chief.

The disadvantage of the Miranda rule is that statements which may be by no means involuntary, made by a defendant who is aware of his "rights," may nonetheless be excluded and a guilty defendant go free as a result. But experience suggests that the totality-of-the-circumstances test which § 3501 seeks to revive is more difficult than Miranda for law enforcement officers to conform to, and for courts to apply in a consistent manner.[2298] The requirement that Miranda warnings be given does not, of course, dispense with the voluntariness inquiry. But as we said in Berkemer v. McCarty,[2299] "[c]ases in which a defendant can make a colorable argument that a self-incriminating statement was 'compelled' despite the fact that the law enforcement authorities adhered to the dictates of Miranda are rare."[2300]

In sum, we conclude that Miranda announced a constitutional rule that Congress may not supersede legislatively. Following the rule of stare decisis, we decline to overrule Miranda ourselves. ****2337** The judgment of the Court of Appeals is therefore

Reversed.

(The dissent of Justice SCALIA, with whom Justice THOMAS joins, is omitted.)

Black Letter Law

Held that Miranda's warning-based approach to determining admissibility of statement made by accused during custodial interrogation was constitutionally based, and could not be in effect overruled by legislative act.

Betts v. Brady

62 S.Ct. 1252

Supreme Court of the United States

BETTS

v.

BRADY, Warden.

No. 837. | Argued April 13, 14, 1942. | Decided June 1, 1942.

Mr. Justice ROBERTS delivered the opinion of the Court.

The petitioner was indicted for robbery in the Circuit Court of Carroll County, Maryland. Due to lack of funds ***457** he was unable to employ counsel, and so informed the judge at his arraignment. He requested that counsel be appointed for him. The judge advised him that this could not be done as it was not the practice in Carroll

[2297] *See, e.g., Patterson v. McLean Credit Union, 491 U.S. 164, 173, 109 S.Ct. 2363, 105 L.Ed.2d 132 (1989)*

[2298] *See, e.g., Haynes v. Washington, 373 U.S., at 515, 83 S.Ct. 1336 ("The line between proper and permissible police conduct and techniques and methods offensive to due process is, at best, a difficult one to draw")*

[2299] *468 U.S. 420, 104 S.Ct. 3138, 82 L.Ed.2d 317 (1984)*

[2300] *Id., at 433, n. 20, 104 S.Ct. 3138*

County to appoint counsel for indigent defendants save in prosecutions for murder and rape.

Without waiving his asserted right to counsel the petitioner pleaded not guilty and ****1254** elected to be tried without a jury. At his request witnesses were summoned in his behalf. He cross-examined the State's witnesses and examined his own. The latter gave testimony tending to establish an alibi. Although afforded the opportunity, he did not take the witness stand. The judge found him guilty and imposed a sentence of eight years.

While serving his sentence, the petitioner filed with a judge of the Circuit Court for Washington County, Maryland, a petition for a writ of habeas corpus alleging that he had been deprived of the right to assistance of counsel guaranteed by the Fourteenth Amendment of the federal Constitution. The writ issued, the cause was heard, his contention was rejected, and he was remanded to the custody of the prison warden.

Some months later a petition for a writ of habeas corpus was presented to Hon. Carroll T. Bond, Chief Judge of the Court of Appeals of Maryland, setting up the same grounds for the prisoner's release as the former petition. The respondent answered, a hearing was afforded, at which an agreed statement of facts was offered by counsel for the parties, the evidence taken at the petitioner's trial was incorporated in the record, and the cause was argued. Judge Bond granted the writ but, for reasons set forth in an opinion, denied the relief prayed and remanded the petitioner to the respondent's custody.

The petitioner applied to this court for certiorari directed to Judge Bond. The writ was issued on account of the importance of the jurisdictional questions involved ***458** and conflicting decisions upon the constitutional question presented. In awarding the writ,[2301] we requested counsel to discuss the jurisdiction of this court, 'particularly (1) whether the decision below is that of a court within the meaning of section 237 of the Judicial Code, and (2) whether state remedies, either by appeal or by application to other judges or any other state court, have been exhausted.'

*****

Was the petitioner's conviction and sentence a deprivation of his liberty without due process of law, in violation of the Fourteenth Amendment, because of the court's refusal to appoint counsel at his request?

The Sixth Amendment of the national Constitution applies only to trials in federal courts. The due process clause of the Fourteenth Amendment does not incorporate, ***462** as such, the specific guarantees found in the Sixth Amendment although a denial by a state of rights or privileges specifically embodied in that and others of the first eight amendments may, in certain circumstances, or in connection with other elements, operate, in a given case, to deprive a litigant of due process of law in violation of the Fourteenth. Due process of law is secured against invasion by the federal Government by the Fifth Amendment and is safeguarded against state action in identical words by the Fourteenth. The phrase formulates a concept less rigid and more fluid than those envisaged in other specific and particular provisions of the Bill of Rights. Its application is less a matter of rule. Asserted denial is to be tested by an appraisal of the totality of facts in a given case. That which may, in one setting, constitute a denial of fundamental fairness, shocking to the universal sense of justice, may, in other circumstances, and in the light of other considerations, fall short of such denial. In the application of such a concept there is always the danger of falling into the habit of formulating the guarantee into a set of hard and fast rules the application of which in a given case may be to ignore the qualifying factors therein disclosed.

[2301] *315 U.S. 791, 62 S.Ct. 639, 86 L.Ed.*

The petitioner, in this instance, asks us, in effect, to apply a rule in the enforcement of the due process clause. He says the rule to be deduced from our former decisions is that, in every case, whatever the circumstances, one charged with crime, who is unable to obtain counsel, must be furnished counsel by the state. Expressions in the ***463** opinions of this court lend color to the argument, but, as the petitioner admits, none of our decisions squarely adjudicates the question now presented.

In Powell v. Alabama,[2302] ignorant and friendless negro youths, strangers in the community, without friends ****1257** or means to obtain counsel, were hurried to trial for a capital offense without effective appointment of counsel on whom the burden of preparation and trial would rest, and without adequate opportunity to consult even the counsel casually appointed to represent them. This occurred in a State whose statute law required the appointment of counsel for indigent defendants prosecuted for the offense charged. Thus the trial was conducted in disregard of every principle of fairness and in disregard of that which was declared by the law of the State a requisite of fair trial. This court held the resulting convictions were without due process of law. It said that, in the light of all the facts, the failure of the trial court to afford the defendants reasonable time and opportunity to secure counsel as a clear denial of due process. The court stated further that 'under the circumstances * * * the necessity of counsel was so vital and imperative that the failure of the trial court to make an effective appointment of counsel was likewise a denial of due process', but added: 'whether this would be so in other criminal prosecutions, or under other circumstances, we need not determine. All that it is necessary now to decide, as we do decide, is that in a capital case, where the defendant is unable to employ counsel, and is incapable adequately of making his own defense because of ignorance, feeblemindedness, illiteracy, or the like, it is the duty of the court, whether requested or not, to assign ***464** counsel for him as a necessary requisite of due process of law; * * *.'

Likewise, in Avery v. Alabama,[2303] the state law required the appointment of counsel. The claim which we felt required examination, as in the Powell case, was that the purported compliance with this requirement amounted to mere lip service. Scrutiny of the record disclosed that counsel had been appointed and the defendant had been afforded adequate opportunity to prepare his defense with the aid of counsel. We, therefore, overruled the contention that due process had been denied.

In Smith v. O'Grady,[2304] the petition for habeas corpus alleged a failure to appoint counsel but averred other facts which, if established, would prove that the trial was a mere sham and pretense, offensive to the concept of due process. There also, state law required the appointment of counsel for one on trial for the offense involved.

Those cases, which are the petitioner's chief reliance, do not rule this. The question we are now to decide is whether due process of law demands that in every criminal case, whatever the circumstances, a state must furnish counsel to an indigent defendant. Is the furnishing of counsel in all cases whatever dictated by natural, inherent, and fundamental principles of fairness? The answer to the question may be found in the common understanding of those who have lived under the Anglo-American system of law. By the Sixth Amendment the people ordained that, in all criminal prosecutions, the accused should 'enjoy the right * * * to have the Assistance of Counsel for his defense.' We have construed the provision to require appointment of counsel in all cases where a defendant is unable to procure the services of an attorney, and where the right has not been intentionally and ***465** competently waived. Though, as we have noted, the amendment lays down no rule for the conduct of the states, the question recurs whether the constraint laid by the amendment upon the

---

[2302] *287 U.S. 45, 53 S.Ct. 55, 65, 77 L.Ed. 158, 84 A.L.R. 527*

[2303] *308 U.S. 444, 60 S.Ct. 321, 84 L.Ed. 377*

[2304] *312 U.S. 329, 61 S.Ct. 572, 85 L.Ed. 859*

national courts expresses a rule so fundamental and essential to a fair trial, and so, to due process of law, that it is made obligatory upon the states by the Fourteenth Amendment. Relevant data on the subject are afforded by constitutional and statutory provisions subsisting in the colonies and the states prior to the inclusion of the Bill of Rights in the national Constitution, and in the constitutional, legislative, and judicial history of the states to the present date. These constitute the most authoritative sources for ascertaining the considered judgment of the citizens of the states upon the question.

The Constitutions of the thirteen original states, as they were at the time of federal union, exhibit great diversity in respect of the right to have counsel in criminal cases. Rhode Island had no constitutional provision on the subject until 1843, North **1258 Carolina and South Carolina had none until 1868. Virginia has never had any. Maryland, in 1776, and New York, in 1777, adopted provisions to the effect that a defendant accused of crime should be 'allowed' counsel. A constitutional mandate that the accused should have a right to be heard by himself and by his counsel was adopted by Pennsylvania in 1776, New Hampshire in 1774, by Delaware in 1782, and by Connecticut in 1818. In 1790 Massachusetts ordained that the defendant should have the right to be heard by himself or his counsel at his election. In 1798 Georgia provided that the accused might be heard by himself or counsel or both. In 1776 New Jersey guaranteed the accused the same privileges of witnesses and counsel as their prosecutors 'are or shall be entitled to.'[2305]

***466** The substance of these provisions of colonial and early state constitutions is explained by the contemporary common law. Originally in England a prisoner was not permitted to be heard by counsel upon the general issue of not guilty on any indictment for treason or felony. The practice of English judges, however, was to permit counsel to advise with a defendant as to the conduct of his case and to represent him in collateral matters and as respects questions of law arising upon the trial. In 1695 the rule was relaxed by statute to the extent of permitting one accused of treason the privilege of being heard by counsel. The rule forbidding the participation of counsel stood, however, as to indictments for felony, until 1836, when a statute accorded the right to defend by counsel against summary convictions and charges of felony. In misdemeanor cases and, after 1695, in prosecutions for treason, the rule was that the defense must be conducted either by the defendant in person or by counsel, but that both might not participate in the trial.

In the light of this common law practice, it is evident that the constitutional provisions to the effect that a defendant should be 'allowed' counsel or should have a right 'to be heard by himself and his counsel', or that he might be heard by 'either or both', at his election, were intended to do away with the rules which denied representation, in whole or in part, by counsel in criminal prosecutions, but were not aimed to compel the state to provide counsel for a defendant. At the least, such a construction by state courts and legislators can not be said to lack reasonable basis.

***467** The statutes in force in the thirteen original states at the time of the adoption of the Bill of Rights are also illuminating. It is of interest that the matter of appointment of counsel for defendants, if dealt with at all, was dealt with by statute rather than by constitutional provision. The contemporary legislation exhibits great diversity of policy.

The constitutions of all the states, presently in force, save that of Virginia, contain ****1259** provisions with respect to the assistance of counsel in criminal trials. Those of nine ***468** states may be said to embody a guarantee textually the same as that of the Sixth Amendment or of like import. In the fundamental law of most states, however, the language used indicates only that a defendant is not to be denied the privilege of representation by counsel of his choice.

[2305] *Art. 16*

In three states the guarantee, whether or not in the exact phraseology of the Sixth Amendment, has been held to require appointment in all cases where the defendant ***469** is unable to procure counsel. In six the provisions (one of which is like the Sixth Amendment) have been held not to require the appointment of counsel for indigent defendants. In eight, provisions, one of which is the same as that of the Sixth Amendment, have evidently not been viewed as requiring such appointment, since the courts have enforced statutes making appointment discretionary, or obligatory ****1260** only in prosecutions for capital offenses or felonies.

In twelve states it seems to be understood that the constitutional provision does not require appointment of ***470** counsel, since statutes of greater or less antiquity call for such appointment only in capital cases or cases of felony or other grave crime, or refer the matter to the discretion of the court. In eighteen states the statutes now require the court to appoint in all cases where defendants are unable to procure counsel. But this has not always been ***471** the statutory requirement in some of those ****1261** states. And it seems to have been assumed by many legislatures that the matter was one for regulation from time to time as deemed necessary, since laws requiring appointment in all cases have been modified to require it only in the case of certain offenses.

This material demonstrates that, in the great majority of the states, it has been the considered judgment of the people, their representatives and their courts that appointment of counsel is not a fundamental right, essential to a fair trial. On the contrary, the matter has generally been deemed one of legislative policy. In the light of this evidence we are unable to say that the concept of due process incorporated in the Fourteenth Amendment obligates the states, whatever may be their own views, to furnish counsel in every such case. Every court has power, if it deems ***472** proper, to appoint counsel where that course seems to be required in the interest of fairness.

The practice of the courts of Maryland gives point to the principle that the states should not be straight-jacketed in this respect, by a construction of the Fourteenth Amendment. Judge Bond's opinion states, and counsel at the bar confirmed the fact, that in Maryland the usual practice is for the defendant to waive a trial by jury. This the petitioner did in the present case. Such trials, as Judge Bond remarks, are much more informal than jury trials and it is obvious that the judge can much better control the course of the trial and is in a better position to see impartial justice done than when the formalities of a jury trial are involved.

In this case there was no question of the commission of a robbery. The State's case consisted of evidence identifying the petitioner as the perpetrator. The defense was an alibi. Petitioner called and examined witnesses to prove that he was at another place at the time of the commission of the offense. The simple issue was the veracity of the testimony for the State and that for the defendant. As Judge Bond says, the accused was not helpless, but was a man forty-three years old, of ordinary intelligence and ability to take care of his own interests on the trial of that narrow issue. He had once before been in a criminal court, pleaded guilty to larceny and served a sentence and was not wholly unfamiliar with criminal procedure. It is quite clear that in Maryland, if the situation had been otherwise and it had appeared that the petitioner was, for any reason, at a serious disadvantage by reason of the lack ***473** of counsel, a refusal to appoint would have resulted in the reversal of a judgment of conviction. Only recently the Court of Appeals has reversed a conviction because it was convinced on the whole record that an accused tried without counsel had been handicapped by the lack of representation.

To deduce from the due process clause a rule binding upon the states in this matter would be to impose upon them, as Judge Bond points out, a requirement without distinction ****1262** between criminal charges of different magnitude or in respect of courts of varying jurisdiction. As he says: 'Charges of small crimes tried before justices of the peace and capital charges tried in the higher courts would equally require the appointment of counsel. Presumably it would be argued that trials in the Traffic Court would require it.' And indeed it was said by petitioner's counsel both below and in this court, that as the Fourteenth Amendment extends the protection of due process to property as well as to life and liberty, if we hold with the petitioner logic would require the furnishing of counsel in civil cases involving property.

An unfair trial is offensive to the common and fundamental ideas of fairness and right, and while want of counsel in a particular case may result in a conviction lacking in such fundamental fairness, we cannot say that the amendment embodies an inexorable command that no trial for any offense, or in any court, can be fairly conducted and justice accorded a defendant who is not represented by counsel.

The judgment is affirmed.

Affirmed.

(The dissent of Mr. Justice BLACK, with whom Mr. Justice DOUGLAS and Mr. Justice MURPHY concur, is omitted.)

Black Letter Law

> Declined to identify appointment of counsel as a fundamental right. No longer good law, but historically defines the reasoning of the court prior to Gideon.

Gideon v. Wainright

83 S.Ct. 792

Supreme Court of the United States

Clarence Earl GIDEON, Petitioner,

v.

Louie L. WAINWRIGHT, Director, Division of Corrections.

No. 155. | Argued Jan. 15, 1963. | Decided March 18, 1963.

Justice BLACK delivered the opinion of the Court.

Petitioner was charged in a Florida state court with having broken and entered a poolroom with intent to commit a misdemeanor. This offense is a felony under ***337** Florida law. Appearing in court without funds and without a lawyer, petitioner asked the court to appoint counsel for him, whereupon the following colloquy took place:

> The COURT: Mr. Gideon, I am sorry, but I cannot appoint Counsel to represent you in this case. Under the laws of the State of Florida, the only time the Court can appoint Counsel to represent a Defendant is when that person is charged with a capital offense. I am sorry, but I will have to deny your request to appoint Counsel to defend you in this case.
>
> The DEFENDANT: The United States Supreme Court says I am entitled to be represented by Counsel.

Put to trial before a jury, Gideon conducted his defense about as well as could ****793** be expected from a layman. He made an opening statement to the jury, cross-examined the State's witnesses, presented witnesses in his own defense, declined to testify himself, and made a short argument 'emphasizing his innocence to the charge contained in the Information filed in this case.' The jury returned a verdict of guilty, and petitioner was sentenced to serve five years in the state prison. Later, petitioner filed in the Florida Supreme Court this habeas corpus petitioner attacking his conviction and sentence on the ground that the trial court's refusal to appoint counsel for him denied him rights 'guaranteed by the Constitution and the Bill of Rights by the United States Government.' Treating the petition for habeas corpus as properly before it, the State Supreme Court, 'upon consideration thereof' but without an opinion, denied all relief. Since 1942, when Betts v. Brady[2306] was decided by a divided ***338** Court, the problem of a defendant's federal constitutional right to counsel in a state court has been a continuing source of controversy and litigation in both state and federal courts. To give this problem another review here, we granted certiorari.[2307] Since Gideon was proceeding in forma pauperis, we appointed counsel to represent him and requested both sides to discuss in their briefs and oral arguments the following: 'Should this Court's holding in Betts v. Brady[2308] be reconsidered?'

I

The facts upon which Betts claimed that he had been unconstitutionally denied the right to have counsel appointed to assist him are strikingly like the facts upon which Gideon here bases his federal constitutional claim. Betts was indicted for robbery in a Maryland state court. On arraignment, he told the trial judge of his lack of funds to hire a lawyer and asked the court to appoint one for him. Betts was advised that it was not the practice in that county to appoint counsel for indigent defendants except in murder and rape cases. He then pleaded not guilty, had witnesses summoned, cross-examined the State's witnesses, examined his own, and chose not to testify himself. He was found guilty by the judge, sitting without a jury, and sentenced to eight years in prison. ***339** Like Gideon, Betts sought release by habeas corpus, alleging that he had been denied the right to assistance of counsel in violation of the Fourteenth Amendment. Betts was denied any relief, and on review this Court affirmed. It was held that a refusal to appoint counsel for an indigent defendant charged with a felony did not necessarily violate the Due Process Clause of the Fourteenth Amendment, which for reasons given the Court deemed to be the only applicable federal constitutional provision. The Court said:

> Asserted denial (of due process) is to be tested by an appraisal of ****794** the totality of facts in a given case. That which may, in one setting, constitute a denial of fundamental fairness, shocking to the universal sense of justice, may, in other circumstances, and in the light of other considerations, fall short of such denial.[2309]

Treating due process as 'a concept less rigid and more fluid than those envisaged in other specific and particular provisions of the Bill of Rights,' the Court held that refusal to appoint counsel under the particular facts and circumstances in the Betts case was not so 'offensive to the common and fundamental ideas of fairness' as to amount to a denial of due process. Since the facts and circumstances of the two cases are so nearly indistinguishable, we think the Betts v. Brady holding if left standing would require us to reject Gideon's claim that the Constitution guarantees him the assistance of counsel. Upon full reconsideration we conclude that Betts v. Brady should be overruled.

[2306] *316 U.S. 455, 62 S.Ct. 1252, 86 L.Ed. 1595*

[2307] *370 U.S. 908, 82 S.Ct. 1259, 8 L.Ed.2d 403*

[2308] *316 U.S. 455, 62 S.Ct. 1252, 86 L.Ed. 1595*

[2309] *316 U.S., at 462, 62 S.Ct., at 1256, 86 L.Ed. 1595*

II

The Sixth Amendment provides, 'In all criminal prosecutions, the accused shall enjoy the right * * * to have the Assistance of Counsel for his defense.' We have construed ***340** this to mean that in federal courts counsel must be provided for defendants unable to employ counsel unless the right is competently and intelligently waived. Betts argued that this right is extended to indigent defendants in state courts by the Fourteenth Amendment. In response the Court stated that, while the Sixth Amendment laid down 'no rule for the conduct of the states, the question recurs whether the constraint laid by the amendment upon the national courts expresses a rule so fundamental and essential to a fair trial, and so, to due process of law, that it is made obligatory upon the states by the Fourteenth Amendment.'[2310] In order to decide whether the Sixth Amendment's guarantee of counsel is of this fundamental nature, the Court in Betts set out and considered '(r)elevant data on the subject * * * afforded by constitutional and statutory provisions subsisting in the colonies and the states prior to the inclusion of the Bill of Rights in the national Constitution, and in the constitutional, legislative, and judicial history of the states to the present date.'[2311] On the basis of this historical data the Court concluded that 'appointment of counsel is not a fundamental right, essential to a fair trial.'[2312] It was for this reason the Betts Court refused to accept the contention that the Sixth Amendment's guarantee of counsel for indigent federal defendants was extended to or, in the words of that Court, 'made obligatory upon the states by the Fourteenth Amendment'. Plainly, had the Court concluded that appointment of counsel for an indigent criminal defendant was 'a fundamental right, essential to a fair trial,' it would have held that the Fourteenth Amendment requires appointment of counsel in a state court, just as the Sixth Amendment requires in a federal court.

***341** We think the Court in Betts had ample precedent for acknowledging that those guarantees of the Bill of Rights which are fundamental safeguards of liberty immune from federal abridgment are equally protected against state invasion by the Due Process Clause of the Fourteenth Amendment. This same principle was recognized, explained, and applied in Powell v. Alabama,[2313] a case upholding the right of counsel, where the Court held that despite sweeping language to the contrary in ****795** Hurtado v. California,[2314] the Fourteenth Amendment 'embraced' those "fundamental principles of liberty and justice which lie at the base of all our civil and political institutions," even though they had been 'specifically dealt with in another part of the Federal Constitution.'[2315] In many cases other than Powell and Betts, this Court has looked to the fundamental nature of original Bill of Rights guarantees to decide whether the Fourteenth Amendment makes them obligatory on the States. Explicitly recognized to be of this 'fundamental nature' and therefore made immune from state invasion by the Fourteenth, or some part of it, are the First Amendment's freedoms of speech, press, religion, assembly, association, and petition for redress of grievances. For the same reason, though not always in precisely the same terminology, the Court has made obligatory on the States the Fifth Amendment's command that ***342** private property shall not be taken for public use without just compensation, the Fourth Amendment's prohibition of unreasonable searches and seizures, and the Eighth's ban on cruel and unusual punishment. On the other hand, this Court in

[2310] *316 U.S., at 465, 62 S.Ct., at 1257, 86 L.Ed. 1595*

[2311] *316 U.S., at 465, 62 S.Ct., at 1257*

[2312] *316 U.S. at 471, 62 S.Ct., at 1261*

[2313] *287 U.S. 45, 53 S.Ct. 55, 77 L.Ed. 158 (1932)*

[2314] *110 U.S. 516, 4 S.Ct. 292, 28 L.Ed. 232 (1884)*

[2315] *287 U.S., at 67, 53 S.Ct., at 63, 77 L.Ed. 158*

Palko v. Connecticut,[2316] refused to hold that the Fourteenth Amendment made the double jeopardy provision of the Fifth Amendment obligatory on the States. In so refusing, however, the Court, speaking through Mr. Justice Cardozo, was careful to emphasize that 'immunities that are valid as against the federal government by force of the specific pledges of particular amendments have been found to be implicit in the concept of ordered liberty, and thus, through the Fourteenth Amendment, become valid as against the states' and that guarantees 'in their origin * * * effective against the federal government alone' had by prior cases 'been taken over from the earlier articles of the Federal Bill of Rights and brought within the Fourteenth Amendment by a process of absorption.'[2317]

We accept Betts v. Brady's assumption, based as it was on our prior cases, that a provision of the Bill of Rights which is 'fundamental and essential to a fair trial' is made obligatory upon the States by the Fourteenth Amendment. We think the Court in Betts was wrong, however, in concluding that the Sixth Amendment's guarantee of counsel is not one of these fundamental rights. Ten years before Betts v. Brady, this Court, after full consideration of all the historical data examined ****796** in Betts, had unequivocally declared that 'the right to the aid of ***343** counsel is of this fundamental character.'[2318] While the Court at the close of its Powell opinion did by its language, as this Court frequently does, limit its holding to the particular facts and circumstances of that case, its conclusions about the fundamental nature of the right to counsel are unmistakable. Several years later, in 1936, the Court reemphasized what it had said about the fundamental nature of the right to counsel in this language:

> We concluded that certain fundamental rights, safeguarded by the first eight amendments against federal action, were also safeguarded against state action by the due process of law clause of the Fourteenth Amendment, and among them the fundamental right of the accused to the aid of counsel in a criminal prosecution.[2319]

And again in 1938 this Court said: "(The assistance of counsel) is one of the safeguards of the Sixth Amendment deemed necessary to insure fundamental human rights of life and liberty. * * * The Sixth Amendment stands as a constant admonition that if the constitutional safeguards it provides be lost, justice will not 'still be done.'"[2320]

In light of these and many other prior decisions of this Court, it is not surprising that the Betts Court, when faced with the contention that 'one charged with crime, who is unable to obtain counsel, must be furnished counsel by the state,' conceded that '(e)xpressions in the opinions of this court lend color to the argument * * *'[2321] The fact is that in deciding as it did—that 'appointment of counsel is not a fundamental right, ***344** essential to a fair trial'—the Court in Betts v. Brady made an abrupt break with its own well-considered precedents. In returning to these old precedents, sounder we believe than the new, we but restore constitutional principles established to achieve a fair system of justice. Not only these precedents but also reason and reflection require us to recognize that in our adversary system of criminal justice, any person haled into court, who is too poor to hire a lawyer, cannot be as-

---

[2316] *302 U.S. 319, 58 S.Ct. 149, 82 L.Ed. 288 (1937)*

[2317] *302 U.S., at 324—325, 326, 58 S.Ct., at 152*

[2318] *Powell v. Alabama, 287 U.S. 45, 68, 53 S.Ct. 55, 63, 77 L.Ed. 158 (1932)*

[2319] *Grosjean v. American Press Co., 297 U.S. 233, 243—244, 56 S.Ct. 444, 446, 80 L.Ed. 660 (1936)*

[2320] *Johnson v. Zerbst, 304 U.S. 458, 462, 58 S.Ct. 1019, 1022, 82 L.Ed. 1461 (1938). To the same effect, see Avery v. Alabama, 308 U.S. 444, 60 S.Ct. 321, 84 L.Ed. 377 (1940), and Smith v. O'Grady, 312 U.S. 329, 61 S.Ct. 572, 85 L.Ed. 859 (1941)*

[2321] *316 U.S., at 462—463, 62 S.Ct., at 1256, 86 L.Ed. 1595*

sured a fair trial unless counsel is provided for him. This seems to us to be an obvious truth. Governments, both state and federal, quite properly spend vast sums of money to establish machinery to try defendants accused of crime. Lawyers to prosecute are everywhere deemed essential to protect the public's interest in an orderly society. Similarly, there are few defendants charged with crime, few indeed, who fail to hire the best lawyers they can get to prepare and present their defenses. That government hires lawyers to prosecute and defendants who have the money hire lawyers to defend are the strongest indications of the wide—spread belief that lawyers in criminal courts are necessities, not luxuries. The right of one charged with crime to counsel may not be deemed fundamental and essential to fair trials in some countries, but it is in ours. From the very beginning, our state and national constitutions and laws have laid great emphasis on procedural and substantive safeguards designed to assure fair trials before impartial tribunals in which every defendant stands equal before the law. This noble ideal cannot be realized if the ****797** poor man charged with crime has to face his accusers without a lawyer to assist him. A defendant's need for a lawyer is nowhere better stated than in the moving words of Mr. Justice Sutherland in Powell v. Alabama:

> The right to be heard would be, in many cases, of little avail if it did not comprehend the right to be ***345** heard by counsel. Even the intelligent and educated layman has small and sometimes no skill in the science of law. If charged with crime, he is incapable, generally, of determining for himself whether the indictment is good or bad. He is unfamiliar with the rules of evidence. Left without the aid of counsel he may be put on trial without a proper charge, and convicted upon incompetent evidence, or evidence irrelevant to the issue or otherwise inadmissible. He lacks both the skill and knowledge adequately to prepare his defense, even though he have a perfect one. He requires the guiding hand of counsel at every step in the proceedings against him. Without it, though he be not guilty, he faces the danger of conviction because he does not know how to establish his innocence.[2322]

The Court in Betts v. Brady departed from the sound wisdom upon which the Court's holding in Powell v. Alabama rested. Florida, supported by two other States, has asked that Betts v. Brady be left intact. Twenty-two States, as friends of the Court, argue that Betts was 'an anachronism when handed down' and that it should now be overruled. We agree.

The judgment is reversed and the cause is remanded to the Supreme Court of Florida for further action not inconsistent with this opinion.

Reversed.

The concurrences of Mr. Justice DOUGLAS, Mr. Justice CLARK, and Mr. Justice Harlan are omitted.)

Black Letter Law

The Court overruled *Betts v. Brady*, returning to the sound wisdom of the Court's holding in *Powell v. Alabama*. The right to counsel at trial under the Sixth Amendment was applied to all of the states through the Fourteenth Amendment.

[2322] *287 U.S., at 68—69, 53 S.Ct., at 64, 77 L.Ed. 158*

Discussion Problem:

13-1. Jason was driving home from "The Sloppy Pelican Bar" on Thursday May 14th, 2013 at 11:35 PM after completing his final exam for Criminal Procedure. The Sloppy Pelican is notorious for its college night Thursdays, and Jason's friend, Trina, owns the bar. Last week on Thursday, the Gulfview Police Department shut down the Sloppy Pelican and arrested Trina for serving alcohol to minors. Jason was also arrested for serving alcohol to minors because the police officers saw him give a 20-year-old girl a beer. They were both indicted and Trina's father, who is a licensed attorney, appeared at her arraignment and filed his Notice of Appearance for the record.

On his drive home on May 14th, two Gulfview police cruisers pulled him over. The officer approached Jason's window and said, "Well, well, well funny seeing you again." The officer continued, "Son, you were swerving in and out of the lanes on Gulfview Boulevard, now be honest with me and we won't bother you too much. How much did you have to drink tonight?" Jason confessed to having two beers but begged the officer not to arrest him and promised to do anything he said. Upon hearing Jason's plea, the officer responded, "Well, we could use your help with something. We heard Trina is still selling beers to minors. We're going to have to drop the last case against her because we don't have enough evidence, but maybe you can help us get out of that situation and we'll help you get out of this one. The officer then proceeded to ask Jason to wear a wire, follow Trina around for the rest of the night, and to try to get her to make incriminating statements. Jason agreed, was wired, and was driven back to the Sloppy Pelican.

While Trina was surprised to see Jason when he returned, the bar was swamped and she asked him to hop behind the bar and help her sell beer to these "kids." Jason assisted Trina in serving up drinks and when he saw Trina serve alcohol to a very young looking girl, he asked the girl, "Hey, how old are you for real?" The bar patron told him that she was 18 but had ID that said she was 21. The college student said, "Trina's cool with it, she knows." Jason went up to Trina and asked, "Trina, do you know that you're selling beer to 18 year olds? That girl over there, she's 18!" Trina replied, "Of course I'm selling them beer, you dummy. They pay me double and I don't ask for IDs. If they're too drunk at the end of the night, I make sure to get them a cab. It's called running a business, Jason." A few moments later, the police officers stormed into the Sloppy Pelican and again arrested Trina for serving alcohol to minors. At her trial for the charge, which carries a 2 year minimum prison sentence, her father/lawyer attempted to suppress the statements made by Trina to Jason that were subsequently overheard and recorded by the police, claiming that the use of the statement violated her Fifth Amendment and Sixth Amendment rights.

You are the state attorney assigned to prosecute Trina. How do you respond to the motion?

-Notes-

Chapter 14: Custody, Interrogation and Invocation

Berkemer v. McCarty

104 S.Ct. 3138

Supreme Court of the United States

Harry J. BERKEMER, Sheriff of Franklin County, Ohio, Petitioner

v.

Richard N. McCARTY.

No. 83-710. | Argued April 18, 1984. | Decided July 2, 1984.

Justice MARSHALL delivered the opinion of the Court.

This case presents two related questions: First, does our decision in Miranda v. Arizona, 384 U.S. 436, 86 S.Ct. 1602, 16 L.Ed.2d 694 (1966), govern the admissibility of statements made during custodial interrogation by a suspect accused of a misdemeanor traffic ***423** offense? Second, does the roadside questioning of a motorist detained pursuant to a traffic stop constitute custodial interrogation for the purposes of the doctrine enunciated in Miranda?

I

A

The parties have stipulated to the essential facts. See App. to Pet. for Cert. A–1. On the evening of March 31, 1980, Trooper Williams of the Ohio State Highway Patrol observed respondent's car weaving in and out of a lane on Interstate Highway 270. After following the car for two miles, Williams forced respondent to stop and asked him to get out of the vehicle. When respondent complied, Williams noticed that he was having difficulty standing. At that point, "Williams concluded that [respondent] would be charged with a traffic offense and, therefore, his freedom to leave the scene was terminated." Id., at A–2. However, respondent was not told that he would be taken into custody. Williams then asked respondent to perform a field sobriety test, commonly known as a "balancing test." Respondent could not do so without falling.

While still at the scene of the traffic stop, Williams asked respondent whether he had been using intoxicants. Respondent replied that "he had consumed two beers and had smoked several joints of marijuana a short time before." Ibid. Respondent's speech was slurred, and Williams had difficulty understanding him. Williams thereupon formally placed respondent under arrest ****3142** and transported him in the patrol car to the Franklin County Jail.

At the jail, respondent was given an intoxilyzer test to determine the concentration of alcohol in his blood.1 The test did not detect any alcohol whatsoever in respondent's system. Williams then resumed questioning respondent ***424** in order to obtain information for inclusion in the State Highway Patrol Alcohol Influence Report. Respondent answered affirmatively a question whether he had been drinking. When then asked if he was under the influence of alcohol, he said, "I guess, barely." Ibid. Williams next asked respondent to indicate on the form whether the marijuana he had smoked had been treated with any chemicals. In the section of the report headed "Remarks," respondent wrote, "No ang[el] dust or PCP in the pot. Rick McCarty." App. 2.

At no point in this sequence of events did Williams or anyone else tell respondent that he had a right to remain silent, to consult with an attorney, and to have an attorney appointed for him if he could not afford one.

B

Respondent was charged with operating a motor vehicle while under the influence of alcohol and/or drugs in violation of Ohio Rev.Code Ann. § 4511.19.[2323] Under Ohio law, that offense is a first-degree misdemeanor and is punishable by fine or imprisonment for up to six months.[2324] Incarceration for a minimum of three days is mandatory.[2325]

Respondent moved to exclude the various incriminating statements he had made to Trooper Williams on the ground that introduction into evidence of those statements would violate the Fifth Amendment insofar as he had not been informed of his constitutional rights prior to his interrogation. When the trial court denied the motion, respondent pleaded "no contest" and was found guilty. He was sentenced to 90 ***425** days in jail, 80 of which were suspended, and was fined $300, $100 of which were suspended.

On appeal to the Franklin County Court of Appeals, respondent renewed his constitutional claim. Relying on a prior decision by the Ohio Supreme Court, which held that the rule announced in Miranda "is not applicable to misdemeanors,"[2326] the Court of Appeals rejected respondent's argument and affirmed his conviction.[2327] The Ohio Supreme Court dismissed respondent's appeal on the ground that it failed to present a "substantial constitutional question."[2328]

Respondent then filed an action for a writ of habeas corpus in the District Court for the Southern District of Ohio. The District Court dismissed the petition, holding that "Miranda warnings do not have to be given prior to in custody interrogation of a suspect arrested for a traffic offense."[2329]

A divided panel of the Court of Appeals for the Sixth Circuit reversed, holding that ****3143** "Miranda warnings must be given to all individuals prior to custodial interrogation, whether the offense investigated be a felony or a misdemeanor traffic offense."[2330] In applying this principle to the facts of the case, the Court of Appeals distinguished between the statements made by respondent before and after his formal arrest. The post-arrest statements, the court ruled, were ***426** plainly inadmissible; because respondent was not warned of his constitutional rights prior to or "[a]t the point that Trooper Williams took [him] to the police station," his ensuing admissions could not be used against him.[2331] The court's treatment of respondent's pre-arrest statements was less clear. It eschewed a holding that "the mere stopping of a motor vehicle triggers Miranda,"[2332] but did not expressly rule that the statements made by respondent at the scene of the traffic stop could be used against him. In the penultimate paragraph of its opinion, the court asserted that "[t]he failure to advise [respondent] of his constitutional rights rendered at least some of his statements inadmissible,"[2333] suggesting that the court was uncertain as to the status of the pre-arrest con-

---

[2323] *(Supp.1983)*

[2324] *§ 2929.21 (1982).*

[2325] *§ 4511.99 (Supp.1983)*

[2326] *State v. Pyle, 19 Ohio St.2d 64, 249 N.E.2d 826 (1969), cert. denied, 396 U.S. 1007 (1970)*

[2327] *State v. McCarty, No. 80AP–680 (Mar. 10, 1981)*

[2328] *State v. McCarty, No. 81–710 (July 1, 1981)*

[2329] *McCarty v. Herdman, No. C–2–81–1118 (Dec. 11, 1981)*

[2330] *McCarty v. Herdman, 716 F.2d 361, 363 (1983) (emphasis in original)*

[2331] *Id., at 364*

[2332] *Ibid.*

[2333] *Ibid. (emphasis added)*

fessions. "Because [respondent] was convicted on inadmissible evidence," the court deemed it necessary to vacate his conviction and order the District Court to issue a writ of habeas corpus. Ibid. However, the Court of Appeals did not specify which statements, if any, could be used against respondent in a retrial.

We granted certiorari to resolve confusion in the federal and state courts regarding the applicability of our ruling in ***427** Miranda to interrogations involving minor offenses and to questioning of motorists ****3144** detained pursuant to traffic stops.[2334]

*428 II

The Fifth Amendment provides: "No person ... shall be compelled in any criminal case to be a witness against himself...." It is settled that this provision governs state as well as federal criminal proceedings.[2335]

In Miranda v. Arizona,[2336] the Court addressed the problem of how the privilege against compelled self-incrimination guaranteed by the Fifth Amendment could be protected from the coercive pressures that can be brought to bear upon a suspect in the context of custodial interrogation. The Court held:

> [T]he prosecution may not use statements, whether exculpatory or inculpatory, stemming from custodial interrogation of [a] defendant unless it demonstrates the use of procedural safeguards effective to secure the privilege against self-incrimination. By custodial interrogation, we mean questioning initiated by law enforcement officers after a person has been taken into custody or otherwise deprived of his freedom of action in any significant way. As for the procedural safeguards to be employed, unless other fully effective means are devised to inform accused persons of their right of silence and to assure a continuous opportunity to exercise it, the ***429** following measures are required. Prior to any questioning, the person must be warned that he has a right to remain silent, that any statement he does make may be used as evidence against him, and that he has a right to the presence of an attorney, either retained or appointed.[2337]

In the years since the decision in Miranda, we have frequently reaffirmed the central principle established by that case: if the police take a suspect into custody and then ask him questions without informing him of the rights enumerated above, his responses cannot be introduced into evidence to establish his guilt.[2338] ****3145**

Petitioner asks us to carve an exception out of the foregoing principle. When the police arrest a person for allegedly committing a misdemeanor traffic offense and then ask him questions without telling him his constitutional rights, petitioner argues, his responses should be admissible against him. We cannot agree.

***430** One of the principal advantages of the doctrine that suspects must be given warnings before being interrogated while in custody is the clarity of that rule.

[2334] *464 U.S. 1038, 104 S.Ct. 697, 79 L.Ed.2d 163 (1984)*

[2335] *Malloy v. Hogan, 378 U.S. 1, 8, 84 S.Ct. 1489, 1493, 12 L.Ed.2d 653 (1964)*

[2336] *384 U.S. 436, 86 S.Ct. 1602, 16 L.Ed.2d 694 (1966)*

[2337] *Id., at 444, 86 S.Ct., at 1612 (footnote omitted)*

[2338] *See, e.g., Estelle v. Smith, 451 U.S. 454, 466–467, 101 S.Ct. 1866, 1875, 68 L.Ed.2d 359 (1981); Rhode Island v. Innis, 446 U.S. 291, 297–298, 100 S.Ct. 1682, 1687–1688, 64 L.Ed.2d 297 (1980) (dictum); Orozco v. Texas, 394 U.S. 324, 326–327, 89 S.Ct. 1095, 1096–1097, 22 L.Ed.2d 311 (1969); Mathis v. United States, 391 U.S. 1, 3–5, 88 S.Ct. 1503, 1504–1505, 20 L.Ed.2d 381 (1968)*

> Miranda's holding has the virtue of informing police and prosecutors with specificity as to what they may do in conducting custodial interrogation, and of informing courts under what circumstances statements obtained during such interrogation are not admissible. This gain in specificity, which benefits the accused and the State alike, has been thought to outweigh the burdens that the decision in Miranda imposes on law enforcement agencies and the courts by requiring the suppression of trustworthy and highly probative evidence even though the confession might be voluntary under traditional Fifth Amendment analysis.[2339]

The exception to Miranda proposed by petitioner would substantially undermine this crucial advantage of the doctrine. The police often are unaware when they arrest a person whether he may have committed a misdemeanor or a felony. Consider, for example, the reasonably common situation in which the driver of a car involved in an accident is taken into custody. Under Ohio law, both driving while under the influence of intoxicants and negligent vehicular homicide are misdemeanors,[2340] while reckless vehicular homicide is a felony.[2341] When arresting a person for causing a collision, the police may not know which of these offenses he may have committed. Indeed, the nature of his offense may depend upon circumstances unknowable to the police, such as whether the suspect has previously committed ***431** a similar offense or has a criminal record of some other kind. It may even turn upon events yet to happen, such as whether a victim of the accident dies. It would be unreasonable to expect the police to make guesses as to the nature of the criminal conduct at issue before deciding how they may interrogate the suspect.

****3146** Equally importantly, the doctrinal complexities that would confront the courts if we accepted petitioner's proposal would be Byzantine. Difficult questions quickly spring to mind: For instance, investigations into seemingly minor offenses sometimes escalate gradually into investigations into more serious matters; at what point in the evolution of an affair of this sort would the police be obliged to give Miranda warnings to a suspect in custody? What evidence would be necessary to establish that an arrest for a misdemeanor offense ***432** was merely a pretext to enable the police to interrogate the suspect (in hopes of obtaining information about a felony) without providing him the safeguards prescribed by Miranda? The litigation necessary to resolve such matters would be time-consuming and disruptive of law enforcement. And the end result would be an elaborate set of rules, interlaced with exceptions and subtle distinctions, discriminating between different kinds of custodial interrogations. Neither the police nor criminal defendants would benefit from such a development.

Absent a compelling justification we surely would be unwilling so seriously to impair the simplicity and clarity of the holding of Miranda. Neither of the two arguments proffered by petitioner constitutes such a justification. Petitioner first contends that Miranda warnings are unnecessary when a suspect is questioned about a misdemeanor traffic offense, because the police have no reason to subject such a suspect to the sort of interrogation that most troubled the Court in Miranda. We cannot agree that the dangers of police abuse are so slight in this context. For example, the offense of driving while intoxicated is increasingly regarded in many jurisdictions as a very serious matter. Especially when the intoxicant at issue is a narcotic drug rather than alcohol, the police sometimes have difficulty obtaining evidence of this crime. Under such circumstances, the incentive for the police to try to induce the defendant to incriminate ***433** himself may well be substantial. Similar incentives are likely to be

[2339] *Fare v. Michael C., 442 U.S. 707, 718, 99 S.Ct. 2560, 2568, 61 L.Ed.2d 197 (1979)*

[2340] *Ohio Rev.Code Ann. §§ 2903.07, 4511.99 (Supp.1983)*

[2341] *§ 2903.06 (Supp.1983)*

present when a person is arrested for a minor offense but the police suspect that a more serious crime may have been committed. See supra, at 3146.

We do not suggest that there is any reason to think improper efforts were made in this case to induce respondent to make damaging admissions. More generally, we have no doubt that, in conducting most custodial interrogations of persons arrested for misdemeanor traffic offenses, the police behave responsibly and do not deliberately exert pressures upon the suspect to confess against his will. But the same might be said of custodial interrogations of persons arrested for felonies. The purposes of the safeguards prescribed by Miranda are to ensure that the police do not coerce or trick captive suspects into **3147 confessing, to relieve the " 'inherently compelling pressures' " generated by the custodial setting itself, " 'which work to undermine the individual's will to resist,' " and as much as possible to free courts from the task of scrutinizing individual cases to try to determine, after the fact, whether particular confessions were voluntary. Those purposes are implicated as much by in-custody questioning of persons suspected of misdemeanors as they are by questioning of persons suspected of felonies.

***434** Petitioner's second argument is that law enforcement would be more expeditious and effective in the absence of a requirement that persons arrested for traffic offenses be informed of their rights. Again, we are unpersuaded. The occasions on which the police arrest and then interrogate someone suspected only of a misdemeanor traffic offense are rare. The police are already well accustomed to giving Miranda warnings to persons taken into custody. Adherence to the principle that all suspects must be given such warnings will not significantly hamper the efforts of the police to investigate crimes.

We hold therefore that a person subjected to custodial interrogation is entitled to the benefit of the procedural safeguards enunciated in Miranda, regardless of the nature or severity of the offense of which he is suspected or for which he was arrested.

The implication of this holding is that the Court of Appeals was correct in ruling that the statements made by respondent at the County Jail were inadmissible. There can be no question that respondent was "in custody" at least as of the moment he was formally placed under arrest and instructed to get into the police car. Because he was not informed of ***435** his constitutional rights at that juncture, respondent's subsequent admissions should not have been used against him.

III

To assess the admissibility of the self-incriminating statements made by respondent prior to his formal arrest, we are obliged to address a second issue concerning the scope of our decision in Miranda: whether the roadside questioning of a motorist detained pursuant to a routine traffic stop should be considered "custodial interrogation." ****3148** Respondent urges that it should, on the ground that Miranda by its terms applies whenever "a person has been taken into custody or otherwise deprived of his freedom of action in any significant way."[2342] ***436** Petitioner contends that a holding that every detained motorist must be advised of his rights before being questioned would constitute an unwarranted extension of the Miranda doctrine.

It must be acknowledged at the outset that a traffic stop significantly curtails the "freedom of action" of the driver and the passengers, if any, of the detained vehicle. Under the law of most States, it is a crime either to ignore a policeman's signal to stop one's car or, once having stopped, to drive away without permission.[2343] Certainly few motorists would feel free either to disobey a directive to pull over or to leave the scene of a traffic stop without being told they might do so.25 Partly for

[2342] *384 U.S., at 444, 86 S.Ct., at 1612 (emphasis added); see id., at 467, 86 S.Ct., at 1624.23*

[2343] *E.g., Ohio Rev.Code Ann. § 4511.02 (1982)*

these reasons, we have long acknowledged that "stopping an automobile and detaining its occupants constitute a 'seizure' ***437** within the meaning of [the Fourth] Amendmen[t], even though the purpose of the stop is limited and the resulting detention quite brief."[2344]

However, we decline to accord talismanic power to the phrase in the Miranda opinion emphasized by respondent. Fidelity to the doctrine announced in Miranda requires that it be enforced strictly, but only ****3149** in those types of situations in which the concerns that powered the decision are implicated. Thus, we must decide whether a traffic stop exerts upon a detained person pressures that sufficiently impair his free exercise of his privilege against self-incrimination to require that he be warned of his constitutional rights.

Two features of an ordinary traffic stop mitigate the danger that a person questioned will be induced "to speak where he would not otherwise do so freely."[2345] First, detention of a motorist pursuant to a traffic stop is presumptively temporary and brief. The vast majority of roadside detentions last only a few minutes. A motorist's expectations, when he sees a policeman's light flashing behind him, are that he will be obliged to spend a short period of time answering questions and waiting while the officer checks his license and registration, that he may then be given a citation, but that in the end he most likely will be allowed to continue on his way. In this respect, ***438** questioning incident to an ordinary traffic stop is quite different from station-house interrogation, which frequently is prolonged, and in which the detainee often is aware that questioning will continue until he provides his interrogators the answers they seek.[2346]

Second, circumstances associated with the typical traffic stop are not such that the motorist feels completely at the mercy of the police. To be sure, the aura of authority surrounding an armed, uniformed officer and the knowledge that the officer has some discretion in deciding whether to issue a citation, in combination, exert some pressure on the detainee to respond to questions. But other aspects of the situation substantially offset these forces. Perhaps most importantly, the typical traffic stop is public, at least to some degree. Passersby, on foot or in other cars, witness the interaction of officer and motorist. This exposure to public view both reduces the ability of an unscrupulous policeman to use illegitimate means to elicit self-incriminating statements and diminishes the motorist's fear that, if he does not cooperate, he will be subjected to abuse. The fact that the detained motorist typically is confronted by only one or at most two policemen further mutes his sense of vulnerability. In short, the atmosphere ***439** surrounding an ordinary traffic stop is substantially less "police dominated" than that surrounding the kinds of interrogation at issue in Miranda itself,[2347] ****3150** and in the subsequent cases in which we have applied Miranda.

In both of these respects, the usual traffic stop is more analogous to a so-called "Terry stop,"[2348] than to a formal arrest. Under the Fourth Amendment, we have held, a policeman who lacks probable cause but whose "observations lead him reasonably to suspect" that a particular person has committed, is committing, or is about to commit a crime, may detain that person briefly in order to "investigate the circumstances that provoke suspicion."[2349] "[T]he stop and inquiry must be 'reasonably

---

[2344] *Delaware v. Prouse, 440 U.S. 648, 653, 99 S.Ct. 1391, 1396, 59 L.Ed.2d 660 (1979) (citations omitted)*

[2345] *Miranda v. Arizona, 384 U.S., at 467, 86 S.Ct., at 1624*

[2346] *See id., at 451, 86 S.Ct., at 1615*

[2347] *See 384 U.S., at 445, 491–498, 86 S.Ct., at 1612, 1636–1640*

[2348] *See Terry v. Ohio, 392 U.S. 1, 88 S.Ct. 1868, 20 L.Ed.2d 889 (1968)*

[2349] *United States v. Brignoni–Ponce, 422 U.S. 873, 881, 95 S.Ct. 2574, 2580, 45 L.Ed.2d 607 (1975)*

related in scope to the justification for their initiation.'"[2350] Typically, this means that the officer may ask the detainee a moderate number of questions to determine his identity and to try to obtain information confirming or dispelling the officer's suspicions. But the detainee is not obliged to respond. And, unless the detainee's answers provide the officer with probable cause to arrest him, he must then be ***440** released. The comparatively nonthreatening character of detentions of this sort explains the absence of any suggestion in our opinions that Terry stops are subject to the dictates of Miranda. The similarly non-coercive aspect of ordinary traffic stops prompts us to hold that persons temporarily detained pursuant to such stops are not "in custody" for the purposes of Miranda.

Respondent contends that to "exempt" traffic stops from the coverage of Miranda will open the way to widespread abuse. Policemen will simply delay formally arresting detained motorists, and will subject them to sustained and intimidating interrogation at the scene of their initial detention.[2351] The net result, respondent contends, will be a serious threat to the rights that the Miranda doctrine is designed to protect.

We are confident that the state of affairs projected by respondent will not come to pass. It is settled that the safeguards prescribed by Miranda become applicable as soon as a suspect's freedom of action is curtailed to a "degree associated with formal arrest."[2352] If a motorist who has been detained pursuant to a traffic stop thereafter is subjected to treatment that renders him "in custody" for practical purposes, he will be entitled to the full panoply of protections prescribed by Miranda.[2353]

****3151 *441** Admittedly, our adherence to the doctrine just recounted will mean that the police and lower courts will continue occasionally to have difficulty deciding exactly when a suspect has been taken into custody. Either a rule that Miranda applies to all traffic stops or a rule that a suspect need not be advised of his rights until he is formally placed under arrest would provide a clearer, more easily administered line. However, each of these two alternatives has drawbacks that make it unacceptable. The first would substantially impede the enforcement of the Nation's traffic laws—by compelling the police either to take the time to warn all detained motorists of their constitutional rights or to forgo use of self-incriminating statements made by those motorists—while doing little to protect citizens' Fifth Amendment rights. The second would enable the police to circumvent the constraints on custodial interrogations established by Miranda.

Turning to the case before us, we find nothing in the record that indicates that respondent should have been given Miranda warnings at any point prior to the time Trooper Williams placed him under arrest. For the reasons indicated above, we reject the contention that the initial stop of respondent's car, by itself, rendered him "in custody." And respondent has failed to demonstrate that, at any time between the initial stop and the arrest, he was subjected to restraints comparable to those associated with a formal arrest. Only a short period of time elapsed between the stop and the arrest. At no point during that interval was respondent ***442** informed that his detention would not be temporary. Although Trooper Williams apparently decided as soon as respondent stepped out of his car that respondent would be taken into custody and charged with a traffic offense, Williams never communicated his intention to respondent. A policeman's unarticulated plan has no bearing on the question whether a suspect was "in custody" at a particular time; the only relevant inquiry is

---

[2350] *Ibid. (quoting Terry v. Ohio, supra, 392 U.S., at 29, 88 S.Ct., at 1884.)*

[2351] *Cf. State v. Roberti, 293 Or. 59, 95, 644 P.2d 1104, 1125 (1982) (Linde, J., dissenting) (predicting the emergence of a rule that "a person has not been significantly deprived of freedom of action for Miranda purposes as long as he is in his own car, even if it is surrounded by several patrol cars and officers with drawn weapons"), withdrawn on rehearing, 293 Or. 236, 646 P. 2d 1341 (1982), cert. pending, No. 82–315*

[2352] *California v. Beheler, 463 U.S. 1121, 1125, 103 S.Ct. 3517, 3520, 77 L.Ed.2d 1275 (1983) (per curiam)*

[2353] *See Oregon v. Mathiason, 429 U.S. 492, 495, 97 S.Ct. 711, 714, 50 L.Ed.2d 714 (1977) (per curiam)*

how a reasonable man in the suspect's position would have understood his situation. Nor do other aspects of the interaction of Williams and respondent support the contention that respondent was exposed to "custodial interrogation" at the scene of the stop. From aught that appears in the stipulation of facts, a single police officer asked respondent a modest number of questions and requested him to perform a simple balancing test at a location visible to passing motorists. Treatment of this sort cannot fairly be characterized as the functional equivalent of formal arrest.

We conclude, in short, that respondent was not taken into custody for the purposes of Miranda until Williams arrested ****3152** him. Consequently, the statements respondent made prior to that point were admissible against him.

IV

We are left with the question of the appropriate remedy. In his brief, petitioner contends that, if we agree with the ***443** Court of Appeals that respondent's post-arrest statements should have been suppressed but conclude that respondent's pre-arrest statements were admissible, we should reverse the Court of Appeals' judgment on the ground that the state trial court's erroneous refusal to exclude the post-arrest admissions constituted "harmless error" within the meaning of Chapman v. California.[2354] Relying on Milton v. Wainwright,[2355] petitioner argues that the statements made by respondent at the police station "were merely recitations of what respondent had already admitted at the scene of the traffic arrest" and therefore were unnecessary to his conviction.[2356] We reject this proposed disposition of the case for three cumulative reasons.

First, the issue of harmless error was not presented to any of the Ohio courts, to the District Court, or to the Court of Appeals. Though, when reviewing a judgment of a federal court, we have jurisdiction to consider an issue not raised below,[2357] we are generally reluctant to do so.[2358]

Second, the admissions respondent made at the scene of the traffic stop and the statements he made at the police station were not identical. Most importantly, though respondent at the scene admitted having recently drunk beer and smoked marijuana, not until questioned at the station did he ***444** acknowledge being under the influence of intoxicants, an essential element of the crime for which he was convicted. This fact assumes significance in view of the failure of the intoxilyzer test to discern any alcohol in his blood.

Third, the case arises in a procedural posture that makes the use of harmless-error analysis especially difficult. This is not a case in which a defendant, after denial of a suppression motion, is given a full trial resulting in his conviction. Rather, after the trial court ruled that all of respondent's self-incriminating statements were admissible, respondent elected not to contest the prosecution's case against him, while preserving his objection to the denial of his pretrial motion. As a result, respondent has not yet had an opportunity to try to impeach the State's evidence or to present evidence of his own. For example, respondent alleges that, at the time of his arrest, he had an injured back and a limp and that those ailments ****3153** accounted for his difficulty getting out of the car and performing the balancing test; because he pleaded "no contest," he never had a chance to make that argument to a jury. It is difficult enough, on the basis of a complete record of a trial and the parties' contentions regarding the relative importance of each portion of the evidence presented, to deter-

---

[2354] *386 U.S. 18, 87 S.Ct. 824, 17 L.Ed.2d 705 (1967)*

[2355] *407 U.S. 371, 92 S.Ct. 2174, 33 L.Ed.2d 1 (1972)*

[2356] *Brief for Petitioner 25*

[2357] *See Carlson v. Green, 446 U.S. 14, 17, n. 2, 100 S.Ct. 1468, 1470 n. 2, 64 L.Ed.2d 15 (1980)*

[2358] *Adickes v. S.H. Kress & Co., 398 U.S. 144, 147, n. 2, 90 S.Ct. 1598, 1603 n. 2, 26 L.Ed.2d 142 (1970)*

mine whether the erroneous admission of particular material affected the outcome. Without the benefit of such a record in this case, we decline to rule that ***445** the trial court's refusal to suppress respondent's post-arrest statements "was harmless beyond a reasonable doubt."[2359]

Accordingly, the judgment of the Court of Appeals is

Affirmed.

Black Letter Law

The Court held that a motorist is in custody, for purposes of interrogation, once he is instructed to get into the police car. Additional questioning after that fact must come only after a proper Miranda warning. Statements made before that point do not require a Miranda warning and should be admissible. Roadside questioning of a motorist detained pursuant to a routine traffic stop does not constitute "custodial interrogation" for purposes of the Miranda rule.

Illinois v. Perkins

110 S.Ct. 2394

Supreme Court of the United States

ILLINOIS, Petitioner

v.

Lloyd PERKINS.

No. 88–1972. | Argued Feb. 20, 1990. | Decided June 4, 1990.

***294** Justice KENNEDY delivered the opinion of the Court.

An undercover government agent was placed in the cell of respondent Perkins, who was incarcerated on charges unrelated to the subject of the agent's investigation. Respondent made statements that implicated him in the crime that the agent sought to solve. ****2396** Respondent claims that the statements should be inadmissible because he had not been given Miranda warnings by the agent. We hold that the statements are admissible. Miranda warnings are not required when the suspect is unaware that he is speaking to a law enforcement officer and gives a voluntary statement.

I

In November 1984, Richard Stephenson was murdered in a suburb of East St. Louis, Illinois. The murder remained unsolved until March 1986, when one Donald Charlton told police that he had learned about a homicide from a fellow inmate at the Graham Correctional Facility, where Charlton had been serving a sentence for burglary. The fellow inmate was Lloyd Perkins, who is the respondent here. Charlton told police that, while at Graham, he had befriended respondent, who told him in detail about a murder that respondent had committed in East St. Louis. On hearing Charlton's account, the police recognized details of the Stephenson murder that were not well known, and so they treated Charlton's story as a credible one.

By the time the police heard Charlton's account, respondent had been released from Graham, but police traced him to a jail in Montgomery County, Illinois, where he was being held pending trial on a charge of aggravated battery, unrelated to the

[2359] *See Chapman v. California, 386 U.S., at 24, 87 S.Ct., at 828*

Stephenson murder. The police wanted to investigate further respondent's connection to the Stephenson murder, but feared that the use of an eavesdropping device would prove impracticable and unsafe. They decided instead to place an undercover agent in the cellblock with respondent and Charlton. The plan was for Charlton and undercover ***295** agent John Parisi to pose as escapees from a work release program who had been arrested in the course of a burglary. Parisi and Charlton were instructed to engage respondent in casual conversation and report anything he said about the Stephenson murder.

Parisi, using the alias "Vito Bianco," and Charlton, both clothed in jail garb, were placed in the cellblock with respondent at the Montgomery County jail. The cellblock consisted of 12 separate cells that opened onto a common room. Respondent greeted Charlton who, after a brief conversation with respondent, introduced Parisi by his alias. Parisi told respondent that he "wasn't going to do any more time" and suggested that the three of them escape. Respondent replied that the Montgomery County jail was "rinky-dink" and that they could "break out." The trio met in respondent's cell later that evening, after the other inmates were asleep, to refine their plan. Respondent said that his girlfriend could smuggle in a pistol. Charlton said: "Hey, I'm not a murderer, I'm a burglar. That's your guys' profession." After telling Charlton that he would be responsible for any murder that occurred, Parisi asked respondent if he had ever "done" anybody. Respondent said that he had and proceeded to describe at length the events of the Stephenson murder. Parisi and respondent then engaged in some casual conversation before respondent went to sleep. Parisi did not give respondent Miranda warnings before the conversations.

Respondent was charged with the Stephenson murder. Before trial, he moved to suppress the statements made to Parisi in the jail. The trial court granted the motion to suppress, and the State appealed. The Appellate Court of Illinois affirmed,[2360] holding that Miranda v. Arizona,[2361] prohibits all undercover contacts with incarcerated suspects that are reasonably likely to elicit an incriminating response.

We granted certiorari,[2362] to decide whether an undercover law enforcement officer must give ***296** Miranda warnings to an incarcerated suspect before asking him questions that may elicit an incriminating response. We now reverse.

**2397 II

In Miranda v. Arizona, supra, the Court held that the Fifth Amendment privilege against self-incrimination prohibits admitting statements given by a suspect during "custodial interrogation" without a prior warning. Custodial interrogation means "questioning initiated by law enforcement officers after a person has been taken into custody...."[2363] The warning mandated by Miranda was meant to preserve the privilege during "incommunicado interrogation of individuals in a police-dominated atmosphere."[2364] That atmosphere is said to generate "inherently compelling pressures which work to undermine the individual's will to resist and to compel him to speak where he would not otherwise do so freely."[2365] "Fidelity to the doctrine announced in Miranda requires that it be enforced strictly, but only in those types of situations in which the concerns that powered the decision are implicated."[2366]

[2360] *176 Ill.App.3d 443, 126 Ill.Dec. 8, 531 N.E.2d 141 (1988)*

[2361] *384 U.S. 436, 86 S.Ct. 1602, 16 L.Ed.2d 694 (1966)*

[2362] *493 U.S. 808, 110 S.Ct. 49, 107 L.Ed.2d 18 (1989)*

[2363] *Id. 384 U.S., at 444, 86 S.Ct., at 1612*

[2364] *Id., at 445, 86 S.Ct., at 1612*

[2365] *Id., at 467, 86 S.Ct., at 1624*

[2366] *Berkemer v. McCarty, 468 U.S. 420, 437, 104 S.Ct. 3138, 3148, 82 L.Ed.2d 317 (1984)*

Conversations between suspects and undercover agents do not implicate the concerns underlying Miranda. The essential ingredients of a "police-dominated atmosphere" and compulsion are not present when an incarcerated person speaks freely to someone whom he believes to be a fellow inmate. Coercion is determined from the perspective of the suspect.[2367] When a suspect considers himself in the company of cellmates and not officers, the coercive atmosphere is lacking.[2368] There is no empirical basis for the assumption that a suspect speaking to those whom he assumes are not officers will feel compelled to speak by the fear ***297** of reprisal for remaining silent or in the hope of more lenient treatment should he confess.

It is the premise of Miranda that the danger of coercion results from the interaction of custody and official interrogation. We reject the argument that Miranda warnings are required whenever a suspect is in custody in a technical sense and converses with someone who happens to be a government agent. Questioning by captors, who appear to control the suspect's fate, may create mutually reinforcing pressures that the Court has assumed will weaken the suspect's will, but where a suspect does not know that he is conversing with a government agent, these pressures do not exist. The state court here mistakenly assumed that because the suspect was in custody, no undercover questioning could take place. When the suspect has no reason to think that the listeners have official power over him, it should not be assumed that his words are motivated by the reaction he expects from his listeners. "[W]hen the agent carries neither badge nor gun and wears not 'police blue,' but the same prison gray" as the suspect, there is no "interplay between police interrogation and police custody."[2369]

Miranda forbids coercion, not mere strategic deception by taking advantage of a suspect's misplaced trust in one he supposes to be a fellow prisoner. As we recognized in Miranda: "[C]onfessions remain a proper element in law enforcement. Any statement given freely and voluntarily without any compelling influences is, of course, admissible in evidence."[2370] Ploys to mislead a suspect or lull him into a false sense of security that do not rise to the level of compulsion or coercion to speak are not within Miranda 's concerns.[2371] ****2398 *298**

Miranda was not meant to protect suspects from boasting about their criminal activities in front of persons whom they believe to be their cellmates. This case is illustrative. Respondent had no reason to feel that undercover agent Parisi had any legal authority to force him to answer questions or that Parisi could affect respondent's future treatment. Respondent viewed the cellmate-agent as an equal and showed no hint of being intimidated by the atmosphere of the jail. In recounting the details of the Stephenson murder, respondent was motivated solely by the desire to impress his fellow inmates. He spoke at his own peril.

The tactic employed here to elicit a voluntary confession from a suspect does not violate the Self–Incrimination Clause. We held in Hoffa v. United States,[2372] that placing an undercover agent near a suspect in order to gather incriminating information was permissible under the Fifth Amendment. In Hoffa, while petitioner Hoffa was on trial, he met often with one Partin, who, unbeknownst to Hoffa, was cooper-

---

[2367] *Rhode Island v. Innis, 446 U.S. 291, 301, 100 S.Ct. 1682, 1689, 64 L.Ed.2d 297 (1980); Berkemer v. McCarty, supra, 468 U.S., at 442, 104 S.Ct., at 3151*

[2368] *Miranda, 384 U.S., at 449, 86 S.Ct., at 1614 ("[T]he 'principal psychological factor contributing to a successful interrogation is privacy—being alone with the person under interrogation' "); id., at 445, 86 S.Ct., at 1612*

[2369] *Kamisar, Brewer v. Williams, Massiah and Miranda: What is "Interrogation"? When Does it Matter?, 67 Geo.L.J. 1, 67, 63 (1978)*

[2370] *384 U.S., at 478, 86 S.Ct., at 1629*

[2371] *Cf. Oregon v. Mathiason, 429 U.S. 492, 495–496, 97 S.Ct. 711, 714, 50 L.Ed.2d 714 (1977) (per curiam); Moran v. Burbine, 475 U.S. 412, 106 S.Ct. 1135, 89 L.Ed.2d 410 (1986) (where police fail to inform suspect of attorney's efforts to reach him, neither Miranda nor the Fifth Amendment requires suppression of prearraignment confession after voluntary waiver)*

[2372] *385 U.S. 293, 87 S.Ct. 408, 17 L.Ed.2d 374 (1966)*

ating with law enforcement officials. Partin reported to officials that Hoffa had divulged his attempts to bribe jury members. We approved using Hoffa's statements at his subsequent trial for jury tampering, on the rationale that "no claim ha[d] been or could [have been] made that [Hoffa's] incriminating statements were the product of any sort of coercion, legal or factual."[2373] In addition, we found that the fact that Partin had fooled Hoffa into thinking that Partin was a sympathetic colleague did not affect the voluntariness of the statements.[2374] The only difference between this case and Hoffa is that the suspect here was incarcerated, but ***299** detention, whether or not for the crime in question, does not warrant a presumption that the use of an undercover agent to speak with an incarcerated suspect makes any confession thus obtained involuntary.

Our decision in Mathis v. United States,[2375] is distinguishable. In Mathis, an inmate in a state prison was interviewed by an Internal Revenue Service agent about possible tax violations. No Miranda warning was given before questioning. The Court held that the suspect's incriminating statements were not admissible at his subsequent trial on tax fraud charges. The suspect in Mathis was aware that the agent was a Government official, investigating the possibility of noncompliance with the tax laws. The case before us now is different. Where the suspect does not know that he is speaking to a government agent there is no reason to assume the possibility that the suspect might feel coerced. (The bare fact of custody may not in every instance require a warning even when the suspect is aware that he is speaking to an official, but we do not have occasion to explore that issue here.)

This Court's Sixth Amendment decisions in Massiah v. United States,[2376] also do not avail respondent. We held in those cases that the government may not use an undercover agent to circumvent the Sixth Amendment right to ****2399** counsel once a suspect has been charged with the crime. After charges have been filed, the Sixth Amendment prevents the government from interfering with the accused's right to counsel.[2377] In the instant case no charges had been filed on the subject of the interrogation, and our Sixth Amendment precedents are not applicable.

Respondent can seek no help from his argument that a bright-line rule for the application of Miranda is desirable. Law enforcement officers will have little difficulty putting into practice our holding that undercover agents need not ***300** give Miranda warnings to incarcerated suspects. The use of undercover agents is a recognized law enforcement technique, often employed in the prison context to detect violence against correctional officials or inmates, as well as for the purposes served here. The interests protected by Miranda are not implicated in these cases, and the warnings are not required to safeguard the constitutional rights of inmates who make voluntary statements to undercover agents.

We hold that an undercover law enforcement officer posing as a fellow inmate need not give Miranda warnings to an incarcerated suspect before asking questions that may elicit an incriminating response. The statements at issue in this case were voluntary, and there is no federal obstacle to their admissibility at trial. We now reverse and remand for proceedings not inconsistent with our opinion.

It is so ordered.

[2373] *Id., at 304, 87 S.Ct., at 414*

[2374] *Ibid. Cf. Oregon v. Mathiason, supra, 429 U.S., at 495–496, 97 S.Ct., at 714 (officer's falsely telling suspect that suspect's fingerprints had been found at crime scene did not render interview "custodial" under Miranda); Frazier v. Cupp, 394 U.S. 731, 739, 89 S.Ct. 1420, 1424, 22 L.Ed.2d 684 (1969); Procunier v. Atchley, 400 U.S. 446, 453–454, 91 S.Ct. 485, 489, 27 L.Ed. 2d 524 (1971)*

[2375] *391 U.S. 1, 88 S.Ct. 1503, 20 L.Ed.2d 381 (1968)*

[2376] *377 U.S. 201, 84 S.Ct. 1199, 12 L.Ed.2d 246 (1964), United States v. Henry, 447 U.S. 264, 100 S.Ct. 2183, 65 L.Ed.2d 115 (1980), and Maine v. Moulton, 474 U.S. 159, 106 S.Ct. 477, 88 L.Ed.2d 481 (1985)*

[2377] *Moulton, supra, at 176, 106 S.Ct., at 487*

Black Letter Law

> The Court held that an undercover law enforcement officer posing as a fellow inmate was not required to give Miranda warnings to an incarcerated suspect before asking questions that could elicit an incriminating response. Conversations between incarcerated suspects and undercover agents posing as fellow inmates do not necessarily implicate the concerns underlying Miranda. Essential elements of a "police-dominated atmosphere" and compulsion are not present when an incarcerated person speaks freely to someone he believes to be a fellow inmate.

Rhode Island v. Innis

100 S.Ct. 1682

Supreme Court of the United States

State of RHODE ISLAND, Petitioner,

v.

Thomas J. INNIS.

No. 78–1076. | Argued Oct. 30, 1979. | Decided May 12, 1980.

Mr. Justice STEWART delivered the opinion of the Court.

In Miranda v. Arizona,[2378] the Court held that, once a defendant in custody asks to speak with a lawyer, all interrogation must cease until a lawyer is present. The issue in this case is whether the respondent was "interrogated" in violation of the standards promulgated in the Miranda opinion.

I

On the night of January 12, 1975, John Mulvaney, a Providence, R.I., taxicab driver, disappeared after being dispatched to pick up a customer. His body was discovered four days later buried in a shallow grave in Coventry, R.I. He had died from a shotgun blast aimed at the back of his head.

On January 17, 1975, shortly after midnight, the Providence police received a telephone call from Gerald Aubin, also a taxicab driver, who reported that he had just been robbed by a man wielding a sawed-off shotgun. Aubin further reported that he had dropped off his assailant near Rhode Island College in a section of Providence known as Mount Pleasant. While at the Providence police station waiting to give a statement, Aubin noticed a picture of his assailant on a bulletin board. Aubin so informed one of the police officers present. The officer prepared a photo array, and again Aubin identified a picture of the same person. That person was the respondent. Shortly thereafter, the Providence police began a search of the Mount Pleasant area.

At approximately 4:30 a. m. on the same date, Patrolman Lovell, while cruising the streets of Mount Pleasant in a patrol ***294** car, spotted the respondent standing in the street facing him. When Patrolman Lovell stopped his car, the respondent walked towards it. Patrolman Lovell then arrested the respondent, who was unarmed, and advised him of his so-called Miranda rights. While the two men waited in the patrol car for other police officers to arrive, Patrolman Lovell did not converse with the respondent other than to respond to the latter's request for a cigarette.

Within minutes, Sergeant Sears arrived at the scene of the arrest, and he also gave the respondent the Miranda warnings. Immediately thereafter, Captain Leyden and other police officers arrived. Captain Leyden advised the respondent of his Mi-

[2378] *384 U.S. 436, 474, 86 S.Ct. 1602, 1627, 16 L.Ed.2d 694*

randa rights. The respondent stated that he understood those rights and wanted to speak with a lawyer. Captain Leyden then directed that the respondent be placed in a "caged wagon," a four-door police car with a wire screen mesh between the front and rear seats, and be driven to the central police station. Three officers, Patrolmen Gleckman, Williams, and McKenna, were assigned to accompany the respondent to the central station. They placed the respondent in the vehicle and shut the doors. Captain Leyden then instructed the officers not to question the respondent or intimidate or coerce him in any way. The three officers then entered the vehicle, and it departed.

While en route to the central station, Patrolman Gleckman initiated a conversation with Patrolman McKenna concerning the missing shotgun. As Patrolman Gleckman later testified:

> A. At this point, I was talking back and forth with Patrolman McKenna stating that I frequent this area while on patrol and [that because a school for handicapped children is located nearby,] there's a lot of handicapped children running around in this area, and God ***295** forbid one of them might find a weapon with shells and they might hurt themselves.[2379]

Patrolman McKenna apparently shared his fellow officer's concern: ****1687** "A. I more or less concurred with him [Gleckman] that it was a safety factor and that we should, you know, continue to search for the weapon and try to find it."[2380] While Patrolman Williams said nothing, he overheard the conversation between the two officers: "A. He [Gleckman] said it would be too bad if the little—I believe he said a girl—would pick up the gun, maybe kill herself."[2381]

The respondent then interrupted the conversation, stating that the officers should turn the car around so he could show them where the gun was located. At this point, Patrolman McKenna radioed back to Captain Leyden that they were returning to the scene of the arrest and that the respondent would inform them of the location of the gun. At the time the respondent indicated that the officers should turn back, they had traveled no more than a mile, a trip encompassing only a few minutes.

The police vehicle then returned to the scene of the arrest where a search for the shotgun was in progress. There, Captain Leyden again advised the respondent of his Miranda rights. The respondent replied that he understood those rights but that he "wanted to get the gun out of the way because of the kids in the area in the school." The respondent then led the police to a nearby field, where he pointed out the shotgun under some rocks by the side of the road.

On March 20, 1975, a grand jury returned an indictment charging the respondent with the kidnaping, robbery, and murder of John Mulvaney. Before trial, the respondent moved to suppress the shotgun and the statements he had ***296** made to the police regarding it. After an evidentiary hearing at which the respondent elected not to testify, the trial judge found that the respondent had been "repeatedly and completely advised of his Miranda rights." He further found that it was "entirely understandable that [the officers in the police vehicle] would voice their concern [for the safety of the handicapped children] to each other." The judge then concluded that the respondent's decision to inform the police of the location of the shotgun was "a waiver, clearly, and on the basis of the evidence that I have heard, and [sic] intelligent waiver, of his [Miranda] right to remain silent." Thus, without passing on

---

[2379]

[2380] *Id., at 53*

[2381] *Id., at 59*

whether the police officers had in fact "interrogated" the respondent, the trial court sustained the admissibility of the shotgun and testimony related to its discovery. That evidence was later introduced at the respondent's trial, and the jury returned a verdict of guilty on all counts.

On appeal, the Rhode Island Supreme Court, in a 3–2 decision, set aside the respondent's conviction.[2382] Relying at least in part on this Court's decision in Brewer v. Williams,[2383] the court concluded that the respondent had invoked his Miranda right to counsel and that, contrary to Mirandas' mandate that, in the absence of counsel, all custodial interrogation then cease, the police officers in the vehicle had "interrogated" the respondent without a valid waiver of his right to counsel. It was the view of the state appellate court that, even though the police officers may have been genuinely concerned about the public safety and even though the respondent had not been addressed personally by the police officers, the respondent nonetheless had been subjected to "subtle coercion" that was the equivalent of "interrogation" within the meaning of the Miranda opinion. Moreover, contrary to the holding of the trial court, the appellate court concluded that the evidence was insufficient to support a finding of waiver. Having ***297** concluded that both the shotgun and testimony relating to its discovery were obtained in violation of the Miranda standards and therefore should not have been admitted into evidence, the Rhode Island Supreme Court held that the respondent was entitled to a new trial.

We granted certiorari to address for the first time the meaning of "interrogation" ****1688** under Miranda v. Arizona.[2384]

II

In its Miranda opinion, the Court concluded that in the context of "custodial interrogation" certain procedural safeguards are necessary to protect a defendant's Fifth and Fourteenth Amendment privilege against compulsory self-incrimination. More specifically, the Court held that "the prosecution may not use statements, whether exculpatory or inculpatory, stemming from custodial interrogation of the defendant unless it demonstrates the use of procedural safeguards effective to secure the privilege against self-incrimination."[2385] Those safeguards included the now familiar Miranda warnings—namely, that the defendant be informed "that he has the right to remain silent, that anything he says can be used against him in a court of law, that he has the right to the presence of an attorney, and that if he cannot afford an attorney one will be appointed for him prior to any questioning if he so desires"—or their equivalent.[2386]

The Court in the Miranda opinion also outlined in some detail the consequences that would result if a defendant sought to invoke those procedural safeguards. With regard to the right to the presence of counsel, the Court noted:

> Once warnings have been given, the subsequent procedure is clear. . . . If the individual states that he wants an attorney, the interrogation must cease until an attorney is present. At that time, the individual must have an opportunity to confer with the attorney and to ***298** have him present during any subsequent questioning. If the individual cannot obtain an

---

[2382] *R.I., 391 A.2d 1158*

[2383] *430 U.S. 387, 97 S.Ct. 1232, 51 L.Ed.2d 424*

[2384] *440 U.S. 934, 99 S.Ct. 1277, 59 L.Ed.2d 492*

[2385] *Id., 384 U.S., at 444, 86 S.Ct., at 1612*

[2386] *Id., at 479, 86 S.Ct., at 1630*

> attorney and he indicates that he wants one before speaking to police, they must respect his decision to remain silent.[2387]

In the present case, the parties are in agreement that the respondent was fully informed of his Miranda rights and that he invoked his Miranda right to counsel when he told Captain Leyden that he wished to consult with a lawyer. It is also uncontested that the respondent was "in custody" while being transported to the police station.

The issue, therefore, is whether the respondent was "interrogated" by the police officers in violation of the respondent's undisputed right under Miranda to remain silent until he had consulted with a lawyer. In resolving this issue, we first define the term "interrogation" under Miranda before turning to a consideration of the facts of this case.

A

The starting point for defining "interrogation" in this context is, of course, the Court's Miranda opinion. There the Court observed that "[b]y custodial interrogation, we mean questioning initiated by law enforcement officers after a person has been taken into custody or otherwise deprived of his freedom of action in any significant way."[2388] This passage and other references throughout the opinion to "questioning" might suggest that the Miranda rules were to apply only to those police interrogation practices that involve express questioning of a defendant while in custody.

***299**We do not, however, construe the Miranda opinion so narrowly. The concern of the Court in Miranda was that the "interrogation environment" created by the interplay of interrogation and custody would "subjugate the individual to the will of his examiner" and thereby undermine the privilege against compulsory self-incrimination.[2389] The police practices that evoked this concern included ****1689** several that did not involve express questioning. For example, one of the practices discussed in Miranda was the use of line-ups in which a coached witness would pick the defendant as the perpetrator. This was designed to establish that the defendant was in fact guilty as a predicate for further interrogation.[2390] A variation on this theme discussed in Miranda was the so-called "reverse line-up" in which a defendant would be identified by coached witnesses as the perpetrator of a fictitious crime, with the object of inducing him to confess to the actual crime of which he was suspected in order to escape the false prosecution.[2391] The Court in Miranda also included in its survey of interrogation practices the use of psychological ploys, such as to "posi[t]" "the guilt of the subject," to "minimize the moral seriousness of the offense," and "to cast blame on the victim or on society."[2392] It is clear that these techniques of persuasion, no less than express questioning, were thought, in a custodial setting, to amount to interrogation.

This is not to say, however, that all statements obtained by the police after a person has been taken into custody are to be considered the product of interrogation. As the Court in Miranda noted:

[2387] *Id., at 473–474, 86 S.Ct., at 1627–1628*

[2388] *Id., at 444, 86 S.Ct., at 1612 (emphasis added)*

[2389] *Id., at 457–458, 86 S.Ct., at 1619*

[2390] *Id., at 453, 86 S.Ct., at 1602*

[2391] *Ibid.*

[2392] *Id., at 450, 86 S.Ct., at 1615*

> Confessions remain a proper element in law enforcement. Any statement given freely and voluntarily without ***300** any compelling influences is, of course, admissible in evidence. The fundamental import of the privilege while an individual is in custody is not whether he is allowed to talk to the police without the benefit of warnings and counsel, but whether he can be interrogated. . . . Volunteered statements of any kind are not barred by the Fifth Amendment and their admissibility is not affected by our holding today.[2393]

It is clear therefore that the special procedural safeguards outlined in Miranda are required not where a suspect is simply taken into custody, but rather where a suspect in custody is subjected to interrogation. "Interrogation," as conceptualized in the Miranda opinion, must reflect a measure of compulsion above and beyond that inherent in custody itself.

We conclude that the Miranda safeguards come into play whenever a person in custody is subjected to either express ***301** questioning or its functional equivalent. That is to say, the term "interrogation" under Miranda refers not only to express questioning, but also to any words or actions on the part of the police (other than those normally attendant to arrest and custody) that the police should know are reasonably likely to elicit an incriminating response ****1690** from the suspect. The latter portion of this definition focuses primarily upon the perceptions of the suspect, rather than the intent of the police. This focus reflects the fact that the Miranda safeguards were designed to vest a suspect in custody with an added measure of protection against coercive police practices, without regard to objective proof of the underlying intent of the police. A practice that the police should know is reasonably likely to evoke an incriminating response from a suspect thus amounts to interrogation. But, since the police surely ***302** cannot be held accountable for the unforeseeable results of their words or actions, the definition of interrogation can extend only to words or actions on the part of police officers that they should have known were reasonably likely to elicit an incriminating response.

B

Turning to the facts of the present case, we conclude that the respondent was not "interrogated" within the meaning of Miranda. It is undisputed that the first prong of the definition of "interrogation" was not satisfied, for the conversation between Patrolmen Gleckman and McKenna included no express questioning of the respondent. Rather, that conversation was, at least in form, nothing more than a dialogue between the two officers to which no response from the respondent was invited.

Moreover, it cannot be fairly concluded that the respondent was subjected to the "functional equivalent" of questioning. It cannot be said, in short, that Patrolmen Gleckman and McKenna should have known that their conversation was reasonably likely to elicit an incriminating response from the respondent. There is nothing in the record to suggest that the officers were aware that the respondent was peculiarly susceptible to an appeal to his conscience concerning the safety of handicapped children. Nor is there anything in the ***303** record to suggest that the police knew that the respondent was unusually disoriented or upset at the time of his arrest.

****1691** The case thus boils down to whether, in the context of a brief conversation, the officers should have known that the respondent would suddenly be moved to make a self-incriminating response. Given the fact that the entire conversation appears to have consisted of no more than a few off hand remarks, we cannot say that the officers should have known that it was reasonably likely that Innis would so respond. This is not a case where the police carried on a lengthy harangue in the

[2393] *Id., at 478, 86 S.Ct., at 1630 (emphasis added)*

presence of the suspect. Nor does the record support the respondent's contention that, under the circumstances, the officers' comments were particularly "evocative." It is our view, therefore, that the respondent was not subjected by the police to words or actions that the police should have known were reasonably likely to elicit an incriminating response from him.

The Rhode Island Supreme Court erred, in short, in equating "subtle compulsion" with interrogation. That the officers' comments struck a responsive chord is readily apparent. Thus, it may be said, as the Rhode Island Supreme Court did say, that the respondent was subjected to "subtle compulsion." But that is not the end of the inquiry. It must also be established that a suspect's incriminating response was the product of words or actions on the part of the police that they should have known were reasonably likely to elicit an incriminating response. This was not established in the present case.

***304** For the reasons stated, the judgment of the Supreme Court of Rhode Island is vacated, and the case is remanded to that court for further proceedings not inconsistent with this opinion.

It is so ordered.

Mr. Justice WHITE, concurring.

I would prefer to reverse the judgment for the reasons stated in my dissenting opinion in Brewer v. Williams,[2394] but given that judgment and the Court's opinion in Brewer, I join the opinion of the Court in the present case.

Mr. CHIEF JUSTICE BURGER, concurring in the judgment.

Since the result is not inconsistent with Miranda v. Arizona,[2395] I concur in the judgment.

The meaning of Miranda has become reasonably clear and law enforcement practices have adjusted to its strictures; I would neither overrule Miranda, disparage it, nor extend it at this late date. I fear, however, that the rationale in Parts II–A and II–B, of the Court's opinion will not clarify the tension between this holding and Brewer v. Williams,[2396] and our other cases. It may introduce new elements of uncertainty; under the Court's test, a police officer, in the brief time available, apparently must evaluate the suggestibility and susceptibility of an accused.[2397] Few, if any, police officers are competent to make the kind of evaluation seemingly contemplated; even a psychiatrist asked to express an expert opinion on these aspects of a suspect in custody would very likely employ extensive questioning and observation to make the judgment now charged to police officers.

***305** Trial judges have enough difficulty discerning the boundaries and nuances flowing from post-Miranda opinions, and we do not clarify that situation today.*

(The dissent of Mr. Justice MARSHALL, with whom Mr. Justice BRENNAN joins, is omitted.)

[2394] *430 U.S. 387, 97 S.Ct. 1232, 51 L.Ed.2d 424 (1977)*

[2395] *384 U.S. 436, 86 S.Ct. 1602, 16 L.Ed.2d 694 (1966)*

[2396] *430 U.S. 387, 97 S.Ct. 1232, 51 L.Ed.2d 424 (1977)*

[2397] *See, e. g., ante, at 1690, n. 8*

Black Letter Law

> The Court held that the Miranda safeguards come into play whenever a person in custody is subjected either to express questioning or to its functional equivalent. For purposes of the Miranda rule, the term "interrogation" refers not only to express questioning but also to any words or actions on the part of the police, other than those normally attendant upon arrest and custody, that the police should know are reasonably likely to elicit an incriminating response from the suspect; the latter portion of this definition focuses primarily on the perceptions of the suspect, rather than on the intent of the police.

Edwards v. Arizona

101 S.Ct. 1880

Supreme Court of the United States

Robert EDWARDS, Petitioner,

v.

State of ARIZONA.

No. 79–5269. | Argued Nov. 5, 1980. | Decided May 18, 1981. | Rehearing Denied June 22, 1981.

Justice WHITE delivered the opinion of the Court.

We granted certiorari in this case,[2398] limited to Q 1 presented in the petition, which in relevant part was "whether the Fifth, Sixth, and Fourteenth Amendments require suppression of a post-arrest confession, which was obtained after Edwards had invoked his right to consult counsel before further interrogation ...."

I

On January 19, 1976, a sworn complaint was filed against Edwards in Arizona state court charging him with robbery, burglary, and first-degree murder. An arrest warrant was issued pursuant to the complaint, and Edwards was arrested at his home later ****1882** that same day. At the police station, he was informed of his rights as required by Miranda v. Arizona.[2399] Petitioner stated that he understood his rights, and was willing to submit to questioning. After ***479** being told that another suspect already in custody had implicated him in the crime, Edwards denied involvement and gave a taped statement presenting an alibi defense. He then sought to "make a deal." The interrogating officer told him that he wanted a statement, but that he did not have the authority to negotiate a deal. The officer provided Edwards with the telephone number of a county attorney. Petitioner made the call, but hung up after a few moments. Edwards then said: "I want an attorney before making a deal." At that point, questioning ceased and Edwards was taken to county jail.

At 9:15 the next morning, two detectives, colleagues of the officer who had interrogated Edwards the previous night, came to the jail and asked to see Edwards. When the detention officer informed Edwards that the detectives wished to speak with him, he replied that he did not want to talk to anyone. The guard told him that "he had" to talk and then took him to meet with the detectives. The officers identified themselves, stated they wanted to talk to him, and informed him of his Miranda rights. Edwards was willing to talk, but he first wanted to hear the taped statement of

[2398] *446 U.S. 950, 100 S.Ct. 2915, 64 L.Ed.2d 807 (1980)*

[2399] *384 U.S. 436, 86 S.Ct. 1602, 16 L.Ed.2d 694 (1966)*

the alleged accomplice who had implicated him. After listening to the tape for several minutes, petitioner said that he would make a statement so long as it was not tape-recorded. The detectives informed him that the recording was irrelevant since they could testify in court concerning whatever he said. Edwards replied: "I'll tell you anything you want to know, but I don't want it on tape." He thereupon implicated himself in the crime.

Prior to trial, Edwards moved to suppress his confession on the ground that his Miranda rights had been violated when the officers returned to question him after he had invoked his right to counsel. The trial court initially granted ***480** the motion to suppress, but reversed its ruling when presented with a supposedly controlling decision of a higher Arizona court. The court stated without explanation that it found Edwards' statement to be voluntary. Edwards was tried twice and convicted. Evidence concerning his confession was admitted at both trials.

On appeal, the Arizona Supreme Court held that Edwards had invoked both his right to remain silent and his right to counsel during the interrogation conducted on the night of January 19. The court then went on to determine, however, that Edwards had waived both rights during the January 20 meeting when he voluntarily gave his statement to the detectives after again being informed that he need not answer questions and that he need not answer without the advice of counsel: "The trial court's finding that the waiver and confession were voluntarily and knowingly made is upheld."

Because the use of Edwards' confession against him at his trial violated his rights under the Fifth and Fourteenth Amendments as construed in Miranda v. Arizona,[2400] ****1883** we reverse the judgment of the Arizona Supreme Court.

*481 II

In Miranda v. Arizona, the Court determined that the Fifth and Fourteenth Amendments' prohibition against compelled self-incrimination required that custodial interrogation be ***482** preceded by advice to the putative defendant that he has the right to remain silent and also the right to the presence of an attorney.[2401] The Court also indicated the procedures to be followed subsequent to the warnings. If the accused indicates that he wishes to remain silent, "the interrogation must cease." If he requests counsel, "the interrogation must cease until an attorney is present."[2402]

Miranda thus declared that an accused has a Fifth and Fourteenth Amendment right to have counsel present during custodial interrogation. Here, the critical facts as found by the Arizona Supreme Court are that Edwards asserted his right to counsel and his right to remain silent on January 19, but that the police, without furnishing him counsel, returned the next morning to confront him and as a result of the meeting secured incriminating oral admissions. Contrary to the holdings of the state courts, Edwards insists that having exercised his right on the 19th to have counsel present during interrogation, he did not validly waive that right on the 20th. For the following reasons, we agree.

First, the Arizona Supreme Court applied an erroneous standard for determining ****1884** waiver where the accused has specifically invoked his right to counsel. It is reasonably clear under our cases that waivers of counsel must not only be voluntary, but must also constitute a knowing and intelligent relinquishment or abandonment of a known right or privilege, a matter which depends in each case "upon the particular

---

[2400] *Supra.*

[2401] *384 U.S., at 479, 86 S.Ct., at 1630*

[2402] *Id., at 474, 86 S.Ct., at 1627*

facts and circumstances surrounding that case, including the background, experience, and conduct of the accused."[2403]

Considering the proceedings in the state courts in the light of this standard, we note that in denying petitioner's motion to suppress, the trial court found the admission to have been "voluntary,"[2404] without separately focusing on whether Edwards had knowingly and intelligently relinquished his right to counsel. The Arizona Supreme Court, in a section of its opinion entitled "Voluntariness of Waiver," stated that in Arizona, confessions are prima facie involuntary and that the State had the burden of showing by a preponderance of the evidence that the confession was freely and voluntarily made. The court stated that the issue of voluntariness should be determined based on the totality of the circumstances as it related to whether an accused's action was "knowing and intelligent and whether his will [was] overborne."[2405] Once the trial court determines that "the confession is voluntary, the finding will not be upset on appeal absent clear and manifest error." Ibid. The court then upheld the trial court's finding that the "waiver and confession were voluntarily and knowingly made."[2406]

In referring to the necessity to find Edwards' confession knowing and intelligent, the State Supreme Court cited Schneckloth v. Bustamonte.[2407] Yet, it is clear that Schneckloth does not control the issue presented in this case. The issue in Schneckloth was under what conditions an individual could be found to have consented to a search and thereby waived his Fourth Amendment rights. The Court declined to impose the "intentional relinquishment or abandonment of a known right or privilege" standard and required only that the consent be voluntary under the totality of the circumstances. The Court specifically noted that the right to counsel was a prime example of those rights requiring the special protection of the knowing and intelligent waiver standard,[2408] but held that "[t]he considerations ***484** that informed the Court's holding in Miranda are simply inapplicable in the present case."[2409] Schneckloth itself thus emphasized that the voluntariness of a consent or an admission on the one hand, and a knowing and intelligent waiver on the other, are discrete inquiries. Here, however sound the conclusion of the state courts as to the voluntariness of Edwards' admission may be, neither the trial court nor the Arizona Supreme Court undertook to focus on whether Edwards understood his right to counsel and intelligently and knowingly relinquished it. It is thus apparent that the decision below misunderstood the requirement for finding a valid waiver of the right to counsel, once invoked.

Second, although we have held that after initially being advised of his Miranda rights, the accused may himself validly waive his rights and respond to interrogation,[2410] the Court has strongly indicated that additional safeguards are necessary when the accused asks for counsel; and we now hold that when an accused has invoked his right to have counsel present during custodial ****1885** interrogation, a valid waiver of that right cannot be established by showing only that he responded to further police-initiated custodial interrogation even if he has been advised of his

---

[2403] *Johnson v. Zerbst, 304 U.S. 458, 464, 58 S.Ct. 1019, 1023, 82 L.Ed. 1461 (1938). See Faretta v. California, 422 U.S. 806, 835, 95 S.Ct. 2525, 2541, 45 L.Ed.2d 562 (1975); North Carolina v. Butler, 441 U.S. 369, 374–375, 99 S.Ct. 1755, 1758, 60 L.Ed.2d 286 (1979);* ****483*** *Brewer v. Williams, 430 U.S. 387, 404, 97 S.Ct. 1232, 1242, 51 L.Ed.2d 424 (1977); Fare v. Michael C., 442 U.S. 707, 724–725, 99 S.Ct. 2560, 2571–2572, 61 L.Ed.2d 197 (1979)*

[2404] *App. 3, 95*

[2405] *122 Ariz., at 212, 594 P.2d, at 78*

[2406] *Ibid.*

[2407] *412 U.S. 218, 226, 93 S.Ct. 2041, 2047, 36 L.Ed.2d 854 (1973)*

[2408] *Id., at 241, 93 S.Ct., at 2055*

[2409] *Id., at 246, 93 S.Ct., at 2057*

[2410] *See North Carolina v. Butler, supra, 441 U.S., at 372–376, 99 S.Ct., at 1757–1759*

rights. We further hold that an accused, such as Edwards, having expressed his desire to deal with the police only through counsel, is not subject to further interrogation by the authorities until counsel has been made available to ***485** him, unless the accused himself initiates further communication, exchanges, or conversations with the police.

Miranda itself indicated that the assertion of the right to counsel was a significant event and that once exercised by the accused, "the interrogation must cease until an attorney is present."[2411] Our later cases have not abandoned that view. In Michigan v. Mosley,[2412] the Court noted that Miranda had distinguished between the procedural safeguards triggered by a request to remain silent and a request for an attorney and had required that interrogation cease until an attorney was present only if the individual stated that he wanted counsel.[2413] In Fare v. Michael C., supra,[2414] the Court referred to Miranda's "rigid rule that an accused's request for an attorney is per se an invocation of his Fifth Amendment rights, requiring that all interrogation cease." And just last Term, in a case where a suspect in custody had invoked his Miranda right to counsel, the Court again referred to the "undisputed right" under Miranda to remain silent and to be free of interrogation "until he had consulted with a lawyer."[2415] We reconfirm these views and, to lend them substance, emphasize that it is inconsistent with Miranda and its progeny for the authorities, at their instance, to reinterrogate an accused in custody if he has clearly asserted his right to counsel.

In concluding that the fruits of the interrogation initiated by the police on January 20 could not be used against Edwards, we do not hold or imply that Edwards was powerless to countermand his election or that the authorities could in no event use any incriminating statements made by Edwards prior to his having access to counsel. Had Edwards initiated the meeting on January 20, nothing in the Fifth and Fourteenth Amendments would prohibit the police from merely listening to his voluntary, volunteered statements and using them against him at the trial. The Fifth Amendment right ***486** identified in Miranda is the right to have counsel present at any custodial interrogation. Absent such interrogation, there would have been no infringement of the right that Edwards invoked and there would be no occasion to determine whether there had been a valid waiver. Rhode Island v. Innis, supra, makes this sufficiently clear.[2416]

****1886** But this is not what the facts of this case show. Here, the officers conducting the interrogation on the evening of January ***487** 19 ceased interrogation when Edwards requested counsel as he had been advised he had the right to do. The Arizona Supreme Court was of the opinion that this was a sufficient invocation of his Miranda rights, and we are in accord. It is also clear that without making counsel available to Edwards, the police returned to him the next day. This was not at his suggestion or request. Indeed, Edwards informed the detention officer that he did not want to talk to anyone. At the meeting, the detectives told Edwards that they wanted to talk to him and again advised him of his Miranda rights. Edwards stated that he would talk, but what prompted this action does not appear. He listened at his own request to part of the taped statement made by one of his alleged accomplices and then made an incriminating statement, which was used against him at his trial. We think it is clear that Edwards was subjected to custodial interrogation on January 20 within the meaning of Rhode Island v. Innis,[2417] and that this occurred at the instance

[2411] *384 U.S., at 474, 86 S.Ct., at 1627*

[2412] *423 U.S. 96, 96 S.Ct. 321, 46 L.Ed.2d 313 (1975)*

[2413] *423 U.S., at 104, n. 10, 96 S.Ct., at 326, n. 10; see also id., at 109–111, 96 S.Ct., at 329–330 (White, J., concurring)*

[2414] *442 U.S., at 719, 99 S.Ct., at 2569*

[2415] *Rhode Island v. Innis, 446 U.S. 291, 298, 100 S.Ct. 1682, 1688, 64 L.Ed.2d 297 (1980)*

[2416] *446 U.S., at 298, n. 2, 100 S.Ct., at 1688, n. 2*

[2417] *supra.*

of the authorities. His statement made without having had access to counsel, did not amount to a valid waiver and hence was inadmissible.

Accordingly, the holding of the Arizona Supreme Court that Edwards had waived his right to counsel was infirm, and the judgment of that court is reversed.

So ordered.

Chief Justice BURGER, concurring in the judgment.

I concur only in the judgment because I do not agree that either any constitutional standard or the holding of Miranda v. Arizona,[2418]—as distinguished from its dicta—calls for a special rule as to how an accused in custody may waive the right to be free from interrogation. The extraordinary protections afforded a person in custody suspected of criminal conduct are not without a valid basis, but ***488** as with all "good" things they can be carried too far. The notion that any "prompting" of a person in custody is somehow evil per se has been rejected.[2419] For me, the inquiry in this setting is whether resumption of interrogation is a result of a voluntary waiver, and that inquiry should be resolved under the traditional standards established in Johnson v. Zerbst[2420]:

> ****1887** A waiver is ordinarily an intentional relinquishment or abandonment of a known right or privilege. The determination of whether there has been an intelligent waiver ... must depend, in each case, upon the particular facts and circumstances surrounding that case, including the background, experience, and conduct of the accused.[2421]

In this case, the Supreme Court of Arizona described the situation as follows: "When the detention officer told Edwards that the detectives were there to see him, he told the officer that he did not wish to speak to anyone. The officer told him that he had to."[2422]

This is enough for me, and on this record the Supreme Court of Arizona erred in holding that the resumption of interrogation was the product of a voluntary waiver, such as I found to be the situation in both Innis[2423] and Brewer v. Williams.[2424]

Justice POWELL, with whom Justice REHNQUIST joins, concurring in the result.

Although I agree that the judgment of the Arizona Supreme Court must be reversed, I do not join the Court's opinion because I am not sure what it means.

***489** I can agree with much of the opinion. It states the settled rule:

> It is reasonably clear under our cases that waivers of counsel must not only be voluntary, but must also constitute a knowing and intelligent relinquishment or abandonment of a known right or privilege, a matter which depends in each case 'upon the particular facts and circumstances

---

[2418] *384 U.S. 436, 86 S.Ct. 1602, 16 L.Ed.2d 694 (1966)*

[2419] *Rhode Island v. Innis, 446 U.S. 291, 100 S.Ct. 1682, 64 L.Ed.2d 297 (1980)*

[2420] *304 U.S. 458, 464, 58 S.Ct. 1019, 1023, 82 L.Ed. 1461 (1938)*

[2421] *Accord, e. g., Fare v. Michael C., 442 U.S. 707, 99 S.Ct. 2560, 61 L.Ed.2d 197 (1979); North Carolina v. Butler, 441 U.S. 369, 99 S.Ct. 1755, 60 L.Ed.2d 286 (1979)*

[2422] *122 Ariz. 206, 209, 594 P.2d 72, 75 (1979) (emphasis added)*

[2423] *Supra, 446 U.S., at 304, 100 S.Ct., at 1691 (concurring opinion)*

[2424] *430 U.S. 387, 417–418, 97 S.Ct. 1232, 1248–1249, 51 L.Ed.2d 424 (1977) (dissenting opinion)*

> surrounding that case, including the background, experience and conduct of the accused.[2425]

I have thought it settled law, as these cases tell us, that one accused of crime may waive any of the constitutional safeguards—including the right to remain silent, to jury trial, to call witnesses, to cross-examine one's accusers, to testify in one's own behalf, and—of course—to have counsel. Whatever the right, the standard for waiver is whether the actor fully understands the right in question and voluntarily intends to relinquish it.

In its opinion today, however, the Court—after reiterating the familiar principles of waiver—goes on to say:

> We further hold that an accused, such as Edwards, having expressed his desire to deal with the police only through counsel, is not subject to further interrogation by the authorities until counsel has been made available to him, unless the accused [has] himself initiate[d] further communication, exchanges, or conversations with the police.[2426]

In view of the emphasis placed on "initiation,"[2427] I find the Court's opinion unclear. If read to create a new per se rule, requiring a threshold inquiry ***490** as to precisely who opened any conversation between an accused and state officials, I cannot agree. I would not superimpose a new element of proof on the established doctrine of waiver of counsel.

Perhaps the Court's opinion can be read as not departing from established doctrine. Accepting the formulation quoted above, two questions are identifiable: (i) was there in fact "interrogation,"[2428] ****1888** and (ii) did the police "initiate" it? Each of these questions is, of course, relevant to the admissibility of a confession. In this case, for example, it is clear that Edwards was taken from his cell against his will and subjected to renewed interrogation. Whether this is described as police-"initiated" interrogation or in some other way, it clearly was questioning under circumstances incompatible with a voluntary waiver of the fundamental right to counsel.

But few cases will be as clear as this one. Communications between police and a suspect in custody are common-place. It is useful to contrast the circumstances of this case with typical, and permissible, custodial communications between police and a suspect who has asked for counsel. For example, police do not impermissibly "initiate" renewed interrogation by engaging in routine conversations with suspects about unrelated matters. And police legitimately may inquire whether a suspect has changed his mind about speaking to them without an attorney.[2429] It is not unusual for a person in custody who previously has expressed an unwillingness to talk or a desire to have a lawyer, to change his mind and even welcome an opportunity to talk. Nothing in the Constitution erects obstacles that preclude police from ascertaining whether a suspect has reconsidered his original decision. As Justice WHITE has observed, this Court consistently has "rejected any paternalistic ***491** rule protecting a

---

[2425] *Johnson v. Zerbst, 304 U.S. 458, 464 [58 S.Ct. 1019, 1023, 82 L.Ed. 1461] (1938). Faretta v. California, 422 U.S. 806, 835 [95 S.Ct. 2525, 2541, 45 L.Ed.2d 562] (1975); North Carolina v. Butler, 441 U.S. 369, 374–375 [99 S.Ct. 1755, 1758, 60 L.Ed. 2d 286] (1979); Brewer v. Williams, 430 U.S. 387, 404 [97 S.Ct. 1232, 1242, 51 L.Ed.2d 424] (1977); Fare v. Michael C., 442 U.S. 707, 724–725 [99 S.Ct. 2560, 2571–2572, 61 L.Ed.2d 197] (1979)." Ante, at 1883–1884*

[2426] *Ante, at 1884–1885 (emphasis added)*

[2427] *See also ante, at 1885, n. 9*

[2428] *see Rhode Island v. Innis, 446 U.S. 291, 100 S.Ct. 1682, 64 L.Ed.2d 297 (1980)*

[2429] *E.g., State v. Turner, 32 Or.App. 61, 65, 573 P.2d 326, 327 (1978); see State v. Crisler, 285 N.W.2d 679, 682 (Minn.1979); State v. Marcum, 24 Wash.App. 441, 445–446, 601 P.2d 975, 978 (1979)*

defendant from his intelligent and voluntary decisions about his own criminal case."[2430]

In sum, once warnings have been given and the right to counsel has been invoked, the relevant inquiry—whether the suspect now desires to talk to police without counsel—is a question of fact to be determined in light of all of the circumstances. Who "initiated" a conversation may be relevant to the question of waiver, but it is not the sine qua non to the inquiry. The ultimate question is whether there was a free and knowing waiver of counsel before interrogation commenced.

If the Court's opinion does nothing more than restate these principles, I am in agreement with it. I hesitate to join the opinion only because of what appears to be an undue and undefined, emphasis on a single element: "initiation." As Justice WHITE has noted, the Court in Miranda v. Arizona,[2431] ***492** imposed a general prophylactic rule that is not manifestly required by anything in the text of the Constitution.[2432] ****1889** Miranda itself recognized, moreover, that counsel's assistance can be waived.[2433] Waiver always has been evaluated under the general formulation of the Zerbst standard quoted above. My concern is that the Court's opinion today may be read as "constitutionalizing" not the generalized Zerbst standard but a single element of fact among the various facts that may be relevant to determining whether there has been a valid waiver.

Black Letter Law

> The Court focused on the applicable standard, finding that the state courts erred by focusing on the voluntariness of the confession rather than on whether the defendant understood his right to counsel and intelligently and knowingly relinquished it.
>
> A valid waiver of invocation of the right must not only be voluntary, but must also constitute a knowing and intelligent relinquishment or abandonment of a known right or privilege, a matter which depends in each case upon particular facts and circumstances surrounding that case, including background, experience, and conduct of the accused.
>
> Once an accused has expressed his desire to deal with police only through counsel, he is not to be subjected to further interrogation until counsel has been made available to him unless accused himself initiates further communications with police.

Michigan v. Mosley

96 S.Ct. 321

Supreme Court of the United States

State of MICHIGAN, Petitioner,

v.

Richard Bert MOSLEY.

No. 74-653. | Argued Oct. 6, 1975. | Decided Dec. 9, 1975.

2430 *Michigan v. Mosley, 423 U.S. 96, 109, 96 S.Ct. 321, 329, 46 L.Ed.2d 313 (1975) (WHITE, J., concurring in result)*

2431 *384 U.S. 436, 86 S.Ct. 1602, 16 L.Ed.2d 694 (1965)*

2432 *Id., at 526, 86 S.Ct., at 1654 (WHITE, J., dissenting); see Michigan v. Tucker, 417 U.S. 433, 443–444, 94 S.Ct. 2357, 2363, 41 L.Ed.2d 182 (1974)*

2433 *384 U.S., at 475, 86 S.Ct., at 1628 (opinion of Warren, C. J.)*

***97** Mr. Justice STEWART delivered the opinion of the Court.

The respondent, Richard Bert Mosley, was arrested in Detroit, Mich., in the early afternoon of April 8, 1971, in connection with robberies that had recently occurred at the Blue Goose Bar and the White Tower Restaurant on that city's lower east side. The arresting officer, Detective James Cowie of the Armed Robbery Section of the Detroit Police Department, was acting on a tip implicating Mosley and three other men in the robberies. After effecting the arrest, Detective Cowie brought Mosley to the Robbery, Breaking and Entering Bureau of the Police Department, located on the fourth floor of the departmental headquarters building. The officer advised Mosley of his rights under this Court's decision in Miranda v. Arizona,[2434] and had him read and sign the department's constitutional rights notification certificate. After filling out the necessary arrest papers, Cowie began questioning Mosley about the robbery of the White Tower Restaurant. When Mosley said he did not want to answer any questions about the robberies, Cowie promptly ceased the interrogation. The completion of the arrest papers and the questioning of Mosley together took approximately 20 minutes. At no time during the questioning did Mosley indicate a desire to consult with a lawyer, and there is no claim that the procedures followed to this point did not fully comply with the strictures of the Miranda opinion. Mosley was then taken to a ninth-floor cell block.

Shortly after 6 p. m., Detective Hill of the Detroit ***98** Police Department Homicide Bureau brought Mosley from the cell block to the fifth-floor office of the Homicide Bureau for questioning about the fatal shooting of a man named Leroy Williams. ****324** Williams had been killed on January 9, 1971, during a holdup attempt outside the 101 Ranch Bar in Detroit. Mosley had not been arrested on this charge or interrogated about it by Detective Cowie. Before questioning Mosley about this homicide, Detective Hill carefully advised him of his "Miranda rights." Mosley read the notification form both silently and aloud, and Detective Hill then read and explained the warnings to him and had him sign the form. Mosley at first denied any involvement in the Williams murder, but after the officer told him that Anthony Smith had confessed to participating in the slaying and had named him as the "shooter," Mosley made a statement implicating himself in the homicide. The interrogation by Detective Hill lasted approximately 15 minutes, and at no time during its course did Mosley ask to consult with a lawyer or indicate that he did not want to discuss the homicide. In short, there is no claim that the procedures followed during Detective Hill's interrogation of Mosley, standing alone, did not fully comply with the strictures of the Miranda opinion.

Mosley was subsequently charged in a one-count information with first-degree murder. Before the trial he moved to suppress his incriminating statement on a number of grounds, among them the claim that under the doctrine of the Miranda case it was constitutionally ***99** impermissible for Detective Hill to question him about the Williams murder after he had told Detective Cowie that he did not want to answer any questions about the robberies. The trial court denied the motion to suppress after an evidentiary hearing, and the incriminating statement was subsequently introduced in evidence against Mosley at his trial. The jury convicted Mosley of first-degree murder, and the court imposed a mandatory sentence of life imprisonment.

On appeal to the Michigan Court of Appeals, Mosley renewed his previous objections to the use of his incriminating statement in evidence. The appellate court reversed the judgment of conviction, holding that Detective Hill's interrogation of Mosley had been a per se violation of the Miranda doctrine. Accordingly, without reaching Mosley's other contentions, the Court remanded the case for a new trial

---

[2434] *384 U.S. 436, 86 S.Ct. 1602, 16 L.Ed.2d 694*

with instructions that Mosley's statement be suppressed as evidence.[2435] After further appeal was denied by the Michigan Supreme Court,[2436] the State filed a petition for certiorari here. We granted the writ because of the important constitutional question presented.[2437]

In the Miranda case this Court promulgated a set of safeguards to protect the there-delineated constitutional rights of persons subjected to custodial police interrogation. In sum, the Court held in that case that unless law enforcement officers give certain specified warnings before ***100** questioning a person in custody,6 and follow certain specified procedures during the course of any subsequent interrogation, any statement made by the person in custody cannot over his objection be admitted in ****325** evidence against him as a defendant at trial, even though the statement may in fact be wholly voluntary.[2438]

Neither party in the present case challenges the continuing validity of the Miranda decision, or of any of the so-called guidelines it established to protect what the Court there said was a person's constitutional privilege against compulsory self-incrimination. The issue in this case, rather, is whether the conduct of the Detroit police that led to Mosley's incriminating statement did in fact violate the Miranda "guidelines," so as to render the statement inadmissible in evidence against Mosley at his trial. Resolution of the question turns almost entirely on the interpretation of a single passage in the Miranda opinion, upon which the Michigan appellate court relied in finding a per se violation of Miranda:

> Once warnings have been given, the subsequent procedure is clear. If the individual indicates in any manner, at any time prior to or during questioning, that he wishes to remain silent, the interrogation must cease. At this point he has shown that he intends to exercise his Fifth Amendment privilege; any statement taken after the person invokes his privilege cannot be other than the product of compulsion, subtle or otherwise. Without the right to cut off questioning, the setting of in-custody ***101** interrogation operates on the individual to overcome free choice in producing a statement after the privilege has been once invoked.[2439]

This passage states that "the interrogation must cease" when the person in custody indicates that "he wishes to remain silent." It does not state under what circumstances, if any, a resumption of questioning is permissible. The passage could be literally read to mean that ***102** a person who has invoked his "right to silence" can never again be subjected to custodial interrogation by any police officer at any time or place on any subject. Another possible construction of the passage would characterize "any statement taken after the person invokes his privilege" as "the product of compulsion" and would therefore mandate its exclusion from evidence, even if it were volunteered by the person in custody without any further interrogation whatever. Or the passage could be interpreted to require only the immediate cessation of questioning, ****326** and to permit a resumption of interrogation after a momentary respite.

It is evident that any of these possible literal interpretations would lead to absurd and unintended results. To permit the continuation of custodial interrogation after a momentary cessation would clearly frustrate the purposes of Miranda by allowing

[2435] *51 Mich.App. 105, 214 N.W.2d 564*

[2436] *392 Mich. 764*

[2437] *419 U.S. 1119, 95 S.Ct. 801, 42 L.Ed.2d 819*

[2438] *See Michigan v. Tucker, 417 U.S. 433, 443, 94 S.Ct. 2357, 2363, 41 L.Ed.2d 182*

[2439] *384 U.S., at 473-474, 86 S.Ct., at 1627*

repeated rounds of questioning to undermine the will of the person being questioned. At the other extreme, a blanket prohibition against the taking of voluntary statements or a permanent immunity from further interrogation, regardless of the circumstances, would transform the Miranda safeguards into wholly irrational obstacles to legitimate police investigative activity, and deprive suspects of an opportunity to make informed and intelligent assessments of their interests. Clearly, therefore, neither this passage nor any other passage in the Miranda opinion can sensibly be read to create a per se proscription of indefinite duration upon any further questioning by any ***103** police officer on any subject, once the person in custody has indicated a desire to remain silent.

A reasonable and faithful interpretation of the Miranda opinion must rest on the intention of the Court in that case to adopt "fully effective means . . . to notify the person of his right of silence and to assure that the exercise of the right will be scrupulously honored . . . ."[2440] The critical safeguard identified in the passage at issue is a person's "right to cut off questioning."[2441] Through the exercise of his option to terminate questioning he can control the time at ***104** which questioning occurs, the subjects discussed, and the duration of the interrogation. The requirement that law enforcement authorities must respect a person's exercise of that option counteracts the coercive pressures of the custodial setting. We therefore conclude that the admissibility of statements obtained after the person in custody has decided to remain silent depends under Miranda on whether his "right to cut off questioning" was "scrupulously honored.

A review of the circumstances leading to Mosley's confession reveals that his ****327** "right to cut off questioning" was fully respected in this case. Before his initial interrogation, Mosley was carefully advised that he was under no obligation to answer any questions and could remain silent if he wished. He orally acknowledged that he understood the Miranda warnings and then signed a printed notification-of-rights form. When Mosley stated that he did not want to discuss the robberies, Detective Cowie immediately ceased the interrogation and did not try either to resume the questioning or in any way to persuade Mosley to reconsider his position. After an interval of more than two hours, Mosley was questioned by another police officer at another location about an unrelated holdup murder. He was given full and complete Miranda warnings at the outset of the second interrogation. He was thus reminded again that he could remain silent and could consult with a lawyer, ***105** and was carefully given a full and fair opportunity to exercise these options. The subsequent questioning did not undercut Mosley's previous decision not to answer Detective Cowie's inquiries. Detective Hill did not resume the interrogation about the White Tower Restaurant robbery or inquire about the Blue Goose Bar robbery, but instead focused exclusively on the Leroy Williams homicide, a crime different in nature and in time and place of occurrence from the robberies for which Mosley had been arrested and interrogated by Detective Cowie. Although it is not clear from the record how much Detective Hill knew about the earlier interrogation, his questioning of Mosley about an unrelated homicide was quite consistent with a reasonable interpretation of Mosley's earlier refusal to answer any questions about the robberies.

This is not a case, therefore, where the police failed to honor a decision of a person in custody to cut off questioning, either by refusing to discontinue the interrogation upon request or by persisting in repeated efforts to ***106** wear down his resistance and make him change his mind. In contrast to such practices, the police here immediately ceased the interrogation, resumed questioning only after the passage of a significant period of time and the provision of a fresh set of warnings, and restricted the second interrogation to a crime that had not been a subject of the earlier interrogation.

[2440] *384 U.S., at 479, 86 S.Ct., at 1630*

[2441] *Id., at 474, 86 S.Ct., at 1627*

The Michigan Court of Appeals viewed this case as factually similar to Westover v. United States,[2442] a companion case to Miranda. But the controlling facts of the two cases are strikingly different.

In Westover, the petitioner was arrested by the Kansas City police at 9:45 p. m. and taken to the police station. Without giving any advisory warnings of any kind to Westover, the police questioned him that night and throughout the next morning about various local robberies. At noon, three FBI agents took over, gave advisory warnings to Westover, and proceeded to question him about two California bank robberies. After two hours of questioning, the petitioner confessed to the California crimes. The Court held that the confession obtained by the FBI was inadmissible because the interrogation leading to the petitioner's statement followed on the heels of prolonged questioning that was commenced and continued ****328** by the Kansas City police without preliminary warnings to Westover of any kind. The Court found that "the federal authorities were the beneficiaries of the pressure applied by the local in-custody interrogation" and that the belated warnings given by the federal officers were "not sufficient to protect" Westover because from his point of view "the warnings came at the end of the interrogation process."[2443]

Here, by contrast, the police gave full "Miranda warnings" to Mosley at the very outset of each interrogation, subjected him to only a brief period of initial questioning, ***107** and suspended questioning entirely for a significant period before beginning the interrogation that led to his incriminating statement. The cardinal fact of Westover the failure of the police officers to give any warnings whatever to the person in their custody before embarking on an intense and prolonged interrogation of him was simply not present in this case. The Michigan Court of Appeals was mistaken, therefore, in believing that Detective Hill's questioning of Mosley was "not permitted" by the Westover decision.[2444]

For these reasons, we conclude that the admission in evidence of Mosley's incriminating statement did not violate the principles of Miranda v. Arizona. Accordingly, the judgment of the Michigan Court of Appeals is vacated, and the case is remanded to that court for further proceedings not inconsistent with this opinion.

It is so ordered.

Judgment vacated and case remanded.

Black Letter Law

The Court held that under the Miranda rule, the admissibility of statements obtained after the person in custody has exercised his right to remain silent depends on whether his "right to cut off questioning" was scrupulously honored. The Court recognized that Miranda does not require all subsequent questioning be undertaken only in the presence of counsel. Admissibility of statements obtained after a person in custody has exercised his right to remain silent depends on whether his "right to cut off questioning" was scrupulously honored; exercise of right to terminate interrogation does not bring forth a per se proscription of indefinite duration on any further questioning by any police officer on any subject.

[2442] *384 U.S. 436, 86 S.Ct. 1602, 16 L.Ed.2d 694*

[2443] *Id., at 496-497, 86 S.Ct., at 1639*

[2444] *51 Mich.App., at 108, 214 N.W.2d, at 566*

Minnick v. Mississippi

111 S.Ct. 486

Supreme Court of the United States

Robert S. MINNICK, Petitioner

v.

MISSISSIPPI.

No. 89–6332. | Argued Oct. 3, 1990. | Decided Dec. 3, 1990.

Justice KENNEDY delivered the opinion of the Court.

To protect the privilege against self-incrimination guaranteed by the Fifth Amendment, we have held that the police must terminate interrogation of an accused in custody if the accused requests the assistance of counsel.[2445] We reinforced the protections of Miranda in Edwards v. Arizona,[2446] which held that once the accused requests counsel, officials may not reinitiate questioning "until counsel has been made available" to him. The issue in the case before us is whether Edwards' protection ceases once the suspect has consulted with an attorney.

***148** Petitioner Robert Minnick and fellow prisoner James Dyess escaped from a county jail in Mississippi and, a day later, broke into a mobile home in search of weapons. In the course of the burglary they were interrupted by the arrival of the trailer's owner, Ellis Thomas, accompanied by Lamar Lafferty and Lafferty's infant son. Dyess and Minnick used the stolen weapons to kill Thomas and the senior Lafferty. Minnick's story is that Dyess murdered one victim and forced Minnick to shoot the other. Before the escapees could get away, two young women arrived at the mobile home. They were held at gunpoint, then bound hand and foot. Dyess and Minnick fled in Thomas' truck, abandoning the vehicle in New Orleans. The fugitives continued to Mexico, where they fought, and Minnick then proceeded alone to California. Minnick was arrested in Lemon Grove, California, on a Mississippi warrant, some four months after the murders.

The confession at issue here resulted from the last interrogation of Minnick while he was held in the San Diego jail, but we first recount the events which preceded it. Minnick was arrested on Friday, August 22, 1986. Petitioner testified that he was mistreated by local police during and after the arrest. The day following the arrest, Saturday, two Federal Bureau of Investigation (FBI) agents came to the jail to interview him. Petitioner testified that he refused to go to the interview, but was told he would "have to go down or else."[2447] The FBI report indicates that the agents read petitioner his Miranda warnings, and that he acknowledged he understood his rights. He refused to sign a rights waiver form, however, and said he would not answer "very many" questions. Minnick told the agents about the jailbreak and the flight, and described how Dyess threatened and beat him. Early in the interview, he sobbed "[i]t was my life or theirs," but otherwise he hesitated to tell what happened at the trailer. The agents reminded him he did not have to answer questions without a lawyer present. According to the report, "Minnick stated 'Come back Monday when I have a lawyer,' ***149** and stated that he would make a more complete statement then with his lawyer present."[2448] The FBI interview ended.

After the FBI interview, an appointed attorney met with petitioner. Petitioner spoke with the lawyer on two or three occasions, though it is not clear from the record whether all of these conferences were in person.

[2445] *Miranda v. Arizona, 384 U.S. 436, 474, 86 S.Ct. 1602, 1627, 16 L.Ed.2d 694 (1966)*

[2446] *451 U.S. 477, 484–485, 101 S.Ct. 1880, 1884–1885, 68 L.Ed.2d 378 (1981)*

[2447] *App. 45*

[2448] *App. 16*

On Monday, August 25, Deputy Sheriff J.C. Denham of Clarke County, Mississippi, came to the San Diego jail to question Minnick. Minnick testified that his jailers again told him he would "have to talk" to Denham **489 and that he "could not refuse."[2449] Denham advised petitioner of his rights, and petitioner again declined to sign a rights waiver form. Petitioner told Denham about the escape and then proceeded to describe the events at the mobile home. According to petitioner, Dyess jumped out of the mobile home and shot the first of the two victims, once in the back with a shotgun and once in the head with a pistol. Dyess then handed the pistol to petitioner and ordered him to shoot the other victim, holding the shotgun on petitioner until he did so. Petitioner also said that when the two girls arrived, he talked Dyess out of raping or otherwise hurting them.

Minnick was tried for murder in Mississippi. He moved to suppress all statements given to the FBI or other police officers, including Denham. The trial court denied the motion with respect to petitioner's statements to Denham, but suppressed his other statements. Petitioner was convicted on two counts of capital murder and sentenced to death.

On appeal, petitioner argued that the confession to Denham was taken in violation of his rights to counsel under the Fifth and Sixth Amendments. The Mississippi Supreme Court rejected the claims. With respect to the Fifth Amendment aspect of the case, the court found "the Edwards bright-line rule as to initiation" inapplicable.[2450] Relying on language in Edwards indicating that the bar on interrogating the accused after a request for counsel *150 applies "'until counsel has been made available to him,'"[2451] the court concluded that "[s]ince counsel was made available to Minnick, his Fifth Amendment right to counsel was satisfied."[2452] The court also rejected the Sixth Amendment claim, finding that petitioner waived his Sixth Amendment right to counsel when he spoke with Denham.[2453] We granted certiorari,[2454] and, without reaching any Sixth Amendment implications in the case, we decide that the Fifth Amendment protection of Edwards is not terminated or suspended by consultation with counsel.

In Miranda v. Arizona,[2455] we indicated that once an individual in custody invokes his right to counsel, interrogation "must cease until an attorney is present"; at that point, "the individual must have an opportunity to confer with the attorney and to have him present during any subsequent questioning." Edwards gave force to these admonitions, finding it "inconsistent with Miranda and its progeny for the authorities, at their instance, to reinterrogate an accused in custody if he has clearly asserted his right to counsel."[2456] We held that "when an accused has invoked his right to have counsel present during custodial interrogation, a valid waiver of that right cannot be established by showing only that he responded to further police-initiated custodial interrogation even if he has been advised of his rights."[2457] Further, an accused who requests an attorney, "having expressed his desire to deal with the police only through counsel, is not subject to further interrogation by the authorities

[2449] *Id., at 45*

[2450] *551 So.2d 77, 83 (1988)*

[2451] *Ibid., quoting Edwards v. Arizona, supra, 451 U.S., at 484–485, 101 S.Ct., at 1885*

[2452] *551 So.2d, at 83*

[2453] *Id., at 83–85*

[2454] *495 U.S. 903, 110 S.Ct. 1921, 109 L.Ed.2d 285 (1990)*

[2455] *supra, 384 U.S., at 474, 86 S.Ct., at 1627*

[2456] *451 U.S., at 485, 101 S.Ct., at 1885*

[2457] *Id., at 484, 101 S.Ct., at 1884–1885*

until counsel has been made available to him, unless the accused himself initiates further communication, exchanges, or conversations with the police."[2458]

Edwards is "designed to prevent police from badgering a defendant into waiving his previously asserted Miranda rights."[2459] ***151** The rule ensures that any statement made in subsequent interrogation is not the result of coercive pressures. Edwards conserves judicial resources which would otherwise be expended in making difficult determinations of voluntariness, and implements the protections ****490** of Miranda in practical and straightforward terms.

The merit of the Edwards decision lies in the clarity of its command and the certainty of its application. We have confirmed that the Edwards rule provides "'clear and unequivocal' guidelines to the law enforcement profession."[2460] Even before Edwards, we noted that Miranda's "relatively rigid requirement that interrogation must cease upon the accused's request for an attorney ... has the virtue of informing police and prosecutors with specificity as to what they may do in conducting custodial interrogation, and of informing courts under what circumstances statements obtained during such interrogation are not admissible. This gain in specificity, which benefits the accused and the State alike, has been thought to outweigh the burdens that the decision in Miranda imposes on law enforcement agencies and the courts by requiring the suppression of trustworthy and highly probative evidence even though the confession might be voluntary under traditional Fifth Amendment analysis."[2461] This pre-Edwards explanation applies as well to Edwards and its progeny.[2462]

The Mississippi Supreme Court relied on our statement in Edwards that an accused who invokes his right to counsel "is not subject to further interrogation by the authorities until counsel has been made available to him...."[2463] We do not interpret this language to mean, as the Mississippi court thought, that the protection of Edwards terminates once counsel has consulted with the suspect. In ***152** context, the requirement that counsel be "made available" to the accused refers to more than an opportunity to consult with an attorney outside the interrogation room.

In Edwards, we focused on Miranda's instruction that when the accused invokes his right to counsel, "the interrogation must cease until an attorney is present,"[2464] agreeing with Edwards' contention that he had not waived his right "to have counsel present during custodial interrogation."[2465] In the sentence preceding the language quoted by the Mississippi Supreme Court, we referred to the "right to have counsel present during custodial interrogation," and in the sentence following, we again quoted the phrase "'interrogation must cease until an attorney is present '" from Miranda.[2466] The full sentence relied on by the Mississippi Supreme Court, moreover, says: "We further hold that an accused, such as Edwards, having expressed his desire to deal with the police only through counsel, is not subject to further interrogation by the authorities until counsel has been made available to him, unless the accused him-

[2458] *Id., at 484–485, 101 S.Ct., at 1885*

[2459] *Michigan v. Harvey, 494 U.S. 344, 350, 110 S.Ct. 1176, 1180, 108 L.Ed.2d 293 (1990). See also Smith v. Illinois, 469 U.S. 91, 98, 105 S.Ct. 490, 494, 83 L.Ed.2d 488 (1984).*

[2460] *Arizona v. Roberson, 486 U.S. 675, 682, 108 S.Ct. 2093, 2098, 100 L.Ed.2d 704 (1988). Cf. Moran v. Burbine, 475 U.S. 412, 425–426, 106 S.Ct. 1135, 1142–1144, 89 L.Ed.2d 410 (1986)*

[2461] *Fare v. Michael C., 442 U.S. 707, 718, 99 S.Ct. 2560, 2568, 61 L.Ed.2d 197 (1979)*

[2462] *Arizona v. Roberson, supra, 486 U.S., at 681–682, 108 S.Ct., at 2098*

[2463] *451 U.S., at 484–485, 101 S.Ct., at 1885*

[2464] *384 U.S., at 474, 86 S.Ct., at 1628 (emphasis added)*

[2465] *451 U.S., at 482, 101 S.Ct., at 1883 (emphasis added)*

[2466] *451 U.S., at 484–485, 101 S.Ct., at 1885 (emphasis added)*

self initiates further communication, exchanges, or conversations with the police."[2467]

Our emphasis on counsel's presence at interrogation is not unique to Edwards. It derives from Miranda, where we said that in the cases before us "[t]he presence of counsel ... would be the adequate protective device necessary to make the process of police interrogation conform to the dictates of the [Fifth Amendment] privilege. His presence would insure that statements made in the government-established atmosphere are not the product of compulsion."[2468] Our cases following Edwards have interpreted the decision to mean that the authorities may not initiate questioning of the accused in counsel's absence. Writing for a plurality of the Court, for instance, then-Justice REHNQUIST described the holding of ****491 *153** Edwards to be "that subsequent incriminating statements made without [Edwards'] attorney present violated the rights secured to the defendant by the Fifth and Fourteenth Amendments to the United States Constitution."[2469] These descriptions of Edwards' holding are consistent with our statement that "[p]reserving the integrity of an accused's choice to communicate with police only through counsel is the essence of Edwards and its progeny."[2470] In our view, a fair reading of Edwards and subsequent cases demonstrates that we have interpreted the rule to bar police-initiated interrogation unless the accused has counsel with him at the time of questioning. Whatever the ambiguities of our earlier cases on this point, we now hold that when counsel is requested, interrogation must cease, and officials may not reinitiate interrogation without counsel present, whether or not the accused has consulted with his attorney.

We consider our ruling to be an appropriate and necessary application of the Edwards rule. A single consultation with an attorney does not remove the suspect from persistent attempts by officials to persuade him to waive his rights, or from the coercive pressures that accompany custody and that may increase as custody is prolonged. The case before us well illustrates the pressures, and abuses, that may be concomitants of custody. Petitioner testified that though he resisted, he was required to submit to both the FBI and the ***154** Denham interviews. In the latter instance, the compulsion to submit to interrogation followed petitioner's unequivocal request during the FBI interview that questioning cease until counsel was present. The case illustrates also that consultation is not always effective in instructing the suspect of his rights. One plausible interpretation of the record is that petitioner thought he could keep his admissions out of evidence by refusing to sign a formal waiver of rights. If the authorities had complied with Minnick's request to have counsel present during interrogation, the attorney could have corrected Minnick's misunderstanding, or indeed counseled him that he need not make a statement at all. We decline to remove protection from police-initiated questioning based on isolated consultations with counsel who is absent when the interrogation resumes.

The exception to Edwards here proposed is inconsistent with Edwards' purpose to protect the suspect's right to have counsel present at custodial interrogation. It is inconsistent as well with Miranda, where we specifically rejected respondent's theory that the opportunity to consult with one's attorney would substantially counteract the compulsion created by custodial interrogation. We noted in Miranda that "[e]ven preliminary advice given to the accused by his own attorney can be swiftly overcome by the secret interrogation process. Thus the need for counsel to protect the Fifth

---

[2467] *Ibid. (emphasis added)*

[2468] *384 U.S., at 466, 86 S.Ct., at 1623. See Fare v. Michael C., supra, 442 U.S., at 719, 99 S.Ct., at 2568*

[2469] *Oregon v. Bradshaw, 462 U.S. 1039, 1043, 103 S.Ct. 2830, 2833, 77 L.Ed.2d 405 (1983) (emphasis added). See also Arizona v. Roberson, supra, 486 U.S., at 680, 108 S.Ct., at 2097 ("The rule of the Edwards case came as a corollary to Miranda's admonition that '[i]f the individual states that he wants an attorney, the interrogation must cease until an attorney is present' "); Shea v. Louisiana, 470 U.S. 51, 52, 105 S.Ct. 1065, 1066, 84 L.Ed.2d 38 (1985) ("In Edwards v. Arizona, ... this Court ruled that a criminal defendant's rights under the Fifth and Fourteenth Amendments were violated by the use of his confession obtained by police-instigated interrogation—without counsel present—after he requested an attorney")*

[2470] *Patterson v. Illinois, 487 U.S. 285, 291, 108 S.Ct. 2389, 2394, 101 L.Ed.2d 261 (1988)*

Amendment privilege comprehends not merely a right to consult with counsel prior to questioning, but also to have counsel present during any questioning if the defendant so desires."[2471]

The exception proposed, furthermore, would undermine the advantages flowing **492 from Edwards' "clear and unequivocal" character. Respondent concedes that even after consultation with counsel, a second request for counsel should reinstate the Edwards protection. We are invited by this formulation to adopt a regime in which Edwards' protection could pass in and out of existence multiple times prior to arraignment, *155 at which point the same protection might reattach by virtue of our Sixth Amendment jurisprudence.[2472] Vagaries of this sort spread confusion through the justice system and lead to a consequent loss of respect for the underlying constitutional principle.

In addition, adopting the rule proposed would leave far from certain the sort of consultation required to displace Edwards. Consultation is not a precise concept, for it may encompass variations from a telephone call to say that the attorney is en route, to a hurried interchange between the attorney and client in a detention facility corridor, to a lengthy in-person conference in which the attorney gives full and adequate advice respecting all matters that might be covered in further interrogations. And even with the necessary scope of consultation settled, the officials in charge of the case would have to confirm the occurrence and, possibly, the extent of consultation to determine whether further interrogation is permissible. The necessary inquiries could interfere with the attorney-client privilege.

Added to these difficulties in definition and application of the proposed rule is our concern over its consequence that the suspect whose counsel is prompt would lose the protection of Edwards, while the one whose counsel is dilatory would not. There is more than irony to this result. There is a strong possibility that it would distort the proper conception of the attorney's duty to the client and set us on a course at odds with what ought to be effective representation.

Both waiver of rights and admission of guilt are consistent with the affirmation of individual responsibility that is a principle of the criminal justice system. It does not detract from this principle, however, to insist that neither admissions nor waivers are effective unless there are both particular and systemic assurances that the coercive pressures of custody were not the inducing cause. The Edwards rule sets forth a specific standard to fulfill these purposes, and we have declined *156 to confine it in other instances.[2473] It would detract from the efficacy of the rule to remove its protections based on consultation with counsel.

Edwards does not foreclose finding a waiver of Fifth Amendment protections after counsel has been requested, provided the accused has initiated the conversation or discussions with the authorities; but that is not the case before us. There can be no doubt that the interrogation in question was initiated by the police; it was a formal interview which petitioner was compelled to attend. Since petitioner made a specific request for counsel before the interview, the police-initiated interrogation was impermissible. Petitioner's statement to Denham was not admissible at trial.

The judgment is reversed, and the case is remanded for further proceedings not inconsistent with this opinion.

It is so ordered.

Justice SOUTER took no part in the consideration or decision of this case.

[2471] *384 U.S., at 470, 86 S.Ct., at 1625 (citation omitted)*

[2472] *see Michigan v. Jackson, 475 U.S. 625, 106 S.Ct. 1404, 89 L.Ed.2d 631 (1986)*

[2473] *See Arizona v. Roberson, 486 U.S. 675, 108 S.Ct. 2093, 100 L.Ed.2d 704 (1988)*

(The dissent of Justice SCALIA, with whom THE CHIEF JUSTICE joins, is omitted.)

Black Letter Law

> The Court held that where accused had requested and been provided counsel, the reinitiation of interrogation that accused was compelled to attend, without counsel, was impermissible. The Fifth Amendment requires that once an accused had requested the assistance of counsel, officials may not reinitiate interrogation without counsel present. Simply because the accused has been afforded the opportunity to meet with his or her attorney, that does not allow to government to reinitiate questioning. The question of waiver must be determined on the particular facts and circumstances surrounding the case, and there is no reason in a case such as this for a per se rule.

North Carolina v. Butler

99 S.Ct. 1755

Supreme Court of the United States

State of NORTH CAROLINA, Petitioner,

v.

Willie Thomas BUTLER.

No. 78–354. | Argued March 27, 1979. | Decided April 24, 1979.

Mr. Justice STEWART delivered the opinion of the Court.

In evident conflict with the present view of every other court that has considered the issue, the North Carolina Supreme Court has held that ****1756** Miranda v. Arizona,[2474] requires that no statement of a person under custodial interrogation may be admitted in evidence against him unless, at the time the statement was made, he explicitly waived the right to the presence of a lawyer. We granted certiorari to consider whether this per se rule reflects a proper understanding of the Miranda decision.[2475]

The respondent was convicted in a North Carolina trial court of kidnaping, armed robbery, and felonious assault. The evidence at his trial showed that he and a man named Elmer Lee had robbed a gas station in Goldsboro, N. C., in December 1976, and had shot the station attendant as he was attempting to escape. The attendant was paralyzed, but survived to testify against the respondent.

The prosecution also produced evidence of incriminating statements made by the respondent shortly after his arrest by Federal Bureau of Investigation agents in the Bronx, N. Y., on the basis of a North Carolina fugitive warrant. Outside the presence of the jury, FBI Agent Martinez testified that at the time of the arrest he fully advised the respondent of the rights delineated in the Miranda case. According to the uncontroverted testimony of Martinez, the agents then took the respondent to the FBI office in nearby New Rochelle, N. Y. There, after the agents determined that the respondent had an 11th grade education and was literate, he was given the Bureau's "Advice of Rights" form ***371** which he read. When asked if he understood his rights, he replied that he did. The respondent refused to sign the waiver at the bottom of the form. He was told that he need neither speak nor sign the form, but that the agents would like him to talk to them. The respondent replied: "I will talk to you but

[2474] *384 U.S. 436, 86 S.Ct. 1602, 16 L.Ed.2d 694*

[2475] *439 U.S. 1046, 99 S.Ct. 720, 58 L.Ed.2d 704*

I am not signing any form." He then made inculpatory statements. Agent Martinez testified that the respondent said nothing when advised of his right to the assistance of a lawyer. At no time did the respondent request counsel or attempt to terminate the agents' questioning.

At the conclusion of this testimony the respondent moved to suppress the evidence of his incriminating statements on the ground that he had not waived his right to the assistance of counsel at the time the statements were made. The court denied the motion, finding that

> [T]he statement made by the defendant, William Thomas Butler, to Agent David C. Martinez, was made freely and voluntarily to said agent after having been advised of his rights as required by the Miranda ruling, including his right to an attorney being present at the time of the inquiry and that the defendant, Butler, understood his ***372** rights; [and] that he effectively waived his rights, including the right to have an attorney present during the questioning by his indication that he was willing to answer questions, having read the rights form together with the Waiver of Rights . . . ."[2476]

The respondent's statements were then admitted into evidence, and the jury ultimately found the respondent guilty of each offense charged.

****1757** On appeal, the North Carolina Supreme Court reversed the convictions and ordered a new trial. It found that the statements had been admitted in violation of the requirements of the Miranda decision, noting that the respondent had refused to waive in writing his right to have counsel present and that there had not been a specific oral waiver. As it had in at least two earlier cases, the court read the Miranda opinion as "provid[ing] in plain language that waiver of the right to counsel during interrogation will not be recognized unless such waiver is 'specifically made' after the Miranda warnings have been given."[2477]

We conclude that the North Carolina Supreme Court erred in its reading of the Miranda opinion. There, this Court said: "If the interrogation continues without the presence of an attorney and a statement is taken, a heavy burden ***373** rests on the government to demonstrate that the defendant knowingly and intelligently waived his privilege against self-incrimination and his right to retained or appointed counsel."[2478]

The Court's opinion went on to say:

> An express statement that the individual is willing to make a statement and does not want an attorney followed closely by a statement could constitute a waiver. But a valid waiver will not be presumed simply from the silence of the accused after warnings are given or simply from the fact that a confession was in fact eventually obtained.[2479]

Thus, the Court held that an express statement can constitute a waiver, and that silence alone after such warnings cannot do so. But the Court did not hold that such an express statement is indispensable to a finding of waiver.

[2476] *App. A–22 to A–23*

[2477] *295 N.C. 250, 255, 244 S.E.2d 410, 413 (1978). See State v. Blackmon, 280 N.C. 42, 49–50, 185 S.E.2d 123, 127–128 (1971); State v. Thacker, 281 N.C. 447, 453–454, 189 S.E.2d 145, 149–150 (1972)*

[2478] *384 U.S., at 475, 86 S.Ct., at 1628*

[2479] *Ibid.*

An express written or oral statement of waiver of the right to remain silent or of the right to counsel is usually strong proof of the validity of that waiver, but is not inevitably either necessary or sufficient to establish waiver. The question is not one of form, but rather whether the defendant in fact knowingly and voluntarily waived the rights delineated in the Miranda case. As was unequivocally said in Miranda, mere silence is not enough. That does not mean that the defendant's silence, coupled with an understanding of his rights and a course of conduct indicating waiver, may never support a conclusion that a defendant has waived his rights. The courts must presume that a defendant did not waive his rights; the prosecution's burden is great; but in at least some cases waiver can be clearly inferred from the actions and words of the person interrogated.

***374** The Court's opinion in Miranda explained the reasons for the prophylactic rules it created:

> ****1758** We have concluded that without proper safeguards the process of in-custody interrogation of persons suspected or accused of crime contains inherently compelling pressures which work to undermine the individual's will to resist and to compel him to speak where he would not otherwise do so freely. In order to combat these pressures and to permit a full opportunity to exercise the privilege against self-incrimination, the accused must be adequately and effectively apprised of his rights and the exercise of those rights must be fully honored.[2480]

The per se rule that the North Carolina Supreme Court has found in Miranda does not speak to these concerns. There is no doubt that this respondent was adequately and effectively apprised of his rights. The only question is whether he waived the exercise of one of those rights, the right to the presence of a lawyer. Neither the state court nor the respondent has offered any reason why there must be a negative answer to that question in the absence of an express waiver. This is not the first criminal case to question whether a defendant waived his constitutional rights. It is an issue with which courts must repeatedly deal. Even when a right so fundamental as that to counsel at trial is involved, the question of waiver must be determined on "the particular facts and circumstances surrounding that case, including the background, ***375** experience, and conduct of the accused."[2481]

We see no reason to discard that standard and replace it with an inflexible per se rule in a case such as this. As stated at the outset of this opinion, it appears that every court that has considered this question has now reached the same conclusion. Ten of the eleven United States Courts of Appeals and the courts of at least 17 States ****1759** have held that an explicit statement ***376** of waiver is not invariably necessary to support a finding that the defendant waived the right to remain silent or the right to counsel guaranteed by the Miranda case. By creating an inflexible rule that no implicit waiver can ever suffice, the North Carolina Supreme Court has gone beyond the requirements of federal organic law. It follows that its judgment cannot stand, since a state court can neither add to nor subtract from the mandates of the United States Constitution.[2482]

Accordingly, the judgment is vacated, and the case is remanded to the North Carolina Supreme Court for further proceedings not inconsistent with this opinion.

It is so ordered.

[2480] *Id., at 467, 86 S.Ct., at 1624*

[2481] *Johnson v. Zerbst, 304 U.S. 458, 464, 58 S.Ct. 1019, 1023, 82 L.Ed. 1461. See also United States v. Washington, 431 U.S. 181, 188, 97 S.Ct. 1814, 1819, 52 L.Ed.2d 238; Schneckloth v. Bustamonte, 412 U.S. 218, 93 S.Ct. 2041, 36 L.Ed.2d 854; Frazier v. Cupp, 394 U.S. 731, 739, 89 S.Ct. 1420, 1424, 22 L.Ed.2d 684*

[2482] *Oregon v. Hass, 420 U.S. 714, 95 S.Ct. 1215, 43 L.Ed.2d 570*

Mr. Justice BRENNAN, with whom Mr. Justice MARSHALL and Mr. Justice STEVENS joins, dissenting.

Miranda v. Arizona,[2483] held that "[n]o effective waiver of the right to counsel during interrogation can be recognized unless specifically made after the warnings we here delineate have been given."[2484] Support for this holding was found in Carnley v. Cochran,[2485] which held that in the absence of an allegation of an "affirmative waiver . . . there is no disputed fact question requiring a hearing." (Emphasis added.)

There is no allegation of an affirmative waiver in this case. As the Court concedes, the respondent here refused to sign the waiver form, and "said nothing when advised of his right to the assistance of a lawyer."[2486] Thus, there was no "disputed fact question requiring a hearing," and the trial court erred in holding one. In the absence of an "affirmative waiver" in the form of an express written or oral statement, the Supreme Court of North Carolina correctly granted a new trial. I would, therefore, affirm its decision.

The rule announced by the Court today allows a finding of waiver based upon "infer[ence] from the actions and words of the person interrogated."[2487] The Court thus shrouds in half-light the question of waiver, allowing courts to construct inferences from ambiguous words and gestures. But the very premise of Miranda requires that ambiguity be interpreted against the interrogator. That premise is the ***378** recognition of the "compulsion inherent in custodial" interrogation,[2488] and of its purpose "to subjugate the individual to the will of [his] examiner."[2489] Under such conditions, only the most explicit waivers of rights can be considered knowingly and freely given.

The instant case presents a clear example of the need for an express waiver requirement. As the Court acknowledges, there is a disagreement over whether respondent ****1760** was orally advised of his rights at the time he made his statement.* The fact that Butler received a written copy of his rights is deemed by the Court to be sufficient basis to resolve the disagreement. But, unfortunately, there is also a dispute over whether Butler could read.[2490] And, obviously, if Butler did not have his rights read to him, and could not read them himself, there could be no basis upon which to conclude that he knowingly waived them. Indeed, even if Butler could read there is no reason to believe that his oral statements, which followed a refusal to sign a written waiver form, were intended to signify relinquishment of his rights.

Faced with "actions and words" of uncertain meaning, some judges may find waivers where none occurred. Others may fail to find them where they did. In the former case, the ***379** defendant's rights will have been violated; in the latter, society's interest in effective law enforcement will have been frustrated. A simple prophylactic rule requiring the police to obtain an express waiver of the right to counsel before proceeding with interrogation eliminates these difficulties. And since the Court agrees that Miranda requires the police to obtain some kind of waiver—whether express or implied—the requirement of an express waiver would impose no burden on the police not imposed by the Court's interpretation. It would merely

---

[2483] *384 U.S. 436, 470, 86 S.Ct. 1602, 1625, 16 L.Ed.2d 694 (1966)*

[2484] *(Emphasis added.)*

[2485] *369 U.S. 506, 516, 82 S.Ct. 884, 890, 8 L.Ed.2d 70 (1962)*

[2486] *Ante, at 1756*

[2487] *Ante, at 1757*

[2488] *384 U.S., at 458, 86 S.Ct. 1602*

[2489] *id., at 457, 86 S.Ct., at 1619*

[2490] *See Tr. of Oral Arg. 22, 23*

make that burden explicit. Had Agent Martinez simply elicited a clear answer from Willie Butler to the question, "Do you waive your right to a lawyer?" this journey through three courts would not have been necessary.

Black Letter Law

The Court held that implied waiver to the Miranda warnings is acceptable and refused to adopt the per se rule applied by the North Carolina court, which required express waiver.

Colorado v. Spring

107 S.Ct. 851

Supreme Court of the United States

COLORADO

v.

SPRING.

No. 85–1517. | Argued Dec. 9, 1986. | Decided Jan. 27, 1987.

Justice POWELL delivered the opinion of the Court.

In Miranda v. Arizona,[2491] the Court held that a suspect's waiver of the Fifth Amendment privilege against self-incrimination is valid only if it is made voluntarily, knowingly, and intelligently.[2492] This case presents the question whether the suspect's awareness of all the crimes about which he may be questioned is relevant to determining the validity of his decision to waive the Fifth Amendment privilege.

I

In February 1979, respondent John Leroy Spring and a companion shot and killed Donald Walker during a hunting trip in Colorado. Shortly thereafter, an informant told agents of the Bureau of Alcohol, Tobacco, and Firearms (ATF) that Spring was engaged in the interstate transportation of stolen firearms. The informant also told the agents that Spring had discussed his participation in the Colorado killing. At the time the ATF agents received this information, Walker's body had not been found and the police had received no report of his disappearance. Based on the information received from the informant relating to the firearms violations, the ATF agents set up an undercover operation to purchase firearms from Spring. On March 30, 1979, ATF agents arrested Spring in Kansas City, Missouri, during the undercover purchase.

***567** An ATF agent on the scene of the arrest advised Spring of his Miranda rights. Spring was advised of his Miranda rights a second time after he was transported to the ATF office in Kansas City. At the ATF office, the agents also advised Spring that he had the right to stop ****854** the questioning at any time or to stop the questioning until the presence of an attorney could be secured. Spring then signed a written form stating that he understood and waived his rights, and that he was willing to make a statement and answer questions.

ATF agents first questioned Spring about the firearms transactions that led to his arrest. They then asked Spring if he had a criminal record. He admitted that he had a juvenile record for shooting his aunt when he was 10 years old. The agents asked if Spring had ever shot anyone else. Spring ducked his head and mumbled, "I shot an-

[2491] *384 U.S. 436, 86 S.Ct. 1602, 16 L.Ed.2d 694 (1966)*

[2492] *Id., at 444, 86 S.Ct., at 1612*

other guy once." The agents asked Spring if he had ever been to Colorado. Spring said no. The agents asked Spring whether he had shot a man named Walker in Colorado and thrown his body into a snowbank. Spring paused and then ducked his head again and said no. The interview ended at this point.

On May 26, 1979, Colorado law enforcement officials visited Spring while he was in jail in Kansas City pursuant to his arrest on the firearms offenses. The officers gave Spring the Miranda warnings, and Spring again signed a written form indicating that he understood his rights and was willing to waive them. The officers informed Spring that they wanted to question him about the Colorado homicide. Spring indicated that he "wanted to get it off his chest." In an interview that lasted approximately 1 ½ hours, Spring confessed to the Colorado murder. During that time, Spring ***568** talked freely to the officers, did not indicate a desire to terminate the questioning, and never requested counsel. The officers prepared a written statement summarizing the interview. Spring read, edited, and signed the statement.

Spring was charged in Colorado state court with first-degree murder. Spring moved to suppress both statements on the ground that his waiver of Miranda rights was invalid. The trial court found that the ATF agents' failure to inform Spring before the March 30 interview that they would question him about the Colorado murder did not affect his waiver of his Miranda rights:

> [T]he questions themselves suggested the topic of inquiry. The questions dealt with 'shooting anyone' and specifically killing a man named Walker and throwing his body in a snowbank in Colorado. The questions were not designed to gather information relating to a subject that was not readily evident or apparent to Spring. Spring had been advised of his right to remain silent, his right to stop answering questions, and to have an Attorney present during interrogation. He did not elect to exercise his right to remain silent or to refuse to answer questions relating to the homicide, nor did he request Counsel during interrogation.[2493]

Accordingly, the trial court concluded that the March 30 statement should not be suppressed on Fifth Amendment grounds. The trial court, however, subsequently ruled that Spring's statement that he "shot another guy once" was irrelevant, and that the context of the discussion did not support the inference that the statement related to the Walker homicide. For that reason, the March 30 statement was not admitted at Spring's trial. The court concluded that the May 26 statement "was made freely, voluntarily, and intelligently, after [Spring's] being properly and fully advised of his rights, and that the statement should not be suppressed, but should ***569** be admitted in evidence."[2494] The May 26 statement was admitted into evidence at trial, and Spring was convicted of first-degree murder.

****855** Spring argued on appeal that his waiver of Miranda rights before the March 30 statement was invalid because he was not informed that he would be questioned about the Colorado murder. Although this statement was not introduced at trial, he claimed that its validity was relevant because the May 26 statement that was admitted against him was the illegal "fruit" of the March 30 statement,[2495] and therefore should have been suppressed. The Colorado Court of Appeals agreed with Spring, holding that the ATF agents "had a duty to inform Spring that he was a suspect, or to readvise him of his Miranda rights, before questioning him about the mur-

[2493] *App. to Pet. for Cert. 4–A*

[2494] *Id., at 5–A*

[2495] *See Wong Sun v. United States, 371 U.S. 471, 83 S.Ct. 407, 9 L.Ed.2d 441 (1963)*

der."[2496] Because they failed to do so before the March 30 interview, "any waiver of rights in regard to questions designed to elicit information about Walker's death was not given knowingly or intelligently."[2497] The court held that the March 30 statement was inadmissible and that the State had failed to meet its burden of proving that the May 26 statement was not the product of the prior illegal statement. The court reversed Spring's conviction and remanded the case for a new trial, directing that if the State sought to introduce the May 26 statement into evidence, the trial court should determine whether the "taint" of ***570** the March 30 statement was sufficiently attenuated to allow introduction of the May 26 statement.

The Colorado Supreme Court affirmed the judgment of the Court of Appeals, although its reasoning differed in some respects.[2498] The court found:

> [T]he validity of Spring's waiver of constitutional rights must be determined upon an examination of the totality of the circumstances surrounding the making of the statement to determine if the waiver was voluntary, knowing and intelligent. No one factor is always determinative in that analysis. Whether, and to what extent, a suspect has been informed or is aware of the subject matter of the interrogation prior to its commencement is simply one factor in the court's evaluation of the total circumstances, although it may be a major or even a determinative factor in some situations.[2499]

The court concluded:

> Here, the absence of an advisement to Spring that he would be questioned about the Colorado homicide, and the lack of any basis to conclude that at the time of the execution of the waiver, he reasonably could have expected that the interrogation would extend to that subject, are determinative factors in undermining the validity of the waiver.[2500]

Justice Erickson, joined by Justice Rovira, dissented as to the resolution of this issue, stating:

> Law enforcement officers have no duty under Miranda to inform a person in custody of all charges being investigated prior to questioning him. All that Miranda requires is that the suspect be advised that he has the right to remain silent, that anything he says can and will be used against him in court, that he has the right to consult with a lawyer and to have the lawyer present during interrogation, and that if he cannot afford a lawyer ***571** one will be appointed to represent him.[2501]

The dissenting justices found "ample evidence to support the trial court's conclusion that Spring waived his Miranda rights" and rejected "the majority's conclusion that Spring's waiver of his Miranda rights on March 30, 1979 was invalid sim-

[2496] *671 P.2d 965, 966 (1983)*

[2497] *Id., at 967*

[2498] *713 P.2d 865 (1985)*

[2499] *Id., at 872–873 (citations omitted)*

[2500] *Id., at 874 (emphasis in original)*

[2501] *Id., at 880 (citations omitted)*

ply because he was not informed of all matters that would be reviewed when he was questioned by the police."[2502] The court **856 remanded the case for further proceedings consistent with its opinion.

We granted certiorari,[2503] to resolve an arguable Circuit conflict3 and to review the Colorado Supreme Court's determination that a suspect's awareness of the possible subjects of questioning is a relevant and sometimes determinative consideration in assessing whether a waiver of the Fifth Amendment privilege is valid. We now reverse.

II

There is no dispute that the police obtained the May 26 confession after complete Miranda warnings and after informing Spring that he would be questioned about the Colorado homicide. The Colorado Supreme Court nevertheless held that the confession should have been suppressed because it was the illegal "fruit" of the March 30 statement. A confession cannot be "fruit of the poisonous tree" if the tree itself is not ***572** poisonous. Our inquiry, therefore, centers on the validity of the March 30 statement.

A

The Fifth Amendment of the United States Constitution provides that no person "shall be compelled in any criminal case to be a witness against himself." This privilege "is fully applicable during a period of custodial interrogation."[2504] In Miranda, the Court concluded that "without proper safeguards the process of in-custody interrogation of persons suspected or accused of crime contains inherently compelling pressures which work to undermine the individual's will to resist and to compel him to speak where he would not otherwise do so freely."[2505] Accordingly, the Court formulated the now-familiar "procedural safeguards effective to secure the privilege against self-incrimination."[2506] The Court's fundamental aim in designing the Miranda warnings was "to assure that the individual's right to choose between silence and speech remains unfettered throughout the interrogation process."[2507]

Consistent with this purpose, a suspect may waive his Fifth Amendment privilege, "provided the waiver is made voluntarily, knowingly and intelligently."[2508] In this case, the law enforcement officials twice informed Spring ***573** of his Fifth Amendment privilege in precisely the manner specified by Miranda. As we have noted, Spring indicated that he understood the enumerated ****857** rights and signed a written form expressing his intention to waive his Fifth Amendment privilege. The trial court specifically found that "there was no element of duress or coercion used to induce Spring's statements [on March 30, 1978]."[2509] Despite the explicit warnings and the finding by the trial court, Spring argues that his March 30 statement was in effect compelled in violation of his Fifth Amendment privilege because he signed the waiver form without being aware that he would be questioned about the Colorado homicide. Spring's argument strains the meaning of compulsion past the breaking point.

[2502] *Id., at 881*

[2503] *476 U.S. 1104, 106 S.Ct. 1961, 90 L.Ed.2d 368 (1986)*

[2504] *Miranda v. Arizona, 384 U.S., at 460–461, 86 S.Ct., at 1620–1621*

[2505] *Id., at 467, 86 S.Ct., at 1624*

[2506] *Id., at 444, 86 S.Ct., at 1612*

[2507] *Id., at 469, 86 S.Ct., at 1625*

[2508] *Id., at 444, 86 S.Ct. at 1612*

[2509] *App. to Pet. for Cert. 3–A*

B

A statement is not "compelled" within the meaning of the Fifth Amendment if an individual "voluntarily, knowingly and intelligently" waives his constitutional privilege.[2510] The inquiry whether a waiver is coerced "has two distinct dimensions."[2511]:

> First the relinquishment of the right must have been voluntary in the sense that it was the product of a free and deliberate choice rather than intimidation, coercion, or deception. Second, the waiver must have been made with a full awareness both of the nature of the right being abandoned and the consequences of the decision to abandon it. Only if the 'totality of the circumstances surrounding the interrogation' reveal both an uncoerced choice and the requisite level of comprehension may a court properly conclude that the Miranda rights have been waived.[2512]

There is no doubt that Spring's decision to waive his Fifth Amendment privilege was voluntary. He alleges no "coercion ***574** of a confession by physical violence or other deliberate means calculated to break [his] will,"[2513] and the trial court found none. His allegation that the police failed to supply him with certain information does not relate to any of the traditional indicia of coercion: "the duration and conditions of detention ..., the manifest attitude of the police toward him, his physical and mental state, the diverse pressures which sap or sustain his powers of resistance and self-control."[2514] Absent evidence that Spring's "will [was] overborne and his capacity for self-determination critically impaired" because of coercive police conduct,[2515] his waiver of his Fifth Amendment privilege was voluntary under this Court's decision in Miranda.

There also is no doubt that Spring's waiver of his Fifth Amendment privilege was knowingly and intelligently made: that is, that Spring understood that he had the right to remain silent and that anything he said could be used as evidence against him. The Constitution does not require that a criminal suspect know and understand every possible consequence of a waiver of the Fifth Amendment privilege.[2516] The Fifth Amendment's guarantee is both simpler and more fundamental: A defendant may not be compelled to be a witness against himself in any respect. The Miranda warnings protect this privilege by ensuring that a suspect knows that he may choose not to talk to law enforcement officers, to talk only with counsel present, or to discontinue talking at any time. The Miranda warnings ensure that a waiver of these rights is knowing and intelligent by ****858** requiring that the suspect be fully advised of this constitutional privilege, including the critical advice that whatever he chooses to say may be used as evidence against him.

***575** In this case there is no allegation that Spring failed to understand the basic privilege guaranteed by the Fifth Amendment. Nor is there any allegation that he misunderstood the consequences of speaking freely to the law enforcement officials.

[2510] *Miranda v. Arizona, supra, at 444, 86 S.Ct., at 1612*

[2511] *Moran v. Burbine, 475 U.S. 412, 421, 106 S.Ct. 1135, 1141, 89 L.Ed.2d 410 (1986)*

[2512] *Ibid. (quoting Fare v. Michael C., 442 U.S. 707, 725, 99 S.Ct. 2560, 2572, 61 L.Ed.2d 197 (1979))*

[2513] *Oregon v. Elstad, 470 U.S. 298, 312, 105 S.Ct. 1285, 1295, 84 L.Ed.2d 222 (1985)*

[2514] *Culombe v. Connecticut, 367 U.S. 568, 602, 81 S.Ct. 1860, 1879, 6 L.Ed.2d 1037 (1961) (opinion of Frankfurter, J.)*

[2515] *Ibid.; see Colorado v. Connelly, 479 U.S. 157, 163–164, 107 S.Ct. 515, ——, 93 L.Ed.2d 473 (1986)*

[2516] *Moran v. Burbine, supra, 475 U.S. at 422, 106 S.Ct., at 1141; Oregon v. Elstad, supra, at 316–317, 105 S.Ct., at 1296–1297*

In sum, we think that the trial court was indisputably correct in finding that Spring's waiver was made knowingly and intelligently within the meaning of Miranda.

III

A

Spring relies on this Court's statement in Miranda that "any evidence that the accused was threatened, tricked, or cajoled into a waiver will ... show that the defendant did not voluntarily waive his privilege."[2517] He contends that the failure to inform him of the potential subjects of interrogation constitutes the police trickery and deception condemned in Miranda, thus rendering his waiver of Miranda rights invalid. Spring, however, reads this statement in Miranda out of context and without due regard to the constitutional privilege the Miranda warnings were designed to protect.

We note first that the Colorado courts made no finding of official trickery. In fact, as noted above, the trial court expressly found that "there was no element of duress or coercion used to induce Spring's statements."[2518] ***576** Spring nevertheless insists that the failure of the ATF agents to inform him that he would be questioned about the murder constituted official "trickery" sufficient to invalidate his waiver of his Fifth Amendment privilege, even if the official conduct did not amount to "coercion." Even assuming that Spring's proposed distinction has merit, we reject his conclusion. This Court has never held that mere silence by law enforcement officials as to the subject matter of an interrogation is "trickery" sufficient to invalidate a suspect's waiver of Miranda rights, and we expressly decline so to hold today.

Once Miranda warnings are given, it is difficult to see how official silence could cause a suspect to misunderstand the nature of his constitutional right—"his right to refuse to answer any question which might incriminate him."[2519] ****859** "Indeed, it seems self-evident that one who is told he is free to refuse to answer questions is in a curious posture to later complain that his answers were compelled."[2520] We have held that a valid waiver does not require that an individual be informed of all information "useful" in making his decision or all information that "might ... affec[t] his decision to confess."[2521] "[W]e have never read the Constitution to require that the police supply a suspect with a flow of information to help him calibrate his self-interest in ***577** deciding whether to speak or stand by his rights."[2522] Here, the additional information could affect only the wisdom of a Miranda waiver, not its essentially voluntary and knowing nature. Accordingly, the failure of the law enforcement officials to inform Spring of the subject matter of the interrogation could not affect Spring's decision to waive his Fifth Amendment privilege in a constitutionally significant manner.

B

This Court's holding in Miranda specifically required that the police inform a criminal suspect that he has the right to remain silent and that anything he says may be used against him. There is no qualification of this broad and explicit warning. The warning, as formulated in Miranda, conveys to a suspect the nature of his constitutional privilege and the consequences of abandoning it. Accordingly, we hold that a

---

[2517] *384 U.S., at 476, 86 S.Ct., at 1629*

[2518] *Supra, at 857*

[2519] *United States v. Washington, 431 U.S. 181, 188, 97 S.Ct. 1814, 1819, 52 L.Ed.2d 238 (1977)*

[2520] *Ibid.*

[2521] *Moran v. Burbine, 475 U.S., at 422, 106 S.Ct., at 1141*

[2522] *Ibid.*

suspect's awareness of all the possible subjects of questioning in advance of interrogation is not relevant to determining whether the suspect voluntarily, knowingly, and intelligently waived his Fifth Amendment privilege.

IV

The judgment of the Colorado Supreme Court is reversed, and the case is remanded for further proceedings not inconsistent with this opinion.

It is so ordered.

(The dissents of Justice MARSHALL, with whom Justice BRENNAN joins, is omitted.)

Black Letter Law

> The Court held that a statement is not "compelled" within the meaning of the Fifth Amendment if an individual "voluntarily, knowingly and intelligently" waives his constitutional privilege. The Court also held that this waiver is not offense specific. The focus is on the constitutional right itself, not the suspected offense.

Discussion Problems:

14-1. On August 4, Lee and Robert were charged with four offenses in the same indictment: conspiracy to commit murder, first-degree premeditated murder while armed. These charges stemmed from a shooting that occurred at approximately 4:00 a.m. on February 23, in the 600 block of Meadows Street, Northwest. The decedent, Billy Michaels, was shot twenty-three times and died from the gunshot wounds. Several eyewitnesses identified the appellants as the shooters.

Lee was first arrested in connection with the Michaels murder. At that time, he was informed of his Miranda rights and signed a form indicating that he was not willing to talk to police without an attorney present. After several months, during which Lee was detained, the government dismissed the charges against him.

Lee was arrested again in May on drug charges. He agreed to cooperate with law enforcement agents and pleaded guilty to distribution of cocaine pursuant to a plea agreement. Until his sentencing about a year later, Lee continued to cooperate with law enforcement authorities, particularly with Bureau of Alcohol, Tobacco and Firearms Special Agent Frank Lopez and Police Detective Anthony Murphy, in the ongoing investigation of criminal activity in the Park Meadows neighborhood.

Approximately 3 years later, Agent Lopez and Detective Murphy visited Lee where he was serving his sentence on the cocaine distribution charge. It was a minimum security facility and Lee was in a work-release program. Lee was summoned by an intercom while taking a GED test to meet with the officers. He was directed to a conference room with a window, a long table and several chairs. After some initial pleasantries, the officers told Lee that they had new evidence relating to the Michaels murder and that they believed he was involved. They provided "a detailed synopsis" of the events before, during and after the murder, including Robert's involvement and the motive for the murder. The agents did not read Lee his Miranda rights, but they notified him that he was not under arrest and did not have to talk to them about the murder. They did indicate, however, that they wanted him to cooperate with them on a new drug investigation and that it could be easier on him if he assisted in the investigation.

Lee confessed to killing Michaels and also implicated Robert in the course of his confession. He also told them that the murder was the result of a "drug-related situation with a person" named Ray Jackson. After Lee indicated that he would cooperate in the new Park Meadows area investigation, the agents told him they would inform the prosecutor and return with a defense attorney to try to reach a plea agreement.

Several months later, Lee was arrested for the murder while still serving his sentence and was subsequently indicted.

Prior to trial Lee's counsel makes a motion to suppress the confessions based upon a violation of his client's 5th, 6th and Due Process rights. Identify and prepare the most valid argument for each of these attempts to suppress.

14-2. Acting on information received earlier in their investigation, Officer Harder and Officer Velloney had probable cause to believe that an individual named "Johnny Rae" was cooking crystal Meth in room 101 of the Lonely Mermaid Inn. They pulled into the motel parking lot, exited their cruiser and headed towards room 101. Officer Harder pulled his sidearm and walked down the sidewalk immediately outside the front door and window to room 101. Looking inside through a hole in the defective closed blinds, he saw what appeared to be a mobile drug laboratory. He also observed a then unknown individual hurriedly packing the pieces of the drug lab into a large box. He kicked in the front door shouting, "freeze – police." He found himself staring into the startled eyes and upraised hands of Johnny Rae. He arrested him, taking him into custody. In response to Officer Harder's questions, Johnny Rae told him all about their mobile lab and how they had previously stored their drugs at 1234 Foxworthy Blvd prior to distribution. Officer Harder then advised him of his Miranda rights and stuck him in the back of his cruiser.

Later that day, Officer Walker rolled up in front of 1234 Foxworthy Blvd. He had a search warrant given by the magistrate based upon the statement made by Johnny Rae. He walked up to the front door and knocked. A young woman with a towheaded child on her hip answered the door. He identified himself as a police officer and asked if he could come in and take a look around. She looked behind her nervously, stuck her head out of the door and in a loud voice said "No, not under any circumstances!", all the while shaking her head up and down in a "Yes" motion and mouthing please help me. Officer Walker grabbed her by arm, pulled her out of the door and then burst through the front door screaming, "Police!" A large, greasy, fat, bearded man holding a sawed off shotgun was standing in the hall. He dropped the shotgun and put both hands on his head.

Officer Walker arrested him, cuffing him in the hallway. The officer advised the man of his Miranda rights. The big guy identified himself as "Bubba Michaels, and told the Officer this was his home and he did not give permission to search it. He then invoked his right to remain silent and asked to speak with his attorney. Officer Walker walked him through the house, discovering a drug-sorting table with methamphetamines, baggies, and bottles in the back bedroom room. He took Bubba out to the cruiser where he locked him in the back He then interviewed the young lady, learning that her name was Linda Lou and that she was the sister of Johnny Rae and the sometime lover of Billy Bob. He spent about 30 minutes with Linda Lou, secured her permission to search the house, and then went back into the house to perform the search.

When Officer Walker returned to the house, he searched the closet in the hallway where he first arrested Bubba. He found a bank bag filled with cash, three sawed off shotguns and a half-kilo of pure heroin underneath the clothes in the closet. He seized the shotguns, remembering a bank robbery last week where sawed off shotguns were the weapons of choice for three robbers, one of whom matched the description of the bearded fat man he currently had locked in his cruiser. When he came back outside, Linda Lou told Officer Walker that Billy Bob held her against her will ever since she came down from Charlottesville, Virginia to visit with her cousin

Johnny Rae. She begged him not to leave her at the home, claiming that Billy Bob's gang would kill her.

While Officer Walker was at 1234 Foxworthy Blvd, Officer Harder and Velloney picked Billy Bob up from a bar and took him to the station. While in the car on the way to the station Billy Bob asked if he should call his attorney. Officer Harder told them him he would get to call his attorney after he had been fingerprinted and processed. Billy Bob was fingerprinted and placed in an interrogation room. Officer Walker suddenly walked into the interrogation room where Billy Bob was waiting and dropped the sawed off shotguns from Foxworthy Blvd on the table. He advised Billy Bob of his rights and told him that he personally did not care if he didn't give it up because Bubba had already sold them down the river, and he was going to prison for bank robbery for the rest of his life, along with his cousin Johnny Rae. Billy Bob waived his rights and confessed to the bank robbery, identifying Bubba Michaels as the ringleader of the robbery and kingpin of their drug operations. All three were placed in a lineup where the bank teller who had been robbed identified Billy Bob and Bubba. Immediately after the lineup, their attorney showed up at the station house and all activities with Billy Bob and Johnny Rae ceased.

You are the prosecuting attorney in this case and have been informed that the defense intends to make a motion to suppress the statements of Johnny Rae, Billy Bob, and Bubba. Your boss has asked you to review these facts and predict how the defense will formulate their argument. She wants your legal memorandum on her desk as quickly as possible.

-Notes-

Chapter 15: Identification Procedures

U.S. v. Wade

87 S.Ct. 1926
Supreme Court of the United States
UNITED STATES, Petitioner,
v.
Billy Joe WADE.
No. 334. | Argued Feb. 16, 1967. | Decided June 12, 1967.

Mr. Justice BRENNAN delivered the opinion of the Court.

The question here is whether courtroom identifications of an accused at trial are to be excluded from evidence because the accused was exhibited to the witnesses before trial at a post-indictment lineup conducted for ***220** identification purposes without notice to and in the absence of the accused's appointed counsel.

The federally insured bank in Eustace, Texas, was robbed on September 21, 1964. A man with a small strip of tape on each side of his face entered the bank, pointed a pistol at the female cashier and the vice president, the only persons in the bank at the time, and forced them to fill a pillowcase with the bank's money. The man then drove away with an accomplice who had been waiting in a stolen car outside the bank. On March 23, 1965, an indictment was returned against respondent, Wade, and two others for conspiring to rob the bank, and against Wade and the accomplice for the robbery itself. Wade was arrested on April 2, and counsel was appointed to represent him on April 26. Fifteen days later an FBI agent, without notice to Wade's lawyer, arranged to have the two bank employees observe a lineup ****1929** made up of Wade and five or six other prisoners and conducted in a courtroom of the local county courthouse. Each person in the line wore strips of tape such as allegedly worn by the robber and upon direction each said something like 'put the money in the bag,' the words allegedly uttered by the robber. Both bank employees identified Wade in the lineup as the bank robber.

At trial the two employees, when asked on direct examination if the robber was in the courtroom, pointed to Wade. The prior lineup identification was then elicited from both employees on cross-examination. At the close of testimony, Wade's counsel moved for a judgment of acquittal or, alternatively, to strike the bank officials' courtroom identifications on the ground that conduct of the lineup, without notice to and in the absence of his appointed counsel, violated his Fifth Amendment privilege against self-incrimination and his Sixth Amendment right to the assistance of counsel. The motion was denied, and Wade was convicted. The ***221** Court of Appeals for the Fifth Circuit reversed the conviction and ordered a new trial at which the in-court identification evidence was to be excluded, holding that, though the lineup did not violate Wade's Fifth Amendment rights, 'the lineup, held as it was, in the absence of counsel, already chosen to represent appellant, was a violation of his Sixth Amendment rights * * *.'[2523] We granted certiorari,[2524] and set the case for oral argument with No. 223, Gilbert v. State of California,[2525] and No. 254, Stovall v. Denno,[2526] which present similar questions. We reverse the judgment of the Court of Appeals

[2523] *358 F.2d 557, 560*

[2524] *385 U.S. 811, 87 S.Ct. 81, 17 L.Ed.2d 53*

[2525] *388 U.S. 263, 87 S.Ct. 1951, 18 L.Ed.2d 1178*

[2526] *386 U.S. 293, 87 S.Ct. 1967, 18 L.Ed.2d 1199*

and remand to that court with direction to enter a new judgment vacating the conviction and remanding the case to the District Court for further proceedings consistent with this opinion.

I

Neither the lineup itself nor anything shown by this record that Wade was required to do in the lineup violated his privilege against self-incrimination. We have only recently reaffirmed that the privilege 'protects an accused only from being compelled to testify against himself, or otherwise provide the State with evidence of a testimonial or communicative nature * * *.'[2527] We there held that compelling a suspect to submit to a withdrawal of a sample of his blood for analysis for alcohol content and the admission in evidence of the analysis report were not compulsion to those ends. That holding was supported by the opinion in Holt v. United States,[2528] in which case a question arose as to whether a blouse belonged to the defendant. A witness testified at trial that the defendant put on the blouse and it had fit him. The defendant argued that the admission of the testimony was error because compelling him to put on the blouse was a violation of his privilege. The Court ***222** rejected the claim as 'an extravagant extension of the Fifth Amendment,' Mr. Justice Holmes saying for the Court: '(T)he prohibition of compelling a man in a criminal court to be witness against himself is a prohibition of the use of physical or moral compulsion to extort communications from him, not an exclusion of his body as evidence when it may be material.'[2529]

The Court in Holt, however, put aside any constitutional questions which might be involved in compelling an accused, as here, to exhibit himself before victims of or witnesses to an alleged crime; the Court stated, 'we need now consider how far a court would go in compelling ****1930** a man to exhibit himself.'[2530]

We have no doubt that compelling the accused merely to exhibit his person for observation by a prosecution witness prior to trial involves no compulsion of the accused to give evidence having testimonial significance. It is compulsion of the accused to exhibit his physical characteristics, not compulsion to disclose any knowledge he might have. It is no different from compelling Schmerber to provide a blood sample or Holt to wear the blouse, and, as in those instances, is not within the cover of the privilege. Similarly, compelling Wade to speak within hearing distance of the witnesses, even to utter words purportedly uttered by the robber, was not compulsion to utter statements of a 'testimonial' nature; he was required to use his voice as an identifying ***223** physical characteristic, not to speak his guilt. We held in Schmerber,[2531] that the distinction to be drawn under the Fifth Amendment privilege against self-incrimination is one between an accused's 'communications' in whatever form, vocal or physical, and 'compulsion which makes a suspect or accused the source of 'real or physical evidence.'[2532] We recognized that 'both federal and state courts have usually held that * * * (the privilege) offers no protection against compulsion to submit to fingerprinting, photography, or measurements, to write or speak for identification, to appear in court, to stand, to assume a stance, to walk, or to make a particular gesture.'[2533] None of these activities becomes testimonial within the scope of the privilege because required of the accused in a pretrial lineup.

[2527] *Schmerber v. State of California, 384 U.S. 757, 761, 86 S.Ct. 1826, 1830, 16 L.Ed.2d 908*

[2528] *218 U.S. 245, 31 S.Ct. 2, 54 L.Ed. 1021*

[2529] *218 U.S., at 252-253, 31 S.Ct. at 6*

[2530] *Id., at 253, 31 S.Ct. at 6*

[2531] *Supra, 384 U.S. at 761, 86 S.Ct. at 1830*

[2532] *Schmerber, supra, at 764, 86 S.Ct. at 1832*

[2533] *Id., at 764, 86 S.Ct. at 1832*

Moreover, it deserves emphasis that this case presents no question of the admissibility in evidence of anything Wade said or did at the lineup which implicates his privilege. The Government offered no such evidence as part of its case, and what came out about the lineup proceedings on Wade's cross-examination of the bank employees involved no violation of Wade's privilege.

II

The fact that the lineup involved no violation of Wade's privilege against self-incrimination does not, however, dispose of his contention that the courtroom identifications should have been excluded because the lineup was conducted without notice to and in the absence of his counsel. Our rejection of the right to counsel claim in Schmerber rested on our conclusion in that case that '(n)o issue of counsel's ability to assist petitioner in respect of any rights he did possess is presented.'[2534] In contrast, in this case it is urged that the assistance of counsel at the lineup was indispensable ***224** to protect Wade's most basic right as a criminal defendant-his right to a fair trial at which the witnesses against him might be meaningfully cross-examined.

The Framers of the Bill of Rights envisaged a broader role for counsel than under the practice then prevailing in England of merely advising his client in 'matters of law,' and eschewing any responsibility for 'matters of fact.' The constitutions in at least 11 of the 13 States expressly or impliedly abolished ****1931** this distinction.[2535] 'Though the colonial provisions about counsel were in accord on few things, they agreed on the necessity of abolishing the facts-law distinction; the colonists appreciated that if a defendant were forced to stand alone against the state, his case was foredoomed.'[2536] This background is reflected in the scope given by our decisions to the Sixth Amendment's guarantee to an accused of the assistance of counsel for his defense. When the Bill of Rights was adopted, there were no organized police forces as we know them today. The accused confronted the prosecutor and the witnesses against him, and the evidence was marshaled, largely at the trial itself. In contrast, today's law enforcement machinery involves critical confrontations of the accused by the prosecution at pretrial proceedings where the results might well settle the accused's fate and reduce the trial itself to a mere formality. In recognition of these realities of modern criminal prosecution, our cases have construed the Sixth Amendment guarantee to apply to 'critical' stages of the proceedings. The guarantee reads: 'In all criminal ***225** prosecutions, the accused shall enjoy the right * * * to have the Assistance of Counsel for his defense.'[2537] The plain wording of this guarantee thus encompasses counsel's assistance whenever necessary to assure a meaningful 'defense.'

As early as Powell v. State of Alabama,[2538] we recognized that the period from arraignment to trial was 'perhaps the most critical period of the proceedings * * *,'[2539] during which the accused 'requires the guiding hand of counsel * * *,'[2540] if the guarantee is not to prove an empty right. That principle has since been applied to require the assistance of counsel at the type of arraignment-for example, that provided by Alabama-where certain rights might be sacrificed or lost: 'What happens there may affect the whole trial. Available defenses may be irretrievably lost, if not then

---

[2534] *384 U.S., at 766, 86 S.Ct. at 1833*

[2535] *Powell v. State of Alabama, 287 U.S. 45, 60-65, 53 S.Ct. 55, 60-62, 77 L.Ed. 158; Note, 73 Yale L.J. 1000, 1030-1033 (1964)*

[2536] *73 Yale L.J., supra, at 1033-1034*

[2537] *(Emphasis supplied.)*

[2538] *Supra*

[2539] *Id., at 57, 53 S.Ct. at 59*

[2540] *Id., at 69, 53 S.Ct. at 64*

and there asserted * * *.'[2541] The principle was also applied in Massiah v. United States,[2542] where we held that incriminating statements of the defendant should have been excluded from evidence when it appeared that they were overheard by federal agents who, without notice to the defendant's lawyer, arranged a meeting between the defendant and an accomplice turned informant. We said, quoting a concurring opinion in Spano v. People of State of New York,[2543] that '(a)nything less * * * might deny a defendant 'effective representation by counsel at the only stage when legal aid and advice would help him.''[2544]

In Escobedo v. State of Illinois,[2545] we drew upon the rationale of Hamilton and Massiah in holding that the right to counsel was guaranteed at the point where the accused, prior to arraignment, was subjected to secret interrogation despite repeated requests to see his lawyer. We again noted the necessity of counsel's presence ***226** if the accused was to have a fair opportunity to present a defense at the trial itself:

> The rule sought by the State here, however, would make the trial no more than an appeal from the interrogation; and the 'right to use counsel at the formal trial (would be) a very hollow thing (if), for all practical purposes, ****1932** the conviction is already assured by pretrial examination'. * * * One can imagine a cynical prosecutor saying: 'Let them have the most illustrious counsel, now. They can't escape the noose. There is nothing that counsel can do for them at the trial.[2546]

Finally in Miranda v. State of Arizona,[2547] the rules established for custodial interrogation included the right to the presence of counsel. The result was rested on our finding that this and the other rules were necessary to safeguard the privilege against self-incrimination from being jeopardized by such interrogation.

Of course, nothing decided or said in the opinions in the cited cases links the right to counsel only to protection of Fifth Amendment rights. Rather those decisions 'no more than (reflect) a constitutional principle established as long ago as Powell v. Alabama * * *.'[2548] It is central to that principle that in addition to counsel's presence at trial, the accused is guaranteed that he need not stand alone against the State at any stage of the prosecution, formal or informal, in court or out, where counsel's absence might derogate from the accused's right to a fair trial. The security of that right is as much the aim of the right to counsel as it is of the other guarantees of the ***227** Sixth Amendment-the right of the accused to a speedy and public trial by an impartial jury, his right to be informed of the nature and cause of the accusation, and his right to be confronted with the witnesses against him and to have compulsory process for obtaining witnesses in his favor. The presence of counsel at such critical confrontations, as at the trial itself, operates to assure that the accused's interests will be protected consistently with our adversary theory of criminal prosecution.[2549]

[2541] *Hamilton v. State of Alabama, 368 U.S. 52, 54, 82 S.Ct. 157, 159, 7 L.Ed.2d 114. See White v. State of Maryland, 373 U.S. 59, 83 S.Ct. 1050, 10 L.Ed.2d 193*

[2542] *377 U.S. 201, 84 S.Ct. 1199, 12 L.Ed.2d 246*

[2543] *360 U.S. 315, 326, 79 S.Ct. 1202, 1209, 3 L.Ed.2d 1265*

[2544] *377 U.S., at 204, 84 S.Ct. at 1202*

[2545] *378 U.S. 478, 84 S.Ct. 1758, 12 L.Ed.2d 977*

[2546] *378 U.S., at 487-488, 84 S.Ct. at 1763*

[2547] *384 U.S. 436, 86 S.Ct. 1602, 16 L.Ed.2d 694*

[2548] *Massiah v. United States, supra, 377 U.S. at 205, 84 S.Ct. at 1202*

[2549] *Cf. Pointer v. State of Texas, 380 U.S. 400, 85 S.Ct. 1065, 13 L.Ed.2d 923*

In sum, the principle of Powell v. Alabama and succeeding cases requires that we scrutinize any pretrial confrontation of the accused to determine whether the presence of his counsel is necessary to preserve the defendant's basic right to a fair trial as affected by his right meaningfully to cross-examine the witnesses against him and to have effective assistance of counsel at the trial itself. It calls upon us to analyze whether potential substantial prejudice to defendant's rights inheres in the particular confrontation and the ability of counsel to help avoid that prejudice.

III

The Government characterizes the lineup as a mere preparatory step in the gathering of the prosecution's evidence, not different-for Sixth Amendment purposes-from various other preparatory steps, such as systematized or scientific analyzing of the accused's fingerprints, blood sample, clothing, hair, and the like. We think there are differences which preclude such stages being characterized as critical stages at which the accused has the right to the presence of his counsel. Knowledge of the techniques of science and technology is sufficiently available, and the variables in techniques few enough, that the accused has the opportunity for a meaningful confrontation of the Government's case at ***228** trial through the ordinary processes of cross-examination of the Government's ****1933** expert witnesses and the presentation of the evidence of his own experts. The denial of a right to have his counsel present at such analyses does not therefore violate the Sixth Amendment; they are not critical stages since there is minimal risk that his counsel's absence at such stages might derogate from his right to a fair trial.

IV

But the confrontation compelled by the State between the accused and the victim or witnesses to a crime to elicit identification evidence is peculiarly riddled with innumerable dangers and variable factors which might seriously, even crucially, derogate from a fair trial. The vagaries of eyewitness identification are well-known; the annals of criminal law are rife with instances of mistaken identification. Mr. Justice Frankfurter once said: 'What is the worth of identification testimony even when uncontradicted? The identification of strangers is proverbially untrustworthy. The hazards of such testimony are established by a formidable number of instances in the records of English and American trials. These instances are recent-not due to the brutalities of ancient criminal procedure.'[2550] A major factor contributing to the high incidence of miscarriage of justice from mistaken identification has been the degree of suggestion inherent in the manner in which the prosecution presents the suspect to witnesses for pretrial identification. A commentator ***229** has observed that '(t)he influence of improper suggestion upon identifying witnesses probably accounts for more miscarriages of justice than any other single factor-perhaps it is responsible for more such errors than all other factors combined.'[2551] Suggestion can be created intentionally or unintentionally in many subtle ways. And the dangers for the suspect are particularly grave when the witness' opportunity for observation was insubstantial, and thus his susceptibility to suggestion the greatest.

Moreover, '(i)t is a matter of common experience that, once a witness has picked out the accused at the line-up, he is not likely to go back on his word later on, so that in practice the issue of identity may (in the absence of other relevant evidence) for all practical purposes be determined there and then, before the trial.'

The pretrial confrontation for purpose of identification may take the form of a lineup, also known as an 'identification parade' or 'show-up,' as in the present case,

[2550] *The Case of Sacco and Vanzetti 30 (1927)*

[2551] *Wall, Eye-Witness Identification in Criminal Cases 26*

or presentation of the suspect alone to the witness, as in Stovall v. Denno.[2552] It is obvious that risks of suggestion attend either form of confrontation and increase the dangers inhering in eyewitness identification. But ***230** as is the ****1934** case with secret interrogations, there is serious difficulty in depicting what transpires at lineups and other forms of identification confrontations. 'Privacy results in secrecy and this in turn results in a gap in our knowledge as to what in fact goes on * * *.'[2553] For the same reasons, the defense can seldom reconstruct the manner and mode of lineup identification for judge or jury at trial. Those participating in a lineup with the accused may often be police officers; in any event, the participants' names are rarely recorded or divulged at trial. The impediments to an objective observation are increased when the victim is the witness. Lineups are prevalent in rape and robbery prosecutions and present a particular hazard that a victim's understandable outrage may excite vengeful or spiteful motives. In any event, neither witnesses nor lineup participants are apt to be alert for conditions prejudicial to the suspect. And if they were, it would likely be of scant benefit to the suspect since neither witnesses nor lineup participants are likely to be schooled in the detection of suggestive influences. Improper influences ***231** may go undetected by a suspect, guilty or not, who experiences the emotional tension which we might expect in one being confronted with potential accusers. Even when he does observe abuse, if he has a criminal record he may be reluctant to take the stand and open up the admission of prior convictions. Moreover any protestations by the suspect of the fairness of the lineup made at trial are likely to be in vain; the jury's choice is between the accused's unsupported version and that of the police officers present. In short, the accused's ***232** inability effectively to reconstruct at trial any unfairness that occurred at the ****1935** lineup may deprive him of his only opportunity meaningfully to attack the credibility of the witness' courtroom identification.

What facts have been disclosed in specific cases about the conduct of pretrial confrontations for identification illustrate both the potential for substantial prejudice to the accused at that stage and the need for its revelation at trial. A commentator provides some striking examples:

> In a Canadian case * * * the defendant had been picked out of a lineup of six men, of which he was the only Oriental. On other cases, a black-haired suspect was placed among a group of light-haired persons, tall suspects have been made to stand with short non-suspects, and, in a case where the perpetrator of the crime was known to be a youth, a suspect under twenty was placed in a lineup with five other persons, all of whom were forty or over.

Similarly state reports, in the course of describing prior identifications admitted as evidence of guilt, reveal ***233** numerous instances of suggestive procedures, for example, that all in the lineup but the suspect were known to the identifying witness, that the other participants in a lineup were grossly dissimilar in appearance to the suspect, that only the suspect was required to wear distinctive clothing which the culprit allegedly wore, that the witness is told by the police that they have caught the culprit after which the defendant is brought before the witness alone or is viewed in jail, that the suspect is pointed out before ****1936** or during a lineup, and that the participants in the lineup are asked to try on an article of clothing which fits only the suspect.

The potential for improper influence is illustrated by the circumstances, insofar as they appear, surrounding the prior identifications in the three cases we decide to-

[2552] *Supra*

[2553] *Miranda v. State of Arizona, supra, 384 U.S. at 448, 86 S.Ct. at 1614*

day. In the present case, the testimony of the identifying ***234** witnesses elicited on cross-examination revealed that those witnesses were taken to the courthouse and seated in the courtroom to await assembly of the lineup. The courtroom faced on a hallway observable to the witnesses through an open door. The cashier testified that she saw Wade 'standing in the hall' within sight of an FBI agent. Five or six other prisoners later appeared in the hall. The vice president testified that he saw a person in the hall in the custody of the agent who 'resembled the person that we identified as the one that had entered the bank.'

The lineup in Gilbert, supra, was conducted in an auditorium in which some 100 witnesses to several alleged state and federal robberies charged to Gilbert made wholesale identifications of Gilbert as the robber in each other's presence, a procedure said to be fraught with dangers of suggestion. And the vice of suggestion created by the identification in Stovall, supra, was the presentation to the witness of the suspect alone handcuffed to police officers. It is hard to imagine a situation more clearly conveying the suggestion to the witness that the one presented is believed guilty by the police.[2554]

The few cases that have surfaced therefore reveal the existence of a process attended with hazards of serious unfairness to the criminal accused and strongly suggest the plight of the more numerous defendants who are unable to ferret out suggestive influences in the ***235** secrecy of the confrontation. We do not assume that these risks are the result of police procedures intentionally designed to prejudice an accused. Rather we assume they derive from the dangers inherent in eyewitness identification and the suggestibility inherent in the context of the pretrial identification. Williams & Hammelmann, in one of the most comprehensive studies of such forms of identification, said, '(T)he fact that the police themselves have, in a given case, little or no doubt that the man put up for identification has committed the offense, and that their chief pre-occupation is with the problem of getting sufficient proof, because he has not 'come clean,' involves a a danger that this persuasion may communicate itself even in a doubtful case to the witness in some way * * *.'[2555]

Insofar as the accused's conviction may rest on a courtroom identification in fact the fruit of a suspect pretrial identification which the accused is helpless to subject to effective scrutiny at trial, the accused is deprived of that right of cross-examination which is an essential safeguard to his right to confront the witnesses against him.[2556] And even though cross-examination is a precious safeguard to a fair trial, it cannot be viewed as an absolute ****1937** assurance of accuracy and reliability. Thus in the present context, where so many variables and pitfalls exist, the first line of defense must be the prevention of unfairness and the lessening of the hazards of eyewitness identification at the lineup itself. The trial which might determine the accused's fate may well not be that in the courtroom but that at the pretrial confrontation, with the State aligned against the accused, the witness the sole jury, and the accused unprotected against the overreaching, intentional or unintentional, and with little or no ***236** effective appeal from the judgment there rendered by the witness-'that's the man.'

Since it appears that there is grave potential for prejudice, intentional or not, in the pretrial lineup, which may not be capable of reconstruction at trial, and since presence of counsel itself can often avert prejudice and assure a meaningful confrontation at trial, there can be ***237** little doubt that for Wade the post-indictment lineup was a critical stage of the prosecution at which he was 'as much entitled to such aid (of counsel) * * * as at the trial itself.'[2557] Thus both Wade and his counsel

---

[2554] *See Frankfurter, The Case of Sacco and Vanzetti 31-32*

[2555] *Identification Parades, Part I, (1963) Crim.L.Rev. 479, 483*

[2556] *Pointer v. State of Texas, 380 U.S. 400, 85 S.Ct. 1065, 13 L.Ed.2d 923*

[2557] *Powell v. State of Alabama, 287 U.S. 45, at 57, 53 S.Ct. 55, at 60, 77 L.Ed. 158*

should have been notified of the impending lineup, and counsel's presence should have been a requisite to conduct of the lineup, absent an 'intelligent waiver.'[2558] No substantial countervailing policy considerations have been advanced against the requirement of the presence of counsel. Concern is expressed that the requirement will forestall prompt identifications and result in obstruction of the confrontations. As for the first, **1938 we note that in the two cases in which the right to counsel is today held to apply, counsel had already been appointed and no argument is made in either case that notice to counsel would have prejudicially delayed the confrontations. Moreover, we leave open the question whether the presence of substitute counsel might not suffice where notification and presence of the suspect's own counsel would result in prejudicial delay. And to refuse to recognize the right to counsel for fear that counsel will obstruct the course of justice is contrary to the ***238** basic assumptions upon which this Court has operated in Sixth Amendment cases. We rejected similar logic in Miranda v. State of Arizona, concerning presence of counsel during custodial interrogation:[2559]

> (A)n attorney is merely exercising the good professional judgment he has been taught. This is not cause for considering the attorney a menace to law enforcement. He is merely carrying out what he is sworn to do under his oath-to protect to the extent of his ability the rights of his client. In fulfilling this responsibility the attorney plays a vital role in the administration of criminal justice under our Constitution.

In our view counsel can hardly impede legitimate law enforcement; on the contrary, for the reasons expressed, law enforcement may be assisted by preventing the infiltration of taint in the prosecution's identification evidence. That result cannot help the guilty avoid conviction but can only help assure that the right man has been brought to justice.

***239** Legislative or other regulations, such as those of local police departments, which eliminate the risks of abuse and unintentional suggestion at lineup proceedings and the impediments to meaningful confrontation at trial may also remove the basis for regarding the stage as 'critical.' But neither Congress nor the ****1939** federal authorities have seen fit to provide a solution. What we hold today 'in no way creates a constitutional straitjacket which will handicap sound efforts at reform, nor is it intended to have this effect.'[2560]

V

We come now to the question whether the denial of Wade's motion to strike the courtroom identification by the bank witnesses at trial because of the absence of his counsel at the lineup required, as the Court of Appeals held, the grant of a new trial at which such evidence is ***240** to be excluded. We do not think this disposition can be justified without first giving the Government the opportunity to establish by clear and convincing evidence that the in-court identifications were based upon observations of the suspect other than the lineup identification.[2561] Where, as here, the admissibility of evidence of the lineup identification itself is not involved, a per se rule of exclusion of courtroom identification would be unjustified.[2562] A rule limited solely to the exclusion of testimony concerning identification at the lineup itself, without

---

[2558] *See Carnley v. Cochran, 369 U.S. 506, 82 S.Ct. 884, 8 L.Ed.2d 70*

[2559] *384 U.S. at 480-481, 86 S.Ct. at 1631, 16 L.Ed.2d 694*

[2560] *Miranda v. State of Arizona, supra, at 467, 86 S.Ct. at 1624*

[2561] *See Murphy v. Waterfront Commission, 378 U.S. 52, 79, n. 18, 84 S.Ct. 1594, 1609, 12 L.Ed.2d 678*

[2562] *See Nardone v. United States, 308 U.S. 338, 341, 60 S.Ct. 266, 267, 84 L.Ed. 307*

regard to admissibility of the courtroom identification, would render the right to counsel an empty one. The lineup is most often used, as in the present case, to crystallize the witnesses' identification of the defendant for future reference. We have already noted that the lineup identification will have that effect. The State may then rest upon the witnesses' unequivocal courtroom identifications, and not mention the pretrial identification as part of the State's case at trial. Counsel is then in the predicament in which Wade's counsel found himself-realizing that possible unfairness at the lineup may be the sole means of attack upon the unequivocal courtroom identification, and having to probe in the dark ***241** in an attempt to discover and reveal unfairness, while bolstering the government witness' courtroom identification by bringing out and dwelling upon his prior identification. Since counsel's presence at the lineup would equip him to attack not only the lineup identification but the courtroom identification as well, limiting the impact of violation of the right to counsel to exclusion of evidence only of identification at the lineup itself disregards a critical element of that right.

We think it follows that the proper test to be applied in these situations is that quoted in Wong Sun v. United States,[2563] "(W)hether, granting establishment of the primary illegality, the evidence to which instant objection is made has been come at by exploitation of that illegality or instead by means sufficiently distinguishable to be purged of the primary taint.'[2564] ****1940** Application of this test in the present context requires consideration of various factors; for example, the prior opportunity to observe the alleged criminal act, the existence of any discrepancy between any pre-lineup description and the defendant's actual description, any identification prior to lineup of another person, the identification by picture of the defendant prior to the lineup, failure to identify the defendant on a prior occasion, and the lapse of time between the alleged act and the lineup identification. It is also relevant to consider those facts which, despite the absence of counsel, are disclosed concerning the conduct of the lineup.

***242** We doubt that the Court of Appeals applied the proper test for exclusion of the in-court identification of the two witnesses. The court stated that 'it cannot be said with any certainty that they would have recognized appellant at the time of trial if this intervening lineup had not occurred,' and that the testimony of the two witnesses 'may well have been colored by the illegal procedure (and) was prejudicial.'[2565] Moreover, the court was persuaded, in part, by the 'compulsory verbal responses made by Wade at the instance of the Special Agent.'[2566] This implies the erroneous holding that Wade's privilege against self-incrimination was violated so that the denial of counsel required exclusion.

On the record now before us we cannot make the determination whether the in-court identifications had an independent origin. This was not an issue at trial, although there is some evidence relevant to a determination. That inquiry is most properly made in the District Court. We therefore think the appropriate procedure to be followed is to vacate the conviction pending a hearing to determine whether the in-court identifications had an independent source, or whether, in any event, the introduction of the evidence was harmless error,[2567] and for the District Court to reinstate the conviction or order a new trial, as may be proper.[2568]

[2563] *371 U.S. 471, 488, 83 S.Ct. 407, 417, 9 L.Ed.2d 441*

[2564] *Maguire, Evidence of Guilt, 221 (1959). See also Hoffa v. United States, 385 U.S. 293, 309, 87 S.Ct. 408, 17 L.Ed.2d 374*

[2565] *358 F.2d, at 560*

[2566] *Ibid.*

[2567] *Chapman v. State of California, 386 U.S. 18, 87 S.Ct. 824, 17 L.Ed.2d 705*

[2568] *See United States v. Shotwell Mfg. Co., 355 U.S. 233, 245-246, 78 S.Ct. 245, 253, 2 L.Ed.2d 234*

***243** The judgment of the Court of Appeals is vacated and the case is remanded to that court with direction to enter a new judgment vacating the conviction and remanding the case to the District Court for further proceedings consistent with this opinion.

It is so ordered.

Judgment of Court of Appeals vacated and case remanded with direction.

THE CHIEF JUSTICE joins the opinion of the Court except for Part I, from which he dissents for the reasons expressed in the opinion of Mr. Justice FORTAS.

Mr. Justice DOUGLAS joins the opinion of the Court except for Part I. On that phase of the case he adheres to the dissenting views in ****1941** Schmerber v. State of California,[2569] since he believes that compulsory lineup violates the privilege against self-incrimination contained in the Fifth Amendment.

Mr. Justice CLARK, concurring.

With reference to the lineup point involved in this case I cannot, for the life of me, see why a lineup is not a critical stage of the prosecution. Identification of the suspect-a prerequisite to establishment of guilt-occurs at this stage, and with Miranda v. State of Arizona[2570] on the books, the requirement of the presence of counsel arises, unless waived by the suspect. I dissented in Miranda but I am bound by it now, as we all are. Schmerber v. State of California[2571] precludes petitioner's claim of self-incrimination. I therefore join the opinion of the Court.

(The dissent and partial concurrence of Mr. Justice BLACK is omitted.)

(The dissent and partial concurrences of Mr. Justice WHITE, whom Mr. Justice HARLAN and Mr. Justice STEWART join, are omitted.)

Black Letter Law

> The Court held that the post-indictment lineup is a critical stage of the prosecution, and as such, the defendant is entitled to the aid of counsel. Both the defendant and counsel must be notified of the impending lineup and counsel must be present, unless the right to counsel has been intelligently waived.

Kirby v. Illinois

92 S.Ct. 1877

Supreme Court of the United States

Thomas KIRBY, etc., Petitioner,

v.

State of ILLINOIS.

No. 70-5061. | Argued Nov. 11, 1971. | Reargued March 20 and 21, 1972. | Decided June 7, 1972.

[2569] *384 U.S. 757, 772-779, 86 S.Ct. 1826, 16 L.Ed.2d 908*

[2570] *384 U.S. 436, 86 S.Ct. 1602, 16 L.Ed.2d 694 (1966)*

[2571] *384 U.S. 757, 86 S.Ct. 1826, 16 L.Ed.2d 908 (1966)*

Mr. Justice STEWART announced the judgment of the Court and an opinion in which THE CHIEF JUSTICE, Mr. Justice BLACKMUN, and Mr. Justice REHNQUIST join.

In United States v. Wade[2572] and Gilbert v. California,[2573] this Court held 'that a post-indictment pretrial lineup at which the accused is exhibited to identifying witnesses is a critical stage of the criminal prosecution; that police conduct of such a lineup without notice to and in the absence of his counsel denies the accused his Sixth (and Fourteenth) Amendment right to counsel and calls in question the admissibility at trial of the in-court identifications of the accused by witnesses who attended the lineup.'[2574] Those cases further held that no 'in-court identifications' are admissible in evidence if their 'source' is a lineup conducted in violation of this constitutional standard. 'Only a per se exclusionary rule as to such testimony can be an effective sanction,' the Court said, 'to assure that law ***684** enforcement authorities will respect the accused's constitutional right to the presence of his counsel at the critical lineup.'[2575] In the present case we are asked to extend the Wade-Gilbert per se exclusionary rule to identification testimony based upon a police station show-up that took place before the defendant had been indicted or otherwise formally charged with any criminal offense.

On February 21, 1968, a man named Willie Shard reported to the Chicago police that the previous day two men had robbed him on a Chicago street of a wallet containing, among other things, traveler's checks and a Social Security card. On February 22, two police officers stopped the petitioner and a companion, Ralph Bean, on West Madison Street in Chicago. When asked for ****1880** identification, the petitioner produced a wallet that contained three traveler's checks and a Social Security card, all bearing the name of Willie Shard. Papers with Shard's name on them were also found in Bean's possession. When asked to explain his possession of Shard's property, the petitioner first said that the traveler's checks were 'play money,' and then told the officers that he had won them in a crap game. The officers then arrested the petitioner and Bean and took them to a police station.

Only after arriving at the police station, and checking the records there, did the arresting officers learn of the Shard robbery. A police car was then dispatched to Shard's place of employment, where it picked up Shard and brought him to the police station. Immediately upon entering the room in the police station where the petitioner and Bean were seated at a table, Shard positively identified them as the men who had ***685** robbed him two days earlier. No lawyer was present in the room, and neither the petitioner nor Bean had asked for legal assistance, or been advised of any right to the presence of counsel.

More than six weeks later, the petitioner and Bean were indicted for the robbery of Willie Shard. Upon arraignment, counsel was appointed to represent them, and they pleaded not guilty. A pretrial motion to suppress Shard's identification testimony was denied, and at the trial Shard testified as a witness for the prosecution. In his testimony he described his identification of the two men at the police station on February 22, and identified them again in the courtroom as the men ***686** who had robbed him on February 20. He was cross-examined at length regarding the circumstances of his identification of the two defendants.[2576] ****1881** The jury found both

[2572] *388 U.S. 218, 87 S.Ct. 1926, 18 L.Ed.2d 1149*

[2573] *388 U.S. 263, 87 S.Ct. 1951, 18 L.Ed.2d 1178*

[2574] *Gilbert v. California, supra, at 272, 87 S.Ct. at 1956*

[2575] *Id., at 273, 87 S.Ct., at 1957*

[2576] *Cf. Pointer v. Texas, 380 U.S. 400, 85 S.Ct. 1065, 13 L.Ed.2d 923*

defendants guilty, and the petitioner's conviction was affirmed on appeal.[2577] The Illinois appellate court held that the admission of Shard's testimony was not error, relying upon an earlier decision of the Illinois Supreme Court, People v. Palmer,[2578] holding that the Wade-Gilbert per se exclusionary rule is not applicable to pre-indictment confrontations. ***687** We granted certiorari, limited to this question.[2579]

I

We note at the outset that the constitutional privilege against compulsory self-incrimination is in no way implicated here. The Court emphatically rejected the claimed applicability of that constitutional guarantee in Wade itself:

> Neither the lineup itself nor anything shown by this record that Wade was required to do in the lineup violated his privilege against self-incrimination. We have only recently reaffirmed that the privilege protects an accused only from being compelled to testify against himself, or otherwise provide the State with evidence of a testimonial or communicative nature . . .[2580]

> We have no doubt that compelling the accused merely to exhibit his person for observation by a prosecution witness prior to trial involves no compulsion of the accused to give evidence having testimonial significance. It is compulsion of the accused ***688** to exhibit his physical characteristics, not compulsion to disclose to any knowledge he might have. . . .[2581]

It follows that the doctrine of Miranda v. Arizona,[2582] has no applicability whatever to the issue before us; for the Miranda decision was based exclusively upon the Fifth and Fourteenth Amendment privilege against compulsory self-incrimination, upon the theory that custodial interrogation is inherently coercive.

The Wade-Gilbert exclusionary rule, by contrast, stems from a quite different constitutional guarantee-the guarantee of the right to counsel contained in the Sixth and Fourteenth Amendments. Unless all semblance of principled constitutional adjudication is to be abandoned, therefore, it is to the decisions construing that guarantee that we must look in determining the present controversy.

In a line of constitutional cases in this Court stemming back to the Court's landmark opinion in Powell v. Alabama,[2583] it has been firmly established that a person's Sixth and Fourteenth Amendment right to counsel attaches only at or after the time that adversary judicial proceedings have been initiated against him.[2584] ****1882**

[2577] *People v. Kirby, 121 Ill.App.2d 323, 257 N.E.2d 589*

[2578] *41 Ill.2d 571, 244 N.E.2d 173*

[2579] *402 U.S. 995, 91 S.Ct. 2178, 29 L.Ed.2d 160*

[2580] *Schmerber v. State of California, 384 U.S. 757, 761, 86 S.Ct. 1826, 1830, 16 L.Ed.2d 908. . . .' 388 U.S., at 221, 87 S.Ct. at 1929*

[2581] *Id., at 222, 87 S.Ct. at 1930*

[2582] *384 U.S. 436, 86 S.Ct. 1602, 16 L.Ed.2d 694*

[2583] *287 U.S. 45, 53 S.Ct. 55, 77 L.Ed. 158*

[2584] *See Powell v. Alabama, supra; Johnson v. Zerbst, 304 U.S. 458, 58 S.Ct. 1019, 82 L.Ed. 1461; Hamilton v. Alabama, 368 U.S. 52, 82 S.Ct. 157, 7 L.Ed.2d 114; Gideon v. Wainwright, 372 U.S. 335, 83 S.Ct. 792, 9 L.Ed.2d 799; White v. Maryland, 373 U.S. 59, 83 S.Ct. 1050, 10 L.Ed.2d 193; Massiah v. United States, 377 U.S. 201, 84 S.Ct. 1199, 12 L.Ed.2d 246; United States v. Wade, 388 U.S. 218, 87 S.Ct. 1926, 18 L.Ed.2d 1149; Gilbert v. California, 388 U.S. 263, 87 S.Ct. 1951, 18 L.Ed.2d 1178; Coleman v. Alabama, 399 U.S. 1, 90 S.Ct. 1999, 26 L.Ed.2d 387*

This is not to say that a defendant in a criminal case has a constitutional right to counsel only at the trial itself. The Powell case makes clear that the right attaches at the time of arraignment, and the Court ***689** has recently held that it exists also at the time of a preliminary hearing.[2585] But the point is that, while members of the Court have differed as to existence of the right to counsel in the contexts of some of the above cases, all of those cases have involved points of time at or after the initiation of adversary judicial criminal proceedings-whether by way of formal charge, preliminary hearing, indictment, information, or arraignment.

The only seeming deviation from this long line of constitutional decisions was Escobedo v. Illinois.[2586] But Escobedo is not apposite here for two distinct reasons. First, the Court in retrospect perceived that the 'prime purpose' of Escobedo was not to vindicate the constitutional right to counsel as such, but, like Miranda, 'to guarantee full effectuation of the privilege against self-incrimination . . .'[2587] Secondly, and perhaps even more important for purely practical purposes, the Court has limited the holding of Escobedo to its own facts,[2588] and those facts are not remotely akin to the facts of the case before us.

The initiation of judicial criminal proceedings is far from a mere formalism. It is the starting point of our whole system of adversary criminal justice. For it is only then that the government has committed itself to prosecute, and only then that the adverse positions of government and defendant have solidified. It is then that a defendant finds himself faced with the prosecutorial forces of organized society, and immersed in the intricacies of substantive and procedural criminal law. ***690** It is this point, therefore, that marks the commencement of the 'criminal prosecutions' to which alone the explicit guarantees of the Sixth Amendment are applicable.[2589]

In this case we are asked to import into a routine police investigation an absolute constitutional guarantee historically and rationally applicable only after the onset of formal prosecutorial ****1883** proceedings. We decline to do so. Less than a year after Wade and Gilbert were decided, the Court explained the rule of those decisions as follows: 'The rationale of those cases was that an accused is entitled to counsel at any 'critical stage of the prosecution,' and that a post-indictment lineup is such a 'critical stage.''[2590] We decline to depart from that rationale today by imposing a per se exclusionary rule upon testimony concerning an identification that took place long before the commencement of any prosecution whatever.

II

What has been said is not to suggest that there may not be occasions during the course of a criminal investigation when the police do abuse identification procedures. Such abuses are not beyond the reach of the Constitution. As the Court pointed out in Wade itself, it is always necessary to 'scrutinize any pretrial confrontation ***691** . . .'[2591] The Due Process Clause of the Fifth and Fourteenth Amendments forbids a lineup that is unnecessarily suggestive and conducive to irreparable mistaken identification.[2592] When a person has not been formally charged with a criminal of-

[2585] *Coleman v. Alabama, supra*

[2586] *378 U.S. 478, 84 S.Ct. 1758, 12 L.Ed.2d 977*

[2587] *Johnson v. New Jersey, 384 U.S. 719, 729, 86 S.Ct. 1772, 1779, 16 L.Ed.2d 882*

[2588] *Johnson v. New Jersey, supra, at 733-734, 86 S.Ct. at 1780*

[2589] *See Powell v. Alabama, 287 U.S., at 66-71, 53 S.Ct., at 63; Massiah v. United States, 377 U.S. 201, 84 S.Ct. 1199, 12 L.Ed. 2d 246; Spano v. New York, 360 U.S. 315, 324, 79 S.Ct. 1202, 1207, 3 L.Ed.2d 1265 (Douglas, J., concurring)*

[2590] *(Emphasis supplied.) Simmons v. United States, 390 U.S. 377, 382-383, 88 S.Ct. 967, 970, 19 L.Ed.2d 1247*

[2591] *388 U.S., at 227, 87 S.Ct. at 1932*

[2592] *Stovall v. Denno, 388 U.S. 293, 87 S.Ct. 1967, 18 L.Ed.2d 1199; Foster v. California, 394 U.S. 440, 89 S.Ct. 1127, 22 L.Ed. 2d 402*

fense, Stovall strikes the appropriate constitutional balance between the right of a suspect to be protected from prejudicial procedures and the interest of society in the prompt and purposeful investigation of an unsolved crime.

The judgment is affirmed.

Mr. Chief Justice BURGER, concurring.

I agree that the right to counsel attaches as soon as criminal charges are formally made against an accused and he becomes the subject of a 'criminal prosecution.' Therefore, I join in the plurality opinion and in the judgment.[2593]

Mr. Justice POWELL, concurring in the result.

As I would not extend the Wade-Gilbert per se exclusionary rule, I concur in the result reached by the Court.

(The dissent of Mr. Justice BRENNAN, with whom Mr. Justice DOUGLAS and Mr. Justice MARSHALL join, is omitted.)

(The dissent of Mr. Justice White is omitted.)

Black Letter Law

> The Court held that lineups occurring "post arrest," but before indictment, are not a critical stage of the prosecution, and a Sixth Amendment right to counsel does not exist for such lineups.

Discussion Problem:

15-1. On May 15, the victim was accosted in her bedroom by an intruder, who held a sharp object to her neck and ordered her to keep her head down. The intruder proceeded to rob and rape the victim. The victim was unable to see the intruder's face during the approximately twenty-minute attack, however, she did hear him speak extensively and was able to notice that he was wearing white shoes and red sweat pants.

Shortly after the victim reported the incident, appellant, wearing red sweat pants and white tennis shoes, was apprehended by police officers in the vicinity of the victim's home. When he was approached by the police, appellant gave his brother's name, and in a subsequent search, the police recovered a razor, a nail clipper, and a nunchuck from appellant's person. On May 22, the police held a "live" voice line-up during which the victim narrowed her selection down to appellant and one other individual. Over two months later, on July 30, after listening to an audio tape of the voice line-up, the victim identified appellant's voice as that of her assailant. Neither appellant nor his attorney was present at the audio tape replay. At the first of the two voice line-ups, with both appellant and his attorney present, five police officers and appellant stood behind the victim and each in turn read a series of threats which the assailant had used. Each participant also read a passage taken from the local newspaper.

At pretrial, appellant unsuccessfully moved to suppress the results of the voice identification. At trial, the State presented an audio-video tape of the voice line-up to the jury. Appellant presented a voice identification expert witness who was allowed to testify as to general standards to measure accuracy in voice identification. Appel-

[2593] *Cf. Coleman v. Alabama, 399 U.S. 1, 21, 90 S.Ct. 1999, 2009, 26 L.Ed.2d 387 (dissenting opinion)*

lant also presented an expert who testified that a sperm sample taken from the victim did not match a sperm sample given by appellant. The State presented expert rebuttal testimony on this issue.

Appellant, analogizing to post-indictment line-up cases, asserts that the absence of his attorney at the audio tape replay violated the right to counsel and further argues that the lack of his presence at the "critical stage" of the replay violates fundamental fairness. For these reasons, appellant contends that the trial court should have suppressed the results of the voice identification procedure

You are an appellate judge writing the majority opinion in this case. Structure your opinion based upon your understanding of the constitutional doctrines applicable to confessions.

-Notes-

Chapter 16: Attenuation of the Taint

Wong Sun v. United States

83 S.Ct. 407

Supreme Court of the United States

WONG SUN and James Wah Toy, Petitioners,

v.

UNITED STATES.

No. 36. | Reargued Oct. 8 and 9, 1962. | Decided Jan. 14, 1963.

Mr. Justice BRENNAN delivered the opinion of the Court.

The petitioners were tried without a jury in the District Court for the Northern District of California under a two-count indictment for violation of the Federal Narcotics ***473** Laws.[2594] They were acquitted under the first count which charged a conspiracy, but convicted under the second ****410** count which charged the substantive offense of fraudulent and knowing transportation and concealment of illegally imported heroin. The Court of Appeals for the Ninth Circuit, one judge dissenting, affirmed the convictions.[2595] We granted certiorari.[2596] We heard argument in the 1961 Term and re-argument this Term.[2597]

About 2 a.m. on the morning of June 4, 1959, federal narcotics agents in San Francisco, after having had one Hom Way under surveillance for six weeks, arrested him and found heroin in his possession. Hom Way, who had not before been an informant, stated after his arrest that he had bought an ounce of heroin the night before from one known to him only as 'Blackie Toy,' proprietor of a laundry on Leavenworth Street.

About 6 a.m. that morning six or seven federal agents went to a laundry at 1733 Leavenworth Street. The sign ***474** above the door of this establishment said 'Oye's Laundry.' It was operated by the petitioner James Wah Toy. There is, however, nothing in the record which identifies James Wah Toy and 'Blackie Toy' as the same person. The other federal officers remained nearby out of sight while Agent Alton Wong, who was of Chinese ancestry, rang the bell. When petitioner Toy appeared and opened the door, Agent Wong told him that he was calling for laundry and dry cleaning. Toy replied that he didn't open until 8 o'clock and told the agent to come back at that time. Toy started to close the door. Agent Wong thereupon took his badge from his pocket and said, 'I am a federal narcotics agent.' Toy immediately 'slammed the door and started running' down the hallway through the laundry to his living quarters at the back where his wife and child were sleeping in a bedroom. Agent Wong and the other federal officers broke open the door and followed Toy down the hallway to the living quarters and into the bedroom. Toy reached into a nightstand drawer. Agent Wong thereupon drew his pistol, pulled Toy's hand out of the drawer, placed him under arrest and handcuffed him. There was nothing in the drawer and a search of the premises uncovered no narcotics.

One of the agents said to Toy '(Hom Way) says he got narcotics from you.' Toy responded, '[n]o, I haven't been selling any narcotics at all. However, I do know somebody who has.' When asked who that was, Toy said, 'I only know him as John-

[2594] *21 U.S.C. s 174, 21 U.S.C.A. s 174*

[2595] *288 F.2d 366*

[2596] *368 U.S. 817, 82 S.Ct. 75, 7 L.Ed.2d 23*

[2597] *370 U.S. 908, 82 S.Ct. 1254, 8 L.Ed.2d 403*

ny. I don't know his last name.' However, Toy described a house on Eleventh Avenue where he said Johnny lived; he also described a bedroom in the house where he said 'Johnny kept about a piece' of heroin, and where he and Johnny had smoked some of the drug the night before. The agents ***475** left immediately for Eleventh Avenue and located the house. They entered and found one Johnny Yee in the bedroom. After a discussion with the agents, Yee took from a bureau drawer several tubes containing in all just less than one ounce of heroin, and surrendered them. Within the hour Yee and Toy were taken to the Office of the Bureau ****411** of Narcotics. Yee there stated that the heroin had been brought to him some four days earlier by petitioner Toy and another Chinese known to him only as 'Sea Dog.'

Toy was questioned as to the identity of 'Sea Dog' and said that 'Sea Dog' was Wong Sun. Some agents, including Agent Alton Wong, took Toy to Wong Sun's neighborhood where Toy pointed out a multifamily dwelling where he said Wong Sun lived. Agent Wong rang a downstairs door bell and a buzzer sounded, opening the door. The officer identified himself as a narcotics agent to a woman on the landing and asked 'for Mr. Wong.' The woman was the wife of petitioner Wong Sun. She said that Wong Sun was 'in the back room sleeping.' Alton Wong and some six other officers climbed the stairs and entered the apartment. One of the officers went into the back room and brought petitioner Wong Sun from the bedroom in handcuffs. A thorough search of the apartment followed, but no narcotics were discovered.

Petitioner Toy and Johnny Yee were arraigned before a United States Commissioner on June 4 on a complaint charging a violation of 21 U.S.C. § 174.[2598] Later that day, each was released on his own recognizance. Petitioner Wong Sun was arraigned on a similar complaint filed the next day and was also released on his own recognizance. ***476** Within a few days, both petitioners and Yee were interrogated at the office of the Narcotics Bureau by Agent William Wong, also of Chinese ancestry. The agent advised each of the three of his right to withhold information which might be used against him, and stated to each that he was entitled to the advice of counsel, though it does not appear that any attorney was present during the questioning of any of the three. The officer also explained to each that no promises or offers of immunity or leniency were being or could be made.

The agent interrogated each of the three separately. After each had been interrogated the agent prepared a statement in English from rough notes. The agent read petitioner Toy's statement to him in English and interpreted certain portions of it for him in Chinese. Toy also read the statement in English aloud to the agent, said there were corrections to be made, and made the corrections in his own hand. Toy would not sign the statement, however; in the agent's words 'he wanted to know first if the other persons involved in the case had signed theirs.' Wong Sun had considerable difficulty understanding the ***477** statement in English and the agent restated its substance in Chinese. Wong Sun refused to sign the statement although he admitted the accuracy of its contents.

Hom Way did not testify at petitioners' trial. The Government offered Johnny Yee as its principal witness but excused him after he invoked the privilege ****412** against self-incrimination and flatly repudiated the statement he had given to Agent William Wong. That statement was not offered in evidence nor was any testimony elicited from him identifying either petitioner as the source of the heroin in his possession, or otherwise tending to support the charges against the petitioners.

The statute expressly provides that proof of the accused's possession of the drug will support a conviction under the statute unless the accused satisfactorily explains the possession. The Government's evidence tending to prove the petitioners' possession (the petitioners offered no exculpatory testimony) consisted of four items which the trial court admitted over timely objections that they were inadmissible as 'fruits' of unlawful arrests or of attendant searches: (1) the statements made orally by peti-

[2598] *21 U.S.C.A. § 174*

tioner Toy in his bedroom at the time of his arrest; (2) the heroin surrendered to the agents by Johnny Yee; (3) petitioner Toy's pretrial unsigned statement; and (4) petitioner Wong Sun's similar statement. The dispute below and here has centered around the correctness of the rulings of the trial judge allowing these items in evidence.

The Court of Appeals held that the arrests of both petitioners were illegal because not based on "probable cause' within the meaning of the Fourth Amendment' nor 'reasonable grounds' within the meaning of the Narcotic ***478** Control Act of 1956. The court said as to Toy's arrest, 'There is no showing in this case that the agent knew Hom Way to be reliable,' and, furthermore, found 'nothing in the circumstances occurring at Toy's premises that would provide sufficient justification for his arrest without a warrant.' 288 F.2d at 369, 370. As to Wong Sun's arrest, the court said 'there is no showing that Johnnie Yee was a reliable informer.' The Court of Appeals nevertheless held that the four items of proof were not the 'fruits' of the illegal arrests and that they were therefore properly admitted in evidence.

The Court of Appeals rejected two additional contentions of the petitioners. The first was that there was insufficient evidence to corroborate the petitioners' unsigned admissions of possession of narcotics. The court held that the narcotics in evidence surrendered by Johnny Yee, together with Toy's statements in his bedroom at the time of arrest corroborated petitioners' admissions. The second contention was that the confessions were ***479** inadmissible because they were not signed. The Court of Appeals held on this point that the petitioners were not prejudiced, since the agent might properly have testified to the substance of the conversations which produced the statements.

We believe that significant differences between the cases of the two petitioners require separate discussion of each. We shall first consider the case of petitioner Toy.

****413 I**

The Court of Appeals found there was neither reasonable grounds nor probable cause for Toy's arrest. Giving due weight to that finding, we think it is amply justified by the facts clearly shown on this record. It is basic that an arrest with or without a warrant must stand upon firmer ground than mere suspicion,[2599] though the arresting officer need not have in hand evidence which would suffice to convict. The quantum of information which constitutes probable cause—evidence which would 'warrant a man of reasonable caution in the belief' that a felony has been committed[2600]—must be measured by the facts of the particular case. The history of the use, and not infrequent abuse, of the power to arrest cautions that a relaxation of the fundamental requirements of probable cause would 'leave law-abiding citizens at the mercy of the officers' whim or caprice.'[2601]

Whether or not the requirements of reliability and particularity of the information on which an officer may act are more stringent where an arrest warrant is absent, they surely cannot be less stringent then where an arrest warrant is obtained. Otherwise, a principal incentive now ***480** existing for the procurement of arrest warrants would be destroyed. The threshold question in this case, therefore, is whether the officers could, on the information which impelled them to act, have procured a warrant for the arrest of Toy. We think that no warrant would have issued on evidence then available.

The narcotics agents had no basis in experience for confidence in the reliability of Hom Way's information; he had never before given information. And yet they

---

[2599] *See Henry v. United States, 361 U.S. 98, 101, 80 S.Ct. 168, 170, 4 L.Ed.2d 134*

[2600] *Carroll v. United States, 267 U.S. 132, 162, 45 S.Ct. 280, 288, 69 L.Ed. 543*

[2601] *Brinegar v. United States, 338 U.S. 160, 176, 69 S.Ct. 1302, 1311, 93 L.Ed. 1879*

acted upon his imprecise suggestion that a person described only as 'Blackie Toy,' the proprietor of a laundry somewhere on Leavenworth Street, had sold one ounce of heroin. We have held that identification of the suspect by a reliable informant may constitute probable cause for arrest where the information given is sufficiently accurate to lead the officers directly to the suspect.[2602] That rule does not, however, fit this case. For aught that the record discloses, Hom Way's accusation merely invited the officers to roam the length of Leavenworth Street (some 30 blocks) in search of one 'Blackie Toy's' laundry—and whether by chance or other ***481** means (the record does not say) they came upon petitioner Toy's laundry, which bore not his name over the door, ****414** but the unrevealing label 'Oye's.' Not the slightest intimation appears on the record, or was made on oral argument, to suggest that the agents had information giving them reason to equate 'Blackie' Toy and James Wah Toy—e.g., that they had the criminal record of a Toy, or that they had consulted some other kind of official record or list, or had some information of some kind which had narrowed the scope of their search to this particular Toy.

It is conceded that the officers made no attempt to obtain a warrant for Toy's arrest. The simple fact is that on the sparse information at the officers' command, no arrest warrant could have issued consistently with Rules 3 and 4 of the Federal Rules of Criminal Procedure.[2603] The arrest warrant procedure serves to insure that the deliberate, impartial judgment of a judicial officer will be interposed ***482** between the citizen and the police, to assess the weight and credibility of the information which the complaining officer adduces as probable cause.[2604] To hold that an officer may act in his own, unchecked discretion upon information too vague and from too untested a source to permit a judicial officer to accept it as probable cause for an arrest warrant, would subvert this fundamental policy.

The Government contends, however, that any defects in the information which somehow took the officers to petitioner Toy's laundry were remedied by events which occurred after they arrived. Specifically, it is urged that Toy's flight down the hall when the supposed customer at the door revealed that he was a narcotics agent adequately corroborates the suspicion generated by Hom Way's accusation. Our holding in Miller v. United States[2605] is relevant here, and exposes the fallacy of this contention. We noted in that case that the lawfulness of an officer's entry to arrest without a warrant 'must be tested by criteria identical with those embodied in 18 U.S.C. § 3109, which deals with entry to execute a search warrant.'[2606] That statute requires that an officer must state his authority and his purpose at the threshold, and be refused admittance, before he may break open the door. We held that when an officer insufficiently or unclearly identifies his office or his mission, the occupant's flight from the door must be regarded as ambiguous conduct. We expressly reserved the question 'whether the unqualified requirements of the rule admit of an exception justifying noncompliance in exigent circumstances.'[2607] In the instant case, Toy's flight from the door afforded no surer an inference of guilty knowledge than did the suspect's conduct in the Miller case. Agent Wong did ****415** eventually disclose that he was a narcotics officer. However, he affirmatively misrepresented his mission at the ***483** outset, by stating that he had come for laundry and dry cleaning. And before

---

[2602] *Draper v. United States, 358 U.S. 307, 79 S.Ct. 329, 3 L.Ed.2d 327*

[2603] *18 U.S.C.A. Giordenello v. United States, 357 U.S. 480, 486, 78 S.Ct. 1245, 2 L.Ed.2d 1503*

[2604] *Cf. Jones v. United States, 362 U.S. 257, 270, 80 S.Ct. 725, 4 L.Ed.2d 697*

[2605] *357 U.S. 301, 78 S.Ct. 1190, 2 L.Ed.2d 1332*

[2606] *357 U.S. at 306, 78 S.Ct. at 1194*

[2607] *357 U.S. at 309, 78 S.Ct. at 1196*

Toy filed, the officer never adequately dispelled the misimpression engendered by his own ruse.[2608]

Moreover, he made no effort at that time, nor indeed at any time thereafter, to ascertain whether the man at the door was the 'Blackie Toy' named by Hom Way. Therefore, this is not the case we hypothesized in Miller where 'without an express announcement of purpose, the facts known to officers would justify them in being virtually certain' that the person at the door knows their purpose.[2609] Toy's refusal to admit the officers and his flight down the hallway thus signified a guilty knowledge no more clearly than it did a natural desire to repel an apparently unauthorized intrusion. Here, as in Miller, ***484** the Government claims no extraordinary circumstances—such as the imminent destruction of vital evidence, or the need to rescue a victim in peril,[2610] which excused the officer's failure truthfully to state his mission before he broke in.

A contrary holding here would mean that a vague suspicion could be transformed into probable cause for arrest by reason of ambiguous conduct which the arresting officers themselves have provoked.[2611] That result would have the same essential vice as a proposition we have consistently rejected—that a search unlawful at its inception may be validated by what it turns up.[2612] Thus we conclude that the Court of Appeals' finding that the officers' uninvited entry into Toy's living quarters was unlawful and that the bedroom arrest which followed was likewise unlawful, was fully justified on the evidence. It remains to be seen what consequences flow from this conclusion.

II.

It is conceded that Toy's declarations in his bedroom are to be excluded ****416** if they are held to be 'fruits' of the agents' unlawful action.

In order to make effective the fundamental constitutional guarantees of sanctity of the home and inviolability of the person,[2613] this Court held nearly half a century ago that evidence seized during an unlawful search could not constitute proof against the victim of the search.[2614] The exclusionary prohibition extends as well to the indirect as the direct products of such invasions.[2615] ***485** Mr. Justice Holmes, speaking for the Court in that case, in holding that the Government might not make use of information obtained during an unlawful search to subpoena from the victims the very documents illegally viewed, expressed succinctly the policy of the broad exclusionary rule:

> The essence of a provision forbidding the acquisition of evidence in a certain way is that not merely evidence so acquired shall not be used before the Court but that it shall not be used at all. Of course this does not mean that the facts thus obtained become sacred and inaccessible. If knowledge of them is gained from an independent source they may be

[2608] *Cf. Gouled v. United States, 255 U.S. 298, 41 S.Ct. 261, 65 L.Ed. 647; Gatewood v. United States, 93 U.S.App.D.C. 226, 209 F.2d 789*

[2609] *357 U.S. at 310, 78 S.Ct. at 1196*

[2610] *See 357 U.S., at 309, 78 S.Ct. 1195*

[2611] *Cf. Henry v. United States, 361 U.S. 98, 104, 80 S.Ct. 168, 172, 4 L.Ed.2d 134*

[2612] *Byars v. United States, 273 U.S. 28, 47 S.Ct. 248, 71 L.Ed. 520; United States v. Di Re, 332 U.S. 581, 595, 68 S.Ct. 222, 228, 92 L.Ed. 210*

[2613] *Boyd v. United States, 116 U.S. 616, 6 S.Ct. 524, 29 L.Ed. 746*

[2614] *Weeks v. United States, 232 U.S. 383, 34 S.Ct. 341, 58 L.Ed. 652*

[2615] *Silverthorne Lumber Co. v. United States, 251 U.S. 385, 40 S.Ct. 182, 64 L.Ed. 319*

> proved like any others, but the knowledge gained by the Government's own wrong cannot be used by it in the way proposed.[2616]

The exclusionary rule has traditionally barred from trial physical, tangible materials obtained either during or as a direct result of an unlawful invasion. It follows from our holding in Silverman v. United States,[2617] that the Fourth Amendment may protect against the overhearing of verbal statements as well as against the more traditional seizure of 'papers and effects.' Similarly, testimony as to matters observed during an unlawful invasion has been excluded in order to enforce the basic constitutional policies.[2618] Thus, verbal evidence which derives so immediately from an unlawful entry and an unauthorized arrest as the officers' action in the present case is no less the 'fruit' of official illegality than the more common tangible fruits of the unwarranted intrusion.[2619] ***486** Nor do the policies underlying the exclusionary rule invite any logical distinction between physical and verbal evidence. Either in terms of deterring lawless conduct by federal officers,[2620] or of closing the doors of the federal courts to any use of evidence unconstitutionally obtained,[2621] the danger in relaxing the exclusionary rules in the case of verbal evidence would seem too great to warrant introducing such a distinction.

The Government argues that Toy's statements to the officers in his bedroom, although closely consequent upon the invasion which we hold unlawful, were nevertheless admissible because they resulted from 'an intervening independent act of a free will.' This contention, however, takes insufficient account of the circumstances. Six or seven officers had broken the door and followed on Toy's heels into the bedroom where his wife and child were sleeping. He had been almost immediately handcuffed and arrested. Under such circumstances it is unreasonable to infer that Toy's response was sufficiently an act of free ****417** will to purge the primary taint of the unlawful invasion.

***487** The Government also contends that Toy's declarations should be admissible because they were ostensibly exculpatory rather than incriminating. There are two answers to this argument. First, the statements soon turned out to be incriminating, for they led directly to the evidence which implicated Toy. Second, when circumstances are shown such as those which induced these declarations, it is immaterial whether the declarations be termed 'exculpatory.' Thus we find no substantial reason to omit Toy's declarations from the protection of the exclusionary rule.

III.

We now consider whether the exclusion of Toy's declarations requires also the exclusion of the narcotics taken from Yee, to which those declarations led the police. The prosecutor candidly told the trial court that 'we wouldn't have found those drugs except that Mr. Toy helped us to.' Hence this is not the case envisioned by this Court where the exclusionary rule has no application because the Government learned of the evidence 'from an independent source.'[2622] Nor is this a case in which the connection between the lawless conduct of the police and the discovery of the chal-

[2616] *251 U.S. at 392, 40 S.Ct. at 183*

[2617] *365 U.S. 505, 81 S.Ct. 679, 5 L.Ed.2d 734*

[2618] *McGinnis v. United States, 1 Cir., 227 F.2d 598*

[2619] *See Nueslein v. District of Columbia, 73 App.D.C. 85, 115 F.2d 690*

[2620] *Rea v. United States, 350 U.S. 214, 76 S.Ct. 292, 100 L.Ed. 233*

[2621] *Elkins v. United States, 364 U.S. 206, 80 S.Ct. 1437, 4 L.Ed.2d 1669*

[2622] *Silverthorne Lumber Co. v. United States, 251 U.S. 385, 392, 40 S.Ct. 182, 183, 64 L.Ed. 319*

lenged evidence has 'become so attenuated as to dissipate the taint.'[2623] We need not hold that all evidence ***488** is 'fruit of the poisonous tree' simply because it would not have come to light but for the illegal actions of the police. Rather, the more apt question in such a case is 'whether, granting establishment of the primary illegality, the evidence to which instant objection is made has been come at by exploitation of that illegality or instead by means sufficiently distinguishable to be purged of the primary taint.'[2624] We think it clear that the narcotics were 'come at by the exploitation of that illegality' and hence that they may not be used against Toy.

IV.

It remains only to consider Toy's unsigned statement. We need not decide whether, in light of the fact that Toy was free on his own recognizance when he made the statement, that statement was a fruit of the illegal arrest.[2625] Since ****418** we have concluded that his declarations in the bedroom and the narcotics surrendered by Yee should not have been admitted in evidence against him, the only proofs remaining to sustain his conviction are his and Wong Sun's unsigned statements. Without scrutinizing the contents of Toy's ambiguous recitals, we conclude that no reference to Toy in Wong Sun's statement constitutes admissible evidence corroborating any admission by Toy. We arrive at this conclusion upon two clear lines of decisions which converge to require it. One line of our decisions establishes that criminal confessions and admissions of guilt require extrinsic corroboration; the other line of precedents holds that an out-of-court declaration made after arrest may not be used at trial against one of the declarant's partners in crime.

It is a settled principle of the administration of criminal justice in the federal courts that a conviction must rest upon firmer ground than the uncorroborated admission or ***489** confession of the accused. We observed in Smith v. United States[2626] that the requirement of corroboration is rooted in 'a long history of judicial experience with confessions and in the realization that sound law enforcement requires police investigations which extend beyond the words of the accused.' In Opper v. United States,[2627] we elaborated the reasons for the requirement:

> In our country the doubt persists that the zeal of the agencies of prosecution to protect the peace, the self-interest of the accomplice, the maliciousness of an enemy or the aberration or weakness of the accused under the strain of suspicion may tinge or warp the facts of the confession. Admissions, retold at a trial, are much like hearsay, that is, statements not made at the pending trial. They had neither the compulsion of the oath nor the test of cross-examination.

It is true that in Smith v. United States,[2628] we held that although 'corroboration is necessary for all elements of the offense established by admissions alone,' extrinsic proof was sufficient which 'merely fortifies the truth of the confession, without independently establishing the crime charged.'[2629] ***490** However, Wong Sun's unsigned confession does not furnish competent corroborative evidence. The second

---

[2623] *Nardone v. United States, 308 U.S. 338, 341, 60 S.Ct. 266, 268, 84 L.Ed. 307*

[2624] *Maguire, Evidence of Guilt, 221 (1959)*

[2625] *Cf. United States v. Bayer, 331 U.S. 532, 67 S.Ct. 1394, 91 L.Ed. 1654*

[2626] *348 U.S. 147, 153, 75 S.Ct. 194, 197, 99 L.Ed. 192*

[2627] *348 U.S. 84, 89—90, 75 S.Ct. 158, 162—163, 99 L.Ed. 101*

[2628] *Supra.*

[2629] *348 U.S. at 156, 75 S.Ct. at 199*

governing principle, likewise well settled in our decisions, is that an out-of-court declaration made after arrest may not be used at trial against one of the declarant's partners in crime. While such a statement is 'admissible against the others **419 where it is in furtherance of the criminal undertaking all such responsibility is at an end when the conspiracy ends.'[2630] We have consistently refused to broaden that very narrow exception to the traditional hearsay rule which admits statements of a codefendant made in furtherance of a conspiracy or joint undertaking.[2631] And where post-conspiracy declarations have been admitted, we have carefully ascertained that limiting instructions kept the jury from considering the contents with respect to the guilt of anyone but the declarant.[2632] We have never ruled squarely on the question presented here, whether a codefendant's statement might serve to corroborate even where it will not suffice to convict. We see *491 no warrant for a different result so long as the rule which regulates the use of out-of-court statements is one of admissibility, rather than simply of weight, of the evidence. The import of our previous holdings is that a co-conspirator's hearsay statements may be admitted against the accused for no purpose whatever, unless made during and in furtherance of the conspiracy. Thus as to Toy the only possible source of corroboration is removed and his conviction must be set aside for lack of competent evidence to support it.

V

We turn now to the case of the other petitioner, Wong Sun. We have no occasion to disagree with the finding of the Court of Appeals that his arrest, also, was without probable cause or reasonable grounds. At all events no evidentiary consequences turn upon that question. For Wong Sun's unsigned confession was not the fruit of that arrest, and was therefore properly admitted at trial. On the evidence that Wong Sun had been released on his own recognizance after a lawful arraignment, and had returned voluntarily several days later to make the statement, we hold that the connection between the arrest and the statement had 'become so attenuated as to dissipate the taint.'[2633] The fact that the statement was unsigned, whatever bearing this may have upon its weight and credibility, does not render it inadmissible; Wong Sun understood and adopted its substance, though he could not comprehend the English words. The petitioner has never suggested any impropriety in the interrogation itself which would require the exclusion of this statement.

We must then consider the admissibility of the narcotics surrendered by Yee. Our holding, supra, that this *492 ounce of heroin was inadmissible against Toy does not compel a like result with respect to Wong Sun. The exclusion of the narcotics as to Toy was required solely by their tainted relationship to information unlawfully obtained from Toy, and not by any official impropriety connected with their surrender by Yee. The seizure of this heroin invaded no right of privacy of person or premises which would entitle Wong Sun to object to its use at his trial.[2634]

**420 However, for the reasons that Wong Sun's statement was incompetent to corroborate Toy's admissions contained in Toy's own statement, any references to Wong Sun in Toy's statement were incompetent to corroborate Wong Sun's admissions. Thus, the only competent source of corroboration for Wong Sun's statement was the heroin itself. We cannot be certain, however, on this state of the record, that the trial judge may not also have considered the contents of Toy's statement as a source of corroboration. Petitioners raised as one ground of objection to the introduc-

---

[2630] *Fiswick v. United States, 329 U.S. 211, 217, 67 S.Ct. 224, 227, 91 L.Ed. 196*

[2631] *See Krulewitch v. United States, 336 U.S. 440, 443—445, 69 S.Ct. 716, 718—719, 93 L.Ed. 790*

[2632] *Lutwak v. United States, 344 U.S. 604, 618—619, 73 S.Ct. 481, 489—490, 97 L.Ed. 593; Delli Paoli v. United States, 352 U.S. 232, 236—237, 77 S.Ct. 294, 297, 1 L.Ed.2d 278*

[2633] *Nardone v. United States, 308 U.S. 338, 341, 60 S.Ct. 266, 84 L.Ed. 307*

[2634] *Cf. Goldstein v. United States, 316 U.S. 114, 62 S.Ct. 1000, 86 L.Ed. 1312*

tion of the statements the claim that each statement, 'even if it were a purported admission or confession or declaration against interest of a defendant * * * would not be binding upon the other defendant.' The trial judge, in allowing the statements in, apparently overruled all of petitioners' objections, including this one. Thus we presume that he considered all portions of both statements as hearing upon the guilt of both petitioners.

We intimate no view one way or the other as to whether the trial judge might have found in the narcotics alone sufficient evidence to corroborate Wong Sun's admissions ***493** that he delivered heroin to Yee and smoked heroin at Yee's house around the date in question. But because he might, as the factfinder, have found insufficient corroboration from the narcotics alone, we cannot be sure that the scales were not tipped in favor of conviction by reliance upon the inadmissible Toy statement. This is particularly important because of the nature of the offense involved here.

Surely, under the narcotics statute, the discovery of heroin raises a presumption that someone—generally the possessor—violated the law. As to him, once possession alone is proved, the other elements of the offense—transportation and concealment with knowledge of the illegal importation of the drug—need not be separately demonstrated, much less corroborated.[2635] Thus particular care ought to be taken in this area, when the crucial element of the accused's possession is proved solely by his own admissions, that the requisite corroboration be found among the evidence which is properly before the trier of facts. We therefore hold that petitioner Wong Sun is also entitled to a new trial.

The judgment of the Court of Appeals is reversed and the case is remanded to the District Court for further proceedings consistent with this opinion.

It is so ordered.

Judgment of Court of Appeals reversed and case remanded to the District Court.

APPENDIX TO OPINION OF THE COURT.

STATEMENT OF JAMES WAH TOY

Taken on June 5, 1959, concerning his knowledge of WONG SUN's narcotic trafficking

I have known WONG SUN for about 3 months. I know him as SEA DOG which is what everyone calls him. ***494** I first met him in Marysville, California, during a Chinese holiday. I drove him back to San Francisco on that occasion. Sometimes he asks me to drive him home and to different places in San Francisco.

Sometime during April or May of this year, he asked me to drive him out to JOHNNY YEE's house, at 11th and Balboa Streets. He asked me to call JOHNNY and tell him we were coming. When ****421** we got there we went into the house and WONG SUN took a paper package out of his pocket and put it on the table. Then both WONG SUN and JOHNNY YEE opened the package. I don't know how much heroin was in it, but I know it was more than 10 spoons. I asked them if I could have some for myself and they said yes. I took a little bit and went across the room and smoked it in a cigarette.

WONG SUN and JOHNNY YEE talked for about 10 or 15 minutes, but they were talking in low tones so that I could not hear what they were saying. I didn't see any money change hands, because I wasn't paying too much attention. WONG SUN and I then left the house and drove. I drove WONG SUN to his home and he gave me $15.00. He said the money was for driving him out there.

[2635] *21 U.S.C. s 174, 21 U.S.C.A. § 174*

I have driven WONG SUN out to JOHNNY YEE's house about 5 times altogether. Each time WONG SUN gave me $10 or $15 for doing it and also, Johnny gave me a little heroin—enough to put in 3 or 4 cigarettes. The last time I drove WONG SUN out to YEE's house was last Tuesday, May 26, 1959. On Wednesday night June 3, 1959, at about 10:00 p.m., I called JOHNNY YEE and told him that 'I'm coming out pretty soon—I don't have anything.' He said okay, so I drove out there. When I got there I went in the house and Johnny gave me a paper of heroin. The bindle had about enough for 5 or 6 cigarettes. I didn't give him any money and he didn't ask for any. He gives it to me just out of friendship. He has given me heroin like this quite a few times. I don't remember how many times. I have known HOM WEI ***495** about 2 or 3 years but I have never dealt in narcotics with him. I have known ED FONG about 1 year and I have never dealt in narcotics with him, either. I have heard people that I know in the Hop Sing Tong Club talk about HOM WEI dealing in narcotics but nothing about ED FONG. I do not know JOHN MOW LIM or BILL FONG. The only connection I have now is JOHNNY YEE.

I have carefully read the foregoing statement, which was made of my own free will, without promise of reward or immunity and not under duress. I have been given ample opportunity to make corrections have initialed or signed each page as evidence thereof and hereby state that this statement is true to the best of my knowledge and belief.

JAMES WAH TOY

JAMES WAH TOY did not wish to sign this statement at this time. He stated he may change his mind at a later date. However, I read this statement to him and in addition he read it also and stated that the contents thereof were true to the best of his knowledge. Corrections made were by JAMES WAH TOY without his initials.

/s/ WILLIAM WONG

William Wong, Narcotic Agent

STATEMENT OF WONG SUN

I met JAMES TOY approximately the middle of March, this year, at Marysville, California, during a Chinese celebration. We returned to San Francisco together and we discussed the possible sale of heroin. I told JMAES that I could get a piece of heroin for $450 from a person known as BILL.

Shortly after returning to San Francisco, JAMES told me he wanted me to get a piece. I asked him who it was ***496** for and he told me it was for JOHNNY. He gave me $450 and I obtained a piece of heroin from BILL. I did this on approximately 8 occasions, however, at least one of these times the heroin was not for JOHNNY—for another friend of JAMES TOY. JOHNNY would pay JAMES $600 for each piece.

On several occasions after I had obtained the piece for JAMES I would drive with him to JOHNNY's house, 606 11th Avenue, and we would go upstairs to the bedroom. There, all three of us would smoke some of the heroin and JAMES would give the piece to JOHNNY. I also went with JAMES on approximately ****422** 3 other occasions when he did not take any heroin and then we smoked at JOHNNY's and we would also get some for our own use.

About 4 days before I was arrested (arrested on June 4, 1959) JAMES called me at home about 7 o'clock in the evening and told me to come by. I went to the laundry and JAMES told me to get a piece. I called BILL and arranged to meet him. JAMES gave me $450 which I gave to BILL when I met him. BILL called me about one hour later at the laundry and I met him. He gave me one piece, which I gave to JAMES, and JAMES immediately thereafter called JOHNNY. We drove to 606—11th Ave. at approximately midnight and JAMES gave the piece to JOHNNY. It was contained in a rubber contraceptive in a small brown paper bag.

Again on June 3rd, the night before I was arrested, I met JAMES at the laundry, prior to 11 o'clock in the evening, and JAMES telephoned JOHNNY at EV—6—9336. Then we went out to JOHNNY's and smoked heroin and also had one paper for our own use later. We were there approximately 1/2 hour and then left.

The laundry mentioned is OYE's LAUNDRY, 1733 Leavenworth Street, which is run by JAMES TOY. I do not know JOHNNY's last name and know him only ***497** through JAMES TOY. As well as the few times at JOHNNY's home, I have seen JOHNNY on a number of occasions at the laundry.

I have carefully read the foregoing statement, consisting of 2 pages which was made of my own free will, without promise of reward or immunity and not under duress. I have been given ample opportunity to make corrections, have initialed or signed each page as evidence thereof and hereby state that this statement is true to the best of my knowledge and belief.

WONG SUN

WONG SUN, being unable to read English, did not sign this statement. However, I read this statement to him and he stated that the contents thereof were true to the best of his knowledge.

/s/ WILLIAM WONG

William Wong, Narcotic Agent

Mr. Justice DOUGLAS, concurring.

While I join the Court's opinion I do so because nothing the Court holds is inconsistent with my belief that there having been time to get a warrant, probable cause alone could not have justified the arrest of petitioner Toy without a warrant.

I adhere to the views I expressed in Jones v. United States.[2636] What I said in the Jones case had been earlier stated by Mr. Justice Jackson, writing for the Court in Johnson v. United States:[2637]

> The point of the Fourth Amendment, which often is not grasped by zealous officers, is not that it denies law enforcement the support of the usual inferences which reasonable men draw from evidence. Its protection ***498** consists in requiring that those inferences be drawn by a neutral and detached magistrate instead of being judged by the officer engaged in the often competitive enterprise of ferreting out crime. Any assumption that evidence sufficient to support a magistrate's disinterested determination to issue a search warrant will justify the officers in making a search without a warrant would reduce the Amendment to a nullity and leave the people's homes secure only in the discretion of police officers.[2638]

[2636] *362 U.S. 257, 273, 80 S.Ct. 725, 737, 4 L.Ed.2d 697*

[2637] *333 U.S. 10, 68 S.Ct. 367, 92 L.Ed. 436 (another narcotics case)*

[2638] *Pp. 13—14, 68 S.Ct. p. 369. And see Chapman v. United States, 365 U.S. 610, 615—616, 81 S.Ct. 776, 779, 5 L.Ed.2d 828*

The Court finds it unnecessary to reach that constitutional question. I mention **423** it only to reiterate that the Johnson case represents the law and is in no way eroded by what we fail to decide today.

Mr. Justice CLARK, with whom Mr. Justice HARLAN, Mr. Justice STEWART and Mr. Justice WHITE join, dissenting.

The Court has made a Chinese puzzle out of this simple case involving four participants: Hom Way, Blackie Toy, Johnny Yee and 'Sea Dog' Sun. In setting aside the convictions of Toy and Sun it has dashed to pieces the heretofore recognized standards of probable cause necessary to secure an arrest warrant or to make an arrest without one. Instead of dealing with probable cause as involving 'probabilities,' 'the factual and practical considerations of everyday life on which reasonable and prudent men, not legal technicians, act,'[2639] the Court sets up rigid, mechanical standards, applying the 20—20 vision of hind-sight in an area where the ambiguity and immediacy inherent in unexpected arrest are present. While probable cause must be based on more than mere suspicion,[2640] it does ***499** not require proof sufficient to establish guilt.[2641] The sole requirement heretofore has been that the knowledge in the hands of the officers at the time of arrest must support a 'man of reasonable caution in the belief' that the subject had committed narcotic offenses.[2642] That decision is faced initially not in the courtroom but at the scene of arrest where the totality of the circumstances facing the officer is weighed against his split-second decision to make the arrest. This is an everyday occurrence facing law enforcement officers, and the unrealistic, enlarged standards announced here place an unnecessarily heavy hand upon them. I therefore dissent.

I

The first character in this affair is Hom Way, who was arrested in possession of narcotics and told the officers early that morning that he had purchased an ounce of heroin on the previous night from Blackie Toy, who operated a laundry on Leavenworth Street. Narcotics agents, armed with this information from a person they had known for six weeks and who was under arrest for possession of narcotics, immediately sought out Blackie Toy, the second character. The laundry was located without difficulty (as far as the record shows) from the information furnished by Hom Way. The Court gratuitously reads into the record its supposition that Hom Way 'merely invited the officers to roam the length of Leavenworth Street (some 30 blocks) in search of one 'Blackie Toy's' laundry.' On the contrary, the identification of 'Blackie' and the directions to his laundry were sufficiently accurate for the officers—two of whom were of Chinese ancestry—to find Blackie at his laundry within an hour. I cannot say in the face of this record that this was a 'roaming' performance ***500** up and down Leavenworth Street. To me it was efficient police work by officers familiar with San Francisco and the habits and practices of its Chinese-American inhabitants. Indeed, the information was much more explicit than that approved by this Court in Draper v. United States.[2643]

There are other indicia of reliability, however. Here the informer, believed by the officers to be reliable,* was under arrest when he implicated himself in the **424** purchase of an ounce of heroin the previous night. Since he was in possession of narcotics and his information related to a narcotics sale in which he was the buyer,

---

[2639] *Brinegar v. United States, 338 U.S. 160, 175, 69 S.Ct. 1302, 1310, 93 L.Ed. 1879 (1949)*

[2640] *Henry v. United States, 361 U.S. 98, 104, 80 S.Ct. 168, 172, 4 L.Ed.2d 134 (1959)*

[2641] *Draper v. United States, 358 U.S. 307, 312, 79 S.Ct. 329, 332, 3 L.Ed.2d 327 (1959)*

[2642] *Carroll v. United States, 267 U.S. 132, 162, 45 S.Ct. 280, 288, 69 L.Ed. 543 (1925)*

[2643] *Supra.*

the officers had good reason to rely on Hom Way's knowledge.[2644] As to his credibility, he was confronted with prosecution for possession of narcotics and well knew that any discrepancies in his story might go hard with him. Furthermore, the statement was a declaration against interest which stripped Hom Way of any explanation for his possession of narcotics and made certain the presumption of 21 U.S.C. § 174. I do not see what stronger and more reliable information one could have to establish probable cause for the arrest without warrant of Blackie Toy.

But even assuming there was no probable cause at this point, the Government produced additional evidence to support the lawfulness of Backie's arrest. In broad daylight, about 6:30 on the same morning that Hom Way was arrested, one of the officers of Chinese ancestry, Agent Alton Wong, knocked on Blackie Toy's laundry door. When Wong told him that he wanted laundry, Blackie ***501** opened the door and advised him to return at 8 a.m. Wong testified that he then 'pulled out (his) badge' and announced that he was a narcotics agent. Blackie slammed the door in Wong's face and ran down the hall of the laundry. Wong broke through the door after him—calling again that he was 'a narcotics Treasury agent.' Only when Blackie reached the family bedroom was Wong able to arrest him, as he reached into a night-stand drawer, apparently looking for narcotics. Agent Wong immediately confronted him with Hom Way's accusation that Blackie Toy had sold him narcotics. Blackie denied selling narcotics, but he did not deny knowing Hom Way and later admitted knowing him. There is no basis in Miller v. United States[2645] for the Court's conclusion that Blackie's flight 'signified a natural desire (by Toy) to repel an apparently unauthorized intrusion. As I see it this is incredible in the light of the record. Nor is there any support in the record that 'before Toy fled, the officer never adequately dispelled the misimpression engendered by his own ruse.' On the contrary the officer's showing of his badge and announcement that he was a narcotics agent immediately put Blackie in flight behind the slamming door. To conclude otherwise takes all prizes as a non sequitur. As he pursued, Wong continued to identify himself as a narcotics agent. I ask, how could he more clearly announce himself and his purpose?

This Court has often held unexplained flight—as here—from an officer to be strong evidence of guilt.[2646] Moreover, as the Government has always emphasized, this is particularly true in narcotics cases where delay may have serious consequences, i.e., the hiding ***502** or destruction of the drugs. This Court noted without disapproval in Miller v. United States,[2647] the state decisions holding that 'justification for noncompliance (with the rule) exists in exigent circumstances, as, for example, when the officers may in good faith believe that the person to be arrested is fleeing or attempting to destroy evidence.[2648] And the Court continued, 'It may be that, without an express announcement of purpose, the facts known to officers would justify them in being virtually certain ****425** that the petitioner already knows their purpose so that an announcement would be a useless gesture.[2649]

The Court places entire reliance on the decision in Miller. I submit that it is inapposite. That case involved interpretation of the law of the District of

---

[2644] *See Rodgers v. United States, 267 F.2d 79 (C.A.9th Cir., 1959), and Thomas v. United States, 281 F.2d 132 (C.A.8th Cir.), cert. denied, 364 U.S. 904, 81 S.Ct. 239, 5 L.Ed.2d 196 (1960)*

[2645] *357 U.S. 301, 78 S.Ct. 1190, 2 L.Ed.2d 1332 (1958)*

[2646] *E.g., Husty v. United States, 282 U.S. 694, 51 S.Ct. 240, 75 L.Ed. 629 (1931); Brinegar v. United States, supra, 338 U.S. at p. 166, n. 7, 69 S.Ct. 1306; see Henry v. United States, supra, where the Court was careful to distinguish its facts from those of 'fleeing men or men acting furtively.' 361 U.S. at 103, 80 S.Ct. at 172*

[2647] *Supra*

[2648] *People v. Maddox, 46 Cal.2d 301, 294 P.2d 6.' 357 U.S. at 309, 78 S.Ct. at 1196*

[2649] *Cf. People v. Martin, 45 Cal.2d 755, 290 P.2d 855; Wilgus, Arrest Without a Warrant, 22 Mich.L.Rev. 541, 798, 802 (1924).' Id. at 310, 78 S.Ct. at 1196*

Columbia.[2650] The arrest was at night, and the door was broken in just as the defendant began to close it. Thus there was no flight but only what the officers believed to be an attempt to bar their entrance. The only identification given by the officers occurred before the defendant opened the door, when 'in a low voice' through the closed door they answered the defendant's query as to who was there by saying, 'Police.'[2651] The facts in Miller differ significantly from this case both in the clarity of identification by the officers and in the character and extent of the defendant's conduct. For that reason, the conclusions that Blackie's flight is evidence to support probable cause and that the officers gave sufficient notice to permit lawful entry are supported rather than weakened by the Court's decision in Miller.

The information from Hom Way and Blackie Toy's unexplained flight cannot be viewed 'in two separate, logic-tight compartments. (T)ogether they composed ***503** a picture meaningful to a trained, experienced observer.'[2652] I submit that the officers as reasonable men properly concluded that the petitioner was the 'Blackie Toy' who Hom Way informed them had committed a felony and that his immediate arrest—as he ran through his hall—was lawful and was imperative in order to prevent his escape. In view of this there is no 'poisonous tree' whose fruits we must evaluate, and Blackie's declaration at the time of the arrest and the narcotics found in Yee's possession are admissible in evidence. The trial court found that evidence sufficiently corroborative of Toy's confession, and the Court of Appeals affirmed. For the same reasons discussed, infra, as to Wong Sun, I see no occasion to overturn these consistent findings of two courts.

II

As to 'Sea Dog,' Wong Sun, there is no disagreement that his confession and the narcotics found in Yee's possession were admissible in evidence against him. The question remains as to whether there was sufficient independent evidence to corroborate the confession. Such evidence 'does not have to prove the offense beyond a reasonable doubt, or even by a preponderance.'[2653] The requirement is satisfied 'if the corroboration merely fortifies the truth of the confession, without independently establishing the crime charged.'[2654] Wong Sun's confession stated in part that about four days before his arrest he and Toy delivered an ounce of heroin to Yee and that on the night before his arrest—the night of June 3, 1959—he and Toy smoked some heroin at Yee's house. On June 4, 1959, the officers found at Yee's residence quantities of heroin totaling 'just less than one ounce.' In light ***504** of this evidence, I am unable to say that the trial court and the Court of Appeals erred in holding that Wong Sun's confession was sufficiently corroborated.

The Court does not reach a contrary conclusion as to corroboration, but it grants Wong Sun a new trial on the ground that the trial court 'may' also 'have considered the contents of Toy's statement as a source of corroboration' of it. This point was not raised as a question here nor was it discussed in the briefs. Despite this the Court goes to some lengths to develop a chain of inferences ****426** in finding prejudicial error. This might be plausible where the case was tried to a jury, as were all the cases cited by the Court. Indeed, I find no case where such presumption of error was applied, as here, to a trial before a judge. The Court admits that the heroin found in Johnny Yee's possession might itself be sufficient corroboration, but it reverses on the excuse that the judge 'may' have considered Toy's confession as well. I see no

---

[2650] *Id. at 306, 78 S.Ct. 1194*

[2651] *Id. at 303, 78 S.Ct. 1192*

[2652] *Christensen v. United States, 104 U.S.App.D.C. 35, 36, 259 F.2d 192, 193 (1958)*

[2653] *Smith v. United States, 348 U.S. 147, 156, 75 S.Ct. 194, 199, 99 L.Ed. 192 (1954)*

[2654] *Ibid; see also Opper v. United States, 348 U.S. 84, 75 S.Ct. 158, 99 L.Ed. 101 (1954)*

reason for this assumption where a federal judge is the trier of the fact, and I would therefore affirm the judgment as to both petitioners.

Black Letter Law

> Case establishing the exception doctrine for the exclusionary rule. The Court held that the rule that regulates use of out-of-court statements is one of admissibility, rather than simply of weight of evidence, and codefendant's statement, which will not suffice to convict, may not serve to corroborate.
>
> Test of excludability is not whether evidence would not have come to light but for illegal actions of police, but whether evidence obtained by exploitation of illegality rather than by means sufficiently distinguishable to be purged of primary taint.

Brown v. Illinois

95 S.Ct. 2254

Supreme Court of the United States

Richard BROWN, Petitioner,

v.

State of ILLINOIS.

No. 73—6650. | Argued March 18, 1975. | Decided June 26, 1975.

Mr. Justice BLACKMUN delivered the opinion of the Court.

This case lies at the crossroads of the Fourth and the Fifth Amendments. Petitioner was arrested without probable cause and without a warrant. He was given, in full, the warnings prescribed by Miranda v. Arizona.[2655] Thereafter, while in custody, he made two inculpatory statements. The issue is whether evidence of those statements was properly admitted, or should have been excluded, in petitioner's subsequent trial for murder in state court. Expressed another way, the issue is whether the statements were to be excluded ***592** as the fruit of the illegal arrest, or were admissible because the giving of the Miranda warnings sufficiently attenuated the taint of the arrest.[2656] The Fourth Amendment, of course, has been held to be applicable to the states through the Fourteenth Amendment.[2657]

I

As petitioner Richard Brown was climbing the last of the stairs leading to the rear entrance of his Chicago apartment in the early evening of May 13, 1968, he happened to glance at the window near the door. He saw, pointed at him through the window, a revolver held by a stranger who was inside the apartment. The man said: 'Don't move, you are under arrest.'[2658] Another man, also with a gun, came up behind Brown and repeated the statement that he was under arrest. It was about 7:45 p.m. The two men turned out to be Detectives William Nolan and William Lenz of the Chicago police force. It is not clear from the record exactly when they advised Brown of their identity, but it is not disputed that they broke into his apartment, searched it, and then arrested Brown, all without probable cause and without any warrant, when he arrived. They later testified that they made the arrest for the pur-

[2655] *384 U.S. 436, 86 S.Ct. 1602, 16 L.Ed.2d 694 (1966)*

[2656] *See Wong Sun v. United States, 371 U.S. 471, 83 S.Ct. 407, 9 L.Ed.2d 441 (1963)*

[2657] *Mapp v. Ohio, 367 U.S. 643, 81 S.Ct. 1684, 6 L.Ed.2d 1081 (1961)*

[2658] *App. 42*

pose of questioning Brown as part of their investigation of the murder of a man named Roger Corpus. Corpus was murdered one week earlier, on May 6, with a .38-caliber revolver in his Chicago West Side second-floor apartment. Shortly thereafter, Detective Lenz obtained petitioners' name, among others, from Corpus' brother. Petitioner and the others were identified as acquaintances of the victim, not as suspects.

***593** On the day of petitioner's arrest, Detectives Lenz and Nolan, armed with a photograph of Brown, and another officer arrived at petitioner's apartment about 5 p.m.[2659] While the third officer covered the front entrance downstairs, the two detectives broke into Brown's apartment and searched it.[2660] Lenz then positioned himself near the rear door and watched through the adjacent window which opened onto the back porch. Nolan sat near the front door. He described the situation at the later suppression hearing:

> After we were there for a while, Detective Lenz told me that somebody was coming up the back stairs. I walked out the front door through the hall and around the corner, and I stayed there behind a door leading on the the back porch. At this time I heard Detective Lenz say, 'Don't move, you are under arrest.' I looked out. I saw Mr. Brown backing away from the window. I walked up behind him, I told him he is under arrest, come back inside the apartment with us.[2661]

****2257** As both officers held him at gunpoint, the three entered the apartment. Brown was ordered to stand against the wall and was searched. No weapon was found.[2662] He was asked his name. When he denied being Richard Brown, Detective Lenz showed him the photograph, informed him that he was under arrest for the murder of Roger Corpus,[2663] handcuffed him,[2664] and escorted him to the squad car.

The two detectives took petitioner to the Maxwell Street police station. During the 20-minute drive Nolan again asked Brown, who then was sitting with him in the back seat of the car, whether his name was Richard Brown and whether he owned a 1966 Oldsmobile. Brown ***594** alternately evaded these questions or answered them falsely.[2665] Upon arrival at the station house Brown was placed in the second-floor central interrogation room. The room was bare, except for a table and four chairs. He was left alone, apparently without handcuffs, for some minutes while the officers obtained the file on the Corpus homicide. They returned with the file, sat down at the table, one across from Brown and the other to his left, and spread the file on the table in front of him.[2666]

The officers warned Brown of his rights under Miranda.[2667] They then informed him that they knew of an incident that had occurred in a poolroom on May 5, when Brown, angry at having been cheated at dice, fired a shot from a revolver into the ceiling. Brown answered: 'Oh, you know about that.'[2668] Lenz informed him that a

[2659] *App. 77, 78*

[2660] *Id., at 86*

[2661] *Id., at 42*

[2662] *Id., at 93*

[2663] *Id., at 16*

[2664] *Id., at 93*

[2665] *Tr. 74*

[2666] *App. 19*

[2667] *Ibid.*

[2668] *Id., at 20*

bullet had been obtained from the ceiling of the poolroom and had been taken to the crime laboratory to be compared with bullets taken from Corpus' body.[2669] Brown responded: 'Oh, you know that, too.'[2670] At this point—it was about 8:45 p.m.—Lenz asked Brown whether he wanted to talk about the Corpus homicide. Petitioner answered that he did. For the next 20 to 25 minutes Brown answered questions put to him by Nolan, as Lenz typed.[2671]

This questioning produced a two-page statement in which Brown acknowledged that he and a man named ***595** Jimmy Claggett visited Corpus on the evening of May 5; that the three for some time sat drinking and smoking marijuana; that Claggett ordered him at gunpoint to bind Corpus' hands and feet with cord from the headphone of a stereo set; and that Claggett, using a .38-caliber revolver sold to him by Brown, shot Corpus three times through a pillow. The statement was signed by Brown.[2672]

About 9:30 p.m. the two detectives and Brown left the station house to look for Claggett in an area of Chicago Brown knew him to frequent. They made a tour of that area but did not locate their quarry. They then went to police headequarters where they endeavored, without success, to obtain a photograph of Claggett. They resumed their search—it was now about 11 p.m.—and they finally observed Claggett crossing at an intersection. Lenz and Nolan arrested him. All four, the two detectives and the two arrested men, returned to the Maxwell Street station about 12:15 a.m.[2673]

Brown was again placed in the interrogation room. He was given coffee and was left alone, for the most part, until 2 a.m. when Assistant State's Attorney Crilly arrived.

Crilly, too, informed Brown of his Miranda rights. After a half hour's conversation, ****2258** a court reporter appeared. Once again the Miranda warnings were given: 'I read him the card.' Id., at 30. Crilly told him that he 'was sure he would be charged with murder.'[2674] Brown gave a second statement, providing a factual account of the murder substantially in accord with his first statement, but containing factual inaccuracies with respect to his personal background. When the statement ***596** was completed, at about 3 a.m., Brown refused to sign it.[2675] An hour later he made a phone call to his mother. At 9:30 that morning, about 14 hours after his arrest, he was taken before a magistrate.

On June 20 Brown and Claggett were jointly indicated by a Cook County grand jury for Corpus' murder. Prior to trial, petitioner moved to suppress the two statements he had made. He alleged that his arrest and detention had been illegal and that the statements were taken from him in violation of his constitutional rights. After a hearing, the motion was denied.[2676]

The case proceeded to trial. The State introduced evidence of both statements. Detective Nolan testified as to the contents of the first,[2677] but the writing itself was

---

[2669] *Ibid.*

[2670] *Id., at 20—21*

[2671] *Id., at 21—23*

[2672] *Id., at 9, 38*

[2673] *Id., at 39*

[2674] *Id., at 32*

[2675] *Id., at 57*

[2676] *R. 46*

[2677] *App. 89—92*

not placed in evidence. The second statement was introduced and was read to the jury in full.[2678] Brown was 23 at the time of the trial.[2679]

The jury found petitioner guilty of murder.[2680] He was sentenced to imprisonment for not less than 15 years nor more than 30 years.[2681]

On appeal, the Supreme Court of Illinois affirmed the judgment of conviction.[2682] The court refused to accept the State's argument that Brown's arrest was lawful. 'Upon review of the record, we conclude that the testimony fails to show that at the time of his apprehension there was probable cause for defendant's arrest, (and) that his arrest was, therefore, unlawful.'[2683] ***597** But it went on to hold in two significant and unembellished sentences:

> (W)e conclude that the giving of the Miranda warnings, in the first instance by the police officer and in the second by the assistant State's Attorney, served to break the causal connection between the illegal arrest and the giving of the statements, and that defendant's act in making the statements was 'sufficiently an act of free will to purge the primary taint of the unlawful invasion.'[2684] We hold, therefore, that the circuit court did not err in admitting the statements into evidence.[2685]

Aside from its reliance upon the presence of the Miranda warnings, no specific aspect of the record or of the circumstances was cited by the court in support of its conclusion. The court, in other words, appears to have held that the Miranda warnings in and of themselves broke the causal chain so that any subsequent statement, even one induced by the continuing effects of unconstitutional custody, was admissible so long as, in the traditional sense, it was voluntary and not coerced in violation of the Fifth and Fourteenth Amendments.

Because of our concern about the implication of our holding in Wong Sun v. United States,[2686] to the facts of Brown's case, we granted certiorari.[2687] ****2259**

II

In Wong Sun, the Court pronounced the principles to be applied where the issue is whether statements and other evidence obtained after an illegal arrest or search should be excluded. In that case, federal agents elicited an oral statement from defendant Toy after forcing entry ***598** at 6 a.m. into his laundry, at the back of which he had his living quarters. The agents had followed Toy down the hall to the bedroom and there had placed him under arrest. The Court of Appeals found that there was no probable cause for the arrest. This Court concluded that that finding was 'amply justified by the facts clearly shown on this record.'[2688] Toy's statement, which

---

[2678] *Tr. 509—528*

[2679] *Id., at 543*

[2680] *R. 80*

[2681] *Id., at 83*

[2682] *56 Ill.2d 312, 307 N.E.2d 356 (1974)*

[2683] *Id., at 315, 307 N.E.2d at 357*

[2684] *Wong Sun v. United States, 371 U.S. 471, at 486, 83 S.Ct. at 416, 9 L.Ed.2d 441*

[2685] *Id., at 317, 307 N.E.2d, at 358*

[2686] *371 U.S. 471, 83 S.Ct. 407, 9 L.Ed.2d 441 (1963)*

[2687] *419 U.S. 894, 95 S.Ct. 172, 42 L.Ed.2d 138 (1974)*

[2688] *371 U.S., at 479, 83 S.Ct., at 413*

bore upon his participation in the sale of narcotics, led the agents to question another person, Johnny Yee, who actually possessed narcotics. Yee stated that heroin had been brought to him earlier by Toy and another Chinese known to him only as 'Sea Dog.' Under questioning, Toy said that 'Sea Dog' was Wong Sun. Toy led agents to a multifamily dwelling where, he said, Wong Sun lived. Gaining admittance to the building through a bell and buzzer, the agents claimed the stairs and entered the apartment. One went into the back room and brought Wong Sun out in handcuffs. After arraignment, Wong Sun was released on his own recognizance. Several days later, he returned voluntarily to give an unsigned confession.

This Court ruled that Toy's declarations and the contraband taken from Yee were the fruits of the agents' illegal action and should not have been admitted as evidence against Toy.[2689] It held that the statement did not result from "an intervening independent act of a free will," and that it was not 'sufficiently an act of free will to purge the primary taint of the unlawful invasion.'[2690] With respect to Wong Sun's confession, however, the Court held that in the light of his lawful arraignment and release on his own recognizance, and of his return voluntarily several days later to make the statement, the connection between his unlawful arrest and the statement 'had 'become so attenuated as to dispute the taint.'[2691] ***599** The Court said:

> We need not hold that all evidence is 'fruit of the poisonous tree' simply because it would not have come to light but for the illegal actions of the police. Rather, the more apt question in such a case is 'whether, granting establishment of the primary illegality, the evidence to which instant objection is made has been come at by exploitation of that illegality or instead by means sufficiently distinguishable to be purged of the primary taint.[2692]

The exclusionary rule thus was applied in Wong Sun primarily to protect Fourth Amendment rights. Protection of the Fifth Amendment right against self-incrimination was not the Court's paramount concern there. To the extent that the question whether Toy's statement was voluntary was considered, it was only to judge whether it 'was sufficiently an act of free will to purge the primary taint of the unlawful invasion.[2693]

The Court in Wong Sun, as is customary, emphasized that application of the exclusionary rule on Toy's behalf protected Fourth Amendment guarantees in two respects: 'in terms of deterring lawless conduct by federal officers,' and by 'closing the doors of the federal courts to any use of evidence unconstitutionally obtained.'[2694] These considerations of deterrence and of judicial integrity, by now, have become rather commonplace ****2260** in the Court's cases.[2695] 'The rule is calculated to prevent, not to repair. Its purpose is to deter—to compel respect for the ***600** constitutional guaranty in the only effectively available way—by removing the incentive to disregard it.'[2696] But '(d)espite its broad deterrent purpose, the exclusion-

---

[2689] *Id., at 484—488, 83 S.Ct., at 416*

[2690] *Id., at 486, 83 S.Ct., at 416*

[2691] *Nardone v. United States, 308 U.S. 338, 341, 60 S.Ct. 266, 84 L.Ed. 307.' Id., at 491, 83 S.Ct., at 419*

[2692] *Maguire, Evidence of Guilt, 221 (1959).' Id., at 487—488, 83 S.Ct., at 417*

[2693] *Id., at 486, 83 S.Ct., at 416 (emphasis added)*

[2694] *Ibid.*

[2695] *See, e.g., United States v. Peltier, 442 U.S. 531, 535—538, 95 S.Ct. 2313, 2316—2318, 45 L.Ed.2d 374; United States v. Calandra, 414 U.S. 338, 347, 94 S.Ct. 613, 619, 38 L.Ed.2d 561 (1974); Terry v. Ohio, 392 U.S. 1, 12—13, 28—29, 88 S.Ct. 1868, 1875, 20 L.Ed.2d 889 (1968)*

[2696] *Elkins v. United States, 364 U.S. 206, 217, 80 S.Ct. 1437, 1444, 4 L.Ed.2d 1669 (1960)*

ary rule has never been interpreted to proscribe the use of illegally seized evidence in all proceedings or against all persons.'[2697]

III

The Illinois courts refrained from resolving the question, as apt here as it was in Wong Sun, whether Brown's statements were obtained by exploitation of the illegality of his arrest. They assumed that the Miranda warnings, by themselves, assured that the statements (verbal acts, as contrasted with physical evidence) were of sufficient free will as to purge the primary taint of the unlawful arrest.[2698]

This Court has described the Miranda warnings as a 'prophylactic rule,'[2699] and as a 'procedural safeguard,'[2700] employed to protect Fifth Amendment rights against 'the compulsion inherent in custodial surroundings.'[2701] The function of the warnings relates to the Fifth Amendment's guarantee against coerced self-incrimination, and the exclusion ***601** of a statement made in the absence of the warnings, it is said, serves to deter the taking of an incriminating statement without first informing the individual of his Fifth Amendment rights.

Although, almost 90 years ago, the Court observed that the Fifth Amendment is in 'intimate relation' with the Fourth,[2702] the Miranda warnings thus far have not been regarded as a means either of remedying or deterring violations of Fourth Amendment rights. Frequently, as here, rights under the two Amendments may appear to coalesce since 'the 'unreasonable searches and seizures' condemned in the Fourth Amendment are almost always made for the purpose of compelling a man to give evidence against himself, which in criminal cases is condemned in the Fifth Amendment.'[2703] The exclusionary rule, however, when utilized to effectuate the Fourth Amendment, serves interests and policies that are distinct from those it serves under the Fifth. It is directed at all unlawful searches and seizures, and not merely those that happen to produce incriminating material or testimony as fruits. In short, exclusion of a confession made without Miranda warnings might be regarded as necessary to effectuate the Fifth Amendment, but it would not be sufficient fully to protect the Fourth. Miranda warnings, and the exclusion of a confession made without them, do ****2261** not alone sufficiently deter a Fourth Amendment violation.

Thus, even if the statements in this case were found to be voluntary under the Fifth Amendment, the Fourth ***602** Amendment issue remains. In order for the causal chain, between the illegal arrest and the statements made subsequent thereto, to be broken. Wong Sun requires not merely that the statement meet the Fifth Amendment standard of voluntariness but that it be 'sufficiently an act of free will to purge the primary taint.'[2704] Wong Sun thus mandates consideration of a statement's admissibility in light of the distinct policies and interests of the Fourth Amendment.

If Miranda warnings, by themselves, were held to attenuate the taint of an unconstitutional arrest, regardless of how wanton and purposeful the Fourth Amendment violation, the effect of the exclusionary rule would be substantially di-

[2697] *United States v. Calandra, 414 U.S., at 348, 94 S.Ct. at 620. See also Michigan v. Tucker, 417 U.S. 433, 446—447, 94 S.Ct. 2357, 2360, 41 L.Ed.2d 182 (1974)*

[2698] *Wong Sun, of course, preceded Miranda*

[2699] *Michigan v. Payne, 412 U.S. 47, 53, 93 S.Ct. 1966, 1969, 36 L.Ed.2d 736 (1973)*

[2700] *Miranda v. Arizona, 384 U.S., at 457, 478, 86 S.Ct. at 1629*

[2701] *Id., at 458, 86 S.Ct. at 1619*

[2702] *Boyd v. United States, 116 U.S. 616, 633, 6 S.Ct. 524, 533, 29 L.Ed. 746 (1886)*

[2703] *Ibid.; see Mapp v. Ohio, 367 U.S., at 646 n. 5, 81 S.Ct. at 1687*

[2704] *371 U.S. at 486, 83 S.Ct. at 416*

luted.[2705] Arrests made without warrant or without probable cause, for questioning or 'investigation,' would be encouraged by the knowledge that evidence derived therefrom could well be made admissible at trial by the simple expedient of giving Miranda warnings. Any incentive to avoid Fourth Amendment violations would be eviscerated by making the warnings, in effect, a 'cure-all,' and the constitutional guarantee against unlawful searches and seizures could ***603** be said to be reduced to 'a form of words.'[2706]

It is entirely possible, of course, as the State here argues, that persons arrested illegally frequently may decide to confess, as an act of free will unaffected by the initial illegality. But the Miranda warnings, alone and per se, cannot always make the act sufficiently a product of free will be break, for Fourth Amendment purposes, the causal connection between the illegality and the confession. They cannot assure in every case that the Fourth Amendment violation has not been unduly exploited.[2707]

While we therefore reject the per se rule which the Illinois courts appear to have accepted, we also decline to adopt any alternative per se or 'but for' rule. The petitioner himself professes not to demand so much.[2708] The question whether a confession is the product of a free will under Wong Sun must be answered on the facts of each case. No single fact is dispositive. The workings of the human mind are too complex, and the possibilities of misconduct too diverse, to permit protection of the Fourth Amendment to turn on such a talismanic test. The Miranda warnings are an important factor, to be sure, in determining whether the confession is obtained by exploitation of an illegal arrest. But they are not the only factor to be considered. The temporal proximity of the arrest and the ****2262** confession, the presence of intervening circumstances,[2709] ***604** and particularly the purpose and flagrancy of the official misconduct are all relevant.[2710] The voluntariness of the statement is a threshold requirement.[2711] And the burden of showing admissibility rests, of course, on the prosecution.

IV

Although the Illinois courts failed to undertake the inquiry mandated by Wong Sun to evaluate the circumstances of this case in the light of the policy served by the exclusionary rule, the trial resulted in a record of amply sufficient detail and depth from which the determination may be made. We therefore decline the suggestion of the United States, as amicus curiae,[2712] to remand the case for further factual findings. We conclude that the State failed to sustain the burden of showing that the evidence in question was admissible under Wong Sun.

Brown's first statement was separated from his illegal arrest by less than two hours, and there was no intervening event of significance whatsoever. In its essentials, his situation is remarkably like that of James Wah Toy in Wong Sun. We could hold Brown's first statement ***605** admissible only if we overrule Wong Sun. We decline to do so. And the second statement was clearly the result and the fruit of the first.

[2705] *See Davis v. Mississippi, 394 U.S. 721, 726—727, 89 S.Ct. 1394, 1397, 22 L.Ed.2d 676 (1969)*

[2706] *See Mapp v. Ohio, 367 U.S., at 648, 81 S.Ct. at 1687*

[2707] *See Westover v. United States, 384 U.S. 436, 496—497, 86 S.Ct. 1602, 1639, 16 L.Ed.2d 694 (1966)*

[2708] *Tr. of Oral Arg. 12, 45, 47*

[2709] *See Johnson v. Louisiana, 406 U.S. 356, 365, 92 S.Ct. 1620, 1626, 32 L.Ed.2d 152 (1972)*

[2710] *See Wong Sun v. United States, 371 U.S., at 491, 83 S.Ct. at 419*

[2711] *Cf. 18 U.S.C. s 3501*

[2712] *See Morales v. New York, 396 U.S. 102, 90 S.Ct. 291, 24 L.Ed.2d 299 (1969)*

The illegality here, moreover, had a quality of purposefulness. The impropriety of the arrest was obvious; awareness of that fact was virtually conceded by the two detectives when they repeatedly acknowledged, in their testimony, that the purpose of their action was 'for investigation' or for 'questioning.'[2713] The arrest, both in design and in execution, was investigatory. The detectives embarked upon this expedition for evidence in the hope that something might turn up. The manner in which Brown's arrest was affected gives the appearance of having been calculated to cause surprise, fright, and confusion. We emphasize that our holding is a limited one. We decide only that the Illinois ****2263** courts were in error in assuming that the Miranda warnings, by themselves, under Wong Sun always purge the taint of an illegal arrest.

The judgment of the Supreme Court of Illinois is reversed and the case is remanded for further proceedings not inconsistent with this opinion.

It is so ordered.

Judgment reversed and case remanded.

***606** Mr. Justice WHITE, concurring in the judgment.

Insofar as the Court holds (1) that despite Miranda warnings the Fourth and Fourteenth Amendments require the exclusion from evidence of statements obtained as the fruit of an arrest which the arresting officers knew or should have known was without probable cause and unconstitutional, and (2) that the statements obtained in this case were in this category, I am in agreement and therefore concur in the judgment.

Mr. Justice POWELL, with whom Mr. Justice REHNQUIST joins, concurring in part.

I join the Court insofar as it holds that the per se rule adopted by the Illinois Supreme Court for determining the admissibility of petitioner's two statements inadequately accommodates the diverse interests underlying the Fourth Amendment exclusionary rule. I would, however, remand the case for reconsideration under the general standards articulated in the Court's opinion and elaborated herein.

A

The issue presented in this case turns on proper application of the policies underlying the Fourth Amendment exclusionary rule, not on the Fifth Amendment or the prophylaxis added to that guarantee by Miranda v. Arizona.[2714] The Court recognized in Wong Sun v. United States[2715] that the Fourth Amendment exclusionary rule applies to statements obtained following an illegal arrest just as it does to tangible evidence seized in a similar manner ***607** or obtained pursuant to an otherwise illegal search and seizure. Wong Sun squarely rejected, however, the suggestion that the admissibility of statements so obtained should be governed by a simple 'but for' test that would render inadmissible all statements given subsequent to an illegal arrest.[2716] In a similar manner, the Court today refrains from according dispositive weight to the single factor of Miranda warnings. I agree with each holding. Neither of the rejected extremes adequately recognizes the competing considerations involved in a determination to exclude evidence after finding that official possession of that evidence was to some degree caused by a violation of the Fourth Amendment.

[2713] *App. 35, 43, 78, 81, 83, 88, 89, 94*

[2714] *384 U.S. 436, 86 S.Ct. 1602, 16 L.Ed.2d 694 (1966)*

[2715] *371 U.S. 471, 83 S.Ct. 407, 9 L.Ed.2d 441 (1963)*

[2716] *Id., at 487—488, 83 S.Ct. at 417*

On this record, I cannot conclude as readily as the Court that admission of the statements here at issue would constitute an effective overruling of Wong Sun.[2717] Although Wong Sun establishes the boundaries within which this case must be decided, the incompleteness of the record leaves me uncertain that it compels the exclusion of petitioner's statements. The statements at issue in Wong Sun were at the temporal extremes in relation to the illegal arrest.[2718] Toy's statement was obtained immediately after ****2264** his pursuit and arrest by six agents. It appears to have been a spontaneous response to a question put to him in the frenzy of that event, and there is no indication that the agents made any attempt to inform him of his right to remain silent. Wong Sun's statement, by contrast, was not given until after he was arraigned and released on his own recognizance. Wong Sun voluntarily returned to the station a few days after the arrest for questioning. His statement was preceded by an official warning of his right ***608** to remain silent and to have counsel if he desired.2 The Court rejected the Government's assertion that Toy's statement resulted from an independent act of free will sufficient to purge the consequences of the illegal arrest. Wong Sun's statement, however, was deemed admissible. Given the circumstances in which Wong Sun's statement was obtained, the Court concluded that 'the connection between the arrest and the statement had 'become so attenuated as to dissipate the taint.''[2719]

Like most cases in which the admissibility of statements obtained subsequent to an illegal arrest is contested, this case concerns statements more removed than that of Toy from the time and circumstances of the illegal arrest. Petitioner made his first statement some two hours following his arrest, after he had been given Miranda warnings. The Court is correct in noting that no other significant intervening event altered the relationship established between petitioner and the officers by the illegal arrest. But the Court's conclusion that admission of this statement could be allowed only by overruling Wong Sun rests either on an overly restrictive interpretation of the attenuation doctrine, to which I cannot subscribe, or on its view that the arrest was made for investigatory purposes, a factual determination that I think more appropriately should have been left for decision in the first instance by the state courts.

B

The Court's rejection in Wong Sun of a 'but for' test, reaffirmed today,[2720] recognizes that in some ***609** circumstances strict adherence to the Fourth Amendment exclusionary rule imposes greater cost on the legitimate demands of law enforcement than can be justified by the rule's deterrent purposes. The notion of the 'dissipation of the taint' attempts to mark the point at which the detrimental consequences of illegal police action become so attenuated that the deterrent effect of the exclusionary rule no longer justifies its cost. Application of the Wong Sun doctrine will generate fact-specific cases bearing distinct differences as well as similarities, and the question of attenuation inevitably is largely a matter of degree. The Court today identifies the general factors that the trial court must consider in making this determination. I think it appropriate, however, to attempt to articulate the possible relationships to those factors in particular, broad categories of cases.

All Fourth Amendment violations are, by constitutional definition, 'unreasonable.' There are, however, significant practical differences that distinguish among violations, differences that measurably assist in identifying the kinds of cases in which disqualifying the evidence is likely to serve the deterrent purposes of the ex-

[2717] *See ante, at 2262*

[2718] *Cf. Collins v. Beto, 348 F.2d 823, 832, 834—836 (CA5 1965) (Friendly, J., concurring)*

[2719] *371 U.S., at 491, 83 S.Ct., at 419*

[2720] *Ante, at 2261—2262*

clusionary rule.[2721] **2265 In my view, the point at which the taint can be said to have dissipated should be related, in the absence of other controlling circumstances, to the nature of that taint.

That police have not succeeded in coercing the accused's confession through willful or negligent misuse of the power of arrest does not remove the fact that they may have tried. The impermissibility of the attempt, and the extent to which such attempts can be deterred by the use of the exclusionary rule, are of primary relevance in determining whether exclusion is an appropriate remedy. *610 The basic purpose of the rule, briefly stated, is to remove possible motivations for illegal arrests. Given this purpose the notion of voluntariness has practical value in deciding whether the rule should apply to statements removed from the immediate circumstances of the illegal arrest. If an illegal arrest merely provides the occasion of initial contact between the police and the accused, and because of time or other intervening factors the accused's eventual statement is the product of his own reflection and free will, application of the exclusionary rule can serve little purpose: the police normally will not make an illegal arrest in the hope of eventually obtaining such a truly volunteered statement. In a similar manner, the role of the Miranda warnings in the Wong Sun inquiry is indirect. To the extent that they dissipate the psychological pressures of custodial interrogation, Miranda warnings serve to assure that the accused's decision to make a statement has been relatively unaffected by the preceding illegal arrest. Correspondingly, to the extent that the police perceive Miranda warnings to have this equalizing potential, their motivation to abuse the power of arrest is diminished. Bearing these considerations in mind, and recognizing that the deterrent value of the Fourth Amendment exclusionary rule is limited to certain kinds of police conduct, the following general categories can be identified.

Those most readily identifiable are on the extremes: the flagrantly abusive violation of Fourth Amendment rights, on the one hand, and 'technical' Fourth Amendment violations, on the other. In my view, these extremes call for significantly different judicial responses.

I would require the clearest indication of attenuation in cases in which official conduct was flagrantly abusive of Fourth Amendment rights. If, for example, the factors *611 relied on by the police in determining to make the arrest were so lacking in indicia of probable cause as to render official belief in its existence entirely unreasonable, or if the evidence clearly suggested that the arrest was effectuated as a pretext for collateral objectives,[2722] or the physical circumstances of the arrest unnecessarily intrusive on personal privacy, I would consider the equalizing potential of Miranda warnings rarely sufficient to dissipate the taint. In such cases the deterrent value of the exclusionary rule is most likely to be effective, and the corresponding mandate to preserve judicial integrity,[2723] most clearly demands that the fruits of official misconduct be denied. I thus would require some demonstrably effective break in the chain of events leading from the illegal arrest to the statement, such as actual consultation with counsel or the accused's presentation before a magistrate for a determination of probable cause, before the taint can be deemed removed.[2724]

**2266 At the opposite end of the spectrum lie 'technical' violations of Fourth Amendment rights where, for example, officers in good faith arrest an individual in reliance on a warrant later invalidated or pursuant to a statute that subsequently is

---

[2721] *Cf. United States v. Calandra, 414 U.S. 338, 347—348, 94 S.Ct. 613, 615, 38 L.Ed.2d 561 (1974); Schneckloth v. Bustamonte, 412 U.S. 218, 250, 93 S.Ct. 2041, 2053, 36 L.Ed.2d 854 (1973) (Powell, J., concurring)*

[2722] *Cf. United States v. Robinson, 414 U.S. 218, 237, 238 n. 2, 94 S.Ct. 467, 470, 38 L.Ed.2d 427 (1973) (Powell, J., concurring)*

[2723] *See United States v. Peltier, 422 U.S. 531, 95 S.Ct. 2313, 45 L.Ed.2d 374 (1975); Michigan v. Tucker, 417 U.S. 433, 450 n. 25, 94 S.Ct. 2357, 2367, 41 L.Ed.2d 182 (1974)*

[2724] *See Gerstein v. Pugh, 420 U.S. 103, 95 S.Ct. 854, 43 L.Ed.2d 54 (1975); cf. Johnson v. Louisiana, 406 U.S. 356, 365, 92 S.Ct. 1620, 1626, 32 L.Ed.2d 152 (1972); Parker v. North Carolina, 397 U.S. 790, 796, 90 S.Ct. 1458, 1462, 25 L.Ed.2d 785 (1970)*

declared unconstitutional.[2725] ***612** As we noted in Michigan v. Tucker:[2726] 'The deterrent purpose of the exclusionary rule necessarily assumes that the police have engaged in willful, or at the very least negligent, conduct which has deprived the defendant of some right.' In cases in which this underlying premise is lacking, the deterrence rationale of the exclusionary rule does not obtain, and I can see no legitimate justification for depriving the prosecution of reliable and probative evidence. Thus, with the exception of statements given in the immediate circumstances of the illegal arrest—a constraint I think is imposed by existing exclusionary-rule law—I would not require more than proof that effective Miranda warnings were given and that the ensuing statement was voluntary in the Fifth Amendment sense. Absent aggravating circumstances, I would consider a statement given at the station house after one has been advised of Miranda rights to be sufficiently removed from the immediate circumstances of the illegal arrest to justify its admission at trial.

Between these extremes lies a wide range of situations that defy ready categorization, and I will not attempt to embellish on the factors set forth in the Court's opinion other than to emphasize that the Wong Sun inquiry always should be conducted with the deterrent purpose of the Fourth Amendment exclusionary rule sharply in focus.[2727] And, in view of the inevitably fact-specific nature of the inquiry, we must place primary reliance on the 'learning, good sense, fairness and courage' of judges who must make the determination in the first instance.[2728]

*613 C

On the facts of record as I view them, it is possible that the police may have believed reasonably that there was probable cause for petitioner's arrest. Although the trial court conducted hearings on petitioner's motion to suppress and received his testimony and that of the arresting officers, its inquiry focused on determining whether petitioner's statements were preceded by adequate Miranda warnings and were made voluntarily. The court did not inquire into the possible justification, actual or perceived, for the arrest. Indeed, numerous questions addressed to the circumstances of the arrest elicited the State's objection, which was sustained.[2729] The Illinois Supreme Court's consideration of the factual basis for its ruling similarly failed to focus on these relevant issues or to rest in any meaningful sense on the factors set forth in the Court's opinion today. After determining that the officers lacked probable cause for petitioner's arrest, the Illinois court concluded simply that examination of the record persuaded it that 'the giving of Miranda warnings . . . served to break the causal connection between the illegal arrest and the giving of the statements.'[2730]

**2267 I am not able to conclude on this record that the officers arrested petitioner solely for the purpose of questioning.[2731] To be sure, there is evidence suggesting, as the Court notes, an investigatory arrest. The strongest evidence on that point is the inconclusive testimony by the arresting officers themselves. But the evidence is conflicting. Responding to questions as to what they told petitioner upon his arrest, the officers testified he was advised that the arrest was for investigation of murder.

[2725] *See United States v. Kilgen, 445 F.2d 287 (CA5 1971)*

[2726] *Supra, 417 U.S., at 447, 94 S.Ct., at 2365*

[2727] *See ALI Model Code of Pre-Arraignment Procedure, Art. 150, p. 54 et seq. and Commentary thereon, p. 375 et seq. (Prop. Off. Draft 1975)*

[2728] *Nardone v. United States, 308 U.S. 338, 342, 60 S.Ct. 266, 268, 84 L.Ed. 307 (1939). See ante, at 2262 n. 10*

[2729] *App. 14—15*

[2730] *56 Ill.2d 312, 317, 307 N.E.2d 356, 358 (1974)*

[2731] *ante, at 2262; see also ante, at 2263 (White, J., concurring in judgment)*

Responding to more pointed questions, ***614** however, one of the arresting officers stated that he informed petitioner that he was being arrested for murder.[2732]

Moreover, other evidence of record indicates that the police may well have believed that probable cause existed to think that petitioner committed the crime of which he ultimately was convicted. As the opinion of the Illinois Supreme Court reveals, petitioner had been identified as an acquaintance of the deceased, and the police had been told that petitioner was seen in the building where the deceased lived on the day of the murder.[2733] It is also plain that the investigation had begun to focus on petitioner. For example, the police had gone to the trouble of obtaining a bullet that petitioner had fired in an unrelated incident for the purpose of comparing it with the bullets that killed the victim.[2734] The officers also obtained petitioner's photograph prior to seeking him out, and the circumstances of petitioner's arrest indicate that their suspicions of him were quite pronounced.

The trial court made no determination as to whether probable cause existed for petitioner's arrest. The Illinois ***615** Supreme Court resolved that issue, but did not consider whether the officers might reasonably, albeit erroneously, have thought that probable cause existed. Rather than decide those matters for the first time at this level, I think it preferable to allow the state courts to reconsider the case under the general guidelines expressed in today's opinions. I ****2268** therefore would remand for reconsideration with directions to conduct such further factual ***616** inquiries as may be necessary to resolve the admissibility issue.

Black Letter Law

The Court held that *Miranda* warnings do not, in and of themselves, cure a Fourth Amendment violation requiring the exclusion of evidence. In other words, the reading of *Miranda* warnings, alone, cannot always make act of confession a product of free will sufficient to break the causal connection between illegality of arrest and confession. As a result, statements stemming from an illegal arrest are not rendered admissible merely because the defendant had been given *Miranda* warnings prior to making statements.

In order to break the causal chain between the illegal arrest and the subsequent confession, thus purging the taint, there must be an intervening act of free will.

Oregon v. Elstad

105 S.Ct. 1285

Supreme Court of the United States

OREGON, Petitioner

v.

Michael James ELSTAD.

No. 83–773. | Argued Oct. 3, 1984. | Decided March 4, 1985.

Justice O'CONNOR delivered the opinion of the Court.

[2732] *See App. 16*

[2733] *56 Ill.2d, at 315, 307 N.E.2d, at 357*

[2734] *App. 20*

This case requires us to decide whether an initial failure of law enforcement officers to administer the warnings required by Miranda v. Arizona[2735] without more, "taints" subsequent admissions made after a suspect has been fully advised of and has waived his Miranda rights. Respondent, Michael James Elstad, was convicted of burglary by an Oregon trial court. The Oregon Court of Appeals reversed, holding that respondent's signed confession, although voluntary, was rendered inadmissible by a prior remark made in response to questioning without benefit of Miranda warnings. We granted certiorari,[2736] and we now reverse.

I

In December 1981, the home of Mr. and Mrs. Gilbert Gross, in the town of Salem, Polk County, Ore., was burglarized. Missing were art objects and furnishings valued at $150,000. A witness to the burglary contacted the Polk County Sheriff's office, implicating respondent Michael Elstad, an 18-year-old neighbor and friend of the Grosses' teenage son. Thereupon, Officers Burke and McAllister went to the home of respondent Elstad, with a warrant for his arrest. Elstad's mother answered the door. She led the officers to her son's room where he lay on his bed, clad in shorts and listening to his stereo. The officers asked him to get dressed and to accompany them into the living room. Officer McAllister asked respondent's mother to step into the kitchen, where he explained that they had a warrant for her ***301** son's arrest for the burglary of a neighbor's residence. Officer Burke remained with Elstad in the living room. He later testified:

> I sat down with Mr. Elstad and I asked him if he was aware of why Detective McAllister and myself were there to talk ****1289** with him. He stated no, he had no idea why we were there. I then asked him if he knew a person by the name of Gross, and he said yes, he did, and also added that he heard that there was a robbery at the Gross house. And at that point I told Mr. Elstad that I felt he was involved in that, and he looked at me and stated, 'Yes, I was there.'[2737]

The officers then escorted Elstad to the back of the patrol car. As they were about to leave for the Polk County Sheriff's office, Elstad's father arrived home and came to the rear of the patrol car. The officers advised him that his son was a suspect in the burglary. Officer Burke testified that Mr. Elstad became quite agitated, opened the rear door of the car and admonished his son: "I told you that you were going to get into trouble. You wouldn't listen to me. You never learn."[2738]

Elstad was transported to the Sheriff's headquarters and approximately one hour later, Officers Burke and McAllister joined him in McAllister's office. McAllister then advised respondent for the first time of his Miranda rights, reading from a standard card. Respondent indicated he understood his rights, and, having these rights in mind, wished to speak with the officers. Elstad gave a full statement, explaining that he had known that the Gross family was out of town and had been paid to lead several acquaintances to the Gross residence and show them how to gain entry through a defective sliding glass door. The statement was typed, reviewed by respondent, read back to him for correction, initialed and signed by Elstad and both officers. As an afterthought, Elstad added and initialed the sentence, "After leaving the house Robby

---

[2735] *384 U.S. 436, 86 S.Ct. 1602, 16 L.Ed.2d 694 (1966)*

[2736] *465 U.S. 1078, 104 S.Ct. 1437, 79 L.Ed.2d 759 (1984)*

[2737] *App. 19–20*

[2738] *Id., at 21*

& I went back to [the] van & Robby handed ***302** me a small bag of grass."[2739] Respondent concedes that the officers made no threats or promises either at his residence or at the Sheriff's office.

Respondent was charged with first-degree burglary. He was represented at trial by retained counsel. Elstad waived his right to a jury, and his case was tried by a Circuit Court Judge. Respondent moved at once to suppress his oral statement and signed confession. He contended that the statement he made in response to questioning at his house "let the cat out of the bag,"[2740] and tainted the subsequent confession as "fruit of the poisonous tree,"[2741] The judge ruled that the statement, "I was there," had to be excluded because the defendant had not been advised of his Miranda rights. The written confession taken after Elstad's arrival at the Sheriff's office, however, was admitted in evidence. The court found:

> [H]is written statement was given freely, voluntarily and knowingly by the defendant after he had waived his right to remain silent and have counsel present which waiver was evidenced by the card which the defendant had signed. [It] was not tainted in any way by the previous brief statement between the defendant and the Sheriff's Deputies that had arrested him.[2742]

Elstad was found guilty of burglary in the first degree. He received a 5-year sentence and was ordered to pay $18,000 in restitution.

Following his conviction, respondent appealed to the Oregon Court of Appeals, relying on Wong Sun and Bayer. The State conceded that Elstad had been in custody when he made his statement, "I was there," and accordingly agreed that this statement was inadmissible as having been given without the prescribed Miranda warnings. But the State maintained that any conceivable "taint" had been dissipated prior to the respondent's written confession by McAllister's careful administration of the requisite warnings. The Court ***303** of Appeals reversed respondent's conviction, identifying the crucial constitutional inquiry as "whether there was a sufficient break in the stream of events between [the] inadmissible statement and the written confession to insulate the latter statement ****1290** from the effect of what went before."[2743] The Oregon court concluded:

> Regardless of the absence of actual compulsion, the coercive impact of the unconstitutionally obtained statement remains, because in a defendant's mind it has sealed his fate. It is this impact that must be dissipated in order to make a subsequent confession admissible. In determining whether it has been dissipated, lapse of time, and change of place from the original surroundings are the most important considerations.[2744]

[2739] *App. 42*

[2740] *Citing United States v. Bayer, 331 U.S. 532, 67 S.Ct. 1394, 91 L.Ed. 1654 (1947)*

[2741] *Citing Wong Sun v. United States, 371 U.S. 471, 83 S.Ct. 407, 9 L.Ed.2d 441 (1963)*

[2742] *App. 45*

[2743] *61 Ore.App. 673, 676, 658 P.2d 552, 554 (1983)*

[2744] *Id., at 677, 658 P.2d, at 554*

Because of the brief period separating the two incidents, the "cat was sufficiently out of the bag to exert a coercive impact on [respondent's] later admissions."[2745]

The State of Oregon petitioned the Oregon Supreme Court for review, and review was declined. This Court granted certiorari to consider the question whether the Self-Incrimination Clause of the Fifth Amendment requires the suppression of a confession, made after proper Miranda warnings and a valid waiver of rights, solely because the police had obtained an earlier voluntary but unwarned admission from the defendant.

II

The arguments advanced in favor of suppression of respondent's written confession rely heavily on metaphor. One metaphor, familiar from the Fourth Amendment context, would require that respondent's confession, regardless of its integrity, voluntariness, and probative value, be suppressed as the "tainted fruit of the poisonous tree" of the Miranda violation. A second metaphor questions whether a ***304** confession can be truly voluntary once the "cat is out of the bag." Taken out of context, each of these metaphors can be misleading. They should not be used to obscure fundamental differences between the role of the Fourth Amendment exclusionary rule and the function of Miranda in guarding against the prosecutorial use of compelled statements as prohibited by the Fifth Amendment. The Oregon court assumed and respondent here contends that a failure to administer Miranda warnings necessarily breeds the same consequences as police infringement of a constitutional right, so that evidence uncovered following an unwarned statement must be suppressed as "fruit of the poisonous tree." We believe this view misconstrues the nature of the protections afforded by Miranda warnings and therefore misreads the consequences of police failure to supply them.

A

Prior to Miranda, the admissibility of an accused's in-custody statements was judged solely by whether they were "voluntary" within the meaning of the Due Process Clause.[2746] If a suspect's statements had been obtained by "techniques and methods offensive to due process,"[2747] or under circumstances in which the suspect clearly had no opportunity to exercise "a free and unconstrained will,"[2748] the statements would not be admitted. The Court in Miranda required suppression of many statements that would have been admissible under traditional due process analysis by presuming that statements made while in custody and without adequate warnings were protected by the Fifth Amendment. The Fifth Amendment, of course, is not concerned with non-testimonial evidence.[2749] Nor is it concerned ***305** with moral and psychological pressures to confess emanating from sources other than official coercion.[2750] Voluntary statements "remain a proper element in law enforcement."[2751]

[2745] *Id., at 678, 658 P.2d, at 555*

[2746] *See, e.g., Haynes v. Washington, 373 U.S. 503, 83 S.Ct. 1336, 10 L.Ed.2d 513 (1963); Chambers v. Florida, 309 U.S. 227, 60 S.Ct. 472, 84 L.Ed. 716 (1940)*

[2747] *Haynes v. Washington, 373 U.S., at 515, 83 S.Ct., at 1344*

[2748] *Id., at 514, 83 S.Ct., at 1343*

[2749] *See Schmerber v. California, 384 U.S. 757, 764, 86 S.Ct. 1826, 1832, 16 L.Ed.2d 908 (1966) (defendant may be compelled to supply blood samples)*

[2750] *See, e.g., California v. Beheler, 463 U.S. 1121, 1125, and n. 3, 103 S.Ct. 3517, 3520, and n. 3, 77 L.Ed.2d 1275 (1983) (per curiam* *****1291*** *); Rhode Island v. Innis, 446 U.S. 291, 303, and n. 10, 100 S.Ct. 1682, 1690, and n. 10, 64 L.Ed.2d 297 (1980); Oregon v. Mathiason, 429 U.S. 492, 495–496, 97 S.Ct. 711, 713–714, 50 L.Ed.2d 714 (1977)*

[2751] *Miranda v. Arizona, 384 U.S., at 478, 86 S.Ct., at 1630*

"Indeed, far from being prohibited by the Constitution, admissions of guilt by wrongdoers, if not coerced, are inherently desirable.... Absent some officially coerced self-accusation, the Fifth Amendment privilege is not violated by even the most damning admissions."[2752] As the Court noted last Term in New York v. Quarles:[2753]

> The Miranda Court, however, presumed that interrogation in certain custodial circumstances is inherently coercive and ... that statements made under those circumstances are inadmissible unless the suspect is specifically informed of his Miranda rights and freely decides to forgo those rights. The prophylactic Miranda warnings therefore are 'not themselves rights protected by the Constitution but [are] instead measures to insure that the right against compulsory self-incrimination [is] protected.'[2754] Requiring Miranda warnings before custodial interrogation provides 'practical reinforcement' for the Fifth Amendment right.

Respondent's contention that his confession was tainted by the earlier failure of the police to provide Miranda warnings and must be excluded as "fruit of the poisonous tree" assumes the existence of a constitutional violation. This figure of speech is drawn from Wong Sun v. United States,[2755] in which the Court held that evidence and witnesses ***306** discovered as a result of a search in violation of the Fourth Amendment must be excluded from evidence. The Wong Sun doctrine applies as well when the fruit of the Fourth Amendment violation is a confession. It is settled law that "a confession obtained through custodial interrogation after an illegal arrest should be excluded unless intervening events break the causal connection between the illegal arrest and the confession so that the confession is 'sufficiently an act of free will to purge the primary taint.'"[2756]

But as we explained in Quarles and Tucker, a procedural Miranda violation differs in significant respects from violations of the Fourth Amendment, which have traditionally mandated a broad application of the "fruits" doctrine. The purpose of the Fourth Amendment exclusionary rule is to deter unreasonable searches, no matter how probative their fruits.[2757] "The exclusionary rule, ... when utilized to effectuate the Fourth Amendment, serves interests and policies that are distinct from those it serves under the Fifth."[2758] Where a Fourth Amendment violation "taints" the confession, a finding of voluntariness for the purposes of the Fifth Amendment is merely a threshold requirement in determining whether the confession may be admitted in evidence.[2759] Beyond this, the prosecution must show a sufficient break in events to undermine the inference that the confession was caused by the Fourth Amendment violation.

The Miranda exclusionary rule, however, serves the Fifth Amendment and ****1292** sweeps more broadly than the Fifth Amendment itself. It may be triggered

---

[2752] *United States v. Washington, 431 U.S. 181, 187, 97 S.Ct. 1814, 1818, 52 L.Ed.2d 238 (1977)*

[2753] *467 U.S. 649, 654, 104 S.Ct. 2626, 2630, 81 L.Ed.2d 550 (1984) (footnote omitted)*

[2754] *Michigan v. Tucker, 417 U.S. 433, 444, 94 S.Ct. 2357, 2364, 41 L.Ed.2d 182 (1974); see Edwards v. Arizona, 451 U.S. 477, 492, 101 S.Ct. 1880, 1888, 68 L.Ed.2d 378 (1981) (POWELL, J., concurring)*

[2755] *371 U.S. 471, 83 S.Ct. 407, 9 L.Ed.2d 441 (1963)*

[2756] *Taylor v. Alabama, 457 U.S. 687, 690, 102 S.Ct. 2664, 2667, 73 L.Ed.2d 314 (1982) (quoting Brown v. Illinois, 422 U.S. 590, 602, 95 S.Ct. 2254, 2261, 45 L.Ed.2d 416 (1975))*

[2757] *Dunaway v. New York, 442 U.S. 200, 216–217, 99 S.Ct. 2248, 2258–2259, 60 L.Ed.2d 824 (1979); Brown v. Illinois, 422 U.S., at 600–602, 95 S.Ct., at 2260–2261*

[2758] *Id., at 601, 95 S.Ct., at 2260*

[2759] *Taylor v. Alabama, supra, 457 U.S., at 690, 102 S.Ct., at 2667*

even in the absence of a Fifth Amendment violation. The Fifth Amendment prohibits ***307** use by the prosecution in its case in chief only of compelled testimony. Failure to administer Miranda warnings creates a presumption of compulsion. Consequently, unwarned statements that are otherwise voluntary within the meaning of the Fifth Amendment must nevertheless be excluded from evidence under Miranda. Thus, in the individual case, Miranda's preventive medicine provides a remedy even to the defendant who has suffered no identifiable constitutional harm.[2760]

But the Miranda presumption, though irrebuttable for purposes of the prosecution's case in chief, does not require that the statements and their fruits be discarded as inherently tainted. Despite the fact that patently voluntary statements taken in violation of Miranda must be excluded from the prosecution's case, the presumption of coercion does not bar their use for impeachment purposes on cross-examination.[2761] The Court in Harris rejected as an "extravagant extension of the Constitution," the theory that a defendant who had confessed under circumstances that made the confession inadmissible, could thereby enjoy the freedom to "deny every fact disclosed or discovered as a 'fruit' of his confession, free from confrontation with his prior statements" and that the voluntariness of his confession would be totally irrelevant.[2762] Where an unwarned statement is preserved for use in situations that fall outside the sweep of the Miranda presumption, "the primary criterion of admissibility ***308** [remains] the 'old' due process voluntariness test."[2763]

In Michigan v. Tucker,[2764] the Court was asked to extend the Wong Sun fruits doctrine to suppress the testimony of a witness for the prosecution whose identity was discovered as the result of a statement taken from the accused without benefit of full Miranda warnings. As in respondent's case, the breach of the Miranda procedures in Tucker involved no actual compulsion. The Court concluded that the unwarned questioning "did not abridge respondent's constitutional privilege. . .but departed only from the prophylactic standards later laid down by this Court in Miranda to safeguard that privilege."[2765] Since there was no actual infringement of the suspect's constitutional rights, the case was not controlled by the doctrine expressed in Wong Sun that fruits of a constitutional violation must be suppressed. In deciding "how sweeping the judicially imposed consequences" of a failure to administer Miranda warnings should be,[2766] the Tucker Court noted that neither the general goal of deterring improper police conduct nor the Fifth Amendment goal of assuring trustworthy evidence would be served by suppression of the witness' testimony. The unwarned confession must, of course, be suppressed, but the Court ruled that introduction of the third-party witness' testimony ****1293** did not violate Tucker's Fifth Amendment rights.

We believe that this reasoning applies with equal force when the alleged "fruit" of a non-coercive Miranda violation is neither a witness nor an article of evidence but the accused's own voluntary testimony. As in Tucker, the absence of any coercion or improper tactics undercuts the twin rationales—trustworthiness and deterrence for a broader rule. Once warned, the suspect is free to exercise his own volition in deciding whether or not to make a statement to the authorities. The Court has often noted: " '[A] living witness is not to be ***309** mechanically equated with the proffer

[2760] *See New York v. Quarles, supra, 467 U.S., at 654, 104 S.Ct., at 2630; Michigan v. Tucker, 417 U.S. 433, 444, 94 S.Ct. 2357, 2363, 41 L.Ed.2d 182 (1974)*

[2761] *Harris v. New York, 401 U.S. 222, 91 S.Ct. 643, 28 L.Ed.2d 1 (1971)*

[2762] *Id., at 225, and n. 2, 91 S.Ct., at 645, and n. 2*

[2763] *Schulhofer, Confessions and the Court, 79 Mich.L.Rev. 865, 877 (1981)*

[2764] *Supra*

[2765] *417 U.S., at 446, 94 S.Ct., at 2364*

[2766] *417 U.S., at 445, 94 S.Ct., at 2364*

of inanimate evidentiary objects illegally seized.... [T]he living witness is an individual human personality whose attributes of will, perception, memory and volition interact to determine what testimony he will give.'"[2767]

Because Miranda warnings may inhibit persons from giving information, this Court has determined that they need be administered only after the person is taken into "custody" or his freedom has otherwise been significantly restrained.[2768] Unfortunately, the task of defining "custody" is a slippery one, and "policemen investigating serious crimes [cannot realistically be expected to] make no errors whatsoever."[2769] If errors are made by law enforcement officers in administering the prophylactic Miranda procedures, they should not breed the same irremediable consequences as police infringement of the Fifth Amendment itself. It is an unwarranted extension of Miranda to hold that a simple failure to administer the warnings, unaccompanied by any actual coercion or other circumstances calculated to undermine the suspect's ability to exercise his free will, so taints the investigatory process that a subsequent voluntary and informed waiver is ineffective for some indeterminate period. Though Miranda requires that the unwarned admission must be suppressed, the admissibility of any subsequent statement should turn in these circumstances solely on whether it is knowingly and voluntarily made.

B

The Oregon court, however, believed that the unwarned remark compromised the voluntariness of respondent's later confession. It was the court's view that the prior answer ***310** and not the unwarned questioning impaired respondent's ability to give a valid waiver and that only lapse of time and change of place could dissipate what it termed the "coercive impact" of the inadmissible statement. When a prior statement is actually coerced, the time that passes between confessions, the change in place of interrogations, and the change in identity of the interrogators all bear on whether that coercion has carried over into the second confession.[2770] The failure of police to administer Miranda warnings does not mean that the statements received have actually been coerced, but only that courts will presume the privilege against compulsory self-incrimination has not been intelligently exercised.[2771] Of the courts that have considered whether a properly warned confession must be suppressed because it was preceded by an unwarned but clearly voluntary admission, the majority have explicitly or implicitly recognized that Westover 's requirement of a break in the stream of ****1294** events is inapposite. In these circumstances, a careful and thorough ***311** administration of Miranda warnings serves to cure the condition that rendered the unwarned statement inadmissible. The warning conveys the relevant information and thereafter the suspect's choice whether to exercise his privilege to remain silent should ordinarily be viewed as an "act of free will."[2772]

The Oregon court nevertheless identified a subtle form of lingering compulsion, the psychological impact of the suspect's conviction that he has let the cat out of the bag and, in so doing, has sealed his own fate. But endowing the psychological effects of voluntary unwarned admissions with constitutional implications would, practically

---

[2767] *United States v. Ceccolini, 435 U.S. 268, 277, 98 S.Ct. 1054, 1060, 55 L.Ed.2d 268 (1978) (emphasis added) (quoting from Smith v. United States, 117 U.S.App.D.C. 1, 3–4, 324 F.2d 879, 881–882 (1963) (Burger, J.) (footnotes omitted), cert. denied, 377 U.S. 954, 84 S.Ct. 1632, 12 L.Ed.2d 498 (1964))*

[2768] *Miranda v. Arizona, 384 U.S., at 478, 86 S.Ct., at 1629*

[2769] *Michigan v. Tucker, supra, 417 U.S., at 446, 94 S.Ct., at 2365*

[2770] *See Westover v. United States, decided together with Miranda v. Arizona, 384 U.S., at 494, 86 S.Ct., at 1638; Clewis v. Texas, 386 U.S. 707, 87 S.Ct. 1338, 18 L.Ed.2d 423 (1967)*

[2771] *See New York v. Quarles, 467 U.S., at 654, and n. 5, 104 S.Ct., at 2630, and n. 5; Miranda v. Arizona, supra, 384 U.S., at 457, 86 S.Ct., at 1618*

[2772] *Wong Sun v. United States, 371 U.S., at 486, 83 S.Ct., at 416*

speaking, disable the police from obtaining the suspect's informed cooperation even when the official coercion proscribed by the Fifth Amendment played no part in either his warned or unwarned confessions. As the Court remarked in Bayer:

> [A]fter an accused has once let the cat out of the bag by confessing, no matter what the inducement, he is never thereafter free of the psychological and practical disadvantages of having confessed. He can never get the cat back in the bag. The secret is out for good. In such a sense, a later confession may always be looked upon as fruit of the first. But this Court has never gone so far as to hold that making a confession under circumstances which preclude its use, perpetually disables the confessor from making a usable one after those conditions have been removed.[2773]

Even in such extreme cases as Lyons v. Oklahoma,[2774] in which police forced a full confession from the accused through unconscionable methods of interrogation, the Court has assumed that the coercive effect of the confession ***312** could, with time, be dissipated.[2775]

This Court has never held that the psychological impact of voluntary disclosure of a guilty secret qualifies as state compulsion or compromises the voluntariness of a subsequent informed waiver. The Oregon court, by adopting this expansive view of Fifth Amendment compulsion, effectively immunizes a suspect who responds to pre-Miranda warning questions from the consequences of his subsequent informed waiver of the privilege of remaining silent.[2776] This immunity comes at a high cost to legitimate law enforcement activity, while adding little desirable protection to the individual's interest in not being compelled to testify against himself.[2777] When neither the initial nor the subsequent admission is coerced, little justification exists for permitting the highly ****1295** probative evidence of a voluntary confession to be irretrievably lost to the fact-finder.

There is a vast difference between the direct consequences flowing from coercion of a confession by physical violence or other deliberate means calculated to break the suspect's will and the uncertain consequences of disclosure of a "guilty secret" freely given in response to an unwarned but non-coercive question, as in this case. Justice BRENNAN's contention that it is impossible to perceive any causal distinction between this case and one involving a confession that is coerced by torture is wholly unpersuasive. Certainly, in ***313** respondent's case, the causal connection between any psychological disadvantage created by his admission and his ultimate decision to cooperate is speculative and attenuated ****1296** at ***314** best. It is difficult to tell with certainty what motivates a suspect to speak. A suspect's confession may be traced to factors as disparate as "a pre-arrest event such as a visit with a minister,"[2778] or an intervening event such as the exchange of words respondent had with his father. We must conclude that, absent deliberately coercive or improper tactics in obtaining the initial statement, the mere fact that a suspect has made an unwarned admission does not warrant a presumption of compulsion. A subsequent administration of Miranda warnings to a suspect who has given a voluntary but unwarned statement ordinarily should suffice to remove the conditions that precluded

---

[2773] *331 U.S., at 540–541, 67 S.Ct., at 1398*

[2774] *322 U.S. 596, 64 S.Ct. 1208, 88 L.Ed. 1481 (1944)*

[2775] *See also Westover v. United States, supra, 384 U.S., at 496, 86 S.Ct., at 1639*

[2776] *See 61 Ore.App., at 679, 658 P.2d, at 555 (Gillette, P.J., concurring)*

[2777] *Cf. Michigan v. Mosley, 423 U.S. 96, 107–111, 96 S.Ct. 321, 328–330, 46 L.Ed.2d 313 (1975) (WHITE, J., concurring in result)*

[2778] *Dunaway v. New York, 442 U.S., at 220, 99 S.Ct., at 2261 (STEVENS, J., concurring)*

admission of the earlier statement. In such circumstances, the finder of fact may reasonably conclude that the suspect made a rational and intelligent choice whether to waive or invoke his rights.

III

Though belated, the reading of respondent's rights was undeniably complete. McAllister testified that he read the Miranda warnings aloud from a printed card and recorded ***315** Elstad's responses. There is no question that respondent knowingly and voluntarily waived his right to remain silent before he described his participation in the burglary. It is also beyond dispute that respondent's earlier remark was voluntary, within the meaning of the Fifth Amendment. Neither the environment nor the manner of either "interrogation" was coercive. The initial conversation took place at midday, in the living room area of respondent's own home, with his mother in the kitchen area, a few steps away. Although in retrospect the officers testified that respondent was then in custody, at the time he made his statement he had not been informed that he was under arrest. The arresting officers' testimony indicates that the brief stop in the living room before proceeding to the station house was not to interrogate the suspect but to notify his mother of the reason for his arrest.[2779]

The State has conceded the issue of custody and thus we must assume that Burke breached Miranda procedures in failing to administer Miranda warnings before initiating the discussion in the living room. This breach may have been the result of confusion as to whether the brief exchange qualified as "custodial interrogation" or it may simply have reflected Burke's reluctance to initiate an alarming police ***316** procedure before McAllister had spoken with respondent's mother. Whatever the reason for Burke's oversight, the incident had none of the earmarks of coercion.[2780] Nor did the officers exploit the unwarned admission to pressure respondent into waiving his right to remain silent.

Respondent, however, has argued that he was unable to give a fully informed waiver of his rights because he was unaware that his prior statement could not be used against him. Respondent suggests that Officer McAllister, to cure this deficiency, should have added an additional warning to those given him at the Sheriff's office. Such a requirement is neither practicable nor constitutionally necessary. In many ****1297** cases, a breach of Miranda procedures may not be identified as such until long after full Miranda warnings are administered and a valid confession obtained.[2781] The standard Miranda warnings explicitly inform the suspect of his right to consult a lawyer before speaking. Police officers are ill-equipped to pinch-hit for counsel, construing the murky and difficult questions of when "custody" begins or whether a given unwarned statement will ultimately be held admissible.[2782]

This Court has never embraced the theory that a defendant's ignorance of the full consequences of his decisions vitiates their voluntariness.[2783] If the prosecution has actually violated the defendant's Fifth Amendment rights by introducing an inadmissible confession at trial, compelling the defendant to testify in rebuttal, the rule announced in Harrison v. United States[2784] precludes use of that testimony ***317** on retrial. "Having 'released the spring' by using the petitioner's unlawfully obtained

---

[2779] *App. 9–10*

[2780] *See Rawlings v. Kentucky, 448 U.S. 98, 109–110, 100 S.Ct. 2556, 2563–2564, 65 L.Ed.2d 633 (1980)*

[2781] *See, e.g., United States v. Bowler, 561 F.2d 1323, 1324–1325 (CA9 1977) (certain statements ruled inadmissible by trial court); United States v. Toral, 536 F.2d 893, 896 (CA9 1976); United States v. Knight, 395 F.2d 971, 974–975 (CA2 1968) (custody unclear)*

[2782] *See Tanner v. Vincent, 541 F.2d 932, 936 (CA2 1976), cert. denied, 429 U.S. 1065, 97 S.Ct. 794, 50 L.Ed.2d 782 (1977)*

[2783] *See California v. Beheler, 463 U.S., at 1125–1126, n. 3, 103 S.Ct., at 3520, n. 3; McMann v. Richardson, 397 U.S. 759, 769, 90 S.Ct. 1441, 1448, 25 L.Ed.2d 763 (1970)*

[2784] *392 U.S. 219, 88 S.Ct. 2008, 20 L.Ed.2d 1047 (1968)*

confessions against him, the Government must show that its illegal action did not induce his testimony."[2785] But the Court has refused to find that a defendant who confesses, after being falsely told that his codefendant has turned State's evidence, does so involuntarily.[2786] The Court has also rejected the argument that a defendant's ignorance that a prior coerced confession could not be admitted in evidence compromised the voluntariness of his guilty plea.[2787] Likewise, in California v. Beheler,[2788] the Court declined to accept defendant's contention that, because he was unaware of the potential adverse consequences of statements he made to the police, his participation in the interview was involuntary. Thus we have not held that the sine qua non for a knowing and voluntary waiver of the right to remain silent is a full and complete appreciation of all of the consequences flowing from the nature and the quality of the evidence in the case.

IV

When police ask questions of a suspect in custody without administering the required warnings, Miranda dictates that the answers received be presumed compelled and that they be excluded from evidence at trial in the State's case in chief. The Court has carefully adhered to this principle, permitting a narrow exception only where pressing public safety concerns demanded.[2789] The Court today in no way retreats from the bright-line rule of Miranda. We do not imply that good faith excuses a failure to administer Miranda warnings; nor do we condone inherently coercive police tactics or methods offensive to due process that render the initial admission involuntary and undermine the suspect's will to invoke his rights once they are read to him. A handful of courts have, however, applied our precedents relating to confessions obtained ***318** under coercive circumstances to situations involving wholly voluntary admissions, requiring a passage of time or break in events before a second, fully warned statement can be deemed voluntary. Far from establishing a rigid rule, we direct courts to avoid one; there is no warrant for presuming coercive effect where the suspect's initial inculpatory statement, though technically in violation ****1298** of Miranda, was voluntary. The relevant inquiry is whether, in fact, the second statement was also voluntarily made. As in any such inquiry, the finder of fact must examine the surrounding circumstances and the entire course of police conduct with respect to the suspect in evaluating the voluntariness of his statements. The fact that a suspect chooses to speak after being informed of his rights is, of course, highly probative. We find that the dictates of Miranda and the goals of the Fifth Amendment proscription against use of compelled testimony are fully satisfied in the circumstances of this case by barring use of the unwarned statement in the case in chief. No further purpose is served by imputing "taint" to subsequent statements obtained pursuant to a voluntary and knowing waiver. We hold today that a suspect who has once responded to unwarned yet uncoercive questioning is not thereby disabled from waiving his rights and confessing after he has been given the requisite Miranda warnings.

The judgment of the Court of Appeals of Oregon is reversed, and the case is remanded for further proceedings not inconsistent with this opinion.

It is so ordered.

[2785] *Id., at 224–225, 88 S.Ct., at 2011*

[2786] *Frazier v. Cupp, 394 U.S. 731, 739, 89 S.Ct. 1420, 1424, 22 L.Ed.2d 684 (1969)*

[2787] *McMann v. Richardson, supra, 397 U.S., at 769, 90 S.Ct., at 1448*

[2788] *Supra*

[2789] *See New York v. Quarles, 467 U.S., at 655–656, 104 S.Ct., at 2631–2632*

(The dissent of Justice BRENNAN, with whom Justice MARSHALL joins, is omitted.)

Justice STEVENS, dissenting.

The Court concludes its opinion with a carefully phrased statement of its holding: ****1322** "We hold today that a suspect who has once responded to unwarned yet uncoercive questioning is not thereby disabled from waiving his rights and confessing after he has been given the requisite Miranda warnings."[2790]

I find nothing objectionable in such a holding. Moreover, because the Court expressly endorses the "bright-line rule of Miranda," which conclusively presumes that incriminating statements obtained from a suspect in custody without administering the required warnings are the product of compulsion,1 and because the Court places so much emphasis on the special facts of this case, I am persuaded that the Court intends its holding to apply only to a narrow category of cases in which the initial questioning of the suspect was made in a totally uncoercive setting and in which the first confession obviously had no influence on the second. I nevertheless ***365** dissent because even such a narrowly confined exception is inconsistent with the Court's prior cases, because the attempt to identify its boundaries in future cases will breed confusion and uncertainty in the administration of criminal justice, and because it denigrates the importance of one of the core constitutional rights that protects every American citizen from the kind of tyranny that has flourished in other societies.

I

The desire to achieve a just result in this particular case has produced an opinion that is somewhat opaque and internally inconsistent. If I read it correctly, its conclusion rests on two untenable premises: (1) that the respondent's first confession was not the product of coercion; and (2) that no constitutional right was violated when respondent was questioned in a tranquil, domestic setting.

***366 **1323** Even before the decision in Miranda v. Arizona,[2791] it had been recognized that police interrogation of a suspect who has been taken into custody is presumptively coercive. That presumption had its greatest force when the questioning occurred in a police station, when it was prolonged, and when there was evidence that the prisoner had suffered physical injury. To rebut the presumption, the prosecutor had the burden of proving the absence of any actual coercion. Because police officers are generally more credible witnesses than prisoners and because it is always difficult for triers of fact to disregard evidence of guilt when addressing a procedural question, more often than not the presumption of coercion afforded only slight protection to the accused.

The decision in Miranda v. Arizona, clarified the law in three important respects. First, it provided the prosecutor with a simple method of overcoming the presumption of coercion. If the police interrogation is preceded by the warning specified in that opinion, the usual presumption does not attach. Second, it provided an important protection to the accused by making the presumption of coercion irrebuttable if the prescribed warnings are not given. Third, the decision ***367** made it clear that a self-incriminatory statement made in response to custodial interrogation was always to be considered "compelled" within the meaning of the Fifth Amendment to the Federal Constitution if the interrogation had not been preceded by appropriate warnings. Thus the irrebuttable presumption of coercion that applies to such a self-incriminato-

---

[2790] *Ante, at 1298*

[2791] *384 U.S. 436, 86 S.Ct. 1602, 16 L.Ed.2d 694 (1966)*

ry statement, like a finding of actual coercion, renders the resulting confession inadmissible as a matter of federal constitutional law.

***368 **1324** In my opinion, the Court's attempt to fashion a distinction between actual coercion "by physical violence or other deliberate means calculated to break the suspect's will,"[2792] and irrebuttably presumed coercion cannot succeed. The presumption is only legitimate if it is assumed that there is always a coercive aspect to custodial interrogation that is not preceded by adequate advice of the constitutional right to remain silent. Although I would not support it, I could understand a rule that refused to apply the presumption unless the interrogation took place in an especially coercive setting—perhaps only in the police station itself—but if the presumption arises whenever the accused has been taken into custody or his freedom has been restrained in any significant way, it will surely be futile to try to develop subcategories of custodial interrogation. Indeed, a major purpose of treating the presumption of coercion as irrebuttable is to avoid the kind of fact-bound inquiry that today's decision will surely engender.

As I read the Court's opinion, it expressly accepts the proposition that routine Miranda warnings will not be sufficient to overcome the presumption of coercion and thereby make a second confession admissible when an earlier confession is tainted by coercion "by physical violence or other ***369** deliberate means calculated to break the suspect's will." Even in such a case, however, it is not necessary to assume that the earlier confession will always "effectively immunize" a later voluntary confession. But surely the fact that an earlier confession was obtained by unlawful methods should add force to the presumption of coercion that attaches to subsequent custodial interrogation and should require the prosecutor to shoulder a heavier burden of rebuttal than in a routine case. Simple logic, as well as the interest in not providing an affirmative incentive to police misconduct, requires that result. I see no reason why the violation of a rule that is as well recognized and easily administered as the duty to give Miranda warnings should not also impose an additional burden on the prosecutor. If we are faithful to the ****1325** holding in ***370** Miranda itself, when we are considering the admissibility of evidence in the prosecutor's case in chief, we should not try to fashion a distinction between police misconduct that warrants a finding of actual coercion and police misconduct that establishes an irrebuttable presumption of coercion.

II

For me, the most disturbing aspect of the Court's opinion is its somewhat opaque characterization of the police misconduct in this case. The Court appears ambivalent on the question whether there was any constitutional violation. This ambivalence is either disingenuous or completely lawless. This Court's power to require state courts to exclude probative self-incriminatory statements rests entirely on the premise that the use of such evidence violates the Federal Constitution. The same constitutional analysis applies ***371** whether the custodial interrogation is actually coercive or irrebuttably presumed to be coercive. If the Court does not accept that premise, it must regard the holding in the Miranda case itself, as well as all of the federal jurisprudence that has evolved from that decision, as nothing more than an illegitimate exercise of raw judicial power. If the Court accepts the proposition that respondent's self-incriminatory statement was inadmissible, it must also acknowledge that the Federal Constitution protected him from custodial police interrogation without first being advised of his right to remain silent.

The source of respondent's constitutional protection is the Fifth Amendment's privilege against compelled self-incrimination that is secured against state invasion by the Due Process Clause of the Fourteenth ****1326** Amendment. Like many other

---

[2792] *Ante, at 1295*

provisions of the Bill of Rights, that provision is merely a procedural safeguard. It is, however, the specific provision that protects all citizens from the kind of custodial interrogation that was once employed by the Star Chamber, by "the Germans of the 1930's and early 1940's," and by some of our own police departments only a few decades ago. ***372** Custodial interrogation that violates that provision of the Bill of Rights is a classic example of a violation of a constitutional right.

I respectfully dissent.

Black Letter Law

> The Court held there is no warrant for presuming coercive effect where a suspect's initial inculpatory statement, though technically in violation of Miranda, was voluntary. The relevant inquiry is whether the second statement was also voluntarily made. If an initial inculpatory statement is voluntarily made while in police custody in his home, the subsequent failure to give Miranda admonitions does not bar admissibility of station house confession, which was made shortly thereafter and preceded by careful admonition and waiver of Miranda rights. Absent deliberately coercive or improper tactics in obtaining an initial statement, the mere fact that a suspect has made an unwarned admission does not warrant a presumption of compulsion, and a subsequent administration of Miranda warnings to a suspect who has given a prior voluntary but unwarned statement ordinarily should suffice to remove the conditions precluded admission of the earlier statement.

Hudson v. Michigan

126 S.Ct. 2159

Supreme Court of the United States

Booker T. HUDSON, Jr., Petitioner,

v.

MICHIGAN.

No. 04–1360. | Argued Jan. 9, 2006. | Reargued May 18, 2006. | Decided June 15, 2006.

Justice SCALIA delivered the opinion of the Court, except as to Part IV.

***588** We decide whether violation of the "knock-and-announce" rule requires the suppression of all evidence found in the search.

I

Police obtained a warrant authorizing a search for drugs and firearms at the home of petitioner Booker Hudson. They discovered both. Large quantities of drugs were found, including cocaine rocks in Hudson's pocket. A loaded gun was lodged between the cushion and armrest of the chair in which he was sitting. Hudson was charged under Michigan law with unlawful drug and firearm possession.

This case is before us only because of the method of entry into the house. When the police arrived to execute the warrant, they announced their presence, but waited only a short time—perhaps "three to five seconds,"[2793]—before turning the knob of the unlocked front door and entering Hudson's home. Hudson moved to suppress all the inculpatory evidence, arguing that the premature entry violated his Fourth Amendment rights.

[2793] *App. 15*

The Michigan trial court granted his motion. On interlocutory review, the Michigan Court of Appeals reversed, relying ***589** on Michigan Supreme Court cases holding that suppression is inappropriate when entry is made pursuant to warrant but without proper " 'knock and announce.'"[2794] The Michigan Supreme Court denied leave to appeal.[2795] Hudson was convicted of drug possession. He renewed his Fourth Amendment claim on appeal, but the Court of Appeals rejected it and affirmed the conviction.[2796] The Michigan Supreme Court again declined review.[2797] We granted certiorari.[2798]

II

The common-law principle that law enforcement officers must announce their presence and provide residents an opportunity to open the door is an ancient one.[2799] Since 1917, when Congress passed the Espionage Act, this traditional protection has been part of federal statutory law,[2800] and is currently codified at 18 U.S.C. § 3109. We applied that statute in Miller v. United States,[2801] and again in Sabbath v. United States.[2802] Finally, in Wilson, we were asked whether the rule was also a command of the Fourth Amendment. Tracing its origins in our English legal heritage,[2803] we concluded that it was.

We recognized that the new constitutional rule we had announced is not easily applied. Wilson and cases following it have noted the many situations in which it is not necessary to knock and announce. It is not necessary when "circumstances presen[t] a threat of physical violence," or if there is "reason to believe that evidence would likely be destroyed if advance notice were given,"[2804] or ****2163** if knocking and ***590** announcing would be "futile,"[2805] We require only that police "have a reasonable suspicion. . .under the particular circumstances" that one of these grounds for failing to knock and announce exists, and we have acknowledged that "[t]his showing is not high."[2806]

When the knock-and-announce rule does apply, it is not easy to determine precisely what officers must do. How many seconds' wait are too few? Our "reasonable wait time" standard,[2807] is necessarily vague. Banks (a drug case, like this one) held that the proper measure was not how long it would take the resident to reach the door, but how long it would take to dispose of the suspected drugs—but that such a time (15 to 20 seconds in that case) would necessarily be extended when, for in-

---

[2794] *App. to Pet. for Cert. 4 (citing People v. Vasquez, 461 Mich. 235, 602 N.W.2d 376 (1999) (per curiam); People v. Stevens, 460 Mich. 626, 597 N.W.2d 53 (1999))*

[2795] *465 Mich. 932, 639 N.W.2d 255 (2001)*

[2796] *App. to Pet. for Cert. 1–2*

[2797] *472 Mich. 862, 692 N.W.2d 385 (2005)*

[2798] *545 U.S. 1138, 125 S.Ct. 2964, 162 L.Ed.2d 886 (2005)*

[2799] *See Wilson v. Arkansas, 514 U.S. 927, 931–932, 115 S.Ct. 1914, 131 L.Ed.2d 976 (1995)*

[2800] *See 40 Stat. 229*

[2801] *357 U.S. 301, 78 S.Ct. 1190, 2 L.Ed.2d 1332 (1958)*

[2802] *391 U.S. 585, 88 S.Ct. 1755, 20 L.Ed.2d 828 (1968)*

[2803] *514 U.S., at 931–936, 115 S.Ct. 1914*

[2804] *Id., at 936, 115 S.Ct. 1914*

[2805] *Richards v. Wisconsin, 520 U.S. 385, 394, 117 S.Ct. 1416, 137 L.Ed.2d 615 (1997)*

[2806] *Ibid.*

[2807] *See United States v. Banks, 540 U.S. 31, 41, 124 S.Ct. 521, 157 L.Ed.2d 343 (2003)*

stance, the suspected contraband was not easily concealed.[2808] If our ex post evaluation is subject to such calculations, it is unsurprising that, ex ante, police officers about to encounter someone who may try to harm them will be uncertain how long to wait.

Happily, these issues do not confront us here. From the trial level onward, Michigan has conceded that the entry was a knock-and-announce violation. The issue here is remedy. Wilson specifically declined to decide whether the exclusionary rule is appropriate for violation of the knock-and-announce requirement.[2809] That question is squarely before us now.

III

A

In Weeks v. United States,[2810] we adopted the federal exclusionary rule for evidence that was unlawfully seized from a home without a warrant in violation of the Fourth Amendment. We began applying the same rule to the States, through the Fourteenth Amendment, in Mapp v. Ohio.[2811]

***591** Suppression of evidence, however, has always been our last resort, not our first impulse. The exclusionary rule generates "substantial social costs,"[2812] which sometimes include setting the guilty free and the dangerous at large. We have therefore been "cautio[us] against expanding" it,[2813] and "have repeatedly emphasized that the rule's 'costly toll' upon truth-seeking and law enforcement objectives presents a high obstacle for those urging [its] application,"[2814] We have rejected "[i]ndiscriminate application" of the rule,[2815] and have held it to be applicable only "where its remedial objectives are thought most efficaciously served,"[2816]—that is, "where its deterrence benefits outweigh its 'substantial social costs,'"[2817]

We did not always speak so guardedly. Expansive dicta in Mapp, for example, suggested wide scope for the exclusionary rule.[2818] ****2164** Whiteley v. Warden, Wyo. State Penitentiary[2819] was to the same effect. But we have long since rejected that approach. As explained in Arizona v. Evans:[2820] "In Whiteley, the Court treated identification of a Fourth Amendment violation as synonymous with application of the exclusionary rule to evidence secured incident to that violation. Subsequent case law has rejected this reflexive application of the exclusionary rule."[2821] We had said as much in Leon, a decade earlier, when we explained that "[w]hether the exclusionary sanction is appropriately imposed in a particular case ... is 'an issue separate from

---

[2808] *Id., at 40–41, 124 S.Ct. 521*

[2809] *514 U.S., at 937, n. 4, 115 S.Ct. 1914*

[2810] *232 U.S. 383, 34 S.Ct. 341, 58 L.Ed. 652 (1914)*

[2811] *367 U.S. 643, 81 S.Ct. 1684, 6 L.Ed.2d 1081 (1961)*

[2812] *United States v. Leon, 468 U.S. 897, 907, 104 S.Ct. 3405 (1984)*

[2813] *Colorado v. Connelly, 479 U.S. 157, 166, 107 S.Ct. 515, 93 L.Ed.2d 473 (1986)*

[2814] *Pennsylvania Bd. of Probation and Parole v. Scott, 524 U.S. 357, 364–365, 118 S.Ct. 2014, 141 L.Ed.2d 344 (1998)*

[2815] *Leon, supra, at 908, 104 S.Ct. 3405*

[2816] *United States v. Calandra, 414 U.S. 338, 348, 94 S.Ct. 613, 38 L.Ed.2d 561 (1974)*

[2817] *Scott, supra, at 363, 118 S.Ct. 2014 (quoting Leon, supra, at 907, 104 S.Ct. 3405)*

[2818] *See, e.g., 367 U.S., at 655, 81 S.Ct. 1684 ("[A]ll evidence obtained by searches and seizures in violation of the Constitution is, by that same authority, inadmissible in a state court")*

[2819] *401 U.S. 560, 568–569, 91 S.Ct. 1031, 28 L.Ed.2d 306 (1971)*

[2820] *514 U.S. 1, 13, 115 S.Ct. 1185, 131 L.Ed.2d 34 (1995)*

[2821] *(Citation omitted.)*

the question whether the Fourth Amendment rights of the party seeking ***592** to invoke the rule were violated by police conduct.'"[2822]

In other words, exclusion may not be premised on the mere fact that a constitutional violation was a "but-for" cause of obtaining evidence. Our cases show that but-for causality is only a necessary, not a sufficient, condition for suppression. In this case, of course, the constitutional violation of an illegal manner of entry was not a but-for cause of obtaining the evidence. Whether that preliminary misstep had occurred or not, the police would have executed the warrant they had obtained, and would have discovered the gun and drugs inside the house. But even if the illegal entry here could be characterized as a but-for cause of discovering what was inside, we have "never held that evidence is 'fruit of the poisonous tree' simply because 'it would not have come to light but for the illegal actions of the police.'"[2823] Rather, but-for cause, or "causation in the logical sense alone,"[2824] can be too attenuated to justify exclusion.[2825] Even in the early days of the exclusionary rule, we declined to

> [H]old that all evidence is 'fruit of the poisonous tree' simply because it would not have come to light but for the illegal actions of the police. Rather, the more apt question in such a case is 'whether, granting establishment of the primary illegality, the evidence to which instant objection is made has been come at by exploitation of that illegality or instead by means sufficiently distinguishable to be purged of the primary taint.'[2826]

***593** Attenuation can occur, of course, when the causal connection is remote.[2827] Attenuation also occurs when, even given a direct causal connection, the interest protected by the constitutional guarantee that has been violated would not be served by suppression of the evidence obtained. "The penalties visited upon the Government, and in turn upon the public, because its officers have violated the law must bear some relation to the purposes which the law is to serve."[2828] Thus, in New York v. Harris, 495 U.S. 14, 110 S.Ct. 1640, 109 L.Ed.2d 13 (1990), where an illegal warrantless arrest was made in Harris's house, we held:

> [S]uppressing [Harris's] statement taken outside the house would not serve the ****2165** purpose of the rule that made Harris' in-house arrest illegal. The warrant requirement for an arrest in the home is imposed to protect the home, and anything incriminating the police gathered from arresting Harris in his home, rather than elsewhere, has been excluded, as it should have been; the purpose of the rule has thereby been vindicated.[2829]

[2822] *468 U.S., at 906, 104 S.Ct. 3405 (quoting Illinois v. Gates, 462 U.S. 213, 223, 103 S.Ct. 2317, 76 L.Ed.2d 527 (1983))*

[2823] *Segura v. United States, 468 U.S. 796, 815, 104 S.Ct. 3380, 82 L.Ed.2d 599 (1984). See also id., at 829, 104 S.Ct. 3380 (STEVENS, J., dissenting) ("We have not ... mechanically applied the [exclusionary] rule to every item of evidence that has a causal connection with police misconduct")*

[2824] *United States v. Ceccolini, 435 U.S. 268, 274, 98 S.Ct. 1054, 55 L.Ed.2d 268 (1978)*

[2825] *Id., at 274–275, 98 S.Ct. 1054*

[2826] *Wong Sun v. United States, 371 U.S. 471, 487–488, 83 S.Ct. 407, 9 L.Ed.2d 441 (1963) (quoting J. Maguire, Evidence of Guilt 221 (1959); emphasis added)*

[2827] *See, e.g., Nardone v. United States, 308 U.S. 338, 341, 60 S.Ct. 266, 84 L.Ed. 307 (1939)*

[2828] *Ceccolini, supra, at 279, 98 S.Ct. 1054*

[2829] *Id., at 20, 110 S.Ct. 1640*

For this reason, cases excluding the fruits of unlawful warrantless searches,[2830] say nothing about the appropriateness of exclusion to vindicate the interests protected by the knock-and-announce requirement. Until a valid warrant has issued, citizens are entitled to shield "their persons, houses, papers, and effects,"[2831] from the government's scrutiny. Exclusion of the evidence obtained by a warrantless search vindicates that entitlement. The interests protected by the knock-and-announce requirement are quite different—and do not include the shielding of potential evidence from the government's eyes.

***594** One of those interests is the protection of human life and limb, because an unannounced entry may provoke violence in supposed self-defense by the surprised resident.[2832] Another interest is the protection of property. Breaking a house (as the old cases typically put it) absent an announcement would penalize someone who "'did not know of the process, of which, if he had notice, it is to be presumed that he would obey it. . . .'"[2833] The knock-and-announce rule gives individuals "the opportunity to comply with the law and to avoid the destruction of property occasioned by a forcible entry."[2834] And thirdly, the knock-and-announce rule protects those elements of privacy and dignity that can be destroyed by a sudden entrance. It gives residents the "opportunity to prepare themselves for" the entry of the police.[2835] "The brief interlude between announcement and entry with a warrant may be the opportunity that an individual has to pull on clothes or get out of bed." Ibid. In other words, it assures the opportunity to collect oneself before answering the door.

What the knock-and-announce rule has never protected, however, is one's interest in preventing the government from seeing or taking evidence described in a warrant. Since the interests that were violated in this case have nothing to do with the seizure of the evidence, the exclusionary rule is inapplicable.

B

Quite apart from the requirement of unattenuated causation, the exclusionary rule has never been applied except "where its deterrence benefits outweigh its 'substantial social costs,'"[2836] ***595** The costs here are considerable. In addition to the grave adverse consequence that exclusion of relevant incriminating evidence always entails (viz., the risk of releasing dangerous criminals into society), imposing that massive ****2166** remedy for a knock-and-announce violation would generate a constant flood of alleged failures to observe the rule, and claims that any asserted Richards justification for a no-knock entry,[2837] had inadequate support.[2838] The cost of entering this lottery would be small, but the jackpot enormous: suppression of all evidence, amounting in many cases to a get-out-of-jail-free card. Courts would experience as never before the reality that "[t]he exclusionary rule frequently requires extensive

[2830] *See, e.g., Boyd v. United States, 116 U.S. 616, 6 S.Ct. 524, 29 L.Ed. 746 (1886); Weeks, 232 U.S. 383, 34 S.Ct. 341; Silverthorne Lumber Co. v. United States, 251 U.S. 385, 40 S.Ct. 182, 64 L.Ed. 319 (1920); Mapp, supra*

[2831] *U.S. Const., Amdt. 4*

[2832] *See, e.g., McDonald v. United States, 335 U.S. 451, 460–461, 69 S.Ct. 191, 93 L.Ed. 153 (1948) (Jackson, J., concurring). See also Sabbath, 391 U.S., at 589, 88 S.Ct. 1755; Miller, 357 U.S., at 313, n. 12, 78 S.Ct. 1190*

[2833] *Wilson, 514 U.S., at 931–932, 115 S.Ct. 1914 (quoting Semayne's Case, 5 Co. Rep. 91a, 91b, 77 Eng. Rep. 194, 195–196 (K.B.1603))*

[2834] *Richards, 520 U.S., at 393, n. 5, 117 S.Ct. 1416. See also Banks, 540 U.S., at 41, 124 S.Ct. 521*

[2835] *Richards, 520 U.S., at 393, n. 5, 117 S.Ct. 1416*

[2836] *Scott, 524 U.S., at 363, 118 S.Ct. 2014 (quoting Leon, 468 U.S., at 907, 104 S.Ct. 3405)*

[2837] *See 520 U.S., at 394, 117 S.Ct. 1416*

[2838] *Cf. United States v. Singleton, 441 F.3d 290, 293–294 (C.A.4 2006)*

litigation to determine whether particular evidence must be excluded."[2839] Unlike the warrant or Miranda requirements, compliance with which is readily determined (either there was or was not a warrant; either the Miranda warning was given, or it was not), what constituted a "reasonable wait time" in a particular case,[2840] (or, for that matter, how many seconds the police in fact waited), or whether there was "reasonable suspicion" of the sort that would invoke the Richards exceptions, is difficult for the trial court to determine and even more difficult for an appellate court to review.

Another consequence of the incongruent remedy Hudson proposes would be police officers' refraining from timely entry after knocking and announcing. As we have observed,[2841] the amount of time they must wait is necessarily uncertain. If the consequences of running afoul of the rule were so massive, officers would be inclined to wait longer than the law requires—producing preventable violence against officers in some cases, and the destruction of evidence in many others.[2842] We deemed these consequences severe enough to produce our unanimous agreement ***596** that a mere "reasonable suspicion" that knocking and announcing "under the particular circumstances, would be dangerous or futile, or that it would inhibit the effective investigation of the crime," will cause the requirement to yield. Richards.[2843]

Next to these "substantial social costs" we must consider the deterrence benefits, existence of which is a necessary condition for exclusion. (It is not, of course, a sufficient condition: "[I]t does not follow that the Fourth Amendment requires adoption of every proposal that might deter police misconduct."[2844]) To begin with, the value of deterrence depends upon the strength of the incentive to commit the forbidden act. Viewed from this perspective, deterrence of knock-and-announce violations is not worth a lot. Violation of the warrant requirement sometimes produces incriminating evidence that could not otherwise be obtained. But ignoring knock-and-announce can realistically be expected to achieve absolutely nothing except the prevention of destruction of evidence and the avoidance of life-threatening resistance by occupants of the premises—dangers which, if there is even "reasonable suspicion" of their existence, suspend the knock-and-announce requirement anyway. Massive deterrence is hardly required.

It seems to us not even true, as Hudson contends, that without suppression there will be no deterrence of knock-and-announce violations at all. Of course even if this assertion were accurate, it would not necessarily justify suppression. Assuming (as the assertion must) that civil suit is not an effective deterrent, one can think of many forms of police misconduct that are similarly "undeterred." When, for example, a confessed suspect in the killing of a police officer, arrested (along with incriminating evidence) in a lawful warranted ****2167** search, is subjected to physical abuse at the station house, would it seriously be suggested that the evidence must be excluded, since that is the only "effective deterrent"? ***597** And what, other than civil suit, is the "effective deterrent" of police violation of an already-confessed suspect's Sixth Amendment rights by denying him prompt access to counsel? Many would regard these violated rights as more significant than the right not to be intruded upon in one's nightclothes—and yet nothing but "ineffective" civil suit is available as a deterrent. And the police incentive for those violations is arguably greater than the incentive for disregarding the knock-and-announce rule.

[2839] *Scott, supra, at 366, 118 S.Ct. 2014*

[2840] *Banks, supra, at 41, 124 S.Ct. 521*

[2841] *See supra, at 2163*

[2842] *See Gates, 462 U.S., at 258, 103 S.Ct. 2317 (White, J., concurring in judgment)*

[2843] *Supra, at 394, 117 S.Ct. 1416*

[2844] *Calandra, 414 U.S., at 350, 94 S.Ct. 613; see also Leon, supra, at 910, 104 S.Ct. 3405*

We cannot assume that exclusion in this context is necessary deterrence simply because we found that it was necessary deterrence in different contexts and long ago. That would be forcing the public today to pay for the sins and inadequacies of a legal regime that existed almost half a century ago. Dollree Mapp could not turn to Rev.Stat. § 1979,[2845] for meaningful relief,[2846] which began the slow but steady expansion of that remedy, was decided the same Term as Mapp. It would be another 17 years before the § 1983 remedy was extended to reach the deep pocket of municipalities.[2847] Citizens whose Fourth Amendment rights were violated by federal officers could not bring suit until 10 years after Mapp, with this Court's decision in Bivens v. Six Unknown Fed. Narcotics Agents.[2848]

Hudson complains that "it would be very hard to find a lawyer to take a case such as this,"[2849] but 42 U.S.C. § 1988(b) answers this objection. Since some civil-rights violations would yield damages too small to justify the expense of litigation, Congress has authorized attorney's fees for civil-rights plaintiffs. This remedy was unavailable in the heydays of our exclusionary-rule jurisprudence, because it is tied to the availability of a cause of action. For years after Mapp, "very few lawyers would even consider representation of persons who had civil rights claims against the police," but now "much has changed. Citizens and lawyers ***598** are much more willing to seek relief in the courts for police misconduct."[2850] The number of public-interest law firms and lawyers who specialize in civil-rights grievances has greatly expanded.

Hudson points out that few published decisions to date announce huge awards for knock-and-announce violations. But this is an unhelpful statistic. Even if we thought that only large damages would deter police misconduct (and that police somehow are deterred by "damages" but indifferent to the prospect of large § 1988 attorney's fees), we do not know how many claims have been settled, or indeed how many violations have occurred that produced anything more than nominal injury. It is clear, at least, that the lower courts are allowing colorable knock-and-announce suits to go forward, unimpeded by assertions of qualified immunity.[2851] As far as we know, civil liability is an ****2168** effective deterrent here, as we have assumed it is in other contexts.[2852]

Another development over the past half-century that deters civil-rights violations is the increasing professionalism of police forces, including a new emphasis on internal police discipline. Even as long ago as 1980 we felt it proper to ***599** "assume" that unlawful police behavior would "be dealt with appropriately" by the authorities,[2853] but we now have increasing evidence that police forces across the United States take the constitutional rights of citizens seriously. There have been "wide-

---

[2845] *42 U.S.C. § 1983*

[2846] *Monroe v. Pape, 365 U.S. 167, 81 S.Ct. 473, 5 L.Ed.2d 492 (1961)*

[2847] *Monell v. New York City Dept. of Social Servs., 436 U.S. 658, 98 S.Ct. 2018, 56 L.Ed.2d 611 (1978)*

[2848] *403 U.S. 388, 91 S.Ct. 1999, 29 L.Ed.2d 619 (1971)*

[2849] *Tr. of Oral Arg. 7*

[2850] *M. Avery, D. Rudovsky, & K. Blum, Police Misconduct: Law and Litigation, p. v (3d ed.2005); see generally N. Aron, Liberty and Justice for All: Public Interest Law in the 1980s and Beyond (1989) (describing the growth of public-interest law)*

[2851] *See, e.g., Green v. Butler, 420 F.3d 689, 700–701 (C.A.7 2005) (denying qualified immunity in a knock-and-announce civil suit); Holland ex rel. Overdorff v. Harrington, 268 F.3d 1179, 1193–1196 (C.A.10 2001) (same); Mena v. Simi Valley, 226 F.3d 1031, 1041–1042 (C.A.9 2000) (same); Gould v. Davis, 165 F.3d 265, 270–271 (C.A.4 1998) (same)*

[2852] *See, e.g., Correctional Services Corp. v. Malesko, 534 U.S. 61, 70, 122 S.Ct. 515, 151 L.Ed.2d 456 (2001) ("[T]he threat of litigation and liability will adequately deter federal officers for Bivens purposes no matter that they may enjoy qualified immunity" (as violators of knock-and-announce do not)); see also Nix v. Williams, 467 U.S. 431, 446, 104 S.Ct. 2501, 81 L.Ed.2d 377 (1984)*

[2853] *United States v. Payner, 447 U.S. 727, 733–734, n. 5, 100 S.Ct. 2439, 65 L.Ed.2d 468 (1980)*

ranging reforms in the education, training, and supervision of police officers."[2854] Numerous sources are now available to teach officers and their supervisors what is required of them under this Court's cases, how to respect constitutional guarantees in various situations, and how to craft an effective regime for internal discipline.[2855] Failure to teach and enforce constitutional requirements exposes municipalities to financial liability.[2856] Moreover, modern police forces are staffed with professionals; it is not credible to assert that internal discipline, which can limit successful careers, will not have a deterrent effect. There is also evidence that the increasing use of various forms of citizen review can enhance police accountability.

In sum, the social costs of applying the exclusionary rule to knock-and-announce violations are considerable; the incentive to such violations is minimal to begin with, and the extant deterrences against them are substantial—incomparably greater than the factors deterring warrantless entries when Mapp was decided. Resort to the massive remedy of suppressing evidence of guilt is unjustified.

IV

A trio of cases—Segura v. United States,[2857] New York v. Harris,[2858] and United ***600** States v. Ramirez[2859]—confirms our conclusion that suppression is unwarranted in this case.

Like today's case, Segura involved a concededly illegal entry. Police conducting a drug crime investigation waited for Segura outside an apartment building; when he arrived, he denied living there. The police arrested him and brought him to the apartment where they suspected illegal activity. An officer knocked. When someone inside opened the door, the police entered, taking Segura with them. They had neither a warrant nor consent to enter, and they did not announce themselves as police—an entry as illegal as can be. Officers then stayed in the apartment for 19 hours awaiting a search warrant.[2860] Once alerted that the search ****2169** warrant had been obtained, the police—still inside, having secured the premises so that no evidence could be removed—conducted a search.[2861] We refused to exclude the resulting evidence. We recognized that only the evidence gained from the particular violation could be excluded,[2862] and therefore distinguished the effects of the illegal entry from the effects of the legal search: "None of the information on which the warrant was secured was derived from or related in any way to the initial entry into petitioners' apartment. . ."[2863] It was therefore "beyond dispute that the information possessed by the agents before they entered the apartment constituted an independent source for the discovery and seizure of the evidence now challenged."[2864]

[2854] *S. Walker, Taming the System: The Control of Discretion in Criminal Justice 1950–1990, p. 51 (1993)*

[2855] *See, e.g., D. Waksman & D. Goodman, The Search and Seizure Handbook (2d ed.2006); A. Stone & S. DeLuca, Police Administration: An Introduction (2d ed.1994); E. Thibault, L. Lynch, & R. McBride, Proactive Police Management (4th ed. 1998)*

[2856] *See Canton v. Harris, 489 U.S. 378, 388, 109 S.Ct. 1197, 103 L.Ed.2d 412 (1989)*

[2857] *468 U.S. 796, 104 S.Ct. 3380, 82 L.Ed.2d 599 (1984)*

[2858] *495 U.S. 14, 110 S.Ct. 1640, 109 L.Ed.2d 13 (1990)*

[2859] *523 U.S. 65, 118 S.Ct. 992, 140 L.Ed.2d 191 (1998)*

[2860] *468 U.S., at 800–801, 104 S.Ct. 3380; id., at 818–819, 104 S.Ct. 3380 (STEVENS, J., dissenting)*

[2861] *Id., at 801, 104 S.Ct. 3380*

[2862] *See id., at 799, 804–805, 104 S.Ct. 3380*

[2863] *Id., at 814, 104 S.Ct. 3380*

[2864] *Ibid.*

If the search in Segura could be "wholly unrelated to the prior entry,"[2865] when the only entry was warrantless, it would be bizarre to treat more harshly the actions in this case, where the only entry was with a warrant. If the probable cause backing a warrant that was issued later in time could be an "independent source" for a search that proceeded after the officers illegally entered and waited, a search warrant ***601** obtained before going in must have at least this much effect.

In the second case, Harris, the police violated the defendant's Fourth Amendment rights by arresting him at home without a warrant, contrary to Payton v. New York,[2866] Once taken to the station house, he gave an incriminating statement.[2867] We refused to exclude it. Like the illegal entry which led to discovery of the evidence in today's case, the illegal arrest in Harris began a process that culminated in acquisition of the evidence sought to be excluded. While Harris's statement was "the product of an arrest and being in custody," it "was not the fruit of the fact that the arrest was made in the house rather than someplace else."[2868] Likewise here: While acquisition of the gun and drugs was the product of a search pursuant to warrant, it was not the fruit of the fact that the entry was not preceded by knock-and-announce.

****2170 *602** United States v. Ramirez, supra, involved a claim that police entry violated the Fourth Amendment because it was effected by breaking a window. We ultimately concluded that the property destruction was, under all the circumstances, reasonable, but in the course of our discussion we unanimously said the following: "[D]estruction of property in the course of a search may violate the Fourth Amendment, even though the entry itself is lawful and the fruits of the search are not subject to suppression."[2869] Had the breaking of the window been unreasonable, the Court said, it would have been necessary to determine whether there had been a "sufficient causal relationship between the breaking of the window and the discovery of the guns to warrant suppression of the evidence."[2870] What clearer expression could there be of the proposition that an impermissible manner of entry does not necessarily trigger the exclusionary rule?

* * *

For the foregoing reasons we affirm the judgment of the Michigan Court of Appeals.

It is so ordered.

*****

(The dissent of Justice BREYER, with whom Justice STEVENS, Justice SOUTER, and Justice GINSBURG join, is omitted.)

Black Letter Law

> The Court held that violation of the requirement that police officers knock-and-announce their presence before executing a search warrant did not require the suppression of all evidence found in the search, since the interests violated had nothing to do with the seizure of the evidence. Whether the exclusionary sanction is appropriately imposed in a particular case, is an issue separate from the question whether the Fourth Amendment rights of the party seeking to invoke the rule were violated by police conduct.

[2865] *Ibid.*

[2866] *445 U.S. 573, 100 S.Ct. 1371, 63 L.Ed.2d 639 (1980)*

[2867] *See 495 U.S., at 15–16, 110 S.Ct. 1640*

[2868] *Id., at 20, 110 S.Ct. 1640*

[2869] *Id., at 71, 118 S.Ct. 992*

[2870] *Id., at 72, n. 3, 118 S.Ct. 992*

Discussion Problems:

16-1. On July 8, the defendant was driving an automobile at the intersection of New South Highway and Northlake Boulevard in Lake Wales, Florida. The vehicle in which the defendant was riding was stopped at a traffic light facing north on New South Highway. Officer Steven Jones was stopped behind the defendant's vehicle. Upon the traffic light turning green, the defendant made a left-hand turn onto Northlake Boulevard. Officer Jones testified that the defendant did not use a left turn signal prior to or during the left-hand turn. Officer Jones also testified that neither he nor the drivers of other vehicles were affected by the defendant's failure to use a turn signal while making that turn. The officer's testimony also indicated that he observed a white light emanating from a crack in the plastic lens covering the tail light of the left rear of the defendant's vehicle. Officer Jones acknowledged that the plastic lens was cracked, but that the light was operating.

Because the defendant failed to use a turn signal in making his left hand turn, and because white light was emanating from a crack in the plastic lens covering the taillight, Officer Jones effected a traffic stop of the defendant's vehicle. Upon being stopped by Officer Jones, the defendant provided the officer with identification. Officer Jones ran a check on the defendant, and learned that there was an outstanding warrant for the defendant's arrest for failure to appear in another proceeding. As a result of the outstanding warrant, the defendant was arrested. A search incident to the defendant's arrest revealed the firearm that formed the basis of the charge against him in this case. A subsequent investigation determined that the warrant, which provided the basis for the defendant's arrest, was issued due to another person's failure to appear. Someone other than the defendant was issued a notice to appear in the other case and wrongfully gave the issuing officer the defendant's name and date of birth. A fingerprint was taken of the individual to whom the notice to appear was issued. It is undisputed the print taken did not match that of the defendant's.

The defendant was charged in this case with possession of a firearm by a convicted felon. He sought to suppress the seizure of the firearm, contending that the traffic stop which preceded the arrest was unlawful and that the warrant which provided the basis for his arrest was wrongfully issued. The trial judge agreed with respondent that the traffic stop was unlawful based upon the Florida Supreme Court's decisions in State v. Riley,[2871] and Doctor v. State.[2872]

You are the trial judge's clerk. She has decided, and communicated to you in chambers, that she is going to apply the attenuation of the taint doctrine to this case, and allow the state to admit the firearm.

As the judge's clerk you have been tasked to draft an order ruling that the firearm is admissible under the attenuation of taint theory. Draft your order so that it includes the relevant case law and facts.

16-2. On November 29, 1995, Officer Jennifer Easterling of the Police Department was patrolling the area of Pontiac and Campbellton in the City. Detective Linda Stanwick had informed Officer Easterling that the defendant was wanted for robbery and he frequented the area of Campbellton and Pontiac. Officer Easterling observed defendant on the west side of Campbellton Street, just north of Pontiac, and took him into custody.

[2871] *638 So.2d 507 (Fla.1994) (failure to use turn signal without driver's conduct creating reasonable safety concern does not constitute violation of statute)*

[2872] *596 So.2d 442 (Fla.1992) (cracked taillight was not violation of law)*

Detective Stanwick was assigned to the investigation of multiple robberies in a five-block radius, including the robbery of Rodrick White. As part of the investigation of the robberies, Detective Easterling spoke with Mr. White. Mr. White told Detective Stanwick that Dominique Gist was the person who robbed him. Gist was arrested and later interviewed by Detective Stanwick. Gist gave Detective Stanwick the defendant's nickname and address and told Detective Stanwick the defendant robbed Mr. White and also was involved in robberies at the gas station at Campbellton and Pontiac. Detective Stanwick ran the description of the suspect to the robberies through the computer. This very general description was consistent with defendant's general description. The officers arrested defendant for the robbery of Mr. White based on the information Gist gave to Detective Stanwick.

The day after defendant's arrest, Detective Stanwick took defendant's picture. Detective Stanwick used this photo in a photographic lineup shown to Mr. White. Mr. White stated he knew defendant and defendant was not the person who robbed him. Detective Stanwick then showed the same photographic lineup to victims of other robberies. Charles Grantham and Manuel Rivero identified defendant as the perpetrator in their robberies.

Defendant was charged with six counts of robbery and two counts of attempted robbery, none of them involving the White robbery for which he was initially arrested.

You are the defendant's counsel and are sitting down to draft a motion to suppress the photographs used to identify your client as the perpetrator of the Grantham & Rivero robberies.

What is your best argument? How will you raise it? What potential responses should you expect from the state?

Chapter 17: Independent Source & Inevitable Discovery

Silverthorne Lumber Co. v. United States

40 S.Ct. 182
Supreme Court of the United States
SILVERTHORNE LUMBER CO., Inc., et al.
v.
UNITED STATES.
No. 358. | Argued Dec. 12, 1919. | Decided Jan. 26, 1920.

***390** Mr. Justice HOLMES delivered the opinion of the Court.

This is a writ of error brought to reverse a judgment of the District Court fining the Silverthorne Lumber Company two hundred and fifty dollars for contempt of court and ordering Frederick W. Silverthorne to be imprisoned until he should purge himself of a similar contempt. The contempt in question was a refusal to obey subpoenas and an order of Court to produce books and documents of the company before the grand jury to be used in regard to alleged violation of the statutes of the United States by the said Silverthorne and his father. One ground of the refusal was that the order of the Court infringed the rights of the parties under the Fourth Amendment of the Constitution of the United States.

The facts are simple. An indictment upon a single specific charge having been brought against the two Silverthornes mentioned, they both were arrested at their homes early in the morning of February 25, and were detained in custody a number of hours. While they were thus detained representatives of the Department of Justice and the United States marshal without a shadow of authority went to the office of their company and made a clean sweep of all the books, papers and documents found there. All the employees were taken or directed to go to the office of the District Attorney of the United States to which also the books, &c., were taken at once. An application was made as soon as might be to the District ***391** Court for a return of what thus had been taken unlawfully. It was opposed by the District Attorney so far as he had found evidence against the plaintiffs in error, and it was stated that the evidence so obtained was before the grand jury. Color had been given by the District Attorney to the approach of those concerned in the act by an invalid subpoena for certain documents relating to the charge in the indictment then on file. Thus the case is not that of knowledge acquired through the wrongful act of a stranger, but it must be assumed that the Government planned or at all events ratified the whole performance. Photographs and copies of material papers were made and a new indictment was framed based upon the knowledge thus obtained. The District Court ordered a return of the originals but impounded the photographs and copies. Subpoenas to produce the originals then were served and on the refusal of the plaintiffs in error to produce them the Court made an order that the subpoenas should be complied with, although it had found that all the papers had been seized in violation of the parties' constitutional rights. The refusal to obey this order is the contempt alleged. The Government now, while in form repudiating and condemning the illegal seizure, seeks to maintain its right to avail itself of the knowledge obtained by that means which otherwise it would not have had.

The proposition could not be presented more nakedly. It is that although of course its seizure was an outrage which the Government now regrets, it may study the papers before it returns them, copy them, and then may use the knowledge that it has gained to call upon the owners in a more regular form to produce them; that the protection of the Constitution covers the physical possession but not any advantages that the Government can gain over the object of its pursuit by doing the forbidden act. Weeks v. United States,[2873] to be sure, had established that laying the papers directly before the grand jury was ***392** unwarranted, but ****183** it is taken to mean only that two steps are required instead of one. In our opinion such is not the law. It reduces the Fourth Amendment to a form of words.[2874] The essence of a provision forbidding the acquisition of evidence in a certain way is that not merely evidence so acquired shall not be used before the Court but that it shall not be used at all. Of course this does not mean that the facts thus obtained become sacred and inaccessible. If knowledge of them is gained from an independent source they may be proved like any others, but the knowledge gained by the Government's own wrong cannot be used by it in the way proposed. The numerous decisions, like Adams v. New York,[2875] holding that a collateral inquiry into the mode in which evidence has been got will not be allowed when the question is raised for the first time at the trial, are no authority in the present proceeding, as is explained in Weeks v. United States.[2876] Whether some of those decisions have gone too far or have given wrong reasons it is unnecessary to inquire; the principle applicable to the present case seems to us plain. It is stated satisfactorily in Flagg v. United States,[2877] it was thought that a different rule applied to a corporation, on the ground that it was not privileged from producing its books and papers. But the rights of a corporation against unlawful search and seizure are to be protected even if the same result might have been achieved in a lawful way.

Judgment reversed.

The CHIEF JUSTICE and Mr. Justice PITNEY dissent.

Black Letter Law

> The rights of a corporation against unlawful search and seizure are to be protected, even if the same result might be achieved by the government in a lawful way.

Nix v. Williams

104 S.Ct. 2501

Supreme Court of the United States

Crispus NIX, Warden, Petitioner

v.

Robert Anthony WILLIAMS.

No. 82-1651. | Argued Jan. 18, 1984. | Decided June 11, 1984.

[2873] 232 U. S. 383, 34 Sup. Ct. 341, 58 L. Ed. 652, L. R. A. 1915B, 834, Ann. Cas. 1915C, 1177.

[2874] 232 U. S. 393, 34 Sup. Ct. 341, 58 L. Ed. 652, L. R. A. 1915B, 834, Ann. Cas. 1915C, 1177

[2875] 192 U. S. 585, 24 Sup. Ct. 372, 48 L. Ed. 575

[2876] 232 U. S. 383, 394, 395, 34 Sup. Ct. 341, 58 L. Ed. 652, L. R. A. 1915B, 834, Ann. Cas. 1915C, 1177

[2877] 233 Fed. 481, 483, 147 C. C. A. 367. In Linn v. United States, 251 Fed. 476, 480, 163 C. C. A. 470

***434** Chief Justice BURGER delivered the opinion of the Court.

We granted certiorari to consider whether, at respondent Williams' second murder trial in state court, evidence pertaining to the discovery and condition of the victim's body was properly admitted on the ground that it would ultimately or inevitably have been discovered even if no violation of any constitutional or statutory provision had taken place.

I

A

On December 24, 1968, 10–year–old Pamela Powers disappeared from a YMCA building in Des Moines, Iowa, where she had accompanied her parents to watch an athletic contest. Shortly after she disappeared, Williams was seen leaving the YMCA carrying a large bundle wrapped in a blanket; a 14–year–old boy who had helped Williams open his car door reported that he had seen "two legs in it and they were skinny and white."

Williams' car was found the next day 160 miles east of Des Moines in Davenport, Iowa. Later several items of clothing belonging to the child, some of Williams' clothing, and an army blanket like the one used to wrap the bundle that Williams carried out of the YMCA were found at a rest stop on ***435** Interstate 80 near Grinnell, between Des Moines and Davenport. A warrant was issued for Williams' arrest.

Police surmised that Williams had left Pamela Powers or her body somewhere between Des Moines and the Grinnell rest stop where some of the young girl's clothing had been found. On December 26, the Iowa Bureau of Criminal Investigation initiated a large-scale search. Two hundred volunteers divided into teams began the search 21 miles east of Grinnell, covering an area several miles to the north and south of Interstate 80. They moved westward from Poweshiek County, in which Grinnell was located, into Jasper County. Searchers were instructed to check all roads, abandoned farm buildings, ditches, culverts, and any other place in which the body of a small child could be hidden.

Meanwhile, Williams surrendered to local police in Davenport, where he was promptly arraigned. Williams contacted a Des Moines attorney who arranged for an attorney in Davenport to meet Williams at the ****2505** Davenport police station. Des Moines police informed counsel they would pick Williams up in Davenport and return him to Des Moines without questioning him. Two Des Moines detectives then drove to Davenport, took Williams into custody, and proceeded to drive him back to Des Moines.

During the return trip, one of the policemen, Detective Leaming, began a conversation with Williams, saying:

> I want to give you something to think about while we're traveling down the road.... They are predicting several inches of snow for tonight, and I feel that you yourself are the only person that knows where this little girl's body is ... and if you get a snow on top of it you yourself may be unable to find it. And since we will be going right past the area [where the body is] on the way into Des Moines, I feel that we could stop and locate the body, that the parents of this little girl should be entitled to a Christian burial for the little girl who was snatched away from them on Christmas [E]ve and murdered.... ***436** [A]fter a snow storm [we may not be] able to find it at all.

Leaming told Williams he knew the body was in the area of Mitchellville—a town they would be passing on the way to Des Moines. He concluded the conversation by saying "I do not want you to answer me.... Just think about it...."

Later, as the police car approached Grinnell, Williams asked Leaming whether the police had found the young girl's shoes. After Leaming replied that he was unsure, Williams directed the police to a point near a service station where he said he had left the shoes; they were not found. As they continued to drive to Des Moines, Williams asked whether the blanket had been found and then directed the officers to a rest area in Grinnell where he said he had disposed of the blanket; they did not find the blanket. At this point Leaming and his party were joined by the officers in charge of the search. As they approached Mitchellville, Williams, without any further conversation, agreed to direct the officers to the child's body.

The officers directing the search had called off the search at 3 p.m., when they left the Grinnell Police Department to join Leaming at the rest area. At that time, one search team near the Jasper County–Polk County line was only two and one-half miles from where Williams soon guided Leaming and his party to the body. The child's body was found next to a culvert in a ditch beside a gravel road in Polk County, about two miles south of Interstate 80, and essentially within the area to be searched.

B
FIRST TRIAL

In February 1969 Williams was indicted for first-degree murder. Before trial in the Iowa court, his counsel moved to suppress evidence of the body and all related evidence including the condition of the body as shown by the autopsy. The ground for the motion was that such evidence was the "fruit" ***437** or product of Williams' statements made during the automobile ride from Davenport to Des Moines and prompted by Leaming's statements. The motion to suppress was denied.

The jury found Williams guilty of first-degree murder; the judgment of conviction was affirmed by the Iowa Supreme Court.[2878] Williams then sought release on habeas corpus in the United States District Court for the Southern District of Iowa. That court concluded that the evidence in question had been wrongly admitted at Williams' trial.[2879] A divided panel of the Court of Appeals for the Eighth Circuit agreed.[2880]

We granted certiorari,[2881] and a divided Court affirmed, holding that Detective Leaming had obtained incriminating statements from Williams by what was viewed as interrogation in violation of his right to counsel.[2882] ****2506** This Court's opinion noted, however, that although Williams' incriminating statements could not be introduced into evidence at a second trial, evidence of the body's location and condition "might well be admissible on the theory that the body would have been discovered in any event, even had incriminating statements not been elicited from Williams."[2883]

[2878] *State v. Williams,* 182 N.W.2d 396 (1970)

[2879] *Williams v. Brewer*, 375 F.Supp. 170 (1974)

[2880] 509 F.2d 227 (1974)

[2881] 423 U.S. 1031, 96 S.Ct. 561, 46 L.Ed.2d 404 (1975)

[2882] *Brewer v. Williams*, 430 U.S. 387, 97 S.Ct. 1232, 51 L.Ed.2d 424 (1977)

[2883] Id., at 407, n. 12, 97 S.Ct., at 1243, n. 12

C
SECOND TRIAL

At Williams' second trial in 1977 in the Iowa court, the prosecution did not offer Williams' statements into evidence, nor did it seek to show that Williams had directed the police to the child's body. However, evidence of the condition of her body as it was found, articles and photographs of her clothing, and the results of post mortem medical and chemical tests on the body were admitted. The trial court concluded that the State had proved by a preponderance of the evidence that, if the search had not been suspended and Williams had not led the police to the victim, her body would have been ***438** discovered "within a short time" in essentially the same condition as it was actually found. The trial court also ruled that if the police had not located the body, "the search would clearly have been taken up again where it left off, given the extreme circumstances of this case and the body would [have] been found in short order."[2884]

In finding that the body would have been discovered in essentially the same condition as it was actually found, the court noted that freezing temperatures had prevailed and tissue deterioration would have been suspended. Id., at 87. The challenged evidence was admitted and the jury again found Williams guilty of first-degree murder; he was sentenced to life in prison.

On appeal, the Supreme Court of Iowa again affirmed.[2885] That court held that there was in fact a "hypothetical independent source" exception to the exclusionary rule:

> After the defendant has shown unlawful conduct on the part of the police, the State has the burden to show by a preponderance of the evidence that (1) the police did not act in bad faith for the purpose of hastening discovery of the evidence in question, and (2) that the evidence in question would have been discovered by lawful means."[2886]

As to the first element, the Iowa Supreme Court, having reviewed the relevant cases, stated:

> The issue of the propriety of the police conduct in this case, as noted earlier in this opinion, has caused the closest possible division of views in every appellate court which has considered the question. In light of the legitimate disagreement among individuals well versed in the law of criminal procedure who were given the opportunity for calm deliberation, it cannot be said that the actions of the police were taken in bad faith.[2887]

***439** The Iowa court then reviewed the evidence de novol and concluded that the State had shown by a preponderance of the evidence that, even if Williams had not guided police to the child's body, it would inevitably have been found by lawful activity of the search party before its condition had materially changed.

[2884] App. 86 (emphasis added)

[2885] 285 N.W.2d 248 (1979)

[2886] Id., at 260

[2887] Id., at 260–261

In 1980 Williams renewed his attack on the state-court conviction by seeking a writ of habeas corpus in the United States District Court for the Southern District of Iowa. The District Court conducted its own independent review of the evidence and concluded, as had the state courts, that the body would inevitably have been found by the searchers in essentially the same condition it was in when Williams led police ****2507** to its discovery. The District Court denied Williams' petition.[2888]

The Court of Appeals for the Eighth Circuit reversed;[2889] an equally divided court denied rehearing en banc.[2890] That court assumed, without deciding, that there is an inevitable discovery exception to the exclusionary rule and that the Iowa Supreme Court correctly stated that exception to require proof that the police did not act in bad faith and that the evidence would have been discovered absent any constitutional violation. In reversing the District Court's denial of habeas relief, the Court of Appeals stated:

> We hold that the State has not met the first requirement. It is therefore unnecessary to decide whether the state courts' finding that the body would have been discovered anyway is fairly supported by the record. It is also unnecessary to decide whether the State must prove the two elements of the exception by clear and ***440** convincing evidence, as defendant argues, or by a preponderance of the evidence, as the state courts held.
>
> The state trial court, in denying the motion to suppress, made no finding one way or the other on the question of bad faith. Its opinion does not even mention the issue and seems to proceed on the assumption—contrary to the rule of law later laid down by the Supreme Court of Iowa—that the State needed to show only that the body would have been discovered in any event. The Iowa Supreme Court did expressly address the issue ... and a finding by an appellate court of a state is entitled to the same presumption of correctness that attaches to trial-court findings under 28 U.S.C. § 2254(d).... We conclude, however, that the state Supreme Court's finding that the police did not act in bad faith is not entitled to the shield of § 2254(d)....[2891]

We granted the State's petition for certiorari,[2892] and we reverse.

II

A

The Iowa Supreme Court correctly stated that the "vast majority" of all courts, both state and federal, recognize an inevitable discovery exception to the exclusionary rule. We ***441** are now urged to adopt and apply the so-called ultimate or inevitable discovery exception to the exclusionary rule.

Williams contends that evidence of the body's location and condition is "fruit of the poisonous tree," i.e., the "fruit" or product of Detective Leaming's

---

[2888] 528 F.Supp. 664 (1981)

[2889] 700 F.2d 1164 (1983)

[2890] Id., at 1175

[2891] Id., at 1169–1170 (footnotes omitted)

[2892] 461 U.S. 956, 103 S.Ct. 2427, 77 L.Ed.2d 1315 (1983)

plea to help the child's parents give her "a Christian burial," which this Court had already held equated to interrogation. He contends that admitting the challenged evidence violated the Sixth Amendment whether it would have been inevitably discovered or not. Williams also contends that, if the inevitable discovery doctrine is constitutionally permissible, it must include a threshold showing of police good faith.

B

The doctrine requiring courts to suppress evidence as the tainted "fruit" of unlawful ****2508** governmental conduct had its genesis in Silverthorne Lumber Co. v. United States.[2893] There, the Court held that the exclusionary rule applies not only to the illegally obtained evidence itself, but also to other incriminating evidence derived from the primary evidence. The holding of Silverthorne was carefully limited, however, for the Court emphasized that such information does not automatically become "sacred and inaccessible."[2894] "If knowledge of [such facts] is gained from an independent source, they may be proved like any others...."[2895]

Wong Sun v. United States,[2896] extended the exclusionary rule to evidence that was the indirect product or "fruit" of unlawful police conduct, but there again the Court emphasized that evidence that has been illegally obtained need not always be suppressed, stating:

> ***442** We need not hold that all evidence is 'fruit of the poisonous tree' simply because it would not have come to light but for the illegal actions of the police. Rather, the more apt question in such a case is 'whether, granting establishment of the primary illegality, the evidence to which instant objection is made has been come at by exploitation of that illegality or instead by means sufficiently distinguishable to be purged of the primary taint.'[2897]

The Court thus pointedly negated the kind of good-faith requirement advanced by the Court of Appeals in reversing the District Court.

Although Silverthorne and Wong Sun involved violations of the Fourth Amendment, the "fruit of the poisonous tree" doctrine has not been limited to cases in which there has been a Fourth Amendment violation. The Court has applied the doctrine where the violations were of the Sixth Amendment.[2898]

The core rationale consistently advanced by this Court for extending the exclusionary rule to evidence that is the fruit of unlawful police conduct has been that this admittedly drastic and socially costly course is needed to deter police from ***443** violations of constitutional and statutory protections. This Court has accepted the argument that the way to ensure such protections is to exclude evidence seized as a result of such violations notwithstanding the high social cost of letting persons obviously guilty go unpunished for their crimes. On this rationale, the prosecution is not to be put in a better position than it would have been in if no illegality had transpired.

[2893] 251 U.S. 385, 40 S.Ct. 182, 64 L.Ed. 319 (1920)

[2894] Id., at 392, 40 S.Ct., at 183

[2895] Ibid. (emphasis added)

[2896] 371 U.S. 471, 83 S.Ct. 407, 9 L.Ed.2d 441 (1963)

[2897] Id., at 487–488, 83 S.Ct., at 417 (emphasis added) (quoting J. Maguire, Evidence of Guilt 221 (1959))

[2898] See *United States v. Wade*, 388 U.S. 218, 87 S.Ct. 1926, 18 L.Ed.2d 1149 (1967), as well as of the Fifth Amendment

By contrast, the derivative evidence analysis ensures that the prosecution is not put in a worse position simply because of some earlier police error or misconduct. The independent source doctrine allows admission of evidence that has been discovered by means wholly independent of any constitutional violation. That doctrine, although closely related to the inevitable discovery doctrine, does not apply here; Williams' statements to Leaming indeed led police to the child's body, but that is not **2509** the whole story. The independent source doctrine teaches us that the interest of society in deterring unlawful police conduct and the public interest in having juries receive all probative evidence of a crime are properly balanced by putting the police in the same, not a worse, position that they would have been in if no police error or misconduct had occurred.[2899] When the challenged evidence has an independent source, exclusion of such evidence would put the police in a worse position than they would have been in absent any error or violation. There ***444** is a functional similarity between these two doctrines in that exclusion of evidence that would inevitably have been discovered would also put the government in a worse position, because the police would have obtained that evidence if no misconduct had taken place. Thus, while the independent source exception would not justify admission of evidence in this case, its rationale is wholly consistent with and justifies our adoption of the ultimate or inevitable discovery exception to the exclusionary rule.

It is clear that the cases implementing the exclusionary rule "begin with the premise that the challenged evidence is in some sense the product of illegal governmental activity."[2900] Of course, this does not end the inquiry. If the prosecution can establish by a preponderance of the evidence that the information ultimately or inevitably would have been discovered by lawful means—here the volunteers' search—then the deterrence rationale has so little basis that the evidence should be received. Anything less would reject logic, experience, and common sense.

***445** The requirement that the prosecution must prove the absence of bad faith, imposed here by the Court of Appeals, would place courts in the position of withholding from juries relevant and undoubted truth that would have been available to police ****2510** absent any unlawful police activity. Of course, that view would put the police in a worse position than they would have been in if no unlawful conduct had transpired. And, of equal importance, it wholly fails to take into account the enormous societal cost of excluding truth in the search for truth in the administration of justice. Nothing in this Court's prior holdings supports any such formalistic, pointless, and punitive approach.

The Court of Appeals concluded, without analysis, that if an absence-of-bad-faith requirement were not imposed, "the temptation to risk deliberate violations of the Sixth Amendment would be too great, and the deterrent effect of the Exclusionary Rule reduced too far."[2901] We reject that view. A police officer who is faced with the opportunity to obtain evidence illegally will rarely, if ever, be in a position to calculate whether the evidence sought would inevitably be discovered[2902]: "[T]he concept of effective deterrence assumes that the police officer consciously realizes the probable consequences of a presumably impermissible course of conduct."[2903]

[2899] See *Murphy v. Waterfront Comm'n of New York Harbor,* 378 U.S. 52, 79, 84 S.Ct. 1594, 1609, 12 L.Ed.2d 678 (1964); *Kastigar v. United States*, 406 U.S. 441, 457, 458–459, 92 S.Ct. 1653, 1663–1664, 32 L.Ed.2d 212 (1972)

[2900] *United States v. Crews*, 445 U.S. 463, 471, 100 S.Ct. 1244, 1250, 63 L.Ed.2d 537 (1980) (emphasis added)

[2901] 700 F.2d, at 1169, n. 5

[2902] Cf. *United States v. Ceccolini*, 435 U.S. 268, 283, 98 S.Ct. 1054, 1064, 55 L.Ed.2d 268 (1978)

[2903] (Opinion concurring in judgment)

On the other hand, when an officer is aware that the evidence will inevitably be discovered, he will try to avoid engaging in ***446** any questionable practice. In that situation, there will be little to gain from taking any dubious "shortcuts" to obtain the evidence. Significant disincentives to obtaining evidence illegally—including the possibility of departmental discipline and civil liability—also lessen the likelihood that the ultimate or inevitable discovery exception will promote police misconduct.[2904] In these circumstances, the societal costs of the exclusionary rule far outweigh any possible benefits to deterrence that a good-faith requirement might produce.

Williams contends that because he did not waive his right to the assistance of counsel, the Court may not balance competing values in deciding whether the challenged evidence was properly admitted. He argues that, unlike the exclusionary rule in the Fourth Amendment context, the essential purpose of which is to deter police misconduct, the Sixth Amendment exclusionary rule is designed to protect the right to a fair trial and the integrity of the fact-finding process. Williams contends that, when those interests are at stake, the societal costs of excluding evidence obtained from responses presumed involuntary are irrelevant in determining whether such evidence should be excluded. We disagree.

Exclusion of physical evidence that would inevitably have been discovered adds nothing to either the integrity or fairness of a criminal trial. The Sixth Amendment right to counsel protects against unfairness by preserving the adversary process in which the reliability of proffered evidence may be tested in cross-examination.[2905] Here, however, Detective Leaming's conduct did nothing to impugn the reliability of the evidence in question—the body of the child and its condition as it was found, articles of clothing found on the body, and the autopsy. No one would seriously contend that the presence of counsel in the police car when Leaming appealed to Williams' ***447** decent human instincts would have had any bearing on the reliability of the body as evidence. Suppression, in these circumstances, would do nothing whatever to promote the integrity of the trial process, but would inflict a wholly unacceptable burden on the administration of criminal justice.

Nor would suppression ensure fairness on the theory that it tends to safeguard the adversary system of justice. To assure the fairness of trial proceedings, this Court has ****2511** held that assistance of counsel must be available at pretrial confrontations where "the subsequent trial [cannot] cure a[n otherwise] one-sided confrontation between prosecuting authorities and the uncounseled defendant."[2906] Fairness can be assured by placing the State and the accused in the same positions they would have been in had the impermissible conduct not taken place. However, if the government can prove that the evidence would have been obtained inevitably and, therefore, would have been admitted regardless of any overreaching by the police, there is no rational basis to keep that evidence from the jury in order to ensure the fairness of the trial proceedings. In that situation, the State has gained no advantage at trial and the defendant has suffered no prejudice. Indeed, suppression of the evidence would operate to undermine the adversary system by putting the State in a worse position than it would have occupied without any police misconduct. Williams' argument that inevitable discovery constitutes impermissible balancing of values is without merit.

More than a half century ago, Judge, later Justice, Cardozo made his seminal observation that under the exclusionary rule "[t]he criminal is to go free because

---

[2904] See *Bivens v. Six Unknown Federal Narcotics Agents*, 403 U.S. 388, 397, 91 S.Ct. 1999, 2005, 29 L.Ed.2d 619 (1971)

[2905] See *United States v. Ash*, 413 U.S. 300, 314, 93 S.Ct. 2568, 2576, 37 L.Ed.2d 619 (1973); *Schneckloth v. Bustamonte*, 412 U.S. 218, 241, 93 S.Ct. 2041, 2055, 36 L.Ed.2d 854 (1973)

[2906] *United States v. Ash*, supra, at 315, 93 S.Ct., at 2576

the constable has blundered."[2907] Prophetically, he went on to consider "how far-reaching in its effect upon society" the exclusionary rule would be when

"[t]he pettiest peace officer would have it in his power through overzeal or indiscretion to confer immunity upon ***448** an offender for crimes the most flagitious."[2908]

Some day, Cardozo speculated, some court might press the exclusionary rule to the outer limits of its logic—or beyond—and suppress evidence relating to the "body of a murdered" victim because of the means by which it was found.[2909] Cardozo's prophecy was fulfilled in Killough v. United States.[2910] But when, as here, the evidence in question would inevitably have been discovered without reference to the police error or misconduct, there is no nexus sufficient to provide a taint and the evidence is admissible.

C

The Court of Appeals did not find it necessary to consider whether the record fairly supported the finding that the volunteer search party would ultimately or inevitably have discovered the victim's body. However, three courts independently reviewing the evidence have found that the body of the child inevitably would have been found by the searchers. Williams challenges these findings, asserting that the record contains only the "post hoc rationalization" that the search efforts would have proceeded two and one-half miles into Polk County where Williams had led police to the body.

When that challenge was made at the suppression hearing preceding Williams' second trial, the prosecution offered the testimony of Agent Ruxlow of the Iowa Bureau of Criminal Investigation. Ruxlow had organized and directed some 200 volunteers who were searching for the child's body.[2911] The searchers were instructed "to check all the roads, the ditches, any culverts.... If they came upon any abandoned farm buildings, they were instructed to go onto the property and search those abandoned farm buildings or any other places where a ***449** small child could be secreted."[2912] Ruxlow testified that he marked off highway maps of Poweshiek and Jasper Counties in grid fashion, divided the volunteers into teams of four to six persons, and assigned each team to search specific grid areas.[2913] Ruxlow also testified that, if the search had not been suspended because of Williams' promised cooperation, it would have continued into Polk County, using the ****2512** same grid system.[2914] Although he had previously marked off into grids only the highway maps of Poweshiek and Jasper Counties, Ruxlow had obtained a map of Polk County, which he said he would have marked off in the same manner had it been necessary for the search to continue.[2915]

The search had commenced at approximately 10 a.m. and moved westward through Poweshiek County into Jasper County. At approximately 3 p.m., after

---

[2907] *People v. Defore*, 242 N.Y. 13, 21, 150 N.E. 585, 587 (1926)

[2908] Id., at 23, 150 N.E., at 588

[2909] Id., at 23–24, 150 N.E., at 588

[2910] 114 U.S.App.D.C. 305, 309, 315 F.2d 241, 245 (1962) (en banc)

[2911] Tr. of Hearings on Motion to Suppress in *State v. Williams*, No. CR 55805, p. 34 (May 31, 1977)

[2912] Id., at 35

[2913] Id., at 34

[2914] Id., at 36, 39–40

[2915] Id., at 39

Williams had volunteered to cooperate with the police, Detective Leaming, who was in the police car with Williams, sent word to Ruxlow and the other Special Agent directing the search to meet him at the Grinnell truck stop and the search was suspended at that time.[2916] Ruxlow also stated that he was "under the impression that there was a possibility" that Williams would lead them to the child's body at that time.[2917] The search was not resumed once it was learned that Williams had led the police to the body,[2918] which was found two and one-half miles from where the search had stopped in what would have been the easternmost grid to be searched in Polk County.[2919] There was testimony that it would have taken an additional three to five hours to discover the body if the search had continued.[2920] The body was found near a culvert, one of the kinds of places the teams had been specifically directed to search.

On this record it is clear that the search parties were approaching the actual location of the body, and we are satisfied, along with three courts earlier, that the volunteer search teams would have resumed the search had Williams ***450** not earlier led the police to the body and the body inevitably would have been found. The evidence asserted by Williams as newly discovered, i.e., certain photographs of the body and deposition testimony of Agent Ruxlow made in connection with the federal habeas proceeding, does not demonstrate that the material facts were inadequately developed in the suppression hearing in state court or that Williams was denied a full, fair, and adequate opportunity to present all relevant facts at the suppression hearing.

The judgment of the Court of Appeals is reversed, and the case is remanded for further proceedings consistent with this opinion.

It is so ordered.

Justice WHITE, concurring.

I join fully in the opinion of the Court. I write separately only to point out that many of Justice Stevens' remarks are beside the point when it is recalled that Brewer v. Williams[2921] was a 5–4 decision and that four Members of the Court, including myself, were of the view that Detective Leaming had done nothing wrong at all, let alone anything unconstitutional. Three of us observed: "To anyone not lost in the intricacies of the prophylactic ***451** rules of Miranda v. Arizona, the result in this case seems utterly senseless...."[2922] It is thus an unjustified reflection on Detective Leaming to say that he "decide to dispense with the requirements of law,"[2923] or that he decided "to take procedural short- ****2513** cuts instead of complying with the law,"[2924] He was no doubt acting as many competent police officers would have acted under similar circumstances and in light of the then-existing law. That five Justices later thought he was mistaken does not call for making him out to be a villain or for a lecture on deliberate police misconduct and its resulting costs to society.

[2916] Id., at 51–52

[2917] Id., at 61

[2918] Id., at 57

[2919] Id., at 39

[2920] Id., at 41

[2921] 430 U.S. 387, 97 S.Ct. 1232, 51 L.Ed.2d 424 (1977)

[2922] Id., at 438, 97 S.Ct., at 1259

[2923] Post, at 2513

[2924] Post, at 2516

Justice STEVENS, concurring in the judgment.

This litigation is exceptional for at least three reasons. The facts are unusually tragic; it involves an unusually clear violation of constitutional rights; and it graphically illustrates the societal costs that may be incurred when police officers decide to dispense with the requirements of law. Because the Court does not adequately discuss any of these aspects of the case, I am unable to join its opinion.

I

In holding that respondent's first conviction had been unconstitutionally obtained, Justice Stewart, writing for the Court, correctly observed:

> The pressures on state executive and judicial officers charged with the administration of the criminal law are great, especially when the crime is murder and the victim a small child. But it is precisely the predictability of those pressures that makes imperative a resolute loyalty to the guarantees that the Constitution extends to us all.[2925]

There can be no denying that the character of the crime may have an impact on the decisional process. As the Court ***452** was required to hold, however, that does not permit any court to condone a violation of constitutional rights. Today's decision is no more an ad hoc response to the pressures engendered by the special facts of the case than was Williams I. It was the majority in Williams I that recognized that "evidence of where the body was found and of its condition might well be admissible on the theory that the body would have been discovered in any event, even had incriminating statements not been elicited from Williams."[2926] It was the author of today's opinion of the Court who characterized this rule of law as a "remarkable" and "unlikely theory."[2927] The rule of law that the Court adopts today has an integrity of its own and is not merely the product of the hydraulic pressures associated with hard cases or strong words.

II

The constitutional violation that gave rise to the decision in Williams I is neither acknowledged nor fairly explained in the Court's opinion. Yet the propriety of admitting evidence relating to the victim's body can only be evaluated if that constitutional violation is properly identified.

Before he was taken into custody, Williams, as a recent escapee from a mental hospital who had just abducted and murdered a small child, posed a special threat to public safety. Acting on his lawyer's advice, Williams surrendered to the Davenport police. The lawyer notified the Des Moines police of Williams' imminent surrender, and police officials, ***453** in the presence of Detective Leaming, agreed that Williams would not be questioned while being brought back from Davenport. Williams was advised of this agreement by ****2514** his attorney. After he was arraigned in Davenport, Williams conferred with another lawyer who was acting as local counsel. This lawyer reminded Williams that he would not be questioned. When Detective Leaming arrived in Davenport, local counsel stressed that the agreement was to be carried out and that Williams was not to be questioned. Detective Leaming then took custody of respondent, and

---

[2925] *Brewer v. Williams*, 430 U.S. 387, 406, 97 S.Ct. 1232, 1243, 51 L.Ed.2d 424 (1977) (Williams I)

[2926] Id., at 407, n. 12, 97 S.Ct., at 1243, n. 12

[2927] Id., at 416–417, n. 1, 97 S.Ct., at 1248–1249, n. 1 (BURGER, C.J., dissenting)

denied counsel's request to ride to Des Moines in the police car with Williams. The "Christian burial speech" occurred during the ensuing trip. As Justice POWELL succinctly observed, this was a case "in which the police deliberately took advantage of an inherently coercive setting in the absence of counsel, contrary to their express agreement."[2928]

The Sixth Amendment guarantees that the conviction of the accused will be the product of an adversarial process, rather than the ex parte investigation and determination by the prosecutor.3 Williams I grew out of a line of cases in which this Court made it clear that the adversarial process protected by the Sixth Amendment may not be undermined by the strategems of the police.

Spano v. New York[2929] dealt with the confession of an uncounseled defendant after prolonged interrogation subsequent to his indictment for first-degree ***454** murder. Four Justices indicated that this questioning violated the Sixth Amendment, noting that to hold otherwise would totally undermine the adversarial process of proof:

> Our Constitution guarantees the assistance of counsel to a man on trial for his life in an orderly courtroom, presided over by a judge, open to the public, and protected by all the procedural safeguards of the law. Surely a Constitution which promises that much can vouchsafe no less to the same man under midnight inquisition in the squad room of a police station.[2930]

As Justice Douglas asked: "[What] use is a defendant's right to effective counsel at every stage of a criminal case if, while he is held awaiting trial, he can be questioned in the absence of counsel until he confesses? In that event the secret trial in the police precincts effectively supplants the public trial guaranteed by the Bill of Rights."[2931]

This view ripened into a holding in Massiah v. United States[2932]: "We hold that the petitioner was denied the basic protections of [the Sixth Amendment] when there was used against him at his trial evidence of his own incriminating words, which federal agents had deliberately elicited from him after he had been indicted and in the absence of his counsel."[2933] Williams I held that Detective Leaming had violated "the clear rule of Massiah" by deliberately eliciting incriminating statements from respondent during the pendency of the adversarial process and outside of that process.[2934] The violation was aggravated by the fact that Detective Leaming had breached a promise to counsel, an act which can only undermine ****2515** the role of counsel in the adversarial process. The ***455** "Christian burial speech" was nothing less than an attempt to substitute an ex parte, inquisitorial process for the clash of adversaries commanded by the Constitution. Thus the now-familiar plaint that "'[t]he criminal is to go free because the constable has blundered,'"[2935] is entirely beside the point. More pertinent is what The Chief Justice wrote for the Court on another occasion: "This is not a

---

[2928] Id., at 414, n. 2, 97 S.Ct., at 1247, n. 2 (concurring opinion)

[2929] 360 U.S. 315, 79 S.Ct. 1202, 3 L.Ed.2d 1265 (1959)

[2930] Id., at 327, 79 S.Ct., at 1209 (Stewart, J., concurring, joined by Douglas and BRENNAN, JJ.)

[2931] Id., at 326, 79 S.Ct., at 1209 (Douglas, J., concurring, joined by Black and BRENNAN, JJ.)

[2932] 377 U.S. 201, 84 S.Ct. 1199, 12 L.Ed.2d 246 (1964)

[2933] Id., at 206, 84 S.Ct., at 1203

[2934] See 430 U.S., at 399–401, 97 S.Ct., at 1239–1241

[2935] Ante, at 2511 (quoting People v. Defore, 242 N.Y. 13, 21, 150 N.E. 585, 587 (1926))

case where, in Justice Cardozo's words, 'the constable ... blundered,' rather, it is one where the 'constable' planned an impermissible interference with the right to the assistance of counsel."[2936]

***456 III**

Once the constitutional violation is properly identified, the answers to the questions presented in this case follow readily. Admission of the victim's body, if it would have been discovered anyway, means that the trial in this case was not the product of an inquisitorial process; that process was untainted by illegality. The good or bad faith of Detective Leaming is therefore simply irrelevant. If the trial process was not tainted as a result of his conduct, this defendant received the type of trial that the Sixth Amendment envisions.[2937] Generalizations about the exclusionary rule employed by the majority, see ante, at 2508–2511, simply do not address the primary question in the case.

The majority is correct to insist that any rule of exclusion not provide the authorities with an incentive to commit violations of the Constitution.[2938] If the inevitable discovery rule provided such an incentive by permitting the prosecution to avoid the uncertainties inherent in its search for evidence, it would undermine the constitutional guarantee itself, and therefore be inconsistent with the deterrent purposes ****2516** of the exclusionary rule. But when the burden of proof on the inevitable discovery question is placed on the prosecution,[2939] it must bear the risk of error in the determination made necessary by its constitutional violation. The uncertainty as to whether the body would ***457** have been discovered can be resolved in its favor here only because, as the Court explains,[2940] petitioner adduced evidence demonstrating that at the time of the constitutional violation an investigation was already under way which, in the natural and probable course of events, would have soon discovered the body. This is not a case in which the prosecution can escape responsibility for a constitutional violation through speculation; to the extent uncertainty was created by the constitutional violation the prosecution was required to resolve that uncertainty through proof. Even if Detective Leaming acted in bad faith in the sense that he deliberately violated the Constitution in order to avoid the possibility that the body would not be discovered, the prosecution ultimately does not avoid that risk; its burden of proof forces it to assume the risk. The need to adduce proof sufficient to discharge its burden, and the difficulty in predicting whether such proof will be available or sufficient, means that the inevitable discovery rule does not permit state officials to avoid the uncertainty they would have faced but for the constitutional violation.

The majority refers to the "societal cost" of excluding probative evidence.[2941] In my view, the more relevant cost is that imposed on society by police officers who decide to take procedural shortcuts instead of complying with the law. What is the consequence of the shortcut that Detective Leaming took when he decided to question Williams in this case and not to wait an hour or so until he arrived in ***458** Des Moines? The answer is years and years of unnecessary but costly litigation. Instead of having a 1969 conviction affirmed in rou-

---

[2936] *United States v. Henry*, 447 U.S. 264, 274–275, 100 S.Ct. 2183, 2188–2189, 65 L.Ed.2d 115 (1980) (footnote and citation omitted)

[2937] See *United States v. Morrison*, 449 U.S. 361, 101 S.Ct. 665, 66 L.Ed.2d 564 (1981); *Weatherford v. Bursey*, 429 U.S. 545, 97 S.Ct. 837, 51 L.Ed.2d 30 (1977); *United States v. Wade*, 388 U.S. 218, 240–243, 87 S.Ct. 1926, 1939–1941, 18 L.Ed.2d 1149 (1967)

[2938] Ante, at 2510

[2939] Ante, at 2509

[2940] Ante, at 2511–2512

[2941] Ante, at 2510

tine fashion, the case is still alive 15 years later. Thanks to Detective Leaming, the State of Iowa has expended vast sums of money and countless hours of professional labor in his defense. That expenditure surely provides an adequate deterrent to similar violations; the responsibility for that expenditure lies not with the Constitution, but rather with the constable.

Accordingly, I concur in the Court's judgment.

(The dissent of Justice BRENNAN, with whom Justice MARSHALL joins, is omitted.)

Black Letter Law

> The Court established an inevitable or ultimate discovery exception to the exclusionary rule. The Court identified a preponderance of the evidence standard for this exception, and did not require the prosecution to prove an absence of bad faith.

Murray v. United States, Carter v. United States

108 S.Ct. 2529

Supreme Court of the United States

Michael F. MURRAY, Petitioner,

v.

UNITED STATES.

James D. CARTER, Petitioner,

v.

UNITED STATES.

Nos. 86–995, 86–1016. | Argued Dec. 8, 1987. | Decided June 27, 1988.

***535** Justice SCALIA delivered the opinion of the Court.

In Segura v. United States,[2942] we held that police officers' illegal entry upon private premises did not require suppression of evidence subsequently discovered at those premises when executing a search warrant obtained on the basis of information wholly unconnected with the initial entry. In these consolidated cases we are faced with the question whether, again assuming evidence obtained pursuant to an independently obtained search warrant, the portion of such evidence that had been observed in plain view at the time of a prior illegal entry must be suppressed.

I

Both cases arise out of the conviction of petitioner Michael F. Murray, petitioner James D. Carter, and others for conspiracy to possess and distribute illegal drugs. Insofar as relevant for our purposes, the facts are as follows: Based on information received from informants, federal law enforcement agents had been surveilling petitioner Murray and several of his co-conspirators. At about 1:45 p.m. on April 6, 1983, they observed Murray drive a truck and Carter drive

[2942] 468 U.S. 796, 104 S.Ct. 3388, 82 L.Ed.2d 599 (1984)

a green camper, into a warehouse in South Boston. When the petitioners drove the vehicles out about 20 minutes later, the surveilling agents saw within the warehouse two individuals and a tractor-trailer rig bearing a long, dark container. Murray and Carter later turned over the truck and camper to other drivers, who were in turn followed and ultimately arrested, and the vehicles lawfully seized. Both vehicles were found to contain marijuana.

After receiving this information, several of the agents converged on the South Boston warehouse and forced entry. They found the warehouse unoccupied, but observed in plain view numerous burlap-wrapped bales that were later found to contain marijuana. They left without disturbing the bales, kept the warehouse under surveillance, and did not reenter it until they had a search warrant. In applying for ***536** the warrant, the agents did not mention the prior entry, and did not rely on any observations made during that entry. When the warrant was issued—at 10:40 p.m., approximately eight hours after the initial entry—the agents immediately reentered the warehouse and seized 270 bales of marijuana and notebooks listing customers for whom the bales were destined.

Before trial, petitioners moved to suppress the evidence found in the warehouse. The District Court denied the motion, rejecting petitioners' arguments that the warrant was invalid because the agents did not inform the Magistrate about their prior warrantless entry, and that the warrant was tainted by that entry.[2943] The First Circuit affirmed, assuming for purposes of its decision that the first entry into the warehouse was unlawful.[2944] Murray and Carter then separately filed petitions for certiorari, which we granted,[2945] ****2533** and have consolidated here.

II

The exclusionary rule prohibits introduction into evidence of tangible materials seized during an unlawful search,[2946] and of testimony concerning knowledge acquired during an unlawful search.[2947] Beyond that, the exclusionary rule also prohibits the introduction of derivative evidence, both tangible and testimonial, that is ***537** the product of the primary evidence, or that is otherwise acquired as an indirect result of the unlawful search, up to the point at which the connection with the unlawful search becomes "so attenuated as to dissipate the taint."[2948]

Almost simultaneously with our development of the exclusionary rule, in the first quarter of this century, we also announced what has come to be known as the "independent source" doctrine.[2949] That doctrine, which has been applied to evidence acquired not only through Fourth Amendment violations but also through Fifth and Sixth Amendment violations, has recently been described as follows:

> [T]he interest of society in deterring unlawful police conduct and the public interest in having juries receive all probative evidence of a crime are properly balanced by putting the police in the same, not a

---

[2943] *United States v. Carter,* No. 83–102–S (Mass., Dec. 23, 1983), App. to Pet. for Cert. 44a–45a

[2944] *United States v. Moscatiello*, 771 F.2d 589 (1985)

[2945] 480 U.S. 916, 107 S.Ct. 1368, 94 L.Ed.2d 685 (1987)

[2946] *Weeks v. United States*, 232 U.S. 383, 34 S.Ct. 341, 58 L.Ed. 652 (1914)

[2947] *Silverman v. United States*, 365 U.S. 505, 81 S.Ct. 679, 5 L.Ed.2d 734 (1961)

[2948] *Nardone v. United States*, 308 U.S. 338, 341, 60 S.Ct. 266, 268, 84 L.Ed. 307 (1939). See *Wong Sun v. United States*, 371 U.S. 471, 484–485, 83 S.Ct. 407, 415–16, 9 L.Ed.2d 441 (1963)

[2949] See *Silverthorne Lumber Co. v. United States*, 251 U.S. 385, 392, 40 S.Ct. 182, 183, 64 L.Ed. 319 (1920)

> worse, position that they would have been in if no police error or misconduct had occurred.... When the challenged evidence has an independent source, exclusion of such evidence would put the police in a worse position than they would have been in absent any error or violation.[2950]

The dispute here is over the scope of this doctrine. Petitioners contend that it applies only to evidence obtained for the first time during an independent lawful search. The Government argues that it applies also to evidence initially discovered during, or as a consequence of, an unlawful search, but later obtained independently from activities untainted by the initial illegality. We think the Government's view has better support in both precedent and policy.

Our cases have used the concept of "independent source" in a more general and a more specific sense. The more general sense identifies all evidence acquired in a fashion untainted ***538** by the illegal evidence-gathering activity. Thus, where an unlawful entry has given investigators knowledge of facts x and y, but fact z has been learned by other means, fact z can be said to be admissible because derived from an "independent source." This is how we used the term in Segura v. United States.[2951] In that case, agents unlawfully entered the defendant's apartment and remained there until a search warrant was obtained. The admissibility of what they discovered while waiting in the apartment was not before us,[2952] but we held that the evidence found for the first time during the execution of the valid and untainted search warrant was admissible because it was discovered pursuant to an "independent source."[2953]

The original use of the term, however, and its more important use for purposes of these cases, was more specific. It was originally applied in the exclusionary rule context, by Justice Holmes, with reference to that particular category of evidence acquired by an untainted search which is identical to the evidence unlawfully acquired—that is, in the example just given, to knowledge of facts x and y derived from an independent source:

> The essence of a provision forbidding the acquisition of evidence in a certain way is that not merely evidence so acquired shall not be used before the Court but that it shall not be used at all. Of course this does not mean that the facts thus obtained become sacred and inaccessible. If knowledge of them is gained from an independent source they may be proved like any others.[2954]

As the First Circuit has observed, "[i]n the classic independent source situation, information which is received through an illegal source is considered to be cleanly obtained when ***539** it arrives through an independent source."[2955] We recently assumed this application of the independent source doctrine (in the Sixth Amendment context) in Nix v. Williams, supra. There incriminating statements obtained in violation of the defendant's right to counsel had led the police

---

[2950] *Nix v. Williams*, 467 U.S. 431, 443, 104 S.Ct. 2501, 2509, 81 L.Ed.2d 377 (1984)

[2951] 468 U.S. 796, 104 S.Ct. 3380, 82 L.Ed.2d 599 (1984)

[2952] Id., at 802–803, n. 4, 104 S.Ct., at 384, n. 4

[2953] Id., at 813–814, 104 S.Ct., at 3389–90. See also *United States v. Wade*, 388 U.S. 218, 240–242, 87 S.Ct. 1926, 1939–40, 18 L.Ed.2d 1149 (1967); ****2534** Costello v. United States, 365 U.S. 265, 280, 81 S.Ct. 534, 542, 5 L.Ed.2d 551 (1961); *Nardone v. United States*, supra, at 341, 60 S.Ct., at 267

[2954] *Silverthorne Lumber*, supra, at [251 U.S.] 392, 40 S.Ct., at 183

[2955] *United States v. Silvestri*, 787 F.2d 736, 739 (1986)

to the victim's body. The body had not in fact been found through an independent source as well, and so the independent source doctrine was not itself applicable. We held, however, that evidence concerning the body was nonetheless admissible because a search had been under way which would have discovered the body, had it not been called off because of the discovery produced by the unlawfully obtained statements.[2956] This "inevitable discovery" doctrine obviously assumes the validity of the independent source doctrine as applied to evidence initially acquired unlawfully. It would make no sense to admit the evidence because the independent search, had it not been aborted, would have found the body, but to exclude the evidence if the search had continued and had in fact found the body. The inevitable discovery doctrine, with its distinct requirements, is in reality an extrapolation from the independent source doctrine: Since the tainted evidence would be admissible if in fact discovered through an independent source, it should be admissible if it inevitably would have been discovered.

Petitioners' asserted policy basis for excluding evidence which is initially discovered during an illegal search, but is subsequently acquired through an independent and lawful source, is that a contrary rule will remove all deterrence to, and indeed positively encourage, unlawful police searches. As petitioners see the incentives, law enforcement officers will routinely enter without a warrant to make sure that what they expect to be on the premises is in fact there. If it is not, they will have spared themselves the time and trouble of getting a warrant; if it is, they can get the warrant and use the evidence despite the unlawful entry.[2957] ***540** We see the incentives differently. An officer with probable cause sufficient to obtain a search warrant would be foolish to enter the premises first in an unlawful manner. By doing so, he would risk suppression of all evidence on the premises, both seen and unseen, since his action would add to the normal burden of convincing a magistrate that there is probable cause the much more onerous burden of convincing a trial court that no information gained from the illegal entry affected either the law enforcement officers' decision to seek a warrant or the magistrate's decision to grant it.[2958] Nor would the officer without sufficient probable cause to obtain a search warrant have any added incentive to conduct an unlawful entry, since whatever he ****2535** finds cannot be used to establish probable cause before a magistrate.

It is possible to read petitioners' briefs as asserting the more narrow position that the "independent source" doctrine does apply to independent acquisition of evidence previously ***541** derived indirectly from the unlawful search, but does not apply to what they call "primary evidence," that is, evidence acquired during the course of the search itself. In addition to finding no support in our precedent,[2959] this strange distinction would produce results bearing no relation to the policies of the exclusionary rule. It would mean, for example, that the government's knowledge of the existence and condition of a dead body, knowledge lawfully acquired through independent sources, would have to be excluded if government agents had previously observed the body during an unlawful search of the defendant's apartment; but not if they had observed a notation that the body was buried in a certain location, producing consequential discovery of the corpse.

III

[2956] Id., 467 U.S., at 448–450, 104 S.Ct., at 2511–12

[2957] Brief for Petitioners 42

[2958] See Part III, infra

[2959] See *Silverthorne Lumber*, 251 U.S., at 392, 40 S.Ct., at 182 (referring specifically to evidence seized during an unlawful search)

To apply what we have said to the present cases: Knowledge that the marijuana was in the warehouse was assuredly acquired at the time of the unlawful entry. But it was also acquired at the time of entry pursuant to the warrant, and if that later acquisition was not the result of the earlier entry there is no reason why the independent source doctrine should not apply. Invoking the exclusionary rule would put the police (and society) not in the same position they would have occupied if no violation occurred, but in a worse one.[2960]

We think this is also true with respect to the tangible evidence, the bales of marijuana. It would make no more sense to exclude that than it would to exclude tangible evidence found upon the corpse in Nix, if the search in that case had not been abandoned and had in fact come upon the body. The First Circuit has discerned a difference between tangible and intangible evidence that has been tainted, in that objects "once seized cannot be cleanly re-seized without returning the objects to private control."[2961] ***542** It seems to us, however, that re-seizure of tangible evidence already seized is no more impossible than rediscovery of intangible evidence already discovered. The independent source doctrine does not rest upon such metaphysical analysis, but upon the policy that, while the government should not profit from its illegal activity, neither should it be placed in a worse position than it would otherwise have occupied. So long as a later, lawful seizure is genuinely independent of an earlier, tainted one (which may well be difficult to establish where the seized goods are kept in the police's possession) there is no reason why the independent source doctrine should not apply.

****2536** The ultimate question, therefore, is whether the search pursuant to warrant was in fact a genuinely independent source of the information and tangible evidence at issue here. This would not have been the case if the agents' decision to seek the warrant was prompted by what they had seen during the initial entry, or if information obtained during that entry was presented to the Magistrate and affected his decision to issue the warrant. On this point the Court of Appeals said the following:

> [W]e can be absolutely certain that the warrantless entry in no way contributed in the slightest either to the issuance of a warrant or to the discovery of the evidence ***543** during the lawful search that occurred pursuant to the warrant.
>
> This is as clear a case as can be imagined where the discovery of the contraband in plain view was totally irrelevant to the later securing of a warrant and the successful search that ensued. As there was no causal link whatever between the illegal entry and the discovery of the challenged evidence, we find no error in the court's refusal to suppress.[2962]

Although these statements can be read to provide emphatic support for the Government's position, it is the function of the District Court rather than the Court of Appeals to determine the facts, and we do not think the Court of Appeals' conclusions are supported by adequate findings. The District Court found that the agents did not reveal their warrantless entry to the Magistrate,[2963] and that they did not include in their application for a warrant any recitation of their

---

[2960] See *Nix v. Williams*, 467 U.S., at 443, 104 S.Ct., at 2508

[2961] *United States v. Silvestri*, 787 F.2d, at 739

[2962] *United States v. Moscatiello*, 771 F.2d, at 603, 604

[2963] App. to Pet. for Cert. 43a

observations in the warehouse.[2964] It did not, however, explicitly find that the agents would have sought a warrant if they had not earlier entered the warehouse. The Government concedes this in its brief.[2965] To be sure, the District Court did determine that the purpose of the warrantless entry was in part "to guard against the destruction of possibly critical evidence,"[2966] and one could perhaps infer from this that the agents who made the entry already planned to obtain that "critical evidence" through a warrant-authorized search. That inference is not, however, clear enough to justify the conclusion that the District Court's findings amounted to a determination of independent source.

Accordingly, we vacate the judgment and remand these cases to the Court of Appeals with instructions that it remand to the District Court for determination whether the ***544** warrant-authorized search of the warehouse was an independent source of the challenged evidence in the sense we have described.

It is so ordered.

Justice MARSHALL, with whom Justice STEVENS and Justice O'CONNOR join, dissenting.

The Court today holds that the "independent source" exception to the exclusionary rule may justify admitting evidence discovered during an illegal warrantless search that is later "rediscovered" by the same team of investigators during a search pursuant to a warrant obtained immediately ****2537** after the illegal search. I believe the Court's decision, by failing to provide sufficient guarantees that the subsequent search was, in fact, independent of the illegal search, emasculates the Warrant Clause and undermines the deterrence function of the exclusionary rule. I therefore dissent.

This Court has stated frequently that the exclusionary rule is principally designed to deter violations of the Fourth Amendment.[2967] By excluding evidence discovered in violation of the Fourth Amendment, the rule "compel[s] respect for the constitutional guaranty in the only effectively available way, by removing the incentive to disregard it."[2968] The Court has crafted exceptions to the exclusionary rule when the purposes of the rule are not furthered by the exclusion. As the Court today recognizes, the independent source exception to the exclusionary rule "allows admission of evidence that has been discovered by means wholly independent of any constitutional violation."[2969] The independent source exception, like the inevitable discovery exception, is primarily ***545** based on a practical view that under certain circumstances the beneficial deterrent effect that exclusion will have on future constitutional violations is too slight to justify the social cost of excluding probative evidence from a criminal trial.[2970] When the seizure of the evidence at issue is "wholly independent of" the constitutional violation, then exclusion arguably will have no effect on a law enforcement officer's incentive to commit an unlawful search.

[2964] Id., at 44a–45a

[2965] Brief for United States 17, n. 5

[2966] App. to Pet. for Cert. 42a

[2967] See, e.g., *United States v. Leon,* 468 U.S. 897, 906, 104 S.Ct. 3405, 3411, 82 L.Ed.2d 677 (1984); *Elkins v. United States*, 364 U.S. 206, 217, 80 S.Ct. 1437, 1444, 4 L.Ed.2d 1669 (1960)

[2968] Id., at 217, 80 S.Ct., at 1444

[2969] *Nix v. Williams*, 467 U.S. 431, 443, 104 S.Ct. 2501, 2508, 81 L.Ed.2d 377 (1984); see *Silverthorne Lumber Co. v. United States*, 251 U.S. 385, 392, 40 S.Ct. 182, 64 L.Ed. 319 (1920)

[2970] See *Nix v. Williams*, supra, 467 U.S., at 444–446, 104 S.Ct., at 2509–10; cf. *United States v. Leon*, supra, 468 U.S., 906–909, 104 S.Ct., at 3411–12

Given the underlying justification for the independent source exception, any inquiry into the exception's application must keep sight of the practical effect admission will have on the incentives facing law enforcement officers to engage in unlawful conduct. The proper scope of the independent source exception, and guidelines for its application, cannot be divined in a factual vacuum; instead, they must be informed by the nature of the constitutional violation and the deterrent effect of exclusion in particular circumstances. In holding that the independent source exception may apply to the facts of these cases, I believe the Court loses sight of the practical moorings of the independent source exception and creates an affirmative incentive for unconstitutional searches. This holding can find no justification in the purposes underlying both the exclusionary rule and the independent source exception.

The factual setting of the instant case is straightforward. Federal Bureau of Investigation (FBI) and Drug Enforcement Agency (DEA) agents stopped two vehicles after they ***546** left a warehouse and discovered bales of marijuana. DEA Supervisor Garibotto and an assistant United States attorney then returned to the warehouse, which had been under surveillance for several hours. After demands that the warehouse door be opened went unanswered, Supervisor Garibotto forced open the door with a tire iron. A number of agents entered the warehouse. No persons were found inside, but the agents saw numerous bales of marijuana in plain view. Supervisor Garibotto then ordered everyone out of the warehouse. Agents did not reenter the ****2538** warehouse until a warrant was obtained some eight hours later. The warehouse was kept under surveillance during the interim.

It is undisputed that the agents made no effort to obtain a warrant prior to the initial entry. The agents had not begun to prepare a warrant affidavit, and according to FBI Agent Cleary, who supervised the FBI's involvement, they had not even engaged in any discussions of obtaining a warrant.[2971] The affidavit in support of the warrant obtained after the initial search was prepared by DEA Agent Keaney, who had tactical control over the DEA agents, and who had participated in the initial search of the warehouse. The affidavit did not mention the warrantless search of the warehouse, nor did it cite information obtained from that search. In determining that the challenged evidence was admissible, the Court of Appeals assumed that the initial warrantless entry was not justified by exigent circumstances and that the search therefore violated the Warrant Clause of the Fourth Amendment.

Under the circumstances of these cases, the admission of the evidence "reseized" during the second search severely undermines the the deterrence function of the exclusionary rule. Indeed, admission in these cases affirmatively encourages illegal searches. The incentives for such illegal conduct are clear. Obtaining a warrant is inconvenient and time consuming. Even when officers have probable cause to support a warrant application, therefore, they have an incentive first ***547** to determine whether it is worthwhile to obtain a warrant. Probable cause is much less than certainty, and many "confirmatory" searches will result in the discovery that no evidence is present, thus saving the police the time and trouble of getting a warrant. If contraband is discovered, however, the officers may later seek a warrant to shield the evidence from the taint of the illegal search. The police thus know in advance that they have little to lose and much to gain by forgoing the bother of obtaining a warrant and undertaking an illegal search.

The Court, however, "see[s] the incentives differently."[2972] Under the Court's view, today's decision does not provide an incentive for unlawful searches, because the officer undertaking the search would know that "his action would

[2971] App. 52

[2972] Ante, at 2534

add to the normal burden of convincing a magistrate that there is probable cause the much more onerous burden of convincing a trial court that no information gained from the illegal entry affected either the law enforcement officers' decision to seek a warrant or the magistrate's decision to grant it."[2973] The Court, however, provides no hint of why this risk would actually seem significant to the officers. Under the circumstances of these cases, the officers committing the illegal search have both knowledge and control of the factors central to the trial court's determination. First, it is a simple matter, as was done in these cases, to exclude from the warrant application any information gained from the initial entry so that the magistrate's determination of probable cause is not influenced by the prior illegal search. Second, today's decision makes the application of the independent source exception turn entirely on an evaluation of the officers' intent. It normally will be difficult for the trial court to verify, or the defendant to rebut, an assertion by officers that they always intended to obtain a warrant, regardless of the results of the illegal search. The testimony of the officers ***548** ****2539** conducting the illegal search is the only direct evidence of intent, and the defendant will be relegated simply to arguing that the officers should not be believed. Under these circumstances, the litigation risk described by the Court seems hardly a risk at all; it does not significantly dampen the incentive to conduct the initial illegal search.

The strong Fourth Amendment interest in eliminating these incentives for illegal entry should cause this Court to scrutinize closely the application of the independent source exception to evidence obtained under the circumstances of the instant cases; respect for the constitutional guarantee requires a rule that does not undermine the deterrence function of the exclusionary rule. When, as here, the same team of investigators is involved in both the first and second search, there is a significant danger that the "independence" of the ***549** source will in fact be illusory, and that the initial search will have affected the decision to obtain a warrant notwithstanding the officers' subsequent assertions to the contrary. It is therefore crucial that the factual premise of the exception—complete independence—be clearly established before the exception can justify admission of the evidence. I believe the Court's reliance on the intent of the law enforcement officers who conducted the warrantless search provides insufficient guarantees that the subsequent legal search was unaffected by the prior illegal search.

To ensure that the source of the evidence is genuinely independent, the basis for a finding that a search was untainted by a prior illegal search must focus, as with the inevitable discovery doctrine, on "demonstrated historical facts capable of ready verification or impeachment."[2974] In the instant cases, there are no "demonstrated historical facts" capable of supporting a finding that the subsequent warrant search was wholly unaffected by the prior illegal search. The same team of investigators was involved in both searches. The warrant was obtained immediately after the illegal search, and no effort was made to obtain a warrant prior to the discovery of the marijuana during the illegal search. The only evidence available that the warrant search was wholly independent is the testimony of the agents who conducted the illegal search. Under these circumstances, the threat that the subsequent search was tainted by the illegal search is too great to allow for the application of the independent source exception. The Court's ***550** contrary holding lends itself to easy abuse, and offers an incentive to bypass the constitutional requirement that probable cause be assessed by a neutral and detached magistrate before ****2540** the police invade an individual's privacy.

[2973] Ibid.

[2974] *Nix v. Williams*, 467 U.S., at 445, n. 5, 104 S.Ct., at 2509, n. 5

The decision in Segura v. United States,[2975] is not to the contrary. In Segura, the Court expressly distinguished between evidence discovered during an initial warrantless entry and evidence that was not discovered until a subsequent legal search. The Court held that under those circumstances, when no information from an illegal search was used in a subsequent warrant application, the warrant provided an independent source for the evidence first uncovered in the second, lawful search.

Segura is readily distinguished from the present cases. The admission of evidence first discovered during a legal search does not significantly lessen the deterrence facing the law enforcement officers contemplating an illegal entry so long as the evidence that is seen is excluded. This was clearly the view of Chief Justice BURGER, joined by Justice O'CONNOR, when he stated that the Court's ruling would not significantly detract from the deterrent effects of the exclusionary rule because "officers who enter illegally will recognize that whatever evidence they discover as a direct result of the entry may be suppressed, as it was by the Court of Appeals in this case."[2976] As I argue above, extending Segura to cover evidence discovered during an initial illegal search will eradicate this remaining deterrence to illegal entry. Moreover, there is less reason to believe that ***551** an initial illegal entry was prompted by a desire to determine whether to bother to get a warrant in the first place, and thus was not wholly independent of the second search, if officers understand that evidence they discover during the illegal search will be excluded even if they subsequently return with a warrant.

In sum, under circumstances as are presented in these cases, when the very law enforcement officers who participate in an illegal search immediately thereafter obtain a warrant to search the same premises, I believe the evidence discovered during the initial illegal entry must be suppressed. Any other result emasculates the Warrant Clause and provides an intolerable incentive for warrantless searches. I respectfully dissent.

Justice STEVENS, dissenting.

While I join Justice MARSHALL's opinion explaining why the majority's extension of the Court's holding in Segura v. United States[2977] "emasculates the Warrant Clause and provides an intolerable incentive for warrantless searches,"[2978] I remain convinced that the Segura decision itself was unacceptable because, even then, it was obvious that it would "provide government agents with an affirmative incentive to engage in unconstitutional violations of the privacy of the home."[2979] I fear that the Court has taken another unfortunate step down the path to a system of "law enforcement unfettered by process concerns."[2980] In due course, I trust it will pause long enough to remember that "the efforts of the courts and their officials to bring the guilty to punishment, praiseworthy as they are, are not to be aided by the sacrifice of those great principles established by years of endeavor and suffering which have resulted in their embodiment in the fundamental law of the land."[2981]

[2975] 468 U.S. 796, 104 S.Ct. 3380, 82 L.Ed.2d 599 (1984)

[2976] Id., at 812, 104 S.Ct., at 3389

[2977] 468 U.S. 796, 104 S.Ct. 3380, 82 L.Ed.2d 599 (1984)

[2978] Ante, at 2540

[2979] 468 U.S., at 817, 104 S.Ct., at 3392 (dissenting opinion)

[2980] Patterson v. Illinois, 487 U.S. 285, 305, 108 S.Ct. 2389, 2402, 101 L.Ed.2d 261 (STEVENS, J., dissenting)

[2981] Weeks v. United States, 232 U.S. 383, 393–394, 34 S.Ct. 341, 344, 58 L.Ed. 652 (1914)

Black Letter Law

> The Court held that the Fourth Amendment does not require the suppression of evidence that is initially discovered during police officers' illegal entry of private premises, and rediscovered during a later search pursuant to a valid warrant that is wholly independent of the initial illegal entry. Marijuana observed in plain view at the time of unlawful entry, and later seized during a subsequent search pursuant to a warrant was admissible under the independent source doctrine. Remand was required to determine whether government agents would have sought warrant if they had not earlier entered the warehouse.

Discussion Problem:

17-1. During the month of August, the defendant made two separate sales of cocaine to a confidential informant, acting at the direction of the County Police. After subsequent police surveillance, a warrant to search the defendant's home was obtained from a District Court judge. The warrant did not contain a "no-knock clause," which authorizes entry, even by force, without first knocking and announcing police presence.

Early on a weekday morning in late September, a large combined task force of law enforcement officers assembled in front of a single-family, colonial style home in a residential area of the County. The task force, which arrived in several cars and trucks, surrounded the home. Eight county deputy sheriffs, wearing black hoods and fatigue style uniforms, battered down the door of the defendant's home with a two handled 'ram,' which is essentially a pipe filled with concrete. Once inside, the task force 'secured the premises' by dispersing throughout the house. Task force officers handcuffed two adults found upstairs in the master bedroom, gathered three small children from other bedrooms, and then herded all five members of the household together in the downstairs family room. The task force leader then summonsed the remaining task force officers to enter and search the entire house.

A clear plastic bag containing 26 grams of cocaine, four smaller baggies containing a total of 6.6 grams of cocaine, $1,369 dollars in U.S. currency, a rental agreement, and a 1986 white Chevy Astro Van were seized in the search. The defendant, who acknowledged that the cocaine seized was his, was arrested and charged with possession with the intent to distribute a controlled dangerous substance.

Before trial, the defendant moves to suppress the evidence seized during the search. He asserts that the search was invalid because the task force, lacking a reasonable suspicion to believe exigent circumstances existed to permit its doing so, failed to knock and announce its presence before entering his home.

You are the state attorney in this case and the judge has asked you to draft a response to the defense's motion, and he has indicated that it would assist the court if you focused on the inevitable discovery approach.

-Notes-

Chapter 18: Good Faith Exception

Massachusetts v. Sheppard

104 S.Ct. 3424
Supreme Court of the United States
MASSACHUSETTS, Petitioner
v.
Osborne SHEPPARD.
No. 82-963. | Argued Jan. 17, 1984. | Decided July 5, 1984.

***983** Justice WHITE delivered the opinion of the Court.

This case involves the application of the rules articulated today in United States v. Leon,[2982] to a situation in ***984** which police officers seize items pursuant to a warrant subsequently invalidated because of a technical error on the part of the issuing judge.

I

The badly burned body of Sandra Boulware was discovered in a vacant lot in the Roxbury section of Boston at approximately 5 a.m., Saturday, May 5, 1979. An autopsy revealed that Boulware had died of multiple compound skull fractures caused by blows to the head. After a brief investigation, the police decided to question one of the victim's boyfriends, Osborne Sheppard. Sheppard told the police that he had last seen the victim on Tuesday night and that he had been at a local gaming house (where card games were played) from 9 p.m. Friday ****3426** until 5 a.m. Saturday. He identified several people who would be willing to substantiate the latter claim.

By interviewing the people Sheppard had said were at the gaming house on Friday night, the police learned that although Sheppard was at the gaming house that night, he had borrowed an automobile at about 3 o'clock Saturday morning in order to give two men a ride home. Even though the trip normally took only 15 minutes, Sheppard did not return with the car until nearly 5 a.m.

On Sunday morning, police officers visited the owner of the car Sheppard had borrowed. He consented to an inspection of the vehicle. Bloodstains and pieces of hair were found on the rear bumper and within the trunk compartment. In addition, the officers noticed strands of wire in the trunk similar to wire strands found on and near the body of the victim. The owner of the car told the officers that when he last used the car on Friday night, shortly before Sheppard borrowed it, he had placed articles in the trunk and had not noticed any stains on the bumper or in the trunk.

On the basis of the evidence gathered thus far in the investigation, Detective Peter O'Malley drafted an affidavit designed to support an application for an arrest warrant and a search warrant authorizing a search of Sheppard's residence. ***985** The affidavit set forth the results of the investigation and stated that the police wished to search for:

> [A] fifth bottle of amaretto liquor, 2 nickel bags of marijuana, a woman's jacket that has been described as black-grey (charcoal), possessions of Sandra D. Boulware, similar type wire and rope that match those on the

[2982] *468 U.S. 897, 104 S.Ct. 3405, 82 L.Ed.2d 677*

body of Sandra D. Boulware, or in the above [T]hunderbird. Blunt instrument that might have been used on the victim. Men's or women's clothing that may have blood, gasoline, burns on them. Items that may have fingerprints of the victim.

Detective O'Malley showed the affidavit to the District Attorney, the District Attorney's first assistant, and a sergeant, who all concluded that it set forth probable cause for the search and the arrest.[2983]

Because it was Sunday, the local court was closed, and the police had a difficult time finding a warrant application form. Detective O'Malley finally found a warrant form previously in use in the Dorchester District. The form was entitled "Search Warrant—Controlled Substance G.L. c. 276 §§ 1 through 3A." Realizing that some changes had to be made before the form could be used to authorize the search requested in the affidavit, Detective O'Malley deleted the subtitle "controlled substance" with a typewriter. He also substituted "Roxbury" for the printed "Dorchester" and typed Sheppard's name and address into blank spaces provided for that information. However, the reference to "controlled substance" was not deleted in the portion of the form that constituted the warrant application and that, when signed, would constitute the warrant itself.

***986** Detective O'Malley then took the affidavit and the warrant form to the residence of a judge who had consented to consider the warrant application. The judge examined the affidavit and stated that he would authorize the search as requested. Detective O'Malley offered the warrant form and stated that he knew the form as presented dealt with controlled substances. He showed the judge where he had crossed out the subtitles. After unsuccessfully searching for a more suitable form, the judge informed O'Malley that he would make the necessary changes so as to provide a proper search warrant. The judge then took the form, made some changes on it, and dated and signed the warrant. However, he did not change the substantive portion of the warrant, which continued to authorize ****3427** a search for controlled substances; nor did he alter the form so as to incorporate the affidavit. The judge returned the affidavit and the warrant to O'Malley, informing him that the warrant was sufficient authority in form and content to carry out the search as requested. O'Malley took the two documents and, accompanied by other officers, proceeded to Sheppard's residence. ***987** The scope of the ensuing search was limited to the items listed in the affidavit, and several incriminating pieces of evidence were discovered. Sheppard was then charged with first-degree murder.

At a pretrial suppression hearing, the trial judge concluded that the warrant failed to conform to the commands of the Fourth Amendment because it did not particularly describe the items to be seized. The judge ruled, however, that the evidence could be admitted notwithstanding the defect in the warrant because the police had acted in good faith in executing what they reasonably thought was a valid warrant.[2984] At the subsequent trial, Sheppard was convicted.

On appeal, Sheppard argued that the evidence obtained pursuant to the defective warrant should have been suppressed. The Supreme Judicial Court of Massachusetts agreed. A plurality of the justices concluded that although "the police conducted the search in a good faith belief, reasonably held, that the search was lawful and authorized by the warrant issued by the judge,"[2985] the evidence had to be excluded because this Court had not recognized a good-faith exception to the exclusionary rule. Two justices combined in a separate concurrence to stress their rejection of the good-faith exception, and one justice dissented, contending that since exclusion of the evi-

---

[2983] *387 Mass. 488, 492, 441 N.E.2d 725, 727 (1982)*

[2984] *App. 35a*

[2985] *387 Mass., at 503, 441 N.E.2d, at 733*

dence in this case would not serve to deter any police misconduct, the evidence should be admitted. We granted certiorari and set the case for argument in conjunction with United States v. Leon.[2986]

II

Having already decided that the exclusionary rule should not be applied when the officer conducting the search acted in ***988** objectively reasonable reliance on a warrant issued by a detached and neutral magistrate that subsequently is determined to be invalid,[2987] the sole issue before us in this case is whether the officers reasonably believed that the search they conducted was authorized by a valid warrant. There is no ****3428** dispute that the officers believed that the warrant authorized the search that they conducted. Thus, the only question is whether there was an objectively reasonable basis for the officers' mistaken belief. Both the trial court,[2988] and a majority of the Supreme Judicial Court,[2989] concluded that there was. We agree.

***989** The officers in this case took every step that could reasonably be expected of them. Detective O'Malley prepared an affidavit which was reviewed and approved by the District Attorney. He presented that affidavit to a neutral judge. The judge concluded that the affidavit established probable cause to search Sheppard's residence,[2990] and informed O'Malley that he would authorize the search as requested. O'Malley then produced the warrant form and informed the judge that it might need to be changed. He was told by the judge that the necessary changes would be made. He then observed the judge make some changes and received the warrant and the affidavit. At this point, a reasonable police officer would have concluded, as O'Malley did, that the warrant authorized a search for the materials outlined in the affidavit.

Sheppard contends that since O'Malley knew the warrant form was defective, he should have examined it to make sure that the necessary changes had been made. However, that argument is based on the premise that O'Malley had a duty to disregard the judge's assurances that the requested search would be authorized and the necessary changes would be made. Whatever an officer may be required to do when he executes a warrant without knowing beforehand what items are to be seized, we refuse to rule that an officer is required ***990** to disbelieve a judge who has just advised him, by word and by action, that the warrant he possesses authorizes him to conduct the search he has requested. In Massachusetts, as in most jurisdictions, the determinations of a judge acting within his jurisdiction, even if erroneous, are valid and binding until they are set aside under some recognized procedure.[2991] If an officer is required to accept at face value the judge's conclusion that a warrant form is invalid, ****3429** there is little reason why he should be expected to disregard assurances that everything is all right, especially when he has alerted the judge to the potential problems.

In sum, the police conduct in this case clearly was objectively reasonable and largely error-free. An error of constitutional dimensions may have been committed with respect to the issuance of the warrant, but it was the judge, not the police officers, who made the critical mistake. "[T]he exclusionary rule was adopted to deter unlawful searches by police, not to punish the errors of magistrates and judges."[2992]

[2986] *468 U.S. 897, 104 S.Ct. 3405, 82 L.Ed.2d 677. 463 U.S. 1205, 103 S.Ct. 3534, 77 L.Ed.2d 1386 (1983)*

[2987] *At 922–923, 104 S.Ct., at 3421*

[2988] *App. 35a*

[2989] *387 Mass., at 503, 441 N.E.2d, at 733; id., at 524–525, 441 N.E.2d, at 745 (Lynch, J., dissenting)*

[2990] *App. 26a*

[2991] *Streeter v. City of Worcester, 336 Mass. 469, 472, 146 N.E.2d 514, 517 (1957); Moll v. Township of Wakefield, 274 Mass. 505, 507, 175 N.E. 81, 82 (1931)*

[2992] *Illinois v. Gates, 462 U.S. 213, 263, 103 S.Ct. 2317, 2346, 76 L.Ed.2d 527 (1983) (WHITE, J., concurring in judgment)*

Suppressing evidence because the ***991** judge failed to make all the necessary clerical corrections despite his assurances that such changes would be made will not serve the deterrent function that the exclusionary rule was designed to achieve. Accordingly, federal law does not require the exclusion of the disputed evidence in this case. The judgment of the Supreme Judicial Court is therefore reversed, and the case is remanded for further proceedings not inconsistent with this opinion.

It is so ordered.

Black Letter Law

The Court held that where police officers, who were advised by a judge that all necessary clerical changes had been made in defective warrant form, and took every step that could reasonably be expected of them, had an objectively reasonable basis for their mistaken belief that a search warrant authorized the search they conducted. The Court refused to apply the exclusionary rule since officers conducting the search acted in objectively reasonable reliance on a warrant issued by a detached and neutral magistrate, which was subsequently determined to be invalid.

United States v. Leon

104 S.Ct. 3405

Supreme Court of the United States

UNITED STATES, Petitioner

v.

Alberto Antonio LEON et al.

No. 82-1771. | Argued Jan. 17, 1984. | Decided July 5, 1984. | Rehearing Denied Sept. 18, 1984.

***900** Justice WHITE delivered the opinion of the Court.

This case presents the question whether the Fourth Amendment exclusionary rule should be modified so as not to bar the use in the prosecution's case in chief of evidence obtained by officers acting in reasonable reliance on a search warrant issued by a detached and neutral magistrate but ultimately found to be unsupported by probable cause. To resolve this question, we must consider once again the tension between the sometimes competing goals of, on the one hand, deterring official misconduct and removing inducements to unreasonable invasions of privacy and, on the other, establishing procedures under which criminal defendants are "acquitted ***901** or convicted on the basis of all the evidence which exposes the truth."[2993]

I

In August 1981, a confidential informant of unproven reliability informed an officer of the Burbank Police Department that two persons known to him as "Armando" and "Patsy" were selling large quantities of cocaine and methaqualone from their residence at 620 Price Drive in Burbank, Cal. The informant also indicated that he had witnessed a sale of methaqualone by "Patsy" at the residence approximately five months earlier and had observed at that time a shoebox containing a large amount of cash that belonged to "Patsy." He further declared that "Armando" and "Patsy" generally kept only small quantities of drugs at their residence and stored the remainder at another location in Burbank.

[2993] *Alderman v. United States, 394 U.S. 165, 175, 89 S.Ct. 961, 967, 22 L.Ed.2d 176 (1969)*

On the basis of this information, the Burbank police initiated an extensive investigation focusing first on the Price Drive residence and later on two other residences as well. Cars parked at the Price Drive residence were determined to belong to respondents Armando Sanchez, who had previously been arrested for possession of marijuana, and Patsy Stewart, who had no criminal record. During the course of the investigation, officers observed an automobile belonging to respondent Ricardo Del Castillo, who had previously been arrested for possession of 50 pounds of marijuana, arrive at the Price Drive residence. The driver of that car entered the house, exited shortly thereafter carrying a small paper sack, and drove away. A check of Del Castillo's probation records led the officers to respondent Alberto Leon, whose telephone number Del Castillo had listed as his employer's. Leon had been arrested in 1980 on drug charges, and a companion had informed the police at that time that Leon was heavily involved in the importation of drugs into this country. Before the current investigation began, the Burbank officers had ***902** learned that an informant had told a Glendale police officer that Leon stored a large quantity of methaqualone at his residence in Glendale. During the course of this investigation, the Burbank officers learned that Leon was living at 716 South Sunset Canyon in Burbank.

Subsequently, the officers observed several persons, at least one of whom had prior drug involvement, arriving at the Price Drive residence and leaving with small packages; observed a variety of other material activity at the two residences as well as at a condominium at 7902 Via Magdalena; and witnessed a variety of relevant activity involving respondents' automobiles. The officers also observed respondents Sanchez and Stewart board separate flights for Miami. The pair later returned to Los Angeles together, consented to a search of their luggage that revealed only a small amount of marijuana, and left the airport. Based on these and other observations summarized in the affidavit,[2994] Officer Cyril Rombach of the Burbank Police Department, an experienced and well-trained narcotics investigator, prepared an application for a warrant to search 620 Price Drive, 716 South Sunset Canyon, 7902 Via Magdalena, and automobiles registered ****3410** to each of the respondents for an extensive list of items believed to be related to respondents' drug-trafficking activities. Officer Rombach's extensive application was reviewed by several Deputy District Attorneys.

A facially valid search warrant was issued in September 1981 by a State Superior Court Judge. The ensuing searches produced large quantities of drugs at the Via Magdalena and Sunset Canyon addresses and a small quantity at the Price Drive residence. Other evidence was discovered at each of the residences and in Stewart's and Del Castillo's automobiles. Respondents were indicted by a grand jury in the District Court for the Central District of California and charged with conspiracy to possess and distribute cocaine and a variety of substantive counts.

***903** The respondents then filed motions to suppress the evidence seized pursuant to the warrant. The District Court held an evidentiary hearing and, while recognizing that the case was a close one,[2995] granted the motions to suppress in part. It concluded that the affidavit was insufficient to establish probable cause, but did not suppress all of the evidence as to all of the respondents because none of the respondents had standing to challenge all of the searches. In ***904** response to a request from the Government, the court made clear that Officer Rombach had acted in good faith, but it rejected the Government's suggestion that the Fourth Amendment exclusionary rule should not apply where evidence is seized in reasonable, good-faith reliance on a search warrant.

[2994] *App. 34*

[2995] *See id., at 131*

The District Court denied the Government's motion for reconsideration,[2996] and a divided panel of the Court of Appeals for the Ninth Circuit affirmed.[2997] The Court of Appeals first concluded that Officer Rombach's affidavit could not establish probable cause to search the Price Drive residence. To the extent that the affidavit set forth facts demonstrating the basis of the informant's knowledge of criminal activity, the information included was fatally stale. The affidavit, moreover, failed to establish the informant's credibility. ****3411** Accordingly, the Court of Appeals concluded that the information provided by the informant was inadequate under both prongs of the two-part test established in Aguilar v. Texas,[2998] and Spinelli v. United States.[2999] The officers' independent investigation neither cured the staleness nor corroborated the details of the informant's declarations. The Court of Appeals then considered whether the affidavit formed a proper basis for the ***905** search of the Sunset Canyon residence. In its view, the affidavit included no facts indicating the basis for the informants' statements concerning respondent Leon's criminal activities and was devoid of information establishing the informants' reliability. Because these deficiencies had not been cured by the police investigation, the District Court properly suppressed the fruits of the search. The Court of Appeals refused the Government's invitation to recognize a good-faith exception to the Fourth Amendment exclusionary rule.[3000]

The Government's petition for certiorari expressly declined to seek review of the lower courts' determinations that the search warrant was unsupported by probable cause and presented only the question "[w]hether the Fourth Amendment exclusionary rule should be modified so as not to bar the admission of evidence seized in reasonable, good-faith reliance on a search warrant that is subsequently held to be defective." We granted certiorari to consider the propriety of such a modification.[3001] Although it undoubtedly is within our power to consider the question whether probable cause existed under the "totality of the circumstances" test announced last Term in Illinois v. Gates,[3002] that question has not been briefed or argued; and it is also within our authority, which we choose to exercise, to take the case as it comes to us, accepting the Court of Appeals' conclusion that probable cause was lacking under the prevailing legal standards.[3003]

We have concluded that, in the Fourth Amendment context, the exclusionary rule can be modified somewhat without jeopardizing its ability to perform its intended functions. Accordingly, we reverse the judgment of the Court of Appeals.

II

Language in opinions of this Court and of individual Justices has sometimes implied that the exclusionary rule is a necessary corollary of the Fourth Amendment,[3004] ***906** or that the rule is required by the conjunction of the Fourth

---

[2996] *Id., at 147*

[2997] *Judgt. order reported at 701 F.2d 187 (1983)*

[2998] *378 U.S. 108, 84 S.Ct. 1509, 12 L.Ed.2d 723 (1964)*

[2999] *393 U.S. 410, 89 S.Ct. 584, 21 L.Ed.2d 637 (1969)*

[3000] *App. to Pet. for Cert. 4a*

[3001] *463 U.S. 1206, 103 S.Ct. 3535, 77 L.Ed.2d 1386 (1983)*

[3002] *462 U.S. 213, 103 S.Ct. 2317, 76 L.Ed.2d 527 (1983)*

[3003] *See this Court's Rule 21.1(a)*

[3004] *Mapp v. Ohio, 367 U.S. 643, 651, 655–657, 81 S.Ct. 1684, 1689, 1691–1692, 6 L.Ed.2d 1081 (1961); Olmstead v. United States, 277 U.S. 438, 462–463, 48 S.Ct. 564, 567, 72 L.Ed. 944 (1928)*

and Fifth Amendments.[3005] These implications need not detain us long. The Fifth Amendment theory has not withstood critical analysis or the test of time,[3006] and the Fourth Amendment "has never been interpreted to proscribe the introduction of illegally seized evidence in all proceedings or against all persons."[3007]

A

The Fourth Amendment contains no provision expressly precluding the use of evidence obtained in violation of its commands, and an examination of its origin and purposes makes clear that the use of fruits of a past unlawful search or seizure "work[s] no new Fourth Amendment wrong."[3008] The wrong condemned by the Amendment is "fully accomplished" by the unlawful search or seizure itself, ibid., and ****3412** the exclusionary rule is neither intended nor able to "cure the invasion of the defendant's rights which he has already suffered."[3009] The rule thus operates as "a judicially created remedy designed to safeguard Fourth Amendment rights generally through its deterrent effect, rather than a personal constitutional right of the party aggrieved."[3010]

Whether the exclusionary sanction is appropriately imposed in a particular case, our decisions make clear, is "an issue separate from the question whether the Fourth Amendment rights of the party seeking to invoke the rule were violated by police conduct."[3011] Only the former question is currently before us, and it must ***907** be resolved by weighing the costs and benefits of preventing the use in the prosecution's case in chief of inherently trustworthy tangible evidence obtained in reliance on a search warrant issued by a detached and neutral magistrate that ultimately is found to be defective.

The substantial social costs exacted by the exclusionary rule for the vindication of Fourth Amendment rights have long been a source of concern. "Our cases have consistently recognized that unbending application of the exclusionary sanction to enforce ideals of governmental rectitude would impede unacceptably the truth-finding functions of judge and jury."[3012] An objectionable collateral consequence of this interference with the criminal justice system's truth-finding function is that some guilty defendants may go free or receive reduced sentences as a result of favorable plea bargains. Particularly ***908** when law enforcement officers have acted in objective good faith or their transgressions have been minor, the magnitude of the benefit conferred on such guilty defendants offends basic concepts of the criminal justice system.[3013] Indiscriminate application of the exclusionary rule, therefore, may well "generat[e] disrespect for the law and administration of justice."[3014] Accordingly, "[a]s with ****3413** any remedial device, the application of the rule has been restricted

---

[3005] *Mapp v. Ohio, supra, 367 U.S., at 661–662, 81 S.Ct., at 1694–1695 (Black, J., concurring); Agnello v. United States, 269 U.S. 20, 33–34, 46 S.Ct. 4, 6–7, 70 L.Ed. 145 (1925)*

[3006] *See Andresen v. Maryland, 427 U.S. 463, 96 S.Ct. 2737, 49 L.Ed.2d 627 (1976)*

[3007] *Stone v. Powell, 428 U.S. 465, 486, 96 S.Ct. 3037, 3048, 49 L.Ed.2d 1067 (1976)*

[3008] *United States v. Calandra, 414 U.S. 338, 354, 94 S.Ct. 613, 623, 38 L.Ed.2d 561 (1974)*

[3009] *Stone v. Powell, supra, 428 U.S., at 540, 96 S.Ct., at 3073 (WHITE, J., dissenting)*

[3010] *United States v. Calandra, supra, 414 U.S., at 348, 94 S.Ct., at 620*

[3011] *Illinois v. Gates, supra, 462 U.S., at 223, 103 S.Ct., at 2324*

[3012] *United States v. Payner, 447 U.S. 727, 734, 100 S.Ct. 2439, 2445, 65 L.Ed.2d 468 (1980)*

[3013] *Stone v. Powell, 428 U.S., at 490, 96 S.Ct., at 3050*

[3014] *Id., at 491, 96 S.Ct., at 3051*

to those areas where its remedial objectives are thought most efficaciously served."[3015]

B

Close attention to those remedial objectives has characterized our recent decisions concerning the scope of the Fourth Amendment exclusionary rule. The Court has, to be sure, not seriously questioned, "in the absence of a more efficacious sanction, the continued application of the rule to suppress evidence ***909** from the [prosecution's] case where a Fourth Amendment violation has been substantial and deliberate...."[3016] Nevertheless, the balancing approach that has evolved in various contexts—including criminal trials—"forcefully suggest[s] that the exclusionary rule be more generally modified to permit the introduction of evidence obtained in the reasonable good-faith belief that a search or seizure was in accord with the Fourth Amendment."[3017]

In Stone v. Powell, supra, the Court emphasized the costs of the exclusionary rule, expressed its view that limiting the circumstances under which Fourth Amendment claims could be raised in federal habeas corpus proceedings would not reduce the rule's deterrent effect,[3018] and held that a state prisoner who has been afforded a full and fair opportunity to litigate a Fourth Amendment claim may not obtain federal habeas relief on the ground that unlawfully obtained evidence had been introduced at his trial.[3019] Proposed extensions of the exclusionary rule to proceedings other than the criminal trial itself have been evaluated and rejected under the same analytic approach. In United States v. Calandra, for example, we declined to allow grand jury witnesses to refuse to answer questions based on evidence obtained from an unlawful search or seizure since "[a]ny incremental deterrent effect which might be achieved by extending the rule to grand jury proceedings is uncertain at best."[3020] Similarly, in United States v. Janis,[3021] we permitted the use in federal civil proceedings of evidence illegally seized by state officials since the likelihood of deterring police misconduct through such an extension of the exclusionary rule was insufficient to outweigh its substantial social costs. In so doing, we declared that, "[i] f ... the exclusionary rule does not result in appreciable deterrence, then, clearly, its use in the instant situation is unwarranted."[3022]

***910** As cases considering the use of unlawfully obtained evidence in criminal trials themselves make clear, it does not follow from the emphasis on the exclusionary rule's deterrent value that "anything which deters illegal searches is thereby commanded by the Fourth Amendment."[3023] In determining whether persons aggrieved solely by the introduction of damaging evidence unlawfully obtained from their co-conspirators or co-defendants could seek suppression, for example, we found that the additional benefits of such an extension of the exclusionary rule would

---

[3015] *United States v. Calandra, supra, 414 U.S., at 348, 94 S.Ct., at 670; see Stone v. Powell, supra, 428 U.S., at 486–487, 96 S.Ct., at 3048–3049; United States v. Janis, 428 U.S. 433, 447, 96 S.Ct. 3021, 3028, 49 L.Ed.2d 1046 (1976)*

[3016] *Franks v. Delaware, 438 U.S. 154, 171, 98 S.Ct. 2674, 2684, 57 L.Ed.2d 667 (1978); Stone v. Powell, supra, 428 U.S., at 492, 96 S.Ct., at 3051*

[3017] *Illinois v. Gates, 462 U.S., at 255, 103 S.Ct., at 2340 (WHITE, J., concurring in judgment)*

[3018] *Id., 428 U.S., at 489–495, 96 S.Ct., at 3050–3052*

[3019] *Cf. Rose v. Mitchell, 443 U.S. 545, 560–563, 99 S.Ct. 2993, 3002–3004, 61 L.Ed.2d 739 (1979)*

[3020] *414 U.S., at 348, 94 S.Ct., at 620*

[3021] *Supra*

[3022] *Id., 428 U.S., at 454, 96 S.Ct., at 3032*

[3023] *Alderman v. United States, 394 U.S., at 174, 89 S.Ct., at 967*

not outweigh its costs.[3024] Standing to invoke the rule has thus been limited to cases in which the prosecution seeks to use the fruits of an illegal search or seizure against the victim of police misconduct.[3025]

Even defendants with standing to challenge the introduction in their criminal ****3414** trials of unlawfully obtained evidence cannot prevent every conceivable use of such evidence. Evidence obtained in violation of the Fourth Amendment and inadmissible in the prosecution's case in chief may be used to impeach a defendant's direct testimony.[3026] A similar assessment of the "incremental furthering" of the ends of the exclusionary rule led us to conclude in United States v. Havens,[3027] that evidence inadmissible in the prosecution's case in chief or otherwise as substantive evidence of guilt may be used to impeach statements made by a defendant in response to "proper cross-examination reasonably suggested by the defendant's direct examination."[3028]

When considering the use of evidence obtained in violation of the Fourth Amendment in the prosecution's case in chief, moreover, we have declined to adopt a per se or "but for" rule ***911** that would render inadmissible any evidence that came to light through a chain of causation that began with an illegal arrest.[3029] We also have held that a witness' testimony may be admitted even when his identity was discovered in an unconstitutional search.[3030] The perception underlying these decisions—that the connection between police misconduct and evidence of crime may be sufficiently attenuated to permit the use of that evidence at trial—is a product of considerations relating to the exclusionary rule and the constitutional principles it is designed to protect.[3031] In short, the "dissipation of the taint" concept that the Court has applied in deciding whether exclusion is appropriate in a particular case "attempts to mark the point at which the detrimental consequences of illegal police action become so attenuated that the deterrent effect of the exclusionary rule no longer justifies its cost."[3032] Not surprisingly in view of this purpose, an assessment of the flagrancy of the police misconduct constitutes an important step in the calculus.[3033]

The same attention to the purposes underlying the exclusionary rule also has characterized decisions not involving the scope of the rule itself. We have not required suppression of the fruits of a search incident to an arrest made in good-faith reliance on a substantive criminal statute that subsequently ***912** is declared unconstitutional.[3034] Similarly, although the Court has been unwilling to conclude that new Fourth Amendment principles are always to have only prospective effect,[3035] ****3415**

[3024] *Id., at 174–175, 89 S.Ct., at 967*

[3025] *Rakas v. Illinois, 439 U.S. 128, 99 S.Ct. 421, 58 L.Ed.2d 387 (1978); Brown v. United States, 411 U.S. 223, 93 S.Ct. 1565, 36 L.Ed.2d 208 (1973); Wong Sun v. United States, 371 U.S. 471, 491–492, 83 S.Ct. 407, 419–420, 9 L.Ed.2d 441 (1963). Cf. United States v. Payner, 447 U.S. 727, 100 S.Ct. 2439, 65 L.Ed.2d 468 (1980)*

[3026] *Walder v. United States, 347 U.S. 62, 74 S.Ct. 354, 98 L.Ed. 503 (1954). See also Oregon v. Hass, 420 U.S. 714, 95 S.Ct. 1215, 43 L.Ed.2d 570 (1975); Harris v. New York, 401 U.S. 222, 91 S.Ct. 643, 28 L.Ed.2d 1 (1971)*

[3027] *446 U.S. 620, 627, 100 S.Ct. 1912, 1916, 64 L.Ed.2d 559 (1980)*

[3028] *Id., at 627–628, 100 S.Ct. at 1916–1917*

[3029] *Brown v. Illinois, 422 U.S. 590, 95 S.Ct. 2254, 45 L.Ed.2d 416 (1975); Wong Sun v. United States, supra, 371 U.S., at 487–488, 83 S.Ct., at 417*

[3030] *United States v. Ceccolini, 435 U.S. 268, 98 S.Ct. 1054, 55 L.Ed.2d 268 (1978)*

[3031] *Dunaway v. New York, 442 U.S. 200, 217–218, 99 S.Ct. 2248, 2259–2260, 60 L.Ed.2d 824 (1979); United States v. Ceccolini, supra, 435 U.S., at 279, 98 S.Ct., at 1061*

[3032] *Brown v. Illinois, supra, 422 U.S., at 609, 95 S.Ct., at 2264 (POWELL, J., concurring in part)*

[3033] *Dunaway v. New York, supra, 442 U.S., at 218, 99 S.Ct., at 2259; Brown v. Illinois, supra, 422 U.S., at 603–604, 95 S.Ct., 2261–2262*

[3034] *Michigan v. DeFillippo, 443 U.S. 31, 99 S.Ct. 2627, 61 L.Ed.2d 343 (1979)*

[3035] *United States v. Johnson, 457 U.S. 537, 560, 102 S.Ct. 2579, 2593, 73 L.Ed.2d 202 (1982)*

no Fourth Amendment decision marking a "clear break with the past" has been applied retroactively.[3036] The propriety ***913** of retroactive application of a newly announced Fourth Amendment principle, moreover, has been assessed largely in terms of the contribution retroactivity might make to the deterrence of police misconduct.[3037]

As yet, we have not recognized any form of good-faith exception to the Fourth Amendment exclusionary rule. But the balancing approach that has evolved during the years of experience with the rule provides strong support for the modification currently urged upon us. As we discuss below, our evaluation of the costs and benefits of suppressing reliable physical evidence seized by officers reasonably relying on a warrant issued by a detached and neutral magistrate leads to the conclusion that such evidence should be admissible in the prosecution's case in chief.

III

A

Because a search warrant "provides the detached scrutiny of a neutral magistrate, ****3416** which is a more reliable safeguard ***914** against improper searches than the hurried judgment of a law enforcement officer 'engaged in the often competitive enterprise of ferreting out crime,'"[3038] we have expressed a strong preference for warrants and declared that "in a doubtful or marginal case a search under a warrant may be sustainable where without one it would fall."[3039] Reasonable minds frequently may differ on the question whether a particular affidavit establishes probable cause, and we have thus concluded that the preference for warrants is most appropriately effectuated by according "great deference" to a magistrate's determination.[3040]

Deference to the magistrate, however, is not boundless. It is clear, first, that the deference accorded to a magistrate's finding of probable cause does not preclude inquiry into the knowing or reckless falsity of the affidavit on which that determination was based.[3041] Second, the courts must also insist that the magistrate purport to "perform his 'neutral and detached' function and not serve merely as a rubber stamp for the police."[3042] A magistrate failing to "manifest that neutrality and detachment demanded of a judicial officer when presented with a warrant application" and who acts instead as "an adjunct law enforcement officer" cannot provide valid authorization for an otherwise unconstitutional search.[3043]

***915** Third, reviewing courts will not defer to a warrant based on an affidavit that does not "provide the magistrate with a substantial basis for determining the existence of probable cause."[3044] "Sufficient information must be presented to the magistrate to allow that official to determine probable cause; his action cannot be a

---

[3036] *See United States v. Peltier, 422 U.S. 531, 95 S.Ct. 2313, 45 L.Ed.2d 374 (1975); Desist v. United States, 394 U.S. 244, 89 S.Ct. 1030, 22 L.Ed.2d 248 (1969); Linkletter v. Walker, 381 U.S. 618, 85 S.Ct. 1731, 14 L.Ed.2d 601 (1965)*

[3037] *United States v. Johnson, supra, 457 U.S., at 560–561, 102 S.Ct., at 2593–2594; United States v. Peltier, supra, 422 U.S., at 536–539, 542, 95 S.Ct., at 2317–2318, 2320*

[3038] *United States v. Chadwick, 433 U.S. 1, 9, 97 S.Ct. 2476, 2482, 53 L.Ed.2d 538 (1977) (quoting Johnson v. United States, 333 U.S. 10, 14, 68 S.Ct. 367, 369, 92 L.Ed. 436 (1948))*

[3039] *United States v. Ventresca, 380 U.S. 102, 106, 85 S.Ct. 741, 744, 13 L.Ed.2d 684 (1965). See Aguilar v. Texas, 378 U.S., at 111, 84 S.Ct., at 1512*

[3040] *Spinelli v. United States, 393 U.S., at 419, 89 S.Ct., at 590. See Illinois v. Gates, 462 U.S., at 236, 103 S.Ct., at 2331; United States v. Ventresca, supra, 380 U.S., at 108–109, 85 S.Ct., at 745–746*

[3041] *Franks v. Delaware, 438 U.S. 154, 98 S.Ct. 2674, 57 L.Ed.2d 667 (1978)*

[3042] *Aguilar v. Texas, supra, 378 U.S., at 111, 84 S.Ct., at 1512. See Illinois v. Gates, supra, 462 U.S., at 239, 103 S.Ct., at 2332*

[3043] *Lo–Ji Sales, Inc. v. New York, 442 U.S. 319, 326–327, 99 S.Ct. 2319, 2324–2325, 60 L.Ed.2d 920 (1979)*

[3044] *Illinois v. Gates, 462 U.S., at 239, 103 S.Ct., at 2332*

mere ratification of the bare conclusions of others."[3045] Even if the warrant application was supported by more than a "bare bones" affidavit, a reviewing court may properly conclude that, notwithstanding the deference that magistrates deserve, the **3417 warrant was invalid because the magistrate's probable-cause determination reflected an improper analysis of the totality of the circumstances,[3046] or because the form of the warrant was improper in some respect.

Only in the first of these three situations, however, has the Court set forth a rationale for suppressing evidence obtained pursuant to a search warrant; in the other areas, it has simply excluded such evidence without considering whether ***916** Fourth Amendment interests will be advanced. To the extent that proponents of exclusion rely on its behavioral effects on judges and magistrates in these areas, their reliance is misplaced. First, the exclusionary rule is designed to deter police misconduct rather than to punish the errors of judges and magistrates. Second, there exists no evidence suggesting that judges and magistrates are inclined to ignore or subvert the Fourth Amendment or that lawlessness among these actors requires application of the extreme sanction of exclusion.

Third, and most important, we discern no basis, and are offered none, for believing that exclusion of evidence seized pursuant to a warrant will have a significant deterrent effect on the issuing judge or magistrate. Many of the factors ***917** that indicate that the exclusionary rule cannot provide an effective "special" or "general" deterrent for individual offending law enforcement officers apply as well to judges or magistrates. And, to the extent that the rule is thought to operate as a "systemic" deterrent on a wider audience, it clearly can have no such effect on individuals empowered to issue search warrants. Judges and magistrates are not adjuncts to the law enforcement team; as neutral judicial officers, they have no stake in the outcome of particular criminal prosecutions. The threat of exclusion thus cannot be expected significantly to deter them. Imposition of the exclusionary sanction is not necessary meaningfully to inform judicial officers of their errors, and we cannot conclude that admitting evidence obtained ****3418** pursuant to a warrant while at the same time declaring that the warrant was somehow defective will in any way reduce judicial officers' professional incentives to comply with the Fourth Amendment, encourage them to repeat their mistakes, or lead to the granting of all colorable warrant requests.

***918 B**

If exclusion of evidence obtained pursuant to a subsequently invalidated warrant is to have any deterrent effect, therefore, it must alter the behavior of individual law enforcement officers or the policies of their departments. One could argue that applying the exclusionary rule in cases where the police failed to demonstrate probable cause in the warrant application deters future inadequate presentations or "magistrate shopping" and thus promotes the ends of the Fourth Amendment. Suppressing evidence obtained pursuant to a technically defective warrant supported by probable cause also might encourage officers to scrutinize more closely the form of the warrant and to point out suspected judicial errors. We find such arguments speculative and conclude that suppression of evidence obtained pursuant to a warrant should be ordered only on a case-by-case basis and only in those unusual cases in which exclusion will further the purposes of the exclusionary rule.

We have frequently questioned whether the exclusionary rule can have any deterrent effect when the offending officers acted in the objectively reasonable belief that their conduct did not violate the Fourth Amendment. "No empirical researcher,

---

[3045] *Ibid. See Aguilar v. Texas, supra 378 U.S., at 114–115, 84 S.Ct., at 1513–1514; Giordenello v. United States, 357 U.S. 480, 78 S.Ct. 1245, 2 L.Ed.2d 1503 (1958); Nathanson v. United States, 290 U.S. 41, 54 S.Ct. 11, 78 L.Ed. 159 (1933)*

[3046] *Illinois v. Gates, supra, 462 U.S., at 238–239, 103 S.Ct., at 2332–2333*

proponent or opponent of the rule, has yet been able to establish with any assurance whether the rule has a deterrent effect...."[3047] But even assuming that the rule effectively ***919** deters some police misconduct and provides incentives for the law enforcement profession as a whole to conduct itself in accord with the Fourth Amendment, it cannot be expected, and should not be applied, to deter objectively reasonable law enforcement activity.

As we observed in Michigan v. Tucker,[3048] and reiterated in United States v. Peltier:[3049]

> The deterrent purpose of the exclusionary rule necessarily assumes that the police have engaged in willful, or at the very least negligent, conduct which has deprived the defendant of some right. By refusing to admit evidence gained as a result of such conduct, the courts hope to instill in those particular investigating officers, or in their future counterparts, a greater degree of care toward the rights of an accused. Where the official action was pursued in complete good faith, however, the deterrence rationale loses much of its force.

The Peltier Court continued:[3050]

> ****3419** If the purpose of the exclusionary rule is to deter unlawful police conduct, then evidence obtained from a search should be suppressed only if it can be said that the law enforcement officer had knowledge, or may properly be charged with knowledge, that the search was unconstitutional under the Fourth Amendment.[3051]

In short, where the officer's conduct is objectively reasonable,

> ***920** [E]xcluding the evidence will not further the ends of the exclusionary rule in any appreciable way; for it is painfully apparent that ... the officer is acting as a reasonable officer would and should act in similar circumstances. Excluding the evidence can in no way affect his future conduct unless it is to make him less willing to do his duty.[3052]

This is particularly true, we believe, when an officer acting with objective good faith has obtained a search warrant from a judge or magistrate and acted within its scope. In most ***921** such cases, there is no police illegality and thus nothing to deter. It is the magistrate's responsibility to determine whether the officer's allegations establish probable cause and, if so, to issue a warrant comporting in form with the requirements of the Fourth Amendment. In the ordinary case, an officer cannot be expected to question the magistrate's probable-cause determination or his judgment that the form of the warrant is technically sufficient. "[O]nce the warrant issues,

---

[3047] *United States v. Janis, 428 U.S., at 452, n. 22, 96 S.Ct., at 3031, n. 22*

[3048] *417 U.S. 433, 447, 94 S.Ct. 2357, 2365, 41 L.Ed.2d 182 (1974)*

[3049] *422 U.S., at 539, 95 S.Ct., at 2318*

[3050] *Id., at 542, 95 S.Ct., at 2320*

[3051] *See also Illinois v. Gates, 462 U.S., at 260–261, 103 S.Ct., at 2344 (WHITE, J., concurring in judgment); United States v. Janis, supra, 428 U.S., at 459, 96 S.Ct., at 3034; Brown v. Illinois, 422 U.S., at 610–611, 95 S.Ct., at 2265–2266 (POWELL, J., concurring in part)*

[3052] *Stone v. Powell, 428 U.S., at 539–540, 96 S.Ct., at 3073–3074 (WHITE, J., dissenting)*

there is literally nothing more the policeman can do in seeking to comply with the law."[3053] Penalizing the officer for the magistrate's error, rather than his own, cannot logically contribute to the deterrence of Fourth Amendment violations.

****3420 *922 C**

We conclude that the marginal or nonexistent benefits produced by suppressing evidence obtained in objectively reasonable reliance on a subsequently invalidated search warrant cannot justify the substantial costs of exclusion. We do not suggest, however, that exclusion is always inappropriate in cases where an officer has obtained a warrant and abided by its terms. "[S]earches pursuant to a warrant will rarely require any deep inquiry into reasonableness,"[3054] for "a warrant issued by a magistrate normally suffices to establish" that a law enforcement officer has "acted in good faith in conducting the search."[3055] Nevertheless, the officer's reliance on the magistrate's probable-cause determination and on the technical sufficiency of the warrant he issues must be objectively reasonable,[3056] and it is clear that in some circumstances ***923** the officer will have no reasonable grounds for believing that the warrant was properly issued.

****3421** Suppression therefore remains an appropriate remedy if the magistrate or judge in issuing a warrant was misled by information in an affidavit that the affiant knew was false or would have known was false except for his reckless disregard of the truth.[3057] The exception we recognize today will also not apply in cases where the issuing magistrate wholly abandoned his judicial role in the manner condemned in Lo–Ji Sales, Inc. v. New York,[3058] in such circumstances, no reasonably well trained officer should rely on the warrant. Nor would an officer manifest objective good faith in relying on a warrant based on an affidavit "so lacking in indicia of probable cause as to render official belief in its existence entirely unreasonable."[3059] Finally, depending on the circumstances of the particular case, a warrant may be so facially deficient—i.e., in failing to particularize the place to be searched or the things to be seized—that the executing officers cannot reasonably presume it to be valid.[3060]

In so limiting the suppression remedy, we leave untouched the probable-cause standard and the various requirements for a valid warrant. Other objections to the modification of ***924** the Fourth Amendment exclusionary rule we consider to be insubstantial. The good-faith exception for searches conducted pursuant to warrants is not intended to signal our unwillingness strictly to enforce the requirements of the Fourth Amendment, and we do not believe that it will have this effect. As we have already suggested, the good-faith exception, turning as it does on objective reasonableness, should not be difficult to apply in practice. When officers have acted pursuant to a warrant, the prosecution should ordinarily be able to establish objective good faith without a substantial expenditure of judicial time.

Nor are we persuaded that application of a good-faith exception to searches conducted pursuant to warrants will preclude review of the constitutionality of the

---

[3053] *Id., 428 U.S., at 498, 96 S.Ct., at 3054 (BURGER, C.J., concurring)*

[3054] *Illinois v. Gates, 462 U.S., at 267, 103 S.Ct., at 2347 (WHITE, J., concurring in judgment)*

[3055] *United States v. Ross, 456 U.S. 798, 823, n. 32, 102 S.Ct. 2157, 2172, n. 32, 72 L.Ed.2d 572 (1982)*

[3056] *Cf. Harlow v. Fitzgerald, 457 U.S. 800, 815–819, 102 S.Ct. 2727, 2737–2739, 73 L.Ed.2d 396 (1982)*

[3057] *Franks v. Delaware, 438 U.S. 154, 98 S.Ct. 2674, 57 L.Ed.2d 667 (1978)*

[3058] *442 U.S. 319, 99 S.Ct. 2319, 60 L.Ed.2d 920 (1979)*

[3059] *Brown v. Illinois, 422 U.S., at 610–611, 95 S.Ct., at 2265–2266 (POWELL, J., concurring in part); see Illinois v. Gates, supra, 462 U.S., at 263–264, 103 S.Ct., at 2345–2346 (WHITE, J., concurring in the judgment)*

[3060] *Cf. Massachusetts v. Sheppard, 468 U.S., at 988–991, 104 S.Ct., at 3428–3430*

search or seizure, deny needed guidance from the courts, or freeze Fourth Amendment law in its present state. There is no need for courts to adopt the inflexible practice of always deciding whether the officers' conduct manifested objective good faith before turning to the question whether the Fourth Amendment has been violated. Defendants seeking suppression of the fruits of allegedly unconstitutional searches or seizures undoubtedly raise live controversies which Art. III empowers federal courts to adjudicate. As cases addressing questions of good-faith immunity under 42 U.S.C. § 1983,[3061] and cases involving the harmless-error doctrine,[3062] make clear, courts have considerable ***925** discretion in conforming their decisionmaking processes to the exigencies of particular cases.

If the resolution of a particular Fourth Amendment question is necessary to guide future action by law enforcement officers and magistrates, nothing will prevent reviewing courts from deciding that question ****3422** before turning to the good-faith issue. Indeed, it frequently will be difficult to determine whether the officers acted reasonably without resolving the Fourth Amendment issue. Even if the Fourth Amendment question is not one of broad import, reviewing courts could decide in particular cases that magistrates under their supervision need to be informed of their errors and so evaluate the officers' good faith only after finding a violation. In other circumstances, those courts could reject suppression motions posing no important Fourth Amendment questions by turning immediately to a consideration of the officers' good faith. We have no reason to believe that our Fourth Amendment jurisprudence would suffer by allowing reviewing courts to exercise an informed discretion in making this choice.

IV

When the principles we have enunciated today are applied to the facts of this case, it is apparent that the judgment of the Court of Appeals cannot stand. The Court of Appeals applied the prevailing legal standards to Officer Rombach's warrant application and concluded that the application could not support the magistrate's probable-cause determination. In so doing, the court clearly informed the magistrate that he ***926** had erred in issuing the challenged warrant. This aspect of the court's judgment is not under attack in this proceeding.

Having determined that the warrant should not have issued, the Court of Appeals understandably declined to adopt a modification of the Fourth Amendment exclusionary rule that this Court had not previously sanctioned. Although the modification finds strong support in our previous cases, the Court of Appeals' commendable self-restraint is not to be criticized. We have now reexamined the purposes of the exclusionary rule and the propriety of its application in cases where officers have relied on a subsequently invalidated search warrant. Our conclusion is that the rule's purposes will only rarely be served by applying it in such circumstances.

In the absence of an allegation that the magistrate abandoned his detached and neutral role, suppression is appropriate only if the officers were dishonest or reckless in preparing their affidavit or could not have harbored an objectively reasonable belief in the existence of probable cause. Only respondent Leon has contended that no reasonably well trained police officer could have believed that there existed probable cause to search his house; significantly, the other respondents advance no comparable argument. Officer Rombach's application for a warrant clearly was supported by much more than a "bare bones" affidavit. The affidavit related the results of an extensive investigation and, as the opinions of the divided panel of the Court of Appeals make clear, provided evidence sufficient to create disagreement among

---

[3061] *Compare O'Connor v. Donaldson, 422 U.S. 563, 95 S.Ct. 2486, 45 L.Ed.2d 396 (1975), with Procunier v. Navarette, 434 U.S. 555, 566, n. 14, 98 S.Ct. 855, 862, n. 14, 55 L.Ed.2d 24 (1978)*

[3062] *Compare Milton v. Wainwright, 407 U.S. 371, 372, 92 S.Ct. 2174, 2175, 33 L.Ed.2d 1 (1972), with Coleman v. Alabama, 399 U.S. 1, 90 S.Ct. 1999, 26 L.Ed.2d 387 (1970)*

thoughtful and competent judges as to the existence of probable cause. Under these circumstances, the officers' reliance on the magistrate's determination of probable cause was objectively reasonable, and application of the extreme sanction of exclusion is inappropriate.

Accordingly, the judgment of the Court of Appeals is

Reversed.

***927** Justice BLACKMUN, concurring.

The Court today holds that evidence obtained in violation of the Fourth Amendment by officers acting in objectively reasonable reliance on a search warrant issued by a neutral and detached magistrate need not be excluded, as a matter of federal law, ****3423** from the case in chief of federal and state criminal prosecutions. In so doing, the Court writes another chapter in the volume of Fourth Amendment law opened by Weeks v. United States.[3063] I join the Court's opinion in this case and the one in Massachusetts v. Sheppard,[3064] because I believe that the rule announced today advances the legitimate interests of the criminal justice system without sacrificing the individual rights protected by the Fourth Amendment. I write separately, however, to underscore what I regard as the unavoidably provisional nature of today's decisions.

As the Court's opinion in this case makes clear, the Court has narrowed the scope of the exclusionary rule because of an empirical judgment that the rule has little appreciable effect in cases where officers act in objectively reasonable reliance on search warrants.[3065] Because I share the view that the exclusionary rule is not a constitutionally compelled corollary of the Fourth Amendment itself,[3066] I see no way to avoid making an empirical judgment of this sort, and I am satisfied that the Court has made the correct one on the information before it. Like all courts, we face institutional limitations on our ability to gather information about "legislative facts," and the exclusionary rule itself has exacerbated the shortage of hard data concerning the behavior of police officers in the absence of such a rule.[3067] Nonetheless, we cannot escape the responsibility to decide the question before us, however imperfect our information may be, and I am prepared to join the Court on the information now at hand.

***928** What must be stressed, however, is that any empirical judgment about the effect of the exclusionary rule in a particular class of cases necessarily is a provisional one. By their very nature, the assumptions on which we proceed today cannot be cast in stone. To the contrary, they now will be tested in the real world of state and federal law enforcement, and this Court will attend to the results. If it should emerge from experience that, contrary to our expectations, the good-faith exception to the exclusionary rule results in a material change in police compliance with the Fourth Amendment, we shall have to reconsider what we have undertaken here. The logic of a decision that rests on untested predictions about police conduct demands no less.

If a single principle may be drawn from this Court's exclusionary rule decisions, from Weeks through Mapp v. Ohio,[3068] to the decisions handed down today, it is that the scope of the exclusionary rule is subject to change in light of changing judicial understanding about the effects of the rule outside the confines of the courtroom. It is

---

[3063] *232 U.S. 383, 34 S.Ct. 341, 58 L.Ed. 652 (1914)*

[3064] *468 U.S. 981, 104 S.Ct. 3424, 82 L.Ed.2d 737 (1984)*

[3065] *See ante, at 3419–3420*

[3066] *See ante, at 3412*

[3067] *See United States v. Janis, 428 U.S. 433, 448–453, 96 S.Ct. 3021, 3029–3031, 49 L.Ed.2d 1046 (1976)*

[3068] *367 U.S. 643, 81 S.Ct. 1684, 6 L.Ed.2d 1081 (1961)*

incumbent on the Nation's law enforcement officers, who must continue to observe the Fourth Amendment in the wake of today's decisions, to recognize the double-edged nature of that principle.

Black Letter Law

> The Court held that the Fourth Amendment exclusionary rule should not be applied so as to bar the use in the prosecution's case in chief of evidence obtained by officers acting in reasonable reliance on a search warrant issued by a detached and neutral magistrate, but ultimately found to be invalid. The Court should apply an objective reasonableness belief standard as to whether the warrant was properly issued, and must also determine if the officer's reliance on the magistrate's probable cause finding was objectively reasonable.

Davis v. United States

131 S.Ct. 2419

Supreme Court of the United States

Willie Gene DAVIS, Petitioner,

v.

UNITED STATES.

No. 09–11328. | Argued March 21, 2011. | Decided June 16, 2011.

Justice ALITO delivered the opinion of the Court.

The Fourth Amendment protects the right to be free from "unreasonable searches and seizures," but it is silent about how this right is to be enforced. To supplement the bare text, this Court created the exclusionary rule, a deterrent sanction that bars the prosecution from introducing evidence obtained by way of a Fourth Amendment violation. The question here is whether to apply this sanction when the police conduct a search in compliance with binding precedent that is later overruled. Because suppression would do nothing to deter police misconduct in these circumstances, and because it would come at a high cost to both the truth and the public safety, we hold that searches conducted in objectively reasonable reliance ***2424** on binding appellate precedent are not subject to the exclusionary rule.

I

The question presented arises in this case as a result of a shift in our Fourth Amendment jurisprudence on searches of automobiles incident to arrests of recent occupants.

A

Under this Court's decision in Chimel v. California,[3069] a police officer who makes a lawful arrest may conduct a warrantless search of the arrestee's person and the area "within his immediate control."[3070] This rule "may be stated clearly enough," but in the early going after Chimel it proved difficult to apply, particularly in cases that involved searches "inside [of] automobile[s] after the arrestees [we]re

[3069] *395 U.S. 752, 89 S.Ct. 2034, 23 L.Ed.2d 685 (1969)*

[3070] *Id., at 763, 89 S.Ct. 2034 (internal quotation marks omitted)*

no longer in [them]."[3071] A number of courts upheld the constitutionality of vehicle searches that were "substantially contemporaneous" with occupants' arrests. Other courts disapproved of automobile searches incident to arrests, at least absent some continuing threat that the arrestee might gain access to the vehicle and "destroy evidence or grab a weapon." In New York v. Belton, this Court granted certiorari to resolve the conflict.[3072]

In Belton, a police officer conducting a traffic stop lawfully arrested four occupants of a vehicle and ordered the arrestees to line up, un-handcuffed, along the side of the thruway.[3073] The officer then searched the vehicle's passenger compartment and found cocaine inside a jacket that lay on the backseat.[3074] This Court upheld the search as reasonable incident to the occupants' arrests. In an opinion that repeatedly stressed the need for a "straightforward," "workable rule" to guide police conduct, the Court announced "that when a policeman has made a lawful custodial arrest of the occupant of an automobile, he may, as a contemporaneous incident of that arrest, search the passenger compartment of that automobile."[3075]

For years, Belton was widely understood to have set down a simple, bright-line rule. Numerous courts read the decision to authorize automobile searches incident to arrests of recent occupants, regardless of whether the arrestee in any particular case was within reaching distance of the vehicle at the time of the search.[3076] Even after the arrestee had stepped out of the vehicle and had been subdued by police, the prevailing understanding was that Belton still authorized a substantially contemporaneous search of the automobile's passenger compartment.

***2425** Not every court, however, agreed with this reading of Belton. In State v. Gant,[3077] the Arizona Supreme Court considered an automobile search conducted after the vehicle's occupant had been arrested, handcuffed, and locked in a patrol car. The court distinguished Belton as a case in which "four unsecured" arrestees "presented an immediate risk of loss of evidence and an obvious threat to [a] lone officer's safety."[3078] The court held that where no such "exigencies exis[t]"—where the arrestee has been subdued and the scene secured—the rule of Belton does not apply.[3079]

This Court granted certiorari in Gant,[3080] and affirmed in a 5–to–4 decision.[3081] Four of the Justices in the majority agreed with the Arizona Supreme Court that Belton 's holding applies only where "the arrestee is unsecured and within reaching distance of the passenger compartment at the time of the search."[3082] The four dissenting Justices, by contrast, understood Belton to have explicitly adopted the simple,

---

[3071] *See New York v. Belton, 453 U.S. 454, 458–459, 101 S.Ct. 2860, 69 L.Ed.2d 768 (1981)*

[3072] *See id., at 459–460, 101 S.Ct. 2860*

[3073] *Id., at 456, 101 S.Ct. 2860; see Brief for Petitioner in New York v. Belton, O.T.1980, No. 80–328, p. 3*

[3074] *Belton, 453 U.S., at 456, 101 S.Ct. 2860*

[3075] *Id., at 459–460, 101 S.Ct. 2860 (footnote omitted)*

[3076] *See Thornton v. United States, 541 U.S. 615, 628, 124 S.Ct. 2127, 158 L.Ed.2d 905 (2004) (SCALIA, J., concurring in judgment) (collecting cases)*

[3077] *216 Ariz. 1, 162 P.3d 640 (2007)*

[3078] *216 Ariz., at 4, 162 P.3d, at 643*

[3079] *216 Ariz., at 4, 162 P.3d, at 643*

[3080] *See 552 U.S. 1230, 128 S.Ct. 1443, 170 L.Ed.2d 274 (2008)*

[3081] *Arizona v. Gant, 556 U.S. 332, 129 S.Ct. 1710, 173 L.Ed.2d 485 (2009)*

[3082] *556 U.S. 129 S.Ct., at 1719*

bright-line rule stated in the Belton Court's opinion.[3083] To limit Belton to cases involving unsecured arrestees, the dissenters thought, was to overrule the decision's clear holding. Gant,[3084] who provided the fifth vote to affirm in Gant, agreed with the dissenters' understanding of Belton 's holding.[3085] Justice SCALIA favored a more explicit and complete overruling of Belton, but he joined what became the majority opinion to avoid "a 4–to–1–to–4" disposition.[3086] As a result, the Court adopted a new, two-part rule under which an automobile search incident to a recent occupant's arrest is constitutional (1) if the arrestee is within reaching distance of the vehicle during the search, or (2) if the police have reason to believe that the vehicle contains "evidence relevant to the crime of arrest."[3087]

B

The search at issue in this case took place a full two years before this Court announced its new rule in Gant. On an April evening in 2007, police officers in Greenville, Alabama, conducted a routine traffic stop that eventually resulted in the arrests of driver Stella Owens (for driving while intoxicated) and passenger Willie Davis (for giving a false name to police). The police handcuffed both Owens and Davis, and they placed the arrestees in the back of separate patrol cars. The police then searched the passenger compartment of Owens's vehicle and found a revolver inside Davis's jacket pocket.

Davis was indicted in the Middle District of Alabama on one count of possession ***2426** of a firearm by a convicted felon.[3088] In his motion to suppress the revolver, Davis acknowledged that the officers' search fully complied with "existing Eleventh Circuit precedent."[3089] Like most courts, the Eleventh Circuit had long read Belton to establish a bright-line rule authorizing substantially contemporaneous vehicle searches incident to arrests of recent occupants.[3090] Davis recognized that the District Court was obligated to follow this precedent, but he raised a Fourth Amendment challenge to preserve "the issue for review" on appeal.[3091] The District Court denied the motion, and Davis was convicted on the firearms charge.

While Davis's appeal was pending, this Court decided Gant. The Eleventh Circuit, in the opinion below, applied Gant 's new rule and held that the vehicle search incident to Davis's arrest "violated [his] Fourth Amendment rights."[3092] As for whether this constitutional violation warranted suppression, the Eleventh Circuit viewed that as a separate issue that turned on "the potential of exclusion to deter wrongful police conduct."[3093] The court concluded that "penalizing the [arresting] officer" for following binding appellate precedent would do nothing to "dete[r] ...

[3083] *556 U.S. 129 S.Ct., at 1727 (opinion of ALITO, J.); see Belton, 453 U.S., at 460, 101 S.Ct. 2860 ("[W]e hold that when a policeman has made a lawful custodial arrest of the occupant of an automobile, he may, as a contemporaneous incident of that arrest, search the passenger compartment of that automobile" (footnote omitted))*

[3084] *Supra, 129 S.Ct., at 1714–1715. Justice SCALIA*

[3085] *556 U.S. 129 S.Ct., at 1724–1725 (concurring opinion)*

[3086] *556 U.S. 129 S.Ct., at 1714–1716*

[3087] *Id., 129 S.Ct., at 1719 (citing Thornton, supra, at 632, 124 S.Ct. 2127 (SCALIA, J., concurring in judgment); internal quotation marks omitted)*

[3088] *See 18 U.S.C. § 922(g)(1)*

[3089] *App. 13–15*

[3090] *See United States v. Gonzalez, 71 F.3d 819, 822, 824–827 (C.A.11 1996) (upholding automobile search conducted after the defendant had been "pulled from the vehicle, handcuffed, laid on the ground, and placed under arrest")*

[3091] *App. 15*

[3092] *598 F.3d 1259, 1263 (CA11 2010)*

[3093] *Id., at 1265 (quoting Herring v. United States, 555 U.S. 135, 137, 129 S.Ct. 695, 172 L.Ed.2d 496 (2009); internal quotation marks omitted)*

Fourth Amendment violations."[3094] It therefore declined to apply the exclusionary rule and affirmed Davis's conviction. We granted certiorari.[3095]

II

The Fourth Amendment protects the "right of the people to be secure in their persons, houses, papers, and effects, against unreasonable searches and seizures." The Amendment says nothing about suppressing evidence obtained in violation of this command. That rule—the exclusionary rule—is a "prudential" doctrine,[3096] created by this Court to "compel respect for the constitutional guaranty."[3097] Exclusion is "not a personal constitutional right," nor is it designed to "redress the injury" occasioned by an unconstitutional search.[3098] The rule's sole purpose, we have repeatedly held, is to deter future Fourth Amendment violations.[3099] Our cases have thus limited the rule's operation to situations in which this purpose is "thought most efficaciously served."[3100] Where suppression fails to yield "appreciable deterrence," exclusion is "clearly ... ***2427** unwarranted."[3101]

Real deterrent value is a "necessary condition for exclusion," but it is not "a sufficient" one.[3102] The analysis must also account for the "substantial social costs" generated by the rule.[3103] Exclusion exacts a heavy toll on both the judicial system and society at large.[3104] It almost always requires courts to ignore reliable, trustworthy evidence bearing on guilt or innocence.[3105] And its bottom-line effect, in many cases, is to suppress the truth and set the criminal loose in the community without punishment.[3106] Our cases hold that society must swallow this bitter pill when necessary, but only as a "last resort."[3107] For exclusion to be appropriate, the deterrence benefits of suppression must outweigh its heavy costs.[3108]

Admittedly, there was a time when our exclusionary-rule cases were not nearly so discriminating in their approach to the doctrine. "Expansive dicta" in several decisions,[3109] suggested that the rule was a self-executing mandate implicit in the Fourth

---

[3094] *598 F.3d, at 1265–1266 (bracketing and internal quotation marks omitted)*

[3095] *562 U.S. 131 S.Ct. 502, 178 L.Ed.2d 368 (2010)*

[3096] *Pennsylvania Bd. of Probation and Parole v. Scott, 524 U.S. 357, 363, 118 S.Ct. 2014, 141 L.Ed.2d 344 (1998)*

[3097] *Elkins v. United States, 364 U.S. 206, 217, 80 S.Ct. 1437, 4 L.Ed.2d 1669 (1960); see Weeks v. United States, 232 U.S. 383, 34 S.Ct. 341, 58 L.Ed. 652 (1914); Mapp v. Ohio, 367 U.S. 643, 81 S.Ct. 1684, 6 L.Ed.2d 1081 (1961)*

[3098] *Stone v. Powell, 428 U.S. 465, 486, 96 S.Ct. 3037, 49 L.Ed.2d 1067 (1976); see United States v. Janis, 428 U.S. 433, 454, n. 29, 96 S.Ct. 3021, 49 L.Ed.2d 1046 (1976) (exclusionary rule "unsupportable as reparation or compensatory dispensation to the injured criminal" (internal quotation marks omitted))*

[3099] *E.g., Herring, supra, at 141, and n. 2, 129 S.Ct. 695; United States v. Leon, 468 U.S. 897, 909, 921, n. 22, 104 S.Ct. 3405, 82 L.Ed.2d 677 (1984); Elkins, supra, at 217, 80 S.Ct. 1437 ("calculated to prevent, not to repair")*

[3100] *United States v. Calandra, 414 U.S. 338, 348, 94 S.Ct. 613, 38 L.Ed.2d 561 (1974)*

[3101] *Janis, supra, at 454, 96 S.Ct. 3021*

[3102] *Hudson v. Michigan, 547 U.S. 586, 596, 126 S.Ct. 2159, 165 L.Ed.2d 56 (2006)*

[3103] *Leon, supra, at 907, 104 S.Ct. 3405*

[3104] *Stone, 428 U.S., at 490–491, 96 S.Ct. 3037*

[3105] *Ibid.*

[3106] *See Herring, supra, at 141, 129 S.Ct. 695*

[3107] *Hudson, supra, at 591, 126 S.Ct. 2159*

[3108] *See Herring, supra, at 141, 129 S.Ct. 695; Leon, supra, at 910, 104 S.Ct. 3405*

[3109] *See Hudson, supra, at 591, 126 S.Ct. 2159*

Amendment itself.[3110] As late as our 1971 decision in Whiteley v. Warden, Wyo. State Penitentiary,[3111] the Court "treated identification of a Fourth Amendment violation as synonymous with application of the exclusionary rule."[3112] In time, however, we came to acknowledge the exclusionary rule for what it undoubtedly is—a "judicially created remedy" of this Court's own making.[3113] We abandoned the old, "reflexive" application of the doctrine, and imposed a more rigorous weighing of its costs and deterrence benefits.[3114] In a line of cases beginning with United States v. Leon,[3115] we also recalibrated our cost-benefit analysis in exclusion cases to focus the inquiry on the "flagrancy of the police misconduct" at issue.[3116]

The basic insight of the Leon line of cases is that the deterrence benefits of exclusion "var[y] with the culpability of the law enforcement conduct" at issue.[3117] When the police exhibit "deliberate," "reckless," or "grossly negligent" disregard for Fourth Amendment rights, the deterrent value of exclusion is strong and tends to outweigh the resulting costs.[3118] But when the police act with an objectively "reasonable good-faith belief" that their conduct is lawful,[3119] or when their conduct involves only simple, "isolated" ***2428** negligence,[3120] the "'deterrence rationale loses much of its force,'" and exclusion cannot "pay its way."[3121]

The Court has over time applied this "good-faith" exception across a range of cases. Leon itself, for example, held that the exclusionary rule does not apply when the police conduct a search in "objectively reasonable reliance" on a warrant later held invalid.[3122] The error in such a case rests with the issuing magistrate, not the police officer, and "punish[ing] the errors of judges" is not the office of the exclusionary rule.[3123]

Other good-faith cases have sounded a similar theme. Illinois v. Krull[3124] extended the good-faith exception to searches conducted in reasonable reliance on subsequently invalidated statutes.[3125] In Arizona v. Evans,[3126] the Court applied the good-faith exception in a case where the police reasonably relied on erroneous in-

---

[3110] *See Olmstead v. United States, 277 U.S. 438, 462, 48 S.Ct. 564, 72 L.Ed. 944 (1928) (remarking on the "striking outcome of the Weeks case" that "the Fourth Amendment, although not referring to or limiting the use of evidence in courts, really forbade its introduction"); Mapp, supra, at 655, 81 S.Ct. 1684 ("[A]ll evidence obtained by searches and seizures in violation of the Constitution is, by that same authority, inadmissible in a state court")*

[3111] *401 U.S. 560, 568–569, 91 S.Ct. 1031, 28 L.Ed.2d 306*

[3112] *Arizona v. Evans, 514 U.S. 1, 13, 115 S.Ct. 1185, 131 L.Ed.2d 34 (1995)*

[3113] *Calandra, supra, at 348, 94 S.Ct. 613*

[3114] *Evans, supra, at 13, 115 S.Ct. 1185; see, e.g., Calandra, supra; Janis, supra; Stone, supra; INS v. Lopez-Mendoza, 468 U.S. 1032, 104 S.Ct. 3479, 82 L.Ed.2d 778 (1984); United States v. Havens, 446 U.S. 620, 100 S.Ct. 1912, 64 L.Ed.2d 559 (1980)*

[3115] *468 U.S. 897, 104 S.Ct. 3405, 82 L.Ed.2d 677*

[3116] *Id., at 909, 911, 104 S.Ct. 3405*

[3117] *Herring, 555 U.S., at 143, 129 S.Ct. 695*

[3118] *Id., at 144, 129 S.Ct. 695*

[3119] *Leon, supra, at 909, 104 S.Ct. 3405 (internal quotation marks omitted)*

[3120] *Herring, supra, at 137, 129 S.Ct. 695*

[3121] *See Leon, supra, at 919, 908, n. 6, 104 S.Ct. 3405 (quoting United States v. Peltier, 422 U.S. 531, 539, 95 S.Ct. 2313, 45 L.Ed.2d 374 (1975))*

[3122] *468 U.S., at 922, 104 S.Ct. 3405*

[3123] *Id., at 916, 104 S.Ct. 3405; see also Massachusetts v. Sheppard, 468 U.S. 981, 990, 104 S.Ct. 3424, 82 L.Ed.2d 737 (1984) (companion case declining to apply exclusionary rule where warrant held invalid as a result of judge's clerical error)*

[3124] *480 U.S. 340, 107 S.Ct. 1160, 94 L.Ed.2d 364 (1987)*

[3125] *Id., at 349–350, 107 S.Ct. 1160 ("legislators, like judicial officers, are not the focus of the rule")*

[3126] *Supra*

formation concerning an arrest warrant in a database maintained by judicial employees.[3127] Most recently, in Herring v. United States,[3128] we extended Evans in a case where police employees erred in maintaining records in a warrant database. "[I]solated," "nonrecurring" police negligence, we determined, lacks the culpability required to justify the harsh sanction of exclusion.[3129]

III

The question in this case is whether to apply the exclusionary rule when the police conduct a search in objectively reasonable reliance on binding judicial precedent. At the time of the search at issue here, we had not yet decided Arizona v. Gant,[3130] and the Eleventh Circuit had interpreted our decision in New York v. Belton,[3131] to establish a bright-line rule authorizing the search of a vehicle's passenger compartment incident to a recent occupant's arrest.[3132] The search incident to Davis's arrest in this case followed the Eleventh Circuit's Gonzalez precedent to the letter. Although the search turned out to be unconstitutional under Gant, all agree that the officers' conduct was in strict compliance with then-binding Circuit law and was not culpable in any way.[3133]

Under our exclusionary-rule precedents, this acknowledged absence of police culpability dooms Davis's claim. Police practices trigger the harsh sanction of exclusion only when they are deliberate enough to yield "meaningfu[l]" deterrence, and culpable enough to be "worth the price paid by the justice system."[3134] The conduct of the officers here was neither of these things. The officers who conducted the search did not violate Davis's Fourth Amendment rights deliberately, recklessly, or with gross negligence.[3135] Nor does this case involve any "recurring or systemic negligence" on the part of law enforcement.[3136] The police acted in strict compliance with binding precedent, ***2429** and their behavior was not wrongful. Unless the exclusionary rule is to become a strict-liability regime, it can have no application in this case.

Indeed, in 27 years of practice under Leon 's good-faith exception, we have "never applied" the exclusionary rule to suppress evidence obtained as a result of non-culpable, innocent police conduct.[3137] If the police in this case had reasonably relied on a warrant in conducting their search,[3138] or on an erroneous warrant record in a government database,[3139] the exclusionary rule would not apply. And if Congress or the Alabama Legislature had enacted a statute codifying the precise holding of the Eleventh Circuit's decision in Gonzalez, we would swiftly conclude that "'[p]enalizing the officer for the legislature's error ... cannot logically contribute to the deter-

---

[3127] *Id., at 14, 115 S.Ct. 1185*

[3128] *555 U.S. 135, 129 S.Ct. 695, 172 L.Ed.2d 496*

[3129] *555 U.S., at 137, 144, 129 S.Ct. 695*

[3130] *556 U.S. 332, 129 S.Ct. 1710, 173 L.Ed.2d 485*

[3131] *453 U.S. 454, 101 S.Ct. 2860, 69 L.Ed.2d 768*

[3132] *Gonzalez, 71 F.3d, at 825*

[3133] *See Brief for Petitioner 49 ("suppression" in this case would "impl[y] no assignment of blame")*

[3134] *Herring, 555 U.S., at 144, 129 S.Ct. 695*

[3135] *See ibid*

[3136] *Ibid*

[3137] *Herring, supra, at 144, 129 S.Ct. 695*

[3138] *See Leon, supra*

[3139] *Herring, supra*

rence of Fourth Amendment violations.'"[3140] The same should be true of Davis's attempt here to "'[p]enaliz[e] the officer for the [appellate judges'] error.'"[3141]

About all that exclusion would deter in this case is conscientious police work. Responsible law-enforcement officers will take care to learn "what is required of them" under Fourth Amendment precedent and will conform their conduct to these rules.[3142] But by the same token, when binding appellate precedent specifically authorizes a particular police practice, well-trained officers will and should use that tool to fulfill their crime-detection and public-safety responsibilities. An officer who conducts a search in reliance on binding appellate precedent does no more than "'ac[t] as a reasonable officer would and should act'" under the circumstances.[3143] The deterrent effect of exclusion in such a case can only be to discourage the officer from "'do[ing] his duty.'"[3144]

That is not the kind of deterrence the exclusionary rule seeks to foster. We have stated before, and we reaffirm today, that the harsh sanction of exclusion "should not be applied to deter objectively reasonable law enforcement activity."[3145] Evidence obtained during a search conducted in reasonable reliance on binding precedent is not subject to the exclusionary rule.

IV

Justice BREYER's dissent and Davis argue that, although the police conduct in this case was in no way culpable, other considerations should prevent the good-faith exception from applying. We are not persuaded.

A

1

The principal argument of both the dissent and Davis is that the exclusionary ***2430** rule's availability to enforce new Fourth Amendment precedent is a retroactivity issue,[3146] not a good-faith issue. They contend that applying the good-faith exception where police have relied on overruled precedent effectively revives the discarded retroactivity regime of Linkletter v. Walker.[3147]

In Linkletter, we held that the retroactive effect of a new constitutional rule of criminal procedure should be determined on a case-by-case weighing of interests. For each new rule, Linkletter required courts to consider a three-factor balancing test that looked to the "purpose" of the new rule, "reliance" on the old rule by law enforcement and others, and the effect retroactivity would have "on the administration of justice."[3148] After "weigh[ing] the merits and demerits in each case," courts decided whether and to what extent a new rule should be given retroactive effect.[3149] In Linkletter itself, the balance of interests prompted this Court to conclude that Mapp

---

[3140] *See Krull, 480 U.S., at 350, 107 S.Ct. 1160*

[3141] *See ibid*

[3142] *Hudson, 547 U.S., at 599, 126 S.Ct. 2159*

[3143] *Leon, 468 U.S., at 920, 104 S.Ct. 3405 (quoting Stone, 428 U.S., at 539–540, 96 S.Ct. 3037 (White, J., dissenting))*

[3144] *468 U.S., at 920, 104 S.Ct. 3405*

[3145] *Id., at 919, 104 S.Ct. 3405*

[3146] *See Griffith v. Kentucky, 479 U.S. 314, 107 S.Ct. 708, 93 L.Ed.2d 649 (1987)*

[3147] *381 U.S. 618, 85 S.Ct. 1731, 14 L.Ed.2d 601 (1965). See post, at 2436 – 2438*

[3148] *381 U.S., at 636, 85 S.Ct. 1731*

[3149] *Id., at 629, 85 S.Ct. 1731*

v. Ohio[3150]—which incorporated the exclusionary rule against the States—should not apply retroactively to cases already final on direct review.[3151] The next year, we extended Linkletter to retroactivity determinations in cases on direct review.[3152]

Over time, Linkletter proved difficult to apply in a consistent, coherent way. Individual applications of the standard "produced strikingly divergent results,"[3153] that many saw as "incompatible" and "inconsistent."[3154] Justice Harlan in particular, who had endorsed the Linkletter standard early on, offered a strong critique in which he argued that "basic judicial" norms required full retroactive application of new rules to all cases still subject to direct review.[3155] Eventually, and after more than 20 years of toil under Linkletter, the Court adopted Justice Harlan's view and held that newly announced rules of constitutional criminal procedure must apply "retroactively to all cases, state or federal, pending on direct review or not yet final, with no exception."[3156]

2

The dissent and Davis argue that applying the good-faith exception in this case is "incompatible" with our retroactivity precedent under Griffith.[3157] We think this argument conflates what are two distinct doctrines.

Our retroactivity jurisprudence is concerned with whether, as a categorical matter, a new rule is available on direct review as a potential ground for relief. Retroactive application under Griffith lifts what would otherwise be a categorical bar to obtaining redress for the government's violation of a newly announced ***2431** constitutional rule.[3158] Retroactive application does not, however, determine what "appropriate remedy" (if any) the defendant should obtain.[3159] Remedy is a separate, analytically distinct issue.[3160] As a result, the retroactive application of a new rule of substantive Fourth Amendment law raises the question whether a suppression remedy applies; it does not answer that question.[3161]

When this Court announced its decision in Gant, Davis's conviction had not yet become final on direct review. Gant therefore applies retroactively to this case. Davis may invoke its newly announced rule of substantive Fourth Amendment law as a basis for seeking relief.[3162] The question, then, becomes one of remedy, and on that issue Davis seeks application of the exclusionary rule. But exclusion of evidence

---

[3150] *367 U.S. 643, 81 S.Ct. 1684, 6 L.Ed.2d 1081*

[3151] *381 U.S., at 639–640, 85 S.Ct. 1731*

[3152] *See Johnson v. New Jersey, 384 U.S. 719, 733, 86 S.Ct. 1772, 16 L.Ed.2d 882 (1966) (holding that Miranda v. Arizona, 384 U.S. 436, 86 S.Ct. 1602, 16 L.Ed.2d 694 (1966), and Escobedo v. Illinois, 378 U.S. 478, 84 S.Ct. 1758, 12 L.Ed.2d 977 (1964), applied retroactively only to trials commenced after the decisions were released)*

[3153] *See Danforth v. Minnesota, 552 U.S. 264, 273, 128 S.Ct. 1029, 169 L.Ed.2d 859 (2008)*

[3154] *Desist v. United States, 394 U.S. 244, 258, 89 S.Ct. 1030, 22 L.Ed.2d 248 (1969) (Harlan, J., dissenting)*

[3155] *394 U.S., at 258–259, 89 S.Ct. 1030; see also Mackey v. United States, 401 U.S. 667, 675–702, 91 S.Ct. 1160, 28 L.Ed.2d 404 (1971) (Harlan, J., concurring in part and dissenting in part)*

[3156] *Griffith, supra, at 328, 107 S.Ct. 708*

[3157] *See post, at 2436 – 2437; Reply Brief for Petitioner 3–7*

[3158] *See Danforth, supra, at 271, n. 5, 128 S.Ct. 1029 (noting that it may "make more sense to speak in terms of the 'redressability' of violations of new rules, rather than the 'retroactivity' of such new rules")*

[3159] *See Powell v. Nevada, 511 U.S. 79, 84, 114 S.Ct. 1280, 128 L.Ed.2d 1 (1994) (noting that it "does not necessarily follow" from retroactive application of a new rule that the defendant will "gain ... relief")*

[3160] *Cf. American Trucking Assns., Inc. v. Smith, 496 U.S. 167, 189, 110 S.Ct. 2323, 110 L.Ed.2d 148 (1990) (plurality opinion) ("[T]he Court has never equated its retroactivity principles with remedial principles")*

[3161] *See Leon, 468 U.S., at 906, 104 S.Ct. 3405 ("Whether the exclusionary sanction is appropriately imposed in a particular case ... is 'an issue separate from the question whether the Fourth Amendment rights of the party seeking to invoke the rule were violated by police conduct'")*

[3162] *See Griffith, supra, at 326, 328, 107 S.Ct. 708*

does not automatically follow from the fact that a Fourth Amendment violation occurred.[3163] The remedy is subject to exceptions and applies only where its "purpose is effectively advanced."[3164]

The dissent and Davis recognize that at least some of the established exceptions to the exclusionary rule limit its availability in cases involving new Fourth Amendment rules. Suppression would thus be inappropriate, the dissent and Davis acknowledge, if the inevitable-discovery exception were applicable in this case.[3165] The good-faith exception, however, is no less an established limit on the remedy of exclusion than is inevitable discovery. Its application here neither contravenes Griffith nor denies retroactive effect to Gant.

It is true that, under the old retroactivity regime of Linkletter, the Court's decisions on the "retroactivity problem in the ***2432** context of the exclusionary rule" did take into account whether "law enforcement officers reasonably believed in good faith" that their conduct was in compliance with governing law.[3166] As a matter of retroactivity analysis, that approach is no longer applicable.[3167] It does not follow, however, that reliance on binding precedent is irrelevant in applying the good-faith exception to the exclusionary rule. When this Court adopted the good-faith exception in Leon, the Court's opinion explicitly relied on Peltier and imported its reasoning into the good-faith inquiry.[3168] That reasonable reliance by police was once a factor in our retroactivity cases does not make it any less relevant under our Leon line of cases.

B

Davis also contends that applying the good-faith exception to searches conducted in reliance on binding precedent will stunt the development of Fourth Amendment law. With no possibility of suppression, criminal defendants will have no incentive, Davis maintains, to request that courts overrule precedent.

1

This argument is difficult to reconcile with our modern understanding of the role of the exclusionary rule. We have never held that facilitating the overruling of precedent is a relevant consideration in an exclusionary-rule case. Rather, we have said time and again that the sole purpose of the exclusionary rule is to deter misconduct by law enforcement.[3169]

We have also repeatedly rejected efforts to expand the focus of the exclusionary rule beyond deterrence of culpable police conduct. In Leon, for example, we made clear that "the exclusionary rule is designed to deter police misconduct rather than to punish the errors of judges."[3170] Krull too noted that "legislators, like judicial officers, are not the focus" of the exclusionary rule.[3171] And in Evans, we said that the

---

[3163] *See Evans, 514 U.S., at 13–14, 115 S.Ct. 1185*

[3164] *Krull, 480 U.S., at 347, 107 S.Ct. 1160*

[3165] *See post, at 2437; Reply Brief for Petitioner 22 ("Doctrines such as inevitable discovery, independent source, attenuated basis, [and] standing ... sharply limit the impact of newly-announced rules")*

[3166] *Peltier, 422 U.S., at 535–537, 95 S.Ct. 2313*

[3167] *See Griffith, 479 U.S. 314, 107 S.Ct. 708, 93 L.Ed.2d 649*

[3168] *See 468 U.S., at 918–919, 104 S.Ct. 3405*

[3169] *See, e.g., Sheppard, 468 U.S., at 990, 104 S.Ct. 3424 (" 'adopted to deter unlawful searches by police' "); Evans, supra, at 14, 115 S.Ct. 1185 ("historically designed as a means of deterring police misconduct")*

[3170] *468 U.S., at 916, 104 S.Ct. 3405; see id., at 918, 104 S.Ct. 3405 ("If exclusion of evidence obtained pursuant to a subsequently invalidated warrant is to have any deterrent effect ... it must alter the behavior of individual law enforcement officers or the policies of their departments")*

[3171] *480 U.S., at 350, 107 S.Ct. 1160*

exclusionary rule was aimed at deterring "police misconduct, not mistakes by court employees."[3172] These cases do not suggest that the exclusionary rule should be modified to serve a ***2433** purpose other than deterrence of culpable law-enforcement conduct.

2

And in any event, applying the good-faith exception in this context will not prevent judicial reconsideration of prior Fourth Amendment precedents. In most instances, as in this case, the precedent sought to be challenged will be a decision of a Federal Court of Appeals or State Supreme Court. But a good-faith exception for objectively reasonable reliance on binding precedent will not prevent review and correction of such decisions. This Court reviews criminal convictions from 12 Federal Courts of Appeals, 50 state courts of last resort, and the District of Columbia Court of Appeals. If one or even many of these courts uphold a particular type of search or seizure, defendants in jurisdictions in which the question remains open will still have an undiminished incentive to litigate the issue. This Court can then grant certiorari, and the development of Fourth Amendment law will in no way be stunted.

Davis argues that Fourth Amendment precedents of this Court will be effectively insulated from challenge under a good-faith exception for reliance on appellate precedent. But this argument is overblown. For one thing, it is important to keep in mind that this argument applies to an exceedingly small set of cases. Decisions overruling this Court's Fourth Amendment precedents are rare. Indeed, it has been more than 40 years since the Court last handed down a decision of the type to which Davis refers.[3173] And even in those cases, Davis points out that no fewer than eight separate doctrines may preclude a defendant who successfully challenges an existing precedent from getting any relief.[3174] Moreover, as a practical matter, defense counsel in many cases will test this Court's Fourth Amendment precedents in the same way that Belton was tested in Gant—by arguing that the precedent is distinguishable.[3175]

At most, Davis's argument might suggest that—to prevent Fourth Amendment law from becoming ossified—the petitioner in a case that results in the overruling of one of this Court's Fourth Amendment precedents should be given the benefit of the victory by permitting the suppression of evidence in that one case. Such a result would undoubtedly be a windfall to this one random litigant. But the exclusionary rule is "not a personal constitutional right."[3176] It is a "judicially created" sanction,[3177] ***2434** specifically designed as a "windfall" remedy to deter future Fourth Amendment violations.[3178] The good-faith exception is a judicially created exception to this judicially created rule. Therefore, in a future case, we could, if necessary, recognize a limited exception to the good-faith exception for a defendant who obtains a judgment over-ruling one of our Fourth Amendment precedents.[3179]

But this is not such a case. Davis did not secure a decision overturning a Supreme Court precedent; the police in his case reasonably relied on binding Circuit

[3172] *514 U.S., at 14, 115 S.Ct. 1185*

[3173] *Chimel v. California, 395 U.S. 752, 89 S.Ct. 2034, 23 L.Ed.2d 685 (overruling United States v. Rabinowitz, 339 U.S. 56, 70 S.Ct. 430, 94 L.Ed. 653 (1950), and Harris v. United States, 331 U.S. 145, 67 S.Ct. 1098, 91 L.Ed. 1399 (1947))*

[3174] *Brief for Petitioner 50*

[3175] *See Brief for Respondent in Arizona v. Gant, O.T.2008, No. 07–542, pp. 22–29*

[3176] *Stone, 428 U.S., at 486, 96 S.Ct. 3037*

[3177] *Calandra, 414 U.S., at 348, 94 S.Ct. 613*

[3178] *See Stone, supra, at 490, 96 S.Ct. 3037*

[3179] *Cf. Friendly, The Bill of Rights as a Code of Criminal Procedure, 53 Cal. L.Rev. 929, 952–953 (1965) ("[T]he same authority that empowered the Court to supplement the amendment by the exclusionary rule a hundred and twenty-five years after its adoption, likewise allows it to modify that rule as the lessons of experience may teach" (internal quotation marks and footnotes omitted))*

precedent.[3180] That sort of blameless police conduct, we hold, comes within the good-faith exception and is not properly subject to the exclusionary rule.

* * *

It is one thing for the criminal "to go free because the constable has blundered."[3181] It is quite another to set the criminal free because the constable has scrupulously adhered to governing law. Excluding evidence in such cases deters no police misconduct and imposes substantial social costs. We therefore hold that when the police conduct a search in objectively reasonable reliance on binding appellate precedent, the exclusionary rule does not apply. The judgment of the Court of Appeals for the Eleventh Circuit is

Affirmed.

Justice SOTOMAYOR, concurring in the judgment.

Under our precedents, the primary purpose of the exclusionary rule is "to deter future Fourth Amendment violations."[3182] Accordingly, we have held, application of the exclusionary rule is unwarranted when it "'does not result in appreciable deterrence.'"[3183] ***2435** In the circumstances of this case, where "binding appellate precedent specifically authorize[d] a particular police practice,"[3184] in accord with the holdings of nearly every other court in the country—application of the exclusionary rule cannot reasonably be expected to yield appreciable deterrence. I am thus compelled to conclude that the exclusionary rule does not apply in this case and to agree with the Court's disposition.

This case does not present the markedly different question whether the exclusionary rule applies when the law governing the constitutionality of a particular search is unsettled. As we previously recognized in deciding whether to apply a Fourth Amendment holding retroactively, when police decide to conduct a search or seizure in the absence of case law (or other authority) specifically sanctioning such action, exclusion of the evidence obtained may deter Fourth Amendment violations:

> If, as the Government argues, all rulings resolving unsettled Fourth Amendment questions should be nonretroactive, then, in close cases, law enforcement officials would have little incentive to err on the side of constitutional behavior. Official awareness of the dubious constitutionality of a practice would be counterbalanced by official certainty that, so long as the Fourth Amendment law in the area remained unsettled, evidence obtained through the questionable practice would be excluded only in the one case definitively resolving the unsettled question.[3185]

The Court of Appeals recognized as much in limiting its application of the good-faith exception it articulated in this case to situations where its "precedent on a given

---

[3180] *See United States v. Gonzalez, 71 F.3d 819*

[3181] *People v. Defore, 242 N.Y. 13, 21, 150 N.E. 585, 587 (1926) (Cardozo, J.)*

[3182] *Ante, at 2426; see, e.g., Herring v. United States, 555 U.S. 135, 141, 129 S.Ct. 695, 172 L.Ed.2d 496 (2009); Illinois v. Krull, 480 U.S. 340, 347–348, 107 S.Ct. 1160, 94 L.Ed.2d 364 (1987)*

[3183] *Arizona v. Evans, 514 U.S. 1, 11, 115 S.Ct. 1185, 131 L.Ed.2d 34 (1995) (quoting United States v. Janis, 428 U.S. 433, 454, 96 S.Ct. 3021, 49 L.Ed.2d 1046 (1976))*

[3184] *Ante, at 2429*

[3185] *United States v. Johnson, 457 U.S. 537, 561, 102 S.Ct. 2579, 73 L.Ed.2d 202 (1982) (footnote omitted)*

point [is] unequivocal."[3186] Whether exclusion would deter Fourth Amendment violations where appellate precedent does not specifically authorize a certain practice and, if so, whether the benefits of exclusion would outweigh its costs are questions unanswered by our previous decisions.

The dissent suggests that today's decision essentially answers those questions, noting that an officer who conducts a search in the face of unsettled precedent "is no more culpable than an officer who follows erroneous 'binding precedent.'"[3187] The Court does not address this issue. In my view, whether an officer's conduct can be characterized as "culpable" is not itself dispositive. We have never refused to apply the exclusionary rule where its application would appreciably deter Fourth Amendment violations on the mere ground that the officer's conduct could be characterized as non-culpable. Rather, an officer's culpability is relevant because it may inform the overarching inquiry whether exclusion would result in appreciable deterrence.[3188] ***2436** Whatever we have said about culpability, the ultimate questions have always been, one, whether exclusion would result in appreciable deterrence and, two, whether the benefits of exclusion outweigh its costs.[3189]

As stated, whether exclusion would result in appreciable deterrence in the circumstances of this case is a different question from whether exclusion would appreciably deter Fourth Amendment violations when the governing law is unsettled. The Court's answer to the former question in this case thus does not resolve the latter one.

(The dissent of Justice BREYER, with whom Justice GINSBURG joins, is omitted.)

Black Letter Law

Held that when the police conduct a search based upon objectively reasonable reliance on binding appellate precedent, the exclusionary rule does not apply. While this case was initially decided under the *Belton* rule, *Gant* occurred after the defendant's conviction. The Court held that the exclusionary rule does not apply retroactively.

Discussion Problems:

18-1. On April 18, Officer Aaron Martingano of the Calusa City Police Department was patrolling his precinct when he observed a vehicle traveling eastbound on a four-lane thoroughfare. The vehicle was straddling the center line of the two eastbound lanes. After following the vehicle for approximately three blocks, Officer Martingano decided to conduct a traffic stop based upon his belief that the driver was violating state traffic law and his suspicion that the driver was intoxicated. After pulling the vehicle over to the side of the road, Officer Martingano approached the vehicle and asked the driver, later identified as McCloud, for his license and insurance information. A passenger, Joseph Rogers, was also in the vehicle.

[3186] *598 F.3d 1259, 1266 (CA11 2010); see id., at 1266–1267 ("[W]e do not mean to encourage police to adopt a ' "let's-wait-until-it's-decided approach" 'to 'unsettled' questions of Fourth Amendment law" (quoting Johnson, 457 U.S., at 561, 102 S.Ct. 2579))*

[3187] *Post, at 2439 (opinion of BREYER, J.)*

[3188] *See ante, at 2427 ("The basic insight of the Leon line of cases is that the deterrence benefits of exclusion var[y] with the culpability of the law enforcement conduct at issue" (internal quotation marks omitted; alteration in original)); see also, e.g., Herring, 555 U.S., at 143, 129 S.Ct. 695 ("The extent to which the exclusionary rule is justified by these deterrence principles varies with the culpability of the law enforcement conduct"); United States v. Leon, 468 U.S. 897, 919, 104 S.Ct. 3405, 82 L.Ed. 2d 677 (1984) ("'Where the official action was pursued in complete good faith, ... the deterrence rationale loses much of its force'" (quoting Michigan v. Tucker, 417 U.S. 433, 447, 94 S.Ct. 2357, 41 L.Ed.2d 182 (1974))).*

[3189] *See, e.g., ante, at 2426 – 2427; Herring, 555 U.S., at 141, 129 S.Ct. 695; Krull, 480 U.S., at 347, 107 S.Ct. 1160*

After McCloud informed him that his license was suspended, Officer Martingano asked McCloud to exit the vehicle and accompany him to the patrol car. McCloud complied and Rogers remained in the front seat of the vehicle. Upon exiting the vehicle, McCloud left the driver's door open, and the door remained open for the duration of the stop. Officer Martingano conducted a pat-down search of McCloud and placed him in the back seat of the patrol car. Officer Martingano then conducted a records check, which indicated McCloud's license was suspended and the vehicle was not registered to McCloud. At that time, Officer Martingano arrested McCloud for driving with a suspended license, placed him in handcuffs, and again placed him in the back seat of the patrol car. After requesting dispatch to contact a wrecker service to tow the vehicle, Officer Martingano asked Rogers to exit the vehicle and sit in the back seat of the patrol car along with McCloud. Rogers did so, and Officer Martingano then searched the passenger compartment of the car.

During the search, Martingano discovered a .25 caliber firearm hidden under a rag in the side pocket of the open door. The firearm was loaded with a magazine containing seven rounds of ammunition. Officer Martingano removed the firearm from the vehicle and took it back to the patrol car in order to secure it. The patrol car was parked directly behind McCloud's vehicle. According to Officer Martingano, when McCloud saw the firearm he stated, "I forgot that was even there." Officer Martingano then advised McCloud of his Miranda rights, and McCloud did not make any additional statements. After the vehicle was impounded, Rogers was released, and McCloud was transported to the police station for booking.

McCloud was charged with being a felon in possession of a firearm in violation of 18 U.S.C. § 922(g)(1). Before the district court, McCloud filed motions to suppress the firearm and exclude his alleged inculpatory statement. The district court denied these motions, concluding the statement was made voluntarily and the search of McCloud's vehicle did not violate the Fourth Amendment because it was properly undertaken as a search incident to lawful arrest.

You are the new associate for the defense team on appeal. Your supervising attorney has asked you to draft a brief based upon the holding in the recent Gant case, which occurred after your client was convicted, and the facts of this case.

18-2. On September 2, 2008 Officer Johnson stopped defendant's car, in which defendant was a passenger, for an equipment violation—namely, that the vehicle had a tinted cover over the license plate. The driver, Michelle Weissman ("Weissman"), was arrested and placed in Officer Johnson's patrol car in handcuffs for failure to have a driver's license. Although initially allowed to remain in the car, defendant was frisked, handcuffed, and placed in a patrol car after a backup officer arrived. The two officers then searched the car incident to the driver's arrest and found a gun and oxycontin in the passenger compartment. Based on his prior training, Officer Johnson testified that he believed he had absolute authority to search the passenger compartment of the car incident to an occupant's arrest. On October 8, 2008 defendant was charged in a single-count indictment with being a felon in possession of a firearm.

On April 2, 2009, defendant entered a guilty plea. Approximately three weeks later, the United States Supreme Court issued its opinion in Arizona v. Gant ("Gant"). On May 5, 2009, defendant filed a motion to withdraw her guilty plea in order to litigate a suppression issue available to defendant following the Supreme Court's issuance of Gant. On January 5, 2010, this Court permitted defendant to withdraw her plea.

Following her plea withdrawal, defendant filed a motion to suppress and request for evidentiary hearing , which this Court referred to a Magistrate.

You are the magistrate's clerk. She has instructed you that she does not want to grant the defense's motion to suppress and has asked you to draft a memorandum considering possible exceptions to the exclusionary rule as the basis for her ruling.

-Notes-

Chapter 19: The Impeachment Exception

Harris v. New York

91 S.Ct. 643
Supreme Court of the United States
Viven HARRIS
v.
NEW YORK.
No. 206. | Argued Dec. 17, 1970. | Decided Feb. 24, 1971.

Mr. Chief Justice BURGER delivered the opinion of the Court.

We granted the writ in this case to consider petitioner's claim that a statement made by him to police under circumstances rendering it inadmissible to establish the prosecution's case in chief under Miranda v. Arizona,[3190] may not be used to impeach his credibility.

The State of New York charged petitioner in a two-count indictment with twice selling heroin to an undercover ***223** police officer. At a subsequent jury trial the officer was the State's chief witness, and he testified as to details of the two sales. A second officer verified collateral details of the sales, and a third offered testimony about the chemical analysis of the heroin.

Petitioner took the stand in his own defense. He admitted knowing the undercover police officer but denied a sale on January 4, 1966. He admitted making a sale of contents of a glassine bag to the officer on January 6 but claimed it was baking powder and part of a scheme to defraud the purchaser.

On cross-examination petitioner was asked seriatim whether he had made specified statements to the police immediately following his arrest on January 7—statements that partially contradicted petitioner's direct testimony at trial. In response to the cross-examination, petitioner testified that he could not remember virtually any of the questions or answers recited by the prosecutor. At the request of petitioner's counsel the written statement from which the prosecutor had read questions and answers in his impeaching process was placed in the record for possible use on appeal; the statement was not shown to the jury.

The trial judge instructed the jury that the statements attributed to petitioner by the prosecution could be considered only in passing on petitioner's credibility and not as evidence of guilt. In closing summations both counsel argued the substance of the impeaching statements. The jury then found petitioner guilty on the second count of the indictment. The New York Court of ****645** Appeals affirmed in a per curiam opinion.[3191]

At trial the prosecution made no effort in its case in chief to use the statements allegedly made by petitioner, ***224** conceding that they were inadmissible under Miranda v. Arizona.[3192] The transcript of the interrogation used in the impeachment, but not given to the jury, shows that no warning of a right to appointed counsel was given before questions were put to petitioner when he was taken into custody. Petitioner makes no claim that the statements made to the police were coerced or involuntary.

[3190] *384 U.S. 436, 86 S.Ct. 1602, 16 L.Ed.2d 694 (1966)*

[3191] *25 N.Y.2d 175, 303 N.Y.S.2d 71, 250 N.E.2d 349 (1969)*

[3192] *384 U.S. 436, 86 S.Ct. 1602, 16 L.Ed.2d 694 (1966)*

Some comments in the Miranda opinion can indeed be read as indicating a bar to use of an uncounseled statement for any purpose, but discussion of that issue was not at all necessary to the Court's holding and cannot be regarded as controlling. Miranda barred the prosecution from making its case with statements of an accused made while in custody prior to having or effectively waiving counsel. It does not follow from Miranda that evidence inadmissible against an accused in the prosecution's case in chief is barred for all purposes, provided of course that the trustworthiness of the evidence satisfies legal standards.

In Walder v. United States,[3193] the Court permitted physical evidence, inadmissible in the case in chief, to be used for impeachment purposes.

It is one thing to say that the Government cannot make an affirmative use of evidence unlawfully obtained. It is quite another to say that the defendant can turn the illegal method by which evidence in the Government's possession was obtained to his own advantage, and provide himself with a shield against contradiction of his untruths. Such an extension of the Weeks doctrine[3194] would be a perversion of the Fourth Amendment. '(T)here is hardly justification for letting the defendant affirmatively resort to perjurious testimony in reliance on the Government's disability to challenge his credibility.'[3195]

***225** It is true that Walder was impeached as to collateral matters included in his direct examination, whereas petitioner here was impeached as to testimony bearing more directly on the crimes charged. We are not persuaded that there is a difference in principle that warrants a result different from that reached by the Court in Walder. Petitioner's testimony in his own behalf concerning the events of January 7 contrasted sharply with what he told the police shortly after his arrest. The impeachment process here undoubtedly provided valuable aid to the jury in assessing petitioner's credibility, and the benefits of this process should not be lost, in our view, because of the speculative possibility that impermissible police conduct will be encouraged thereby. Assuming that the exclusionary rule has a deterrent effect on proscribed police conduct, sufficient deterrence flows when the evidence in question is made unavailable to the prosecution in its case in chief.

Every criminal defendant is privileged to testify in his own defense, or to refuse to do so. But that privilege cannot be construed to include the right to commit perjury.[3196] Having voluntarily taken the stand, petitioner was under an obligation to speak truthfully and accurately, and the prosecution here did no more than utilize the traditional truth-testing devices of the adversary ****646** process. Had ***226** inconsistent statements been made by the accused to some third person, it could hardly be contended that the conflict could not be laid before the jury by way of cross-examination and impeachment.

The shield provided by Miranda cannot be perverted into a license to use perjury by way of a defense, free from the risk of confrontation with prior inconsistent utterances. We hold, therefore, that petitioner's credibility was appropriately impeached by use of his earlier conflicting statements.

Affirmed.

Mr. Justice BLACK dissents.

[3193] *347 U.S. 62, 74 S.Ct. 354, 98 L.Ed. 503 (1954)*

[3194] *Weeks v. United States, 232 U.S. 383, 34 S.Ct. 341, 58 L.Ed. 652*

[3195] *347 U.S., at 65, 74 S.Ct., at 356*

[3196] *See United States v. Knox, 396 U.S. 77, 90 S.Ct. 363, 24 L.Ed.2d 275 (1969); cf. Dennis v. United States, 384 U.S. 855, 86 S.Ct. 1840, 16 L.Ed.2d 973 (1966)*

Mr. Justice BRENNAN, with whom Mr. Justice DOUGLAS and Mr. Justice MARSHALL, join, dissenting.

It is conceded that the question-and-answer statement used to impeach petitioner's direct testimony was, under Miranda v. Arizona,[3197] constitutionally inadmissible as part of the State's direct case against petitioner. I think that the Constitutional also denied the State the use of the statement on cross-examination to impeach the credibility of petitioner's testimony given in his own defense. The decision in Walder v. United States,[3198] is not, as the Court today holds, dispositive to the contrary. Rather, that case supports my conclusion.

The State's case against Harris depended upon the jury's belief of the testimony of the undercover agent that petitioner 'sold' the officer heroin on January 4 and again on January 6. Petitioner took the stand and flatly denied having sold anything to the officer on January 4. He countered the officer's testimony as to the January 6 sale with testimony that he had sold the officer two glassine bags containing what appeared to be heroin, but that actually the bags contained only baking powder intended to deceive the officer in order to obtain $12. ***227** The statement contradicted petitioner's direct testimony as to the events of both days. The statement's version of the events on January 4 was that the officer had used petitioner as a middleman to buy some heroin from a third person with money furnished by the officer. The version of the events on January 6 was that petitioner had again acted for the officer in buying two bags of heroin from a third person for which petitioner received $12 and a part of the heroin. Thus, it is clear that the statement was used to impeach petitioner's direct testimony not on collateral matters but on matters directly related to the crimes for which he was on trial.

Walder v. United States was not a case where tainted evidence was used to impeach an accused's direct testimony on matters directly related to the case against him. In Walder the evidence was used to impeach the accused's testimony on matters collateral to the crime charged. Walder had been indicted in 1950 for purchasing and possessing heroin. When his motion to suppress use of the narcotics as illegally seized was granted, the Government dismissed the prosecution. ****647** Two years later Walder was indicted for another narcotics violation completely unrelated to the 1950 one. Testifying in his own defense, he said on direct examination that he had never in his life possessed narcotics. On cross-examination he denied that law enforcement officers had seized narcotics from his home two years earlier. The Government was then permitted to introduce the testimony of one of the officers involved in the 1950 seizure, that when he had raided Walder's home at that time he had seized narcotics there. ***228** The Court held that on facts where 'the defendant went beyond a mere denial of complicity in the crimes of which he was charged and made the sweeping claim that he had never dealt in or possessed any narcotics,'[3199] the exclusionary rule of Weeks v. United States,[3200] would not extend to bar the Government from rebutting this testimony with evidence, although tainted, that petitioner had in fact possessed narcotics two years before. The Court was careful, however, to distinguish the situation of an accused whose testimony, as in the instant case, was a 'denial of complicity in the crimes of which he was charged,' that is, where illegally obtained evidence was used to impeach the accused's direct testimony on matters directly related to the case against him. As to that situation, the Court said:

> Of course, the Constitution guarantees a defendant the fullest opportunity to meet the accusation against him. He must be free to deny all the ele-

---

[3197] *384 U.S. 436, 86 S.Ct. 1602, 16 L.Ed.2d 694 (1966)*

[3198] *347 U.S. 62, 74 S.Ct. 354, 98 L.Ed. 503 (1954)*

[3199] *347 U.S., at 65, 74 S.Ct., at 356*

[3200] *232 U.S. 383, 34 S.Ct. 341, 58 L.Ed. 652 (1914)*

> ments of the case against him without thereby giving leave to the Government to introduce by way of rebuttal evidence illegally secured by it, and therefore not available for its case in chief.[3201]

From this recital of facts it is clear that the evidence used for impeachment in Walder was related to the earlier 1950 prosecution and had no direct bearing on 'the elements of the case' being tried in 1952. The evidence tended solely to impeach the credibility of the defendant's direct testimony that he had never in his life possessed heroin. But that evidence was completely unrelated to the indictment on trial and did not in any way interfere with his freedom to deny all elements of that case against him. In contrast, here, the evidence used for impeachment, a statement concerning the details of the very sales alleged in the indictment, was directly related to the case against petitioner.

***229** While Walder did not identify the constitutional specifics that guarantee 'a defendant the fullest opportunity to meet the accusation against him * * * (and permit him to) be free to deny all the elements of the case against him,' in my view Miranda v. Arizona,[3202] identified the Fifth Amendment's privilege against self-incrimination as one of those specifics. ***230** That ****648** privilege has been extended against the States.[3203] It is fulfilled only when an accused is guaranteed the right 'to remain silent unless he chooses to speak in the unfettered exercise of his own will,'[3204] The choice of whether to testify in one's own defense must therefore be 'unfettered,' since that choice is an exercise of the constitutional privilege.[3205] Griffin held that comment by the prosecution upon the accused's failure to take the stand or a court instruction that such silence is evidence of guilt is impermissible because it 'fetters' that choice-' (i)t cuts down on the privilege by making its assertion costly.'[3206] For precisely the same reason the constitutional guarantee forbids the prosecution to use a tainted statement to impeach the accused who takes the stand: The prosecution's use of the tainted statement 'cuts down on the privilege by making its assertion costly.'[3207] Thus, the accused is denied an 'unfettered' choice when the decision whether to take the stand is burdened by the risk that an illegally obtained prior statement may be introduced to impeach his direct testimony denying complicity in the crime charged against him. We settled this proposition in Miranda where we said:

> The privilege against self-incrimination protects the individual from being compelled to incriminate himself in any manner * * *. (S)tatements merely intended to be exculpatory by the defendant are often used to impeach his testimony at trial * * *. These statements are incriminating in any meaningful sense of the word and may not be used without the full warnings and effective waiver required for ***231** any other statement.[3208]

This language completely disposes of any distinction between statements used on direct as opposed to cross-examination. ****649** 'An incriminating statement is as

---

[3201] *347 U.S., at 65, 74 S.Ct., at 356*

[3202] *384 U.S. 436, 86 S.Ct. 1602, 16 L.Ed.2d 694 (1966)*

[3203] *Malloy v. Hogan, 378 U.S. 1, 84 S.Ct. 1489, 12 L.Ed.2d 653 (1964)*

[3204] *Id., at 8, 84 S.Ct., at 1493 (emphasis added)*

[3205] *Griffin v. California, 380 U.S. 609, 85 S.Ct. 1229, 14 L.Ed.2d 106 (1965)*

[3206] *Id., at 614, 85 S.Ct., at 1233*

[3207] *Ibid*

[3208] *384 U.S., at 476-477, 86 S.Ct., at 1629 (emphasis added)*

incriminating when used to impeach credibility as it is when used as direct proof of guilt and no constitutional distinction can legitimately be drawn.'[3209]

The objective of deterring improper police conduct is only part of the larger objective of safeguarding the integrity of our adversary system. The 'essential mainstay' of that system[3210] is the privilege against self-incrimination, which for ***232** that reason has occupied a central place in our jurisprudence since before the Nation's birth. Moreover, 'we may view the historical development of the privilege as one which groped for the proper scope of governmental power over the citizen. * * * All these policies point to one overriding thought: the constitutional foundation underlying the privilege is the respect a government * * * must accord to the dignity and integrity of its citizens.'[3211] These values are plainly jeopardized if an exception against admission of tainted statements is made for those used for impeachment purposes. Moreover, it is monstrous that courts should aid or abet the law-breaking police officer. It is abiding truth that '(n)othing can destroy a government more quickly than its failure to observe its own laws, or worse, its disregard of the charter of its own existence.'[3212] Thus even to the extent that Miranda was aimed at deterring police practices in disregard of the Constitution, I fear that today's holding will seriously undermine the achievement of that objective. The Court today tells the police that they may freely interrogate an accused incommunicado and without counsel and know that although any statement they obtain in violation of Miranda cannot be used on the State's direct case, it may be introduced if the defendant has the temerity to testify in his own defense. This goes far toward undoing much of the progress made in conforming police methods to the Constitution. I dissent.

Black Letter Law

> *In this case, the defendant had not been advised of his rights to counsel and to remain silent prior to making a statement, but the statement otherwise satisfied legal standards for admissibility.*

United States v. Havens

100 S.Ct. 1912

Supreme Court of the United States

UNITED STATES, Petitioner,

v.

J. Lee HAVENS.

No. 79–305. | Argued March 19, 1980. | Decided May 27, 1980. | Rehearing Denied Aug. 11, 1980. | See 448 U.S. 911, 101 S.Ct. 25.

Mr. Justice WHITE delivered the opinion of the Court.

The petition for certiorari filed by the United States in this criminal case presented a single question: whether evidence suppressed as the fruit of an unlawful search and seizure may nevertheless be used to impeach a defendant's false trial testimony, given in response to proper cross-examination, where the evidence does not

[3209] *People v. Kulis, 18 N.Y.2d 318, 324, 274 N.Y.S.2d 873, 876, 221 N.E.2d 541, 543 (1966) (dissenting opinion)*

[3210] *Miranda v. Arizona, 384 U.S., at 460, 86 S.Ct. 1602*

[3211] *Ibid*

[3212] *Mapp v. Ohio, 367 U.S. 643, 659, 81 S.Ct. 1684, 1694, 6 L.Ed.2d 1081 (1961)*

squarely contradict the defendant's testimony on direct examination. We issued the writ.[3213]

****1914 I**

Respondent was convicted of importing, conspiring to import, and intentionally possessing a controlled substance, cocaine. According to the evidence at his trial, Havens and John McLeroth, both attorneys from Ft. Wayne, Ind., boarded a flight from Lima, Peru, to Miami, Fla. In Miami, a customs officer searched McLeroth and found cocaine sewed into makeshift pockets in a T-shirt he was wearing under his outer ***622** clothing. McLeroth implicated respondent, who had previously cleared customs and who was then arrested. His luggage was seized and searched without a warrant. The officers found no drugs but seized a T-shirt from which pieces had been cut that matched the pieces that had been sewn to McLeroth's T-shirt. The T-shirt and other evidence seized in the course of the search were suppressed on motion prior to trial.

Both men were charged in a three-count indictment, but McLeroth pleaded guilty to one count and testified against Havens. Among other things, he asserted that Havens had supplied him with the altered T-shirt and had sewed the makeshift pockets shut. Havens took the stand in his own defense and denied involvement in smuggling cocaine. His direct testimony included the following:

> Q. And you heard Mr. McLeroth testify earlier as to something to the effect that this material was taped or draped around his body and so on, you heard that testimony?
>
> A. Yes, I did.
>
> Q. Did you ever engage in that kind of activity with Mr. McLeroth and Augusto or Mr. McLeroth and anyone else on that fourth visit to Lima, Peru?
>
> A. I did not.[3214]

On cross-examination, Havens testified as follows:

> Q. Now, on direct examination, sir, you testified that on the fourth trip you had absolutely nothing to do with the wrapping of any bandages or tee shirts or anything involving Mr. McLeroth; is that correct?
>
> A. I don't—I said I had nothing to do with any wrapping or bandages or anything, yes. I had nothing to do with anything with McLeroth in connection with this cocaine matter.
>
> Q. And your testimony is that you had nothing to ***623** do with the sewing of the cotton swatches to make pockets on that tee shirt?
>
> A. Absolutely not.
>
> Q. Sir, when you came through Customs, the Miami International Airport, on October 2, 1977, did you have in your suitcase Size 38–40 medium tee shirts?[3215]

[3213] *444 U.S. 962, 100 S.Ct. 447, 62 L.Ed.2d 374 (1979)*

[3214] *App. 34*

[3215] *Id., at 35*

An objection to the latter question was overruled and questioning continued:

Q. On that day, sir, did you have in your luggage a Size 38–40 medium man's tee shirt with swatches of clothing missing from the tail of that tee shirt?

A. Not to my knowledge.

Q. Mr. Havens, I'm going to hand you what is Government's Exhibit 9 for identification and ask you if this tee shirt was in your luggage on October 2nd, 1975 [sic]?

A. Not to my knowledge. No.[3216]

Respondent Havens also denied having told a Government agent that the T-shirts found in his luggage belonged to McLeroth.

On rebuttal, a Government agent testified that Exhibit 9 had been found in respondent's suitcase and that Havens claimed the T-shirts found in his bag, including Exhibit 9, belonged to McLeroth. Over objection, the T-shirt was then admitted into evidence, the jury being instructed that the rebuttal evidence should be considered only for impeaching Havens' credibility.

The Court of Appeals reversed, relying on Agnello v. United States[3217] and ****1915** Walder v. United States.[3218] The court held that illegally seized evidence may be used for impeachment only if the evidence contradicts a particular statement made by a defendant in the course of his direct examination.[3219] We reverse.

***624 II**

In Agnello v. United States,[3220] a defendant charged with conspiracy to sell a package of cocaine testified on direct examination that he had possessed the packages involved but did not know what was in them. On cross-examination, he denied ever having seen narcotics and ever having seen a can of cocaine which was exhibited to him and which had been illegally seized from his apartment. The can of cocaine was permitted into evidence on rebuttal. Agnello was convicted and his conviction was affirmed by the Court of Appeals. This Court reversed, holding that the Fourth Amendment required exclusion of the evidence. The Court pointed out that "[i]n his direct examination, Agnello was not asked and did not testify concerning the can of cocaine" and "did nothing to waive his constitutional protection or to justify cross-examination in respect of the evidence claimed to have been obtained by the search."[3221] The Court also said, quoting from Silverthorne Lumber Co. v. United States,[3222] that the exclusionary rule not only commands that illegally seized evidence "shall not be used before the Court but that it shall not be used at all."[3223]

[3216] *Id., at 46*

[3217] *269 U.S. 20, 46 S.Ct. 4, 70 L.Ed. 145 (1925)*

[3218] *347 U.S. 62, 74 S.Ct. 354, 98 L.Ed. 503 (1954)*

[3219] *592 F.2d 848 (CA5 1979)*

[3220] *Supra*

[3221] *269 U.S., at 35, 46 S.Ct., at 7*

[3222] *251 U.S. 385, 392, 40 S.Ct. 182, 183, 64 L.Ed. 319 (1920)*

[3223] *269 U.S., at 35, 46 S.Ct., at 7*

The latter statement has been rejected in our later cases, however, and Agnello otherwise limited. In Walder v. United States,[3224] the use of evidence obtained in an illegal search and inadmissible in the Government's case in chief was admitted to impeach the direct testimony of the defendant. This Court approved, saying that it would pervert the rule of Weeks v. United States,[3225] to hold otherwise. Similarly, in Harris v. New York[3226] and Oregon v. Hass,[3227] statements taken in violation of Miranda v. Arizona,[3228] and unusable by the prosecution as part of its own case, were held admissible to impeach statements made by the defendant in the course of his direct testimony. Harris ***625** also made clear that the permitted impeachment by otherwise inadmissible evidence is not limited to collateral matters.[3229]

These cases were understood by the Court of Appeals to hold that tainted evidence, inadmissible when offered as part of the Government's main case, may not be used as rebuttal evidence to impeach a defendant's credibility unless the evidence is offered to contradict a particular statement made by a defendant during his direct examination; a statement made for the first time on cross-examination may not be so impeached. This approach required the exclusion of the T-shirt taken from Havens' luggage because, as the Court of Appeals read the record, Havens was asked nothing on his direct testimony about the incriminating T-shirt or about the contents of his luggage; the testimony about the T-shirt, which the Government desired to impeach first appeared on cross-examination, not on direct.

It is true that Agnello involved the impeachment of testimony first brought out on cross-examination and that in Walder, Harris, and Hass, the testimony impeached was given by the defendant while testifying on direct examination. In our view, however, a flat rule permitting only statements on direct examination to be impeached misapprehends the underlying rationale of Walder, Harris and Hass. These cases repudiated the statement in Agnello that no use at all may be made of illegally obtained evidence. Furthermore, in Walder, the Court said that in Agnello, the Government had "smuggled in" the impeaching opportunity ****1916** in the course of cross-examination. The Court also relied on the statement in Agnello[3230] that Agnello had done nothing "to justify cross-examination in respect of the evidence claimed to have been obtained by the search." The implication of Walder is that Agnello was a case of cross-examination having too tenuous a connection with any subject opened upon direct examination to permit impeachment by tainted evidence.

***626** In reversing the District Court in the case before us, the Court of Appeals did not stop to consider how closely the cross-examination about the T-shirt and the luggage was connected with matters gone into in direct examination. If these questions would have been suggested to a reasonably competent cross-examiner by Havens' direct testimony, they were not "smuggled in"; and forbidding the Government to impeach the answers to these questions by using contrary and reliable evidence in its possession fails to take account of our cases, particularly Harris and Hass. In both cases, the Court stressed the importance of arriving at the truth in criminal trials, as well as the defendant's obligation to speak the truth in response to proper questions. We rejected the notion that the defendant's constitutional shield against having illegally seized evidence used against him could be "perverted into a license to use perjury by way of a defense, free from the risk of confrontation with

---

[3224] *Supra*

[3225] *232 U.S. 383, 34 S.Ct. 341, 58 L.Ed. 652 (1914)*

[3226] *401 U.S. 222, 91 S.Ct. 643, 28 L.Ed.2d 1 (1971)*

[3227] *420 U.S. 714, 95 S.Ct. 1215, 43 L.Ed.2d 570 (1975)*

[3228] *384 U.S. 436, 86 S.Ct. 1602, 16 L.Ed.2d 694 (1966)*

[3229] *401 U.S., at 225, 91 S.Ct., at 645*

[3230] *Supra, at 35, 46 S.Ct., at 7*

prior inconsistent utterances."[3231] Both cases also held that the deterrent function of the rules excluding unconstitutionally obtained evidence is sufficiently served by denying its use to the government on its direct case. It was only a "speculative possibility" that also making it unavailable to the government for otherwise proper impeachment would contribute substantially in this respect.[3232]

Neither Harris nor Hass involved the impeachment of assertedly false testimony first given on cross-examination, but the reasoning of those cases controls this one. There is no gainsaying that arriving at the truth is a fundamental goal of our legal system.[3233] We have repeatedly insisted that when defendants testify, they must testify truthfully or suffer the consequences. This is true even though a defendant is compelled to testify against his will.[3234] It is essential, ***627** therefore, to the proper functioning of the adversary system that when a defendant takes the stand, the government be permitted proper and effective cross-examination in an attempt to elicit the truth. The defendant's obligation to testify truthfully is fully binding on him when he is cross-examined. His privilege against self-incrimination does not shield him from proper questioning.[3235] He would unquestionably be subject to a perjury prosecution if he knowingly lies on cross-examination.[3236] In terms of impeaching a defendant's seemingly false statements with his prior inconsistent utterances or with other reliable evidence available to the government, we see no difference of constitutional magnitude between the defendant's statements on direct examination and his answers to questions put to him on cross-examination that are plainly within the scope of the defendant's direct examination. Without this opportunity, the normal function of cross-examination would be severely impeded.

We also think that the policies of the exclusionary rule no more bar impeachment here than they did in Walder, Harris, and Hass. In those cases, the ends of the exclusionary rules were thought adequately implemented ****1917** by denying the government the use of the challenged evidence to make out its case in chief. The incremental furthering of those ends by forbidding impeachment of the defendant who testifies was deemed insufficient to permit or require that false testimony go unchallenged, with the resulting impairment of the integrity of the fact-finding goals of the criminal trial. We reaffirm this assessment of the competing interests, and hold that a defendant's statements made in response to proper cross-examination reasonably suggested by the defendant's direct examination are subject to otherwise proper impeachment ***628** by the government, albeit by evidence that has been illegally obtained and that is inadmissible on the government's direct case, or otherwise, as substantive evidence of guilt.

In arriving at its judgment, the Court of Appeals noted that in response to defense counsel's objection to the impeaching evidence on the ground that the matter had not been "covered on direct," the trial court had remarked that "[i]t does not have to be covered on direct." The Court of Appeals thought this was error since in its view illegally seized evidence could be used only to impeach a statement made on direct examination. As we have indicated, we hold a contrary view; and we do not understand the District Court to have indicated that the Government's question, the answer to which is sought to be impeached, need not be proper cross-examination in the first instance. The Court of Appeals did not suggest that either the cross-examina-

---

[3231] *401 U.S., at 226, 91 S.Ct., at 646. See also Oregon v. Hass, supra, at 722, 723, 95 S.Ct., at 1221*

[3232] *Harris v. New York, supra, at 225, 91 S.Ct., at 645. Oregon v. Hass, supra, at 723, 95 S.Ct., at 1221*

[3233] *Oregon v. Hass, supra, at 722, 95 S.Ct., at 1221*

[3234] *Bryson v. United States, 396 U.S. 64, 72, 90 S.Ct. 355, 360, 24 L.Ed.2d 264 (1969); United States v. Knox, 396 U.S. 77, 90 S.Ct. 363, 24 L.Ed.2d 275 (1969)*

[3235] *Brown v. United States, 356 U.S. 148, 154–155, 78 S.Ct. 622, 626, 2 L.Ed.2d 589 (1958)*

[3236] *Cf. United States v. Apfelbaum, 445 U.S. 115, 100 S.Ct. 948, 63 L.Ed.2d 250 (1980); Bryson v. United States, supra; United States v. Knox, supra; United States v. Wong, 431 U.S. 174, 97 S.Ct. 1823, 52 L.Ed.2d 231 (1977)*

tion or the impeachment of Havens would have been improper absent the use of illegally seized evidence, and we cannot accept respondent's suggestions that because of the illegal search and seizure, the Government's questions about the T-shirt were improper cross-examination. McLeroth testified that Havens had assisted him in preparing the T-shirt for smuggling. Havens, in his direct testimony, acknowledged McLeroth's prior testimony that the cocaine "was taped or draped around his body and so on" but denied that he had "ever engage[d] in that kind of activity with Mr. McLeroth. . . . " This testimony could easily be understood as a denial of any connection with McLeroth's T-shirt and as a contradiction of McLeroth's testimony. Quite reasonably, it seems to us, the Government on cross-examination called attention to his answers on direct and then asked whether he had anything to do with sewing the cotton swatches on McLeroth's T-shirt. This was cross-examination growing out of Havens' direct testimony; and, as we hold above, the ensuing impeachment did not violate Havens' constitutional rights.

***629** We reverse the judgment of the Court of Appeals and remand the case to that court for further proceedings consistent with this opinion.

So ordered.

Mr. Justice BRENNAN, joined by Mr. Justice MARSHALL and joined in Part I by Mr. Justice STEWART and Mr. Justice STEVENS, dissenting.

The Court upholds the admission at trial of illegally seized evidence to impeach a defendant's testimony deliberately elicited by the Government under the cover of impeaching an accused who takes the stand in his own behalf. I dissent. Criminal defendants now told that prosecutors are licensed to insinuate otherwise inadmissible evidence under the guise of cross-examination no longer have the unfettered right to elect whether or not to testify in their own behalf. Not only is today's decision an unwarranted departure from prior controlling cases, but, regrettably, it is yet another element in the trend to depreciate the constitutional protections guaranteed the criminally accused.

I

The question before us is not of first impression. The identical issue was confronted in Agnello v. United States,[3237] which determined—contrary to the instant decision—that it was constitutionally impermissible to admit evidence obtained in ****1918** violation of the Fourth Amendment to rebut a defendant's response to a matter first raised during the Government's cross-examination. Subsequently, Walder v. United States,[3238] affirmed the introduction of unlawfully acquired evidence to impeach an accused's false assertions about previous conduct that had been offered during direct testimony. But Walder took pains to draw the distinction between its own holding and Agnello, noting that "the defendant [Walder] went beyond a mere denial of complicity in the crimes of which he was charged and made the sweeping ***630** [and untrue] claim that he had never dealt in or possessed any narcotics."[3239] In "shar[p] contras[t]," in Agnello, "the Government . . . tried to smuggle [the tainted evidence] . . . in on cross-examination," and "elicit[ed] the expected denial. . . ."[3240]

The Court's recent decisions have left Agnello undisturbed. Harris v. New York[3241] allowed the government to use inadmissible uncounseled statements to im-

[3237] *269 U.S. 20, 46 S.Ct. 4, 70 L.Ed. 145 (1925)*

[3238] *347 U.S. 62, 74 S.Ct. 354, 98 L.Ed. 503 (1954)*

[3239] *347 U.S., at 65, 74 S.Ct., at 356*

[3240] *347 U.S., at 66, 74 S.Ct., at 356*

[3241] *401 U.S. 222, 91 S.Ct. 643, 28 L.Ed.2d 1 (1971)*

peach direct examination. So, too, Oregon v. Hass[3242] reaffirmed Harris in the context of impeachment of the defendant's direct testimony. Significantly, neither decision intimated that Agnello had lost vitality, or that the distinction emphasized by Walder had been effaced.

The Court's opinion attempts to discredit Agnello by casting a strawman as its holding, and then demolishing the pitiful scarecrow of its own creation. Specifically, the Court cites Agnello's quotation of language from Silverthorne Lumber Co. v. United States[3243] that "illegally seized evidence 'shall not . . . be used at all,'"[3244] and then refers to the subsequent decisions that indeed permit limited use of that evidence for impeachment. But the actual principle of Agnello, as discerned by Walder, is that the Government may not employ its power of cross-examination to predicate the admission of illegal evidence. In other words, impeachment by cross-examination about—or introduction of—suppressible evidence must be warranted by defendant's statements upon direct questioning. That principle is not at all inconsistent with later cases holding that the defendant may not take advantage of evidentiary suppression to advance specific perjurious claims as part of his direct case.

Nor is it correct to read Agnello as turning upon the tenuity of the link between the cross-examination involved there and the subject matter of the direct examination.[3245] The cross-examination about Agnello's previous connection with cocaine was reasonably related to his direct testimony that he lacked knowledge that the commodity he was transporting ***631** was cocaine.[3246] For "[t]he possession by Frank Agnello of the can of cocaine which was seized tended to show guilty knowledge and criminal intent on his part . . .."[3247] Thus, the constitutional flaw found in Agnello was that the introduction of the tainted evidence had been prompted by statements of the accused first elicited upon cross-examination. And the case was so read in Walder v. United States. That decision specifically stated that a defendant "must be free to deny all the elements of the case against him without thereby giving leave to the Government to introduce by way of rebuttal evidence illegally secured by it, and therefore not available for its case in chief."[3248] Since as a matter of the law of evidence it would be perfectly permissible to cross-examine a defendant as to his denial of complicity in the crime, the quoted passage in Walder must be understood to impose a further condition before the prosecutor may refer to tainted evidence—that is, some particular direct testimony by the accused that relies upon "the Government's disability to challenge his credibility."[3249]

In fact, the Court's current interpretation of Agnello and Walder simply trivializes ****1919** those decisions by transforming their Fourth Amendment holdings into nothing more than a constitutional reflection of the common-law evidentiary rule of relevance.

Finally, the rationale of Harris v. New York and Oregon v. Hass does not impel the decision at hand. The exclusionary rule exception established by Harris and Hass may be fairly easily cabined by defense counsel's willingness to forgo certain areas of questioning. But the rule prescribed by the Court in this case passes control of the exception to the Government, since the prosecutor can lay the predicate for admitting otherwise suppressible evidence with his own questioning. To be sure, the Court re-

---

[3242] *420 U.S. 714, 95 S.Ct. 1215, 43 L.Ed.2d 570 (1975)*

[3243] *251 U.S. 385, 392, 40 S.Ct. 182, 183, 64 L.Ed. 319 (1920)*

[3244] *Ante, at 1915*

[3245] *Ante, at 1916*

[3246] *269 U.S., at 29–30, 46 S.Ct., at 5*

[3247] *Id., at 35, 46 S.Ct., at 7*

[3248] *347 U.S., at 65, 74 S.Ct., at 356*

[3249] *Ibid*

quires that cross-examination be "proper"; however, traditional evidentiary principles accord parties fairly considerable latitude in cross-examining ***632** opposing witnesses.[3250] In practical terms, therefore, today's holding allows even the moderately talented prosecutor to "work in . . . evidence on cross-examination [as it would] in its case in chief . . .."[3251] To avoid this consequence, a defendant will be compelled to forgo testifying on his own behalf.

"[T]he Constitution guarantees a defendant the fullest opportunity to meet the accusation against him."[3252] Regrettably, surrender of that guarantee is the price the Court imposes for the defendant to claim his right not to be convicted on the basis of evidence obtained in violation of the Constitution. I cannot agree that one constitutional privilege must be purchased at the expense of another.

II

The foregoing demonstration of its break with precedent provides a sufficient ground to condemn the present ruling—unleashing, as it does, a hitherto relatively confined exception to the exclusionary rule. But I have a more fundamental difference with the Court's holding here, which culminates ***633** the approach taken in Harris v. New York, and Oregon v. Hass. For this sequence of decisions undercuts the constitutional canon that convictions cannot be procured by governmental lawbreaking.[3253]

"'[I]t is monstrous that courts should aid or abet the law-breaking police officer.'"[3254] And what is especially troubling about these cases is the mode of analysis employed by the Court. In each, the judgment that tainted evidence may be admitted has been bottomed upon a determination that the "incremental furthering" of constitutional ends would not be sufficient to warrant exclusion of otherwise probative evidence.[3255]

Of course, "[t]here is no gainsaying that arriving at the truth is a fundamental goal of our legal system."[3256] But it is also undeniable that promotion of that objective must be consonant with other ****1920** ends, in particular those enshrined in our Constitution. I still hope that the Court would not be prepared to acquiesce in torture or other police conduct that "shocks the conscience" even if it demonstrably advanced the fact-finding process. At any rate, what is important is that the Constitution does not countenance police misbehavior, even in the pursuit of truth. The processes of our judicial system may not be fueled by the illegalities of government authorities.[3257]

Nevertheless, the Court has undertaken to strike a "balance" between the "policies" it finds in the Bill of Rights and the "competing interes[t]" in accurate trial determinations.[3258] This balancing effort is completely freewheeling. Far from applying criteria intrinsic to the Fourth and Fifth Amendments, the Court resolves suc-

---

[3250] *See C. McCormick, Law of Evidence §§ 21–24 (2d ed. 1972)*

[3251] *Walder v. United States, 347 U.S., at 66, 74 S.Ct., at 356*

[3252] *Id., at 65, 74 S.Ct., at 356; see Harris v. New York, supra, at 229–230, 91 S.Ct., at 647 (BRENNAN, J., dissenting)*

[3253] *See Harris v. New York, 401 U.S., at 226–232, 91 S.Ct., at 646–49 (BRENNAN, J., dissenting); Oregon v. Hass, 420 U.S., at 724–725, 95 S.Ct., at 1222 (BRENNAN, J., dissenting)*

[3254] *Id., at 724, 95 S.Ct., at 1222, quoting Harris v. New York, supra, 401 U.S., at 232, 91 S.Ct., at 649 (BRENNAN, J., dissenting)*

[3255] *Ante, at 1917; see Oregon v. Hass, supra, 420 U.S., at 721, 95 S.Ct., at 1220; Harris v. New York, supra, 401 U.S., at 225, 91 S.Ct., at 645*

[3256] *Ante, at 1916*

[3257] *See, e. g., Mapp v. Ohio, 367 U.S. 643, 81 S.Ct. 1684, 6 L.Ed.2d 1081 (1961)*

[3258] *Ante, at 1917*

ceeding cases simply by declaring that so much exclusion is enough to deter ***634** police misconduct.[3259] That hardly conforms to the disciplined analytical method described as "legal reasoning," through which judges endeavor to formulate or derive principles of decision that can be applied consistently and predictably.

Ultimately, I fear, this ad hoc approach to the exclusionary rule obscures the difference between judicial decision making and legislative or administrative policymaking. More disturbingly, by treating Fourth and Fifth Amendment privileges as mere incentive schemes, the Court denigrates their unique status as constitutional protections. Yet the efficacy of the Bill of Rights as the bulwark of our national liberty depends precisely upon public appreciation of the special character of constitutional prescriptions. The Court is charged with the responsibility to enforce constitutional guarantees; decisions such as today's patently disregard that obligation.

Accordingly, I dissent.

Black Letter Law

> The Court held that a defendant's statements made in response to proper cross-examination reasonably suggested by defendant's direct examination are subject to otherwise proper impeachment by the Government, to include using evidence illegally obtained and otherwise inadmissible. Such cross examinations are not limited to questions, but could also include the admissibility of otherwise suppressed evidence.

James v. Illinois

110 S.Ct. 648

Supreme Court of the United States

Darryl JAMES, Petitioner

v.

ILLINOIS.

No. 88-6075. | Argued Oct. 3, 1989. | Decided Jan. 10, 1990.

Justice BRENNAN delivered the opinion of the Court.

The impeachment exception to the exclusionary rule permits the prosecution in a criminal proceeding to introduce illegally ***309** obtained evidence to impeach the defendant's own testimony. The Illinois Supreme Court extended this exception to permit the prosecution to impeach the testimony of all defense witnesses with illegally obtained evidence.[3260] Finding this extension inconsistent with the balance of values underlying our previous applications of the exclusionary rule, we reverse.

I

On the night of August 30, 1982, eight young boys returning home from a party were confronted by a trio of other boys who demanded money. When the eight boys refused to comply, one member of the trio produced a gun and fired into the larger group, killing one boy and seriously injuring another. When the police arrived, the remaining members of the larger group provided eyewitness accounts of the event and descriptions of the perpetrators.

[3259] *Ante, at 1916–1917; see Oregon v. Hass, supra, 420 U.S., at 721, 95 S.Ct., at 1220; Harris v. New York, supra, 401 U.S., at 225, 91 S.Ct., at 645; cf. Stone v. Powell, 428 U.S. 465, 486–489, 96 S.Ct. 3037, 3048–50, 49 L.Ed.2d 1067 (1976); United States v. Calandra, 414 U.S. 338, 350–352, 94 S.Ct. 613, 621–622, 38 L.Ed.2d 561 (1974)*

[3260] *123 Ill.2d 523, 124 Ill.Dec. 35, 528 N.E.2d 723 (1988)*

The next evening, two detectives of the Chicago Police Department took 15-year-old Darryl James into custody as a suspect in the shooting. James was found at his mother's beauty parlor sitting under a hair dryer; when he emerged, his hair was black and curly. After placing James in their car, the detectives questioned him about his prior hair color. He responded that the previous day his hair had been reddish brown, long, and combed straight back. The detectives questioned James again later at the police station, and he further stated that he had gone to the beauty parlor in order to have his hair "dyed black and curled in order to change his appearance."[3261]

The State subsequently indicted James for murder and attempted murder. Prior to trial, James moved to suppress the statements regarding his hair, contending that they were the fruit of a Fourth Amendment violation because the detectives lacked probable cause for his warrantless arrest. After an evidentiary hearing, the trial court sustained this ***310** motion and ruled that the statements would be inadmissible at trial.

At trial, five members of the larger group of boys testified for the State, and each made an in-court identification of the defendant. Each testified that the person responsible for the shooting had "reddish" hair, worn shoulder length in a slicked-back "butter" style. Each also recalled having seen James several weeks earlier at a parade, at which time James had the aforementioned hair color and style. At trial, however, his hair was black and worn in a "natural" style. Despite the discrepancy between the witnesses' description and his present appearance, the witnesses stood firm in their conviction that James had been present and had fired the shots.

James did not testify in his own defense. He called as a witness Jewel Henderson, a friend of his family. Henderson testified that on the day of the shooting she had taken James to register for high school and that, at that time, his hair was black. The State then sought, over James' objection, to introduce his illegally obtained statements as a means of impeaching the credibility of Henderson's testimony. After determining that the suppressed statements had been made voluntarily, ****651** the trial court overruled James' objection. One of the interrogating detectives then reported James' prior admissions that he had reddish hair the night of the shooting and he dyed and curled his hair the next day in order to change his appearance. James ultimately was convicted of both murder and attempted murder and sentenced to 30 years' imprisonment.

On appeal, the Illinois Appellate Court reversed James' convictions and ordered a new trial.[3262] The appellate court held that the exclusionary rule barred admission of James' illegally obtained statements for the purpose of impeaching a defense witness' testimony and that the resulting constitutional error was not harmless. However, the Illinois Supreme Court reversed. ***311** The court reasoned that, in order to deter the defendant from engaging in perjury "by proxy," the impeachment exception to the exclusionary rule ought to be expanded to allow the State to introduce illegally obtained evidence to impeach the testimony of defense witnesses other than the defendant himself. The court therefore ordered James' convictions reinstated. We granted certiorari.[3263]

II

"There is no gainsaying that arriving at the truth is a fundamental goal of our legal system."[3264] But various constitutional rules limit the means by which government may conduct this search for truth in order to promote other values embraced by

---

[3261] *App. 11*

[3262] *153 Ill.App.3d 131, 106 Ill.Dec. 327, 505 N.E.2d 1118 (1987)*

[3263] *489 U.S. 1010, 109 S.Ct. 1117, 103 L.Ed.2d 180 (1989)*

[3264] *United States v. Havens, 446 U.S. 620, 626, 100 S.Ct. 1912, 1916, 64 L.Ed.2d 559 (1980)*

the Framers and cherished throughout our Nation's history. "Ever since its inception, the rule excluding evidence seized in violation of the Fourth Amendment has been recognized as a principal mode of discouraging lawless police conduct.... [W]ithout it the constitutional guarantee against unreasonable searches and seizures would be a mere 'form of words.'"[3265] The occasional suppression of illegally obtained yet probative evidence has long been considered a necessary cost of preserving overriding constitutional values: "[T]here is nothing new in the realization that the Constitution sometimes insulates the criminality of a few in order to protect the privacy of us all."[3266]

This Court has carved out exceptions to the exclusionary rule, however, where the introduction of reliable and probative evidence would significantly further the truth-seeking function of a criminal trial and the likelihood that admissibility of such evidence would encourage police misconduct is but a "speculative possibility."[3267] ***312** One exception to the rule permits prosecutors to introduce illegally obtained evidence for the limited purpose of impeaching the credibility of the defendant's own testimony. This Court first recognized this exception in Walder v. United States,[3268] permitting the prosecutor to introduce into evidence heroin obtained ****652** through an illegal search to undermine the credibility of the defendant's claim that he had never possessed narcotics. The Court explained that a defendant

> [M]ust be free to deny all the elements of the case against him without thereby giving leave to the Government to introduce by way of rebuttal evidence illegally secured by it, and therefore not available for its case in chief. Beyond that, however, there is hardly justification for letting the defendant affirmatively resort to perjurious testimony in reliance on the Government's disability to challenge his credibility.[3269]

In Harris v. New York, supra, and Oregon v. Hass,[3270] the Court applied the exception to permit prosecutors to impeach defendants using incriminating yet voluntary and reliable statements elicited in violation of Miranda requirements. Finally, in United States v. Havens,[3271] the Court expanded the exception to permit ***313** prosecutors to introduce illegally obtained evidence in order to impeach a defendant's "answers to questions put to him on cross-examination that are plainly within the scope of the defendant's direct examination."[3272]

This Court insisted throughout this line of cases that "evidence that has been illegally obtained ... is inadmissible on the government's direct case, or otherwise, as substantive evidence of guilt."[3273] However, because the Court believed that permitting the use of such evidence to impeach defendants' testimony would further the goal of truth-seeking by preventing defendants from perverting the exclusionary rule "'into a license to use perjury by way of a defense,'"[3274] and because the Court fur-

---

[3265] *Terry v. Ohio, 392 U.S. 1, 12, 88 S.Ct. 1868, 1875, 20 L.Ed.2d 889 (1968), quoting Mapp v. Ohio, 367 U.S. 643, 655, 81 S.Ct. 1684, 1691, 6 L.Ed.2d 1081 (1961)*

[3266] *Arizona v. Hicks, 480 U.S. 321, 329, 107 S.Ct. 1149, 1154-55, 94 L.Ed.2d 347 (1987)*

[3267] *Harris v. New York, 401 U.S. 222, 225, 91 S.Ct. 643, 645-46, 28 L.Ed.2d 1 (1971)*

[3268] *347 U.S. 62, 74 S.Ct. 354, 98 L.Ed. 503 (1954)*

[3269] *Id., at 65, 74 S.Ct., at 356*

[3270] *420 U.S. 714, 95 S.Ct. 1215, 43 L.Ed.2d 570 (1975)*

[3271] *Supra*

[3272] *Id., 446 U.S., at 627, 100 S.Ct., at 1916*

[3273] *Id., at 628, 100 S.Ct., at 1917*

[3274] *Id., at 626, 100 S.Ct., at 1916 (citation omitted)*

ther believed that permitting such use would create only a "speculative possibility that impermissible police conduct will be encouraged thereby,"[3275] the Court concluded that the balance of values underlying the exclusionary rule justified an exception covering impeachment of defendants' testimony.

III

In this case, the Illinois Supreme Court held that our balancing approach in Walder and its progeny justifies expanding the scope of the impeachment exception to permit prosecutors to use illegally obtained evidence to impeach the credibility of defense witnesses. We disagree. Expanding the class of impeachable witnesses from the defendant alone to all defense witnesses would create different incentives affecting the behavior of both defendants and law enforcement officers. As a result, this expansion would not promote the truth-seeking function to the same extent as did creation of the original exception, and yet it would significantly undermine ***314** the deterrent effect of the general exclusionary rule. Hence, we believe that this proposed expansion would frustrate rather than further the purposes underlying the exclusionary rule.

The previously recognized exception penalizes defendants for committing perjury by allowing the prosecution to expose their perjury through impeachment using illegally obtained evidence. Thus defendants are discouraged in the first instance from "affirmatively resort[ing] to perjurious testimony."[3276] But the exception leaves defendants free to testify truthfully on their own behalf; they can offer probative and exculpatory evidence ****653** to the jury without opening the door to impeachment by carefully avoiding any statements that directly contradict the suppressed evidence. The exception thus generally discourages perjured testimony without discouraging truthful testimony.

In contrast, expanding the impeachment exception to encompass the testimony of all defense witnesses would not have the same beneficial effects. First, the mere threat of a subsequent criminal prosecution for perjury is far more likely to deter a witness from intentionally lying on a defendant's behalf than to deter a defendant, already facing conviction for the underlying offense, from lying on his own behalf. Hence the Illinois Supreme Court's underlying premise that a defendant frustrated by our previous impeachment exception can easily find a witness to engage in "perjury by proxy" is suspect.

More significantly, expanding the impeachment exception to encompass the testimony of all defense witnesses likely would chill some defendants from presenting their best defense ***315** and sometimes any defense at all-through the testimony of others. Whenever police obtained evidence illegally, defendants would have to assess prior to trial the likelihood that the evidence would be admitted to impeach the otherwise favorable testimony of any witness they call. Defendants might reasonably fear that one or more of their witnesses, in a position to offer truthful and favorable testimony, would also make some statement in sufficient tension with the tainted evidence to allow the prosecutor to introduce that evidence for impeachment. First, defendants sometimes need to call "reluctant" or "hostile" witnesses to provide reliable and probative exculpatory testimony, and such witnesses likely will not share the defendants' concern for avoiding statements that invite impeachment through contradictory evidence. Moreover, defendants often cannot trust even "friendly" witnesses to testify without subjecting themselves to impeachment, simply due to insufficient care or attentiveness. This concern is magnified in those occasional situations when defendants must call witnesses to testify despite having had only a limited opportunity to consult with or prepare them in advance. For these reasons, we have

[3275] *Harris, supra, 401 U.S., at 225, 91 S.Ct., at 645*

[3276] *Walder, supra, 347 U.S., at 65, 74 S.Ct., at 356*

recognized in a variety of contexts that a party "cannot be absolutely certain that his witnesses will testify as expected."[3277] As a result, *316 an expanded impeachment exception likely would chill some **654 defendants from calling witnesses who would otherwise offer probative evidence.

*317 This realization alters the balance of values underlying the current impeachment exception governing defendants' testimony. Our prior cases make clear that defendants ought not be able to "pervert" the exclusion of illegally obtained evidence into a shield for perjury, but it seems no more appropriate for the State to brandish such evidence as a sword with which to dissuade defendants from presenting a meaningful defense through other witnesses. Given the potential chill created by expanding the impeachment exception, the conceded gains to the truth-seeking process from discouraging or disclosing perjured testimony would be offset to some extent by the concomitant loss of probative witness testimony. Thus, the truth-seeking rationale supporting the impeachment of defendants in Walder and its progeny does not apply to other witnesses with equal force.

Moreover, the proposed expansion of the current impeachment exception would significantly weaken the exclusionary rule's deterrent effect on police misconduct. This Court has characterized as a mere "speculative possibility"[3278] the likelihood that permitting prosecutors to impeach defendants with illegally obtained *318 evidence would encourage police misconduct. Law enforcement officers will think it unlikely that the defendant will first decide to testify at trial and will also open the door inadvertently to admission of any illegally obtained evidence. Hence, the officers' incentive to acquire evidence through illegal means is quite weak.

In contrast, expanding the impeachment exception to all defense witnesses would significantly **655 enhance the expected value to the prosecution of illegally obtained evidence. First, this expansion would vastly increase the number of occasions on which such evidence could be used. Defense witnesses easily outnumber testifying defendants, both because many defendants do not testify themselves and because many if not most defendants call multiple witnesses on their behalf. Moreover, due to the chilling effect identified above,[3279] illegally obtained evidence holds even greater value to the prosecution for each individual witness than for each defendant. The prosecutor's access to impeachment evidence would not just deter perjury; it would also deter defendants from calling witnesses in the first place, thereby keeping from the jury much probative exculpatory evidence. For both of these reasons, police officers and their superiors would recognize that obtaining evidence through illegal means stacks the deck heavily in the prosecution's favor. It is thus far more than a "speculative possibility" that police misconduct will be encouraged by permitting such use of illegally obtained evidence.

The United States argues that this result is constitutionally acceptable because excluding illegally obtained evidence solely from the prosecution's case in chief would still provide a quantum of deterrence sufficient to protect the privacy interests underlying the exclusionary rule. We disagree. Of course, a police officer might in certain situations believe that obtaining particular evidence through illegal means, resulting *319 in its suppression from the case in chief, would prevent the prosecution from establishing a prima facie case to take to a jury. In such situations, the officer likely would be deterred from obtaining the evidence illegally for fear of jeopardizing the entire case. But much if not most of the time, police officers confront opportunities to obtain evidence illegally after they have already legally obtained (or know that they have other means of legally obtaining) sufficient evidence to sustain a prima facie case. In these situations, a rule requiring exclusion of illegally obtained

[3277] *Brooks v. Tennessee, 406 U.S. 605, 609, 92 S.Ct. 1891, 1893, 32 L.Ed.2d 358 (1972)*

[3278] *Harris v. New York, 401 U.S., at 225, 91 S.Ct., at 645*

[3279] *See supra, at 653-654*

evidence from only the government's case in chief would leave officers with little to lose and much to gain by overstepping constitutional limits on evidence gathering. Narrowing the exclusionary rule in this manner, therefore, would significantly undermine the rule's ability "to compel respect for the constitutional guaranty in the only effectively available way-by removing the incentive to disregard it."[3280] So long as we are committed to protecting the people from the disregard of their constitutional rights during the course of criminal investigations, inadmissibility of illegally obtained evidence must remain the rule, not the exception.

IV

The cost to the truth-seeking process of evidentiary exclusion invariably is perceived more tangibly in discrete prosecutions than is the protection of privacy values through deterrence of future police misconduct. When defining the precise scope of the exclusionary rule, however, we must focus on systemic effects of proposed exceptions to ensure ***320** that individual liberty from arbitrary or oppressive police conduct does not succumb to the inexorable pressure to introduce all incriminating evidence, no matter how obtained, in each and every criminal case. Our previous recognition of an impeachment exception limited to the testimony of defendants ****656** reflects a careful weighing of the competing values. Because expanding the exception to encompass the testimony of all defense witnesses would not further the truth-seeking value with equal force but would appreciably undermine the deterrent effect of the exclusionary rule, we adhere to the line drawn in our previous cases.

Accordingly, we hold that the Illinois Supreme Court erred in affirming James' convictions despite the prosecutor's use of illegally obtained statements to impeach a defense witness' testimony. The court's judgment is reversed, and the case is remanded for further proceedings not inconsistent with this opinion.

It is so ordered.

Justice STEVENS, concurring.

While I join the opinion of the Court, certain comments in the dissent prompt this postscript. The dissent answers the wrong question when it states that "[t]he interest in protecting the truth-seeking function of the criminal trial is every bit as strong in this case as in our earlier cases."[3281] This is self-evident. The State always has a strong interest in the truth-seeking function. The proper question, however, is whether the admission of the illegally obtained evidence in this case would sufficiently advance the truth-seeking function to overcome the loss to the deterrent value of the exclusionary rule. With respect to this issue, the dissent overestimates the benefit of the exclusionary rule even to the defendant bent on presenting perjured testimony and exaggerates the injury that exclusion of unlawfully obtained evidence causes to the truth-seeking function.

In "contested criminal trials,"[3282] the urge to win can unfortunately lead each side to overstate its case. As ***321** the Court properly observes, the ability of the dishonest defendant to procure false testimony is tempered by the availability of the illegally obtained evidence for use in a subsequent perjury prosecution of the defense witness.[3283] A witness who is not on trial faces a far different calculus than one whose testimony can mean the difference between acquittal and a prison sentence. He or she will think long and hard before accepting a defendant's invitation to know-

---

[3280] *Elkins v. United States, 364 U.S. 206, 217, 80 S.Ct. 1437, 1444, 4 L.Ed.2d 1669 (1960)*

[3281] *Post, at 658*

[3282] *Post, at 659*

[3283] *Ante, at 652-653*

ingly offer false testimony that is directly contradicted by the State's evidence. The dissent ignores this "hard reality,"[3284] in presuming that a defense witness will offer false testimony when that testimony is immunized from rebuttal at trial.

While the dissent assumes false testimony or, at least, faulty recollection with respect to defense witnesses, it is unwilling to entertain the same assumption with respect to the prosecution's witnesses. The evidentiary issue in this case involves the testimony of a police officer about a statement that he allegedly heard the defendant make at the time of his arrest. An officer whose testimony provides the foundation for admission of an oral statement or physical evidence may be influenced by his interest in effective law enforcement or may simply have faulty recollection. It is only by giving 100-percent credence to every word of the officer's testimony that the dissent can so categorically state that "the defendant himself revealed the witness' testimony to be false,"[3285] that "James ... said his hair was previously red,"[3286] or that information presented to the jury was "known to be untrue."[3287] That assumption is no more warranted in the case of prosecution witnesses than the opposite assumption is warranted in the case of defense witnesses.

In this case, in which the guilty verdict is supported by the testimony of five eyewitnesses, it is highly probable that these characterizations are accurate. But the testimony of those five witnesses, on which the dissenters rely for their conclusion that any error committed by the trial court was ***322** harmless,[3288] would also seem to be sufficient to obviate the need to rely on ****657** the officer's rebuttal to discredit the witness Henderson's testimony. Were the officer's testimony not so corroborated, it would surely be improper to presume-as the dissenters do-that the conflict between the testimony of the officer and Henderson should necessarily be resolved in the officer's favor or that exclusion of the evidence would result in a decision by jurors who are "positively misled."[3289]

Justice KENNEDY, with whom THE CHIEF JUSTICE, Justice O'CONNOR, and Justice SCALIA join, dissenting.

To deprive the prosecution of probative evidence acquired in violation of the law may be a tolerable and necessary cost of the exclusionary rule. Implementation of the rule requires us to draw certain lines to effect its purpose of deterring unlawful conduct. But the line drawn by today's opinion grants the defense side in a criminal case broad immunity to introduce whatever false testimony it can produce from the mouth of a friendly witness. Unless petitioner's conviction is reversed, we are told, police would flout the Fourth Amendment, and as a result, the accused would be unable to offer any defense. This exaggerated view leads to a drastic remedy: The jury cannot learn that defense testimony is inconsistent with probative evidence of undoubted value. A more cautious course is available, one that retains Fourth Amendment protections and yet safeguards the truth-seeking function of the criminal trial.

Our precedents establish that the exclusionary rule does not apply where the interest in pursuing truth or other important values outweighs any deterrence of un-

[3284] *Post, at 659*

[3285] *Post, at 658*

[3286] *Post, at 660, n. 2*

[3287] *Post, at 659*

[3288] *Post, at 661*

[3289] *Post, at 658*

lawful conduct that the rule might achieve.[3290] One instance is a defendant's attempt to take advantage by presenting testimony in outright contradiction of excluded ***323** facts, secure in the knowledge that the inconsistency will not be revealed to the jury. As we said over 35 years ago:

> It is one thing to say that the Government cannot make an affirmative use of evidence unlawfully obtained. It is quite another to say that the defendant can turn the illegal method by which evidence in the Government's possession was obtained to his own advantage, and provide himself with a shield against contradiction of his untruths. Such an extension of the Weeks[3291] doctrine would be a perversion of the Fourth Amendment.[3292]

Under this rationale, our consistent rule has been that a defendant's testimony is subject to rebuttal by contradicting evidence that otherwise would be excluded. The principle applies to suppressed physical evidence, as in Walder itself and United States v. Havens[3293] and to statements obtained in violation of the law, so long as the statements are voluntary and reliable.[3294]

Petitioner argues that the rationale of these cases is confined to "impeachment" of testimony presented by the defendant himself because these cases involve only "impeachment by self-contradiction."[3295] The theory, it seems, is that excluded evidence introduced in opposition to the defendant's testimony impeaches by means of the contradiction itself; the substantive truth or falsity of the suppressed evidence is irrelevant. Our cases do not bear this reading. In Havens, the defendant was charged as an accomplice in the smuggling of narcotics. A codefendant hid the drugs in a ****658** T-shirt constructed with special pockets. The pockets were made of patches cut from another T-shirt found in the defendant's luggage during an illegal search. When the defendant denied having possessed the T-shirts, the cut ***324** T-shirt, which had been excluded at the outset, was admitted as rebuttal evidence. We upheld its admission.[3296] There was no "self-contradiction" involved, for the rebuttal of the defendant's testimony could only have been based on the jury's belief in the substantive truth of the fact that the altered T-shirt was used in the smuggling, and that it belonged to the defendant. The same was true in Walder, where we upheld the admission of illegally seized heroin from an unrelated investigation to impeach the defendant's statement that he had never possessed the drug. In sum, our cases show that introduction of testimony contrary to excluded but reliable evidence subjects the testimony to rebuttal by that evidence.

I agree with the majority that the resolution of this case depends on a balance of values that informs our exclusionary rule jurisprudence. We weigh the "'likelihood of ... deterrence against the costs of withholding reliable information from the truth-seeking process.'"[3297] The majority adopts a sweeping rule that the testimony of wit-

---

[3290] *See, e.g., Illinois v. Krull, 480 U.S. 340, 347-348, 107 S.Ct. 1160, 1165-1166, 94 L.Ed.2d 364 (1987); United States v. Leon, 468 U.S. 897, 906-907, 104 S.Ct. 3405, 3411-3412, 82 L.Ed.2d 677 (1984); Stone v. Powell, 428 U.S. 465, 486-489, 96 S.Ct. 3037, 3048-3050, 49 L.Ed.2d 1067 (1976); United States v. Calandra, 414 U.S. 338, 347-348, 94 S.Ct. 613, 619-620, 38 L.Ed.2d 561 (1974)*

[3291] *Weeks v. United States, 232 U.S. 383, 34 S.Ct. 341, 58 L.Ed. 652 (1914)*

[3292] *Walder v. United States, 347 U.S. 62, 65, 74 S.Ct. 354, 356, 98 L.Ed. 503 (1954)*

[3293] *446 U.S. 620, 100 S.Ct. 1912, 64 L.Ed.2d 559 (1980)*

[3294] *See Oregon v. Hass, 420 U.S. 714, 95 S.Ct. 1215, 43 L.Ed.2d 570 (1975); Harris v. New York, 401 U.S. 222, 91 S.Ct. 643, 28 L.Ed.2d 1 (1971)*

[3295] *Brief for Petitioner 13*

[3296] *See 446 U.S., at 623, 628, 100 S.Ct., at 1914-15, 1917*

[3297] *Ante, at 651, n. 1 (quoting Illinois v. Krull, supra, 480 U.S., at 347, 107 S.Ct., at 1166)*

nesses other than the defendant may never be rebutted with excludable evidence. I cannot draw the line where the majority does.

The interest in protecting the truth-seeking function of the criminal trial is every bit as strong in this case as in our earlier cases that allowed rebuttal with evidence that was inadmissible as part of the prosecution's case in chief. Here a witness who knew the accused well took the stand to testify about the accused's personal appearance. The testimony could be expected to create real doubt in the minds of jurors concerning the eyewitness identifications by persons who did not know the accused. To deprive the jurors of knowledge that statements of the defendant himself revealed the witness' testimony to be false would result in a decision by triers of fact who were not just kept in the dark as to excluded evidence, but positively misled. The potential for harm to the truth-seeking process resulting from the majority's new rule ***325** in fact will be greater than if the defendant himself had testified. It is natural for jurors to be skeptical of self-serving testimony by the defendant. Testimony by a witness said to be independent has the greater potential to deceive. And if a defense witness can present false testimony with impunity, the jurors may find the rest of the prosecution's case suspect, for ineffective and artificial cross-examination will be viewed as a real weakness in the state's case. Jurors will assume that if the prosecution had any proof the statement was false, it would make the proof known. The majority does more than deprive the prosecution of evidence. The state must also suffer the introduction of false testimony and appear to bolster the falsehood by its own silence.

The majority's fear that allowing the jury to know the whole truth will chill defendants from putting on any defense seems to me far too speculative to justify the rule here announced. No restriction on the defense results if rebuttal of testimony by witnesses other than the defendant is confined to the introduction of excludable evidence that is in direct contradiction of the testimony. If mere "tension with the tainted evidence,"[3298] opened the door to introduction of all the evidence subject to suppression, then the majority's fears might be justified. But in this context rebuttal can and should be confined to situations where there is direct conflict, which is to say where, within reason, the witness' testimony and the excluded testimony cannot both be true.

****659 *326** Also missing from the majority's analysis is the almost certain knowledge that the testimony immunized from rebuttal is false. The majority's apparent assumption that defense witnesses protected by today's rule have only truth-telling in mind strikes me as far too sanguine to support acceptance of a rule that controls the hard reality of contested criminal trials. The majority expresses the common sense of the matter in saying that presentation of excluded evidence must sometimes be allowed because it "penalizes defendants for committing perjury."[3299]

In some cases, of course, false testimony can result from faulty recollection. But the majority's ironclad rule is one that applies regardless of the witness' motives, and may be misused as a license to perjure. Even if the witness testifies in good faith, the defendant and his lawyer, who offer the testimony, know the facts. Indeed, it is difficult here to imagine the defense attorney's reason for asking Henderson about petitioner's hair color if he did not expect her to cast doubt on the eyewitness identification of petitioner by giving a description of petitioner's hair color contrary to that contained in his own (suppressed) statement.

The suggestion that the threat of a perjury prosecution will provide sufficient deterrence to prevent false testimony.[3300] ***327** A heightened proof requirement ap-

[3298] *Ante, at 653*

[3299] *Ante, at 652*

[3300] *Ante, at 320-321 (opinion of BRENNAN, J.); ante, at 656 (opinion of STEVENS, J.), is not realistic. See generally Dunn v. United States, 442 U.S. 100, 108, 99 S.Ct. 2190, 2195, 60 L.Ed.2d 743 (1979) (describing proof of perjury as "exceptionally difficult")*

plies in Illinois and other States, making perjury convictions difficult to sustain.[3301] Where testimony presented on behalf of a friend or family member is involved, the threat that a future jury will convict the witness may be an idle one.

The damage to the truth seeking process caused by the majority's rule is certain to be great whether the testimony is perjured or merely false. In this case there can be little doubt of the falsity, since petitioner's description of his own hair was at issue. And as a general matter the alternative to rebuttal is endorsement of judicial proceedings conducted in reliance on information known to be untrue. Suppressed evidence is likely to consist of either voluntary statements by the defendant himself or physical evidence. Both have a high degree of reliability, and testimony in direct conflict to such evidence most often will represent an attempt to place ****660** falsehoods before the jury.

***328** The suggestion that all this is so far beyond the control of the defendant that he will put on no defense is not supported. As to sympathetic witnesses, such as the family friend here, it should not be too hard to assure the witness does not volunteer testimony in contradiction of the facts. The defendant knows the content of the suppressed evidence. Even in cases where the time for consultation is limited, the defense attorney can take care not to elicit contradicting testimony. And in the case of truly neutral witnesses, or witnesses hostile to the accused, it is hard to see the danger that they will present false testimony for the benefit of the defense.

The majority's concerns may carry greater weight where contradicting testimony is elicited from a defense witness on cross-examination. In that situation there might be a concern that the prosecution would attempt to produce such testimony as the foundation to put excluded evidence before the jury. We have found that possibility insufficient to justify immunity for a defendant's own false testimony on cross-examination.[3302] As to cross-examination of other witnesses, perhaps a different rule could be justified. Rather than wait for an appropriate case to consider this or similar measures, however, the majority opts for a wooden rule immunizing all defense testimony from rebuttal, without regard to knowledge that the testimony introduced at the behest of the defendant is false or perjured.

I also cannot agree that admission of excluded evidence on rebuttal would lead to the "disregard of ... constitutional rights," by law enforcement officers[3303] that the majority fears. This argument has been raised in our previous cases in this area of the law.[3304] To date we have rejected it. Now the specter appears premised on an assumption that a single slip of the tongue by any defense witness will open the door to ***329** any suppressed evidence at the prosecutor's disposal. If this were so, the majority's concern that officers would be left with little to lose from conducting an illegal search would be understandable. And the argument might hold more force if, as the majority speculates,[3305] police confront the temptation to seize evidence illegally "much if not most of the time" after gathering sufficient evidence to present proof of guilt beyond a reasonable doubt in the case in chief. Again, however, I disagree with the predictions.

It is unrealistic to say that the decision to make an illegal search turns on a precise calculation of the possibilities of rebuttal at some future trial. There is no reason to believe a police officer, unschooled in the law, will assess whether evidence already in his possession would suffice to survive a motion for acquittal fol-

---

[3301] *See People v. Alkire, 321 Ill. 28, 151 N.E. 518 (1926); People v. Harrod, 140 Ill.App.3d 96, 94 Ill.Dec. 490, 488 N.E.2d 316 (1986)*

[3302] *United States v. Havens, 446 U.S. 620, 100 S.Ct. 1912, 64 L.Ed.2d 559 (1980)*

[3303] *Ante, at 655*

[3304] *See Havens, supra, at 633-634, 100 S.Ct., at 1919-1920 (BRENNAN, J., dissenting); Hass, 420 U.S., at 725, 95 S.Ct., at 1222 (BRENNAN, J., dissenting); Harris, 401 U.S., at 232, 91 S.Ct., at 649 (BRENNAN, J., dissenting)*

[3305] *Ante, at 655*

lowing the case in chief. The officer may or may not even know the identity of the ultimate defendant. He certainly will not know anything about potential defense ****661** witnesses, much less what the content of their testimony might be. What he will know for certain is that evidence from an illegal search or arrest (which may well be crucial to securing a conviction) will be lost to the case in chief. Our earlier assessments of the marginal deterrent effect are applicable here. "Assuming that the exclusionary rule has a deterrent effect on proscribed police conduct, sufficient deterrence flows when the evidence in question is made unavailable ***330** to the prosecution in its case in chief."[3306]

In this case, the defense witness, one Jewel Henderson, testified that petitioner's hair was black on the date of the offense. Her statement, perjured or not, should not have been offered to the jurors without giving them the opportunity to consider the unequivocal and contradicting description by the person whose own hair it was. I would allow the introduction of petitioner's statement that his hair was red on the day of the shootings. The result is consistent with our line of cases from Walder to Havens and compelled by their reasoning.

The prosecution, it is true, did not limit itself to petitioner's description of his hair color. It went beyond this to introduce petitioner's statement that he went to the beauty shop to "change his appearance."[3307] The prosecutor used this statement to suggest that petitioner had a guilty mind and an intention to evade capture by disguise. This goes beyond what was necessary to rebut Henderson's testimony and raises many of the concerns expressed in the majority opinion. Nonetheless, there was overwhelming evidence of petitioner's guilt in this case, including the testimony of five eyewitnesses. In view of these circumstances, I agree with the Illinois Supreme Court that any error as to the additional statements or the prosecutor's argument had no effect on petitioner's trial and may be considered harmless.

Where the jury is misled by false testimony, otherwise subject to flat contradiction by evidence illegally seized, the protection of the exclusionary rule is "'perverted into a license to use perjury by way of a defense, free from the risk of confrontation with prior inconsistent utterances.'"[3308] The perversion is the same where the perjury is by proxy. I would affirm the judgment of the Illinois Supreme Court.

Black Letter Law

The Court held that the impeachment exception to the exclusionary rule (that permits prosecution in criminal proceedings to introduce illegally obtained evidence to impeach a defendant's own testimony) would not be expanded to permit prosecution to impeach testimony of all defense witnesses with illegally obtained evidence.

Discussion Problem:

19-1. On September 4, 1994, police in Calusa, Florida, stopped a vehicle in which Billy Bob was a passenger and Michael "Bubba" Loving ("Bubba Loving") was the driver. Incident to that stop, the police officers searched Billy Bob for weapons and discovered cash and small amounts of marijuana and crack cocaine. Subsequent state drug charges against Billy Bob were dismissed after a Florida Superior Court judge ruled that the officers lacked justification to search him and suppressed the seized evidence.

[3306] *Harris, supra, at 225, 91 S.Ct., at 645*

[3307] *App. 11*

[3308] *Havens, supra, 446 U.S., at 626, 100 S.Ct., at 1916 (quoting Harris, supra, 401 U.S., at 226, 91 S.Ct., at 646)*

Pursuant to further investigation, federal agents arrested Billy Bob in Calusa on April 18, 1995. That same day, a grand jury returned a one-count indictment charging Billy Bob and Penelope Horowitz with conspiring to traffic drugs from July to December in Florida and Georgia. Horowitz eventually pleaded guilty while Billy Bob proceeded to trial.

At trial, the government sought to show that, throughout the indictment period, Billy Bob traveled between Lawrence, Georgia, and Calusa, Florida to manage sales of crack cocaine out of Horowitz's Calusa residence.

In its case in chief, the government presented six witnesses who testified about their involvement with Billy Bob. Raul Oregano testified that Billy Bob initially sold drugs for him in Lawrence, but then became interested in selling in Calusa, another locale in which Oregano conducted his drug business. Oregano stated that although he rejected Billy Bob's offer to become a partner in his Calusa business, he did drive Billy Bob to Calusa to meet Horowitz. To Oregano's dismay, Billy Bob then began to compete with him in the Calusa drug trade.

Most of the other witnesses testified that they saw Billy Bob in Horowitz's residence (where they bought crack cocaine), and/or that they bought the drug directly from Billy Bob at that location. In particular, Marlane Hornbuckle testified that she first met Billy Bob in May in Lawrence, at which time she drove him to her apartment in Calusa. She stated that he carried at least 200 bags of crack cocaine on that trip, intending that she sell it in Calusa. Hornbuckle testified that soon thereafter, she moved into Horowitz's apartment out of which they sold crack cocaine. She indicated that Billy Bob stayed in their living room at least three days a week and that, two or three times during each of those days, she would obtain from him a batch of twenty bags of crack cocaine to sell.

Michael Loving testified that his brother, Bubba Loving, told him that Billy Bob operated out of Horowitz's residence. He stated that Billy Bob was at Horowitz's residence at least two or three times per week, and that he bought crack cocaine many times from Billy Bob at that location. Three other witnesses, Bruce Moody, Scott Poulin, and Karla Lovell, testified that they regularly purchased crack cocaine out of Horowitz's apartment and that they either bought directly from Billy Bob or they saw him there when they bought from Horowitz.

There was testimony to the effect that Billy Bob would exchange crack cocaine for travel between Lawrence and Calusa. Hornbuckle testified that she drove Billy Bob from Lawrence to Calusa at least five times and that various people, including Bubba Loving, Horowitz and Lovell, also drove him to and from Lawrence and Calusa. Moody testified that he drove Billy Bob twice to Lawrence from Florida. Lovell testified that on two occasions she picked up Billy Bob in Lawrence and transported him to Calusa, where, she said, he would stay for about a week.

On the second day of his trial, Billy Bob testified in his own defense. Defense counsel began Billy Bob's direct examination with the following question: "Billy, yesterday there were six witnesses that testified directly about your supposed involvement in a crack ring. We'll go through this list and ask you whether you know these people in any way." In response to counsel's subsequent questions, Billy Bob testified: "Of the witnesses who testified yesterday, I can assure you, I can swear before God that I have only seen two of them, [Hornbuckle and Oregano]."

As to Hornbuckle, he testified that the first time he saw her was in prison after his April 1995 arrest. He stated that the events to which Hornbuckle testified "didn't happen" and that he never gave or sold crack cocaine to her. As to Oregano, he stated that, although he had seen Oregano several times, he neither sold crack cocaine for him nor knew that he was "involved in this kind of business." Additionally, Billy Bob denied knowing either Bubba Loving or Horowitz, his indicted co-conspirator.

Concerning his whereabouts during the indictment period (July to December), Billy Bob testified that he split his time between Atlanta and Gainsville. He stated that, during this time, he was devoted full-time to his business of promoting bluegrass music in the Gainsville area. When asked if he went to Florida during the indictment period, Billy Bob replied that he traveled there only once to see his attorney. When asked if he had any friends or associates in Calusa, he replied that he had a "woman friend" there.

During cross-examination by the prosecutor, Billy Bob maintained that he did not know Bubba Loving and that he traveled to Calusa only once during the indictment period-to meet only with his attorney. When pressed, however, he acknowledged that he traveled to Calusa once again during that time, again to see his attorney, and that he also once went to a fast food restaurant near Calusa to meet his woman friend. The prosecutor then inquired, "And on any of these occasions that you went to Calusa to see your lawyer ... did you possess crack cocaine?"

At this point, defense counsel objected and a sidebar conference was held. Anticipating that the question would lead to further inquiry into the September Calusa arrest (during which evidence was unlawfully seized), counsel argued that the subject was "very prejudicial" and, in any event, irrelevant to the charged conspiracy.

You are the trial judge. How do you rule? Why? Assume that the counsel will ask for a written ruling on this issue. Lay out the structure of the ruling that you want your clerk to draft. Be sure to identify any specific case law they need to address.

-Notes-

3rd Edition Acknowledgements

This book is part of my own small effort to continue to produce casebooks that are student focused, user friendly and competitively priced. As always I write for the people in my life who matter most, my wife Pamela, children Laura and Charles, and the students for whom it is written.

The work of my research assistants on this edition was herculean - I could not have completed it without their hard work, sage discussions and excellent advice. MaryAnn Jaghab and Stephanie Boussias are to be commended for all that they brought to this project. It would have been impossible to complete without them.

We stand on the shoulders of everyone that ever crosses our lives, and I have been blessed in that regard as well. The mistakes within, and I am sure that there are many (mostly grammatical I hope), are of course, my own.

Enjoy!

Charles H. Rose III
December 2016

1st Edition Acknowledgements

Few things in life are ever done in a vacuum, and this book is no exception. While it has been a labor of love, it would have never been possible without the love and support of my wife Pamela, my two children, Laura and Charlie, and the students for whom it is written. I particularly want to thank my research assistants, Leslie Rae Newton, Jamie Combee, and Victoria San Pedro for their invaluable assistance in bringing this book to life. The text passed through their capable hands, and is much the better for it.

We stand on the shoulders of everyone that ever crosses our lives, and I have been blessed in that regard as well. The mistakes within, and I am sure that there are many (mostly grammatical I hope), are of course, my own.

Enjoy!

Charles H. Rose III
June 2013

By the Author

Books with Practice Ready Press

Everyday Evidence: A Practical Approach (enhanced)

The Federal And Florida Rules of Evidence, 2nd Edition

Federal Criminal Procedure: Cases that Matter, 1st Edition

Federal Criminal Procedure: Cases that Matter, 2nd Edition

Federal Criminal Procedure: Cases that Matter, 3rd Edition

Persuasive Openings: Storytelling in the Courtroom (enhanced)

Total TV v. 4 Geeks & a Gal, 1st Edition (case file)

Persuasive Openings: Storytelling in the Courtroom

Books with WEST Publishing

Fundamental Trial Advocacy, 3rd Edition

Fundamental Trial Advocacy, 2nd Edition

Fundamental Trial Advocacy, 1st Edition

Fundamental Pretrial Advocacy, 2nd Edition

Fundamental Pretrial Advocacy, 1st Edition

Mastering Trial Advocacy, 1st Edition

Mastering Trial Advocacy: Cases, Problems, & Exercises

Advocacy Case Files, 1st Edition

Evidence in Context: Evidentiary Problems & Exercises, 1st Edition

Jury Selection: The Law, Art and Science of Jury Selection, 3rd Edition (co-author)

Books with Matthew Bender (LEXIS)

Military Crimes & Defenses, 2nd Edition (co-author)

Military Crimes & Defenses, 1st Edition (co-author)

Books with ASPEN Publishing

Evidence Practice Under the Rules, 4th Edition (co-author)

Evidence Practice Under the Rules, 3rd Edition (co-author)

Copyright

This book is a work of non-fiction. The organization and presentation of these U.S. Supreme Court cases is designed to present the information in a structure that maximizes learning. The discussion problems within are based upon real appellate cases or the febrile imaginings of a law professor.

Third Edition

Print Edition (c) December 2016

ISBN-10:

ISBN-13:

Publisher

Practice Ready Press

United States

6261 14th Avenue South

Suite 201

Gulfport, Florida 33707

www.practice-ready-press.com

Phone: 813-924-4717

Made in the USA
Monee, IL
13 September 2026

62981007R10420